THE FEMINIST PHILOSOPHY READER

Alison Bailey and Chris Cuomo

Boston   Burr Ridge, IL   Dubuque, IA   New York   San Francisco   St. Louis
Bangkok   Bogotá   Caracas   Kuala Lumpur   Lisbon   London   Madrid   Mexico City
Milan   Montreal   New Delhi   Santiago   Seoul   Singapore   Sydney   Taipei   Toronto

The McGraw-Hill Companies

McGraw-Hill
Higher Education

Published by McGraw-Hill, an imprint of The McGraw-Hill Companies, Inc., 1221 Avenue of the Americas, New York, NY 10020. Copyright © 2008. All rights reserved. No part of this publication may be reproduced or distributed in any form or by any means, or stored in a database or retrieval system, without the prior written consent of The McGraw-Hill Companies, Inc., including, but not limited to, in any network or other electronic storage or transmission, or broadcast for distance learning.

This book is printed on acid-free paper.

1 2 3 4 5 6 7 8 9 0 DOC/DOC 0 9 8 7

ISBN: 978-0-07-340739-5
MHID: 0-07-340739-9

Publisher: *Lisa Moore*
Sponsoring Editor: *Mark Georgiev*
Marketing Manager: *Pamela Cooper*
Editorial Coordinators: *Sora Kim and Briana Porco*
Production Editor: *Chanda Feldman*
Manuscript Editor: *Jean Dal Porto*
Design Manager: *Cassandra Chu*
Cover Designer: *Ayelet Arbel*
Art Editor: *Emma Ghiselli*
Production Supervisor: *Tandra Jorgensen*
Composition: *10/12 Times New Roman by ICC Macmillan, Inc.*
Printing: *45# New Era Matte, R. R. Donnelley & Sons, Inc.*

Cover: © Royalty-Free/CORBIS
Credits: *The credits section for this book begins on page 881 and is considered an extension of the copyright page.*

Library of Congress Cataloging-in-Publication Data

Bailey, Alison.
   The feminist philosophy reader / Alison Bailey, Chris Cuomo. — 1st ed.
       p. cm.
   Includes bibliographical references and index.
   ISBN-13: 978-0-07-340739-5 (alk. paper)
   ISBN-10: 0-07-340739-9 (alk. paper)
  1. Feminist theory.   I. Cuomo, Chris J.   II. Title.
HQ1190.B34 2008
305.4201—dc22

                                        2007030064

The Internet addresses listed in the text were accurate at the time of publication. The inclusion of a Web site does not indicate an endorsement by the authors or McGraw-Hill, and McGraw-Hill does not guarantee the accuracy of the information presented at these sites.

www.mhhe.com

CONTENTS

This book is dedicated to our Mothers
Bonnie Powers Cuomo
and
Judith Stanton Bailey
(1933–2000)

PREFACE

Feminism sparked one of the most important and influential theoretical endeavors of the last fifty years, and feminist philosophical contributions to that effort have been profound. Today the number of scholarly works and publications, university courses, conferences, and organizations dedicated to feminist philosophy is impressive indeed. In addition to articulating and investigating key questions and issues concerning sexism and its vicissitudes, feminist philosophers have brought new insights to nearly every area of the discipline of philosophy, from ethics to philosophy of science, from political theory to aesthetics to the study of historical philosophical figures. But twenty years ago, when we were graduate students, we read and assembled photocopied packets of readings for our courses. This was the only way to provide students with a thorough survey of the most significant and engaging articles in the field.

Today there are many more textbooks on feminist philosophy, but most anthologies focus on specific areas of inquiry, such as ethics, political theory, or epistemology. After years of reading, teaching, and winnowing through the literature, we are now delighted to present a reader that captures a few of the more defining moments in feminist philosophy, from the earliest second wave to the post-9/11 present. Our emphasis is on the field as it emerged in the United States and Europe, out of both feminist movements and academic communities, and most of the essays included here first appeared in English. The chapters focus on central issues in feminism, such as the meanings of privilege and oppression, sex, gender, sexuality, race, nation, and some of the core areas of philosophy, including ethics, epistemology, politics, and ontology. Theoretical methods represented include analytic, continental, psychoanalytic, postmodern, and postcolonial, and a few things in between. This volume reflects the view that feminism's foundational concerns necessarily include racism, heterosexism, and other forms of oppression and injustice. And although this text was also shaped by historical factors, including our own limitations and the hegemonic influence of Anglophone philosophy and American feminist theory, we hope to have presented a pluralist and inclusive reading of what history has provided.

The Feminist Philosophy Reader will introduce some readers to feminist theory, and others to the discipline of Philosophy. Brief essays at the beginning of each chapter provide overviews of the general issues and methods connecting the various selections. Because the work presented here is both practically significant and theoretically sophisticated, we believe students at many different levels will find it informative, useful, and perhaps challenging as well. The table of contents is structured in relation to several primary themes, but there is a phenomenal amount of conversation, common ground, and creative tension among the essays overall. A number of innovative courses in feminist philosophy could be built around the text. Each chapter also includes a list of resources for further reading and films that complement the topics addressed in each section.

Writing philosophy is commonly considered a solo pursuit, but that impression hides the fact that all philosophy is generated out of historical influences, conversations, communities, and cross-pollinations. Feminist philosophy is no exception. In fact, phallocratic and other marginalizing traditions in the discipline of philosophy have made it necessary for feminists and other "outsiders" to create and nurture intellectual spaces where critical and resistant understandings can develop. It is quite unlikely that a volume such as this would have been possible without those spaces, including organizations such as the Society for Women in Philosophy, the International Association of Women Philosophers, and the National Women's Studies Association, all founded in the 1970s, and still going strong today. We are indebted to those legacies of feminist creativity and resistance, and the webs of relation, support, and knowledge they have fostered. And we are deeply grateful to the authors included in this volume, along with the generations of feminist intellectuals who comprised their surrounding communities, and all the contemporary theorists and activists who comprise ours.

Alison Bailey and Chris Cuomo
July 2007

ACKNOWLEDGMENTS

Special thanks go to the people who helped us in the preparation of this text, including Kate Smith and Drew Anastasia for their tireless search, photocopy, and collating missions; to Rozel White and Becca Chase of the Illinois State University Women's and Gender Studies Program; to Hara Bastas for helpful research; to members of the University of Cincinnati Departments of Women's Studies and Philosophy; to Cicely Robinson-Jones for last-minute mailing and faxing; and to members of the Institute for Women's Studies and the Department of Philosophy at the University of Georgia, for their continued support of this project. Thanks also to the College of Arts and Science at Illinois State University for the subvention funds that allowed us expand the content of the volume.

We are also deeply grateful to the many students in our Feminist Philosophy courses throughout the years, who helped us develop this reader in many ways, and whose interest and enthusiasm continues to inspire us. Thanks especially to those in recent classes, who offered helpful input on the material and structure of this reader.

Thanks to the many anonymous readers and reviewers who provided honest, careful, and attentive feedback on our introductions and selections, and who generously shared their own ideas and insights with us.

Thanks to Jon-David Hague, whose vision helped initiate this volume, and to the rest of the McGraw-Hill team, who brought their terrific expertise to its production: Sora Lisa Kim, Briana Porco, Mark Georgiev, Chanda Feldman, Jean Dal Porto, and Fred Courtright.

Endless gratitude to Karen Schlanger, for her unwavering support and interest in this project, for her patience, and for fabulous meals during our marathon work sessions in Cincinnati. And special thanks to our friend William Edward Morris, for the book's clear and simple title.

CHAPTER 1

A FEMINIST TURN IN PHILOSOPHY

CHRIS CUOMO / ALISON BAILEY

What is the use of studying philosophy if all that it does for you is to enable you to talk with some plausibility about some abstruse questions of logic, etc., and if it does not improve your thinking about the important questions of everyday life?
—LUDWIG WITTGENSTEIN

If you have wondered about the meanings or relevance of feminism, or if you are interested in women's intellectual traditions, or in connections among race, class, gender, and sexuality, or if you would like to know more about general philosophical methods and contemporary controversies, you have selected the right book. But we should alert you—studying feminist philosophy does require some courage. Serious attention to the pervasive human problem of women's subordination can lead to deep questioning of just about anything. Commerce, religion, government, morality, science—all tend to reflect the perspectives and interests of those with more power and reinforce their sense of superiority, while keeping others in subordinate roles and substandard locations. Gender distinctions and hierarchies have long been fundamental features of social existence, and so they inform most understandings of what it means to be human, and infuse nearly every institution and every sort of relationship. Feminist investigations of sexism and its myriad effects began as critical explorations of women's "second class" positions vis-à-vis men, but as you will see, those explorations have led to intense philosophical examination of the conditions of violence and subjection, analyses of many specific social norms and practices, and further inquiries into the deep relations of embodiment, power, and identity.

At the heart of feminism is a moral judgment from the perspectives of the subjugated— usually women—and an argument that the systematic mistreatment and devaluation of females cross-culturally is a paradigmatic human harm with grave and pervasive consequences. Feminism is therefore also a positive judgment that with emancipation for women will come widespread human improvement. Feminist philosophy is grounded in the premise that in patriarchal, sexist, or male-dominated contexts, women's wisdom on the matters that affect them is crucial. However, in such contexts, "woman" is seen as a diverse social category, not a universal experience or body type, because women and their interests are immeasurably diverse. Instead of promoting a female essence, feminist philosophers investigate the patterns, histories, and systemic nature of women's oppression and feminist resistances. Yet the practical and moral mission of feminism remains at the core of its more abstract projects. Feminist philosophy is built on the hope that intellectual understanding can lead to ethical and political improvement in our own lives, and in bigger and wider realities as well.

The authors included in this volume utilize the tools of philosophy—deep conceptual interrogation, self-reflexive critical dialogue, phenomenology, and precise argumentation—to foster resistance to oppression, and to help engender fruitful alternatives. In addition to investigating the primary topics of feminism (such as sexism, gender, racism, sexuality, mothering, and rape), feminist thinkers generate compelling insights concerning many core questions in philosophy. When viewed through feminist lenses, perennial philosophical puzzles, such as the meaning of goodness and evil, the importance of rights, the reliability of knowledge, and the possibility of positive change broaden and take on new relevance. Feminists have also been at the forefront of investigating the fact that different forms of oppression are deeply related and indebted to each other. It is therefore not surprising that in the last half century or so, feminist philosophers have made valuable contributions to our knowledge about some of the most basic and influential aspects of modern and postmodern life. As it turns out, there are few areas of philosophy where critical questions about history, power, and perspective are not somehow germane.

But feminist philosophy goes beyond a simple application of "traditional" philosophical methods to "new" sets of topics and questions. It also develops innovative methods for bringing marginalized and revolutionary perspectives to the forefront. Questions about the *matters* and the *methods* of feminism are deeply entwined, for the prejudices of sexist worldviews inform conceptions of intellectual virtues, and christen some methods as more "rigorous" or scientific than others. Feminist philosophers discuss methods in relation to values and ethics, as well as epistemological ideals. For example, the inclusion of the perspectives, interests, and voices of women in theories about women benefits both accuracy and democratic ideals, and exemplifies the view that the moral and epistemological dimensions of research can augment each other.

Questioning false and unjustly biased premises and starting points is a hallmark of feminist philosophy. As you will see throughout this volume, a very common philosophical premise rejected by feminists is the ideal of the "universal" human subject, or knower, who is fundamentally independent, constitutionally isolated from others, ideally unemotional, and driven by the maximization of his own interests. Feminist philosophers show that such conceptions of selves are not universal truths, but projections of particular masculinist cultural ideals. In contrast, by initiating questions about subjectivity and knowledge from the perspectives of women, feminists find that the patterns and inevitabilities of human life tend more toward interdependence than independence, and toward a need for mutual caretaking that is severely compromised by oppressive relations. Articulating and examining the implications of the foundational importance of relationality in human experience raises compelling questions, such as how should we conceive of individual blameworthiness if moral beings are inevitably primarily "social"? Or, how can we best negotiate the conflicts that arise when we are physiologically inclined toward dependence, yet socially inclined to be independent?

Perhaps most importantly, feminists apply their own methods reflexively and self critically. Understanding the production of knowledge to be fundamentally social and historical, feminist philosophy provides an abundance of evidence that any perspective is partial and interested. And so feminist theories must acknowledge and address their own partiality. This is one reason why feminist philosophers have so often approached their work as a communal endeavor, and a site for intellectual cross-pollination. Notably, the philosophers represented here display a strong sense of political and intellectual community. Yet, perhaps because there is so much at stake, struggles between feminists over appropriate responses to conditions and histories of oppression can get quite heated. Some would say feminists have raised the philosophical and political practice of "reflective equilibrium" to a high art. As predominantly white and Euro-American feminists criticize the hidden prejudices and problematic biases in the history of "male-stream" philosophy, so women of color and outsiders to the academy question theories developed by privileged academic women, whose own experiences are often rather cloistered, and whose comforts systematically depend on the exploitation of others. As the Euro-American dominance of the field indicates, feminist philosophies have been shaped by the interests and perspectives of privileged women who inevitably write from their own cultural and class biases, despite their attempts to be "inclusive." A primary warning of feminism is that the solipsisms of the privileged are often disastrous, and so such issues must always be addressed. Feminist philosophy may not always live up to its own high ideals, but the fact that its methodologies tend to encourage pluralism (openness to all relevant viewpoints), democracy, and self-reflexivity, and that it is motivated by ethics of caring and solidarity, helps feminism maintain its noteworthy integrity and success amidst diversity.

ENGAGING TRADITIONS

Another project of feminist philosophy has been to recover and study the work of forgotten women philosophers, a radical act in itself. Most of today's scholars describe philosophy as something born in ancient Greece, but of course if we think of philosophy as a distinct human practice rather than a specific intellectual tradition, no one knows where philosophy first began, or how the practices of philosophical inquiry first developed. In some sense, feminist philosophy is probably nearly as old as resistance to patriarchy or sexism, for becoming a resistant or revolutionary subject often includes "getting philosophical" about the state of oppression suffered by one's class, and about whatever keeps the dominant group or groups in positions of power. Whether or not they had the power to publish or distribute their work, women intellectuals throughout the ages and in nearly every context have probably presented critical

arguments addressing masculine domination and related issues. In many cultures philosophy has also been a professional activity housed in institutions of education, government, religion, science, and art, but philosophy can occur anywhere, and grassroots political movements tend to have their own philosophers, whether or not those individuals are people who write books or give lectures or have jobs in academia.

As far as the Western canon goes, we know that influential and brilliant female (and some male) thinkers have been questioning sexist practices and engaging in philosophical discourse about sexual equality since before Sappho. In *A History of Women Philosophers*, Mary Ellen Waithe lists sixteen women philosophers from the classical world, seventeen from 500–1600, and over thirty from 1600–1900. While women philosophers are not necessarily feminist philosophers, it is an understatement to say that there is a strong historical correlation between women intellectuals and feminist ideas, for the correlation is enormous, and the pantheon of feminist and "pre-feminist" philosophers throughout history is well worth recalling. Hypatia of Alexandria, a very influential mathematician of the fifth century, was put to death by a mob in 415 CE, because of her political and religious alliances. In *The Book of the City of Ladies* (1405), Christine de Pisan defended women against stereotypes of them as lacking intellect, virtue, and strength. Princess Elizabeth of Bohemia corresponded with René Descartes on the problems generated by his theory of substance dualism. Sor Juana Inés de la Cruz's *La Respuesta* (1690) appealed to natural law theory to bring out the inconsistencies in the church's position that scholarly activities were improper for women. The contributions Harriet Taylor Mill made to *On Liberty* (1869) and *Principles of Political Economy* (1848) were acknowledged by John Stuart Mill, but for many years were ignored by historical scholars. The work of black philosophers such as W. E. B. DuBois, Eugene Clay Holmes, and Alain L. Locke suffered similar disciplinary erasure. Women philosophers and social reformers of the early twentieth century, including Jane Addams, Jessie Taft, Charlotte Perkins Gilman, and Anna Julia Cooper, were influential in the development and dissemination of American pragmatism. In 1963, Hannah Arendt published a work of philosophical nonfiction, *Eichmann in Jerusalem: A Report on the Banality of Evil,* which has had an enormous impact on modern and contemporary understandings of the lessons of the Holocaust, and the problem of human evil.

In addition to recovering and reclaiming historical works that are of particular interest, feminist philosophers also reconsider and reinterpret works from traditional philosophical canons. To name just a few well-known examples, feminists have drawn on Karl Marx and Friedrick Engels's accounts of class exploitation through labor in capitalism to help explain women's subordination through sexual divisions of labor, John Rawls's theory of justice to clarify the requirements of democracy, and Michel Foucault's discussions of the relationships between disciplinary institutions and bodily practices to theorize the reproduction and performance of sexuality and gender. The field of feminist philosophy includes a great wealth of work on canonical philosophers. For example, a well-known book series that offers feminist reinterpretations of the "Western philosophical tradition" includes collections on thirty major figures from different contexts and historical eras.

But this is not to say that the relationship between feminist and traditional philosophy is a happy one. Scholars looking for blatantly derogatory remarks about women and non-Europeans need not dig very deep in the history of philosophy. In *Generation of Animals,* Aristotle offered a "biological" explanation for women's inferiority, arguing that because heat is a fundamental principle of perfection in animals, and women have a cooler nature, women are monstrosities in comparison to the proper (male) human form. (Tuana 1993, 18–19). Despite John Locke's philosophical attachment to the idea of democracy, he held investments in the slave-trading Royal African Company, and assisted in the writing of the slave constitution of Carolina. Immanuel Kant is renowned for his philosophies of ethics, reason, and existence, but he was also a founding theorist of the modern concept of race, and his comments on women and non-whites in *Observations on the Feeling of the Beautiful and Sublime* (1764) are notoriously degrading. Kant held that women have strong inborn feelings for all that is beautiful, and they therefore should not trouble themselves with intellectual matters: "A woman therefore will learn no geometry. . . . The fair can leave Descartes to his vortices to whirl forever, without troubling themselves."[1] Of African peoples, Kant remarked, "So fundamental is the difference between [the black and white] races of man . . . it appears to be as great in regard to mental capacities as in color" so that "a clear proof that what [a Negro] said was stupid" was that "this fellow was quite black from head to foot."[2] Clearly, for Kant, some peoples had more personhood than others. Arthur Schopenhauer's "On Women" described women as having no sense of justice, due to their "defective powers in reasoning and deliberation," as they are "dependent not upon strength but upon craft; and hence their instinctive capacity for cunning, and their ineradicable tendency to say what is not true" (Witt 2004). In a passage from *Being and Nothingness* that reads like a chauvinistic cliché, Jean Paul Sartre wrote that "one of the most fundamental tendencies of human reality [is] the tendency to fill. . . . A good part of our life is passed in plugging holes, in filling empty places. . . . It is only from this standpoint that we can pass on to sexuality. The obscenity for the feminine sex is that everything which 'gapes open.'"[3]

---

[1] Descartes, cited in Clack, 1998, 147.
[2] From Kant's *Observations on the Feeling of the Beautiful and Sublime,* trans. John T. Goldthwait. Berkeley: University of California Press, 1960, pp. 111–113. Cited in Mills, 1997.
[3] For a specific discussion of this view of female sexuality see Irigaray, in this volume. For more disturbing examples of misogyny and racism in the history of Western philosophy, see Nancy Tuana (1992 and 1993), Charlotte Witt (2004), Beverley Clack (1999), and Andrew Vallis (2005).

Passages and works such as these from the history of philosophy indicate the prevalence of prejudicial views, as well as the fact that teachers and scholars throughout the ages have mostly been quite unperturbed by them. They merit feminist attention because they lead to more thorough understandings of influential philosophical traditions (for example, how racism is embedded within them), and because they may expose relationships between ideas, cultural values, and major and minor misuses of power. Overall, contemporary feminist philosophers mine the history of philosophy in search of clues and tools that might further feminism's critical and liberatory projects. It is interesting to note how many of the philosophers who have been criticized for their misogyny, racism, and xenophobia have also provided valuable resources for feminist thought. Perhaps we should take this to be testament both to the usefulness of philosophy, and to the resourcefulness of feminism.

A FEMINIST TURN

The work highlighted in this volume focuses less on the history of philosophy, and more on the meanings and implications of feminism itself, and on feminist analyses of relevant philosophical and political issues. These essays represent a specific academic and intellectual tradition that emerged, especially but not exclusively in North America and Europe, from women's, civil rights, labor, antiwar, black power, and anti-imperialist movements for social change, and that continues to evolve today in relation to specific social realities, and in complex conversation with other critical and cultural discourses. This turn toward feminist topics, questions, and methods in the discipline of philosophy has had radical impacts on the discipline as we know it, by introducing the position that power, privilege, and social identities are philosophically fundamental issues, and by improving the intellectual and professional climate for scholars who find questions about

gender, race, difference, sexuality, etc., to be of interest.

Many factors contributed to the development of the field of feminist philosophy in the 1970s. Greatly expanded numbers of women, working class students, and students of color had entered the academy in the 1950s and 1960s, and the role of students and intellectuals in social movements of the sixties made the academy a highly significant site for political innovation and struggle. The growing awareness that women's contributions had been systematically erased or de-emphasized in nearly every academic discipline, along with growing impatience over differential treatment, sexual harassment, and sexist academic cultures, resulted in fiery demands for change in institutions of higher learning.

Ironically, a book written by someone exceedingly close to the masculinist tradition of European thought marked a turning point in feminist philosophy. Simone de Beauvoir's *The Second Sex,* first published as *Le Deuxieme Sexe* in 1949 (and published in English in 1953), is considered by many to be a founding text of modern feminism. Beauvoir's project was to ask how patterns of female subordination are formed in relation to specific cultural and metacultural views about femininity, and to examine relationships between those patterns and the inevitable conflicts and constructs of human existence. The text is interdisciplinary, drawing on sociological, biological, and historical data, although Beauvoir's guiding framework is philosophical and existentialist. Her central themes and arguments, regarding cross-cultural patterns of female oppression, comparisons between women's oppression and other forms of "otherness," and the idea that "woman is not born, but made," remain extremely influential today, especially in Western feminisms. As the most extensive feminist philosophical work published in its day, *The Second Sex* provides a unique model, reference point, and foil for feminist thinkers. In the discipline of philosophy the book has come to symbolize the beginning of a shift toward the instantiation of feminist philosophy in its own terms. In addition to the influence of *The Second Sex,* Beauvoir's persona as a well-known "independent" woman intellectual (she was a lifelong lover with Jean-Paul Sartre, but they never married) was inspirational to a generation of activist intellectuals who strongly identified with her personal and philosophical commitments.

In the early 1970s feminist philosophy gained momentum as a field in the new interdisciplinary area of Women's Studies, which inspired many women (and a few men) in the academy to expand their research and teaching to include data on women and girls, hidden histories, and attention to feminist topics and inquiries. Yet at first there was precious little work that addressed contemporary issues from feminist perspectives using the particular tools and methods of philosophy. When courses on "Women and Philosophy" were first offered, teachers drew from the work of historical figures such as Mary Wollstonecraft, Charlotte Perkins Gilman, Emma Goldman, Jane Addams, and texts such as Fredrick Engles's *Origin of the Family* (1884), and John Stuart and Harriet Taylor Mill's *On the Subjection of Women* (1869). *The Second Sex* was one of the few contemporary philosophical works available, although many professors also taught the work of movement writers like Ti-Grace Atkinson, Shulamith Firestone, Francis Beale, and Barbara Deming. Several anthologies of feminist political thought had just been published—Robin Morgan's *Sisterhood Is Powerful: An Anthology of Writings from the Women's Liberation Movement* (1970), Toni Cade Bambara's *Black Woman* (1970), and Alice Rossi's *The Feminist Papers: From Adams to de Beauvoir* (1973), a collection of European and American feminist writings from 1770 to the early 1950s.

Out of a hunger for better course material and an interest in developing explicitly feminist philosophical works, scholar-activists carved a space for feminist philosophy by creating contexts for presenting and discussing feminist works, and then publishing, teaching, and distributing those works. They also created professional organizations and institutions to build communities of engagement and support, including most notably the Society for Women in Philosophy and the academic journal *Hypatia.* The growth of feminist culture, such as bookstore and coffeehouse movements, also contributed to the flourishing of feminist thought and theory throughout the 1980s, and created a lively if short-lived sense that a fruitful and productive bridging of academic and nonacademic political discourses was possible. For better or worse, like most areas of political theorizing, in recent years feminist philosophy has become more firmly ensconced in the academy.

By now an abundance of compelling and pertinent work has been published by feminist philosophers, and the field has evolved into a recognized subfield of the academic discipline, a prominent discourse in feminist theory, a major voice in critical studies, and an unusually activist intellectual community. Feminist philosophers have provided a wealth of ideas about resisting and transforming oppressive systems and the values that sustain them. Contemporary feminist philosophy does not shy away from making practical suggestions, or from using its institutional power to help create positive change. Although there is no denying that the interests and perspectives of privileged writers have shaped the development of feminist thought throughout history, one of the great tenets of philosophy is that we try to face up to uncomfortable truths. As the rules and norms of gender are always diverse and subtly shifting, feminism is also constantly under construction in multiple venues, and so feminist philosophy continues to play a vital and dynamic role in charting the paths of ongoing movements for social justice.

The nine sections of this book address issues and questions that have been central in the development of feminist philosophy in its own terms. The first four sections are constructed around core concepts—oppression and resistance, sex and gender, sexualities, and race and racism. These concepts are important because they are much more than words and ideas—they are lived by all of us, in idiosyncratic ways but also in response to powerful and deeply engrained social patterns. The remaining five sections are organized around areas of philosophical inquiry—postcoloniality and transnationality, ethics, politics, epistemology, and ontology. Although there are many other topics that could be included in an anthology of feminist philosophy, we hope to have provided a fairly wide and deep survey of the field. For further exploration we have included references and media resources so that you may go on to develop your own feminist knowledge in the matters that interest you.

FOR FURTHER READING

Addelson, Kathryn Pyne. "Feminist Philosophy and the Women's Movement." *Hypatia* 9(3) (1994): 216–25.

Alanen, Lilli, and Charlotte Witt, eds. *Feminist Reflections on the History of Philosophy.* Dordrecht: Kluwer Academic, 2004.

Alcoff, Linda Martín. "Philosophy Matters: A Review of Recent Work in Feminist Philosophy. *Signs: Journal of Women in Culture and Society* 25(3)(2000): 841–82.

Alcoff, Linda Martín. *Singing in the Fire: Stories of Women in Philosophy.* Rowman and Littlefield, 2003.

Alcoff, Linda Martín, and Eva Feder Kittay, eds. *The Blackwell Guide to Feminist Philosophy.* Boston: Blackwell Publishing, Ltd., 2006.

Allen, Jeffner, and Iris Young. *Thinking Muse: Feminism and Modern French Philosophy.* Bloomington, IN: Indiana University Press, 1989.

Anzaldúa, Gloria E., and Cherrie Moraga, eds. *This Bridge Called My Back: Writings by Radical Women of Color.* 2nd ed. Berkeley, CA: Third Woman Press, 2002.

Bambara, Toni Cade. *The Black Woman: An Anthology.* New York: New American Library, 1970.

Barthe, Else. M., ed. *Women Philosophers: A Bibliography of Books through 1990.* Bowling Green, OH: Bowling Green State University Press, 1997.

Bell, Linda. *Beyond the Margins: Reflections of a Feminist Philosopher.* New York: SUNY Press, 2003.

Card, Claudia. "The Feistiness of Feminism." In *Feminist Ethics,* edited by Claudia Card. Lawrence, KS: University of Kansas Press, 1991.

Clack, Beverley, ed. *Misogyny in the Western Philosophical Tradition: A Reader.* New York: Routledge, 1999.

Cudd, Ann E. Analyzing Backlash to Progressive Social Movements. *APA Newsletter on Feminism and Philosophy* (99)1(1999): 2.

Deutscher, Penelope. *Yielding Gender: Feminism, Deconstruction, and the History of Philosophy.* London: Routledge, 1997.

Ferguson, Ann. "Twenty Years of Feminist Philosophy." *Hypatia* 9(3)(1994): 97–216.

Firestone, Shulamith. *The Dialectic of Sex: The Case for a Feminist Revolution.* New York: Bantam Books, 1970.

Fricker, Miranda, and Jennifer Hornsby, eds. *The Cambridge Companion to Feminism and Philosophy.* Cambridge: Cambridge University Press, 2000.

Gardner, Catherine Villanueva. *Rediscovering Women Philosophers: Philosophical Genre and the Boundaries of Philosophy.* Boulder, CO: Westview Press, 2000.

Gatens, Moira. "The Feminist Critique of Philosophy." In her *Feminism and Philosophy: Perspectives on Difference and Equality.* Bloomington, IN: Indiana University Press, 1991.

Griffiths, Morwenna, and Margaret Whitford, eds. *Feminist Perspectives in Philosophy.* Bloomington, IN: Indiana University Press, 1988.

Grimshaw, Jean. *Philosophy and Feminist Thinking.* Minneapolis, MN: University of Minnesota Press, 1986.

Harris, Leonard, ed. *Philosophy Born of Struggle: Anthology of Afro-American Philosophy from 1917.* Dubuque, IA: Kendall/Hunt Publishing Unit, 1983.

Holland, Nancy J. *Is Women's Philosophy Possible?* Savage, MD: Rowman and Littlefield, 1990.

Hutchings, Noël, and William D. Rumsey, eds. *The Collaborative Bibliography of Women in Philosophy.* Charlottesville, VA: Philosophy Documentation Center, 1997.

Jaggar, Alison, and Iris Young, eds. *A Companion to Feminist Philosophy.* Boston: Blackwell Publishing, Ltd., 2000.

Lloyd, Genevieve. *Feminism and the History of Philosophy.* New York: Oxford University Press, 2001.

Malcolm, Norman, *Ludwig Wittgenstein: A Memoir.* 2nd ed. Oxford: Oxford University Press, 1984.

McAlister, Linda López. "On the Possibility of Feminist Philosophy." *Hypatia* 9(3)(1994): 188–96.

McAlister, Linda López, ed. *Hypatia's Daughters: Fifteen Hundred Years of Women Philosophers.* Bloomington, IN: Indiana University Press, 1996.

Mill, John Stuart. *The Subjection of Women.* Edited by Sue Mansfield. Arlington Heights, IL: Croft Classics, 1980.

Millet, Kate. *Sexual Politics.* Urbana, IL: University of Illinois Press, 2000 (1970).

Mills, Charles M. *Blackness Visible: Essays on Philosophy and Race.* Ithaca: Cornell University Press, 1997.

Mills, Charles M. *The Racial Contract.* Ithaca, NY: Cornell University Press, 1997.

Morgan, Robin. *Sisterhood Is Powerful: An Anthology of Writings from the Women's Liberation Movement.* New York: Vintage Books, 1970.

Rich, Adrienne. "Disloyal to Civilization: Feminism, Racism, Gynephobia." In her *On Lies, Secrets and Silence.* New York: Norton, 1979.

Rossi, Alice, ed. *The Feminist Papers: From Adams to de Beauvoir.* New York: Bantam, 1973.

Roth, Benita. 1999. "Race, Class and the Emergence of Black Feminism in the 1960s and 1970s," *Womanist Theory and Research,* Vol. 3(1)(1999):

Scheman, Naomi. "Undoing Philosophy as Feminist." In her *Engenderings: Constructions of Knowledge, Authority, and Privilege.* New York: Routledge, 1993.

Scheman, Naomi. "The Unavoidability of Gender." In her *Engenderings: Constructions of Knowledge, Authority, and Privilege.* New York: Routledge, 1993.

Schott, Robin. *Discovering Feminist Philosophy.* Lanham, MD: Rowman and Littlefield, 2003.

Tong, Rosemarie. *Feminist Thought: A More Comprehensive Introduction.* Boulder, CO: Westview Press, 1998.

Tougas, Cecile T., and Sara Ebernrick, eds. *Presenting Women Philosophers.* Philadelphia: Temple University Press, 2000.

Tuana, Nancy. *Woman and the History of Philosophy.* New York: Paragon House, 1992.

Tuana, Nancy. *The Less Noble Sex: Scientific, Religious, and Philosophical Conceptions of Women's Nature.* Bloomington, IN: Indiana University Press, 1993.

Vallis, Andrew. *Race and Racism in Modern Philosophy.* Ithaca, NY: Cornell University Press, 2005.

Vetterinling-Braggin, Frederick Ellison, and Jane English. *Feminism and Philosophy.* Totowa, NJ: Littlefield, Adams and Co., 1977.

Waithe, Mary Ellen, ed. *A History of Women Philosophers,* Volumes I–IV. New York: Springer Publishing, 1987–1991.

Witt, Charlotte. "Feminist History of Philosophy." In *Feminist Reflections on the History of Philosophy,* edited by Lilli Alanen and Charlotte Witt. Boston: Kluwer Academic Publishers, 2004.

CHAPTER 2

OPPRESSION AND RESISTANCE

Feminism is a response to the fact of female oppression, and so this journey in feminist philosophy focuses on interrogations of subordination and exploitation patterns related to sexual difference and other corresponding forms of social stratification, degradation, privilege, and harm. As you will see, a central task of feminist philosophy has been to examine women's oppression and the possibilities for resistance and positive change. In arguing that women are indeed oppressed, feminists have drawn from traditional political theories, analyses of class oppression, theories of race and racism, accounts of identity formation and sexuality, and many other sources. But by focusing on the particulars of sexism as a distinct and nearly universal (though diverse) form of human harm, feminism contributes to more general analyses of what oppression is, how it works, and how it might be overcome. In other words, by providing greater understanding of women's positions, needs, and experiences, feminist philosophy contributes to our most basic and general understanding of social stratification, power, and human capacities.

In contrast to the work presented here, earlier liberal feminist philosophies theorized oppression by emphasizing the unjust distribution of political and legal rights according to sex, the problems with gender roles that relegate women to private spheres, and the sexist biases structuring institutions of education, medicine, and the law. But they often took the goal of feminist politics to be equality with privileged men, and failed to question norms of personhood that were based on idealized notions of universal, independent, utility-maximizing "rational man." In contrast, neo-Marxist and radical feminists understood female subordination in relation to economic domination, especially in marriage and familial relationships. They also saw the double-sided significance of consciousness and bodily disciplines, such as sexuality, as aspects of human experience that can both enable freedom and reproduce oppression. Some held that, like the proletariat, women constituted a separate "sex class" whose liberation would result from economic revolution, equalization of labor, and fundamental changes in the family.

Although analogies with slavery and racism were common in their arguments, too often white feminist scholars understood "woman" as a universal category, or took their own cultures to be paradigmatic. Sometimes their work was explicitly exclusionary or elitist; other times it merely failed to acknowledge or address the diversity of female experience. Before the 1980s, it was not unusual for feminists with class, racial, and sexual privilege to describe their plight as though it were universal, or to discuss women of color and lesbians in distancing or derogatory ways. By the 1980s, the work of several women and lesbians of color came to scholarly prominence in the United States through the bridge created by the thriving feminist publishing and bookstore movement of that era. The influence of those writers on feminist theory, activism, and practice was profound. In addition to raising political consciousness about racism and homophobia, Audre Lorde, Barbara Smith, Gloria Anzaldúa, and many others argued that feminism must address multifaceted and interwoven systems of domination, exploitation, and violence. The oppressions that females experience take myriad forms, and different systems of oppression, such as racism and sexism, are not merely analogous—they are deeply connected. The category "women" therefore includes members of oppressed and oppressor groups. Any one woman may be located in complex relation to various groups, so feminist theories and practices must respond to relationships among multiple and interwoven identities and forms of oppression. As Audre Lorde wrote, "To imply . . . that all women suffer the same oppression simply because we are women is to lose sight of the many tools of patriarchy. It is to ignore how those tools are used by women against each other." Identities and subject positions are complicated and multiplex, involving class, race, nation, physical ability, sexuality, and the like, and feminism must be attentive to that complexity.

This chapter includes several influential essays that examine the logic of sex-based oppression, relationships between different forms of oppression, the function of privilege in maintaining oppression, and strategies for resistance. While they draw on different philosophical and political inspirations, these works have in common the aim of developing specifically feminist analyses of sexist oppression, rather than simply applying preexisting critical frameworks to questions about women.

Gayle Rubin's classic "The Traffic in Women: Notes on the 'Political Economy' of Sex," is an early attempt to develop a full account of the origins and oppressive nature of the sex/gender system. She believes Marxism alone is inadequate for developing such an account, because women's usefulness to capitalism (i.e., reproductive labor and unpaid housework) cannot explain *why* women are in subordinate social roles. As Rubin points out, women are oppressed in noncapitalist societies, and gang rape, foot binding, and the use of chastity belts cannot be explained by capitalist needs to generate surplus value. She argues that sexual difference itself is a social product, not secondary to economic material life, but fundamental in its own right. Rubin draws on anthropological theories of kinship as an observable empirical template for the sex/gender system, and psychoanalytic accounts of how the sex/gender system is reproduced in children's development, to articulate a more satisfying historical and cross-cultural explanation of male dominance.

Influenced more by analytic philosophy of language than anthropological or historical studies, and therefore more concerned about understanding the necessary and sufficient conditions of categorical subjugation, Marilyn Frye's landmark "Oppression" aims to develop an accurate and politically useful understanding of the concept. She argues that one of the reasons people fail to see or understand oppression is that they focus on particular attitudes, events, and actions that strike them as harmful, but do not see these in relation to the social and political systems that create and enable them. Frye identifies a key aspect of oppression in the "double binds" members of oppressed groups commonly experience. That is, they are faced daily with situations in which their options are reduced to choices that all expose them to penalty, censure, or deprivation. Frye's metaphor of the birdcage illustrates how sexist barriers are systematically related to one another, although it can be difficult to see the broader interwoven system when focused only on one aspect, such as feminine beauty norms. But when we begin to see how different damaging norms are interrelated, the facts of oppression become clear.

Audre Lorde's well-known "The Master's Tools Will Never Dismantle the Master's House," originally written as a presentation for a Women's Studies conference, challenged the newly developing world of academic feminism to reconsider its own replication of oppressive norms, to work harder to realize its own hopes of being antiracist and multicultural, and to take lesbian experiential knowledge about "redemptive" female possibilities to heart. In making her criticisms of privileged white women public, Lorde helped insert broader politics of identity, and moral attentiveness to intragroup differences in general, into feminist academic and political consciousness. Her claim that survival and flourishing depend upon facing fears and turning presumed weaknesses into strengths captures a very influential feminist philosophical perspective on the psychology of domination and liberation, and on the ever-present possibility of feminist revolution through creativity and critical thought.

Sandra Lee Bartky's "On Psychological Oppression" also evokes philosophical and experiential connections between sexism and racism to identify and elaborate on the "internal" dimensions of women's oppression. Drawing on Frantz Fanon's account of black men's psychic alienation under racism and colonialism (itself an elaboration of Marxist theories of alienation), Bartky presents a similar analysis of the psychic alienation women experience in patriarchies. Psychological oppression weighs on the mind of the oppressed, because members of oppressed groups internalize the distorted and degrading conceptions of them that are presented by dominant cultures. For women there are three key modes of psychological alienation that can result in a diminishment of autonomy and self-esteem: stereotyping, cultural domination, and sexual objectification. Bartky gives clear examples of different women's experiences of each of these modes, and demonstrates

how fragmentation and mystification underscore oppression's debilitating effects. She concludes that psychological oppression typically involves the unique double bind of living in a culture that affirms women's human status while simultaneously denying them adequate agency, autonomy, and cultural expression.

If oppression creates and systematically conveys undeserved harms, we might think of privileges as the unearned and therefore "undeserved" benefits automatically granted to beneficiaries of oppressive systems. The existence of such benefits may be inherently unjust, because they are the result of plunder, slavery, coercion, threat, and the like. In addition, the unfair and unequal distribution of benefits creates forms of life that in turn reproduce themselves by passing the benefits on to designated others, thereby maintaining the unequal and unfair distribution of goods and harms. A common example is the fact that generations who benefited economically from slavery in the antebellum United States have been able to pass that wealth down to their descendents with complete impunity, while the descendents of the people whose unpaid labor created that wealth are still disproportionately living in poverty.

Understanding privilege is an important part of a theory of oppression, for power is unconsciously and intentionally maintained and passed on through such benefits. But while it can sometimes be easy to see others' unfair advantages, it can be difficult to recognize one's own. In "White Privilege and Male Privilege," Peggy McIntosh begins with a basic observation: male students in her Women's Studies classes are willing to admit that women are oppressed as a sex, but are rarely willing to admit their own sex privilege. Raising similar questions about privilege based on race and sexuality, she makes an informal list of the daily effects of privilege she enjoys. Making an important distinction between earned strength and unearned power conferred systemically, McIntosh shows how some privileges appear to be strengths when in fact they are just permission to dominate, and other privileges are social norms that ought to be available to everyone. Privilege is like an invisible weightless knapsack packed with tools, passports, and other special provisions that allow those who are male, white, or straight to move through the world with ease, while others suffer from lacking the same. McIntosh concludes that heterosexism, racism, and sexism have distinct and interlocking advantages associated with them, and that acknowledging their unseen dimensions is the first step toward change.

The emphasis of María Lugones' work is on the practices and strategies of resistance, and associated complex skills that oppressed folks are able to develop, despite the overwhelming influence of subjugating power. In "Playfulness, 'World'-Traveling, and Loving Perception," she explores the role that arrogant perception (an idea developed by Marilyn Frye) plays in preventing identification, communication, and love across differences. Women with privilege are trained to be arrogant perceivers, thereby keeping their gaze fixed on those with power, and impeding their ability to connect in resistance with women who inhabit different "worlds" of sense. In developing resistant and useful concepts of "worlds," "travel," and "playfulness," Lugones shows us how we can enact disloyalty to arrogant perceivers, including our own tendencies to perceive others arrogantly. We may thereby disrupt harmful constructions of reality, and fracture the barriers that make deep and lasting coalitions so difficult to maintain.

THE TRAFFIC IN WOMEN: NOTES ON THE "POLITICAL ECONOMY" OF SEX

Gayle Rubin

The literature on women—both feminist and anti-feminist—is a long rumination on the question of the nature and genesis of women's oppression and social subordination. The question is not a trivial one, since the answers given it determine our visions of the future, and our evaluation of whether or not it is realistic to hope for a sexually egalitarian society. More importantly, the analysis of the causes of women's oppression forms the basis for any assessment of just what would have to be changed in order to achieve a society without gender hierarchy. Thus, if innate male aggression and dominance are at the root of female oppression, then the feminist program would logically require either the extermination of the offending sex, or else a eugenics project to modify its character. If sexism is a by-product of capitalism's relentless appetite for profit, then sexism would wither away in the advent of a successful socialist revolution. If the world historical defeat of women occurred at the hands of an armed patriarchal revolt, then it is time for Amazon guerrillas to start training in the Adirondacks.

It lies outside the scope of this paper to conduct a sustained critique of some of the currently popular explanations of the genesis of sexual inequality—theories such as the popular evolution exemplified by *The Imperial Animal,* the alleged overthrow of prehistoric matriarchies, or the attempt to extract all of the phenomena of social subordination from the first volume of *Capital.* Instead, I want to sketch some elements of an alternate explanation of the problem.

Marx once asked: "What is a Negro slave? A man of the black race. The one explanation is as good as the other. A Negro is a Negro. He only becomes a slave in certain relations. A cotton

spinning jenny is a machine for spinning cotton. It becomes *capital* only in certain relations. Torn from these relationships it is no more capital than gold in itself is money or sugar is the price of sugar." One might paraphrase: What is a domesticated woman? A female of the species. The one explanation is as good as the other. A woman is a woman. She only becomes a domestic, a wife, a chattel, a playboy bunny, a prostitute, or a human dictaphone in certain relations. Torn from these relationships, she is no more the helpmate of man than gold in itself is money . . . etc. What then are these relationships by which a female becomes an oppressed woman? The place to begin to unravel the system of relationships by which women become the prey of men is in the overlapping works of Claude Lévi-Strauss and Sigmund Freud. The domestication of women, under other names, is discussed at length in both of their *oeuvres.* In reading through these works, one begins to have a sense of a systematic social apparatus which takes up females as raw materials and fashions domesticated women as products. Neither Freud nor Lévi-Strauss sees his work in this light, and certainly neither turns a critical glance upon the processes he describes. Their analyses and descriptions must be read, therefore, in something like the way in which Marx read the classical political economists who preceded him (on this, see Althusser and Balibar, 1970:11–69). Freud and Lévi-Strauss are in some sense analogous to Ricardo and Smith: They see neither the implications of what they are saying, nor the implicit critique which their work can generate when subjected to a feminist eye. Nevertheless, they provide conceptual tools with which one can build descriptions of the part of social life which is the locus of the oppression of women, of sexual minorities, and of certain aspects of human personality within individuals. I call that part of social life the "sex/gender system," for lack of a more elegant term. As a preliminary definition, a "sex/gender system" is the set of arrangements by which a society transforms biological sexuality into products of human activity, and in which these transformed sexual needs are satisfied.

The purpose of this essay is to arrive at a more fully developed definition of the sex/gender system, by way of a somewhat idiosyncratic and exegetical reading of Lévi-Strauss and Freud. I use the word "exegetical" deliberately. The dictionary defines "exegesis" as a "critical explanation or analysis; especially, interpretation of the Scriptures." At times, my reading of Lévi-Strauss and Freud is freely interpretive, moving from the explicit content of a text to its presuppositions and implications. My reading of certain psychoanalytic texts is filtered through a lens provided by Jacques Lacan, whose own interpretation of the Freudian scripture has been heavily influenced by Lévi-Strauss.[1]

I will return later to a refinement of the definition of a sex/gender system. First, however, I will try to demonstrate the need for such a concept by discussing the failure of classical Marxism to fully express or conceptualize sex oppression. This failure results from the fact that Marxism, as a theory of social life, is relatively unconcerned with sex. In Marx's map of the social world, human beings are workers, peasants, or capitalists; that they are also men and women is not seen as very significant. By contrast, in the maps of social reality drawn by Freud and Lévi-Strauss, there is a deep recognition of the place of sexuality in society, and of the profound differences between the social experience of men and women.

MARX

There is no theory which accounts for the oppression of women—in its endless variety and monotonous similarity, cross-culturally and throughout history—with anything like the explanatory power of the Marxist theory of class oppression. Therefore, it is not surprising that there have been numerous attempts to apply Marxist analysis to the question of women. There are many ways of doing this. It has been argued that women are a reserve labor force for capitalism, that women's generally lower wages provide extra surplus to a capitalist employer, that women serve the ends of capitalist consumerism in their roles as administrators of family consumption, and so forth.

However, a number of articles have tried to do something much more ambitious—to locate the oppression of women in the heart of the capitalist dynamic by pointing to the relationship between housework and the reproduction of labor (see Benston, 1969; Dalla Costa, 1972; Larguia and Dumoulin, 1972; Gerstein, 1973; Vogel, 1973; Secombe, 1974; Gardiner, 1974; Rowntree, M. & J., 1970). To do this is to place women squarely in the definition of capitalism, the process in which capital is produced by the extraction of surplus value from labor by capital.

Briefly; Marx argued that capitalism is distinguished from all other modes of production by its unique aim: the creation and expansion of capital. Whereas other modes of production might find their purpose in making useful things to satisfy human needs, or in producing a surplus for a ruling nobility, or in producing to insure sufficient sacrifice for the edification of the gods, capitalism produces capital. Capitalism is a set of social relations—forms of property, and so forth—in which production takes the form of turning money, things, and people into capital. And capital is a quantity of goods or money which, when exchanged for labor, reproduces and augments itself by extracting unpaid labor, or surplus value, from labor and into itself.

> The result of the capitalist production process is neither a mere product (use-value) nor a *commodity,* that is, a use-value which has exchange value. Its result, its product, is the creation of *surplus-value* for capital, and consequently the actual *transformation* of money or commodity into capital. . . ."
> (Marx, 1969:399; italics in the original)

[1] Moving between Marxism, structuralism, and psychoanalysis produces a certain clash of epistemologies. In particular, structuralism is a can from which worms crawl out all over the epistemological map. Rather than trying to cope with this problem, I have more or less ignored the fact that Lacan and Lévi-Strauss are among the foremost living ancestors of the contemporary French intellectual revolution (see Foucault, 1970). It would be fun, interesting, and, if this were France, essential, to start my argument from the center of the structuralist maze and work my way out from there, along the lines of a "dialectical theory of signifying practices" (see Hefner, 1974).

The exchange between capital and labor which produces surplus value, and hence capital, is highly specific. The worker gets a wage; the capitalist gets the things the worker has made during his or her time of employment. If the total value of the things the worker has made exceeds the value of his or her wage, the aim of capitalism has been achieved. The capitalist gets back the cost of the wage, plus an increment—surplus value. This can occur because the wage is determined not by the value of what the laborer makes, but by the value of what it takes to keep him or her going—to reproduce him or her from day to day, and to reproduce the entire work force from one generation to the next. Thus, surplus value is the difference between what the laboring class produces as a whole, and the amount of that total which is recycled into maintaining the laboring class.

> The capital given in exchange for labour power is converted into necessaries, by the consumption of which the muscles, nerves, bones, and brains of existing labourers are reproduced, and new labourers are begotten . . . the individual consumption of the labourer, whether it proceed within the workshop or outside it, whether it be part of the process of production or not, forms therefore a factor of the production and reproduction of capital; just as cleaning machinery does. . . . (Marx, 1972: 572)
>
> Given the individual, the production of labour-power consists in his reproduction of himself or his maintenance. For his maintenance he requires a given quantity of the means of subsistence. . . . Labour-power sets itself in action only by working. But thereby a definite quantity of human muscle, brain, nerve, etc., is wasted, and these require to be restored. . . . (Ibid.: 171)

The amount of the difference between the reproduction of labor power and its products depends, therefore, on the determination of what it takes to reproduce that labor power. Marx tends to make that determination on the basis of the quantity of commodities—food, clothing, housing, fuel—which would be necessary to maintain the health, life, and strength of a worker. But these commodities must be consumed before they can be sustenance, and they are not immediately in consumable form when they are purchased by the wage. Additional labor must be performed upon these things before they can be turned into people. Food must be cooked, clothes cleaned, beds made, wood chopped, etc. Housework is therefore a key element in the process of the reproduction of the laborer from whom surplus value is taken. Since it is usually women who do housework, it has been observed that it is through the reproduction of labor power that women are articulated into the surplus value nexus which is the *sine qua non* of capitalism.[2] It can be further argued that since no wage is paid for housework, the labor of women in the home contributes to the ultimate quantity of surplus value realized by the capitalist. But to explain women's usefulness to capitalism is one thing. To argue that this usefulness explains the genesis of the oppression of women is quite another. It is precisely at this point that the analysis of capitalism ceases to explain very much about women and the oppression of women.

Women are oppressed in societies which can by no stretch of the imagination be described as capitalist. In the Amazon valley and the New Guinea highlands, women are frequently kept in their place by gang rape when the ordinary mechanisms of masculine intimidation prove insufficient. "We tame our women with the banana," said one Mundurucu man (Murphy, 1959:195). The ethnographic record is littered with practices whose effect is to keep women "in their place"—men's cults, secret initiations, arcane male knowledge, etc. And pre-capitalist, feudal Europe was hardly a society in which there was no sexism. Capitalism has taken over, and rewired, notions of male and female which predate it by centuries. No analysis of the

---

[2]A lot of the debate on women and housework has centered around the question of whether or not housework is "productive" labor. Strictly speaking, housework is not ordinarily "productive" in the technical sense of the term (I. Gough, 1972; Marx, 1969:387-413). But this distinction is irrelevant to the main line of the argument. Housework may not be "productive," in the sense of directly producing surplus value and capital, and yet be a crucial element in the production of surplus value and capital.

reproduction of labor power under capitalism can explain foot-binding, chastity belts, or any of the incredible array of Byzantine, fetishized indignities, let alone the more ordinary ones, which have been inflicted upon women in various times and places. The analysis of the reproduction of labor power does not even explain why it is usually women who do domestic work in the home, rather than men.

In this light it is interesting to return to Marx's discussion of the reproduction of labor. What is necessary to reproduce the worker is determined in part by the biological needs of the human organism, in part by the physical conditions of the place in which it lives, and in part by cultural tradition. Marx observed that beer is necessary for the reproduction of the English working class, and wine necessary for the French.

> . . . *the number and extent of his [the worker's] so-called necessary wants, as also the modes of satisfying them, are themselves the product of historical development,* and depend therefore to a great extent on the degree of civilization of a country, more particularly on the conditions under which, and consequently on the habits and degree of comfort in which, the class of free labourers has been formed. *In contradistinction therefore to the case of other commodities, there enters into the determination of the value of labour power a historical and moral element.* . . . (Marx, 1972:171, my italics)

It is precisely this "historical and moral element" which determines that a "wife" is among the necessities of a worker, that women rather than men do housework, and that capitalism is heir to a long tradition in which women do not inherit, in which women do not lead, and in which women do not talk to god. It is this "historical and moral element" which presented capitalism with a cultural heritage of forms of masculinity and femininity. It is within this "historical and moral element" that the entire domain of sex, sexuality, and sex oppression is subsumed. And the briefness of Marx's comment only serves to emphasize the vast area of social life which it covers and leaves unexamined. Only by subjecting this "historical and moral element" to analysis can the structure of sex oppression be delineated.

ENGELS

In *The Origin of the Family, Private Property, and the State,* Engels sees sex oppression as part of capitalism's heritage from prior social forms. Moreover, Engels integrates sex and sexuality into his theory of society. *Origin* is a frustrating book. Like the nineteenth-century tomes on the history of marriage and the family which it echoes, the state of the evidence in *Origin* renders it quaint to a reader familiar with more recent developments in anthropology. Nevertheless, it is a book whose considerable insight should not be overshadowed by its limitations. The idea that the "relations of sexuality" can and should be distinguished from the "relations of production" is not the least of Engels' intuitions:

> According to the materialistic conception, the determining factor in history is, in the final instance, the production and reproduction of immediate life. *This again, is of a twofold character: on the one hand, the production of the means of existence of food, clothing, and shelter and the tools necessary for that production; on the other side, the production of human beings themselves,* the propagation of the species. The social organization under which the people of a particular historical epoch and a particular country live is determined by both kinds of production: by the stage of development of labor on the one hand, and of the family on the other. . . . (Engels, 1972:71–72; my italics)

This passage indicates an important recognition—that a human group must do more than apply its activity to reshaping the natural world in order to clothe, feed, and warm itself. We usually call the system by which elements of the natural world are transformed into objects of human consumption the "economy." But the needs which are satisfied by economic activity even in the richest, Marxian sense, do not exhaust fundamental human requirements. A human group must also reproduce itself from generation to generation.

The needs of sexuality and procreation must be satisfied as much as the need to eat, and one of the most obvious deductions which can be made from the data of anthropology is that these needs are hardly ever satisfied in any "natural" form, any more than are the needs for food. Hunger is hunger, but what counts as food is culturally determined and obtained. Every society has some form of organized economic activity. Sex is sex, but what counts as sex is equally culturally determined and obtained. Every society also has a sex/gender system—a set of arrangements by which the biological raw material of human sex and procreation is shaped by human, social intervention and satisfied in a conventional manner, no matter how bizarre some of the conventions may be.[3]

---

[3] That some of them are pretty bizarre, from our point of view, only demonstrates the point that sexuality is expressed through the intervention of culture (see Ford and Beach, 1972). Some examples may be chosen from among the exotica in which anthropologists delight. Among the Banaro, marriage involves several socially sanctioned sexual partnerships. When a woman is married, she is initiated into intercourse by the sib-friend of her groom's father. After bearing a child by this man, she begins to have intercourse with her husband. She also has an institutionalized partnership with the sib-friend of her husband. A man's partners include his wife, the wife of his sib-friend, and the wife of his sib-friend's son (Thurnwald, 1916). Multiple intercourse is a more pronounced custom among the Marind Anim. At the time of marriage, the bride has intercourse with all of the members of the groom's clan, the groom coming last. Every major festival is accompanied by a practice known as *otiv-bombari,* in which semen is collected for ritual purposes. A few women have intercourse with many men, and the resulting semen is collected in coconut-shell buckets. A Marind male is subjected to multiple homosexual intercourse during initiation (Van Baal, 1966). Among the Etoro, heterosexual intercourse is taboo for between 205 and 260 days a year (Kelly, 1974). In much of New Guinea, men fear copulation and think that it will kill them if they engage in it without magical precautions (Glasse, 1971; Meggitt, 1970). Usually, such ideas of feminine pollution express the subordination of women. But symbolic systems contain internal contradictions, whose logical extensions sometimes lead to inversions of the propositions on which a system is based. In New Britain, men's fear of sex is so extreme that rape appears to be feared by men rather than women. Women run after the men, who flee from them, women are the sexual aggressors, and it is bridegrooms who are reluctant (Goodale and Chowning, 1971). Other interesting sexual variations can be found in Yalmon (1963) and K. Gough (1959).

The realm of human sex, gender, and procreation has been subjected to, and changed by, relentless social activity for millennia. Sex as we know it—gender identity, sexual desire and fantasy, concepts of childhood—is itself a social product. We need to understand the relations of its production, and forget, for awhile, about food, clothing, automobiles, and transistor radios. In most Marxist tradition, and even in Engels' book, the concept of the "second aspect of material life" has tended to fade into the background, or to be incorporated into the usual notions of "material life." Engels' suggestion has never been followed up and subjected to the refinement which it needs. But he does indicate the existence and importance of the domain of social life which I want to call the sex/gender system.

Other names have been proposed for the sex/gender system. The most common alternatives are "mode of reproduction" and "patriarchy." It may be foolish to quibble about terms, but both of these can lead to confusion. All three proposals have been made in order to introduce a distinction between "economic" systems and "sexual" systems, and to indicate that sexual systems have a certain autonomy and cannot always be explained in terms of economic forces. "Mode of reproduction," for instance, has been proposed in opposition to the more familiar "mode of production." But this terminology links the "economy" to production, and the sexual system to "reproduction." It reduces the richness of either system, since "productions" and "reproductions" take place in both. Every mode of production involves reproduction—of tools, labor, and social relations. We cannot relegate all of the multi-faceted aspects of social reproduction to the sex system. Replacement of machinery is an example of reproduction in the economy. On the other hand, we cannot limit the sex system to "reproduction" in either the social or biological sense of the term. A sex/gender system is not simply the reproductive moment of a "mode of production." The formation of gender identity is an example of production in the realm of the sexual system. And a sex/gender system involves more than the "relations of procreation," reproduction in the biological sense.

The term "patriarchy" was introduced to distinguish the forces maintaining sexism from other social forces, such as capitalism. But the use of "patriarchy" obscures other distinctions. Its use is analagous to using capitalism to refer to all modes of production, whereas the usefulness of the term "capitalism" lies precisely in that it distinguishes between the different systems by which societies are provisioned and organized. Any society will have some system of "political economy." Such a system may be egalitarian or socialist. It may be class stratified, in which case the oppressed class may consist of serfs, peasants, or slaves. The oppressed class may consist of wage laborers, in which case the system is properly labeled "capitalist." The power of the term lies in its implication that, in fact, there are alternatives to capitalism.

Similarly, any society will have some systematic ways to deal with sex, gender, and babies. Such a system may be sexually egalitarian, at least in theory, or it may be "gender stratified," as seems to be the case for most or all of the known examples. But it is important—even in the face of a depressing history—to maintain a distinction between the human capacity and necessity to create a sexual world, and the empirically oppressive ways in which sexual worlds have been organized. Patriarchy subsumes both meanings into the same term. Sex/gender system, on the other hand, is a neutral term which refers to the domain and indicates that oppression is not inevitable in that domain, but is the product of the specific social relations which organize it.

Finally, there are gender-stratified systems which are not adequately described as patriarchal. Many New Guinea societies (Enga, Maring, Bena Bena, Huli, Melpa, Kuma, Gahuku-Gama, Fore, Marind Anim, ad nauseum; see Berndt, 1962; Langness, 1967; Rappaport, 1975; Read, 1952; Meggitt, 1970; Glasse, 1971; Strathern, 1972; Reay, 1959; Van Baal, 1966; Lindenbaum, 1973) are viciously oppressive to women. But the power of males in these groups is not founded on their roles as fathers or patriarchs, but on their collective adult maleness, embodied in secret cults, men's houses, warfare, exchange networks, ritual knowledge, and various initiation procedures. Patriarchy is a specific form of male dominance, and the use of the term ought to be confined to the Old Testament-type pastoral nomads from whom the term comes, or groups like them. Abraham was a Patriarch—one old man whose absolute power over wives, children, herds, and dependents was an aspect of the institution of fatherhood, as defined in the social group in which he lived.

Whichever term we use, what is important is to develop concepts to adequately describe the social organization of sexuality and the reproduction of the conventions of sex and gender. We need to pursue the project Engels abandoned when he located the subordination of women in a development within the mode of production.[4] To do this, we can imitate Engels in his method rather than in his results. Engels approached the task of analyzing the "second aspect of material life" by way of an examination of a theory of kinship systems. Kinship systems are and do many things. But they are made up of, and reproduce, concrete forms of socially organized sexuality. Kinship systems are observable and empirical forms of sex/gender systems.

KINSHIP
(ON THE PART PLAYED BY SEXUALITY IN THE TRANSITION FROM APE TO "MAN")

To an anthropologist, a kinship system is not a list of biological relatives. It is a system of categories and statuses which often contradict actual genetic relationships. There are dozens of examples in

---

[4] Engels thought that men acquired wealth in the form of herds and, wanting to pass this wealth to their own children, overthrew "mother right" in favor of patrilineal inheritance. "The overthrow of mother right was the *world historical defeat of the female sex*. The man took command in the home also; the woman was degraded and reduced to servitude; she became the slave of his lust and a mere instrument for the production of children" (Engels, 1972:120–21; italics in original).As has been often pointed out women do not necessarily have significant social authority in societies practicing matrilineal inheritance (Schneider and Gough, 1962).

which socially defined kinship statuses take precedence over biology. The Nuer custom of "woman marriage" is a case in point. The Nuer define the status of fatherhood as belonging to the person in whose name cattle bridewealth is given for the mother. Thus, a woman can be married to another woman, and be husband to the wife and father of her children, despite the fact that she is not the inseminator (Evans-Pritchard, 1951:107–09).

In pre-state societies, kinship is the idiom of social interaction, organizing economic, political, and ceremonial, as well as sexual, activity. One's duties, responsibilities, and privileges vis-à-vis others are defined in terms of mutual kinship or lack thereof. The exchange of goods and services, production and distribution, hostility and solidarity, ritual and ceremony, all take place within the organizational structure of kinship. The ubiquity and adaptive effectiveness of kinship has led many anthropologists to consider its invention, along with the invention of language, to have been the developments which decisively marked the discontinuity between semi-human hominids and human beings (Sahlins, 1960; Livingstone, 1969; Lévi-Strauss, 1969).

While the idea of the importance of kinship enjoys the status of a first principle in anthropology, the internal workings of kinship systems have long been a focus for intense controversy. Kinship systems vary wildly from one culture to the next. They contain all sorts of bewildering rules which govern whom one may or may not marry. Their internal complexity is dazzling. Kinship systems have for decades provoked the anthropological imagination into trying to explain incest taboos, cross-cousin marriage, terms of descent, relationships of avoidance or forced intimacy, clans and sections, taboos on names—the diverse array of items found in descriptions of actual kinship systems. In the nineteenth century, several thinkers attempted to write comprehensive accounts of the nature and history of human sexual systems (see Fee, 1973). One of these was *Ancient Society,* by Lewis Henry Morgan. It was this book which inspired Engels to write *The Origin of the Family, Private Property, and the State*. Engels' theory is based upon Morgan's account of kinship and marriage.

In taking up Engels' project of extracting a theory of sex oppression from the study of kinship, we have the advantage of the maturation of ethnology since the nineteenth century. We also have the advantage of a peculiar and particularly appropriate book, Lévi-Strauss' *The Elementary Structures of Kinship*. This is the boldest twentieth-century version of the nineteenth-century project to understand human marriage. It is a book in which kinship is explicitly conceived of as an imposition of cultural organization upon the facts of biological procreation. It is permeated with an awareness of the importance of sexuality in human society. It is a description of society which does not assume an abstract, genderless human subject. On the contrary, the human subject in Lévi-Strauss's work is always either male or female, and the divergent social destinies of the two sexes can therefore be traced. Since Lévi-Strauss sees the essence of kinship systems to lie in an exchange of women between men, he constructs an implicit theory of sex oppression. Aptly, the book is dedicated to the memory of Lewis Henry Morgan.

"VILE AND PRECIOUS MERCHANDISE"

—Monique Wittig

The Elementary Structures of Kinship is a grand statement on the origin and nature of human society. It is a treatise on the kinship systems of approximately one-third of the ethnographic globe. Most fundamentally, it is an attempt to discern the structural principles of kinship. Lévi-Strauss argues that the application of these principles (summarized in the last chapter of *Elementary Structures*) to kinship data reveals an intelligible logic to the taboos and marriage rules which have perplexed and mystified Western anthropologists. He constructs a chess game of such complexity that it cannot be recapitulated here. But two of his chess pieces are particularly relevant to women—the "gift" and the incest taboo, whose dual articulation adds up to his concept of the exchange of women.

The Elementary Structures is in part a radical gloss on another famous theory of primitive social organization, Mauss' *Essay on the Gift* (See also Sahlins, 1972:Chap. 4). It was Mauss who first theorized as to the significance of one of the most striking features of primitive societies: the extent to which giving, receiving, and reciprocating gifts dominates social intercourse. In such societies, all sorts of things circulate in exchange—food, spells, rituals, words, names, ornaments, tools, and powers.

> Your own mother, your own sister, your own pigs, your own yams that you have piled up, you may not eat. Other people's mothers, other people's sisters, other people's pigs, other people's yams that they have piled up, you may eat. (Arapesh, cited in Lévi-Strauss, 1969:27)

In a typical gift transaction, neither party gains anything. In the Trobriand Islands, each household maintains a garden of yams and each household eats yams. But the yams a household grows and the yams it eats are not the same. At harvest time, a man sends the yams he has cultivated to the household of his sister; the household in which he lives is provisioned by his wife's brother (Malinowski, 1929). Since such a procedure appears to be a useless one from the point of view of accumulation or trade, its logic has been sought elsewhere. Mauss proposed that the significance of gift giving is that it expresses, affirms, or creates a social link between the partners of an exchange. Gift giving confers upon its participants a special relationship of trust, solidarity, and mutual aid. One can solicit a friendly relationship in the offer of a gift; acceptance implies a willingness to return a gift and a confirmation of the relationship. Gift exchange may also be the idiom of competition and rivalry. There are many examples in which one person humiliates another by giving more than can be reciprocated. Some political systems, such as the Big Man systems of highland New Guinea, are based on exchange which is unequal on the material plane. An aspiring Big Man

wants to give away more goods than can be reciprocated. He gets his return in political prestige.

Although both Mauss and Lévi-Strauss emphasize the solidary aspects of gift exchange, the other purposes served by gift giving only strengthen the point that it is an ubiquitous means of social commerce. Mauss proposed that gifts were the threads of social discourse, the means by which such societies were held together in the absence of specialized governmental institutions. "The gift is the primitive way of achieving the peace that in civil society is secured by the state. . . . Composing society, the gift was the liberation of culture" (Sahlins, 1972:169,175).

Lévi-Strauss adds to the theory of primitive reciprocity the idea that marriages are a most basic form of gift exchange, in which it is women who are the most precious of gifts. He argues that the incest taboo should best be understood as a mechanism to insure that such exchanges take place between families and between groups. Since the existence of incest taboos is universal, but the content of their prohibitions variable, they cannot be explained as having the aim of preventing the occurrence of genetically close matings. Rather, the incest taboo imposes the social aim of exogamy and alliance upon the biological events of sex and procreation. The incest taboo divides the universe of sexual choice into categories of permitted and prohibited sexual partners. Specifically, by forbidding unions within a group it enjoins marital exchange between groups.

> The prohibition on the sexual use of a daughter or a sister compels them to be given in marriage to another man, and at the same time it establishes a right to the daughter or sister of this other man. . . . The woman whom one does not take is, for that very reason, offered up. (Lévi-Strauss, 1969:51)

> The prohibition of incest is less a rule prohibiting marriage with the mother, sister, or daughter, than a rule obliging the mother, sister, or daughter to be given to others. It is the supreme rule of the gift. . . . (Ibid.:481)

The result of a gift of women is more profound than the result of other gift transactions, because the relationship thus established is not just one of reciprocity, but one of kinship. The exchange partners have become affines, and their descendents will be related by blood: "Two people may meet in friendship and exchange gifts and yet quarrel and fight in later times, but intermarriage connects them in a permanent manner" (Best, cited in Lévi-Strauss, 1969:481). As is the case with other gift giving, marriages are not always so simply activities to make peace. Marriages may be highly competitive, and there are plenty of affines who fight each other. Nevertheless, in a general sense the argument is that the taboo on incest results in a wide network of relations, a set of people whose connections with one another are a kinship structure. All other levels, amounts, and directions of exchange—including hostile ones—are ordered by this structure. The marriage ceremonies recorded in the ethnographic literature are moments in a ceaseless and ordered procession in which women, children, shells, words, cattle names, fish, ancestors, whale's teeth, pigs, yams, spells, dances, mats, etc., pass from hand to hand, leaving as their tracks the ties that bind. Kinship is organization, and organization gives power. But who is organized?

If it is women who are being transacted, then it is the men who give and take them who are linked, the woman being a conduit of a relationship rather than a partner to it.[5] The exchange of women does not necessarily imply that women are objectified, in the modern sense, since objects in the primitive world are imbued with highly personal qualities. But it does imply a distinction between gift and giver. If women are the gifts, then it is men who are the exchange partners. And it is the partners, not the presents, upon whom reciprocal exchange confers its quasi-mystical power of social linkage. The relations of such a system are such that women are in no position to realize the benefits of their own circulation. As long as the relations specify that men exchange women, it is men who are the beneficiaries of the product of such exchanges—social organization.

> The total relationship of exchange which constitutes marriage is not established between a man and a woman, but between two groups of men, and the woman figures only as one of the objects in the exchange, not as one of the partners. . . . This remains true even when the girl's feelings are taken into consideration, as, moreover, is usually the case. In acquiescing to the proposed union, she precipitates or allows the exchange to take place, she cannot alter its nature. . . . (Lévi-Strauss in ibid.:115)[6]

To enter into a gift exchange as a partner, one must have something to give. If women are for men to dispose of, they are in no position to give themselves away.

> "What woman," mused a young Northern Melpa man, "is ever strong enough to get up and say, 'Let us make *moka*, let us find wives and pigs, let us give our daughters to men, let us wage war, let us kill our enemies!' No indeed not! . . . they are little rubbish things who stay at home simply, don't you see?" (Strathern, 1972:161)

What women indeed! The Melpa women of whom the young man spoke can't get wives, they *are* wives, and what they get are husbands, an entirely different matter. The Melpa women can't give their daughters to men, because they do not have the same rights in their daughters that their male kin have, rights of bestowal (although *not* of ownership).

---

[5] "What, would you like to marry your sister? What is the matter with you? Don't you want a brother-in-law? Don't you realize that if you marry another man's sister and another man marries your sister, you will have at least two brothers-in-law, while if you marry your own sister you will have none? With whom will you hunt, with whom will you garden, whom will you go visit?" (Arapesh, cited in Lévi-Strauss, 1969:485).

[6] This analysis of society as based on bonds between men by means of women makes the separatist responses of the women's movement thoroughly intelligible. Separatism can be seen as a mutation in social structure, as an attempt to form social groups based on unmediated bonds between women. It can also be seen as a radical denial of men's "rights" in women, and as a claim by women of rights in themselves.

The "exchange of women" is a seductive and powerful concept. It is attractive in that it places the oppression of women within social systems, rather than in biology. Moreover, it suggests that we look for the ultimate locus of women's oppression within the traffic in women, rather than within the traffic in merchandise. It is certainly not difficult to find ethnographic and historical examples of trafficking in women. Women are given in marriage, taken in battle, exchanged for favors, sent as tribute, traded, bought, and sold. Far from being confined to the "primitive" world, these practices seem only to become more pronounced and commercialized in more "civilized" societies. Men are of course also trafficked—but as slaves, hustlers, athletic stars, serfs, or as some other catastrophic social status, rather than as men. Women are transacted as slaves, serfs, and prostitutes, but also simply as women. And if men have been sexual subjects—exchangers—and women sexual semi-objects—gifts—for much of human history, then many customs, clichés, and personality traits seem to make a great deal of sense (among others, the curious custom by which a father gives away the bride).

The "exchange of women" is also a problematic concept. Since Lévi-Strauss argues that the incest taboo and the results of its application constitute the origin of culture, it can be deduced that the world historical defeat of women occurred with the origin of culture, and is a prerequisite of culture. If his analysis is adopted in its pure form, the feminist program must include a task even more onerous than the extermination of men; it must attempt to get rid of culture and substitute some entirely new phenomena on the face of the earth. However, it would be a dubious proposition at best to argue that if there were no exchange of women there would be no culture, if for no other reason than that culture is, by definition, inventive. It is even debatable that "exchange of women" adequately describes all of the empirical evidence of kinship systems. Some cultures, such as the Lele and the Luma, exchange women explicitly and overtly. In other cultures, the exchange of women can be

inferred. In some—particularly those hunters and gatherers excluded from Lévi-Strauss's sample—the efficacy of the concept becomes altogether questionable. What are we to make of a concept which seems so useful and yet so difficult?

The "exchange of women" is neither a definition of culture nor a system in and of itself. The concept is an acute, but condensed, apprehension of certain aspects of the social relations of sex and gender. A kinship system is an imposition of social ends upon a part of the natural world. It is therefore "production" in the most general sense of the term: a molding, a transformation of objects (in this case, people) to and by a subjective purpose (for this sense of production, see Marx, 1971a:80-99). It has its own relations of production, distribution, and exchange, which include certain "property" forms in people. These forms are not exclusive, private property rights, but rather different sorts of rights that various people have in other people. Marriage transactions—the gifts and material which circulate in the ceremonies marking a marriage—are a rich source of data for determining exactly who has which rights in whom. It is not difficult to deduce from such transactions that in most cases women's rights are considerably more residual than those of men.

Kinship systems do not merely exchange women. They exchange sexual access, genealogical statuses, lineage names and ancestors, rights and *people*—men, women, and children—in concrete systems of social relationships. These relationships always include certain rights for men, others for women. "Exchange of women" is a shorthand for expressing that the social relations of a kinship system specify that men have certain rights in their female kin, and that women do not have the same rights either to themselves or to their male kin. In this sense, the exchange of women is a profound perception of a system in which women do not have full rights to themselves. The exchange of women becomes an obfuscation if it is seen as a cultural necessity, and when it is used as the single tool with which an analysis of a particular kinship system is approached.

If Lévi-Strauss is correct in seeing the ex-change of women as a fundamental principle of kinship, the subordination of women can be seen as a product of the relationships by which sex and gender are organized and produced. The economic oppression of women is derivative and secondary. But there is an "economics" of sex and gender, and what we need is a political economy of sexual systems. We need to study each soci-ety to determine the exact mechanisms by which particular conventions of sexuality are produced and maintained. The "exchange of women" is an initial step toward building an arsenal of concepts with which sexual systems can be described.

DEEPER INTO THE LABYRINTH

More concepts can be derived from an essay by Lévi-Strauss, "The Family," in which he in-troduces other considerations into his analy-sis of kinship. In *The Elementary Structures of Kinship,* he describes rules and systems of sexual combination. In "The Family," he raises the issue of the preconditions necessary for marriage sys-tems to operate. He asks what sort of "people" are required by kinship systems, by way of an analysis of the sexual division of labor.

Although every society has some sort of divi-sion of tasks by sex, the assignment of any particu-lar task to one sex or the other varies enormously. In some groups, agriculture is the work of women, in others, the work of men. Women carry the heavy burdens in some societies, men in others. There are even examples of female hunters and warriors, and of men performing child-care tasks. Lévi-Strauss concludes from a survey of the division of labor by sex that it is not a biological specialization, but must have some other purpose. This purpose, he argues, is to insure the union of men and women by making the smallest viable economic unit con-tain at least one man and one woman.

> The very fact that it [the sexual division of labor] varies endlessly according to the society selected for consideration shows that . . . it is the mere fact of its existence which is mysteriously required,

the form under which it comes to exist being ut-terly irrelevant, at least from the point of view of any natural necessity . . . the sexual division of la-bor is nothing else than a device to institute a re-ciprocal state of dependency between the sexes. (Lévi-Strauss, 1971:347-48)

The division of labor by sex can therefore be seen as a "taboo": a taboo against the sameness of men and women, a taboo dividing the sexes into two mutually exclusive categories, a taboo which ex-acerbates the biological differences between the sexes and thereby *creates* gender. The division of labor can also be seen as a taboo against sexual arrangements other than those containing at least one man and one woman, thereby enjoining het-erosexual marriage.

The argument in "The Family" displays a radical questioning of all human sexual arrange-ments, in which no aspect of sexuality is taken for granted as "natural" (Hertz, 1960, constructs a similar argument for a thoroughly cultural ex-planation of the denigration of left-handedness). Rather, all manifest forms of sex and gender are seen as being constituted by the imperatives of social systems. From such a perspective, even *The Elementary Structures of Kinship* can be seen to assume certain preconditions. In purely logical terms, a rule forbidding some marriages and commanding others presupposes a rule en-joining marriage. And marriage presupposes in-dividuals who are disposed to marry.

It is of interest to carry this kind of deductive enterprise even further than Lévi-Strauss does, and to explicate the logical structure which un-derlies his entire analysis of kinship. At the most general level, the social organization of sex rests upon gender, obligatory heterosexuality, and the constraint of female sexuality.

Gender is a socially imposed division of the sexes. It is a product of the social relations of sex-uality. Kinship systems rest upon marriage. They therefore transform males and females into "men" and "women," each an incomplete half which can only find wholeness when united with the other. Men and women are, of course, different. But they are not as different as day and night, earth and sky, yin and yang, life and death. In fact, from the standpoint of nature, men and women are closer to each other than either is to anything else—for instance, mountains, kangaroos, or coconut palms. The idea that men and women are more different from one another than either is from anything else must come from somewhere other than nature. Furthermore, although there is an average difference between males and females on a variety of traits, the range of variation of those traits shows considerable overlap. There will always be some women who are taller than some men, for instance, even though men are on the average taller than women. But the idea that men and women are two mutually exclusive categories must arise out of something other than a nonexistent "natural" opposition.[7] Far from being an expression of natural differences, exclusive gender identity is the suppression of natural similarities. It requires repression: in men, of whatever is the local version of "feminine" traits; in women, of the local definition of "masculine" traits. The division of the sexes has the effect of repressing some of the personality characteristics of virtually everyone, men and women. The same social system which oppresses women in its relations of exchange, oppresses everyone in its insistence upon a rigid division of personality.

Furthermore, individuals are engendered in order that marriage be guaranteed. Lévi-Strauss comes dangerously close to saying that heterosexuality is an instituted process. If biological and hormonal imperatives were as overwhelming as popular mythology would have them, it would hardly be necessary to insure heterosexual unions by means of economic interdependency. Moreover, the incest taboo presupposes a prior, less articulate taboo on homosexuality. A prohibition against *some* heterosexual unions assumes a taboo against

non-heterosexual unions. Gender is not only an identification with one sex; it also entails that sexual desire be directed toward the other sex. The sexual division of labor is implicated in both aspects of gender—male and female it creates them, and it creates them heterosexual. The suppression of the homosexual component of human sexuality, and by corollary, the oppression of homosexuals, is therefore a product of the same system whose rules and relations oppress women.

In fact, the situation is not so simple, as is obvious when we move from the level of generalities to the analysis of specific sexual systems. Kinship systems do not merely encourage heterosexuality to the detriment of homosexuality. In the first place, specific forms of heterosexuality may be required. For instance, some marriage systems have a rule of obligatory cross-cousin marriage. A person in such a system is not only heterosexual, but "cross-cousin-sexual." If the rule of marriage further specifies matrilateral cross-cousin marriage, then a man will be "mother's-brother's-daughter-sexual" and a woman will be "father's-sister's-son-sexual."

On the other hand, the very complexities of a kinship system may result in particular forms of institutionalized homosexuality. In many New Guinea groups, men and women are considered to be so inimical to one another that the period spent by a male child *in utero* negates his maleness. Since male life force is thought to reside in semen, the boy can overcome the malevolent effects of his fetal history by obtaining and consuming semen. He does so through a homosexual partnership with an older male kinsman (Kelly, 1974; see also Van Baal, 1966; Williams, 1936).

In kinship systems where bridewealth determines the statuses of husband and wife, the simple prerequisites of marriage and gender may be overridden. Among the Azande, women are monopolized by older men. A young man of means may, however, take a boy as wife while he waits to come of age. He simply pays a bridewealth (in spears) for the boy, who is thereby turned into a wife (Evans-Pritchard, 1970). In Dahomey, a woman

---

[7] "The woman shall not wear that which pertaineth unto a man, neither shall a man put on a woman's garment: for all that do so *are* abomination unto the LORD thy God" (Deuteronomy, 22:5; emphasis not mine).

could turn herself into a husband if she possessed the necessary bridewealth (Herskovitz, 1937).

The institutionalized "transvesticism" of the Mohave permitted a person to change from one sex to the other. An anatomical man could become a woman by means of a special ceremony, and an anatomical woman could in the same way become a man. The transvestite then took a wife or husband of her/his own anatomical sex and opposite social sex. These marriages, which we would label homosexual, were heterosexual ones by Mohave standards, unions of opposite socially defined sexes. By comparison with our society, this whole arrangement permitted a great deal of freedom. However, a person was not permitted to be some of both genders—he/she could be either male female, but not a little of each (Devereaux, 1937; see also McMurtrie, 1914; Sonenschein, 1966).

In all of the above examples, the rules of gender division and obligatory heterosexuality are present even in their transformations. These two rules apply equally to the constraint of both male and female behavior and personality. Kinship systems dictate some sculpting of the sexuality of both sexes. But it can be deduced from *The Elementary Structures of Kinship* that more constraint is applied to females when they are pressed into the service of kinship than to males. If women are exchanged, in whatever sense we take the term, marital debts are reckoned in female flesh. A woman must become the sexual partner of some man to whom she is owed as return on a previous marriage. If a girl is promised in infancy, her refusal to participate as an adult would disrupt the flow of debts and promises. It would be in the interests of the smooth and continuous operation of such a system if the woman in question did not have too many ideas of her own about whom she might want to sleep with. From the standpoint of the system, the preferred female sexuality would be one which responded to the desire of others, rather than one which actively desired and sought a response.

This generality, like the ones about gender and heterosexuality, is also subject to considerable

variation and free play in actual systems. The Lele and the Kuma provide two of the clearest ethnographic examples of the exchange of women. Men in both cultures are perpetually engaged in schemes which necessitate that they have full control over the sexual destinies of their female kinswomen. Much of the drama in both societies consists in female attempts to evade the sexual control of their kinsmen. Nevertheless, female resistance in both cases is severely circumscribed (Douglas, 1963; Reay, 1959).

One last generality could be predicted as a consequence of the exchange of women under a system in which rights to women are held by men. What would happen if our hypothetical woman not only refused the man to whom she was promised, but asked for a woman instead? If a single refusal were disruptive, a double refusal would be insurrectionary. If each woman is promised to some man, neither has a right to dispose of herself. If two women managed to extricate themselves from the debt nexus, two other women would have to be found to replace them. As long as men have rights in women which women do not have in themselves, it would be sensible to expect that homosexuality in women would be subject to more suppression than in men.

In summary, some basic generalities about the organization of human sexuality can be derived from an exegesis of Lévi-Strauss's theories of kinship. These are the incest taboo, obligatory heterosexuality, and an asymmetric division of the sexes. The asymmetry of gender—the difference between exchanger and exchanged—entails the constraint of female sexuality. Concrete kinship systems will have more specific conventions, and these conventions vary a great deal. While particular socio-sexual systems vary, each one is specific, and individuals within it will have to conform to a finite set of possibilities. Each new generation must learn and become its sexual destiny, each person must be encoded with its appropriate status within the system. It would be extraordinary for one of us to calmly assume that we would conventionally marry a mother's brother's daughter, or a father's sister's son. Yet there are groups in which such a marital future is taken for granted.

Anthropology, and descriptions of kinship systems, do not explain the mechanisms by which children are engraved with the conventions of sex and gender. Psychoanalysis, on the other hand, is a theory about the reproduction of kinship. Psychoanalysis describes the residue left within individuals by their confrontation with the rules and regulations of sexuality of the societies to which they are born.

PSYCHOANALYSIS AND ITS DISCONTENTS

The battle between psychoanalysis and the women's and gay movements has become legendary. In part, this confrontation between sexual revolutionaries and the clinical establishment has been due to the evolution of psychoanalysis in the United States, where clinical tradition has fetishized anatomy. The child is thought to travel through its organismic stages until it reaches its anatomical destiny and the missionary position. Clinical practice has often seen its mission as the repair of individuals who somehow have become derailed en route to their "biological" aim. Transforming moral law into scientific law, clinical practice has acted to enforce sexual convention upon unruly participants. In this sense, psychoanalysis has often become more than a theory of the mechanisms of the reproduction of sexual arrangements; it has been one of those mechanisms. Since the aim of the feminist and gay revolts is to dismantle the apparatus of sexual enforcement, a critique of psychoanalysis has been in order.

But the rejection of Freud by the women's and gay movements has deeper roots in the rejection by psychoanalysis of its own insights. Nowhere are the effects on women of male-dominated social systems better documented than within the clinical literature. According to the Freudian orthodoxy, the attainment of "normal" femininity extracts severe costs from women. The theory of gender acquisition could have been the basis of a critique

of sex roles. Instead, the radical implications of Freud's theory have been radically repressed. This tendency is evident even in the original formulations of the theory, but it has been exacerbated over time until the potential for a critical psychoanalytic theory of gender is visible only in the symptomatology of its denial—an intricate rationalization of sex roles as they are. It is not the purpose of this paper to conduct a psychoanalysis of the psychoanalytic unconscious; but I do hope to demonstrate that it exists. Moreover, the salvage of psychoanalysis from its own motivated repression is not for the sake of Freud's good name. Psychoanalysis contains a unique set of concepts for understanding men, women, and sexuality. It is a theory of sexuality in human society. Most importantly, psychoanalysis provides a description of the mechanisms by which the sexes are divided and deformed, of how bisexual, androgynous infants are transformed into boys and girls.[8] Psychoanalysis is a feminist theory *manqué*.

THE OEDIPUS HEX

Until the late 1920s, the psychoanalytic movement did not have a distinctive theory of feminine development. Instead, variants of an "Electra" complex in women had been proposed, in which female experience was thought to be a mirror image of the Oedipal complex described for males. The boy loved his mother, but gave her up out of fear of the father's threat of castration. The girl, it was thought, loved her father, and gave him up out

---

[8] "In studying women we cannot neglect the methods of a science of the mind, a theory that attempts to explain how women become women and men, men. The borderline between the biological and the social which finds expression in the family is the land psychoanalysis sets out to chart, the land where sexual distinction originates." (Mitchell, 1971:167)

"What is the *object* of psychoanalysis? . . . but the '*effects*,' prolonged into the surviving adult, of the extraordinary adventure which from birth the liquidation of the Oedipal phase transforms a small animal conceived by a man and a woman into a small human child . . . the 'effects' still present in the survivors of the forced 'humanization' of the small human animal into a *man* or a *woman*. . . ." (Althusser, 1969:57, 59; italics in original)

of fear of maternal vengeance. This formulation assumed that both children were subject to a biological imperative toward heterosexuality. It also assumed that the children were already, before the Oedipal phase, "little" men and women.

Freud had voiced reservations about jumping to conclusions about women on the basis of data gathered from men. But his objections remained general until the discovery of the pre-Oedipal phase in women. The concept of the pre-Oedipal phase enabled both Freud and Jeanne Lampl de Groot to articulate the classic psychoanalytic theory of femininity.[9] The idea of the pre-Oedipal phase in women produced a dislocation of the biologically derived presuppositions which underlay notions of an "Electra" complex. In the pre-Oedipal phase, children of both sexes were psychically indistinguishable, which meant that their differentiation into masculine and feminine children had to be explained, rather than assumed. Pre-Oedipal children were described as bisexual. Both sexes exhibited the full range of libidinal attitudes, active and passive. And for children of both sexes, the mother was the object of desire.

In particular, the characteristics of the pre-Oedipal female challenged the ideas of a primordial heterosexuality and gender identity. Since the girl's libidinal activity was directed toward the mother, her adult heterosexuality had to be explained:

> It would be a solution of ideal simplicity if we could suppose that from a particular age onwards the elementary influence of the mutual attraction between the sexes makes itself felt and impels the small woman towards men. . . . But we are not going to find things so easy; we scarcely know whether we are to believe seriously in the power of which poets talk so much and with such enthusiasm but which cannot be further dissected analytically. (Freud, 1965:119)

Moreover, the girl did not manifest a "feminine" libidinal attitude. Since her desire for the mother was active and aggressive, her ultimate accession to "femininity" had also to be explained:

> In conformity with its peculiar nature, psychoanalysis does not try to describe what a woman is . . . but sets about enquiring how she comes into being, how a woman develops out of a child with a bisexual disposition. (Ibid.:116)

In short, feminine development could no longer be taken for granted as a reflex of biology. Rather, it had become immensely problematic. It is in explaining the acquisition of "femininity" that Freud employs the concepts of penis envy and castration which have infuriated feminists since he first introduced them. The girl turns from the mother and represses the "masculine" elements of her libido as a result of her recognition that she is castrated. She compares her tiny clitoris to the larger penis, and in the face of its evident superior ability to satisfy the mother, falls prey to penis envy and a sense of inferiority. She gives up her struggle for the mother and assumes a passive feminine position vis-à-vis the father. Freud's account can be read as claiming that femininity is a consequence of the anatomical differences between the sexes. He has therefore been accused of biological determinism. Nevertheless, even in his most anatomically stated versions of the female castration complex, the "inferiority" of the woman's genitals is a product of the situational context: the girl feels less "equipped" to possess and satisfy the mother.

---

[9]The psychoanalytic theories of femininity were articulated in the context of a debate which took place largely in the *International Journal of Psychoanalysis* and *The Psychoanalytic Quarterly* in the late 1920s and early 1930s. Articles representing the range of discussion include: Freud, 1961a, 1961b, 1965; Lampl de Groot, 1933, 1948; Deutsch, 1948a, 1948b; Horney, 1973; Jones, 1933. Some of my dates are of reprints; for the original chronology, see Chasseguet-Smirgel (1970: introduction). The debate was complex, and I have simplified it. Freud, Lampl de Groot, and Deutsch argued that femininity developed out of a bisexual, "phallic" girl-child; Horney and Jones argued for an innate femininity. The debate was not without its ironies. Horney defended women against penis envy by postulating that women are born and not made; Deutsch, who considered women to be made and not born, developed a theory of feminine masochism whose best rival is *Story of O*. I have attributed the core of the "Freudian" version of female development equally to Freud and to Lampl de Groot. In reading through the articles, it has seemed to me that the theory is as much (or more) hers as it is his.

If the pre-Oedipal lesbian were not confronted by the heterosexuality of the mother, she might draw different conclusions about the relative status of her genitals.

Freud was never as much of a biological determinist as some would have him. He repeatedly stressed that all adult sexuality resulted from psychic, not biologic, development. But his writing is often ambiguous, and his wording leaves plenty of room for the biological interpretations which have been so popular in American psychoanalysis. In France, on the other hand, the trend in psychoanalytic theory has been to de-biologize Freud, and to conceive of psychoanalysis as a theory of information rather than organs. Jacques Lacan, the instigator of this line of thinking, insists that Freud never meant to say anything about anatomy, and that Freud's theory was instead about language and the cultural meanings imposed upon anatomy. The debate over the "real" Freud is extremely interesting, but it is not my purpose here to contribute to it. Rather, I want to rephrase the classic theory of femininity in Lacan's terminology, after introducing some of the pieces on Lacan's conceptual chessboard.

KINSHIP, LACAN, AND THE PHALLUS

Lacan suggests that psychoanalysis is the study of the traces left in the psyches of individuals as a result of their conscription into systems of kinship.

> Isn't it striking that Lévi-Strauss, in suggesting that implication of the structures of language with that part of the social laws which regulate marriage ties and kinship, is already conquering the very terrain in which Freud situates the unconscious? (Lacan, 1968:48)

> For where on earth would one situate the determinations of the unconsciousness if it is not in those nominal cadres in which marriage ties and kinship are always grounded. . . . And how would one apprehend the analytical conflicts and their Oedipean prototype outside the engagements which have fixed, long before the subject came into the world, not only his destiny, but his identity itself? (Ibid.:126)

> This is precisely where the Oedipus complex . . . may be said, in this connection, to mark the limits which our discipline assigns to subjectivity: that is to say, what the subject can know of his unconscious participation in the movement of the complex structures of marriage ties, by verifying the symbolic effects in his individual existence of the tangential movement towards incest. . . . (Ibid.:40)

Kinship is the culturalization of biological sexuality on the societal level; psychoanalysis describes the transformation of the biological sexuality of individuals as they are enculturated.

Kinship terminology contains information about the system. Kin terms demarcate statuses, and indicate some of the attributes of those statuses. For instance, in the Trobriand Islands a man calls the women of his clan by the term for "sister." He calls the women of clans into which he can marry by a term indicating their marriageability. When the young Trobriand male learns these terms, he learns which women he can safely desire. In Lacan's scheme, the Oedipal crisis occurs when a child learns of the sexual rules embedded in the terms for family and relatives. The crisis begins when the child comprehends the system and his or her place in it; the crisis is resolved when the child accepts that place and accedes to it. Even if the child refuses its place, he or she cannot escape knowledge of it. Before the Oedipal phase, the sexuality of the child is labile and relatively unstructured. Each child contains all of the sexual possibilities available to human expression. But in any given society, only some of these possibilities will be expressed, while others will be constrained. When the child leaves the Oedipal phase, its libido and gender identity have been organized in conformity with the rules of the culture which is domesticating it.

The Oedipal complex is an apparatus for the production of sexual personality. It is a truism to say that societies will inculcate in their young the character traits appropriate to carrying on the business of society. For instance, E. P. Thompson (1963) speaks of the transformation of the personality structure of the English working class, as artisans were changed into good industrial workers. Just as the social forms of labor demand certain kinds of personality, the social forms of sex and gender demand certain kinds of people. In the most general terms, the Oedipal complex is a machine which fashions the appropriate forms of sexual individuals (see also the discussion of different forms of "historical individuality" in Althusser and Balibar, 1970:112, 251–53).

In the Lacanian theory of psychoanalysis, it is the kin terms that indicate a structure of relationships which will determine the role of any individual or object within the Oedipal drama. For instance, Lacan makes a distinction between the "function of the father" and a particular father who embodies this function. In the same way, he makes a radical distinction between the penis and the "phallus," between organ and information. The phallus is a set of meanings conferred upon the penis. The differentiation between phallus and penis in contemporary French psychoanalytic terminology emphasizes the idea that the penis could not and does not play the role attributed to it in the classical terminology of the castration complex.[10]

In Freud's terminology, the Oedipal complex presents two alternatives to a child: to have a penis or to be castrated. In contrast, the Lacanian theory of the castration complex leaves behind all reference to anatomical reality:

> The theory of the castration complex amounts to having the male organ play a dominant role—this time as a symbol—*to the extent that its absence or presence transforms an anatomical difference into a major classification of humans, and to the extent that, for each subject, this presence or absence is not taken for granted, is not reduced purely and simply to a given, but is the problematical result of an intra- and intersubjective process* (the subject's assumption of his own sex). (Laplanche and Pontalis, in Mehlman, 1972:198-99; my italics)

The alternative presented to the child may be rephrased as an alternative between having, or not having, the phallus. Castration is not having the (symbolic) phallus. Castration is not a real "lack," but a meaning conferred upon the genitals of a woman:

> Castration may derive support from . . . the apprehension in the Real of the absence of the penis in women—but even this supposes a symbolization of the object, since the Real is full, and "lacks" nothing. Insofar as one finds castration in the genesis of neurosis, it is never real but symbolic. . . . (Lacan, 1968:271)

The phallus is, as it were, a distinctive feature differentiating "castrated" and "noncastrated." The presence or absence of the phallus carries the differences between two sexual statuses, "man" and "woman" (see Jakobson and Halle, 1971, on distinctive features). Since these are not equal, the phallus also carries a meaning of the dominance of men over women, and it may be inferred that "penis envy" is a recognition thereof. Moreover, as long as men have rights in women which women do not have in themselves, the phallus also carries the meaning of the difference between "exchanger" and "exchanged," gift and giver. Ultimately, neither the classical Freudian nor the rephrased Lacanian theories of the Oedipal process make sense unless at least this much of the paleolithic relations of sexuality are still with us. We still live in a "phallic" culture.

Lacan also speaks of the phallus as a symbolic object which is exchanged within and between families (see also Wilden, 1968:303–305). It is interesting to think about this observation in terms of primitive marriage transactions and exchange networks. In those transactions, the exchange of women is usually one of many cycles of exchange. Usually, there are other objects circulating as well

---

[10] I have taken my position on Freud somewhere between the French structuralist interpretations and American biologistic ones, because I think that Freud's wording is similarly somewhere in the middle. He does talk about penises, about the "inferiority" of the clitoris, about the psychic consequences of anatomy. The Lacanians, on the other hand, argue from Freud's text that he is unintelligible if his words are taken literally, and that a thoroughly nonanatomical theory can be deduced as Freud's intention (see Althusser, 1969). I think that they are right; the penis is walking around too much for its role to be taken literally. The detachability of the penis, and its transformation in fantasy (e.g., penis = feces = child = gift), argue strongly for a symbolic interpretation. Nevertheless, I don't think that Freud was as consistent as either I or Lacan would like him to have been, and some gesture must be made to what he said, even as we play with what he must have meant.

as women. Women move in one direction, cattle, shells, or mats in the other. In one sense, the Oedipal complex is an expression of the circulation of the phallus in intrafamily exchange, an inversion of the circulation of women in interfamily exchange. In the cycle of exchange manifested by the Oedipal complex, the phallus passes through the medium of women from one man to another—from father to son, from mother's brother to sister's son, and so forth. In this family *Kula* ring, women go one way, the phallus the other. It is where we aren't. In this sense, the phallus is more than a feature which distinguishes the sexes: it is the embodiment of the male status, to which men accede, and in which certain rights inhere—among them, the right to a woman. It is an expression of the transmission of male dominance. It passes through women and settles upon men.[11] The tracks which it leaves include gender identity, the division of the sexes. But it leaves more than this. It leaves "penis envy," which acquires a rich meaning of the disquietude of women in a phallic culture.

OEDIPUS REVISITED

We return now to the two pre-Oedipal androgynes, sitting on the border between biology and culture. Lévi-Strauss places the incest taboo on that border, arguing that its initiation of the exchange of women constitutes the origin of society. In this sense, the incest taboo and the exchange of women are the content of the original social contract (see Sahlins, 1972: Chap. 4). For individuals, the Oedipal crisis occurs at the same divide, when the incest taboo initiates the exchange of the phallus.

The Oedipal crisis is precipitated by certain items of information. The children discover the differences between the sexes, and that each child must become one or the other gender. They also discover the incest taboo, and that some sexuality is prohibited—in this case, the mother is unavailable to either child because she "belongs" to the father. Lastly, they discover that the two genders do not have the same sexual "rights" or futures.

In the normal course of events, the boy renounces his mother for fear that otherwise his father would castrate him (refuse to give him the phallus and make him a girl). But by this act of renunciation, the boy affirms the relationships which have given mother to father and which will give him, if he becomes a man, a woman of his own. In exchange for the boy's affirmation of his father's right to his mother, the father affirms the phallus in his son (does not castrate him). The boy exchanges his mother for the phallus, the symbolic token which can later be exchanged for a woman. The only thing required of him is a little patience. He retains his initial libidinal organization and the sex of his original love object. The social contract to which he has agreed will eventually recognize his own rights and provide him with a woman of his own.

What happens to the girl is more complex. She, like the boy, discovers the taboo against incest and the division of the sexes. She also discovers some unpleasant information about the gender to which she is being assigned. For the boy, the taboo on incest is a taboo on certain women. For the girl, it is a taboo on all women. Since she is in a homosexual position vis-à-vis the mother, the rule of heterosexuality which dominates the scenario makes her position excruciatingly untenable. The mother, and all women by extension, can only be properly beloved by someone "with a penis" (phallus). Since the girl has no "phallus," she has no "right" to love her mother or

---

[11] The pre-Oedipal mother is the "phallic mother," e.g., she is believed to possess the phallus. The Oedipal-inducing information is that the mother does not possess the phallus. In other words, the crisis is precipitated by the "castration" of the mother, by the recognition that the phallus only passes through her, but does not settle on her. The "phallus" must pass through her, since the relationship of a male to every other male is defined through a woman. A man is linked to a son by a mother, to his nephew by virtue of a sister, etc. Every relationship between male kin is defined by the woman between them. If power is a male prerogative, and must be passed on, it must go through the woman-in-between. Marshall Sahlins (personal communication) once suggested that the reason women are so often defined as stupid, polluting, disorderly, silly, profane, or whatever, is that such categorizations define women as "incapable" of possessing the power which must be transferred through them.

another woman, since she is herself destined to some man. She does not have the symbolic token which can be exchanged for a woman.

If Freud's wording of this moment of the female Oedipal crisis is ambiguous, Lampl de Groot's formulation makes the context which confers meaning upon the genitals explicit:

> . . . *if the little girl comes to the conclusion that such an organ is really indispensable to the possession of the mother, she experiences* in addition to the narcissistic insults common to both sexes still another blow, namely *a feeling of inferiority about her genitals.* (Lampl de Groot, 1933:497; my italics)

The girl concludes that the "penis" is indispensable for the possession of the mother because only those who possess the phallus have a "right" to a woman, and the token of exchange. She does not come to her conclusion because of the natural superiority of the penis either in and of itself, or as an instrument for making love. The hierarchical arrangement of the male and female genitals is a result of the definitions of the situation—the rule of obligatory heterosexuality and the relegation of women (those without the phallus, castrated) to men (those with the phallus).

The girl then begins to turn away from the mother, and to the father.

> To the girl, it [castration] is an accomplished fact, which is irrevocable, but the recognition of which compels her finally to renounce her first love object and to taste to the full the bitterness of its loss . . . the father is chosen as a love-object, the enemy becomes the beloved. . . . (Lampl de Groot, 1948:213)

This recognition of "castration" forces the girl to redefine her relationship to herself, her mother, and her father.

She turns from the mother because she does not have the phallus to give her. She turns from the mother also in anger and disappointment, because the mother did not give her a "penis" (phallus). But the mother, a woman in a phallic culture, does not have the phallus to give away (having gone through the Oedipal crisis herself a generation earlier). The girl then turns to the father because

only he can "give her the phallus," and it is only through him that she can enter into the symbolic exchange system in which the phallus circulates. But the father does not give her the phallus in the same way that he gives it to the boy. The phallus is affirmed in the boy, who then has it to give away. The girl never gets the phallus. It passes through her, and in its passage is transformed into a child. When she "recognizes her castration," she accedes to the place of a woman in a phallic exchange network. She can "get" the phallus—in intercourse, or as a child—but only as a gift from a man. She never gets to give it away.

When she turns to the father, she also represses the "active" portions of her libido:

> The turning away from her mother is an extremely important step in the course of a little girl's development. It is more than a mere change of object . . . hand in hand with it there is to be observed a marked lowering of the active sexual impulses and a rise of the passive ones. . . . The transition to the father object is accomplished with the help of the passive trends in so far as they have escaped the catastrophe. The path to the development of femininity now lies open to the girl. (Freud, 1961b:239)

The ascendance of passivity in the girl is due to her recognition of the futility of realizing her active desire, and of the unequal terms of the struggle. Freud locates active desire in the clitoris and passive desire in the vagina, and thus describes the repression of active desire as the repression of clitoral eroticism in favor of passive vaginal eroticism. In this scheme, cultural stereotypes have been mapped onto the genitals. Since the work of Masters and Johnson, it is evident that this genital division is a false one. Any organ—penis, clitoris, vagina—can be the locus of either active or passive eroticism. What is important in Freud's scheme, however, is not the geography of desire, but its self-confidence. It is not an organ which is repressed, but a segment of erotic possibility. Freud notes that "more constraint has been applied to the libido when it is pressed into the service of the feminine function . . ." (Freud, 1965:131). The girl has been robbed.

If the Oedipal phase proceeds normally and the girl "accepts her castration," her libidinal structure and object choice are now congruent with the female gender role. She has become a little woman—feminine, passive, heterosexual. Actually, Freud suggests that there are three alternate routes out of the Oedipal catastrophe. The girl may simply freak out, repress sexuality altogether, and become asexual. She may protest, cling to her narcissism and desire, and become either "masculine" or homosexual. Or she may accept the situation, sign the social contract, and attain "normality."

Karen Horney is critical of the entire Freud/Lampl de Groot scheme. But in the course of her critique she articulates its implications:

> . . . when she [the girl] first turns to a man (the father), it is in the main only by way of the narrow bridge of resentment . . . we should feel it a contradiction if the relation of woman to man did not retain throughout life some tinge of this enforced substitute for that which was really desired. . . . The same character of something remote from instinct, secondary and substitutive, would, even in normal women, adhere to the wish for motherhood. . . . The special point about Freud's viewpoint is rather that it sees the wish for motherhood not as an innate formation, but as something that can be reduced psychologically to its ontogenetic elements and draws its energy originally from homosexual or phallic instinctual elements. . . . It would follow, finally, that women's whole reaction to life would be based on a strong subterranean resentment. (Horney, 1973:148–49)

Horney considers these implications to be so far-fetched that they challenge the validity of Freud's entire scheme. But it is certainly plausible to argue instead that the creation of "femininity" in women in the course of socialization is an act of psychic brutality, and that it leaves in women an immense resentment of the suppression to which they were subjected. It is also possible to argue that women have few means for realizing and expressing their residual anger. One can read Freud's essays on femininity as descriptions of how a group is prepared psychologically, at a tender age, to live with its oppression.

There is an additional element in the classic discussions of the attainment of womanhood. The girl first turns to the father because she must, because she is "castrated" (a woman, helpless, etc.). She then discovers that "castration" is a prerequisite to the father's love, that she must be a woman for him to love her. She therefore begins to desire "castration," and what had previously been a disaster becomes a wish.

> Analytic experience leaves no room for doubt that the little girl's first libidinal relation to her father is masochistic, and the masochistic wish in its earliest distinctively feminine phase is: "I want to be castrated by my father." (Deutsch, 1948a:228)

Deutsch argues that such masochism may conflict with the ego, causing some women to flee the entire situation in defense of their self-regard. Those women to whom the choice is "between finding bliss in suffering or peace in renunciation" (ibid.:231) will have difficulty in attaining a healthy attitude to intercourse and motherhood. Why Deutsch appears to consider such women to be special cases, rather than the norm, is not clear from her discussion.

The psychoanalytic theory of femininity is one that sees female development based largely on pain and humiliation, and it takes some fancy footwork to explain why anyone ought to enjoy being a woman. At this point in the classic discussions biology makes a triumphant return. The fancy footwork consists in arguing that finding joy in pain is adaptive to the role of women in reproduction, since childbirth and defloration are "painful." Would it not make more sense to question the entire procedure? If women, in finding their place in a sexual system, are robbed of libido and forced into a masochistic eroticism, why did the analysts not argue for novel arrangements, instead of rationalizing the old ones?

Freud's theory of femininity has been subjected to feminist critique since it was first published. To the extent that it is a rationalization of female subordination, this critique has been justified. To the extent that it is a description of a process which subordinates women, this critique is a mistake. As a description of how phallic culture domesticates women, and the effects in women of their domestication, psychoanalytic theory has no parallel (see also Mitchell, 1971 and 1974; Lasch, 1974). And since psychoanalysis is a theory of gender, dismissing it would be suicidal for a political movement dedicated to eradicating gender hierarchy (or gender itself). We cannot dismantle something that we underestimate or do not understand. The oppression of women is deep; equal pay, equal work, and all of the female politicians in the world will not extirpate the roots of sexism. Lévi-Strauss and Freud elucidate what would otherwise be poorly perceived parts of the deep structures of sex oppression. They serve as reminders of the intractability and magnitude of what we fight, and their analyses provide preliminary charts of the social machinery we must rearrange.

WOMEN UNITE TO OFF THE OEDIPAL RESIDUE OF CULTURE

The precision of the fit between Freud and Lévi-Strauss is striking. Kinship systems require a division of the sexes. The Oedipal phase divides the sexes. Kinship systems include sets of rules governing sexuality. The Oedipal crisis is the assimilation of these rules and taboos. Compulsory heterosexuality is the product of kinship. The Oedipal phase constitutes heterosexual desire. Kinship rests on a radical difference between the rights of men and women. The Oedipal complex confers male rights upon the boy, and forces the girl to accommodate herself to her lesser rights.

This fit between Lévi-Strauss and Freud is by implication an argument that our sex/gender system is still organized by the principles outlined by Lévi-Strauss, despite the entirely nonmodern character of his data base. The more recent data on which Freud bases his theories testifies to the endurance of these sexual structures. If my reading of Freud and Lévi-Strauss is accurate, it suggests that the feminist movement must attempt to resolve the Oedipal crisis of culture by reorganizing the domain of sex and gender in such a way that each individual's Oedipal experience would be less destructive. The dimensions of such a task are difficult to imagine, but at least certain conditions would have to be met.

Several elements of the Oedipal crisis would have to be altered in order that the phase not have such disastrous effects on the young female ego. The Oedipal phase institutes a contradiction in the girl by placing irreconcilable demands upon her. On the one hand, the girl's love for the mother is induced by the mother's job of child care. The girl is then forced to abandon this love because of the female sex role—to belong to a man. If the sexual division of labor were such that adults of both sexes cared for children equally, primary object choice would be bisexual. If heterosexuality were not obligatory, this early love would not have to be suppressed, and the penis would not be overvalued. If the sexual property system were reorganized in such a way that men did not have overriding rights in women (if there was no exchange of women) and if there were no gender, the entire Oedipal drama would be a relic. In short, feminism must call for a revolution in kinship.

The organization of sex and gender once had functions other than itself—it organized society. Now, it only organizes and reproduces itself. The kinds of relationships of sexuality established in the dim human past still dominate our sexual lives, our ideas about men and women, and the ways we raise our children. But they lack the functional load they once carried. One of the most conspicuous features of kinship is that it has been systematically stripped of its functions—political, economic, educational, and organizational. It has been reduced to its barest bones—*sex and gender.*

Human sexual life will always be subject to convention and human intervention. It will never be completely "natural," if only because our species is social, cultural, and articulate. The wild profusion of infantile sexuality will always be tamed. The confrontation between immature and helpless infants and the developed social life of their elders will probably always leave some residue of disturbance. But the mechanisms and aims of this process need not be largely independent of conscious choice. Cultural evolution provides us with the opportunity to seize control of the means of sexuality, reproduction, and socialization, and to make conscious decisions to liberate human sexual life from the archaic relationships which deform it. Ultimately, a thorough-going feminist revolution would liberate more than women. It would liberate forms of sexual expression, and it would liberate human personality from the straightjacket of gender.

"DADDY, DADDY, YOU BASTARD, I'M THROUGH."

—Sylvia Plath

In the course of this essay I have tried to construct a theory of women's oppression by borrowing concepts from anthropology and psychoanalysis. But Lévi-Strauss and Freud write within an intellectual tradition produced by a culture in which women are oppressed. The danger in my enterprise is that the sexism in the tradition of which they are a part tends to be dragged in with each borrowing. "We cannot utter a single destructive proposition which has not already slipped into the form, the logic, and the implicit postulations of precisely what it seeks to contest" (Derrida, 1972:250). And what slips in is formidable. Both psychoanalysis and structural anthropology are, in one sense, the most sophisticated ideologies of sexism around.[12]

For instance, Lévi-Strauss sees women as being like words, which are misused when they are not "communicated" and exchanged. On the last page of a very long book, he observes that this creates something of a contradiction in women, since women are at the same time "speakers" and "spoken." His only comment on this contradiction is this:

But woman could never become just a sign and nothing more, since even in a man's world she is still a person, and since insofar as she is defined as a

sign she must be recognized as a generator of signs. In the matrimonial dialogue of men, woman is never purely what is spoken about; for if women in general represent a certain category of signs, destined to a certain kind of communication, each woman preserves a particular value arising from her talent, before and after marriage, for taking her part in a duet. In contrast to words, which have wholly become signs, woman has remained at once a sign and a value. *This explains why the relations between the sexes have preserved that affective richness, ardour and mystery which doubtless originally permeated the entire universe of human communications.* (Lévi-Strauss, 1969:496; my italics)

This is an extraordinary statement. Why is he not, at this point, denouncing what kinship systems do to women, instead of presenting one of the greatest rip-offs of all time as the root of romance?

A similar insensitivity is revealed within psychoanalysis by the inconsistency with which it assimilates the critical implications of its own theory. For instance, Freud did not hesitate to recognize that his findings posed a challenge to conventional morality:

We cannot avoid observing with critical eyes, and we have found that it is impossible to give our support to conventional sexual morality or to approve highly of the means by which society attempts to arrange the practical problems of sexuality in life.

---

[12] Parts of Wittig's *Les Guérillères* (1973) appear to be tirades against Lévi-Strauss and Lacan. For instance:

Has he not indeed written, power and the possession of women, leisure and the enjoyment of women? He writes that you are currency, an item of exchange. He writes, barter, possession and acquisition of women and merchandise. Better for you to see your guts in the sun and utter the death rattle than to live a life that anyone can appropriate. What belongs to you on this earth? Only death. No power on earth can take that away from you. And—consider explain tell yourself—if happiness consists in the possession of something, then hold fast to this sovereign happiness—to die. (Wittig, 1973:115–16; see also 106–107; 113–14; 134)

The awareness of French feminists of Lévi-Strauss and Lacan is most clearly evident in a group called "Psychoanalyse et Politique" which defined its task as a feminist use and critique of Lacanian psychoanalysis.

We can demonstrate with ease that what the world calls its code of morals demands more sacrifices than it is worth, and that its behavior is neither dictated by honesty nor instituted with wisdom. (Freud, 1943:376–77; my emphasis)

Nevertheless, when psychoanalysis demonstrates with equal facility that the ordinary components of feminine personality are masochism, self-hatred, and passivity,[13] a similar judgment is *not* made. Instead, a double standard of interpretation is employed. Masochism is bad for men, essential to women. Adequate narcissism is necessary for men, impossible for women. Passivity is tragic in man, while lack of passivity is tragic in a woman.

It is this double standard which enables clinicians to try to accommodate women to a role whose destructiveness is so lucidly detailed in their own theories. It is the same inconsistent attitude which permits therapists to consider lesbianism as a problem to be cured, rather than as the resistance to a bad situation that their own theory suggests.[14]

There are points within the analytic discussions of femininity where one might say, "This is oppression of women," or "We can demonstrate with ease that what the world calls femininity demands more sacrifices than it is worth." It is precisely at such points that the implications of the theory are ignored, and are replaced with formulations whose purpose is to keep those implica-

tions firmly lodged in the theoretical unconscious. It is at these points that all sorts of mysterious chemical substances, joys in pain, and biological aims are substituted for a critical assessment of the costs of femininity. These substitutions are the symptoms of theoretical repression, in that they are not consistent with the usual canons of psychoanalytic argument. The extent to which these rationalizations of femininity go against the grain of psychoanalytic logic is strong evidence for the extent of the need to suppress the radical and feminist implications of the theory of femininity (Deutsch's discussions are excellent examples of this process of substitution and repression).

The argument which must be woven in order to assimilate Lévi-Strauss and Freud into feminist theory is somewhat tortuous. I have engaged it for several reasons. First, while neither Lévi-Strauss nor Freud questions the undoubted sexism endemic to the systems they describe, the questions which ought to be posed are blindingly obvious. Secondly, their work enables us to isolate sex and gender from "mode of production," and to counter a certain tendency to explain sex oppression as a reflex of economic forces. Their work provides a framework in which the full weight of sexuality and marriage can be incorporated into an analysis of sex oppression. It suggests a conception of the women's movement as analogous to, rather than isomorphic with, the working-class movement, each addressing a different source of human discontent. In Marx's vision, the working-class movement would do more than throw off the burden of its own exploitation. It also had the potential to change society, to liberate humanity, to create a classless society. Perhaps the women's movement has the task of effecting the same kind of social change for a system of which Marx had only an imperfect apperception. Something of this sort is implicit in Wittig (1973)—the dictatorship of the Amazon *guérillères* is a temporary means for achieving a genderless society.

The sex/gender system is not immutably oppressive and has lost much of its traditional function. Nevertheless, it will not wither away in the

---

[13] "Every woman adores a fascist."—Sylvia Plath

[14] One clinician, Charlotte Wolff (1971) has taken the psychoanalytic theory of womanhood to its logical extreme and proposed that lesbianism is a healthy response to female socialization.

> Women who do not rebel against the status of object have declared themselves defeated as persons in their own rights. (Wolff, 1971:65)

> The lesbian girl is the one who, by all means at her disposal, will try to find a place of safety inside and outside the family, through her fight for equality with the male. She will not, like other women, play up to him: indeed, she despises the very idea of it. (Ibid.:59)

> The lesbian was and is unquestionably in the avant-garde of the fight for equality of the sexes, and for the psychical liberation of women. (Ibid.:66)

It is revealing to compare Wolff's discussion with the articles on lesbianism in Marmor, 1965.

absence of opposition. It still carries the social burden of sex and gender, of socializing the young, and of providing ultimate propositions about the nature of human beings themselves. And it serves economic and political ends other than those it was originally designed to further (cf. Scott, 1965). The sex/gender system must be reorganized through political action.

Finally, the exegesis of Lévi-Strauss and Freud suggests a certain vision of feminist politics and the feminist utopia. It suggests that we should not aim for the elimination of men, but for the elimination of the social system which creates sexism and gender. I personally find a vision of an Amazon matriarchate, in which men are reduced to servitude or oblivion (depending on the possibilities for parthenogenetic reproduction), distasteful and inadequate. Such a vision maintains gender and the division of the sexes. It is a vision which simply inverts the arguments of those who base their case for inevitable male dominance on ineradicable and *significant* biological differences between the sexes. But we are not only oppressed *as* women, we are oppressed by having to *be* women, or men as the case may be. I personally feel that the feminist movement must dream of even more than the elimination of the oppression of women. It must dream of the elimination of obligatory sexualities and sex roles. The dream I find most compelling is one of an androgynous and genderless (though not sexless) society; in which one's sexual anatomy is irrelevant to who one is, what one does, and with whom one makes love.

THE POLITICAL ECONOMY OF SEX

It would be nice to be able to conclude here with the implications for feminism and gay liberation of the overlap between Freud and Lévi-Strauss. But I must suggest, tentatively, a next step on the agenda: a Marxian analysis of sex/gender systems. Sex/gender systems are not ahistorical emanations of the human mind; they are products of historical human activity.

We need, for instance, an analysis of the evolution of sexual exchange along the lines of Marx's discussion in *Capital* of the evolution of money and commodities. There is an economics and a politics to sex/gender systems which is obscured by the concept of "exchange of women." For instance, a system in which women are exchangeable only for one another has different effects on women than one in which there is a commodity equivalent for women.

> That marriage in simple societies involves an "exchange" is a somewhat vague notion that has often confused the analysis of social systems. The extreme case is the exchange of "sisters," formerly practiced in parts of Australia and Africa. Here the term has the precise dictionary meaning of "to be received as an equivalent for," "to give and receive reciprocally." From quite a different standpoint the virtually universal incest prohibition means that marriage systems necessarily involve "exchanging" siblings for spouses, giving rise to a reciprocity that is purely notional. But in most societies marriage is mediated by a set of intermediary transactions. If we see these transactions as simply implying immediate or long-term reciprocity, then the analysis is likely to be blurred. . . . The analysis is further limited if one regards the passage of property simply as a symbol of the transfer of rights, for then the nature of the objects handed over . . . is of little importance. . . . Neither of these approaches is wrong; both are inadequate. (Goody, 1973:2)

There are systems in which there is no equivalent for a woman. To get a wife, a man must have a daughter, a sister, or other female kinswoman in whom he has a right of bestowal. He must have control over some female flesh. The Lele and Kuma are cases in point. Lele men scheme constantly in order to stake claims in some as yet unborn girl, and scheme further to make good their claims (Douglas, 1963). A Kuma girl's marriage is determined by an intricate web of debts, and she has little say in choosing her husband. A girl is usually married against her will, and her groom shoots an arrow into her thigh to symbolically prevent her from running away. The young wives almost always do run away, only to be returned to their new husbands by an elaborate conspiracy enacted by their kin and affines (Reay, 1959).

In other societies, there is an equivalent for women. A woman can be converted into bridewealth, and bridewealth can be in turn converted into a woman. The dynamics of such systems vary accordingly, as does the specific kind of pressure exerted upon women. The marriage of a Melpa woman is not a return for a previous debt. Each transaction is self-contained, in that the payment of a bridewealth in pigs and shells will cancel the debt. The Melpa woman therefore has more latitude in choosing her husband than does her Kuma counterpart. On the other hand, her destiny is linked to bridewealth. If her husband's kin are slow to pay, her kin may encourage her to leave him. On the other hand, if her consanguineal kin are satisfied with the balance of payments, they may refuse to back her in the event that she wants to leave her husband. Moreover, her male kinsmen use the bridewealth for their own purposes, in *moka* exchange and for their own marriages. If a woman leaves her husband, some or all of the bridewealth will have to be returned. If, as is usually the case, the pigs and shells have been distributed or promised, her kin will be reluctant to back her in the event of marital discord. And each time a woman divorces and remarries, her value in bridewealth tends to depreciate. On the whole, her male consanguines will lose in the event of a divorce, unless the groom has been delinquent in his payments. While the Melpa woman is freer as a new bride than a Kuma woman, the bridewealth system makes divorce difficult or impossible (Strathern, 1972).

In some societies, like the Nuer, bridewealth can only be converted into brides. In others, bridewealth can be converted into something else, like political prestige. In this case, a woman's marriage is implicated in a political system. In the Big Man systems of Highland New Guinea, the material which circulates for women also circulates in the exchanges on which political power is based. Within the political system, men are in constant need of valuables to disburse, and they are dependent upon input. They depend not only upon their immediate partners, but upon the partners of their partners, to several degrees of remove. If a

man has to return some bridewealth he may not be able to give it to someone who planned to give it to someone else who intended to use it to give a feast upon which his status depends. Big Men are therefore concerned with the domestic affairs of others, whose relationship with them may be extremely indirect. There are cases in which headmen intervene in marital disputes involving indirect trading partners in order that *moka* exchanges not be disrupted (Bulmer, 1969:11). The weight of this entire system may come to rest upon one woman kept in a miserable marriage.

In short, there are other questions to ask of a marriage system than whether or not it exchanges women. Is the woman traded for a woman, or is there an equivalent? Is this equivalent only for women, or can it be turned into something else? If it can be turned into something else, is it turned into political power or wealth? On the other hand, can bridewealth be obtained only in marital exchange, or can it be obtained from elsewhere? Can women be accumulated through amassing wealth? Can wealth be accumulated by disposing of women? Is a marriage system part of a system of stratification?[15]

These last questions point to another task for a political economy of sex. Kinship and marriage are always parts of total social systems, and are always tied into economic and political arrangements.

> Lévi-Strauss . . . rightly argues that the structural implications of a marriage can only be understood if we think of it as one item in a whole series of transactions between kin groups. So far, so good. But in none of the examples which he provides in his book does he carry this principle far enough. The reciprocities of kinship obligation are not merely symbols of alliance, they are also economic transactions, political transactions, charters to rights of domicile and land use. No useful picture of "how a kinship system works" can be provided unless these several aspects or implications of the kinship organization are considered simultaneously. (Leach, 1971:90)

---

[15] Another line of inquiry would compare bridewealth systems to dowry systems. Many of these questions are treated in Goody and Tambiah, 1973.

Among the Kachin, the relationship of a tenant to a landlord is also a relationship between a son-in-law and a father-in-law. "The procedure for acquiring land rights of any kind is in almost all cases tantamount to marrying a woman from the lineage of the lord" (ibid.:88). In the Kachin system, bridewealth moves from commoners to aristocrats, women moving in the opposite direction.

> From an economic aspect the effect of matrilateral cross-cousin marriage is that, on balance, the headman's lineage constantly pays wealth to the chief's lineage in the form of bridewealth. The payment can also, from an analytical point of view, be regarded as a rent paid to the senior landlord by the tenant. The most important part of this payment is in the form of consumer goods—namely cattle. The chief converts this perishable wealth into imperishable prestige through the medium of spectacular feasting. The ultimate consumers of the goods are in this way the original producers, namely, the commoners who attend the feast. (Ibid.:89)

In another example, it is traditional in the Trobriands for a man to send a harvest gift—*urigubu*—of yams to his sister's household. For the commoners, this amounts to a simple circulation of yams. But the chief is polygamous, and marries a woman from each subdistrict within his domain. Each of these subdistricts therefore sends *urigubu* to the chief, providing him with a bulging storehouse out of which he finances feasts, craft production, and *kula* expeditions. This "fund of power" underwrites the political system and forms the basis for chiefly power (Malinowski, 1970).

In some systems, position in a political hierarchy and position in a marriage system are intimately linked. In traditional Tonga, women married up in rank. Thus, low-ranking lineages would send women to higher ranking lineages. Women of the highest lineage were married into the "house of Fiji," a lineage defined as outside the political system. If the highest ranking chief gave his sister to a lineage other than one which had no part in the ranking system, he would no longer be the highest ranking chief. Rather, the lineage of his sister's son would outrank his own.

In times of political rearrangement, the demotion of the previous high-ranking lineage was formalized when it gave a wife to a lineage which it had formerly outranked. In traditional Hawaii, the situation was the reverse. Women married down, and the dominant lineage gave wives to junior lines. A paramount would either marry a sister or obtain a wife from Tonga. When a junior lineage usurped rank, it formalized its position by giving a wife to its former senior line.

There is even some tantalizing data suggesting that marriage systems may be implicated in the evolution of social strata, and perhaps in the development of early states. The first round of the political consolidation which resulted in the formation of a state in Madagascar occurred when one chief obtained title to several autonomous districts through the vagaries of marriage and inheritance (Henry Wright, personal communication). In Samoa, legends place the origin of the paramount title—the *Tafa'ifa*—as a result of intermarriage between ranking members of four major lineages. My thoughts are too speculative, my data too sketchy, to say much on this subject. But a search ought to be undertaken for data which might demonstrate how marriage systems intersect with large-scale political processes like state-making. Marriage systems might be implicated in a number of ways: in the accumulation of wealth and the maintenance of differential access to political and economic resources; in the building of alliances; in the consolidation of high-ranking persons into a single closed strata of endogamous kin.

These examples—like the Kachin and the Trobriand ones—indicate that sexual systems cannot, in the final analysis, be understood in complete isolation. A full-bodied analysis of women in a single society, or throughout history, must take *everything* into account: the evolution of commodity forms in women, systems of land tenure, political arrangements, subsistence technology, etc. Equally important, economic and political analyses are incomplete if they do not consider women, marriage, and sexuality. Traditional concerns of anthropology and social science—such as the evolution of social stratification and the origin of the state—must be reworked to include the implications of matrilateral cross-cousin marriage, surplus extracted in the form of daughters, the conversion of female labor into male wealth, the conversion of female lives into marriage alliances, the contribution of marriage to political power, and the transformations which all of these varied aspects of society have undergone in the course of time.

This sort of endeavor is, in the final analysis, exactly what Engels tried to do in his effort to weave a coherent analysis of so many of the diverse aspects of social life. He tried to relate men and women, town and country, kinship and state, forms of property, systems of land tenure, convertibility of wealth, forms of exchange, the technology of food production, and forms of trade, to name a few, into a systematic historical account. Eventually, someone will have to write a new version of *The Origin of the Family, Private Property and the State,* recognizing the mutual interdependence of sexuality, economics, and politics without underestimating the full significance of each in human society.

BIBLIOGRAPHY

Althusser, Louis. "Freud and Lacan." *New Left Review* 55(1969): 48–65.

———, and Balibar, Etienne. *Reading Capital*. London: New York Left Books, 1970.

Benston, Margaret. "The Political Economy of Women's Liberation." *Monthly Review* 21, no. 4(1969): 13–27.

Berndt, Ronald. *Excess and Restraint*. Chicago: University of Chicago Press, 1962.

Bulmer, Ralph. "Political Aspects of the Moka Ceremonial Exchange System Among the Kyaka People of the Western Highlands of New Guinea." *Oceania* 31, no. 1(1969): 1–13.

Chassetguet-Smirgel, J. *Female Sexuality*. Ann Arbor: University of Michigan Press, 1970.

Dalla Costa, Mariarosa, and Selma James. *The Power of Women and the Subversion of the Community*. Bristol: Falling Wall Press, 1972.

Derrida, Jacques. "Structure, Sign, and Play in the Discourse of the Human Sciences." In *The Structuralist Controversy,* edited by R. Macksey and E. Donato. Baltimore: Johns Hopkins Press, 1972.

Deutsch, Helene. "The Significance of Masochism in the Mental Life of Women." In *The Psychoanalytic Reader*, edited by R. Fleiss. New York: International Universities Press, 1948a.

———"On Female Homosexuality." In *The Psychoanalytic Reader*, edited by R. Fleiss. New York: International Universities Press, 1948b.

Devereaux, George. "Institutionalized Homosexuality Among Mohave Indians." *Human Biology* 9(1937): 498–529.

Douglas, Mary. *The Lele of Kasai*. London: Oxford University Press, 1963.

Engels, Frederick. *The Origin of Family, Private Property and the State,* edited by Eleanor Leacock. New York: International Universities Press, 1972.

Evans-Pritchard, E. E. *Kinship and Marriage Among the Nuer*. London: Oxford University Press, 1951.

———"Sexual Inversion Among the Azande." *American Anthropologist* 72(1970): 1428–34.

Fee, Elizabeth. "The Sexual Politics of Victorian Social Anthropology." *Feminist Studies* (Winter/ Spring)(1973): 23–29.

Ford, Clellan, and Frank Beach. *Patterns of Sexual Behavior*. New York: Harper, 1972.

Foucault, Michel. *The Order of Things*. New York: Pantheon, 1970.

Freud, Sigmund. *A General Introduction to Psychoanalysis*. Garden City, NY: Garden City Publishing Company, 1943.

———"Some Psychical Consequences of the Anatomical Distinction Between the Sexes." In *The Complete Works of Sigmund Freud*, vol. 19, edited by J. Strachey. London: Hogarth, 1961a.

———"Female Sexuality." In *The Complete Works of Sigmund Freud*, vol. 21, edited by J. Strachey. London: Hogarth, 1961b.

———"Feminity." In *New Introductory Lectures in Psychoanalysis*, edited by J. Strachey. New York: W.W. Norton, 1965.

Gardiner, Jean. "Political Economy of Female Labor in Capitalist Society." Unpublished Manuscript, 1974.

Gerstein, Ira. "Domestic Work and Capitalism." *Radical America 7,* nos. 4 and 5(1973): 101–28.

Glasse, R. M. "The Mask of Venery." Paper read at the 70th Annual Meeting of the American Anthropologist Association, New York City, December 1971.

Goodale, Jane, and Ann Chowing. "The Contaminating Woman." Paper read at the 70th Annual Meeting of the American Anthropologist Association, 1971.

Goody, Jack, and S. J. Tambiah. *Bridewealth and Dowry*. Cambridge, England: Cambridge University Press, 1973.

Gough, Ian. "Marx and Productive Labor." *New Left Review* 76(1972): 47–72.

Gough, Kathleen. "The Nayars and the Definition of Marriage." *Journal of the Royal Anthropological Institute* 89(1959): 23–24.

Hefner, Robert. "The Tel Quel Ideology: Material Practice Upon Material Practice." *Substance* 8(1974): 127–38.

Herskovitz, Melville. "A Note on 'Women Marriage' in Dahomey." *Africa* 10, no. 3(1937): 335–41.

Hertz, Robert. *Death and the Right Hand*. Glencoe: Free Press, 1960.

Horney, Karen. "The Denial of the Vagina." In Karen Horney, *Feminine Psychology,* edited by Harold Kelman. New York: W.W. Norton, 1973.

Jakobson, Roman, and Morris Halle. "*Fundamentals of Language*" The Hague: Mouton, 1971.

Jones, Ernest. "The Phallic Phase." *International Journal of Psychoanalysis* 14(1933): 1–33.

Kelly, Raymond. "Witchcraft and Sexual Relations: An Explanation of the Social and Semantic Implications of the Structure of Belief." Paper read at the 73rd Annual Meeting of the American Anthropological Association, Mexico City, 1974.

Lacan, Jacques. "The Function of Language in Psychoanalysis." In Anthony Wilden: *The Language of the Self.* Baltimore, MD: Johns Hopkins University Press, 1968.

Lampl de Groot, Jeane. "Problems of Femininity." *Psychoanalytic Quarterly* 2(1933): 489–518.

———"The Evolution of the Oedipus Complex." In *The Psychoanalytic Reader,* edited by R. Fleiss. New York: International University Press, 1948.

Langness, L. L. "Sexual Antagonism in the New Guinea Highlands: A Bena Bena Example." *Oceania* 37, no. 3(1967): 161–77.

Larguia, Isabel, and John Dumolin. "Towards a Science of Women's Liberation." *NACLA Newsletter* 6, no. 10(1972): 3–20.

Lasch, Christopher. "Freud and Women." *New York Review of Books* 21, no. 15(1974): 12–17.

Leach, Edmund. *Rethinking Anthropology*. New York: Humanities Press, 1971.

Lévi-Strauss, Claude. *The Elementary Structures of Kinship*. Boston: Beacon Press, 1969.

———"The Family." In *Man, Culture, and Society,* edited by H. Shapiro. London: Oxford University Press, 1971.

Lindenbaum, Shirley. "A Wife Is the Hand of Man." Paper read at the 72nd Annual Meeting of the American Anthropological Association, 1973.

Livingstone, Frank. "Genetics, Ecology and the Origins of Incest and Exogamy." *Current Anthropology* 10, no. 1(1969): 45–49.

Malinowski, Bronislaw. *The Family Amongst Australian Aborigines*. London: University of London Press, 1913.

———*The Sexual Life of Savages*. London: Routledge and Kegan Paul, 1929.

———"The Primitive Economics of the Trobriand Islanders." In *Cultures of the Pacific,* edited by T. Harding and B. Wallace. New York: Free Press, 1970.

Marx, Karl. *Theories of Surplus Value, Part 1*. Moscow: Progress Publishers, 1969.

———*Pre-Capitalist Economic Formations*. New York: International Publishers, 1971a.

———*Wage-Labor and Capital*. New York: International Publishers, 1971b.

———*Capitol*, vol. 1. New York: International Publishers, 1972.

McMurtrie, Douglas. "A Legend of Lesbian Love Among North American Indians." *Urologic and Cutaneous Review* (April)(1914): 192–93.

Meggitt, M. J. "Male-Female Relationships in the Highlands of New Guinea." *American Anthropologist* 66, no. 4, part 2(1964): 204–24.

Mehlman, Jeffrey. *French Freud: Structural Studies in Psychoanalysis*. New Haven: Yale French Studies # 48, 1972.

Mitchell, Juliet. *Women's Estate*. New York: Vintage, 1971.

———*Psychoanalysis and Feminism*. New York: Pantheon, 1974.

Murphy, Robert. "Social Structure and Sex Antagonism." *Southwestern Journal of Anthropology* 15, no. 1(1959): 81–96.

Rappaport Roy, and Georgeda Buchbinder. "Fertility and Death Among the Maring. In *Sex Roles in the New Guinea Highlands*, edited by Paula Brown and G. Buchbinder. Cambridge, MA: Harvard University Press, 1976.

Read, Kenneth. "The Nama Cult of the Central Highlands, New Guinea." *Oceania* 23, no. 1(1952): 1–25.

Reay, Marie. *The Kuma.* London: Cambridge University Press, 1959.

Rowntree, M. and J. "More on the Political Economy of Women's Liberation." *Monthly Review* 21, no. 8(1970): 26–32.

Sahlins, Marshall. "The Origin of Society." *Scientific American* 203, no. 3(1960a): 76–86.

————"Political Power and the Economy in Primitive Society." In *Essays in the Science of Culture,* edited by Robert Dole and Robert Caneiro. New York: Crowell, 1960b.

————*Stone Age Economics.* Chicago: Aldine-Atherton, 1972.

Schneider, David, and Kathleen Gough, eds. *Matrilineal Kinship.* Berkley: University of California Press, 1961.

Scott, John Finley. "The Role of Collegiate Sororities in Maintaining Class and Ethnic Endogamy." *American Sociological Review* 30, no. 4(1965): 415–26.

Secombe, Wally. "Housework Under Capitalism." *New Left Review* 83(1973): 3–24.

Sonenschein, David. "Homosexuality as a Subject of Anthropological Investigation." *Anthropological Quarterly* 2(1966): 73–82.

Strathem, Marilyn. *Women in Between.* New York: Seminar, 1972.

Thompson, E. P. *The Making of the English Working Class.* New York: Vintage, 1963.

Thurnwald, Richard. "Banaro Society." Memoirs of the American Anthropological Association 3, no. 4(1916): 251–391.

Van Baal, J. *Dema.* The Hague: Nijhoff, 1966.

Vogel, Lise. "The Earthly Family." *Radical America* 7, nos. 4 and 5(1973): 9–50.

Wilden, Anthony. *The Language of the Self.* Baltimore: Johns Hopkins Press, 1968.

Williams, F. E. *Papuans of the Trans-Fly.* Oxford: Clarendon, 1936.

Wittig, Monique. *Les Guérillères.* New York: Avon, 1973.

Wolf, Charlotte. *Love between Women.* London: Duckworth, 1971.

Yalmon, Nur. "On the Purity of Women in the Castes of Ceylon and Malabar." *Journal of the Royal Anthropological Institute* 93, no. 1(1963): 25–58.

OPPRESSION

Marilyn Frye

It is a fundamental claim of feminism that women are oppressed. The word 'oppression' is a strong word. It repels and attracts. It is dangerous and dangerously fashionable and endangered. It is much misused, and sometimes not innocently.

The statement that women are oppressed is frequently met with the claim that men are oppressed too. We hear that oppressing is oppressive to those who oppress as well as to those they oppress. Some men cite as evidence of their oppression their much advertised inability to cry. It is tough, we are told, to be masculine. When the stresses and frustrations of being a man are cited as evidence that oppressors are oppressed by their oppressing, the word 'oppression' is being stretched to meaninglessness; it is treated as though its scope includes any and all human experience of limitation or suffering, no matter the cause, degree or consequence. Once such usage has been put over on us, then if ever we deny that any person or group is oppressed, we seem to imply that we think they never suffer and have no feelings. We are accused of insensitivity; even of bigotry. For women, such accusation is particularly intimidating, since sensitivity is one of the few virtues that has been assigned to us. If we are found insensitive, we may fear we have no redeeming traits at all and perhaps are not real women. Thus are we silenced before we begin: the name of our situation drained of meaning and our guilt mechanisms tripped.

But this is nonsense. Human beings can be miserable without being oppressed, and it is perfectly consistent to deny that a person or group is oppressed without denying that they have feelings or that they suffer.

We need to think clearly about oppression, and there is much that mitigates against this. I do not want to undertake to prove that women are oppressed (or that men are not), but I want to make clear what is being said when we say it. We need this word, this concept, and we need it to be sharp and sure.

I

The root of the word 'oppression' is the element 'press'. *The press of the crowd; pressed into military service; to press a pair of pants; printing press; press the button.* Presses are used to mold things or flatten them or reduce them in bulk, sometimes to reduce them by squeezing out the gasses or liquids in them. Something pressed is something caught between or among forces and barriers which are so related to each other that jointly they restrain, restrict or prevent the thing's motion or mobility. Mold. Immobilize. Reduce.

The mundane experience of the oppressed provides another clue. One of the most characteristic and ubiquitous features of the world as experienced by oppressed people is the double bind—situations in which options are reduced to a very few and all of them expose one to penalty, censure or deprivation. For example, it is often a requirement upon oppressed people that we smile and be cheerful. If we comply, we signal our docility and our acquiescence in our situation. We need not, then, be taken note of. We acquiesce in being made invisible, in our occupying no space. We participate in our own erasure. On the other hand, anything but the sunniest countenance exposes us to being perceived as mean, bitter, angry or dangerous. This means, at the least, that we may be found "difficult" or unpleasant to work with, which is enough to cost one one's livelihood; at worst, being seen as mean, bitter, angry

or dangerous has been known to result in rape, arrest, beating and murder. One can only choose to risk one's preferred form and rate of annihilation.

Another example: It is common in the United States that women, especially younger women, are in a bind where neither sexual activity nor sexual inactivity is all right. If she is heterosexually active, a woman is open to censure and punishment for being loose, unprincipled or a whore. The "punishment" comes in the form of criticism, snide and embarrassing remarks, being treated as an easy lay by men, scorn from her more restrained female friends. She may have to lie and hide her behavior from her parents. She must juggle the risks of unwanted pregnancy and dangerous contraceptives. On the other hand, if she refrains from heterosexual activity, she is fairly constantly harassed by men who try to persuade her into it and pressure her to "relax" and "let her hair down"; she is threatened with labels like "frigid," "uptight," "man-hater," "bitch" and "cocktease." The same parents who would be disapproving of her sexual activity may be worried by her inactivity because it suggests she is not or will not be popular, or is not sexually normal. She may be charged with lesbianism. If a woman is raped, then if she has been heterosexually active she is subject to the presumption that she liked it (since her activity is presumed to show that she likes sex), and if she has not been heterosexually active, she is subject to the presumption that she liked it (since she is supposedly "repressed and frustrated"). Both heterosexual activity and heterosexual nonactivity are likely to be taken as proof that you wanted to be raped, and hence, of course, weren't *really* raped at all. You can't win. You are caught in a bind, caught between systematically related pressures.

Women are caught like this, too, by networks of forces and barriers that expose one to penalty, loss or contempt whether one works outside the home or not, is on welfare or not, bears children or not, raises children or not, marries or not, stays married or not, is heterosexual, lesbian, both or neither. Economic necessity; confinement to racial and/or sexual job ghettos; sexual harassment; sex discrimination; pressures of competing expectations and judgments about *women, wives* and *mothers* (in the society at large, in racial and ethnic subcultures and in one's own mind); dependence (full or partial) on husbands, parents or the state; commitment to political ideas; loyalties to racial or ethnic or other "minority" groups; the demands of self-respect and responsibilities to others. Each of these factors exists in complex tension with every other, penalizing or prohibiting all of the apparently available options. And nipping at one's heels, always, is the endless pack of little things. If one dresses one way, one is subject to the assumption that one is advertising one's sexual availability; if one dresses another way, one appears to "not care about oneself" or to be "unfeminine." If one uses "strong language," one invites categorization as a whore or slut; if one does not, one invites categorization as a "lady"—one too delicately constituted to cope with robust speech or the realities to which it presumably refers.

The experience of oppressed people is that the living of one's life is confined and shaped by forces and barriers which are not accidental or occasional and hence avoidable, but are systematically related to each other in such a way as to catch one between and among them and restrict or penalize motion in any direction. It is the experience of being caged in: all avenues, in every direction, are blocked or booby trapped.

Cages. Consider a birdcage. If you look very closely at just one wire in the cage, you cannot see the other wires. If your conception of what is before you is determined by this myopic focus, you could look at that one wire, up and down the length of it, and be unable to see why a bird would not just fly around the wire any time it wanted to go somewhere. Furthermore, even if, one day at a time, you myopically inspected each wire, you still could not see why a bird would have trouble going past the wires to get anywhere. There is no physical property of any one wire, *nothing* that the closest scrutiny could discover, that will reveal how a bird could be inhibited or harmed by it except in the most accidental way. It is only

when you step back, stop looking at the wires one by one, microscopically, and take a macroscopic view of the whole cage, that you can see why the bird does not go anywhere; and then you will see it in a moment. It will require no great subtlety of mental powers. It is perfectly *obvious* that the bird is surrounded by a network of systematically related barriers, no one of which would be the least hindrance to its flight, but which, by their relations to each other, are as confining as the solid walls of a dungeon.

It is now possible to grasp one of the reasons why oppression can be hard to see and recognize: one can study the elements of an oppressive structure with great care and some good will without seeing the structure as a whole, and hence without seeing or being able to understand that one is looking at a cage and that there are people there who are caged, whose motion and mobility are restricted, whose lives are shaped and reduced.

The arresting of vision at a microscopic level yields such common confusion as that about the male door-opening ritual. This ritual, which is remarkably widespread across classes and races, puzzles many people, some of whom do and some of whom do not find it offensive. Look at the scene of the two people approaching a door. The male steps slightly ahead and opens the door. The male holds the door open while the female glides through. Then the male goes through. The door closes after them. "Now how," one innocently asks, "can those crazy womenslibbers say that is oppressive? The guy *removed* a barrier to the lady's smooth and unruffled progress." But each repetition of this ritual has a place in a pattern, in fact in several patterns. One has to shift the level of one's perception in order to see the whole picture.

The door-opening pretends to be a helpful service, but the helpfulness is false. This can be seen by noting that it will be done whether or not it makes any practical sense. Infirm men and men burdened with packages will open doors for able-bodied women who are free of physical burdens. Men will impose themselves awkwardly and jostle everyone in order to get to the door first. The act is not determined by convenience or grace. Furthermore, these very numerous acts of unneeded or even noisome "help" occur in counterpoint to a pattern of men not being helpful in many practical ways in which women might welcome help. What *women* experience is a world in which gallant princes charming commonly make a fuss about being helpful and providing small services when help and services are of little or no use, but in which there are rarely ingenious and adroit princes at hand when substantial assistance is really wanted either in mundane affairs or in situations of threat, assault or terror. There is no help with the (his) laundry; no help typing a report at 4:00 a.m.; no help in mediating disputes among relatives or children. There is nothing but advice that women should stay indoors after dark, be chaperoned by a man, or when it comes down to it, "lie back and enjoy it."

The gallant gestures have no practical meaning. Their meaning is symbolic. The door-opening and similar services provided are services which really are needed by people who are for one reason or another incapacitated—unwell, burdened with parcels, etc. So the message is that women are incapable. The detachment of the acts from the concrete realities of what women need and do not need is a vehicle for the message that women's actual needs and interests are unimportant or irrelevant. Finally, these gestures imitate the behavior of servants toward masters and thus mock women, who are in most respects the servants and caretakers of men. The message of the false helpfulness of male gallantry is female dependence, the invisibility or insignificance of women, and contempt for women.

One cannot see the meanings of these rituals if one's focus is riveted upon the individual event in all its particularity, including the particularity of the individual man's present conscious intentions and motives and the individual woman's conscious perception of the event in the moment. It seems sometimes that people take a deliberately myopic view and fill their eyes with things seen microscopically

in order not to see macroscopically. At any rate, whether it is deliberate or not, people can and do fail to see the oppression of women because they fail to see macroscopically and hence fail to see the various elements of the situation as systematically related in larger schemes.

As the cageness of the birdcage is a macroscopic phenomenon, the oppressiveness of the situations in which women live our various and different lives is a macroscopic phenomenon. Neither can be *seen* from a microscopic perspective. But when you look macroscopically you can see it—a network of forces and barriers which are systematically related and which conspire to the immobilization, reduction and molding of women and the lives we live.

II

The image of the cage helps convey one aspect of the systematic nature of oppression. Another is the selection of occupants of the cages, and analysis of this aspect also helps account for the invisibility of the oppression of women.

It is as a woman (or as a Chicana/o or as a Black or Asian or lesbian) that one is entrapped.

"Why can't I go to the park; you let Jimmy go!"
"Because it's not safe for girls."

"I want to be a secretary, not a seamstress; I don't want to learn to make dresses."

"There's no work for negroes in that line; learn a skill where you can earn your living."[1]

When you question why you are being blocked, why this barrier is in your path, the answer has not to do with individual talent or merit, handicap or failure; it has to do with your membership in some category understood as a "natural" or "physical" category. The "inhabitant" of the "cage" is not an individual but a group, all those of a certain category. If an individual is oppressed, it is in virtue of being a member of a group or category of people that is systematically reduced, molded, immobilized. Thus, to recognize a person as oppressed, one has to see that individual *as* belonging to a group of a certain sort.

There are many things which can encourage or inhibit perception of someone's membership in the sort of group or category in question here. In particular, it seems reasonable to suppose that if one of the devices of restriction and definition of the group is that of physical confinement or segregation, the confinement and separation would encourage recognition of the group as a group. This in turn would encourage the macroscopic focus which enables one to recognize oppression and encourages the individuals' identification and solidarity with other individuals of the group or category. But physical confinement and segregation of the group as a group is not common to all oppressive structures, and when an oppressed group is geographically and demographically dispersed the perception of it as a group is inhibited. There may be little or nothing in the situations of the individuals encouraging the macroscopic focus which would reveal the unity of the structure bearing down on all members of that group.*

A great many people, female and male and of every race and class, simply do not believe that *woman* is a category of oppressed people, and I think that this is in part because they have been fooled by the dispersal and assimilation of women throughout and into the systems of class and race which organize men. Our simply being dispersed makes it difficult for women to have knowledge of each other and hence difficult to recognize the shape of our common cage. The dispersal and assimilation of women throughout economic classes and races also divides us against each other practically and economically and thus attaches *interest* to the inability to see: for some, jealousy of their benefits, and for some, resentment of the others' advantages.

To get past this, it helps to notice that in fact women of all races and classes *are* together in a ghetto of sorts. There is a women's place, a sector, which is inhabited by women of all classes and races, and it is not defined by geographical boundaries but by function. The function is the service of men and men's interests as men define them, which includes the bearing and rearing of children. The details of the service and the working conditions vary by race and class, for men of different races and classes have different interests, perceive their interests differently, and express their needs and demands in different rhetorics, dialects and languages. But there are also some constants.

Whether in lower, middle or upper-class home or work situations, women's service work always includes personal service (the work of maids, butlers, cooks, personal secretaries),* sexual service (including provision for his genital sexual needs and bearing his children, but also including "being nice," "being attractive for him," etc.), and ego service (encouragement, support, praise, attention). Women's service work also is characterized everywhere by the fatal combination of responsibility and powerlessness: we are held responsible and we hold ourselves responsible for good outcomes for men and children in almost every respect though we have in almost no case power adequate to that project. The details of the subjective experience of this servitude are local. They vary with economic class and race and ethnic tradition as well as the personalities of the men in question. So also are the details of the forces which coerce our tolerance of this servitude particular to the different situations in which different women live and work.

All this is not to say that women do not have, assert and manage sometimes to satisfy our own interests, nor to deny that in some cases and in some respects women's independent interests do

---

*Coerced assimilation is in fact one of the *policies* available to an oppressing group in its effort to reduce and/or annihilate another group. This tactic is used by the U.S. government, for instance, on the American Indians.

*At higher class levels women may not *do* all these kinds of work, but are generally still responsible for hiring and supervising those who do it. These services are still, in these cases, women's responsibility.

overlap with men's. But at every race/class level and even across race/class lines men do not serve women as women serve men. "Women's sphere" may be understood as the "service sector," taking the latter expression much more widely and deeply than is usual in discussions of the economy.

III

It seems to be the human condition that in one degree or another we all suffer frustration and limitation, all encounter unwelcome barriers, and all are damaged and hurt in various ways. Since we are a social species, almost all of our behavior and activities are structured by more than individual inclination and the conditions of the planet and its atmosphere. No human is free of social structures, nor (perhaps) would happiness consist in such freedom. Structure consists of boundaries, limits and barriers; in a structured whole, some motions and changes are possible, and others are not. If one is looking for an excuse to dilute the word 'oppression', one can use the fact of social structure as an excuse and say that everyone is oppressed. But if one would rather get clear about what oppression is and is not, one needs to sort out the sufferings, harms and limitations and figure out which are elements of oppression and which are not.

From what I have already said here, it is clear that if one wants to determine whether a particular suffering, harm or limitation is part of someone's being oppressed, one has to look at it *in context* in order to tell whether it is an element in an oppressive structure: one has to see if it is part of an enclosing structure of forces and barriers which tends to the immobilization and reduction of a group or category of people. One has to look at how the barrier or force fits with others and to whose benefit or detriment it works. As soon as one looks at examples, it becomes obvious that not everything which frustrates or limits a person is oppressive, and not every harm or damage is due to or contributes to oppression.

If a rich white playboy who lives off income from his investments in South African diamond mines should break a leg in a skiing accident at Aspen and wait in pain in a blizzard for hours before he is rescued, we may assume that in that period he suffers. But the suffering comes to an end; his leg is repaired by the best surgeon money can buy and he is soon recuperating in a lavish suite, sipping Chivas Regal. Nothing in this picture suggests a structure of barriers and forces. He is a member of several oppressor groups and does not suddenly become oppressed because he is injured and in pain. Even if the accident was caused by someone's malicious negligence, and hence someone can be blamed for it and morally faulted, that person still has not been an agent of oppression.

Consider also the restriction of having to drive one's vehicle on a certain side of the road. There is no doubt that this restriction is almost unbearably frustrating at times, when one's lane is not moving and the other lane is clear. There are surely times, even, when abiding by this regulation would have harmful consequences. But the restriction is obviously wholesome for most of us most of the time. The restraint is imposed for our benefit, and does benefit us; its operation tends to encourage our *continued* motion, not to immobilize us. The limits imposed by traffic regulations are limits most of us would cheerfully impose on ourselves given that we knew others would follow them too. They are part of a structure which shapes our behavior, not to our reduction and immobilization, but rather to the protection of our continued ability to move and act as we will.

Another example: The boundaries of a racial ghetto in an American city serve to some extent to keep white people from going in, as well as to keep ghetto dwellers from going out. A particular white citizen may be frustrated or feel deprived because s/he cannot stroll around there and enjoy the "exotic" aura of a "foreign" culture, or shop for bargains in the ghetto swap shops. In fact, the existence of the ghetto, of racial segregation, does deprive the white person of knowledge and harm her/his character by nurturing unwarranted feelings of superiority. But this does not make the white person in this situation a member of an oppressed race or a person oppressed because of her/his race. One must look at the barrier. It limits the activities and the access of those on both sides of it (though to different degrees). But it is a product of the intention, planning and action of whites for the benefit of whites, to secure and maintain privileges that are available to whites generally, as members of the dominant and privileged group. Though the existence of the barrier has some bad consequences for whites, the barrier does not exist in systematic relationship with other barriers and forces forming a structure oppressive to whites; quite the contrary. It is part of a structure which oppresses the ghetto dwellers and thereby (and by white intention) protects and furthers white interests as dominant white culture understands them. This barrier is not oppressive to whites, even though it is a barrier to whites.

Barriers have different meanings to those on opposite sides of them, even though they are barriers to both. The physical walls of a prison no more dissolve to let an outsider in than to let an insider out, but for the insider they are confining and limiting while to the outsider they may mean protection from what s/he takes to be threats posed by insiders—freedom from harm or anxiety. A set of social and economic barriers and forces separating two groups may be felt, even painfully, by members of both groups and yet may mean confinement to one and liberty and enlargement of opportunity to the other.

The service sector of the wives/mommas/assistants/girls is almost exclusively a woman-only sector; its boundaries not only enclose women but to a very great extent keep men out. Some men sometimes encounter this barrier and experience it as a restriction on their movements, their activities, their control or their choices of "lifestyle." Thinking they might like the simple nurturant life (which they may imagine to be quite free of stress, alienation and hard work), and feeling deprived since it seems closed to them, they thereupon announce the discovery that they are oppressed, too, by "sex roles." But that barrier is erected and maintained by men, for the benefit of men. It consists of cultural and economic forces and pressures in a culture and economy controlled by men in which, at every economic level and in all racial and ethnic subcultures, economy, tradition—and even ideologies of liberation—work to keep at least local culture and economy in male control.*

The boundary that sets apart women's sphere is maintained and promoted by men generally for the benefit of men generally, and men generally do benefit from its existence, even the man who bumps into it and complains of the inconvenience. That barrier is protecting his classification and status as a male, as superior, as having a right to sexual access to a female or females. It protects a kind of citizenship which is superior to that of females of his class and race, his access to a wider range of better paying and higher status work, and his right to prefer unemployment to the degradation of doing lower status or "women's" work.

If a person's life or activity is affected by some force or barrier that person encounters, one may not conclude that the person is oppressed simply because the person encounters that barrier or force; nor simply because the encounter is unpleasant, frustrating or painful to that person at that time; nor simply because the existence of the barrier or force, or the processes which maintain or apply it, serve to deprive that person of something of value. One must look at the barrier or force and answer certain questions about it. Who constructs and maintains it? Whose interests are served by its existence? Is it part of a structure which tends

---

* Of course this is complicated by race and class. Machismo and "Black manhood" politics seem to help keep Latin or Black men in control of more cash than Latin or Black women control; but these politics seem to me also to ultimately help keep the larger economy in *white* male control.

to confine, reduce and immobilize some group? Is the individual a member of the confined group? Various forces, barriers and limitations a person may encounter or live with may be part of an oppressive structure or not, and if they are, that person may be on either the oppressed or the oppressor side of it. One cannot tell which by how loudly or how little the person complains.

IV

Many of the restrictions and limitations we live with are more or less internalized and self-monitored, and are part of our adaptations to the requirements and expectations imposed by the needs and tastes and tyrannies of others. I have in mind such things as women's cramped postures and attenuated strides and men's restraint of emotional self-expression (except for anger). Who gets what out of the practice of those disciplines, and who imposes what penalties for improper relaxations of them? What are the rewards of this self-discipline?

Can men cry? Yes, in the company of women. If a man cannot cry, it is in the company of men that he cannot cry. It is men, not women, who require this restraint; and men not only require it, they reward it. The man who maintains a steely or tough or laid-back demeanor (all are forms which suggest invulnerability) marks himself as a member of the male community and is esteemed by other men. Consequently, the maintenance of that demeanor contributes to the man's self-esteem. It is felt as good, and he can feel good about himself. The way this restriction fits into the structures of men's lives is as one of the socially required behaviors which, if carried off, contribute to their acceptance and respect by significant others and to their own self-esteem. It is to their benefit to practice this discipline.

Consider, by comparison, the discipline of women's cramped physical postures and attenuated stride. This discipline can be relaxed in the company of women; it generally is at its most strenuous in the company of men. Like men's emotional restraint, women's physical restraint is required by men. But unlike the case of men's emotional restraint, women's physical restraint is not rewarded. What do we get for it? Respect and esteem and acceptance? No. They mock us and parody our mincing steps. We look silly, incompetent, weak and generally contemptible. Our exercise of this discipline tends to low esteem and low self-esteem. It does not benefit us. It fits in a network of behaviors through which we constantly announce to others our membership in a lower caste and our unwillingness and/or inability to defend our bodily or moral integrity. It is degrading and part of a pattern of degradation.

Acceptable behavior for both groups, men and women, involves a required restraint that seems in itself silly and perhaps damaging. But the social effect is drastically different. The woman's restraint is part of a structure oppressive to women; the man's restraint is part of a structure oppressive to women.

V

One is marked for application of oppressive pressures by one's membership in some group or category. Much of one's suffering and frustration befalls one partly or largely because one is a member of that category. In the case at hand, it is the category, *woman*. Being a woman is a major factor in my not having a better job than I do; being a woman selects me as a likely victim of sexual assault or harassment; it is my being a woman that reduces the power of my anger to a proof of my insanity. If a woman has little or no economic or political power, or achieves little of what she wants to achieve, a major causal factor in this is that she is a woman. For any woman of any race or economic class, being a woman is significantly attached to whatever disadvantages and deprivations she suffers, be they great or small.

None of this is the case with respect to a person's being a man. Simply being a man is not what stands between him and a better job; whatever assaults and harassments he is subject to, being male is not what selects him for victimization; being male is not a factor which would make his anger impotent—quite the opposite. If a man has little or no material or political power, or achieves little of what he wants to achieve, his being male is no part of the explanation. Being male is something he has going *for* him, even if race or class or age or disability is going against him.

Women are oppressed, *as women*. Members of certain racial and/or economic groups and classes, both the males and the females, are oppressed *as*

members of those races and/or classes. But men are not oppressed *as men*.

. . . and isn't it strange that any of us should have been confused and mystified about such a simple thing?

NOTE

1. This example is derived from *Daddy Was a Number Runner,* by Louise Meriwether (Prentice-Hall. Englewood Cliffs, New Jersey. 1970). p. 144.

THE MASTER'S TOOLS WILL NEVER DISMANTLE THE MASTER'S HOUSE*

Audre Lorde

I AGREED TO TAKE PART in a New York University Institute for the Humanities conference a year ago, with the understanding that I would be commenting upon papers dealing with the role of difference within the lives of american women: difference of race, sexuality, class, and age. The absence of these considerations weakens any feminist discussion of the personal and the political.

It is a particular academic arrogance to assume any discussion of feminist theory without examining our many differences, and without a significant input from poor women, Black and Third World women, and lesbians. And yet, I stand here as a Black lesbian feminist, having been invited to comment within the only panel at this conference where the input of Black feminists and lesbians is represented. What this says about the vision of this conference is sad, in a country where racism, sexism, and homophobia are inseparable. To read this program is to assume that lesbian and Black

women have nothing to say about existentialism, the erotic, women's culture and silence, developing feminist theory, or heterosexuality and power. And what does it mean in personal and political terms when even the two Black women who did present here were literally found at the last hour? What does it mean when the tools of a racist patriarchy are used to examine the fruits of that same patriarchy? It means that only the most narrow perimeters of change are possible and allowable.

The absence of any consideration of lesbian consciousness or the consciousness of Third World women leaves a serious gap within this conference and within the papers presented here. For example, in a paper on material relationships between women, I was conscious of an either/or model of nurturing which totally dismissed my knowledge as a Black lesbian. In this paper there was no examination of mutuality between women, no systems of shared support, no interdependence as exists between lesbians and women-identified women. Yet it is only in the patriarchal model of nurturance that women "who attempt to emancipate themselves pay perhaps too high a price for the results," as this paper states.

For women, the need and desire to nurture each other is not pathological but redemptive, and it is within that knowledge that our real power is

*Comments at "The Personal and the Political Panel," Second Sex Conference, New York, September 29, 1979.

rediscovered. It is this real connection which is so feared by a patriarchal world. Only within a patriarchal structure is maternity the only social power open to women.

Interdependency between women is the way to a freedom which allows the *I* to *be,* not in order to be used, but in order to be creative. This is a difference between the passive *be* and the active *being.*

Advocating the mere tolerance of difference between women is the grossest reformism. It is a total denial of the creative function of difference in our lives. Difference must be not merely tolerated, but seen as a fund of necessary polarities between which our creativity can spark like a dialectic. Only then does the necessity for interdependency become unthreatening. Only within that interdependency of different strengths, acknowledged and equal, can the power to seek new ways of being in the world generate, as well as the courage and sustenance to act where there are no charters.

Within the interdependence of mutual (nondominant) differences lies that security which enables us to descend into the chaos of knowledge and return with true visions of our future, along with the concomitant power to effect those changes which can bring that future into being. Difference is that raw and powerful connection from which our personal power is forged.

As women, we have been taught either to ignore our differences, or to view them as causes for separation and suspicion rather than as forces for change. Without community there is no liberation, only the most vulnerable and temporary armistice between an individual and her oppression. But community must not mean a shedding of our differences, nor the pathetic pretense that these differences do not exist.

Those of us who stand outside the circle of this society's definition of acceptable women; those of us who have been forged in the crucibles of difference—those of us who are poor, who are lesbians, who are Black, who are older—know that *survival is not an academic skill.* It is learning

how to stand alone, unpopular and sometimes reviled, and how to make common cause with those others identified as outside the structures in order to define and seek a world in which we can all flourish. It is learning how to take our differences and make them strengths. *For the master's tools will never dismantle the master's house.* They may allow us temporarily to beat him at his own game, but they will never enable us to bring about genuine change. And this fact is only threatening to those women who still define the master's house as their only source of support.

Poor women and women of Color know there is a difference between the daily manifestations of marital slavery and prostitution because it is our daughters who line 42nd Street. If white american feminist theory need not deal with the differences between us, and the resulting difference in our oppressions, then how do you deal with the fact that the women who clean your houses and tend your children while you attend conferences on feminist theory are, for the most part, poor women and women of Color? What is the theory behind racist feminism?

In a world of possibility for us all, our personal visions help lay the groundwork for political action. The failure of academic feminists to recognize difference as a crucial strength is a failure to reach beyond the first patriarchal lesson. In our world, divide and conquer must become define and empower.

Why weren't other women of Color found to participate in this conference? Why were two phone calls to me considered a consultation? Am I the only possible source of names of Black feminists? And although the Black panelist's paper ends on an important and powerful connection of love between women, what about interracial cooperation between feminists who don't love each other?

In academic feminist circles, the answer to these questions is often, "We did not know who to ask." But that is the same evasion of responsibility, the same cop-out, that keeps Black women's art out of women's exhibitions, Black women's work out of most feminist publications except for the occasional "Special Third World Women's Issue," and Black women's texts off your reading lists. But as Adrienne Rich pointed out in a recent talk, white feminists have educated themselves about such an enormous amount over the past ten years, how come you haven't also educated yourselves about Black women and the differences between us—white and Black—when it is key to our survival as a movement?

Women of today are still being called upon to stretch across the gap of male ignorance and to educate men as to our existence and our needs. This is an old and primary tool of all oppressors to keep the oppressed occupied with the master's concerns. Now we hear that it is the task of women of Color to educate white women—in the face of tremendous resistance—as to our existence, our differences, our relative roles in our joint survival. This is a diversion of energies and a tragic repetition of racist patriarchal thought.

Simone de Beauvoir once said: "It is in the knowledge of the genuine conditions of our lives that we must draw our strength to live and our reasons for acting."

Racism and homophobia are real conditions of all our lives in this place and time. *I urge each one of us here to reach down into that deep place of knowledge inside herself and touch that terror and loathing of any difference that lives there. See whose face it wears.* Then the personal as the political can begin to illuminate all our choices.

ON PSYCHOLOGICAL OPPRESSION

Sandra Lee Bartky

In *Black Skin, White Masks,* Frantz Fanon offers an anguished and eloquent description of the psychological effects of colonialism on the colonized, a "clinical study" of what he calls the "psychic alienation of the black man." "Those who recognize themselves in it," he says, "will have made a step forward."[1] Fanon's black American readers saw at once that he had captured the corrosive effects not only of classic colonial oppression but of domestic racism too, and that his study fitted well the picture of black America as an internal colony. Without wanting in any way to diminish the oppressive and stifling realities of black experience that Fanon reveals, let me say that I, a white woman, recognize myself in this book too, not only in my "shameful livery of white incomprehension,"[2] but as myself the victim of a "psychic alienation" similar to the one Fanon has described. In this paper I shall try to explore that moment of recognition, to reveal the ways in which the psychological effects of sexist oppression resemble those of racism and colonialism.

To oppress, says Webster, is "to lie heavy on, to weigh down, to exercise harsh dominion over." When we describe a people as oppressed, what we have in mind most often is an oppression that is economic and political in character. But recent liberation movements, the black liberation movement and the women's movement in particular, have brought to light forms of oppression that are not immediately economic or political. It is possible to be oppressed in ways that need involve neither physical deprivation, legal inequality, nor economic exploitation;[3] one can be oppressed psychologically—the "psychic alienation" of which Fanon speaks. To be psychologically oppressed is to be weighed down in your mind; it is to have a harsh dominion exercised over your self-esteem. The psychologically oppressed become their own oppressors; they come to exercise harsh dominion over their own self-esteem. Differently put, psychological oppression can be regarded as the "internalization of intimations of inferiority."[4]

Like economic oppression, psychological oppression is institutionalized and systematic; it serves to make the work of domination easier by breaking the spirit of the dominated and by rendering them incapable of understanding the nature of those agencies responsible for their subjugation. This allows those who benefit from the established order of things to maintain their ascendancy with more appearance of legitimacy and with less recourse to overt acts of violence than they might otherwise require. Now, poverty and powerlessness can destroy a person's self-esteem, and the fact that one occupies an inferior position in society is all too often racked up to one's being an inferior sort of person. Clearly, then, economic and political oppression are themselves psychologically oppressive. But there are unique modes of psychological oppression that can be distinguished from the usual forms of economic and political domination. Fanon offers a series of what are essentially phenomenological descriptions of psychic alienation.[5] In spite of considerable overlapping, the experiences of oppression he describes fall into three categories: stereotyping, cultural domination, and sexual objectification. These, I shall contend, are some of the ways in which the terrible messages of inferiority can be delivered even to those who may enjoy certain material benefits; they are special modes of psychic alienation. In what follows, I shall examine some of the ways in which American women—white women and women of color—are stereotyped, culturally dominated, and sexually objectified. In the course of the discussion, I shall argue that our ordinary concept of oppression needs to be altered and expanded, for it is too restricted to encompass what an analysis of psychological oppression reveals about the nature of oppression in general. Finally, I shall be concerned throughout to show how both fragmentation and mystification are present in each mode of psychological oppression, although in varying degrees: fragmentation, the splitting of the whole person into parts of a person which, in stereotyping, may take the form of a war between a "true" and "false" self—or, in sexual objectification, the form of an often coerced and degrading identification of a person with her body; mystification, the systematic obscuring of both the reality and agencies of psychological oppression so that its intended effect, the depreciated self, is lived out as destiny, guilt, or neurosis.

The stereotypes that sustain sexism are similar in many ways to those that sustain racism. Like white women, black and brown persons of both sexes have been regarded as childlike, happiest when they are occupying their "place"; more intuitive than rational, more spontaneous than deliberate, closer to nature, and less capable of substantial cultural accomplishment. Black men and women of all races have been victims of sexual stereotyping: the black man and the black woman, like the "Latin spitfire," are lustful and hotblooded; they are thought to lack the capacities for instinctual control that distinguish people from animals. What is seen as an excess in persons of color appears as a deficiency in the white woman; comparatively frigid, she has been, nonetheless, defined by her sexuality as well, here her reproductive role or function. In regard to capability and competence, black women have, again, an excess of what in white women is a deficiency. White women have been seen as incapable and incompetent: no matter, for these are traits of the truly feminine woman. Black women, on the other hand, have been seen as overly capable, hence, as unfeminine bitches who threaten, through their very competence, to castrate their men.

Stereotyping is morally reprehensible as well as psychologically oppressive on two counts, at least. First, it can hardly be expected that those who hold a set of stereotyped beliefs about the sort of person I am will understand my needs or even respect my rights. Second, suppose that I, the object of some stereotype, believe in it myself—for why should I not believe what everyone else believes? I may then find it difficult to achieve what existentialists call an authentic choice of self, or what some psychologists have regarded as a state of self-actualization. Moral philosophers have quite correctly placed a high value, sometimes the highest value, on the development of autonomy and moral agency. Clearly, the economic and political domination of women—our concrete powerlessness—is what threatens our autonomy most. But stereotyping, in its own way, threatens our self-determination too. Even when economic and political obstacles on the path to autonomy are removed, a depreciated alter ego still blocks the way. It is hard enough for me to determine what sort of person I am or ought to try to become without being shadowed by an alternate self, a truncated and inferior self that I have, in some sense, been doomed to be all the time. For many, the prefabricated self triumphs over a more authentic self which, with work and encouragement, might sometime have emerged. For the talented few, retreat into the *imago* is raised to the status of art or comedy. Muhammad Ali has made himself what he could scarcely escape being made into—a personification of Primitive Man; while Zsa Zsa Gabor is not so much a woman as the parody of a woman.

Female stereotypes threaten the autonomy of women not only by virtue of their existence but also by virtue of their content.[6] In the conventional portrait, women deny their femininity when they undertake action that is too self-regarding or independent. As we have seen, black women are condemned (often by black men) for supposedly having done this already; white women stand under an injunction not to follow their example. Many women in many places lacked (and many still lack) the elementary right to choose our own mates; but for some women even in our own society today, this is virtually the only major decision we are thought capable of making without putting our womanly nature in danger; what follows ever after is or ought to be a properly feminine submission to the decisions of men. We cannot be autonomous, as men are thought to be autonomous, without in some sense ceasing to be women. When one considers how interwoven are traditional female stereotypes with traditional female roles—and these, in turn, with

the ways in which we are socialized—all this is seen in an even more sinister light: White women, at least, are psychologically conditioned not to pursue the kind of autonomous development that is held by the culture to be a constitutive feature of masculinity.

The truncated self I am to be is not something manufactured out there by an anonymous Other which I encounter only in the pages of *Playboy* or the *Ladies' Home Journal;* it is inside of me, a part of myself. I may become infatuated with my feminine persona and waste my powers in the more or less hopeless pursuit of a *Vogue* figure, the look of an *Essence* model, or a home that "expresses my personality." Or I may find the parts of myself fragmented and the fragments at war with one another. Women are only now learning to identify and struggle against the forces that have laid these psychic burdens upon us. More often than not, we live out this struggle, which is really a struggle against oppression, in a mystified way: What we are enduring we believe to be entirely intrapsychic in character, the result of immaturity, maladjustment, or even neurosis.

Tyler, the great classical anthropologist, defined culture as all the items in the general life of a people. To claim that women are victims of cultural domination is to claim that all the items in the general life of our people—our language, our institutions, our art and literature, our popular culture—are sexist; that all, to a greater or lesser degree, manifest male supremacy. There is some exaggeration in this claim, but not much. Unlike the black colonial whom Fanon describes with such pathos, women *qua* women are not now in possession of an alternate culture, a "native" culture which, even if regarded by everyone, including ourselves, as decidedly inferior to the dominant culture, we could at least recognize as our own. However degraded or distorted an image of ourselves we see reflected in the patriarchal culture, the culture of our men is still our culture. Certainly in some respects, the condition of women is like the condition of a colonized people. But we are not a colonized people; we have never been more than half a people.[7]

This lack of cultural autonomy has several important consequences for an understanding of the condition of women. A culture has a global character; hence, the limits of my culture are the limits of my world. The subordination of women, then, because it is so pervasive a feature of my culture, will (if uncontested) appear to be natural—and because it is natural, unalterable. Unlike a colonized people, women have no memory of a "time before": a time before the masters came, a time before we were subjugated and ruled. Further, since one function of cultural identity is to allow me to distinguish those who are like me from those who are not, I may feel more kinship with those who share my culture, even though they oppress me, than with the women of another culture, whose whole experience of life may well be closer to my own than to any man's.

Our true situation in regard to male supremacist culture is one of domination and exclusion. But this manifests itself in an extremely deceptive way; mystification once more holds sway. Our relative absence from the "higher" culture is taken as proof that we are unable to participate in it ("Why are there no great women artists?"). Theories of the female nature must then be brought forward to try to account for this.[8] The splitting or fragmenting of women's consciousness which takes place in the cultural sphere is also apparent. While remaining myself, I must at the same time transform myself into that abstract and "universal" subject for whom cultural artifacts are made and whose values and experience they express. This subject is not universal at all, however, but *male.* Thus, I must approve the taming of the shrew, laugh at the mother-in-law or the dumb blonde, and somehow identify with all those heroes of fiction from Faust to the personae of Norman Mailer and Henry Miller, whose *Bildungsgeschichten* involve the sexual exploitation of women. Women of color have, of course, a special problem: The dominant cultural subject is not only male, but *white,* so their cultural alienation is doubled; they are expected to assimilate cultural motifs that are not only masculinist but racist.[9]

Women of all races and ethnicities, like Fanon's "black man," are subject not only to stereotyping and cultural depreciation but to sexual objectification as well. Even though much has been written about sexual objectification in the literature of the women's movement, the notion itself is complex, obscure, and much in need of philosophical clarification. I offer the following preliminary characterization of sexual objectification: A person is sexually objectified when her sexual parts or sexual functions are separated out from the rest of her personality and reduced to the status of mere instruments or else regarded as if they were capable of representing her. On this definition, then, the prostitute would be a victim of sexual objectification, as would the *Playboy* bunny, the female breeder, and the bathing beauty.

To say that the sexual part of a person is regarded as if it could represent her is to imply that it cannot, that the part and the whole are incommensurable. But surely there are times, in the sexual embrace perhaps, when a woman might want to be regarded as nothing but a sexually intoxicating body and when attention paid to some other aspect of her person—say, to her mathematical ability—would be absurdly out of place. If sexual relations involve some sexual objectification, then it becomes necessary to distinguish situations in which sexual objectification is oppressive from the sorts of situations in which it is not.[10] The identification of a person with her sexuality becomes oppressive, one might venture, when such an identification becomes habitually extended into every area of her experience. To be routinely perceived by others in a sexual light on occasions when such a perception is inappropriate is to have one's very being subjected to that compulsive sexualization that has been the traditional lot of both white women and black men and women of color generally.

"For the majority of white men," says Fanon, "the Negro is the incarnation of a genital potency beyond all moralities and prohibitions."[11] Later in *Black Skin, White Masks,* he writes that "the Negro is the genital."[12]

One way to be sexually objectified, then, is to be the object of a kind of perception, unwelcome and inappropriate, that takes the part for the whole. An example may make this clearer. A young woman was recently interviewed for a teaching job in philosophy by the academic chairman of a large department. During most of the interview, so she reported, the man stared fixedly at her breasts. In this situation, the woman is a bosom, not a job candidate. Was this department chairman guilty only of a confusion between business and pleasure? Scarcely. He stares at her breasts for his sake, not hers. Her wants and needs not only play no role in the encounter but, because of the direction of his attention, she is discomfited, feels humiliated, and performs badly. Not surprisingly, she fails to get the job. Much of the time, sexual objectification occurs independently of what women want; it is something done to us against our will. It is clear from this example that the objectifying perception that splits a person into parts serves to elevate one interest above another. Now it stands revealed not only as a way of perceiving, but as a way of maintaining dominance as well. It is not clear to me that the sexual and nonsexual spheres of experience can or ought to be kept separate forever (Marcuse, for one, has envisioned the eroticization of all areas of human life); but as things stand now, sexualization is one way of fixing disadvantaged persons in their disadvantage, to their clear detriment and within a narrow and repressive eros.

Consider now a second example of the way in which that fragmenting perception, which is so large an ingredient in the sexual objectification of women, serves to maintain the dominance of men. It is a fine spring day, and with an utter lack of self-consciousness, I am bouncing down the street. Suddenly I hear men's voices. Catcalls and whistles fill the air. These noises are clearly sexual in intent and they are meant for me; they come from across the street. I freeze. As Sartre would say, I have been petrified by the gaze of the Other. My face flushes and my motions become stiff and self-conscious. The body which only a moment before I inhabited with such ease now floods my consciousness. I have been made into an object. While it is true that for these men I am nothing but, let us say, a "nice piece of ass," there is more involved in this encounter than their mere fragmented perception of me. They could, after all, have enjoyed me in silence. Blissfully unaware, breasts bouncing, eyes on the birds in the trees, I could have passed by without having been turned to stone. But I must be *made* to know that I am a "nice piece of ass": I must be made to see myself as they see me. There is an element of compulsion in this encounter, in this being-made-to-be-aware of one's own flesh; like being made to apologize, it is humiliating. It is unclear what role is played by sexual arousal or even sexual connoisseurship in encounters like these. What I describe seems less the spontaneous expression of a healthy eroticism than a ritual of subjugation.

Sexual objectification as I have characterized it involves two persons: the one who objectifies and the one who is objectified. But the observer and the one observed can be the same person. I can, of course, take pleasure in my own body as another might take pleasure in it and it would be naive not to notice that there are delights of a narcissistic kind that go along with the status "sex object." But the extent to which the identification of women with their bodies feeds an essentially infantile narcissism—an attitude of mind in keeping with our forced infantilization in other areas of life—is, at least for me, an open question. Subject to the evaluating eye of the male connoisseur, women learn to evaluate themselves first and best. Our identities can no more be kept separate from the appearance of our bodies than they can be kept separate from the shadow-selves of the female stereotype. "Much of a young woman's identity is already defined in her kind of attractiveness and in the selectivity of her search for the man (or men) by whom she wishes to be sought."[13] There is something obsessional in the preoccupation of many women with their bodies, although the magnitude of the obsession will vary somewhat with the presence or absence in a woman's life of other sources of self-esteem and with her capacity to gain a living independent of her looks. Surrounded on all sides by images of perfect female beauty—for, in modern advertising, the needs of capitalism and the traditional values of patriarchy are happily married—of course we fall short. The narcissism encouraged by our identification with the body is shattered by these images. Whose nose is not the wrong shape, whose hips are not too wide or too narrow? Anyone who believes that such concerns are too trivial to weigh very heavily with most women has failed to grasp the realities of the feminine condition.

The idea that women ought always to make themselves as pleasing to the eye as possible is very widespread indeed. It was dismaying to come across this passage in a paper written by an eminent Marxist humanist in defense of the contemporary women's movement:

> There is no reason why a woman's liberation activist should not try to look pretty and attractive. One of the universal human aspirations of all times was to raise reality to the level of art, to make the world more beautiful, to be more beautiful within given limits. Beauty is a value in itself; it will always be respected and will attract—to be sure various forms of beauty but not to the exclusion of physical beauty. A woman does not become a sex object in herself, or only because of her pretty appearance. She becomes a sexual object in relationship, when she allows a man to treat her in a certain depersonalizing, degrading way; and vice versa, a woman does not become a sexual subject by neglecting her appearance.[14]

It is not for the sake of mere men that we women—not just we women, but we women's liberation activists—ought to look "pretty and attractive,"

but for the sake of something much more exalted: for the sake of beauty. This preoccupation with the way we look and the fear that women might stop trying to make themselves pretty and attractive (so as to "raise reality to the level of art") would be a species of objectification anywhere; but it is absurdly out of place in a paper on women's emancipation. It is as if an essay on the black liberation movement were to end by admonishing blacks not to forget their natural rhythm, or as if Marx had warned the workers of the world not to neglect their appearance while throwing off their chains.

Markovic's concern with women's appearance merely reflects a larger cultural preoccupation. It is a fact that women in our society are regarded as having a virtual duty "to make the most of what we have." But the imperative not to neglect our appearance suggests that we can neglect it, that it is within our power to make ourselves look better—not just neater and cleaner, but prettier, and more attractive. What is presupposed by this is that we don't look good enough already, that attention to the ordinary standards of hygiene would be insufficient, that there is something wrong with us as we are. Here, the "intimations of inferiority" are clear: Not only must we continue to produce ourselves as beautiful bodies, but the bodies we have to work with are deficient to begin with. Even within an already inferiorized identity (i.e., the identity of one who is principally and most importantly a body), I turn out once more to be inferior, for the body I am to be, never sufficient unto itself, stands forever in need of plucking or painting, of slimming down or fattening up, of firming or flattening.

The foregoing examination of three modes of psychological oppression, so it appears, points up the need for an alteration in our ordinary concept of oppression. Oppression, I believe, is ordinarily conceived in too limited a fashion. This has placed undue restrictions both on our understanding of what oppression itself is and on the categories of persons we might want to classify as oppressed. Consider, for example, the following paradigmatic case of oppression:

> And the Egyptians made the children of Israel to serve with rigor; and they made their lives bitter with hard bondage, in mortar and in brick, and in all manner of service in the field; all their service wherein they made them serve, was with rigor.[15]

Here the Egyptians, one group of persons, exercise harsh dominion over the Israelites, another group of persons. It is not suggested that the Israelites, however great their sufferings, have lost their integrity and wholeness *qua* persons. But psychological oppression is dehumanizing and depersonalizing; it attacks the person in her personhood. I mean by this that the nature of psychological oppression is such that the oppressor and oppressed alike come to doubt that the oppressed have the capacity to do the sorts of things that only persons can do, to be what persons, in the fullest sense of the term, can be. The possession of autonomy, for example, is widely thought to distinguish persons from nonpersons; but some female stereotypes, as we have seen, threaten the autonomy of women. Oppressed people might or might not be in a position to exercise their autonomy, but the psychologically oppressed may come to believe that they lack the capacity to be autonomous whatever their position.

Similarly, the creation of culture is a distinctly human function, perhaps the most human function. In its cultural life, a group is able to affirm its values and to grasp its identity in acts of self-reflection. Frequently, oppressed persons, cut off from the cultural apparatus, are denied the exercise of this function entirely. To the extent that we are able to catch sight of ourselves in the dominant culture at all, the images we see are distorted or demeaning. Finally, sexual objectification leads to the identification of those who undergo it with what is both human and not quite human—the body. Thus, psychological oppression is just what Fanon said it was—"psychic alienation"—the estrangement or separating of a person from some of the essential attributes of personhood.

Mystification surrounds these processes of human estrangement. The special modes of psychological oppression can be regarded as some of the many ways in which messages of inferiority are delivered to those who are to occupy an inferior position in society. But it is important to remember that messages of this sort are neither sent nor received in an unambiguous way. We are taught that white women and (among others) black men and women are deficient in those capacities that distinguish persons from nonpersons, but at the same time we are assured that we are persons after all. *Of course* women are persons; *of course* blacks are human beings. Who but the lunatic fringe would deny it? The Antillean Negro, Fanon is fond of repeating, is a *Frenchman*. The official ideology announces with conviction that "all men are created equal"; and in spite of the suspect way in which this otherwise noble assertion is phrased, we women learn that they mean to include us after all.

It is itself psychologically oppressive both to believe and at the same time not to believe that one is inferior—in other words, to believe a contradiction. Lacking an analysis of the larger system of social relations which produced it, one can only make sense of this contradiction in two ways. First, while accepting in some quite formal sense the proposition that "all men are created equal," I can believe, inconsistently, what my oppressors have always believed: that some types of persons are less equal than others. I may then live out my membership in my sex or race in *shame;* I am "only a woman" or "just a nigger." Or, somewhat more consistently, I may reject entirely the belief that my disadvantage is generic; but having still to account for it somehow, I may locate the cause squarely within myself, a bad destiny of an entirely private sort—a character flaw, an "inferiority complex," or a neurosis.

Many oppressed persons come to regard themselves as uniquely unable to satisfy normal criteria of psychological health or moral adequacy. To believe that my inferiority is a function of the kind of person I am may make me ashamed of being one of *this* kind. On the other hand, a lack I share with many others just because of an accident of birth would be unfortunate indeed, but at least I would not have to regard myself as having failed uniquely to measure up to standards that people like myself are expected to meet. It should be pointed out, however, that both of these "resolutions"—the ascription of one's inferiority to idiosyncratic or else to generic causes—produces a "poor self-image," a bloodless term of the behavioral sciences that refers to a very wide variety of possible ways to suffer.[16]

To take one's oppression to be an inherent flaw of birth, or of psychology, is to have what Marxists have characterized as "false consciousness." Systematically deceived as we are about the nature and origin of our unhappiness, our struggles are directed inward toward the self, or toward other similar selves in whom we may see our deficiencies mirrored, not outward upon those social forces responsible for our predicament. Like the psychologically disturbed, the psychologically oppressed often lack a viable identity. Frequently we are unable to make sense of our own impulses or feelings, not only because our drama of fragmentation gets played out on an inner psychic stage, but because we are forced to find our way about in a world which presents itself to us in a masked and deceptive fashion. Regarded as persons, yet depersonalized, we are treated by our society the way the parents of some schizophrenics are said by R. D. Laing to treat their children—professing love at the very moment they shrink from their children's touch.

In sum, then, to be psychologically oppressed is to be caught in the double bind of a society which both affirms my human status and at the same time bars me from the exercise of many of those typically human functions that bestow this status. To be denied an autonomous choice of self, forbidden cultural expression, and condemned to the immanence of mere bodily being is to be cut off from the sorts of activities that define what it is to be human. A person whose being has been subjected to these cleavages may be described as "alienated." Alienation in any form causes a rupture within the human person, an estrangement from self, a "splintering

of human nature into a number of misbegotten parts."[17] Any adequate theory of the nature and varieties of human alienation, then, must encompass psychological oppression—or, to use Fanon's term once more, "psychic alienation."

Much has been written about alienation, but it is Marx's theory of alienation that speaks most compellingly to the concerns of feminist political theory. Alienation for Marx is primarily the alienation of labor. What distinguishes human beings from animals is "labor"—for Marx, the free, conscious, and creative transformation of nature in accordance with human needs. But under capitalism, workers are alienated in production, estranged from the products of their labor, from their own productive activity, and from their fellow workers.

Human productive activity, according to Marx, is "objectified" in its products. What this means is that we are able to grasp ourselves reflectively primarily in the things we have produced; human needs and powers become concrete "in their products as the amount and type of change which their exercise has brought about."[18] But in capitalist production, the capitalist has a right to appropriate what workers have produced. Thus, the product goes to augment capital, where it becomes part of an alien force exercising power over those who produced it. An "objectification" or extension of the worker's self, the product is split off from this self and turned against it. But workers are alienated not only from the products they produce but from their own laboring activity as well, for labor under capitalism is not, as labor should be, an occasion for human self-realization but mere drudgery which "mortifies the body and ruins the mind."[19] The worker's labor "is therefore not voluntary, but coerced; it is forced labor. It is therefore not the satisfaction of a need; it is merely a means to satisfy needs external to it."[20] When the free and creative productive activity that should define human functioning is reduced to a mere means to sustain life, to "forced labor," workers suffer fragmentation and loss of self. Since labor is the most characteristic human life activity, to be alienated from one's own labor is to be estranged from oneself.

In many ways, psychic alienation and the alienation of labor are profoundly alike. Both involve a splitting off of human functions from the human person, a forbidding of activities thought to be essential to a fully human existence. Both subject the individual to fragmentation and impoverishment. Alienation is not a condition into which someone might stumble by accident; it has come both to the victim of psychological oppression and to the alienated worker from without, as a usurpation by someone else of what is, by rights, *not his to usurp*.[21] Alienation occurs in each case when activities which not only belong to the domain of the self but define, in large measure, the proper functioning of this self, fall under the control of others. To be a victim of alienation is to have a part of one's being stolen by another. Both psychic alienation and the alienation of labor might be regarded as varieties of alienated productivity. From this perspective, cultural domination would be the estrangement or alienation of production in the cultural sphere; while the subjective effects of stereotyping as well as the self-objectification that regularly accompanies sexual objectification could be interpreted as an alienation in the production of one's own person.

All the modes of oppression—psychological, political, and economic—and the kinds of alienation they generate serve to maintain a vast system of privilege—privilege of race, of sex, and of class. Every mode of oppression within the system has its own part to play, but each serves to support and to maintain the others. Thus, for example, the assault on the self-esteem of white women and of black persons of both sexes prepares us for the historic role that a disproportionate number of us are destined to play within the process of production: that of a cheap or reserve labor supply. Class oppression, in turn, encourages those who are somewhat higher in the hierarchies of race or gender to cling to a false sense of superiority—a poor compensation indeed. Because of the interlocking character of the modes of oppression, I think it highly unlikely that any form of oppression will disappear entirely until the system of oppression as a whole is overthrown.

NOTES

1. Frantz Fanon, *Black Skins, White Masks* (New York: Grove Press, 1967), p. 12.
2. Ibid.
3. For an excellent comparison of the concepts of exploitation and oppression, see Judith Farr Tormey, "Exploitation, Oppression and Self-Sacrifice," in *Women and Philosophy,* ed. Carol C. Gould and Marx W. Wartofsky (New York: G. P. Putnam's Sons, 1976), pp. 206–221.
4. Joyce Mitchell Cook, paper delivered at Philosophy and the Black Liberation Struggle Conference, University of Illinois, Chicago Circle, November 19–20, 1970.
5. Fanon's phenomenology of oppression, however, is almost entirely a phenomenology of the oppression of colonized *men*. He seems unaware of the ways in which the oppression of women by their men in the societies he examines is itself similar to the colonization of natives by Europeans. Sometimes, as in *A Dying Colonialism* (New York: Grove Press, 1968), he goes so far as to defend the clinging to oppressive practices, such as the sequestration of women in Moslem countries, as an authentic resistance by indigenous people to Western cultural intrusion. For a penetrating critique of Fanon's attitude toward women, see Barbara Burris, "Fourth World Manifesto," in *Radical Feminism,* ed. A. Koedt, E. Levine, and A. Rapone (New York: Quadrangle, 1973), pp. 322–357.
6. I have in mind Abraham Maslow's concept of autonomy, a notion which has the advantage of being neutral as regards the controversy between free will and determinism. For Maslow, the sources of behavior of autonomous or "psychologically free"

individuals are more internal than reactive:

> Such people become far more self-sufficient and self-contained. The determinants which govern them are now primarily inner ones. . . . They are the laws of their own inner nature, their potentialities and capacities, their talents, their latent resources, their creative impulses, their needs to know themselves and to become more and more integrated and unified, more and more aware of what they really are, of what they really want, of what their call or vocation or fate is to be. *Toward a Psychology of Being,* 2d ed. ([New York: D. Van Nostrand Co., 1968], p. 35).

It would be absurd to suggest that most men are autonomous in this sense of the term. Nevertheless, insofar as there are individuals who resemble this portrait, I think it likelier that they will be men than women—at least white women. I think it likely that more white men than white women *believe* themselves to be autonomous; this belief, even if false, is widely held, and this in itself has implications that are important to consider. Whatever the facts may be in regard to men's lives, the point to remember is this: women have been thought to have neither the capacity nor the right to aspire to an ideal of autonomy, an ideal to which there accrues, whatever its relation to mental health, an enormous social prestige.

7. Many feminists would object vigorously to my claim that there has been no female culture (see, e.g., Burris, "Fourth World Manifesto"). I am not claiming that women have had no enclaves within the dominant culture, that we have never made valuable contributions to the larger culture, or even that we have never dominated any avenue of cultural expression—one would have to think only of the way in which women have dominated certain forms of folk art (e.g., quilting). What I am claiming is that none of this adds up to a "culture," in the sense in which we speak of Jewish culture, Arapesh culture, or Afro-American culture. Further, the fact that many women are today engaged in the self-conscious attempt to create a female culture testifies, I think, to the situation regarding culture being essentially as I describe it.

8. The best-known modern theory of this type is, of course, Freud's. He maintains that the relative absence of women from the higher culture is the consequence of a lesser ability to sublimate libidinal drives. See "Femininity" in *New Introductory Lectures in Psychoanalysis* (New York: W. W. Norton, 1933).

9. I take it that something like this forms the backdrop to the enjoyment of the average movie. It is daunting to consider the magnitude of the task of neutralization or transformation of hostile cultural messages that must fall constantly to the average female, non-white or even working class white male TV watcher or moviegoer. The pleasure we continue to take in cultural products that may disparage us remains, at least to me, something of a mystery.

10. There might be some objection to regarding ordinary sexual relations as involving sexual objectification, since this use of the term seems not to jibe with its use in more ordinary contexts. For Hegel, Marx, and Sartre, "objectification" is an important moment in the dialectic of consciousness. My decision to treat ordinary sexual relations or even sexual desire alone as involving some objectification is based on a desire to remain within this tradition. Further, Sartre's phenomenology of sexual desire in *Being and Nothingness* (New York: Philosophical Library, 1966) draws heavily on a concept of objectification in an unusually compelling description of the experienced character of that state:

> The caress by realizing the Other's incarnation reveals to me my own incarnation; that is, I make myself flesh in order to impel the Other to realize for herself and for-me her own flesh, and my caresses cause my

flesh to be born for me in so far as it is for the Other flesh causing her to be born as flesh. I make her enjoy my flesh through her flesh in order to compel her to feel herself flesh. And so possession truly appears as a double reciprocal incarnation. (p. 508)

What I call "objectification," Sartre here calls "incarnation," a refinement not necessary for my purposes. What he calls "sadism" is incarnation without reciprocity. Most of my examples of sexual objectification would fall into the latter category.

11. Fanon, *Black Skin, White Masks,* p. 177. Eldridge Cleaver sounds a similar theme in *Soul on Ice* (New York: Dell, 1968). The archetypal white man in American society, for Cleaver, is the "Omnipotent Administrator," the archetypal black man the "Super-Masculine Menial."

12. P. 180.

13. Erik Erikson, "Inner and Outer Space: Reflections on Womanhood," *Daedalus,* Vol. 93, 1961, pp. 582–606.

14. Mihailo Markovic, "Women's Liberation and Human Emancipation," in *Women and Philosophy,* pp. 165–166. In spite of this lapse and some questionable opinions concerning the nature of female sexuality, Markovic's paper is a most compelling defense of the claim that the emancipation of women cannot come about under capitalism.

15. Exod. 1:13–14.

16. The available clinical literature on the psychological effects of social inferiority supports this claim. See William H. Grier and Price M. Cobbs, *Black Rage* (New York: Grosset & Dunlap, 1969); Pauline Bart, "Depression in Middle-Aged Women," in *Women in Sexist Society,* ed. Vivian Gornick and Barbara Moran (New York: New American Library, 1971), pp. 163–186; also Phyllis Chesler, *Women and Madness.* (New York: Doubleday, 1972).

17. Bertell Ollman, *Alienation: Marx's Conception of Man in Capitalist Society* (London and New York: Cambridge University Press, 1971), p. 135.

18. Ibid., p. 143.

19. Karl Marx, *The Economic and Philosophical Manuscripts of 1844,* ed. Dirk J. Struik (New York: International Publishers, 1964), p. 111.

20. Ibid.

21. The use of the masculine possessive pronoun is deliberate.

WHITE PRIVILEGE AND MALE PRIVILEGE

A Personal Account of Coming to See Correspondences through Work in Women's Studies (1988)

Peggy McIntosh

Through work to bring materials and perspectives from Women's Studies into the rest of the curriculum, I have often noticed men's unwillingness to grant that they are overprivileged in the curriculum, even though they may grant that women are disadvantaged. Denials that amount to taboos surround the subject of advantages that men gain from women's disadvantages. These denials protect male privilege from being fully recognized, acknowledged, lessened, or ended.

Thinking through unacknowledged male privilege as a phenomenon with a life of its own, I realized that since hierarchies in our society are interlocking, there was most likely a phenomenon of white privilege that was similarly denied and protected, but alive and real in its effects. As a white person, I realized I had been taught about racism as something that puts others at a disadvantage, but had been taught not to see one of its corollary aspects, white privilege, which puts me at an advantage.

I think whites are carefully taught not to recognize white privilege, as males are taught not to recognize male privilege. So I have begun in an untutored way to ask what it is like to have white privilege. This paper is a partial record of my personal observations and not a scholarly analysis. It is based on my daily experiences within my particular circumstances.

I have come to see white privilege as an invisible package of unearned assets that I can count on cashing in each day, but about which I was "meant" to remain oblivious. White privilege is like an invisible weightless knapsack of special provisions, assurances, tools, maps, guides, codebooks, passports, visas, clothes, compass, emergency gear, and blank checks.

Since I have had trouble facing white privilege, and describing its results in my life, I saw parallels here with men's reluctance to acknowledge male privilege. Only rarely will a man go beyond acknowledging that women are disadvantaged to acknowledging that men have unearned advantage, or that unearned privilege has not been good for men's development as human beings, or for society's development, or that privilege systems might ever be challenged and *changed*.

I will review here several types or layers of denial that I see at work protecting, and preventing awareness about, entrenched male privilege. Then I will draw parallels, from my own experience, with the denials that veil the facts of white privilege. Finally, I will list forty-six ordinary and daily ways in which I experience having white privilege, by contrast with my African American colleagues in the same building. This list is not intended to be generalizable. Others can make their own lists from within their own life circumstances.

Writing this paper has been difficult, despite warm receptions for the talks on which it is based. For describing white privilege makes one newly accountable. As we in Women's Studies

work reveal male privilege and ask men to give up some of their power, so one who writes about having white privilege must ask, "Having described it, what will I do to lessen or end it?"

The denial of men's overprivileged state takes many forms in discussions of curriculum change work. Some claim that men must be central in the curriculum because they have done most of what is important or distinctive in life or in civilization. Some recognize sexism in the curriculum but deny that it makes male students seem unduly important in life. Others agree that certain *individual* thinkers are male oriented but deny that there is any *systemic* tendency in disciplinary frameworks or epistemology to overempower men as a group. Those men who do grant that male privilege takes institutionalized and embedded forms are still likely to deny that male hegemony has opened doors for them personally. Virtually all men deny that male overreward alone can explain men's centrality in all the inner sanctums of our most powerful institutions. Moreover, those few who will acknowledge that male privilege systems have overempowered them usually end up doubting that we could dismantle these privilege systems. They may say they will work to improve women's status, in the society or in the university, but they can't or won't support the idea of lessening men's. In curricular terms, this is the point at which they say that they regret they cannot use any of the interesting new scholarship on women because the syllabus is full. When the talk turns to giving men less cultural room, even the most thoughtful and fair-minded of the men I know will tend to reflect, or fall back on, conservative assumptions about the inevitability of present gender relations and distributions of power, calling on precedent or sociobiology and psychobiology to demonstrate that male domination is natural and follows inevitably from evolutionary pressures. Others resort to arguments from "experience" or religion or social responsibility or wishing and dreaming.

After I realized, through faculty development work in Women's Studies, the extent to which men work from a base of unacknowledged privilege, I understood that much of their oppressiveness was unconscious. Then I remembered the frequent charges from women of color that white women whom they encounter are oppressive. I began to understand why we are justly seen as oppressive, even when we don't see ourselves that way. At the very least, obliviousness of one's privileged state can make a person or group irritating to be with. I began to count the ways in which I enjoy unearned skin privilege and have been conditioned into oblivion about its existence, unable to see that it put me "ahead" in any way, or put my people ahead, overrewarding us and yet also paradoxically damaging us, or that it could or should be changed.

My schooling gave me no training in seeing myself as an oppressor, as an unfairly advantaged person, or as a participant in a damaged culture. I was taught to see myself as an individual whose moral state depended on her individual moral will. At school, we were not taught about slavery in any depth; we were not taught to see slaveholders as damaged people. Slaves were seen as the only group at risk of being dehumanized. My schooling followed the pattern which Elizabeth Minnich has pointed out: whites are taught to think of their lives as morally neutral, normative, and average, and also ideal, so that when we work to benefit others, this is seen as work that will allow "them" to be more like "us." I think many of us know how obnoxious this attitude can be in men.

After frustration with men who would not recognize male privilege, I decided to try to work on myself at least by identifying some of the daily effects of white privilege in my life. It is crude work, at this stage, but I will give here a list of special circumstances and conditions I experience that I did not earn but that I have been made to feel are mine by birth, by citizenship, and by virtue of being a conscientious law-abiding "normal" person of goodwill. I have chosen those conditions that I think in my case *attach somewhat more to skin-color privilege* than to class, religion, ethnic status, or geographical location,

though these other privileging factors are intricately intertwined. As far as I can see, my Afro-American co-workers, friends, and acquaintances with whom I come into daily or frequent contact in this particular time, place, and line of work cannot count on most of these conditions.

1. I can, if I wish, arrange to be in the company of people of my race most of the time.
2. I can avoid spending time with people whom I was trained to mistrust and who have learned to mistrust my kind or me.
3. If I should need to move, I can be pretty sure of renting or purchasing housing in an area which I can afford and in which I would want to live.
4. I can be reasonably sure that my neighbors in such a location will be neutral or pleasant to me.
5. I can go shopping alone most of the time, fairly well assured that I will not be followed or harassed by store detectives.
6. I can turn on the television or open to the front page of the paper and see people of my race widely and positively represented.
7. When I am told about our national heritage or about "civilization," I am shown that people of my color made it what it is.
8. I can be sure that my children will be given curricular materials that testify to the existence of their race.
9. If I want to, I can be pretty sure of finding a publisher for this piece on white privilege.
10. I can be fairly sure of having my voice heard in a group in which I am the only member of my race.
11. I can be casual about whether or not to listen to another woman's voice in a group in which she is the only member of her race.
12. I can go into a book shop and count on finding the writing of my race represented, into a supermarket and find the staple foods that fit with my cultural traditions, into a hairdresser's shop and find someone who can deal with my hair.

13. Whether I use checks, credit cards, or cash, I can count on my skin color not to work against the appearance that I am financially reliable.

14. I could arrange to protect our young children most of the time from people who might not like them.

15. I did not have to educate our children to be aware of systemic racism for their own daily physical protection.

16. I can be pretty sure that my children's teachers and employers will tolerate them if they fit school and workplace norms; my chief worries about them do not concern others' attitudes toward their race.

17. I can talk with my mouth full and not have people put this down to my color.

18. I can swear, or dress in secondhand clothes, or not answer letters, without having people attribute these choices to the bad morals, the poverty, or the illiteracy of my race.

19. I can speak in public to a powerful male group without putting my race on trial.

20. I can do well in a challenging situation without being called a credit to my race.

21. I am never asked to speak for all the people of my racial group.

22. I can remain oblivious to the language and customs of persons of color who constitute the world's majority without feeling in my culture any penalty for such oblivion.

23. I can criticize our government and talk about how much I fear its policies and behavior without being seen as a cultural outsider.

24. I can be reasonably sure that if I ask to talk to "the person in charge," I will be facing a person of my race.

25. If a traffic cop pulls me over or if the IRS audits my tax return, I can be sure I haven't been singled out because of my race.

26. I can easily buy posters, postcards, picture books, greeting cards, dolls, toys, and children's magazines featuring people of my race.

27. I can go home from most meetings of organizations I belong to feeling somewhat tied in, rather than isolated, out of place, outnumbered, unheard, held at a distance, or feared.

28. I can be pretty sure that an argument with a colleague of another race is more likely to jeopardize her chances for advancement than to jeopardize mine.

29. I can be fairly sure that if I argue for the promotion of a person of another race, or a program centering on race, this is not likely to cost me heavily within my present setting, even if my colleagues disagree with me.

30. If I declare there is a racial issue at hand, or there isn't a racial issue at hand, my race will lend me more credibility for either position than a person of color will have.

31. I can choose to ignore developments in minority writing and minority activist programs, or disparage them, or learn from them, but in any case, I can find ways to be more or less protected from negative consequences of any of these choices.

32. My culture gives me little fear about ignoring the perspectives and powers of people of other races.

33. I am not made acutely aware that my shape, bearing, or body odor will be taken as a reflection on my race.

34. I can worry about racism without being seen as self-interested or self-seeking.

35. I can take a job with an affirmative action employer without having my co-workers on the job suspect that I got it because of my race.

36. If my day, week, or year is going badly, I need not ask of each negative episode or situation whether it has racial overtones.

37. I can be pretty sure of finding people who would be willing to talk with me and advise me about my next steps, professionally.

38. I can think over many options, social, political, imaginative, or professional, without asking whether a person of my race would be accepted or allowed to do what I want to do.

39. I can be late to a meeting without having the lateness reflect on my race.

40. I can choose public accommodation without fearing that people of my race cannot get in or will be mistreated in the places I have chosen.

41. I can be sure that if I need legal or medical help, my race will not work against me.

42. I can arrange my activities so that I will never have to experience feelings of rejection owing to my race.

43. If I have low credibility as a leader, I can be sure that my race is not the problem.

44. I can easily find academic courses and institutions that give attention only to people of my race.

45. I can expect figurative language and imagery in all of the arts to testify to experiences of my race.

46. I can choose blemish cover or bandages in "flesh" color and have them more or less match my skin.

I repeatedly forgot each of the realizations on this list until I wrote it down. For me, white privilege has turned out to be an elusive and fugitive subject. The pressure to avoid it is great, for in facing it I must give up the myth of meritocracy. If these things are true, this is not such a free country; one's life is not what one makes it; many doors open for certain people through no virtues of their own. These perceptions mean also that my moral condition is not what I had been led to believe. The appearance of being a good citizen rather than a troublemaker comes in large part from having all sorts of doors open automatically because of my color.

A further paralysis of nerve comes from literary silence protecting privilege. My clearest memories of finding such analysis are in Lillian Smith's unparalleled *Killers of the Dream* and Margaret Andersen's review of Karen and Mamie Fields' *Lemon Swamp*. Smith, for example, wrote about walking toward black children on the street and knowing they would step into the gutter; Andersen contrasted the pleasure that she, as a white child, took on summer driving trips to the south with Karen Fields' memories of driving in a closed car stocked with all necessities lest, in stopping, her black family should suffer "insult, or worse." Adrienne Rich also recognizes and writes about daily experiences of privilege, but in my observation, white women's writing in this area is far more often on systemic racism than on our daily lives as light-skinned women.[1]

In unpacking this invisible knapsack of white privilege, I have listed conditions of daily experience that I once took for granted, as neutral, normal, and universally available to everybody, just as I once thought of a male-focused curriculum as the neutral or accurate account that can speak for all. Nor did I think of any of these perquisites as bad for the holder. I now think that we need a more finely differentiated taxonomy of privilege, for some of these varieties are only what one would want for everyone in a just society, and others give license to be ignorant, oblivious, arrogant, and destructive. Before proposing some more finely tuned categorization, I will make some observations about the general effects of these conditions on my life and expectations.

In this potpourri of examples, some privileges make me feel at home in the world. Others allow me to escape penalties or dangers that others suffer. Through some, I escape fear, anxiety, insult, injury, or a sense of not being welcome, not being real. Some keep me from having to hide, to be in disguise, to feel sick or crazy, to negotiate each transaction from the position of being an outsider or, within my group, a person who is suspected of having too close links with a dominant culture. Most keep me from having to be angry.

I see a pattern running through the matrix of white privilege, a pattern of assumptions that were passed on to me as a white person. There was one main piece of cultural turf; it was my own turf, and I was among those who could control the turf. I could measure up to the cultural standards and take advantage of the many options I saw around me to make what the culture would call a success of my life. *My skin color was an asset for any move I was educated to want to make.* I could think of myself as "belonging" in major ways and of making social systems work for me. I could freely disparage, fear, neglect, or be oblivious to anything outside of the dominant cultural forms. Being of the main culture, I could also criticize it fairly freely. My life was reflected back to me frequently enough so that I felt, with regard to my race, if not to my sex, like one of the real people.

Whether through the curriculum or in the newspaper, the television, the economic system, or the general look of people in the streets, I received daily signals and indications that my people counted and that others *either didn't exist or must be trying, not very successfully, to be like people of my race.* I was given cultural permission not to hear voices of people of other races or a tepid cultural tolerance for hearing or acting on such voices. I was also raised not to suffer seriously from anything that darker-skinned people might say about my group, "protected," though perhaps I should more accurately say *prohibited,* through the habits of my economic class and social group, from living in racially mixed groups or being reflective about interactions between people of differing races.

In proportion as my racial group was being made confident, comfortable, and oblivious, other groups were likely being made unconfident, uncomfortable, and alienated. Whiteness protected me from many kinds of hostility, distress, and violence, which I was being subtly trained to visit in turn upon people of color.

For this reason, the word "privilege" now seems to me misleading. Its connotations are too positive to fit the conditions and behaviors which "privilege systems" produce. We usually think of privilege as being a favored state, whether earned, or conferred by birth or luck. School graduates are reminded they are privileged and urged to use their (enviable) assets well. The word "privilege" carries the connotation of being something everyone must want. Yet some of the conditions I have described here work to systemically overempower certain groups. Such privilege simply *confers dominance,* gives permission to control, because of one's race or sex. The kind of privilege

that gives license to some people to be, at best, thoughtless and, at worst, murderous should not continue to be referred to as a desirable attribute. Such "privilege" may be widely desired without being in any way beneficial to the whole society.

Moreover, though "privilege" may confer power, it does not confer moral strength. Those who do not depend on conferred dominance have traits and qualities that may never develop in those who do. Just as Women's Studies courses indicate that women survive their political circumstances to lead lives that hold the human race together, so "underprivileged" people of color who are the world's majority have survived their oppression and lived survivors' lives from which the white global minority can and must learn. In some groups, those dominated have actually become strong through *not* having all of these unearned advantages, and this gives them a great deal to teach the others. Members of so-called privileged groups can seem foolish, ridiculous, infantile, or dangerous by contrast.

I want, then, to distinguish between earned strength and unearned power conferred systemically. Power from unearned privilege can look like strength when it is, in fact, permission to escape or to dominate. But not all of the privileges on my list are inevitably damaging. Some, like the expectation that neighbors will be decent to you, or that your race will not count against you in court, should be the norm in a just society and should be considered as the entitlement of everyone. Others, like the privilege not to listen to less powerful people, distort the humanity of the holders as well as the ignored groups. Still others, like finding one's staple foods everywhere, may be a function of being a member of a numerical majority in the population. Others have to do with not having to labor under pervasive negative stereotyping and mythology.

We might at least start by distinguishing between positive advantages that we can work to spread, to the point where they are not advantages at all but simply part of the normal civic and social fabric, and negative types of advantage that unless rejected will always reinforce our present hierarchies. For example, the positive "privilege" of belonging, the feeling that one belongs within the human circle, as Native Americans say, fosters development and should not be seen as privilege for a few. It is, let us say, an entitlement that none of us should have to earn; ideally it is an *unearned entitlement.* At present, since only a few have it, it is an *unearned advantage* for them. The negative "privilege" that gave me cultural permission not to take darker-skinned Others seriously can be seen as arbitrarily conferred dominance and should not be desirable for anyone. This paper results from a process of coming to see that some of the power that I originally saw as attendant on being a human being in the United States consisted in *unearned advantage* and *conferred dominance,* as well as other kinds of special circumstance not universally taken for granted.

In writing this paper I have also realized that white identity and status (as well as class identity and status) give me considerable power to choose whether to broach this subject and its trouble. I can pretty well decide whether to disappear and avoid and not listen and escape the dislike I may engender in other people through this essay, or interrupt, answer, interpret, preach, correct, criticize, and control to some extent what goes on in reaction to it. Being white, I am given considerable power to escape many kinds of danger or penalty as well as to choose which risks I want to take.

There is an analogy here, once again, with Women's Studies. Our male colleagues do not have a great deal to lose in supporting Women's Studies, but they do not have a great deal to lose if they oppose it either. They simply have the power to decide whether to commit themselves to more equitable distributions of power. They will probably feel few penalties whatever choice they make; they do not seem, in any obvious short-term sense, the ones at risk, though they and we are all at risk because of the behaviors that have been rewarded in them.

Through Women's Studies work I have met very few men who are truly distressed about sys-temic, unearned male advantage and conferred dominance. And so one question for me and others like me is whether we will be like them, or whether we will get truly distressed, even outraged, about unearned race advantage and conferred dominance and if so, what we will do to lessen them. In any case, we need to do more work in identifying how they actually affect our daily lives. We need more down-to-earth writing by people about these taboo subjects. We need more understanding of the ways in which white "privilege" damages white people, for these are not the same ways in which it damages the victimized. Skewed white psyches are an inseparable part of the picture, though I do not want to confuse the kinds of damage done to the holders of special assets and to those who suffer the deficits. Many, perhaps most, of our white students in the United States think that racism doesn't affect them because they are not people of color; they do not see "whiteness" as a racial identity. Many men likewise think that Women's Studies does not bear on their own existences because they are not female; they do not see themselves as having gendered identities. Insisting on the universal "effects" of "privilege" systems, then, becomes one of our chief tasks, and being more explicit about the *particular* effects in particular contexts is another. Men need to join us in this work.

In addition, since race and sex are not the only advantaging systems at work, we need to similarly examine the daily experience of having age advantage, or ethnic advantage, or physical ability, or advantage related to nationality, religion, or sexual orientation. Professor Marnie Evans suggested to me that in many ways the list I made also applies directly to heterosexual privilege. This is a still more taboo subject than race privilege: the daily ways in which heterosexual privilege makes some persons comfortable or powerful, providing supports, assets, approvals, and rewards to those who live or expect to live in heterosexual pairs. Unpacking that content is still more difficult, owing to the deeper imbeddedness of heterosexual advantage and dominance and stricter taboos surrounding these.

But to start such an analysis I would put this observation from my own experience: the fact that I live under the same roof with a man triggers all kinds of societal assumptions about my worth, politics, life, and values and triggers a host of unearned advantages and powers. After recasting many elements from the original list I would add further observations like these:

1. My children do not have to answer questions about why I live with my partner (my husband).
2. I have no difficulty finding neighborhoods where people approve of our household.
3. Our children are given texts and classes that implicitly support our kind of family unit and do not turn them against my choice of domestic partnership.
4. I can travel alone or with my husband without expecting embarrassment or hostility in those who deal with us.
5. Most people I meet will see my marital arrangements as an asset to my life or as a favorable comment on my likability, my competence, or my mental health.
6. I can talk about the social events of a weekend without fearing most listeners' reactions.
7. I will feel welcomed and "normal" in the usual walks of public life, institutional and social.
8. In many contexts, I am seen as "all right" in daily work on women because I do not live chiefly with women.

Difficulties and dangers surrounding the task of finding parallels are many. Since racism, sexism, and heterosexism are not the same, the advantages associated with them should not be seen as the same. In addition, it is hard to isolate aspects of unearned advantage that derive chiefly from social class, economic class, race, religion, region, sex, or ethnic identity. The oppressions are both distinct and interlocking, as the Combahee River Collective statement of 1977 continues to remind us eloquently.[2]

One factor seems clear about all of the interlocking oppressions. They take both active forms that we can see and embedded forms that members of the dominant group are taught not to see. In my class and place, I did not see myself as racist because I was taught to recognize racism only in individual acts of meanness by members of my group, never in invisible systems conferring racial dominance on my group from birth. Likewise, we are taught to think that sexism or heterosexism is carried on only through intentional, individual acts of discrimination, meanness, or cruelty, rather than in invisible systems conferring unsought dominance on certain groups. Disapproving of the systems won't be enough to change them. I was taught to think that racism could end if white individuals changed their attitudes; many men think sexism can be ended by individual changes in daily behavior toward women. But a man's sex provides advantage for him whether or not he approves of the way in which dominance has been conferred on his group. A "white" skin in the United States opens many doors for whites whether or not we approve of the way dominance has been conferred on us. Individual acts can palliate, but cannot end, these problems. To redesign social systems, we need first to acknowledge their colossal unseen dimensions. The silences and denials surrounding privilege are the key political tool here. They keep the thinking about equality or equity incomplete, protecting unearned advantage and conferred dominance by making these taboo subjects. Most talk by whites about equal opportunity seems to me now to be about equal opportunity to try to get into a position of dominance while denying that *systems* of dominance exist.

Obliviousness about white advantage, like obliviousness about male advantage, is kept strongly inculturated in the United States so as to maintain the myth of meritocracy, the myth that democratic choice is equally available to all. Keeping most people unaware that freedom of confident action is there for just a small number of people props up those in power and serves to keep power in the hands of the same groups that have most of it already. Though systemic change takes many decades, there are pressing questions for me and I imagine for some others like me if we raise our daily consciousness on the perquisites of being light-skinned. What will we do with such knowledge? As we know from watching men, it is an open question whether we will choose to use unearned advantage to weaken invisible privilege systems and whether we will use any of our arbitrarily awarded power to try to reconstruct power systems on a broader base.

NOTES

1. Andersen, Margaret, "Race and the Social Science Curriculum: A Teaching and Learning Discussion." *Radical Teacher,* November, 1984, pp. 17–20. Smith, Lillian, *Killers of the Dream,* New York: W.W. Norton, 1949.
2. "A Black Feminist Statement," The Combahee River Collective, in G. Hull, P. Scott, B. Smith, Eds., *All the Women Are White, All the Blacks Are Men, But Some of Us Are Brave: Black Women's Studies,* Old Westbury, NY: The Feminist Press, 1982, pp. 13–22.

PLAYFULNESS, "WORLD"-TRAVELLING, AND LOVING PERCEPTION

María Lugones

This is a paper about cross-cultural and cross-racial loving that emphasizes the need to understand and affirm the plurality in and among women as central to feminist ontology and epistemology. Love is seen not as fusion and erasure of difference but as incompatible with them. Love reveals plurality. Unity—not to be confused with solidarity—is understood as conceptually tied to domination. This paper weaves two aspects of life together. My coming to consciousness as a daughter and my coming to consciousness as a woman of color have made this weaving possible. This weaving reveals the possibility and complexity of a pluralistic feminism, a feminism that affirms the plurality in each of us and among us as richness and as central to feminist ontology and epistemology.

The paper describes the experience of 'outsiders' to the mainstream of, for example, White/Anglo organization of life in the U.S. and stresses

a particular feature of the outsider's existence: The outsider has necessarily acquired flexibility in shifting from the mainstream construction of life where she is constructed as an outsider to other constructions of life where she is more or less 'at home.' This flexibility is necessary for the outsider but it can also be willfully exercised by the outsider or by those who are at ease in the mainstream. I recommend this willful exercise which I call "world"-travelling and I also recommend that the willful exercise be animated by an attitude that I describe as playful.

As outsiders to the mainstream, women of color in the U.S. practice "world"-travelling, mostly out of necessity. I affirm this practice as a skillful, creative, rich, enriching and, given certain circumstances, as a loving way of being and living. I recognize that much of our travelling is done unwillfully to hostile White/Anglo "worlds." The hostility of these "worlds" and the compulsory nature of the "travelling" have obscured for us the enormous value of this aspect of our living and its connection to loving. Racism has a vested interest in obscuring and devaluing the complex skills involved in it. I recommend that we affirm this travelling across "worlds" as partly constitutive of crosscultural and cross-racial loving. Thus I recommend to women of color in the U.S. that we learn to love each other by learning to travel to each other's "worlds."

Hypatia vol 2, no 2 (Summer 1987). © By María Lugones.

On the other hand, the paper makes a connection between what Marilyn Frye has named "arrogant perception" and the failure to identify with persons that one views arrogantly or has come to see as the products of arrogant perception. A further connection is made between this failure of identification and a failure of love, and thus between loving and identifying with another person. The sense of love is not the one Frye has identified as both consistent with arrogant perception and as promoting unconditional servitude. "We can be taken in by this equation of servitude with love," Frye (1983, 73) says, "because we make two mistakes at once; we think, of both servitude and love that they are selfless or unselfish." Rather, the identification of which I speak is constituted by what I come to characterize as playful "world" travelling. To the extent that we learn to perceive others arrogantly or come to see them only as products of arrogant perception and continue to perceive them that way, we fail to identify with them—fail to love them—in this particularly deep way.

IDENTIFICATION AND LOVE

As a child, I was taught to perceive arrogantly. I have also been the object of arrogant perception. Though I am not a White/Anglo woman, it is clear to me that I can understand both my childhood training as an arrogant perceiver and my having been the object of arrogant perception without any reference to White/Anglo men, which is some indication that the concept of arrogant perception can be used cross-culturally and that White/Anglo men are not the only arrogant perceivers. I was brought up in Argentina watching men and women of moderate and of considerable means graft the substance[1] of their servants to themselves. I also learned to graft my mother's substance to my own. It was clear to me that both men and women were the victims of arrogant perception and that arrogant perception was systematically organized to break the spirit of all women and of most men. I valued my rural 'gaucho' ancestry because its ethos has always been one of independence in

poverty through enormous loneliness, courage and self-reliance. I found inspiration in this ethos and committed myself never to be broken by arrogant perception. I can say all of this in this way only because I have learned from Frye's "In and Out of Harm's Way, Arrogance and Love." She has given me a way of understanding and articulating something important in my own life.

Frye is not particularly concerned with women as arrogant perceivers but as the objects of arrogant perception. Her concern is, in part, to enhance our understanding of women "untouched by phallocratic machinations" (Frye 1983, 53), by understanding the harm done to women through such machinations. In this case she proposes that we could understand women untouched by arrogant perception through an understanding of what arrogant perception does to women. She also proposes an understanding of what it is to love women that is inspired by a vision of women unharmed by arrogant perception. To love women is, at least in part, to perceive them with loving eyes. "The loving eye is a contrary of the arrogant eye" (Frye 1983, 75).

I am concerned with women as arrogant perceivers because I want to explore further what it is to love women. I want to explore two failures of love: my failure to love my mother and White/Anglo women's failure to love women across racial and cultural boundaries in the U.S. As a consequence of exploring these failures I will offer a loving solution to them. My solution modifies Frye's account of loving perception by adding what I call playful "world"-travel.

It is clear to me that at least in the U.S. and Argentina women are taught to perceive many other women arrogantly. Being taught to perceive arrogantly is part of being taught to be a woman of a certain class in both the U.S. and Argentina, it is part of being taught to be a White/Anglo woman in the U.S., and it is part of being taught to be a woman in both places to be both the agent and the object of arrogant perception. My love for my mother seemed to me thoroughly imperfect as I was growing up because I was unwilling to become what I had been taught to see my mother as being. I thought that to love her was consistent with my abusing her (using, taking for granted, and demanding her services in a far reaching way that, since four other people engaged in the same grafting of her substance onto themselves, left her little of herself to herself) and was to be in part constituted by my identifying with her, my seeing myself in her. To love her was supposed to be of a piece with both my abusing her and with my being open to being abused. It is clear to me that I was not supposed to love servants. I could abuse them without identifying with them, without seeing myself in them. When I came to the U.S. I learned that part of racism is the internalization of the propriety of abuse without identification. I learned that I could be seen as a being to be used by White/Anglo men and women without the possibility of identification, i.e., without their act of attempting to graft my substance onto theirs, rubbing off on them at all. They could remain untouched, without any sense of loss.

So, women who are perceived arrogantly can perceive other women arrogantly in their turn. To what extent those women are responsible for their arrogant perceptions of other women is certainly open to question, but I do not have any doubt that many women have been taught to abuse women in this particular way. I am not interested in assigning responsibility. I am interested in understanding the phenomenon so as to understand a loving way out of it.

There is something obviously wrong with the love that I was taught and something right with my failure to love my mother in this way. But I do not think that what is wrong is my profound desire to identify with her, to see myself in her, what is wrong is that I was taught to identify with a victim of enslavement. What is wrong is that I was taught to practice enslavement of my mother and to learn to become a slave through this practice. There is something obviously wrong with my having been taught that love is consistent with abuse, consistent with arrogant perception. Notice that the love I was taught is the love that

Frye (1983, 73) speaks of when she says "We can be taken in by this equation of servitude with love." Even though I could both abuse and love my mother, I was not supposed to love servants. This is because in the case of servants one is and is supposed to be clear about their servitude and the "equation of servitude with love" is never to be thought clearly in those terms. So, I was not supposed to love and could not love servants. But I could love my mother because deception (in particular, self-deception) is part of this "loving." Servitude is called abnegation and abnegation is not analyzed any further. Abnegation is not instilled in us through an analysis of its nature but rather through a heralding of it as beautiful and noble. We are coaxed, seduced into abnegation not through analysis but through emotive persuasion. Frye makes the connection between deception and this sense of "loving" clear. When I say that there is something obviously wrong with the loving that I was taught, I do not mean to say that the connection between this loving and abuse is obvious. Rather, I mean that once the connection between this loving and abuse has been unveiled, there is something obviously wrong with the loving given that it is obvious that it is wrong to abuse others.

I am glad that I did not learn my lessons well, but it is clear that part of the mechanism that permitted my not learning well involved a separation from my mother. I saw us as beings of quite a different sort. It involved an abandoning of my mother while I longed not to abandon her. I wanted to love my mother, though, given what I was taught, "love" could not be the right word for what I longed for.

I was disturbed by my not wanting to be what she was. I had a sense of not being quite integrated, my self was missing because I could not identify with her, I could not see myself in her, I could not welcome her world. I saw myself as separate from her, a different sort of being, not quite of the same species. This separation, this lack of love, I saw, and I think that I saw correctly, as a lack in myself (not a fault, but a lack). I also see that if this was a lack of love, love cannot be what I was taught. Love has to be rethought, made anew.

There is something in common between the relation between myself and my mother as someone I did not use to be able to love and the relation between myself or other women of color in the U.S. and White/Anglo women: there is a failure of love. I want to suggest here that Frye has helped me understand one of the aspects of this failure, the directly abusive aspect. But I also think that there is a complex failure of love in the failure to identify with another woman, the failure to see oneself in other women who are quite different from oneself. I want to begin to analyze this complex failure.

Notice that Frye's emphasis on independence in her analysis of loving perception is not particularly helpful in explaining this failure. She says that in loving perception, "the object of the seeing is another being whose existence and character are logically independent of the seer and who may be practically or empirically independent in any particular respect at any particular time" (Frye 1983, 77). But this is not helpful in allowing me to understand how my failure of love toward my mother (when I ceased to be her parasite) left me not quite whole. It is not helpful since I saw her as logically independent from me. It also does not help me to understand why the racist or ethnocentric failure of love of White/ Anglo women—in particular of those White/Anglo women who are not pained by their failure— should leave me not quite substantive among them. Here I am not particularly interested in cases of White women's parasitism onto women of color but more pointedly in cases where the failure of identification is the manifestation of the "relation." I am particularly interested here in those many cases in which White/Anglo women do one or more of the following to women of color: they ignore us, ostracize us, render us invisible, stereotype us, leave us completely alone, interpret us as crazy. All of this *while we are in their midst.* The more independent I am, the more

independent I am left to be. Their world and their integrity do not require me at all. There is no sense of self-loss in them for my own lack of solidity. But they rob me of my solidity through indifference, an indifference they can afford and which seems sometimes studied. (All of this points of course toward separatism in communities where our substance is seen and celebrated, where we become substantive through this celebration. But many of us have to work among White/Anglo folk and our best shot at recognition has seemed to be among White/Anglo women because many of them have expressed a *general* sense of being pained at their failure of love.)

Many times White/Anglo women want us out of their field of vision. Their lack of concern is a harmful failure of love that leaves me independent from them in a way similar to the way in which, once I ceased to be my mother's parasite, she became, though not independent from all others, certainly independent from me. But of course, because my mother and I wanted to love each other well, we were not whole in this independence. White/Anglo women are independent from me, I am independent from them, I am independent from my mother, she is independent from me, and none of us loves each other in this independence.

I am incomplete and unreal without other women. I am profoundly dependent on others without having to be their subordinate, their slave, their servant.

Frye (1983, 75) also says that the loving eye is "the eye of one who knows that to know the seen, one must consult something other than one's own will and interests and fears and imagination." This is much more helpful to me so long as I do not understand Frye to mean that I should not consult my own interests nor that I should exclude the possibility that my self and the self of the one I love may be importantly tied to each other in many complicated ways. Since I am emphasizing here that the failure of love lies in part in the failure to identify and since I agree with Frye that one "must consult something other than one's own will and interests and fears and imagination," I will proceed to try to explain what I think needs to be consulted. To love my mother was not possible for me while I retained a sense that it was fine for me and others to see her arrogantly. Loving my mother also required that I see with her eyes, that I go into my mother's world, that I see both of us as we are constructed in her world, that I witness her own sense of herself from within her world. Only through this travelling to her "world" could I identify with her because only then could I cease to ignore her and to be excluded and separate from her. Only then could I see her as a subject even if one subjected and only then could I see at all how meaning could arise fully between us. We are fully dependent on each other for the possibility of being understood and without this understanding we are not intelligible, we do not make sense, we are not solid, visible, integrated, we are lacking. So travelling to each other's "worlds" would enable us to *be* through *loving* each other.

Hopefully the sense of identification I have in mind is becoming clear. But if it is to become clearer, I need to explain what I mean by a "world" and by "travelling" to another "world."

In explaining what I mean by a "world" I will not appeal to travelling to other women's worlds. Rather I will lead you to see what I mean by a "world" the way I came to propose the concept to myself through the kind of ontological confusion about myself that we, women of color, refer to half-jokingly as "schizophrenia" (we feel schizophrenic in our goings back and forth between different "communities") and through my effort to make some sense of this ontological confusion.

"WORLDS" AND "WORLD" TRAVELLING

Some time ago I came to be in a state of profound confusion as I experienced myself as both having and not having a particular attribute. I was sure I had the attribute in question and, on the other hand, I was sure that I did not have it. I remain convinced that I both have and do not have this attribute. The attribute is playfulness. I am sure that I am a playful person. On the other hand, I can say, painfully, that I am not a playful person. I am not a playful person in certain worlds. One of the things I did as I became confused was to call my friends, far away people who knew me well, to see whether or not I was playful. Maybe they could help me out of my confusion. They said to me, "Of course you are playful" and they said it with the same conviction that I had about it. Of course I am playful. Those people who were around me said to me, "No, you are not playful. You are a serious woman. You just take everything seriously." They were just as sure about what they said to me and could offer me every bit of evidence that one could need to conclude that they were right. So I said to myself "Okay, maybe what's happening here is that there is an attribute that I do have but there are certain worlds in which I am not at ease and it is because I'm not at ease in those worlds that I don't have that attribute in those worlds. But what does that mean?" I was worried both about what I meant by "worlds" when I said "in some worlds I do not have the attribute" and what I meant by saying that lack of ease was what led me not to be playful in those worlds. Because you see, if it was just a matter of lack of ease, I could work on it.

I can explain some of what I mean by a "world." I do not want the fixity of a definition at this point, because I think the term is suggestive and I do not want to close the suggestiveness of it too soon. I can offer some characteristics that serve to distinguish between a "world," a utopia, a possible world in the philosophical sense, and a world-view. By a "world" I do not mean a utopia at all. A utopia does not count as a world in my sense. The "worlds" that I am talking about are possible. But a possible world is not what I mean by a "world" and I do not mean a world-view, though something like a world-view is involved here.

For something to be a "world" in my sense it has to be inhabited at present by some flesh and blood people. That is why it cannot be a utopia. It may also be inhabited by some imaginary people. It may be inhabited by people who are dead or people that the inhabitants of this "world" met in some other "world" and now have in this "world" in imagination.

A "world" in my sense may be an actual society given its dominant culture's description and construction of life, including a construction of the relationships of production, of gender, race, etc. But a "world" can also be such a society given a non-dominant construction, or it can be such a society or *a* society given an idiosyncratic construction. As we will it is problematic to say that these are all constructions of the same society. But they are different "worlds."

A "world" need not be a construction of a whole society. It may be a construction of a tiny portion of a particular society. It may be inhabited by just a few people. Some "worlds" are bigger than others.

A "world" may be incomplete in that things in it may not be altogether constructed or some things may be constructed negatively (they are not what 'they' are in some other "world"). Or the "world" may be incomplete because it may have references to things that do not quite exist in it, references to things like Brazil, where Brazil is not quite part of that "world". Given lesbian feminism, the construction of 'lesbian' is purposefully and healthily still up in the air, in the process of becoming. What it is to be a Hispanic in this country is, in a dominant Anglo construction, purposefully incomplete. Thus one cannot really answer questions of the sort "What is a Hispanic?", "Who counts as a Hispanic?", "Are Latinos, Chicanos, Hispanos, black dominicans, white cubans, korean-colombians, italian-argentinians hispanic?" What it is to be a 'hispanic' in the varied so-called hispanic communities in the U.S. is also up in the air. We have not yet decided whether there is something like a 'hispanic' in our varied "worlds." So, a "world" may be an incomplete visionary non-utopian construction of life or it may be a traditional construction of life. A traditional Hispano

construction of Northern New Mexican life is a "world." Such a traditional construction, in the face of a racist, ethnocentrist, money-centered anglo construction of Northern New Mexican life is highly unstable because Anglos have the means for imperialist destruction of traditional Hispano "worlds."

In a "world" some of the inhabitants may not understand or hold the particular construction of them that constructs them in that "world." So, there may be "worlds" that construct me in ways that I do not even understand. Or it may be that I understand the construction, but do not hold it of myself. I may not accept it as an account of myself, a construction of myself. And yet, I may be *animating* such a construction.

One can "travel" between these "worlds" and one can inhabit more than one of these "worlds" at the very same time. I think that most of us who are outside the mainstream of, for example, the U.S. dominant construction or organization of life are "world travellers" as a matter of necessity and of survival. It seems to me that inhabiting more than one "world" at the same time and "travelling" between "worlds" is part and parcel of our experience and our situation. One can be at the same time in a "world" that constructs one as stereotypically latin, for example, and in a "world" that constructs one as latin. Being stereotypically latin and being simply latin are different simultaneous constructions of persons that are part of different "worlds." One animates one or the other or both at the same time without necessarily confusing them, though simultaneous enactment can be confusing if one is not on one's guard.

In describing my sense of a "world," I mean to be offering a description of experience, something that is true to experience even if it is ontologically problematic. Though I would think that any account of identity that could not be true to this experience of outsiders to the mainstream would be faulty even if ontologically unproblematic. Its ease would constrain, erase, or deem aberrant experience that has within it significant insights into non-imperialistic understanding between people.

Those of us who are "world"-travellers have the distinct experience of being different in different "worlds" and of having the capacity to remember other "worlds" and ourselves in them. We can say "That is me there, and I am happy in that "world." So, the experience is of being a different person in different "worlds" and yet of having memory of oneself as different without quite having the sense of there being any underlying "I." So I can say "that is me there and I am so playful in that "world." I say "That is *me* in that "world" not because I recognize myself in that person, rather the first person statement is non-inferential. I may well recognize that that person has abilities that I do not have and yet the having or not having of the abilities is always an "I have . . ." and "I do not have . . . ", i.e. it is always experienced in the first person.

The shift from being one person to being a different person is what I call "travel." This shift may not be willful or even conscious, and one may be completely unaware of being different than one is in a different "world," and may not recognize that one is in a different "world." Even though the shift can be done willfully, it is not a matter of acting. One does not pose as someone else, one does not pretend to be, for example, someone of a different personality or character or someone who uses space or language differently than the other person. Rather one is someone who has that personality or character or uses space and language in that particular way. The "one" here does not refer to some underlying "I." One does not *experience* any underlying "I."

BEING AT EASE IN A "WORLD"

In investigating what I mean by "being at ease in a "world" I will describe different ways of being at ease. One may be at ease in one or in all of these ways. There is a maximal way of being at ease, viz, being at ease in all of these ways. I take this maximal way of being at ease to be

somewhat dangerous because it tends to produce people who have no inclination to travel across "worlds" or have no experience of "world" travelling.

The first way of being at ease in a particular "world" is by being a fluent speaker in that "world." I know all the norms that there are to be followed, I know all the words that there are to be spoken. I know all the moves. I am confident.

Another way of being at ease is by being normatively happy. I agree with all the norms, I could not love any norms better. I am asked to do just what I want to do or what I think I should do. At ease.

Another way of being at ease in a "world" is by being humanly bonded. I am with those I love and they love me too. It should be noticed that I may be with those I love and be at ease because of them in a "world" that is otherwise as hostile to me as "worlds" get.

Finally one may be at ease because one has a history with others that is shared, especially daily history, the kind of shared history that one sees exemplified by the response to the "Do you remember poodle skirts?" question. There you are, with people you do not know at all. The question is posed and then they all begin talking about their poodle skirt stories. I have been in such situations without knowing what poodle skirts, for example, were and I felt so ill at ease because it was not *my* history. The other people did not particularly know each other. It is not that they were humanly bonded. Probably they did not have much politically in common either. But poodle skirts were in their shared history.

One may be at ease in one of these ways or in all of them. Notice that when one says meaningfully "This is *my* world," one may not be at ease in it. Or one may be at ease in it only in some of these respects and not in others. To say of some "world" that it is "*my* world" is to make an evaluation. One may privilege one or more "worlds" in this way for a variety of reasons for example because one experiences oneself as an agent in a fuller sense than one experiences "oneself" in other "worlds." One may disown a "world" because one has first person memories of a person who is so thoroughly dominated that she has no sense of exercising her own will or has a sense of having serious difficulties in performing actions that are willed by herself and no difficulty in performing actions willed by others. One may say of a "world" that it is "my world" because one is at ease in it, i.e., being at ease in a "world" may be the basis for the evaluation.

Given the clarification of what I mean by a "world," "world"-travel, and being at ease in a "world," we are in a position to return to my problematic attribute, playfulness. It may be that in this "world" in which I am so unplayful, I am a different person than in the "world" in which I am playful. Or it may be that the "world" in which I am unplayful is constructed in such a way that I could be playful in it. I could practice, even though that "world" is constructed in such a way that my being playful in it is kind of hard. In describing what I take a "world" to be, I emphasized the first possibility as both the one that is truest to the experience of "outsiders" to the mainstream and as ontologically problematic because the "I" is identified in some sense as one and in some sense as a plurality. I identify myself as myself through memory and I retain myself as different in memory. When I travel from one "world" to another, I have this image, this memory of myself as playful in this other "world." I can then be in a particular "world" and have a double image of myself as, for example, playful and as not playful. But this is a very familiar and recognizable phenomenon to the outsider to the mainstream in some central cases when in one "world" I animate, for example, that "world's" caricature of the person I am in the other "world." I can have both images of myself and to the extent that I can materialize or animate both images at the same time I become an ambiguous being. This is very much a part of trickery and foolery. It is worth remembering that the trickster and the fool are significant characters in many

non-dominant or outsider cultures. One then sees any particular "world" with these double edges and sees absurdity in them and so inhabits oneself differently. Given that latins are constructed in Anglo "worlds" as stereotypically intense—intensity being a central characteristic of at least one of the anglo stereotypes of latins—and given that many latins, myself included, are genuinely intense, I can say to myself "I am intense" and take a hold of the double meaning. And furthermore, I can be stereotypically intense or be the real thing and, if you are Anglo, you do not know when I am which *because* I am Latin-American. As Latin-American I am an ambiguous being, a two-imaged self. I can see that gringos see me as stereotypically intense because I am, as a Latin-American, constructed that way but I may or may not *intentionally* animate the stereotype or the real thing knowing that you may not see it in anything other than in the stereotypical construction. This ambiguity is funny and is not just funny, it is survival-rich. We can also make the picture of those who dominate us funny precisely because we can see the double edge, we can see them doubly constructed, we can see the plurality in them. So we know truths that only the fool can speak and only the trickster can play out without harm. We inhabit "worlds" and travel across them and keep all the memories.

Sometimes the "world"-traveller has a double image of herself and each self includes as important ingredients of itself one or more attributes that are *incompatible* with one or more of the attributes of the other self; for example being playful and being unplayful. To the extent that the attribute is an important ingredient of the self she is in that "world," i.e., to the extent that there is a particularly good fit between that "world" and her having that attribute in it and to the extent that the attribute is personality or character central, that "world" would have to be changed if she is to be playful in it. It is not the case that if she could come to be at ease in it, she would be her own playful self. Because the attribute is personality or character central and there is such a good fit between that "world" and her being constructed with that attribute as central, *she* cannot become playful, she is unplayful. To become playful would be for her to become a contradictory being. So I am suggesting that the lack of ease solution cannot be a solution to my problematic case. My problem is not one of lack of ease. I am suggesting that I can understand my confusion about whether I am or am not playful by saying that I am both and that I am different persons in different "worlds" and can remember myself in both as I am in the other. I am a plurality of selves. This is to understand my confusion because *it is to come to see it as a piece* with much of the rest of my experience as an outsider in some of the "worlds" that I inhabit and of a piece with significant aspects of the experience of non-dominant people in the "worlds" of their dominators.

So, though I may not be at ease in the "worlds" in which I am not constructed playful, it is not that I am not playful *because* I am not at ease. The two are compatible. But lack of playfulness is not caused by lack of ease. Lack of playfulness is not symptomatic of lack of ease but of lack of health. I am not a healthy being in the "worlds" that construct me unplayful.

PLAYFULNESS

I had a very personal stake in investigating this topic. Playfulness is not only the attribute that was the source of my confusion and the attitude that I recommend as the loving attitude in travelling across "worlds," I am also scared of ending up a serious human being, someone with no multi-dimensionality, with no fun in life, someone who is just someone who has had the fun constructed out of her. I am seriously scared of getting stuck in a "world" that constructs me that way. A world that I have no escape from and in which I cannot be playful.

I thought about what it is to be playful and what it is to play and I did this thinking in a "world" in which I only remember myself as

playful and in which all of those who know me as playful are imaginary beings, a "world" in which I am scared of losing my memories of myself as playful or having them erased from me. Because I live in such a "world," after I formulated my own sense of what it is to be playful and to play I decided that I needed to "go to the literature." I read two classics on the subject Johan Huizinga's *Homo Ludens* and Hans-Georg Gadamer's chapter on the concept of play in his *Truth and Method*. I discovered, to my amazement, that what I thought about play and playfulness, if they were right, was absolutely wrong. Though I will not provide the arguments for this interpretation of Gadamer and Huizinga here, I understood that both of them have an agonistic sense of 'play.' Play and playfulness have, ultimately, to do with contest, with winning, losing, battling. The sense of playfulness that I have in mind has nothing to do with those things. So, I tried to elucidate both senses of play and playfulness by contrasting them to each other. The contrast helped me see the attitude that I have in mind as the loving attitude in travelling across "worlds" more clearly.

An agonistic sense of playfulness is one in which *competence* is supreme. You better know the rules of the game. In agonistic play there is risk, there is *uncertainty,* but the uncertainty is about who is going to win and who is going to lose. There are rules that inspire hostility. The attitude of *playfulness is conceived as secondary to or derivative from play*. Since play is agon, then the only conceivable playful attitude is an agonistic one (the attitude does not turn an activity into play, but rather presupposes an activity that is play). One of the paradigmatic ways of playing for both Gadamer and Huizinga is role-playing. In role-playing, the person who is a participant in the game has a *fixed conception of him or herself*. I also think that the players are imbued with *self-importance* in agonistic play since they are so keen on winning given their own merits, their very own competence.

When considering the value of "world"-travelling and whether playfulness is the loving attitude to have while travelling, I recognized the agonistic attitude as inimical to travelling across "worlds." The agonistic traveller is a conqueror, an imperialist. Huizinga, in his classic book on play, interprets Western civilization as play. That is an interesting thing for Third World people to think about. Western civilization has been interpreted by a white western man as play in the agonistic sense of play. Huizinga reviews western law, art, and many other aspects of western culture and sees agon in all of them. Agonistic playfulness leads those who attempt to travel to another "world" with this attitude to failure. Agonistic travellers fail consistently in their attempt to travel because what they do is to try to conquer the other "world." The attempt is not an attempt to try to erase the other "world." That is what assimilation is all about. Assimilation is the destruction of other people's "worlds." So, the agonistic attitude, the playful attitude given western man's construction of playfulness, is not a healthy, loving attitude to have in travelling across "worlds." Notice that given the agonistic attitude one *cannot* travel across "worlds," though one can kill other "worlds" with it. So for people who are interested in crossing racial and ethnic boundaries, an arrogant western man's construction of playfulness is deadly. One cannot cross the boundaries with it. One needs to give up such an attitude if one wants to travel.

So then, what is the loving playfulness that I have in mind? Let me begin with one example. We are by the river bank. The river is very, very low. Almost dry. Bits of water here and there. Little pools with a few trout hiding under the rocks. But mostly is wet stones, grey on the outside. We walk on the stones for awhile. You pick up a stone and crash it onto the others. As it breaks, it is quite wet inside and it is very colorful, very pretty, I pick up a stone and break it and run toward the pieces to see the colors. They are beautiful. I laugh and bring the pieces back to you and you are doing the same with your pieces. We keep on crashing stones for hours, anxious to see the beautiful new colors. We are playing. The playfulness of our activity

does not presuppose that there is something like "crashing stones" that is a particular form of play with its own rules. Rather *the attitude that carries us through the activity, a playful attitude, turns the activity into play.* Our activity has no rules, though it is certainly intentional activity and we both understand what we are doing. The playfulness that gives meaning to our activity includes uncertainty, but in this case the uncertainty is an *openness to surprise.* This is a particular metaphysical attitude that does not expect the world to be neatly packaged, ruly. Rules may fail to explain what we are doing. We are not self-important, we are not fixed in particular constructions of ourselves, which is part of saying that we are *open to self-construction.* We may not have rules, and when we do have rules, *there are no rules that are to us sacred.* We are not worried about competence. We are not wedded to a particular way of doing things. While playful we have not abandoned ourselves to, nor are we stuck in, any particular "world." We *are there creatively.* We are not passive.

Playfulness is, in part, an openness to being a fool, which is a combination of not worrying about competence, not being self-important, not taking norms as sacred and finding ambiguity and double edges a source of wisdom and delight.

So, positively, the playful attitude involves openness to surprise, openness to being a fool, openness to self-construction or reconstruction and to construction or reconstruction of the "worlds" we inhabit playfully. Negatively, playfulness is characterized by uncertainty, lack of self-importance, absence of rules or a not taking rules as sacred, a not worrying about competence and a lack of abandonment to a particular construction of oneself, others and one's relation to them. In attempting to take a hold of oneself and of one's relation to others in a particular "world," one may study, examine and come to understand oneself. One may then see what the possibilities for play are for the being one is in that "world." One may even decide to inhabit that self fully in order to understand it better and find its creative possibilities. All of this is just self-reflection and it is quite different from resigning or abandoning oneself to the particular construction of oneself that one is attempting to take a hold of.

CONCLUSION

There are "worlds" we enter at our own risk, "worlds" that have agon, conquest, and arrogance as the main ingredients in their ethos. These are "worlds" that we enter out of necessity and which would be foolish to enter playfully in either the agonistic sense or in my sense. In such "worlds" we are not playful.

But there are "worlds" that we can travel to lovingly and travelling to them is part of loving at least some of their inhabitants. The reason why I think that travelling to someone's "world" is a way of identifying with them is because by travelling to their "world" we can understand *what it is to be them and what it is to be ourselves in their eyes*. Only when we have travelled to each other's "worlds" are we fully subjects to each other (I agree with Hegel that self-recognition requires other subjects, but I disagree with his claim that it requires tension or hostility).

Knowing other women's "worlds" is part of knowing them and knowing them is part of loving them. Notice that the knowing can be done in greater or lesser depth, as can the loving. Also notice that travelling to another's "world"–is not the same as becoming intimate with them. Intimacy is constituted in part by a very deep knowledge of the other self and "world" travelling is only part of having this knowledge. Also notice that some people, in particular those who are outsiders to the mainstream, can be known only to the extent that they are known in several "worlds" and as "world"-travellers.

Without knowing the other's "world," one does not know the other, and without knowing the other, one is really alone in the other's presence because the other is only dimly present to one.

Through travelling to other people's "worlds" we discover that there are "worlds" in which those who are the victims of arrogant perception are really subjects, lively beings, resistors, constructors of visions even though in the mainstream construction they are animated only by the arrogant perceiver and are pliable, foldable, file-awayable, classifiable. I always imagine the Aristotelian slave as pliable and foldable at night or after he or she cannot work anymore (when he or she dies as a tool). Aristotle tells us nothing about the slave *apart from the master*. We know the slave only through the master. The slave is a tool of the master. After working hours he or she is folded and placed in a drawer till the next morning. My mother was apparent to me mostly as a victim of arrogant perception. I was loyal to the arrogant perceiver's construction of her and thus disloyal to her in assuming that she was exhausted by that construction. I was unwilling to be like her and thought that identifying with her, seeing myself in her necessitated that I become like her. I was wrong both in assuming that she was exhausted by the arrogant perceiver's construction of her and in my understanding of identification, though I was not wrong in thinking that identification was part of loving and that it involved in part my seeing myself in her. I came to realize through travelling to her "world" that she is not foldable and pliable, that she is not exhausted by the mainstream argentinian patriarchal construction of her. I came to realize that there are "worlds" in which she shines as a creative being. Seeing myself in her through travelling to her "world" has meant seeing how different from her I am in her "world."

So, in recommending "world"-travelling and identification through "world"-travelling as part of loving other women, I am suggesting disloyalty to arrogant perceivers, including the arrogant perceiver in ourselves, and to their constructions of women. In revealing agonistic playfulness as incompatible with "world"-travelling, I am revealing both its affinity with imperialism and arrogant perception and its incompatibility with loving and loving perception.

NOTE

1. Grafting the substance of another to oneself is partly constitutive of arrogant perception. See M. Frye (1983, 66).

REFERENCES

Frye, Marilyn. 1983. *The Politics of Reality. Essays in Feminist Theory.* Trumansburg, NY: Crossing Press.

Gadamer, Hans-George. 1975. *Truth and Method.* New York: Seabury Press.

Huizinga, Johan. 1968. *Homo Ludens.* Buenos Aires, Argentina: Emece Editores.

FOR FURTHER READING

Bailey, Alison. "Privilege: Expanding on Marilyn Frye's 'Oppression.'" *The Journal of Social Philosophy,* 29(3)(1998): 104–19.

Bartky, Sandra. *Femininity and Domination.* New York: Routledge, 1990.

Carbado, Devon. "Straight Out of the Closet: Men, Feminism and Heterosexual Privilege." In his *Black Men on Race, Gender and Sexuality.* New York: New York University Press, 1999.

Fanon, Frantz. *Black Skin, White Masks.* New York: Grove Press, 1991(1967).

Frankenberg, Ruth. *White Women, Race Matters: The Social Construction of Whiteness.* Minneapolis: University of Minnesota Press, 1993.

Frye, Marilyn. *The Politics of Reality: Essays in Feminist Theory.* Freedom, CA: The Crossing Press. 1983.

Goldman, Emma. *The Traffic in Women and Other Essays on Feminism.* Albion, CA: Time Change Press, 1970.

Hartmann, Heidi. "The Unhappy Marriage of Marxism and Feminism: Towards a More Progressive Union." In *Women and Revolution: A Discussion of the Unhappy Marriage of Marxism and Feminism,* edited by Lydia Sargent. Boston: South End Press, 1983.

Heldke, Lisa, and Peg O'Connor, eds. *Oppression, Privilege, and Resistance: Theoretical Perspectives on Racism, Sexism, and Heterosexism.* New York: McGraw-Hill, 2004.

Kimmel, Michael, and Abby Ferber, eds. *Privilege: A Reader.* Boulder, CO: Westview Press, 2003.

Lorde, Audre. *Sister Outsider: Essays and Speeches.* Freedom, CA.: The Crossing Press, 1984.

Lugones, María. *Pilgrimages/Peregrinajes: Theorizing Coalition against Multiple Oppressions.* Lanham, MD: Rowman and Littlefield, 2003.

Pharr, Suzanne. *Homophobia: Weapon of Sexism.* Inverness, CA: Chardon Press, 1988.

Rothenberg, Paula S., ed. *White Privilege: Essential Readings on the Other Side of Racism.* New York: Worth Publishers, 2002.

Rothenberg, Paula S., ed. *Race, Class and Gender in the United States.* 6th ed. New York: Worth Publishers, 2004.

Young, Iris. "The Five Faces of Oppression." In her *Justice and the Politics of Difference.* Princeton: Princeton University Press, 1990.

MEDIA RESOURCES

Frantz Fanon: Black Skin, White Mask. DVD. Directed by Isaac Julien and produced by Mark Nash for the Arts Council of England. (UK, 1996). This film provides an essential background for Sandra Bartky's essay on psychological oppression in this section. Jean-Paul Sartre recognized Fanon as the figure "through whose voice the Third World finds and speaks for itself." The film explores Fanon's two major works, *Black Skin, White Masks* and *The Wretched of the Earth,* as pioneering studies of the psychological impact of racism on both colonized and colonizer. Available: California Newsreel, http://www.newsreel.org/, or 877–811–7495.

Guerrillas in Our Midst. VHS. Produced and directed by Amy Harrison (US, 1993). The Guerrilla Girls are anonymous and savvy groups of art terrorists who have succeeded in exposing the racism and sexism of the art world since the mid-1980s. Their witty and brave tactics have changed the face of cultural and political activism. This is a delightful example of feminist resistance to visual culture. Available: Women Make Movies, www.wmm.com, or 212–925–0606.

The Color Line and the Bus Line. VHS. ABC Nightline (US, 1996). Part of ABC's series "Race in America." This episode tells the story of Cynthia Wiggins, an African-American single mother, and her commute to work at a shopping mall in Buffalo, New York. Viewers come to see how her death is caused by institutionalized racism. This video is a stunning illustration of Marilyn Frye's thesis that oppression must be viewed macroscopically to be understood. Available: The ABC store, www.abcnewsstore.com/store/index.cfm?fuseaction=customer.product&productcode=N960524S01&category code=TOP100, or 1–800–505–6139.

The Edge of Each Other's Battles: The Vision of Audre Lorde, VHS. Produced and directed by Jennifer Abod (US, 2002). A moving documentary tribute to legendary black lesbian feminist poet. Lorde inspired several generations of activists with her poetry, serving as a catalyst for change and uniting the communities of which she was a part: black arts and black liberation, women's liberation, and lesbian and gay liberation. Amazing footage from the I Am Your Sister Conference, which brought together 1,200 activists from 23 countries. The video powerfully brings Lorde's legacy to life and conveys the spirit, passion, and intensity that remains her trademark. Available: Women Make Movies, www.wmm.com, or 212–925–0606.

Women Organize! VHS/DVD. Produced and directed by Joan E. Biren and the Union Institute Center for Women (US, 2000). A video portrait of five women organizers from diverse backgrounds who are involved in the global and local struggles for racial, social, and economic injustice, including work with high school girls in low-income neighborhoods, Asian immigrant communities, and black lesbians working against homophobia. Available: Women Make Movies, www.wmm.com, or 212–925–0606.

CHAPTER 3

SEX AND GENDER

To claim that women are oppressed or mistreated is to assume that there are people, readily identifiable as women, who have something in common just about everywhere they exist. But how much do "women" really have in common, beyond the fact that they are subjected to norms, roles, and constraints imposed by categorizations that mark femaleness, and define it as "other" and "less" than maleness? How should we understand the differences and commonalities among systems of sexual difference, and how should we understand the aspects of sex and gender that are relevant in our own lives and histories? Are they constantly under cultural construction, sturdily supported by evolutionary biology, or a mixture of both?

Some believe that the category "woman" is identical to the category "female," but most feminist thinkers challenge the assumption that what it means to be a woman in any context is totally reducible to biological differences from men. Instead, they argue that sex and gender differences are also products of hegemonic norms defining sexual divisions of labor, dominant masculine and subordinate feminine roles, and more. Because some aspects of what it means to be a

woman or man are more physical or more cultural than others, it can be helpful to distinguish reproductive types from cultural categories. Biological femaleness is considered a category of *sex,* and femininity—what it means to be a normal or proper female in a particular context—is a category of *gender*. Feminists note that even bare "biological" descriptions of bodies are laden with cultural influences, and cultural norms of gender can be very deeply embodied.

There are reproductive physical similarities among "female human persons," of course, but as Anne Fausto-Sterling argues in this chapter, when we look through the lenses of medicine and human experience, we find a variety of body types rather than a strict bifurcation between women and men. To look only for similarities in women's lives or experiences, at the expense of noticing differences, is to ignore the ways categories of sex and gender are shaped by racism, colonialism, class, etc., and how privileged women benefit from certain versions of femininity. What it means to be a woman means different things in different communities, and women are therefore subject to different roles and regulations. One example is the way ideal white Western female sexuality has historically been described as innocent or chaste, while women of color are characterized as having voracious sexual appetites. Another is the fact that some lesbians would say they are not women, while others would think it is obvious that they are women.

Given patterns of oppression, philosophy can help us to uncover and dissect conceptual and practical trends and patterns so as to better address them. In addition, Western philosophy can be said to have a fetish for categories and analyses of the meanings of categories. For feminist philosophy, foundational and categorical questions involve relationships between the meanings of difference (especially, but not only, sex and gender difference), the existence of pervasive and complex patterns of mistreatment and injustice, and the potential for liberation, resistance, or positive movement. But because terms marking sex and gender cover terrifically large and diverse categories, claims about "women" and "men" tend to be falsely universalizing. Instead of simply looking for universal truths about "women" and "men," feminist philosophers therefore typically find it more useful to critically consider at the practices and discourses that give meaning to sex and gender, in particular places and particular times. For so long, categories and traits of sex and gender have been described as natural, and hence have been used to describe domination and subordination as inevitable, justified, or even good. Examinations of the philosophical, scientific, and cultural meanings of sex and gender, and their relationships to various other forms of oppression, are therefore foundational to feminism.

Historically, such feminist investigations have drawn on other theoretical engagements with matters of exploitation, categorical subjugation, and social "otherness," including liberal, antislavery, Marxist, postcolonial, and other leftist philosophical and literary movements. Many would say that feminist philosophy emerged as an academic presence through European existentialism, with the publication of Simone de Beauvoir's

The Second Sex. Arguing famously that "one is not born a woman, but rather, becomes one," Beauvoir presented a multidisciplinary study of the pervasiveness of women's mistreatment and second-class position, and the meanings and roles attributed to females and femininity. Her introduction, anthologized here, explores why and how "woman" is regarded as the perpetual other to the masculine norm, and how solidarity among women is short-circuited by conservative roles and institutions. Beauvoir's work is canonical for its historical significance. Her examination of the ways sex difference mirrors other oppressive frameworks helped generate a line of political and philosophical inquiry that remains central today.

Judith Butler revisits the question of what it means to "become" a woman with a precise articulation of the idea that gender is not something we *have,* but something we *do.* In "Performative Acts and Gender Constitution," she describes gender as the highly stylized performance of acts whose constant and disciplined repetition over time create the effect of a solid and substantial identity. Even more deeply, bodily disciplines, repetitions, and critical disruptions in turn make and remake sex difference itself. The very idea of a sex/gender schema—the idea there are two "natural" sexes that predictably give rise to two corresponding genders—is therefore a cultural invention, crafted through social sanctions and taboos, in the service of reproductive interests. The categories of "sex," "gender," and "sexuality" are not stable fixed natural kinds, but expressions of enforced cultural performances that acquire whatever stability and coherence they have within what Butler calls the "heterosexual matrix."

In "Reconstructing Black Masculinity," bell hooks illustrates the fact that dichotomous gender norms are not universal by examining the ways specific contemporary norms of black masculinity have been shaped by racism, capitalism, sexism, and hegemonic white cultural standards. Central to her discussion is a description of the shift from a nineteenth-century emphasis on patriarchal status, characterized by black men's roles as providers and protectors, to current hypermasculine models of black manhood, marked in U.S. pop culture by obsessions with violence and sexual conquest. Hooks traces stereotypes of black masculinity, and black feminist responses to them, in black power movement discourses, black nationalist ideologies, and the artistic work of Eddie Murphy and Spike Lee, the last of which she analyzes in her own inimitable style. Hooks shows how particular performances of black manhood erode solidarity between black women and men, weaken black communities, and prevent the development of creative strategies for confronting and resisting white supremacy, internalized sexism, and homophobia.

One may have little trouble grasping the idea that genders as cultural products are diverse, constructed, and dynamic, but it can be more difficult to extend this understanding to categories of sex. Most contemporary cultures are deeply committed to the idea that there exist only two sexes, and that female and male are natural complements and opposites. In the words of Judith Lorber, "gender is so pervasive that we assume it is bred into our genes" (1994). But the emerging recognition of intersex persons, and the insights of queer theory, challenge those basic assumptions. The acknowledgment of bodies and identities that do not easily fit into existing categories of sex leads us to look at the extent to which dichotomous biological categories are also socially determined. Ann Fausto-Sterling's essay, "Should There Only Be Two Sexes?" presents empirical, medical, moral, and political arguments for accepting the real spectrum of human sex variation, and especially the existence of intersex or sexually ambiguous bodies, rather than disciplining bodies into a strict two-party sex system. She rejects the convention of surgically assigning a sex to intersex infants, who have some mixture of male and female primary sex characteristics, and imagines a better future where conceptions of sex and gender identity are far more open and

flexible for everyone. An excellent example of theory tied to practice, Fausto-Sterling's analysis is deeply influenced by the experiences of individuals who have suffered grievous harms from commonplace medical interventions, activists who are working to end unnecessary genital surgery on infants, and transgendered and genderqueer folks who have carved out healthy and satisfying identities outside and betwixt the two-party sex system.

Giving voice to newly articulate bodily practices and gender politics, in "Transgender Butch: Butch/FTM Border Wars and the Masculine Continuum," Judith Halberstam self-reflexively engages questions about politics of representation of transsexual, transgender butch, and lesbian butch bodies. By tracing the connections and discontinuities between these terms, as categories but also as real communities with various perspectives and interests, she addresses many of the "thorny questions of identity raised by the public emergence of the female-to-male transsexual." One compelling point of contrast is the fact that trans men are typically described as females with "the wrong body," who have intense desire for re-embodiment as males, where butch lesbians are associated with more casual and playful masculine inclinations from within confidently and unquestionably female bodies. In discussing these and other contrasts and conversations, Halberstam illuminates the impact of evolving female masculinities on male masculinities, transgendered possibilities, queer butch identities, and feminist lesbian politics.

Conceptual attention to sex and gender has long been central to Western feminism, but even when they are taken to be immeasurably diverse, those categories are not considered so important or illuminating by feminists everywhere. For example, Oyèrónké Oyěwùmí argues that Western feminist attention to embodied gender is rooted in specific cultural hierarchies, and epistemologies that privilege visual ways of making sense of the world. In "Visualizing the Body: Western Theories and African Subjects," she argues that influential groups in the West have always asserted their superiority and attempted to justify domination over others through claims that they possess superior bodies. Social order is thus described as accurately reflecting natural endowment, as evidenced through particular bodily types. It is no secret that Western philosophy is filled with examples of arguments that deny women citizenship in the polis or bar them from higher education because of female bodily features. Oyĕwùmí believes that the Western feminist focus on sex difference is a legacy of the belief that social differences are bodily, but this way of organizing social reality is not universal. In Yorùbá society, social relations, rather than bodily types, determine social roles, and Yorùbá culture privileges a multiplicity of senses (especially hearing) over what we can see. By centralizing a Yorùbá perspective, Oyĕwùmí raises some stunning questions about Western thought's exaggerated emphasis on the body, and Western feminisms' own assumptions about the relevance of sex.

INTRODUCTION TO *THE SECOND SEX*

Simone de Beauvoir
Translated and edited by H. M. Parshley

For a long time I have hesitated to write a book on woman. The subject is irritating, especially to women; and it is not new. Enough ink has been spilled in the quarrelling over feminism, now practically over, and perhaps we should say no more about it. It is still talked about, however, for the voluminous nonsense uttered during the last century seems to have done little to illuminate the problem. After all, is there a problem? And if so, what is it? Are there women, really? Most assuredly the theory of the eternal feminine still has its adherents who will whisper in your ear: 'Even in Russia women still are *women*'; and other erudite persons—sometimes the very same—say with a sigh: 'Woman is losing her way, woman is lost.' One wonders if women still exist, if they will always exist, whether or not it is desirable that they should, what place they occupy in this world, what their place should be. 'What has become of women?' was asked recently in an ephemeral magazine.[1]

But first we must ask: what is a woman? '*Tota mulier in utero,*' says one, 'woman is a womb.' But in speaking of certain women, connoisseurs declare that they are not women, although they are equipped with a uterus like the rest. All agree in recognizing the fact that females exist in the human species; today as always they make up about one half of humanity. And yet we are told that femininity is in danger; we are exhorted to be women, remain women, become women. It would appear, then, that every female human being is not necessarily a woman; to be so considered she must share in that mysterious and threatened reality known as femininity. Is this attribute something secreted by the ovaries? Or is it a Platonic essence, a product of the philosophic imagination? Is a rustling petticoat enough to bring it down to earth? Although some women try zealously to incarnate this essence, it is hardly patentable. It is frequently described in vague and dazzling terms that seem to have been borrowed from the vocabulary of the seers, and indeed in the times of St. Thomas it was considered an essence as certainly defined as the somniferous virtue of the poppy.

But conceptualism has lost ground. The biological and social sciences no longer admit the existence of unchangeably fixed entities that determine given characteristics, such as those ascribed to woman, the Jew, or the Negro. Science regards any characteristic as a reaction dependent in part upon a *situation*. If today femininity no longer exists, then it never existed. But does the word *woman*, then, have no specific content? This is stoutly affirmed by those who hold to the philosophy of the enlightenment, of rationalism, of nominalism; women, to them, are merely the human beings arbitrarily designated by the word *woman*. Many American women particularly are prepared to think that there is no longer any place for woman as such; if a backward individual still takes herself for a woman, her friends advise her to be psychoanalyzed and thus get rid of this obsession. In regard to a work, *Modern Woman: The Lost Sex,* which in other respects has its irritating features, Dorothy Parker has written: 'I cannot be just to books which treat of woman as woman.... My idea is that all of us, men as well as women, should be regarded as human beings.' But nominalism is a rather inadequate doctrine, and the antifemininists have had no trouble in showing that women simply *are not* men. Surely woman is, like man, a human being; but such a declaration is abstract. The fact is that every concrete human being is always a singular, separate individual. To decline to accept such notions as the eternal feminine, the black soul, the Jewish character, is not to deny that Jews, Negroes, women exist today—this denial does not represent a liberation for those concerned,

---

[1] *Franchise,* dead today.

but rather a flight from reality. Some years ago a well-known woman writer refused to permit her portrait to appear in a series of photographs especially devoted to women writers; she wished to be counted among the men. But in order to gain this privilege she made use of her husband's influence! Women who assert that they are men lay claim none the less to masculine consideration and respect. I recall also a young Trotskyite standing on a platform at a boisterous meeting and getting ready to use her fists, in spite of her evident fragility. She was denying her feminine weakness; but it was for love of a militant male whose equal she wished to be. The attitude of defiance of many American women proves that they are haunted by a sense of their femininity. In truth, to go for a walk with one's eyes open is enough to demonstrate that humanity is divided into two classes of individuals whose clothes, faces, bodies, smiles, gaits, interests, and occupations are manifestly different. Perhaps these differences are superficial, perhaps they are destined to disappear. What is certain is that right now they do most obviously exist.

If her functioning as a female is not enough to define woman, if we decline also to explain her through 'the eternal feminine', and if nevertheless we admit, provisionally, that women do exist, then we must face the question: what is a woman?

To state the question is, to me, to suggest, at once, a preliminary answer. The fact that I ask it is in itself significant. A man would never get the notion of writing a book on the peculiar situation of the human male.[2] But if I wish to define myself, I must first of all say: 'I am a woman'; on this truth must be based all further discussion. A man never begins by presenting himself as an individual of a certain sex; it goes without saying that he is a man. The terms *masculine* and *femi-*

nine are used symmetrically only as a matter of form, as on legal papers. In actuality the relation of the two sexes is not quite like that of two electrical poles, for man represents both the positive and the neutral, as is indicated by the common use of *man* to designate human beings in general; whereas woman represents only the negative, defined by limiting criteria, without reciprocity. In the midst of an abstract discussion it is vexing to hear a man say: 'You think thus and so because you are a woman'; but I know that my only defense is to reply: 'I think thus and so because it is true,' thereby removing my subjective self from the argument. It would be out of the question to reply: 'And you think the contrary because you are a man', for it is understood that the fact of being a man is no peculiarity. A man is in the right in being a man; it is the woman who is in the wrong. It amounts to this: just as for the ancients there was an absolute vertical with reference to which the oblique was defined, so there is an absolute human type, the masculine. Woman has ovaries, a uterus; these peculiarities imprison her in her subjectivity, circumscribe her within the limits of her own nature. It is often said that she thinks with her glands. Man superbly ignores the fact that his anatomy also includes glands, such as the testicles, and that they secrete hormones. He thinks of his body as a direct and normal connection with the world, which he believes he apprehends objectively, whereas he regards the body of woman as a hindrance, a prison, weighed down by everything peculiar to it. 'The female is a female by virtue of a certain *lack* of qualities,' said Aristotle; 'we should regard the female nature as afflicted with a natural defectiveness.' And St. Thomas for his part pronounced woman to be an 'imperfect man', an 'incidental' being. This is symbolized in Genesis where Eve is depicted as made from what Bossuet called 'a supernumerary bone' of Adam.

Thus humanity is male and man defines woman not in herself but as relative to him; she is not regarded as an autonomous being. Michelet writes: 'Woman, the relative being . . .' And

---

[2] The Kinsey Report [Alfred C. Kinsey and others: *Sexual Behavior in the Human Male* (W. B. Saunders Co., 1948)] is no exception, for it is limited to describing the sexual characteristics of American men, which is quite a different matter.

Benda is most positive in his *Rapport & Uriel:* 'The body of man makes sense in itself quite apart from that of woman, whereas the latter seems wanting in significance by itself . . . Man can think of himself without woman. She cannot think of herself without man.' And she is simply what man decrees; thus she is called 'the sex', by which is meant that she appears essentially to the male as a sexual being. For him she is sex—absolute sex, no less. She is defined and differentiated with reference to man and not he with reference to her; she is the incidental, the inessential as opposed to the essential. He is the Subject, he is the Absolute—she is the Other.[3]

The category of the *Other* is as primordial as consciousness itself. In the most primitive societies, in the most ancient mythologies, one finds the expression of a duality—that of the Self and the Other. This duality was not originally attached to the division of the sexes; it was not dependent upon any empirical facts. It is revealed in such works as that of Granet on Chinese thought and those of Dumézil on the East Indies and Rome. The feminine element was at first no more involved in such pairs as Varuna-Mitra, Uranus-Zeus, Sun-Moon, and Day-Night than it was in the contrasts between Good and Evil, lucky and unlucky auspices, right

and left, God and Lucifer. Otherness is a fundamental category of human thought.

Thus it is that no group ever sets itself up as the One without at once setting up the Other over against itself. If three travelers chance to occupy the same compartment, that is enough to make vaguely hostile 'others' out of all the rest of the passengers on the train. In small-town eyes all persons not belonging to the village are 'strangers' and suspect; to the native of a country all who inhabit other countries are 'foreigners'; Jews are 'different' for the anti-Semite, Negroes are 'inferior' for American racists, aborigines are 'natives' for colonists, proletarians are the 'lower class' for the privileged.

Lévi-Strauss, at the end of a profound work on the various forms of primitive societies, reaches the following conclusion: 'Passage from the state of Nature to the state of Culture is marked by man's ability to view biological relations as a series of contrasts; duality, alternation, opposition, and symmetry, whether under definite or vague forms, constitute not so much phenomena to be explained as fundamental and immediately given data of social reality.'[4] These phenomena would be incomprehensible if in fact human society were simply a *Mitsein* or fellowship based on solidarity and friendliness. Things become clear, on the contrary, if, following Hegel, we find in consciousness itself a fundamental hostility toward every other consciousness; the subject can be posed only in being opposed—he sets himself up as the essential, as opposed to the other, the inessential, the object.

But the other consciousness, the other ego, sets up a reciprocal claim. The native traveling abroad is shocked to find himself in turn regarded as a 'stranger' by the natives of neighbouring countries. As a matter of fact, wars, festivals, trading, treaties, and contests among tribes, nations, and classes tend to deprive the concept *Other*

---

[3] E. Lévinas expresses this idea most explicitly in his essay *Temps et l'Autre.* 'Is there not a case in which otherness, alterity [*altérité*], unquestionably marks the nature of a being, as its essence, an instance of otherness not consisting purely and simply in the opposition of two species of the same genus? I think that the feminine represents the contrary in its absolute sense, this contrariness being in no wise affected by any relation between it and its correlative and thus remaining absolutely other. Sex is not a certain specific difference. . . no more is the sexual difference a mere contradiction. . . . Nor does this difference lie in the duality of two complementary terms, for two complementary terms imply a pre-existing whole. . . . Otherness reaches its full flowering in the feminine, a term of the same rank as consciousness but of opposite meaning.'

I suppose that Lévinas does not forget that woman, too, is aware of her own consciousness, or ego. But it is striking that he deliberately takes a man's point of view, disregarding the reciprocity of subject and object. When he writes that woman is mystery, he implies that she is mystery for man. Thus his description, which is intended to be objective, is in fact an assertion of masculine privilege.

[4] See C. Lévi-Strauss; *Les Structures élémentaires de la parenté.* My thanks are due to C. Lévi-Strauss for his kindness in furnishing me with the proofs of his work.

of its absolute sense and to make manifest its relativity; willy-nilly, individuals and groups are forced to realize the reciprocity of their relations. How is it, then, that this reciprocity has not been recognized between the sexes, that one of the contrasting terms is set up as the sole essential, denying any relativity in regard to its correlative and defining the latter as pure otherness? Why is it that women do not dispute male sovereignty? No subject will readily volunteer to become the object, the inessential; it is not the Other who, in defining himself as the Other, establishes the One. The Other is posed as such by the One in defining himself as the One. But if the Other is not to regain the status of being the One, he must be submissive enough to accept this alien point of view. Whence comes this submission in the case of woman?

There are, to be sure, other cases in which a certain category has been able to dominate another completely for a time. Very often this privilege depends upon inequality of numbers – the majority imposes its rule upon the minority or persecutes it. But women are not a minority, like the American Negroes or the Jews; there are as many women as men on earth. Again, the two groups concerned have often been originally independent; they may have been formerly unaware of each other's existence, or perhaps they recognized each other's autonomy. But a historical event has resulted in the subjugation of the weaker by the stronger. The scattering of the Jews, the introduction of slavery into America, the conquests of imperialism are examples in point. In these cases the oppressed retained at least the memory of former days; they possessed in common a past, a tradition, sometimes a religion or a culture.

The parallel drawn by Bebel between women and the proletariat is valid in that neither ever formed a minority or a separate collective unit of mankind. And instead of a single historical event it is in both cases a historical development that explains their status as a class and accounts for the membership of *particular individuals* in that

class. But proletarians have not always existed, whereas there have always been women. They are women in virtue of their anatomy and physiology. Throughout history they have always been subordinated to men,[5] and hence their dependency is not the result of a historical event or a social change—it was not something that *occurred.* The reason why otherness in this case seems to be an absolute is in part that it lacks the contingent or incidental nature of historical facts. A condition brought about at a certain time can be abolished at some other time, as the Negroes of Haiti and others have proved; but it might seem that a natural condition is beyond the possibility of change. In truth, however, the nature of things is no more immutably given, once for all, than is historical reality. If woman seems to be the inessential which never becomes the essential, it is because she herself fails to bring about this change. Proletarians say 'We'; Negroes also. Regarding themselves as subjects, they transform the bourgeois, the whites, into 'others'. But women do not say 'We', except at some congress of feminists or similar formal demonstration; men say 'women', and women use the same word in referring to themselves. They do not authentically assume a subjective attitude. The proletarians have accomplished the revolution in Russia, the Negroes in Haiti, the Indo-Chinese are battling for it in Indo-China; but the women's effort has never been anything more than a symbolic agitation. They have gained only what men have been willing to grant; they have taken nothing, they have only received.

The reason for this is that women lack concrete means for organizing themselves into a unit which can stand face to face with the correlative unit. They have no past, no history, no religion of their own; and they have no such solidarity of work and interest as that of the proletariat. They are not even promiscuously herded together in the way that creates community feeling among the

---

[5] With rare exceptions, perhaps, like certain matriarchal rulers, queens, and the like.—Tr

American Negroes, the ghetto Jews, the workers of Saint-Denis, or the factory hands of Renault. They live dispersed among the males, attached through residence, housework, economic condition, and social standing to certain men—fathers or husbands—more firmly than they are to other women. If they belong to the bourgeoisie, they feel solidarity with men of that class, not with proletarian women; if they are white, their allegiance is to white men, not to Negro women. The proletariat can propose to massacre the ruling class, and a sufficiently fanatical Jew or Negro might dream of getting sole possession of the atomic bomb and making humanity wholly Jewish or black; but woman cannot even dream of exterminating the males. The bond that unites her to her oppressors is not comparable to any other. The division of the sexes is a biological fact, not an event in human history. Male and female stand opposed within a primordial *Mitsein,* and woman has not broken it. The couple is a fundamental unity with its two halves riveted together, and the cleavage of society along the line of sex is impossible. Here is to be found the basic trait of woman: she is the Other in a totality of which the two components are necessary to one another.

One could suppose that this reciprocity might have facilitated the liberation of woman. When Hercules sat at the feet of Omphale and helped with her spinning, his desire for her held him captive; but why did she fail to gain a lasting power? To revenge herself on Jason, Medea killed their children; and this grim legend would seem to suggest that she might have obtained a formidable influence over him through his love for his offspring. In *Lysistrata* Aristophanes gaily depicts a band of women who joined forces to gain social ends through the sexual needs of their men; but this is only a play. In the legend of the Sabine women, the latter soon abandoned their plan of remaining sterile to punish their ravishers. In truth woman has not been socially emancipated through man's need—sexual desire and the desire for offspring—which makes the male dependent for satisfaction upon the female.

Master and slave, also, are united by a reciprocal need, in this case economic, which does not liberate the slave. In the relation of master to slave the master does not make a point of the need that he has for the other; he has in his grasp the power of satisfying this need through his own action; whereas the slave, in his dependent condition, his hope and fear, is quite conscious of the need he has for his master. Even if the need is at bottom equally urgent for both, it always works in favor of the oppressor and against the oppressed. That is why the liberation of the working class, for example, has been slow.

Now, woman has always been man's dependent, if not his slave; the two sexes have never shared the world in equality. And even today woman is heavily handicapped, though her situation is beginning to change. Almost nowhere is her legal status the same as man's, and frequently it is much to her disadvantage. Even when her rights are legally recognized in the abstract, long-standing custom prevents their full expression in the mores. In the economic sphere men and women can almost be said to make up two castes; other things being equal, the former hold the better jobs, get higher wages, and have more opportunity for success than their new competitors. In industry and politics men have a great many more positions and they monopolize the most important posts. In addition to all this, they enjoy a traditional prestige that the education of children tends in every way to support, for the present enshrines the past—and in the past all history has been made by men. At the present time, when women are beginning to take part in the affairs of the world, it is still a world that belongs to men—they have no doubt of it at all and women have scarcely any. To decline to be the Other, to refuse to be a party to the deal—this would be for women to renounce all the advantages conferred upon them by their alliance with the superior caste. Man-the-sovereign will provide woman-the-liege with material protection and will undertake the moral justification of her existence; thus she can evade at once both economic risk and the metaphysical risk of a liberty in which ends and aims must be contrived without assistance. Indeed, along with the ethical urge of each individual to affirm his subjective existence, there is also the temptation to forgo liberty and become a thing. This is an inauspicious road, for he who takes it—passive, lost, ruined—becomes henceforth the creature of another's will, frustrated in his transcendence and deprived of every value. But it is an easy road; on it one avoids the strain involved in undertaking an authentic existence. When man makes of woman the *Other,* he may, then, expect her to manifest deep-seated tendencies toward complicity. Thus, woman may fail to lay claim to the status of subject because she lacks definite resources, because she feels the necessary bond that ties her to man regardless of reciprocity, and because she is often very well pleased with her role as the *Other.*

But it will be asked at once: how did all this begin? It is easy to see that the duality of the sexes, like any duality, gives rise to conflict. And doubtless the winner will assume the status of absolute. But why should man have won from the start? It seems possible that women could have won the victory; or that the outcome of the conflict might never have been decided. How is it that this world has always belonged to the men and that things have begun to change only recently? Is this change a good thing? Will it bring about an equal sharing of the world between men and women?

These questions are not new, and they have often been answered. But the very fact that woman *is the Other* tends to cast suspicion upon all the justifications that men have ever been able to provide for it. These have all too evidently been dictated by men's interest. A little-known feminist of the seventeenth century, Poulain de la Barre, put it this way: 'All that has been written about women by men should be suspect, for the men are at once judge and party to the lawsuit.' Everywhere, at all times, the males have displayed their satisfaction in feeling that they are the lords of creation. 'Blessed be God . . . that He did not make me a woman,' say the Jews in their morning

prayers, while their wives pray on a note of resignation: 'Blessed be the Lord, who created me according to His will.' The first among the blessings for which Plato thanked the gods was that he had been created free, not enslaved; the second, a man, not a woman. But the males could not enjoy this privilege fully unless they believed it to be founded on the absolute and the eternal; they sought to make the fact of their supremacy into a right. 'Being men, those who have made and compiled the laws have favored their own sex, and jurists have elevated these laws into principles', to quote Poulain de la Barre once more.

Legislators, priests, philosophers, writers, and scientists have striven to show that the subordinate position of woman is willed in heaven and advantageous on earth. The religions invented by men reflect this wish for domination. In the legends of Eve and Pandora men have taken up arms against women. They have made use of philosophy and theology, as the quotations from Aristotle and St. Thomas have shown. Since ancient times satirists and moralists have delighted in showing up the weaknesses of women. We are familiar with the savage indictments hurled against women throughout French literature. Montherlant, for example, follows the tradition of Jean de Meung, though with less gusto. This hostility may at times be well founded, often it is gratuitous; but in truth it more or less successfully conceals a desire for self-justification. As Montaigne says, 'It is easier to accuse one sex than to excuse the other.' Sometimes what is going on is clear enough. For instance, the Roman law limiting the rights of woman cited 'the imbecility, the instability of the sex' just when the weakening of family ties seemed to threaten the interests of male heirs. And in the effort to keep the married woman under guardianship, appeal was made in the sixteenth century to the authority of St. Augustine, who declared that 'woman is a creature neither decisive nor constant', at a time when the single woman was thought capable of managing her property. Montaigne understood clearly how arbitrary and unjust was woman's appointed lot: 'Women are not in the wrong when they decline to accept the rules laid down for them, since the men make these rules without consulting them. No wonder intrigue and strife abound.' But he did not go so far as to champion their cause.

It was only later, in the eighteenth century, that genuinely democratic men began to view the matter objectively. Diderot, among others, strove to show that woman is, like man, a human being. Later John Stuart Mill came fervently to her defense. But these philosophers displayed unusual impartiality. In the nineteenth century the feminist quarrel became again a quarrel of partisans. One of the consequences of the industrial revolution was the entrance of women into productive labor, and it was just here that the claims of the feminists emerged from the realm of theory and acquired an economic basis, while their opponents became the more aggressive. Although landed property lost power to some extent, the bourgeoisie clung to the old morality that found the guarantee of private property in the solidity of the family. Woman was ordered back into the home the more harshly as her emancipation became a real menace. Even within the working class the men endeavored to restrain woman's liberation, because they began to see the women as dangerous competitors – the more so because they were accustomed to work for lower wages.

In proving woman's inferiority, the antifeminists then began to draw not only upon religion, philosophy, and theology, as before, but also upon science—biology, experimental psychology, etc. At most they were willing to grant 'equality in difference' to the *other* sex. That profitable formula is most significant; it is precisely like the 'equal but separate' formula of the Jim Crow laws aimed at the North American Negroes. As is well known, this so-called equalitarian segregation has resulted only in the most extreme discrimination. The similarity just noted is in no way due to chance, for whether it is a race, a caste, a class, or a sex that is reduced to a position of inferiority, the methods of justification are the same. 'The eternal feminine' corresponds to 'the black soul' and to 'the Jewish character'. True, the Jewish problem is on the whole very different from the other two—to the anti-Semite the Jew is not so much an inferior as he is an enemy for whom there is to be granted no place on earth, for whom annihilation is the fate desired. But there are deep similarities between the situation of woman and that of the Negro. Both are being emancipated today from a like paternalism, and the former master class wishes to 'keep them in their place'—that is, the place chosen for them. In both cases the former masters lavish more or less sincere eulogies, either on the virtues of 'the good Negro' with his dormant, childish, merry soul—the submissive Negro—or on the merits of the woman who is 'truly feminine'—that is, frivolous, infantile, irresponsible—the submissive woman. In both cases the dominant class bases its argument on a state of affairs that it has itself created. As George Bernard Shaw puts it, in substance, 'The American white relegates the black to the rank of shoeshine boy; and he concludes from this that the black is good for nothing but shining shoes.' This vicious circle is met with in all analogous circumstances; when an individual (or a group of individuals) is kept in a situation of inferiority, the fact is that he *is* inferior. But the significance of the verb to *be* must be rightly understood here; it is in bad faith to give it a static value when it really has the dynamic Hegelian sense of 'to have become'. Yes, women on the whole *are* today inferior to men; that is, their situation affords them fewer possibilities. The question is: should that state of affairs continue?

Many men hope that it will continue; not all have given up the battle. The conservative bourgeoisie still see in the emancipation of women a menace to their morality and their interests. Some men dread feminine competition. Recently a male student wrote in the *Hebdo-Latin*: 'Every woman student who goes into medicine or law robs us of a job.' He never questioned his rights in this world. And economic interests are not the only ones concerned. One of the benefits that oppression confers upon the oppressors is that the most humble among them is made to *feel* superior; thus, a 'poor white' in the South can console himself with the thought that he is not a 'dirty nigger'—and the more prosperous whites cleverly exploit this pride.

Similarly, the most mediocre of males feels himself a demi-god as compared with women. It was much easier for M. de Montherlant to think himself a hero when he faced women (and women chosen for his purpose) than when he was obliged to act the man among men—something many women have done better than he, for that matter. And in September 1948, in one of his articles in the *Figaro littéraire,* Claude Mauriac—whose great originality is admired by all—could[6] write regarding woman: '*We* listen on a tone [*sic!*] of polite indifference . . . to the most brilliant among them, well knowing that her wit reflects more or less luminously ideas that come from *us*.' Evidently the speaker referred to is not reflecting the ideas of Mauriac himself, for no one knows of his having any. It may be that she reflects ideas originating with men, but then, even among men there are those who have been known to appropriate ideas not their own; and one can well ask whether Claude Mauriac might not find more interesting a conversation reflecting Descartes, Marx, or Gide rather than himself. What is really remarkable is that by using the questionable *we* he identifies himself with St. Paul, Hegel, Lenin, and Nietzsche, and from the lofty eminence of their grandeur looks down disdainfully upon the bevy of women who make bold to converse with him on a footing of equality. In truth, I know of more than one woman who would refuse to suffer with patience Mauriac's 'tone of polite indifference'.

I have lingered on this example because the masculine attitude is here displayed with disarming ingenuousness. But men profit in many more subtle ways from the otherness, the alterity of woman. Here is miraculous balm for those afflicted with an inferiority complex, and indeed

no one is more arrogant toward women, more aggressive or scornful, than the man who is anxious about his virility. Those who are not fear-ridden in the presence of their fellow men are much more disposed to recognize a fellow creature in woman; but even to these the myth of Woman, the Other, is precious for many reasons.[7] They cannot be blamed for not cheerfully relinquishing all the benefits they derive from the myth, for they realize what they would lose in relinquishing woman as they fancy her to be, while they fail to realize what they have to gain from the woman of tomorrow. Refusal to pose oneself as the Subject, unique and absolute, requires great self-denial. Furthermore, the vast majority of men make no such claim explicitly. They do not *postulate* woman as inferior, for today they are too thoroughly imbued with the ideal of democracy not to recognize all human beings as equals.

In the bosom of the family, woman seems in the eyes of childhood and youth to be clothed in the same social dignity as the adult males. Later on, the young man, desiring and loving, experiences the resistance, the independence of the woman desired and loved; in marriage, he respects woman as wife and mother, and in the concrete events of conjugal life she stands there before him as a free being. He can therefore feel that social subordination as between the sexes no longer exists and that on the whole, in spite of differences, woman is an equal. As, however, he observes some points of inferiority—the most important being unfitness for the professions— he attributes these to natural causes. When he is in a co-operative and benevolent relation with

---

[6] Or at least he thought he could.

[7] A significant article on this theme by Michel Carrouges appeared in No. 292 of the *Cahiers du Sud.* He writes indignantly: 'Would that there were no woman-myth at all but only a cohort of cooks, matrons, prostitutes, and bluestockings serving functions of pleasure or usefulness!' That is to say, in his view woman has no existence in and for herself; he thinks only of her *function* in the male world. Her reason for existence lies in man. But then, in fact, her poetic 'function' as a myth might be more valued than any other. The real problem is precisely to find out why woman should be defined with relation to man.

woman, his theme is the principle of abstract equality, and he does not base his attitude upon such inequality as may exist. But when he is in conflict with her, the situation is reversed: his theme will be the existing inequality, and he will even take it as justification for denying abstract equality.[8]

So it is that many men will affirm as if in good faith that women *are* the equals of man and that they have nothing to clamor for, while *at the same time* they will say that women can never be the equals of man and that their demands are in vain. It is, in point of fact, a difficult matter for man to realize the extreme importance of social discriminations which seem outwardly insignificant but which produce in woman moral and intellectual effects so profound that they appear to spring from her original nature. The most sympathetic of men never fully comprehend woman's concrete situation. And there is no reason to put much trust in the men when they rush to the defense of privileges whose full extent they can hardly measure. We shall not, then, permit ourselves to be intimidated by the number and violence of the attacks launched against women, nor to be entrapped by the self-seeking eulogies bestowed on the 'true woman', nor to profit by the enthusiasm for woman's destiny manifested by men who would not for the world have any part of it.

We should consider the arguments of the feminists with no less suspicion, however, for very often their controversial aim deprives them of all real value. If the 'woman question' seems trivial, it is because masculine arrogance has made of it a 'quarrel'; and when quarreling one no longer reasons well. People have tirelessly sought to prove that woman is superior, inferior, or equal to man. Some say that, having been created after Adam, she is evidently

a secondary being; others say on the contrary that Adam was only a rough draft and that God succeeded in producing the human being in perfection when He created Eve. Woman's brain is smaller; yes, but it is relatively larger. Christ was made a man; yes, but perhaps for his greater humility. Each argument at once suggests its opposite, and both are often fallacious. If we are to gain understanding, we must get out of these ruts; we must discard the vague notions of superiority, inferiority, equality which have hitherto corrupted every discussion of the subject and start afresh.

Very well, but just how shall we pose the question? And, to begin with, who are we to propound it at all? Man is at once judge and party to the case; but so is woman. What we need is an angel—neither man nor woman—but where shall we find one? Still, the angel would be poorly qualified to speak, for an angel is ignorant of all the basic facts involved in the problem. With a hermaphrodite we should be no better off, for here the situation is most peculiar; the hermaphrodite is not really the combination of a whole man and a whole woman, but consists of parts of each and thus is neither. It looks to me as if there are, after all, certain women who are best qualified to elucidate the situation of woman. Let us not be misled by the sophism that because Epimenides was a Cretan he was necessarily a liar; it is not a mysterious essence that compels men and women to act in good or in bad faith, it is their situation that inclines them more or less toward the search for truth. Many of today's women, fortunate in the restoration of all the privileges pertaining to the estate of the human being, can afford the luxury of impartiality—we even recognize its necessity. We are no longer like our partisan elders; by and large we have won the game. In recent debates on the status of women the United Nations has persistently maintained that the equality of the sexes is now becoming a reality, and already some of us have never had to sense in our femininity an inconvenience or an obstacle. Many problems appear to us to be more pressing than those which concern us in

---

[8] For example, a man will say that he considers his wife in no wise degraded because she has no gainful occupation. The profession of housewife is just as lofty, and so on. But when the first quarrel comes, he will exclaim: 'Why, you couldn't make your living without me!'

particular, and this detachment even allows us to hope that our attitude will be objective. Still, we know the feminine world more intimately than do the men because we have our roots in it, we grasp more immediately than do men what it means to a human being to be feminine; and we are more concerned with such knowledge. I have said that there are more pressing problems, but this does not prevent us from seeing some importance in asking how the fact of being women will affect our lives. What opportunities precisely have been given us and what withheld? What fate awaits our younger sisters, and what directions should they take? It is significant that books by women on women are in general animated in our day less by a wish to demand our rights than by an effort toward clarity and understanding. As we emerge from an era of excessive controversy, this book is offered as one attempt among others to confirm that statement.

But it is doubtless impossible to approach any human problem with a mind free from bias. The way in which questions are put, the points of view assumed, presuppose a relativity of interest; all characteristics imply values, and every objective description, so called, implies an ethical background. Rather than attempt to conceal principles more or less definitely implied, it is better to state them openly at the beginning. This will make it unnecessary to specify on every page in just what sense one uses such words as *superior, inferior, better, worse, progress, reaction,* and the like. If we survey some of the works on woman, we note that one of the points of view most frequently adopted is that of the public good, the general interest; and one always means by this the benefit of society as one wishes it to be maintained or established. For our part, we hold that the only public good is that which assures the private good of the citizens; we shall pass judgment on institutions according to their effectiveness in giving concrete opportunities to individuals. But we do not confuse the idea of private interest with that of happiness, although that is another common point of view. Are not women of the harem more happy than women voters? Is not the housekeeper

happier than the working-woman? It is not too clear just what the word *happy* really means and still less what true values it may mask. There is no possibility of measuring the happiness of others, and it is always easy to describe as happy the situation in which one wishes to place them.

In particular those who are condemned to stagnation are often pronounced happy on the pretext that happiness consists in being at rest. This notion we reject, for our perspective is that of existentialist ethics. Every subject plays his part as such specifically through exploits or projects that serve as a mode of transcendence; he achieves liberty only through a continual reaching out toward other liberties. There is no justification for present existence other than its expansion into an indefinitely open future. Every time transcendence falls back into immanence, stagnation, there is a degradation of existence into the *'en-soi'*—the brutish life of subjection to given conditions—and of liberty into constraint and contingence. This downfall represents a moral fault if the subject consents to it; if it is inflicted upon him, it spells frustration and oppression. In both cases it is an absolute evil. Every individual concerned to justify his existence feels that his existence involves an undefined need to transcend himself, to engage in freely chosen projects.

Now, what peculiarly signalizes the situation of woman is that she—a free and autonomous being like all human creatures—nevertheless finds herself living in a world where men compel her to assume the status of the Other. They propose to stabilize her as object and to doom her to immanence since her transcendence is to be overshadowed and forever transcended by another ego (*conscience*) which is essential and sovereign. The drama of woman lies in this conflict between the fundamental aspirations of every subject (ego)—who always regards the self as the essential—and the compulsions of a situation in which she is the inessential. How can a human being in woman's situation attain fulfillment? What roads are open to her? Which are blocked? How can independence be recovered in a state of dependency? What circumstances limit woman's liberty and how can they be overcome? These are the fundamental questions on which I would fain throw some light. This means that I am interested in the fortunes of the individual as defined not in terms of happiness but in terms of liberty.

Quite evidently this problem would be without significance if we were to believe that woman's destiny is inevitably determined by physiological, psychological, or economic forces. Hence I shall discuss first of all the light in which woman is viewed

by biology, psychoanalysis, and historical materialism. Next I shall try to show exactly how the concept of the 'truly feminine' has been fashioned—why woman has been defined as the Other—and what have been the consequences from man's point of view. Then from woman's point of view I shall describe the world in which women must live; and thus we shall be able to envisage the difficulties in their way as, endeavoring to make their escape from the sphere hitherto assigned them, they aspire to full membership in the human race.

PERFORMATIVE ACTS AND GENDER CONSTITUTION: AN ESSAY IN PHENOMENOLOGY AND FEMINIST THEORY

Judith Butler

Philosophers rarely think about acting in the theatrical sense, but they do have a discourse of 'acts' that maintains associative semantic meanings with theories of performance and acting. For example, John Searle's 'speech acts,' those verbal assurances and promises which seem not only to refer to a speaking relationship, but to constitute a moral bond between speakers, illustrate one of the illocutionary gestures that constitutes the stage of the analytic philosophy of language. Further, 'action theory,' a domain of moral philosophy, seeks to understand what it is 'to do' prior to any claim of what one *ought* to do. Finally, the phenomenological theory of 'acts,' espoused by Edmund Husserl, Maurice Merleau-Ponty and George Herbert Mead, among others, seeks to explain the mundane way in which social agents *constitute* social reality through language, gesture, and all manner of symbolic social sign. Though phenomenology sometimes appears to assume the existence of a choosing and constituting agent prior to language

(who poses as the sole source of its constituting acts), there is also a more radical use of the doctrine of constitution that takes the social agent as an *object* rather than the subject of constitutive acts.

When Simone de Beauvoir claims, "one is not born, but, rather, *becomes* a woman," she is appropriating and reinterpreting this doctrine of constituting acts from the phenomenological tradition.[1] In this sense, gender is in no way a stable identity or locus of agency from which various acts proceed; rather, it is an identity tenuously constituted in time—an identity instituted through a *stylized repetition of acts.* Further, gender is instituted through the stylization of the body and, hence, must be understood as the mundane way in which bodily gestures, movements, and enactments of various kinds constitute the illusion of an abiding gendered self. This formulation moves the conception of gender off the ground of a substantial model of identity to one that requires a conception of a constituted *social temporality.* Significantly, if gender is instituted through acts which are internally discontinuous, then the *appearance of substance* is precisely that, a constructed identity, a performative

---

[1] For a further discussion of Beauvoir's feminist contribution to phenomenological theory, see my "Variations on Sex and Gender: Beauvoir's *The Second Sex*," *Yale French Studies* 172 (1986).

accomplishment which the mundane social audience, including the actors themselves, come to believe and to perform in the mode of belief. If the ground of gender identity is the stylized repetition of acts through time, and not a seemingly seamless identity, then the possibilities of gender transformation are to be found in the arbitrary relation between such acts, in the possibility of a different sort of repeating, in the breaking or subversive repetition of that style.

Through the conception of gender acts sketched above, I will try to show some ways in which reified and naturalized conceptions of gender might be understood as constituted and, hence, capable of being constituted differently. In opposition to theatrical or phenomenological models which take the gendered self to be prior to its acts, I will understand constituting acts not only as constituting the identity of the actor, but as constituting that identity as a compelling illusion, an object of *belief.* In the course of making my argument, I will draw from theatrical, anthropological, and philosophical discourses, but mainly phenomenology, to show that what is called gender identity is a performative accomplishment compelled by social sanction and taboo. In its very character as performative resides the possibility of contesting its reified status.

I. SEX/GENDER: FEMINIST AND PHENOMENOLOGICAL VIEWS

Feminist theory has often been critical of naturalistic explanations of sex and sexuality that assume that the meaning of women's social existence can be derived from some fact of their physiology. In distinguishing sex from gender, feminist theorists have disputed causal explanations that assume that sex dictates or necessitates certain social meanings for women's experience. Phenomenological theories of human embodiment have also been concerned to distinguish between the various physiological and biological causalities that structure bodily existence and the *meanings* that embodied existence assumes

in the context of lived experience. In Merleau-Ponty's reflections in *The Phenomenology of Perception* on "the body in its sexual being," he takes issue with such accounts of bodily experience and claims that the body is "an historical idea" rather than "a natural species."[2] Significantly, it is this claim that Simone de Beauvoir cites in *The Second Sex* when she sets the stage for her claim that "woman," and by extension, any gender, is an historical situation rather than a natural fact.[3]

In both contexts, the existence and facticity of the material or natural dimensions of the body are not denied, but reconceived as distinct from the process by which the body comes to bear cultural meanings. For both Beauvoir and Merleau-Ponty, the body is understood to be an active process of embodying certain cultural and historical possibilities, a complicated process of appropriation which any phenomenological theory of embodiment needs to describe. In order to describe the gendered body, a phenomenological theory of constitution requires an expansion of the conventional view of acts to mean both that which constitutes meaning and that through which meaning is performed or enacted. In other words, the acts by which gender is constituted bear similarities to performative acts within theatrical contexts. My task, then, is to examine in what ways gender is constructed through specific corporeal acts, and what possibilities exist for the cultural transformation of gender through such acts.

Merleau-Ponty maintains not only that the body is an historical idea but a set of possibilities to be continually realized. In claiming that the body is an historical idea, Merleau-Ponty means that it gains its meaning through a concrete and historically mediated expression in the world. That the body is a set of possibilities signifies (a) that its appearance in the world, for perception, is not predetermined by some manner of interior

---

[2] Maurice Merleau-Ponty, "The Body in its Sexual Being," in *The Phenomenology of Perception,* trans. Colin Smith (Boston: Routledge and Kegan Paul, 1962).
[3] Simone de Beauvoir, *The Second Sex,* trans. H. M. Parshley (New York: Vintage, 1974), 38.

essence, and (b) that its concrete expression in the world must be understood as the taking up and rendering specific of a set of historical possibilities. Hence, there is an agency which is understood as the process of rendering such possibilities determinate. These possibilities are necessarily constrained by available historical conventions. The body is not a self-identical or merely factic materiality; it is a materiality that bears meaning, if nothing else, and the manner of this bearing is fundamentally dramatic. By dramatic I mean only that the body is not merely matter but a continual and incessant *materializing* of possibilities. One is not simply a body, but, in some very key sense, one does one's body and, indeed, one does one's body differently from one's contemporaries and from one's embodied predecessors and successors as well.

It is, however, clearly unfortunate grammar to claim that there is a 'we' or an 'I' that does its body, as if a disembodied agency preceded and directed an embodied exterior. More appropriate, I suggest, would be a vocabulary that resists the substance metaphysics of subject-verb formations and relies instead on an ontology of present participles. The 'I' that is its body is, of necessity, a mode of embodying, and the 'what' that it embodies is possibilities. But here again the grammar of the formulation misleads, for the possibilities that are embodied are not fundamentally exterior or antecedent to the process of embodying itself. As an intentionally organized materiality, the body is always an embodying *of* possibilities both conditioned and circumscribed by historical convention. In other words, the body *is* a historical situation, as Beauvoir has claimed, and is a manner of doing, dramatizing, and *reproducing* a historical situation.

To do, to dramatize, to reproduce, these seem to be some of the elementary structures of embodiment. This doing of gender is not merely a way in which embodied agents are exterior, surfaced, open to the perception of others. Embodiment clearly manifests a set of strategies or what Sartre would perhaps have called a style of being

or Foucault, "a stylistics of existence." This style is never fully self-styled, for living styles have a history, and that history conditions and limits possibilities. Consider gender, for instance, as *a corporeal style,* an 'act,' as it were, which is both intentional and performative, where 'performative' itself carries the double-meaning of 'dramatic' and 'non-referential.'

When Beauvoir claims that 'woman' is a historical idea and not a natural fact, she clearly underscores the distinction between sex, as biological facticity, and gender, as the cultural interpretation or signification of that facticity. To be female is, according to that distinction, a facticity which has no meaning, but to be a woman is to have *become* a woman, to compel the body to conform to an historical idea of 'woman,' to induce the body to become a cultural sign, to materialize oneself in obedience to an historically delimited possibility, and to do this as a sustained and repeated corporeal project. The notion of a 'project', however, suggests the originating force of a radical will, and because gender is a project which has cultural survival as its end, the term *'strategy'* better suggests the situation of duress under which gender performance always and variously occurs. Hence, as a strategy of survival, gender is a performance with clearly punitive consequences. Discrete genders are part of what 'humanizes' individuals within contemporary culture; indeed, those who fail to do their gender right are regularly punished. Because there is neither an 'essence' that gender expresses or externalizes nor an objective ideal to which gender aspires; because gender is not a fact, the various acts of gender creates the idea of gender, and without those acts, there would be no gender at all. Gender is, thus, a construction that regularly conceals its genesis. The tacit collective agreement to perform, produce, and sustain discrete and polar genders as cultural fictions is obscured by the credibility of its own production. The authors of gender become entranced by their own fictions whereby the construction compels one's belief in its necessity and naturalness. The historical possibilities materialized through various corporeal styles are nothing other than those punitively regulated cultural fictions that are alternately embodied and disguised under duress.

How useful is a phenomenological point of departure for a feminist description of gender? On the surface it appears that phenomenology shares with feminist analysis a commitment to grounding theory in lived experience, and in revealing the way in which the world is produced through the constituting acts of subjective experience. Clearly, not all feminist theory would privilege the point of view of the subject (Kristeva once objected to feminist theory as 'too existentialist'[4]), and yet the feminist claim that the personal is political suggests, in part, that subjective experience is not only structured by existing political arrangements, but effects and structures those arrangements in turn. Feminist theory has sought to understand the way in which systemic or pervasive political and cultural structures are enacted and reproduced through individual acts and practices, and how the analysis of ostensibly personal situations is clarified through situating the issues in a broader and shared cultural context. Indeed, the feminist impulse, and I am sure there is more than one, has often emerged in the recognition that my pain or my silence or my anger or my perception is finally not mine alone, and that it delimits me in a shared cultural situation which in turn enables and empowers me in certain unanticipated ways. The personal is thus implicitly political inasmuch as it is conditioned by shared social structures, but the personal has also been immunized against political challenge to the extent that public/private distinctions endure. For feminist theory, then, the personal becomes an expansive category, one which accommodates, if only implicitly, political structures usually viewed as public. Indeed, the very meaning of the political expands as well. At its best, feminist theory involves a dialectical expansion

of both of these categories. My situation does not cease to be mine just because it is the situation of someone else, and my acts, individual as they are, nevertheless reproduce the situation of my gender, and do that in various ways. In other words, there is, latent in the personal is political formulation of feminist theory, a supposition that the life-world of gender relations is constituted, at least partially, through the concrete and historically mediated *acts* of individuals. Considering that "the" body is invariably transformed into his body or her body, the body is only known through its gendered appearance. It would seem imperative to consider the way in which this gendering of the body occurs. My suggestion is that the body becomes its gender through a series of acts which are renewed, revised, and consolidated through time. From a feminist point of view, one might try to reconceive the gendered body as the legacy of sedimented acts rather than a predetermined or foreclosed structure, essence or fact, whether natural, cultural, or linguistic.

The feminist appropriation of the phenomenological theory of constitution might employ the notion of an *act* in a richly ambiguous sense. If the personal is a category which expands to include the wider political and social structures, then the *acts* of the gendered subject would be similarly expansive. Clearly, there are political acts which are deliberate and instrumental actions of political organizing, resistance collective intervention with the broad aim of instating a more just set of social and political relations. There are thus acts which are done in the name of women, and then there are acts in and of themselves, apart from any instrumental consequence, that challenge the category of women itself. Indeed, one ought to consider the futility of a political program which seeks radically to transform the social situation of women without first determining whether the category of woman is socially constructed in such a way that to be a woman is, by definition, to be in an oppressed situation. In an understandable desire to forge bonds of solidarity, feminist discourse has often

---

[4] Julia Kristeva, *Histoire d'amour* (Paris: Editions Denoel 1983), 242.

relied upon the category of woman as a universal presupposition of cultural experience which, in its universal status, provides a false ontological promise of eventual political solidarity. In a culture in which the false universal of 'man' has for the most part been presupposed as coextensive with humanness itself, feminist theory has sought with success to bring female specificity into visibility and to rewrite the history of culture in terms which acknowledge the presence, the influence, and the oppression of women. Yet, in this effort to combat the invisibility of women as a category feminists run the risk of rendering visible a category which may or may not be representative of the concrete lives of women. As feminists, we have been less eager, I think, to consider the status of the category itself and, indeed, to discern the conditions of oppression which issue from an unexamined reproduction of gender identities which sustain discrete and binary categories of man and woman.

When Beauvoir claims that woman is an "historical situation," she emphasizes that the body suffers a certain cultural construction, not only through conventions that sanction and proscribe how one acts one's body, the 'act' or performance that one's body is, but also in the tacit conventions that structure the way the body is culturally perceived. Indeed, if gender is the cultural significance that the sexed body assumes, and if that significance is codetermined through various acts and their cultural perception, then it would appear that from within the terms of culture it is not possible to know sex as distinct from gender. The reproduction of the category of gender is enacted on a large political scale, as when women first enter a profession or gain certain rights, or are reconceived in legal or political discourse in significantly new ways. But the more mundane reproduction of gendered identity takes place through the various ways in which bodies are acted in relationship to the deeply entrenched or sedimented expectations of gendered existence. Consider that there is a sedimentation of gender norms that produces the peculiar phenomenon of

a natural sex, or a real woman, or any number of prevalent and compelling social fictions, and that this is a sedimentation that over time has produced a set of corporeal styles which, in reified form, appear as the natural configuration of bodies into sexes which exist in a binary relation to one another.

II. BINARY GENDERS AND THE HETEROSEXUAL CONTRACT

To guarantee the reproduction of a given culture, various requirements, well-established in the anthropological literature of kinship, have instated sexual reproduction within the confines of a heterosexually-based system of marriage which requires the reproduction of human beings in certain gendered modes which, in effect, guarantee the eventual reproduction of that kinship system. As Foucault and others have pointed out, the association of a natural sex with a discrete gender and with an ostensibly natural 'attraction' to the opposing sex/gender is an unnatural conjunction of cultural constructs in the service of reproductive interests.[5] Feminist cultural anthropology and kinship studies have shown how cultures are governed by conventions that not only regulate and guarantee the production, exchange, and consumption of material goods, but also reproduce the bonds of kinship itself, which require taboos and a punitive regulation of reproduction to effect that end. Levi-Strauss has shown how the incest taboo works to guarantee the channeling of sexuality into various modes of heterosexual marriage,[6] Gayle Rubin has argued convincingly that the incest taboo produces certain kinds of

---

[5] See Michel Foucault, *The History of Sexuality: An Introduction,* trans. Robert Hurley (New York: Random House, 1980), 154: "the notion of 'sex' made it possible to group together, in an artificial unity, anatomical elements, biological functions, conducts, sensations, and pleasures, and it enabled one to make use of this fictitious unity as a causal principle . . .".

[6] See Claude Levi-Strauss, *The Elementary Structures of Kinship* (Boston: Beacon Press, 1965).

discrete gendered identities and sexualities.[7] My point is simply that one way in which this system of compulsory heterosexuality is reproduced and concealed is through the cultivation of bodies into discrete sexes with 'natural' appearances and 'natural' heterosexual dispositions. Although the ethnocentric conceit suggests a progression beyond the mandatory structures of kinship relations as described by Levi-Strauss, I would suggest, along with Rubin, that contemporary gender identities are so many marks or "traces" of residual kinship. The contention that sex, gender, and heterosexuality are historical products which have become conjoined and reified as natural over time has received a good deal of critical attention not only from Michel Foucault, but Monique Wittig, gay historians, and various cultural anthropologists and social psychologists in recent years.[8] These theories, however, still lack the critical resources for thinking radically about the historical sedimentation of sexuality and sex-related constructs if they do not delimit and describe the mundane manner in which these constructs are produced, reproduced, and maintained within the field of bodies.

Can phenomenology assist a feminist reconstruction of the sedimented character of sex, gender, and sexuality at the level of the body? In the first place, the phenomenological focus on the various acts by which cultural identity is constituted and assumed provides a felicitous starting point for the feminist effort to understand the mundane manner in which bodies get crafted into genders. The formulation of the body as a mode of dramatizing or enacting possibilities offers a way to understand how a cultural convention is embodied and enacted. But it seems difficult, if

not impossible, to imagine a way to conceptualize the scale and systemic character of women's oppression from a theoretical position which takes constituting acts to be its point of departure. Although individual acts do work to maintain and reproduce systems of oppression, and, indeed, any theory of personal political responsibility presupposes such a view, it doesn't follow that oppression is a sole consequence of such acts. One might argue that without human beings whose various acts, largely construed, produce and maintain oppressive conditions, those conditions would fall away, but note that the relation between acts and conditions is neither unilateral nor unmediated. There are social contexts and conventions within which certain acts not only become possible but become conceivable as acts at all. The transformation of social relations becomes a matter, then, of transforming hegemonic social conditions rather than the individual acts that are spawned by those conditions. Indeed, one runs the risk of addressing the merely indirect, if not epiphenomenal, reflection of those conditions if one remains restricted to a politics of acts.

But the theatrical sense of an "act" forces a revision of the individualist assumptions underlying the more restricted view of constituting acts within phenomenological discourse. As a given temporal duration within the entire performance, "acts" are a shared experience and 'collective action.' Just as within feminist theory the very category of the personal is expanded to include political structures, so is there a theatrically-based and, indeed, less individually-oriented view of acts that goes some of the way in defusing the criticism of act theory as 'too existentialist.' The act that gender is, the act that embodied agents *are* inasmuch as they dramatically and actively embody and, indeed, *wear* certain cultural significations, is clearly not one's act alone. Surely, there are nuanced and individual ways of *doing* one's gender, but *that* one does it, and that one does it *in accord with* certain sanctions and proscriptions, is clearly not a fully individual matter. Here again, I don't mean to minimize the effect of certain gender norms which originate

[7] Gayle Rubin, "The Traffic in Women: Notes on the 'Political Economy' of Sex," in *Toward an Anthropology of Women,* ed. Rayna R. Reiter (New York: Monthly Review Press, 1975), 178–85.

[8] See my "Variations on Sex and Gender: Beauvoir, Wittig, and Foucault," in *Feminism as Critique,* ed. Seyla Benhabib and Drucila Cornell (London: Basil Blackwell, 1987 [distributed by University of Minnesota Press]).

within the family and are enforced through certain familial modes of punishment and reward and which, as a consequence, might be construed as highly individual, for even there family relations recapitulate, individualize, and specify pre-existing cultural relations; they are rarely, if ever, radically original. The act that one does, the act that one performs, is, in a sense, an act that has been going on before one arrived on the scene. Hence, gender is an act which has been rehearsed, much as a script survives the particular actors who make use of it, but which requires individual actors in order to be actualized and reproduced as reality once again. The complex components that go into an act must be distinguished in order to understand the kind of acting in concert and acting in accord which acting one's gender invariably is.

In what senses, then, is gender an act? As anthropologist Victor Turner suggests in his studies of ritual social drama, social action requires a performance which is *repeated*. This repetition is at once a reenactment and reexperiencing of a set of meanings already socially established; it is the mundane and ritualized form of their legitimation.[9] When this conception of social performance is applied to gender, it is clear that although there are individual bodies that enact these significations

by becoming stylized into gendered modes, this "action" is immediately public as well. There are temporal and collective dimensions to these actions, and their public nature is not inconsequential; indeed, the performance is effected with the strategic aim of maintaining gender within its binary frame. Understood in pedagogical terms, the performance renders social laws explicit.

As a public action and performative act, gender is not a radical choice or project that reflects a merely individual choice, but neither is it imposed or inscribed upon the individual, as some post-structuralist displacements of the subject would contend. The body is not passively scripted with cultural codes, as if it were a lifeless recipient of wholly pre-given cultural relations. But neither do embodied selves pre-exist the cultural conventions which essentially signify bodies. Actors are always already on the stage, within the terms of the performance. Just as a script may be enacted in various ways, and just as the play requires both text and interpretation, so the gendered body acts its part in a culturally restricted corporeal space and enacts interpretations within the confines of already existing directives.

Although the links between a theatrical and a social role are complex and the distinctions not easily drawn (Bruce Wilshire points out the limits of the comparison in *Role-Playing and Identity: The Limits of Theatre as Metaphor*[10]), it seems clear that, although theatrical performances can meet with political censorship and scathing criticism, gender performances in non-theatrical contexts are governed by more clearly punitive and regulatory social conventions. Indeed, the sight of a transvestite onstage can compel pleasure and applause while the sight of the same transvestite on the seat next to us on the bus can compel fear, rage, even violence. The conventions which mediate proximity and identification in these two instances are clearly quite different. I want to

---

[9] See Victor Turner, *Dramas, Fields, and Metaphors* (Ithaca: Cornell University Press, 1974). Clifford Geertz suggests in "Blurred Genres: The Refiguration of Thought," in *Local Knowledge, Further Essays in Interpretive Anthropology* (New York: Basic Books, 1983), that the theatrical metaphor is used by recent social theory in two, often opposing, ways. Ritual theorists like Victor Turner focus on a notion of social drama of various kinds as a means for settling internal conflicts within a culture and regenerating social cohesion. On the other hand, symbolic action approaches, influenced by figures as diverse as Emile Durkheim, Kenneth Burke, and Michel Foucault, focus on the way in which political authority and questions of legitimation are thematized and settled within the terms of performed meaning. Geertz himself suggests that the tension might be viewed dialectically; his study of political organization in Bali as a "theatre-state" is a case in point. In terms of an explicitly feminist account of gender as performative, it seems clear to me that an account of gender as ritualized, public performance must be combined with an analysis of the political sanctions and taboos under which that performance may and may not occur within the public sphere free of punitive consequence.

---

[10] Bruce Wilshire, *Role-Playing and Identity: The Limits of Theatre as Metaphor* (Boston: Routledge and Kegan Paul, 1981).

make two different kinds of claims regarding this tentative distinction. In the theatre, one can say, 'this is just an act,' and de-realize the act, make acting into something quite distinct from what is real. Because of this distinction, one can maintain one's sense of reality in the face of this temporary challenge to our existing ontological assumptions about gender arrangements; the various conventions which announce that 'this is only a play' allows strict lines to be drawn between the performance and life. On the street or in the bus, the act becomes dangerous, if it does, precisely because there are no theatrical conventions to delimit the purely imaginary character of the act, indeed, on the street or in the bus, there is no presumption that the act is distinct from a reality; the disquieting effect of the act is that there are no conventions that facilitate making this separation. Clearly, there is theatre which attempts to contest or, indeed, break down those conventions that demarcate the imaginary from the real (Richard Schechner brings this out quite clearly in *Between Theatre and Anthropology*[11]). Yet in those cases one confronts the same phenomenon, namely, that the act is not contrasted with the real, but *constitutes* a reality that is in some sense new, a modality of gender that cannot readily be assimilated into the pre-existing categories that regulate gender reality. From the point of view of those established categories, one may want to claim, but oh, this is *really* a girl or a woman, or this is *really* a boy or a man, and further that the *appearance* contradicts the *reality* of the gender, that the discrete and familiar reality must be there, nascent, temporarily unrealized, perhaps realized at other times or other places. The transvestite, however, can do more than simply express the distinction between sex and gender, but challenges, at least implicitly, the distinction between appearance and reality that structures a good deal of popular thinking about gender identity. If the 'reality' of gender is constituted by the performance itself, then there is no recourse to an essential and unrealized 'sex' or 'gender' which gender performances ostensibly express. Indeed, the transvestite's gender is as fully real as anyone whose performance complies with social expectations.

Gender reality is performative which means, quite simply, that it is real only to the extent that it is performed. It seems fair to say that certain kinds of acts are usually interpreted as expressive of a gender core or identity, and that these acts either conform to an expected gender identity or contest that expectation in some way. That expectation, in turn, is based upon the perception of sex, where sex is understood to be the discrete and factic datum of primary sexual characteristics. This implicit and popular theory of acts and gestures as *expressive* of gender suggests that gender itself is something prior to the various acts, postures, and gestures by which it is dramatized and known; indeed, gender appears to the popular imagination as a substantial core which might well be understood as the spiritual or psychological correlate of biological sex.[12] If gender attributes, however, are not expressive but performative, then these attributes effectively constitute the identity they are said to express or reveal. The distinction between expression and performativeness is quite crucial, for if gender attributes and acts, the various ways in which a body shows or produces its cultural signification, are performative, then there is no preexisting identity by which an act or attribute might be measured; there would be no true or false, real or distorted acts of gender,

---

[11] Richard Schechner, *Between Theatre and Anthropology* (Philadelphia: University of Pennsylvania Press, 1985). See especially, "News, Sex, and Performance," 295–324.

[12] In *Mother Camp* (Prentice-Hall, 1974), Anthropologist Esther Newton gives an urban ethnography of drag queens in which she suggests that all gender might be understood on the model of drag. In *Gender: An Ethnomethodological Approach* (Chicago: University of Chicago Press, 1978), Suzanne J. Kessler and Wendy McKenna argue that gender is an "accomplishment" which requires the skills of constructing the body into a socially legitimate artifice.

and the postulation of a true gender identity would be revealed as a regulatory fiction. That gender reality is created through sustained social performances means that the very notions of an essential sex, a true or abiding masculinity or femininity, are also constituted as part of the strategy by which the performative aspect of gender is concealed.

As a consequence, gender cannot be understood as a *role* which either expresses or disguises an interior 'self,' whether that 'self' is conceived as sexed or not. As performance which is performative, gender is an 'act,' broadly construed, which constructs the social fiction of its own psychological interiority. As opposed to a view such as Erving Goffman's which posits a self which assumes and exchanges various 'roles' within the complex social expectations of the 'game' of modern life,[13] I am suggesting that this self is not only irretrievably 'outside,' constituted in social discourse, but that the ascription of interiority is itself a publically regulated and sanctioned form of essence fabrication. Genders, then, can be neither true nor false, neither real nor apparent. And yet, one is compelled to live in a world in which genders constitute univocal signifiers, in which gender is stabilized, polarized, rendered discrete and intractable. In effect, gender is made to comply with a model of truth and falsity which not only contradicts its own performative fluidity, but serves a social policy of gender regulation and control. Performing one's gender wrong initiates a set of punishments both obvious and indirect, and performing it well provides the reassurance that there is an essentialism of gender identity after all. That this reassurance is so easily displaced by anxiety, that culture so readily punishes or marginalizes those who fail to perform the illusion of gender essentialism should be sign enough that on some level there is social knowledge that the truth or falsity of gender is only socially compelled and in no sense ontologically necessitated.[14]

III. FEMINIST THEORY: BEYOND AN EXPRESSIVE MODEL OF GENDER

This view of gender does not pose as a comprehensive theory about what gender is or the manner of its construction, and neither does it prescribe an explicit feminist political program. Indeed, I can imagine this view of gender being used for a number of discrepant political strategies. Some of my friends may fault me for this and insist that any theory of gender constitution has political presuppositions and implications, and that it is impossible to separate a theory of gender from a political philosophy of feminism. In fact, I would agree, and argue that it is primarily political interests which create the social phenomena of gender itself, and that without a radical critique of gender constitution feminist theory fails to take stock of the way in which oppression structures the ontological categories through which gender is conceived. Gayatri Spivak has argued that feminists need to rely on an operational essentialism, a false ontology of women as a universal in order to advance a feminist political program.[15] She knows that the category of 'women' is not fully expressive, that the multiplicity and discontinuity of the referent mocks and rebels against the univocity of the sign, but suggests it could be used for strategic purposes. Kristeva suggests something similar, I think, when she prescribes that feminists use the category of women as a political tool without

---

[13] See Erving Goffmann, *The Presentation of Self in Everyday Life* (Garden City: Doubleday, 1959).

[14] See Michel Foucault's edition of *Herculine Barbin: The Journals of a Nineteenth Century French Hermaphrodite,* trans. Richard McDougall (New York: Pantheon Books, 1984), for an interesting display of the horror evoked by intersexed bodies. Foucault's introduction makes clear that the medical delimitation of univocal sex is yet another wayward application of the discourse on truth-as-identity. See also the work of Robert Edgerton in *American Anthropologist* on the cross-cultural variations of response to hermaphroditic bodies.

[15] Remarks at the Center for Humanities, Wesleyan University, Spring, 1985.

attributing ontological integrity to the term, and adds that, strictly speaking, women cannot be said to exist.[16] Feminists might well worry about the political implications of claiming that women do not exist, especially in light of the persuasive arguments advanced by Mary Anne Warren in her book, *Gendercide*.[17] She argues that social policies regarding population control and reproductive technology are designed to limit and, at times, eradicate the existence of women altogether. In light of such a claim, what good does it do to quarrel about the metaphysical status of the term, and perhaps, for clearly political reasons, feminists ought to silence the quarrel altogether.

But it is one thing to use the term and know its ontological insufficiency and quite another to articulate a normative vision for feminist theory which celebrates or emancipates an essence, a nature, or a shared cultural reality which cannot be found. The option I am defending is not to redescribe the world from the point of view of women. I don't know what that point of view is, but whatever it is, it is not singular, and not mine to espouse. It would only be half-right to claim that I am interested in how the phenomenon of a men's or women's point of view gets constituted, for while I do think that those points of views are, indeed, socially constituted, and that a reflexive genealogy of those points of view is important to do, it is not primarily the gender episteme that I am interested in exposing, deconstructing, or reconstructing. Indeed, it is the presupposition of the category of woman itself that requires a critical genealogy of the complex institutional and discursive means by which it is constituted. Although some feminist literary critics suggest that the presupposition of sexual difference is necessary for all discourse, that position reifies sexual difference as the founding moment of culture and precludes an analysis not only of

how sexual difference is constituted to begin with but how it is continuously constituted, both by the masculine tradition that preempts the universal point of view, and by those feminist positions that construct the univocal category of 'women' in the name of expressing or, indeed, liberating a subjected class. As Foucault claimed about those humanist efforts to liberate the criminalized subject, the subject that is freed is even more deeply shackled than originally thought.[18]

Clearly, though, I envision the critical genealogy of gender to rely on a phenomenological set of presuppositions, most important among them the expanded conception of an "act" which is both socially shared and historically constituted, and which is performative in the sense I previously described. But a critical genealogy needs to be supplemented by a politics of performative gender acts, one which both redescribes existing gender identities and offers a prescriptive view about the kind of gender reality there ought to be. The redescription needs to expose the reifications that tacitly serve as substantial gender cores or identities, and to elucidate both the act and the strategy of disavowal which at once constitute and conceal gender as we live it. The prescription is invariably more difficult, if only because we need to think a world in which acts, gestures, the visual body, the clothed body, the various physical attributes usually associated with gender, *express nothing*. In a sense, the prescription is not utopian, but consists in an imperative to acknowledge the existing complexity of gender which our vocabulary invariably disguises and to bring that complexity into a dramatic cultural interplay without punitive consequences.

Certainly, it remains politically important to represent women, but to do that in a way that does not distort and reify the very collectivity the theory is supposed to emancipate. Feminist theory which presupposes sexual difference as

---

[16] Julia Kristeva, "Woman Can Never Be Defined", trans. Marilyn A. August, in *New French Feminisms,* ed. Elaine Marks and Isabelle de Courtivron (New York: Schocken, 1981).

[17] Mary Anne Warren, *Gendercide: The Implications of Sex Selection* (New Jersey: Rowman and Allanheld, 1985).

[18] Ibid.; Michel Foucault, *Discipline and Punish: The Birth of the Prison,* trans. Alan Sheridan (New York: Vintage Books, 1978).

the necessary and invariant theoretical point of departure clearly improves upon those humanist discourses which conflate the universal with the masculine and appropriate all of culture as masculine property. Clearly, it is necessary to reread the texts of western philosophy from the various points of view that have been excluded, not only to reveal the particular perspective and set of interests informing those ostensibly transparent descriptions of the real, but to offer alternative descriptions and prescriptions; indeed, to establish philosophy as a cultural practice, and to criticize its tenets from marginalized cultural locations. I have no quarrel with this procedure, and have clearly benefited from those analyses. My only concern is that sexual difference not become a reification which unwittingly preserves a binary restriction on gender identity and an implicitly heterosexual framework for the description of gender, gender identity, and sexuality. There is, in my view, nothing about femaleness that is waiting to be expressed; there is, on the other hand, a good deal about the diverse experiences of women that is being expressed and still needs to be expressed, but caution is needed with respect to that theoretical language, for it does not simply report a pre-linguistic experience, but constructs that experience as well as the limits of its analysis. Regardless of the pervasive character of patriarchy and the prevalence of sexual difference as an operative cultural distinction, there is nothing about a binary gender system that is given. As a corporeal field of cultural play, gender is a basically innovative affair, although it is quite clear that there are strict punishments for contesting the script by performing out of turn or through unwarranted improvisations. Gender is not passively scripted on the body, and neither is it determined by nature, language, the symbolic, or the overwhelming history of patriarchy. Gender is what is put on, invariably, under constraint, daily and incessantly, with anxiety and pleasure, but if this continuous act is mistaken for a natural or linguistic given, power is relinquished to expand the cultural field bodily through subversive performances of various kinds.

RECONSTRUCTING BLACK MASCULINITY

bell hooks

Black and white snapshots of my childhood always show me in the company of my brother. Less than a year older than me, we looked like twins and for a time in life we did everything together. We were inseparable. As young children, we were brother and sister, comrades, in it together. As adolescents, he was forced to become a boy and I was forced to become a girl. In our southern black Baptist patriarchal home, being a boy meant learning to be tough, to mask one's feelings, to stand one's ground and fight—being a girl meant learning to obey, to be quiet, to clean, to recognize that you had no ground to stand on.

I was tough, he was not. I was strong willed, he was easygoing. We were both a disappointment. Affectionate, full of good humor, loving, my brother was not at all interested in becoming a patriarchal boy. This lack of interest generated a fierce anger in our father.

We grew up staring at black and white photos of our father in a boxing ring, playing basketball, with the black infantry he was part of in World War II. He was a man in uniform, a man's man, able to hold his own. Despising his one son for not wanting to become the strong silent type (my brother loved to talk, tell jokes, and make us happy), our father let him know early on that he was no son to him, real sons wanted to be like their fathers. Made to feel inadequate, less than male in his childhood, one boy in a house full of six sisters, he became forever haunted by the idea of patriarchal masculinity. All that he had questioned in his childhood was sought after in his early adult life in order to become a man's man—phallocentric, patriarchal, and masculine. In traditional black communities when one tells a grown male to "be a man," one is urging him to aspire to a masculine identity rooted in the patriarchal ideal. Throughout black male history in the United States there have been black men who were not at all interested in the patriarchal ideal. In the black community of my childhood, there was no monolithic standard of black masculinity. Though the patriarchal ideal was the most esteemed version of manhood, it was not the only version. No one in our house talked about black men being no good, shiftless, trifling. Head of the household, our father was a "much man," a provider, lover, disciplinarian, reader, and thinker. He was introverted, quiet, and slow to anger, yet fierce when aroused. We respected him. We were in awe of him. We were afraid of his power, his physical prowess, his deep voice, and his rare unpredictable but intense rage. We were never allowed to forget that, unlike other black men, our father was the fulfillment of the patriarchal masculine ideal.

Though I admired my father, I was more fascinated and charmed by black men who were not obsessed with being patriarchs: by Felix, a hobo who jumped trains, never worked a regular job, and had a missing thumb; by Kid, who lived out in the country and hunted the rabbits and coons that came to our table; by Daddy Gus, who spoke in hushed tones, sharing his sense of spiritual mysticism. These were the men who touched my heart. The list could go on. I remember them because they loved folks, especially women and children. They were caring and giving. They were black men who chose alternative lifestyles, who questioned the *status quo,* who shunned a ready made patriarchal identity and invented themselves. By knowing them, I have never been tempted to ignore the complexity of black male experience and identity. The generosity of spirit that characterized who they were and how they lived in the world lingers in my memory. I write this piece to honor them, knowing as I do now that it was no simple matter for them to choose

against patriarchy, to choose themselves, their lives. And I write this piece for my brother in hopes that he will recover one day, come back to himself, know again the way to love, the peace of an unviolated free spirit. It was this peace that the quest for an unattainable life-threatening patriarchal masculine ideal took from him.

When I left our segregated southern black community and went to a predominately white college, the teachers and students I met knew nothing about the lives of black men. Learning about the matriarchy myth and white culture's notion that black men were emasculated, I was shocked. These theories did not speak to the world I had most intimately known, did not address the complex gender roles that were so familiar to me. Much of the scholarly work on black masculinity that was presented in the classroom then was based on material gleaned from studies of urban black life. This work conveyed the message that black masculinity was homogenous. It suggested that all black men were tormented by their inability to fulfill the phallocentric masculine ideal as it has been articulated in white supremacist capitalist patriarchy. Erasing the realities of black men who have diverse understandings of masculinity, scholarship on the black family (traditionally the framework for academic discussion of black masculinity) puts in place of this lived complexity a flat, one-dimensional representation.

The portrait of black masculinity that emerges in this work perpetually constructs black men as "failures" who are psychologically "fucked up," dangerous, violent, sex maniacs whose insanity is informed by their inability to fulfill their phallocentric masculine destiny in a racist context. Much of this literature is written by white people, and some of it by a few academic black men. It does not interrogate the conventional construction of patriarchal masculinity or question the extent to which black men have historically internalized this norm. It never assumes the existence of black men whose creative agency has enabled them to subvert norms and develop ways of thinking about masculinity that challenge patriarchy. Yet, there has never been a time in the history of the United States when black folks, particularly black men, have not been enraged by the dominant culture's stereotypical, fantastical representations of black masculinity. Unfortunately, black people have not systematically challenged these narrow visions, insisting on a more accurate "reading" of black male reality. Acting in complicity with the *status quo,* many black people have passively absorbed narrow representations of black masculinity, perpetuated stereotypes, myths, and offered one-dimensional accounts. Contemporary black men have been shaped by these representations.

No one has yet endeavored to chart the journey of black men from Africa to the so called "new world" with the intent to reconstruct how they saw themselves. Surely the black men who came to the American continent before Columbus, saw themselves differently from those who were brought on slave ships, or from those few who freely immigrated to a world where the majority of their brethren were enslaved. Given all that we know of the slave context, it is unlikely that enslaved black men spoke the same language, or that they bonded on the basis of shared "male" identity. Even if they had come from cultures where gender difference was clearly articulated in relation to specific roles that was all disrupted in the "new world" context. Transplanted African men, even those who were coming from cultures where sex roles shaped the division of labor, where the status of men was different and most often higher than that of females, had imposed on them the white colonizer's notions of manhood and masculinity. Black men did not respond to this imposition passively. Yet it is evident in black male slave narratives that black men engaged in racial uplift were often most likely to accept the norms of masculinity set by white culture.

Although the gendered politics of slavery denied black men the freedom to act as "men" within the definition set by white norms, this notion of manhood did become a standard used to measure black male progress. Slave narratives document ways black men thought about manhood. The narratives of Henry "Box" Brown, Josiah Henson, Frederick Douglass, and a host of other black men reveal that they saw "freedom" as that change in status that would enable them to fulfill the role of chivalric benevolent patriarch. Free, they would be men able to provide for and take care of their families. Describing how he wept as he watched a white slave overseer beat his mother, William Wells Brown lamented, "Experience has taught me that nothing can be more heart-rending than for one to see a dear and beloved mother or sister tortured, and to hear their cries and not be able to render them assistance. But such is the position which an American slave occupies." Frederick Douglass did not feel his manhood affirmed by intellectual progress. It was affirmed when he fought man to man with the slave overseer. This struggle was a "turning point" in Douglass' life: "It rekindled in my breast the smoldering embers of liberty. It brought up my Baltimore dreams and revived a sense of my own manhood. I was a changed being after that fight. I was nothing before—I was a man now." The image of black masculinity that emerges from slave narratives is one of hardworking men who longed to assume full patriarchal responsibility for families and kin.

Given this aspiration and the ongoing brute physical labor of black men that was the backbone of slave economy (there were more male slaves than black female slaves, particularly before breeding became a common practice), it is really amazing that stereotypes of black men as lazy and shiftless so quickly became common in public imagination. In these 19th and early 20th-century representations, black men were cartoon-like creatures only interested in drinking and having a good time. Such stereotypes were an effective way for white racists to erase the significance of black male labor from public consciousness. Later on, these same stereotypes were evoked as reasons to deny black men jobs. They are still evoked today.

Male "idleness" did not have the same significance in African and Native American cultures that it had in the white mindset. Many 19th-century Christians saw all forms of idle activity as evil, or at least a breeding ground for wrong-doing. For Native Americans and Africans, idle time was space for reverie and contemplation. When slavery ended, black men could once again experience that sense of space. There are no studies which explore the way Native American cultures altered notions of black masculinity, especially for those black men who lived as Indians or who married Indian wives. Since we know there were many tribes who conceived of masculine roles in ways that were quite different from those of whites, black men may well have found African ideas about gender roles affirmed in Native traditions.

There are also few confessional narratives by black men that chronicle how they felt as a group when freedom did not bring with it the opportunity for them to assume a "patriarchal" role. Those black men who worked as farmers were often better able to assume this role than those who worked as servants or who moved to cities. Certainly, in the mass migration from the rural south to the urban north, black men lost status. In southern black communities there were many avenues for obtaining communal respect. A man was not respected solely because he could work, make money, and provide. The extent to which a given black man absorbed white society's notion of manhood likely determined the extent of his bitterness and despair that white supremacy continually blocked his access to the patriarchal ideal.

Nineteenth century black leaders were concerned about gender roles. While they believed that men should assume leadership positions in the home and public life, they were also concerned about the role of black women in racial uplift. Whether they were merely paying lip-service to the cause of women's rights or were true believers, exceptional individual black men advocated equal rights for black women. In his work, Martin Delaney continually stressed that both genders needed to work in the interest of racial

uplift. To him, gender equality was more a way to have greater involvement in racial uplift than a way for black women to be autonomous and independent. Black male leaders like Martin Delaney and Frederick Douglass were patriarchs, but as benevolent dictators they were willing to share power with women, especially if it meant they did not have to surrender any male privilege. As co-editors of the *North Star,* Douglass and Delaney had a masthead in 1847 which read "right is of no sex—truth is of no color . . ." The 1848 meeting of the National Negro Convention included a proposal by Delaney stating: "Whereas we fully believe in the equality of the sexes, therefore, resolved that we hereby invite females hereafter to take part in our deliberation." In Delaney's 1852 treatise *The Condition, Elevation, Emigration, and Destiny of the Colored People of the United States, Politically Considered,* he argued that black women should have full access to education so that they could be better mothers, asserting:

> The potency and respectability of a nation or people, depends entirely upon the position of their women; therefore, it is essential to our elevation that the female portion of our children be instructed in all the arts and sciences pertaining to the highest civilization.

In Delaney's mind, equal rights for black women in certain public spheres such as education did not mean that he was advocating a change in domestic relations whereby black men and women would have co-equal status in the home.

Most 19th-century black men were not advocating equal rights for women. On one hand, most black men recognized the powerful and necessary role black women had played as freedom fighters in the movement to abolish slavery and other civil rights efforts, yet on the other hand they continued to believe that women should be subordinate to men. They wanted black women to conform to the gender norms set by white society. They wanted to be recognized as "men," as patriarchs, by other men, including white men. Yet they could not assume this position if black women were not willing to conform to prevailing sexist gender norms.

Many black women who had endured white supremacist patriarchal domination during slavery did not want to be dominated by black men after manumission. Like black men, they had contradictory positions on gender. On one hand they did not want to be "dominated," but on the other hand they wanted black men to be protectors and providers. After slavery ended, enormous tension and conflict emerged between black women and men as folks struggled to be self-determining. As they worked to create standards for community and family life, gender roles continued to be problematic.

Black men and women who wanted to conform to gender role norms found that this was nearly impossible in a white racist economy that wanted to continue its exploitation of black labor. Much is made, by social critics who want to further the notion that black men are symbolically castrated, of the fact that black women often found work in service jobs while black men were unemployed. The reality, however, was that in some homes it was problematic when a black woman worked and the man did not, or when she earned more than he, yet, in other homes, black men were quite content to construct alternative roles. Critics who look at black life from a sexist standpoint advance the assumption that black men were psychologically devastated because they did not have the opportunity to slave away in low paying jobs for white racist employers when the truth may very well be that those black men who wanted to work but could not find jobs, as well as those who did not want to find jobs, may simply have felt relieved that they did not have to submit to economic exploitation. Concurrently, there were black women who wanted black men to assume patriarchal roles and there were some who were content to be autonomous, independent. And long before contemporary feminist movement sanctioned the idea that men could remain home and rear children while women worked, black women and men had such arrangements and were happy with them.

Without implying that black women and men lived in gender utopia, I am suggesting that black sex roles, and particularly the role of men, have been more complex and problematized in black life than is believed. This was especially the case when all black people lived in segregated neighborhoods. Racial integration has had a profound impact on black gender roles. It has helped to promote a climate wherein most black women and men accept sexist notions of gender roles. Unfortunately, many changes have occurred in the way black people think about gender, yet the shift from one standpoint to another has not been fully documented. For example: To what extent did the civil rights movement, with its definition of freedom as having equal opportunity with whites, sanction looking at white gender roles as a norm black people should imitate? Why has there been so little positive interest shown in the alternative lifestyles of black men? In every segregated black community in the United States there are adult black men married, unmarried, gay, straight, living in households where they do not assert patriarchal domination and yet live fulfilled lives, where they are not sitting around worried about castration. Again it must be emphasized that the black men who are most worried about castration and emasculation are those who have completely absorbed white supremacist patriarchal definitions of masculinity.

Advanced capitalism further changed the nature of gender roles for all men in the United States. The image of the patriarchal head of the household, ruler of this mini-state called the "family," faded in the 20th century. More men than ever before worked for someone else. The state began to interfere more in domestic matters. A man's time was not his own; it belonged to his employer, and the terms of his rule in the family were altered. In the old days, a man who had no money could still assert tyrannic rule over family and kin, by virtue of his patriarchal status, usually affirmed by Christian belief systems. Within a burgeoning capitalist economy, it was wage-earning power that determined the extent to which a man would rule over a household, and even that rule was limited by the power of the state. In *White Hero, Black Beast,* Paul Hoch describes the way in which advanced capitalism altered representations of masculinity:

> The concept of masculinity is dependent at its very root on the concepts of sexual repression and private property. Ironically, it is sexual repression and economic scarcity that give masculinity its main significance as a symbol of economic status and sexual opportunity. The shrinkage of the concept of man into the narrowed and hierarchical conceptions of masculinity of the various work and consumption ethics also goes hand in hand with an increasing social division of labor, and an increasing shrinkage of the body's erogenous potentials culminating in a narrow genital sexuality. As we move from the simpler food-gathering societies to the agricultural society to the urbanized work and warfare society, we notice that it is a narrower and narrower range of activities that yield masculine status.

In feminist terms, this can be described as a shift from emphasis on patriarchal status (determined by one's capacity to assert power over others in a number of spheres based on maleness) to a phallocentric model, where what the male does with his penis becomes a greater and certainly a more accessible way to assert masculine status. It is easy to see how this served the interests of a capitalist state which was indeed depriving men of their rights, exploiting their labor in such a way that they only indirectly received the benefits, to deflect away from a patriarchal power based on ruling others and to emphasize a masculine status that would depend solely on the penis.

With the emergence of a fierce phallocentrism, a man was no longer a man because he provided care for his family, he was a man simply because he had a penis. Furthermore, his ability to use that penis in the arena of sexual conquest could bring him as much status as being a wage earner and provider. A sexually defined masculine ideal rooted in physical domination and sexual possession of women could be accessible to all men. Hence, even unemployed black men could gain status, could be seen as the embodiment of masculinity, within a phallocentric framework. Barbara Ehrenreich's *The Hearts of Men* chronicles white

male repudiation of a masculine ideal rooted in a notion of patriarchal rule requiring a man to marry and care for the material well-being of women and children and an increasing embrace of a phallocentric "playboy" ideal. At the end of the chapter "Early Rebels," Ehrenreich describes rites of passage in the 1950s which led white men away from traditional nonconformity into a rethinking of masculine status:

> . . . not every would-be male rebel had the intellectual reserves to gray gracefully with the passage of the decade. They drank beyond excess, titrating gin with coffee in their lunch hours, gin with Alka-Seltzer on the weekends. They had stealthy affairs with secretaries, and tried to feel up their neighbors' wives at parties. They escaped into Mickey Spillane mysteries, where naked blondes were routinely perforated in a hail of bullets, or into Westerns, where there were no women at all and no visible sources of white-collar employment. And some of them began to discover an alternative, or at least an entirely new style of male rebel who hinted, seductively, that there was an alternative. The new rebel was the playboy.

Even in the restricted social relations of slavery black men had found a way to practice the fine art of phallocentric seduction. Long before white men stumbled upon the "playboy" alternative, black vernacular culture told stories about that non-working man with time on his hands who might be seducing somebody else's woman. Blues songs narrate the "playboy" role. Ehrenreich's book acknowledges that the presence of black men in segregated black culture and their engagement in varied expressions of masculinity influenced white men:

> The Beat hero, the male rebel who actually walks away from responsibility in any form, was not a product of middle-class angst. The possibility of walking out, without money or guilt, and without ambition other than to see and do everything, was not even imminent in the middle-class culture of the early fifties . . . The new bohemianism of the Beats came from somewhere else entirely, from an

underworld and an underclass invisible from the corporate "crystal palace" or suburban dream houses.

Alternative male lifestyles that opposed the *status quo* were to be found in black culture.

White men seeking alternatives to a patriarchal masculinity turned to black men, particularly black musicians. Norman Podhoretz's 1963 essay "My Negro Problem—And Ours" names white male fascination with blackness, and black masculinity:

> Just as in childhood I envied Negroes for what seemed to me their superior masculinity, so I envy them today for what seems to be their superior physical grace and beauty. I have come to value physical grace very highly and I am now capable of aching with all my being when I watch a Negro couple on the dance floor, or a Negro playing baseball or basketball. They are on the kind of terms with their own bodies that I should like to be on with mine, and for that precious quality they seem blessed to me.

Black masculinity, as fantasized in the racist white imagination, is the quintessential embodiment of man as "outsider" and "rebel." They were the ultimate "traveling men" drifting from place to place, town to town, job to job.

Within segregated black communities, the "traveling" black man was admired even as he was seen as an indictment of the failure of black men to achieve the patriarchal masculine ideal. Extolling the virtues of traveling black men in her novels, Toni Morrison sees them as "truly masculine in the sense of going out so far where you're not supposed to go and running toward confrontations rather than away from them." This is a man who takes risks, what Morrison calls a "free man":

> This is a man who is stretching, you know, he's stretching, he's going all the way within his own mind and within whatever his outline might be. Now that's the tremendous possibility for masculinity among black men. And you see it a lot . . . They may end up in sort of twentieth-century, contemporary terms being also unemployed. They may

be in prison. They may be doing all sorts of things. But they are adventuresome in that regard.

Within white supremacist capitalist patriarchy, rebel black masculinity has been idolized and punished, romanticized yet vilified. Though the traveling man repudiates being a patriarchal provider, he does not necessarily repudiate male domination.

Collectively, black men have never critiqued the dominant culture's norms of masculine identity, even though they have reworked those norms to suit their social situation. Black male sociologist Robert Staples argues that the black male is "in conflict with the normative definition of masculinity," yet this conflict has never assumed the form of complete rebellion. Assuming that black men are "crippled emotionally" when they cannot fully achieve the patriarchal ideal, Staples asserts: "This is a status which few, if any, black males have been able to achieve. Masculinity, as defined in this culture, has always implied a certain autonomy and mastery of one's environment." Though Staples suggests, "the black male has always had to confront the contradiction between the normative expectation attached to being male in this society and proscriptions on his behavior and achievement of goals," implicit in his analysis is the assumption that black men could only internalize this norm and be victimized by it. Like many black men, he assumes that patriarchy and male domination is not a socially constructed social order but a "natural" fact of life. He therefore cannot acknowledge that black men could have asserted meaningful agency by repudiating the norms white culture was imposing.

These norms could not be repudiated by black men who saw nothing problematic or wrong minded about them. Staples, like most black male scholars writing about black masculinity, does not attempt to deconstruct normative thinking, he laments that black men have not had full access to patriarchal phallocentrism. Embracing the phallocentric ideal, he explains black male rape of women by seeing it as a reaction against their inability to be "real men" (i.e., assert legitimate domination over women). Explaining rape, Staples argues:

> In the case of black men, it is asserted that they grow up feeling emasculated and powerless before reaching manhood. They often encounter women as authority figures and teachers or as the head of their household. These men consequently act out their feelings of powerlessness against black women in the form of sexual aggression. Hence, rape by black men should be viewed as both an aggressive and political act because it occurs in the context of racial discrimination which denies most black men a satisfying manhood.

Staples does not question why black women are the targets of black male aggression if it is white men and a white racist system which prevents them from assuming the "patriarchal" role. Given that many white men who fully achieve normal masculinity rape, his implied argument that black men would not rape if they could be patriarchs seems ludicrous. And his suggestion that they would not rape if they could achieve a "satisfying manhood" is pure fantasy. Given the context of this paragraph, it is safe to assume that the "satisfying manhood" he evokes carries with it the phallocentric right of men to dominate women, however benevolently. Ultimately, he is suggesting that if black men could legitimately dominate women more effectively they would not need to coerce them outside the law. Growing up in a black community where there were individual black men who critiqued normative masculinity, who repudiated patriarchy and its concomitant support of sexism, I fully appreciate that it is a tremendous loss that there is little known of their ideas about black masculinity. Without documentation of their presence, it has been easier for black men who embrace patriarchal masculinity, phallocentrism, and sexism to act as though they speak for all black men. Since their representations of black masculinity are in complete agreement with white culture's assessment, they do not threaten or challenge white domination; they reinscribe it.

Contemporary black power movement made synonymous black liberation and the effort to create a social structure wherein black men could assert themselves as patriarchs, controlling community, family, and kin. On one hand, black men expressed contempt for white men yet they also envied them their access to patriarchal power. Using a "phallocentric" stick to beat white men, Amiri Baraka asserted in his 1960s essay "american sexual reference: black male":

> Most American white men are trained to be fags. For this reason it is no wonder that their faces are weak and blank, left without the hurt that reality makes—anytime. That red flush, those silk blue faggot eyes ... They are the 'masters' of the world, and their children are taught this as God's fingerprint, so they can devote most of their energies to the nonrealistic, having no use for the real. They devote their energies to the nonphysical, the nonrealistic, and become estranged from them. Even their wars move to the stage where whole populations can be destroyed by pushing a button. ... can you, for a second imagine the average middle class white man able to do somebody harm? Alone? Without the technology that at this moment still has him rule the world: Do you understand the softness of the white man, the weakness ...

This attack on white masculinity, and others like it, did not mean that black men were attacking normative masculinity, they were simply pointing out that white men had not fulfilled the ideal. It was a case of "will the real man please stand up." And when he stood up, he was, in the eyes of black power movement, a black male.

This phallocentric idealization of masculinity is most powerfully expressed in the writings of George Jackson. Throughout *Soledad Brother,* he announces his uncritical acceptance of patriarchal norms, especially the use of violence as a means of social control. Critical of nonviolence as a stance that would un-man black males, he insisted:

> The symbol of the male here in North American has always been the gun, the knife, the club. Violence

is extolled at every exchange: the TV, the motion pictures, the best-seller lists. The newspapers that sell best are those that carry the boldest, bloodiest headlines and most sports coverage. To die for king and country is to die a hero.

Jackson felt black males would need to embrace this use of violence if they hoped to defeat white adversaries. And he is particularly critical of black women for not embracing these notions of masculinity:

> I am reasonably certain that I draw from every black male in this country some comments to substantiate that his mother, the black female, attempted to aid his survival by discouraging his violence or by turning it inward. The blacks of slave society, U.S.A., have always been a matriarchal subsociety. The implication is clear, black mama is going to have to put a sword in that brother's hand and stop that "be a good boy" shit.

A frighteningly fierce misogyny informs Jackson's rage at black women, particularly his mother. Even though he was compelled by black women activists and comrades to reconsider his position on gender, particularly by Angela Davis, his later work, *Blood In My Eye,* continues to see black liberation as a "male thing," to see revolution as a task for men:

> At the end of this massive collective struggle, we will uncover a new man, the unpredictable culmination of the revolutionary process. He will be better equipped to wage the real struggle, the permanent struggle after the revolution—the one for new relationships between men.

Although the attitudes expressed by Baraka and Jackson appear dated, they have retained their ideological currency among black men through time. Black female critiques of black male phallocentrism and sexism have had little impact on black male consciousness. Michele Wallace's *Black Macho and the Myth of the Super Woman* was the first major attempt by a black woman to speak from a feminist standpoint about black male sexism. Her analysis of black masculinity was based primarily on her experience in

the urban northern cities, yet she wrote as if she were speaking comprehensively about collective black experience. Even so, her critique was daring and courageous. However, like other critics she evoked a monolithic homogenous representation of black masculinity. Discussing the way black male sexism took precedence over racial solidarity during Shirley Chisolm's presidential campaign, Wallace wrote:

> The black political forces in existence at the time—in other words, the black male political forces—did not support her. In fact, they actively opposed her nomination. The black man in the street seemed either outraged that she dared to run or simply indifferent.
>
> Ever since then it has really baffled me to hear black men say that black women have no time for feminism because being black comes first. For them, when it came to Shirley Chisholm, being black no longer came first at all. It turned out that what they really meant all along was that the black man came before the black woman.

Chisholm documented in her autobiography that sexism stood in her way more than racism. Yet she also talks about the support she received from her father and her husband for her political work. Commenting on the way individuals tried to denigrate this support by hinting that there was something wrong with her husband, Chisholm wrote: "Thoughtless people have suggested that my husband would have to be a weak man who enjoys having me dominate him. They are wrong on both counts." Though fiercely critical of sexism in general and black male sexism in particular, Chisholm acknowledged the support she had received from black men who were not advancing patriarchy. Any critique of "black macho," of black male sexism, that does not acknowledge the actions of black men who subvert and challenge the *status quo* can not be an effective critical intervention. If feminist critics ignore the efforts of individual black men to oppose sexism, our critiques seem to be self-serving, appear to be anti-male rather than anti-sexist. Absolutist portraits that imply that all black men are irredeemably sexist, inherently supportive of male domination, make it appear that there is no way to change this, no alternative, no other way to be. When attention is focused on those black men who oppose sexism, who are disloyal to patriarchy, even if they are exceptions, the possibility for change, for resistance is affirmed. Those representations of black gender relationships that perpetually pit black women and men against one another deny the complexity of our experiences and intensify mutually destructive internecine gender conflict.

More than ten years have passed since Michele Wallace encouraged black folks to take gender conflict as a force that was undermining our solidarity and creating tension. Without biting her tongue, Wallace emphatically stated:

> I am saying, among other things, that for perhaps the last fifty years there has been a growing distrust, even hatred, between black men and black women. It has been nursed along not only by racism on the part of whites but also by an almost deliberate ignorance on the part of blacks about the sexual politics of their experience in this country.

The tensions Wallace describes between black women and men have not abated, if anything they have worsened. In more recent years they have taken the public form of black women and men competing for the attention of a white audience. Whether it be the realm of job hunting or book publishing, there is a prevailing sense within white supremacist capitalist patriarchy that black men and women cannot both be in the dominant culture's limelight. While it obviously serves the interests of white supremacy for black women and men to be divided from one another, perpetually in conflict, there is no overall gain for black men and women. Sadly, black people collectively refuse to take seriously issues of gender that would undermine the support for male domination in black communities.

Since the 1960s black power movement had worked over-time to let sisters know that they should assume a subordinate role to lay the groundwork for an emergent black patriarchy that would elevate the status of black males, women's liberation movement has been seen as a threat. Consequently, black women were and are encouraged to think that any involvement with feminism was/is tantamount to betraying the race. Such thinking has not really altered over time. It has become more entrenched. Black people responded with rage and anger to Wallace's book, charging that she was a puppet of white feminists who were motivated by vengeful hatred of black men, but they never argued that her assessment of black male sexism was false. They critiqued her harshly because they sincerely believed that sexism was not a problem in black life and that black female support of black patriarchy and phallocentrism might heal the wounds inflicted by racist domination. As long as black people foolishly cling to the rather politically naive and dangerous assumption that it is in the interests of black liberation to support sexism and male domination, all our efforts to decolonize our minds and transform society will fail.

Perhaps black folks cling to the fantasy that phallocentrism and patriarchy will provide a way out of the havoc and wreckage wreaked by racist genocidal assault because it is an analysis of our current political situation that places a large measure of the blame on the black community, the black family, and, most specifically, black women. This way of thinking means that black people do not have to envision creative strategies for confronting and resisting white supremacy and internalized racism. Tragically, internecine gender conflict between black women and men strengthens white supremacist capitalist patriarchy. Politically behind the times where gender is concerned, many black people lack the skills to function in a changed and changing world. They remain unable to grapple with a contemporary reality where male domination is consistently challenged and under siege. Primarily it is white male advocates of feminist politics who do the scholarly work that shows the crippling impact of contemporary patriarchy on men, particularly those groups of men who do not receive maximum benefit from this system. Writing about the way patriarchal masculinity undermines the ability of males to construct self and identity with their well-being in mind, creating a life-threatening masculinist sensibility, these works rarely discuss black men.

Most black men remain in a state of denial, refusing to acknowledge the pain in their lives that is caused by sexist thinking and patriarchal, phallocentric violence that is not only expressed by male domination over women but also by internecine conflict among black men. Black people must question why it is that, as white culture has responded to changing gender roles and feminist movement, they have turned to black culture and particularly to black men for articulations of misogyny, sexism, and phallocentrism. In popular culture, representations of black masculinity equate it with brute phallocentrism, woman-hating, a pugilistic "rapist" sexuality, and flagrant disregard for individual rights. Unlike the young George Jackson who, however wrong-minded, cultivated a patriarchal masculinist ethic in the interest of providing black males with a revolutionary political consciousness and a will to resist race and class domination, contemporary young black males espousing a masculinist ethic are not radicalized or insightful about the collective future of black people. Public figures such as Eddie Murphy, Arsenio Hall, Chuck D., Spike Lee, and a host of other black males blindly exploit the commodification of blackness and the concomitant exotification of phallocentric black masculinity.

When Eddie Murphy's film *Raw* (which remains one of the most graphic spectacles of black male phallocentrism) was first shown in urban cities, young black men in the audience gave black power salutes. This film not only did not address the struggle of black people to resist racism, Murphy's evocation of homosocial bonding with rich white men against "threatening" women who want to take their money conveyed his conservative politics. *Raw* celebrates a pugilistic eroticism, the logic of which tells young men that women do not want to hear declarations of love but want to be "fucked to death." Women are represented strictly in misogynist

terms—they are evil; they are all prostitutes who see their sexuality solely as a commodity to be exchanged for hard cash, and after the man has delivered the goods they betray him. Is this the "satisfying masculinity" black men desire or does it expose a warped and limited vision of sexuality, one that could not possibly offer fulfillment or sexual healing? As phallocentric spectacle, *Raw* announces that black men are controlled by their penises ("it's a dick thing") and asserts a sexual politic that is fundamentally anti-body.

If the black male cannot "trust" his body not to be the agent of his victimization, how can he trust a female body? Indeed, the female body, along with the female person, is constructed in *Raw* as threatening to the male who seeks autonomous selfhood since it is her presence that awakens phallocentric response. Hence her personhood must be erased; she must be like the phallus, a "thing." Commenting on the self-deception that takes place when men convince themselves and one another that women are not persons, in her essay on patriarchal phallocentrism "The Problem That Has No Name," Marilyn Frye asserts:

> The rejection of females by phallists is both morally and conceptually profound. The refusal to perceive females as persons is conceptually profound because it excludes females from that community whose conceptions of things one allows to influence one's concepts—it serves as a police lock on a closed mind. Furthermore, the refusal to treat women with the respect due to persons is in itself a violation of a moral principle that seems to many to be the founding principle of all morality. This violation of moral principle is sustained by an active manipulation of circumstances that is systematic and habitual and unacknowledged. The exclusion of women from the conceptual community simultaneously excludes them from the moral community.

Black male phallocentrism constructs a portrait of woman as immoral, simultaneously suggesting that she is irrational and incapable of reason. Therefore, there is no need for black men to listen to women or to assume that women have knowledge to share.

It is this representation of womanhood that is graphically evoked in Murphy's film *Harlem Nights*. A dramatization of black male patriarchal fantasies, this film reinvents the history of Harlem so that black men do not appear as cowards unable to confront racist white males but are reinscribed as tough, violent; they talk shit and take none. Again, the George Jackson revolutionary political paradigm is displaced in the realm of the cultural. In this fantasy, black men are as able and willing to assert power "by any means necessary" as are white men. They are shown as having the same desires as white men; they long for wealth, power to dominate others, freedom to kill with impunity, autonomy, and the right to sexually possess women. They embrace notions of hierarchal rule. The most powerful black man in the film, Quick (played by Murphy), always submits to the will of his father. In this world where homosocial black male bonding is glorified and celebrated, black women are sex objects. The only woman who is not a sex object is the post-menopausal mama/matriarch. She is dethroned so that Quick can assert his power, even though he later (again submitting to the father's will) asks her forgiveness. *Harlem Nights* is a sad fantasy, romanticizing a world of misogynist homosocial bonding where everyone is dysfunctional and no one is truly cared for, loved, or emotionally fulfilled.

Despite all the male bluster, Quick, a quintessential black male hero, longs to be loved. Choosing to seek the affections of an unavailable and unattainable black woman (the mistress of the most powerful white man), Quick does attempt to share himself, to drop the masculine mask and be "real" (symbolized by his willingness to share his real name). Yet the black woman he chooses rejects him, only seeking his favors when she is ordered to by the white man who possesses her. It is a tragic vision of black heterosexuality. Both black woman and black man are unable to respond fully to one another because they are so preoccupied with the white power structure, with the white man. The most valued black woman "belongs" to a white man who willingly exchanges her sexual favors in the interest of business. Desired by black and white men alike (it is their joint lust that renders her more valuable, black men desire her because white men desire her and *vice versa*), her internalized racism and her longing for material wealth and power drive her to act in complicity with white men against black men. Before she can carry out her mission to kill him, Quick shoots her after they have had sexual intercourse. Not knowing that he has taken the bullets from her gun, she points it, telling him that her attack is not personal but "business." Yet when he kills her he makes a point of saying that it is "personal." This was a very sad moment in the film, in that he destroys her because she rejects his authentic need for love and care.

Contrary to the phallocentric representation of black masculinity that has been on display throughout the film, the woman-hating black men are really shown to be in need of love from females. Orphaned, Quick, who is "much man" seeking love, demonstrates his willingness to be emotionally vulnerable, to share only to be rejected, humiliated. This drama of internecine conflict between black women and men follows the conventional sexist line that sees black women as betraying black men by acting in complicity with white patriarchy. This notion of black female complicity and betrayal is so fixed in the minds of many black men they are unable to perceive any flaws in its logic. It certainly gives credence to Michele Wallace's assertion that black people do not have a clear understanding of black sexual politics. Black men who advance the notion that black women are complicit with white men make this assessment without ever invoking historical documentation. Indeed, annals of history abound that document the opposite assumption, showing that black women have typically acted in solidarity with black men. While it may be accurate to argue that sexist black women are complicit with white supremacist capitalist patriarchy, so are sexist black men. Yet most black men continue to deny their complicity.

Spike Lee's recent film *Mo' Better Blues* is another tragic vision of contemporary black heterosexuality. Like *Harlem Nights,* it focuses on a world of black male homosocial bonding where black women are seen primarily as sex objects. Even when they have talent, as the black female jazz singer Clarke does, they must still exchange their sexual favors for recognition. Like Quick, Bleek, the black hero, seeks recognition of his value in heterosexual love relations. Yet he is unable to see the "value" of the two black women who care for him. Indeed, scenes where he makes love to Clarke and alternately sees her as Indigo and *vice versa* suggest the dixie cup sexist mentality (i.e., all women are alike). And even after his entire world has fallen apart he never engages in a self-critique that might lead him to understand that phallocentrism (he is constantly explaining himself by saying "it's a dick thing") has blocked his ability to develop a mature adult identity, has rendered him unable to confront pain and move past denial. Spike Lee's use of Murphy's phrase establishes a continuum of homosocial bonding between black men that transcends the cinematic fiction.

Ironically, the film suggests that Bleek's nihilism and despair can only be addressed by a rejection of a playboy, "dick thing" masculinity and the uncritical acceptance of the traditional patriarchal role. His life crisis is resolved by the reinscription of a patriarchal paradigm. Since Clarke is no longer available, he seeks comfort with Indigo, pleads with her to "save his life." Spike Lee, like Murphy to some extent, exposes the essential self-serving narcissism and denial of community that is at the heart of phallocentrism. He does not, however, envision a radical alternative. The film suggests Bleek has no choice and can only reproduce the same family narrative from which he has emerged, effectively affirming the appropriateness of a nuclear family paradigm where women as mothers restrict black masculinity, black male creativity, and fathers hint at the possibility of freedom. Domesticity represents a place where one's life is "safe" even though one's creativity is contained. The nightclub represents a world outside the home where creativity flourishes and with

it an uninhibited eroticism, only that world is one of risk. It is threatening.

The "love supreme" (Coltrane's music and image is a motif throughout the film) that exists between Indigo and Bleek appears shallow and superficial. No longer sex object to be "boned" whenever Bleek desires, her body becomes the vessel for the reproduction of himself *via* having a son. Self-effacing, Indigo identifies Bleek's phallocentrism by telling him he is a "dog," but ultimately she rescues the "dog." His willingness to marry her makes up for dishonesty, abuse, and betrayal. The redemptive love Bleek seeks cannot really be found in the model Lee offers and as a consequence this film is yet another masculine fantasy denying black male agency and capacity to assume responsibility for their personal growth and salvation. The achievement of this goal would mean they must give up phallocentrism and envision new ways of thinking about black masculinity.

Even though individual black women adamantly critique black male sexism, most black men continue to act as though sexism is not a problem in black life and refuse to see it as the force motivating oppressive exploitation of women and children by black men. If any culprit is identified, it is racism. Like Staples' suggestion that the explanation of why black men rape is best understood in a context where racism is identified as the problem, any explanation that evokes a critique of black male phallocentrism is avoided. Black men and women who espouse cultural nationalism continue to see the struggle for black liberation largely as a struggle to recover black manhood. In her essay "Africa On My Mind: Gender, Counter Discourse and African-American Nationalism," E. Frances White shows that overall black nationalist perspectives on gender are rarely rooted purely in the Afrocentric logic they seek to advance, but rather reveal their ties to white paradigms:

In making appeals to conservative notions of appropriate gender behavior, African-American nationalists reveal their ideological ties to other nationalist movements, including European and Euro-American bourgeois nationalists over the past 200 years. These parallels exist despite the different class and power base of these movements.

Most black nationalists, men and women, refuse to acknowledge the obvious ways patriarchal phallocentric masculinity is a destructive force in black life, the ways it undermines solidarity between black women and men, or how it is life-threatening to black men. Even though individual black nationalists like Haki Madhubuti speak against sexism, progressive Afrocentric thinking does not have the impact that the old guard message has. Perhaps it provides sexist black men with a sense of power and agency (however illusory) to see black women, and particularly feminist black women, as the enemy that prevents them from fully participating in this society. For such fiction gives them an enemy that can be confronted, attacked, annihilated, an enemy that can be conquered, dominated.

Confronting white supremacist capitalist patriarchy would not provide sexist black men with an immediate sense of agency or victory. Blaming black women, however, makes it possible for black men to negotiate with white people in all areas of their lives without vigilantly interrogating those interactions. A good example of this displacement is evident in Brent Staples' essay "The White Girl Problem." Defending his "politically incorrect taste in women" (i.e., his preference for white female partners), from attacking black women, Staples never interrogates his desire. He does not seek to understand the extent to which white supremacist capitalist patriarchy determines his desire. He does not want desire to be politicized. And of course his article does not address white female racism or discuss the fact that a white person does not have to be anti-racist to desire a black partner. Many inter-racial relationships have their roots in racist constructions of the Other. By focusing in a stereotypical way on black women's anger, Staples can avoid these issues and depoliticize the politics of black

and white female interactions. His essay would have been a needed critical intervention had he endeavored to explore the way individuals maintain racial solidarity even as they bond with folks outside their particular group.

Solidarity between black women and men continues to be undermined by sexism and misogyny. As black women increasingly oppose and challenge male domination, internecine tensions abound. Publicly, many of the gender conflicts between black women and men have been exposed in recent years with the increasingly successful commodification of black women's writing. Indeed, gender conflict between sexist black male writers and those black female writers who are seen as feminists has been particularly brutal. Black male critic Stanley Crouch has been one of the leading voices mocking and ridiculing black women. His recently published collection of essays, *Notes of A Hanging Judge,* includes articles that are particularly scathing in their attacks on black women.

His critique of Wallace's *Black Macho* is mockingly titled "Aunt Jemima Don't Like Uncle Ben" (notice that the emphasis is on black women not liking black men, hence the caption already places accountability for tensions on black women). The title deflects attention away from the concrete critique of sexism in *Black Macho* by making it a question of personal taste. Everyone seems eager to forget that it is possible for black women to love black men and yet unequivocally challenge and oppose sexism, male domination, and phallocentrism. Crouch never speaks to the issues of black male sexism in his piece and works instead to make Wallace appear an "unreliable" narrator. His useful critical comments are thus undermined by the apparent refusal to take seriously the broad political issues Wallace raises. His refusal to acknowledge sexism, expressed as "black macho," is a serious problem. It destroys the possibility of genuine solidarity between black women and men, makes it appear that he is really angry at Wallace and other black women because he is fundamentally anti-feminist and unwilling to challenge male domination. Crouch's stance epitomizes the attitude of contemporary black male writers who are either uncertain about their political response to feminism or are adamantly anti-feminist. Much black male anti-feminism is linked to a refusal to acknowledge that the phallocentric power black men wield over black women is "real" power, the assumption being that only the power white men have that black men do not have is real.

If, as Frederick Douglass maintained, "power concedes nothing without a demand," the black women and men who advocate feminism must be ever vigilant, critiquing and resisting all forms of sexism. Some black men may refuse to acknowledge that sexism provides them with forms of male privilege and power, however relative. They do not want to surrender that power in a world where they may feel otherwise quite powerless. Contemporary emergence of a conservative black nationalism which exploits a focus on race to both deny the importance of struggling against sexism and racism simultaneously is both an overt attack on feminism and a force that actively seeks to reinscribe sexist thinking among black people who have been questioning gender. Commodification of blackness that makes phallocentric black masculinity marketable makes the realm of cultural politics a propagandistic site where black people are rewarded materially for reactionary thinking about gender. Should we not be suspicious of the way in which white culture's fascination with black masculinity manifests itself? The very images of phallocentric black masculinity that are glorified and celebrated in rap music, videos, and movies are the representations that are evoked when white supremacists seek to gain public acceptance and support for genocidal assault on black men, particularly youth.

Progressive Afrocentric ideology makes this critique and interrogates sexism. In his latest book, *Black Men: Obsolete, Single, Dangerous,* Haki Madhubuti courageously deplores all forms of sexism, particularly black male violence against women. Like black male political figures of the past, Madhubuti's support of gender equality and his critique of sexism is not linked to an overall questioning of gender roles and a repudiation of all forms of patriarchal domination, however benevolent. Still, he has taken the important step of questioning sexism and calling on black people to explore the way sexism hurts and wounds us. Madhubuti acknowledges black male misogyny:

> The "fear" of women that exists among many Black men runs deep and often goes unspoken. This fear is cultural. Most men are introduced to members of the opposite sex in a superficial manner, and seldom do we seek a more in depth or informed understanding of them . . . Women have it rough all over the world. Men must become informed listeners.

Woman-hating will only cease to be a norm in black life when black men collectively dare to oppose sexism. Unfortunately, when all black people should be engaged in a feminist movement that addresses the sexual politics of our communities, many of us are tragically investing in old gender norms. At a time when many black people should be reading Madhubuti's *Black Men, Sister Outsider, The Black Women's Health Book, Feminist Theory: From Margin to Center,* and a host of other books that seek to explore black sexual politics with compassion and care, folks are eagerly consuming a conservative tract, *The Blackman's Guide To Understanding The Blackwoman* by Shahrazad Ali. This work actively promotes black male misogyny, coercive domination of females by males, and, as a consequence, feeds the internecine conflict between black women and men. Though many black people have embraced this work there is no indication that it is having a positive impact on black communities, and there is every indication that it is being used to justify male dominance, homophobic assaults on black gay people, and rejection of black styles that emphasize our diasporic connection to Africa and the Caribbean. Ali's book romanticizes black patriarchy, demanding that black women "submit" to black male domination in lieu of changes in society that would make it possible for black men to be more fulfilled.

Calling for a strengthening of black male phallocentric power (to be imposed by force if need be), Ali's book in no way acknowledges sexism. When writing about black men, her book reads like an infantile caricature of the Tarzan fantasy. Urging black men to assert their rightful position as patriarchs, she tells them: "Rise Blackman, and take your rightful place as ruler of the universe and everything in it. Including the black woman." Like *Harlem Nights,* this is the stuff of pure fantasy. That black people, particularly the underclass, are turning to escapist fantasies that can in no way adequately address the collective need of African Americans for renewed black liberation struggle is symptomatic of the crisis we are facing. Desperately clinging to ways of thinking and being that are detrimental to our collective well-being obstructs progressive efforts for change.

More black men have broken their silence to critique Ali's work than have ever offered public support of feminist writing by black women. Yet it does not help educate black people about the ways feminist analysis could be useful in our lives for black male critics to act as though the success of this book represents a failure on the part of feminism. Ali's sexist, homophobic, self-denigrating tirades strike a familiar chord because so many black people who have not decolonized their minds think as she does. Though black male critic Nelson George critiques Ali's work, stating that it shows "how little Afrocentrism respects the advances of African-American women," he suggests that it is an indication of how "unsuccessful black feminists have been in forging alliance with this ideologically potent community." Statements like this one advance the notion that feminist education is the sole task of black women. It also rather neatly places George outside either one of these potent communities. Why does he not seize the critical moment to bring to public awareness the feminist visions of Afrocentric black women? All too

often, black men who are indirectly supportive of feminist movement act as though black women have a personal stake in eradicating sexism that men do not have. Black men benefit from feminist thinking and feminist movement too.

Any examination of the contemporary plight of black men reveals the way phallocentrism is at the root of much black-on-black violence, undermines family relations, informs the lack of preventive health care, and even plays a role in promoting drug addiction. Many of the destructive habits of black men are enacted in the name of "manhood." Asserting their ability to be "tough," to be "cool," black men take grave risks with their lives and the lives of others. Acknowledging this in his essay "Cool Pose! The Proud Signature of Black Survival," Richard Majors argues that "cool" has positive dimensions even though it "is also an aggressive assertion of masculinity." Yet, he never overtly critiques sexism. Black men may be reluctant to critique phallocentrism and sexism, precisely because so much black male "style" has its roots in these positions; they may fear that eradicating patriarchy would leave them without the positive expressive styles that have been life-sustaining. Majors is clear, however, that a "cool pose" linked to aggressive phallocentrism is detrimental to both black men and the people they care about:

> Perhaps black men have become so conditioned to keeping up their guard against oppression from the dominant white society that this particular attitude and behavior represents for them their best safeguard against further mental or physical abuse. However, this same behavior makes it very difficult for these males to let their guard down and show affection . . .

Elsewhere, he suggests "that the same elements of cool that allow for survival in the larger society may hurt black people by contributing to one of the more complex problems facing black people today—black-on-black crime." Clearly, black men need to employ a feminist analysis that will address the issue of how to construct a life-sustaining black masculinity that does not have its roots in patriarchal phallocentrism.

refused additional operations. Thus, in those studies of vaginoplasty for which evaluation of surgical success includes clear criteria and reporting, the surgery has a high failure rate.

Studies of hypospadias surgery reveal good news, bad news, and news of uncertain valence. The good news is that adult men who have undergone hypospadias surgery reached important sexual milestones—for example, age of first intercourse—at the same age as men in control groups (who had undergone inguinal, but not genital, surgery as children). Nor did they differ from control groups in sexual behavior or functioning. The bad news is that these men were more timid about seeking sexual contact, possibly because they had more negative feelings about their genital appearance. Furthermore, the greater the number of operations men had, the higher their level of sexual inhibition.[47] Surgery was least successful for men with severe hypospadias, who could often have normal erections but found that problems such as spraying during urination and ejaculation persisted.[48]

And the news of uncertain valence? It all depends on whether you think strict adherence to prescribed gender role signifies psychological health. One study, for example, found that boys who had been hospitalized more often for hypospadias-related problems showed higher levels of "cross-gender" behavior.[49] For intersex management teams, such as one that aims explicitly "to prevent the development of cross-gender identification in children born with . . . ambiguous genitalia," such results might signify failure.[50] On the other hand, practitioners have found that even when they follow Money's management principles to the T, as many as 13 percent of all intersex kids—not just boys with hypospadias—end up straying from the treatment's strict gender demands. This distresses psychologists who adhere to the two-party system.[51] But to those of us who believe gender is quite varied anyway, gender variability among intersexual children does not constitute bad news.

THE RIGHT TO REFUSE

Modern management manuals devote a great deal of thought to how to get parents to go along with suggested treatments. Clearly it is a matter of great delicacy. And so it must be, because parents *can* be intractable. Sometimes they assert their own views about their child's sex and about the degree of surgical alteration they will permit. In the 1990s, Helena Harmon-Smith's son was born with both an ovary and a testis, and doctors wanted to turn him into a girl. Harmon-Smith refused. "He had parts I didn't have," she wrote, and "he is a beautiful child."[52] Harmon-Smith did not see the need for surgical intervention, but against her express instructions, a surgeon removed her son's gonads. In response she has become an activist, founding a support group for parents called Hermaphrodite Education and Listening Post (HELP).

Recently Harmon-Smith published instructions, in the form of Ten Commandments, for physicians who encounter the birth of an intersexual child. The Commandments include: Thou shalt "not make drastic decisions in the first year"; thou shalt "not isolate the family from information or support"; thou shalt "not isolate the patient in an intensive care unit" but shalt "allow the patient to stay on a regular ward."[53] Kessler suggests a new script to be used in announcing the birth of an XX child affected by CAH: Congratulations. "You have a beautiful baby girl. The size of her clitoris and her fused labia provided us with a clue to an underlying medical problem that we might need to treat. Although her clitoris is on the large size it is definitely a clitoris. . . . The important thing about a clitoris is how it functions, not how it looks. She's lucky. Her sexual partners will find it easy to locate her clitoris."[54]

Parental resistance is not new. In the 1930s Hugh Hampton Young described two cases in which parents refused to let doctors perform surgery on their intersexual children. Gussie, aged fifteen, had been raised as a girl. After admission to a hospital (the reason for hospitalization is unclear), Young learned (from performing a surgical examination under general anesthesia) that Gussie had a testis on one side, an enlarged clitoris/penis, a vagina, and an underdeveloped fallopian tube and uterus but no ovary. While the child was on the operating table, they decided to bring the testis down into the scrotum/enlarged labium. They then told the mother that the child was not a girl, but a boy, advised her to change h/her name to Gus and to have h/her return for further "normalizing" surgery.

The mother's response was outraged and swift: "She became greatly incensed, and asserted that her child was a girl, that she didn't want a boy, and that she would continue to bring up the patient as a girl."[55] Parental resistance put Young on the spot. He had already created a new body with an external testicle. Ought he to accommodate the mother's insistence that Gus remain Gussie? And if so, how? Should he offer to remove the penis and testicle, even though that would leave Gussie without any functioning gonad? Should he attempt to manipulate h/her hormonal productions? These questions remained unanswered; the child never returned to the hospital. In a similar case the parents refused to allow even exploratory surgery and, following an initial external examination of the child, never returned. Young was left to ponder the possibilities that lay beyond his control. "Should," he wondered, "this patient be allowed to grow up as a male . . . even if [surgery] shows the gonads to be female?"[56]

Young also discussed several cases of adult hermaphrodites who refused not only treatment but the chance to get a full "scientific" explanation of their "condition." George S., for example, raised as a girl, ran away from home at age fourteen, dressing and living as a man. Later s/he married as a man, but found it too hard to support a wife. So s/he emigrated from England to America, dressed again as a woman, and became some man's "mistress," although s/he also continued to be the male partner in intercourse with women. H/her fully developed breasts caused

embarrassment and s/he asked Young to remove them. When Young refused to do so without operating to discover h/her "true" sex, the patient vanished. Another of Young's patients, Francies Benton, made h/her living as an exhibit in a circus freak show. The advertisement read "male and female in one. One body—two people." Benton had no interest in changing h/her lifestyle, but sought Young's expertise to satisfy h/her curiosity and to provide medical testimony verifying the truth of h/her advertising claims.[57]

Dogma has it that without medical care, especially early surgical intervention, hermaphrodites are doomed to a life of misery. Yet there are few empirical investigations to back up this claim.[58] In fact, the studies gathered to build a case for medical treatment often do just the opposite. Francies Benton, for example, "had not worried over his condition, did not wish to be changed, and was enjoying life."[59] Claus Overzier, a physician at the Medical Clinic at the University of Mainz, Germany, reports that in the majority of cases the psychological behavior of patients agreed only with their sex of rearing and not with their body type. And in many of these cases, body type was not "smoothed over" to conform to sex of rearing. In only fifteen percent of his ninety-four cases were patients discontented with their legal sex; and in each of these it was a "female" who wished to become a "male." Even Dewhurst and Gordon, who are adamant about the importance of very early treatment, acknowledged great success in "changing the sex" of older patients. They reported on twenty cases of children reclassified into a different sex after the supposedly critical period of eighteen months. They deemed all the reclassifications "successful," wondering whether sex "re-registration can be recommended more readily than has been suggested so far."[60] Rather than emphasize this positive finding, however, they stressed the practical difficulties involved with late sex changes.

Sometimes patients refuse treatment despite strikingly visible consequences, such as beard growth in females. Randolf et al. discuss one girl who "has adamantly refused further surgery in spite of the disfiguring prominence of her clitoris,"[61] while Van der Kamp et al. report that nine out of ten adult women who had undergone vaginal reconstruction felt that such operations should not be done until early adolescence.[62] Finally, Bailez et al. report on an individual's refusal of a fourth operation needed to achieve a vaginal opening suitable for intercourse.[63]

Intersexual children who grow up with genitalia that seem to contradict their assigned gender identities are not doomed to lives of misery. Laurent and I turned up more than eighty examples (published since 1950) of adolescents and adults who grew up with visibly anomalous genitalia. In only one case was an individual deemed potentially psychotic, but that was connected to a psychotic parent and not to sexual ambiguity. The case summaries make clear that children adjust to the presence of anomalous genitalia and manage to develop into functioning adults, many of whom marry and have active and apparently satisfying sex lives. Striking instances include men with small penises who have active marital sex lives without penetrative intercourse.[64] Even proponents of early intervention recognize that adjustment to unusual genitalia is possible. Hampson and Hampson, in presenting data on more than 250 postadolescent hermaphrodites, wrote: "The surprise is that so many ambiguous-looking patients were able, *appearance notwithstanding,* to grow up and achieve a rating of psychologically healthy, or perhaps only mildly non-healthy."[65]

The clinical literature is highly anecdotal. There exist no consistent or arguably scientific standards for evaluating the health and psychological well-being of the patients in question. But despite the lack of quantitative data, our survey reveals a great deal. Although they grew up with malformations such as small phalluses, sexual precocity, pubertal breast development, and periodic hematuria (blood in the urine; or in these cases menstrual blood), the majority of intersexual children raised as males assumed lifestyles characteristic of heterosexually active

adult males. Fifty-five intersexual children grew up as females. Despite genital anomalies that included the presence of a penis, an enlarged clitoris, bifid scrota, and/or virilizing puberty, most assumed the roles and activities of heterosexually active females.

Two interesting differences appear between the group raised as males (RAM) and the one raised as females (RAF). First, only a minority of the RAF's chose to feminize their masculinized genitalia during adolescence or adulthood, while well over half of the RAM's elected surgery to masculinize their feminized bodies. Second, 16 percent of the RAF's decided as adolescents or adults to change their identities from female to male. Individuals who initiated such changes adjusted successfully—and often with expressed delight—to their new identities. In contrast, only 6 percent of the RAM's wished to change from male to female. In other words, males appear to be more anxious to change their feminized bodies than females are to change their masculinized ones. In a culture that prizes masculinity, this is hardly surprising. Again we see that it is possible to visualize the medical and biological only by peering through a cultural screen.[66]

REVISITING THE FIVE SEXES

Those who defend current approaches to the management of intersexuality can, at best, offer a weak case for continuing the status quo. Many patients are scarred—both psychologically and physically—by a process heavy on surgical prowess and light on explanation, psychological support, and full disclosure. We stand now at a fork in the road. To the right we can walk toward reaffirmation of the naturalness of the number 2 and continue to develop new medical technology, including gene "therapy" and new prenatal interventions to ensure the birth of only two sexes. To the left, we can hike up the hill of natural and cultural variability. Traditionally, in European and American culture we have defined two genders, each with a range of permissible behaviors; but things have begun to change. There are househusbands and women fighter pilots. There are feminine lesbians and gay men both buff and butch. Male to female and female to male transsexuals render the sex/gender divide virtually unintelligible.

All of which brings me back to the five sexes. I imagine a future in which our knowledge of the body has led to resistance against medical surveillance,[67] in which medical science has been placed at the service of gender variability, and genders have multiplied beyond currently fathomable limits. Suzanne Kessler suggests that "gender variability can . . . be seen . . . in a new way—as an expansion of what is meant by male and female."[68] Ultimately, perhaps, concepts of masculinity and femininity might overlap so completely as to render the very notion of gender difference irrelevant.

In the future, the hierarchical divisions between patient and doctor, parent and child, male and female, heterosexual and homosexual will dissolve. The critical voices of people discussed in this chapter all point to cracks in the monolith of current medical writings and practice. It is possible to envision a new ethic of medical treatment, one that permits ambiguity to thrive, rooted in a culture that has moved beyond gender hierarchies. In my utopia, an intersexual's major medical concerns would be the potentially life-threatening conditions that sometimes accompany intersex development, such as salt imbalance due to adrenal malfunction, higher frequencies of gonadal tumors, and hernias. Medical intervention aimed at synchronizing body image and gender identity would only rarely occur before the age of reason. Such technological intervention would be a cooperative venture among physician, patient, and gender advisers. As Kessler has noted, the unusual genitalia of intersexuals could be considered to be "intact" rather than "deformed"; surgery, seen now as a creative gesture (surgeons "create" a vagina), might be seen as destructive (tissue is destroyed and removed) and thus necessary only when life is at stake.[69]

Accepted treatment approaches damage both mind and body. And clearly, it is possible for healthy adults to emerge from a childhood in which genital anatomy does not completely match sex of rearing. But still, the good doctors are skeptical.[70] So too are many parents and potential parents. It is impossible not to personalize the argument. What if you had an intersexual child? Could you and your child become pioneers in a new management strategy? Where, in addition to the new intersexual rights activists, might you look for advice and inspiration?

The history of transsexualism offers food for thought. In European and American culture we understand transsexuals to be individuals who have been born with "good" male or "good" female bodies. Psychologically, however, they envision themselves as members of the "opposite" sex. A transsexual's drive to have his/her body conform with his/her psyche is so strong that many seek medical aid to transform their bodies hormonally and ultimately surgically, by removal of their gonads and transformation of their external genitalia. The demands of self-identified transsexuals have contributed to changing medical practices, forcing recognition and naming of the phenomenon. Just as the idea that homosexuality is an inborn, stable trait did not emerge until the end of the nineteenth century, the transsexual did not fully emerge as a special type of person until the middle of the twentieth. Winning the right to surgical and legal sex changes, however, exacted a price: the reinforcement of a two-gender system.[71] By requesting surgery to make their bodies match their gender, transsexuals enacted the logical extreme of the medical profession's philosophy that within an individual's body, sex and gender must conform. Indeed, transsexuals had little choice but to view themselves within this framework if they wanted to obtain surgical help. To avoid creating a "lesbian" marriage, physicians in gender clinics demanded that married transsexuals divorce before their surgery. Afterwards, they could legally change their birth certificates to reflect their new status.

Within the past ten to twenty years, however, the edifice of transsexual dualism has developed large cracks. Some transsexual organizations have begun to support the concept of *transgenderism,* which constitutes a more radical re-visioning of sex and gender.[72] Whereas traditional transsexuals might describe a male transvestite—a man dressing in women's clothing—as a transsexual on the road to becoming a complete female, transgenderists accept "kinship among those with gender-variant identities. Transgenderism supplants the dichotomy of transsexual and transvestite with a concept of continuity." Earlier generations of transsexuals did not want to depart from gender norms, but rather to blend totally into their new gender role. Today, however, many argue that they need to come out as transsexuals, permanently assuming a transsexual identity that is neither male nor female in the traditional sense.[73]

Within the transgender community (which has its own political organizations and even its own electronic bulletin board on the Internet), gender variations abound. Some choose to become women while keeping their male genitals intact. Many who have undergone surgical transformation have taken up homosexual roles. For example, a male-to-female transsexual may come out as a lesbian (or a female-to-male as a gay male). Consider Jane, born a physiological male, now in her late thirties, living with her wife (whom she married when her name was still John). Jane takes hormones to feminize herself, but they have not yet interfered with her ability to have erections and intercourse as a man:

> From her perspective, Jane has a lesbian relationship with her wife (Mary). Yet she also uses her penis for pleasure. Mary does not identify herself as a lesbian, although she maintains love and attraction for Jane, whom she regards as the same person she fell in love with although this person has changed physically. Mary regards herself as heterosexual . . . although she defines sexual intimacy with her spouse Jane as somewhere between lesbian and heterosexual.[74]

Does acceptance of gender variation mean the concept of gender would disappear entirely? Not necessarily. The transgender theorist Martine Rothblatt proposes a chromatic system of gender that would differentiate among hundreds of different personality types. The permutations of her suggested seven levels each of aggression, nurturance, and eroticism could lead to 343 ($7 \times 7 \times 7$) shades of gender. A person with a mauve gender, for example, would be "a low-intensity nurturing person with a fair amount of eroticism but not much aggressiveness."[75] Some might find Rothblatt's system silly or unnecessarily complex. But her point is serious and begins to suggest ways we might raise intersex children in a culture that recognizes gender variation.

Is it so unreasonable to ask that we focus more clearly on variability and pay less attention to gender conformity? The problem with gender, as we now have it, is the violence—both real and metaphorical—we do by generalizing. No woman or man fits the universal gender stereotype. "It might be more useful," writes the sociologist Judith Lorber, ". . . to group patterns of behavior and only then look for identifying markers of the people likely to enact such behaviors."[76]

Were we in Europe and America to move to a multiple sex and gender role system (as it seems we might be doing), we would not be cultural pioneers. Several Native American cultures, for example, define a third gender, which may include people whom we would label as homosexual, transsexual, or intersexual but also people we would label as male or female.[77] Anthropologists have described other groups, such as the Hijras of India, that contain individuals whom we in the West would label intersexes, transsexuals, effeminate men, and eunuchs. As with the varied Native American categories, the Hijras vary in their origins and gender characteristics.[78] Anthropologists debate about how to interpret Native American gender systems. What is important, however, is that the existence of other systems suggests that ours is not inevitable.

I do not mean to romanticize other gender systems; they provide no guarantee of social equality. In several small villages in the Dominican Republic and among the Sambia, a people residing in the highlands of Papua, New Guinea, a genetic mutation causing a deficiency in the enzyme 5-α-reductase occurs with fairly high frequency.[79] At birth, XY children with 5-α-reductase deficiency have a tiny penis or clitoris, undescended testes, and a divided scrotum. They can be mistaken for girls, or their ambiguity may be noticed. In adolescence, however, naturally produced testosterone causes the penises of XY teenagers deficient in 5-α-reductase to grow; their testes descend, their vaginal lips fuse to form a scrotum, their bodies become hairy, bearded, and musclebound.[80]

And in both the Dominican Republic and New Guinea, DHT-deficient children—who in the United States are generally operated on immediately—are recognized as a third sex.[81] The Dominicans call it *guevedoche,* or "penis at twelve," while the Sambians use the word *kwolu-aatmwol,* which suggests a person's transformation "into a male thing."[82] In both cultures, the DHT-deficient child experiences ambivalent sex-role socialization. And in adulthood s/he most commonly—but not necessarily with complete success—self-identifies as a male. The anthropologist Gil Herdt writes that, at puberty, "the transformation may be from female—possibly ambiguously reared—to male-aspiring third sex, who is, in certain social scenes, categorized with adult males."[83]

While these cultures know that sometimes a third type of child is born, they nevertheless recognize only two gender roles. Herdt argues that the strong preference in these cultures for maleness, and the positions of freedom and power that males hold, make it easy to understand why in adulthood the *kwolu-aatmwol* and the *guevedoche* most frequently chose the male over the female role. Although Herdt's work provides us with a perspective outside our own cultural framework, only further studies will clarify how members of a third sex manage in cultures that acknowledge three categories of body but offer only a two-gender system.

TOWARD THE END OF GENDER TYRANNY: GETTING THERE FROM HERE

Simply recognizing a third category does not assure a flexible gender system. Such flexibility requires political and social struggle. In discussing my "five sexes" proposal Suzanne Kessler drives home this point with great effect:

> The limitation with Fausto-Sterling's proposal is that legitimizing other sets of genitals . . . still gives genitals primary signifying status and ignores the fact that in the everyday world gender attributions are made without access to genital inspection . . . what has primacy in everyday life is the gender that is performed, regardless of the flesh's configuration under the clothes.

Kessler argues that it would be better for intersexuals and their supporters to turn everyone's focus away from genitals and to dispense with claims to a separate intersexual identity. Instead, she suggests, men and women would come in a wider assortment. Some women would have large clitorises or fused labia, while some men would have "small penises or misshapen scrota—phenotypes with no particular clinical or identity meaning."[84] I think Kessler is right, and this is why I am no longer advocating using discrete categories such as herm, merm, and ferm, even tongue in cheek.

The intersexual or transgender person who presents a social gender—what Kessler calls "cultural genitals"—that conflicts with h/her physical genitals often risks h/her life. In a recent court case, a mother charged that her son, a transvestite, died because paramedics stopped treating him after discovering his male genitals. The jury awarded her $2.9 million in damages. While it is heartening that a jury found such behavior unacceptable, the case underscores the high risk of gender transgression.[85] "Transgender warriors," as Leslie Feinberg calls them, will continue to be in danger until we succeed in moving them onto the "acceptable" side of the imaginary line separating "normal, natural, holy" gender from the "abnormal, unnatural, sick [and] sinful."[86]

A person with ovaries, breasts, and a vagina, but whose "cultural genitals" are male also faces difficulties. In applying for a license or passport, for instance, one must indicate "M" or "F" in the gender box. Suppose such a person checks "F" on his or her license and then later uses the license for identification. The 1998 murder in Wyoming of homosexual Matthew Shepherd makes clear the possible dangers. A masculine-presenting female is in danger of violent attack if she does not "pass" as male. Similarly, she can get into legal trouble if stopped for a traffic violation or passport control, as the legal authority can accuse her of deception—masquerading as a male for possibly illegal purposes. In the 1950s, when police raided lesbian bars, they demanded that women be wearing three items of women's clothing in order to avoid arrest.[87] As Feinberg notes, we have not moved very far beyond that moment.

Given the discrimination and violence faced by those whose cultural and physical genitals don't match, legal protections are needed during the transition to a gender-diverse utopia. It would help to eliminate the "gender" category from licenses, passports, and the like. The transgender activist Leslie Feinberg writes: "Sex categories should be removed from all basic identification papers—from driver's licenses to passports—and since the right of each person to define their own sex is so basic, it should be eliminated from birth certificates as well."[88] Indeed, why are physical genitals necessary for identification? Surely attributes both more visible (such as height, build, and eye color) and less visible (fingerprints and DNA profiles) would be of greater use.

Transgender activists have written "An International Bill of Gender Rights" that includes (among ten gender rights) "the right to define gender identity, the right to control and change one's own body, the right to sexual expression and the right to form committed, loving relationships and enter into marital contracts."[89] The legal bases for such rights are being hammered

out in the courts as I write, through the establishment of case law regarding sex discrimination and homosexual rights.[90]

Intersexuality, as we have seen, has long been at the center of debates over the connections among sex, gender, and legal and social status. A few years ago the Cornell University historian Mary Beth Norton sent me the transcripts of legal proceedings from the General Court of the Virginia Colony. In 1629, one Thomas Hall appeared in court claiming to be both a man and a woman. Because civil courts expected one's dress to signify one's sex, the examiner declared Thomas was a woman and ordered her to wear women's clothing. Later, a second examiner overruled the first, declaring Hall a man who should, therefore, wear men's clothing. In fact, Thomas Hall had been christened Thomasine and had worn women's clothing until age twenty-two, when he joined the army. Afterward s/he returned to women's clothing so that s/he could make a living sewing lace. The only references to Hall's anatomy say that he had a man's part as big as the top of his little finger, that he did not have the use of this part, and that—as Thomasine herself put it—she had "a peece of an hole." Finally, the Virginia Court, accepting Thomas(ine)'s gender duality, ordered that "it shall be published that the said Hall is a man *and* a woman, that all inhabitants around may take notice thereof and that he shall go clothed in man's apparel, only his head will be attired in a Coiffe with an apron before him."[91]

Today the legal status of operated intersexuals remains uncertain.[92] Over the years the rights of royal succession, differential treatment by social security or insurance laws, gendered labor laws, and voting limitations would all have been at stake in declaring an intersex legally male or female. Despite the lessening of such concerns, the State remains deeply interested in regulating marriage and the family. Consider the Australian case of an XX intersex born with an ovary and fallopian tube on the right side, a small penis, and a left testicle. Reared as a male, he sought surgery in adulthood to masculinize his penis and deal with his developed breasts. The physicians in charge of his case agreed he should remain a male, since this was his psychosexual orientation. He later married, but the Australian courts annulled the union. The ruling held that in a legal system that requires a person to be either one or the other, for the purpose of marriage, he could be neither male nor female (hence the need for the right to marry in the Bill of Gender Rights).[93]

As usual, the debates over intersexuality are inextricable from those over homosexuality; we cannot consider the challenges one poses to our gender system without considering the parallel challenge posed by the other. In considering the potential marriage of an intersexual, the legal and medical rules often focus on the question of homosexual marriage. In the case of *Corbett v. Corbett 1970,* April Ashley, a British transsexual, married one Mr. Corbett, who later asked the court to annul the marriage because April was really a man. April argued that she was a social female and thus eligible for marriage. The judge, however, ruled that the operation was pure artifact, imposed on a clearly male body. Not only had April Ashley been born a male, but her transforming surgery had not created a vagina large enough to permit penile penetration. Furthermore, sexual intercourse was "the institution on which the family is built, and in which the capacity for natural hetero-sexual intercourse is an essential element." "Marriage," the judge continued, "is a relationship which depends upon sex and not gender."[94]

An earlier British case had annulled a marriage between a man and a woman born without a vagina. The husband testified that he could not penetrate more than two inches into his wife's artificial vagina. Furthermore, he claimed even that channel was artificial, not the biological one due him as a true husband. The divorce commissioner agreed, citing a much earlier case in which the judge ruled, "I am of the opinion that no man ought to be reduced to this state of quasi-natural connexion."[95]

Both British judges declared marriage without the ability for vaginal-penile sex to be illegal,

one even adding the criterion that two inches did not a penetration make. In other countries—and even in the several U.S. states that ban anal and oral contact between both same-sex and opposite-sex partners and those that restrict the ban to homosexual encounters[96]—engaging in certain types of sexual encounters can result in felony charges. Similarly, a Dutch physician discussed several cases of XX intersexuals, raised as males, who married females. Defining them as biological females (based on their two X chromosomes and ovaries), the physician called for a discussion of the legality of the marriages. Should they be dissolved "notwithstanding the fact that they are happy ones?" Should they "be recognized legally and ecclesiastically?"[97]

If cultural genitals counted for more than physical genitals, many of the dilemmas just described could be easily resolved. Since the mid-1960s the International Olympic Committee has demanded that all female athletes submit to a chromosome or DNA test, even though some scientists urge the elimination of sex testing.[98] Whether we are deciding who may compete in the women's high jump or whether we should record sex on a newborn's birth certificate, the judgment derives primarily from social conventions. Legally, the interest of the state in maintaining a two-gender system focuses on questions of marriage, family structure, and sexual practices. But the time is drawing near when even these state concerns will seem arcane to us.[99] Laws regulating consensual sexual behavior between adults had religious and moral origins. In the United States, at least, we are supposed to experience complete separation of church and state. As our legal system becomes further secularized (as I believe it will), it seems only a matter of time before the last laws regulating consensual bedroom behavior will become unconstitutional.[100] At that moment the final legal barriers to the emergence of a wide range of gender expression will disappear.

The court of the Virginia Colony required Thomas/Thomasine to signal h/her physical genitals by wearing a dual set of cultural genitals. Now, as then, physical genitals form a poor basis for deciding the rights and privileges of citizenship. Not only are they confusing; they are not even publicly visible. Rather, it is social gender that we see and read. In the future, hearing a birth announced as "boy" or "girl" might enable new parents to envision for their child an expanded range of possibilities, especially if their baby were among the few with unusual genitals. Perhaps we will come to view such children as especially blessed or lucky. It is not so far-fetched to think that some can become the most desirable of all possible mates, able to pleasure their partners in a variety of ways. One study of men with unusually small penises, for example, found them to be "characterized by an experimental attitude to positions and methods." Many of these men attributed "partner sexual satisfaction and the stability of their relationships to their need to make extra effort including non-penetrating techniques."[101]

My vision is utopian, but I believe in its possibility. All of the elements needed to make it come true already exist, at least in embryonic form. Necessary legal reforms are in reach, spurred forward by what one might call the "gender lobby": political organizations that work for women's rights, gay rights, and the rights of transgendered people. Medical practice has begun to change as a result of pressure from intersexual patients and their supporters. Public discussion about gender and homosexuality continues unabated with a general trend toward greater tolerance for gender multiplicity and ambiguity. The road will be bumpy, but the possibility of a more diverse and equitable future is ours if we choose to make it happen.

NOTES

1. Fausto-Sterling 1993a. The piece was reprinted on the Op-Ed page of the *New York Times* under the title "How Many Sexes Are There?" Fausto-Sterling 1994.
2. This is the same organization that tried to close down the Off Broadway play "Corpus Christi" (by Terence McNally) during the fall season of 1998 in New York City.
3. Rights 1995 Section 4, p. 11. The syndicated columnist E. Thomas McClanahan took up the attack as well. "What the heck," he wrote, "why settle for five genders? Why not press for an even dozen?" (McClanahan 1995 p. B6). Pat Buchanan also joined the chorus: "They say there aren't two sexes, there are five genders. . . . I tell you this: God created man and woman—I don't care what Bella Abzug says" (quoted in *The Advocate,* October 31, 1995). Columnist Marilyn vos Savant writes: "There are men and there are women—no matter how they're constructed . . . and that's that" (vos Savant 1996 p. 6).
4. Money 1994.
5. Scott's novel won the Lambda Literary Award in 1995. She specifically acknowledged my work on her web site.
6. See, for example, Rothblatt 1995; Burke 1996; and Diamond 1996.
7. Spence has been writing for some time about the impossibility of these terms. See, e.g., Spence 1984 and 1985.
8. For activists working for change see the Intersex Society of North America (http://www.isna.org) and Chase 1998a, b; and Harmon-Smith 1998. For academics in addition to myself, see Kessler 1990; Dreger 1993; Diamond and Sigmundson 1997a, b; Dreger 1998b; Kessler 1998; Preves 1998; Kipnis and Diamond 1998; Dreger 1998c. For physicians who are moving toward (or embracing) the new paradigm see Schober 1998; Wilson and Reiner 1998; and Phornphutkul et al. 1999. More cautiously, Meyer-Bahlburg suggests modest changes in medical practice, including giving more thought to gender assignment (an "optimal gender policy"), elimination of nonconsensual surgery for mild degrees of genital abnormalities, and provision of more support services for intersex persons and their parents. He also calls for obtaining more data on long-term outcomes (Meyer-Bahlburg 1998).
9. See comments by Chase (1998a and 1998b). Chase has repeatedly tried to get the attention of mainstream American feminists through venues like *Ms.* Magazine and the academic journal *Signs,* but has been unable to stir their interest in the question of genital surgery on American newborns. It seems it is much more comfortable to confront the practices of other cultures than it

is our own. The surgeon Justine Schober writes: "To this date, no studies of clitoral surgery address the long term results of erotic sexual sensitivity" (Schober 1998, p. 550). Costa et al. 1997 report that of eight clitorectomized patients, two reported no orgasm during intercourse. Some who report orgasm find it much diminished compared to before surgery. Others find it so difficult to achieve that it becomes not worth the trouble.

10. Thankfully, some physicians are open to new ideas. Mine have struck a chord with one local pediatric endocrinologist, and we have presented a case and the new thinking about how to manage intersexual births in a Grand Rounds. The surgeon discussed here did not attend, but one other surgeon did.

   One local surgeon, although a colleague in the Brown Medical School, has never acknowledged my many communications. These included copies of publications such *as Hermaphrodites with Attitude* and *Alias* (a newsletter of the AIS Support Group), as well as drafts of my own writing, for which I solicited feedback. After reading an article in an in-house newsletter delineating the "standard" surgical approaches to intersexuality, Cheryl Chase and I wrote asking for a chance to present the emerging alternative thinking on the topic. The surgeon replied (to Chase, with only a *cc* rather than direct address to me) that the publication was limited to members of the Department of Pediatrics. "We do not wish our publication to become a forum for expression of ideas, be they medical or otherwise," the letter read.

11. In this chapter I discuss only evaluations of genital surgery. Some forms of intersexuality involve chromosomal and/or hormonal changes without affecting visible genital components. While these conditions receive medical attention, especially hormonal treatments, surgery is never involved because there are many fewer doubts about gender assignment. In the vast majority of these cases, the children involved have mental and emotional functions within a normal range. This is not to say that they encounter no difficulties because of their differences—only that the difficulties are surmountable. For recent literature on Turner Syndrome and other gender chromosome anomalies, see: Raboch et al. 1987; McCauley and Urquiza 1988; Sylven et al. 1993;

Bender et al. 1995; Cunniff et al. 1995; Toublanc et al. 1997; and Boman et al. 1998.

12. Many of these details were conveyed to me by personal communication, but Chase's story is now widely documented. See, for example, Chase 1998a.

13. Chase's story of doctors refusing to tell her the truth even once she had reached adulthood are repeated over and over in the stories of hundreds of adult intersexuals. These may be found scattered in newsletters, media interviews, and academic books and articles, many of which I cite in this chapter. The sociologist Sharon Preves has interviewed forty adult intersexuals and is beginning to publish her results. In one article she recounts Flora's experience of visiting a genetic counselor at age twenty-four, who said, "I'm obliged to tell you that certain details of your condition have not been divulged to you, but I cannot tell you what they are because they would upset you too much" (Preves 1999, p. 37).

14. Cheryl Chase to Anne Fausto-Sterling (personal correspondence, 1993).

15. Chase 1998, p. 200. For more on HELP, see Harmon and Smith 1998 and visit their web site: http://www.help@jaxnet.com. Their address is P.O. Box 26292, Jacksonville, FL 32226.

16. Chase uses the following quote from an AIS support group newsletter. "Our first impression of ISNA was that they were perhaps a bit too angry and militant to gain the support of the medical profession. However, we have to say that, having read [political analyses of intersexuality by ISNA, Kessler, Fausto-Sterling, and Holmes], we feel that the feminist concepts relating to the patriarchal treatment of intersexuality are extremely interesting and do make a lot of sense" (Chase 1998, p. 200).

17. The intersexual rights movement has become international. For an example of "coming out" in Germany, see Tolmein and Bergling 1999. For other foreign organizations, consult the ISNA web page: http://www.isna.org.

18. For example, the surgeon John Gearhart and colleagues published a paper in which they measured nerve responses during phallic reconstruction. In their six-case study, they

were able to monitor nerve responses in the phallus even after surgery. They wrote: "Our study clearly shows that modern techniques of genital reconstruction allow for preservation of nerve conduction in the dorsal neurovascular bundle and may permit normal sexual function in adulthood" (Gearhart et al. 1995, p. 486). (Note that their study was done on infants, and not enough time has elapsed for adult follow-up studies.) Both in a private letter and a letter to the *Journal of Urology* (Chase 1995), Cheryl Chase disputed the implications of their research with case studies of her own, collected from ISNA members. She cited the absence or diminishment of orgasm in adults whose nervous transmission was normal. Gearhart and colleagues responded by calling for long-term follow-up studies. In another article, Chase points out how surgical techniques are constructed as moving targets. Criticism can always be deflected by claiming that newer techniques have solved the problem. Given that it can take decades for some of the problems to emerge, this is indeed a dilemma (Chase 1998a; Kipnis and Diamond 1998).

19. Costa et al. 1997 and Velidedeoglu et al. 1997 list clitorectomy and clitoral recession as alternatives to clitoroplasty, coldly noting that "clitorectomy results in loss of a sensate clitoris" (p. 215).

20. The cancer story is not unusual. A number of adult intersexuals recount how, during their teen years, they believed they were dying of cancer. Moreno's story is recounted in Moreno 1998.

21. Ibid., p. 208. This sentiment is echoed by yet another ISNA activist, Morgan Holmes, a vibrant woman in her late twenties. To prevent a miscarriage, doctors had treated her mother with progestin, a masculinizing hormone, and Morgan was born with an enlarged clitoris. When she was seven, doctors performed a clitoral reduction. As with Cheryl Chase, no one talked about the operation, but Holmes remembers it. Although the surgery did not render her inorgasmic, her sexual function was severely affected. Like Chase, Holmes chose to go public. In her Master's thesis, analyzing her own case in the context of feminist theories on the construction and meanings of gender, she writes passionately about lost possibilities:

"I like to imagine, if my body had been left intact and my clitoris had grown at the same rate as the rest of my body, what would my lesbian relationships have been like? What would my current heterosexual relationship be like? What if—as a woman—I could assume a penetrative role . . . with both women and men? When the doctors initially assured my father that I would grow up to have 'normal sexual function,' they did not mean that they could guarantee that my amputated clitoris would be sensitive or that I would be able to achieve orgasm . . . . What was being guaranteed was that I would not grow up to confuse the issue of who (man) fucks whom (woman). These possibilities . . . were negated in a reasonably simple two-hour operation. All the things I might have grown up to do, all the possibilities went down the hall with my clitoris to the pathology department. Me and my remains went to the recovery room and have not yet emerged" (Holmes 1994, p. 53).

22. Baker 1981; Elias and Annas 1988; Goodall 1991.

23. Anonymous 1994a.

24. Anonymous 1994b.

25. The fastest way to locate these organizations and the rich support and information they provide is via the Internet. The web address is http://www. isna.org. ISNA stands for Intersex Society of North America and their mailing address is: PO Box 3070, Ann Arbor, MI 48106-3070.

26. One woman writes: "When I discovered I had AIS the pieces finally fit together. But what fell apart was my relationship with both my family and physicians. It was not learning about chromosomes or testes that caused enduring trauma, it was discovering that I had been told lies. I avoided all medical care for the next 18 years. I have severe osteoporosis as a result of a lack of medical attention. This is what lies produce" (Groveman 1996, p. 1,829). This issue of the *Canadian Medical Association Journal* contains several letters with similar sentiments written by AIS women outraged that the CMAJ had awarded second prize in a medical student essay contest on medical ethics to an essay defending the ethics of lying to AIS patients. The essay was published in an earlier issue (Natarajan 1996). For many more stories see the issues of ISNA's (see previous

note) newsletter, "Hermaphrodites with Attitude," the newsletter of ALIAS, an AIS support group (email aissg@aol.com), the journal *Chrysalis* 2:5 (fall 1997/winter 1998), and Moreno 1998. For further discussion of ethical decision making, see Rossiter and Diehl 1998 and Catlin 1998.

27. Meyer-Bahlburg writes: "Although current surgical procedures of clitoral recession, if done well, appear to preserve the glans clitoris and its innervation, we are still in need of controlled long-term follow-up studies that assess in detail the quality of clitoral functioning in adults who have undergone such procedures [clitoral surgery] in infancy or childhood" (Meyer-Bahlburg 1998, p. 12).

28. The most recent full-length book on the clitoris is old, by medical standards—dating from 1976 (Lowry and Lowry 1976). For a roadmap of changing conventions in clitoral representations, see Moore and Clarke 1995. A rare anatomical study of the clitoris concludes that "current anatomical descriptions of female human urethral and genital anatomy are inaccurate" (O'Connell et al. 1998, p. 1,892). For a more complete drawing of the clitoris based on these recent findings, see Williamson and Nowak 1998. Furthermore, new aspects of female genital anatomy and physiology continue to be described. See Kellogg and Parra 1991 and Ingelman-Sundberg 1997.

    Perhaps the best and least known text depicting female sexual anatomy is Dickinson 1949. Dickinson is remarkable because he draws the variability, often in composite drawings, which give a vibrant sense of anatomical variation. Unfortunately, his drawings have been ignored in the more standard anatomical texts. For attempts to standardize clitoral size in newborns, see Tagatz et al. 1979; Callegari et al. 1987; Oberfield et al. 1989; and Phillip et al. 1996.

29. Failure to attend to genital variability, especially in children, has made it difficult to use anatomical markers to document sexual abuse in children. Here we seem to be caught in a vicious circle. Our taboos on acknowledging infantile and immature genitalia mean that we really haven't looked at them very systematically. This means that we have no "objective" way to document the very thing we fear: sexual abuse of children. It also leaves us ill-equipped

to have sensible conversations with intersex children and their parents about their own anatomical differences. See, for example, McCann et al. 1990; Berenson et al. 1991; Berenson et al. 1992; Emans 1992; and Gardner 1992.

30. See, for example, a new, computerized image reproduced on p. 288 of Moore and Clarke 1995. This image labels only the glans and some nerves. The shaft is barely visible and the crura are unlabeled. Compare this to feminist publications such as *Our Bodies, Ourselves.* Modern anatomy CD's for popular use barely mention the clitoris and show no labeled pictures of it (see, for example, Bodyworks by Softkey).

31. Newman et al. 1992b (p. 182) write: "Long term results of operations that eliminate erectile tissue are yet to be systematically evaluated."

32. Newman et al. (1992b) mention one of nine patients with pain with orgasm; p. 8 following clitoral recession. Randolf et al. (1981) write: "A second effort at recession is worthwhile and can be satisfactorily accomplished in spite of old scar" (p. 884). Lattimer (1961), in his description of the recession operation, refers to "the midline scar," which ends up hidden from view in the folds of the labia majora. Allen et al. (1982) cite 4/8 clitoral recessions complaining of painful erections. Nihoul-Fekete (1981) says that clitorectomy leaves painful stumps; about recession clitoroplasty, she writes: "Clitoral sensitivity is retained, except in cases where postoperative necrosis resulted from excessive dissection of the vascular pedicles" (p. 255).

33. Nihoul-Fekete et al. 1982.

34. Allen et al. 1982, p. 354.

35. Newman et al. (1992b) write that patients who underwent extensive vaginal and clitoral surgery have "sexual function ranging from satisfactory to poor" (p. 650). Allen et al. (1982) write that they limited vaginoplasties in infants, waiting until puberty for the full operation "rather than provoke dense scarring and vaginal stenosis following an aggressive procedure at an earlier age" (p. 354). Nihoul-Fekete (1981) mentions as a goal keeping the vagina free of an annular scar; on vaginoplasties: "Complications arise from poor healing with resultant stenosis of the vaginal opening" (p. 256). Dewhurst and Gordon (1969) write that if the fused labial folds are

divided before bowel and bladder continence is achieved, "it may be followed by imperfect healing and perhaps scarring later" (p. 41).

36. Nihoul-Fekete 1981.

37. A debate continues over whether it is best to perform these early in childhood or wait until adolescence or adulthood. As with hypospadias surgery, there are many varieties of surgery for vaginal reconstruction. For a brief history of them, see Schober 1998.

38. On stenosis or vaginal narrowing: 3 out of 10 moderate to severe introital stenosis; 5 out of 10 moderate to severe vaginal stenosis (van der Kamp et al. 1992). Operations before 1975—of 33: 8 vaginal stenosis, 3 small vaginal orifice, 1 labial adhesions; 1 penile fibrosis. Of 25 post 1975: 3 vaginal stenosis, 1 labial adhesions (Lobe et al. 1987); 8 out of 14 with vaginal pullthrough type vaginoplasties developed severe stenosis (Newman et al. 1992b); 8 out of 13 early vaginoplasties: stenosis caused by scarring (p. 601) (Sotiropoulos et al. 1976). Migeon says that girls with vaginal operations "have scar tissue from surgery. They experience difficult penetration. These girls suffer" (in Hendricks 1993). Nihoul-Fekete et al. (1982) report 10/16 clitoral recessions in which postpubertal patients reported hypersensitivity of the clitoris.

39. Bailez et al. 1992, p. 681.

40. Colapinto 1997.

41. One recent evaluation of the psychological health of intersex children found: "dilating the vagina at a younger age appeared to lead to severe psychological problems because it was experienced as a violation of the body integrity" (Slijper et al. 1998) p. 132.

42. Colapinto 1997; Money and Lamacz 1987.

43. Bailez et al. 1992.

44. Newman et al. 1992a, p. 651. The data from Allen et al.—that seven of their eight patients required more than one surgery to complete clitoroplasty—suggests that multiple operations may be the rule rather than the exception (Allen et al. 1982). Innes-Williams 1981, p. 243.

45. Additional data on multiple surgeries follow: Randolf et al. 1981: 8 out of 37 required second operations to make clitoral recession "work." Lobe et al. 1987: 13 out of 58 patients required

more than two operations; it seems likely from their discussion that many more of the 58 required two operations, but the data are not given. Allen et al (1982): 7 out of 8 clitoroplasties needed additional surgery. Van der Kamp et al. (1982): 8 out of 10 patients required two or more surgeries. Sotiropoulos et al. 1976: 8 out of 13 early vaginoplasties required second operations. Jones and Wilkins (1961): 40 percent of patients required second surgery with vaginoplasties. Nihoul-Fekete et al. (1982) report 33 percent of their early vaginoplasties required later additional surgery. Newman et al. (1992a): 2 out of 9 required second recession operations; 1/9 required second vaginoplasty. Azziz et al. (1986): 30/78 repeat (second and third times) surgeries for vaginoplasties; success of vaginoplasties was only 34.3 percent when done on children younger than four years of age. Innes-Williams (1981) writing about operations for hypospadias: recommends for intersexes two operations and says that poor technique or poor wound healing can mean further (third or more) surgery. See also Alizai et al. 1999.

The number of surgeries can rise to as high as 20. In one study of 73 hypospadias patients the mean number of operations was 3.2, while the range ran from 1 to 20. See reports by Mureau, Slijper et al. 1995a, 1995b, 1995c.

46. Mulaikal et al. 1987.

47. The psychological results of hypospadias surgery may differ in different cultures. A series of studies done in the Netherlands, for example, where male circumcision is uncommon, found that dissatisfaction with genital appearance resulted in part from the circumcised appearance following hypospadias surgery (Mureau, Slijper et al. 1995a, 1995b, 1995c; Mureau 1997; Mureau et al. 1997). For an earlier study, see Eberle et al. (1993), who found persistent cases of sexual ambiguity (seen as a bad thing) in 11 percent of their hypospadias patients. Duckett found "this study most disturbing for those of us who offer an optimistic outlook for our patients with hypospadias" (Duckett 1993, p. 1,477).

48. Miller and Grant 1997. For more on the effects of hypospadias, see Kessler 1998, pp. 70–73.

49. Sandberg and Meyer-Bahlburg 1995. See also Berg and Berg 1983, who report increased

uncertainty about gender identity and masculinity but no increase in homosexuality among
men with hypospadias.

50. Slijper et al. 1998, p. 127.
51. Ibid.
52. Harmon-Smith, personal communication. For
    more on HELP and other support groups, con-
    sult the ISNA Web page: http://www.isna.org.
53. Harmon-Smith 1998. The full commandments
    are:

    1) DO NOT tell the family to not name "the
       child"! Doing so only isolates them, and
       makes them begin to see their baby as an
       "abnormality."
    2) DO encourage the family to call their
       child by a nickname (Honey, Cutie,
       Sweetie, or even "little one") or by a
       non-gender-specific name.
    3) DO NOT refer to the patient as "the child."
       Doing so makes parents begin to see their
       child as an object, not a person.
    4) DO call the patient by nickname/name cho-
       sen by the parents. It may be uncomfortable
       at first but will help the parents greatly. Ex-
       ample: "How is your little sweetie doing
       today?"
    5) DO NOT isolate the patient in a NICU.
       This scares the parents and makes them
       feel something is very wrong with
       their child. It isolates the family and
       prevents siblings, aunts, uncles and even
       grandparents from visiting and it starts a
       process within the family of treating the
       new member differently.
    6) DO allow the patient to stay on a regular
       ward. Admit patients to the children's wing,
       perhaps in a single room. Then visitors are
       allowed, and bonding within the family can
       begin.
    7) DO connect the family with an information
       or support group. There are many available:
       National Organization for Rare Disorders
       (NORD); Parent to Parent; HELP: AIS
       support group; Intersex Society of North
       America; even March of Dimes or Easter
       Seals.
    8) DO NOT isolate the family from informa-
       tion or support. Do not assume they will
       not understand or will be more upset if they

learn about other disorders or related problems. Let the parents decide what information they want or need. Encourage them to
seek out who can give them information
and share experiences.

    9) DO encourage the family to see a counselor
       or therapist. Do not only refer them to a
       genetic counselor; they will need emotional
       support as well as genetic information.
       Refer them to a family counselor, therapist
       or social worker familiar with family crisis
       intervention/therapy.
    10) DO NOT make drastic decisions in the
        first year. The parents need time to adjust
        to this individual child. They will need to
        understand the condition and what their
        specific child needs. Allow them time to get
        over being presented with new information
        and ideas. Let them understand that their
        child is not a condition that must conform to
        a set schedule but an individual. DO NOT
        schedule the first surgery before the patient
        even leaves the hospital. This will foster fear
        in the parents that this is life threatening and
        they have an abnormal or damaged child.

54. Kessler 1998, p. 129.
55. Young 1937, p. 154. For a more recent exam-
    ple, see several cases of parental refusal of sex
    reassignment following traumatic injury to their
    sons' penises in Gilbert et al. 1993.
56. Young 1937, p. 158.
57. Recently academics have begun to analyze the
    phenomenon of displaying extraordinary bodies
    as a form of public entertainment. For an entree
    into this literature, see Thomson 1996.
58. Kessler 1990.
59. Young 1937, p. 146.
60. Dewhurst and Gordon 1963, p. 77.
61. Randolf et al. 1981, p. 885.
62. Van der Kamp et al. 1992.
63. Bailez et al. 1992, p. 886. "A number of
    mothers reported their husbands were actually
    opposed to surgery," and they cite one patient
    whose surgery was postponed because the
    family wanted the child to participate in the
    decision-making process (Hendricks 1993).
    Migeon reports on others who stop taking
    medication that prevents virilization. Jones and
    Wilkins (1961) report a patient who accepted
    hysterectomy and mastectomy but refused

genital operations, even though he had to pee sitting down. Azziz et al. (1986) report on sixteen patients requiring repeat operations to achieve goal of comfortable intercourse, five never followed through on having them. Lubs et al. (1959) talk of a sixteen-year-old patient with genital abnormalities: "The family felt she should not be subject to further examination and would permit no studies to be carried out" (p. 1,113). Van Seters and Slob (1988) describe a case of micropenis in which the father refused surgery until the boy was old enough to decide for himself. Hurtig et al. (1983) discuss noncompliance with taking antimasculinizing drugs in two of four patients they studied. Hampson (1955) mentions a few parents who have refused recommendations of sex change surgery, "assured by their own thoroughgoing conviction of the boyness of their son or the girlness of their daughter" (p. 267). Beheshti et al. (1983) mention two cases in which parents refused gender reassignment.

64. Van Seters and Slob (1988). For more on the ability of children with micropenises, raised as males to adjust to the male sexual role, see Reilly and Woodhouse 1989.

65. Hampson and Hampson 1961, pp. 1,428–29; emphasis added.

66. Because of the small sample size, these numbers do not reach statistical significance, it could be random chance that the numbers came out this way. I expand upon my prejudice to the contrary in this paragraph.

67. Actually, this moment is already here, as the agendas of ISNA and other organizations attest.

68. Kessler 1998, p. 131.

69. Ibid., p. 40

70. Despite medical skepticism, ISNA's message is making inroads. A recent article from a nursing journal discussed ISNA's viewpoint and noted that "it is important to help parents focus on their infant as a whole rather than on the infant's condition. The nurse can emphasize a child's features that are unrelated to gender, such as 'what beautiful eyes the baby has,' or 'your baby has a nose just like daddy's' " (Parker 1998, p. 22). See also the editorial in the same issue (Haller 1998).

71. There is a significant and fascinating literature on transsexuality. See, for instance, Hausman

1992 and 1995; Bloom 1994; Bollin 1994; and Devor 1997.

72. Major work on transgender theory and practice includes Feinberg 1996 and 1998; Ekins and King 1997; Bornstein 1994 and Atkins 1998. Also, browse issues of the journal *Chrysalis: The Journal of Transgressive Gender Identities*.

73. Bolin 1994, pp. 461, 473.

74. Ibid., p. 484.

75. Rothblatt 1995, p. 115.

76. Lorber 1993, p. 571.

77. See also the discussion in chapter 1. Also, Herdt 1994a, b; Besnier 1994; Roscoe 1991 and 1994; Diedrich 1994; and Snarch 1992.

78. An ascetic sect, the Hijras are invested with the divine powers of the goddess; they dance and perform at the birth of male children and at marriages, and also serve the goddess at her temple (Nanda 1986, 1989, and 1994).

79. Without the enzyme the body cannot transform the hormone testosterone into a related form—dihydrotestosterone (DHT). In the embryo, DHT mediates the formation of the male external genitalia.

80. For a thorough recent review of the biology, see Quigley et al. 1995 and Griffin and Wilson 1989.

81. This form of androgen insensitivity is often misdiagnosed, and irreparable surgery, such as removal of the testes, is performed. When the potential difficulties go "unmanaged" until puberty, more satisfactory options are available for an affected individual. See the discussion on p. 1,929 of Griffin and Wilson 1989, and a case discussed in Holmes et al. 1992.

82. Herdt and Davidson 1988; Herdt 1990b and 1994a, b.

83. Herdt 1994, p. 429.

84. Kessler 1998, p. 90.

85. Press 1998.

86. Rubin 1984, p. 282.

87. Kennedy and Davis 1993.

88. Feinberg 1996, p. 125.

89. For a complete statement of the International Bill of Gender Rights, see pp. 165–169 of Feinberg 1996.

90. For a thorough and thoughtful treatment of the legal issues (which by extrapolation might apply to intersexuals), see Case 1995. For a discussion of how legal decisions construct the

heterosexual and homosexual subject, see Halley 1991, 1993, and 1994.

91. In Norton 1996, pp. 187–88.

92. As sex reassignment surgery became more common in the 1950s, doctors worried about their personal liability. Even though physicians obtained parental approval, could a child—upon reaching the age of majority—sue the surgeon "for charges ranging from malpractice to assault and battery or even mayhem"? Despite "this disagreeable quirk in the law," the worried physician writing this passage felt he ought not shrink from "handling these unfortunate children . . . in whatever way seems . . . to be most suitable and humane" (Gross and Meeker 1955, p. 321).

   In 1957, Dr. E. C. Hamblen, reiterating the fear of lawsuit, sought the aid of a law clinic at Duke University. One suggested solution, which never saw the light of day, was to set up state boards or commissions "on sex assignment or reassignment, comparable to boards of eugenics which authorize sterilization." Hamblen hoped such action could protect a physician whose position he feared "might be precarious, indeed, if legal action subsequently resulted in a jury trial" (Hamblen 1957, p. 1,240). After this early flurry of self-concern, the medical literature falls silent on the question of the patient's right to sue. Perhaps doctors have relied both on their near certainty that current medical approaches to intersexuality are both morally and medically correct and on the realization that the vast majority of their patients would never choose to go public about such intimate matters. In the post–Lorena Bobbit era, however, it seems only a matter of time until some medical professional confronts the civil claims of a genitally altered intersexual.

93. O'Donovan 1985. For an up-to-date review of the legal status of the intersexual, see Greenberg 1999.

94. O'Donovan 1985, p. 15; Ormrod 1992.

95. Edwards 1959, p. 118.

96. Halley 1991.

97. Ten Berge 1960, p. 118.

98. See de la Chapelle 1986; Ferguson-Smith et al. 1992; Holden 1992; Kolata 1992; Serrat and Garcia de Herreros 1993; Unsigned 1993.

99. I never would have guessed, when I first drafted this chapter in 1993, that in 1998 homosexual marriages would be on the ballots in two states. Although it lost in both cases, clearly the issue is now open to discussion. I believe it is a matter of time before the debate will be joined again, with different results.

100. Rhode Island repealed its antisodomy law in 1998, the same year that a similar law was found unconstitutional in the state of Georgia.

101. Reilly and Woodhouse 1989, p. 571; see also Woodhouse 1994.

TRANSGENDER BUTCH: BUTCH/FTM BORDER WARS AND THE MASCULINE CONTINUUM

Judith Halberstam

THE WRONG BODY

In 1995 the BBC broadcast a series called *The Wrong Body*. One episode in the series dealt with a young person called Fredd, a biological female, who claimed to have been born into the wrong body. Nine-year-old Fredd claimed that "she" was really a male and demanded that his family, friends, teachers, and other social contacts deal with him as a boy. The program followed Fredd's quest for gender reassignment over a period of three years until at age twelve, Fredd trembled on the verge of female puberty. Fredd expressed incredible anxiety about the possibility that his efforts to be resocialized as a male were to be thwarted by the persistence of the flesh, and he sought hormone-blocking drugs to stave off the onset of puberty and testosterone shots to produce desired male secondary characteristics in and on his body. The BBC program dealt with

Fredd's condition as a medical problem that presented certain ethical conundrums when it came to prescribing treatment. Should Fredd be forced to be a woman before he could decide to become a man? Could a twelve year old know enough about embodiment, gender, and sexuality to demand a sex change? What were the implications of Fredd's case for other seemingly commonplace cases of tomboyism?

Over the three-year period covered by the documentary, Fredd spent a considerable amount of time attending a child psychiatrist. We watched as Fredd carefully reeducated his doctor about the trials and tribulations of gender dysphoria and led his doctor through the protocols of gender reassignment, making sure that the doctor used the correct gender pronouns and refusing to allow the doctor to regender him as female. The doctor suggested at various moments that Fredd may be experiencing a severe stage of tomboy identification and that he may change his mind about his gender identity once his sexuality developed within a female adolescent growing spurt. Fredd firmly distinguished for the doctor between sexuality and gender and insisted that his sexual preference would make no difference to his sense of a core male gender identity. The doctor sometimes referred to Fredd by his female name and was calmly corrected as Fredd maintained a consistent and focused sense of himself as male and as a boy. Fredd's case made for a rivetting documentary, and although the BBC interviewers did not push in these directions, questions about childhood cross-identification, about the effects of visible transsexualities, and about early childhood gender selection all crowded in on the body of this young person. What gender is Fredd as he waits for his medical authorization to begin hormones? What kind of refusal of gender and what kind of confirmation of conventional gender does Fredd's battle with the medical authorities represent? Finally, what do articulations of the notion of a wrong body and the persistent belief in the possibility of a "right" body register

in relation to the emergence of other genders, transgenders?

In this essay, I take up some of the questions raised by contemporary discussions of transsexuality about the relations between identity, embodiment, and gender. In an extended consideration of the differences and continuities between transsexual, transgender, and lesbian masculinities, I approach the thorny questions of identity raised by the public emergence of the female-to-male transsexual (FTM) in the last decade or so. If some female-born people now articulate clear desires to become men, what is the effect of their transitions on both male masculinity and on the category of butch? What will be the effect of a visible transsexual population on young people who cross-identify? Will more tomboys announce their transsexual aspirations if the stigma is removed from the category?

In the last part of this century, the invention of transsexuality as a medical category has partly drained gender variance out of the category of homosexuality and located gender variance very specifically within the category of transsexuality. I want to analyze here the surprising continuities and unpredictable discontinuities between gender variance that retains the birth body (for example, butchness) and gender variance that necessitates sex reassignment. Medical descriptions of transsexuality throughout the last forty years have been preoccupied with a discourse of "the wrong body" that describes transsexual embodiment in terms of an error of nature whereby gender identity and biological sex are not only discontinuous but catastrophically at odds. The technological availabilities of surgeries to reassign gender have made the option of gender transition available to those who understand themselves to be tragically and severely at odds with their bodies, and particularly for male-to-female transsexuals (MTFS), these surgical transitions have been embraced by increasing numbers of gender-variant people. The recent visibility of female-to-male transsexuals has immensely complicated the discussions around transsexuality because gender transition from female to male allows biological women to access male privilege within their reassigned genders. Although few commentators would be so foolish as to ascribe FTM transition solely to the aspiration for mobility within a gender hierarchy, the fact is that gender reassignment for FTMS does have social and political consequences.

If we study the fault lines between masculine women and transsexual men, we discover, I point out, that as transsexual men become associated with real and desperate desires for reembodiment, so butch women become associated with a playful desire for masculinity and a casual form of gender deviance. Although homosexuality was removed from the DSM III manual in 1973, transsexuality remains firmly in the control of medical and psychological technologies.[1] However, all too often, such a fact is used to argue that more cultural anxiety focuses on the transsexual than on the homosexual. I believe that the confusing overlaps between some forms of transsexuality and some gender-deviant forms of lesbianism have created not only definitional confusion for so-called medical experts but also a strange struggle between FTMS and lesbian butches who accuse each other of gender normativity. I am attempting here to unravel some of the most complicated of these arguments.

I use the term "transgender butch" to describe a form of gender transitivity that could be crucial to many butches' sense of embodiment, sexual subjectivity, and even gender legitimacy. As the visibility of a transsexual community grows at the end of the twentieth century and as FTMS become increasingly visible within that community, questions about the viability of queer butch identities become unavoidable. Some lesbians seem to see FTMS as traitors to a "woman's" movement who cross over and become the enemy. Some FTMS see lesbian feminism as a discourse that has demonized FTMS and their masculinity. Some butches consider FTMS to be butches who believe in anatomy, and some FTMS consider butches to be FTMS who are too afraid to make the "transition" from female to male. The border wars between

transgender butches and FTMS presume that masculinity is a limited resource, available to only a few in ever decreasing quantities. Or else we see masculinity as a set of protocols that should be agreed on in advance. Masculinity, of course, is what we make it; it has important relations to maleness, increasingly interesting relations to transsexual maleness, and a historical debt to lesbian butchness. At least one of the issues I want to take up here is what model of masculinity is at stake in debates between butches and FTMS and what, if anything, separates butch masculinity from transsexual masculinities. I will examine some of the identifications that we have argued about (the stone butch in particular) and attempt to open dialogue between FTM and butch subject positions that allows for cohabitation in the territories of queer gender. I will also look at the language of these arguments and try to call attention to the importance of the metaphors of border, territory, crossing, and transitivity.

Recently, transsexual communities have become visible in many urban areas, and a transsexual activist response to transphobia (as separate from homophobia and not assimilable under the banner "queer") has animated demands for special health care considerations and legal rights. Although one might expect the emergence of transsexual activism to fulfill the promise of a "queer" alliance between sexual minorities by extending the definition of sexual minority beyond gay and lesbian, in fact there is considerable antipathy between gays and lesbians and transsexuals, and the term "queer" has not managed to bridge the divide. Whereas transsexuals seem suspicious of a gay and lesbian hegemony under the queer banner, gays and lesbians fear that some forms of transsexualism represent a homophobic restoration of gender normativity. But there is possibly another group in this standoff who maintain the utility of queer definition without privileging either side of the gay/lesbian versus transsexual divide. This group may be identified as transgender or gender-queer. The gender-queer position, often also called queer theory or postmodernism, has been cast in many different theoretical locations as the blithe opponent of the real, the player who fails to understand the life-and-death struggle around gender definition. While I contest such a characterization of the transgender position, I do want to consider what kind of symbolic burden we force on the transsexual body within postmodernism and how such bodies resist or defy the weight of signifying the technological constructions of otherness.

TRANSGENDER BUTCH

As a nontranssexual who has written about transsexuality, I would like to comment in this section about the important skirmishes between FTM and butch theorists, my role in those skirmishes, and the kinds of knowledge they produce.

In 1994 I published an essay called "F2M: The Making of Female Masculinity" in a volume called *The Lesbian Postmodern.*[2] The avowed intention of the article was to examine the various representations of transsexual bodies and transgender butch bodies that surfaced around 1990 to 1991, largely within lesbian contexts. The essay was speculative and concentrated on films, videos, and narratives about gender-ambiguous characters. Much to my surprise, the essay was regarded with much suspicion and hostility by some members of FTM International, a San Francisco-based transsexual men's group; these reactions caused me to look carefully at the kinds of assumptions I was making about transsexuality and about the kinds of continuities or overlaps that I presumed between the categories of FTM and butch. My intention here is not to apologize for that essay or simply to explain again my position; rather, I want to use the constructive criticism I received about that article to reconsider the various relations and nonrelations between FTM and butch subjectivities and bodies. Ultimately, I believe that "F2M" was actually trying to carve out a subject position that we might usefully call transgender butch to signify the transition that the identity requires from female identity to masculine embodiment. At present, the moniker "FTM" names a radical shift in both identity and body base within the context of transsexuality that by comparison makes "butch" look like a stable signifier. But the shifts and accommodations made in most cross-gender identifications, whether aided by surgery or hormones or not, involve a great deal of instability and transitivity. Transgender butch conveys some of this movement.

In "F2M," I attempted to describe the multiple versions of masculinity that seemed to be emerging simultaneously out of both lesbian and transsexual contexts. My project was not a fact-finding ethnography about FTM; nor did it examine the mechanics, trials, tribulations, benefits, and necessities of body alteration. Rather, I asked discursive and possibly naive questions such as: Why, in this age of gender transitivity, when many queers and feminists have agreed that gender is a social construct, is transsexuality a widespread phenomenon? Why has there been so little discussion of the shared experiences of masculine lesbians and FTMs? And, finally, why are we not in what Sandy Stone has called a "post-transsexual era"?[3] My questions presumed that some forms of transsexuality represented gender essentialism, but from this assertion, some people understood me to be saying that butchness was postmodern and subversive whereas transsexualism was dated and deluded. I think, rather, that I was trying to create a theoretical and cultural space for the transgender butch that did not presume transsexuality as its epistemological frame. I was also implicitly examining the possibility of the non-operated-upon transgender person.

My article was received, as I suggested, as a clumsy and ignorant attack on the viability of FTM transsexuality, and there was a small debate about it in the pages of the *FTM Newsletter.* The editor, James Green, took me to task for speaking for FTMS, and in a review essay, a writer called Isabella cast me in the role of the lesbian feminist who wanted transsexuals to disappear within some postmodern proliferation of queer identities.[4] Isabella noted that I focused on film and video in my essay (on representations, in other words, as opposed to "real" accounts), and she accused me of failing to integrate the real lives and words of "the successfully integrated post-op FTM" into my theory.[5] She went on to suggest that I was not interested in the reality of transsexuality because "it is the fluidity, the creation and dissolution of gender 'fictions' that is so fascinating" (14).

Another more recent article critiquing "F2M" also accused the essay of advocating some simple celebratory mode of border crossing. In "No Place like Home: The Transgendered Narrative of Leslie Feinberg's *Stone Butch Blues,*" Jay Prosser sets up "F2M" as a prime example of queer theory's fixation on the transgender body.[6] This article pits queer theory against transgender identity in a polemic: queer theory represents gender within some notion of postmodern fluidity and fragmentation, but transgender theory eschews such theoretical free fall and focuses instead on "subjective experience" (490). Queer theories of gender, in Prosser's account, emphasize the performative, and transgender theories emphasize narrative. Queer theories of gender are constructivist, and transgender theories are essentialist. Ultimately, Prosser proposes that transgender be separated from "genetic queerness" to build a transgender community (508).

My essay also found a supporter in the *FTM Newsletter.* Jordy Jones, an FTM performance artist from San Francisco, responded to some of the criticisms of my article by suggesting that the notion that I had advanced of gender as a fiction did not necessarily erase the real-life experiences of transsexuals; rather, he suggested, it describes the approximate relation between concepts and bodies.[7] Furthermore, Jones objected to the very idea that transsexual experience could be represented in any totalizing or universal way:

> Not everyone who experiences gender dysphoria experiences it in the same way, and not everyone deals with it in the same way. Not all transgendered individuals take hormones, and not everyone who takes hormones is transgendered. I have a

(genetically female) friend who identifies as male and passes perfectly. He's never had a shot. I certainly know dykes who are butcher than I could ever be, but who wouldn't consider identifying as anything other than women. (15)

Jones, eloquently and forcefully, articulates here the limits of a monolithic model of transsexuality. His description of the wild variability of masculinities and identifications across butch and transsexual bodies refuses any notion of a butch-FTM continuum on the one hand, but on the other hand, it acknowledges the ways in which butch and FTM bodies are read against and through each other for better or for worse. Jones's understanding of transgender variability produces an almost fractal model of cross-gender identifications that can never return to the binary models of before and after, or transsexual and nontranssexual, or butch and FTM.

Needless to say, I have learned a great deal from these various interactions and textual conversations, and I want to use them here to resituate "F2M: The Making of Female Masculinity" in terms of a continuing "border war," to use Gayle Rubin's term, between butches and FTMS. Here, I try again to create an interpretive model of transgender butchness that refuses to invest in the notion of some fundamental antagonism between lesbian and FTM subjectivities. This is not to ignore, however, the history of lesbian feminist opposition to transsexuals, which has been well documented by Sandy Stone. In "A Post-transsexual Manifesto," Stone shows how Janice Raymond and other feminists in the 1970s and 1980s (Mary Daly, for example) saw male-to-female transsexuals as phallocratic agents who were trying to infiltrate women-only space.[8] More recently, some lesbians have voiced their opposition to FTM transsexuals and characterized them as traitors and as women who literally become the enemy.[9] More insidiously, lesbians have tended to erase FTMS by claiming transsexual males as lesbians who lack access to a liberating lesbian discourse. So, for example, Billie Tipton, the jazz musician who lived his life as a man and who married a woman, is often represented within lesbian history as a lesbian woman forced to hide her gender to advance within his profession rather than as a transsexual man living within his chosen gender identity. In "The Politics of Passing," for example, Elaine K. Ginsberg rationalizes Tipton's life: "He lived his professional life as a man, presumably because his chosen profession was not open to women.[10] Many revisionist accounts of transgender lives rationalize them out of existence in this way or through the misuse of female pronouns and do real damage to the project of mapping transgender histories.

So while it is true that transgender and transsexual men have been wrongly folded into lesbian history, it is also true that the distinctions between some transsexual identities and some lesbian identities may at times become quite blurry. Many FTMS do come out as lesbians before they come out as transsexuals (many, it must also be said, do not). And for this reason alone, one cannot always maintain hard and fast and definitive distinctions between lesbians and transsexuals. In the collection *Dagger: On Butch Women,* for example, the editors include a chapter of interviews with FTMS as part of their survey of an urban butch scene.[11] The five FTMS in the interview testify to a period of lesbian identification. Shadow admits that "the dyke community's been really great, keeping me around for the last 12 years" (154); Mike says that he never really identified as female but that he did "identif[y] as a lesbian for a while" because "being a dyke gave me options" (155). Similarly, Billy claims that he feels neither male nor female but that he did "go through the whole lesbian separatist bullshit" (155). Like Shadow, Eric feels that for a while, "the lesbian place was really good for me" (156), and finally Sky suggests that although certain individuals in the dyke community are hostile to him, "I'm forty years old and I've been involved with dykes for nearly half my life. I'm not going to give that up" (158). Obviously, these FTM voices are quite particular and in no way represent a consensus or

even a dominant version of the relations between FTM and dyke communities. Also, these versions of FTM history have been carefully chosen to fit into a collection of essays about lesbian masculinities. However, these transgender men do articulate one very important line of affiliation between transsexualities and lesbian identities. Many transgender men, quite possibly, successfully identify as butch in a queer female community before they decide to transition. Once they have transitioned, many transsexual men want to maintain their ties to their queer lesbian communities. Much transsexual discourse now circulating tries to cast the lesbian pasts of FTMS as instances of mistaken identities or as an effort to find temporary refuge within some queer gender-variant notion of "butchness."[12]

In this FTM chapter of *Dagger,* just to complicate matters further, the transgender men also tell of finding the limits of lesbian identification. Billy, for one, hints at the kinds of problems some pretransition transgender men experience when they identify as lesbians. Billy recalls: "I've had this problem for ten years now with women being attracted to my boyishness and my masculinity, but once they get involved with me they tell me I'm too male" (156). Billy crosses the line for many of his lovers because he wants a real moustache and a real beard and does not experience his masculinity as temporary or theatrical. Billy's experience testifies to the ways in which masculinity within some lesbian contexts presents a problem when it becomes too "real," or when some imaginary line has been crossed between play and seriousness. This also makes lesbian masculinity sound like a matter of degree. Again, this kind of limited understanding of lesbian masculinity has a history within lesbian feminism. As many historians have pointed out, male identification was an accusation leveled at many butches in the early days of lesbian feminism, and so it is hardly surprising to find a residue of this charge in the kinds of judgments made against FTMS by lesbians in contemporary settings.[13] The real problem with this notion of

lesbian and transgender masculinities lies in the way it suggests a masculine continuum that looks something like this:
Androgyny—Soft Butch—Butch—Stone Butch — Transgender Butch—FTM Not Masculine———————————————Very Masculine.

Such a model clearly has no interpretive power when we return to Jordy Jones's catalog of transgender variety. For Jones, the intensity of masculinity was not accounted for by transsexual identification. Furthermore, as Jones points out, "not everyone who experiences gender dysphoria deals with it in the same way"; gender dysphoria can be read all the way along the continuum, and it would not be accurate to make gender dysphoria the exclusive property of transsexual bodies or to surmise that the greater the gender dysphoria, the likelier a transsexual identification. At the transgender end of the spectrum, the continuum model miscalculates the relation between bodily alteration and degree of masculinity; at the butch end, the continuum model makes it seem as if butchness is sometimes just an early stage of transsexual aspiration. Stone butchness, for example, is very often seen as a compromise category between lesbian and FTM and is therefore defined by sexual dysfunction rather than sexual practice. As a compromise category, stone butch may be seen as a last-ditch effort to maintain masculinity within female embodiment: the expectation, of course, is that such an effort will fail and the stone butch will become fully functional once she takes steps toward transitioning to be a transsexual man.

In the essay "Stone Butch Now" (as opposed to stone butch in the 1950s), Heather Findlay interviews stone butches about their various modes of gender and sexual identification. For the purposes of the article, stone butch occupies "a gray area" between lesbian and FTM.[14] One of Findlay's informants simply calls him/herself Jay and relates that s/he is considering transitioning.[15] Jay tries to define the difference between being stone and being transsexual: "As a stone butch you have a sense of humor about your discomfort in the

world. As an FTM, however, you lose that sense of humor. Situations that were funny suddenly get very tragic" (44). Obviously, in this comment, Jay already seems to be speaking from the perspective of an FTM. To do so, s/he must cast the stone butch as playful in comparison to the seriousness of the FTM transsexual. The stone butch laughs at her gender discomfort whereas the FTM finds his discomfort to be a source of great pain. The stone butch manages her gender dysphoria, according to such a model, but the FTM cannot. Again, these oppositions between FTM and butch come at the expense of a complex butch subjectivity and also work to totalize both categories in relation to a set of experiences. As other stone butches interviewed in the article attest, being stone may mean moving in and out of gender comfort and may mean a very unstable sense of identification with lesbianism or femaleness. To separate the category of FTM from the category of butch, Jay must assign butch to femaleness and FTM to maleness.

The places where the divisions between butch and FTM become blurry have less to do with the identity politics of lesbian feminism and more to do with embodiment. As Jordy Jones suggests, many individuals who take hormones may not be transgendered, and many transgendered men may not take hormones. In fact, although in "F2M" I tried to make visible some of the gender fictions that prop up contemporary gender binarism, in the disputes between different groups of queers, we see that the labels "butch" and "transsexual" mark another gender fiction, the fiction of clear distinctions. In "F2M" I used the refrain "There are no transsexuals. We are all transsexuals" to point to the inadequacy of such a category in an age of profound gender trouble. I recognize, of course, the real and particular history of the transsexual and of transsexual surgery, hormone treatment, and transsexual rights discourse. I also recognize that there are huge and important differences between genetic females who specifically identify as transsexual and genetic females who feel comfortable with female masculinity. There are real and physical differences between female-born men who take hormones, have surgery, and live as men and female-born butches who live some version of gender ambiguity. But there are also many situations in which those differences are less clear than one might expect, and there are many butches who pass as men and many transsexuals who present as gender ambiguous and many bodies that cannot be classified by the options transsexual and butch. We are not all transsexual, I admit, but many bodies are gender strange to some degree or another, and it is time to complicate on the one hand the transsexual models that assign gender deviance only to transsexual bodies and gender normativity to all other bodies, and on the other hand the hetero-normative models that see transsexuality as the solution to gender deviance and homosexuality as a pathological perversion.

FEMALE-TO-MALE

While many female-to-male transsexuals (FTMS) live out their masculinity in deliberately ambiguous bodies, many others desire complete transitions from female to male (and these people I will call transsexual males or transsexual men). Some of those transgender people who retain the label "FTM" (rather than becoming "men") have mastectomies and hysterectomies and take testosterone on a regular basis and are quite satisfied with the male secondary characteristics that such treatments produce. These transgender subjects are not attempting to slide seamlessly into manhood, and their retention of the FTM label suggests the emergence of a new gender position marked by this term. However, another strand of male transsexualism has produced a new discourse on masculinity that depends in part on startlingly conservative pronouncements about the differences between themselves and transgender butches. These conservative notions are betrayed in the tendency of some transsexual males to make distinct gender assignations to extremely and deliberately gender-ambiguous bodies, and this tendency has a history within transsexual male autobiography;

indeed, the denigration of the category "butch" is a standard feature of the genre.

In Mario Martino's autobiography *Emergence* (1977), Martino goes to great lengths to distinguish himself from lesbians and from butches in particular as he negotiates the complications of pretransition identifications. Before his transition, Mario falls in love with a young woman; s/he tells the girlfriend, Becky: "You and I are not lesbians. We relate to each other as man to woman, woman to man."[16] One day, Becky comes home from work and asks: "Mario, what's a butch?" (141). Mario writes, "I could actually feel my skin bristle" (141). Becky tells Mario that the head nurse on the ward where Becky works asked her about her "butch," and in effect she wants to know the difference between Mario and a butch. Mario gives her a simple answer: "A butch is the masculine member of a lesbian team. That would make you the feminine member. But, Becky, honest-to-God, I don't feel that we're lesbians. I still maintain I should have been a male" (141). Becky seems satisfied with the answer, but the question itself plagues Mario long into the night: "The word *butch* magnified itself before my eyes. *Butch* implied female—and I had never thought of myself as such" (142). In *Emergence,* lesbianism haunts the protagonist and threatens to swallow his gender specificity and disallow his transsexuality. Unfortunately, as we see in the passages I have quoted, Martino's efforts to disentangle his maleness from lesbian masculinity tend to turn butchness into a stable female category and tend to overemphasize the differences between butch womanhood and transsexual manhood.

Another transsexual autobiography also magnifies the gulf between butch and transsexual male to markout the boundaries of transsexual masculinity. In *Dear Sir or Madam,* Mark Rees obsessively marks out his difference from lesbians. On attending a lesbian club before transition, sometime in the early 1960s, he feels assured in his sense of difference because, he notes, "the women there didn't want to be men; they were happy in their gender role."[17] He goes on to identify lesbianism in terms of two feminine women whose attraction is based on sameness, not difference. It is hard to imagine what Rees thinks he saw when he entered the lesbian bar. In the 1960s, butch-femme would still have been a cultural dominant in British lesbian bar culture, and it is unlikely that the scene that presented itself to Rees was a kind of "Bargirls" scene of lipstick lesbians. What probably characterized the scene before him was an array of gender-deviant bodies in recognizable butch-femme couplings. Because he needs to assert a crucial difference between himself and lesbians, Rees tries to deny the possibility of cross-identifying butch women.

In his desperation to hold the terms "lesbian" and "transsexual" apart, however, Rees goes one step further than just making lesbianism into a category for women who were "happy in their gender role." He also marks out the difference in terms of sexual aim as well as sexual and gender identity; he focuses, in other words, on the partner of the transsexual male for evidence of the distinctiveness of transsexual maleness. Rees claims to find a medical report confirming that lesbians and transsexuals are totally different. The report suggests that transsexuals "do not see themselves as lesbians before treatment, hate their partners seeing their bodies. It added that the partners of female-to-males are normal heterosexual women, not lesbians, and see their lovers as men, in spite of their lack of a penis. The partners were feminine, many had earlier relations with genetic males and often experienced orgasms with their female-to-male partners for the first time" (*Dear Sir or Madam,* 59). This passage should signal some of the problems attendant on this venture of making transsexual man and transgender butch into totally separate entities. Although one is extremely sympathetic to the sense of being misidentified, the need to stress the lack of identification inevitably leads to a conservative attempt to reorder the sex and gender categories that are in danger of becoming scrambled. Here Rees attempts to locate difference in the desires of the transsexual male's partner and unwittingly makes

a distinction between these women as "normal heterosexual women" and lesbians. Lesbianism suddenly becomes a category of pathology next to the properly heterosexual and gender-normative aims of the transsexual man and his feminine partner. Furthermore, this "normal heterosexual woman" finds her perfect mate in the transsexual man and indeed, we are told, often experiences orgasm with him "for the first time."

Rees's categorical distinctions between lesbians and partners of transsexual men and both his and Martino's horror of the slippage between homosexual and transsexual also echo in various informal bulletins that circulate on transsexual discussion lists on the Internet. In some bulletins, transsexual men send each other tips on how to pass as a man, and many of these tips focus almost obsessively on the care that must be taken by the transsexual man not to look like a butch lesbian. Some tips tell guys[18] to dress preppy as opposed to the standard jeans and leather jacket look of the butch; in other instances, transsexual men are warned against certain haircuts (punk styles or crew cuts) that are supposedly popular among butches. These tips, obviously, steer the transsexual man away from transgression or alternative masculine styles and toward a conservative masculinity. One wonders whether another list of tips should circulate advising transsexual men of how not to be mistaken for straight, or worse a Republican or a banker. Most of these lists seem to place no particular political or even cultural value on the kinds of masculinity they mandate.[19]

Finally, in relation to the conservative project of making concrete distinctions between butch women and transsexual males, such distinctions all too often serve the cause of hetero-normativity by consigning homosexuality to pathology and by linking transsexuality to a new form of heterosexuality. In a popular article on transsexual men that appeared in the *New Yorker,* for example, reporter Amy Bloom interviews several transsexual men and some sex reassignment surgeons to try to uncover the motivations and mechanics of so-called "high intensity transsexualism."[20]

Bloom comments on the history of transsexual-ism, the process of transition, and the multiple, highly invasive surgeries required for sex reas-signment from female to male. She interviews a young white transsexual male who sees his trans-sexualism as a birth defect that needs correction and several older white transsexual males, one Latino transsexual man, and one black trans-sexual man, who have varying accounts of their gender identities. Bloom spends much time de-tailing the looks of the men she interviews: a young transsexual man, Lyle, is "a handsome, shaggy graduating senior," and James Green is a chivalrous man with a "Jack Nicholson smile" (40); Loren Cameron is "a not uncommon type of handsome, cocky, possibly gay man" with "a tight, perfect build" (40); Luis is a "slightly built, gentle South American man" (40). So what, you might think, these are some important descrip-tions of what transsexual men look like. They look, in fact, like other men, and Bloom quickly admits that she finds herself in flirtatious hetero-sexual dynamics with her charming companions, dynamics that quickly shore up the essential dif-ferences between men and women. Bloom, for example, reports that she was sitting in her rental car with James Green and could not find the dim-mer switch for the headlights; when James finds it for her, she comments: "He looks at me exactly as my husband has on hundreds of occasions: af-fectionate, pleased, a little charmed by this blind spot of mine" (40). Later, over dinner with Green, she notices: "He does not say, 'Gee, this is a lot of food,' or anything like that. Like a man he just starts eating" (40).

Bloom's descriptions of her interviewees and her accounts of her interactions with them raise questions about mainstream attitudes toward male transsexuals versus mainstream attitudes toward masculine lesbians. Would Bloom, in a similar ar-ticle on butch lesbians, comment so approvingly on their masculinity? Would she notice a woman's muscular build, another butch's wink, another's "Jack Nicholson smile"? Would she be aware of their eating habits, their mechanical aptitudes? The

answer, of course, is a resounding "no," and indeed I find confirmation for my suspicions further down the page. Bloom reflects on her meetings with these handsome transsexual men as follows:

> I expected to find psychologically disturbed, male-identified women so filled with self-loathing that it had even spilled into their physical selves, lead-ing them to self-mutilating, self-punishing surgery. Maybe I would meet some very butch lesbians, in ties and jackets and chest binders, who could not, would not accept their female bodies. I didn't meet these people. I met men. (41)

What a relief for Bloom that she was spared inter-action with those self-hating masculine women and graced instead by the dignified presence of men! Posttransition, we must remember at all times, many transsexual men become heterosex-ual men, living so-called normal lives, and for folks like Amy Bloom, this is a cause for some celebration.

In her interaction with a black transsexual man, Bloom asks questions that actually raise some interesting issues, however. Michael, un-like James and Loren, is not part of an urban FTM community; he lives a quiet and somewhat secre-tive life and shies away from anything that may reveal his transsexuality. Michael finds a degree of acceptance from his family and coworkers and strives for nothing more than this tolerance. He articulates his difference from some other transsexuals:

> I was born black. I don't expect people to like me, to accept me. Some transsexuals, especially the white MTF's—they're in shock after the transition. Loss of privilege, loss of status; they think people should be thrilled to work side by side with them. Well, people do not go to work in mainstream America hoping for an educational experience. I didn't expect anyone to be happy to see me—I just expected, I demanded a little tolerance. (49)

Michael is the only person in the whole article to mention privilege and the change in social status experienced by transsexuals who pass. He clearly identifies the differences between transsexuals in terms of race and class, and he speaks of lowered expectations on account of a lifetime of experiencing various forms of intolerance. Bloom makes little comment on Michael's testimony, and she does not make a connection between what he says and what the other white men say. But Michael's experience is crucial to the politics of transsexualism. In America there is a huge difference between becoming a black man or a man of color and becoming a white man, and these differences are bound to create gulfs within transsexual communities and will undoubtedly resonate in the border wars between butches and transsexual men. The politics of transsexuality, quite obviously, reproduce other political struggles in other locations, and while some transsexuals find strength in the notion of identity politics, others find their identities and loyalties divided by their various affiliations. As in so many other identity-based activist projects, one axis of identification is a luxury most people cannot afford.

We are presently in the midst of a "reverse discourse" of transsexuality. In *The History of Sexuality,* Michel Foucault analyzes the strategic production of sexualities and sexual identities, and he proposes a model of a "reverse discourse" to explain the web of relations between power, discourse, sexuality, and resistance. He argues that resistance is always already embedded in power "as an irreducible opposite" and that therefore resistance cannot come from an outside; the multiplicity of power means that there is no opposite, no site of resistance where power has not already been.[21] There is, Foucault suggests, a "reverse discourse" in which one empowers a category that might have been used to oppress one—one transforms a debased position into a challenging presence. As a reverse discourse takes shape around the definitions of transsexual and transgender, it is extremely important to recognize the queerness of these categories, their instability and their interpretability. While identity obviously continues to be the best basis for political organizing, we have seen within various social movements

of the last decade that identity politics must give way to some form of coalition if a political movement is to be successful. The current discourse in some transsexual circles, therefore, of setting up gay and lesbian politics and communities as the enemy to transgender definition is as pernicious as the gay and lesbian tendencies to ignore the specificities of transsexual political needs and demands.[22] Furthermore, the simple opposition of transsexual versus gay and lesbian masks many other lines of affiliation and coalition that already exist within multiple queer communities: it masks, for example, that the gay/lesbian versus transsexual/transgender opposition is very much a concern in white queer contexts but not necessarily in queer communities of color. Many immigrant queer groups have successfully integrated transgender definition into their conceptions of community.[23]

THE RIGHT BODY?

My intent is not to vilify male transsexualism as simply a reconsolidation of dominant masculinity. But I do want to point carefully to the places where such a reconsolidation threatens to take place. In academic conversations, transsexualism has been used as both the place of gender transgression and the marker of gender conservatism. Obviously, transsexualism is neither essentially transgressive nor essentially conservative, and perhaps it becomes a site of such contestation because it is not yet clear what the politics of transsexualism will look like. Indeed, the history of FTM transsexuality is still being written, and as FTM communities emerge in urban settings, it becomes clear that their relations to the history of medicine, the history of sexuality, and the history of gender are only now taking shape. One attempt to chart this history in relation to a more general history of transsexualism and medical technology reveals what we might call the essentially contradictory politics of transsexualism. In *Changing Sex,* Bernice Hausman meticulously details the dependence of the category "transsexual" on medical technologies and in turn the dependence of the very concept of gender on the emergence of the transsexual. Several times in the book, Hausman rejects the notion that we can read gender as an ideology without also considering it as a product of technological relations. This argument marks a crucial contribution to the study of gender and technology, but unfortunately Hausman quite simply tends to attribute too much power to the medical configuration of transsexual definition. She claims that the transsexual and the doctor codependently produce transsexual definitions and that therefore transsexual agency can be read "through their doctor's discourses." She develops this notion of an interdependent relationship between transsexuals and medical technology to build to a rather astounding conclusion:

> By demanding technological intervention to "change sex," transsexuals demonstrate that their relationship to technology is a dependent one . . . demanding sex change is therefore part of what constructs the subject as a transsexual: it is the mechanism through which transsexuals come to identify themselves under the sign of transsexualism and construct themselves as subjects. Because of this we can read transsexuals' agency through their doctor's discourses, as the demand for sex change was instantiated as the primary symptom (and sign) of the transsexual.[24]

Sex change itself has become a static signifier in this paragraph, and no distinction is upheld between FTM sex change and MTF sex change. No power is granted to the kinds of ideological commitments that doctors may have that influence their thinking about making vaginas versus making penises, and because sex change rhetoric has been mostly used in relation to MTF bodies, the FTM and his relation to the very uncertain process of sex change, demanding sex change, and completing sex change is completely lost.

Hausman's book, I should stress, is careful and historically rich and will undoubtedly change the way that gender is conceived in relation to transsexual and nontranssexual bodies. But the particular border wars between butches and transsexual

men that concern me both here and in my earlier essay have been lost in a study of this kind. Future studies of transsexuality and of lesbianism must attempt to account for historical moments when the difference between gender deviance and sexual deviance is hard to discern.[25] The history of inversion and of people who identified as inverts (Radclyffe Hall, for example) still represents a tangle of cross-identification and sexual preference that is neither easily separated nor comfortably accounted for under the heading of "lesbian." There is not, furthermore, one history to be told here (the history of medical technology) about one subject (the transsexual). There are many histories of bodies that escape and elude medical taxonomies, of bodies that never present themselves to the physician's gaze, of subjects who identify within categories that emerge as a consequence of sexual communities and not in relation to medical or psychosexual research.

Because these categories are so difficult to disentangle, perhaps, a new category has emerged in recent years, "transgender." Transgender describes a gender identity that is at least partially defined by transitivity but that may well stop short of transsexual surgery. Inevitably, the term becomes a catchall, and this somewhat lessens its effect. Toward the end of her book, Hausman attempts to stave off criticisms of her work that may be based on an emergent notion of transgenderism. She acknowledges that transgender discourse seems to counter her claims that transsexuals are produced solely within medical discourse and that this discourse actually suggests "a fundamental antipathy to the regulatory mode of medical surveillance" (*Changing Sex,* 195). Hausman manages to discount such an effect of transgender discourse by arguing that "the desire to celebrate and proliferate individual performances as a way to destabilize 'gender' at large is based on liberal humanist assumptions of self-determination" (197). This is an easy dismissal of a much more complicated and ongoing project. Transgender discourse in no way argues that people should just pick up new genders and eliminate old ones or proliferate at will because gendering is available as a self-determining practice; rather, transgender discourse asks only that we recognize the nonmale and nonfemale genders already in circulation and presently under construction.

BORDER WARS

Because the production of gender and sexual deviance takes place in multiple locations (the doctor's office, the operating room, the sex club, the bedroom, the bathroom) and because the discourses to which gender and sexual deviance are bound also emerge in many different contexts (medical tracts, queer magazines, advice columns, films and videos, autobiographies), the categories of transsexual, transgender, and butch are constantly under construction. However, in the border wars between butches and transsexual men, transsexuals are often cast as those who cross borders (of sex, gender, bodily coherence), and butches are left as those who stay in one place, possibly a border space of nonidentity. The terminology of "border war" is both apt and problematic for this reason. On the one hand, the idea of a border war sets up some notion of territories to be defended, ground to be held or lost, permeability to be defended against. On the other hand, a border war suggests that the border is at best slippery and permeable. As I mentioned earlier, in "No Place like Home," Prosser critiques queer theory for fixing on "the transgendered crossing in order to denaturalize gender" (484), and he claims that queer border crossing positions itself against "the homeliness of identity politics" (486). For Prosser, such a move leaves the transsexual man with no place to go and leaves him languishing in the "uninhabitable space—the borderlands in between, where passing as either gender might prove quite a challenge" (488–89). Whereas queers might celebrate the space in between, Prosser suggests, the transsexual rushes onward to find the space beyond, "the promise of home on the other side"

(489). "Home," as one might imagine in relation to Prosser's model, is represented as the place in which one finally settles into the comfort of one's true and authentic gender.

Prosser thinks that queer theory (specifically, actually, my earlier essay "F2M") celebrates the in-between space as full of promise and "freedom and mobility for the subject" ("No Place like Home," 499), whereas transsexual theory embraces place, location, and specificity. The queer butch, in other words, represents fluidity to the transsexual man's stability, and stability (staying in a female body) to the transsexual man's fluidity (gender crossing). Prosser makes little or no recognition of the trials and tribulations that confront the butch who for whatever reasons (concerns about surgery or hormones, feminist scruples, desire to remain in a lesbian community, lack of funds, lack of successful phalloplasty models) decides to make a home in the body with which she was born. Even more alarming, he makes little or no recognition of the fact that many FTMS also live and die in those inhospitable territories in between. It is true that many transsexuals do transition to go somewhere, to be somewhere, and to leave geographies of ambiguity behind. However, many post-op MTFS are in between because they cannot pass as women; many FTMS who pass fully clothed have bodies that are totally ambiguous; some transsexuals cannot afford all the surgeries necessary to full sex reassignment (if there is such a thing), and these people make their home where they are; some transsexual folks do not define their transsexuality in relation to a strong desire for penises or vaginas, and they may experience the desire to be trans or queer more strongly than the desire to be male or female.

If the borderlands are uninhabitable for some transsexuals who imagine that home is just across the border, imagine what a challenge they present to those subjects who do not believe that such a home exists, either metaphorically or literally. Prosser's cartography of gender relies on a belief in the two territories of male and female, divided by a flesh border and crossed by surgery and endocrinology. The queer cartography that he rejects prefers the charting of hybridity: queer hybridity is far from the ludic and giddy mixing that Prosser imagines and more of a recognition of the dangers of investing in comforting but tendentious notions of home. Some bodies are never at home, some bodies cannot simply cross from A to B, some bodies recognize and live with the inherent instability of identity.

So far, I have noted the ways in which transsexual males and butch lesbians regard each other with some suspicion and the ways in which the two categories blur and separate. I have argued against stable and coherent definitions of sexual identity and tried to suggest the ways in which the lines between the transsexual and the gender-deviant lesbian inevitably crisscross each other and intersect, even producing a new category: transgender. I want to turn now to the rhetoric itself in the debate between transsexuals and butches to try to identify some of the dangers in demanding discrete and coherent sexual and gender identities. Much of the rhetoric surrounding transsexualism plays with the sense of transitivity and sees transsexuality as a passage or journey. Along the way, predictably enough, borders are crossed, and one leaves a foreign country to return, as we saw in Prosser's essay, to the home of one's true body.

If we return for the moment to the BBC series *The Wrong Body,* it offers an interesting example of the power of this kind of rhetoric. In one remarkable confrontation between Fredd and his psychiatrist, the psychiatrist used an extended simile to try to express his understanding of the relation of Fredd's female and male gender identities. He said: "You, Fredd, are like someone who has learned to speak French perfectly and who immigrates to France and lives there as a Frenchman. But just because you speak French and learn to imitate Frenchness and live among French people, you are still English." Fredd countered with: "No, I don't just speak French having moved there, I AM French." In this exchange, the doctor deploys what has become a common metaphor for transsexualism as a crossing of national borders from one place to another, from one state to another, from one gender to another. Fredd rejects such a rhetorical move and insists that his expression of his boy self is not a transition but rather the expression of a self that he has always inhabited. That Fredd is young and indeed preadolescent allows him to articulate his transsexualism very differently from many adult transsexuals. He is passing into manhood not from one adult body to another but from an almost pregendered body into a fully gendered male body. The rhetoric of passing and crossing and transitioning has only a limited use for him.

Metaphors of travel and border crossings are inevitable within a discourse of transsexuality. But they are also laden with the histories of other identity negotiations, and they carry the burden of national and colonial discursive histories. What does it mean, then, to discuss gender variance and gender transitivity as a journey from one country to another or from a foreign country toward home or from illegal status to naturalized citizenship? How useful or how limiting are metaphors of the border and crossing and belonging to questions of gender identity? How does gender transitivity rely on the stability of other identity markers?

Within discussions of postmodernism, the transsexual body has often come to represent contradictory identity per se in the twentieth century and has been discussed using precisely the rhetoric of colonialism. Whereas Janice Raymond identified the transsexual body in 1979 as part of a patriarchal empire intent on colonizing female bodies and feminist souls,[26] Sandy Stone responded in her "Posttranssexual Manifesto" by allowing the "empire" to "strike back" and calling for a "counterdiscourse" within which the transsexual might speak as transsexual. Whereas Bernice Hausman reads transsexual autobiographies as evidence that to a certain extent "transsexuals are the dupes of gender,"[27] Jay Prosser sees these narratives as "driven by the attempt to realize the fantasy of belonging in the sexed body and the world."[28] Many contemporary discussions of plastic surgery and body manipulation take transsexuality as a privileged signifier of the productive effects of body manipulation, and many theories of postmodern subjectivity understand the fragmentation of the body in terms of a paradigmatic transsexuality. Transsexuality, in other words, seems burdened not only by an excess of meaning but also by the weight of contradictory and competing discourses. If we sort through the contradictions, we find transsexuals represented as "empire" and the subaltern, as gender dupes and gender deviants, and as consolidated identities and fragmented bodies.

Jay Prosser, as we saw, critiques postmodern queer theory in particular for fixing on "the transgendered crossing in order to denaturalize gender" ("No Place like Home," 484), and he claims that queer affirmations of the "trans journey" celebrate "opposition to a narrative centered upon home" (486). Female-to-male transsexual theorist Henry Rubin provides an even more polarized opposition than the queer versus transgender split produced by Prosser. For Rubin, the division that is most meaningful is between transsexuals and transgenders: "Although it is often assumed that 'transgender' is an umbrella term that refers to cross-dressers, drag queens, butch dykes, gender blenders, and transsexuals, among others, there is a tension between transsexual and transgenders."[29] For Rubin, the tension lies between the transsexual's quest for "home,' a place of belonging to one sex or the other," and the transgender quest for "a world without gender" (7). According to such logic, the transgender person is just playing with gender and trying to deconstruct the naturalness of gender, but the transsexual bravely reaffirms the notion of stable gender and fortifies the reality of biology. The people who fall under the "umbrella" of transgender definition represent for Rubin a nonserious quest for gender instability that comes at the expense of a transsexual quest for "a place of belonging." To hold up what might seem an unlikely division between transgender and transsexual, Rubin models his argument on the various debates about lesbian identity. In the

1970s, it became quite common for women to call themselves "lesbian" as a mark of solidarity rather than a statement of sexual practice, and Rubin suggests that transgenders are like political lesbians. Again, such an argument collapses the historical differences between the lesbian sex debates and contemporary identity skirmishes, and it also renders transgenders as well-meaning, but transsexuals as the real thing.

The contradictions of cross-identification and its mobilities are further exemplified in a highly renowned autobiographical transsexual text, Jan Morris's *Conundrum*. Jan Morris was at one time known as James Morris, a travel writer and, in the 1950s, foreign correspondent for the *London Times*. Morris uses her skills as a travel writer to take the metaphor of travel and migration to its logical end in relation to questions of gender transition. She describes every aspect of her transition from male to female as a journey and characterizes not only gender identity in terms of countries but also national identities in terms of gender. "I was a child of imperial times," writes Morris at one point to explain her impression of "Black Africa" as "everything I wanted not to be."[30] While cities like Venice represent the feminine (and therefore a desired female self) to the pretranssexual James Morris, Black Africa represents a masculinity that scares him because it is "alien" and "vicious." In this transsexual autobiography, the space in between male and female is represented as monstrous. Jan Morris describes herself between genders as "a kind of nonhuman, a sprite or monster" (114), and the space of gender is described as "identity itself."

Morris, world traveler and travel writer, understands national identity in much the same way that she understands gender identity; national identities are stable, legible, and all established through the ruling consciousness of empire. Accordingly, Morris collates different reactions to her gender ambiguity according to country: "Americans," she tells us, "generally assumed me to be female" (111); however, in a manner reminiscent of a whole history of colonial travel narratives, Morris tells us casually: "Among the guileless people, the problem was minimal. They simply asked. After a flight from Darjeeling to Calcutta, for instance, during which I had enjoyed the company of an Indian family, the daughter walked over to me at the baggage counter and asked . . . 'whether you are a boy or a girl' " (111). In her essay on transsexuality, Sandy Stone does mention the "Oriental" quality of Morris's travel narrative, and Marjorie Garber upgrades this assessment to "Orientalist" in her discussion of Morris's description of her sex change in Casablanca. In general, however, there has been little consideration of this transsexual autobiography as a colonial artifact, as, indeed, a record of a journey that does not upend either gender conventionality or the conventions of the travelogue.[31] Ultimately, *Conundrum* is a rather unremarkable modernist narrative about the struggle to maintain identity in the face of a crumbling empire. It is, paradoxically, a narrative of change that struggles to preserve the status quo. I want to stress that Morris's narrative in no way represents "*the* transsexual autobiography." Plenty of other transsexual fictions and autobiographies contradict Morris's travelogue, and many such narratives combine a profound sense of dislocation with a brave attempt to make do with the status of unbelonging. The narrative of the female-to-male transsexual, furthermore, differs in significant ways from, and in no way mirrors, the narrative of the male-to-female. Morris's book serves less as a representative narrative and more as a caution against detaching the metaphors of travel and home and migration from the actual experience of immigration in a world full of borders.

Indeed, we might do well to be wary of such a unidirectional politics of home and of such divisions between sexual minorities. As Fredd's story shows, transsexuality requires often long periods of transition, periods within which one must live between genders. The place where transgender ends and transsexual begins is not as clear as either Morris's text or Rubin's essay

assumes, and the spaces between genders, which some queer theory claims, do not represent giddy zones of mobility and freedom but represent lives reconciled to gender, queerness and bodies committed to making do with the essential discomforts of embodiment. Although the language of home and location in Prosser's and Henry Rubin's essays sounds unimpeachable, as in the Morris text, there is little or no recognition here of the danger of transposing an already loaded conceptual frame—place, travel, location, home, borders—onto another contested site. In *Conundrum,* the equation of transsexuality with travel, and gender with place, produced a colonialist narrative in which both gender identity and national identity are rendered immutable and essential. Of the male, Morris writes: "It is this feeling of unfluctuating control, I think, that women cannot share, and it springs of course not from the intellect or the personality . . . but specifically from the body" (82). On becoming female, she comments: "My body then was made to push and initiate, it is made now to yield and accept, and the outside change has had its inner consequences" (153). The politics of home for Morris are simply the politics of colonialism, and the risk of essentialism that she takes by changing sex turns out to be no risk at all. The language that Prosser and Rubin use to defend their particular transsexual project from queer appropriations runs the risk not only of essence and even colonialism but, in their case, of using the loaded language of migration and homecoming to ratify new, distinctly unqueer models of manliness.

Analyses of transsexual subjectivity by critics such as Prosser and Rubin, I am arguing, are implicated in the colonial framework that organizes Morris's account of transsexuality, if only because both texts seem unaware of the discussions of borders and migration that have raged in other theoretical locations. In Chicano/a studies and postcolonial studies in particular, the politics of migration have been fiercely debated, and what has emerged is a careful refusal of the dialectic of home and border. If home has represented the comfort of place and the politics of location and the stability of belonging within such a dialectic, the border has stood for the politics of displacement, the hybridity of identity and the economics of undocumented labor. There is little to be gained theoretically or materially from identifying either home or border as the true place of resistance. In the context of a discussion of Asian American theater, Dorinne Kondo notes "home for many people on the margins is what we cannot not want."[32] In this context, home represents the belated construction of a safe haven in the absence of such a place in the present or the past. Home becomes a mythic site, a place to anchor some racial and ethnic identities even as those identities are wrenched out of context or pressured into assimilation. But for the queer subject, or what Gloria Anzaldúa calls the border dweller, home is what the person living in the margins cannot want: "She leaves the familiar and safe home ground to venture into the unknown and possibly dangerous terrain. This is her home/ this thin edge of/of barbwire."[33] Clearly, home can be a fantasy space, a remembered place of stable origin and a nostalgic dream of community; it can as easily be a space of exclusion whose very comforts depend on the invisible labor of migrant border dwellers. To move back to the debate around transsexualism and queers, the journey home for the transsexual may come at the expense of a recognition that others are permanently dislocated.

When nine-year-old Fredd rejects his doctor's simile of naturalized citizenship for his transsexual condition, Fredd rejects both the history of the rhetorical containment of transsexuality within conventional medical taxonomies and a recent attempt to translate the rhetoric of transsexuality into the language of home and belonging. Fredd does not, however, reject the popular formulation of being a "boy trapped in a girl's body," and he holds on to his fantasy of male adulthood even as his body begins to betray him. We might do well to work on other formulations of gender and body, right body, and right gender to provide

children such as Fredd, queer cross-identifying children, with futures and bodies that seem habitable. Obviously, the metaphor of crossing over and indeed migrating to the right body from the wrong body merely leaves the politics of stable gender identities, and therefore stable gender hierarchies, completely intact. The BBC program avoided the more general questions raised by the topic of transsexuality by emphasizing Fredd's individual needs and his urgent desire for maleness. When Fredd was shown in dialogue with other transsexual men, the group as a whole expressed their desire simply to be "normal" boys and men and to live like other male subjects. None of the group expressed homosexual desires, and all expected to live "normal lives" in the future once their sex reassignment surgery was complete.

Transsexuality currently represents an immensely complicated web of identifications and embodiments and gendered phenomena and cannot reduce down to Fredd's narrative of prepubescent angst or Jan Morris's narrative of colonial melancholy. However, as "transgender" becomes a popularly recognized term for cross-identification, the sexual politics of transgenderism and transsexualism must be carefully considered. Because much of the discussion currently circulates around the male-to-female experience of transsexuality, we have yet to consider the gender politics of transitioning from female to male. In this section, I have tried to argue that wholesale adoptions of the rhetoric of home and migration within some transsexual aesthetic practices alongside the rejection of a queer border politics can have the uncanny effect of using postcolonial rhetorics to redeem colonial texts (such as Morris's) or of using formulations of home and essence advanced by feminists of color to ratify the location of white transsexual men. Such rhetoric also assumes that the proper solution to "painful wrong embodiment" (Prosser) is moving to the right body, where "rightness" may as easily depend on whiteness or class privilege as it does on being regendered. Who, we might ask, can afford to dream of a right body? Who believes that such a body exists? Finally, as long as migration and borders and home remain metaphorical figures within such discourse, transsexuals and transgendered people who actually are border dwellers or who really do work as undocumented laborers or who really have migrated from their homelands never to return must always remain just outside discourse, invisible and unrecognized, always inhabiting the wrong body.

CONCLUSION

As Gayle Rubin remarks in her essay on the varieties of butchness: "Butches vary in how they relate to their female bodies" ("Thinking Sex," 470). She goes on to show that "forms of masculinity are molded by experiences and expectations of class, race, ethnicity, religion, occupation, age, subculture, and individual personality" (470). Rubin also casts the tensions between butches and FTMS as border wars (she calls them "frontier fears") and notes that the border between these two modes of identification is permeable at least in part because "no system of classification can successfully catalogue or explain the infinite vagaries of human diversity" (473). Rubin's conclusion in this essay advocates gender and sexual (and other kinds of) diversity not only as a political strategy but as simply the only proper response to the enormous range of masculinities and genders that we produce.

I also want to argue against monolithic models of gender variance that seem to emerge from the loaded and intense discussions between and among transgender butches and transsexual males at present, and I also want to support some call for diversity. However, at the same time, it is important to stress that not all models of masculinity are equal, and as butches and transsexuals begin to lay claims to the kinds of masculinities they have produced in the past and are generating in the present, it is crucial that we also pay careful attention to the function of homophobia and sexism in particular within the new masculinities. There are transsexuals, and we are not all transsexuals; gender is not fluid,

and gender variance is not the same wherever we may find it. Specificity is all. As gender-queer practices and forms continue to emerge, presumably the definitions of "gay," "lesbian," and "transsexual" will not remain static, and we will produce new terms to delineate what they cannot. In the meantime, gender variance, like sexual variance, cannot be relied on to produce a radical and oppositional politics simply by virtue of representing difference. Radical interventions come from careful consideration of racial and class constructions of sexual identities and gender identities and from a consideration of the politics of mobility outlined by that potent prefix "trans." Who, in other words, can afford transition, whether that transition be a move from female to male, a journey across the border and back, a holiday in the sun, a trip to the moon, a passage to a new body, a one-way ticket to white manhood? Who, on the other hand, can afford to stay home, who can afford to make a home, build a new home, move homes, have no home, leave home? Who can afford metaphors? I suggest we think carefully, butches and FTMS alike, about the kinds of men or masculine beings that we become and lay claim to: alternative masculinities, ultimately, will fail to change existing gender hierarchies to the extent to which they fail to be feminist, antiracist, and queer.

NOTES

1. For more on this see Phyllis Burke, *Gender Shock: Exploding the Myths of Male and Female* (New York: Doubleday, 1996), 60–66.
2. Judith Halberstam, "F2M: The Making of Female Masculinity," in *The Lesbian Postmodern,* ed. Laura Doan (New York: Columbia University Press, 1994), 210–28.
3. Sandy Stone, "The 'Empire' Strikes Back: A Posttranssexual Manifesto," in *Body Guards: The Cultural Politics of Gender Ambiguity,* ed. Julia Epstein and Kristina Straub (New York: Routledge, 1993), 280–304.
4. See *FTM International Newsletter* 29 (January 1995).

5. Isabella, "Review Essay," *FTM Newsletter* 29 (January 1995): 13–14.

6. Jay Prosser, "No Place like Home: The Transgendered Narrative of Leslie Feinberg's *Stone Butch Blues,*" *Modern Fiction Studies* 41, nos. 3–4 (1995). I should say here that I find Prosser's work challenging and provocative, and I believe that his book on transsexual body narratives will be a crucial intervention into transgender discourse. My disagreements with Prosser are particular to this article. See Prosser, *Second Skins: The Body Narratives of Transsexuals* (New York: Columbia University Press, 1998).

7. Jordy Jones, "Another View of F2M," *FTM Newsletter* 29 (January 1995): 14–15.

8. See Stone, "Empire Strikes Back."

9. An example of an article that represented this kind of hostile attitude toward FTMS by lesbians appeared in the *Village Voice* in response to the horrifying murders of transgender man Brando Teena, his girlfriend Lisa Lewis, and another friend, Philip DeVine (see Donna Minkowitz, "Gender Outlaw," *Village Voice,* 19 April 1994, 24–30). Many people wrote to the *Village Voice* charging Minkowitz with insensitivity to the chosen gender of Teena.

10. See Elaine K. Ginsberg, "Introduction: The Politics of Passing," in *Passing and the Fictions of Identity,* ed. Elaine K. Ginsberg (Durham, N.C.: Duke University Press, 1996), 3. Ginsberg also blurs the lines between racial and gendered passing in this essay and makes the two analogous, thereby losing the very different social and political structures of gender and race.

11. Deva, "FTM/Female-to-Male: An Interview with Mike, Eric, Billy, Sky, and Shadow," in *Dagger: On Butch Women,* ed. Lily Burana, Roxxie, and Linnea Due (Pittsburgh and San Francisco: Cleis Press, 1994), 154–67.

12. For an example of this tendency see Henry Rubin, *Female to Male Transsexuals: A Phenomenological Study* (Chicago: University of Chicago Press, forthcoming).

13. See also Elizabeth Lapovsky Kennedy and Madeline Davis, *Boots of Leather, Slippers of Gold: The History of a Lesbian Community* (New York: Routledge, 1993).

14. Heather Findlay, "Stone Butch Now," *Girlfriends Magazine,* March/April, 1995, 45.

15. I have maintained the female gender pronouns used in the article here until I refer to Jay as FTM, and then I use male pronouns.

16. Mario Martino, with harriett, *Emergence: A Transsexual Autobiography* (New York: Crown Publishers, 1977), 132.

17. Mark Rees, *Dear Sir or Madam: The Autobiography of a Female-to-Male Transsexual* (London: Cassell, 1996), 59.

18. "Guys" is an insider term used between FTMS and within transsexual circles.

19. Unfortunately, I cannot provide a citation for such a list because the lists are often anonymous and circulate only within a limited list with no intention of becoming public.

20. Amy Bloom, "The Body Lies," *New Yorker* 70, no. 21 (18 July 1994): 38–49.

21. Michel Foucault, *The History of Sexuality, Volume 1: An Introduction,* trans. Robert Hurley (New York: Vintage, 1980), 96.

22. Again, this is difficult to document, if only because transsexual discourse is still in the making. I am thinking of one particular conference I attended on transsexual and transgender issues in which a group of transsexual panelists insistently defined their political strategies in opposition to gay and lesbian political aims, which they considered to be mainstream and transsexual insensitive: "Transformations" Conference, CLAGS, Thursday, 2 May 1996.

23. For example, one critic comments on the effect of immigration on the Filipino third gender category of *bakla* (see Martin Manalansan, "Under the Shadows of Stonewall: Gay Transnational Politics and the Diasporic Dilemma," in *Worlds Aligned: Politics and Culture in the Shadow of Capital,* ed. David Lloyd and Lisa Lowe [Durham, N.C.: Duke University Press, 1997]).

24. Bernice Hausman, *Changing Sex: Transsexualism, Technology, and the Idea of Gender* (Durham, N.C.: Duke University Press, 1995), 110.

25. Hausman, to her credit, does look at this shared history in a section on early-twentieth-century sexology. She studies the language of inversion and claims: 'Transsexual' is not a term that can accurately be used to describe subjects exhibiting cross-sex behaviors prior to the technical capacity for sex reassignment . . . there is no transsexuality without the surgeon" (117).

26. Raymond, *Transsexual Empire.*

27. Hausman, *Changing Sex,* 140.

28. Prosser, "No Place like Home," 489.

29. Henry S. Rubin, "Do You Believe in Gender?" *Sojourner* 21, no. 6 (February 1996): 7–8.

30. Jan Morris, *Conundrum: An Extraordinary Narrative of Transsexualism* (New York: Henry Holt, 1986), 99.

31. Stone, "Empire Strikes Back"; Marjorie Garber, "The Chic of Araby: Transvestism, Transsexualism, and the Erotics of Cultural Appropriation," in *Body Guards: The Cultural Politics of Gender Ambiguity,* ed. Julia Epstein and Kristina Straub (New York: Routledge, 1994), 223–47.

32. Dorinne Kondo, "The Narrative Production of 'Home,' Community, and Political Identity in Asian American Theater," in *Displacement, Diaspora, and Geographies of Identity,* ed. Smadar Lavie and Ted Swedenburg (Durham, N.C.: Duke University Press, 1996), 97.

33. Gloria Anzaldúa, *Borderlands/La Frontera: The New Mestiza* (San Francisco: Spinsters/Aunt Lute Foundation, 1987), 13.

VISUALIZING THE BODY: WESTERN THEORIES AND AFRICAN SUBJECTS

Oyèrónké Oyĕwùmí

The idea that biology is destiny—or, better still, destiny is biology—has been a staple of Western thought for centuries.[1] Whether the issue is who is who in Aristotle's polis[2] or who is poor in the late twentieth-century United States, the notion that difference and hierarchy in society are biologically determined continues to enjoy credence even among social scientists who purport to explain human society in other than genetic terms. In the West, biological explanations appear to be especially privileged over other ways of explaining differences of gender, race, or class. Difference is expressed as degeneration. In tracing the genealogy of the idea of degeneration in European thought, J. Edward Chamberlain and Sander Gilman noted the way it was used to define certain kinds of difference, in the nineteenth century in particular. "Initially, degeneration brought together two notions of difference, one scientific—a deviation from an original type—and the other moral, a deviation from a norm of behavior. But they were essentially the same notion, of a fall from grace, *a deviation from the original type.*"[3] Consequently, those in positions of power find it imperative to establish their superior biology as a way of affirming their privilege and dominance over "Others." Those who are different are seen as genetically inferior, and this, in turn, is used to account for their disadvantaged social positions.

The notion of society that emerges from this conception is that society is constituted by bodies and as bodies—male bodies, female bodies, Jewish bodies, Aryan bodies, black bodies, white bodies, rich bodies, poor bodies. I am using the word "body" in two ways: first, as a metonymy for biology and, second, to draw attention to the sheer physicality that seems to attend being in Western culture. I refer to the corporeal body as well as to metaphors of the body.

The body is given a logic of its own. It is believed that just by looking at it one can tell a person's beliefs and social position or lack thereof. As Naomi Scheman puts it in her discussion of the body politic in premodern Europe:

The ways people knew their places in the world had to do with their bodies and the histories of those bodies, and when they violated the prescriptions for those places, their bodies were punished, often spectacularly. One's place in the body politic was as natural as the places of the organs in one's body, and political disorder [was] as unnatural as the shifting and displacement of those organs.[4]

Similarly, Elizabeth Grosz remarks on what she calls the "depth" of the body in modern Western societies:

> Our [Western] body forms are considered expressions of an interior, not inscriptions on a flat surface. By constructing a soul or psyche for itself, the "civilized body" forms libidinal flows, sensations, experiences, and intensities into needs, wants. . . . The body becomes a text, a system of signs to be deciphered, read, and read into. Social law is incarnated, "corporealized" [;] correlatively, bodies are textualized, read by others as expressive of a subject's psychic interior. A storehouse of inscriptions and messages between [the body's] external and internal boundaries . . . generates or constructs the body's movements into "behavior," which then [has] interpersonally and socially identifiable meanings and functions within a social system.[5]

Consequently, since the body is the bedrock on which the social order is founded, the body is always *in* view and *on* view. As such, it invites a *gaze,* a gaze of difference, a gaze of differentiation—the most historically constant being the gendered gaze. There is a sense in which phrases such as "the social body" or "the body politic" are not just metaphors but can be read literally. It is not surprising, then, that when the body politic needed to be purified in Nazi Germany, certain kinds of bodies had to be eliminated.[6]

The reason that the body has so much presence in the West is that the world is primarily perceived by sight.[7] The differentiation of human bodies in terms of sex, skin color, and cranium size is a testament to the powers attributed to "seeing." The gaze is an invitation to differentiate. Different approaches to comprehending reality, then, suggest epistemological differences between societies. Relative to Yorùbá society, which is the focus of this book, the body has an exaggerated presence in the Western conceptualization of society. The term "worldview," which is used in the West to sum up the cultural logic of a society, captures the West's privileging of the visual. It is Eurocentric to use it to describe cultures that may privilege

other senses. The term "world-sense" is a more inclusive way of describing the conception of the world by different cultural groups. In this study, therefore, "worldview" will only be applied to describe the Western cultural sense, and "world-sense" will be used when describing the Yorùbá or other cultures that may privilege senses other than the visual or even a combination of senses.

The foregoing hardly represents the received view of Western history and social thought. Quite the contrary: until recently, the history of Western societies has been presented as a documentation of rational thought in which ideas are framed as the agents of history. If bodies appear at all, they are articulated as the debased side of human nature. The preferred focus has been on the mind, lofty and high above the foibles of the flesh. Early in Western discourse, a binary opposition between body and mind emerged. The much-vaunted Cartesian dualism was only an affirmation of a tradition[8] in which the body was seen as a trap from which any rational person had to escape. Ironically, even as the body remained at the center of both sociopolitical categories and discourse, many thinkers denied its existence for certain categories of people, most notably themselves. "Bodylessness" has been a precondition of rational thought. Women, primitives, Jews, Africans, the poor, and all those who qualified for the label "different" in varying historical epochs have been considered to be the embodied, dominated therefore by instinct and affect, reason being beyond them. They are the Other, and the Other is a body.[9]

In pointing out the centrality of the body in the construction of difference in Western culture, one does not necessarily deny that there have been certain traditions in the West that have attempted to explain differences according to criteria other than the presence or absence of certain organs: the possession of a penis, the size of the brain, the shape of the cranium, or the color of the skin. The Marxist tradition is especially noteworthy in this regard in that it emphasized social relations as an explanation for class inequality. However, the critique of Marxism as androcentric by numerous feminist writers suggests that this paradigm is also implicated in Western somatocentricity.[10] Similarly, the establishment of disciplines such as sociology and anthropology, which purport to explain society on the bases of human interactions, seems to suggest the relegation of biological determinism in social thought. On closer examination, however, one finds that the body has hardly been banished from social thought, not to mention its role in the constitution of social status. This can be illustrated in the discipline of sociology. In a monograph on the body and society, Bryan Turner laments what he perceives as the absence of the body in sociological inquiries. He attributes this phenomenon of "absent bodies"[11] to the fact that "sociology emerged as a discipline which took the social meaning of human interaction as its principal object of inquiry, claiming that the meaning of social actions can never be reduced to biology or physiology."[12]

One could agree with Turner about the need to separate sociology from eugenics and phrenology. However, to say that bodies have been absent from sociological theories is to discount the fact that the social groups that are the subject matter of the discipline are essentially understood as rooted in biology. They are categories based on perceptions of the different physical presence of various body-types. In the contemporary U.S., so long as sociologists deal with so-called social categories like the underclass, suburbanites, workers, farmers, voters, citizens, and criminals (to mention a few categories that are historically and in the cultural ethos understood as representing specific body-types), there is no escape from biology. If the social realm is determined by the kinds of bodies occupying it, then to what extent is there a social realm, given that it is conceived to be biologically determined? For example, no one hearing the term "corporate executives" would assume them to be women; and in the 1980s and 1990s, neither would anyone spontaneously associate whites with the terms "underclass" or "gangs"; indeed,

if someone were to construct an association between the terms, their meanings would have to be shifted. Consequently, any sociologist who studies these categories cannot escape an underlying biological insidiousness.

This omnipresence of biologically deterministic explanations in the social sciences can be demonstrated with the category of the criminal or criminal type in contemporary American society. Troy Duster, in an excellent study of the resurgence of overt biological determinism in intellectual circles, berates the eagerness of many researchers to associate criminality with genetic inheritance; he goes on to argue that other interpretations of criminality are possible:

> The prevailing economic interpretation explains crime rates in terms of access to jobs and unemployment. A cultural interpretation tries to show differing cultural adjustments between the police and those apprehended for crimes. A political interpretation sees criminal activity as political interpretation, or pre-revolutionary. A conflict interpretation sees this as an interest conflict over scarce resources.[13]

Clearly, on the face of it, all these explanations of criminality are nonbiological; however, as long as the "population" or the social group they are attempting to explain—in this case criminals who are black and/or poor—is seen to represent a genetic grouping, the underlying assumptions about the genetic predisposition of that population or group will structure the explanations proffered whether they are body-based or not. This is tied to the fact that because of the history of racism, the underlying research question (even if it is unstated) is not why certain individuals commit crimes: it is actually why black people have such a propensity to do so. The definition of what is criminal activity is very much tied up with who (black, white, rich, poor) is involved in the activity.[14] Likewise, the police, as a group, are assumed to be white. Similarly, when studies are done of leadership in American society, the researchers "discover" that most people in leadership positions are white males; no matter what account these researchers give for this result, their statements will be read as explaining the predisposition of this group to leadership.

The integrity of researchers is not being questioned here; my purpose is not to label any group of scholars as racist in their intentions. On the contrary, since the civil rights movement, social-scientific research has been used to formulate policies that would abate if not end discrimination against subordinated groups. What must be underscored, however, is how knowledge-production and dissemination in the United States are inevitably embedded in what Michael Omi and Howard Winant call the "everyday common sense of race—a way of comprehending, explaining and acting in the world."[15] Race, then, is a fundamental organizing principle in American society. It is institutionalized, and it functions irrespective of the action of individual actors.

In the West, social identities are all interpreted through the "prism of heritability,"[16] to borrow Duster's phrase. Biological determinism is a filter through which all knowledge about society is run. As mentioned in the preface, I refer to this kind of thinking as body-reasoning;[17] it is a bio-logic interpretation of the social world. The point, again, is that as long as social actors like managers, criminals, nurses, and the poor are presented as groups and not as individuals, and as long as such groupings are conceived to be genetically constituted, then there is no escape from biological determinism.

Against this background, the issue of gender difference is particularly interesting in regard to the history and the constitution of difference in European social practice and thought. The lengthy history of the embodiment of social categories is suggested by the myth fabricated by Socrates to convince citizens of different ranks to accept whatever status was imposed upon them. Socrates explained the myth to Glaucon in these terms:

> Citizens, we shall say to them in our tale, you are brothers, yet God has framed you differently. Some of you have the power of command, and in the composition of these he has mingled gold, where-fore also they have the greatest honor; others he has made silver, to be auxiliaries; others again who are to be husbandmen and craftsmen he has composed of brass and iron; and the species will generally be preserved in the children. . . . An Oracle says that when a man of brass or iron guards the state, it will be destroyed. Such is the tale; is there any possibility of making our citizens believe in it?

Glaucon replies, "Not in the present generation; there is no way of accomplishing this; but their sons may be made to believe in the tale, and their sons' sons, and posterity after them."[18] Glaucon was mistaken that the acceptance of the myth could be accomplished only in the next generation: the myth of those born to rule was already in operation; mothers, sisters, and daughters—women—were already excluded from consideration in any of those ranks. In a context in which people were ranked according to association with certain metals, women were, so to speak, made of wood, and so were not even considered. Stephen Gould, a historian of science, calls Glaucon's observation a prophecy, since history shows that Socrates' tale has been promulgated and believed by subsequent generations.[19] The point, however, is that even in Glaucon's time, it was more than a prophecy: it was already a social practice to exclude women from the ranks of rulers.

Paradoxically, in European thought, despite the fact that society was seen to be inhabited by bodies, only women were perceived to be embodied; men had no bodies—they were walking minds. Two social categories that emanated from this construction were the "man of reason" (the thinker) and the "woman of the body," and they were oppositionally constructed. The idea that the man of reason often had the woman of the body on his mind was clearly not entertained. As Michel Foucault's *History of Sexuality* suggests, however, the man of ideas often had the woman and indeed other bodies on his mind.[20]

In recent times, thanks in part to feminist scholarship, the body is beginning to receive the attention it deserves as a site and as material for the explication of European history and thoughts.[21] The distinctive contribution of feminist discourse to our understanding of Western societies is that it makes explicit the gendered (therefore embodied) and male-dominant nature of all Western institutions and discourses. The feminist lens disrobes the man of ideas for all to see. Even discourses like science that were assumed to be objective have been shown to be male-biased.[22] The extent to which the body is implicated in the construction of sociopolitical categories and epistemologies cannot be overemphasized. Dorothy Smith has written that in Western societies "a man's body gives credibility to his utterance, whereas a woman's body takes it away from hers."[23] Writing on the construction of masculinity, R. W. Connell notes that the body is inescapable in its construction and that a stark physicalness underlies gender categories in the Western worldview: "In our [Western] culture, at least, the physical sense of maleness and femaleness is central to the cultural interpretation of gender. Masculine gender is (among other things) a certain feel to the skin, certain muscular shapes and tensions, certain postures and ways of moving, certain possibilities in sex."[24]

From the ancients to the moderns, gender has been a foundational category upon which social categories have been erected. Hence, gender has been ontologically conceptualized. The category of the citizen, which has been the cornerstone of much of Western political theory, was male, despite the much-acclaimed Western democratic traditions.[25] Elucidating Aristotle's categorization of the sexes, Elizabeth Spelman writes: "A woman is a female who is free; a man is a male who is a citizen."[26] Women were excluded from the category of citizens because "penis possession"[27] was one of the qualifications for citizenship. Lorna Schiebinger notes in a study of the origins of modern science and women's exclusion from European scientific institutions that "differences between the two sexes were reflections of a set of dualistic principles that penetrated the cosmos as well as the bodies of men

and women."[28] Differences and hierarchy, then, are enshrined on bodies; and bodies enshrine differences and hierarchy. Hence, dualisms like nature/culture, public/private, and visible/invisible are variations on the theme of male/female bodies hierarchically ordered, differentially placed in relation to power, and spatially distanced one from the other.[29]

In the span of Western history, the justifications for the making of the categories "man" and "woman" have not remained the same. On the contrary, they have been dynamic. Although the boundaries are shifting and the content of each category may change, the two categories have remained hierarchical and in binary opposition. For Stephen Gould, "the justification for ranking groups by inborn worth has varied with the tide of Western history. Plato relied on dialectic, the church upon dogma. For the past two centuries, scientific claims have become the primary agent of validating Plato's myth."[30] The constant in this Western narrative is the centrality of the body: two bodies on display, two sexes, two categories persistently viewed—one in relation to the other. That narrative is about the unwavering elaboration of the body as the site and cause of differences and hierarchies in society. In the West, so long as the issue is difference and social hierarchy, then the body is constantly positioned, posed, exposed, and reexposed as their cause. Society, then, is seen as an accurate reflection of genetic endowment—those with a superior biology inevitably are those in superior social positions. No difference is elaborated without bodies that are positioned hierarchically. In his book *Making Sex*,[31] Thomas Laqueur gives a richly textured history of the construction of sex from classical Greece to the contemporary period, noting the changes in symbols and the shifts in meanings. The point, however, is the centrality and persistence of the body in the construction of social categories. In view of this history, Freud's dictum that anatomy is destiny was not original or exceptional; he was just more explicit than many of his predecessors.

SOCIAL ORDERS AND BIOLOGY: NATURAL OR CONSTRUCTED?

The idea that gender is socially constructed—that differences between males and female are to be located in social practices, not in biological facts—was one important insight that emerged early in second-wave feminist scholarship. This finding was understandably taken to be radical in a culture in which difference, particularly gender difference, had always been articulated as natural and, therefore, biologically determined. Gender as a social construction became the cornerstone of much feminist discourse. The notion was particularly attractive because it was interpreted to mean that gender differences were not ordained by nature; they were mutable and therefore changeable. This in turn led to the opposition between social constructionism and biological determinism, as if they were mutually exclusive.

Such a dichotomous presentation is unwarranted, however, because the ubiquity of biologically rooted explanations for difference in Western social thought and practices is a reflection of the extent to which biological explanations are found compelling.[32] In other words, so long as the issue is difference (whether the issue is why women breast-feed babies or why they could not vote), old biologies will be found or new biologies will be constructed to explain women's disadvantage. The Western preoccupation with biology continues to generate constructions of "new biologies" even as some of the old biological assumptions are being dislodged. In fact, in the Western experience, social construction and biological determinism have been two sides of the same coin, since both ideas continue to reinforce each other. When social categories like gender are constructed, new biologies of difference can be invented. When biological interpretations are found to be compelling, social categories do derive their legitimacy and power from biology. In short, the social and the biological feed on each other.

The biologization inherent in the Western articulation of social difference is, however, by no means universal. The debate in feminism about what roles and which identities are natural and what aspects are constructed only has meaning in a culture where social categories are conceived as having no independent logic of their own. This debate, of course, developed out of certain problems; therefore, it is logical that in societies where such problems do not exist, there should be no such debate. But then, due to imperialism, this debate has been universalized to other cultures, and its immediate effect is to inject Western problems where such issues originally did not exist. Even then, this debate does not take us very far in societies where social roles and identities are not conceived to be rooted in biology. By the same token, in cultures where the visual sense is not privileged, and the body is not read as a blueprint of society, invocations of biology are less likely to occur because such explanations do not carry much weight in the social realm. That many categories of difference are socially constructed in the West may well suggest the mutability of categories, but it is also an invitation to endless constructions of biology—in that there is no limit to what can be explained by the body-appeal. Thus biology is hardly mutable; it is much more a combination of the Hydra and the Phoenix of Greek mythology. Biology is forever mutating, not mutable. Ultimately, the most important point is not that gender is socially constructed but the extent to which biology itself is socially constructed and therefore inseparable from the social.

The way in which the conceptual categories sex and gender functioned in feminist discourse was based on the assumption that biological and social conceptions could be separated and applied universally. Thus sex was presented as the natural category and gender as the social construction of the natural. But, subsequently, it became apparent that even sex has elements of construction. In many feminist writings thereafter, sex has served as the base and gender as the superstructure.[33] In spite of all efforts to separate the two, the distinction between sex and gender is a red herring. In Western conceptualization, gender cannot exist without sex since the body sits squarely at the base of both categories. Despite the preeminence of feminist social constructionism, which claims a social deterministic approach to society, biological foundationalism,[34] if not reductionism, is still at the center of gender discourses, just as it is at the center of all other discussions of society in the West.

Nevertheless, the idea that gender is socially constructed is significant from a cross-cultural perspective. In one of the earliest feminist texts to assert the constructionist thesis and its need for cross-cultural grounding, Suzanne J. Kessler and Wendy McKenna wrote that "by viewing gender as a social construction, it is possible to see descriptions of other cultures as evidence for alternative but equally real conceptions of what it means to be woman or man."[35] Yet, paradoxically, a fundamental assumption of feminist theory is that women's subordination is universal. These two ideas are contradictory. The universality attributed to gender asymmetry suggests a biological basis rather than a cultural one, given that the human anatomy is universal whereas cultures speak in myriad voices. That gender is socially constructed is said to mean that the criteria that make up male and female categories vary in different cultures. If this is so, then it challenges the notion that there is a biological imperative at work. From this standpoint, then, gender categories are mutable, and as such, gender then is denaturalized.

In fact, the categorization of women in feminist discourses as a homogeneous, bio-anatomically determined group which is always constituted as powerless and victimized does not reflect the fact that gender relations are social relations and, therefore, historically grounded and culturally bound. If gender is socially constructed, then gender cannot behave in the same way across time and space. If gender is a social construction, then we must examine the various cultural/architectural sites where it was constructed, and we must acknowledge that variously located actors (aggregates, groups, interested parties) were part of the construction. We must further acknowledge that if gender is

a social construction, then there was a specific time (in different cultural/architectural sites) when it was "constructed" and therefore a time before which it was not. Thus, gender, being a social construction, is also a historical and cultural phenomenon. Consequently, it is logical to assume that in some societies, gender construction need not have existed at all.

From a cross-cultural perspective, the significance of this observation is that one cannot assume the social organization of one culture (the dominant West included) as universal or the interpretations of the experiences of one culture as explaining another one. On the one hand, at a general, global level, the constructedness of gender does suggest its mutability. On the other hand, at the local level—that is, within the bounds of any particular culture—gender is mutable only if it is socially constructed as such. Because, in Western societies, gender categories, like all other social categories, are constructed with biological building blocks, their mutability is questionable. The cultural logic of Western social categories is founded on an ideology of biological determinism: the conception that biology provides the rationale for the organization of the social world. Thus, as pointed out earlier, this cultural logic is actually a "bio-logic."

THE "SISTERARCHY": FEMINISM AND ITS "OTHER"

From a cross-cultural perspective, the implications of Western bio-logic are far-reaching when one considers the fact that gender constructs in feminist theory originated in the West, where men and women are conceived oppositionally and projected as embodied, genetically derived social categories.[36] The question, then, is this: On what basis are Western conceptual categories exportable or transferable to other cultures that have a different cultural logic? This question is raised because despite the wonderful insight about the social construction of gender, the way cross-cultural data have been used by many feminist writers undermines the notion that differing cultures may construct social categories differently. For one thing, if different cultures necessarily always construct gender as feminism proposes that they do *and must,* then the idea that gender is socially constructed is not sustainable.

The potential value of Western feminist social constructionism remains, therefore, largely unfulfilled, because feminism, like most other Western theoretical frameworks for interpreting the social world, cannot get away from the prism of biology that necessarily perceives social Rubin hierarchies as natural. Consequently, in cross-cultural gender studies, theorists impose Western categories on non-Western cultures and then project such categories as natural. The way in which dissimilar constructions of the social world in other cultures are used as "evidence" for the constructedness of gender and the insistence that these cross-cultural constructions are gender categories as they operate in the West nullify the alternatives offered by the non-Western cultures and undermine the claim that gender is a social construction.

Western ideas are imposed when non-Western social categories are assimilated into the gender framework that emerged from a specific sociohistorical and philosophical tradition. An example is the "discovery" of what has been labeled "third gender"[37] or "alternative genders"[38] in a number of non-Western cultures. The fact that the African "woman marriage,"[39] the Native American "berdache,"[40] and the South Asian "hijra"[41] are presented as gender categories incorporates them into the Western bio-logic and gendered framework without explication of their own sociocultural histories and constructions. A number of questions are pertinent here. Are these social categories seen as gendered in the cultures in question? From whose perspective are they gendered? In fact, even the appropriateness of naming them "third gender" is questionable since the Western cultural system, which uses biology to map the social world, precludes the possibility of more than two genders because gender is the elabora-

tion of the perceived sexual dimorphism of the human body into the social realm. The trajectory of feminist discourse in the last twenty-five years has been determined by the Western cultural environment of its founding and development.

Thus, in the beginning of second-wave feminism in Euro-America, sex was defined as the biological facts of male and female bodies, and gender was defined as the social consequences that flowed from these facts. In effect, each society was assumed to have a sex/gender system.[42] The most important point was that sex and gender are inextricably bound. Over time, sex tended to be understood as the base and gender as the superstructure. Subsequently, however, after much debate, even sex was interpreted as socially constructed. Kessler and McKenna, one of the earliest research teams in this area, wrote that they "use gender, rather than sex, even when referring to those aspects of being a woman (girl) or man (boy) that have been viewed as biological. This will serve to emphasize our position that the element of social construction is primary in all aspects of being male or female."[43] Judith Butler, writing almost fifteen years later, reiterates the interconnectedness of sex and gender even more strongly:

> It would make no sense, then, to define gender as the cultural interpretation of sex, if sex itself is a gendered category. Gender ought not to be conceived merely as a cultural inscription of meaning on a pregiven surface (a juridical conception); gender must also designate the very apparatus of production whereby the sexes themselves are established. As a result, gender is not to culture as sex is to nature; gender is also the discursive/cultural means by which "sexed nature" or "a natural sex" is produced.[44]

Given the inseparability of sex and gender in the West, which results from the use of biology as an ideology for mapping the social world, the terms "sex" and "gender," as noted earlier, are essentially synonyms. To put this another way: since in Western constructions, physical bodies are always social bodies, there is really no distinction between sex and gender.[45] In Yorùbá society, in contrast, social relations derive their legitimacy from social facts, not from biology. The bare biological facts of pregnancy and parturition count only in regard to procreation, where they must. Biological facts do not determine who can become the monarch or who can trade in the market. In indigenous Yorùbá conception, these questions were properly social questions, not biological ones; hence, the nature of one's anatomy did not define one's social position. Consequently, the Yorùbá social order requires a different kind of map, not a gender map that assumes biology as the foundation for the social.

The splitting of hairs over the relationship between gender and sex, the debate on essentialism, the debates about differences among women,[46] and the preoccupation with gender bending/blending[47] that have characterized feminism are actually feminist versions of the enduring debate on nature versus nurture that is inherent in Western thought and in the logic of its social hierarchies. These concerns are not necessarily inherent in the discourse of society as such but are a culture-specific concern and issue. From a cross-cultural perspective, the more interesting point is the degree to which feminism, despite its radical local stance, exhibits the same ethnocentric and imperialistic characteristics of the Western discourses it sought to subvert. This has placed serious limitations on its applicability outside of the culture that produced it. As Kathy Ferguson reminds us: "The questions we can ask about the world are enabled, and other questions disabled, by the frame that orders the questioning. *When we are busy arguing about the questions that appear within a certain frame, the frame itself becomes invisible; we become enframed within it.*"[48] Though feminism in origin, by definition, and by practice is a universalizing discourse, the concerns and questions that have informed it are Western (and its audience too is apparently assumed to be composed of just Westerners, given that many of the theorists tend to use the first-person plural "we" and "our culture" in their writings). As such, feminism remains enframed by the tunnel vision and the bio-logic of other Western discourses.

Yorùbá society of southwestern Nigeria suggests a different scenario, one in which the body is not always enlisted as the basis for social classification. From a Yorùbá stance, the body appears to have an exaggerated presence in Western thought and social practice, including feminist theories. In the Yorùbá world, particularly in pre-nineteenth-century[49] Ọ̀yọ̀ culture, society was conceived to be inhabited by people in relation to one another. That is, the "physicality" of maleness or femaleness did not have social antecedents and therefore did not constitute social categories. Social hierarchy was determined by social relations. As noted earlier, how persons were situated in relationships shifted depending on those involved and the particular situation. The principle that determined social organization was seniority, which was based on chronological age. Yorùbá kinship terms did not denote gender, and other nonfamilial social categories were not gender-specific either. What these Yorùbá categories tell us is that the body is not always in view and on view for categorization. The classic example is the female who played the roles of *ọba* (ruler), *ọmọ* (offspring), *ọkọ, aya, ìyá* (mother), and *aláwo* (diviner-priest) all in one body. None of these kinship and nonkinship social categories are gender-specific. One cannot place persons in the Yorùbá categories just by looking at them. What they are heard to say may be the most important cue. Seniority as the foundation of Yorùbá social intercourse is relational and dynamic; unlike gender, it is not focused on the body.[50]

If the human body is universal, why does the body appear to have an exaggerated presence in the West relative to Yorùbáland? A comparative research framework reveals that one major difference stems from which of the senses is privileged in the apprehension of reality—sight in the West and a multiplicity of senses anchored by hearing in Yorùbáland. The tonality of Yorùbá language predisposes one toward an apprehension of reality that cannot marginalize the auditory.

Consequently, relative to Western societies, there is a stronger need for a broader contextualization in order to make sense of the world.[51] For example, Ifá divination, which is also a knowledge system in Yorùbáland, has both visual and oral components.[52] More fundamentally, the distinction between Yorùbá and the West symbolized by the focus on different senses in the apprehension of reality involves more than perception—for the Yorùbá, and indeed many other African societies, it is about "a particular presence in the world—a world conceived of as a whole in which all things are linked together."[53] It concerns the many worlds human beings inhabit; it does not privilege the physical world over the metaphysical. A concentration on vision as the primary mode of comprehending reality promotes what can be seen over that which is not apparent to the eye; it misses the other levels and the nuances of existence. David Lowe's comparison of sight and the sense of hearing encapsulates some of the issues to which I wish to draw attention. He writes:

> Of the five senses, hearing is the most pervasive and penetrating. I say this, although many, from Aristotle in *Metaphysics* to Hans Jonas in *Phenomenon of Life,* have said that sight is most noble. But sight is always directed at what is straight ahead. . . . And sight cannot turn a corner, at least without the aid of a mirror. On the other hand, sound comes to one, surrounds one for the time being with an acoustic space, full of timbre and nuances. It is more proximate and suggestive than sight. Sight is always the perception of the surface from a particular angle. But sound is that perception able to penetrate beneath the surface. . . . Speech is the communication connecting one person with another. Therefore, the quality of sound is fundamentally more vital and moving than that of sight.[54]

Just as the West's privileging of the visual over other senses has been clearly demonstrated, so too the dominance of the auditory in Yorùbáland can be shown.

In an interesting paper appropriately entitled "The Mind's Eye," feminist theorists Evelyn Fox Keller and Christine Grontkowski make the following observation: "We [Euro-Americans] speak of knowledge as illumination, knowing as seeing, truth as light. How is it, we might ask, that vision came to seem so apt a model for knowledge? And having accepted it as such, how has the metaphor colored our conceptions of knowledge?"[55] These theorists go on to analyze the implications of the privileging of sight over other senses for the conception of reality and knowledge in the West. They examine the linkages between the privileging of vision and patriarchy, noting that the roots of Western thought in the visual have yielded a dominant male logic.[56] Explicating Jonas's observation that "to get the proper view, we take the proper distance,"[57] they note the passive nature of sight, in that the subject of the gaze is passive. They link the distance that seeing entails to the concept of objectivity and the lack of engagement between the "I" and the subject—the Self and the Other.[58] Indeed, the Other in the West is best described as another body—separate and distant.

Feminism has not escaped the visual logic of Western thought. The feminist focus on sexual difference, for instance, stems from this legacy. Feminist theorist Nancy Chodorow has noted the primacy and limitations of this feminist concentration on difference:

> For our part as feminists, even as we want to eliminate gender inequality, hierarchy, and difference, we expect to find such features in most social settings. . . . We have begun from the assumption that *gender is always a salient* feature of social life, and we do not have theoretical approaches that emphasize sex similarities over differences.[59]

Consequently, the assumption and deployment of patriarchy and "women" as universals in many feminist writings are ethnocentric and demonstrate the hegemony of the West over other cultural groupings.[60] The emergence of patriarchy as a form of social organization in Western history is a function of the differentiation between male and female bodies, a difference rooted in the visual, a difference that cannot be reduced to biology and that has to be understood as being constituted within particular historical and social realities. I am not suggesting that gender categories are necessarily limited to the West, particularly in the contemporary period. Rather, I am suggesting that discussions of social categories should be defined and grounded in the local milieu, rather than based on "universal" findings made in the West. A number of feminist scholars have questioned the assumption of universal patriarchy. For example, the editors of a volume on Hausa women of northern Nigeria write: "A preconceived assumption of gender asymmetry actually distorts many analyses, since it precludes the exploration of gender as a fundamental component of social relations, inequality, processes of production and reproduction, and ideology."[61] Beyond the question of asymmetry, however, a preconceived notion of gender as a universal social category is equally problematic. If the investigator assumes gender, then gender categories will be found whether they exist or not.

Feminism is one of the latest Western theoretical fashions to be applied to African societies. Following the one-size-fits-all (or better still, the Western-size-fits-all) approach to intellectual theorizing, it has taken its place in a long series of—Western paradigms—including Marxism, functionalism, structuralism, and poststructuralism—imposed on African subjects. Academics have become one of the most effective international hegemonizing forces, producing not homogenous social experiences but a homogeny of hegemonic forces. Western theories become tools of hegemony as they are applied universally, on the assumption that Western experiences define the human. For example, a study of Gã residents of a neighborhood in Accra, Ghana, starts thus: "Improving our analysis of women and class formation is necessary to refine our perceptions."[62] Women? What women? Who qualifies to be women in this cultural setting, and on what bases are they to be identified? These questions are legitimate ones to raise if researchers take the constructedness of social categories seriously and take into account local conceptions

of reality. The pitfalls of preconceived notions and ethnocentricity become obvious when the author of the study admits:

> Another bias I began with I was forced to change. Before starting fieldwork I was not particularly interested in economics, causal or otherwise. But by the time I had tried an initial presurvey, . . . the overweening importance of trading activities in pervading every aspect of women's lives made a consideration of economics imperative. And when the time came to analyze the data in depth, the most cogent explanations often were economic ones. I started out to work with women; I ended by working with traders.[63]

Why, in the first place, did Claire Robertson, the author of this study, start with women, and what distortions were introduced as a result? What if she had started with traders? Would she have ended up with women? Beginnings are important; adding other variables in midstream does not prevent or solve distortions and misapprehensions. Like many studies on Africans, half of Robertson's study seems to have been completed—and categories were already in place—before she met the Gã people. Robertson's monograph is not atypical in African studies; in fact, it is one of the better ones, particularly because unlike many scholars, she is aware of some of her biases. The fundamental bias that many Westerners, including Robertson, bring to the study of other societies is "body-reasoning," the assumption that biology determines social position. Because "women" is a body-based category, it tends to be privileged by Western researchers over "traders," which is non-body-based. Even when traders are taken seriously, they are embodied such that the trader category, which in many West African societies is non-gender-specific, is turned into "market women," as if the explanation for their involvement in this occupation is to be found in their breasts, or to put it more scientifically, in the X chromosome.[64] The more the Western bio-logic is adopted, the more this body-based framework is inscribed conceptually and into the social reality.

Different modes of apprehending knowledge yield dissimilar emphases on types and the nature of evidence for making knowledge-claims. Indeed, this also has implications for the organization of social structure, particularly the social hierarchy that undergirds who knows and who does not. I have argued that Western social hierarchies such as gender and race are a function of the privileging of the visual over other senses in Western culture. It has also been noted that the Yorùbá frame of reference was based more on a combination of senses anchored by the auditory. Consequently, the promotion in African studies of concepts and theories derived from the Western mode of thought at best makes it difficult to understand African realities. At worse, it hampers our ability to build knowledge about African societies.

NOTES

1. Compare Thomas Laqueur's usage: "Destiny Is Anatomy," which is the title of chapter 2 of his *Making Sex: Body and Gender from the Greeks to Freud* (Cambridge, Mass.: Harvard University Press, 1990).
2. Elizabeth Spelman, *Inessential Woman: Problems of Exclusion in Feminist Thought* (Boston: Beacon Press, 1988), 37.
3. J. Edward Chamberlain and Sander Gilman, *Degeneration: The Darker Side of Progress* (New York: Columbia University Press, 1985), 292.
4. Naomi Scheman, *Engenderings: Constructions of Knowledge, Authority, and Privilege* (New York: Routledge, 1993), 186.
5. Elizabeth Grosz, "Bodies and Knowledges: Feminism and the Crisis of Reason," in *Feminist Epistemologies,* ed. Linda Alcoff and Elizabeth Potter (New York: Routledge, 1994), 198; emphasis added.
6. Scheman, *Engenderings.*
7. See, for example, the following for accounts of the importance of sight in Western thought: Hans Jonas, *The Phenomenon of Life* (New York: Harper and Row, 1966); Donald Lowe, *History of Bourgeois Perception* (Chicago: University of Chicago Press, 1982).
8. Compare the discussion in Nancy Scheper-Hughes and Margaret Lock, "The Mindful Body: A Prolegomenon to Future Work in Medical Anthropology," *Medical Anthropology Quarterly,* n.s., 1 (March 1987): 7–41.
9. The work of Sander Gilman is particularly illuminating on European conceptions of difference and otherness. See *Difference and Pathology: Stereotypes of Sexuality, Race, and Madness* (Ithaca, N.Y.: Cornell University Press, 1985); *On Blackness without Blacks: Essays on the Image of the Black in Germany* (Boston: G. K. Hall, 1982); *The Case of Sigmund Freud: Medicine and Identity* (Baltimore: Johns Hopkins University Press, 1993); *Jewish Self-Hatred: Anti-Semitism and the Hidden Language of the Jews* (Baltimore: Johns Hopkins University Press, 1986).
10. See, for example, the following: Linda Nicholson, "Feminism and Marx," in *Feminism as Critique: On the Politics of Gender,* ed. Seyla Benhabib and Drucilla Cornell (Minneapolis: University of Minnesota Press, 1986); Michele Barrett, *Women's Oppression Today* (London: New Left Books, 1980); Heidi Hartmann, "The Unhappy Marriage of Marxism and Feminism: Towards a More Progressive Union," in *Women and Revolution: A Discussion of the Unhappy Marriage of Marxism and Feminism,* ed. Lydia Sargent (Boston: South End Press, 1981).
11. Bryan Turner, "Sociology and the Body," in *The Body and Society: Explorations in Social Theory* (Oxford: Blackwell, 1984), 31.
12. Ibid.
13. Troy Duster, *Backdoor to Eugenics* (New York: Routledge, 1990).
14. Ibid.
15. Michael Omi and Howard Winant, *Racial Formation in the United States from the 1960s to the 1980s* (New York: Routledge, 1986). Compare also the discussion of the pervasiveness of race over other variables, such as class, in the analysis of the Los Angeles riot of 1992. According to Cedric Robinson, "Mass media and official declarations subsumed the genealogy of the Rodney King Uprisings into the antidemocratic narratives of race which dominate American culture. Urban unrest, crime, and poverty are discursive economies which signify

race while erasing class" ("Race, Capitalism and the Anti-Democracy," paper presented at the Inter-disciplinary Humanities Center, University of California–Santa Barbara, winter 1994).

16. Duster (*Backdoor*) points to the widely held notion that diseases as well as money "run in families."

17. Compare Cornel West's concept of racial reasoning in *Race Matters* (New York: Vantage, 1993).

18. Cited in Stephen Gould, *The Mismeasure of Man* (New York: Norton, 1981), 19.

19. Ibid.

20. A recent anthology questions the dominant self-representation of Jews as "the People of the Book" and in the process attempts to document a relatively less common image of Jews as "the People of the Body." The editor of the volume makes an interesting point about "the [Jewish] thinker" and his book. He comments that the thinker's book "is evocative of . . . wisdom and the pursuit of knowledge. In this way, the image of the Jew (who is always male) poring over a book is always misleading. He appears to be elevated in spiritual pursuit. But if we could peer over his shoulders and see what his text says, he may in fact be reading about matters as erotic as what position to take during sexual intercourse. What is going on in 'the thinker's' head or more interestingly in his loins?" (Howard Elberg-Schwartz, "People of the Body," introduction to *People of the Body: Jews and Judaism from an Embodied Perspective* [Albany: State University of New York Press, 1992]). The somatocentric nature of European discourses suggests that the phrase the "People of the Body" may have a wider reach.

21. Attention to the body has not been smooth-sailing in feminism either. See Elizabeth Grosz, *Volatile Bodies: Toward a Corporeal Feminism* (Bloomington:Indiana University Press, 1994).

22. Virginia Woolf had summed up the feminist position succinctly: "Science it would seem is not sexless; she is a man, a father infected too" (quoted in Hillary Rose, "Hand, Brain, and Heart: A Feminist Epistemology for the Natural Sciences," *Signs* 9, no. 1 [1983]: 73–90). See also the following: Sandra Harding, *The Science Question in Feminism* (Ithaca, N.Y.: Cornell University Press, 1986); idem, ed., *The Racial Economy of Science* (Bloomington: Indiana University Press, 1993); Donna J. Haraway, *Primate Visions: Gender, Race, and Nature in the World of Modern Science* (New York: Routledge, 1989); and Margaret Wertheim *Pythagoras' Trousers: God Physics and the Gender Wars* (New York: Random House, 1995).

23. Dorothy E. Smith, *The Everyday World as Problematic: A Feminist Sociology* (Boston: Northeastern University Press, 1987), 30.

24. R. W. Connell, *Masculinities* (London: Polity Press, 1995), 53.

25. Susan Okin, *Women in Western Political Thought* (Princeton, N.J.: Princeton University Press, 1979); Elizabeth Spelman, *Inessential Woman: Problems of Exclusion in Feminist Thought* (Boston: Beacon Press, 1988).

26. Quoted in Laqueur, *Making Sex,* 54.

27. Ibid.

28. Lorna Schiebinger, *The Mind Has No Sex? Women in the Origins of Modern Science* (Cambridge, Mass.: Harvard University Press, 1989), 162.

29. For an account of some of these dualisms, see "Hélène Cixous," in *New French Feminisms: An Anthology,* ed. Elaine Marks and Isabelle de Courtivron (Amherst, Mass.: University of Massachusetts Press, 1980).

30. Gould, *Mismeasure of Man,* 20.

31. Laqueur, *Making Sex.*

32. See Suzanne J. Kessler and Wendy McKenna, *Gender: An Ethnomethodological Approach* (New York: John Wiley and Sons, 1978).

33. For elucidation, see Jane F. Collier and Sylvia J. Yanagisako, eds., *Gender and Kinship: Essays toward a Unified Analysis* (Stanford, Calif.: Stanford University Press, 1987).

34. Linda Nicholson has also explicated the pervasiveness of biological foundationalism in feminist thought. See "Interpreting Gender," in *Signs* 20 (1994): 79–104.

35. Kessler and McKenna, *Gender.*

36. In the title of this section, I use the term "sisterarchy." In using the term, I am referring to the well-founded allegations against Western feminists by a number of African, Asian, and Latin American feminists that despite the notion that the "sisterhood is global," Western women are at the top of the hierarchy of the sisterhood; hence it is actually

a "sisterarchy." Nkiru Nzegwu uses the concept in her essay "O Africa: Gender Imperialism in Academia," in *African Women and Feminism: Reflecting on the Politics of Sisterhood,* ed. Oyèrónké Oyĕwùmí (Trenton, N.J.: African World Press, forthcoming).

37. Lorber, *Paradoxes of Gender,* 17–18.

38. Ibid.

39. See Ifi Amadiume, *Male Daughters, Female Husbands: Gender and Sex in an African Society* (London: Zed Books, 1987), for an account of this institution in Igboland of southeastern Nigeria. See also Melville J. Herskovitz, "A Note on 'Woman Marriage' in Dahomey," *Africa* 10 (1937):335–41, for an earlier allusion to its wide occurrence in Africa.

40. Kessler and McKenna, *Gender,* 24–36.

41. Serena Nanda, "Neither Man Nor Woman: The Hijras of India," in *Gender in Cross-cultural Perspective,"* ed. Caroline Brettell and Carolyn Sargent (Englewood Cliffs, N.J.: Prentice Hall, 1993).

42. Gayle Rubin, "The Traffic in Women," in *Toward an Anthropology of Women,* ed. Rayna R. Reiter (New York: Monthly Review Press, 1975).

43. Kessler and McKenna, *Gender,* 7; Laqueur, *Making Sex.*

44. Judith Butler, *Gender Trouble: Feminism and the Subversion of Identity* (New York: Routledge, 1990), 7.

45. In her study (*Male Daughters*) of the Igbo society of Nigeria, anthropologist Ifi Amadiume introduced the idea of "gender flexibility" to capture the real separability of gender and sex in that African society. I, however, think that the "woman to woman" marriages of Igboland invite a more radical interrogation of the concept of gender, an interrogation that "gender flexibility" fails to represent. For one thing, the concept of gender as elaborated in the literature is a dichotomy, a duality grounded on the sexual dimorphism of the human body. Here, there is no room for flexibility.

46. The "race and gender literature" is grounded on notions of differences among women.

47. See, for example, Holly Devor, *Gender Blending: Confronting the Limits of Duality* (Bloomington: Indiana University Press, 1989); Rebecca Gordon, "Delusions of Gender,"

Women's Review of Books 12, no. 2 (November 1994): 18–19.

48. Kathy Ferguson, *The Man Question: Visions of Subjectivity in Feminist Theory* (Berkeley: University of California Press), 7.

49. My use of the nineteenth century as a benchmark is merely to acknowledge the emerging gender configurations in the society; the process must have started earlier, given the role of the Atlantic slave trade in the dislocation of Yorùbáland.

50. See chapter 2 for a full account of Yorùbá worldsense as it is mapped onto social hierarchies.

51. This is not an attempt on my part to partake of some of the reductionist discussion about the "orality" of African societies in relation to "writing" in the West; nor is it the intention of this book to set up a binary opposition between the West and Yorùbáland, on the one hand, and writing and orality, on the other, as some scholars have done. There is a huge literature on writing and orality. A good entry point into the discourse, though it is an overly generalized account, is Walter Ong, *Orality and Literacy: The Technologizing of the Word* (New York: Methuen, 1982). For a recent account of some the issues from an African perspective, see Samba Diop, "The Oral History and Literature of Waalo, Northern Senegal: The Master of the Word in Wolof Tradition" (Ph.D. diss., Department of Comparative Literature, University of California–Berkeley, 1993).

52. See Wande Abimbola, *Ifa: An Exposition of the Ifa Literary Corpus* (Ìbàdàn: Oxford University Press, 1976).

53. Amadou Hampate Ba, "Approaching Africa," in *African Films: The Context of Production,* ed. Angela Martin (London: British Film Institute, 1982), 9.

54. Lowe, *History of Bourgeois Perception,* 7.

55. Evelyn Fox Keller and Christine Grontkowski, "The Mind's Eye," in *Discovering Reality: Feminist Perspectives on Epistemology. Metaphysics, Methodology, and Philosophy of Science,* ed. Sandra Harding and Merrill B. Hintikka (Boston: Reidel, 1983), 208.

56. Ibid.

57. Jonas, *Phenomenon of Life,* 507.

58. Keller and Grontkowski, "The Mind's Eye."

59. Nancy Chodorow, *Feminism and Psychoanalytic Theory* (New Haven: Yale University Press, 1989), 216.

60. See Amadiume, *Male Daughters;* and Valerie Amos and Pratibha Parma, "Challenging Imperial Feminism," *Feminist Review* (July 1984): 3–20.

61. Catherine Coles and Beverly Mack, eds., *Hausa Women in the Twentieth Century* (Madison: University of Wisconsin Press, 1991), 6.

62. Claire Robertson, *Sharing the Same Bowl: A Socioeconomic History of Women and Class in Accra, Ghana* (Bloomington: Indiana University Press, 1984), 23.

63. Ibid., 25.

64. For example, Bessie House-Midamba and Felix K. Ekechi, *African Market Women's Economic Power: The Role of Women in African Economic Development* (Westport, Conn.: Greenwood Press, 1995); Gracia Clark, *Onions Are My Husband: Accumulation by West African Market Women* (Chicago: University of Chicago Press, 1994).

FOR FURTHER READING

Beauvoir, Simone. *The Second Sex,* translated by H. M. Parshley. New York: Vintage Books, 1989 (1946).

Butler, Judith. *Gender Trouble: Feminism and the Subversion of Identity.* New York: Routledge, 1990.

Butler, Judith. "Imitation and Gender Subordination." In her *Inside/Out: Lesbian Theories, Gay Theories,* edited by Diana Fuss. New York: Routledge, 1991.

Chodorow, Nancy. *Reproduction of Mothering.* Berkeley: University of California Press, 1978.

Dreger, Alice Domurat. *Hermaphrodites and the Medical Invention of Sex.* Cambridge: Harvard University Press, 1998.

Fausto-Sterling, Anne. *Sexing the Body: Gender Politics and the Construction of Sexuality.* New York: Basic Books, 2000.

Feinberg, Leslie. *Transgender Liberation: A Movement Whose Time Has Come.* New York: World View Forum, 1992.

Fuss, Diana. *Essentially Speaking: Feminism, Nature and Difference.* New York: Routledge, 1989.

Gatens, Moira. "Psychoanalysis and French Feminisms." In her *Feminism and Philosophy: Perspectives on Difference and Equality.* Bloomington, IN: Indiana University Press, 1991.

Grosz, Elizabeth. *Sexual Subversions.* East Melbourne, Australia: Allen and Unwin Academic, 1989.

Irigaray, Luce. *Speculum of the Other Woman,* translated by Gillian C. Gill. Ithaca: Cornell University Press, 1985.

Irigaray, Luce. *The Sex Which Is Not One,* translated by Catherine Porter. Ithaca: Cornell University Press, 1985.

Lorber, Judith. "Night to His Day: The Social Construction of Gender." In her *Paradoxes of Gender.* New Haven: Yale University Press, 1994.

Lorde, Audre. *Sister Outsider: Essays and Speeches.* Freedom, CA.: The Crossing Press, 1984.

May, Larry, and Robert Strikwerda. *Rethinking Masculinity: Philosophical Explorations in Light of Feminism.* Lanham, MD: Rowman and Littlefield, 1996.

Mitchell, Juliet. *Psychoanalysis and Feminism.* New York: Pantheon, 1974.

Nicholson, Linda. "Gender." In *A Companion to Feminist Philosophy,* edited by Alison M. Jaggar and Iris Marion Young. Malden, MA: Blackwell Publishers, Inc., 1998.

Oyěwùmí, Oyèrónké. "Visualizing the Body: Western Theories and African Subjects." In her *The Invention of Women: Making an African Sense of Western Gender Discourses.* Minneapolis: University of Minnesota, 1997.

Rubin, Gayle. "Of Catamites and Kings: Reflections on Butch, Gender, and Boundaries." In *The Persistent Desire: A Femme-Butch Reader,* edited by Joan Nestle. Boston: Alyson Publications, 1992.

Prosser, Jay. "Transgender." In *Lesbian and Gay Studies: A Critical Introduction,* edited by Andy Medhurst and Sally R. Munt. London: Cassell, 1997.

Prosser, Jay. *Second Skins.* New York: Columbia University Press, 1998.

Stone, Sandy. "The Empire Strikes Back: A Posttranssexual Manifesto." In *Body Guards: The Cultural Politics of Gender Ambiguity,* edited by Julia Epstein and Kristina Straub. New York: Routledge, 1993.

West, Candace, and Don Zimmerman. "Doing Gender." *Gender and Society* 1(1987): 125–51.

Whitford, Margaret. *Luce Irigaray: Philosophy in the Feminine.* New York: Routledge, 1991.

Zita, Jacqueline N. *Body Talk: Philosophical Reflections on Sex and Gender.* Columbia University Press, 1998.

MEDIA RESOURCES

A Boy Named Sue. VHS. Directed by Julie Wyman (US, 2000). Documentary chronicling the transformation of a transsexual named Theo from a woman to a man over the course of six years. Available: Women Make Movies, www.wmm.com, or 212–925–0606.

bell hooks: Cultural Criticism & Transformation. VHS Produced and directed by Sut Jhally. Edited by Sut Jhally, Mary Patierno, and Harriet Hirshorn (US 1997). In this two-part video series, bell hooks makes a compelling argument for the transformative power of cultural criticism. Part One addresses critical thinking as transformation, the power of representations, her use of the phrase "White Supremacist Capitalist Patriarchy," and what it means to be an enlightened witness. In Part Two, she demonstrates the value of cultural studies in concrete analysis through such subjects as the OJ Simpson case, black female bodies, Madonna, Spike Lee, and Gangsta rap. The aim of cultural analysis, she argues, should be the production of enlightened witnesses—audiences who engage with the representations of cultural life knowledgeably and vigilantly. Available: Media Education Foundation, http://www.mediaed.org/index_html, or 800–897–0089.

Is It a Boy or Girl? VHS. Directed by Cheryl Chase (US, 2000). Investigation into the medical treatment of intersexuals. Available: Intersex Society of North America, http://www.isna.org/, Fax: 801–348–5350.

Outlaw. VHS. Directed by Alisa Lebow (US, 1994). The story of Leslie Feinberg, a self-identified gender outlaw who has spent most of her life passing for a man. Available: Women Make Movies, www.wmm.com, or 212–925–0606.

Tough Guise: Violence, Media and the Crisis in Masculinity. DVD. Directed by Sut Jhally and produced by Susan Ericsson and Sanjay Talreja (US, 1999). While the social construction of femininity has been widely examined, the dominant role of masculinity has until recently remained largely invisible. *Tough Guise* is the first educational video to systematically examine the relationship between pop-cultural imagery and the social construction of masculine identities in the United States at the dawn of the twenty-first century. A good video to watch with the bell hook's essay on masculinity. Available: Media Education Foundation: http://www.mediaed.org/index_html, or 800–897–0089.

Tongues Untied. VHS/DVD. Directed by Marlon Riggs (US, 1990). Marlon Riggs, with assistance from other gay black men, especially poet Essex Hemphill, celebrates black men loving black men as a revolutionary act. A moving portrait of black masculinities. Available: California Newsreel: http://www.newsreel.org/, or 877–811–7495.

Venus Boys. DVD. Directed by Gabrielle Baur (US, 2002). A cinematic journey through the world of female masculinities. Women become men—some just for a night, others for the rest of their lives. This is a wonderful film about people who create intermediate sexual identities. A perfect film to see before you read Judith Halberstam's essay on female masculinities. Available at many local, and through most online, video stores.

CHAPTER 4

SEXUALITIES

The term sexuality refers to a broad range of behaviors and practices, but also to identities, layers of consciousness, realms of fantasy, aesthetic sensibilities—and social and political systems—that are powerful and pervasive. Feminists typically regard sexuality from a sense that "the personal is political," by analyzing desire and intimate relationships in light of the social contexts that shape them, promoting women's sexual empowerment as a fundamental value, and investigating the sexual politics embedded in many other areas of life. Like conversations about the meanings of gender or race, feminist philosophies of sexuality can be traced in relation to specific political histories. The "sexual revolution" of the 1960s and 1970s, including legalized contraception and abortion, sexual liberation movements, and the advent of the birth control pill, irreversibly changed the sexual landscape for many. In France, feminist intellectuals developed analyses of Western philosophical and literary theories, highlighting the absence of women in Western discourse, and the total "projection of male libidinal economy in all patriarchal systems," including language, capitalism, socialism, and religion. Their response was to explore female libido, "as a first step in discovering what might be the relationships between woman's body, as she interiorizes it, and woman's language" (Marks and de Courtivron, xii). Early work in contemporary feminist philosophy in North America was directly influenced by consciousness-raising groups and newly energized lesbian and bisexual communities, where women's sexual experiences and knowledge also got serious and sustained attention. Feminist movements contributed to the development of greater self-knowledge, and more authentic, gratifying, and adventurous sexual practices and identities for many women.

By the early 1980s the critical conversation had expanded greatly, as the field of Women's Studies grew and feminist theorists began to write on rape, sexual slavery, harassment, pornography, reproductive liberties, and motherhood. Sexuality was also widely discussed as an area for fostering women's political, physical, and spiritual freedom and well-being. Despite some very heated "splits" between lesbians and straight feminists, lesbian philosophy flourished in many circles. In the United States, discussions of lesbian sexuality, separatism, and ethics provided new venues for developing theoretical alternatives to heteropatriarchal ideas.[1] In a landmark essay first published in 1980, Adrienne Rich challenged the idea that heterosexuality is normal and universal, and that women are innately attracted to men. Instead, Rich argued that the ubiquitous ideology that requires female bonding with males indicates that heterosexuality is more likely a product of social conditioning than an innate desire. Her conclusion that heterosexuality is therefore best characterized as a compulsory institution designed to perpetuate male privilege and dominance was extremely influential.

In the later 1980s and 90s the AIDS crisis, coupled with a growing religious "family values" movement, shifted public discussions of sexuality from liberation and freedom to danger and sin. In the United States, political and religious leaders capitalized on the crisis by denouncing sexual freedom and autonomy, and initiating "culture wars" against gay and lesbian communities, feminists, avante-garde artists, and pro-choice organizations.[2] At the same time, funds were funneled away from domestic social welfare programs, dramatically reducing poor and rural women's access to prenatal care, contraception, and abortion. Controversies over morality, free speech, and the definition of acceptable cultural standards raged in headlines, the courts, and college campuses. Feminist and queer navigations of these political sea changes were complicated and intense. Eventually, feminist and lesbian communities became polarized into two camps over sexual ethics and the "feminist acceptability" of pornography, sadomasochism, sex work, transsexuality, and sex with men. Several of the readings in this chapter discuss those "feminist

sex wars," which unearthed an incredible range of challenging philosophical, political, and practical questions and issues.

By the end of the twentieth century, feminist philosophy had made the topics of sexuality, pleasure, violence, and bodily experience quite visible in the discipline. It is sobering to realize that even in the wake of Freud, male philosophers have generally taken their own sexual cultures for granted, and assumed the naturalness of women's sexual subordination. In response, feminists have delved into questions about women's sexual exploitation and disempowerment, and explorations of female-centered sexualities, as rich and open areas for philosophical investigation and innovation.

The title of Luce Irigaray's "This Sex Which Is Not One" refers to female sexuality conceived in its own terms, rather than in reference to masculine parameters. Irigaray rejects the "dominant phallic economy" reproduced by theories such as Freud's and Lacan's, which define woman as a lack and offer nothing of substance concerning female anatomy, pleasure, or possibility. Instead, women's sexuality should be thought of as plurality, for two labia are nearly always in a state of self-caress, and women's bodies have multiple, subtle sites of arousal. Phallic economies alienate women from their own pleasure, and instill in them the desire to possess the phallus vicariously, or to fill a void through maternity. Instead, women require their own "imaginary" and language to realize their sexualities. Renunciations of heterosexuality may be instrumental, but Irigaray is not very optimistic about the liberatory potential of lesbian love or separatism, which she thinks are likely to be simplistic reversals of male domination.

Jessica Benjamin deploys the tools of psychoanalysis to explore how misguided notions of ideal love link female desire to submission rather than freedom. In "A Desire of One's Own," she argues that such notions of ideal love emerge from the daughter's impossible wish to be like the powerful father and be loved by him, because in

---

[1] Of foundational importance in this regard was the work of active lesbian members of Midwest SWIP, including Joyce Trebilcot, Marilyn Frye, Claudia Card, Jackie Anderson, María Lugones, Sarah Hoagland, Jeffner Allen, and Victoria Davion.
[2] The phrase "culture war" was popularized by Patrick Buchanan during his 1992 campaign speech to the Republican National Convention when he proclaimed that conservatives must declare a cultural revolution—"a war for the nation's soul."

heteropatriarchal gender arrangements individuation requires separation from mothers, and the phallus exclusively represents sexual subjectivity and agency. Feminine desire is therefore inevitably associated with passivity and envy, and women lack a "desire of their own." The cultivation of female desire could be enabled by developmental opportunities to identify with both parents as subjects of desire, but Benjamin believes we must also articulate models of desire that do not depend on the phallus. She suggests that the intersubjective nature of erotic interaction and mutual recognition provides an alternative conception of self, where female desire may be found.

In "Sexualities," Catherine MacKinnon expresses less optimism about the liberatory possibilty of authentic female sexuality. She too rejects accepted models of sexuality, such as the theories of Freud and Kinsey, which see it as an innate and unconditioned drive differentiated by gender through heterosexual intercourse. But she concludes that sexuality itself is a product of oppressive male power, because "woman," "the female sex," and "female sexuality" are defined through male desire, arousal, and satisfaction, and women's sexuality is constructed in response to what men want. MacKinnon argues that the domination of women by men, including rape, pornography, sexual harassment, and domestic violence, is inscribed onto the very practices of heterosexuality. Pornography in particular tells the truth about sex: it permits men to have whatever they want sexually. The construction of sexuality under patriarchy forms the basis for social, economic, political, and religious domination of women.

Ann Ferguson's essay "Sex War: The Debate between Radical and Libertarian Feminists," presents a philosophical analysis of the arguments typical on either "side" of the feminist controversies that raged in the 1980s, over pornography, sadomasochism, and other practices associated with objectification and domination. Identifying essentialism and oversimplification in the arguments on either side, Ferguson also

questions the common tendency to consider sexuality in universal terms, removed from its historical and cultural context and influences. Her suggestions for employing a coherent yet pluralist feminist sexual morality include the development of feminist erotica and sex education, and acknowledgment that feminist sexuality can include "risky" practices, such as capitalist-produced pornography, prostitution, and nuclear family relations between male breadwinners and female housewives.

In "Questioning Censorship," the collective Kiss and Tell considers the relationships between power, freedom, and silence in a dialogue on the meanings of censorship and political correctness. The work reprinted here questions objectivity and cultural appropriation, and performs a contemporary feminist tendency to boldly explore contradictory impulses concerning sexual desire, politics, playfulness, and critique. Their dialogical reflection on the repressive power of language and law provides a useful model of artistic philosophical interchange that is truth-seeking and serious about justice, yet open-ended, self-critical, and unapologetic about erotic desire.

In "Toward a Genealogy of Black Female Sexuality: The Problem of Silence," Evelynn Hammonds points to the absence of black women's voices in contemporary discussions of sexual politics in the United States, and asks why black feminists have failed to develop a suitable analysis of their own sexualities. In addressing the problem of silence, she outlines several issues that have shaped the political terrain. Historically, European colonial exploitation and degradation linked the image of the prostitute and the black female, and in the Victorian era black female sexuality was defined in opposition to "the cult of true womanhood"—an imagined ideal of white female sexuality that characterized aristocratic ladies as pure, passionless, and chaste, and black women as impure, immoral, and promiscuous. Those binaries both exposed and pathologized black women. While some black feminist intellectuals presented cogent analyses of the relationships between racism and sexuality, other reformers resisted racist characterizations by representing themselves as exceptionally moral, which provided some protection but also reinforced damaging norms. Hammonds shows how the legacy of silence regarding black female sexuality persists despite changing material conditions, making it nearly impossible to disrupt dominant discourses that vilify black women. She characterizes the work of Audre Lorde and other lesbian writers as evidence that it is possible for black women to disrupt silence and articulate positive affirming sexualities and strategies of resistance.

Chris Cuomo's "Religion and the Right to be Gay" argues that justice for LGBT folks is not merely a matter of dispelling false beliefs and stereotypes. Because anti-gay practices and polices are often based on subjective values and charges of sinfulness, legal protections are needed to prevent members of religious groups from enforcing their religion's punishments and exclusions on those who do not subscribe to their religious rules or beliefs. In order to clarify the meaning and significance of such protections, Cuomo looks at the roots of homophobia, and the relationships between sexual identities and actions.

THIS SEX WHICH IS NOT ONE

Luce Irigaray
Translated by **Catherine Porter**
with **Carolyn Burke**

Female sexuality has always been conceptualized on the basis of masculine parameters. Thus the opposition between "masculine" clitoral activity and "feminine" vaginal passivity, an opposition which Freud—and many others—saw as stages, or alternatives, in the development of a sexually "normal" woman, seems rather too clearly required by the practice of male sexuality. For the clitoris is conceived as a little penis pleasant to masturbate so long as castration anxiety does not exist (for the boy child), and the vagina is valued for the "lodging" it offers the male organ when the forbidden hand has to find a replacement for pleasure-giving.

In these terms, woman's erogenous zones never amount to anything but a clitoris-sex that is not comparable to the noble phallic organ, or a hole-envelope that serves to sheathe and massage the penis in intercourse: a non-sex, or a masculine organ turned back upon itself, self-embracing.

About woman and her pleasure, this view of the sexual relation has nothing to say. Her lot is that of "lack," "atrophy" (of the sexual organ), and "penis envy," the penis being the only sexual organ of recognized value. Thus she attempts by every means available to appropriate that organ for herself: through her somewhat servile love of the father-husband capable of giving her one, through her desire for a child-penis, preferably a boy, through access to the cultural values still reserved by right to males alone and therefore always masculine, and so on. Woman lives her own desire only as the expectation that she may

at last come to possess an equivalent of the male organ.

Yet all this appears quite foreign to her own pleasure, unless it remains within the dominant phallic economy. Thus, for example, woman's autoeroticism is very different from man's. In order to touch himself, man needs an instrument: his hand, a woman's body, language . . . And this self-caressing requires at least a minimum of activity. As for woman, she touches herself in and of herself without any need for mediation, and before there is any way to distinguish activity from passivity. Woman 'touches herself' all the time, and moreover no one can forbid her to do so, for her genitals are formed of two lips in continuous contact. Thus, within herself, she is already two—but not divisible into one(s)—that caress each other.

This autoeroticism is disrupted by a violent break-in: the brutal separation of the two lips by a violating penis, an intrusion that distracts and deflects the woman from this "self-caressing" she needs if she is not to incur the disappearance of her own pleasure in sexual relations. If the vagina is to serve *also,* but *not only,* to take over for the little boy's hand in order to assure an articulation between autoeroticism and heteroeroticism in intercourse (the encounter with the totally other always signifying death), how, in the classic representation of sexuality, can the perpetuation of autoeroticism for woman be managed? Will woman not be left with the impossible alternative between a defensive virginity, fiercely turned in upon itself, and a body open to penetration that no longer knows, in this "hole" that constitutes its sex, the pleasure of its own touch? The more or less exclusive—and highly anxious—attention paid to erection in Western sexuality proves to what extent the imaginary that governs it is foreign to the feminine. For the most part, this sexuality offers nothing but imperatives dictated by male rivalry: the "strongest" being the one who has the best "hard-on," the longest, the biggest, the stiffest penis, or even the one who "pees the farthest" (as in little boys' contests). Or

This text was originally published as "Ce sexe qui n'en est pas un," in *Cahiers du Grif,* no. 5. English translation: "This Sex Which Is Not One," trans. Claudia Reeder, in *New French Feminisms,* eds. Elaine Marks and Isabelle de Courtivron (New York, 1981), pp. 99–106.

else one finds imperatives dictated by the enactment of sadomasochistic fantasies, these in turn
governed by man's relation to his mother: the desire to force entry, to penetrate, to appropriate for
himself the mystery of this womb where he has
been conceived, the secret of his begetting, of his
"origin." Desire/need, also to make blood flow
again in order to revive a very old relationship—
intrauterine, to be sure, but also prehistoric—to
the maternal.

Woman, in this sexual imaginary, is only a
more or less obliging prop for the enactment of
man's fantasies. That she may find pleasure there
in that role, by proxy, is possible, even certain.
But such pleasure is above all a masochistic prostitution of her body to a desire that is not her own,
and it leaves her in a familiar state of dependency
upon man. Not knowing what she wants, ready
for anything, even asking for more, so long as
he will "take" her as his "object" when he seeks
his own pleasure. Thus she will not say what she
herself wants; moreover, she does not know, or
no longer knows, what she wants. As Freud admits, the beginnings of the sexual life of a girl
child are so "obscure," so "faded with time," that
one would have to dig down very deep indeed to
discover beneath the traces of this civilization, of
this history, the vestiges of a more archaic civilization that might give some clue to woman's sexuality. That extremely ancient civilization would
undoubtedly have a different alphabet, a different language . . . Woman's desire would not be
expected to speak the same language as man's;
woman's desire has doubtless been submerged by
the logic that has dominated the West since the
time of the Greeks.

Within this logic, the predominance of the
visual, and of the discrimination and individuali-
zation of form, is particularly foreign to female
eroticism. Woman takes pleasure more from
touching than from looking, and her entry into
a dominant scopic economy signifies, again, her
consignment to passivity: she is to be the beautiful object of contemplation. While her body
finds itself thus eroticized, and called to a double

movement of exhibition and of chaste retreat in
order to stimulate the drives of the "subject," her
sexual organ represents *the horror of nothing to
see.* A defect in this systematics of representation and desire. A "hole" in its scoptophilic lens.
It is already evident in Greek statuary that this
nothing-to-see has to be excluded, rejected, from
such a scene of representation. Woman's genitals
are simply absent, masked, sewn back up inside
their "crack."

This organ which has nothing to show for itself also lacks a form of its own. And if woman
takes pleasure precisely from this incomplete-
ness of form which allows her organ to touch
itself over and over again, indefinitely, by itself,
that pleasure is denied by a civilization that privileges phallomorphism. The value granted to the
only definable form excludes the one that is in
play in female autoeroticism. The *one* of form,
of the individual, of the (male) sexual organ, of
the proper name, of the proper meaning . . . supplants, while separating and dividing, that contact of *at least two* (lips) which keeps woman in
touch with herself, but without any possibility
of distinguishing what is touching from what is
touched.

Whence the mystery that woman represents in
a culture claiming to count everything, to number
everything by units, to inventory everything as
individualities. *She is neither one nor two.* Rigorously speaking, she cannot be identified either
as one person, or as two. She resists all adequate
definition. Further, she has no "proper" name.
And her sexual organ, which is not *one* organ, is
counted as *none.* The negative, the underside, the
reverse of the only visible and morphologically
designatable organ (even if the passage from
erection to detumescence does pose some problems): the penis.

But the "thickness" of that "form," the layer-
ing of its volume, its expansions and contractions
and even the spacing of the moments in which
it produces itself as form—all this the feminine
keeps secret. Without knowing it. And if woman
is asked to sustain, to revive, man's desire, the

request neglects to spell out what it implies as to the value of her own desire. A desire of which she is not aware, moreover, at least not explicitly. But one whose force and continuity are capable of nurturing repeatedly and at length all the masquerades of "feminity" that are expected of her.

It is true that she still has the child, in relation to whom her appetite for touch, for contact, has free rein, unless it is already lost, alienated by the taboo against touching of a highly obsessive civilization. Otherwise her pleasure will find, in the child, compensations for and diversions from the frustrations that she too often encounters in sexual relations per se. Thus maternity fills the gaps in a repressed female sexuality. Perhaps man and woman no longer caress each other except through that mediation between them that the child—preferably a boy—represents? Man, identified with his son, rediscovers the pleasure of maternal fondling; woman touches herself again by caressing that part of her body: her baby-penis-clitoris.

What this entails for the amorous trio is well known. But the Oedipal interdiction seems to be a somewhat categorical and factitious law—although it does provide the means for perpetuating the authoritarian discourse of fathers—when it is promulgated in a culture in which sexual relations are impracticable because man's desire and woman's are strangers to each other. And in which the two desires have to try to meet through indirect means, whether the archaic one of a sense-relation to the mother's body, or the present one of active or passive extension of the law of the father. These are regressive emotional behaviors, exchanges of words too detached from the sexual arena not to constitute an exile with respect to it: "mother" and "father" dominate the interactions of the couple, but as social roles. The division of labor prevents them from making love. They produce or reproduce. Without quite knowing how to use their leisure. Such little as they have, such little indeed as they wish to have. For what are they to do with leisure? What substitute for amorous resource are they to invent? Still . . .

Perhaps it is time to return to that repressed entity, the female imaginary. So woman does not have a sex organ? She has at least two of them, but they are not identifiable as ones. Indeed, she has many more. Her sexuality, always at least double, goes even further: it is *plural.* Is this the way culture is seeking to characterize itself now? Is this the way texts write themselves/are written now? Without quite knowing what censorship they are evading? Indeed, woman's pleasure does not have to choose between clitoral activity and vaginal passivity, for example. The pleasure of the vaginal caress does not have to be substituted for that of the clitoral caress. They each contribute, irreplaceably, to woman's pleasure. Among other caresses . . . Fondling the breasts, touching the vulva, spreading the lips, stroking the posterior wall of the vagina, brushing against the mouth of the uterus, and so on. To evoke only a few of the most specifically female pleasures. Pleasures which are somewhat misunderstood in sexual difference as it is imagined—or not imagined, the other sex being only the indispensable complement to the only sex.

But *woman has sex organs more or less everywhere.* She finds pleasure almost anywhere. Even if we refrain from invoking the hystericization of her entire body, the geography of her pleasure is far more diversified, more multiple in its differences, more complex, more subtle, than is commonly imagined—in an imaginary rather too narrowly focused on sameness.

"She" is indefinitely other in herself. This is doubtless why she is said to be whimsical, incomprehensible, agitated, capricious . . . not to mention her language, in which "she" sets off in all directions leaving "him" unable to discern the coherence of any meaning. Hers are contradictory words, somewhat mad from the standpoint of reason, inaudible for whoever listens to them with ready-made grids, with a fully elaborated code in hand. For in what she says, too, at least when she dares, woman is constantly touching herself. She steps ever so slightly aside from herself with a murmur, an exclamation, a whisper, a sentence left unfinished . . . When she returns, it is to set off again from elsewhere. From another point of pleasure, or of pain. One would have to listen with another ear, as if hearing *an "other meaning" always in the process of weaving itself, of embracing itself with words, but also of getting rid of words in order not to become fixed, congealed in them.* For if "she" says something, it is not, it is already no longer, identical with what she means. What she says is never identical with anything, moreover; rather, it is contiguous. *It touches (upon).* And when it strays too far from that proximity, she breaks off and starts over at "zero": her body-sex.

It is useless, then, to trap women in the exact definition of what they mean, to make them repeat (themselves) so that it will be clear; they are already elsewhere in that discursive machinery where you expected to surprise them. They have returned within themselves. Which must not be understood in the same way as within yourself. They do not have the interiority that you have, the one you perhaps suppose they have. Within themselves means *within the intimacy of that silent, multiple, diffuse touch.* And if you ask them insistently what they are thinking about, they can only reply: Nothing. Everything.

Thus what they desire is precisely nothing, and at the same time everything. Always something more and something else besides that *one*— sexual organ, for example—that you give them, attribute to them. Their desire is often interpreted, and feared, as a sort of insatiable hunger, a voracity that will swallow you whole. Whereas it really involves a different economy more than anything else, one that upsets the linearity of a project, undermines the goal-object of a desire, diffuses the polarization toward a single pleasure, disconcerts fidelity to a single discourse . . .

Must this multiplicity of female desire and female language be understood as shards, scattered remnants of a violated sexuality? A sexuality denied? The question has no simple answer. The rejection, the exclusion of a female imaginary certainly puts woman in the position of experiencing herself only fragmentarily, in the little-structured margins of a dominant ideology, as waste, or excess, what is left of a mirror invested by the (masculine) "subject" to reflect himself, to copy himself. Moreover, the role of "femininity" is prescribed by this masculine specula(riza)tion and corresponds scarcely at all to woman's desire, which may be recovered only in secret, in hiding, with anxiety and guilt.

But if the female imaginary were to deploy itself, if it could bring itself into play otherwise than as scraps, uncollected debris, would it represent itself, even so, in the form of *one* universe? Would it even be volume instead of surface? No. Not unless it were understood, yet again, as a privileging of the maternal over the feminine. Of a phallic maternal, at that. Closed in upon the jealous possession of its valued product. Rivaling man in his esteem for productive excess. In such a race for power, woman loses the uniqueness of her pleasure. By closing herself off as volume, she renounces the pleasure that she gets from the *non-suture of her lips:* she is undoubtedly a mother, but a virgin mother, the role was assigned to her by mythologies long ago. Granting her a certain social power to the extent that she is reduced, with her own complicity, to sexual impotence.

(Re-)discovering herself, for a woman, thus could only signify the possibility of sacrificing no one of her pleasures to another, of identifying herself with none of them in particular, *of never being simply one.* A sort of expanding universe to which no limits could be fixed and which would not be incoherence nonetheless—nor that polymorphous perversion of the child in which the erogenous zones would lie waiting to be regrouped under the primacy of the phallus.

Woman always remains several, but she is kept from dispersion because the other is already within her and is autoerotically familiar to her. Which is not to say that she appropriates the other for herself, that she reduces it to her own property. Ownership and property are doubtless quite foreign to the feminine. At least sexually. But not *nearness.* Nearness so pronounced that it makes all discrimination of identity, and thus all forms of property, impossible. Woman derives pleasure from what is *so near that she cannot have it, nor have herself.* She herself enters into a ceaseless exchange of herself with the other without any possibility of identifying either. This puts into question all prevailing economies: their calculations are irremediably stymied by woman's pleasure, as it increases indefinitely from its passage in and through the other.

However, in order for woman to reach the place where she takes pleasure as woman, a long detour by way of the analysis of the various systems of oppression brought to bear upon her is assuredly necessary. And claiming to fall back on the single solution of pleasure risks making her miss the process of going back through a social practice that *her* enjoyment requires.

For woman is traditionally a use-value for man, an exchange value among men; in other words, a commodity. As such, she remains the guardian of material substance, whose price will be established, in terms of the standard of their work and of their need/desire, by "subjects": workers, merchants, consumers. Women are marked phallically by their fathers, husbands, procurers. And this branding determines their value in sexual commerce. Woman is never anything but the locus of a more or less competitive exchange between two men, including the competition for the possession of mother earth.

How can this object of transaction claim a right to pleasure without removing her/itself from established commerce? With respect to other merchandise in the marketplace, how could this commodity maintain a relationship other than one of aggressive jealousy? How could material substance enjoy her/itself without provoking the consumer's anxiety over the disappearance of his nurturing ground? How could that exchange— which can in no way be defined in terms "proper" to woman's desire—appear as anything but a pure mirage, mere foolishness, all too readily obscured by a more sensible discourse and by a system of apparently more tangible values?

A woman's development, however radical it may seek to be, would thus not suffice to liberate woman's desire. And to date no political theory or political practice has resolved, or sufficiently taken into consideration, this historical problem, even though Marxism has proclaimed its importance. But women do not constitute, strictly speaking, a class, and their dispersion among several classes makes their political struggle complex, their demands sometimes contradictory.

There remains, however, the condition of underdevelopment arising from women's submission by and to a culture that oppresses them, uses them, makes of them a medium of exchange, with very little profit to them. Except in the quasi monopolies of masochistic pleasure, the domestic labor force, and reproduction. The powers of slaves? Which are not negligible powers, moreover. For where pleasure is concerned, the master is not necessarily well served. Thus to reverse the relation, especially in the economy of sexuality, does not seem a desirable objective.

But if women are to preserve and expand their autoeroticism, their homo-sexuality, might not the renunciation of heterosexual pleasure correspond once again to that disconnection from power that is traditionally theirs? Would it not involve a new prison, a new cloister, built of their own accord? For women to undertake tactical strikes, to keep themselves apart from men long enough to learn to defend their desire, especially through speech, to discover the love of other women while sheltered from men's imperious choices that put them in the position of rival commodities, to forge for themselves a social status that compels recognition, to earn their living in order to escape from the condition of prostitute . . . these are certainly indispensable stages in the escape from their proletarization on the exchange market. But if their aim were simply to reverse the order of things, even supposing this to be possible, history would repeat itself in the long run, would revert to sameness: to phallocratism. It would leave room neither for women's sexuality, nor for women's imaginary, nor for women's language to take (their) place.

A DESIRE OF ONE'S OWN: PSYCHOANALYTIC FEMINISM AND INTERSUBJECTIVE SPACE

Jessica Benjamin

The question of woman's desire actually runs parallel to the question of power. We have often had cause to wonder whether the feminist focus on personal life, and for that matter the preoccupation with inner life that characterizes psychoanalysis, is fated to surrender the great issues of power. That would mean that the revaluation of things feminine in fact perpetuates the split between transcendence and immanence that Simone de Beauvoir saw as the great divide between the sexes. And yet, the challenge to this kind of split may be the greatest theoretical insight that feminism has to offer. Feminist thought is caught between three tasks: to redeem what has been devalued in women's domain, to conquer the territory that has been reserved to men, and to resolve and transcend the opposition between these spheres by reformulating the relationship between them. The structural tension between male and female categories and the difficulty of reformulating it are as pertinent to the problems of sexuality as to those of politics.

Consider again the origins of the idea that "the personal is political." It grew and flourished from within the high-flown rhetoric of revolutionary idealism as a critique of the ideal of sacrifice for the greater good that is intimately connected with the vision of individual transcendence through social struggle. As Carol Gilligan has pointed out in a discussion of *the Aeneid,* the notion of social responsibility conceived as duty or obligation has gone hand in hand with the representation of the self as separate, bounded, and autonomous.[1] This notion of sacrifice is inextricably associated with the idea that one is responsible only for one's self and that one can consider the web

of immediate personal connections as less important than, for example, the abstract, universal cause of humanity, the founding of Rome, or the liberation of the oppressed.

It should be obvious that the reason women began to question this conception of struggle and sacrifice, to claim that the personal was also political, came from their very inability to detach themselves from such personal ties, especially from their responsibilities to children. They were not as able to devalue such attachments as were men. In de Beauvoir's terms, that could be seen only in the negative: women were trapped in immanence while men could heroically struggle for transcendence, for the personal glory that comes with sacrifice and valor. Indeed, what has always seemed curious about de Beauvoir's feminism is her agreement with the male idealization of individual transcendence and sacrifice over personal connection and responsibility. The doctrine of "the personal is political" not only meant the affirmation of personal responsibilities as equal to abstract ones; it also meant the rejection of this idealization, the awareness that it had fostered submission and passivity and hero worship on the part of women.

With the emergence of women's liberation, women began to reflect on the contradictory position in which they found themselves; more skeptical about detachment, less committed to idealizing absolute separation, women were yet ready to idealize the man who represented and gave them vicarious access to transcendence. Women's defense of personal attachment had been double-edged—at once a critique of heroism and a reflection of woman's need to be close to her hero and to his project, thus compliance with, as well as a challenge to, male idealized independence. Suddenly, in a kind of euphoric moment of demystification, this contradiction became visible and unsupportable.

De Beauvoir herself did much to analyze and demystify the wish for vicarious transcendence, woman's hope that the idealized other will give "her possession of herself and of the universe he represents."[2] Here she quotes a patient of Janet's, who expresses with un-selfconscious ardor the yearning for what I call ideal love:

> All my foolish acts and all the good things I have done have the same cause: an aspiration for a perfect and ideal love in which I can give myself completely, entrust my being to another, God, man, or woman, so superior to me that I will no longer need to think what to do in life. . . . Someone to obey blindly and with confidence . . . who will bear me up and lead me gently and lovingly toward perfection. How I envy the ideal love of Mary Magdalene and Jesus: to be the ardent disciple of an adored and worthy master; to live and die for him, my idol. (pp. 716–19)

The subject of this paper is woman's propensity toward ideal love. Ideal love typifies the curious role of women in both criticizing and complying with the elevation of masculine individuality and the devaluation of femininity. I shall argue that ideal love is the key to understanding the intricate relationship between woman's desire and woman's submission. I will try to show how the critique of individualism that has been developing within psychoanalytic feminism leads us to explore another level of an old problem, the problem of woman's desire. Today we may consider this problem with the greater clarity that derives from an analysis of the gender split, and with the resolve to confront not only the idealization of masculinity but also the reactive revaluation of femininity—a femininity whose character has been constituted as the other, the opposite, the excluded.

According to current developments in psychoanalytic feminism, the salient feature of male individuality is that it grows out of the repudiation of the primary identification with and dependency on the mother. That leads to an individuality that stresses, as Nancy Chodorow has argued, difference as denial of commonality, separation as denial of connection; and that is made up of a series of dualisms, of mutually exclusive poles, where independence seems to exclude all dependency rather than be character-

ized by a balance of separation and connection.[3] The critique of this form of individualism is the contribution of the evolving integration of object relations theory with feminism that began with Chodorow's work. Central to this critique of dualism, cogently elaborated by Evelyn Fox Keller in relation to scientific thought, is the awareness that the idealization of a particular form of one-sided autonomy permeates the Western notion of the individual as thinking subject, as explorer of the world. I have argued that this idealization is profoundly embedded in all modern social activity and forms of knowledge; it informs the traditions of Western rationality and underlies the instrumental character that stamps that rationality.[4]

Elsewhere I have tried to show how the one-sided autonomy that denies dependency characteristically leads to domination.[5] Since the child continues to need the mother, since man continues to need woman, the absolute assertion of independence requires possessing and controlling the needed object. The intention is not to do without her but to make sure that her alien otherness is either assimilated or controlled, that her own subjectivity nowhere asserts itself in a way that could make his dependency upon her a conscious insult to his sense of freedom. In his discussion of the ideal subject in philosophical idealism, Herbert Marcuse explains:

> Self-sufficiency and independence of all that is other and alien is the sole guarantee of the subject's freedom. What is not dependent on any other person or thing, what possesses itself, is free. . . . Having excludes the other. . . . Relating to the other in such a way that the subject really reaches and is united with him counts as loss and dependence.[6]

Naturally, Marcuse identifies this form of individuality with the bourgeois era, with the possessive individualism of specific property relations. Historically, that identification—based on Marx's ideas about the interaction of economics and ideology—has been the springboard for the critique of the autonomous individual. In Max

Weber's view, the precondition of this individuality and its consummation in the Protestant ethic can be located in the essential rationality of the Occident.[7] To these frameworks, feminist theory added an analysis of psychological and social core of this individual in the domination of woman by man. Thus, the missing piece in analyzing Western rationality and individualism is the structure of gender domination. This structure is materialized—in a way that occludes its gender roots—in the instrumentalism that pervades our economic and social relations. A feminist analysis reveals this apparent gender neutrality of instrumental rationality to be a mystification, parallel, if you like, to the mystification of commodity fetishism—an illusion created by the gender relations themselves.

In psychoanalysis, it becomes more apparent that the celebration of individuality is a gender-related project. Indeed, the feminist critique of individualism has taken psychoanalysis itself to task both for its tendency to make independence and separateness the goal of development (as in the view that the ego develops from oneness to separateness) and for the idea that femininity is defined by the lack of the penis. As Chodorow has pointed out, these two coordinates of Freudian thought are interconnected, drawn from the plane of the masculine experience of individuation. In fact, the idealization of separation and the idealization of the phallus go together. We see that in Juliet Mitchell's argument that the phallus is the representative of the principle of individuation. The father and his phallus intervene to spring the child from the dyadic trap, the oneness with mother, forcing the child to individuate.[8] This theme has been reiterated in myriad forms; indeed, the relationship to the father's phallus may be the indissoluble lump in the batter for a feminist version of psychoanalysis.[9] It presents us with the dilemma that desire and power, symbolically speaking, are one. And the consequences for the girl are, as Mitchell put it, "no phallus, no power, except those winning ways of getting one" (p. 96).

The logic of this position can only succumb to a massive critique of a whole set of assumptions in Freudian thought: that individuality is defined by separateness; that separation is brought about through paternal intervention (read authority); that the father's phallus, which forbids incest, is the prime mover of separation; that the girl's lack of the phallus relegates her to a passive, envious relationship to father and phallus; that this position, in which the girl is deprived of her own agency and desire, is the hallmark of femininity. Against each of these assertions, persuasive evidence has been cited and arguments have been mounted. New ways of looking at self and other emerged, in fact, before the recent wave of feminism. What psychoanalytic feminists have done is to locate the problem in the structure of gender relations, thus offering a materialist explanation for the misapprehensions in Freudian thought, and for the insistent sticky pull of orthodoxy that every critic must still confront. The critique of psychoanalysis as ideology ultimately goes beyond the idea of bias to the idea of real appearance: it shows how the sexual fallacies reflect the real appearance of gender relations.

Briefly, a critical feminist psychoanalytic theory offers the following answers. We argue that individuality is properly, ideally, a balance of separation and connectedness, of the capacities for agency and relatedness. We rely on infancy research that suggests that the self does not proceed from oneness to separateness, but evolves by simultaneously differentiating and recognizing the other, by alternating between "being with" and being distinct.[10] We say that once we shift from the oedipal perspective that Mitchell uses to the preoedipal one, it is clear that the impulse toward separation is present from the start, that no outside agitator is required. We maintain that the vital issue is whether the mother herself is able to recognize the child's subjectivity, and later whether the child can recognize the mother. Thus, we dispute the necessity of the patriarchal mode of separation.

Perhaps most important, we begin with a new position on femininity; we argue that long before the oedipal phase and the emergence of penis envy, the little girl has consolidated her feminine gender identity on the basis of her identification with her mother. Freud's argument that such identification is not truly feminine, that only the penis wish and the passive love of the father are feminine, seems simply implausible. It gives way before the explanatory power of the alternate model of gender evolution—that the girl sustains her primary identification with the mother and that the boy must break that identity and switch to the father.[11] It is this break in identification that brings about the attitude of repudiation and distance toward primary connectedness, nurturance, and intimacy that characterizes the male model of independence, the male idealization of autonomy. Thus, maternal identification theory leans toward the revaluation of the mother, whose influence Freud neglected in favor of the father, and is less likely than the theory of phallic monism to emphasize the negativity of the female condition.

Yet this position, precisely because of its emphasis on the mother, is vulnerable to the objection that it disregards the Freudian argument, not so easily explained away, that women lack a desire of their own. The problem of desire is more likely to be addressed by feminists who work in the Lacanian tradition, which begins with the phallus as the central organizer of gender.[12] The idea of desire suggests power and activity, even as, it would seem, does the image of male desire, the phallus. Freud cautioned against the easy equation of femininity with passivity and masculinity with activity, yet he found that the circuitous path to femininity culminates in the acceptance of passivity. Thus, Mitchell herself has proposed that we accept Freud's understanding of feminine passivity in representing desire. Only by acknowledging the power of the phallus, she argues, can we finally confront the negativity of our condition and understand the origins of woman's submission, the deep unconscious roots of patriarchy.

Indeed, we must admit that we are still unable to produce a female image or symbol that would counterbalance the monopoly of the phallus in representing desire. Woman's sexuality is primarily portrayed through her object status, her ability to attract. The closest we have come to an image of feminine activity is motherhood and fertility. But the mother is not culturally articulated as a sexual subject, one who actively desires something for herself—quite the contrary.[13] And once sexuality is cut loose from reproduction, once woman is no longer mother, we are at a loss for an image of woman's sexual agency. What is woman's desire?

The idea that little girls develop their gender identity through identification with the mother is persuasive. But it does not entirely solve the problem that penis envy was meant to explain.[14] The fact is, as Dinnerstein has described it, that the little girl's sexuality is muted by the fact that the woman she must identify with, her mother, is so profoundly desexualized (Dinnerstein sees the girl, like the boy, as complicit in this desexualization, because it is a way of reacting against the mother's omnipotence; thus, as mother, she must deny her own sexuality). The reasons for the desexualization of the mother—the fear of her power and the need to control her, the source of goodness—have often been discussed. But there is a reason beyond the wishes of the child in each of us, one that arises from the current practice of motherhood, that is, the frequent depression of the isolated mother, the "housewife's syndrome." To be a subject of desire, a sexual agent, implies a control over one's own destiny, a freedom to will, that mothers often lack. Their power over their children is not to be mistaken for the freedom to act on their own wishes and impulses, to be author and agent in their own lives. The mother's sexual feelings, with their threat of selfishness, passion, and uncontrollability, are a disturbing possibility that even psychoanalysts would relegate to the "unnatural."

Briefly, then, the power of the mother cannot, as in the case of the father, be described as the power of a sexual subject. Ironically, psychoanalytic thought often depicts the power the mother has over her child with the emblem of the phallus. In this view, the child does not know that the mother's power is not the power of a subject until desire, especially genital desire, begins to enter the picture. Thus, it is the "phallic" mother who is powerful in the preoedipal era and the "castrated" mother who is repudiated by the boy in the oedipal era. According to this theory, the little girl loves her phallic mother actively but turns away from her when she discovers that she can get the phallus only from her father, whom she agrees to love passively.[15] Hence, Freud argued, for woman desire is constituted by the effort to get the missing phallus, an effort that leads her irrevocably into the passive position of being the object for the father, the male subject. In this sense, woman has no active desire; instead, she is doomed to envy the embodiment of desire, which forever eludes her since only a man can possess it. Desire in women thus appears as envy, and only as envy. For Freud, what woman lacks is a desire of her own.

Let us acknowledge the real problem, the partial truth of this gloomy view.[16] So far, women do not have an equivalent image of desire; the existing equation of masculinity with desire, and femininity with object-of-desire, reflects a condition that does exist; it is not merely a biased view. It is a real appearance—real, yes, but only apparently essential, rather a manifestation of deeper causes. This condition, then, is not inevitable but has come into being through forces we intend to understand and counteract. We need not deny the contribution of anatomical reality in shaping the current condition of femininity; we only have to argue that how biological givens are psychically organized is partly the work of culture, of social arrangements, which we can change or redirect. To begin to think about such changes, we need to understand the complex unconscious forces that contribute to our current gender arrangements.

In this case we are asking, What are the deeper causes to which we might attribute woman's lack of sexual subjectivity? How does woman's desire become alienated into forms of submission and dependency? How does it come about that femininity appears inextricably linked to passivity, even to masochism, or that women seek their desire in another, hope to have it recognized and recognizable through the subjectivity of an other?

The danger of the position that sees identification with the mother as the source of femininity is that we will accept, even idealize, the deprivation to which women have been subjected. We may detect in some contemporary feminist thought the incipient rejection of sexuality as a component of woman's autonomy. That would mean avoiding a confrontation with the aspects of masculinity we wish to appropriate, making sexuality and desire the right of the stronger. The idealization of motherhood, which can be traced through popular culture to both antifeminist and feminist cultural politics, can be seen as an attempt to preserve a sphere of influence and agency, the power of the apron strings. But all these tendencies are united by the tendency to naturalize woman's desexualization and lack of agency in the world. Two dangers arise from a one-sided revaluing of woman's position: freedom and desire might remain unchallenged male domain, leaving us to be righteous and deeroticized, intimate, caring, and self-sacrificing; or we might ignore the power of sexual imagery and the unconscious relationships represented by it. Then we would fail to understand the psychology of male domination, the force of desire that substantiates power, the adoration that creates it ever anew.

The theory of maternal identification does provide us with a new starting point, but it has to be further developed in order to confront the problem of woman's desire. It must struggle with the unconscious and the exclusive power of the phallus in representing desire. With what shall we represent our desire? I believe that the new theory of gender identification can yet point the way out of the dilemma of penis envy; that we do not, as Mitchell claimed in her allegiance to Freud, have to wait until some other principle of individuation and desire appears in the society of the future. Briefly, I will argue that what Freud saw as the little girl's early masculine orientation really reflects the wish of the toddler—of both sexes—to identify with the father, who is perceived as a representative of the outside world.

Psychoanalysis has accepted the importance of the boy's early love for the father in forming his sense of agency and desire; it has not assigned equal importance to the girl's early love. This early love of the father is an ideal love; that is, it is full of the idealization that such a little child forms not merely because the father is big but because the father appears to be the solution to a series of conflicts that occur at this point in development. This idealization becomes the basis for future relationships of ideal love, the submission to a powerful other who seems to embody the agency and desire one lacks in oneself, someone who can be a mirror of one's ideal image of the self.

Critics of Freud have long argued that the father and his phallus have the power they do because of their ability to stand for difference and separation from the mother. The phallus is not intrinsically the symbol of desire but becomes so because of the child's search for a pathway to individuation. As long as the traditional sexual division of labor persists, the child will turn to the father as the "knight in shining armor"[17] who represents freedom, the outside world, will, agency, and desire. But the way in which the father represents all of that is given by the interaction of the child's own internal psychological workings with social and cultural conditions. As each phase of infancy has been analyzed in terms of the infant's own contribution to interaction, the different responses of mothers and fathers can be schematized for each phase. Thus, we can see the creation of composite gender representations through accumulated experience in each

phase. For example, it has been noted that in early infancy the father plays more exuberantly and wildly with the baby, jiggling and whooping, while the mother, absorbed with caretaking and responsibility, feeling less separate from the child she has borne, is less playful.[18] In the child's earliest perceptions, then, the father may stand for outsideness, novelty, stimulation, and excitement; the mother for soothing, holding, and containment.

The importance of the father as a figure of excitement becomes crucial only at the point where the child begins to experience differentiation—the process of sorting out self and other and becoming more autonomous—in a more conflictual way. This point, according to the most powerful psychoanalytic paradigm of early development, Margaret Mahler's separation-individuation theory, occurs around the second half of the second year of life.[19] The Rapprochement phase, as she has called it, might be seen as the great fall from grace. At this point, the child's awareness of its separate existence intensifies, with the child becoming conscious of its dependency. The child is confronted with this truth: mother is not an extension of myself; since we are separate, I possess only my own limited powers; everything she does for me is not under my control, not a reflection of my will. This blow to the child's narcissism has to be repaired by parental confirmation of the child's independence. Thus emerges a fundamental paradox: the need to be recognized as independent by the very person you once depended upon. The underlying question is whether the price of selfhood is going to be the loss of the mother's love, or, conversely, whether the price of love is to be the inhibition of autonomy.

What is really wanted at this point in life is recognition of one's desire, that one *is* a subject of desire, an agent who can will things and make them happen. And at this very point, early in life, where desire enters in, the first realizations of gender difference begin to take hold in the psyche. That is, coincidentally, the period of "core gender identity formation," in Robert Stoller's term. And it is the point at which the father's difference from the mother first becomes crucial. What is interesting is that little boys seem to get through this phase with more bravado and less depression than girls. If boys tend to escape the depression associated with Rapprochement, it is because they are able to deny the feeling of helplessness that comes with the realization of separateness. Mahler says they do so by virtue of their greater "motor-mindedness," which helps sustain the buoyancy of their body ego feelings, their pleasure in active aggressive strivings.[20] In light of the well-known fascination of little boys with motor vehicles, that could be called the tendency to brmm brmm brmm one's way through Rapprochement.

Feminists have argued that the mother's greater identification with the daughter and her willingness to bolster the son's independence are responsible for the differences between boy and girl toddlers' reactions to Rapprochement.[21] That may be true. But equally important is that boys seem to resolve the conflict of independence with the mother by turning to someone else. And this other is conventionally the father, or male substitute or symbol, who can be a different object of identification. At this point, when the child is discovering its own desire and agency, the father's position as the one who was outside, who was exciting, becomes crucial. The father, as Ernest Abelin has argued, becomes the subject of desire in whom the child wishes to recognize himself.[22] Importantly, in this phase of life excitement begins to be felt not as emanating from the object (she, it is so attractive) but as a property of the self, one's own inner desire. The father now becomes the symbolic figure who represents just such an owner of desire, desire for the mother (Abelin makes much of the fact that the desire is toward the mother; I am inclined to think it more diffuse, but that may vary with the mother's ability to juggle availability to the demanding husband and son). This recognition of himself in the father also enables the boy to deny the helplessness felt at this phase, to feel that he is power-

ful like his father. Paternal identification thus has a defensive aspect—the son denies dependency and dissociates himself from his previous tie—that later stamps this ideal image of the father.

The child is in conflict between the desire to hold on to the mother and the desire to fly away, and wants to solve this problem by becoming independent without experiencing loss. The great desire of the child is to be recognized in all its triumphant willing. The solution to this dilemma is to split—to assign the contradictory strivings to different objects. Schematically, the mother can become the object of desire, the father the subject of desire in whom one recognizes oneself. This "way out" of the internal conflict around dependency is usually realized fully only in boys, for only in boys is this identification with the father encouraged by mother and father alike. Both children have the wish to separate and experience themselves as subjects of desire, but only boys seem to have full access to a vehicle for this wish. The vehicle has both defensive and constructive aspects: on the one hand, it enables the child to separate, avoiding the Rapprochement conflict and denying feelings of helplessness; on the other, it helps consolidate a representation of desire, excitement, and the outside world with which the child can identify.

The ideal love of the child for the father reflects the child's longing to be recognized by a powerful other as being like him. Psychoanalysts have called the period preceding this one, where the child is elated about his new abilities and locomotion, a "love affair with the world." In Rapprochement, the love affair with the world becomes a love affair with the father, indeed, a homoerotic love affair. The boy's identificatory love for the father, his wish to be recognized as like him, is the erotic force behind separation. Desire is intrinsically linked, at this point, to the idea of freedom. But the separation that is presumably occurring actually takes place in the context of a powerful connection. Indeed, identification is the chief mode of connecting with others in this phase, as the well-known phenomenon of parallel play suggests. The longing for this ideal love, this identificatory love of the child for the father, is the basis of the idealization of the father and male power, as well as of the cultural construction of the autonomous individual that I referred to earlier. But it is an idealization untainted with submission as long as the wonderful, exciting father says, "Yes, you are like me."

Thus, I believe that the key to the missing desire in women is in one sense the missing father. Being the I who desires is routed through identification with him. Why has the discussion of the father-daughter relationship been so thin compared to that of the father-son relationship?[23] The psychoanalytic commonplace is that the boy has one object (the mother), and the girl has two (mother and father). But at times we are tempted to think that the boy has two and the girl has none. I believe that behind the missing phallus, the envy that has been attributed to women, is the longing for just such a homoerotic bond, just such an ideal love. That is why we find so many stories of woman's love being directed to a hero such as she herself would be, accompanied by the wish for disciplehood and submission to an ideal. We can also explain the identification with little boys that Freud found in women's masochistic fantasies ("A Child Is Being Beaten"[24]) by reference to the longing for this homoerotic, ideal love. It is the wish to be like the powerful father, and to be loved by him, that appears in this alien form. The more common variety of ideal love, a woman's adoration of heroic men who sacrifice love for freedom, can thus be traced back to this phase of life and the disappointments a girl usually suffers. When Bogart tells Bergman that in this world the troubles of a few little people don't amount to a hill of beans, and he walks off into the sunset with the French colonel to join the resistance, we have the whole story.

I will draw several conclusions from this model. Historically, the gap left in the girl's subjectivity by the missing father appeared as a lack, which the theory of penis envy emerged to fill.

On the level of real life, when the desire to identify is blocked, envy takes its place. Unlike jealousy, envy is about being, not having, and should be read as a signal of thwarted identification. On the other hand, under the present gender system, the girl's wish to identify with the father, even if it is satisfied, leads to myriad problems. As long as the mother is not articulated as a sexual agent, identification with the father's agency and desire must appear illegitimate and stolen; furthermore, it conflicts with the cultural image of woman-as-sexual-object and with the girl's maternal identification. It will not correspond with what she knows about her mother's position in her father's eyes.[25]

The "real" solution to this dilemma of woman's desire is much further-reaching and has to do with the need for a mother who *is* articulated as a sexual subject, who is an agent, who does express desire. Thus, psychoanalytic feminism rejects both the idea that the mother cannot be a figure of separation and a subject of desire for her children, and the idea that the father cannot offer himself as a figure of identification for the daughter. We therefore challenge the structure of heterosexuality as it is formed through the differential meanings of mother and father, rooted in the early acquisition of gender, and shaped by the earliest splitting of the psyche.

Yet, even this early phase of gender is less rigid than the oedipal organization that comes after it. In the second and third years of life, gender is still loose, contradictory, and vague. The child is still interested in identifying with both parents, in being everything. My point is not that gender can or should be eliminated but that along with a conviction of gender identity, the individual ideally integrates and expresses male and female aspects of selfhood. This integration then allows flexibility in the expression of gender and one's own individual will. That could be called an argument for androgyny or bisexuality—not a rejection of gender but a vision of reconciling the gendered self with the self that is bi-, or supra-, or nongendered.

In making this argument for gender flexibility, I am aware that I am crossing the frontier into defending, rather than merely explicating, the early magical and narcissistic wishes against the oedipal reality principle. It is not my intention wholly to deny the critique of narcissism and early splitting made by Otto Kernberg or Christopher Lasch in particular. I am not saying that individuals should not grow up, should bask in preoedipal unreality. But this period, if all goes well, is precisely not characterized by more intense splitting of opposites, especially when it comes to gender. Rather, I believe that the magical hope of reconciling gender oppositions that children of this age possess appears wholly unrealistic only in the light of our present cultural schisms. If our interest is in gender structures rather than ego pathology, it is worth questioning the conventional psychoanalytic position that splitting is more of a problem in preoedipal than in oedipal life.

What hampers the crossing over and intermingling, the abrogation of boundaries that ideally should exist alongside gender structures? The verdict is that the derogation of the female side of these polarities in every case leads to a hardening of the opposition between aspects of male and female individuality as now constructed.[26] The taboo on maternal sexual agency, the defensive mode of separation where the father is used to deny the mother, the idealization of the male figure in identificatory love, and the confirmation that the price of freedom is the relinquishment of nurturance and dependency—each of these reflects the derogation of femininity. The oedipal sexual organization now defines the form of our parenting arrangements, our cultural imagery, and our separation of public and private spheres. In this sense, gender structures are not merely materialized or reproduced through parenting, but are embedded in social and cultural life at all levels. At each level, the division between male and female accentuates the irreconcilability of opposites. In every case, the male side of the pole, particularly the emphatic autonomy that denies interdependence and mutuality, has been idealized.

The upshot of this analysis is that the paradigm of sexual repression now appears secondary to another overarching concept whose significance has outgrown its original position in the Freudian edifice: the idea of splitting. In splitting, two complementary elements that should be held in tension are instead set up as opposites, with one side idealized and the other devalued. Thus, at the broader level, psychoanalytic feminism does not merely challenge the splitting of nurturance and freedom in the division of parenting (as in the exciting father and the holding mother); it also points to the dualistic mentality that inheres in our culture.[27]

But still one question remains: does woman have a desire of her own, one that is distinct in its form or content from that of man? Would something different come of identifying with the mother as subject of desire instead of with the father as subject of desire? I can argue with some confidence that a great difference would result from the opportunity to identify with both parents as subjects of desire, rather than repeating the triangular pattern where one is the agent, the other is the object. But reaching further, is there an alternate mode of representing woman's desire that does not occur through the phallus?

Although I have argued against attributing primary importance to the phallus in producing the conventional organization of gender and sexuality, I should like now to return to its symbolic significance. The phallus still has the power to represent desire, to represent the idealized force of paternal liberation. While we can now see that the phallus acquires its power not only as a defensive reaction to maternal power but also as a figure of excitement that contrasts with maternal holding and containment, we must still answer the question, What alternative to the phallus is there? Is there another relationship to desire than the one represented by the idealized phallus? Even if we question the existing gender division, seeing it as the source of the unique status of the phallus in representing desire, we must consider Mitchell's argument that until that division is overcome, there is no other way to represent desire or difference or separation. Is she right, or can we discern the rudiments of another form of representing desire, woman's desire, in the here and now of patriarchal culture?

There is a line of thought that answers this question by offering a female representation of desire derived from the image of our organs. This representation would have to be formed at the same symbolic level on which the phallus works. But the representational level, which has been organized and dominated by the phallus, keeps the female body in its place as object. Agency is not restored to woman by aestheticizing her body—that has already been done in spades. For the symbolic level of the psyche seems to be occupied and organized by phallic structures. The representation of woman's sexuality does not seem to have its own symbolic structures but rather seems to be incorporated into the system organized by phallic structures. That is why women appeared to Freud to be defined by their absence of phallic or masculine structures.

Finding woman's desire, I believe, requires finding an alternative to the phallic structures, to the symbolic mode. And that means *an alternative mode of structuring the psyche, not just a symbol to replace the phallus.* The phallic mode includes the whole constellation of using the father as a vehicle for separation, of internalizing the father qua phallus as a representation of agency and desire. The problem is to find another psychic mode rather than just a female counterpart to the phallic symbol. I have tried to develop a notion of this other mode using the concept of *intersubjectivity.*

Intersubjectivity refers to what happens between individuals, and within the individual-with-others, rather than within the individual psyche. The mode of representing intrapsychic events, the symbolic use of the body that psychoanalysis discovered, does not distinguish between real and imagined, inside and outside, introjective-projective processes and interaction. It does not distinguish between you as an independently

existing subject and you as a fantasy extension of my wishes and desires. Similarly, it does not distinguish between I as independently existing and desiring and I as merely embodying your wishes, agency, and desire. It does not distinguish when I am really the subject, with a desire of my own. Thus, Mitchell can speak of the child wishing to represent the phallus for the mother as if this fantasy of being something for the other constituted desire in its essential aspect.[28] The intersubjective mode assumes the possibility of a context with others in which desire is constituted for the self. It thus assumes the paradox that in being with the other, I may experience the most profound sense of self.

If it is clear that the intrapsychic mode is also the phallic mode, that it has heretofore dominated the representation of desire and activity, then we might speculate that the intersubjective mode is distinct from phallic organization and provides a different arena for experiencing will, agency, and desire. The intrapsychic mode operates at the level of subject-object experience, where the other's actual independent subjectivity is not relevant. Alternatively, the intersubjective mode, where two subjects meet, where both woman and man can be subject, may point to a locus for woman's independent desire, a relationship to desire that is not represented by the phallus.

Since there is no elaboration of this alternative to the phallic order equal to it in conceptual clarity and richness, I can only propose an exploration. First, the intersubjective mode refers to aspects of the self that each individual brings with her from infancy—agency and receptivity toward the world. While this self needs the other's response to develop, it exists a priori, before the response. It requires response and recognition, but is not called into being by them. This capacity for connection and agency later meshes with symbolic structures, but it is not created by them. Second, the intersubjective mode acknowledges that the other person really exists in the here and now, not merely in the symbolic dimension. What he or she actually does, matters. So depending on how things go between me and you, either I can really get through to you and you to me and there can be real recognition, or we can go along each encapsulated in our subjective bubble, having fantasies about one another. According to D. W. Winnicott, this moment of really getting through, of really recognizing the other as existing outside the self and not just as a bundle of my own projections, is the decisive aspect of differentiation.[29]

This moment, which Winnicott sees as created by destruction, occurs when the other is truly placed outside the control of fantasy. That is, one destroys the object in fantasy and discovers that it still exists in reality; it survives, setting a limit to the power of fantasy and self. To me it seems that the clarity of such a moment, the heightened awareness of both self and other, the reciprocal recognition that intensifies the self's freedom of expression, is actually the goal of erotic union. That is not to say that fantasy, phallic symbolic processes, and the pleasure principle are extraneous to the goal but that in love they are organized by the self-other recognition rather than the other way around. The desire for the heightened sense of self is the central meaning of getting pleasure *with* the other. Here the desire to lose the self in the other and really to be known for oneself can coalesce. Receptivity, knowing or taking in the other, becomes a mode of activity in its own right. My point is that this set of experiences— experiences of recognition—is not adequately represented by the concepts and symbols we have used for intrapsychic life, for identificatory or instinctual relationships, for ideal or object love.

Winnicott tried to grasp this set of experiences by using spatial metaphors, by describing a space that contains and a space in which we create. This space begins between mother and baby—he calls it the holding environment—and expands into what he calls the transitional area, the child's area of play, creativity, and fantasy.[30] The transitional space is suffused with the mother's protection and one's own freedom to create and imagine and discover. The central experience to which Winnicott refers is being and playing *alone* in the presence

of the other; to be truly alone with oneself paradoxically requires this sense of the other's being there.[31] Given safety without intrusion, the infant can be in a state of relaxation—that well-known inward gaze—where its own impulses or drives are experienced as coming from within and feeling real. It is in this way, through the unobtrusive mediation of the other, that drives become one's own desire.

This intermediate terrain may and even should be experienced as within one's own body self, as well, and the body may come to be such a metaphor of transitional fantasy. The interior of the body and the space between bodies form an elusive pattern, a plane whose edge is ever-shifting. Winnicott often quoted a line of poetry by Tagore—"On the seashore of endless worlds children play"—that expressed what he thought about play and the transitional area. This image suggests something that both forms a boundary and opens up into endless possibility; it evokes a particular kind of holding, similar to the first bodily holding by the mother. It refers to a presymbolic sense of self as having resources, a sense of self that evolves through relationships that validate what we can do for ourselves. The confidence in one's inner resources is also founded in the experience of the other's integrity and separateness, her ability to tolerate and create limits for our impulses, which permits us the freedom of spontaneous interaction. The awareness of one's own intentions, the ability to express them through action, and the confidence that they are one's *own,* evolve through the flow of recognition between two persons.

The self that develops and accumulates through such experiences of recognition is a different modality that sometimes works with, but sometimes is at cross-purposes to, the symbolized ego of phallic structuring. It is essential to retain this sense of the complementary, as well as the contrasting, relationship of these modes. Otherwise, one falls into the trap of choosing between them, grasping one side of a contradiction that must remain suspended to be clarifying. But even if we can sketch the idea of the intersubjective dimension, can we describe a mode of representing desire unique to intersubjectivity? And are we justified in linking this desire with women, with femininity as now constituted and known? I suggest that the intersubjective mode of desire has its counterpart in spatial rather than symbolic representation, and that this mode does have something to do with female experience. I would have to say that Erik Erikson was not all wrong in his intuitions about inner space, though he was wrong in some of the conclusions he drew from them.[32] I would also add that the idea of inner space or spatial representation of desire can be associated with subjectivity only when the interior is not merely an object to be discovered or a receptacle in which to put things. Rather, inner space should be understood as part of a continuum that includes the space between the I and the you, as well as the space within me; and, further, the space within should be understood as a receptacle only insofar as it refers to the receptivity of the subject.

Winnicott has suggested that the lines between the two psychic modes correspond to gender lines, that the classic view of oral and anal stages "arises out of consideration of the pure male element," whereas the "pure female element has nothing to do with drive." It has, rather, to do with "*being,* and this forms the basis of self-discovery . . . the capacity to develop an inside, to be a container."[33] We could read that negatively, as has often been done, equating this notion of being, of inside, of container, with passivity and lack of desire. But I think that would be wrong. Rather, I think it points to the side of the self preoccupied not with gender but with whether the drives I feel are really my own, whether they come from within me, and whether I can contain them (bear them without losing or injuring myself). In other words, it is about the *relationship* of the self to desire.

Ideally, this relationship is formed through a wide series of experiences and identifications that are not restricted by rigid gender formulas.

I have argued that girls should get what boys get from their father—recognition of agency, curiosity, movement toward the outside—and that they should get it from their mothers as well as their fathers. All of that contributes to the conviction of owning one's desire. I am arguing here for simultaneity and equality, not exclusion and the privileging of either male or female sets of experiences, capacities, and relationships.

I should like to explore further the possibility that femininity has been based not only on the lack of male experience but also on access to a different kind of experiences. Furthermore, these experiences are not merely the excluded opposites to male experience, the familiar half of the dualistic equation (if male equals rational, female equals irrational). Here, I think, the key is the idea of *self-discovery* that is associated with having an inside. This experience has been less well articulated in our culture and has never achieved the rich elaboration that we have for phallic structures. We can thus only begin to evaluate what woman's capacity for developing her inside, for self-discovery, might mean. Donna Bassin has argued that woman's inner space provides a metaphor of equal importance to "phallic activity and its representations, which serve as structures of knowing and creating the world."[34] The opportunity to explore one's own inner life as a creative activity, rather than waiting to be found by the phallic explorer, is one of the possible gifts of psychoanalysis to women, particularly the form of psychoanalysis that stresses not the analyst's mutative interpretations (the analyst brings the hidden unconscious to light) but the analyst's creation of an environment in which transitional experience is possible, where play and creativity can occur (the analyst provides a crucible in which experience can be transformed in the process of self-discovery). The persisting interest women have had in psychoanalysis despite its frequent antifeminist stance testifies to that possibility, to the hope of the inward journey.

Returning to the contrasting figures of infancy, the holding mother and the exciting father, we can now see the equal importance of each: recognition in and by the exciting other, and the holding that allows the self to experience desire as truly inner. So it is not merely the recognizing response of the exuberant and excited father that ignites the child's own sense of activity and desire. An important component of women's fantasy life centers around the wish for a holding other whose presence does not violate one's space but permits the experience of one's own desire, who recognizes it when it emerges of itself. This experience of inner space is in turn associated with the space between self and other: the holding environment and transitional experience. The sense of having an inside is dependent upon a sense of the space in between inside and outside—again the paradox that we need to experience being alone in the presence of the other.

The emphasis for a woman is likely to be on finding her *own, inner* desire because of the fear of impingement, intrusion, and violation. These fears, in turn, may be seen as the counterpart to a wish, the wish to submit to or to incorporate the phallus, the instrument of penetration, in order finally to be found. Woman's desire to be found and known can be symbolically apprehended as the reception of the penis. But the wish to be found and known, the desire for access to one's own interior that has found no external representation, also implies the dimension of the self's experience with the holding other. Here the spatial metaphor comes into play. A woman who had experienced incestuous violation in early puberty dreamed often of rooms. Her need to use the therapeutic environment as a space in which she could experience aloneness without fear of intrusion, control, or responsibility for the other, was an important theme. Once when she was looking forward to an overseas business trip, she announced that the best part would be to be alone in her hotel room where no one could call her. Here she would be held, safe, and alone with her thoughts; in this room of her own, this full rather than empty aloneness, she could look into herself.

I was interested to find that Carol Gilligan has made a similar point about women's desire in her analysis of the Psyche myth. The myth, as told by Apulius, contains a description of women's sexual awakening occurring in a state of benign aloneness. Gilligan points to the image of female self-discovery: Psyche is carried by the wind and laid in a bed of flowers, there left to herself. She contrasts this self-discovery with Psyche's previous state, when, adulated for her beauty, she was the idealized object: "You ought to have wept for me then," Psyche told her father, "for it was as though I had become dead."[35]

The women I have seen in clinical practice who present such images of spatial containment and inner space also have masochistic fantasies in which surrender is called forth by the other's power to penetrate, to know, and to control their desire. Yet in these fantasies we gradually discern a strand of seeking recognition for a force that originates within, a force imbued with the authenticity of *inner* desire. It seems to me that what is experientially female is the association of desire with a space, a place within the self, from which this force can emerge. This space is in turn connected to the space between self and the other. Ideally, in the psychoanalytic process the analysand gains access to transitional experience. As play in this transitional space develops, spatial metaphors may articulate the search for a desire of one's own. In them, a union or balance of holding and excitement is finally achieved. Within this space one's own desire can emerge, not as borrowed but as authentically one's own. It is thus not a different desire but a difference relation of self to other that is at stake.

The fantasy of submission in ideal love is that of being released into abandon by another who remains in control. Here I would argue that the freedom and abandon called forth by this powerful, controlling other represent an alienated version of the safe space that permits self-discovery, aloneness in the presence of the other.[36] Too often woman's desire has been known through these alien offshoots of idealization: submission and envy.

No doubt what we see in early ideal love reveals another profound truth: the pathway to desire leads through freedom. Woman's desire, I believe, can be found not through the current emphasis on *freedom from:* as autonomy or separation from a powerful other, guaranteed by identification with an opposing power. Rather, we are seeking a relationship to desire in the *freedom to:* freedom to be both with and distinct from the other. This relationship can be grasped in terms of intersubjective reality, where subject meets subject. The phallus as emblem of desire has represented the one-sided individuality of subject meeting object, a complementarity that idealizes one side and devalues the other. The discovery of our own desire will proceed, I believe, through the mode of thought that can suspend and reconcile such opposition, the dimension of recognition between self and other.

NOTES

1. Carol Gilligan, "Remapping the Moral Domain: New Images of Self in Relationship," paper presented at the Conference on Reconstructing Individualism, Stanford Humanities Center, February 1984, printed in *Reconstructing Individualism: Autonomy, Individuality, and the Self in Western Thought,* ed. Thomas C. Heller, Morton Sosna, and David Willberry (Stanford University Press).

2. Simone de Beauvoir, *The Second Sex,* trans. H. M. Parshley (New York: Vintage, 1974), p. 717.

3. These and other illuminating distinctions are laid out in Nancy Chodorow's "Gender, Relation and Difference in Psychoanalytic Perspective," in *The Future of Difference,* ed. Hester Eisenstein and Alice Jardine (Boston: G. K. Hall, 1980), pp. 3–19.

4. See Nancy Chodorow, *The Reproduction of Mothering: Psychoanalysis and the Sociology of Gender (Berkeley:* University of California Press, 1978), and Evelyn Fox Keller, *Reflections on Gender and Science* (New Haven: Yale University Press, 1985). See also Carol Gilligan, *In a Different Voice: Psychological Theory and Women's Development* (Cambridge: Harvard University Press, 1982). Although quite different in emphasis, these books share a common intention, and I have benefited from reading and discussing with each of these authors. The decisive perspective is the idea of a necessary balance between individuation and sociability as mutually interdependent experiences, as first formulated by Chodorow: "Differentiation is not distinctness and separateness, but a particular way of being connected to others" ("Gender, Relation and Difference," p. 11); Chodorow has amplified this perspective in "Toward a Relational Individualism: The Mediation of Self through Psychoanalysis," paper presented at the Conference on Reconstructing Individualism, Stanford Humanities Center, February 1984. Dorothy Dinnerstein's critique of female mothering in *The Mermaid and the Minotaur: Sexual and Human Malaise* (New York: Harper and Row, 1976) has been very influential, although less explicitly critical of psychoanalytic theory or the concept of the individual. See also Jane Flax, "Political Philosophy and the Patriarchal Unconscious," in *Discovering Reality: Feminist Perspectives on Epistemology, Metaphysics, Methodology, and the Philosophy of Science,* ed. Sandra Harding and Merrill E. Hintikka (Boston: Reidel, 1983), and Seyla Benhabib, "The Generalized and the Concrete Other: Visions of the Autonomous Self," paper presented at the Conference on Women and Morality, SUNY-Stonybrook, March 1985. I have explored the theme of individualism and instrumental rationality in "Authority and the Family Revisited; or A World without Fathers?" *New German Critique,* no. 13 (Winter 1978), pp. 35–57, and the psychoanalytic perspective on development in "The Oedipal Riddle: Authority, Autonomy, and the New Narcissism," in *The Problem of Authority in America,* ed. John P. Diggins and Mark E. Kann (Philadelphia: Temple University Press, 1981), pp. 195–224.

5. Jessica Benjamin, "Master and Slave: The Fantasy of Erotic Domination," in *Powers of Desire: The Politics of Sexuality,* ed. Ann Snitow, Christine Stansell, and Sharon Thompson (New York: Monthly Review Press, 1983), pp. 280–99.

6. Herbert Marcuse, "Philosophy and Critical Theory," in his *Negations: Essays in Critical Theory,* trans. Jeremy J. Shapiro (Boston: Beacon, 1968), pp. 134–58.

7. Max Weber's thesis is elucidated in his *The Prot-estant Ethic and the Spirit of Capitalism,* trans. T. Parsons (New York: Charles Scribner, 1958).

8. Juliet Mitchell, *Psychoanalysis and Feminism: Freud, Reich, Laing, and Women* (New York: Pantheon, 1974), pp. 392–93.

9. For example, Janine Chassequet-Smirgel refers to it as "the patriarchal law of separa-tion" in "Perversion and the Universal Law," *International Journal of Psycho-Analysis* 10 (1983):293–301, and explains that the phallus, by reminding the boy of his insufficiency and the father's exclusive possession of the mother, affirms that law.

10. This complex issue cannot be elaborated here. The most interesting summary and innovative perspective on the meaning of the new infancy research is Daniel Stern's "The Early Development of Schemas of Self, of Other, and of Various Experiences of 'Self with Other,' " in *Reflections on Self Psychology,* ed. Joseph Lichtenberg and Samuel Kaplan (Hillsdale, N. J.: Analytic Press, 1983), pp. 49–84.

11. This perspective originated with Robert Stoller's research and theorizing; see his *Sex and Gender* (New York: Science House, 1968), and "The Sense of Femaleness" (1968), in *Psychoanalysis and Women,* ed. Jean Baker Miller (Baltimore: Penguin, 1973). Its consequences were elabo-rated in feminist terms by Chodorow in *The Reproduction of Mothering.*

12. See Mitchell's *Psychoanalysis and Feminism, and* more recently her introduction to *Feminine Sexuality: Jacques Lacan and the "Ecole Freudienne,"* ed. Juliet Mitchell and Jacqueline Rose, trans. Jacqueline Rose (New York: Norton, 1982), pp. 1–26. See also Jane Gallop's *The Daughter's Seduction: Feminism and Psycho-analysis* (Ithaca: Cornell University Press, 1982).

13. Nancy Chodorow and Susan Contratto in "The Fantasy of the Perfect Mother" (in *Rethinking the Family: Some Feminist Questions,* ed. Barrie Thorne with Marilyn Yalom [New York: Longman, 1982], pp. 54–76) explicate clearly the relationship between the fantasy that the mother is all-powerful and the denial of her sexuality, both dependent on viewing the mother from the perspective of the child. Contratto also critiques current views of asexual motherhood in "Maternal Sexuality and Asexual Motherhood," in *Women, Sex, and Sexuality,* ed. Catharine R. Stimpson and Ethel Spector Person (Chicago: University of Chicago Press, 1980), pp. 224–40.

14. Jacqueline Rose, in her introduction to *Feminine Sexuality,* argues that gender identity theory as used by Chodorow "displaces" the concepts of the unconscious and of bisexuality. This dismissal of object relations theory appears to contain a misapprehension of the process of identification, which proceeds through the unconscious fantasies of the child, but is as-sociated with specific phases of cognitive and affective development that have been empiri-cally documented. Thus, it misses the qualita-tively distinct aspect of sexual experience and identification in the preoedipal phase that is not captured by oedipal categories. Moreover, it assumes that only the structuralist version of the unconscious—an abstract category in which representation of the world subsumes experience in the world—deserves the dignity of the term. This level of abstraction may have its own uses. But the global rejection of maternal identifica-tion theory by Rose and other feminist Lacanians only hinders the analysis of the specific difficulty that confronts the girl in the effort to reconcile gender identity and sexuality.

15. Sigmund Freud, "Some Psychical Conse-quences of the Anatomical Distinction between the Sexes" (1926), *Standard Edition,* vol. 19, pp. 248–60, and "Female Sexuality" (1931), *Standard Edition,* vol. 21, pp. 225–46.

16. A discussion of the differing meanings of sexual inhibition and identity for men and women can be found in Ethel Spector Person's "Sexuality as the Mainstay of Identity: Psychoanalytic Perspec-tives," in Stimpson and Person, *Women, Sex, and Sexuality,* pp. 36–61.

17. This phrase is apparently Margaret Mahler's, quoted in Ernest L. Abelin, "Triangulation, the Role of the Father and the Origins of Core Gender Identity during the Rapprochement Subphase," in *Rapprochement: The Critical Subphase of Separation-Individuation,* ed. Ruth F. Lax, Sheldon Bach, and J. Alexis Burland (New York: Jason Aronson, 1980), p. 152. The most persuasive discussions of father and phallus as ways of defending against maternal

power can be found in Janine Chassequet-Smirgel's anthology, *Female Sexuality: New Psychoanalytic Views* (Ann Arbor: Michigan University Press, 1970) and her "Freud and Female Sexuality," *International Journal of Psychoanalysis,* 57, pp. 275–286.

18. For a number of articles on this difference, see *Father and Child: Developmental and Clinical Perspectives,* ed. Stanley H. Cath, Alan R. Gurwitt, and John Munder Ross (Boston: Little, Brown, 1982).

19. Margaret S. Mahler, Fred Pine, and Anni Bergman, *The Psychological Birth of the Human Infant: Symbiosis and Individuation* (New York: Basic Books, 1975).

20. Ibid., pp. 213–14.

21. See Jane Flax, "Mother-Daughter Relationships: Psychodynamics, Politics, and Philosophy," in Eisenstein and Jardine, *The Future of Difference,* pp. 20–40. More generally, Chodorow argues in *The Reproduction of Mothering* that mothers bind their daughters by virtue of greater identification, and separate from boys by conferring the status of heterosexual love object upon them.

22. This thesis was developed and elaborated by Ernest Abelin in several notable articles, including "Triangulation," see note 17 above. Freud also noted the intensity of the preoedipal boy's identification with the father, whom he takes as his ideal, and indeed Freud states that identification is the earliest form of love ("Group Psychology and the Analysis of the Ego" [1921], *Standard Edition,* vol. 18, pp. 67–143).

23. This point has also been made by Doris Bernstein. Her work is a notable exception; see "The Female Superego: A Different Perspective," *International Journal of Psycho-analysis* 64, pt. 2 (1983): 187–201. For a similarly exceptional account, see also Ricki Levenson, "Intimacy, Autonomy, and Gender: Developmental Differences and Their Reflection in Adult Relationships," *Journal of the American Academy of Psychoanalysis* 12 (1984):529–44.

24. Sigmund Freud, "A Child Is Being Beaten" (1919), *Standard Edition,* vol. 17, pp. 159–72.

25. The conflict between paternal identification and paternal object love becomes infinitely more complicated in the oedipal period than I can here describe. It would seem that the more the idealization of the father is sustained, the less likely is the daughter's persuasion of a right to her own desire. For example, if the oedipal father of adolescence, a period when the issues become more explicit, discourages or forbids manifest sexuality in his daughter, that blocks both separation from and identification with him and encourages submission and idealization. As Miriam Johnson ("Fathers and 'Femininity' in Daughters: A Review of the Research," *Sociology and Social Research* 67 [1983]:1–17) notes, the daughter's tie to the father, if sexualized, is more likely to discourage autonomy.

26. See Chodorow, "Gender, Relation and Difference," and Keller, *Reflections.*

27. Keller's *Reflections* has contributed a great deal to the theme of sustaining a tension rather than splitting opposites. See also Gilligan's remarks on the essential tension in "Remapping the Moral Domain," Linda Gordon's comments on sustaining the tension of opposing tendencies in historical research, and my elucidation of the balance of differentiation and its breakdown in "Master and Slave" (see note 5 above).

28. See Mitchell, *Psychoanalysis and Feminism,* pp. 396–97, and her introduction to *Feminine Sexuality.* Desire is thus by its very nature "insoluble," Mitchell argues. Lacanian desire—always a desire for what is not—would seem to be the impediment to ever reaching the other, and thus finally at odds with love, with the meeting of two minds, two bodies. Desire is then a kind of addiction to the ideal.

29. This analysis proceeds from the principal text of D. W. Winnicott on differentiation, in which he makes a similar distinction between the self as isolated and the intersubjective self; see "The Use of an Object and Relating through Identifications," in *Playing and Reality* (London: Penguin, 1974), pp. 101–111. An excellent interpretation of Winnicott's theory, to which I am indebted, is Michael Eigen's "The Area of Faith in Winnicott, Lacan, and Bion," *International Journal of Psycho-analysis* 62 (1981):413–33.

30. See D. W. Winnicott's "Transitional Objects and Transitional Phenomena," and the other essays in *Playing and Reality.*

31. D. W. Winnicott, "The Capacity to Be Alone" (1958), in his *The Maturational Processes and*

the Facilitating Environment: Studies in the
Theory of Emotional Development (New York:
International Universities Press, 1965). Elsa First
provided a very helpful account of the signifi-
cance of this text in her paper at the New York
Freudian Society, March 1985.

32. Erik Erikson, "Womanhood and the Inner
    Space," in Identity, Youth, and Crisis (New York:
    W. W. Norton, 1968), pp. 261–94.

33. D. W. Winnicott, "Creativity and Its Origins," in
    his Playing and Reality, p. 97.

34. Donna Bassin, "Woman's Images of Inner Space:
    Data towards Expanded Interpretive Catego-
    ries," International Review of Psycho-analysis 9
    (1982):200.

35. Carol Gilligan, "The Psychology of Love," Semi-
    nar on Sex and Consumerism, New York Institute
    for the Humanities, March 1985.

36. This idea has been developed by Emmanuel
    Ghent in "Masochism, Submission, Surrender,"
    Colloquium, New York University Postdoctoral
    Psychology Program, December 1983.

SEXUALITY

Catherine A. Mackinnon

What is it about women's experience that produces a distinctive perspective on social reality?
How is an angle of vision and an interpretive
hermeneutics of social life created in the group,
women? What happens to women to give them a
particular interest in social arrangements, something to have a consciousness of? How are the
qualities we know as male and female socially
created and enforced on an everyday level? Sexual objectification of women—first in the world,
then in the head, first in visual appropriation,
then in forced sex, finally in sexual murder[1]—
provides answers.

Male dominance is sexual. Meaning: men in
particular, if not men alone, sexualize hierarchy;
gender is one. As much as a sexual theory of gender as a gendered theory of sex, this is the theory
of sexuality that has grown out of consciousness
raising. Recent feminist work, both interpretive and empirical, on rape, battery, sexual harassment, sexual abuse of children, prostitution
and pornography, support it.[2] These practices,
taken together, express and actualize the distinctive power of men over women in society; their
effective permissibility confirms and extends
it. If one believes women's accounts of sexual

use and abuse by men;[3] if the pervasiveness of
male sexual violence against women substanti-
ated in these studies is not denied, minimized, or
excepted as deviant or episodic;[4] if the fact that
only 7.8 percent of women in the United States
are not sexually assaulted or harassed in their
lifetime is considered not ignorable or inconsequential;[5] if the women to whom it happens are
not considered expendable; if violation of women
is understood as sexualized on some level—then
sexuality itself can no longer be regarded as un-
implicated. Nor can the meaning of practices of
sexual violence be categorized away as violence
not sex. The male sexual role, this information
and analysis taken together suggest, centers on
aggressive intrusion on those with less power.
Such acts of dominance are experienced as sexually arousing, as sex itself.[6] They therefore are.
The new knowledge on the sexual violation of
women by men thus frames an inquiry into the
place of sexuality in gender and of gender in
sexuality.

A feminist theory of sexuality based on these
data locates sexuality within a theory of gender inequality, meaning the social hierarchy of
men over women. To make a theory feminist, it
is not enough that it be authored by a biological
female, nor that it describe female sexuality as
different from (if equal to) male sexuality, or as
if sexuality in women ineluctably exists in some

realm beyond, beneath, above, behind—in any event, fundamentally untouched and unmoved by—an unequal social order. A theory of sexuality becomes feminist methodologically, meaning feminist in the post-marxist sense, to the extent it treats sexuality as a social construct of male power: defined by men, forced on women, and constitutive of the meaning of gender. Such an approach centers feminism on the perspective of the subordination of women to men as it identifies sex—that is, the sexuality of dominance and submission—as crucial, as a fundamental, as on some level definitive, in that process. Feminist theory becomes a project of analyzing that situation in order to face it for what it is, in order to change it.

Focusing on gender inequality without a sexual account of its dynamics, as most work has, one could criticize the sexism of existing theories of sexuality and emerge knowing that men author scripts to their own advantage, women and men act them out; that men set conditions, women and men have their behavior conditioned; that men develop developmental categories through which men develop, and women develop or not; that men are socially allowed selves hence identities with personalities into which sexuality is or is not well integrated, women being that which is or is not integrated, that through the alterity of which a self experiences itself as having an identity; that men have object relations, women are the objects of those relations; and so on. Following such critique, one could attempt to invert or correct the premises or applications of these theories to make them gender neutral, even if the reality to which they refer looks more like the theories—once their gender specificity is revealed—than it looks gender neutral. Or, one could attempt to enshrine a distinctive "women's reality" as if it really were permitted to exist as something more than one dimension of women's response to a condition of powerlessness. Such exercises would be revealing and instructive, even deconstructive, but to limit feminism to correcting sex bias by acting in theory as if male

power did not exist in fact, including by valorizing in writing what women have had little choice but to be limited to becoming in life, is to limit feminist theory the way sexism limits women's lives: to a response to terms men set.

A distinctively feminist theory conceptualizes social reality, including sexual reality, on its own terms. The question is, what are they? If women have been substantially deprived not only of their own experience but of terms of their own in which to view it, then a feminist theory of sexuality which seeks to understand women's situation in order to change it must first identify and criticize the construct "sexuality" as a construct that has circumscribed and defined experience as well as theory. This requires capturing it in the world, in its situated social meanings, as it is being constructed in life on a daily basis. It must be studied in its experienced empirical existence, not just in the texts of history (as Foucault does), in the social psyche (as Lacan does), or in language (as Derrida does). Sexual meaning is not made only, or even primarily, by words and in texts. It *is* made in social relations of power in the world, through which process gender is also produced. In feminist terms, the fact that male power has power means that the interests of male sexuality construct what sexuality as such means, including the standard way it *is* allowed and recognized to be felt and expressed and experienced, in a way that determines women's biographies, including sexual ones. Existing theories, until they grasp this, will not only misattribute what they call female sexuality to women as such, as if it were not imposed on women daily; they will also participate in enforcing the hegemony of the social construct "desire," hence its product, "sexuality," hence its construct "woman," on the world.

The gender issue, in this analysis, becomes the issue of what is taken to be "sexuality"; what sex means and what *is* meant by sex, when, how, with whom, and with what consequences to whom. Such questions are almost never systematically confronted, even in discourses that purport feminist awareness. What sex is—how it comes to be attached and attributed to what it is, embodied and practiced as it is, contextualized in the ways it is, signifying and referring to what it does—is taken as a baseline, a given, except in explanations of what happened when it is thought to have gone wrong. It is as if "erotic," for example, can be taken as having an understood referent, although it is never defined, except to imply that it is universal yet individual, ultimately variable and plastic, essentially indefinable but overwhelmingly positive. "Desire," the vicissitudes of which are endlessly extolled and philosophized in culture high and low, is not seen as fundamentally problematic or as calling for explanation on the concrete, interpersonal operative level, unless (again) it is supposed to be there and is not. To list and analyze what seem to be the essential elements for male sexual arousal, what has to be there for the penis to work, seems faintly blasphemous, like a pornographer doing market research. Sex is supposed both too individual and too universally transcendent for that. To suggest that the sexual might be continuous with something other than sex itself—something like politics—is seldom done, is treated as detumescent, even by feminists. It is as if sexuality comes from the stork.

Sexuality, in feminist light, is not a discrete sphere of interaction or feeling or sensation or behavior in which preexisting social divisions may or may not be played out. It is a pervasive dimension of social life, one that permeates the whole, a dimension along which gender occurs and through which gender is socially constituted; it is a dimension along which other social divisions, like race and class, partly play themselves out. Dominance eroticized defines the imperatives of its masculinity, submission eroticized defines its femininity. So many distinctive features of women's status as second class—the restriction and constraint and contortion, the servility and the display, the self-mutilation and requisite presentation of self as a beautiful thing, the enforced passivity, the humiliation—are made

into the content of sex for women. Being a thing for sexual use is fundamental to it. This approach identifies not just a sexuality that is shaped under conditions of gender inequality but reveals this sexuality itself to be the dynamic of the inequality of the *sexes*. It is to argue that the excitement at reduction of a person to a thing, to less than a human being, as socially defined, is its fundamental motive force. It is to argue that sexual difference is a function of sexual dominance. It is to argue a sexual theory of the distribution of social power by gender, in which this sexuality that is sexuality is substantially what makes the gender division be what it is, which is male dominant, wherever it is, which is nearly everywhere.

Across cultures, in this perspective, sexuality is whatever a given culture or subculture defines it as. The next question concerns its relation to gender as a division of power. Male dominance appears to exist cross-culturally, if in locally particular forms. Across cultures, is whatever defines women as "different" the same as whatever defines women as "inferior" the same as whatever defines women's "sexuality"? Is that which defines gender inequality as merely the sex difference also the content of the erotic, cross-culturally? In this view, the feminist theory of sexuality is its theory of politics, its distinctive contribution to social and political explanation. To explain gender inequality in terms of "sexual politics"[7] is to advance not only a political theory of the sexual that defines gender but also a sexual theory of the political to which gender is fundamental.

In this approach, male power takes the social form of what men as a gender want sexually, which centers on power itself, as socially defined. In capitalist countries, it includes wealth. Masculinity is having it; femininity is not having it. [Masculinity precedes male as femininity precedes female, and male sexual desire defines both.] Specifically, "woman" is defined by what male desire requires for arousal and satisfaction and is socially tautologous with "female sexuality" and "the female sex." In the permissible ways a woman can be treated, the ways that are socially considered not violations but appropriate to her nature, one finds the particulars of male sexual interests and requirements. [In the concomitant sexual paradigm, the ruling norms of sexual attraction and expression are fused with gender identity formation and affirmation, such that sexuality equals heterosexuality equals the sexuality of (male) dominance and (female) submission.]

Post-Lacan, actually post-Foucault, it has become customary to affirm that sexuality is socially constructed.[8] Seldom specified is what, socially, it is constructed of, far less who does the constructing or how, when, or where.[9] When capitalism is the favored social construct, sexuality is shaped and controlled and exploited and repressed by capitalism; not, capitalism creates sexuality as we know it. When sexuality is a construct of discourses of power, gender is never one of them; force is central to its deployment but through repressing it, not through constituting it; speech is not concretely investigated for its participation in this construction process. Power is everywhere therefore nowhere, diffuse rather than pervasively hegemonic. "Constructed" seems to mean influenced by, directed, channeled, as a highway constructs traffic patterns. Not: Why cars? Who's driving? Where's everybody going? What makes mobility matter? Who can own a car? Are all these accidents not very accidental? Although there are partial exceptions (but disclaimers notwithstanding) the typical model of sexuality which is tacitly accepted remains deeply Freudian[10] and essentialist: sexuality is an innate *sui generis* primary natural prepolitical unconditioned[11] drive divided along the biological gender line, centering on heterosexual intercourse, that is, penile intromission, full actualization of which is repressed by civilization. Even if the sublimation aspect of this theory is rejected, or the reasons for the repression are seen to vary (for the survival of civilization or to maintain fascist control or to keep capitalism moving), sexual expression is implicitly seen as the expression of something that is to a significant extent pre-social and is socially denied its full force. Sexuality remains largely pre-cultural and universally invariant, social only in that it needs society to take socially specific forms. The impetus itself is a hunger, an appetite founded on a need; what it is specifically hungry for and how it is satisfied is then open to endless cultural and individual variance, like cuisine, like cooking.

Allowed/not allowed is this sexuality's basic ideological axis. The fact that sexuality is ideologically bounded is known. That these are its axes, central to the way its "drive" is driven, and that this is fundamental to gender and gender is fundamental to it, is not.[12] Its basic normative assumption is that whatever is considered sexuality should be allowed to be "expressed." Whatever is called sex is attributed a normatively positive valence, an affirmative valuation. This *ex cathedra* assumption, affirmation of which appears indispensable to one's credibility on any subject that gets near the sexual, means that sex as such (whatever it is) is good—natural, healthy, positive, appropriate, pleasurable, wholesome, fine, one's own, and to be approved and expressed. This, sometimes characterized as "sex-positive," is, rather obviously, a value judgment.

Kinsey and his followers, for example, clearly thought (and think) the more sex the better. Accordingly, they trivialize even most of those cases of rape and child sexual abuse they discern as such, decry women's sexual refusal as sexual inhibition, and repeatedly interpret women's sexual disinclination as "restrictions" on men's natural sexual activity, which left alone would emulate (some) animals.[13] Followers of the neo-Freudian derepression imperative have similarly identified the frontier of sexual freedom with transgression of social restraints on access, with making the sexually disallowed allowed, especially male sexual access to anything. The struggle to have everything sexual allowed in a society we are told would collapse if it were, creates a sense of resistance to, and an aura of danger around, violating the powerless. If we knew the boundaries were phony, existed only to eroticize the targeted transgressable, would penetrating them feel less sexy? Taboo and crime may serve to eroticize what would otherwise feel about as much like dominance as taking candy from a baby. Assimilating actual powerlessness to male prohibition, to male power, provides the appearance of resistance, which makes overcoming possible, while never undermining the reality of power, or its dignity, by giving the powerless actual power. The point is, allowed/not allowed becomes the ideological axis along which sexuality is experienced when and because sex—gender and sexuality—is about power.

One version of the derepression hypothesis that purports feminism is: civilization having been male dominated, female sexuality has been repressed, not allowed. Sexuality as such still centers on what would otherwise be considered the reproductive act, on intercourse: penetration of the erect penis into the vagina (or appropriate substitute orifices), followed by thrusting to male ejaculation. If reproduction actually had anything to do with what sex was for, it would not happen every night (or even twice a week) for forty or fifty years, nor would prostitutes exist. "We had sex three times" typically means the man entered the woman three times and orgasmed three times. Female sexuality in this model refers to the presence of this theory's "sexuality," or the desire to be so treated, in biological females; "female" is somewhere between an adjective and a noun, half possessive and half biological ascription. Sexual freedom means women are allowed to behave as freely as men to express this sexuality, to have it allowed, that is (hopefully) shamelessly and without social constraints to initiate genital drive satisfaction through heterosexual intercourse.[14] Hence, the liberated woman. Hence, the sexual revolution.

The pervasiveness of such assumptions about sexuality throughout otherwise diverse methodological traditions is suggested by the following comment by a scholar of violence against women:

> If women were to escape the culturally stereotyped role of disinterest in and resistance to sex and to take on an assertive role in expressing their own sexuality, rather than leaving it to the assertiveness of men, it would contribute to the reduction of rape . . . First, and most obviously, voluntary sex would be available to more men, thus reducing the "need" for rape. Second, and probably more important, it would help to reduce the confounding of sex and aggression.[15]

In this view, somebody must be assertive for sex to happen. Voluntary sex—sexual equality—means equal sexual aggression. If women freely expressed "their own sexuality," more heterosexual intercourse would be initiated. Women's "resistance" to sex is an imposed cultural stereotype, not a form of political struggle. Rape is occasioned by women's resistance, not by men's force; or, male force, hence rape, is created by women's resistance to sex. Men would rape less if they got more voluntarily compliant sex from women. Corollary: the force in rape is not sexual to men.

Underlying this quotation lurks the view, as common as it is tacit, that if women would just accept the contact men now have to rape to get— if women would stop resisting or (in one of the pornographers' favorite scenarios) become sexual aggressors—rape would wither away. On one level, this is a definitionally obvious truth. When a woman accepts what would be rape if she did not accept it, what happens is sex. If women were to accept forced sex as sex, "voluntary sex would be available to more men." If such a view is not implicit in this text, it is a mystery how women equally aggressing against men sexually would eliminate, rather than double, the confounding of sex and aggression. Without such an assumption, only the confounding of sexual aggression with gender would be eliminated. If women no longer resisted male sexual aggression, the confounding of sex with aggression would, indeed, be so epistemologically complete that it would be eliminated. No woman would ever be sexually violated, because sexual violation would be sex. The situation might resemble the one evoked by a society categorized as "rape-free" in part because the men assert there is no rape there: "our women never resist."[16] Such pacification also occurs in "rape-prone" societies like the United States, where some force may be perceived as force, but only above certain threshold standards.

While intending the opposite, some feminists have encouraged and participated in this type of analysis by conceiving rape as violence, not sex.[17] While this approach gave needed emphasis to rape's previously effaced elements of power and dominance, it obscured its elements of sex. Aside from failing to answer the rather obvious question, if it is violence not sex, why didn't he just hit her? this approach made it impossible to see that violence is sex when it is practiced as sex.[18] This is obvious once what sexuality is, is understood as a matter of what it means and how it is interpreted. To say rape is violence not sex preserves the "sex is good" norm by simply distinguishing forced sex as "not sex," whether it means sex to the perpetrator or even, later, to the victim, who has difficulty experiencing sex without reexperiencing the rape. Whatever is sex cannot be violent; whatever is violent cannot be sex. This analytic wish-fulfillment makes it possible for rape to be opposed by those who would save sexuality from the rapists while leaving the sexual fundamentals of male dominance intact.

While much previous work on rape has analyzed it as a problem of inequality between the sexes but not as a problem of unequal sexuality on the basis of gender,[19] other contemporary explorations of sexuality that purport to be feminist lack comprehension either of gender as a form of social power or of the realities of sexual violence. For instance, the editors of *Powers of Desire* take sex "as a central form of expression, one that defines identity and is seen as a primary source of energy and pleasure."[20] This may be how it "is seen," but it is also how the editors, operatively, see it. As if women choose sexuality as definitive of identity. As if it is as much a form of women's "expression" as it is men's. As if violation and abuse are not equally central to sexuality as women live it.

The *Diary* of the Barnard conference on sexuality pervasively equates sexuality with "pleasure." "Perhaps the overall question we need to ask is: how do women . . . negotiate sexual pleasure?"[21] As if women under male supremacy have power to. As if "negotiation" is a form of freedom. As if pleasure and how to get it, rather than dominance and how to end it, is the "overall" issue sexuality presents feminism. As if women do just need a good fuck. In these texts, taboos are treated as real restrictions—as things that really are not allowed—instead of as guises under which hierarchy is eroticized. The domain of the sexual is divided into "restriction, repression, and danger" on the one hand and "exploration, pleasure, and agency" on the other.[22] This division parallels the ideological forms through which dominance and submission are eroticized, variously socially coded as heterosexuality's male/female, lesbian culture's butch/femme, and sadomasochism's top/bottom.[23] Speaking in role terms, the one who pleasures in the illusion of freedom and security within the reality of danger is the "girl"; the one who pleasures in the reality of freedom and security within the illusion of danger is the "boy". That is, the *Diary* uncritically adopts as an analytic tool the central dynamic of the phenomenon it purports to be analyzing. Presumably, one is to have a sexual experience of the text.

The terms of these discourses preclude or evade crucial feminist questions. What do sexuality and gender inequality have to do with each other? How do dominance and submission become sexualized, or, why is hierarchy sexy? How does it get attached to male and female? Why does sexuality center on intercourse, the reproductive act by physical design? Is masculinity the enjoyment of violation, femininity the enjoyment of being violated? Is that the social meaning of intercourse? Do "men love death"?[24] Why? What is the etiology of heterosexuality in women? Is its pleasure women's stake in subordination?

Taken together and taken seriously, feminist inquiries into the realities of rape, battery, sexual harassment, incest, child sexual abuse, prostitution, and pornography answer these questions by suggesting a theory of the sexual mechanism. Its script, learning, conditioning, developmental logos, imprinting of the microdot, its *deus ex machina,* whatever sexual process term defines sexual arousal itself, is force, power's expression. Force is sex, not just sexualized; force is the desire dynamic, not just a response to the desired object when desire's expression is frustrated. Pressure, gender socialization, withholding benefits, extending indulgences, the how-to books, the sex therapy are the soft end; the fuck, the fist, the street, the chains, the poverty are the hard end. Hostility and contempt, or arousal of master to slave, together with awe and vulnerability, or arousal of slave to master—these are the emotions of this sexuality's excitement. "Sadomasochism is to sex what war is to civil life: the magnificent experience," wrote Susan Sontag.[25] "[I]t is hostility—the desire, overt or hidden, to harm another person—that generates and enhances sexual excitement," wrote Robert Stoller.[26] Harriet Jacobs a slave, speaking of her systematic rape by her master, wrote, "It seems less demeaning to give one's self, than to submit to compulsion."[27] It is clear from the data that the force in sex and the sex in force is a matter of simple empirical description—unless one accepts that force in sex is not force anymore, it is just sex; or, if whenever a woman is forced it is what she really wants, or it or she does not matter; or, unless prior aversion or sentimentality substitutes what one wants sex to be, or will condone or countenance as sex, for what is actually happening.

To be clear: what is sexual is what gives a man an erection. Whatever it takes to make a penis shudder and stiffen with the experience of its potency is what sexuality means culturally. Whatever else does this, fear does, hostility does, hatred does, the helplessness of a child or a student or an infantilized or restrained or vulnerable woman does, revulsion does, death does. Hierarchy, a

constant creation of person/thing, top/bottom, dominance/subordination relations, does. What is understood as violation, conventionally penetration and intercourse, defines the paradigmatic sexual encounter. The scenario of sexual abuse is: you do what I say. These textualities and these relations, situated within as well as creating a context of power in which they can be lived out, become sexuality. All this suggests that what is called sexuality is the dynamic of control by which male dominance—in forms that range from intimate to institutional, from a look to a rape—eroticizes and thus defines man and woman, gender identity and sexual pleasure. It is also that which maintains and defines male supremacy as a political system. Male sexual desire is thereby simultaneously created and serviced, never satisfied once and for all, while male force is romanticized, even sacralized, potentiated and naturalized, by being submerged into sex itself.

In contemporary philosophical terms, nothing is "indeterminate" in the post-structuralist sense here; it is all too determinate.[28] Nor does its reality provide just one perspective on a relativistic interpersonal world that could mean anything or its opposite.[29] The reality of pervasive sexual abuse and its erotization does not shift relative to perspective, although whether or not one will see it or accord it significance may. Interpretation varies relative to place in sexual abuse, certainly; but the fact that women are sexually abused as women, located in a social matrix of sexualized subordination, does not go away because it is often ignored or authoritatively disbelieved or interpreted out of existence. Indeed, some ideological supports for its persistence rely precisely upon techniques of social indeterminacy: no language but the obscene to describe the unspeakable, denial by the powerful casting doubt on the facticity of the injuries, actually driving its victims insane. Indeterminacy, in this light, is a neo-Cartesian mind game that raises acontextualized interpretive possibilities that have no real social meaning or real possibility of any, thus dissolving the ability to criticize the oppressiveness of actual meanings without making space for new ones. The feminist point is simple. Men are women's material conditions. If it happens to women, it happens.

Women often find ways to resist male supremacy and to expand their spheres of action. But they are never free of it. Women also embrace the standards of women's place in this regime as "our own" to varying degrees and in varying voices—as affirmation of identity and right to pleasure, in order to be loved and approved and paid, in order just to make it through another day. This, not inert passivity, is the meaning of being a victim.[30] The term is not moral: who is to blame or to be pitied or condemned or held responsible. It is not prescriptive: what we should do next. It is not strategic: how to construe the situation so it can be changed. It is not emotional: what one feels better thinking. It is descriptive: who does what to whom and gets away with it.

Thus the question Freud never asked is the question that defines sexuality in a feminist perspective: what do men want? Pornography provides an answer. Pornography permits men to have whatever they want sexually. It is their "truth about sex."[31] It connects the centrality of visual objectification to both male sexual arousal, and male models of knowledge and verification, objectivity with objectification. It shows how men see the world, how in seeing it they access and possess it, and how this is an act of dominance over it. It shows what men want and gives it to them. From the testimony of the pornography, what men want is: women bound, women battered, women tortured, women humiliated, women degraded and defiled, women killed. Or, to be fair to the soft core, women sexually accessible, have-able, there for them, wanting to be taken and used, with perhaps just a little light bondage. Each violation of women—rape, battery, prostitution, child sexual abuse, sexual harassment—is made sexuality, made sexy, fun, and liberating of women's true nature in the pornography. Each specifically victimized and vulnerable group of women, each tabooed target group—Black women, Asian women, Latin

women, Jewish women, pregnant women, disabled women, retarded women, poor women, old women, fat women, women in women jobs, prostitutes, little girls—distinguishes pornographic genres and subthemes classified according to diverse customers' favorite degradation. Women are made into and coupled with anything considered lower than human: animals, objects, children, and (yes) other women. Anything women have claimed as their own—motherhood, athletics, traditional men's jobs, lesbianism, feminism—is made specifically sexy, dangerous, provocative, punished, made men's in pornography.

Pornography is a means through which sexuality is socially constructed, a site of construction, a domain of exercise. It constructs women as things for sexual use and constructs its consumers to desperately want women, to desperately want possession and cruelty and dehumanization. Inequality itself, subjection itself, hierarchy itself, objectification itself, with self-determination ecstatically relinquished, is the apparent consent of women's sexual desire and desirability. "The major theme of pornography as a genre," writes Andrea Dworkin, "is male power."[32] Women are in pornography to be violated and taken, men to violate and take them, either on screen or by camera or pen, on behalf of the viewer. Not that sexuality in life or in media never expresses love and affection; only that love and affection are not what is sexualized in this society's actual sexual paradigm, as pornography testifies to it. Violation of the powerless, intrusion on women, is. The milder forms, possession and use, the mildest of which is visual objectification, are. This sexuality of observation, visual intrusion and access, of entertainment, makes sex largely a spectator sport for its participants.

If pornography has not become sex to and from the male point of view, it is hard to explain why the pornography industry makes a known ten billion dollars a year selling it as sex mostly to men; why it is used to teach sex to child prostitutes, to recalcitrant wives and girlfriends and daughters, to medical students, and to sex offenders; why it is nearly universally classified as a subdivision of "erotic literature"; why it is protected and defended as if it were sex itself.[33] And why a prominent sexologist fears that enforcing the views of feminists against pornography in society would make men "erotically inert wimps."[34] No pornography, no male sexuality.

A feminist critique of sexuality in this sense is advanced in Andrea Dworkin's *Pornography: Men Possessing Women.* Building on her earlier identification of gender inequality as a system of social meaning,[35] an ideology lacking basis in anything other than the social reality its power constructs and maintains, she argues that sexuality is a construct of that power, given meaning by, through, and in pornography. In this perspective, pornography is not harmless fantasy or a corrupt and confused misrepresentation of otherwise natural healthy sex, nor is it fundamentally a distortion, reflection, projection, expression, representation, fantasy, or symbol of it. Through pornography, among other practices, gender inequality becomes both sexual and socially real. Pornography "reveals that male pleasure is inextricably tied to victimizing, hurting, exploiting." "Dominance in the male system is pleasure." Rape is "the defining paradigm of sexuality," to avoid which boys choose manhood and homophobia.[36]

Women, who are not given a choice, are objectified; or, rather, "the object is allowed to desire, if she desires to be an object."[37] Psychology sets the proper bounds of this objectification by terming its improper excesses "fetishism," distinguishing the uses from the abuses of women.[38] Dworkin shows how the process and content of women's definition as women, as an under-class, are the process and content of their sexualization as objects for male sexual use. The mechanism is (again) force, imbued with meaning because it is the means to death;[39] and death is the ultimate sexual act, the ultimate making of a person into a thing.

Why, one wonders at this point, is intercourse "sex" at all? In pornography, conventional intercourse is one act among many; penetration is crucial but can be done with anything; penis is crucial but not necessarily in the vagina. Actual pregnancy is a minor subgenetic theme, about as important in pornography as reproduction is in rape. Thematically, intercourse is incidental in pornography, especially when compared with force, which is primary. From pornography one learns that forcible violation of women is the essence of sex. Whatever is that and does that is sex. Everything else is secondary. Perhaps the reproductive act is considered sexual because it is considered an act of forcible violation and defilement of the female distinctively as such, not because it "is" sex a priori.

To be sexually objectified means having a social meaning imposed on your being that defines you as to be sexually used, according to your desired uses, and then using you that way. Doing this is sex in the male system. Pornography is a sexual practice of this because it exists in a social system in which sex in life is no less mediated than it is in representation. There is no irreducible essence, no "just sex." If sex is a social construct of sexism, men have sex with their image of a woman. Pornography creates an accessible sexual object, the possession and consumption of which is male sexuality, to be possessed and consumed as which is female sexuality. This is not because pornography depicts objectified sex, but because it creates the experience of a sexuality which is itself objectified. The appearance of choice or consent, with their attribution to inherent nature, is crucial in concealing the reality of force. Love of violation, variously termed female masochism and consent, comes to define female sexuality,[40] legitimating this political system by concealing the force on which it is based.

In this system, a victim, usually female, always feminized, is "never forced, only actualized."[41] Women whose attributes particularly fixate men—such as women with large breasts—are seen as full of sexual desire. Women men want, want men. Women fake vaginal orgasms, the only "mature" sexuality, because men demand that women enjoy vaginal penetration.[42]

Raped women are seen as asking for it: if a man wanted her, she must have wanted him. Men force women to become sexual objects, "that thing which causes erection, then hold themselves helpless and powerless when aroused by her.[43] Men who sexually harass say women sexually harass them. They mean they are aroused by women who turn them down. This elaborate projective system of demand characteristics—taken to pinnacles like fantasizing a clitoris in a woman's throat[44] so that men can enjoy forced fellatio in real life, assured that women do too—is surely a delusional structure deserving of serious psychological study. Instead, it is women who resist it who are studied, seen as in need of explanation and adjustment, stigmatized as inhibited and repressed and asexual. The assumption that in matters sexual women really want what men want from women, makes male force against women in sex invisible. It makes rape sex. Women's sexual "reluctance, dislike, and frigidity," women's puritanism and prudery in the face of this sex, is "the silent rebellion of women against the force of the penis . . . an ineffective rebellion, but a rebellion nonetheless."[45]

Nor is homosexuality without stake in this gendered sexual system. Putting to one side the obviously gendered content of expressly adopted roles, clothing, and sexual mimicry, to the extent the gender of a sexual object is crucial to arousal, the structure of social power which stands behind and defines gender is hardly irrelevant, even if it is rearranged. Some have argued that lesbian sexuality—meaning here simply women having sex with women, not with men—solves the problem of gender by eliminating men from women's voluntary sexual encounters.[46] Yet women's sexuality remains constructed under conditions of male supremacy; women remain socially defined as women in relation to men; the definition of women as men's inferiors remains sexual even if not heterosexual, whether men are present at the time or not. To the extent gay men choose men because they are men, the meaning of masculinity is affirmed as well as undermined. It may also

be that sexuality is so gender marked that it carries dominance and submission with it, whatever the gender of its participants.

Each structural requirement of this sexuality as revealed in pornography is professed in recent defenses of sadomasochism, described by proponents as that sexuality in which "the basic dynamic . . . is the power dichotomy."[47] Exposing the prohibitory underpinnings on which this violation model of the sexual depends, one advocate says: "We select the most frightening, disgusting or unacceptable activities and transmute them into pleasure." The relational dynamics of sadomasochism do not even negate the paradigm of male dominance, but conform precisely to it: the ecstasy in domination ("I like to hear someone ask for mercy or protection"); the enjoyment of inflicting psychological as well as physical torture ("I want to see the confusion, the anger, the turn-on, the helplessness"); the expression of belief in the inferior's superiority belied by the absolute contempt ("the bottom must be my superior . . . playing a bottom who did not demand my respect and admiration would be like eating rotten fruit"); the degradation and consumption of women through sex ("she feeds me the energy I need to dominate and abuse her"); the health and personal growth rationale ("it's a healing process"); the anti-puritan radical therapy justification ("I was taught to dread sex . . . It is shocking and profoundly satisfying to commit this piece of rebellion, to take pleasure exactly as I want it, to exact it like tribute"); the bipolar doublethink in which the top enjoys "sexual service" while "the will to please is the bottom's source of pleasure." And the same bottom line of all top-down sex: "I want to be in control." The statements are from a female sadist. The good news is, it is not biological.

As pornography connects sexuality with gender in social reality, the feminist critique of pornography connects feminist work on violence against women with its inquiry into women's consciousness and gender roles. It is not only that women are the principal targets of rape, which by conservative definition happens to almost half of all women at least once in their lives. It is not only that over one-third of all women are sexually molested by older trusted male family members or friends or authority figures as an early, perhaps initiatory, interpersonal sexual encounter. It is not only that at least the same percentage, as adult women, are battered in homes by male intimates. It is not only that about one-fifth of American women have been or are known to be prostitutes, and most cannot get out of it. It is not only that 85 percent of working women will be sexually harassed on the job, many physically, at some point in their working lives.[48] All this documents the extent and terrain of abuse and the effectively unrestrained and systematic sexual aggression by less than one-half of the population against the other more than half. It suggests that it is basically allowed.

It does not by itself show that availability for this treatment defines the identity attributed to that other half of the population; or, that such treatment, all this torment and debasement, is socially considered not only rightful but enjoyable, and is in fact enjoyed by the dominant half; or, that the ability to engage in such behaviors defines the identity of that half. And not only of that half. Now consider the content of gender roles. All the social requirements for male sexual arousal and satisfaction are identical with the gender definition of "female." All the essentials of the male gender role are also the qualities sexualized as "male" in male dominant sexuality. If gender is a social construct, and sexuality is a social construct, and the question is, of what is each constructed, the fact that their contents are identical—not to mention that the word *sex* refers to both—might be more than a coincidence.

As to gender, what is sexual about pornography is what is unequal about social life. To say that pornography sexualizes gender and genders sexuality means that it provides a concrete social process through which gender and sexuality become functions of each other. Gender and sexuality, in this view, become two different shapes

taken by the single social equation of male with dominance and female with submission. Feeling this as identity, acting it as role, inhabiting and presenting it as self, is the domain of gender. Enjoying it as the erotic, centering upon when it elicits genital arousal, is the domain of sexuality. Inequality is what is sexualized through pornography; it is what is sexual about it. The more unequal, the more sexual. The violence against women in pornography is an expression of gender hierarchy, the extremity of the hierarchy expressed and created through the extremity of the abuse, producing the extremity of the male sexual response. Pornography's multiple variations on and departures from the male dominant/female submissive sexual/gender theme are not exceptions to these gender regularities. They affirm them. The capacity of gender reversals (dominatrixes) and inversions (homosexuality) to stimulate sexual excitement is derived precisely from their mimicry or parody or negation or reversal of the standard arrangement. This affirms rather than undermines or qualifies the standard sexual arrangement as the standard sexual arrangement, the definition of sex, the standard from which all else is defined, that in which sexuality as such inheres.

Male sexuality is apparently activated by violence against women and expresses itself in violence against women to a significant extent. If violence is seen as occupying the most fully achieved end of a dehumanization continuum on which objectification occupies the least express end, one question that is raised is whether some form of hierarchy—the dynamic of the continuum—is currently essential for male sexuality to experience itself. If so, and if gender is understood to be a hierarchy, perhaps the sexes are unequal so that men can be sexually aroused. To put it another way, perhaps gender must be maintained as a social hierarchy so that men will be able to get erections; or, part of the male interest in keeping women down lies in the fact that it gets men up. Maybe feminists are considered castrating because equality is not sexy.

Recent inquiries into rape support such suspicions. Men often rape women, it turns out, because they want to and enjoy it. The act, including the dominance, is sexually arousing, sexually affirming, and supportive of the perpetrator's masculinity.

Add this to rape's pervasiveness and permissibility, together with the belief that it is both rare and impermissible. Combine this with the similarity between the patterns, rhythms, roles, and emotions, not to mention acts, which make up rape (and battery) on the one hand and intercourse on the other. All this makes it difficult to sustain the customary distinctions between pathology and normalcy, paraphilia and nomophilia, violence and sex, in this area. Some researchers have previously noticed the centrality of force to the excitement value of pornography but have tended to put it down to perversion. Robert Stoller, for example, observes that pornography today depends upon hostility, voyeurism, and sadomasochism and calls perversion "the erotic form of hatred."[49] If the perverse in this context is seen not as the other side of a bright normal/abnormal line but as an undiluted expression of a norm that permeates many ordinary interactions, hatred of women—that is, misogyny—becomes a dynamic of sexual excitement itself.

All women live in sexual objectification the way fish live in water. With no alternatives, the strategy to acquire self-respect and pride is: I chose it.

Consider the conditions under which this is done. This is a culture in which women are socially expected—and themselves necessarily expect and want—to be able to distinguish the socially, epistemologically, indistinguishable. Rape and intercourse are not authoritatively separated by any difference between the physical acts or amount of force involved but only legally, by a standard that centers on the man's interpretation of the encounter. Thus, although raped women, that is, most women, are supposed to be able to feel every day and every night that they have some meaningful determining part in having their sex life—their life, period—not be a series of rapes, the most they provide is the raw data for the man to see as he sees it. And he has been seeing pornography. Similarly, "consent" is supposed to be the crucial line between rape and intercourse, but the legal standard for it is so passive, so acquiescent, that a woman can be dead and have consented under it. The mind fuck of all of this makes liberalism's complicitous collapse into "I chose it" feel like a strategy for sanity. It certainly makes a woman at one with the world.

The general theory of sexuality emerging from this feminist critique does not consider sexuality to be an inborn force inherent in individuals, nor cultural in the Freudian sense, in which sexuality exists in a cultural context but in universally invariant stages and psychic representations.[50] It appears instead to be culturally specific, even if so far largely invariant because male supremacy is largely universal, if always in specific forms. Although some of its abuses (like prostitution) are accentuated by poverty, it does not vary by class, although class is one hierarchy it sexualizes. Sexuality becomes, in this view, social and relational, constructing and constructed of power. Infants, though sensory, cannot be said to possess sexuality in this sense because they have not had the experiences (and do not speak the language) that give it social meaning. Since sexuality *is* its social meaning, infant erections, for example, are clearly sexual in the sense that this society centers its sexuality on them, but to relate to a child as though his erections mean what adult erections have been conditioned to mean is a form of child abuse. Such erections have the meaning they acquire in social life only to observing adults.

At risk of further complicating the issues, perhaps it would help to think of women's sexuality as women's like Black culture is Blacks': it is, and it is not. The parallel cannot be precise in part because, owing to segregation, Black culture developed under more autonomous conditions than women, intimately integrated with men by force, have had. Still, both can be experienced as a source of strength, joy, expression, and as an affirmative badge of pride.[51] Both remain nonetheless stigmatic in the sense of a brand, a restriction, a definition as less. This *is* not because of any intrinsic content or value, but because the social reality is that their shape, qualities, texture, imperative, and very existence are a response to powerlessness. They exist as they do because of lack of choice. They are created out of social conditions of oppression and exclusion. They may be part of a strategy for survival or even of change. But, as is, they are not the whole world, and it is the whole world that one is entitled to. This is why interpreting female sexuality as an expression of women's agency and autonomy, as if sexism did not exist, *is* always denigrating and bizarre and reductive, as it would be to interpret Black culture as if racism did not exist. As if Black culture just arose freely and spontaneously on the plantations and in the ghettos of North America, adding diversity to American pluralism.

So long as sexual inequality remains unequal and sexual, attempts to value sexuality as women's, possessive as if women possess it, will remain part of limiting women to it, to what women are now defined as being. Outside of truly rare and contrapuntal glimpses (which most people think they live almost their entire sex life within), to seek an equal sexuality without political transformation is to seek equality under conditions of inequality. Rejecting this, and rejecting the glorification of settling for the best that inequality has to offer or has stimulated the resourceful to invent, are what Ti-Grace Atkinson meant to reject when she said: "I do not know any feminist worthy of that name who, if forced to choose between freedom and sex, would choose sex. She'd choose freedom every time." [52]

NOTES

1. See Jane Caputi, *The Age of Sex Crime* (Bowling Green, Ohio: Bowling Green State University Popular Press, 1987); Deborah Cameron and Elizabeth Frazer, *The Lust to Kill: A Feminist*

Investigation of Sexual Murder (New York: New York University Press, 1987).

2. A few basic citations from the massive body of work on which this chapter draws are:

On Rape: Diana E. H. Russell and Nancy Howell, "The Prevalence of Rape in the United States Revisited," *Signs: Journal of Women in Culture and Society* 8 (Summer 1983): 668–695; D. Russell, *Rape in Marriage* (New York: Macmillan 1982); Lorenne M. G. Clark and Debra Lewis, *The Politics of Rape: The Victim's Perspective* (New York: Stein & Day, 1975); Andrea Medea and Kathleen Thompson, *Against Rape* (New York: Farrar, Straus and Giroux, 1974); Susan Brownmiller, *Against Our Will: Men, Women, and Rape* (New York: Simon and Schuster, 1975); Irene Frieze, "Investigating the Causes and Consequences of Marital Rape," *Signs: Journal of Women in Culture and Society* 8 (Spring 1983): 532–553; Nancy Gager and Cathleen Schurr, *Sexual Assault: Confronting Rape in America* (New York: Grosset & Dunlap, 1976); Gary LaFree, "Male Power and Female Victimization: Towards a Theory of Interracial Rape," *American Journal of Sociology* 88 (1982): 311–328; Martha Butt, "Cultural Myths and Supports for Rape," *Journal of Personality and Social Psychology* 38 (1980): 217–230; Kalamu ya Salaam, "Rape: A Radical Analysis from the African-American Perspective," in *Our Women Keep Our Skies from Falling* (New Orleans: Nkombo, 1980); J. Check and N. Malamuth, "An Empirical Assessment of Some Feminist Hypotheses about Rape," *International Journal of Women's Studies* 8 (1985): 414–423.

On Battery: D. Martin, *Battered Wives* (San Francisco: Glide Productions, 1976); S. Steinmerz, *The Cycle of Violence: Assertive, Aggressive, and Abusive Family Interaction* (New York: Praeger, 1977); R. Emerson Dobash and Russell Dobash, *Violence against Wives: A Case against the Patriarchy* (New York: Free Press, 1979); R. Langley and R. Levy, *Wife Beating: The Silent Crisis* (New York: E. P. Dutton, 1977); Evan Stark, Anne Flitcraft, and William Frazier, "Medicine and Patriarchal Violence: The Social Construction of a 'Private' Event," *International Journal of Health Services* 9 (1979): 461–493; Lenore Walker, *The Battered Woman* (New York: Harper & Row, 1979).

On Sexual Harassment: Merit Systems Protection Board, *Sexual Harassment in the Federal Workplace: Is it a Problem?* (Washington, D. C.: U. S. Government Printing Office, 1981); C. A, MacKinnon, *Sexual Harassment of Working Women* (New Haven: Yale University Press, 1979); Donna Benson and Gregg Thomson, "Sexual Harassment on a University Campus: The Confluence of Authority Relations, Sexual Interest, and Gender Stratification," *Social Problems* 29 (1982): 236–251; Phyllis Crocker and Anne E. Simon, "Sexual Harassment in Education," 10 *Capital University Law Review* 541 (1981).

On Incest and Child Sexual Abuse: D. Finkelhor, *Sexually Victimized Children* (New York: Free Press, 1979); J. Herman, *Father-Daughter Incest* (Cambridge, Mass.: Harvard University Press, 1981); D. Finkelhor, *Child Sexual Abuse: Theory and Research* (New York: Free Press, 1984); A. Jaffe, L. Dynneson, and R. Ten-Bensel, "Sexual Abuse of Children. An Epidemologic Study," *American Journal of Diseases of Children* 129 (1975): 689–695; K. Brady, *Father's Days: A True Story of Incest* (New York: Seaview Books, l979); L. Armstrong, *Kiss Daddy Goodnight* (New York: Hawthorn Press, 1978); S. Burler, *Conspiracy of Silence: The Trauma of Incest* (San Francisco: New Glide Publications, 1978); A. Burgess, N. Groth, L. Homstrom, and S. Sgroi, *Sexual Assault of Children and Adolescents* (Lexington, Mass.: Lexington Books, 1978); F. Rush, *The Best-Kept Secret: Sexual Abuse of Children* (Englewood Cliffs, N.J.: Prentice-Hall, 1980); Diana E. H. Russell, "The Prevalence and Seriousness of Incestuous Abuse: Stepfathers v. Biological Fathers," *Child Abuse and Neglect: The International Journal* 8 (1984): *15–22;* idem, "The Incidence and Prevalence of Intrafamilial and Extrafamilial Sexual Abuse of Female Children," ibid. 7 (1983): 133–146; idem, *The Secret Trauma: Incestuous Abuse of Women and Girls* (New York: Basic Books, 1986).

On Prostitution: Kathleen Barry, *Female Sexual Slavery* (Englewood Cliffs, N. J.: Prentice Hall, 1979); M. Griffin, "Wives, Hookers and the Law," 10 *Student Lawyer* 18–21 (January 1982); J. James and J. Meyerding, "Early Sexual Experience as a Factor in Prostitution," *Archives*

of Sexual Behavior 7 (1978): 31–42; United Nations Economic and Social Council, Commission on Human Rights, Sub-Commission on Prevention of Discrimination and Protection of Minorities, Working Group on Slavery, *Suppression of the Traffic in Persons and of the Exploitation of the Prostitution of Others, E/Cn.4/AC.2/5* (New York, 1976); Jennifer James, *The Politics of Prostitution* (Seattle: Social Research Associates, 1975); Kate Millett, *The Prostitution Papers* (New York: Avon Books, 1973).

On Pornography: L. Lederer, ed., *Take Back the Night: Women on Pornography* (New York: William Morrow, 1980): Andrea Dworkin, *Pornography: Men Possessing Women* (New York: Perigee, 1981); Linda Lovelace and Michael McGrady, *Ordeal* (Secaucus, N.J.: Citadel Press, 1980); P. Bogdanovich, *The Killing of the Unicorn: Dorothy Stratten, 1960–1980* (New York: William Morrow, 1984); M. Langelan, "The Political Economy of Pornography," *Aegis: Magazine on Ending Violence against Women 32* (August 1981): 5–7. D. Leidholdr, "Where Pornography Meets Fascism," *WIN New.* March 15, 1983, pp. 18–22; E. Donnerstein. "Erotica and Human Aggression," in *Aggression: Theoretical and Empirical Review,* ed. R. Green and E. Donnerstein (New York: Academic Press, 1983); idem, "Pornography: Its Effects on Violence Against Women," in *Pornography and Sexual Aggression,* ed. N. Malamuth and E. Donnerstein (Orlando. Fla.: Academic Press, 1984); Geraldine Finn, "Against Sexual Imagery, Alternative or Otherwise" (Paper presented at Symposium on Images of Sexuality in Art and Media, Ottawa, March 13–16, 1985); Diana E. H. Russell, "Pornography and Rape: A Causal Model," *Political Psychology* 9 (1988): 41–74; M. McManus, ed., *Final Report of the Attorney General's Commission on Pornography* (Nashville: Rutledge Hill Press, 1986).

See Generally: Diana E. H. Russell, *Sexual Exploitation: Rape, Child Sexual Abuse, and Workplace Sexual Harassment* (Beverly Hills: Russell Sage, 1984); D. Russell and N. Van de Ven, *Crimes Against Women: Proceedings of the International Tribunal* (Millbrae, Calif.: Les Femmes, 1976); E. Stanko, *Intimate Intrusions: Women's Experience of Male Violence* (London:

Routledge & Kegan Paul, 1985); Ellen Morgan, *The Erotization of Male Dominance/Female Submission (Pittsburgh:* Know, 1975): Adrienne Rich, "Compulsory Heterosexuality and Lesbian Existence," *Signs: Journal of Women in Culture and Society* 5 (Summer 1980): 631–660; J. Long Laws and P. Schwartz, *Sexual Scripts: The Social Construction of Female Sexuality* (Hinsdale. Ill.: Dryden Press, 1977); L. Phelps, "Female Sexual Alienation," in *Women: A Feminist Perspective,* ed. J. Freeman (Palo Alto, Calif.: Mayfield, 1979); Shere Hite, *The Hite Report: A Nationwide Survey of Female Sexuality* (New York: Macmillan, 1976); Andrea Dworkin, *Intercourse* (New York: Free Press, 1987). Recent comparative work provides confirmation and contrasts: Pat Caplan, ed., *The Cultural Construction of Sexuality* (New York: Tavistock, 1987); Marjorie Shostak, *Nisa: The Life and Words of a !Kung Woman* (New York: Vintage Books, 1983).

3. Freud's decision to disbelieve women's accounts of being sexually abused as children was apparently central in the construction of the theories of fantasy and possibly also of the unconscious. That is, to some degree, his belief that the sexual abuse in his patients' accounts did not occur created the need for a theory like fantasy, like unconscious, to explain the reports. See Rush, *The Best-Kept Secret;* Jeffrey M. Masson, *The Assault on Truth: Freud's Suppression of the Seduction Theory (New* York: Farrar, Straus and Giroux, 1984). One can only speculate on the course of the modern psyche (not to mention modern history) had the women been believed.

4. E. Schur, *Labeling Women Deviant: Gender, Stigma, and Social Control* (Philadelphia: Temple University Press, 1984) (a superb review of studies which urges a "continuum" rather than a "deviance" approach to issues of sex inequality).

5. This figure was calculated at my request by Diana E. H. Russell on the random-sample data base of 930 San Francisco households discussed in *The Secret Trauma,* pp. 20–37, and *Rape in Marriage,* pp. 27–41. The figure includes all the forms of rape or other sexual abuse or harassment surveyed, noncontact as well as contact, from gang rape by strangers and marital rape to obscene phone calls, unwanted sexual advances on the street, unwelcome requests to pose for

pornography, and subjection to peeping toms and sexual exhibitionists (flashers).

6. S. D. Smithyman, "The Undetected Rapist" (Ph. D. diss., Claremont Graduate School, 1978); N. Groth, *Men Who Rape: The Psychology of the Offender* (New York: Plenum Press, 1979); D. Scully and J. Marolla, "'Riding the Bull at Gilley's': Convicted Rapists Describe the Rewards of Rape," *Social Problems* 32 (1985): 251. (The manuscript subtitle was "Convicted Rapists Describe the Pleasure of Raping.")

7. Kate Millett, *Sexual Politics* (Garden City, N. Y.: Doubleday, 1970).

8. Jacques Lacan, *Feminine Sexuality,* trans. Jacqueline Rose, ed. Juliet Mitchell and Jacqueline Rose (New York: Norton, 1982); Michel Foucault. *The History of Sexuality,* vol. 1: An Introduction (New York: Random House, 1980); idem, *Power/Knowledge,* ed. C. Gordon (New York: Pantheon, 1980).

See generally (including materials reviewed in) R. Padgug, "Sexual Matters; On Conceptualizing Sexuality in History," *Radical History Review* 70 (Spring/Summer 1979), e.g., p. 9; M. Vicinus, "Sexuality and Power: A Review of Current Work in the History of Sexuality," *Feminist Studies* 8 (Spring 1982): 133–155; S. Ortner and H. Whitehead, *Sexual Meanings: The Cultural Construction of Gender and Sexuality* (Cambridge: Cambridge University Press, 1981); Red Collective, *The Politics of Sexuality in Capitalism* (London: Black Rose Press, 1978; J. Weeks, *Sex, Politics, and Society: The Regulation of Sexuality since 1800* (New York: Longman, 1981); J. D'Emilio, *Sexual Politics, Sexual Communities: The Making of a Homosexual Minority in the United States 1940–1970* (Chicago: University of Chicago Press, 1983); A. Snitow, C. Stansell, and S. Thompson, eds., Introduction to *Powers of Desire: The Politics of Sexuality* (New York: Monthly Review Press, 1983); E. Dubois and L. Gordon, "Seeking Ecstasy on the Battlefield: Danger and Pleasure in Nineteenth-Century Feminist Social Thought," *Feminist Studies* 9 (Spring 1983): 7–25.

9. An example is Jeffrey Weeks, *Sexuality and Its Discontents* (London: Routledge & Kegan Paul, 1985).

10. Luce Irigaray's critique of Freud in *Speculum of the Other Women* (Ithaca; Cornell University

Press, 1974) acutely shows how Freud constructs sexuality from the male point of view, with woman as deviation from the norm. But she, too, sees female sexuality not as constructed by male dominance but only repressed under it.

11. For those who think that such notions are atavisms left behind by modern scientists, see one entirely typical conceptualization of "sexual pleasure, a powerful unconditioned stimulus and reinforcer" in N. Malamuth and B. Spinner, "A Longitudinal Content Analysis of Sexual Violence in the Best-Selling Erotic Magazines," *Journal of Sex Research* 16 (August 1980): 226. See also B. Ollman's discussion of Wilhelm Reich in *Social and Sexual Revolution* (Boston: South End Press, 1979), esp. pp. 186–187.

12. Foucault's contributions to such an analysis and his limitations are discussed illuminatingly in Frigga Haug, ed., *Female Sexualization,* trans. Erica Carter (London: Verso, 1987), pp. 190–198.

13. A. Kinsey, W. Pomeroy, C. Martin, and P. Gebhard, *Sexual Behavior in the Human Female* (Philadelphia: W. B. Saunders, 1953); A. Kinsey, W. Pomeroy, and C. Martin, *Sexual Behavior in the Human Male* (Philadelphia: W. B. Saunders, 1948). See the critique of Kinsey in Dworkin, *Pornography,* pp. 179–198.

14. Examples include: D. English, "The Politics of Porn: Can Feminists Walk the Line?" *Mother Jones,* April 1980, pp. 20–23, 43–44, 48–50; D. English, A. Hollibaugh, and G. Rubin, "Talking Sex: A Conversation on Sexuality and Feminism," *Socialist Review* 58 (July–August) 1981; J. B. Elshtain, "The Victim Syndrome: A Troubling Turn in Feminism," *The Progressive,* June 1982, pp. 40–47; Ellen Willis, *Village Voice,* November 12, 1979. This approach also tends to characterize the basic ideology of "human sexuality courses" as analyzed by C. Vance in Snitow, Stansell, and Thompson, *Powers of Desire,* pp. 371–384. The view of sex so promulgated is distilled in the following quotation, coming after an alliterative list, probably intended to be humorous, headed "determinants of sexuality" (on which "power" does not appear, although every other word begins with p): "Persistent puritanical pressures promoting propriety, purity, and prudery are opposed by a powerful, prime-val, procreative passion to plunge his pecker into

her pussy"; "Materials from Course on Human Sexuality," College of Medicine and Dentistry of New Jersey, Rutgers Medical School, January 29 February 2, 1979, p. 39.

15. A third reason is also given: "to the extent that sexism in societal and family structure is responsible for the phenomena of 'compulsive masculinity' and structured antagonism between the sexes, the elimination of sexual inequality would reduce the number of 'power trip' and 'degradation ceremony' motivated rapes," M. Straus, "Sexual Inequality, Cultural Norms, and Wife-Beating," *Victimology: An International Journal* 1 (1976): 54–76. Note that these structural factors seem to be considered nonsexual, in the sense that "power trip" and "degradation ceremony" motivated rapes are treated as not erotic to the perpetrators *because* of the elements of dominance and degradation, nor is "structured antagonism" seen as an erotic element of rape or sex (or family).

16. P. R. Sanday, "The Socio-Cultural Context of Rape: A Cross-Cultural Study," *Journal of Social Issues* 87, no. 4 (1981): 16. See also M. Lewin, "Unwanted Intercourse: The Difficulty of Saying 'No,'" *Psychology of Women Quarterly* 9 (1985): 184–192.

17. Susan Brownmiller, *Against Our Will,* originated this approach, which has since become ubiquitous.

18. Annie McCombs helped me express this thought; letter to *Off Our Backs* (Washington, D. C., October 1984), p. 34.

19. Brownmiller, *Against Our Will,* did analyze rape as something men do to women, hence as a problem of gender, even though her concept of gender is biologically based. See, e.g., her pp. 4–6, and discussion in chap. 3. An exception is Clark and Lewis, *Rape.*

20. Snitow, Stansell, and Thompson, Introduction to *Powers of Desire,* p. 9.

21. C. Vance, "Concept Paper: Toward a Politics of Sexuality," in *Diary of a Conference on Sexuality,* ed. H. Alderfer, B. Jaker, and M. Nelson (Record of the planning committee of the conference "The Scholar and the Feminist IX: Toward a Politics of Sexuality," April 24, 1982), p. 27: to address "women's sexual pleasure, choice, and autonomy, acknowledging that

sexuality is simultaneously a domain of restriction, repression and danger as well as a domain of exploration, pleasure and agency." Parts of the *Diary,* with the conference papers, were later published in C. Vance, ed., *Pleasure and Danger: Exploring Female Sexuality* (London: Routledge & Kegan Paul, 1984).

22. Vance, "Concept Paper," p. 38.

23. For example see A. Hollibaugh and C. Moraga, "What We're Rollin' Around in Bed With: Sexual Silences in Feminism," in Snitow, Stansell, and Thompson, *Powers of Desire,* pp. 394–405, esp. 398; Samois, *Coming to Power* (Berkeley, Calif.: Alyson Publications, 1983).

24. Andrea Dworkin, "Why So-called Radical Men Love and Need Pornography," in Lederer, *Take Back the Night,* p. 148.

25. Susan Sontag, "Fascinating Fascism," in *Under the Sign of Saturn* (New York: Farrar, Straus and Giroux, 1980), p. 103.

26. Robert Stoller, *Sexual Excitement: Dynamics of Erotic Life* (New York: Pantheon Books, 1979), p. 6.

27. Harriet Jacobs, quoted in Rennie Simson, "The Afro-American Female: The Historical Context of the Construction of Sexual Identity," in Snitow, Stansell, and Thompson, *Powers of Desire,* p. 231. Jacobs subsequently resisted by hiding in an attic cubbyhole "almost deprived of light and air, and with no space to move my limbs, for nearly seven years" to avoid him.

28. A similar rejection of indeterminacy can be found in Linda Alcoff, "Cultural Feminism versus Post-Structuralism: The Identity Crisis in Feminist Theory," *Signs: Journal of Women in Culture and Society* 13 (Spring 1988): 419–420. The article otherwise misdiagnoses the division in feminism as that between so-called cultural feminists and post-structuralism, when the division is between those who take sexual misogyny seriously as a mainspring to gender hiearchy and those who wish, liberal-fashion, to affirm "differences" without seeing that sameness/ difference is a dichotomy of exactly the sort that post-structuralism purports to deconstruct.

29. See Sandra Harding, "Introduction: Is There a Feminist Method?" in *Feminism and Methodology* (Bloomington: Indiana University Press, 1987), pp. 1–14.

30. One of the most compelling accounts of active victim behavior is provided in *Give Sorrow Words: Maryse Holder's Letters from Mexico,* intro. Kate Millett (New York: Grove Press, 1980). Ms. Holder wrote a woman friend of her daily, frantic, and always failing pursuit of men, sex, beauty, and feeling good about herself: "Fuck fucking, will *feel* self-respect" (p. 94). She was murdered soon after by an unknown assailant.

31. This phrase comes from Michel Foucault, "The West and the Truth of Sex," *Substance* 5 (1978): 20. Foucault does not criticize pornography in these terms.

32. Dworkin, *Pornography,* p. 24.

33. J. Cook, "The X-Rated Economy," *Forbes,* September 18, 1978, p. 18; Langelan, "The Political Economy of Pornography," p. 5; *Public Hearings on Ordinances to Add Pornography as Discrimination Against Women* (Minneapolis, December 12–13, 1983); F. Schauer, "Response: Pornography and the First Amendment," 40, *University of Pittsburgh Law Review, 605,* 616 (1979).

34. John Money, professor of medical psychology and pediatrics, Johns Hopkins Medical Institutions, letter to Clive M. Davis, April 18, 1948. The same view is expressed by Al Goldstein, editor of *Screw,* a pornographic newspaper, concerning antipornography feminists, termed "nattering nabobs of sexual negativism": "We must repeat to ourselves like a mantra: sex is good; nakedness is a joy; an erection is beautiful . . . Don't let the bastards get you limp"; "Dear Playboy," *Playboy, June* 1985, p. 12.

35. Andrea Dworkin, "The Root Cause," in *Our Blood: Prophesies and Discourses on Sexual Politics* (New York: Harper & Row, 1976), pp. 96–111.

36. Dworkin, *Pornography* pp. 69, 136, and chap. 2, "Men and Boys." "In practice, fucking is an act of possession—simultaneously an act of ownership, taking, force, it is conquering; it expresses in intimacy power over and against, body to body, person to thing. 'The sex act' means penile intromission followed by penile thrusting, or fucking. The woman is acted on, the man acts and through action expresses sexual power, the power of masculinity. Fucking requires that the male act on one who has less power and this

valuation is so deep, so completely implicit in the act, that the one who is fucked is stigmatized as feminine during the act even when not anatomically female. In the male system, sex is the penis, the penis is sexual power, its use in fucking is manhood," p. 23.

37. Ibid., p. 109.

38. Ibid., pp. 113–128.

39. Ibid., p. 174.

40. Freud believed that the female nature was inherently masochistic; Sigmund Freud, Lecture XXXIII, "The Psychology of Women," in *New Introductory Lectures on Psychoanalysis* (London: Hogarth Press. 1933). Helene Deutsch, Marie Bonaparte, Sandor Rado, Adolf Grunberger, Melanie Klein, Helle Thorning, Georges Bataille, Theodore Reik, Jean-Paul Sartre, and Simone de Beauvoir all described some version of female masochism in their work, each with a different theoretical account for virtually identical observations. See Helene Deutsch, "The Significance of Masochism in the Mental Life of Women," *International Journal of Psychoanalysis* 11 (1930); 48–60; idem in *The Psychology of Women (New* York: Grune & Stratton, 1944). Several are summarized by Janine Chasseguet-Smirgel, ed., in her Introduction to *Female Sexuality: New Psychoanalytic Views* (Ann Arbor: University of Michigan Press, 1970); Theodore Reik, *Masochism in Sex and Society* (New York: Grove Press, 1962), p. 217; Helle Thorning, "The Mother-Daughter Relationship and Sexual Ambivalence," *Heresies* 12 (1979): 3–6; Georges Bataille, *Death and Sensuality* (New York: Walker and Co., 1962); Jean-Paul Sartre, "Concrete Relations with Others," in *Being and Nothingness: An Essay on Phenomenological Ontology,* trans. Hazel E. Barnes (New York: Philosophical Library (1956), pp. 361–430. Betsey Belote stated: "masochistic and hysterical behavior is so similar to the concept of 'femininity' that the three are not clearly distinguishable"; "Masochistic Syndrome, Hysterical Personality, and the Illusion of the Healthy Woman," in *Female Psychology: The Emerging Self,* ed. Sue Cox (Chicago; Science Research Associates, 1976), p. 347. See also S. Bartky, "Feminine Masochism and the Politics of Personal Transformation," *Women's Studies International Forum* 7 (1984):

327–328. Andrea Dworkin writes: "I believe that freedom for women must begin in the repudiation of our own masochism . . . I believe that ridding ourselves of our own deeply entrenched masochism, which takes so many tortured forms, is the first priority; it is the first deadly blow that we can strike against systematized male dominance," *Our Blood,* p. 111.

41. Dworkin, *Pornography,* p. 146.

42. Anne Koedt, "The Myth of the Vaginal Organism," in *Notes from the Second Year: Women's Liberation* (New York: Radical Feminism, 1970); Ti-Grace Atkinson, *Amazon Odyssey: The First Collection of Writing by the Political Pioneer of the Women's Movement* (New York: Links Books, 1974); Phelps, "Female Sexual Alienation."

43. Dworkin, *Pornography,* p. 22.

44. This is the plot of *Deep Throat,* the pornographic film Linda "Lovelace" was forced to make. It may be the largest-grossing pornography film in the history of the world (McManus, *Final Report,* p. 345). That this plot is apparently enjoyed to such a prevalent extent suggests that it appeals to something extant in the male psyche.

45. Dworkin, "The Root Cause," p. 56.

46. A prominent if dated example is Jill Johnston, *Lesbian Nation: The Feminist Solution* (New York: Simon and Schuster, 1973).

47. This and the following quotations in this paragraph are from P. Califia, "A Secret Side of Lesbian Sexuality," *The Advocate* (San Francisco), December 27, 1979, pp. 19–21, 27–28.

48. The statistics in this paragraph are drawn from the sources referenced in note 2, above, as categorized by topic. Kathleen Barry defines "female sexual slavery" as a condition of prostitution which one cannot get out of.

49. Robert Stoller, *Perversion: The Erotic Form of Hatred* (New York: Pantheon, 1975), p. 87.

50. This is also true of Foucault, *The History of Sexuality.* Foucault understands that sexuality must be discussed with method, power, class, and the law. Gender, however, eludes him. So he cannot distinguish between the silence about sexuality that Victorianism has made into a noisy discourse and the silence that has *been* women's sexuality under conditions of subordination by and to men. Although he purports to grasp sexuality, including desire itself, as social, he

does not see the content of its determination as a sexist social order that eroticizes potency as male and victimization as female. Women are simply beneath significant notice.

51. On sexuality, see, e.g., A. Lorde, *Uses of the Erotic: The Erotic as Power* (Brooklyn, N. Y.: Out and Out Books, 1978); and Haunani-Kay Trask, *Eros and Power: The Promise of Feminist Theory* (Philadelphia: University of Pennsylvania Press, 1986). Both creatively attempt such a reconstitution. Trask's work suffers from an underlying essentialism in which the realities of sexual abuse are not examined or seen as constituting women's sexuality as such. Thus, a return to mother and body can be urged as social bases for reclaiming a feminist eros. Another

reason the parallel cannot be at all precise is that Black women and their sexuality make up both Black culture and women's sexuality, inhabiting both sides of the comparison. In other words, parallels which converge and interact are not parallels. The comparison may nonetheless be heuristically useful both for those who understand one experience but not the other and for those who can compare two dimensions of life which overlap and resonate together at some moments and diverge sharply in dissonance at others.

52. Ti-Grace Atkinson, "Why I'm against S/M Liberation," in *Against Sadomasochism: A Radical Feminist Analysis,* ed. F. Linden, D. Pagano, D. Russell, and S. Star (Palo Alto, Calif.: Frog in the Well, 1982), p. 91.

SEX WAR: THE DEBATE BETWEEN RADICAL AND LIBERTARIAN FEMINISTS

Ann Ferguson

In the last four years, there has been an increasing polarization of American feminists into two camps on issues of feminist sexual morality. The first camp, the radical feminists, holds that sexuality in a male-dominant society involves danger—that is, that sexual practices perpetuate violence against women. The opposing camp, self-styled "anti-prudes," I term "libertarian feminists," for whom the key feature of sexuality is the potentially liberating aspects of the exchange of pleasure between consenting partners. As thus constituted these are not exclusive positions: obviously it is quite consistent to hold that contemporary sexual practices involve both danger and pleasure.[1]

What accounts, then, for the current dichotomy, indeed the bitter opposition, between radical- and libertarian-feminist positions on sexual morality? I would argue that there are both historical and philosophical differences between the two camps. Historically, radical feminists have been those who are members of or who identify with a lesbian-feminist community that rejects male-dominated heterosexual sex. Radical feminists tend to condemn sadomasochism, pornography, prostitution, cruising (promiscuous sex with strangers), adult/child sexual relations, and sexual role playing (e.g., butch/femme relationships). They reject such practices because of implicit and explicit analyses that tie dominant/subordinate

---

[1] It is important to note that feminists in the first phase of the women's movement during the late 1960s did not make this distinction in thinking about sexuality; they emphasized both

a defense of women's right to pleasure (female orgasms) and legal protection from one of the dangers of heterosexual intercourse: unwanted pregnancies (i.e., the right to abortion). During the second phase in the early 1970s, feminists emphasized women's right to sexual pleasure with women (lesbian feminism). It is only in the third phase of the movement, when the goals of sexual pleasure have become culturally legitimated to a greater extent, that many feminists have begun to emphasize the violence and danger of heterosexual institutions like pornography.

power relations to the perpetuance of male dominance.[2] Libertarian feminists, on the other hand,
tend to be heterosexual feminists or lesbian feminists who support any sort of consensual sexuality that brings the participants pleasure, including
sadomasochism, pornography, role-oriented sex,
cruising, and adult/child sexual relations. These
issues have come to a head recently in disagreements regarding radical feminists' condemnation
of pornography and sadomasochistic sexuality,
particularly by such groups as Women against
Pornography and Women against Violence against
Women. Some of the spokeswomen for libertarian
feminism are self-identified "S/M" lesbian feminists who argue that the moralism of the radical
feminists stigmatizes sexual minorities such as
butch/femme couples, sadomasochists, and man/
boy lovers, thereby legitimizing "vanilla sex" lesbians and at the same time encouraging a return
to a narrow, conservative, "feminine" vision of
ideal sexuality.[3]

A problem with the current debate between
radical and libertarian feminists is that their

opposing positions do not exhaust the possible
feminist perspectives on sexual pleasure, sexual
freedom, and danger. Both sides are working with
a number of philosophical assumptions about the
nature of sexuality, power, and freedom that have
never been properly developed and defended.
Consequently, each side claims the other ignores an important aspect of sexuality and sexual
freedom. But both can be seen to be vulnerable
from a third perspective that I shall call a (not
the) socialist-feminist perspective. Although I do
not have space here to develop that perspective
adequately, I hope to advance the debate between
the two theoretical positions in the women's
movement on sexual morality by presenting and
critiquing their underlying paradigms of sexuality, social power, and sexual freedom.

TWO PARADIGMS CONTRASTED

Radical feminists' views on sexuality include the
following:

1. Heterosexual sexual relations generally are
   characterized by an ideology of sexual objectification (men as subjects/masters; women
   as objects/slaves) that supports male sexual
   violence against women.
2. Feminists should repudiate any sexual
   practice that supports or "normalizes" male
   sexual violence.
3. As feminists we should reclaim control over
   female sexuality by developing a concern
   with our own sexual priorities, which differ
   from men's—that is, more concern with
   intimacy and less with performance.
4. The ideal sexual relationship is between fully
   consenting, equal partners who are emotionally involved and do not participate in polarized roles.

From these four aspects of the radical-feminist
sexual ideology, one can abstract the following

---

[2] See Robin Linden, Darlene Pagano, Diana Russell, and
Susan Leigh Star, eds., *Against SadoMasochism* (East Palo
Alto, Calif.: Frog in the Well Press, 1982); Susan Brown-
miller, *Against Our Will: Men, Women and Rape* (New York:
Simon & Schuster, 1976); Kathleen Barry, *Female Sexual
Slavery* (Englewood Cliffs, N.J.: Prentice-Hall, Inc., 1979);
Andrea Dworkin, *Pornography: Men Possessing Women*
(New York: G. P. Putnam's Sons, 1981); Susan Griffin, *Por-
nography and Silence: Culture's Revolt against Nature* (New
York: Harper & Row, 1982); Laura Lederer, ed., *Take Back
the Night: Women on Pornography* (New York: Dell Publish-
ing Co., 1981); and Nancy Myron and Charlotte Bunch, eds.,
Lesbianism and the Women's Movement (Baltimore: Diana
Press, 1975).

[3] See Pat Califia, "Feminism and Sadomasochism," *Her-
esies 12* 3, no. 4 (1981): 30–34; Gayle Rubin, "The Leather
Menace: Comments on Politics and S/M," in *Coming to
Power: Writings and Graphics on Lesbian S/M,* ed. SAMOIS
(Boston: Alyson Publications, 1982); Gayle Rubin, Deirdre
English, and Amber Hollibaugh, "Talking Sex: A Conversa-
tion on Sexuality and Feminism," *Socialist Review 58* 11,
no. 4 (July/August 1981): 43–62; and Gayle Rubin, "Sexual
Politics, the New Right and the Sexual Fringe," in *The Age
Taboo: Gay Male Sexuality, Power and Consent,* ed. Daniel
Tsang (Boston: Alyson Publications, 1981).

theoretical assumptions about sexuality, social power, and sexual freedom:

5. Human sexuality is a form of expression between people that creates bonds and communicates emotion (the primacy of intimacy theory).
6. Theory of Social Power: In patriarchal societies sexuality becomes a tool of male domination through sexual objectification. This is a social mechanism that operates through the institution of masculine and feminine roles in the patriarchal nuclear family. The attendant ideology of sexual objectification is sadomasochism, that is, masculinity as sadistic control over women and femininity as submission to the male will.
7. Sexual freedom requires the sexual equality of partners and their equal respect for one another both as subject and as body. It also requires the elimination of all patriarchal institutions (e.g., the pornography industry, the patriarchal family, prostitution, and compulsory heterosexuality) and sexual practices (sadomasochism, cruising, and adult/child and butch/femme relationships) in which sexual objectification occurs.

The libertarian-feminist paradigm can be summarized in a manner that brings out in sharp contrast its emphasis and that of the radical-feminist paradigm:

1. Heterosexual as well as other sexual practices are characterized by repression. The norms of patriarchal bourgeois sexuality repress the sexual desires and pleasures of everyone by stigmatizing sexual minorities, thereby keeping the majority "pure" and under control.
2. Feminists should repudiate any theoretical analyses, legal restrictions, or moral judgments that stigmatize sexual minorities and thus restrict the freedom of all.
3. As feminists we should reclaim control over female sexuality by demanding the right to practice whatever gives us pleasure and satisfaction.

4. The ideal sexual relationship is between fully consenting, equal partners who negotiate to maximize one another's sexual pleasure and satisfaction by any means they choose.

The general paradigms of sexuality, social power, and sexual freedom one can draw from this sexual ideology are:

5. Human sexuality is the exchange of physical erotic and genital sexual pleasures (the primacy of pleasure theory).
6. Theory of Social Power: Social institutions, interactions, and discourses distinguish the normal/legitimate/healthy from the abnormal/illegitimate/unhealthy and privilege certain sexual expressions over others, thereby institutionalizing sexual repression and creating a hierarchy of social power and sexual identities.
7. Sexual freedom requires oppositional practices, that is, transgressing socially respectable categories of sexuality and refusing to draw the line on what counts as politically correct sexuality.

CRITIQUE OF RADICAL AND LIBERTARIAN FEMINISMS

Radical feminists assert the value of emotional intimacy in sexual interactions while libertarian feminists emphasize pleasure. But neither emotions nor physical pleasures can be isolated and discussed in a vacuum. These values can be judged only in a specific historical context since there is no one universal function that can be posited for sexuality. Physical pleasures, emotional intimacy, reproduction—each of these takes priority for different cultures, classes, races at different times in their histories.

Thus we must reject both the radical-feminist view that patriarchy has stolen our essentially emotional female sexuality and the libertarian-feminist view that sexual repression has denied women erotic pleasure. Both of these positions are essentialist. It has been true in recent Western patriarchal cultures that the goal of female sexuality, emotional intimacy, has for "respectable" women been differentiated from the goal of male sexuality, physical pleasure. But not all societies, and not even all classes and races within these Western cultures, have organized sexuality into such a dichotomized system. So when the two camps accuse each other of being "female" or "male" identified, respectively, they are treating historically developed gender identities as if they were human universals.

The problem with both radical and libertarian theories is that they describe social power in too simple a fashion. There may be, in fact, no universal strategy for taking back sexual power. Although the radical feminists are right that sexual objectification characterizes patriarchally constructed heterosexuality, their account is overdrawn. We need a more careful study of sexual fantasies and their effects. Even when fantasies involve images of dominance and submission, they may empower some women to enjoy sex more fully, a phenomenon that, by enhancing connections to one's body, develops self-affirmation. Nonetheless, in order to test the possibility of a different type of sexual practice that would provide mental affirmation as well, we do need to develop an alternative feminist sexual fantasy therapy for women, and for men, that does not involve such images.

Libertarian feminists are ingenuous in their insistence that any consensual sexual activity should be acceptable to feminists. This begs the question, for any feminist position has to examine the concept of *consent* itself in order to explore hidden power structures that place women in unequal (hence coercive) positions. That some avowed feminists think they consent to sado-masochism and to the consumption of pornography does not indicate that the true conditions for consent are present. Libertarians must show why these cases differ from the battered wife and "happy housewife" syndromes—something they have not yet convincingly done.

Pornography is an especially difficult topic, in part because the distinction between erotica and pornography is dependent on the context, that is,

on the gender, class, and culture of the audience. Pornographic practices, discourses, and images primarily directed at men reduce women to sex objects. But there are other contradictory popular discourses directed primarily at women or mixed audiences—for example, the literature of romance, "PG" movies, and television soap operas.

If we look at the whole entire system of such ideological sexual communications, we find a set of conflicting assumptions. These assumptions constitute a distinctive blend of liberal individualist and patriarchal ideals peculiar to advanced capitalist patriarchal societies. On the one hand, the ideology of romantic love permeates much erotica, assuming that sexual liaisons should be between peers who each have a right to equal sexual pleasure. On the other hand, it is also true that in much sexually explicit material the message is what Andrea Dworkin and Kathleen Barry call "cultural sadism"—that is, that men should initiate and control sex and women should submit to it (men are consumers, women providers, of sex).

Libertarian and radical feminists each choose to emphasize opposing sides of these contradictions. I argue, instead, that we should develop feminist erotica and sex education that aims to make people conscious of these contradictions in order to encourage new forms of feminist fantasy production. This erotica and education must emerge in a variety of contexts (high school courses, soap operas, and Harlequin novels as well as avant-garde art) and be geared to all types of audiences. This means avoiding the sexual vanguardism of either radicals or libertarians, who interact primarily within closed countercultural communities (lesbian feminists, middle-class radicals, and other sexual minorities).[4]

---

[4]The criticism of vanguard politics is not meant to imply that oppositional subcultures are irrelevant in a feminist strategy for social change. To the contrary, lesbian-feminist and alternative feminist networks are a necessity, both for survival and as a challenge to dominant sexual and social ideologies. The point is that social change within the dominant culture's practices is not successfully accomplished by vanguard sexual politics among isolated subcultural groups.

To further resolve this dilemma I think we must adopt a transitional feminist sexual morality that distinguishes between basic, risky, and forbidden sexual practices.[5] Forbidden sexual practices are those in which relations of dominance and submission are so explicit that feminists hold they should be illegal. Such practices include incest, rape, domestic violence, and sexual relations between very young children and adults. The difference between a forbidden and a risky practice is an epistemological one: that is, a practice is termed "risky" if it is suspected of leading to dominant/subordinate relationships, although there is no conclusive proof of this, while forbidden practices are those for which there is such evidence. Sadomasochism, capitalist-produced pornography, prostitution, and nuclear family relations between male breadwinners and female housewives are all risky practices from a feminist point of view. This does not mean that feminists do not have a right to engage in these practices. But since there is conflicting evidence concerning their role in structures of male dominance, they cannot be listed as basic feminist practices, that is, those we would advise our children to engage in. Basic feminist practices can include both casual and more committed sexual love, co-parenting, and communal relationships. They are distinguished by self-conscious negotiation and equalization of the partners in terms of the different relations of power (economic, social [e.g., age, gender], etc.) that hold between them. A feminist morality should be pluralist with respect to basic and risky practices. That is, feminists should be free to choose between basic and risky practices without fear of moral condemnation from other feminists.

CONCLUSIONS

Our contemporary sexual practices are characterized both by dominant/submissive power relations and by potential for liberation. In order to avoid the oversimplifications of the radical and libertarian positions on sexuality, we need a paradigm that can be historicized. Elsewhere I suggest the use of "modes of sex/affective production."[6] Conceiving of contemporary public patriarchy as a developing system allows us to explore the contradictions in our contemporary sexual identities, sexual ideologies, and sex/affective institutions.[7] Our vision of a sexually liberated society should situate genital sexual practices in a wider complex of sex/affective relationships. Parent-child and kinship-friendship networks are all implicated in sexual equalization, as are class and race power dynamics.[8] A completely elaborated feminist sexual morality must explore these relations in much greater detail than we have to date.

*Departments of Philosophy and Women's Studies
University of Massachusetts, Amherst*

---

[5]I develop these distinctions somewhat further in Ann Ferguson, "The Sex Debate within the Women's Movement: A Socialist-Feminist View," *Against the Current* (September/October 1983), pp. 10–16.

[6]This concept is related to what Gayle Rubin calls "sex/gender systems" ("The Traffic in Women: Notes toward a 'Political Economy' of Sex," in *Toward an Anthropology of Women,* ed. Rayna Rapp Reiter [New York: Monthly Review Press, 1975]). I develop the concept further to include the production and exchange of sexuality, nurturance, and affection in "Women as a New Revolutionary Class in the U.S.A.," in *Between Labor and Capital,* ed. Pat Walker (Boston: South End Press, 1979).

[7]See Ann Ferguson and Nancy Folbre, "The Unhappy Marriage of Capitalism and Patriarchy," in *Women and Revolution: A Discussion of the Unhappy Marriage of Marxism and Feminism,* ed. Lydia Sargent (Boston: South End Press, 1981); and Ann Ferguson, "Patriarchy, Sexual Identity, and the Sexual Revolution," in Ann Ferguson, Jacquelyn N. Zita, and Kathryn Pyne Addelson, "Viewpoint: On 'Compulsory Heterosexuality and Lesbian Existence': Defining the Issues," *Signs: Journal of Women in Culture and Society* 7, no. 1 (Autumn 1981): 158–72.

[8]Ann Ferguson, "On Conceiving Motherhood and Sexuality: A Feminist Materialist Perspective," in *Mothering: Essays in Feminist Theory,* ed. Joyce Trebilcot (Totowa, N.J.: Rowman & Allenheld, 1984).

KISS AND TELL: QUESTIONING CENSORSHIP

**Persimmon Blackbridge,
Lizard Jones, and
Susan Stewart**

*For me, freedom of speech and censorship exist
within the discourse of power. To censor requires the
power to impose one's views, ideologies, realities,
and the power to silence others. How can I have
freedom of speech when I am continually silenced by
sexism, racism, and homophobia?*
—Agnes Huang[1]

BAN CENSORSHIP

LIZARD: I cannot make sense of the censorship
debates. I mean, I know where I stand on certain things, but in the context of the censorship
discussion as it is framed, my stands are contradictory. I try to make everything go together
and end up going around in circles, worrying at
the same arguments in the same succession.

I'm sick of it. The word "censorship" should
be banned. It is too loaded, and is used to mean
too many different things.

[1] Agnes Huang, letter to authors, January 1994.

Feminist activists use "censorship" in a particular political discourse, namely the discussion of sexual representation. It has a sort of
political short-hand to it, and "anti-censorship
feminist" carries with it a host of political
positions. It puts you on one side of a once
impossibly sharp fence.

We in Kiss & Tell are anti-censorship feminists
by default. As lesbian art makers, we have no
choice: our desires and our art have put us
here. Our culture is continually silenced, our
sexuality erased. Our work has been seized,
refused, banned. And it is only anti-censorship
activists who seem to care.

But being anti-censorship is twisted around
in sordid ways. Neo-Nazis and Holocaust
deniers lie to glorify the most repressive and
brutally *pro*-censorship regime of recent European history, and they defend themselves by
saying they are *anti*-censorship. Politics may
make strange bedfellows, but I will not ally
myself with these people. That's clear enough
for me.

PERSIMMON: And then there are our alliances
with liberals. I was at a forum recently where
a civil liberties activist spoke proudly about
his organization's principles. His group, he
said, believed so strongly in freedom of speech

HOMETOWN

*Hometown, USA. As pinched and dry as ever. The same heat, the same dust, the same brown moun-
tains closing in. The same low buildings under a new coat of made-up history. Kitty's Saloon, with its
tired waitresses in Old West drag. Peso Pete's Western Souvenirs, with its window display of five-and-
dime racism. Mac's Liquor. The Pinky Laundromat. Home. Coming back here was not a smart idea.*

    *Any friends I once had in this place had all run, like I had run, as soon as they could scrape
together bus fare to somewhere else. I had no relatives here who were still speaking to me. This was
not a town that loved its lesbian daughters.*

    *All I had was this dumb idea that since I was going to be a couple of hundred miles away in the
state capital for a weekend conference on censorship, I might as well spend a few days visiting the
land of my birth. To reconnect with my roots? To ponder my past? To buy an Authentic Western Shirt
for only $12.98 plus tax?*

KISS AND TELL (*Continued*)

that they would defend society's rejects whom no one else would touch: homosexuals and Nazis. The way he talked had a whole row of lesbians flinching. And this guy is supposed to be on our side.

He was firmly against censorship, and painted a glowing picture of the alternative, a "free market of ideas" where all would join the fray of democratic debate, and theories that were racist and sexist and selfish and mean would eventually be seen for what they are, and be consigned to the rubbish heap of history.

The pure anti-censorship position is very appealing because it's so clear. It's the "just say no" approach. You don't have to make judgements and draw fine lines between this and that, and see all the ways it can backfire and figure out what to do about them. But when has the marketplace been free? And why haven't those ancient stereotypes hawked by hate mongers disappeared yet? The market isn't free, it's stacked against some of us. Until gay-bashing, synagogue-burning, and racist murders are a thing of the past, I'll keep supporting laws against hate-literature.

Does this put me on the pro-censorship side of the fence? According to some civil libertarians it does. But it's a stupid fence. It cuts my life up in ways that don't make sense. What is ignored is power: who has it and who doesn't.

STRANGE IDEAS: OPINION AS CENSORSHIP

PERSIMMON: Censorship is a word some people use every time someone disagrees with them, especially if that someone has made a political criticism of their work. For example, some people say, "If you call my work sexist/racist/homophobic/etc. you are censoring me."

Someone saying you shouldn't do something isn't the same as someone forcibly preventing you. Yes, criticism can be very painful to hear. Often when people have political criticisms of my work, I feel hurt, misunderstood, silenced. I feel like I never want to open my mouth again. But as you can see, here I am, opening my mouth. Criticism has not, in fact, silenced me.

People have a right to protest, and a right to a say in their own representation. I can't equate that with Canada Customs seizing books. Canada Customs has the power to stop hundreds

---

HOMETOWN (*Continued*)

I was staying at the Bucking Bronco Motel. It was like any motel anywhere. My room was small and barren and smelled like air conditioning. I was kept awake half the night by a pair of bucking broncos next door. They checked out in the morning looking fresh and rested and very pleased with themselves. I was so happy for them.

After I unglued my eyelids and unspiked my hair, I moseyed on down to the corner cafe for breakfast. The waitress brought me a cup of that watery stuff they think is coffee in the USA. It didn't work. When my breakfast special arrived, I asked for a cup of tea. Oh Canada. If you leave the tea bag in long enough you can get a reliable hit of caffeine as it eats away your stomach lining. She brought me presweetened ice tea. Back in the USA. How could I have forgotten so many of our quaint national customs?

I was just finishing my home fries when She walked in. Why am I even surprised any more?

"Howdy partner," she said with a wide cowboy grin.

of gay and lesbian books from coming into Canada, and they do. The homophobia implicit in their decisions is backed by a long history of laws, institutions, and social norms which discriminate against us. But when a lesbian group in Northampton, Massachusetts protested against DRAWING THE LINE, saying it promoted violence against women, they had neither the power of the state nor the power of social sanction to use against us. They were angry, they were protesting, but they were not censors.

SUSAN: Politically Correct, the very phrase sends my mind into paroxysms of confusion—oh what tangled webs we weave.

When I was a fresh-faced activist, back in the seventies, these words actually meant something. That is, I could count on them meaning a very specific thing, political ethics. Political correctness in those days was a useful teaching tool for young, naive, and politically inept newcomers like myself. It served as a method of analysis, understanding, and consciousness raising that suggested possible attitude and behaviour changes. For example, "It's not politically correct to buy California grapes because farm workers are being exploited," or, "It's politically incorrect to use sexist slurs even if they were meant as a joke."

Later the words lost their gloss and progressive people dropped the phrase because it had taken on the additional meanings of political rigidity, dogma, and limitation. It seemed to have outlived its original usefulness. Political correctness became something to joke about, and in lesbian circles it also became something to react against. Many lesbians challenged the notion of political correctness as a way to extend boundaries and explore taboo territories. I can still remember when wearing lipstick was a rebellious act in lesbian/feminist circles, to say nothing about packing a dildo and the fine art of penetration. The thrills of being incorrect were sweet indeed.

So where has the Right been all these years and why the new spin on this term? Are they really so behind the times or am I missing something here?

It seems there is a lot of mileage to be gotten from twisting the meaning of this language around and using it as a verbal smart-bomb. A challenge to hate-literature suddenly becomes a threat to freedom of expression, or equity legislation becomes discrimination against white males. And all because of the

---

"Don't," I said. "Just don't."
She parked her butt on the stool next to mine. "You're in a fun mood," she said.
"Try Disney World," I said.
The waitress brought her coffee, which she sipped with apparent relish.
"So, are you going to show me your old house and all that?" she asked.
"No."
"How about the reservoir where you first kissed Sally Stanley?"
"How do you know about that?"
"Oh, well . . . you hear things. She's working on a disabled dykes' newsletter in Chicago these days. Very tough gal, Sally."
"You're making that up!"

KISS AND TELL (*Continued*)

repressive forces of political correctness? I hadn't realized that we had become such a threat. Nor could I have imagined that concepts that once spoke of integrity and fairness would be turned against us in such a lethal and transparently malicious way.

KISS & TELL: What does it mean these days to say someone is "politically correct"? Sometimes it means there's left-wing political content in their artwork. Sometimes it means they talk a lot about the importance of political art. Sometimes it means they trash all art that isn't political. Sometimes it means they don't laugh at sexist jokes. Sometimes it means they get mad at sexist jokes. Sometimes it means their use of language is nervously careful and spiked with guilt. Sometimes it means they put down everyone who hasn't been educated in the same political language as they have. Sometimes it means they speak up when they think something's wrong.

The term "politically correct" is the right-wing popular culture counterpart of those great put-downs of the old Left, like "running dog lackey of the bourgeoisie." It's a name-calling term, vague and imprecise, a smear tactic rather than a concrete description of someone's actions or attitudes. When someone is called politically correct, it carries a host of unspoken implications, which may not apply to the actual situation in question.

It's a big crossover item—it's in gay and lesbian magazines as well as straight ones, and it's no longer useful. The term is used too often to trivialize dissent. If you call us politically correct, we don't know what you mean. At this point in time, given the constant use of the term in mainstream media, we'll probably think it means we're left-wing political artists and you don't think we should be, which is your tough luck. But it might be an important insight into ways that we behave which are really obnoxious. Why not drop the term and be clear about specific criticisms? Otherwise, we're just smearing each other with the right-wing's shit.

PERSIMMON: Why do I read the newspaper? It just drives me crazy. Like this little item from the front page of the *Vancouver Sun:* "Political correctness poses a greater threat to freedom of speech than any government undertaking, Supreme Court Justice John Sopinka said Thursday."[2] And he should know. He wrote

---

[2] Geoff Baker, "Judge's View: Political Correctness 'threat to free speech'," *Vancouver Sun,* 29 October 1993, p. 1.

HOMETOWN (*Continued*)

"Maybe so, maybe not. You'll never know, will you?" She tried the grin again. She was good, but no match for me and my evil mood.

I paid the bill and left a tip for the waitress. It wasn't her fault.

Out on the street, the heat struck like a slap in the face. The sidewalk lurched under my feet but Her arm was around me, holding me up. I clung to her until the street stopped spinning.

Coming back here was not a smart idea.

When my lungs remembered how to breathe, she discreetly removed her arm from my waist. Don't scare the horses. We walked through downtown, all two blocks of it. Halifax was enthralled with the Western Wear stores. She wanted boots, belts, fringed shirts, all the tourist lures. I wouldn't play.

We turned onto a straggling side street and passed my old grade school, scene of so many golden childhood memories. If I pointed it out to Halifax, she'd just want to look closer, walk around, ask me questions I didn't want to answer. I said nothing.

the majority opinion in the Butler decision. Yes, that same Butler decision that has been applied so consistently against gay and lesbian materials. But never mind that! What you should really be worrying about is political correctness. Tell me more, Justice Sopinka!

"... he also warned that if judges are forced to work under constant fear of being rebuked for every action and utterance that falls from their bench, it 'may result in decisions that are politically correct, but may not be legally and factually correct.'" The utterances alluded to include a particular series of wildly sexist remarks made by judges, in court, that some feminists saw as lacking in judicial impartiality.

The nerve of those women, rebuking our judges like that! Don't they know that judges are delicate creatures? They can't stand being rebuked, they just buckle under the strain. Yes, our legal system is in great danger. And our arts system too—it's already fallen, and lies helpless under the heel of the "politically correct"!

If all my information came from the mainstream media, I'd think that art today is wholly dominated by stern, self-righteous people of colour together with an army of shrill and simplistic white queers—as well as the occasional fat, middle-aged feminist. We run it all! It's amazing!

We have such power that we can silence anyone who disagrees with us! All art must conform to our rigid and narrow standards of political correctness! We control the galleries, the critics, the granting agencies! University administrators quake in fear and fall all over themselves to do our bidding! There are only a few brave and lonely souls who dare to lift their voices against the totalitarian rule of the politically correct. But at great personal risk, they *do* speak out, every day, in the *Vancouver Sun, Macleans, Newsweek, the New Yorker,* the *CBC,* the *Globe and Mail,* network TV, the *New York Times* . . .

But my delusions of grandeur are burst every time I put down the paper and look around me. We don't run the world. W. P. Kinsella[3] is still a best-seller. He hasn't been silenced by First Nations writers who suggest that they also deserve access to publishing, promotion, and

---

[3]W.P. Kinsella is a white Canadian writer who has been widely criticized by First Nations people for inaccurate and stereotypical portrayals of their cultures.

We turned down another street and there was my ex-home. I glanced at it casually and said nothing. It had a new porch, new curtains, new paint, new people. But the same old garage, spiders in the dark, the old smell of oil spilled one summer and cleaned up with sand, grit on my cheek, his hand on the back of my neck, pressing my face into the concrete floor.

My eyes filled with whirling black spots. Everything was getting smaller and farther away, and I was trying to breathe a brick wall. My knees wanted to give way, but Halifax was pulling me along the street, down the block, around the corner, away.

"Walk," she ordered. "Come on."

I was walking reasonably well on my own steam by the time we got back to the Bucking Bronco. Some ecologically sensitive person had turned off the air conditioner. My room was hot and dark. I lay down on the bed and she lay beside me, stroking my hair. That was nice. Maybe I'd go to sleep and wake up in Vancouver.

KISS AND TELL (*Continued*)

distribution. White straight men still get more shows, more grants, more reviews.

It's not that things haven't changed. They have. Fifteen years ago I was one of the few openly lesbian students at my art school, and we were taught that political art is bad art. Nowadays, that same school has one or two arts-and-contemporary-issues classes every semester. There are small but vocal groups of students who refuse to be invisible as queers, single mothers, people of colour, and/or disabled people.

But there has also been very palpable backlash against these groups in response to the gains they have made. There has been graphic death-threat graffiti against lesbians and gay men, in the toilets and halls of that liberal art school. There have been chilling personal attacks against the only First Nations teacher in the school, written on the walls of that teacher's classroom. The new usage of the term "politically correct" is one of the more polite manifestations of the backlash from the Right, which *sees* the changes of the last few decades as an overwhelming threat.

LIZARD: When I read about neo-Nazis complaining about their "curtailed freedom of expression," or "censored" academics who can no longer even promote sexual harassment (poor things), or men who refuse to be "silenced" by women talking about violence against women, I am struck dumb. I am so angry that I can barely respond enough to say I think this is crap. I feel powerless and furious.

There's no arguing about it, because there's no common basis for argument, there's not anything to agree on, the two ways of thinking are so different, it would *be* like arguing with someone from Mars who had learned the language but didn't understand the concepts. It reminds me of trying to argue with my parents when I was a child. They always had a comeback that seemed rational but *made no sense*. It didn't deal with anything that I was talking about.

These people I read about in the paper are not my parents. But they do have power, and I threaten it. And they are fighting back in the same indescribably frustrating way as my parents did, by saying they make sense, by being oh so reasonable and calm when really they are lashing out with the biggest weapons they can muster. And they are formidable weapons—the universities, the media, public funding, corporate power.

HOMETOWN (**Continued**)

"So that was where you used to live, eh?" she said after a while. The bitch is too bright. I can't keep anything from her.

"I don't want to talk about it," I said.

"Okay."

She kissed my cheek and then my lips. I stared at the wall. My eyes were adjusting to the dark and I could just make out the pattern of the wallpaper. She snuggled closer to me, nuzzling my neck. Her hand brushed across my breasts, very soft, then down to my belly. Then back to my breasts. My nipples were hard. I lay frozen. She touched me again, again. Every touch went straight to my cunt. Her soft hands filled me with a terrible pain. I had never been so turned on in my life.

"Stop it," I whispered.

"Hmmm?"

"Stop it!" This time it was very loud. She stopped.

But don't think I am fooled for one minute. I grew up with this. I grew up with the myth that there is such a thing as total objectivity, you just need the right judge. That there are universal principles that result in total equality. And anyone who doesn't agree with the particular ways they are interpreted is subversive.

For example, the principle is that professors should be allowed to express themselves. I agree. But when I apply this principle to real life, I don't agree with the interpretations I read. I have questions. Are those professors being *prevented* from expressing themselves? Are they willing to take responsibility for what they are saying? Can they deal with challenges to their authority? Do they believe everyone has the same right to self-expression as they do? If so, are they willing to hand over their lecture platforms? How much immunity from political debate comes with tenure?

But if you ask these questions, the comeback is that professors should be allowed to express themselves. I am tired of this predictability masquerading as an original response. It's the backlash, and we predicted it, and it's here. Think of something new to say.

I am tired of sloppy thinking masquerading as the "rational" side. I am tired of having statements by women's groups, anti-racist activists, disabled speakers, or lesbian artists be dismissed as hysterical, dogmatic, and narrow-minded (of all things). I can't think of a way to argue because it's the ultimate doublespeak, by people who think they control the power of the word.

WHOSE UNIVERSE?

KISS & TELL: Equality is one of the "universal" principles of Euro-American liberalism. It was considered a universal principle way back when the only people allowed to vote on this continent were white male property owners. It was considered a universal principle when many people on this continent were living in slavery. Obviously, these universal principles are applied in particular ways, depending on who is involved, when and where. Some people are more equal than others.

These days, equality is still invoked in strange ways. For many people it means treating everyone exactly the same regardless of their circumstances and histories. As Anatole France said, "The law in its majestic equality forbids the rich as well as the poor to sleep under bridges, to beg in the streets, and to steal bread."

"What's wrong?" she asked.

"Fuck you," I said. It was all I could think of, so I said it again. Halifax leaned back on her elbow and looked at me.

"I get the impression you're not into sex right now," she said.

"Oh fuck off . . . just . . . don't . . . You act like you're taking care of me and then you start . . . all that." The words didn't really make sense but they were spilling out. "You jerk. You creep. Just fuck off. Go away."

"I'm sorry," she said. "I thought you were into it."

"Stop acting nice. You don't care how I feel. Just go away!"

She got off the bed and sat on the luggage rack by the door. "I'm not trying to change the topic from how insensitive I was, but is there something else going on?"

"No," I said.

KISS AND TELL (*Continued*)

Under this definition of equality, affirmative action is called "reverse discrimination" because it doesn't pretend we're all the same. But ignoring our differences and our present-day lack of equality serves to entrench inequality.

"Universal" equality was recently invoked by a Canadian Legion branch that denied entrance to a group of Sikh veterans because they wouldn't take off their turbans. It wasn't racism, we were told; no one in their branch is allowed to wear "headgear" in the building. Everyone was being treated equally, and the Sikh veterans had the choice to either break their religious requirements or not take part in Remembrance Day ceremonies at the Legion. All people, regardless of race, are equally required to comply with that branch's interpretation of obscure Anglo customs, or stay out. And that's supposed to be equality.

The same kind of retreat to "universal" principles that calls affirmative action "reverse discrimination" is often used to dismiss the issue of cultural appropriation in art. Cultural appropriation refers to the practice of artists, writers, social scientists, and so on from a dominant culture building careers on images, stories, or information taken from cultures whose own art, writing, and social sciences are at the same time being suppressed. A clear example of this was given by Maria Campbell at the series of forums *Telling Our Own Story:*

> Much of the history of our people has been written by non-Native people. A few years ago in Alberta, a special department was set up in the University of Alberta and millions of dollars was poured into this ings and the history of our people. These were called "the Riel Papers." Not one penny of that was ever spent on encouraging Metis writers to do the work.[4]

People who argue against the practice of cultural appropriation are often called censors simply for asking dominant culture artists to act more responsibly. Campbell says:

> I know I keep hearing the word censorship. I hear it over and over when I talk about this and I think it's got nothing to do with censorship, it's got to do with ethics. I think it is stealing and there is no way you can get away from that.[5]

---

[4] Maria Campbell, quoted by Kerrie Charnley in the Final Report of a series of forums called "Telling Our Own Story: Appropriation and Indigenous Writers and Performing Artists," 1990, p. 13.

[5] Maria Campbell, quoted in "Telling Our Own Story" Final Report, p. 20.

HOMETOWN (*Continued*)

"*Was it something to do with seeing your old house?*"
"*No," I said.*
"*Okay," she said. She sat there, quietly, watching me. I could hear a motorcycle in the distance. Or maybe a car with a bad muffler. The light in the room was pearly and soft with dark edges, sunshine through beige fibreglass curtains.*
"*It was the garage," I said.*
"*When you were a kid?*"
"*Yeah.*"
"*Who was it?*"
"*Some guy. A stranger.*"
"*Do you want to tell me about it?*"

Arguments against cultural appropriation are rooted in specific situations in a specific time in history, past and present. They are not universal principles applied equally, across the board, in every situation for all time.

For example, in British Columbia, First Nations people were at one time arrested for participating in potlatch ceremonies. Many works of art were confiscated in those raids, art which later turned up in museums or the homes of white collectors. Later, institutions like the Vancouver Art Gallery refused to buy the work of First Nations artists who used traditional styles, saying it was anthropology, not art.[6] At the same time, the Gallery was buying work by white artists who used traditional First Nations forms and imagery in combination with European styles.

Often First Nations images or stories are used by white artists without any understanding of their context and meaning. Sometimes they are not only misunderstood, but misused, mistold, in ways that perpetuate oppressive stereotypes. In some First Nations cultures, there are images and stories that are

the exclusive property of particular families or clans. For anyone else to use them is an act similar to plagiarism or violating copyright law. All this (and more) is behind many First Nations people's demand for accountability from white artists in Canada. It has to do with a specific historical situation, where people's work has been stolen, where certain artists have been shut out while others profit, where harmful stereotypes are reinforced, where copyrights are broken and important cultural symbols are treated with ignorant disrespect.

People who call this position "censorship" often misrepresent (and misunderstand) it. They talk as if critics of cultural appropriation were setting up a Universal Principle of Cultural No Trespassing that states: "No one is allowed to make art based on the art forms of cultures not their own." Then they argue against that principle. They give examples of what would happen if it were applied equally to everyone. It would mean a Japanese musician shouldn't play Bach. It would mean a Hungarian dancer shouldn't perform an Irish jig.

These examples clearly show that any Universal Principle of Cultural No Trespassing is ridiculous. But they don't involve histories of invasion and present-day realities of suppression and exploitation. Cultural No Trespassing

---

[6] This policy, in place for decades, has now been changed, in response to the many arguments put forth by First Nations artists and theorists.

"No," I said.

"Okay. Whatever you want to do. You're in charge."

I lay there, silent and stiff. She managed to look cool and relaxed on the rickety luggage rack, like she was ready to sit there for hours. She can always outwait me. It's not fair. I sat up.

"What I feel like doing is fucking," I said.

"Okay," she said. She crossed the room and sat on the side of the bed.

I moved away from her, as much as I could on the undersized motel mattress.

"But I also feel like yelling at you," I said.

"That's fine too."

"Yeah, well you're not my therapist! If I wanted a therapist I'd go get one, and I sure as hell wouldn't sleep with her, so don't pull that shit on me."

KISS AND TELL (*Continued*)

has *never* been what critics of cultural appropriation are arguing for. It's not an issue of Universal Principles. It's not about what has to happen everywhere, always and forever. It's about particular situations in particular places, and how we can move those situations on in a better direction.

> I don't think anyone of us can claim to know the answers. I don't come here with answers for this question of appropriation or what we should be doing about it. All I know is that I see the damage that has happened with our people. And I can see that there is misrepresentation and there are lies that are being perpetuated and that's hurting not only our people but hurting all peoples. Because lies always destroy and cause chaos and replace truth, and we concern ourselves with that.
>
> —Jeannette Armstrong[7]

WHOSE FREEDOM?

KISS & TELL: Black feminist theorist bell hooks' book of media and cultural criticism, *Black Looks,* was seized by Canada Customs as

---

[7] Jeannette Armstrong, quoted in "Telling Our Own Story" Final Report (see note 4), pp. 19–20.

possible hate literature and therefore not allowed into Canada.

Meanwhile, efforts to get the Canadian military to deal with internal racism are met with cries of censorship. When the right of people with social privilege to say whatever they want, anytime, anywhere, is challenged, freedom of speech is vigorously defended.

What this society considers to be fundamental truths, rights, and principles have been defined and refined over decades, centuries. The people who have been central in formulating these definitions have been white European men of the middle and upper classes. Their biases are reflected in these concepts. Their point of view is seen as universal rather than particular and limited.

One of the most blatant examples is how Man was for so long assumed to include women, so that what was true of men became the Universal and what was true of women was just a subcategory, a deviation from the norm.

PERSIMMON: I remember when I first started seeing the world from the point of view of women. I had been female all 20 years of my life, but in subtle and far-reaching ways, I still saw men as central and women as a subgroup.

HOMETOWN (*Continued*)

"Damn right I'm not your fucking therapist," she said. "Thank god!"

"I'd never have you for a therapist," I said.

She tried not to laugh and failed. I tried to be offended and failed.

"Jerk face," I said, pulling her down on the bed with me.

"Asshole," she said. "What do you want? You want to pretend sex is always easy? Sometimes stuff comes up in sex and some of it isn't just straight-up fun. If that makes you want to go away, fine, go away. But I'd rather talk, or cry, or fuck our way through it. That's not therapy, it's real life. I want you. Get it?"

I sighed and buried my face in her neck. She smelled of sweat and sex and sunscreen.

"It wasn't a stranger, it was my father," I said.

She started to say something, but I pushed her away from me. Then I pushed her off the bed. She lay on the floor, looking startled. I leaned over the edge of the bed and kissed her. Somehow in the middle of the kiss she ended up lying on top of me.

To abandon that perspective was a wild and difficult shift.

Some ways of thinking are so ingrained that it's hard to even notice them, particularly when we're on the comfortable side of the power imbalance. Challenges to this ideology are often unheard or ignored, because the biases of our so-called universal truths are also the biases of most people who hold power, publish books, make laws.

In the white world, we act as if "race" is about people of colour, and white people's experience is apart from race. We don't notice our whiteness. We think it's all-pervasive and invisible, like air. But everyone else notices.

I notice how straight people forget that they're straight—for hours, days, years at a time. What luxury! Noticing that, I still forget I'm white. "As lesbians . . ." I say, and then I have to go back and think about it. Is it a lesbian thing or just a white lesbian thing? It's like trying to see when the eye doctor puts those weird drops in your eyes. It's like trying to wake up from a dream. But I'm working on it. The benefits of learning to see the world (and my own life) from a wider, more flexible, more realistic perspective are obvious.

As a lesbian, I'm quite familiar with straight perspectives on the world. I don't have to struggle to take them into account. I'm surrounded by images of heterosexuality. I learn to read myself into those pictures, change their meaning to include me. It's a subversive thing, but it doesn't challenge the right of hets to be seen as the universal norm, representing all people, while lesbians are different, particular, special (as in special rights, special-interest groups, special needs).

I grew up and live in a culture that encourages me to forget some things and won't allow me to forget others. In this book, my identity as a woman and a lesbian are always in the foreground, my identity as a Euro-Canadian comes in and out of focus, and having learning disabilities virtually disappears (even though the act of writing calls that identity up over and over). Parts of my identity jump out or are forgotten, depending on what I'm writing about. I can't always tell when that means I'm writing from a cultural blind spot, and when I'm just writing from a specific point of view.

But do I have to keep chopping up my identities, with some parts visible, others masquerading as universal, and still others dismissed as irrelevant? Do we have to always speak as this fragment and that fragment? Does this

---

"You're in charge," she whispered.
"Touch me," I said.
She touched me, slow and soft like before.
"Hit me," I said.
Halifax paused for a fraction of a second and then slapped me hard across my face. The sudden pain shocked through my body and I cried out, clinging to her.
She looked into my face, searching. "You're so beautiful," she said and slapped me again.
"No, don't!" I flinched away from her.
She stayed where she was. "You're in charge."
I caught my breath. "Yes," I said. "Okay." I let the thought turn in my mind. "Get me a drink of water," I said.
She brought me a glass of water.

KISS AND TELL (*Continued*)

language have the words to speak our simultaneous selves?

COVERT CENSORSHIP

PERSIMMON: In 1990, I spoke at the Canadian Museums Association Conference in Edmonton about right-wing attempts to cut funding to lesbian and gay artists. Many gay and lesbian arts administrators came up and introduced themselves to me over the weekend. But there were other people in town that weekend who weren't so warmly welcomed—a Native delegation from North Dakota was petitioning a local museum for the return of stolen artworks of deep religious significance. Their petition was turned down. The museum said it owned their heritage.

As I looked around that weekend, I saw that there were very few people of colour at that conference of influential arts administrators. There were far more white queers than there were people of colour—straight, gay, or whatever. The censorship of exclusion was alive and well, and at that level of the art world, white gays and lesbians were not the main target of it.

LIZARD: There are writers who have empowered me by articulating censorship issues in terms of problems I understand. Among them is U.S. writer and artist Carol Jacobsen,[8] who discusses covert censorship. It's the kind of censorship oppressed groups experience, where no one bans the work, exactly, it's just that it's not good enough to be published, or not appropriate for this gallery, or not the kind of job our print shop wants right now.

Toronto writer Marlene Nourbese Philip, in her 1989 essay "The Disappearing Debate,"[9] articulates the conflict between two anti-censorship battles: fighting for freedom of speech for individual writers, and fighting against systemic racism in publishing. Nourbese Philip sets her argument in the context of the debate then raging across Canada about the Women's Press' anti-racist guidelines.[10] Other examples are only too easy to find. In Canada in the 1990s,

---

[8] Carol Jacobsen, "Redefining Censorship: A Feminist View," *Art Journal* 50, no. 4 (1991): 42–55.

[9] Marlene Nourbese Philip, "The Disappearing Debate, Or, How the Discussion of Racism Has Been Taken Over by the Censorship Issue," in her *Frontiers,* (Stratford, Ontario: The Mercury Press, 1992), 269–86.

[10] In 1989 the Women's Press in Toronto rejected three stories from an anthology because they felt the stories were racist. They followed up the action by printing anti-racist guidelines for their writers.

HOMETOWN (*Continued*)

"Okay, kneel by the bed," I told her. She obeyed. Amazing. I was trying not to grin, but it was hard. I drank some water and then, on a second's impulse, I threw the rest in her face. She knelt there, water dripping down her neck. She looked very serious and sweet.

"Get on the bed," I said.

She obeyed. We lay together, kissing and feeling each other, till that terrible lovely pain rose in me again.

"Tie me up," I said.

She went to my suitcase and pulled out four long leather straps that I had certainly never packed.

She stretched me out on the bed, tying my wrists and ankles to the iron bedstead. She lay on top of me, touching my bound body softly, kissing my mouth. I wanted to hold her, touch her, but I was tied to the bed. A wild helplessness filled my chest, like panic, but sweeter.

"freedom of speech" is somehow seen as a *more* universal or fundamental principle than freedom from racism.

In her essay, Nourbese Philip dismantles the notion (especially appealing to white male artists) of an unfettered imagination driven inexorably by the muse, out of the artist's control, which must not be held to account by political concerns. She says:

> The imagination, I maintain, is both free and unfree. Free in that it can wander wheresoever it wishes, unfree in that it is profoundly affected and shaped by the societies in which we live.[11]

THE CENSORSHIP FENCE

LIZARD: I have been dragged kicking and screaming to an anti-censorship position. I did not start out here. I found the analysis logically compelling but politically lacking. I felt the anti-censorship position ignored a lot of things. For one thing, I was expected to believe that images are only symptoms, never causes, and never dangerous. It is a short step from that to building an alliance with Jim Keegstra,[12] and I refuse.

Over the censorship fence I have watched the pro-legislative reform feminists with some curiosity. Maybe it will work, I thought. Maybe they will really be able to stop sexism and leave sex intact. It seemed clear that any such legislation would be used against lesbians and gays, but a part of me wanted to believe otherwise, wanted to believe that it could work.

But it doesn't work. Right from the start, the most dire lesbian predictions have come true. The first implementation of Butler was the seizure of a lesbian magazine (*Bad Attitude*) at a gay bookstore (Glad Day Books in Toronto). Since then, Butler has been used against lesbians and gays over and over again.

So do we want to give up on law reform altogether, or do we want to keep pushing for the protection of laws, knowing the government has a different agenda from ours?

---

[11] Marlene Nourbese Philip, "The Disappearing Debate," 278.

[12] Jim Keegstra was a high school history teacher who in the 1980s taught his students that the Holocaust never happened. He used freedom of speech arguments to defend his actions.

When I was moaning under her, she got up and went back to my suitcase. She pulled out a knife.

"Don't!" I said. She stopped. I waited. She waited. I could see the pearly light on her cheekbones, the line of her shoulders, her breasts under the tight T-shirt, her legs spread casually wide.

"No, it's okay," I said. "Do it."

She cut the buttons off my shirt, one by one, and opened it; cut my bra into pieces and threw it on the floor. She slit open my pants and pulled them off. It was a sharp knife. I could tell. I lay there, tied open, exposed. She sat back, her eyes cruising my body. I waited. She waited.

My mouth was dry. My heart was pounding, pounding.

"Please," I said, and she slowly moved toward me. With the back of the knife blade, she stroked my nipples, first one, then the other, over and over. Fear and desire fought in my throat. My body was slick with sweat. My breath came fast and ragged.

KISS AND TELL (*Continued*)

What about the people who are hurt by the laws? What about the people who are hurt by the lack of laws? Are we going to weigh their relative pain and decide? Who is going to decide?

KISS & TELL: The censorship debate has forged unthinkable alliances. There are the women who built a common front with the political Right to make the Butler decision. And there are the Noam Chomskys[13] of the world, who insist that we anti-censorship activists have to protect books by neo-fascists like LePen in order to be consistent. In both cases we have been told that distasteful as these alliances are, they are necessary.

But maybe these alliances are only necessary if the world is divided in two by the present censorship fence. The discussion of censorship,

criticism, affirmative action, regulation, reform, and imagery is much more complicated than this debate allows. There are other ways to look at it, that make more sense, that make the pieces fit better.

When we talk about censorship we need to talk about power—who has it, and what are they doing with it? We have to look at each instance and weigh the power imbalances. Who has the power to speak? Who has the power to impose silence? Who has the law on their side? Who has economic power on their side? Who has media control on their side? Who has gallery control on their side? Who will go to jail? Who is trying to redress what?

In Canada today, we are not equal. Many people are not free to speak, free from discrimination, free from poverty. Freedom and equality aren't abstract concepts separate from daily life. They can't be laid over the power imbalances of our present system without being distorted beyond all meaning. The fight against censorship only makes sense when these realities are not denied.

---

[13] Noam Chomsky, in the film *Manufacturing Consent,* by Mark Achbar and Peter Wintonick (co-produced by Necessary Illusions and the National Film Board, 1992).

HOMETOWN (*Continued*)

She leaned over to the bedside table and pulled out a package of latex gloves. Maybe someone left them there, along with the Gideon's Bible. She pulled one on. It was shiny silver. Safer sex with style. She untied me, retied me ass up. I could feel her eyes on me. There was no way to hide. The back of her blade caressed my butt, and then suddenly the edge, swift and sharp. I gasped and twisted my tied body so I could see her over my shoulder. Her face was hard and beautiful. She parted the cheeks of my ass and her knife whispered across my crack. Slowly, she slipped a finger up my ass, and then out. My cunt was open, wet, yearning toward her, but she ignored it. Her fingers were slick with lube from somewhere, nowhere. Two fingers now up my tight hot hole, burning inside me, filling me with fire. I couldn't breathe. She pushed into me, slowly, slowly, taking me moaning, crying, tied writhing on the harsh sheets. The impossibly slow strokes, her knife, her mouth. She had me, held me, hurt me. I was hers.

CLAIMING THE RIGHT TO BE QUEER

Chris Cuomo

It is difficult to get a clear sense of the state of lesbian and gay politics today.[1] Many public, cultural, and familial spaces have been transformed (or at least many are now *in*formed) by gay-friendly perspectives, yet in other places oppressive sexual norms remain exceedingly powerful, and very idea of being out can send shivers down spines. In the U.S., lesbian, gay, bisexual and transgendered people seem to experience greater comfort and freedom overall, but homophobic violence and vitriol are still quite common. The National Gay and Lesbian Task Force recently reported that more than 90 percent of gay men and lesbians have been victims of violence or harassment in some form on the basis of their sexual orientation; greater than one in five gay men and nearly one in ten lesbians have been punched, hit, or kicked; a quarter of all gays have had objects thrown at them; a third have been chased; a third have been sexually harassed; and nearly one-seventh have been spit on.[2] There are now thirty or so state laws and nearly three hundred municipal and county ordinances prohibiting

discrimination based on sexual orientation in the U.S., but new roadblocks against gay legal rights continue to arise. Whether or not such contradictory trends are surprising, they merit serious philosophical and political attention.

Especially in relation to so much positive change, understanding the persistence of homophobia and related violence is crucial for the well-being of lesbian, gay, and bisexual people. The fact that gay politics in America seem so often to be a dance of two-steps-forward-one-step-back raises important questions about the nature of homophobia, and about what sorts of legislative and cultural strategies will help secure gay political equality in the coming decades. More broadly, beyond the realm of "gay rights," better understanding of homophobic values and violence, and how to overcome them, may be helpful for developing progressive political strategies and priorities in contexts where communities seem deeply divided over issues involving fundamental values.

Among queer folk and our allies, it is commonly stated that the roots of America's failure to extend full justice to its lesbian and gay members are false but widely and deeply held beliefs or negative stereotypes, such as the belief that lesbians and gay men are predatory or diseased, or the belief that homoerotic orientations are a relatively recent or culturally specific invention. Despite the fact that passionate false beliefs are notoriously intractable and dangerous, if anti-gay sentiment is based on false belief there is reason for hope regarding long-term progress for lesbian and gay political rights and equality. Education and the cultural work of dispelling stereotypes and conveying more accurate information are precisely where strategies such as coming out, and cultivating greater visibility and inclusion, are focused, and in many ways those strategies are quite successful.

According to one popular view, which I will call the "enlightenment" view, it is a very positive development that, in spite of persistent homophobia, lesbians, gay men, and bisexuals are now more visible in the social landscape. The enlightenment view is based on the reasonable notion that with

---

[1] This essay expands upon an argument first presented in my "Dignity and the Right to be Lesbian or Gay," *Philosophical Studies,* 132(1): 75–85. Regarding terminology, the category names available for referring to sexual minorities, nonheterosexual identities, and counterhegemonic forms of gender are highly contested and always in flux. My argument here focuses on lesbian and gay sexual identities, but because the central subjects of "lesbian and gay politics" in the U.S. and elsewhere include bisexual and transgendered people, I also utilize "queer" and the abbreviation LGBT, as umbrella terms (although transgendered folks are not necessarily gay). Also, as my main questions involve social movements that aim for political rights for specific groups, my discussions of "sexualities" primarily involve lesbian and gay *identities,* rather than pleasures or desires, for of course anyone may experience queer pleasures and desires.

[2] Mohr, R. (2005). *The Long Arc of Justice: Lesbian and Gay Marriage, Equality, and Rights.* (New York: Columbia University Press), 22.

greater visibility comes an increased sense of normalcy, and holds that education and awareness are able to dispel false beliefs, and will eventually result in social progress and greater justice. Accordingly, persistent homophobia and accompanying paradoxes of political progress and regress exist because backlash is always possible concerning matters that challenge influential norms of gender, and because the work of coming out and accurately representing gay and lesbian lives is an ongoing project. Yet the enlightenment view remains optimistic, for even homophobic representations can contribute to the wider acknowledgement of human sexual diversity. As one gay philosopher writes, "the more the Right has to talk about things gay, the more the taboos against them evaporate."[3]

But what if persistent homophobia is not always a matter of false beliefs, such as beliefs that gay people are predatory or diseased, but is instead sometimes a subjective judgment based on a true belief? If I think that drinking alcohol is sinful, and I see that you drink a glass of wine every night, I will have a subjective negative judgment based on my accurate belief about what you drink. Similarly, while some anti-gay sentiment is based on false beliefs, persistent homophobia can also be based on true beliefs about gay people, such as the view that gay people have sex with, or are positively inclined toward sexual pleasures involving, others of their same sex or gender. For the homophobe this accurate belief is coupled with the subjective judgment that gay peoples' desires, pleasures, or actions are wrong, or sinful. If people with that subjective judgment are much more powerful than gay or gay-positive folks, and if their religious views are given priority in shaping the laws that apply to everyone, their views about what is sinful will have undue influence in the common culture. Education is a good way to dispel false beliefs, but if subjective judgments about accurate observations are the issue, social justice for lesbians, gay men, and bisexuals may depend not only on eradicating false beliefs, but also on defusing the moral judgments of homophobes, limiting their influence

in public contexts, and building up the community that does not judge us negatively. Homophobes are not necessarily wrong about the facts of the matter. What is at issue are their judgments, and the power their judgments have—especially in a democracy that maintains a healthy separation between state and church.

The enlightenment view's emphasis on education and dispelling false beliefs about LGBT lives does address some politically important needs. However, it is incomplete. Because it focuses on education and gaining acceptance, it fails to strongly oppose the dominant culture's terms of acceptance and the fictions that bolster those terms, such as the notion that religious morality, or one groups notion of sin, trumps more universal ethical claims, such as a general human right to sexual freedom.[4] Because subjective judgments are "justified" by specific ideas about what it means to be a normal human being, what sexuality is, and what human history indicates about all of that, reducing prejudice against lesbian and gay sexualities and people requires deep questioning of prevalent conceptions of sexual history and "normalcy." At the very least, as many lesbian and gay theorists have emphasized, disarming homophobia calls for frank analyses of human sexualities in general—not just homosexualities—and the historical, social, and cultural contexts in which they are formed and maintained. Because the enlightenment view focuses on education and gaining acceptance, it fails to strongly oppose the dominant culture's terms of acceptance, its own fictions about itself, and its refusal to promote sexual freedom in general.

THE POWER OF PROTECTION

Legal protection for gay and lesbian people and interests is called for whether homophobia is the result of false beliefs, or subjective judgments based in particular cultural or religious views. Perhaps most importantly, establishing protected

---

[3] Mohr, p. 7.

[4] Like most human freedoms, a general right to sexual freedom would apply primarily to consensual adults.

class status makes members of marginalized groups "equal under the law," and provides tools for addressing discriminatory policies in institutions. Legal protections are also needed to prevent members of religious groups from enforcing their religion's punishments and exclusions on others. Data and experience show that sexual minorities are subject to undue harm and discrimination, not the least of which is the great suffering of LGBT and questioning youth in homophobic contexts, which is well-documented in dramatically increased rates of harassment and suicide. In addition, the real costs of delegitimizing same-sex conjugal partnerships, including lost pensions, income and estate tax benefits, insurance benefits, etcetera, and the absence of rights concerning health care decisions, adoption, inheritance, and even visitation in hospitals, are infamously unfair. As philosopher Richard Mohr argues, continued homophobic mistreatment "justifies the application to gay people of the moral sense of minority, and in turn ought to invoke the constitutional norms the culture thinks appropriate for minority status, especially enhanced constitutional equal protection of the sort currently afforded by the Supreme Court to blacks, ethnic minorities, and religious minorities."[5]

Currently the U.S. Equal Employment Opportunity Commission admits that they "do not prohibit discrimination and harassment based on sexual orientation . . . although other federal agencies and many states and municipalities do"[6] (this is a shift from Bill Clinton-era federal practice, which did prohibit discrimination based on sexual orientation). Although we do not presently see majority support for a queer civil rights amendment to the U.S. Constitution, establishing protected class status through the inclusion of LGBT folks in local and statewide civil rights ordinances remains an important and often-successful progressive legislative strategy (In 2007 there are around 300 such laws on the

books).[7] Given the preponderance of homophobia and its harms, establishing legal protections against antigay discrimination, as a response to specific histories of injustice and with the goal of promoting equal treatment under the law and in public institutions, is generally seen as a necessary step toward justice for all.

Group-protective legislation that prohibits and punishes discrimination can go hand in hand with gay-positive cultural politics that aim to increase visibility and smash stereotypes, for protected group status can create greater safety and a public sense of acceptability, which provides more room for queer self-representation in wider cultures. In turn, more accurate or sympathetic presentations of gay lives can help raise consciousness for some, undermine damaging myths and stereotypes, and reinforce legal protections. Nonetheless, while it is often hoped that protected class status *leads to* greater social acceptability by creating a more hospitable environment, protected status will not be granted unless there is *already* a sufficient degree of acceptance of the group in question, and a good deal of concern for their wellbeing. Advocates for group protections therefore face the difficult joint tasks of proving that group members need legal protection due to particular unjustified harms, while also showing that members of the group in question are sufficiently similar to the status quo to deserve fully equal treatment in all public institutional policies. Because there are pervasive beliefs that derided sexualities render some people essentially unworthy of equal treatment, and even justify harming and punishing them, arguments that queers are sufficiently similar to the status quo will remain controversial. It is therefore tempting to minimize or draw attention away from the very thing that sets the group apart,

---

[5] Mohr, p. 86.
[6] http://www.eeoc.gov/facts/fs-orientation_parent_marital_political.html

[7] Anti-discrimination laws vary widely. Some only prohibit discrimination in public employment, others include discrimination in public accommodations, private employment, education, housing, credit, and/or union practices. See National Gay and Lesbian Task Force, (n.d.) States, cities, and counties with civil rights ordinances, policies or proclamations prohibiting discrimination on the basis of sexual orientation. Retrieved August 31, 2006, from http://www.thetaskforce.org/theissues/issue.cfm?issueID=18.

which is also the thing that ought to be protected from attack or degradation.

What is the best approach for establishing protected group status for lesbians and gay men? Because these efforts typically happen at the local level and involve public political campaigns, the processes and conceptual schemes used can be quite influential in shaping more queer-positive cultures. In the U.S., protected status has been granted to groups based on histories of unjustified and categorical discrimination and harm (due to age, disability, national origin, race, sex), or in order to remedy or protect against other forms of discrimination that are considered fundamentally unjustified (such as discrimination based on religion, veteran status, or retaliation). Arguments for group legal protections are often built on the position that gay, lesbian, and bisexual folks are "relevantly like other minority groups—blacks, the Irish, women, Jews, the handicapped, Mormons, and others—traditionally thought deserving of protection from governmental discrimination," and therefore deserving of equal protection under the law.[8] Analogies are most commonly made with gender and racial discrimination, because those are paradigm areas where civil rights law has been somewhat successful, and because legal protections against sexism and racism are based on the view that it is not permissible to punish people or treat them unfairly simply because of who they are—because of immutable characteristics that have historically and unjustly placed them in a devalued category. Racism and sexism are about body types, relatively "fixed" characteristics and involuntary identities, not about what people do. In fact, a very troubling aspect of both sexism and racism is that one may be subject to them no matter what one does or accomplishes. In contrast, people with gay identities are presented with the option of an action that could change them, because theoretically those identities can be renounced or sublimated in a way that a racial identity cannot. While racism, sexism, and homophobia are interrelated and historically similar,

they are also very distinct. If homophobia is often based on negative subjective judgments about gay actions, rather than body types or fixed characteristics, then instead of (or in addition to) being strongly similar to racism, homophobia may have much in common with unlawful discrimination against *voluntary* features, such as religion, creed, or marital status. I will argue below that, like religion, sexual identity is based on foundational actions, and homophobia targets these actions. Defending the legitimacy of these actions should therefore be a focus of gay-positive politics.

QUEER ACTS

Analogies with sexism and racism, along with the enlightenment view that the root cause of anti-gay sentiment is false beliefs about queers, support the view that homophobia is about who we *are* rather than what we *do*. If homophobia is based on false beliefs about who we are, the focus of gay politics should be to show that we are deserving people, rather than to fight for the right to do as we please. And homophobia and hence gay inequality cannot be simply about sex acts, for there are no definitive lesbian and gay sex acts (if there were, then straights who deviate could not remain straight), and it seems rather obvious that persons are subject to harm just for being perceived as being gay, regardless of actual sexual behaviors. Nonetheless, we should not be so quick to decide that queer inequality is about who we are, rather than what we do, *or that we can make an analytical distinction between being and doing.* Personally, the more significant and painful homophobia I experience is typically of the "love the sinner, hate the sin" sort, where it's precisely my supposedly deviant behavior, or my comfort with my own deviancy, that is judged negatively by folks who otherwise want very much to give me the benefit of the doubt, because they do recognize my dignity or value as a person. Regarding sexuality (and probably many other facets of human life), who we are and what we do are mutually constituted.

In his book *The Long Arc of Justice: Lesbian and Gay Marriage, Equality, and Rights,* Richard

---

[8] Mohr, p. 74.

Mohr argues for the view the heart of homophobia is a categorical denial of dignity, rather than blame for despised actions, and the main evidence he provides is an analysis of popular gay names and slurs. He writes that "No widespread anti-gay slur gives any indication that its censure is directed at sex acts rather than despised social status," and further:

> Many slang pejoratives explicitly denote homosexual status rather than homosexual acts. Put-downs of gay men nominally based on charges of effeminacy are of this sort. They put down gay men not as performers of sodomy but as having a low status derivative from the low status in which society holds women, and additionally from the sense that they have betrayed their socially assigned gender status. To be sure betrayal is a willful action, but it is not the willfulness of being a queen that is the brunt of slurs like sissy. It is the challenge that the queen's status presents to socially managed gender distinctions that is condemned . . . The queen's very existence is a challenge to the status "real manhood." Action has little to do with the perceived threat.(18)

But what exactly is the "queen's status," apart from queeny action, behaviors, inclinations, desires, and tendencies, including gender bending and blending, suggestions of stereotypical feminine receptivity in a male body, and the like? Regarding sexuality and sexual identity, certainly there is not such a strong distinction between doing and being. To be queer is to be a queer body, is to be a body who acknowledges queer pleasure and desire, and who claims that pleasure and desire as part of one's identity, at least somewhere. This acknowledgement or claiming is the willful act despised by homophobes and prized by gay-positive communities. If someone sees you claim queer desire, they are justified in thinking that you may be queer, and perhaps in calling you a queer. This is not because of what you are, but because of what you've done. Yet I'm suggesting that that doing is better conceived as an affirmation than a sex act.

Queer inequalities are built on particular legacies and histories, and in the American record,

labeling actions perverse or "sinful" is a common justification for the social degradation and punishment of those who participate in or prize them. One under-analyzed example is the harsh judgment and punishment waged against native peoples throughout the Americas in response to the gender and sexual diversity evident in indigenous cultures.[9] That harsh judgment served a key role in the Euro-Christian conquest of this continent, not least significantly because for the Spanish, punishment for perversity provided a rationale for taking native lands, as well as for murder, mutilation, and cultural genocide. As anthropologist Walter Williams writes, "Sixteenth century Spanish writings on Native American gender diversity were part of a moral discourse in which the justification for conquest came to hinge on the 'rationality' of the natives, and sodomy and deviance from hierarchical and dualistic gender norms were irrefutable evidence of irrationality"—of being sub-human. For example, in the mid sixteenth century "a Spanish official sang the praises of Vasco Nunez de Balboa, who on his expedition through Panama in 1513, 'saw men dressed like women, learnt that they were sodomites, and threw the king and forty others to be eaten by his dogs, a fine action of an honorable and Catholic Spaniard.'"[10]

Harsh punishment for sexual deviance continues today with the anti-gay-marriage crusade, the persistence of the troubling "ex-gay" movement, and the preponderance of abstinence-based education, which has entered a new phase of targeting lesbian, gay, and bisexual youth with "preventative" measures and "conversion" tactics (A recent report describes a case involving a 5-year-old boy who was subjected to conversion

---

[9] See for example Smith, A. (2005). *Conquest: Sexual Violence and American Indian Genocide.* (Boston: South End Press); Roscoe, W. (2000). *Changing Ones: Third and Fourth Genders in Native North America.* (New York: Palgrave); Jacobs, S., Wesley, T., and Lang, S. (Eds) (1997); *Two-Spirit People: Native American Gender Identity, Sexuality, and Spirituality.* (Chicago: University of Illinois Press); Williams, W. (1986). *The Spirit and the Flesh: Sexual Diversity in American Indian Culture.* (Boston: Beacon Press).
[10] Williams, 137.

therapy to address "prehomosexuality.")[11] All are testament to the notion that homophobes are quite obsessed in what gay folks *do,* and that our *beings* are cast as hateful because of our doings. In the online literature of the virulently anti-gay Parents Rights Coalition, based in Waltham, Mass, we find another example:

> We attempt to stop childhood molestation and "gay" affirmation during adolescence by keeping the homosexual agenda out of schools. Children attend gay-straight alliances with the intent to learn about their sexuality. Once there, "gay" is presented as a valid choice for any questioning youth. . . . Our concern is for the physical safety of gays, which requires that we advocate against the idea that "gay" is an equally valid "life choice." *The dangers of being gay come from the behaviors associated with gayness* rather than the supposed harassment from "homophobes." Anal intercourse, anal-oral stimulation, domestic violence, drug use, "fisting," fellatio, fecal ingestion, promiscuity, oral-sex, sadomasochism, and sodomy are all dangerous to the human body and *ought never be practiced,* let alone suggested in high school. (emphasis in original)[12]

We see in this rhetoric a very precise equation of being gay with "gay" acts. But note that *all of the sex acts mentioned in the list are regularly performed by straight people,* so the definitive act that is considered sinful is not merely a sex act. What is particularly interesting here is the an emphasis on the core and most despised gay act: the act of affirmation, of deciding that it is okay to be gay, of saying yes to whatever it is that leads one to think that one might be queer. As the author states, "We advocate against the idea that 'gay' is an equally valid 'life choice.' . . ." The definitive act is a yes-saying, an affirmation of a positive inclination toward a certain sort of action.

Conceiving of queer sexuality a form of yes-saying makes available a way of thinking about queerness as a choice (the choice to affirm) that does not depend on overly ambitious claims about the voluntariness of sexual desire (something that lesbians and gay men have been arguing about for decades). It also helps explain some of the significance of coming out, especially what we refer to as "coming out to oneself." Everyone with queer potential has the option of saying yes to one's own queerness, at least somewhere, and coming out is part of that yes-saying. To *be* lesbian, gay, or bisexual is to make and claim some queer affirmation. While there is a sense in which such actions may be internal, there is plenty of philosophical work to recommend the view that queer affirmations are best described as actions, because they are performative assertions of agency and will.

The act of accepting one's own queerness—saying yes to it somewhere in one's experience or consciousness—is quite necessary for "being" gay or lesbian. Homoerotic impulses are rampant in the species, and heterosexuality as an identity could not be maintained unless queer desires and acts could be effectively disavowed with proclamations and counterevidence in the form of heterosexual acts and commitments. Sexual identities and actions are inextricably connected, although the relevant actions are not reducible to sex acts. Even if erotic desire and arousal are commonly experienced as involuntary, arousal and desire are not the sum total of identity or being. In response to oppressive, repressive, and discriminatory histories, lesbians, gay men, and bisexuals demand equality so as to freely and legitimately express, not simply so as to be. Or, queer being is inextricable from queer doing. Arguments for protected status for sexual minorities should therefore probably be closer to arguments for religious freedom than sex or race equality. Like religion, sexual identity requires a foundational yes-saying, an action, an affirmation of a positive inclination toward a certain sort of action.

There are other strong analogies between sexual cultures and religious beliefs or creeds, because both are matters of pronounced beliefs and commitments that are relatively subjective and private.

---

[11] Cianciotto, J. and Cahill, S. (2006). *Youth in the Crosshairs: The Third Wave of Ex-Gay Activism.* New York: National Gay and Lesbian Task Force Policy Institute.

[12] Whiteman, S. (n.d.) "A Discussion on Homosexuality." Retrieved August 31, 2006, from http://www.parentsrightscoalition.org/Writings/Statement.htm.

Even when one seems to be born into a religious sect, certain voluntary actions are required for a religious identity. In order to be Mormon one must "accept Christ as one's personal savior," and pledge to help convert others to being Mormon. It makes no sense to think of religion as an immutable or involuntary category, yet religious preferences are clear grounds for categorical protections. Indeed, religious freedom, and religious affiliation as a protected class, require the right to *do,* to affirm one's beliefs through appropriate actions, not simply the right to *be.* Under Title VII, "Employers may not treat employees or applicants less- or more-favorably because of their religious beliefs or practices. Employers must reasonably accommodate employees' sincerely held religious beliefs or practices unless doing so would impose an undue hardship on the employer. And employers must permit employees to engage in religious expression, unless the religious expression would impose an undue hardship on the employer." Title VII's categorical protection of religious expression is clearly about voluntary and optional actions.

While illegal actions may warrant unequal treatment, actions that are considered socially or morally valuable are *protected* by the law. One person's sin may be another person's valued and life-affirming behavior (i.e., eating meat, driving a car, drinking alcohol), which is one reason why separations of state and church are fundamental for democracy. Yet, because many legal norms do have religious backgrounds, the growth of democracy calls for ongoing vigilance in identifying the inappropriate traces of religious prejudice in the law. Should it be illegal to believe that it is okay to be gay, and to act accordingly?

DIGNITY AND THE RIGHT TO "BE" QUEER

As I mentioned earlier, Richard Mohr describes queer inequality as rooted in denials of queer personhood, or dignity, and he rejects the view that homophobia is rooted in negative judgments about queer acts. In contrast, I have argued here that sub-jective judgments about queer acts are often at the heart of homophobia, and that the most despised act is the affirmation of queer self-acceptance and the celebration of queer pleasures. Yet as I have also tried to emphasize throughout, I do not reject the enlightenment view completely. In fact, I cannot help but think that there is something distinct about dignity that Mohr fears we'll lose sight of if we focus exclusively on sexual freedom as the goal of lesbian and gay politics. On the positive side, Mohr seems to believe that there is something distinctly valuable about dignity as a political goal that will be missed if we overemphasize sex.

An example that Mohr rightly highlights as paradigmatic of the denial of queer equality is the indignity of offering the consolation prize of "civil unions" rather than marriage for same-sex couples. Restating an analysis that feminist and gay theorists have long deployed, Mohr describes the legal institution of marriage as a ritual that draws into being a social form as it ratifies that very form, for it is a rite of passage that defines men and women as legally distinct from each other, and heterosexual pair bonding as the only legally protected form of family. Laws maintaining the exclusivity of heterosexual marriage are designed to maintain heterosexual supremacy, as anti-miscegenation laws maintained white supremacy. Prohibitions on gay marriage and the offer of a separate, secondary class of civil unions not only deny sanctification to lesbian and gay unions and families—they also draw lesbians and gay men into complicity with the institutionalization of heterosexual supremacy. For these reasons Mohr sees the full right to gay marriage as a remedy that would establish an important freedom but also help establish dignity, by removing the indignity of that secondary status, and forced complicity with legal structures that maintain our inequality.

There is clearly something like a "homophobic gaze" that is similar to the sexist or racist gaze, that creates a serious and persistent form of harm that is more subtle than outright violence, and that is not reducible to a denial of rights and therefore cannot simply be "protected" by the law. It is the part of oppression that gets under the skin and into the psyche, that can undermine flourishing even for those with great material comfort and the full exercise of liberty. It may even be the part of oppression that makes oppressed folks with economic and other social privileges less likely to continue to struggle for justice, for the homophobic denial of our dignity is quite tiresome, and leaves many longing for zones of freedom and autonomy that approximate the freedoms enjoyed by those who are completely at ease in straight worlds. I've argued here that homophobia is often a response to positive affirmations of sexual and gender diversity, but it does not follow that free expressions of such affirmations are equivalent to enjoying appropriate respect from others.

But how much do others' feelings about my dignity impact my sense of equality or inequality, if I am free to act as I please, where and when I please? Conversely, if I lack sexual liberties, does it help matters much if I am held in high moral regard? As a woman, I'm inclined to believe it helps somewhat, but not very much. To help illustrate the significance of denials of dignity, and to bolster his argument that being is more significant than doing, Richard Mohr describes a racist joke that plays on the fact that people of color with superior accomplishments can still be viewed as lesser, even naturally debased, beings.[13] The racist assumption is that race makes the person of color fundamentally unequal regardless of what she does, and assigns her a status lower than the average white person, although her accomplishments are higher. Accomplishments alone are not sufficient to ensure that others will treat you with dignity. But how much would racist names matter if people of color had more social and political power overall? Compare for example with another put-down that Mohr briefly discusses: "The derogatory terms that have male genitalia as their metaphoric vehicles, such as "prick," are not in fact putdowns of men as men but are simply equivalents to 'bozo.' Real men are unassailable."[14]

Actually, the term "prick" often is a putdown of a man as a man. Nonetheless, "prick" doesn't wound the way "nigger," "fag," and "cunt" can, because men typically have enough social privilege (at least as men) not to care about what less powerful folks call them. Dignity is closely connected to social power. Yet harsh judgment can be harmful to one's sense of dignity, even for those who enjoy a terrific range of social freedoms, and so it is certainly important not to lose sight of the political importance and requirements of dignity.

SOME SUGGESTIONS

The enlightenment view holds that the most important political work for LGBT communities and our allies is to address homophobia with education, and more accurate representations of queer lives. That work is crucial, especially because of its importance in bolstering dignity, and creating useful models and zones of safety for gay, lesbian, bisexual, and questioning youth (and of course it is always a good idea to be on the side of accuracy). However, because homophobia can be based on accurate beliefs, and because religious views that label gay affirmations "sinful" are hegemonic, enlightenment strategies are not enough. In addition to movements to dispel false negative stereotypes, sexual liberation therefore calls for movements that proclaim and protect our right to be queer, which necessary includes the right to do queer things. Queer dignity can only be established in relation to the full freedom to perform gay acts, definitive and otherwise. I therefore call on our friends and allies to adopt a new set of mantras. Rather than telling your homophobic friends and family members that you know lots of gay people and they are totally nice, normal, moral people, please consider also telling them that regardless of who you know or what you think of them, you think it is perfectly fine to be gay, and that a lesbian has as much right to be a lesbian as anyone has to become "born again." It probably would not hurt for queer folks to also see how comfortable *we* are with the idea that it is always and everywhere okay to be what we want to be.

[13] Mohr, p. 19.
[14] Mohr, p. 20.

In this essay I have raised five points for consideration. 1) The political perspective that I've called the "enlightenment view," has real limits, as it tends to reduce the problem of homophobia to a preponderance of false beliefs, and to prioritize acceptability over sexual freedoms. 2) Instead we need to also direct significant political attention to defusing the moral judgments of homophobes, and reducing their influence in our common cultures. 3) While sexual identity is commonly thought of as a form of "being," regarding sexuality it is fallacious to assume a stark dichotomy between "being" and "doing." 4) The most significant acts defining queer identities are the acceptance and affirmations of one's own queer pleasures and desires. 5) Rather than looking to similarities with race and gender, in arguing for protected group status for LGBT folks, it may be quite politically useful to focus on commonalities between religion and sexual identity, for both depend on professed beliefs, rather than immutable characteristics.

Queer politics are not just about convincing others that we are worthy of full equality under the law. Political action and activism, including fights for rights, are ways to claim space in the realm of legitimate and valued life forms. The fact that religious opinion is continually allowed to trump basic sexual freedom may be altered somewhat if we begin to assert that prima facie, sexual identities are as legitimate as religious identities. Where free expression and diversity are allowed to flourish, the sort of consciousness-raising and familiarity that promotes mutual respect for dignity across difference becomes more possible, and the harsh judgments of stereotypes and religious prejudices have less power. I'd say that any way you slice it, full equality requires dignity, but for contemporary subjects (at least), dignity and sexual freedoms are inseparable. Equality is the demand for enough space and enough power to regularly experience both.

TOWARD A GENEALOGY OF BLACK FEMALE SEXUALITY: THE PROBLEMATIC OF SILENCE

Evelynn M. Hammonds

To name ourselves rather than be named we must first see ourselves. For some of us this will not be easy. So long unmirrored, we may have forgotten how we look. Nevertheless, we can't theorize in a void; we must have evidence.
LORRAINE O'GRADY, "OLYMPIA'S MAID"[1]

Sexuality has become one of the most visible, contentious and spectacular features of modern life in the United States during this century. Controversies over sexual politics and sexual behavior reveal other tensions in U.S. society, particularly those around changing patterns of work, family organization, disease control, and gender relations. In the wake of Anita Hill's allegations of sexual harassment by Supreme Court nominee Clarence Thomas and the more recent murder charges brought against football star O. J. Simpson, African Americans continue to be used as the terrain upon which contested notions about race, gender, and sexuality are worked out. Yet, while black men have increasingly been the focus of debates about sexuality in the academy and in the media, the specific ways in which black women figure in these discourses has remained largely unanalyzed and untheorized.

In this essay, I will argue that the construction of black women's sexuality, from the nineteenth century to the present, engages three sets of issues. First, there is the way black women's sexuality has been constructed in a binary opposition to that of white women: it is rendered simultaneously invisible, visible (exposed), hypervisible, and pathologized in dominant discourses.

Secondly, I will describe how resistance to these dominant discourses has been coded and lived by various groups of black women within black communities at different historical moments. Finally, I will discuss the limitations of these strategies of resistance in disrupting dominant discourses about black women's sexuality and the implications of this for black women with AIDS.

In addressing these questions, I am specifically interested in interrogating the writing of black feminist theorists on black women's sexuality. As sociologist Patricia Hill Collins has noted, while black feminist theorists have written extensively on the impact of such issues as rape, forced sterilization, and homophobia on black women's sexuality, "when it comes to other important issues concerning the sexual politics of Black womanhood, . . . Black feminists have found it almost impossible to say what has happened to Black women."[2] To date, there has been no full-length historical study of African American women's sexuality in the United States. In this essay, I will examine some of the reasons why black feminists have failed to develop a complex, historically specific analysis of black women's sexuality.

Black feminist theorists have almost universally described black women's sexuality, when viewed from the vantage of the dominant discourses, as an absence. In one of the earliest and most compelling discussions of black women's sexuality, literary critic Hortense Spillers wrote, "Black women are the beached whales of the sexual universe, unvoiced, misseen, not doing, awaiting *their* verb."[3] For writer Toni Morrison, black women's sexuality is one of the "unspeakable things unspoken" of the African American experience. Black women's sexuality is often described in metaphors of speechlessness, space, or vision; as a "void" or empty space that is simultaneously ever-visible (exposed) and invisible, where black women's bodies are always already colonized. In addition, this always already colonized black female body has so much sexual potential it has none at all.[4] Historically, black women have reacted to the repressive force

of the hegemonic discourses on race and sex that constructed this image with silence, secrecy, and a partially self-chosen invisibility.[5]

Black feminist theorists—historians, literary critics, sociologists, legal scholars, and cultural critics—have drawn upon a specific historical narrative which purportedly describes the factors that have produced and maintained perceptions of black women's sexuality (including their own). Three themes emerge in this history. First, the construction of the black female as the embodiment of sex and the attendant invisibility of black women as the unvoiced, unseen—everything that is not white. Secondly, the resistance of black women both to negative stereotypes of their sexuality and to the material effects of those stereotypes on black women's lives. And, finally, the evolution of a "culture of dissemblance" and a "politics of silence" by black women on the issue of their sexuality.

COLONIZING BLACK WOMEN'S BODIES

By all accounts, the history of discussions of black women's sexuality in Western thought begins with the Europeans' first contact with peoples on the African continent. As Sander Gilman argued in his widely cited essay "Black Bodies, White Bodies: Toward an Iconography of Female Sexuality in Late Nineteenth-Century Art, Medicine, and Literature,"[6] the conventions of human diversity that were captured in the iconography of the period linked the image of the prostitute and the black female through the Hottentot female. The Hottentot female most vividly represented in this iconography was Sarah Bartmann, known as the "Hottentot Venus." This southern African black woman was crudely exhibited and objectified by European audiences and scientific experts because of what they regarded as unusual aspects of her physiognomy—her genitalia and buttocks. Gilman argued that Sarah Bartmann, along with other black females brought from southern Africa, became the central image for the black female in Europe through the nineteenth century. The "primitive" genitalia of these women were defined by European commentators as the sign of their "primitive" sexual appetites. Thus, the black female became the antithesis of European sexual mores and beauty and was relegated to the lowest position on the scale of human development. The image of the black female constructed in this period reflected everything the white female was not, or, as art historian Lorraine O'Grady has put it, "White is what woman is [was]; not-white (and the stereotypes not-white gathers in) is what she had better not be."[7] Gilman shows that by the end of the nineteenth century European experts in anthropology, public health, medicine, biology, and psychology had concluded, with ever-increasing "scientific" evidence, that the black female embodied the notion of uncontrolled sexuality.

In addition, as white European elites' anxieties surfaced over the increasing incidence of sexually transmitted diseases, especially syphilis, high rates of these diseases among black women were used to define them further as a source of corruption and disease. It was the association of prostitutes with disease that provided the final link between the black female and the prostitute. Both were bearers of the stigmata of sexual difference and deviance. Gilman concluded that the construction of black female sexuality as inherently immoral and uncontrollable was a product of nineteenth century biological sciences. Ideologically, these sciences reflected European males' fear of difference in the period of colonialism, and their consequent need to control and regulate the sexuality of those rendered "other."

Paula Giddings, following Gilman, pointed out that the negative construction of black women's sexuality as revealed by the Bartmann case also occurred at a time when questions about the entitlement of nonenslaved blacks to citizenship was being debated in the United States. In part, the contradiction presented by slavery was resolved in the U.S. by ascribing certain inherited characteristics to blacks, characteristics that made them unworthy of citizenship; foremost among these was the belief in the unbridled sexuality of black people and specifically that of black women.[8] Thus, racial difference was linked to sexual difference in order to maintain white male supremacy during the period of slavery.

During slavery, the range of ideological uses for the image of the always-already sexual black woman was extraordinarily broad and familiar. This stereotype was used to justify the enslavement, rape, and sexual abuse of black women by white men; the lynching of black men; and, not incidentally, the maintenance of a coherent biological theory of human difference based on fixed racial typologies. Because African American women were defined as property, their social, political, and legal rights barely exceeded those of farm animals—indeed, they were subjected to the same forms of control and abuse as animals. For black feminist scholars, the fact that black women emerged under slavery as speaking subjects at all is worthy of note.[9] And it is the fact that African American women of this period do speak to the fact of their sexual exploitation that counts as their contestation to the dominant discourses of the day. Indeed, as Hazel Carby has described, black women during slavery were faced with having to develop ways to be recognized within the category of woman by whites by asserting a positive value to their sexuality that could stand in both public and private.[10]

THE POLITICS OF "RECONSTRUCTING WOMANHOOD"[11]

As the discussion of sex roles and sexuality began to shift among whites in the U.S. by the end of the nineteenth century, the binary opposition which characterized black and white female sexuality was perpetuated by both Victorian sexual ideology and state practices of repression. White women were characterized as pure, passionless, and de-sexed, while black women were the epitome of immorality, pathology, impurity, and sex itself. "Respectability" and "sexual control" were set against "promiscuity" in the discourse of middle-class whites, who viewed the lifestyles of black people and the new white immigrants in urban centers as undermining the moral values of the country.[12] Buttressed by the doctrine of the Cult of True Womanhood, this binary opposition seemed to lock black women forever outside the ideology of womanhood so celebrated in the Victorian era. As Beverly Guy Sheftall notes, black women were painfully aware that "they were devalued no matter what their strengths might be, and that the Cult of True Womanhood was not intended to apply to them no matter how intensely they embraced its values."[13]

In the late-nineteenth century, with increasing exploitation and abuse of black women despite the legal end of slavery, U.S. black women reformers recognized the need to develop different strategies to counter negative stereotypes of their sexuality which had been used as justifications for the rape, lynching, and other abuses of black women by whites. More than a straightforward assertion of a normal female sexuality and a claim to the category of protected womanhood was called for in the volatile context of Reconstruction where, in the minds of whites, the political rights of black men were connected to notions of black male sexual agency.[14] Politics, sexuality, and race were already inextricably linked in the U.S., but the problematic established by this link reached new heights of visibility during the period of Reconstruction through the increased lynchings of black men and women by the early decades of the twentieth century.

One of the most cogent analyses by a black woman about the connections between politics and sex in this period was made by Ida B. Wells. Wells understood that the history of the condoned murders of blacks was "a direct consequence of blacks having been granted a political right, the franchise, without being given the means to protect or maintain that right."[15] Wells argued that the cry of "rape" had come to mean any alliance between a "white woman and a colored man," and state and civilian responses were confined entirely to the protection of women who happened to be white.[16] Her

analysis of lynching, as Hazel Carby has argued, provided a "detailed dissection of how patriarchal power manipulated sexual ideologies to effect political and economic subordination."[17] On the other hand, educator and activist Anna Julia Cooper emphasized that the interrelated practices of racism and sexism were connected to the consequences of U.S. imperialism. In both instances, these activists argued that African American women had to organize themselves politically to effect their inclusion in the category of protected womanhood. The antilynching movement then became the catalyst for the establishment of the black women's club movement.

Wells is particularly important for my discussion because she demonstrated how the discourses of rape and lynching were categories through which the negative rendering of the sexuality of black people was maintained. Carby, in her discussion of this movement, makes much of the fact that issues surrounding the representation of black female sexuality became the centerpiece of the club movement. These club women strove to break the binary that they had been forced to occupy with white women by asserting that "an injury to one woman is an injury to all women."[18] The primary goal of these women was to retrieve and reconstruct a notion of womanhood that, in the economic and political arena, was being constructed as irredeemably pathologized. Secondarily, they wanted to enlist white women in the destruction of the binary which, they argued, contributed to the oppression of white women as well.

THE POLITICS OF SILENCE

Although some of the strategies used by these black women reformers might have initially been characterized as resistance to dominant and increasingly hegemonic constructions of their sexuality, by the early twentieth century, they had begun to promote a public silence about sexuality which, it could be argued, continues to the present.[19] This "politics of silence," as described by historian Evelyn Brooks Higginbotham, emerged as a political strategy by black women reformers who hoped by their silence and by the promotion of proper Victorian morality to demonstrate the lie of the image of the sexually immoral black woman.[20] Historian Darlene Clark Hine argues that the "culture of dissemblance" which this politics engendered was seen as a way for black women to "protect the sanctity of inner aspects of their lives."[21] She defines this culture as "the behavior and attitudes of Black women that created the appearance of openness and disclosure but actually shielded the truth of their inner lives and selves from their oppressors." "Only with secrecy," Hine argues, "thus achieving a self-imposed invisibility, could ordinary Black women accrue the psychic space and harness the resources needed to hold their own."[22] And by the projection of the image of a "super moral" black woman, they hoped to garner greater respect, justice, and opportunity for all black Americans. Of course, as Higginbotham notes, there were problems with this strategy. First, it did not achieve its goal of ending the negative stereotyping of black women. And second, some middle-class black women engaged in policing the behavior of poor and working-class women and others who deviated from a Victorian norm, in the name of protecting the "race."[23] Black women reformers were responding to the ways in which any black woman could find herself "exposed" and characterized in racist sexual terms no matter what the truth of her individual life; they saw any so-called deviant individual behavior as a threat to the race as a whole. But the most enduring and problematic aspect of this "politics of silence" is that in choosing silence, black women have also lost the ability to articulate any conception of their sexuality.

Yet, this last statement is perhaps too general. Carby notes that during the 1920s, black women in the U.S. risked having all representations of black female sexuality appropriated as primitive and exotic within a largely racist society.[24] She continues, "Racist sexual ideologies proclaimed black women to be rampant sexual beings, and in response black women writers either focused on defending their morality or displaced sexuality onto another terrain."[25] As many black feminist literary and cultural critics have noted, the other terrain on which black women's sexuality was displaced was music, notably the blues. The early blues singers—who were most decidedly not middle class—have been called "pioneers who claimed their sexual subjectivity through their songs and produced a Black women's discourse on Black sexuality."[26] At a moment when middle-class black women's sexuality was "completely underwritten to avoid endorsing sexual stereotypes," the blues women defied and exploited those stereotypes.[27] Yet, ultimately, neither silence nor defiance was able to dethrone negative constructions of black female sexuality. Nor could these strategies allow for the unimpeded expression of self-defined black female sexualities. Such approaches did not allow African American women to gain control over their sexuality.

In previous eras, black women had articulated the ways in which active practices of the state—the definition of black women as property, the sanctioned rape and lynching of black men and women, the denial of the vote—had been supported by a specific ideology about black female sexuality (and black male sexuality). These state practices effaced any notion of differences among and between black women, including those of class, color, and educational and economic privilege; all black women were designated as the same. The assertion of a supermoral black female subject by black women activists did not completely efface such differences nor did it directly address them. For black women reformers of this period, grounded in particular religious traditions, to challenge the negative stereotyping of black women directly meant continuing to reveal the ways in which state power was complicit in the violence against black people. The appropriation of respectability and the denial of sexuality was, therefore, a nobler path to emphasizing that the story of black women's immorality was a lie.[28]

Without more detailed historical studies of black female sexuality in each period, we do not know the extent of this "culture of dissemblance," and many questions remain unanswered.[29] Was it expressed differently in rural and in urban areas; in the north, west, or south? How was it maintained? Where and how was it resisted? How was it shaped by class, color, economic, and educational privilege? And furthermore, how did it change over time? How did something that was initially adopted as a political strategy in a specific historical period become so ingrained in black life as to be recognizable as a culture? Or was it? In the absence of detailed historical studies we can say little about the ways social constructions of sexuality change in tandem with changing social conditions in specific historical moments within black communities.

PERSISTENT LEGACIES: THE POLITICS OF COMMODIFICATION

This legacy of silence has persisted despite the changing material conditions of African American women. And from even this very incomplete history, we can see that black women's sexuality is ideologically situated between race and gender, where the black female subject is not seen and has no voice. Methodologically, black feminists have found it difficult even to characterize this juncture, this point of erasure where African American women are located. As legal scholar Kimberlé Crenshaw puts it, "Existing within the overlapping margins of race and gender discourse and the empty spaces between, it is a location whose very nature resists telling."[30] And this silence about sexuality is enacted individually and collectively by black women and by black feminist theorists writing about black women. In addition, institutions such as black churches and historically black colleges have also contributed to the maintenance of silence about sexuality.

It should not surprise us that black women are silent about sexuality. The imposed production of silence and the removal of any alternatives to the production of silence, reflect the deployment of power against racialized subjects "wherein those who could speak did not want to and those who did want to speak were prevented from doing

so."[31] It is this deployment of power at the level of the social and the individual which has to be historicized. It seems clear that what is needed is a methodology that allows us to contest rather than reproduce the ideological system that has, up to now, defined the terrain of black women's sexuality. Hortense Spillers made this point over a decade ago when she wrote: "Because black American women do not participate, as a category of social and cultural agents, in the legacies of symbolic power, they maintain no allegiances to a strategic formation of texts, or ways of talking about sexual experience, that even remotely resemble the paradigm of symbolic domination, except that such paradigm has been their concrete disaster."[32] To date, largely through the work of black feminist literary critics, we know more about the elision of sexuality by black women than we do about the possible varieties of expression of sexual desire.[33] Thus, what we have is a very narrow view of black women's sexuality. Certainly it is true, as Crenshaw notes, that "in feminist contexts, sexuality represents a central site of the oppression of women; rape and the rape trial are its dominant narrative trope. In antiracist discourse, sexuality is also a central site upon which the repression of blacks has been premised; the lynching narrative is embodied as its trope."[34] Sexuality is also, as Carole Vance defines it, "simultaneously a domain of restriction, repression, and danger as well as a domain of exploration, pleasure, and agency."[35] In the past the restrictive, repressive, and dangerous aspects of black female sexuality have been emphasized by black feminist writers, while pleasure, exploration, and agency have gone underanalyzed.

I want to suggest that contemporary black feminist theorists have not taken up this project in part because of their own status in the academy. Reclaiming the body as well as subjectivity is a process that black feminist theorists in the academy must go through themselves while they are doing the work of producing theory. Black feminist theorists are themselves engaged in a process of fighting to reclaim the body—the maimed, immoral, black female body—which can be and is still being used by others to discredit them as producers of knowledge and as speaking subjects. Legal scholar Patricia J. Williams illuminates my point: "No matter what degree of professional I am, people will greet and dismiss my black femaleness as unreliable, untrustworthy, hostile, angry, powerless, irrational, and probably destitute."[36] When reading student evaluations, she finds comments about her teaching and her body: "I marvel, in a moment of genuine bitterness, that anonymous student evaluations speculating on dimensions of my anatomy are nevertheless counted into the statistical measurement of my teaching proficiency."[37] The hypervisibility of black women academics and the contemporary fascination with what bell hooks calls the "commodification of Otherness"[38] means that black women today find themselves precariously perched in the academy. Ann du Cille notes:

> Mass culture, as hooks argues, produces, promotes, and perpetuates the commodification of Otherness through the exploitation of the black female body. In the 1990s, however, the principal sites of exploitation are not simply the cabaret, the speakeasy, the music video, the glamour magazine; they are also the academy, the publishing industry, the intellectual community.[39]

In tandem with the notion of silence, contemporary black women writers have repeatedly drawn on the notion of the "invisible" to describe aspects of black women's lives in general and sexuality in particular. Audre Lorde writes that "within this country where racial difference creates a constant, if unspoken distortion of vision, Black women have on the one hand always been highly visible, and on the other hand, have been rendered invisible through the depersonalization of racism."[40] The hypervisibility of black women academics means that visibility, too, can be used to control the intellectual issues that black women can and cannot speak about. Already threatened with being sexualized and rendered inauthentic as knowledge producers in the academy by students and colleagues alike, this avoidance of theorizing

about sexuality can be read as one contemporary manifestation of their structured silence. I want to stress here that the silence about sexuality on the part of black women academics is no more a "choice" than was the silence practiced by early twentieth-century black women. This production of *silence* instead of *speech* is an effect of the institutions such as the academy which are engaged in the commodification of Otherness.

The "politics of silence" and the "commodification of Otherness" are not simply abstractions. These constructs have material effects on black women's lives. In shifting the site of theorizing about black female sexuality from the literary or legal terrain to that of medicine and the control of disease, we can see some of these effects. In the AIDS epidemic, the experiences and needs of black women have gone unrecognized. I have argued elsewhere that the set of controlling images of black women with AIDS has foregrounded stereotypes of these women that have prevented them from being embraced by the public as people in need of support and care. The AIDS epidemic *is* being used to "inflect, condense and rearticulate the ideological meanings of race, sexuality, gender, childhood, privacy, morality, and nationalism."[41] Black women with AIDS are largely poor and working-class; many are single mothers; they are constantly represented with regard to their drug use and abuse and uncontrolled sexuality. The supposedly "uncontrolled sexuality" of black women is one of the key features in the representation of black women in the AIDS epidemic.

The position of black women in this epidemic was dire from the beginning and worsens with each passing day. Silence, erasure, and the use of images of immoral sexuality abound in narratives about the experiences of black women with AIDS. Their voices are not heard in discussions of AIDS, while intimate details of their lives are exposed to justify their victimization. In the "war of representation" that is being waged through this epidemic, black women are the victims that are the "other" of the "other," the deviants of the deviants, irrespective of their sexual identities or practices. The representation of black women's sexuality in narratives about AIDS continues to demonstrate the disciplinary practices of the state against black women. The presence of disease is now used to justify denial of welfare benefits, treatment, and some of the basic rights of citizenship, such as privacy for black women and their children. Given the absence of black feminist analyses or a strong movement (such as the one Ida B. Wells led against lynching), the relationship between the treatment of black women in the AIDS epidemic and state practices has not been articulated. While white gay male activists are using the ideological space framed by this epidemic to contest the notion that homosexuality is "abnormal" and to preserve the right to live out their homosexual desires, black women are rendered silent. The gains made by gay activists will do nothing for black women if the stigma continues to be attached to their sexuality. Black feminist critics must work to find ways to contest the historical construction of black female sexualities by illuminating how the dominant view was established and maintained and how it can be disrupted. This work might very well save some black women's lives.

Visibility, in and of itself, is not my only goal, however. Several writers, including bell hooks, have argued that one answer to the silence on the issue of black female sexuality is for black women to see themselves, to mirror themselves. The appeal to the visual and the visible *is* deployed as an answer to the legacy of silence and repression. Mirroring as a way of negating a legacy of silence needs to be explored in much greater depth than it has been to date by black feminist theorists. An appeal to the visual is not uncomplicated or innocent, however. As theorists, we have to ask how vision *is* structured and, following that, we have to explore how difference is established, how it operates, and how it constitutes subjects who *see* and *speak* in the world. This we must apply to the ways in which black women are seen and not seen by the dominant society and also how they see themselves

in a different landscape. But in overturning the "politics of silence," the goal cannot be merely to be seen. As I have argued, visibility, in and of itself, does not erase a history of silence nor does it challenge the structure of power and domination—symbolic and material—that determines what can and cannot be seen. The goal should be to develop a "politics of articulation" that would build on the interrogation of what makes it possible for black women to speak and act.

As this essay was being written, the current Surgeon General of the United States, Joycelyn Elders, a black woman was removed from her position by President Clinton. The reason given for her ouster was her "outspoken" views on health policies relating to sex education. Elders was the third black woman in as many years, following law professors Anita Hill and Lani Guinier, for whom issues about the visibility, "outspokenness," and sexuality of black women took center stage. Though there are striking differences in the events surrounding these three women, there are equally striking similarities. Hill, Guinier, and Elders were vilified in the public press for speaking out on issues that ran counter to powerful interests of the state: Hill on sexual harassment, Guinier on the rights of minority voters, and Elders on sex education. The response to them was that on these issues—sexual harassment, voting rights, and sex—black women were to be seen and not heard; exposed and victimized but not given serious protection from slander in the expression of their views. The media spectacle surrounding these three women sent a powerful message that the negative representations of black women (especially on issues related to sexuality in the cases of Hill and Elders), produced and maintained by state practices could still be used to justify the silencing of black women. The hypervisibility of these women in the media did not allow their views to challenge the charges put against them. Thus, the question remains: how can black feminists dislodge the negative stereotyping of their sexuality and the attendant denials of citizenship and protection?

Developing a complex analysis of black female sexuality is critical to this project. Black feminist theorizing about black female sexuality has, with a few exceptions (Cheryl Clarke, Jewelle Gomez, Barbara Smith, and Audre Lorde), been focused relentlessly on heterosexuality. The historical narrative that dominates discussions of black female sexuality does not address even the possibility of a black lesbian sexuality or of a lesbian or queer subject. Spillers confirms this point when she notes that "the sexual realities of black American women across the spectrum of sexual preference and widened sexual styles tend to be a missing dialectical feature of the entire discussion."[42] Discussions of black lesbian sexuality have most often focused on differences from or equivalencies with white lesbian sexualities, with "black" added to delimit the fact that black lesbians share a history with other black women. However, this addition tends to obfuscate rather than illuminate the subject position of black lesbians. One obvious example of distortion is that black lesbians do not experience homophobia in the same way as white lesbians do. Here, as with other oppressions, the homophobia experienced by black women is always shaped by racism. What has to be explored and historicized is the specificity of black lesbian experience. I want to understand in what way black lesbians are "outsiders" within black communities. This I think, would force us to examine the construction of the "closet" by black lesbians. Although this is the topic for another essay, I want to suggest here that if we accept the existence of the "politics of silence" as an historical legacy shared by all black women, then certain expressions of black female sexuality will be rendered as dangerous, for individuals and for the collectivity. It follows, then, that the culture of dissemblance makes it acceptable for some heterosexual black women to cast black lesbians as proverbial traitors to the race.[43] And this, in turn, explains why black lesbians—whose "deviant" sexuality is framed within an already existing deviant sexuality—have been wary of embracing the status of "traitor," and the potential loss of community such an embrace engenders.[44]

Of course, while some black lesbians have hidden the truth of their lives, others have developed forms of resistance to the formulation of lesbian as traitor within black communities. Audre Lorde is one obvious example. Lorde's claiming of her black and lesbian difference "forced both her white and Black lesbian friends to contend with her historical agency in the face of [this] larger racial/sexual history that would reinvent her as dead."[45] I would also argue that Lorde's writing, with its focus on the erotic, on passion and desire, suggests that black lesbian sexualities can be read as one expression of the reclamation of the despised black female body. Therefore, the works of Lorde and other black lesbian writers, because they foreground the very aspects of black female sexuality that are submerged—namely, female desire and agency—are critical to our theorizing of black female sexualities. Since silence about sexuality is being produced by black women and black feminist theorists, that silence itself suggests that black women do have some degree of agency. A focus on black lesbian sexualities implies that another discourse—other than silence—can be produced. Black lesbian sexualities are not simply identities. Rather they represent discursive and material terrains where there exists the possibility for the active production of speech, desire, and agency. Black lesbians theorizing sexuality is a site that disrupts silence and imagines a positive affirming sexuality. I am arguing here for a different level of engagement between black heterosexual and black lesbian women as the basis for the development of a black feminist praxis that articulates the ways in which invisibility, otherness, and stigma are produced and re-produced on black women's bodies. And ultimately my hope is that such an engagement will produce black feminist analyses which detail strategies for differently located black women to shape interventions that embody their separate and common interests and perspectives.

NOTES

1. Lorraine O'Grady, "Olympia's Maid: Reclaiming Black Female Subjectivity," *Afterimage* (Summer, 1992): 14.

2. Patricia Hill Collins, *Black Feminist Thought: Knowledge, Consciousness and the Politics of Empowerment* (Boston: Unwin Hyman, 1990), p. 164.

3. Hortense Spillers, "Interstices: A Small Drama of Words," in Carole S. Vance, ed., *Pleasure and Danger,* pp. 73–100.

4. Ibid.

5. Darlene Clark Hine, "Rape and the Inner Lives of Black Women in the Middle West: Preliminary Thoughts on the Culture of Dissemblance," *Signs* 14, no. 4 (1989): 915–20.

6. Sander L. Gilman, "Black Bodies, White Bodies: Toward an Iconography of Female Sexuality in Late Nineteenth Century Art, Medicine, and Literature," *Critical Inquiry* 12, no. 1 (Autumn 1985): 204–42.

7. O'Grady, "Olympia's Maid."

8. Paula Giddings, "The Last Taboo," in Toni Morrison, ed., *Race-ing Justice, En-gendering Power: Essays on Anita Hill, Clarence Thomas and the Construction of Social Reality* (New York: Pantheon Books, 1992), p. 445.

9. See the studies of Harriet Jacobs and Linda Brent.

10. Hazel Carby, *Reconstructing Womanhood: The Emergence of the Black Female Novelist* (New York: Oxford University Press, 1987), pp. 40–61.

11. This heading is taken from the title of Carby's book cited above.

12. Giddings, "The Last Taboo."

13. Beverly Guy-Sheftall, *Daughters of Sorrow: Attitudes Toward Black Women, 1880–1920.* Black Women in United States History, vol. 11 (Brooklyn: Carlson Publishing, 1990), p. 90.

14. Martha Hodes, "The Sexualization of Reconstruction Politics: White Women and Black Men in the South after the Civil War," in John C. Fout and Maura S. Tantillo, eds., *American Sexual Politics: Sex Gender and Race since the Civil War* (Chicago: The University of Chicago Press, 1993), pp. 60–61.

15. Carby, *Reconstructing Womanhood,* p. 113.

16. Ibid.

17. Ibid., p. 114.

18. Ibid., p. 118.

19. See Evelyn Brooks Higginbotham, "African-American Women's History and the Meta-language of Race," *Signs* 17, no. 2 (1992): 251–74; Elsa Barkley Brown, "Negotiating and Transforming the Public Sphere: African American Political Life in the Transition From Slavery to Freedom," *Public Culture* 7, no. 1 (Fall 1994): 107–46; as well as Hine, Giddings, and Carby.

20. Higginbotham, "African American Women's History," p. 262.

21. Hine, "Rape and the Inner Lives," p. 915.

22. Ibid.

23. See Carby, "Policing the Black Woman's Body." Elsa Barkley Brown argues that the desexualization of black women was not just a middle-class phenomenon imposed on working-class women. Though many working-class women resisted Victorian attitudes toward womanhood and developed their own notions of sexuality and respectability, some, also from their own experiences, embraced a desexualized image. Brown, "Negotiating and Transforming the Public Sphere," p. 144.

24. Hazel Carby, *Reconstructing Womanhood,* p.174.

25. Ibid.

26. Ann Du Cille, "Blues Notes on Black Sexuality: Sex and the Texts of Jessie Fauset and Nella Larsen," *Journal of the History of Sexuality* 3, no. 3 (1993): 419. See also Hazel Carby, " 'It Just Be's Dat Way Sometime': The Sexual Politics of Black Women's Blues," in Ellen DuBois and Vicki Ruiz, eds., *Unequal Sisters: A Multicultural Reader in U.S. Women's History* (New York: Routledge, 1990).

27. Here, I am paraphrasing Du Cille, "Blues Notes," p. 443.

28. Evelyn Brooks Higginbotham, *Righteous Discontent: The Women's Movement in the Black Baptist Church, 1880–1920* (Cambridge, Mass.: Harvard University Press, 1993).

29. The historical narrative discussed here is very incomplete. To date, there are no detailed historical studies of black women's sexuality.

30. Kimberle Crenshaw, "Whose Story Is It Anyway?: Feminist and Antiracist Appropriations of Anita Hill," in Morrison, ed., *Race-ing Justice, En-gendering Power,* p. 403.

31. Abdul JanMohamed, "Sexuality on/of the Racial Border: Foucault, Wright, and the Articulation of Racialized Sexuality," in Domna Stanton, ed., *Discourses of Sexuality: From Aristotle to AIDS* (Ann Arbor: University of Michigan Press, 1992), p. 105.

32. Spillers, "Interstices," p. 80.

33. See analyses of novels by Nella Larsen and Jessie Fauset by Carby, McDowell, and others.

34. Crenshaw, "Whose Story Is It Anyway?" p. 405.

35. Carole S. Vance, "Pleasure and Danger: Towards a Politics of Sexuality," in Carole S. Vance (ed.), *Pleasure and Danger: Exploring Female Sexuality,* London: Pandora Press, 1989.

36. Patricia J. Williams, *The Alchemy of Race and Rights* (Cambridge: Harvard University Press, 1991), p. 95.

37. Ibid.

38. bell hooks, *Black Looks: Race, and Representation* (Boston: South End Press, 1992), p. 21.

39. Ann du Cille, "The Occult of True Black Womanhood: Critical Demeanor and Black Feminist Studies," *Signs* 19, no. 3 (1994): 591–629.

40. Karla Scott, as quoted in Teresa De Lauretis, "The Practice of Love: Lesbian Sexuality and Perverse Desire" (Bloomington: Indiana University Press, 1994), p. 36.

41. Simon Watney, *Policing Desire: Pornography, AIDS and the Media* (Minneapolis: University of Minnesota Press, 1989), p. ix.

42. Spillers, *Ibid.,* "Interstices."

43. In a group discussion of two novels written by black women, Jill Nelson's *Volunteer Slavery* and Audre Lorde's *Zami,* a black woman remarked that while she thought Lorde's book was better written than Nelson's, she was disturbed that Lorde spoke so much about sex, and "aired all of her dirty linen in public." She held to this view even after it was pointed out to her that Nelson's book also included descriptions of her sexual encounters.

44. I am reminded of my mother's response when I "came out" to her. She asked me why, given that I was already black and had a nontraditional profession for a woman, I would want to take on one more thing to make my life difficult. My mother's point, which is echoed by many black women, is that in announcing my homosexuality, I was choosing to alienate myself from the black community.

45. See Scott, quoted in Teresa De Lauretis, *The Practice of Love: Lesbian Sexuality and Perverse Desire* (Bloomington: Indiana University Press, 1994), p. 36.

FOR FURTHER READING

Allen, Jeffner, ed. *Lesbian Philosophies and Cultures.* Albany, NY: State University of New York Press, 1990.

Boston Women's Health Collective. *Our Bodies, Ourselves: For the New Century.* New York: Simon and Schuster, 1998.

Califia, Pat. *Speaking Sex to Power: The Politics of Queer Sex.* San Francisco: Cleis Press, 2002.

Cohen, Cheryl H. "The Feminist Sexuality Debate: Ethics and Politics." *Hypatia* 1(2) (1986): 71–86.

Collins, Patricia Hill. *Black Sexual Politics: African Americans, Gender and the New Racism.* New York: Routledge, 2004.

De Lauretis, Teresa. *The Practice of Love: Lesbian Sexuality and Perverse Desire.* Bloomington: Indiana University Press, 1994.

Dworkin, Andrea. *Intercourse.* New York: Free Press, 1987.

Firestone, Shulamith. *The Dialectic of Sex: The Case for a Feminist Revolution.* New York: Bantam, 1970.

Foucault, Michel. *The History of Sexuality, Volume One: An Introduction.* New York: Pantheon, 1978.

Frye, Marilyn. "Lesbian Sex." *Sinister Wisdom* 35 (1988): 46–54.

Frye, Marilyn. "Willful Virgin *or* Do You Have to Be a Lesbian to Be a Feminist?" In her *Willful Virgin: Essays in Feminism.* Freedom, CA: The Crossing Press, 1992.

Garry, Ann. "The Philosopher as Teacher: Why Are Sex and Love Philosophically Interesting?" *Metaphilosophy* 11(2) (1980): 165–77.

Hoagland, Sarah Lucia. *Lesbian Ethics: Toward New Value.* Palo Alto, CA.: Institute of Lesbian Studies, 1988.

Hopkins, Patrick. "Gender Treachery: Homophobia, Masculinity, and Threatened Identities." In *Rethinking Masculinity: Philosophical Explorations in Light of Feminism,* edited by Larry May, Robert Strikwerda, and Patrick Hopkins, 2nd ed. Lanham, MD: Rowman and Littlefield, 1996.

Kitzinger, Celia, and Sue Wilkinson. *Heterosexuality: A "Feminism and Psychology" Reader.* London: Sage, 1993.

Kitzinger, Celia, and Sue Wilkinson. "Virgins and Queers: Rehabilitating Heterosexuality?" *Gender and Society* 8(3) (1993): 444–62.

Lorde, Audre. "Uses of the Erotic: The Erotic as Power. In her *Sister Outsider: Essays and Speeches.* Freedom, CA: The Crossing Press, 1983.

Mackinnon, Catherine. *Feminism Unmodified: Discourses on Life and Law.* Cambridge, MA: Harvard University Press, 1987.

Mackinnon, Catherine A. *Toward a Feminist Theory of The State.* Cambridge, MA: Harvard University Press, 1989.

Marks, Elaine, and Isabelle de Courtivron. *New French Feminisms.* New York: Schocken Books, 1980.

Moraga, Cherríe. "From a Long Line of Venditas." In her *Loving in the War Years: Lo Que Nunca Pasó por sus Labios.* Boston: South End Press, 1983.

Rich, Adrienne. "Compulsory Heterosexuality and Lesbian Existence." In *Signs: A Journal of Women and Culture* 5(4) (1980): 631–60.

Rubin, Gayle. "Thinking Sex: Notes for a Radical Theory of the Politics of Sexuality." In *Pleasure and Danger: Exploring Female Sexuality,* edited by Carole S. Vance. London: Pandora Press, 1989.

Sedgwick, Eve. *Tendencies.* Durham, NC: Duke University Press, 1993.

Segal, Lynne. "Rethinking Heterosexuality: Women with Men." In her *Straight Sex: Rethinking the Politics of Pleasure.* Berkeley: University of California Press, 1994.

Snitow, Ann, Christine Stansell, and Sharon Thompson, eds. *Powers of Desire: The Politics of Sexuality.* New York: Monthly Review Press, 1983.

Wittig, Monique. *The Straight Mind and Other Essays.* Boston: Beacon, 1992.

Zita, Jacqueline. *Body Talk: Philosophical Reflections on Sex and Gender.* New York: Columbia, 1998.

Zita, Jacqueline. "Sexualities." In *A Companion to Feminist Philosophy,* edited by Alison M. Jaggar and Iris Marion Young. Oxford: Blackwell, 1998.

MEDIA RESOURCES

Silence: In Search of Black Female Sexuality in America. DVD. Directed and produced by Mya Baker (US, 2004). A perfect companion to the Evelynn Hammonds essay. This collection of interviews, film clips, personal accounts, and expert insights takes us on a journey throughout American history, exposing the exploitation of black women's sexuality and black women's attempts to break the silence around their sexuality. Available: National Film Network, http://www.nationalfilmnetwork.com, or 1–800–431–4586.

The Pill. VHS. Produced and directed by Stephen Ives, Ben Loeterman (US, 2005). In May 1960, the FDA approved the sale of a pill that arguably would have a greater impact on American culture than any other drug in the nation's history. For women across the country, the contraceptive pill was liberating: it allowed them to pursue careers, fueled the feminist and pro-choice movements, and encouraged more open attitudes towards sex. Available through PBS Videos: http://www.pbs.org/.

The Education of Shelby Knox. DVD/VHS. Directed by Marion Lipschutz and Rose Rosenblatt (US, 2005). At 15, Shelby pledges celibacy until marriage, but because her hometown of Lubbock, Texas, has one of the highest teen pregnancy and STI rates in the state, she also spearheads a campaign for comprehensive sex education in the high schools, opposing the established "abstinence only" curriculum. When the campaign broadens with a fight for a gay-straight alliance club in the high school, Shelby confronts her parents and her faith as she begins to understand how deeply personal beliefs can inform political action. Available: InCite Pictures, www.incite-pictures.com, or 212–216–9315.

CHAPTER 5

RACE AND RACISM

Contemporary feminist antiracist politics spring from earlier movements for social and political reform. Some of the earliest feminist writing in the United States emerged from movements against slavery and lynching. For example, in the 1820s and 1830s, leading white suffragists Frances Wright and Sarah and Angelina Grimké argued that white women ought to use their natural moral superiority to abolish the "social cancer" of slavery. And, in the latter half of that century, black women intellectuals such as Anna Julia Cooper and Ida B. Wells Barnett wrote and lectured on the practical and conceptual connections between racist violence, the subjection of women, and the need for universal liberal education. Feminist movements of the 1960s and 1970s were also closely connected to struggles for civil rights. Many influential feminist thinkers from that period, including Florynce Kennedy, Audre Lorde, Cherrie Moraga, and Barbara Smith, emphasized the deep and inextricable links between sexism, racism, homophobia, and class-based oppression. And, although they wouldn't characterize themselves strictly as feminists, activists Anna Mae Pictou Aquash (American Indian Movement) and Dolores Huerta (United Farm Workers), worked to call attention to the continued violence of colonialism and capitalism against indigenous peoples and migrant workers. Feminist thinkers were certainly aware of these movements and paid close attention to them.

Despite the intertwined struggles against racism and sexism, feminist theories and movements too often reflect and reinscribe the unjust hierarchies they set out to dismantle. White feminists' comparisons between racism and sexism falsely assumed that these systems of domination were conceptually separable, and that analyses of sexism modeled on white women's lives could be extended universally to all women. Even now it is disappointing, but not surprising, that most feminist philosophy remains conceptually white-centered and Eurocentric, and most feminist philosophers are white. By "white-centered," we mean that the most valued ways of understanding the world, making moral judgments, and expressing ideas are grounded in white peoples' lives and experiences, and that these experiences and patterns are routinely falsely characterized as universally human and good.

Despite the overwhelming impact of race on social reality in the United States, and the fact that some of the most important antiracist thinkers of the twentieth century had training in philosophy (e.g., W. E. B. DuBois, Alain Locke, Angela Davis, and Cornel West), until very recently the discipline, outside of applied ethics, has given extremely little attention to questions of race. In its quest for certainty, Western philosophy continues to generate what it imagines to be colorless and genderless explanations and conceptual frameworks, leaving questions of race to social scientists, historians, and literary theorists. Although feminist work on race and racism has increased dramatically over the past thirty years, feminist philosophers have also contributed their share to "white solipsism": Adrienne Rich's term for the tendency "to think, imagine and speak as if whiteness described the world."[1] Feminist philosophers continue to cling to traditional analytic approaches that favor coherence, orderly arguments, and conceptual abstractions over approaches that are grounded in women's diverse experiences.

Race remains inevitably present in philosophical inquiry: it shapes the puzzles philosophers are keen on solving, the problems they find pressing, and the very structure and language of inquiry. The fact that so many philosophers have theorized as if bodies don't matter, or as if human experience were homogenous, is surely a marker of privilege. In fact, many of the racist comments and observations made by key figures in philosophy have been typically characterized as distracting asides, rather than as important sites for engagement. As a case in point, the entry on John Locke in *The Encyclopedia of Philosophy* suggests that instead of treating the contradictions between Locke's political ideals about freedom and his views on slavery as philosophically important or interesting, it is recommended that

his comments be "mercifully passed over" by readers.[2]

Regarding the importance of race, racism, and the experiences of women of color in feminist theorizing, the terrain began to shift in the early 1980s, due in part to the publication of several landmark collections: Gloría Anzaldúa and Cherríe Moraga's *This Bridge Called My Back: Radical Writings by Women of Color* (1981), Barbara Smith's collection *Home Girls: A Black Feminist Anthology* (1983), and *All the Women Are White, All the Blacks Are Men, But Some of Us Are Brave* (1982), edited by Gloria T. Hull, Patricia Bell Scott, and Barbara Smith. Among others, these books brought the perspectives and scholarly contributions of women of color to the fore, and challenged white feminists to question their assumptions that all women share a common experience of sexual difference, onto which race and class can be layered. Elizabeth Spelman's *Inessential Woman* (1988) is an early effort to identify, make visible, and correct that assumption regarding race. Her essay "Gender and Race: The Ampersand Problem in Feminist Thought" addresses a crucial flaw in white feminist thinking: the idea that race, gender, and class are conceptually separable units that can be pulled apart and reconnected like the beads of a pop-bead necklace. Using textual examples from white feminists' work, Spelman illustrates how additive analyses undermine philosophical understandings of how race/racism, and sex/sexism are deeply enmeshed.

False simplistic ideas about race and gender create more than conceptual damage—they can shape feminist policies in ways that continue to harm women of color. Kimberlé Crenshaw's essay provides a clear example of how to avoid white solipsism and pop-bead thinking in ways that are attentive to nonwhite women's experiences. Using the example of domestic violence,

---

[1] Rich, Adrienne. Disloyal to civilization: Feminism, racism, gynephobia. In *On lies, secrets and silence.* New York: Norton, 1979, 299.

[2] Clapp, James Gordon. John Locke. *Encyclopedia of philosophy*, vol. IV. New York: MacMillan Publishing Company, Inc., 1967, 499.

she explains how social services have presupposed a similarity among women's lives, and how existing services are easily gerrymandered in an attempt to accommodate the needs of women of color, immigrants, and poor women. Instead, she argues, services should be reformed in light of empirical studies that identify the ways domestic violence services in particular either help or harm women seeking shelter. Crenshaw's notion of "intersectionality" replaces the additive analysis criticized by Spelman, and provides a more accurate description of the multiple ways women experience domestic violence.

Thinking at the intersections presupposes that we know just what it means to have a race; for this reason philosophers need to examine race as an ontological category. As is clearly stated in the American Anthropological Association's "Statement on 'Race,'" scientists attentive to cultural history and diversity have long recognized that races are socially constructed: that is, races are politically, legally, and culturally real, and not biological natural kinds. This means that finding answers to our political questions will require both empirical studies of women's lives and metaphysical investigations into the nature of race and how it connects with gender as a form of identity. One important philosophical question along these lines addresses the relation between the social construction of race and purity.

In the United States nearly everyone is aware of the "one-drop rule," or the idea that any amount of African-American ancestry "makes" a person black. This cultural and legal marker is contained by white anxiety about racial purity. In "Purity, Impurity, and Separation," María Lugones carefully spells out the connections between the logic of purity and the politics of domination underlying in racism and colonialism. Her discussion gives us a deeper understanding of the problematic "pop-bead" metaphysics Spelman describes. People who struggle daily against multiple oppressions frequently describe themselves as being torn between two or more identities, or as having multiple personalities. For example,

Native American feminists can be in tribal solidarity with men of their nation while working against colonialism, but may find themselves at odds with one another on gender issues. Oppression makes it difficult to see all facets of our identity at once. Purity obfuscates multiplicity though "split-separation" which either homogenizes identities into fictitious emulsified wholes, or creates the experience of fragmentation. Resistance and transformation, Lugones concludes, require making multiplicity visible by embracing more "curdled logics."

Racial categories based on the logic of purity continue to have a horrifying impact on indigenous communities. In her essay "Some Kind of Indian," M. Annette Jaimes explains how European racial schemas have given rise to "blood quantum" policies that define tribal membership in ways that are divisive to indigenous solidarity and conflict with tribal notions of membership based on elaborate kinship systems. Jaimes uses historical examples to demonstrate how colonial constructions of native identity have been used to cheat indigenous people out of their lands, regulate native populations, limit fishing quotas and water rights, and restrict who counts as Native artisans.

Women of color have always been attentive to the ways unearned advantages accompanying white privilege come at their expense. Making privilege visible to whites raises important questions about the political contributions privileged subjects can make to discussions of oppression and resistance. In "Locating Traitorous Identities: Toward a View of Privilege-Cognizant White Character," Alison Bailey explores what it might mean to be a "race traitor," that is, a member of a privileged group who is unfaithful to the worldviews she or he is expected to hold (e.g., male feminists, white antiracists). Using Sandra Harding's account of traitorous identities, Bailey offers an alternative characterization of traitors as privilege-cognizant whites who refuse to animate the scripts they are expected to perform. Blending Aristotle's account of character formation and María Lugones's concept of world-traveling, she articulates a notion of "traitorous scripts" and explains how animating them helps to cultivate and maintain a traitorous character that is useful for antiracist projects.

Still, white feminists' philosophical attention to racism often takes place in safe theoretical spaces where whiteness is centered, and as a result these conversations sometimes fail to challenge directly the irreconcilable material differences between white women and women of color. Aileen Moreton-Robinson shows how indigenous women have challenged white feminist authority in Australia by bringing different methods and priorities to political work, such as an emphasis on cultural integrity, self-determination, land rights, and services. She holds that white Australian feminists cannot ignore existing power relations between themselves and Indigenous feminists, and structural relations between white and Indigenous societies. White women benefit from histories of colonization and continuing neocolonial relations. Therefore, white women must relinquish power, including their power in feminist movements, and give more attention to those who are most in need, and most harmed by the legacies of colonialism.

GENDER & RACE: THE AMPERSAND PROBLEM IN FEMINIST THOUGHT

Elizabeth V. Spelman

You don't really want Black folks, you are just looking for yourself with a little color to it.
—BERNICE JOHNSON REAGON

As a discussion of gender and gender relations is really, even if obscurely, about a particular group of women and their relation to a particular group of men, it is unlikely to be applicable to any other group of women. At the same time, the particular race and class identity of those referred to simply as "women" becomes explicit when we see the inapplicability of statements about "women" to women who are not of that race or class.

Some of these points are illustrated tellingly in an article in the *New York Times* about how "women and Blacks" have fared in the U.S. military.[1] The author of the article does not discuss women who are Black or Blacks who are women. Indeed, it is clear that the "women" referred to are white, the "Blacks" referred to are male, even though, in a chart comparing the numbers and the placement of "women" and "Blacks," a small note appears telling the reader that Black women are included in the category "Blacks."[2] There are several things to note about the sexual and racial ontology of the article. The racial identity of those identified as "women" does not become explicit until reference is made to Black women, at which point it also becomes clear that the category "women" excludes Black women. In the contrast between "women" and "Blacks" the usual contrast between "men" and "women" is dropped, even though the distinction is in effect between a group of men and a group of women. But the men in question are not called men. They are called "Blacks."

It is not easy to think about gender, race, and class in ways that don't obscure or underplay their effects on one another. The crucial question

is how the links between them are conceived. So, for example, we see that de Beauvoir tends to talk about comparisons between sex and race, or between sex and class, or between sex and culture; she describes what she takes to be comparisons between sexism and racism, between sexism and classism, between sexism and anti-Semitism. In the work of Chodorow and others influenced by her, we observe a readiness to look for links between sexism and other forms of oppression depicted as distinct from sexism. In both examples, we find an additive analysis of the various elements of identity and of various forms of oppression: there's sex *and* race *and* class; there's sexism *and* racism *and* classism. In both examples, attempts to bring in elements of identity other than gender, to bring in kinds of oppression other than sexism, still have the effect of obscuring the racial and class identity of those described as "women," still make it hard to see how women not of a particular race and class can be included in the description.

In this essay we shall examine in more detail how additive analyses of identity and of oppression can work against an understanding of the relations between gender and other elements of identity, between sexism and other forms of oppression. In particular we will see how some very interesting and important attempts to link sexism and racism themselves reflect and perpetuate racism. Ironically, the categories and methods we may find most natural and straightforward to use as we explore the connections between sex and race, sexism and racism, confuse those connections rather than clarify them.

As has often been pointed out, what have been called the first and second waves of the women's movement in the United States followed closely on the heels of women's involvement in the nineteenth-century abolitionist movement and the twentieth-century civil rights movement. In both centuries, challenges to North American racism served as an impetus to, and model for, the feminist attack on sexist institutions, practices, and ideology. But this is not to say that all antiracists were antisexists, or that all antisexists were antiracists. Indeed, many abolitionists of the nineteenth century and civil rights workers of the twentieth did not take sexism seriously, and we continue to learn about the sad, bitter, and confusing history of women who in fighting hard for feminist ends did not take racism seriously.[3]

Recent feminist theory has not totally ignored white racism, though white feminists have paid much less attention to it than have Black feminists. Much of feminist theory has reflected and contributed to what Adrienne Rich has called "white solipsism": the tendency "to think, imagine, and speak as if whiteness described the world."[4] While solipsism is "not the consciously held belief that one race is inherently superior to all others, it is a tunnel-vision which simply does not see nonwhite experience or existence as precious or significant, unless in spasmodic, impotent guilt-reflexes, which have little or no long-term, continuing momentum or political usefulness."[5]

In this essay I shall focus on what I take to be instances and sustaining sources of this tendency in recent theoretical works by, or of interest to, feminists. In particular, I examine certain ways of comparing sexism and racism in the United States, as well as habits of thought about the source of women's oppression and the possibility of our liberation. I hope that exposing some of the symptoms of white solipsism—especially in places where we might least expect to find them—will help to eliminate tunnel vision and to widen the descriptive and explanatory scope of feminist theory. Perhaps we might hasten the day when it will no longer be necessary for anyone to have to say, as Audre Lorde has, "How difficult and time-consuming it is to have to reinvent the pencil every time you want to send a message."[6]

I shall not explicitly be examining class and classism, though at a number of points I suggest ways in which considerations of class and classism affect the topic at hand. Many of the questions I raise about comparisons between sexism and racism could also be raised about comparison between sexism and classism or racism and classism.

I

It is perhaps inevitable that comparisons of sexism and racism include, and often culminate in, questions about which form of oppression is more "fundamental."[7] Whether or not one believes that this way of thinking will bear any strategic or theoretic fruit, such comparisons have come to inform analyses of the nature of sexism and the nature of racism. To begin, I will examine some recent claims that sexism is more fundamental than racism, a highly ambiguous argument. In many instances the evidence offered in support turns out to refute the claim; and this way of comparing sexism and racism often presupposes the nonexistence of Black women, insofar as neither the description of sexism nor that of racism seems to apply to them. This is a bitter irony indeed, since Black women are the victims of both sexism and racism.

We need to ask first what "more fundamental" means in a comparison of racism and sexism. It has meant or might mean several different though related things:[8]

It is harder to eradicate sexism than it is to eradicate racism.

There might be sexism without racism but not racism without sexism: any social and political changes that eradicate sexism will eradicate racism, but social and political changes that eradicate racism will not eradicate sexism.

Sexism is the first form of oppression learned by children.

Sexism predates racism.

Sexism is the cause of racism.

Sexism is used to justify racism.

Sexism is the model for racism.

We can trace these arguments in the work of two important feminist theorists: Kate Millett in

Sexual Politics and Shulamith Firestone in *The Dialectic of Sex.* It is worth remembering that these authors did not ignore race and racism. But their treatments of the subjects enable us to see that as long as race is taken to be independent of sex, racism as independent of sexism, we are bound to give seriously misleading descriptions of gender and gender relations.

In *Sexual Politics,* Kate Millett seems to hold that sexism is more fundamental than racism in three senses: it is "sturdier" than racism and so presumably is harder to eradicate; it has a more "pervasive ideology" than racism, and so those who are not racists may nevertheless embrace sexist beliefs; and it provides our culture's "most fundamental concept of power."[9] But as Margaret Simons has pointed out, Millett ignores the fact that Black women and other women of color do not usually describe their own lives as ones in which they experience sexism as more fundamental than racism.[10] There is indeed something very peculiar about the evidence Millett offers in behalf of her view that sexism is the more endemic oppression.

On the one hand, she states that everywhere men have power over women. On the other hand, she notes with interest that some observers have described as an effect of racism that Black men do not have such power over Black women, and that only when racism is eradicated will Black men assume their proper position of superiority. She goes on to argue that "the military, industry, technology, universities, science, political office, and finance—in short, every avenue of power within the society, including the coercive force of the police, is entirely in male hands."[11] But surely that is white male supremacy. Since when did Black males have such institutionally based power, in what Millett calls "our culture"? She thus correctly describes as sexist the hope that Black men could assume their "proper authority" over Black women, but her claim about the pervasiveness of sexism is belied by her reference to the lack of authority of Black males.

There is no doubt that Millett is right to view as sexist the hope that racial equity will

be established when Black males have authority over Black females, but it also is correct to describe as racist the hope—not uncommonly found in feminist arguments—that sexual equity will be established when women can be presidents or heads of business. That is no guarantee that they will not be running racist countries and corporations. As Elizabeth F. Hood said: "Many white women define liberation as the access to those thrones traditionally occupied by white men—positions in the kingdoms which support racism."[12] Of course, one might insist that any truly antisexist vision also is an antiracist vision, for it requires the elimination of all forms of oppression against all women, white or Black.[13] But, similarly, it can be said that any truly antiracist vision would have to be antisexist, for it requires the elimination of all forms of oppression against all Blacks and other people of color, women or men.

In arguing for the position in *The Dialectic of Sex* that racism is "extended sexism," Shulamith Firestone provides another variation on the view that sexism is more fundamental:

> Racism is sexism extended. . . . Let us look at race relations in America, a macrocosm of the hierarchical relations within the nuclear family: the white man is father, the white woman wife-and-mother, her status dependent on his; the blacks, like children, are his property, their physical differentiation branding them the subservient class, in the same way that children form so easily distinguishable a servile class vis-à-vis adults. The power hierarchy creates the psychology of racism, just as, in the nuclear family, it creates the psychology of sexism.[14]

It is clear that Firestone sees sexism as the model for racism; as the cause of racism, so that racism cannot disappear unless sexism does; and as the historical precursor of racism. Moreover, with this model she sees the goal of the Black man (male child) to be to usurp the power of the white man (father), which means that the restoration of the authority of the Black man will involve his domination of women.[15] Hence sexism according to Firestone is more fundamental than racism, in the sense that the eradication of racism is portrayed as compatible with the continuation of sexism.

Here, as in the case of Millett, the evidence Firestone offers actually undermines her claim. First of all, she points out, and her analogy to the family requires, that the Black man is not really "the *real* man."[16] However much the Black man tries to act like the white man, and however much his treatment of Black women resembles the white man's treatment of white women and Black women, he isn't really The Man. Now if this is so, it seems odd to claim that sexism is more fundamental than racism, since according to Firestone's own account the Black man's identity as a man is obscured or erased by his identity as a Black. Thus according to her own account, the racial identity of being an inferior assigned him by racists is more fundamental than the sexual identity of being a superior assigned him by sexists.

Firestone also claims that "the All-American Family is predicated on the existence of the black ghetto whorehouse. The rape of the black community in America makes possible the existence of the family structure of the larger white community."[17] But to say in these ways that racism makes sexism possible is to say that in the absence of racism, sexism could not exist—surely just the opposite of the claim that sexism is more fundamental than racism, the claim Firestone wishes to establish.

II

If Millett's and Firestone's accounts tend to ignore facts about the status of Black men, other similar accounts ignore the existence of Black women. In the process of comparing racism and sexism, Richard Wasserstrom describes the ways in which women and Blacks have been stereotypically conceived of as less fully developed than white men: In the United States, "men and women are taught to see men as independent, capable, and powerful; men and women are taught to see women as dependent, limited in abilities, and passive."[18] But who is taught to see Black men as "independent, capable, and powerful," and by whom are they taught? Are Black men taught that? Black women? White men? White women? Similarly, who is taught to see Black women as "dependent, limited in abilities, and passive"? If this stereotype is so prevalent, why then have Black women had to defend themselves against the images of matriarch and whore?

Wasserstrom continues:

> As is true for race, it is also a significant social fact that to be a female is to be an entity or creature viewed as different from the standard, fully developed person who is male as well as white. But to be female, as opposed to being black, is not to be conceived of as simply a creature of less worth. That is one important thing that differentiates sexism from racism: the ideology of sex, as opposed to the ideology of race, is a good deal more complex and confusing. Women are both put on a pedestal and deemed not fully developed persons.[19]

He leaves no room for the Black woman. For a Black woman cannot be "female, as opposed to being Black"; she is female *and* Black. Since Wasserstrom's argument proceeds from the assumption that one is either female or Black, it cannot be an argument that applies to Black women. Moreover, we cannot generate a composite image of the Black women from Wasserstrom's argument, since the description of women as being put on a pedestal, or being dependent, never generally applied to Black women in the United States and was never meant to apply to them.

Wasserstrom's argument about the priority of sexism over racism has an odd result, which stems from the erasure of Black women in his analysis. He wishes to claim that in this society sex is a more fundamental fact about people than race. Yet his description of women does not apply to the Black woman, which implies that being Black is a more fundamental fact about her than being a woman and hence that her sex is not a more fundamental fact about her than her race. I am not saying that Wasserstrom actually believes this is true, but that paradoxically the terms of his theory force him into that position. If the terms of one's theory require that a person is either female or Black, clearly there is no room to describe someone who is both.

A similar erasure of the Black woman, through failure to note how sexist stereotypes are influenced by racist ones, is found in Laurence Thomas's comparison of sexism and racism.[20] Like Wasserstrom, Thomas believes that sexism is more deeply ingrained in our culture. Racist attitudes, he says, are easier to give up than sexist ones for two reasons: First, "sexism, unlike racism, readily lends itself to a morally unobjectionable description," and second, "the positive self-concept of men has been more centrally tied to their being sexists than has been the positive self-concept of whites to their being racists."[21]

Thomas argues that it is not morally objectionable that "a natural outcome of a sexist conception of women" is the role of men as benefactors of women—part of men's role vis-à-vis women is to "protect women and to provide them with the comforts of life."[22] But at best, Thomas's claim about the man's role as benefactor of woman only applies to men and women of the same race (and probably of the same class). It is of course difficult to explain how claims about roles are established, but the history of race relations in the United States surely makes ludicrous the idea that the role of white men is to be the benefactors of Black women—to "protect" them and to "provide them with the comforts of life." This neither describes what white men have done, nor what they have been told they ought to have done, with respect to Black women.

Thomas's description of sexism in relations between women and men leaves out the reality of racism in relations between Blacks and whites. If he wishes to insist that his analysis was only meant to apply to same-race sexual relations, then he cannot continue to speak unqualifiedly about relations between men and women. My point is not that Black men cannot in any way be sexist to white or to Black women, for indeed they can, just as white women can be racist to Black men or to Black women. My point, rather, is that a theory of sexism that describes men's and women's roles can itself reflect the racist society in which it develops, insofar as it is based on an erasure of the realities of white racism.

Thomas also holds that sexism is more central to the positive self-concept of men than racism has been to the positive self-concept of whites. He claims that, although being benefactors of women is essential to men's self-esteem as "real" men, for whites it is not necessary to own slaves or to hate Blacks in order to be "really" white.[23] Once again, we have to see what happens to Thomas's claim when we put "Black" or "white" in front of "men" or "women" in his formula: "For white men, being benefactors of Black women is essential to their self-esteem as 'real' men." That is false. Indeed, in a racist society, white men's self-esteem requires the opposite position and attitude toward Black women.

Reflection on this leads to doubts about the second part of Thomas's claim—that whites don't have to be racists in order to be "really" white. Does he mean to say that in our society a white man feels no threat to his self-esteem if a Black man gets the job for which they both are candidates? That a white man feels no threat to his self-esteem if a Black man marries the white woman the white man is hoping to marry? That a white man feels no threat to his self-esteem if he lives in a neighborhood with Blacks? Certainly not all white men's self-esteem is so threatened. But this is a racist society, and generally, the self-esteem of white people is deeply influenced by their difference from and supposed superiority to Black people.[24] Those of us who are white may not think of ourselves as racists, because we do not own slaves or hate Blacks, but that does not mean that much of what props up our sense of self is not based on the racism that unfairly distributes benefits and burdens to whites and Blacks.

For example, think for a moment about a case of self-esteem that seems on the surface most unlikely to be supported by racism: the self-esteem that might be thought to attend sincere and serious philosophical reflection on the problems of racism. How could this be said to be based on racism, especially if the philosopher is trying to eliminate racism? As the editors of the *Philosophical Forum* in an issue on philosophy and the Black experience pointed out, "Black people have to a disproportionate extent supplied the labor which has made possible the cultivation of philosophical inquiry."[25] A disproportionate amount of the labor that makes it possible for some people to have philosophy as a profession has been done by Blacks and others under conditions that can only be described as racist. If the connection between philosophy and racism is not very visible, that invisibility itself is a product of racism. Any feminist would recognize a similar point about sexism: it is only in footnotes and prefaces that we see a visible connection made between a man's satisfaction in having finished an article or book and a woman's having made that completion possible.[26]

At several points early in his essay, Thomas says that he is going to consider the "way in which sexism and racism each conceives of its object: woman and Blacks, respectively."[27] But there are many difficulties in talking about sexism and racism in this way, some of which we have noted, and others to which we now turn.

III

First of all, sexism and racism do not have different "objects" in the case of Black women. It is highly misleading to say, without further explanation, that Black women experience "sexism and racism." For to say merely that suggests that Black women experience one form of oppression, as Blacks (the same thing Black men experience) and that they experience another form of oppression, as women (the same thing white women experience). While it is true that images and institutions that are described as sexist affect both Black and white women,

they are affected in different ways, depending upon the extent to which they are affected by other forms of oppression. Thus, as noted earlier, it will not do to say that women are oppressed by the image of the "feminine" woman as fair, delicate, and in need of support and protection by men. As Linda Brent succinctly puts it, "That which commands admiration in the white woman only hastens the degradation of the female slave."[28] More specifically, as Angela Davis reminds us, "the alleged benefits of the ideology of femininity did not accrue" to the Black female slave—she was expected to toil in the fields for just as long and hard as the Black male was.[29]

Reflection on the experience of Black women also shows that it is not as if one form of oppression is merely piled upon another. As Barbara Smith has remarked, the effect of multiple oppression "is not merely arithmetic."[30] This additive method informs Gerda Lerner's analysis of the oppression of Black women under slavery: "Their work and duties were the same as that of the men, while childbearing and rearing fell upon them as an added burden."[31] But as Angela Davis has pointed out, the mother/housewife role (even the words seem inappropriate) doesn't have the same meaning for women who experience racism as it does for those who are not so oppressed:

> In the infinite anguish of ministering to the needs of the men and children around her (who were not necessarily members of her immediate family), she was performing the only labor of the slave community which could not be directly and immediately claimed by the oppressor.[32]

The meaning and the oppressive nature of the "housewife" role has to be understood in relation to the roles against which it is contrasted. The work of mate/mother/nurturer has a different meaning depending on whether it is contrasted to work that has high social value and ensures economic independence or to labor that is forced, degrading, and unpaid. All of these factors are left out in a simple additive analysis. How one form of oppression is experienced is influenced by and influences how another form is experienced. An additive analysis treats the oppression of a Black woman in a society that is racist as well as sexist as if it were a further burden when, in fact, it is a different burden. As the work of Davis, among others, shows, to ignore the difference is to deny the particular reality of the Black woman's experience.

If sexism and racism must be seen as interlocking, and not as piled upon each other, serious problems arise for the claim that one of them is more fundamental than the other. As we saw, one meaning of the claim that sexism is more fundamental than racism is that sexism causes racism: racism would not exist if sexism did not, while sexism could and would continue to exist even in the absence of racism. In this connection, racism is sometimes seen as something that is both derivative from sexism and in the service of it: racism keeps women from uniting in alliance against sexism. This view has been articulated by Mary Daly in *Beyond God the Father*. According to Daly, sexism is the "root and paradigm" of other forms or oppression such as racism. Racism is a "deformity *within* patriarchy…. It is most unlikely that racism will be eradicated as long as sexism prevails."[33]

Daly's theory relies on an additive analysis, and we can see again why such an analysis fails to describe adequately Black women's experience. Daly's analysis makes it look simply as if both Black women and white women experience sexism, while Black women also experience racism. Black women, Daly says, must come to see what they have in common with white women—shared sexist oppression—and see that they are all "pawns in the racial struggle, which is basically not the struggle that will set them free as women."[34] But insofar as she is oppressed by racism in a sexist context and sexism in a racist context, the Black woman's struggle cannot be compartmentalized into two struggles—one as a Black and one as a woman.

Indeed, it is difficult to imagine why a Black woman would think of her struggles this way except in the face of demands by white women or by Black men that she do so. This way of speaking about her struggle is required by a theory that insists not only that sexism and racism are distinct but that one might be eradicated before the other. Daly rightly points out that the Black woman's struggle can easily be, and has usually been, subordinated to the Black man's struggle in antiracist organizations. But she does not point out that the Black woman's struggle can easily be, and usually has been, subordinated to the white woman's struggle in antisexist organizations.

Daly's line of thought also promotes the idea that, were it not for racism, there would be no important differences between Black and white women. Since, according to her view, sexism is the fundamental form of oppression and racism works in its service, the only significant differences between Black and white women are differences that men (Daly doesn't say whether she means white men or Black men or both) have created and that are the source of antagonism between women. What is really crucial about us is our sex; racial distinctions are one of the many products of sexism, of patriarchy's attempt to keep women from uniting. According to Daly, then, it is through our shared sexual identity that we are oppressed together; it is through our shared sexual identity that we shall be liberated together.

This view not only ignores the role women play in racism and classism, but it seems to deny the positive aspects of racial identities. It ignores the fact that being Black is a source of pride, as well as an occasion for being oppressed. It suggests that once racism is eliminated, Black women no longer need be concerned about or interested in their Blackness—as if the only reason for paying attention to one's Blackness is that it is the source of pain and sorrow and agony. The assumption that there is nothing positive about having a Black history and identity is racism pure and simple. Recall the lines of Nikki Giovanni:

> and I really hope no white person ever has cause to write about me
>
> because they never understand Black love is Black wealth and they'll
>
> probably talk about my hard childhood
>
> and never understand that
>
> all the while I was quite happy.[35]

Or recall the chagrin of the central character in Paule Marshall's story "Reena," when she discovered that her white boyfriend could only see her Blackness in terms of her suffering and not as something compatible with taking joy and pleasure in life.[36] I think it is helpful too in this connection to remember the opening lines of Pat Parker's "For the white person who wants to know how to be my friend":

> The first thing you do is to forget that i'm Black.
> Second, you must never forget that i'm Black.[37]

Perhaps it does not occur to feminists who are white that celebrating being white has anything to do with our celebrating being women. But that may be so because celebrating being white is already taken care of by the predominantly white culture in which we live in North America. Certainly feminist theory and activity on the whole have recognized that it is possible, if difficult, to celebrate being a woman without at the same time conceiving of woman in terms of the sexist imagery and lore of the centuries. (That celebrating womanhood is a tricky business we know from the insidiousness of the "two-sphere" ideology of the nineteenth century and of the image of the "total woman"—in Daly's wonderful phrase, the "totaled woman"—of the twentieth century: as if by celebrating what men tell us we are, the burden magically disappears because we embrace it.) But just as it is possible and desirable to identify oneself as a woman and yet think of and describe oneself in ways that are not sexist, so it is possible and desirable to

identify oneself as a Black woman and yet think of oneself in ways that are not racist.

In sum, according to an additive analysis of sexism and racism, all women are oppressed by sexism; some women are further oppressed by racism. Such an analysis distorts Black women's experiences of oppression by failing to note important differences between the contexts in which Black women and white women experience sexism. The additive analysis also suggests that a woman's racial identity can be "subtracted" from her combined sexual and racial identity: "We are all women." But this does not leave room for the fact that different women may look to different forms of liberation just because they are white or Black women, rich or poor women, Catholic or Jewish women.

IV

Feminist leaders such as Elizabeth Cady Stanton used racist arguments in pleas to better the condition of "women." Though such blatant racism is not as likely to appear in contemporary feminism, that doesn't mean that visions of a nonsexist world will also be visions of a nonracist world. In the rest of the essay I will explore how some ways of conceiving women's oppression and liberation contribute to the white solipsism of feminist theory.

Feminist theorists as politically diverse as Simone de Beauvoir, Betty Friedan, and Shulamith Firestone have described the conditions of women's liberation in terms that suggest that the identification of woman with her body has been the source of our oppression, and hence that the source of our liberation lies in sundering that connection.[38] For example, de Beauvoir introduces *The Second Sex* with the comment that woman has been regarded as "womb"; and she later observes that woman is thought of as planted firmly in the world of "immanence," that is, the physical world of nature, her life defined by the dictates of her "biologic fate."[39] In contrast, men live in the world of "transcendence," actively using their minds to create "values, mores, religions.[40] Theirs is the world of culture as opposed to the world of nature. Among Friedan's central messages is that women should be allowed and encouraged to be "culturally" as well as "biologically" creative, because the former activities, in contrast to childbearing and rearing, are "mental" and are of "highest value to society"—"mastering the secrets of atoms, or the stars, composing symphonies, pioneering a new concept in government or society."[41]

This view comes out especially clearly in Firestone's work. According to her, the biological difference between women and men is at the root of women's oppression. It is woman's body—in particular, our body's capacity to bear children—that makes, or makes possible, the oppression of women by men. Hence we must disassociate ourselves from our bodies—most radically—by making it possible, or even necessary, to conceive and bear children outside the womb, and by otherwise generally disassociating our lives from the thankless tasks associated with the body.[42]

In predicating women's liberation on a disassociation from our bodies, Firestone oddly enough joins the chorus of male voices that has told us over the centuries about the disappointments entailed in being embodied creatures. What might be called "somatophobia" (fear of and disdain for the body) is part of a centuries-long tradition in Western culture. As de Beauvoir so thoroughly described in *The Second Sex,* the responsibility for being embodied creatures has been assigned to women: we have been associated, indeed virtually identified, with the body; men (or some men) have been associated and virtually identified with the mind. Women have been portrayed as possessing bodies in a way men have not. It is as if women essentially, men only accidentally, have bodies. It seems to me that Firestone's (as well as Friedan's and de Beauvoir's) prescription for women's liberation does not challenge the negative attitude toward the body; it only hopes to end the association between the body, so negatively characterized, and women.

I think the somatophobia we see in the work of Firestone and others is a force that contributes

to white solipsism in feminist thought, in at least three related ways. First, insofar as feminists ignore, or indeed accept, negative views of the body in prescriptions for women's liberation, we will also ignore an important element in racist thinking. For the superiority of men to women (or, as we have seen, of some men to some women) is not the only hierarchical relationship that has been linked to the superiority of the mind to the body. Certain kinds, or "races," of people have been held to be more body-like than others, and this has meant that they are perceived as more animal-like and less god-like. For example, in *The White Man's Burden,* Winthrop Jordan describes ways in which white Englishmen portrayed black Africans as beastly, dirty, highly sexual beings.[43] Lillian Smith tells us in *Killers of the Dream* how closely run together were her lessons about the evil of the body and the evil of Blacks.[44]

We need to examine and understand somatophobia and look for it in our own thinking, for the idea that the work of the body and for the body has no part in real human dignity has been part of racist as well as sexist ideology. That is, oppressive stereotypes of "inferior races" and of women (notice that even in order to make the point in this way, we leave up in the air the question of how we shall refer to those who belong to both categories) have typically involved images of their lives as determined by basic bodily functions (sex, reproduction, appetite, secretions, and excretions) and as given over to attending to the bodily functions of others (feeding, washing, cleaning, doing the "dirty work"). Superior groups, we have been told from Plato on down, have better things to do with their lives. It certainly does not follow from the presence of somatophobia in a person's writings that she or he is a racist or a sexist. But disdain for the body historically has been symptomatic of sexist and racist (as well as classist) attitudes.

Human groups know that the work of the body and for the body is necessary for human existence, and they make provisions for that necessity. Thus even when a group views its liberation in terms of being free of association with, or responsibility for, bodily tasks, its own liberation is likely to be predicated on the oppression of other groups—those assigned to do the body's work. For example, if feminists decide that women are not going to be relegated to doing such work, who do we think is going to do it? Have we attended to the role that racism and classism historically have played in settling that question? We may recall why Plato and Aristotle thought philosophers and citizens needed leisure from this kind of work and who they thought ought to do it.

Finally, if one thinks—as de Beauvoir, Friedan, and Firestone do—that the liberation of women requires abstracting the notion of woman from the notion of woman's body, then one might logically think that the liberation of Blacks requires abstracting the notion of a Black person from the notion of a black body. Since the body, or at least certain of its aspects, may be thought to be the culprit, the solution may seem to be: Keep the person and leave the occasion for oppression behind. Keep the woman, somehow, but leave behind her woman's body; keep the Black person but leave the Blackness behind. Once one attempts to stop thinking about oneself in terms of having a body, then one not only will stop thinking in terms of characteristics such as womb and breast, but also will stop thinking in terms of skin and hair. We would expect to find that any feminist theory based in part on a disembodied view of human identity would regard blackness (or any other physical characteristic that may serve as a centering post for one's identity) as of temporary and negative importance.

Once the concept of woman is divorced from the concept of woman's body, conceptual room is made for the idea of a woman who is no particular historical woman—she has no color, no accent, no particular characteristics that require having a body. She is somehow all and only woman; that is her only identifying feature. And so it will seem inappropriate or beside the point to think of women in terms of any physical characteristics,

especially if their oppression has been rationalized by reference to those characteristics.

None of this is to say that the historical and cultural identity of being Black or white is the same thing as, or is reducible to, the physical feature of having black or white skin. Historical and cultural identity is not constituted by having a body with particular identifying features, but it cannot be comprehended without such features and the significance attached to them.

V

Adrienne Rich was perhaps the first well-known contemporary white feminist to have noted "white solipsism" in feminist theorizing and activity. I think it is no coincidence that she also noticed and attended to the strong strain of somatophobia in feminist theory. *Of Woman Born* updates the connection between somatophobia and misogyny/gynephobia that Simone de Beauvoir described at length in *The Second Sex.*[45] But unlike de Beauvoir or Firestone, Rich refuses to throw out the baby with the bathwater: she sees that the historical negative connection between woman and body (in particular, between woman and womb) can be broken in more than one way. Both de Beauvoir and Firestone wanted to break it by insisting that women need be no more connected—in thought or deed—with the body than men have been. In their view of embodiment as a liability, de Beauvoir and Firestone are in virtual agreement with the patriarchal cultural history they otherwise question. Rich, however, insists that the negative connection between woman and body be broken along other lines. She asks us to think about whether what she calls "flesh-loathing" is the only attitude it is possible to have toward our bodies. Just as she explicitly distinguishes between motherhood as experience and motherhood as institution, so she implicitly asks us to distinguish between embodiment as experience and embodiment as institution. Flesh-loathing is part of the well-entrenched beliefs, habits, and practices epitomized in the treatment of pregnancy as a disease. But we need not experience our flesh, our body, as loathsome.

I think it is not a psychological or historical accident that having examined the way women view their bodies, Rich also focused on the failure of white women to see Black women's experiences as different from their own. For looking at embodiment is one way (though not the only one) of coming to recognize and understand the particularity of experience. Without bodies we could not have personal histories. Nor could we be identified as woman or man, Black or white. This is not to say that reference to publicly observable bodily characteristics settles the question of whether someone is woman or man, Black or white; nor is it to say that being woman or man, Black or white, just means having certain bodily characteristics (that is one reason some Blacks want to capitalize the term; "Black" refers to a cultural identity, not simply a skin color). But different meanings are attached to having certain characteristics, in different places and at different times and by different people, and those differences affect enormously the kinds of lives we lead or experiences we have. Women's oppression has been linked to the meanings assigned to having a woman's body by male oppressors. Blacks' oppression has been linked to the meanings assigned to having a black body by white oppressors. (Note how insidiously this way of speaking once again leaves unmentioned the situation for Black women.) We cannot hope to understand the meaning of a person's experiences, including her experiences of oppression, without first thinking of her as embodied, and second thinking about the particular meanings assigned to that embodiment. If, because of somatophobia, we think and write as if we are not embodied, or as if we would be better off if we were not embodied, we are likely to ignore the ways in which different forms of embodiment are correlated with different kinds of experience.

Rich—unlike de Beauvoir—asks us to reflect on the culturally assigned differences between having a Black or a white body, as well as on the differences between having the body of a woman or of a man. Other feminists have reflected on the meaning of embodiment and recognized the connection between flesh-loathing and woman-hatred, but they have only considered it far enough to try to divorce the concept of woman from the concept of the flesh. In effect, they have insisted that having different bodies does not or need not mean men and women are any different as humans; and having said that, they imply that having different colored bodies does not mean that Black women and white women are any different. Such statements are fine if interpreted to mean that the differences between woman and man, Black and white, should not be used against Black women and white women and Black men. But not paying attention to embodiment and to the cultural meanings assigned to different forms of it is to encourage sexblindness and colorblindness. These blindnesses are vicious when they are used to support the idea that all experience is male experience or that all experience is white experience. Rich does not run away from the fact that women have bodies, nor does she wish that women's bodies were not so different from men's. That healthy regard for the ground of our differences from men is logically connected to—though of course does not ensure—a healthy regard for the ground of the differences between Black women and white women.

> "Colorblindness" . . . implies that I would look at a Black woman and see her as white, thus engaging in white solipsism to the utter erasure of her particular reality.[46]

Colorblindness denies the particularity of the Black woman and rules out the possibility both that her history has been different and that her future might be different in any significant way from the white woman's.

VI

I have been discussing the ways in which some aspects of feminist theory exhibit what Adrienne Rich has called "white solipsism." In particular,

I have been examining ways in which some prominent claims about the relation between sexism and racism ignore the realities of racism. I have also suggested that there are ways of thinking about women's oppression and about women's liberation that reflect and encourage white solipsism, but that thinking differently about women and about sexism might lead to thinking differently about Blackness and about racism.

First, we have to continue to reexamine the traditions which reinforce sexism and racism. Though feminist theory has recognized the connection between somatophobia and misogyny/gynephobia, it has tended to challenge the misogyny without challenging the somatophobia, and without fully appreciating the connection between somatophobia and racism.

Second, we have to keep a cautious eye on discussions of racism versus sexism. They keep us from seeing ways in which what sexism means and how it works is modulated by racism, and ways in which what racism means is modulated by sexism. Most important, discussions of sexism versus racism tend to proceed as if Black women—to take one example—do not exist. None of this is to say that sexism and racism are thoroughly and in every context indistinguishable. Certain political and social changes may point to the conclusion that some aspects of racism will disappear sooner than some aspects of sexism (see, for example, the statistics Diane Lewis cites in "A Response to Inequality: Black Women, Racism, and Sexism.")[47] Other changes may point to the conclusion that some aspects of sexism will disappear sooner than some aspects of racism (e.g., scepticism about the possible effects of passage of the ERA on the lives of Black women in the ghetto). And there undoubtedly is disagreement about when certain changes should be seen as making any dent in sexism or racism at all. But as long as Black women and other women of color are at the bottom of the economic heap (which clearly we cannot fully understand in the absence of a class analysis), and as long as our

descriptions of sexism and racism themselves reveal racist and sexist perspectives, it seems both empirically and conceptually premature to make grand claims about whether sexism or racism is "more fundamental." For many reasons, then, it seems wise to proceed very cautiously in this inquiry.

Third, it is crucial to sustain a lively regard for the variety of women's experiences. On the one hand, what unifies women and justifies us in talking about the oppression of women is the overwhelming evidence of the worldwide and historical subordination of women to men. On the other, while it may be possible for us to speak about women in a general way, it also is inevitable that any statement we make about women in some particular place at some particular time is bound to suffer from ethnocentrism if we try to claim for it more generality than it has. So, for example, to say that the image of woman as frail and dependent is oppressive is certainly true. But it is oppressive to white women in the United States in quite a different way than it is oppressive to Black women, for the sexism Black women experience is in the context of their experience of racism. In Toni Morrison's *The Bluest Eye,* the causes and consequences of Pecola's longing to have blue eyes are surely quite different from the causes and consequences of a white girl with brown eyes having a similar desire.[48] More to the point, the consequences of *not* having blue eyes are quite different for the two. Similarly, the family may be the locus of oppression for white middle-class women, but to claim that it is the locus of oppression for all women is to ignore the fact that for Blacks in America the family has been a source of resistance against white oppression.[49]

In short, the claim that all women are oppressed is fully compatible with, and needs to be explicated in terms of, the many varieties of oppression that different populations of women have been subject to. After all, why should oppressors settle for uniform kinds of oppression, when to oppress their victims in many different ways—consciously or unconsciously—makes it more likely that the oppressed groups will not perceive it to be in their interest to work together?

Finally, it is crucial not to see Blackness only as the occasion for oppression—any more than one sees being a woman only as the occasion for oppression. No one ought to expect the forms of our liberation to be any less various than the forms of our oppression. We need to be at least as generous in imagining what women's liberation will be like as our oppressors have been in devising what women's oppression has been.

NOTES

1. Halloran, "Women, Blacks, Spouses Transforming the Military."

2. See also Gloria T. Hull, Patricia Bell Scott, and Barbara Smith, eds., *All the Women Are White, All the Blacks Are Men, But Some of Us Are Brave: Black Women's Studies* (Old Westbury, N.Y.: Feminist Press, 1982).

3. See Eleanor Flexner, *Century of Struggle* (New York: Atheneum, 1972), especially chapter 13, on the inhospitality of white women's organizations to Black women, as well as Aileen S. Kraditor's *The Ideas of the Woman Suffrage Movement, 1890–1920* (Garden City, N.Y.: Doubleday, 1971). See also DuBois, *Feminism and Suffrage;* Sara Evans, *Personal Politics* (New York: Vintage, 1979), on sexism in the civil rights movement; Dorothy Sterling, *Black Foremothers* (Old Westbury, N.Y.: Feminist Press, 1979), 147, on Alice Paul's refusal to grant Mary Church Terrell's request that Paul endorse enforcement of the Nineteenth Amendment for all women; Davis, *Women, Race, and Class;* Bettina Aptheker, *Women's Legacy: Essays on Race, Sex, and Class in American History* (Amherst: University of Massachusetts Press, 1982); Paula Giddings, *When and Where I Enter: The Impact of Black Women on Race and Sex in America* (New York: Morrow, 1984).

4. Adrienne Rich, "Disloyal to Civilization: Feminism, Racism, Gynephobia," in her *On Lies, Secrets, and Silence* (New York: Norton, 1979), 299 and passim. In the philosophical literature, solipsism is the view according to which it is only one's self that is knowable, or it is only one's self that constitutes the world. Strictly speaking, of course, Rich's use of the phrase "white solipsism" is at odds with the idea of there being only the self, insofar as it implies that there are other white people; but she is drawing from the idea of there being only one perspective on the world—not that of one person, but of one "race." (For further comment on the concept of race, see references in note 23 below.)

5. Ibid., 306.

6. Audre Lorde, "Man Child: A Black Lesbian Feminist's Response," *Conditions* 4 (1979): 35. My comments about racism apply to the racism directed against Black people in the United States. I do not claim that all my arguments apply to the racism experienced by other people of color.

7. See Margaret A. Simons, "Racism and Feminism: A Schism in the Sisterhood," *Feminist Studies* 5, no. 2 (1979): 384–401.

8. A somewhat similar list appears in Alison M. Jaggar and Paula Rothenberg's introduction to part 2 of *Feminist Frameworks,* 2d ed. (New York: McGraw-Hill, 1984), 86.

9. Kate Millett, *Sexual Politics* (New York: Ballantine, 1969), 33–34.

10. Simons, "Racism and Feminism."

11. Millett, *Sexual Politics*, 33–34.

12. Elizabeth F. Hood, "Black Women, White Women: Separate Paths to Liberation," *Black Scholar,* April 1978, 47.

13. This is precisely the position we found Richards attacking.

14. Shulamith Firestone, *The Dialectic of Sex* (New York: Bantam, 1970), 108.

15. Ibid., 117–18.

16. Ibid., 115. Emphasis in the original.

17. Ibid., 116.

18. Richard A. Wasserstrom, "Racism and Sexism," in *Philosophy and Women,* ed. Sharon Bishop and Marjorie Weinzweig (Belmont, Cal.: Wadsworth, 1979), 8. Reprinted from "Racism, Sexism, and Preferential Treatment: An

Approach to the Topics," *UCLA Law Review* (February 1977): 581–615.

19. Ibid.

20. Laurence Thomas, "Sexism and Racism: Some Conceptual Differences," *Ethics* 90 (1980): 239–50.

21. I shall here leave aside the question of whether Thomas succeeds in offering a description of sexism that is not of something morally objectionable (see B. C. Postow's reply to Thomas, "Thomas on Sexism," *Ethics* 90 [1980]: 251–56). I shall also leave aside the question of to whom such a description is or is not morally objectionable, as well as the question of how its moral objectionableness is to be measured.

22. Thomas, "Sexism and Racism," 239 and passim.

23. Thomas says that "one very important reason" for this lack of analogy is that racial identity, unlike sexual identity, is "more or less settled by biological considerations" (ibid., 248). If Thomas means by this that there are such things as "races," and that the question of what race one belongs to is settled by biology, one must point out in reply that it is far from clear that this is so. See Ashley Montagu, "The Concept of Race: Part 1," *American Anthropologist* 64, no. 5 (1962), reprinted in *Anthropology: Contemporary Perspectives,* ed. David E. Hunter and Philip Whitten (Boston: Little, Brown, 1975), 83–95; and Frank B. Livingstone, "On the Nonexistence of Human Races," *The Concept of Race*, ed. Ashley Montagu (New York: Collier, 1964), reprinted in Hunter and Whitten. The existence of racism does not require that there are races; it requires the belief that there are races.

24. This is the kind of superiority that de Beauvoir described.

25. *Philosophical Forum,* 9, no. 2–3 (1977–78): 113.

26. See Carol Christ and Judith Plaskow Goldenberg, "For the Advancement of My Career: A Form Critical Study in the Art of Acknowledgement," *Bulletin of the Council for Religious Studies* (June 1972), for a marvelous study of the literary form of the "acknowledgement to the wife." See also the gruesomely delightful "Collecting Scholar's Wives," by Marilyn Hoder-Salmon, in *Feminist Studies* 4, no. 3 (n.d.): 107–14.

27. Thomas, "Sexism and Racism," 242–43.

28. Linda Brent, "The Trials of Girlhood," in *Root of Bitterness,* ed. Nancy F. Cott (New York: Dutton, 1972), 201.

29. Angela Y. Davis, "Reflections on the Black Woman's Role in the Community of Slaves," *Black Scholar* 3 (1971): 7.

30. Barbara Smith, "Notes For Yet Another Paper on Black Feminism, or Will the Real Enemy Please Stand Up," *Conditions* 5 (1979): 123–32. See also "The Combahee River Collective Statement," *Capitalist Patriarchy and the Case for Socialist Feminism,* ed. Zillah Eisenstein (New York: Monthly Review Press, 1979), 362–72.

31. Gerda Lerner, ed., *Black Woman in White America* (New York: Vintage, 1973), 15.

32. Davis, "Reflections on the Black Woman's Role," 7. Davis revises this slightly in *Women, Race, and Class.*

33. Mary Daly, *Beyond God the Father* (Boston: Beacon Press, 1975), 56–57.

34. Ibid.

35. Nikki Giovanni, "Nikki Rosa," in *The Black Woman,* ed. Toni Cade (New York: New American Library, 1980), 16.

36. Paule Marshall, "Reena," in *The Black Woman,* 28.

37. Pat Parker, *Womanslaughter* (Oakland: Diana Press, 1978), 13.

38. Spelman, "Woman as Body."

39. De Beauvoir, *The Second Sex*, xii, 57.

40. Ibid., 119.

41. Friedan, *The Feminine Mystique,* 247–77.

42. Firestone, *The Dialectic of Sex,* chap. 10.

43. Winthrop P. Jordan, *The White Man's Burden* (New York: Oxford University Press, 1974), chap. 1.

44. Smith, *Killers of the Dream,* 83–98.

45. Adrienne Rich, *Of Woman Born* (New York: Norton, 1976).

46. Rich, "Disloyal to Civilization," 300.

47. Diane Lewis, "A Response to Inequality: Black Women, Racism, and Sexism," *Signs* 3, no. 2 (1977): 339–61.

48. Toni Morrison, *The Bluest Eye* (New York: Pocketbooks, 1972).

49. See, for example, Carol Stack, *All Our Kin* (New York: Harper and Row, 1974).

MAPPING THE MARGINS: INTERSECTIONALITY, IDENTITY POLITICS, AND VIOLENCE AGAINST WOMEN OF COLOR

Kimberlé Williams Crenshaw

INTRODUCTION

Over the last two decades, women have organized against the almost routine violence that shapes their lives.[1] Drawing from the strength of shared experience, women have recognized that the political demands of millions speak more powerfully than do the pleas of a few isolated voices. This politicization in turn has transformed the way we understand violence against women. For example, battering and rape, once seen as private (family matters) and aberrational (errant sexual aggression), are now largely recognized as part of a broad-scale system of domination that affects women as a class.[2] This process of recognizing as social and systemic what was formerly perceived as isolated and individual has also characterized the identity politics of African-Americans, other people of color, and gays and lesbians, among others. For all these groups, identity-based politics has been a source of strength, community, and intellectual development.

The embrace of identity politics, however, has been in tension with dominant conceptions of social justice. Race, gender, and other identity categories are most often treated in mainstream liberal discourse as vestiges of bias or domination—that is, as intrinsically negative frameworks in which social power works to exclude or marginalize those who are different. According to this understanding, our liberatory objective should be to empty such categories of any social significance. Yet implicit in certain strands of feminist and racial liberation movements, for example, is the view that the social power in delineating difference need not be the power of domination; it can instead be the source of social empowerment and reconstruction.

The problem with identity politics is not that it fails to transcend difference, as some critics charge, but rather the opposite—that it frequently conflates or ignores intragroup differences. In the context of violence against women, this elision of difference in identity politics is problematic, fundamentally because the violence that many women experience is often shaped by other dimensions of their identities, such as race and class. Moreover, ignoring difference *within* groups contributes to tension *among* groups, another problem of identity politics which bears on efforts to politicize violence against women. Feminist efforts to politicize experiences of women and antiracist efforts to politicize experiences of people of color have frequently proceeded as though the issues and experiences they each detail occur on mutually exclusive terrains. Although racism and sexism readily intersect in the lives of real people, they seldom do in feminist and antiracist practices. Thus, when the practices expound identity as "woman" *or* "person of color" as an either/or proposition, they relegate the identity of women of color to a location that resists telling.

My objective in this article is to advance the telling of that location by exploring the race and gender dimensions of violence against women of color. Contemporary feminist and antiracist discourses have failed to consider intersectional identities such as women of color.[3] Focusing on one dimension of male violence against women—battering—I consider how the experiences of women of color are frequently the product of intersecting patterns of racism and sexism,[4] and how these experiences tend not to be represented within the discourses either of feminism or of antiracism. Because of their intersectional identity as both women *and* of color within discourses shaped to respond to one *or* the other, women of color are marginalized within both.

I used the concept of intersectionality to denote the various ways in which race and gender interact to shape the multiple dimensions of black women's employment experiences.[5] My objective there was to illustrate that many of the experiences black women face are not subsumed within the traditional boundaries of race or gender discrimination as these boundaries are currently understood, and that the intersection of racism and sexism factors into black women's lives in ways that cannot be captured wholly by looking separately at the race or gender dimensions of those experiences. I build on those observations here by exploring the various ways in which race and gender intersect in shaping structural, political, and representational aspects of violence against women of color.[6]

I should say at the outset that intersectionality is not being offered here as some new, totalizing theory of identity. Nor do I mean to suggest that violence against women of color can be explained only through the specific frameworks of race and gender considered here.[7] Indeed, factors I address only in part or not at all, such as class or sexuality, are often as critical in shaping the experiences of women of color. My focus on the intersections of race and gender only highlights the need to account for multiple grounds of identity when considering how the social world is constructed.

I have divided the issues presented in this article into three categories. In Part I, I discuss structural intersectionality, the ways in which the location of women of color at the intersection of race and gender makes our actual experience of domestic violence, rape, and remedial reform qualitatively different from that of white women. I shift the focus in Part II to political intersectionality, where I analyze how feminist and antiracist politics have both, paradoxically, often helped to marginalize the issue of violence against women of color. Finally, I address the implications of the intersectional approach within the broader scope of contemporary identity politics.

I. STRUCTURAL INTERSECTIONALITY

A. Structural Intersectionality and Battering

I observed the dynamics of structural intersectionality during a brief field study of battered women's shelters located in minority communities in Los Angeles. In most cases, the physical assault that leads women to these shelters is merely the most immediate manifestation of the subordination they experience. Many women who seek protection are unemployed or underemployed, and a good number of them are poor. Shelters serving these women cannot afford to address only the violence inflicted by the batterer; they must also confront the other multilayered and routinized forms of domination that often converge in these women's lives, hindering their ability to create alternatives to the abusive relationships that brought them to shelters in the first place. Many women of color, for example, are burdened by poverty, child care responsibilities, and the lack of job skills. These burdens, largely the consequence of gender and class oppression, are then compounded by the racially discriminatory employment and housing practices often faced by women of color, as well as by the disproportionately high unemployment among people of color that makes battered women of color less able to depend on the support of friends and relatives for temporary shelter.

Where systems of race, gender, and class domination converge, as they do in the experiences of battered women of color, intervention strategies based solely on the experiences of women who do not share the same class or race backgrounds will be of limited help to women who face different obstacles because of race and class. Such was the case in 1990 when Congress amended the marriage fraud provisions of the Immigration and Nationality Act to protect immigrant women who were battered or exposed to extreme cruelty by the U.S. citizens or permanent residents these women immigrated to the United States to marry. Under the marriage fraud provisions of the act, a person who immigrated to the United States in order to marry a U.S. citizen or permanent resident had to remain "properly" married for two years before even applying for permanent resident status,[8] at which time applications for the immigrant's permanent status were required of both spouses.[9] Predictably, under these circumstances, many immigrant women were reluctant to leave even the most abusive of partners for fear of being deported. When faced with the choice between protection from their batterers and protection against deportation, many immigrant women chose the latter. Reports of the tragic consequences of this double subordination put pressure on Congress to include in the Immigration Act of 1990 a provision amending the marriage fraud rules to allow for an explicit waiver for hardship caused by domestic violence.[10] Yet many immigrant women, particularly immigrant women of color, have remained vulnerable to battering because they are unable to meet the conditions established for a waiver. The evidence required to support a waiver "can include, but is not limited to, reports and affidavits from police, medical personnel, psychologists, school officials, and social service agencies."[11] For many immigrant women, limited access to these resources can make it difficult for them to obtain the evidence needed for a waiver. Cultural barriers, too, often further discourage immigrant women from reporting or escaping battering situations. Tina Shum, a family counselor at a social service agency, points out that "[t]his law sounds so easy to apply, but there are cultural complications in the Asian community that make even these requirements difficult. . . . Just to find the opportunity and courage to call us is an accomplishment for many."[12] The typical immigrant spouse, she suggests, may live "[i]n an extended family where several generations live together, there may be no privacy on the telephone, no opportunity to leave the house and no understanding of public

phones."[13] As a consequence, many immigrant women are wholly dependent on their husbands as their link to the world outside their homes.

Immigrant women are also vulnerable to spousal violence because so many of them depend on their husbands for information regarding their legal status. Many women who are now permanent residents continue to suffer abuse under threats of deportation by their husbands. Even if the threats are unfounded, women who have no independent access to information will still be intimidated by such threats. Further, even though the domestic violence waiver focuses on immigrant women whose husbands are U.S. citizens or permanent residents, there are countless women married to undocumented workers (or are themselves undocumented) who suffer in silence for fear that the security of their entire families will be jeopardized should they seek help or otherwise call attention to themselves.

Language barriers present another structural problem that often limits opportunities of non-English-speaking women to take advantage of existing support services. Such barriers limit access not only to information about shelters but also to the security that shelters provide. Some shelters turn non-English-speaking women away for lack of bilingual personnel and resources.

These examples illustrate how patterns of subordination intersect in women's experience of domestic violence. Intersectional subordination need not be intentionally produced; in fact, it is frequently the consequence of the imposition of one burden interacting with preexisting vulnerabilities to create yet another dimension of disempowerment. In the case of the marriage fraud provisions of the Immigration and Nationality Act, the imposition of a policy specifically designed to burden one class—immigrant spouses seeking permanent resident status—exacerbated the disempowerment of those already subordinated by other structures of domination. By failing to take into account immigrant spouses' vulnerability to domestic violence, Congress positioned these women to absorb the simultaneous impact of its anti-immigration policy and their spouses' abuse.

The enactment of the domestic violence waiver of the marriage fraud provisions similarly illustrates how modest attempts to respond to certain problems can be ineffective when the intersectional location of women of color is not considered in fashioning the remedy. Cultural identity and class both affect the likelihood that a battered spouse could take advantage of the waiver. Although the waiver is formally available to all women, the terms of the waiver make it inaccessible to some. Immigrant women who are socially, culturally, or economically privileged are more likely to be able to marshall the resources needed to satisfy the waiver requirements. Those immigrant women who are least able to take advantage of the waiver—women who are socially or economically the most marginal—are the ones most likely to be women of color.

II. POLITICAL INTERSECTIONALITY

The concept of political intersectionality highlights the fact that women of color are situated within at least two subordinated groups that frequently pursue conflicting political agendas. The need to split one's political energies between two sometimes-opposing groups is a dimension of intersectional disempowerment which men of color and white women seldom confront. Indeed, their specific raced *and* gendered experiences, although intersectional, often define as well as confine the interests of the entire group. For example, racism as experienced by people of color who are of a particular gender—male—tends to determine the parameters of antiracist strategies, just as sexism as experienced by women who are of a particular race—white—tends to ground the women's movement. The problem is not simply that both discourses fail women of color by not acknowledging the "additional" issue of race or of patriarchy but, rather, that the discourses are often inadequate even to the discrete tasks of articulating the full dimensions of racism and

sexism. Because women of color experience racism in ways not always the same as those experienced by men of color and sexism in ways not always parallel to experiences of white women, antiracism and feminism are limited, even on their own terms.

Among the most troubling political consequences of the failure of antiracist and feminist discourses to address the intersections of race and gender is the fact that, to the extent that they can forward the interest of "people of color" and "women," respectively, one analysis often implicitly denies the validity of the other. The failure of feminism to interrogate race means that feminism's resistance strategies will often replicate and reinforce the subordination of people of color, likewise, the failure of antiracism to interrogate patriarchy means that antiracism will frequently reproduce the subordination of women. These mutual elisions present a particularly difficult political dilemma for women of color. Adopting either analysis constitutes a denial of a fundamental dimension of our subordination and precludes the development of a political discourse that more fully empowers women of color.

A. The Politicization of Domestic Violence

That the political interests of women of color are obscured and sometimes jeopardized by political strategies that ignore or suppress intersectional issues is illustrated by my experiences in gathering information for this article. I attempted to review Los Angeles Police Department statistics reflecting the rate of domestic violence interventions by precinct, because such statistics can provide a rough picture of arrests by racial group, given the degree of racial segregation in Los Angeles.[14] The LAPD, however, would not release the statistics. A representative explained that the statistics were not released, in part, because domestic violence activists—both within and outside the LAPD—feared that statistics reflecting the extent of domestic violence in minority communities might be selectively interpreted and publicized in ways that would undermine long-term efforts to force the LAPD to address domestic violence as a serious problem. Activists were worried that the statistics might permit opponents to dismiss domestic violence as a minority problem and, therefore, not deserving of aggressive action.

The informant also claimed that representatives from various minority communities opposed the release of these statistics. They were concerned, apparently, that the data would unfairly represent black and brown communities as unusually violent, potentially reinforcing stereotypes that might be used in attempts to justify oppressive police tactics and other discriminatory practices. These misgivings are based on the familiar and not-unfounded premise that certain minority groups—especially black men—have already been stereotyped as uncontrollably violent. Some worry that attempts to make domestic violence an object of political action may only serve to confirm such stereotypes and undermine efforts to combat negative beliefs about the black community.

This account sharply illustrates how women of color can be erased by the strategic silences of antiracism and feminism. The political priorities of both have been defined in ways that suppress information that could facilitate attempts to confront the problem of domestic violence in communities of color.

1. Domestic Violence and Antiracist Politics
Within communities of color, efforts to stem the politicization of domestic violence are often grounded in attempts to maintain the integrity of the community. The articulation of this perspective takes different forms. Some critics allege that feminism has no place within communities of color, that the issues are internally divisive, and that they represent the migration of white women's concerns into a context in which they are not merely irrelevant but harmful. At its most extreme, this rhetoric denies that gender violence is a problem in the community and characterizes any effort to politicize gender subordination as itself a community problem. This is

the position taken by Shahrazad Ali in her controversial book, *The Blackman's Guide to Understanding the Blackwoman.*[15] In this stridently antifeminist tract, Ali draws a positive correlation between domestic violence and the liberation of African-Americans. Ali blames the deteriorating conditions within the black community on the insubordination of black women and on the failure of black men to control them.[16] She goes so far as to advise black men to physically chastise black women when they are "disrespectful."[17] While she cautions that black men must use moderation in disciplining "their" women, she argues that they must sometimes resort to physical force to reestablish the authority over black women that racism has disrupted.

Ali's premise is that patriarchy is beneficial for the black community, and that it must be strengthened through coercive means if necessary.[18] Yet the violence that accompanies this will to control is devastating, not just for the black women who are victimized but for the entire black community.[19] The recourse to violence to resolve conflicts establishes a dangerous pattern for children raised in such environments and contributes to many other pressing problems.[20] It has been estimated that nearly 40 percent of all homeless women and children have fled violence in the home,[21] and an estimated 63 percent of young men between the ages of eleven and twenty who are imprisoned for homicide have killed their mothers' batterers.[22] Moreover, while gang violence, homicide, and other forms of black-on-black crime have increasingly been discussed within African-American politics, patriarchal ideas about gender and power preclude the recognition of domestic violence as yet another compelling form of black-on-black crime.

Efforts such as Ali's to justify violence against women in the name of black liberation are indeed extreme.[23] The more common problem is that the political or cultural interests of the community are interpreted in a way that precludes full public recognition of the problem of domestic violence. While it would be misleading to suggest that white Americans have come to terms with the degree of violence in their own homes, it is nonetheless the case that race adds yet another dimension to sources of suppression of the problem of domestic violence within nonwhite communities. People of color often must weigh their interests in avoiding issues that might reinforce distorted public perceptions against the need to acknowledge and address intracommunity problems. Yet the cost of suppression is seldom recognized, in part because the failure to discuss the issue shapes perceptions of how serious the problem is in the first place.

The controversy over Alice Walker's novel *The Color Purple* can be understood as an intracommunity debate about the political costs of exposing gender violence within the black community. Some critics chastised Walker for portraying black men as violent brutes. One critic lambasted Walker's portrayal of Celie, the emotionally and physically abused protagonist who finally triumphs in the end; the critic contended that Walker had created in Celie a black woman whom she couldn't imagine existing in any black community she knew or could conceive of.[24]

The claim that Celie was somehow an inauthentic character might be read as a consequence of silencing discussion of intracommunity violence. Celie may be unlike any black woman we know because the real terror experienced daily by minority women is routinely concealed in a misguided (though perhaps understandable) attempt to forestall racial stereotyping. Of course, it is true that representations of black violence—whether statistical or fictional—are often written into a larger script that consistently portrays black and other minority communities as pathologically violent. The problem, however, is not so much the portrayal of violence itself as it is the absence of other narratives and images portraying a fuller range of black experience. Suppression of some of these issues in the name of antiracism imposes real costs: where information about violence in minority communities is not available, domestic violence is unlikely to be addressed as a serious issue.

The political imperatives of a narrowly focused antiracist strategy support other practices that isolate women of color. For example, activists who have attempted to provide support services to Asian- and African-American women report intense resistance from those communities. At other times, cultural and social factors contribute to suppression. Nilda Remonte, director of Everywoman's Shelter in Los Angeles, points out that in the Asian community, saving the honor of the family from shame is a priority. Unfortunately, this priority tends to be interpreted as obliging women not to scream rather than obliging men not to hit.

Race and culture contribute to the suppression of domestic violence in other ways as well. Women of color are often reluctant to call the police, a hesitancy likely due to a general unwillingness among people of color to subject their private lives to the scrutiny and control of a police force that is frequently hostile. There is also a more generalized community ethic against public intervention, the product of a desire to create a private world free from the diverse assaults on the public lives of racially subordinated people. The home is not simply a man's castle in the patriarchal sense: it may also function as a safe haven from the indignities of life in a racist society. However, but for this "safe haven" in many cases, women of color victimized by violence might otherwise seek help.

There is also a general tendency within antiracist discourse to regard the problem of violence against women of color as just another manifestation of racism. In this sense, the relevance of gender domination within the community is reconfigured as a consequence of discrimination against men. Of course, it is probably true that racism contributes to the cycle of violence, given the stress that men of color experience in dominant society; it is therefore more than reasonable to explore the links between racism and domestic violence. Yet the chain of violence is more complex and extends beyond this single link. Racism is linked to patriarchy to the extent that racism denies men of color the power and privilege that dominant men enjoy. When violence is understood as an acting-out of being denied male power in other spheres, it seems counterproductive to embrace constructs that implicitly link the solution to domestic violence to the acquisition of greater male power. The more promising political imperative is to challenge the legitimacy of such power expectations by exposing their dysfunctional and debilitating effect on families and communities of color. Moreover, while understanding links between racism and domestic violence is an important component of any effective intervention strategy, it is also clear that women of color need not await the ultimate triumph over racism before they can expect to live violence-free lives.

2. Race and the Domestic Violence Lobby Not only do race-based priorities function to obscure the problem of violence suffered by women of color; feminist concerns often suppress minority experiences as well. Strategies for increasing awareness of domestic violence within the white community tend to begin by citing the commonly shared assumption that battering is a minority problem. The strategy then focuses on demolishing this straw man, stressing that spousal abuse also occurs in the white community. Countless first-person stories begin with a statement like, "I was not supposed to be a battered wife." That battering occurs in families of all races and all classes seems to be an ever-present theme of antiabuse campaigns. First-person anecdotes and studies, for example, consistently assert that battering cuts across racial, ethnic, economic, educational, and religious lines. Such disclaimers seem relevant only in the presence of an initial, widely held belief that domestic violence occurs primarily in minority or poor families. Indeed, some authorities explicitly renounce the "stereotypical myths" about battered women; a few commentators have even transformed the message that battering is not *exclusively* a problem of the poor or minority communities into a claim that it *equally* affects all races and classes. Yet these comments seem less concerned with exploring domestic abuse within "stereotyped" communities than with removing the stereotype as an obstacle to exposing battering within white middle- and upper-class communities.[25]

Efforts to politicize the issue of violence against women challenge beliefs that violence occurs only in homes of Others. While it is unlikely that advocates and others who adopt this rhetorical strategy intend to exclude or ignore the needs of poor and colored women, the underlying premise of this seemingly univeralistic appeal is to keep the sensibilities of dominant social groups focused on the experiences of those groups. Indeed, as subtly suggested by the opening comments of Senator David Boren (Dem.-Okla.) in support of the Violence Against Women Act of 1991, the displacement of the Other as the presumed victim of domestic violence works primarily as a political appeal to rally white elites. Boren said: "Violent crimes against women are not limited to the streets of the inner cities, but also occur in homes in the urban and rural areas across the country. Violence against women affects not only those who are actually beaten and brutalized, but indirectly affects all women. Today, our wives, mothers, daughters, sisters, and colleagues are held captive by fear generated from these violent crimes—held captive not for what they do or who they are, but solely because of gender."[26] Rather than focusing on and illuminating how violence is disregarded when the home is somehow Other, the strategy implicit in Senator Boren's remarks functions instead to politicize the problem only within the dominant community. This strategy permits white women victims to come into focus, but it does little to disrupt the patterns of neglect that permitted the problem to continue as long as it was imagined to be a minority problem. Minority women's experience of violence is ignored, except to the extent that it gains white support for domestic violence programs in the white community.

Senator Boren and his colleagues no doubt believe that they have provided legislation and resources that will address the problems of all women victimized by domestic violence. Yet despite their universalizing rhetoric of "all" women, they were able to empathize with female victims of domestic violence only by looking past the plight of Other women and by recognizing the familiar faces of their own. The strength of the appeal to "protect our women" must be its race and class specificity. After all, it has always been someone's wife, mother, sister, or daughter who has been abused, even when the violence was stereotypically black or brown, and poor. The point here is not that the Violence Against Women Act is particularistic on its own terms, but that unless the senators and other policymakers ask why violence remained insignificant as long as it was understood as a minority problem, it is unlikely that women of color will share equally in the distribution of resources and concern. It is even more unlikely, however, that those in power will be forced to confront this issue. As long as attempts to politicize domestic violence focus on convincing whites that this is not a "minority" problem but *their* problem, any authentic and sensitive attention to the experiences of black and other minority women probably will continue to be regarded as jeopardizing the movement.

While Senator Boren's statement reflects a self-consciously political presentation of domestic violence, an episode of the CBS news program *48 Hours* shows how similar patterns of othering nonwhite women are apparent in journalistic accounts of domestic violence as well.[27] The program presented seven women who were victims of abuse. Six were interviewed at some length along with their family members, friends, supporters, and even detractors. The viewer got to know something about each of these women. These victims were humanized. Yet the seventh woman, the only nonwhite one, never came into focus. She was literally unrecognizable throughout the segment, first introduced by photographs showing her face badly beaten and later shown with her face electronically altered in the videotape of a hearing at which she was forced to

testify. Other images associated with this woman included shots of a bloodstained room and blood-soaked pillows. Her boyfriend was pictured handcuffed while the camera zoomed in for a close-up of his bloodied sneakers. Of all the presentations in the episode, hers was the most graphic and impersonal. The overall point of the segment "featuring" this woman was that battering might not escalate into homicide if battered women would only cooperate with prosecutors. However, in focusing on its own agenda and failing to explore why this woman refused to cooperate, the program diminished this woman, communicating, however subtly, that she was responsible for her own victimization.

Unlike the other women, all of whom, again, were white, this black woman had no name, no family, no context. The viewer sees her only as victimized and uncooperative. She cries when shown pictures; she pleads not to be forced to view the bloodstained room and her disfigured face. The program does not help the viewer to understand her predicament. The possible reasons she did not want to testify—fear, love, or possibly both—are never suggested. Most unfortunately, she, unlike the other six, is given no epilogue. While the fates of the other women are revealed at the end of the episode, we discover nothing about the black woman. She, like the Others she represents, is simply left to herself and soon forgotten.

I offer this description to suggest that Other women are silenced as much by being relegated to the margin of experience as by total exclusion. Tokenistic, objectifying, voyeuristic inclusion is at least as disempowering as complete exclusion. The effort to politicize violence against women will do little to address black and other minority women if their images are retained simply to magnify the problem rather than to humanize their experiences. Similarly, the antiracist agenda will not be advanced significantly by forcibly suppressing the reality of battering in minority communities. As the *48 Hours* episode makes clear, the images and stereotypes we fear are indeed readily available, and they are frequently deployed in ways that do not generate sensitive understanding of the nature of domestic violence in minority communities.

3. Race and Domestic Violence Support Services

Women working in the field of domestic violence have sometimes reproduced the subordination and marginalization of women of color by adopting policies, priorities, or strategies of empowerment that either elide or wholly disregard the particular intersectional needs of women of color. While gender, race, and class intersect to create the particular context in which women of color experience violence, certain choices made by "allies" can reproduce intersectional subordination within the very resistance strategies developed to respond to the problem.

This problem is starkly illustrated by the inaccessibility of domestic violence support services for many non-English-speaking women. In a letter written to the deputy commissioner of the New York State Department of Social Services, Diana Campos, director of Human Services for Programas de Ocupaciones y Desarrollo Económico Real, Inc. (PODER), detailed the case of a Latina in crisis who was repeatedly denied accommodation at a shelter because she could not prove that she was English-proficient. The woman had fled her home with her teenaged son, believing her husband's threats to kill them both. She called the domestic violence hotline administered by PODER, seeking shelter for herself and her son. However, because most shelters would not accommodate the woman with her son, they were forced to live on the streets for two days. The hotline counselor was finally able to find an agency that would take both the mother and her son, but when the counselor told the intake coordinator at the shelter that the woman spoke limited English, the coordinator told her that they could not take anyone who was not English-proficient. When the woman in crisis called back and was told of the shelter's "rule," she replied that she could understand English if spoken to her slowly. As

Campos explains, Mildred, the hotline counselor, told Wendy, the intake coordinator

> that the woman said that she could communicate a little in English. Wendy told Mildred that they could not provide services to this woman because they have house rules that the woman must agree to follow. Mildred asked her, "What if the woman agrees to follow your rules? Will you still not take her?" Wendy responded that all of the women at the shelter are required to attend [a] support group and they would not be able to have her in the group if she could not communicate. Mildred mentioned the severity of this woman's case. She told Wendy that the woman had been wandering the streets at night while her husband is home, and she had been mugged twice. She also reiterated the fact that this woman was in danger of being killed by either her husband or a mugger. Mildred expressed that the woman's safety was a priority at this point, and that once in a safe place, receiving counseling in a support group could be dealt with.[28]

The intake coordinator restated the shelter's policy of taking only English-speaking women, and stated further that the woman would have to call the shelter herself for screening. If the woman could communicate with them in English, she might be accepted. When the woman called the PODER hotline later that day, she was in such a state of fear that the hotline counselor who had been working with her had difficulty understanding her in Spanish. The woman had been slipping back into her home during the day when her husband was at work. She remained in a heightened state of anxiety because he was returning shortly, and she would be forced to go back out into the streets for yet another night. Campos directly intervened at this point, calling the executive director of the shelter. A counselor called back from the shelter. As Campos reports, the counselor told her that

> they did not want to take the woman in the shelter because they felt that the woman would feel isolated. I explained that the son agreed to translate for his mother during the intake process. Furthermore, that we would assist them in locating a Spanish-speaking

battered women's advocate to assist in counseling her. Marie stated that utilizing the son was not an acceptable means of communication for them, *since it further victimized the victim.* In addition, she stated that they had similar experiences with women who were non-English-speaking, and that the women eventually just left because they were not able to communicate with anyone. I expressed my extreme concern for her safety and reiterated that we would assist them in providing her with the necessary services until we could get her placed someplace where they had bilingual staff.[29]

After several more calls, the shelter finally agreed to take the woman. The woman called once more during the negotiation; however, once a plan was in place, the woman never called back. Said Campos, "After so many calls, we are now left to wonder if she is alive and well, and if she will ever have enough faith in our ability to help her to call us again the next time she is in crisis."[30]

Despite this woman's desperate need, she was unable to receive the protection afforded English-speaking women, due to the shelter's rigid commitment to exclusionary policies. Perhaps even more troubling than the shelter's lack of bilingual resources was its refusal to allow a friend or relative to translate for the woman. This story illustrates the absurdity of a feminist approach that makes the ability to attend a support group without a translator a more significant consideration in the distribution of resources than the risk of physical harm on the street. The point is not that the shelter's image of empowerment is empty but, rather, that it was imposed without regard to the disempowering consequences for women who didn't match the kind of client the shelter's administrators imagined. Thus, they failed to accomplish the basic priority of the shelter movement—to get the woman out of danger.

Here the woman in crisis was made to bear the burden of the shelter's refusal to anticipate and provide for the needs of non-English-speaking women. Said Campos, "It is unfair to impose more stress on victims by placing them in the position of having to demonstrate their

proficiency in English in order to receive services that are readily available to other battered women."[31] The problem is not easily dismissed as one of well-intentioned ignorance. The specific issue of monolingualism and the monistic view of women's experience that set the stage for this tragedy were not new issues in New York. Indeed, several women of color have reported that they had repeatedly struggled with the New York State Coalition Against Domestic Violence over language exclusion and other practices that marginalized the interests of women of color.[32] Yet despite repeated lobbying, the coalition did not act to incorporate the specific needs of nonwhite women into its central organizing vision.

Some critics have linked the coalition's failure to address these issues to the narrow vision of coalition that animated its interaction with women of color in the first place. The very location of the coalition's headquarters in Woodstock, New York—an area where few people of color live—seemed to guarantee that women of color would play a limited role in formulating policy. Moreover, efforts to include women of color came, it seems, as something of an afterthought. Many were invited to participate only after the coalition was awarded a grant by the state to recruit women of color. However, as one "recruit" said, "they were not really prepared to deal with us or our issues. They thought that they could simply incorporate us into their organization without rethinking any of their beliefs or priorities and that we would be happy."[33] Even the most formal gestures of inclusion were not to be taken for granted. On one occasion when several women of color attended a meeting to discuss a special task force on women of color, the group debated all day over including the issue on the agenda.[34]

The relationship between the white women and the women of color on the board was a rocky one from beginning to end. Other conflicts developed over differing definitions of feminism. For example, the board decided to hire a Latina staffperson to manage outreach programs to the Latino community, but the white members of the hiring committee rejected candidates favored by Latina committee members who did not have recognized feminist credentials. As Campos pointed out, by measuring Latinas against their own biographies, the white members of the board failed to recognize the different circumstances under which feminist consciousness develops and manifests itself within minority communities. Many of the women who interviewed for the position were established activists and leaders within their own community, a fact in itself suggesting that these women were probably familiar with the specific gender dynamics in their communities and were accordingly better qualified to handle outreach than were other candidates with more conventional feminist credentials.[35]

The coalition ended a few months later, when the women of color walked out.[36] Many of these women returned to community-based organizations, preferring to struggle over women's issues within their communities rather than struggle over race and class issues with white middle-class women. Yet as illustrated by the case of the Latina who could find no shelter, the dominance of a particular perspective and set of priorities within the shelter community continues to marginalize the needs of women of color.

The struggle over which differences matter and which do not is neither abstract nor insignificant. Indeed, these conflicts are about more than difference as such; they raise critical issues of power. The problem is not simply that women who dominate the antiviolence movement are different from women of color but, rather, that they frequently have the power to determine, either through material resources or rhetorical resources, whether the intersectional differences of women of color will be incorporated at all into the basic formulation of policy. Thus, the struggle over incorporating these differences is not a petty or superficial conflict about who gets to sit at the head of the table. In the context of violence, it is sometimes a deadly serious matter of who will survive—and who will not.[37]

B. Political Intersectionalities in Rape

In the previous sections, I have used intersectionality to describe or frame various relationships between race and gender. I have used it as a way to articulate the interaction of racism and patriarchy generally. I have also used intersectionality to describe the location of women of color both within overlapping systems of subordination and at the margins of feminism and antiracism. When race and gender factors are examined in the context of rape, intersectionality can be used to map the ways in which racism and patriarchy have shaped conceptualizations of rape, to describe the unique vulnerability of women of color to these converging systems of domination, and to track the marginalization of women of color within antiracist and antirape discourses.[38]

1. Racism and Sexism in Dominant Conceptualizations of Rape Generations of critics and activists have criticized dominant conceptualizations of rape as racist and sexist. These efforts have been important in revealing the way in which representations of rape both reflect and reproduce race and gender hierarchies in American society. Black women, at once women and people of color, are situated within both groups, each of which has benefited from challenges to sexism and racism, respectively; yet the particular dynamics of gender and race relating to the rape of black women have received scant attention. Although antiracist and antisexist assaults on rape have been politically useful to black women, at some level, the monofocal antiracist and feminist critiques have also produced a political discourse that disserves black women.

Historically, the dominant conceptualization of rape as quintessentially involving a black offender and a white victim has left black men subject to legal and extralegal violence. The use of rape to legitimize efforts to control and discipline the black community is well established, and the casting of all black men as potential threats to the sanctity of white womanhood is a familiar construct that antiracists confronted and attempted to dispel over a century ago.

Feminists have attacked other dominant, essentially patriarchal, conceptions of rape, particularly as represented through law. The early emphasis of rape law on the propertylike aspect of women's chastity resulted in less solicitude for rape victims whose chastity had been in some way devalued. Some of the most insidious assumptions were written into the law, including the early common law notion that a woman alleging rape must be able to show that she resisted to the utmost in order to prove that she was raped rather than seduced. Women themselves were put on trial, as judge and jury scrutinized their lives to determine whether they were innocent victims or women who essentially got what they were asking for. Legal rules thus functioned to legitimize a good/bad woman dichotomy, and women who led sexually autonomous lives were usually the least likely to be vindicated if they were raped.

Today, long after the most egregious discriminatory laws have been eradicated, constructions of rape in popular discourse and in criminal law continue to manifest vestiges of these racist and sexist themes. As Valerie Smith notes, "a variety of cultural narratives that historically have linked sexual violence with racial oppression continue to determine the nature of public response" to interracial rapes.[39] Smith reviews the well-publicized case of a jogger who was raped in New York's Central Park to expose how the public discourse on the assault "made the story of sexual victimization inseparable from the rhetoric of racism."[40] Smith contends that in dehumanizing the rapists as "savages," "wolves," and "beasts," the press "shaped the discourse around the event in ways that inflamed pervasive fears about black men."[41] Given the chilling parallels between the media representations of the Central Park rape and the sensationalized coverage of similar allegations that in the past frequently culminated in lynchings, one could hardly be surprised when Donald Trump took out a full-page ad in four

New York newspapers demanding that New York "Bring Back the Death Penalty, Bring Back Our Police."[42]

Other media spectacles suggest that traditional gender-based stereotypes that oppress women continue to figure in the popular construction of rape. In Florida, for example, a controversy was sparked by a jury's acquittal of a man accused of a brutal rape because, in the jurors' view, the woman's attire suggested that she was asking for sex. Even the press coverage of William Kennedy Smith's rape trial involved a considerable degree of speculation regarding the sexual history of his accuser.

The racism and sexism written into the social construction of rape are merely contemporary manifestations of rape narratives emanating from a historical period when race and sex hierarchies were more explicitly policed. Yet another is the devaluation of black women and the marginalization of their sexual victimizations. This was dramatically shown in the special attention given to the rape of the Central Park jogger during a week in which twenty eight other cases of first-degree rape or attempted rape were reported in New York. Many of these rapes were as horrific as the rape in Central Park, yet all were virtually ignored by the media. Some were gang rapes, and in a case that prosecutors described as "one of the most brutal in recent years," a woman was raped, sodomized, and thrown fifty feet off the top of a four-story building in Brooklyn. Witnesses testified that the victim "screamed as she plunged down the air shaft. . . . She suffered fractures of both ankles and legs, her pelvis was shattered and she suffered extensive internal injuries."[43] This rape survivor, like most of the other forgotten victims that week, was a woman of color.

In short, during the period when the Central Park jogger dominated the headlines, many equally horrifying rapes occurred. None, however, elicited the public expressions of horror and outrage that attended the Central Park rape. To account for these different responses, Smith suggests a sexual hierarchy in operation that holds certain female bodies in higher regard than others.[44] Statistics from prosecution of rape cases suggest that this hierarchy is at least one significant, albeit often-overlooked, factor in evaluating attitudes toward rape.[45] A study of rape dispositions in Dallas, for example, showed that the average prison term for a man convicted of raping a black woman was two years,[46] as compared to five years for the rape of a Latina and ten years for the rape of a white woman.[47] A related issue is the fact that African-American victims of rape are the least likely to be believed.[48] The Dallas study and others like it also point to a more subtle problem: neither the antirape nor the antiracist political agenda has focused on the black rape victim. This inattention stems from the way the problem of rape is conceptualized within antiracist and antirape reform discourses. Although the rhetoric of both agendas formally includes black women, racism is generally not problematized in feminism, and sexism is not problematized in antiracist discourses. Consequently, the plight of black women is relegated to a secondary importance: the primary beneficiaries of policies supported by feminists and others concerned about rape tend to be white women, and the primary beneficiaries of the black community's concern over racism and rape tend to be black men. Ultimately, the reformist and rhetorical strategies that have grown out of antiracist and feminist rape reform movements have been ineffective in politicizing the treatment of black women.

2. Race and the Antirape Lobby Feminist critiques of rape have focused on the way that rape law has reflected dominant rules and expectations that tightly regulate the sexuality of women. In the context of the rape trial, the formal definition of rape as well as the evidentiary rules applicable in a rape trial discriminate against women by measuring the rape victim against a narrow norm of acceptable sexual conduct for women. Deviation from that norm tends to turn women into illegitimate rape victims, leading to rejection of their claims.

Historically, legal rules dictated, for example, that rape victims must have resisted their assailants in order for their claims to be accepted. Any abatement of struggle was interpreted as the woman's consent to the intercourse, under the logic that a real rape victim would protect her honor virtually to the death. While utmost resistance is not formally required anymore, rape law continues to weigh the credibility of women against narrow normative standards of female behavior. A woman's sexual history, for example, is frequently explored by defense attorneys as a way of suggesting that a woman who consented to sex on other occasions was likely to have consented in the case at issue. Past sexual conduct as well as the specific circumstances leading up to the rape are often used to distinguish the moral character of the "legitimate" rape victim from women who are regarded as morally debased or in some other way "responsible" for their own victimization.

This type of feminist critique of rape law has informed many of the fundamental reform measures enacted in antirape legislation, including increased penalties for convicted rapists and changes in evidentiary rules to preclude attacks on the woman's moral character. These reforms limit the tactics attorneys might use to tarnish the image of the rape victim, but they operate within preexisting social constructs that distinguish victims from nonvictims on the basis of their sexual character. Thus, these reforms, while beneficial, do not challenge the background cultural narratives that undermine the credibility of black women.

Because black women face subordination based on both race and gender, reforms of rape law and judicial procedures which are premised on narrow conceptions of gender subordination may not address the devaluation of black women. Much of the problem results from the way that certain gender expectations for women intersect with certain sexualized notions of race—notions that are deeply entrenched in American culture. Sexualized images of African-Americans go all the way back to Europeans' first engagement with Africans. Blacks have long been portrayed as more sexual, more earthy, more gratification-oriented; these sexualized images of race intersect with norms of women's sexuality, norms that are used to distinguish good women from bad, madonnas from whores. Thus, black women are essentially prepackaged as bad women in cultural narratives about good women who can be raped and bad women who cannot. The discrediting of black women's claims is the consequence of a complex intersection of a gendered sexual system, one that constructs rules appropriate for good and bad women, and a race code that provides images defining the allegedly essential nature of black women. If these sexual images form even part of the cultural imagery of black women, then the very representation of a black female body at least suggests certain narratives that may make black women's rape either less believable or less important. These narratives may explain why rapes of black women are less likely to result in convictions and long prison terms than are rapes of white women.

Rape law reform measures that do not in some way engage and challenge the narratives that are read onto black women's bodies are unlikely to affect the way that cultural beliefs oppress black women in rape trials. While the degree to which legal reform can directly challenge cultural beliefs that shape rape trials is limited, the very effort to mobilize political resources toward addressing the sexual oppression of black women can be an important first step in drawing greater attention to the problem. One obstacle to such an effort has been the failure of most antirape activists to analyze specifically the consequences of racism in the context of rape. In the absence of a direct attempt to address the racial dimensions of rape, black women are simply presumed to be represented in and benefited by prevailing feminist critiques.

3. Antiracism and Rape Antiracist critiques of rape law focus on how the law operates primarily to condemn rapes of white women by black men. While the heightened concern with protecting white women against black men has been primarily criticized as a form of discrimination against black men, it just as surely reflects devaluation of black women; this disregard for black women results from an exclusive focus on the consequences of the problem for black men.[49] Of course, rape accusations historically have provided a justification for white terrorism against the black community, generating a legitimating power of such strength that it created a veil virtually impenetrable to appeals based on either humanity or fact. Ironically, while the fear of the black rapist was exploited to legitimate the practice of lynching, rape was not even alleged in most cases. The well-developed fear of black sexuality served primarily to increase white tolerance for racial terrorism as a prophylactic measure to keep blacks under control. Within the African-American community, cases involving race-based accusations against black men have stood as hallmarks of racial injustice. The prosecution of the Scottsboro boys and the Emmett Till tragedy, for example, triggered African-American resistance to the rigid social codes of white supremacy. To the extent that rape of black women is thought to dramatize racism, it is usually cast as an assault on black manhood, demonstrating his inability to protect black women. The direct assault on black womanhood is less frequently seen as an assault on the black community.

The sexual politics that this limited reading of racism and rape engenders continues to play out today, as illustrated by the Mike Tyson rape trial. The use of antiracist rhetoric to mobilize support for Tyson represented an ongoing practice of viewing with considerable suspicion rape accusations against black men and interpreting sexual racism through a male-centered frame. The historical experience of black men has so completely occupied the dominant conceptions of racism and rape that there is little room to squeeze in the experiences of black women. Consequently, racial solidarity was continually raised as a rallying point on behalf of Tyson, but never on behalf of Desiree Washington, Tyson's black accuser. Leaders ranging from Benjamin Hooks to Louis Farrakhan expressed their support for Tyson, *yet* no established black leader voiced any concern for Washington. Thus, the fact that black men have often been falsely accused of raping white women underlies the antiracist defense of black men accused of rape even when the accuser herself is a black woman.

As a result of this continual emphasis on black male sexuality as the core issue in antiracist critiques of rape, black women who raise claims of rape against black men are not only disregarded but also sometimes vilified within the African-American community. One can only imagine the alienation experienced by a black rape survivor such as Desiree Washington when the accused rapist is embraced and defended as a victim of racism while she is, at best, disregarded and, at worst, ostracized and ridiculed. In contrast, Tyson was the beneficiary of the long-standing practice of using antiracist rhetoric to deflect the injury suffered by black women victimized by black men. Some defended the support given to Tyson on the ground that all African-Americans can readily imagine their sons, fathers, brothers, or uncles being wrongly accused of rape; yet daughters, mothers, sisters, and aunts also deserve at least a similar concern, since statistics show that black women are more likely to be raped than black men are to be falsely accused of it. Given the magnitude of black women's vulnerability to sexual violence, it is not unreasonable to expect as much concern for black women who are raped as is expressed for the men who are accused of raping them.

Black leaders are not alone in their failure to empathize with or rally around black rape victims. Indeed, some black women were among Tyson's staunchest supporters and Washington's harshest critics.[50] The media widely noted the lack of sympathy black women had for Washington; Barbara Walters used the observation as a way of challenging Washington's credibility, going so far as to press her for a reaction.[51] The most troubling revelation was that many of the women who did not support Washington also doubted Tyson's story. These women did not sympathize with Washington because they believed that she had no business being in Tyson's hotel room at 2:00 A.M. A typical response was offered by one young black woman who stated, "She asked for it, she got it, it's not fair to cry rape."

Indeed, some of the women who expressed their disdain for Washington acknowledged that they encountered the threat of sexual assault almost daily.[52] Yet it may be precisely this threat—along with the relative absence of rhetorical strategies challenging the sexual subordination of black women—that animated their harsh criticism. In this regard, black women who condemned Washington were quite like all other women who seek to distance themselves from rape victims as a way of denying their own vulnerability. Prosecutors who handle sexual assault cases acknowledge that they often exclude women as potential jurors because women tend to empathize least with the victim.[53] To identify too closely with victimization may reveal their own vulnerability.[54] Consequently, women often look for evidence that the victim brought the rape on herself, usually by breaking social rules that are generally held applicable only to women. And when the rules classify women as dumb, loose, or weak, on the one hand, and smart, discriminating, and strong, on the other, it is not surprising that women who cannot step outside the rules to critique them would attempt to validate themselves within them. The position of most black women on this issue is particularly problematic, first, because of the extent to which they are consistently reminded that they are the group most vulnerable to sexual victimization, and, second, because most black women share the African-American community's general resistance to explicitly feminist analysis when it appears to run up against long-standing narratives that construct black men as the primary victims of sexual racism.

C. Rape and Intersectionality in Social Science

The marginalization of black women's experiences within the antiracist and feminist critiques of rape law are facilitated by social science studies that fail to examine the ways in which racism and sexism converge. Gary LaFree's *Rape and Criminal Justice: The Social Construction of Sexual Assault* is a classic example.[55] Through a study of rape prosecutions in Minneapolis, LaFree attempts to determine the validity of two prevailing claims regarding rape prosecutions. The first claim is that black defendants face significant racial discrimination;[56] the second is that rape laws serve to regulate the sexual conduct of women by withholding from rape victims the ability to invoke sexual assault law when they have engaged in nontraditional behavior.[57] LaFree's compelling study concludes that law constructs rape in ways that continue to manifest both racial and gender domination.[58] Although black women are positioned as victims of both the racism and the sexism that LaFree so persuasively details, his analysis is less illuminating than might be expected, because black women fall through the cracks of his dichotomized theoretical framework.

1. Racial Domination and Rape   LaFree confirms the findings of earlier studies which show that race is a significant determinant in the ultimate disposition of rape cases. He finds that black men accused of raping white women were treated most harshly, while black offenders accused of raping black women were treated most leniently.[59] These effects held true even after controlling for other factors such as injury to the victim and acquaintance between victim and assailant: "Compared to other defendants, blacks who were suspected of assaulting white women received more serious charges, were more likely to have their cases filed as felonies, were more likely to receive prison sentences if convicted, were more likely to be incarcerated in the state penitentiary (as opposed to a jail or minimum-security facility), and received longer sentences on the average."[60]

LaFree's conclusions that black men are differentially punished depending on the race of the victim do not, however, contribute much to understanding the plight of black rape victims. Part of the problem lies in the author's use of "sexual stratification" theory, which posits both that women are differently valued according to their race and that there are certain "rules of sexual access" governing who may have sexual contact with whom in this sexually stratified market.[61] According to the theory, black men are discriminated against in that their forced "access" to white women is more harshly penalized than their forced "access" to black women.[62] LaFree's analysis focuses on the harsh regulation of access by black men to white women, but is silent about the relative subordination of black women to white women. The emphasis on differential access to women is consistent with analytical perspectives that view racism primarily in terms of the inequality between men. From this prevailing viewpoint, the problem of discrimination is that white men can rape black women with relative impunity while black men cannot do the same with white women.[63] Black women are considered victims of discrimination only to the extent that white men can rape them without fear of significant punishment. Rather than being viewed as victims of discrimination in their own right, they become merely the means by which discrimination against black men can be recognized. The inevitable result of this orientation is that efforts to fight discrimination tend to ignore the particularly vulnerable position of black women, who must both confront racial bias *and* challenge their status as instruments, rather than beneficiaries, of the civil rights struggle.

Where racial discrimination is framed by LaFree primarily in terms of a contest between black and white men over women, the racism experienced by black women will only be seen in terms of white male access to them. When rape of black women by white men is eliminated as a factor in the analysis, whether for statistical or other reasons, racial discrimination against black women no longer matters, since LaFree's analysis involves comparing the "access" of white and black men to white women. Yet discrimination against black women does not result simply from white men raping them with little sanction and being punished less than black men who rape white women, nor from white men raping them but not being punished as white men who rape white women would be. Black women are also discriminated against because intraracial rape of white women is treated more seriously than is intraracial rape of black women. However, the differential protection that black and white women receive against intraracial rape is not seen as racist because intraracial rape does not involve a contest between black and white men. In other words, the way the criminal justice system treats rapes of black women by black men and rapes of white women by white men is not seen as raising issues of racism, because black and white men are not involved with each other's women.

In sum, black women who are raped are racially discriminated against because their rapists, whether black or white, are less likely to be charged with rape; and, when charged and convicted, their rapists are less likely to receive significant jail time than are the rapists of white women. While sexual stratification theory does posit that women are stratified sexually by race, most applications of the theory focus on the inequality of male agents of rape rather than on the inequality of rape victims, thus marginalizing the racist treatment of black women by consistently portraying racism in terms of the relative power of black and white men.

In order to understand and treat the victimization of black women as a consequence of racism and of sexism, it is necessary to shift the analysis away from the differential access of men, and more toward the differential protection of women. Throughout his analysis, LaFree fails to do so.

His sexual stratification thesis—in particular, its focus on the comparative power of male agents of rape—illustrates how the marginalization of black women in antiracist politics is replicated in social science research. Indeed, the thesis leaves unproblematized the racist subordination of less valuable objects (black women) to more valuable objects (white women), and it perpetuates the sexist treatment of women as property extensions of "their" men.

2. Rape and Gender Subordination   Although LaFree does attempt to address gender-related concerns of women in his discussion of rape and the social control of women, his theory of sexual stratification fails to focus sufficiently on the effects of stratification on women.[64] LaFree quite explicitly uses a framework that treats race and gender as separate categories, but he gives no indication that he understands how black women may fall between categories, or within both. The problem with LaFree's analysis lies not in its individual observations, which can be insightful and accurate, but rather in his failure to connect them and to develop a broader, deeper perspective. His two-track framework makes for a narrow interpretation of the data because it leaves untouched the possibility that these two tracks may intersect. Further, it is those who exist at the intersection of gender and race discrimination—black women—who suffer from this fundamental oversight.

LaFree attempts to test the feminist hypothesis that "the application of law to nonconformist women in rape cases may serve to control the behavior of all women."[65] This inquiry is important, he explains, because "if women who violate traditional sex roles and are raped are unable to obtain justice through the legal system, then the law may be interpreted as an institutional arrangement for reinforcing women's gender-role conformity."[66] He finds that "acquittals were more common and final sentences were shorter when nontraditional victim behavior was alleged."[67] Thus, LaFree concludes, the victim's moral character was more important than victim injury—indeed, was second only to the defendant's character. Overall, 82.3 percent of the traditional victim cases resulted in convictions and average sentences of 43.38 months; only 50 percent of nontraditional victim cases led to convictions, with an average term of 27.83 months. The effects of traditional and nontraditional behavior by black women are difficult to determine from the information given and must be inferred from LaFree's passing comments. For example, he notes that black victims were evenly divided between traditional and nontraditional gender roles. This observation, together with the lower rate of conviction for men accused of raping blacks, suggests that gender-role behavior was not as significant in determining case disposition as it was in cases involving white victims. Indeed, LaFree explicitly notes that "the victim's *race* was . . . [a]n important predictor of jurors' case evaluations."[68]

> Jurors were less likely to believe in a defendant's guilt when the victim was black. Our interviews with jurors suggested that part of the explanation for this effect was that jurors . . . [w]ere influenced by stereotypes of black women as more likely to consent to sex or as more sexually experienced and hence less harmed by the assault. In a case involving the rape of a young black girl, one juror argued for acquittal on the grounds that a girl her age from "that kind of neighborhood" probably wasn't a virgin anyway.[69]

LaFree also notes that "[o]ther jurors were simply less willing to believe the testimony of black complainants."[70] One white juror is quoted as saying: "Negroes have a way of not telling the truth. They've a knack for coloring the story. So you know you can't believe everything they say."[71]

Despite explicit evidence that the race of the victim is significant in determining the disposition of rape cases, LaFree concludes that rape law functions to penalize nontraditional behavior in women. LaFree fails to note that racial identification may in some cases serve as a proxy for nontraditional behavior. That is, rape law serves not only to penalize actual examples of nontradi-

tional behavior but also to diminish and devalue women who belong to groups in which nontraditional behavior is perceived as common. For the black rape victim, the disposition of her case may often turn less on her behavior than on her identity. LaFree misses the point that although white and black women have shared interests in resisting the madonna/whore dichotomy altogether, they nevertheless experience its oppressive power differently. Black women continue to be judged by who they are, not by what they do.

3. Compounding the Marginalizations of Rape   LaFree offers clear evidence that racial and sexual hierarchies subordinate black women to white women, as well as to men—both black and white. However, the different effects of rape law on black women are scarcely mentioned in LaFree's conclusions. In a final section, LaFree treats the devaluation of black women as an aside—one without apparent ramifications for rape law. He concludes: "The more severe treatment of black offenders who rape white women *(or, for that matter, the milder treatment of black offenders who rape black women)* is probably best explained in terms of racial discrimination within a broader context of continuing social and physical segregation between blacks and whites."[72] Implicit throughout LaFree's study is the assumption that blacks who are subjected to social control are black *men*. Moreover, the social control to which he refers is limited to securing the boundaries between black males and white females. His conclusion that race differentials are best understood within the context of social segregation as well as his emphasis on the interracial implications of boundary enforcement overlook the intraracial dynamics of race and gender subordination. When black men are leniently punished for raping black women, the problem is *not* "best explained" in terms of social segregation, but in terms of both the race- and gender-based devaluation of black women. By failing to examine the sexist roots of such lenient punishment, LaFree and other writers sensitive to racism ironically repeat the mistakes of those who ignore race as a factor in such cases. Both groups fail to consider directly the situation of black women.

Studies like LaFree's do little to illuminate how the interaction of race, class, and nontraditional behavior affects the disposition of rape cases involving black women. Such an oversight is especially troubling given evidence that many cases involving black women are dismissed outright. Over 20 percent of rape complaints were recently dismissed as "unfounded" by the Oakland Police Department, which did not even interview many, if not most, of the women involved.[73] Not coincidentally, the vast majority of the complainants were black and poor; many of them were substance abusers or prostitutes. Explaining their failure to pursue these complaints, the police remarked that "those cases were hopelessly tainted by women who are transient, uncooperative, untruthful or not credible as witnesses in court."[74]

The effort to politicize violence against women will do little to address the experiences of black and other nonwhite women until the ramifications of racial stratification among women are acknowledged. At the same time, the antiracist agenda will not be furthered by suppressing the reality of intraracial violence against women of color. The effect of both these marginalizations is that women of color have no ready means to link their experiences with those of other women. This sense of isolation compounds efforts to politicize sexual violence within communities of color and perpetuates the deadly silence surrounding these issues.

D. Implications

With respect to the rape of black women, race and gender converge in ways that are only vaguely understood. Unfortunately, the analytical frameworks that have traditionally informed both antirape and antiracist agendas tend to focus only on single issues. They are thus incapable of developing solutions to the compound marginalization of black women victims, who, yet again, fall into the void between concerns about women's issues and concerns about racism. This dilemma is complicated by the role that cultural images play in the treatment of black women victims. That is, the most critical aspects of these problems may revolve less around the political agendas of separate race- and gender-sensitive groups, and more around the social and cultural devaluation of women of color. The stories our culture tells about the experience of women of color present another challenge—and a further opportunity—to apply and evaluate the usefulness of the intersectional critique.

III. CONCLUSION

This article has presented intersectionality as a way of framing the various interactions of race and gender in the context of violence against women of color. Yet intersectionality might be more broadly useful as a way of mediating the tension between assertions of multiple identity and the ongoing necessity of group politics. It is helpful in this regard to distinguish intersectionality from the closely related perspective of antiessentialism, from which women of color have critically engaged white feminism for the absence of women of color, on the one hand, and for speaking for women of color, on the other. One rendition of this antiessentialist critique—that feminism essentializes the category "woman"—owes a great deal to the postmodernist idea that categories we consider natural or merely representational are actually socially constructed in a linguistic economy of difference. While the descriptive project of postmodernism—questioning the ways in which meaning is socially constructed—is generally sound, this critique sometimes misreads the meaning of social construction and distorts its political relevance.

One version of antiessentialism, embodying what might be called the vulgarized social construction thesis, is that since all categories are socially constructed, there is no such thing as, say, blacks or women, and thus it makes no sense to continue reproducing those categories by organizing around them.[75] Even the Supreme Court has gotten into this act. In *Metro Broadcasting, Inc. v. FCC,*[76] the court conservatives, in rhetoric that oozes vulgar constructionist smugness, proclaimed that any set-aside designed to increase the voices of minorities on the airwaves was itself based on a racist assumption that skin color is in some way connected to the likely content of one's broadcast.[77]

To say that a category such as race or gender is socially constructed is not to say that that category has no significance in our world. On the contrary, a large and continuing project for subordinated people—and indeed, one of the projects for which postmodern theories have been very helpful—is thinking about the way in which power has clustered around certain categories and is exercised against others. This project attempts to unveil the processes of subordination and the various ways in which those processes are experienced by people who are subordinated and people who are privileged by them. It is, then, a project that presumes that categories have meaning and consequences. This project's most pressing problem, in many if not most cases, is not the existence of the categories but, rather, the particular values attached to them and the way those values foster and create social hierarchies.

This is not to deny that the process of categorization is itself an exercise of power; the story is much more complicated and nuanced than that. First, the process of categorizing—or, in identity terms, naming—is not unilateral. Subordinated people can and do participate, sometimes even subverting the naming process in empowering ways. One need only think about the historical subversion of the category "black" or the current transformation of "queer" to understand that categorization is not a one-way street. Clearly, there is unequal power, but there is nonetheless some degree of agency that people can and do exert in the politics of naming. Moreover, it is impor-tant to note that identity continues to be a site of resistance for members of different subordinated groups. We all can recognize the distinction between the claims "I am black" and the claim "I am a person who happens to be black." "I am black" takes the socially imposed identity and empowers it as an anchor of subjectivity; "I am black" becomes not simply a statement of resistance but also a positive discourse of self-identification, intimately linked to celebratory statements like the black nationalist "black is beautiful." "I am a person who happens to be black," on the other hand, achieves self-identification by straining for a certain universality (in effect, "I am first a person") and for a concomitant dismissal of the imposed category ("black") as contingent, circumstantial, nondeterminant. There is truth in both characterizations, of course, but they function quite differently, depending on the political context. At this point in history, a strong case can be made that the most critical resistance strategy for disempowered groups is to occupy and defend a politics of social location rather than to vacate and destroy it.

Vulgar constructionism thus distorts the possibilities for meaningful identity politics by conflating at least two separate but closely linked manifestations of power. One is the power exercised simply through the process of categorization; the other, the power to cause that categorization to have social and material consequences. While the former power facilitates the latter, the political implications of challenging one over the other matter greatly. We can look at debates over racial subordination throughout history and see that, in each instance, there was a possibility of challenging either, the construction of identity or the system of subordination based on that identity. Consider, for example, the segregation system in *Plessy v. Ferguson.*[78] At issue were multiple dimensions of domination, including categorization, the sign of race, and the subordination of those so labeled. There were at least two targets for Plessy to challenge: the construction of identity ("What is a black?"), and the system of subordination based on that identity ("Can blacks and whites sit together on a train?"). Plessy actually made both arguments, one against the coherence of race as a category, the other against the subordination of those deemed to be black. In his attack on the former, Plessy argued that the segregation statute's application to him, given his mixed race status, was inappropriate. The court refused to see this as an attack on the coherence of the race system and instead responded in a way that simply reproduced the black/white dichotomy that Plessy was challenging. As we know, Plessy's challenge to the segregation system was not successful either. In evaluating various resistance strategies today, it is useful to ask which of Plessy's challenges would have been best for him to have won—the challenge against the coherence of the racial categorization system or the challenge to the practice of segregation?

The same question can be posed for *Brown v. Board of Education.*[79] Which of two possible arguments was politically more empowering—that segregation was unconstitutional because the racial categorization system on which it was based was incoherent, or that segregation was unconstitutional because it was injurious to black children and oppressive to their communities? While it might strike some as a difficult question, for the most part, the dimension of racial domination that has been most vexing to African-Americans has not been the social categorization as such but, rather, the myriad ways in which those of us so defined have been systematically subordinated. With particular regard to problems confronting women of color, when identity politics fail us, as they frequently do, it is not primarily because those politics take as natural certain categories that are socially constructed—instead, it is because the descriptive content of those categories and the narratives on which they are based have privileged some experiences and excluded others.

Along these lines, consider the controversy involving Clarence Thomas and Anita Hill. During the Senate hearings for the confirmation of Clarence Thomas to the Supreme Court, Anita Hill, in bringing allegations of sexual harassment against Thomas, was rhetorically disempowered in part because she fell between the dominant interpretations of feminism and antiracism. Caught between the competing narrative tropes of rape (advanced by feminists), on the one hand, and lynching (advanced by Thomas and his antiracist supporters), on the other, the race and gender dimensions of her position could not be told. This dilemma could be described as the consequence of antiracism's having essentialized blackness and feminism's having essentialized womanhood. However, recognizing as much does not take us far enough, for the problem is not simply linguistic or philosophical in nature; rather, it is specifically political: the narratives of gender are based on the experience of white, middle-class women, and the narratives of race are based on the experience of black men. The solution does not merely entail arguing for the multiplicity of identities or challenging essentialism generally. Instead, in Hill's case, for example, it would have been necessary to assert those crucial aspects of her location which were erased, even by many of her advocates—that is, to state what difference her difference made.

If, as this analysis asserts, history and context determine the utility of identity politics, how then do we understand identity politics today, especially in light of our recognition of multiple dimensions of identity? More specifically, what does it mean to argue that gender identities have been obscured in antiracist discourses, just as race identities have been obscured in feminist discourses? Does that mean we cannot talk about identity? Or instead, that any discourse about identity has to acknowledge how our identities are constructed through the intersection of multiple dimensions? A beginning response to these questions requires us first to recognize that the organized identity groups in which we find ourselves are in fact coalitions, or at least potential coalitions waiting to be formed.

In the context of antiracism, recognizing the ways in which the intersectional experiences of women of color are marginalized in prevailing conceptions of identity politics does not require that we give up attempts to organize as communities of color. Rather, intersectionality provides a basis for reconceptualizing race as a coalition between men and women of color. For example, in the area of rape, intersectionality provides a way of explaining why women of color must abandon the general argument that the interests of the community require the suppression of any confrontation around intraracial rape. Intersectionality may provide the means for dealing with other marginalizations as well. For example, race can also be a coalition of straight and gay people of color, and thus serve as a basis for critique of churches and other cultural institutions that reproduce heterosexism.

With identity thus reconceptualized it may be easier to understand the need for—and to summon—the courage to challenge groups that are after all, in one sense, "home" to us, in the name of the parts of us that are not made at home. This takes a great deal of energy and arouses intense anxiety. The most one could expect is that we will dare to speak against internal exclusions and marginalizations, that we might call attention to how the identity of "the group" has been centered on the intersectional identities of a few. Recognizing that identity politics takes place at the site where categories intersect thus seems more fruitful than challenging the possibility of talking about categories at all. Through an awareness of intersectionality, we can better acknowledge and ground the differences among us and negotiate the means by which these differences will find expression in constructing group politics.

NOTES

1. Feminist academics and activists have played a central role in forwarding an ideological and institutional challenge to the practices that condone and perpetuate violence against women.

See generally S. Brownmiller, *Against Our Will: Men, Women and Rape* (1975); L. M. G. Clark and D. J. Lewis, *Rape: The Price of Coercive Sexuality* (1977); R. E. Dobash and R. Dobash, *Violence against Wives: A Case against the Patriarchy* (1979); N. Gager and C. Schurr, *Sexual Assault: Confronting Rape in America* (1976); D. E. H. Russell, *The Politics of Rape: The Victim's Perspective* (1974); E. A. Stanko, *Intimate Intrusions: Women's Experience of Male Violence* (1985); L. E. Walker, *Terrifying Love: Why Battered Women Kill and How Society Responds* (1989); L. E. Walker, *The Battered Woman Syndrome* (1984); L. E. Walker, *The Battered Woman* (1979).

2. See, for example, S. Schechter, *Women and Male Violence: The Visions and Struggles of the Battered Women's Movement* (1982) (arguing that battering is a means of maintaining women's subordinate position); S. Brownmiller, *supra* note 1 (arguing that rape is a patriarchal practice that subordinates women to men); E. Schneider, "The Violence of Privacy," 23 *Conn. L. Rev.*, 973, 974 (1991) (discussing how "concepts of privacy permit, encourage and reinforce violence against women"); S. Estrich, "Rape," 95 *Yale L. J.* 1087 (1986) (analyzing rape law as one illustration of sexism in criminal law); see also C. A. Mackinnon, *Sexual Harassment of Working Women: A Case of Sex Discrimination,* 143–213 (1979) (arguing that sexual harassment should be redefined as sexual discrimination actionable under Title VII, rather than viewed as misplaced sexuality in the workplace).

3. Although the objective of this article is to describe the intersectional location of women of color and their marginalization within dominant resistance discourses, I do not mean to imply that the disempowerment of women of color is singularly or even primarily caused by feminist and antiracist theorists or activists. Indeed, I hope to dispel any such simplistic interpretations by capturing, at least in part, the way that prevailing structures of domination shape various discourses of resistance. As I have noted elsewhere, "People can only demand change in ways that reflect the logic of the institutions they are challenging. Demands for change that do not reflect . . . dominant ideology . . . will probably

be ineffective"; Crenshaw, *Race, Reform, and Retrenchment: Transformation and Legitimation in Antidiscrimination Law,* at 1367. Although there are significant political and conceptual obstacles to moving against structures of domination with an intersectional sensibility, my point is that the effort to do so should be a central theoretical and political objective of both antiracism and feminism.

4. Although this article deals with violent assault perpetrated by men against women, women are also subject to violent assault by women. Violence among lesbians is a hidden but significant problem. One expert reported in a study of 90 lesbian couples that roughly 46 percent of lesbians have been physically abused by their partners; J. Garcia, "The Cost of Escaping Domestic Violence: Fear of Treatment in a Largely Homophobic Society May Keep Lesbian Abuse Victims from Calling for Help," *Los Angeles Times* (May 6, 1991), 2; see also K. Lobel, ed., *Naming the Violence: Speaking Out about Lesbian Battering* (1986); R. Robson, "Lavender Bruises: Intralesbian Violence, Law and Lesbian Legal Theory," 20 *Golden Gate U. L. Rev.,* 567 (1990). There are clear parallels between violence against women in the lesbian community and violence against women in communities of color. Lesbian violence is often shrouded in secrecy for reasons similar to those which have suppressed the exposure of heterosexual violence in communities of color—fear of embarrassing other members of the community, which is already stereotyped as deviant, and fear of being ostracized from the community. Despite these similarities, there are nonetheless distinctions between male abuse of women and female abuse of women that, in the context of patriarchy, racism, and homophobia, warrant more focused analysis than is possible here.

5. K. Crenshaw, "Demarginalizing the Intersection of Race and Sex," *U. Chi. Legal F.,* 139 (1989).

6. I explicitly adopt a black feminist stance in this survey of violence against women of color. I do this cognizant of several tensions that such a position entails. The most significant one stems from the criticism that while feminism purports to speak for women of color through its invocation of the term "woman," the feminist perspective excludes women of color because it is based upon the experiences and interests of a certain subset of women. On the other hand, when white feminists attempt to include other women, they often add our experiences into an otherwise unaltered framework. It is important to name the perspective from which one constructs her analysis; and for me, that is as a black feminist. Moreover, it is important to acknowledge that the materials that I incorporate in my analysis are drawn heavily from research on black women. On the other hand, I see my own work as part of a broader collective effort among feminists of color to expand feminism to include analyses of race and other factors such as class, sexuality, and age. I have attempted therefore to offer my sense of the tentative connections between my analysis of the intersectional experiences of black women and the intersectional experiences of other women of color. I stress that this analysis is not intended to include falsely nor to exclude unnecessarily other women of color.

7. I consider intersectionality a provisional concept linking contemporary politics with postmodern theory. In mapping the intersections of race and gender, the concept does engage dominant assumptions that race and gender are essentially separate categories. By tracing the categories to their intersections, I hope to suggest a methodology that will ultimately disrupt the tendencies to see race and gender as exclusive or separable. While the primary intersections that I explore here are between race and gender, the concept can and should be expanded by factoring in issues such as class, sexual orientation, age, and color.

8. 8 U.S.C. § 1186a (1988). The marriage fraud amendments provide that an alien spouse "shall be considered, at the time of obtaining the status of an alien lawfully admitted for permanent residence, to have obtained such status on a conditional basis subject to the provisions of this section"; § 1186a(a)(1). An alien spouse with permanent resident status under this conditional basis may have her status terminated if the attorney general finds that the marriage was "improper" (§ 1186a(b)(1)), or if she fails to file a petition or fails to appear at the personal interview (§ 1186a(c)(2)(A)).

9. The marriage fraud amendments provided that for the conditional resident status to be removed "the alien spouse and the petitioning spouse (if not deceased) *jointly* must submit to the Attorney General . . . a petition which requests the removal of such conditional basis and which states, under penalty of perjury, the facts and information"; § 1186a(b)(1)(A) (emphasis added). The amendments provided for a waiver, at the attorney general's discretion, if the alien spouse was able to demonstrate that deportation would result in extreme hardship, or that the qualifying marriage was terminated for good cause; § 1186a(c)(4). However, the terms of this hardship waiver have not adequately protected battered spouses. For example, the requirement that the marriage be terminated for good cause may be difficult to satisfy in states with no-fault divorces; E. P. Lynsky, "Immigration Marriage Fraud Amendments of 1986: Till Congress Do Us Part," 41 *U. Miami L. Rev.,* 1087, 1095 n. *47*(1987) (student author) (citing J. B. Ingber and R. L. Prischet, "The Marriage Fraud Amendments," in S. Mailman, ed., *The New Simpson-Rodino Immigration Law of 1986,* 564–65 (1986).

10. Immigration Act of 1990, Pub. L. No. 101–649, 104 Stat. 4978. The act, introduced by Rep. Louise Slaughter (Dem.–N.Y.), provides that a battered spouse who has conditional permanent resident status can be granted a waiver for failure to meet the requirements if she can show that "the marriage was entered into in good faith and that after the marriage the alien spouse was battered by or was subjected to extreme mental cruelty by the U.S. citizen or permanent resident spouse"; H.R. Rep. No. 723(I), 101st Cong., 2d Sess. 78 (1990), reprinted in 1990 U.S.C.C.A.N. 6710, 6758; see also 8 C.F.R. § 216.5(3) (1992) (regulations for application for waiver based on claim of having been battered or subjected to extreme mental cruelty).

11. H.R. Rep. No. 723(I), *supra* note 10, at 79, reprinted in 1990 U.S.C.C.A.N. 6710, 6759.

12. D. Hodgin, "'Mail-Order' Brides Marry Pain to Get Green Cards," *Washington Post,* October 16, 1990, at E5.

13. *Id.*

14. Most crime statistics are classified by sex or race but none are classified by sex and race. Because we know that most rape victims are women, the racial breakdown reveals, at best, rape rates for black women. Yet even given this head start, rates for other nonwhite women are difficult to collect. While there are some statistics for Latinas, statistics for Asian and Native American women are virtually nonexistent; cf. G. Chezia Carraway, "Violence Against Women of Color," 43 *Stan. L. Rev.,* 1301 (1993).

15. S. Ali, *The Blackman's Guide to Understanding the Blackwoman* (1989). Ali's book sold quite well for an independently published title, an accomplishment no doubt due in part to her appearances on the Phil Donahue, Oprah Winfrey, and Sally Jesse Raphael television talk shows. For public and press reaction, see D. Gillism, "Sick, Distorted Thinking," *Washington Post* (Oct. 11, 1990), D3; L. Williams, "Black Woman's Book Starts a Predictable Storm," *New York Times* (Oct. 2, 1990), C11; see also P. Cleacue, *Mad at Miles: A Black Woman's Guide to Truth* (1990). The title clearly styled after Ali's, *Mad at Miles* responds not only to issues raised by Ali's book, but also to Miles Davis's admission in his autobiography, *Miles: The Autobiography* (1989), that he had physically abused, among other women, his former wife, actress Cicely Tyson.

16. Ali suggests that the Blackwoman "certainly does not believe that her disrespect for the Blackman is destructive, nor that her opposition to him has deteriorated the Black nation"; S. Ali, *supra* note 15, at viii. Blaming the problems of the community on the failure of the black woman to accept her "real definition," Ali explains that "[n]o nation can rise when the natural order of the behavior of the male and the female have been altered against their wishes by force. No species can survive if the female of the genus disturbs the balance of her nature by acting other than herself"; *id.* at 76.

17. Ali advises the Blackman to hit the Blackwoman in the mouth, "[b]ecause it is from that hole, in the lower part of her face, that all her rebellion culminates into words. Her unbridled tongue is a main reason she cannot get along with the Blackman. She often needs a reminder"; *id.* at 161. Ali warns that "if [the Blackwoman] ignores

the authority and superiority of the Blackman, there is a penalty. When she crosses this line and becomes viciously insulting it is time for the Blackman to soundly slap her in the mouth"; *id.*

18. In this regard, Ali's arguments bear much in common with those of neoconservatives who attribute many of the social ills plaguing black America to the breakdown of patriarchal family values; see, for example, W. Raspberry, "If We Are to Rescue American Families, We Have to Save the Boys," *Chicago Tribune* (July 19, 1989), C15; G. F. Will, "Voting Rights Won't Fix It," *Washington Post* (Jan. 23, 1986), A23; G. F. Will, "'White Racism' Doesn't Make Blacks Mere Victims of Fate," *Milwaukee Journal* (Feb. 21, 1986), 9. Ali's argument shares remarkable similarities to the controversial "Moynihan Report" on the black family, so called because its principal author was now-Senator Daniel P. Moynihan (Dem.–N.Y.). In the infamous chapter entitled "The Tangle of Pathology," Moynihan argued that "the Negro community has been forced into a matriarchal structure which, because it is so out of line with the rest of American society, seriously retards the progress of the group as a whole, and imposes a crushing burden on the Negro male and, in consequence, on a great many Negro women as well"; Office of Policy Planning and Research, U.S. Department of Labor, *The Negro Family: The Case for National Action,* 29 (1965), reprinted in L. Rainwater and W. L. Yancey, *The Moynihan Report and the Politics of Controversy* 75 (1967). A storm of controversy developed over the book, although few commentators challenged the patriarchal discourse embedded in the analysis. Bill Moyers, then a young minister and speechwriter for President Lyndon B. Johnson, firmly believed that the criticism directed at Moynihan was unfair. Some twenty years later, Moyers resurrected the Moynihan thesis in a special television program, *The Vanishing Family: Crisis in Black America.* (CBS television broadcast, Jan. 25, 1986). The show first aired in January 1986 and featured several African-American men and women who had become parents but were unwilling to marry. See A. Linger, "Hardhitting Special About Black Families," *Christian Science Monitor* (Jan. 23, 1986), 23. Many saw the Moyers show as a vindication of Moynihan. President Reagan took the opportunity to introduce an initiative to revamp the welfare system a week after the program aired; M. Barone, "Poor Children and Politics," *Washington Post* (Feb. 10, 1986), A1. Said one official, "Bill Moyers has made it safe for people to talk about this issue, the disintegrating black family structure"; R. Pear, "President Reported Ready to Propose Overhaul of Social Welfare System," *New York Times* (Feb. 1, 1986), A12. Critics of the Moynihan/Moyers thesis have argued that it scapegoats the black family generally and black women in particular. For a series of responses, see "Scapegoating the Black Family," *The Nation* (July 24, 1989) (special issue, edited by Jewell Handy Gresham and Margaret B. Wilkerson, with contributions from Margaret Burnham, Constance Clayton, Dorothy Height, Faye Wattleton, and Marian Wright Edelman). For an analysis of the media's endorsement of the Moynihan/Moyers thesis, see C. Ginsburg, *Race and Media: The Enduring Life of the Moynihan Report* (1989).

19. Domestic violence relates directly to issues that even those who subscribe to Ali's position must also be concerned about. The socioeconomic condition of black males has been one such central concern. Recent statistics estimate that 25 percent of black males in their twenties are involved in the criminal justice systems; see D. G. Savage, "Young Black Males in Jail or in Court Control Study Says," *Los Angeles Times* (Feb. 27, 1990), A1; *Newsday* (Feb. 27, 1990), 15; "Study Shows Racial Imbalance in Penal System," *New York Times* (Feb. 27, 1990), A18. One would think that the linkages between violence in the home and the violence on the streets would alone persuade those like Ali to conclude that the African-American community cannot afford domestic violence and the patriarchal values that support it.

20. A pressing problem is the way domestic violence reproduces itself in subsequent generations. It is estimated that boys who witness violence against women are ten times more likely to batter female partners as adults; *Women and Violence: Hearings before the Senate Comm. on the Judiciary on Legislation to Reduce the Growing Problem of Violent Crime against Women,* 101st Cong.,

2d Sess., pt. 2, at 89 (1991) (testimony of Charlotte Fedders). Other associated problems for boys
who witness violence against women include
higher rates of suicide, violent assault, sexual
assault, and alcohol and drug use; *id.,* pt. 2, at
131 (statement of Sarah M. Buel, assistant district
attorney, Massachusetts, and supervisor, Harvard
Law School Battered Women's Advocacy Project).

21. *Id.* at 142 (statement of Susan Kelly-Dreiss, discussing several studies in Pennsylvania linking
homelessness to domestic violence).

22. *Id.* at 143 (statement of Susan Kelly-Dreiss).

23. Another historical example includes Eldridge
Cleaver, who argued that he raped white women
as an assault upon the white community. Cleaver
"practiced" on black women first; E. Cleaver,
Soul on Ice, 14–15 (1968). Despite the appearance of misogyny in both works, each professes
to worship black women as "queens" of the black
community. This "queenly subservience" parallels closely the image of the "woman on a pedestal" against which white feminists have railed.
Because black women have been denied pedestal
status within dominant society, the image of the
African queen has some appeal to many African-
American women. Although it is not a feminist
position, there are significant ways in which the
promulgation of the image directly counters the
intersectional effects of racism and sexism that
have denied African-American women a perch in
the "gilded cage."

24. T. Harris, *"On The Color Purple,* Stereotypes,
and Silence," 18 *Black Am. Lit. F.,* 155 (1984).

25. On January 14, 1991, Sen. Joseph Biden (Dem.–
DeL.) introduced Senate Bill 15, the Violence
Against Women Act of 1991, comprehensive
legislation addressing violent crime confronting
women; S. 15, 102d Cong., 1st Sess. (1991). The
bill consists of several measures designed to create safe streets, safe homes, and safe campuses
for women. More specifically, Title III of the bill
creates a civil rights remedy for crimes of violence motivated by the victim's gender, *id.* § 01.
Among the findings supporting the bill were "(1)
crimes motivated by the victim's gender constitute bias crimes in violation of the victim's right
to be free from discrimination on the basis of
gender," and "(2) current law [does not provide a
civil rights remedy] for gender crimes committed

on the street or in the home"; S. Rep. No. 197,
102d Cong., 1st Sess. 27 (1991).

26. 137 Cong. Rec. S611 (daily ed. Jan. 14, 1991)
(statement of Senator Boren). Sen. William
Cohen (Dem.–Me.) followed with a similar
statement, noting "that rapes and domestic assaults are not limited to the streets of our inner
cities or to those few highly publicized cases
that we read about in the newspapers or see
on the evening news. Women throughout the
country, in our nation's urban areas and rural
communities, are being beaten and brutalized in
the streets and in their homes. It is our mothers,
wives, daughters, sisters, friends, neighbors,
and coworkers who are being victimized; and in
many cases, they are being victimized by family
members, friends, and acquaintances"; *id.* (statement of Senator Cohen).

27. *48 Hours,* "Till Death Do Us Part" (CBS television broadcast, Feb. 6, 1991).

28. Letter of Diana M. Campos, director of Human
Services, PODER, to Joseph Semidei, deputy
commissioner, New York State Department of
Social Services (Mar. 26, 1992).

29. *Id.* (emphasis added).

30. *Id.*

31. *Id.*

32. Roundtable Discussion on Racism and the
Domestic Violence Movement (April 2, 1992)
(transcript on file with the *Stanford Law Review).* The participants in the discussion—Diana
Campos, director, Bilingual Outreach Project of
the New York State Coalition Against Domestic
Violence; Elsa A. Rios, project director, Victim Intervention Project (a community-based
project in East Harlem, New York, serving
battered women); and Haydee Rosario, a social
worker with the East Harlem Council for Human Services and a Victim Intervention Project
volunteer—recounted conflicts relating to race
and culture during their association with the New
York State Coalition Against Domestic Violence,
a state oversight group that distributed resources
to battered women's shelters throughout the state
and generally set policy priorities for the shelters
that were part of the coalition.

33. *Id.*

34. *Id.*

35. *Id.*

36. Ironically, the specific dispute that led to the walkout concerned the housing of the Spanish-language domestic violence hotline. The hotline was initially housed at the coalition's head-quarters, but languished after a succession of coordinators left the organization. Latinas on the coalition board argued that the hotline should be housed at one of the community service agencies, while the board insisted on maintaining control of it. The hotline is now housed at PODER; *id.*

37. Said Campos, "It would be a shame that in New York state a battered woman's life or death were dependent upon her English language skills"; D. M. Campos, *supra* note 28.

38. The discussion in the following section focuses rather narrowly on the dynamics of a black-white sexual hierarchy. I specify African-Americans in part because, given the centrality of sexuality as a site of racial domination of African-Americans, any generalizations that might be drawn from this history seem least applicable to other racial groups. To be sure, the specific dynamics of racial oppression experienced by other racial groups are likely to have a sexual component as well. Indeed, the repertoire of racist imagery that is commonly associated with different racial groups each contain a sexual stereotype as well. These images probably influence the way that rapes involving other minority groups are perceived both inter-nally and in society at large, but they are likely to function in different ways.

39. V. Smith, "Split Affinities: The Case of Inter-racial Rape," in M. Hirsch and E. F Keller, eds., *Conflicts in Feminism,* 271, 274 (1990).

40. *Id.* at 276–78.

41. Smith cites the use of animal images to char-acterize the accused black rapists, including descriptions such as: "'a wolfpack of more than a dozen young teenagers' and '[t]here was a full moon Wednesday night. A suitable backdrop for the howling of wolves. A vicious pack ran ram-pant through Central Park. . . . This was bestial brutality.'" An editorial in the *New York Times* was entitled "The Jogger and the Wolf Pack"; *id.* at 277 (citations omitted).

Evidence of the ongoing link between rape and racism in American culture is by no means unique to media coverage of the Central Park jogger case. In December 1990, the George Washington University student newspaper, *The Hatchet,* printed a story in which a white student alleged that she had been raped at knife-point by two black men on or near the campus; the story caused considerable racial tension. Shortly after the report appeared, the wom-an's attorney informed the campus police that his client had fabricated the attack. After the hoax was uncovered, the woman said that she hoped the story "would highlight the problems of safety for women"; F. Banger, "False Rape Report Upsetting Campus," *New York Times* (Dec. 12, 1990), A2; see also L. Payne, "A Rape Hoax Stirs Up Hate," *New York Newsday* (Dec. 16, 1990), 6.

42. W. C. Troft, "Deadly Donald," UP (Apr. 30, 1989). Donald Trump explained that he spent $85,000 to take out these ads because "I want to hate these muggers and murderers. They should be forced to suffer and, when they kill, they should be executed for their crimes"; "Trump Calls for Death to Muggers," *Los Angeles Times* (May 1, 1989), A2. But cf. "Leaders Fear 'Lynch' Hysteria in Re-sponse to Trump Ads," UPI (May 6, 1989) (com-munity leaders feared that Trump's ads would fan "the flames of racial polarization and hatred"); C. Fuchs Epstein, "Cost of Full Page Ad Could Help Fight Causes of Urban Violence," *New York Times* (May 15, 1989), A18 ("Mr. Trump's proposal could well lead to further violence").

43. R. D. McFadden, "2 Men Get 6 to 18 Years for Rape in Brooklyn," *New York Times* (Oct. 2, 1990), B2. The woman "lay half naked, moaning and crying for help until a neighbor heard her" in the air shaft; "Community Rallies to Support Victim of Brutal Brooklyn Rape," *New York Daily News* (June 26, 1989), 6. The victim "suf-fered such extensive injuries that she had to learn to walk again. . . . She faces years of psychologi-cal counseling"; McFadden, *supra.*

44. Smith points out that "[t]he relative invisibility of black women victims of rape also reflects the differential value of women's bodies in capitalist societies. To the extent that rape is constructed as a crime against the property of privileged white men, crimes against less valuable women—women of color, working-class women, and lesbians, for example—mean less or mean differ-ently than those against white women from the

middle and upper classes"; Smith, *supra* note 39, at 275–76.

45. "Cases involving black offenders and black victims were treated the least seriously"; G. D. LaFree, *Rape and Criminal Justice: The Social Construction of Sexual Assault* (1989). LaFree also notes, however, that "the race composition of the victim-offender dyad" was not the only predictor of case dispositions; *id.* at 219–20.

46. "Race Tilts the Scales of Justice. Study: Dallas Punishes Attacks on Whites More Harshly," *Dallas Times Herald* (Aug. 19, 1990), A1. A study of 1988 cases in Dallas County's criminal justice system concluded that rapists whose victims were white were punished more severely than those whose victims were black or Hispanic. The *Dallas Times Herald,* which had commissioned the study, reported that "[t]he punishment almost doubled when the attacker and victim were of different races. Except for such interracial crime, sentencing disparities were much less pronounced"; *id.*

47. *Id.* Two criminal law experts, Iowa law professor David Baldus and Carnegie-Mellon University professor Alfred Blumstein "said that the racial inequities might be even worse than the figures suggest"; *id.*

48. *See* G. LaFree, *supra* note 45, at 219–20 (quoting jurors who doubted the credibility of black rape survivors); see also H. Field and L. Bienen, *Jurors and Rape: A Study in Psychology and Law 141* (1980), at 117–18.

49. The statistic that 89 percent of all men executed for rape in this country were black is a familiar one. *Furman v. Georgia,* 408 U.S. 238, 364 (1972) (Marshall, J., concurring). Unfortunately, the dominant analysis of racial discrimination in rape prosecutions generally does not discuss whether any of the rape *victims* in these cases were black; see J. Wriggins, "Rape, Racism, and the Law," 6 *Harv. Women's L. J.,* 103, 113 (1983) (student author).

50. See M. Rosenfeld, "After the Verdict, the Doubts: Black Women Show Little Sympathy for Tyson's Accuser," *Washington Post* (Feb. 13, 1992), D1; A. Johnson, "Tyson Rape Case Strikes a Nerve Among Blacks," *Chicago Tribune* (Mar. 29, 1992), C1; S. P. Kelly, "Black Women Wrestle with Abuse Issue: Many Say Choosing Racial

over Gender Loyalty Is Too Great a Sacrifice," *Chicago Star Tribune* (Feb. 18, 1992), A1.

51. 20/20 (ABC television broadcast, Feb. 21, 1992).

52. According to a study by the Bureau of Justice, black women are significantly more likely to be raped than white women, and women in the 16–24 age group are two to three times more likely to be victims of rape or attempted rape than women in any other age group; see R. J. Ostrow, "Typical Rape Victim Called Poor, Young," *Los Angeles Times* (Mar. 25, 1985), 8.

53. See P. Tyre, "What Experts Say About Rape Jurors," *New York Newsday* (May 19, 1991), 10 (reporting that "researchers had determined that jurors in criminal trials side with the complainant or defendant whose ethnic, economic and religious background most closely resembles their own. The exception to the rule . . . is the way women jurors judge victims of rape and sexual assault"). Linda Fairstein, a Manhattan prosecutor, states, "too often women tend to be very critical of the conduct of other women, and they often are not good jurors in acquaintance-rape cases"; M. Carlson, "The Trials of Convicting Rapists," *Time* (Oct. 14, 1991), 11.

54. As sex crimes prosecutor Barbara Eganhauser notes, even young women with contemporary lifestyles often reject a woman's rape accusation out of fear. "To call another woman the victim of rape is to acknowledge the vulnerability in yourself. They go out at night, they date, they go to bars, and walk alone. To deny it is to say at the trial that women are not victims"; Tyre, *supra* note 53.

55. G. LaFree, *supra* note 45.

56. *Id.* at 49–50.

57. *Id.* at 50–51.

58. *Id.* at 237–40.

59. LaFree concludes that recent studies finding no discriminatory effect were inconclusive because they analyzed the effects of the defendant's race independently of the race of victim. The differential race effects in sentencing are often concealed by combining the harsher sentences given to black men accused of raping white women with the more lenient treatment of black men accused of raping black women; *id.* at 117, 140. Similar results were found in another study: see A. Walsh, "The Sexual Stratification Hypothesis and Sexual Assault in Light of the Changing

Conceptions of Race," 25 *Criminology,* 153, 170 (1987) ("sentence severity mean for blacks who assaulted whites, which was significantly in excess of mean for whites who assaulted whites, was masked by the lenient sentence severity mean for blacks who assaulted blacks").

60. G. LaFree, *supra* note 45, at 139–40.

61. Sexual stratification, according to LaFree, refers to the differential valuation of women according to their race and to the creation of "rules of sexual access" governing who may have contact with whom. Sexual stratification also dictates what the penalty will be for breaking these rules: the rape of a white woman by a black man is seen as a trespass on the valuable property rights of white men and is punished most severely; *id.* at 48–49. The fundamental propositions of the sexual stratification thesis have been summarized as follows: (1) Women are viewed as the valued and scarce property of the men of their own race. (2) White women, by virtue of membership in the dominant race, are more valuable than black women. (3) The sexual assault of a white by a black threatens both the white man's "property rights" and his dominant social position. This dual threat accounts for the strength of the taboo attached to interracial sexual assault. (4) A sexual assault by a male of any race upon members of the less valued black race is perceived as nonthreatening to the status quo and therefore less serious. (5) White men predominate as agents of social control. Therefore, they have the power to sanction differentially according to the perceived threat to their favored social position; Walsh, *supra* note 59, at 155.

62. I use the term "access" guardedly because it is an inapt euphemism for rape. On the other hand, rape is conceptualized differently depending on whether certain race-specific rules of sexual access are violated. Although violence is not explicitly written into the sexual stratification theory, it does work itself into the rules, in that sexual intercourse which violates the racial access rules is presumed to be coercive rather than voluntary; see, for example, *Sims v. Balkam,* 136 S.E. 2d 766, 769 (Ga. 1964) (describing the rape of a white woman by a black man as "a crime more horrible than death"); *Story v. State,* 59 So.

480 (Ala. 1912) ("The consensus of public opinion, unrestricted to either race, is that a white woman prostitute is yet, though lost of virtue, above the even greater sacrifice of the voluntary submission of her person to the embraces of the other race"); Wriggins, *supra* note 49, at 125, 127.

63. This traditional approach places black women in a position of denying their own victimization, requiring them to argue that it is racist to punish black men more harshly for raping white women than for raping black women. However, in the wake of the Mike Tyson trial, it seems that many black women are prepared to do just that; see notes 50–52 *supra* and accompanying text.

64. G. LaFree, *supra* note 45, at 148. LaFree's transition between race and gender suggests that the shift might not loosen the frame enough to permit discussion of the combined effects of race and gender subordination on black women. LaFree repeatedly separates race from gender, treating them as wholly distinguishable issues; see, for example, *id.* at 147.

65. *Id.*

66. *Id.* at 151. LaFree interprets nontraditional behavior to include drinking, drug use, extramarital sex, illegitimate children, and "having a reputation as a 'partier,' a 'pleasure seeker' or someone who stays out late at night"; *id.* at 201.

67. *Id.* at 204.

68. *Id.* at 219 (emphasis added). While there is little direct evidence that prosecutors are influenced by the race of the victim, it is not unreasonable to assume that since race is an important predictor of conviction, prosecutors determined to maintain a high conviction rate might be less likely to pursue a case involving a black victim than a white one. This calculus is probably reinforced when juries fail to convict in strong cases involving black victims. For example, the acquittal of three white St. John's University athletes for the gang rape of a Jamaican schoolmate was interpreted by many as racially influenced. Witnesses testified that the woman was incapacitated during much of the ordeal, having ingested a mixture of alcohol given to her by a classmate who subsequently initiated the assault. The jurors insisted that race played no role in their decision to acquit. "There was no

race, we all agreed to it," said one juror; "They were trying to make it racial but it wasn't," said another; "Jurors: 'It Wasn't Racial,'" *New York Newsday* (July 25, 1991), at 4. Yet it is possible that race did influence on some level their belief that the woman consented to what by all accounts, amounted to dehumanizing conduct; see, for example, C. Agus, "Whatever Happened to 'The Rules,'" *New York Newsday* (July 28, 1991), 11 (citing testimony that at least two of the assailants hit the victim in the head with their penises). The jury nonetheless thought, in the words of its foreman, that the defendants' behavior was "obnoxious" but not criminal; see S. H. Schanberg, "Those 'Obnoxious' St. John's Athletes," *New York Newsday* (July 30, 1991), 79. One can imagine a different outcome had the races of the parties only been reversed. Rep. Charles Rangel (Dem.–N.Y.) called the verdict "a rerun of what used to happen in the South"; J. M. Brodie, "The St. John's Rape Acquittal: Old Wounds That Just Won't Go Away," *Black Issues in Higher Educ.* (Aug. 15, 1991), 18. Denise Snyder, executive director of the D.C. Rape Crisis Center, commented: "It's a historical precedent that white men can assault black women and get away with it. Woe be to the black man who assaults white women. All the prejudices that existed a hundred years ago are dormant and not so dormant, and they rear their ugly heads in situations like this. Contrast this with the Central Park jogger who was an upper-class white woman"; J. Mann, "New Age, Old Myths," *Washington Post* (July 26, 1991), C3 (quoting Snyder); see K Bumiller, "Rape as a Legal Symbol: An Essay on Sexual Violence and Racism," 42 *U. Miami L. Rev.,* 75, 88 ("The cultural meaning of rape is rooted in a symbiosis of racism and sexism that has tolerated the acting out of male aggression against women and, in particular, black women").

69. *Id.* at 219–20 (citations omitted). Anecdotal evidence suggests that this attitude exists among some who are responsible for processing rape cases. Fran Weinman, a student in my seminar on race, gender, and the law, conducted a field study at the Rosa Parks Rape Crisis Center. During her study, she counseled and accompanied a twelve-year-old black rape survivor who

became pregnant as a result of the rape. The girl was afraid to tell her parents, who discovered the rape after she became depressed and began to slip in school. Police were initially reluctant to interview the girl. Only after the girl's father threatened to take matters into his own hands did the police department send an investigator to the girl's house. The city prosecutor indicated that the case wasn't a serious one, and was reluctant to prosecute the defendant for statutory rape even though the girl was underage; the prosecutor reasoned, "After all, she looks sixteen." After many frustrations, the girl's family ultimately decided not to pressure the prosecutor any further and the case was dropped; see F. Weinman, "Racism and the Enforcement of Rape Law," 13–30 (1990) (unpublished manuscript) (on file with the *Stanford Law Review).*

70. G. LaFree, *supra* note 45, at 220.

71. *Id.*

72. *Id.* at 239 (emphasis added). The lower conviction rates for those who rape black women may be analogous to the low conviction rates for acquaintance rape. The central issue in many rape cases is proving that the victim did not consent. The basic presumption in the absence of explicit evidence of lack of consent is that consent exists. Certain evidence is sufficient to disprove that presumption, and the quantum of evidence necessary to prove nonconsent increases as the presumptions warranting an inference of consent increase. Some women—based on their character, identity, or dress—are viewed as more likely to consent than other women. Perhaps it is the combination of the sexual stereotypes about black people along with the greater degree of familiarity presumed to exist between black men and black women that leads to the conceptualization of such rapes as existing somewhere between acquaintance rape and stranger rape.

73. C. Cooper, Nowhere to Turn for Rape Victims: High Proportion of Cases Tossed Aside by Oakland Police, *S. F. Examiner,* Sept. 16, 1990, at A10.

74. *Id.* Advocates point out that because investigators work from a profile of the kind of case likely to get a conviction, people left out of that profile

are people of color, prostitutes, drug users, and people raped by acquaintances. This exclusion results in "a whole class of women . . . systematically being denied justice. Poor women suffer the most"; *id.*

75. I do not mean to imply that all theorists who have made antiessentialist critiques have lapsed into vulgar constructionism. Indeed, antiessentialists avoid making these troubling moves and would no doubt be receptive to much of the critique set forth herein. I use the phrase "vulgar constructionism" to distinguish between those antiessentialist critiques that leave room for identity politics and those that do not.

76. 110 S. Ct. 2997 (1990).

77. The FCC's choice to employ a racial criterion embodies the related notions that a particular and distinct viewpoint inheres in certain racial groups and that a particular applicant, by virtue of race or ethnicity alone, is more valued than other applicants because the applicant is "likely to provide [that] distinct perspective." The policies directly equate race with belief and behavior, for they establish race as a necessary and sufficient condition of securing the preference. . . . The policies impermissibly value individuals because they presume that persons think in a manner associated with their race; *id.* at 3037 (O'Connor, J., joined by Rehnquist, C. J., and Scalia and Kennedy, J. J., dissenting) (internal citations omitted).

78. 163 U.S. 537 (1896).

79. 397 U.S. 483 (1954).

AMERICAN ANTHROPOLOGICAL ASSOCIATION STATEMENT ON "RACE" (MAY 17, 1998)

The following statement was adopted by the Executive Board of the American Anthropological Association, acting on a draft prepared by a committee of representative American anthropologists. It does not reflect a consensus of all members of the AAA, as individuals vary in their approaches to the study of "race." We believe that it represents generally the contemporary thinking and scholarly positions of a majority of anthropologists.

In the United States both scholars and the general public have been conditioned to viewing human races as natural and separate divisions within the human species based on visible physical differences. With the vast expansion of scientific knowledge in this century, however, it has become clear that human populations are not unambiguous, clearly demarcated, biologically distinct groups. Evidence from the analysis of genetics (e.g., DNA) indicates that most physical variation, about 94%, lies *within* so-called racial groups. Conventional geographic "racial" groupings differ from one another only in about 6% of their genes. This means that there is greater variation within "racial" groups than between them. In neighboring populations there is much overlapping of genes and their phenotypic (physical) expressions. Throughout history whenever different groups have come into contact, they have interbred. The continued sharing of genetic materials has maintained all of humankind as a single species.

Physical variations in any given trait tend to occur gradually rather than abruptly over geographic areas. And because physical traits are inherited independently of one another, knowing the range of one trait does not predict the presence of others. For example, skin color varies largely from light in the temperate areas in the north to dark in the tropical areas in the south; its intensity is not related to nose shape or hair texture. Dark skin may be associated with frizzy or kinky hair or curly or wavy or straight hair, all of which are found among different indigenous peoples in tropical regions. These facts render any attempt to establish lines of division among biological populations both arbitrary and subjective.

Historical research has shown that the idea of "race" has always carried more meanings than mere physical differences; indeed, physical variations in the human species have no meaning except the social ones that humans put on them. Today scholars in many fields argue that "race" as it is understood in the United States of America was a social mechanism invented during the 18th century to refer to those populations brought together in colonial America: the English and other European settlers, the conquered Indian peoples, and those peoples of Africa brought in to provide slave labor.

From its inception, this modern concept of "race" was modeled after an ancient theorem of the Great Chain of Being, which posited natural categories on a hierarchy established by God or nature. Thus "race" was a mode of classification linked specifically to peoples in the colonial situation. It subsumed a growing ideology of inequality devised to rationalize European attitudes and treatment of the conquered and enslaved peoples. Proponents of slavery in particular during the 19th century used "race" to justify the retention of slavery. The ideology magnified the differences among Europeans, Africans, and Indians, established a rigid hierarchy of socially exclusive categories, underscored and bolstered unequal rank and status differences, and provided the rationalization that the inequality was natural or God-given. The different physical traits of African-Americans and Indians became markers or symbols of their status differences.

As they were constructing US society, leaders among European-Americans fabricated the cultural/behavioral characteristics associated with each "race," linking superior traits with Europeans and negative and inferior ones to blacks and Indians. Numerous arbitrary and fictitious beliefs about the different peoples were institutionalized and deeply embedded in American thought.

Early in the 19th century the growing fields of science began to reflect the public consciousness about human differences. Differences among the "racial" categories were projected to their greatest extreme when the argument was posed that Africans, Indians, and Europeans were separate species, with Africans the least human and closer taxonomically to apes.

Ultimately "race" as an ideology about human differences was subsequently spread to other areas of the world. It became a strategy for dividing, ranking, and controlling colonized people used by colonial powers everywhere. But it was not limited to the colonial situation. In the latter part of the 19th century it was employed by Europeans to rank one another and to justify social, economic, and political inequalities among their peoples. During World War II, the Nazis under Adolf Hitler enjoined the expanded ideology of "race" and "racial" differences and took them to a logical end: the extermination of 11 million people of "inferior races" (e.g., Jews, Gypsies, Africans, homosexuals, and so forth) and other unspeakable brutalities of the Holocaust.

"Race" thus evolved as a worldview, a body of prejudgments that distorts our ideas about human differences and group behavior. Racial beliefs constitute myths about the diversity in the human species and about the abilities and behavior of people homogenized into "racial" categories. The myths fused behavior and physical features together in the public mind, impeding our comprehension of both biological variations and cultural behavior, implying that both are genetically determined. Racial myths bear no relationship to the reality of human capabilities or behavior. Scientists today find that reliance on such folk beliefs about human differences in research has led to countless errors.

At the end of the 20th century, we now understand that human cultural behavior is learned, conditioned into infants beginning at birth, and always subject to modification. No human is born with a built-in culture or language. Our temperaments, dispositions, and personalities, regardless of genetic propensities, are developed within sets of meanings and values that we call "culture." Studies of infant and early childhood learning and behavior attest to the reality of our cultures in forming who we are.

It is a basic tenet of anthropological knowledge that all normal human beings have the capacity to learn any cultural behavior. The American experience with immigrants from hundreds of different language and cultural backgrounds who have acquired some version of American culture traits and behavior is the clearest evidence of this fact. Moreover, people of all physical variations have learned different cultural behaviors and continue to do so as modern transportation moves millions of immigrants around the world.

How people have been accepted and treated within the context of a given society or culture has a direct impact on how they perform in that society. The "racial" worldview was invented to assign some groups to perpetual low status, while others were permitted access to privilege, power, and wealth. The tragedy in the United States has been that the policies and practices stemming from this worldview succeeded all too well in constructing unequal populations among Europeans, Native Americans, and peoples of African descent. Given what we know about the capacity of normal humans to achieve and function within any culture, we conclude that present-day inequalities between so-called "racial" groups are not consequences of their biological inheritance but products of historical and contemporary social, economic, educational, and political circumstances.

[Note: For further information on human biological variations, see the statement prepared and issued by the American Association of Physical Anthropologists, 1996 (AJPA 101:569–570).]

AAA POSITION PAPER ON "RACE": COMMENTS?

As a result of public confusion about the meaning of "race," claims as to major biological differences among "races" continue to be advanced. Stemming from past AAA actions designed to address public misconceptions on race and intelligence, the need was apparent for a clear AAA statement on the biology and politics of race that would be educational and informational. Rather than wait for each spurious claim to be raised, the AAA Executive Board determined that the Association should prepare a statement for approval by the Association and elicit member input.

Commissioned by the Executive Board of the American Anthropological Association, a position paper on race was authored by Audrey Smedley *(Race in North America: Origin and Evolution of a Worldview,* 1993) and thrice reviewed by a working group of prominent anthropologists: George Armelagos, Michael Blakey, C. Loring Brace, Alan Goodman, Faye Harrison, Jonathan Marks, Yolanda Moses, and Carol Mukhopadhyay. A draft of the current paper was published in the September 1997 *Anthropology Newsletter* and posted onto the AAA website http://www.aaanet.org for a number of months, and member comments were requested. While Smedley assumed authorship of the final draft, she received comments not only from the working group but also from the AAA membership and other interested readers. The paper above was adopted by the AAA Executive Board on May 17, 1998, as an official statement of AAA's position on "race."

As the paper is considered a *living statement,* AAA members', other anthropologists', and public comments are invited. Your comments may be sent via mail or e-mail to Peggy Overbey, Director of Government Relations, American Anthropological Association, 4350 N. Fairfax Dr., Suite 640, Arlington, VA 22201.

SOME KIND OF INDIAN: ON RACE, EUGENICS, AND MIXED-BLOODS

M. Annette Jaimes

ONE "RED RACE" OF PEOPLE

In this ahistorical era of heightened contradiction and controversy over American citizenry and national character, American Indian tribes have insisted persistently that they, and not the U.S. government, hold the right to define tribal membership and therefore Indian identification, as differentiated from their U.S. citizenship. Traditionally, most tribes have determined their members by cultural rather than political criteria, and as Native nationhoods. This is in contrast to any "scientific" approach with a racial construct used to determine "blood quantum" formulations. Actually, there is no factual evidence that indigenous peoples of the Americas, before the European conquest, applied a concept of race to their traditional membership, which, in fact, included "whites" as well as "mixed-bloods" via naturalization and adoption. After the conquest and forced assimilation, one does run across references in Indian dialogue that a particular group sees itself as a national entity, in terms of its communal conceptualization of nationhood as "a people." Yet, this is not the same as the perception and promotion of themselves as a distinct "race" of people that has come forth in federal Indian policy-making. A famous Shawnee leader Tecumseh, for example, did refer to a "red race" of Native people, and others used terms such as full-blood, mixed-blood, and halfbreed.[1] However, it is the position of this paper that such terms meant different things to the Natives and non-Natives.

Euroamericans designated all "New World" Indians as one single "race," predicated on ideas of "purity of race" and culture. This ideal later resulted in a tropism of a race construct linked with ethnicity and nationality. A group of intellectual reformers, calling themselves "Friends of the Indians," in contrast to those among the military and government leaders who wanted to keep on killing Indians in the nineteenth century, went so far as to declare Indians "blank slates" in order to build a case for their "Americanization" as lower status citizens.[2] This Eurocentric preoccupation with and construction of "race" can be found in the nineteenth-century racial–racist doctrines that were based on prevailing pseudoscientific theories, especially at times in the mid-1800s when "white" scientists measured skulls of Natives, called *Crania Americana,* to compare and contrast with other racial types to justify "a case for Indian inferiority."[3] Such blatant pseudoscience was meant to establish a theoretical framework that ordered and explained human variety, as well as to distinguish superior races from inferior ones. In this racial hierarchy, Indians were in competition with African-Black Americans as the lowest "race of mankind," in what was referred to as "the great chain of being" by Eurocentric social scientists.[4] Such racist orthodoxy has since been soundly disputed as European pseudoscience, which the Euroamericans took to quite readily as a rationale for racial oppression of colonized peoples as "groups of color." It overlooked those eighteenth-century patriarchal ideals of the Enlightenment, among western Europeans, that espoused all humankind as one brotherhood. However, the biblical origin myths prevailed in espousing a "Christian-derived" parentage among them that envisioned a "white" Adam and Eve. In this essay, I address the areas of traditional Native identity in contrast to the later U.S. colonization, eugenics coding that has contributed to American racisms, the status of "mixed-blood" identities in Indian–Tribal demographics, and I close with who is *Indigenous to the Americas.*

TRADITIONAL NATIVE IDENTITY
AND U.S. COLONIZATION

"New World" Indians were considered "savages" and "heathens" by the Spanish, at the same time the Spaniards were burning "heretics" during the Inquisition, to justify their imperial aims. By the seventeenth century, entire peoples indigenous to this hemisphere had been wiped out, with their cultures for the most part destroyed. Such racistly based pogroms ignored the physical and cultural diversity that was evident among Native groups.

In pre-Columbian times, traditional Native peoples designated their societies, more often than not, on matrilineal descendancy, with few exceptions to patrilineal descendancy in tracing their ancestry. Both led to elaborate kinship traditions through clan structures or moieties. (These clans respected the plant and animal worlds as living and spirit entities, in what cultural anthropologists call "animism" and "totemism.")[5] Generally speaking, more indigenous cultures trace relationship through the mother than through the father. These communal societies also had spheres of matrifocal and/or patrifocal influence and decision making among their members; some spheres were designated by age as well as gender, especially delegating leadership and authority among senior members as elders. Women among the oldest Southwest tribes (i.e., Pimas/Maricopas, Hopis) had decision-making control in the education of the younger generations as well as in agrarian activities, whereas the men had more visible influence in religious ceremonies; all members participated in communal rituals. Yet, it is unlikely that traditional Native societies were matriarchies, as some feminists—Native as well as non-Native—attempt to claim,[6] the majority among them were matrilineal because it was much easier to trace a child from its mother. These kinship systems, consequently, allowed for much influence and power for decision making among the women in what are the closest models to egalitarianism among many Native societies.

In contemporary times, membership has been determined by some tribes to require birth on the reservation whereas some hold to a grandfather clause that accepts all identified as members before a certain date regardless of other factors. Assimilationist "policies," in contrast to traditional customs, have been influenced by mandated federal rules and regulations, which are primarily implemented by the Bureau of Indian Affairs (BIA).[7] Therefore, a variety of internally deduced cultural and kinship criteria are used to determine tribal membership. This may or may not coincide with the government's externally imposed policies of Indian identification process—primarily blanket-policies—implemented and regulated by several agencies of the federal government.

This conflict about identification has resulted in pressure for tribal councils to have "civil rights codes" written into their Indian Reorganization Act (IRA) constitutions (mandated by congressional legislation in 1934), and at times has intruded upon the exercise of tribal sovereignty in their internal affairs. The conflict becomes even more complex when, as in the case of *Santa Clara Pueblo v. Martinez* (436 US 49, 1978), a male-dominated leadership among a Pueblo society in New Mexico was able to take membership away from one of its women and her children because she had married a Navajo man outside of the tribe. This case reflects a "trickle-down patriarchy" as a result of IRA reorganization forced upon the Pueblo people by the U.S. government. The pre-IRA tradition of matrilineality that existed among the Santa Clara people, would have prevented this legal decision by a skewed male-dominated leadership on the Pueblo council.[8]

This usurpation of indigenous sovereignty in North America has a long history that involved European-spawned racial theories which led to federal Indian policy. The "blood quantum" stipulation first emerged from the interpretations of the General (Dawes) Allotment Act of 1887, which congressionally mandated the requirement that all eligible Indian individuals for allotments must be at least "one half or more Indian blood."[9] Such restrictive determination of who can identify as an "Indian" for federal entitlements has been fraught with inconsistencies and contradictions found in federal Indian policy throughout the twentieth century. These conflicts of policy have escalated during Republican administrations, particularly during the Reagan–Bush years.

> The blood-quantum mechanism most typically used by the federal government to assign identification to [Indian] individuals over the years is as racist as any conceivable policy. . . . The restriction of federal entitlement funds to cover only the relatively few Indians who meet quantum requirements, essentially a cost-cutting policy at its inception, has served to exacerbate tensions over the identity issue among Indians. . . . Thus, a bitter divisiveness has been built into Indian communities and national policies, sufficient to preclude achieving the internal unity necessary to offer any serious challenge to the status quo.[10]

The Allotment Act was designed to break up the communal land base of the particular tribes by dividing up land parcels among individual members. It was meant to coerce them into "white man's civilization" and rationalize their Christian salvation from "savagery." As a result of this act, there was even a campaign for non-Indian men to marry Indian women among the allotees, because the landholdings would revert to the husband's control as patriarch of the family. In some cases, this led to the early death of the Indian wife, giving clear transfer of title to the "white" male spouse.[11] The hidden agenda in this legislation, which soon became apparent, was to coopt the land for non-Indian use and eventual ownership, as those Indians who "failed" as farmers and went into debt would either lease or sell their land parcels to non-Indians. This in turn led to the checkerboarding of non-Indian holdings among the Indian allotments; Cherokee communities in Oklahoma are a case in point. A drastic consequence of the allotment campaign in this forced assimilation, has cost Indian peoples at least two-thirds of their land base which has been expropriated by the federal government, under a "trusteeship" for the Indians, with cooperation from individual non-Indians. This has resulted in an estimated 100 out of 150 million acres being stolen by non-Indians with government complicity. Once all "blooded" Indians were "allotted," the federal government quickly opened up "surplus" land to non-Indian settlement; in addition, natural resources on Native lands were claimed by the federal government.[12]

Because of the imposed exclusion policy on Native Americans, most tribes today have succumbed to a required enrollment process and recordkeeping in order to insure federal recognition, as well as federal funding. These quasi-national entities may designate a different requirement of "blood quantum" than the BIA criteria of "quarter-blood," or none at all; the BIA reduced this standard from the "half-blood" quantum required in the Allotment Act as a result of the pressure to acknowledge the high degree of intermixing among American Indians. The Cherokees of Oklahoma are often represented as not requiring any "blood quantum" standard, which has contributed to their high membership population (240,000). The tribal registrar has indicated, however, that to apply for tribal membership, a person must first meet certain BIA criteria (as noted on the Cherokee membership application) that require a "Certificate of Degree of Indian Blood."[13] According to the latest data on American Indian tribes, Cherokees have recently surpassed the Navajo–Diné population (200,000) in numbers, but not in landbase.[14] Yet, the Cherokees are restricted to tracing their Indian descendancy through the controversial 1887 Dawes rolls (as listed in the Allotment Act), prepared by the federal government for designated allotments among "eligible" members on tribal rolls. As reported in the 1928 *Merriam Report,* these tribal rolls included many non-Indians who were listed as the result of the chicanery of "white" BIA commissioners. Marriages were arranged with "whites" causing

Cherokee allotees to eventually lose their lands due to intermarriage. These practices led to the dispossession of traditional Indians from their homeland, as well as to the cultural deprivation of Oklahoma Cherokees.[15]

There are also the varying degrees of "blood quantum" requirements, to none-at-all among the Sioux (Lakotas, Dakotas, Hunkpapas, and Santees). The most recent tribe to remove the blood quantum requirement in its tribal constitution is the Osage in Oklahoma, but tribal enrollees have to have ancestors on the 1906 Osage rolls.[16]

Throughout the twentieth century, traditional kinship systems among Native cultures and their societies still survive, even if discreetly practiced, as can be attested to by cultural anthropologists and more recently sociologists, as well as by the tribal members themselves.[17] These kinship traditions are also in the context of what they hold in common as Native Nations with other indigenous peoples to the Americas, such as the Northwest fishing societies and the Pueblos of the Southwest, as well as *los Indios* of Central and South America. This is so even though a systemic and effective campaign has tried to diffuse and confuse these "Indian Identity" issues. At a 1969 congressional hearing, it was stated in testimony: "Questions of identity often trouble modern Indian youth, especially those of mixed Indian and white ancestry. Is being Indian a matter of adopted life-style and point of view, they wonder, or of physical appearance and the amount of genetic Indian-ness, which is traced by reconstructing a family tree?"[18] Therefore, what contributes to the confusion are the various methods used to define and enumerate American Indians as a federal entitlement population in the United States. These include: legal definitions, such as enrollment in an American Indian tribe; self-declaration, as in more liberal U.S. census enumerations; community recognition, for example, by other Indians or tribal members; recognition by non-Indians; biological definitions, such as blood quantum (which is being

condemned as a racist and genocidal policy by international human rights tribunals initiated by indigenous peoples); cultural definitions (which may include subjective determination, such as knowing one's native language or "acting" like an "Indian").[19]

Other systematic strategies in this colonization process are used to dispossess the Indians from their lands, and it was the allotment years that preceded a grander scheme of western expansionism. As illustration, the Allotment Act clearly demonstrates other economic determinants than the mere overflow of cash from the federal treasury into the use of blood quantum to negate Native individuals out of existence. The huge windfall of land expropriated by the United States, as a result of this act, was only the tip of the iceberg. For instance, in constricting the acknowledged size of Indian populations, the government could technically meet its obligations to reserve first rights to water usage for non-Indian agricultural, ranching, municipal, and industrial use in the arid West. The same principle pertains to the assignment of fishing quotas in the Pacific Northwest, a matter directly related to the development of a lucrative non-Indian fishing industry in that bioregion.[20]

Such racially constructed policy is indicative of an advanced stage of U.S. postmodernist colonization in the state of Native America. These race politics are succinctly stated by Rayna Green, curator of Native American Studies at the Smithsonian Institute: "There is a kind of 'ethnic cleansing' going on. . . ."[21] She was referring to the politics of "Indian Identity" over issues of who can or cannot claim to be "recognized" as a "legitimate" American Indian these days, which is interpreted from the amended Indian Arts and Crafts Act of 1990 (P.L. 101-644-1104 *Stat.* 4662) for self-serving ends. (This was actually her response to being targeted by "Indian Identity police," herself, for not being an "enrolled" Cherokee. However, the tribal chair of the Cherokee Nation, Wilma Mankiller, has come out in support of Green as a respected individual, regardless of her "unenrolled" Cherokee status, who has done much good for the Cherokee people.)

Individual attacks on nonfederally–recognized Indians, who have neither BIA certification nor tribal affiliation, are a kind of race-baiting with tragic consequences of ethno-racism and autogenocide among Native peoples, even though many of those targeted have documentation that traces their family trees to Native descendancy. Those who cannot "prove" they are Indian are also being accused of "ethnic fraud" by some self-serving Indian spokespersons and organizations.[22] Such charges seem to be underlined with neofascist tendencies and motives among the accusers. Questions arise as to whether or not a Native individual or group need be identified as Indian by geneology, as in kinship relations, and/or by culture. These identity questions come at a time when many Native cultures are under seige by mainstream society and their lifeways are threatened. This matter is not so much a problem among those who are trying to pass themselves off as "Indians," as it is among neoconservative tribal elite cultural brokers who are guilty of corruption brought on by Indian and tribal partisan politics. Hence, these campaigns to discredit Indians are based more on disinformation, rumor-mongering, and just plain mean-spiritedness that presume the person under attack is guilty until she or he can prove otherwise. Those individuals and families who are victimized in this way have decisions imposed upon them because they are out of favor with those in control, and these arbitrary decisions are often sanctioned by the BIA technocrats and federal authorities.

EUGENICS CODING AND AMERICAN RACISMS

Eugenics coding is not new to the Eurocentric historiography and the United States is no exception. Other groups of color and creed have been defined in racialist terms, for example, Africans were coded by "blood" to designate their ability to be "good" and "strong" slaves and to serve as "beasts of burden." Even after the Civil War and the emancipation of the African slaves in U.S. society, the "one-drop rule" still prevailed to determine if an individual was to be racially classified as a Negro. An attorney, Brian Begue, made this statement in an appellate court, "If you're a little bit white, you're black. If you're a little bit black, you're still black."[23]

This "one-drop rule" is the antithesis of how American Indians or Native Americans are determined, based on blood quantum formulations that require the minimum BIA standard of quarter-blood for federal recognition, and more recently tribal membership among some groups. In this process anything below that quantum disqualifies individuals from their Native ancestry and heritage. In 1972, intertribal organizations in the United States wrote a manifesto entitled *Twenty Points* that listed grievances as a result of U.S. colonization among disenfranchised and dispossessed Native Americans. One of these points denounced the BIA implementation of blood quantum criteria as a racist and genocidal policy to terminate the rights of Native peoples as individuals and tribal groups.[24] Some Native groups advocate that the blood quantum degree should be increased, from "quarter-blood" to "half-blood" (as called for in the 1887 Allotment Act); some tribal spokespersons now advocate a "racially pure" Indian people among their own tribes. This goes against current research on "genetic markers" which indicates a high degree of racial mixing among Native populations to North America, which was even evident in pre-Columbian times.[25] It would also violate traditional kinship taboos that prohibit incest while encouraging exogamy among Native Nations. Tribal entities with small population, such as the Turtle Mountain Chippewa tribe (in North Dakota), would be most affected with all the attendant health problems due to inbreeding. In the state of Hawaii, the 50 percent blood quantum has prevailed since its imposition by the United States authorities, to determine who are eligible to call themselves Native Hawaiian. A "People's Tribunal" on Native Hawaiian sovereignty was held in Hawaii in the summer of 1993. After hearing several days of testimony among the indigenous population of the Islands, nine notable international judges recommended that "Blood quantum standards of identification should be immediately suspended."[26] As Haunani Kay Trask states, "We [the Native Hawaiians] are the only population that are defined racially on the Islands. . . . We traditionally determined our membership by geneology that is connected with the land, and which is different than race."[27] These racist and genocidal polices had nothing to do with indigenous traditions and kinship structures of a land-based culture and nationhood that were manifested in Native spirituality until the coming of the racially preoccupied "white" Europeans.

This xenophobic perception of distinct and absolute races (those of Western European stock are deemed "superior" in contrast to "inferior" ones), which is predicated on skin color and other physical traits, has the underlying but unproven assumption of a "purity of racial blood." This assumption also was manifested in Nazi Germany with horrifying consequences and tragedy, to those who did not fit the ideal of the German "super race." In what he calls *The Nazi Connection,* Stefan Kuhl makes astonishing links with Nazi race policies and American eugenicists as collaborators in what is known as the International Eugenics Movement.[28] Historical analysis of Adolf Hitler's leadership has correlated the Fuehrer's recorded interest in the earlier U.S. genocidal campaign that targeted early Native peoples as a model for his "Jewish Solution" during World War II.[29] Ward Churchill's treatise for "a functional definition of genocide" has laid out the premise that the containment policy in South Africa's Apartheid against the indigenous peoples in that country was also influenced by the United States–established reservation system.[30]

In the history of United States racism, the color lines were drawn on southern Europeans and Asian groups who were targeted for entry and citizenship restrictions by immigration quotas. These restrictions were invoked when large numbers of Asian-American immigrants posed a threat of the diffusion of "white" American citizens during this country's growth years.[31] U.S. miscegenation laws on the books discouraged Euroamericans from marrying persons of "color." These were officially struck down in 1968, as a result of civil rights legislation (of which some has been dismantled). But there is evidence that some states, especially in the South and more recently in the Pacific Northwest, covertly and illegally implement them.[32] During World War II and into the 1960s, America's Indians were mainly out of sight while contained on the reservations, or they were visible as alcoholics on skidrow only, especially the male population coming back from the war and suffering post-combat experiences.[33] Among the latter, many Indian veterans became recipients of federal programs in the 1960s, ironically to assist them in making the transition from reservation to urban life in the big cities, at the expense of relinquishing their tribal community status among their own peoples.

Postindustrial, high-tech modernization is an advanced stage of *institutional racism* that permeates the whole of American society. This is manifested in its salience as well as signification of race, gender, and class distinctions in hierarchical and elitist structures. In U.S. historiography, a strain of American racism unique to this country is predicated on Eurocentric myths interpreted from biblical scripture that a "chosen" people are meant to have dominion over nature and others as they subdue the Earth (Genesis 1: 28).[34] This can be called theological racism, but the Anglo-Americans who settled in this country called it their "manifest destiny," to justify the conquest and colonization of early indigenous peoples and their lands to the Americas, within the context of the arrogant "Doctrine of Discovery" of European imperialism. This "Christian nationalism" evolved to rationalize imperialism by a Protestant crusade in the United States.[35] A biological ideology to justify this race teleology was later extrapolated from Newtonian physics and Darwinian economics, but it has been debunked as pseudoscientism.

As a first-class power with Second and even Third World people among its "ethnic minorities," the United States is guilty in its mistreatment of all groups of people who do not meet "white" ideals of physical characteristics and "moral" character. In its mainstream xenophobia and racism against others the United States is also guilty of violating basic human rights; it has been particularly avaricious in targeting indigenous peoples with visible acts of genocide and ethnocide that can be correlated with ecocide.

There is an increasing amount of documentation on what is being calling *environmental racism,* because Indian lands have been targeted first for military sites, uranium mining, and toxic waste dumps. In the Southwest, the Four Corners area and Black Mesa, among the Diné and Hopi in Arizona, and Acoma and Laguna Pueblo in New Mexico were declared "national sacrifice areas" in the 1970s by the Nixon Administration,[36] and Native inhabitants were treated as expendable people on their own homelands. This game plan can also be linked with the *ecological racism* that denies Native groups their first-rights claims to water and other natural resources found on their designated landbases.[37] There is also the destruction by prodevelopment schemes, such as highway construction, that cause land erosion, stream deterioration and flooding of communities and sacred sites on Native lands.

At the same time, a prevailing Eurocentric mind-set laments the passing of traditional Native peoples and their cultures, as in bygone days, while proclaiming that these groups are participating in their own demise by getting in the way of "progress."[38] There is no other word for this than genocide, both cultural and biological. Indigenous peoples throughout the globe and especially in Third World countries find themselves under siege of prodevelopment agendas. Any indigenous group resisting its own destruction by the corporate domination and coercion of the

prodevelopment technological paradigm is stigmatized as backward and primitive. This insidious prejudice negates Native peoples' environmental rights by referring to them as "ecological noble savages," a phrase inspired by romantic literati of the past and taken up by present-day satirists.[39]

Those tribal groups who succumb to prodevelopment schemes, which often involve Indian gaming, find they are denigrated for not behaving like "Indians" by environmental fundamentalists and others who do not want the competition. These tribal decisions are often made in order to build some kind of self-sufficiency after long years of poverty and colonization in the United States. On the other hand, there is a highly visible group of "cultural brokers" in the Indian world who have a record of opportunism, as well as "progressive" tribal leaders, who succumb to "economic bribery" at the expense of the well-being of their Native constituency. In one such recent scenario, the Mescalero Apache tribal council negotiated a nuclear dump site in their community, against the protests of their own people.[40] This is a Catch 22 that Native peoples face in the dialectics of their survival.

Currently, facts are coming to light that the United States is still on the path of imperialist designs for conquest and colonization, which first led to the subjugation of this hemisphere's original inhabitants in the formation of its race-conscious nationalism. As the only superpower in the world, the United States collaborates with transnational corporations and second- and third-rate world powers in super schemes (i.e., NAFTA [North American Free Trade Agreement] and the Trilateral Commission); the mainstream citizenry and well-being of this planet are threatened by its predatory pursuit of the profit motive.[41]

It is all too evident that American racisms are alive and well in U.S. social and political institutions. Even more insidious signs are on the horizon, as Native peoples in North America, among other indigenous peoples worldwide, are now being subjected to genetic research. This extension of the eugenics movement is being called the "Human Genome Diversity Project,"[42] as the latest form of racism on the globe. Selected Native groups are being targeted as intact biological, cultural, and land-based entities, and as "threatened" peoples; this means that such groups are soon-to-be extinct as biological and cultural gene pools. There are scientists who claim they are interested in preserving these groups for future study by soliciting DNA data sampling and collection from human subjects among their membership. At the same time, these same scientists do not seem concerned that these groups are facing their physical demise as distinct peoples and cultures. This kind of research is still predicated on the racist doctrines of *scientific racism.* This is a science of bigotry, that also has unethical aims because one of its major objectives is to patent the data accumulated as genetic resource data as the "intellectual property" of the geneticists.

The eugenics "experts" have already experimented with the genetic engineering of plants and animals,[43] which leads one to ponder what they have in store for humans. This is the "virtual reality" context from which genetic research is operating, and at the expense and exploitation of Native peoples as merely biological and cultural entities. Many Native human rights activists are concerned about this project which they call the "Vampire Project"[44] (because the best genetic sample is a subject's blood).

Indigenous delegations to the United Nations are beginning to suspect a new kind of racism that is continuing the genocide, ethnocide, and ecocide of these populations and their habitats. Some even suspect that the intent is to remove the Native peoples as final barriers to corporate development, which also includes land seizures and the intellectual property rights that indigenous peoples hold about agrarian and ecological knowledge.[45] The Human Genome Diversity Project is being initiated and backed by private transcorporate enterprises, and has been designated as a separate project from the larger Human Genome Project that is sampling the human species at large. Hence *genetic racism* is manifesting itself today under the guise of medical research to find cures for terminal diseases and to prolong human life. This is all happening in an era of human overpopulation and "endangered species," and yet there are predictions of human cloning and "designer babies" in the continuing search for the perfect human and ultimate immortality. A new eugenics is on the scene, but with more awareness from the past in raising questions as to *who* will have access to this data and power and *why,* and for *what* worthy or wicked purpose it will be eventually and inevitably used.

MIXED-BLOOD IDENTITIES

Miscegenation is a necessary topic in any discussion about race, especially because debates are often predicated on the strange Eurocentric assumption about the "purity" of the races. Miscegenation got the attention of the Spanish and Portuguese sovereigns when their own citizens persisted in intermixing with the Native population of the "New World." But those liaisons were often not recognized by the Roman Catholic authorities as legitimate marriages. Such indirectly sanctioned illegitimacy can be correlated with a pecking order in determining occupation that was to be used as a racist strategy for slave labor. This is documented in historical annals on the Spanish and other European social systems, which stratify the hierarchy of racial castes.[46] According to more modern prevailing attitudes on miscegenation, someone who is born of two diverse "races" is of marginal status and will therefore develop a marginal personality. It is assumed that these individuals will have difficulty in reconciling the two cultures from whence they come and that these difficulties will therefore contribute to their marginalization and even alienation.[47] The underlying presumption in this context is that "marginal" people have no ethics or moral conscience because they are not committed devotees, enthusiasts, or patriots of either social system. This presumption is also grounded in the presumed superiority of the national ideology referred to as the "Protestant Ethic" and Western Christianity in general, among Euroamerican immigrants to the United States.

In this racial–racist construction, it is also important to provide a context of how so-called mixed-bloods were perceived in pre-Columbian times. As noted before, there is no evidence that early indigenous peoples to this hemisphere based their membership on any construct of "race." The obsession with race was brought over with Eurocentric ideas that also subordinated women.

The Native cultures did acknowledge diversity in physical characteristics, but were more concerned with cultural differences between themselves and others. There was a strong sense of nationhood that can even be described as ethnocentrism among all Native Nations, but this was not predicated on any racial criteria. It was not until the importation of pseudoscientific ideas of race (with other Eurocentric ideas such as sexism), that racially designated sub-categories proliferated—mulattos, quadroons, mestizos, métis, creoles, half-breeds, and so forth—as hybrid categories. Among Native Americans, intermixing has led to mixed-blood categories, such as the Red–Black Indians among Cherokees, Lumbees, and other southeastern tribes, as well as the mestizo (of Spanish and Indian mixings) Indians of the Southwest and Mexico, and the métis (of French and Indian mixing, or Indian and white) among the northern Nations of the United States and Canada.

In analyzing "color, race, and caste in the evolution of Red–Black peoples," Jack Forbes quotes early Spanish and Portuguese sources on the origins of such biracial terms as mestizo and mulatto. Forbes also traces the growth of racism and disdain for "mixed-bloods," from simply describing status in occupation and citizenry to derogatory stereotypes.[48] The Spaniards were notorious for these racial classifications, and more than thirty categories were designated as interracial categories among their populace.[49] An ecclesiastical policy was even developed for how the church authorities determined who was bio-

logically an ideal Christian, that included being of "pure" race, which they called limpiezas de sangre (purity of blood).[50]

This xenophobia projected on "mixed-bloods" is confused with a purity in culture as well as race, which is manifested in nationalist pride and other political ideologies. Such myths have led to and even directly espouse "ethnic cleansing" in volatile parts of the world today, as in the current Serbian war raging against the Croatians in Eastern Europe.

The Lumbees of North Carolina have state recognition, but are still in the process of pursuing federal recognition. For the first time, tribal leaders among federally recognized groups have been solicited to cast their votes in this process, and a majority voted against the Lumbees. There are several theories as to what was behind this and even talk of ethnoracism among the already-recognized groups. And even though it looks like the Lumbees, among the Red–Black Indians, might attain a pseudotribal status from the federal government, they have been criticized for having too open an enrollment policy in determining their tribal membership. In the Southwest, several tribal peoples can rightfully claim a tricultural description as a result of early missionization by the Spanish Roman Catholics, and later the Protestant settlers. Among these Native peoples are the Pimas, Apaches, Yaquis, and T'Ono O'dom (formerly Papagos) in Arizona, as well as the Pueblo societies of New Mexico, and the southern California Mission Band Rancherias.

Russell Thornton also has written about the high degree of intermarriage and miscegenation among American Indians since the European conquest. He writes that this intermixing actually changed the physical and genetic makeup of Indian populations. He states, "In many if not most instances, mixing with nontribal or non-Indian populations was a result of the depopulation of American Indians, whereby the number of potential mates had been severely restricted (such as epidemics)."[51] Thornton seems to have overlooked the probability, which Forbes considers, that the indigenous peoples in some parts of the Americas had already been intermixing with other "racial" and cultural groups, years before the European invaders had reached their shores. This would then account for already recognized physical diversity among Native populations, and what some would refer to as racial strains or genetic markers.

Today, American Indians still have to deal with the Euroamerican treatment of "mixed-bloods" in the historiography, which still has racist consequences. Traditionally, an individual could become a member of a tribal society by kinship and intermarriage, or adoption and naturalization, no matter what the "racial" pedigree. Later, Euroamericans saw advantages to pitting "confused half-breeds" against the so-called fullbloods who were resisting the western expansion into Indian lands. There was even a period when "mixed-blood" leadership was handpicked by "white" Americans, to thwart the traditional leadership, because the thinking was that a "mixed-blood" was more likely than a "full-blood" to cooperate and assimilate to "white" men's ways. Actually, a solution to the "Indian problem" among liberal educators and policy makers, who called themselves "Friends of the Indians," encouraged intermarriage between Indians and whites to facilitate the assimilation of the latter.[52] But for the most part, and especially in recent times, "mixed-bloods" find themselves doubly marginalized in any society, because they are not fully accepted in any designated "race" or ethnic group. As Vine Deloria Jr., senior Native (Lakota) scholar, insightfully wrote in 1977: "No Indian tribe today can claim a pure blood stock as if this requirement necessarily guaranteed 'Indianness'"[53] Deloria has since been working on a book about "Indian Treaty Making," that includes intertribal treaties made between Native Nations before those with the United States. He has noted that some treaties between Europeans and Indians had sections (some since removed) specific to the protection of "mixed-blood" members by the Indian leaders.[54]

There have been notable exceptions, however, to the thinking, based on racist assumptions, that "mixed-bloods" are easy assimilationists and that "fullbloods" are less able to be coopted. It can even be argued that what Indians meant by "fullbloods" was very different from what non-Indians meant because it had more to do with cultural criteria for determining tribal membership. Two historical cases are the famed Quanah Parker, a "half-breed" Comanche, and Captain Jack, a "mixed-blood" leader among the Modocs and Klamaths. Parker's mother was a "white" Protestant who was kidnapped by the Comanches when she was nine years old. She was later married to a prominent male leader in the tribal nation.[55] Both respected men used their leadership to resist European encroachment by negotiating for their people with the "whites." In modern times notable Native "mixed-bloods" have made their mark in Indian history. Among the more well-known were Will Rogers (Cherokee), the famed comic and satirist, and D'Arcy McNickle (Salish and Kootenai), a notable historical novelist. Both of these individuals were accorded full membership status among their respective tribal nations. But today we are witnessing a growing number of Native peoples with "mixed-blood" ancestry and heritage being denied their Indian identity by federal mandate via the BIA.

These divisive matters have now escalated to the point that many among the younger generations are denied federal services because of federal Indian policy that has closed their tribal rolls, terminated whole tribes, and even declared some extinct. This can happen to individuals even if they do meet blood quantum standards. Therefore, this can be perceived as discrimination against "mixed-bloods." Such issues also need to be put into the context that it has been estimated there is at least 50 percent intermarriage among Native Americans (with men slightly higher than women) who marry outside of their tribe, either other Indians (in intertribal relations) or "whites."[56] Intertribal relations have been in practice since pre-Columbian times, because exogamy was encouraged for political and biological reasons. Because these are highly politicized times, political motivations can determine, even among Indians themselves, why a particular group or an individual might not be "recognized" by the tribe and/or "certified" by the federal government.[57] Such decisions can be made for political expediency, that is at the expense of a tribe's or pueblo's cultural integrity, based on kinship traditions such as matrilineality (as in the legal case, *Martinez v. Santa Clara Pueblo, 1978).* Those with "mixed-blood identities" among Native Americans are hit even harder by this, because they do not fit into the rigid racial–racist categories in the census. This problematic situation is encouraging a growing trend among "mixed-blood" groups to challenge the imposed race categories.[58]

A contrast to U.S. Indian policy is Canadian government policy that recognizes its primarily landless métis populations and organizations, as having certain aboriginal rights. Métis, however, are considered a separate category that distinguishes them from Reserve Indians as tribal groups in Canada. In the province of Quebec, they are referred to as French métis because they speak a French patois and are Roman Catholics. (In the United States "mixed-blood" groups are lumped with other "ethnic minorities.") However, these same métis groups, especially the women, criticize the Canadian government because they are at a disadvantage when compared with land-based Reserve Indians.[59]

What also needs to be challenged in this arena is that the hybridization that exists among most of us is not negative or denigrating, but rather is an attribute we can take pride in as nonracist and universal in our affinity with biological and cultural diversity. The reality is, however, that a distinct "race" or a "pure" race of people cannot be proven, scientifically or otherwise. Therefore, the majority if not all of humanity at this time, are probably of "mixed-blood" descendancy as well as heritage, as a result of human inclination and capacity for intermixing and intermarriage.

INDIGENOUS TO THE AMERICAS

These intense years have brought American Indians through the twentieth century, to a mood of backslide toward reactionary politics. Even while the Clinton Administration proclaims a new day for Indians, new stratagems are at play for dispossessing Indians further, with colonial "identities" that are symptomatic of race and genetics that is correlated with nationalist issues and affairs. Indians are now being told to give up the last vestiges of their "Indianness," in order to compete like everyone else, for they have never fully had liberation from the European invasion. It is a fact of Indian life that the U.S. government still controls their homelands, and they are the most regulated and controlled population caught in a rat maze of federal and state bureaucracy. Indians live in what has been called a "settler state" that has imposed colonization on its traditional indigenous peoples.[60] The oppressive conditions of this colonization have created a federal dependency spawned from a racist paternalism and divisiveness about "Indian Identity." Government policies have made Native peoples subject to removal and relocation, and threatened cultural and political domains. Traditional Native peoples and their approach to life have stood in the way of development in mining and other profit-motive ventures, which have proven hazardous to the inhabitants' health, as well as the ecology of their natural environment.[61] An international perspective is needed for the Native peoples' situational affairs, as well as for local, regional, and national agendas, in order to connect the Indians' historical legacy with the present blight so that a more promising future for younger generations can be created.

With this historical legacy and the current state of affairs throughout Native America, it appears that for the Indians to survive in this country they must first perish, as is the lot of all mythological creatures. Yet, we can challenge this negation of us as relics of the past, and become the universal people we are meant to be. To accomplish this, we must resist the forces of our homogenization that are patriotic coercion for American nation-alism. We need a call for our decolonization in alliance with other disenfranchised and dispos-sessed peoples. And we need to never lose sight of who we are in the circle we call humanity. This has nothing to do with race and racism, but is rooted historically in our cultural identity with the land and the environment.[62]

We also need to restore a strong sense of who we are as Native individuals and cultural groups in our own right. This is particularly urgent be-cause there is a growing number of urban-based "ethnic" Indians, estimated at 60 percent of all Indians, and rising. Most Native American popu-lations are found in the Western states; metro-politan Los Angeles is home to the largest Native population, at about 100,000, with Chicago next in line. The population of tribal-based Indi-ans is dropping. The largest land-based groups are in the Southwest, with the exception of the Oklahoma Cherokees.[63] There is evidence that the neoconservative federally recognized tribal leadership in alliance with the Washington D.C. cultural brokers, are advocating the adoption of more restrictive qualifications for tribally rec-ognized members among Native Americans. The federal government continues to determine rigid and inhumane racist categories that deny "mixed-blood" heritage in present times, even though such undesignated groups were tradition-ally considered members of the nations in pre-Columbian times. We question how some tribal leaders determine who gets on their tribal rolls and who gets taken off; at times these policies have appeared to be more influenced by tribal partisan politics than by the protection of mem-bership rights. This is creating a problem in Indian and tribal identity politics, which is be-coming the concern of human rights activists, as well as those who perceive a conflict in regard to democratic ideals and rights. Tribal leaders are now being pressured to include "civil rights codes" in their tribes' constitutions, which pro-hibit decisions about tribal membership that dis-criminate based on "race, creed, and/or national

origin, as articulated in the U.S. Constitution and its Bill of Rights."[64] It is my assessment that gen-der should also be included among these rights because of noted court cases of tribal patriarchy, in which predominantly male-dominated tribal councils deny Native women and their offspring tribal status. These inequities are a result of U.S. colonization, and particularly due to the Indian Reorganization of tribal governance in 1934.

Haunani Kay Trask made this insightful as-sessment on the subject: "When you divide a peo-ple by race, you divide the people, themselves, from each other."[65] It is in this way we give up our ontology that is the ethos of our very exist-ence, as *Indigenous to the Americas.* Granted that legal and entitlement considerations have come down to a recent "federal deficit" issue as part of the economic crisis in United States. Tribes and intertribal Indian organizations, until recently, were advocating more open policies to tribal en-rollment and BIA certification. There has been abuse in this process, but it is probably a regional problem due to administrative mismanagement and even bureaucratic corruption. However, these problems do not require generic legisla-tion via federal policy and congressional laws. Such McCarthyite tactics violate the human laws of Native individuals and groups who still trace their Indian identity through kinship and geneol-ogy, in stark contrast to any nationalist ideology based on racial constructs and racist formula-tions. As Vine Deloria once stated: "We should just drop the definitions, and concentrate on the development of programs for Indians wherever they are instead of keeping the myth alive that we follow very proper rules in determining who is eligible for federal service."[66] In this context, there is a need for resolutions of the ideological issues raised in terms of legal constructions of who is an American Indian and how that corre-lates with federal and state entitlements.

There is also a need to challenge the ahistori-cism that exists in U.S. society, in order to ac-knowledge and comprehend the historiography of U.S. colonization put upon Tribal and Native groups of this continent. This understanding must also extend to how that U.S.–Indian construction is manifested in federal Indian policy in contrast to international human rights for indigenous peoples of the Americas. This is part of the decolonization process that is presently in motion, and what can be perceived as an indigenous liberation movement. Intertribal and regional organizations, such as the Confederated Chapters of the American Indian Movement, are the vanguard of this more global movement.[67] Their agendas focus on the decentralization of leadership within their own ranks as well as grassroots Native environmentalism to resist genocide, ethnocide, and ecocide while restoring ecological balance to their habitats and the planet—as Mother Earth. These liberation struggles also include the Native peoples in Third World countries as well as the United States and Canada.

On the basis of this research I make the following recommendations: (1) include community recognition, off as well as on reservation areas; (2) determine the definitions of a Tribal–Native community predicated on cultural traditions and indigenous rights that are predicated on cultural integrity; (3) reject the BIA Blood Quantum altogether, and replace it with a broader scope of kinship traditions that includes exogamy, naturalization, and adoption, as well as matrilineal or patrilineal ancestral lineage; (4) allow traditional Native peoples to determine tribal membership, which would acknowledge their landless and nonfederally recognized relations, and include a population among those who are referred to as "mixed-blood." These recommendations need an international vision that would also address the need for the U.S. federal and state system to assist in the maintenance of traditional Native communities as cultural enclaves with indigenous rights. They would also assist in the restoration of groups who can claim grievances of acts of genocide and ethnocide on Native populations, which involve eugenics coding imposed upon them. This last recommendation also recognizes the impact of ecocide that has been wrought on Native lands as

bioregional spheres in the natural environment, as a result of government and corporate intervention and exploitation of those homelands.[68] Indigenous groups should also be able to continue to solicit redress in international arenas, such as human rights forums, to hold the U.S. authorities accountable for past wrongdoing while the government makes amends by restitution and reparation to its colonized populations. Only then will Euroamerican imperialism and hegemony be confronted so the people, Native and non-Native among us, will be able to heal the wounds of our past and present for the sake of our future.

NOTES

1. On Tecumseh and a "Pan-Indian Federation," see Glenn Tucker, *Tecumseh: Vision of Glory* (Indianapolis: Bobbs-Merrill, 1959); also, a soon-to-be published paper by Rachel Buff, "Tecumseh, Tenskwatawa, and the National Popular: Myth, Historiography, and Popular Memory," *Historical Reflections, Cross-Cultural Contact,* special issue.

2. Alexandra Harmon, "When an Indian is not an Indian?. 'Friends of the Indian' and the Problem of Indian Identity," *Journal of Ethnic Studies* 18. no. 2 (1991): 95–123. Harmon bases her primary research on the *Proceedings of the 7th Annual Meeting of the Lake Mohonk Conference of Friends of the Indian (1886, 1889),* in Lake Mohonk, N.Y.

3. See Stephen Jay Gould, *The Mismeasure of Man* (New York: Norton, 1981), pp. 50–60, on "Morton's Skulls," as a case of pseudoscientific racism that was later debunked for skewed research in the study of "craniometrics."

4. Ibid, pp. 98–103. The 1900s was the height of "scientific" racism that was predicated on American eugenics as well as the racial-racist doctrines of German social scientists of the time.

5. See Baird J. Callicott. *In Defense of the Land Ethic* (Binghamton: State University of New York Press, 1989), pp. 177–219, on American Indian Environmental Ethics and the Ojibways as illustration of attitudes towards nature, and an American Indian land wisdom.

6. Paula Gunn Allen, *The Sacred Hoop: Recovering the Feminine in American Indian Traditions* (Boston: Beacon Press, 1986). The author refers to native cultures as "matriarchies" and characterized as "gynocentric" in her pandering generalizations to feminism.

7. Established in 1820, within the U.S. (Continental) Office of War, the bureau is now under the auspices of the Department of the Interior. It has been criticized by Indians as a vehicle for colonist oppression; however, many Indians see it as a necessary evil because it symbolizes the federal obligations, which are based on treaties and other agreements. See M. A. Jaimes, "American Indian Identification/Eligibility Policy in Federal Indian Service Programs," chapter 3. on BIA Origins, pp. 40–50 (Ph.D. dissertation, Arizona State University, 1990).

8. M. A. Jaimes with Theresa Halsey, "American Indian Women: At the Center of Indigenous Resistance in North America," *The State of Native America,* ed. M. A. Jaimes (Boston: South End Press, 1992), pp. 311–44.

9. M. A. Jaimes, "Federal Indian Identification Policy: A Usurpation of Indigenous Sovereignty in North America," in Jaimes, pp. 123–38. *The General Allotment Act of 1887,* also known as the *Dawes Act,* is described by W. Churchill and G. Morris, "Table: Indian Laws and Cases," in Jaimes, p. 14.

10. Jaimes in Jaimes, *State of Native America,* p. 136.

11. Jack Weatherford. *Native Roots* (New York: Crown, 1991), pp. 19–36. For a fictional account, see Linda Hogan's excellent novel, *Mean Spirit* (New York: Atheneum, 1990), a story about a "white" man who married an Indian woman for her allotment, which led to her murder.

12. Ward Churchill, *Struggle for the Land* (Monroe, Maine: Common Courage Press, 1992–1993)—the theft of Indian lands is a main premise of this book.

13. *Cherokee Nation Application Form Letter* (p. 1. not dated), signed by R. Lee Fleming, Tribal Registrar, states:

> This letter is in reference to your inquiry concerning Cherokee Registration. To be eligible for Tribal membership with the Cherokee Nation, you must apply and be able to present necessary evidence. This evidence is a Certificate of Degree of Indian Blood (CDIB), issued by the Bureau of Indian Affairs.

14. "Cherokees Experience Population Boom," *The Circle,* Tulsa, Okla., February 18, 1994, 16.

15. Lynda Dixon Shaver, "Oklahoma Indians and the Cultural Deprivation of an Oklahoma Cherokee Family," presented at the Speech and Communication Association meeting, November 1993, Miami, Fla.

16. Shelly Davis, "Osage Adopt Constitution: U.S. Declared First Constitution Obsolete in 1881," in *News from Indian Country* (from Pawhuska, Okla.), February 1994, 15.

17. Edward Valandra, a graduate student working on his master's thesis in political science at the University of Colorado at Boulder, and former tribal council member for the Roseland Oglala Tribal Nation, has provided keen insights into the continuing practices of traditional kinship among his peoples in South Dakota. See also M. A. Jaimes's dissertation, "An American Indian International Perspective," pp. 159–69.

18. Peter Nabokov, ed., *Native American Testimony: A Chronicle of Indian–White Relations from Prophecy to the Present* (New York: Penguin Books, 1991), pp. 411–12; taken from 1969 Congressional hearings in Indian Education.

19. Russell Thornton, *American Indian Holocaust Survival: A Population History since 1492* (Norman: University of Oklahoma Press, 1987), p. 224. Quote is summary by James L. Simmons, 1977.

20. Jaimes in Jaimes, *State of Native America,* pp. 127–29.

21. Quote from Rayna Green on "ethnic cleansing" in Jerry Reynolds, "Indian Writers, Part II: The Good, the Bad, and the Ugly." *Indian Country Today,* Rapid City, S. Dakota, Sept. 15, 1993.

22. Elizabeth Cook-Lynn, ed., "Meeting of Indian Professors Takes Up Issues of 'Ethnic' Fraud." *Wicazo Sa Review* 1, no. 11 (Spring 1993): 57–59. Assessment of "ethnic fraud" position taken by the American Indian Professoriate organization 1993 meeting at Arizona State University, Tempe, Ariz.; the position was spearheaded by Lakota ethnocentric Bea Medicine. The problem is that

such inclusive claims to "documented abuse" on which this organization predicates its exclusionary position can be contradicted with violations that target those who have legitimate claims to being American Indian. It is therefore my assessment that the latter as exclusive abuse is more abusive, which leads me to conclude that the inconsistency of this policy is more about "Indian Identity" baiting motivated by professional self-interest in federal times of economic recession than not.

23. "The One-Drop Rule Defined" statement quotes Calvin Trillin, "American Chronicles: Black or White," *New Yorker* April 4, 1986, 76–78, about the Phipps case (*Jane Doe v. State of Louisiana,* 1983).

24. The "Twenty Points," 1973 statement in "On the Trail of Broken Treaties," is from "BIA, I'm Not Your Indian Anymore," *Akwesasne Notes,* Mohawk Nation, Roosevelt, N.Y. See also R. Burnett and J. Kostner, *The Road to Wounded Knee* (New York: Bantam Books, 1974); and "TREATY: The Campaign of Russell Means for the Presidency of the Oglala Sioux Tribe," *Porcupine,* S. Dakota, 1982.

25. See Emoke Szathmary, about research on "genetic markers" in his "Genetics of Aboriginal North Americans," *Evolutionary Anthropology* 1, no. 6 (1993): 202–20.

26. Native Hawaiian Peoples' International Tribunal, *Kanaka, Maoli Nation, Plaintiff, v. United States of America, Defendant,* held on the Hawaiian Islands, August 12–21, 1993, Interim Report on "Summary of Recognitions, Findings, and Recommendations" (to be followed by a complete final text from tribunal judges and rapporteur).

27. Haunani Kay Trask, taped presentation of "Native Hawaiian Sovereignty Rights and Indigenous Structures," from Feb. 22, 1994, University of Colorado at Boulder. See also H. K. Trask, *From a Native Daughter* (Monroe, Maine: Common Courage Press, 1993). This indigenous manifesto for Native Hawaiian liberation was presented as a documented testimony to the Native Hawaiian Peoples' International Tribunal, cited in note 26.

28. Stefan Kuhl, *The Nazi Connection: Eugenics, American Racism, and German National Socialism* (New York: Oxford University Press, 1994).

29. Hermann Raushning, *The Voice of Destruction* (New York: Putnam & Sons, 1940), esp. chapter 16, "Magic, Black and White" pp. 230–42.

30. Ward Churchill, "Genocide: Towards a Functional Definition," *Alternative Press* 2, no. 3 (July 1986): 403–30. See also Churchill, "In the Matter of Julius Streicher" on "Applying Nuremburg Precedents in the U.S.," in *Indians Are Us?,* ed. W. Churchill (Monroe, Maine: Common Courage Press, 1994), pp. 73–87; and M. A. Jaimes's citation of Churchill's work in *The State of Native America,* pp. 1–12.

31. M. Omi and H. Winant, *Racial Formation in the United States: From the 1960s to the 1980s* (New York: Routledge and Kegan Paul, 1986), pp. 105–43.

32. There is evidence that these racist practices are still in evidence, albeit in more covert manifestation as "institutional racism," which is still rooted in the southern United States with some such laws still on the books, but it is not exclusive to that region. Even more overt racism is evident in parts of the Northwest in Washington and Oregon, as well as along the economically eroded midwestern "Farmer's Belt," with particular emphasis in Idaho where paramilitary strongholds among the "white supremacy" racist groups are taking hold.

33. Tom Holm, "Patriots and Pawns; State Use of American Indians in the Military and the Process of Nativization in the U.S.," in Jaimes, pp. 345–70.

34. "And God blessed them, and God said onto them, 'Be fruitful, and multiply, and replenish the earth, and subdue it: and have dominion over the fish of the sea, and over the fowl of the air, and over every living thing that moveth upon the earth.'" Genesis 1:28, King James Translation of the Bible. This biblical reference is linked with the Spanish Sovereign Crown's "Doctrine of Discovery" that rationalized Spanish imperialism, later to be used as an international code by other imperialist seapowers beginning in the fifteenth century in the "New World." See J. H. Elliot, *Imperial Spain, 1469–1716* (New York: Penguin Books, 1990), p. 107.

35. Rudolf Acuna, *Occupied America,* 3rd ed. (New York: Harper Collins, 1988), p. 21, the Protestant Crusade, and pp. 202–76, Mexican American deportations. In addition, other respective seminal texts are Reginal Horsman, *Race and Manifest Destiny* (Cambridge, Mass.: Harvard University

Press, 1981) on U.S. racial nationalism; Richard Drinnon, *Facing West* (New York: Schocken Books, 1980/1990) on the metaphysics of Indian-hating and Empire-building.

36. President Richard M. Nixon, before the Watergate scandal, was known for asserting to his cabinet that certain parts of the United States (at the time sitting on Indian reservation lands in Arizona and New Mexico) were to be unofficially declared "national sacrifice areas (NSAs)." These targeted areas included "expendable" Native peoples and their cultural communities on those lands, for the sake of prodevelopment interests around uranium and other mining operational enterprises (i.e., Peabody Coal Co.). For reference see W. Churchill and W. LaDuke, "Native North America: The Political Economy of Radioactive Colonialism," in Jaimes, pp. 241–66.

37. Marianna Guerrero, "American Indian Water Rights: The Blood of Life in Native North America," in Jaimes, pp. 189–216. This "water theft" premise is the thesis of her essay.

38. Eugene Linden, "Lost Tribes, Lost Knowledge," *Time,* September 23, 1991, 46–56; this cover story is about the "nomadic" Penans, Sarawak, and Malaysians in Borneo, Papua, New Guinea; the Aleuts, Unalaska, Alaska in the Aleutian Islands; Bayanga Pygmies in Central Africa; and Lacandan in Chiapas, Mexico, among indigenous peoples worldwide.

39. K. H. Redford, "The Ecological Nobel Savage" on the "Tasaday Hoax." *Cultural Survival Quarterly* 15, no. 1 (1991): 46–48.

40. Bunty Anquoe, "Mescalero Apache Sign Agreement to Establish Facility for Nuclear Waste," *Indian Country Today* (Rapid City, S. Dakota) 13, no. 33 (Feb. 10, 1994): Al–A2. This case is really about money and what is being called "economy bribery." Therefore, Valerie Taliman ("Nuclear Guinea Pigs," *The Circle* [February 1994], p. 7) is more appropriate to assessing these kinds of economic enterprises that are hazardous to the health and environment of those living close to a "hosted" toxic dump site.

41. Ward Churchill, "Since Predator Came: A Survey of Native America Since 1492," *The Current Wisdom* 1, no. 1 (1992): 24–28.

42. On the "Human Genome Diversity Project," see "Summary of Planning Workshop 3(B)"

on "Ethical and Human Rights Implications," regarding the methods of research sampling, Stanford University, Stanford, Calif., cover letter dated May 17, 1994, and signed by Jean Dobie, Assistant Director, Morrison Institute for Populations and Resources Studies (involved in "selected dissemination of report"). This summation comprises more than 30 pages with an unattached tentative list of more than 600 indigenous groups targeted for DNA sampling worldwide (about 65 in North America, the United States, and Canada), with the data bank reputed to be in Los Alamos, New Mexico. It also lists thirteen participants of this session who are among the leading "genetic experts," several of whom are affiliated with the National Institutes of Health. This project is also indicated to be sponsored by private corporations, and it is different from the government-sponsored Human Genome Project that is collecting DNA samples for a larger data bank from the human population at large.

43. Vandana Shiva, *The Violence of the Green Movement: Third World Agriculture, Ecology and Politics* (Zed Books and Third World Network, 1991). This "genetic engineering" in the plant world is a main premise in her work, which emphasizes the case of India. Of particular note is the chapter on "Miracle Seeds and the Destruction of Genetic Diversity," pp. 61–102. Another article which is pretty lame in comparison to Shiva's work on the issue of indigenous agrarian knowledge is by S. H. Davis, "Hard Choices: Indigenous Economic Development and Intellectual Property Rights." *Akwe:kon (All of Us)* 10, no. 4 (Winter 1993): 19–25 (from Cornell University, Ithaca, N.Y.).

44. Sharon Venne, an international human rights activist for indigenous peoples and a Cree delegate to the United Nations since 1981, has shared this assessment with me. She was referring to the Human Rights proceedings at the "Working Group for Indigenous Populations (Peoples)," Geneva, Switzerland, 1993, at which she was a participant. She credits another delegate with the term "the Vampire Project" for referring to the "Human Genome Project" because it prefers blood samples to hair follicles and cheek scrapings for DNA genetic data.

45. 1993 Working Group; Venne and others from the international human rights arena asked such questions as, "Why (by what criteria) are the Native people and their respective cultures targeted on this list as "threatened" peoples in the first place? If this is in fact the case, what is being humanely done to assist them in this genocide, ethnocide, and ecocide?" Such queries have prompted the indigenous non-governmental organizations of the United Nations to submit a declaration to cease and desist in the genetic research that is already underway. As Venne points out, the problem with this scenario is that while one area of the United Nations puts forth a declaration in protest, in another area of the monolithic, duplicitous bureaucracy, other agencies are funding the global project.

46. William Stanton, *The Leopard Spots: Scientific Attitudes Toward Race in America, 1819–59* (Chicago: University of Chicago, 1960). Of particular note is Stanton's "The Problem of the Free Hybrid," pp. 189–91.

47. Ibid.

48. Jack D. Forbes, *Black Africans and Native Americans; Color, Race, and Caste in the Evolution of Red–Black Peoples* (New York: Basil Blackwell, 1988). See also bell hooks, *Black Looks: Race and Representation* (Boston: South End Press, 1992); especially noted is her chapter "Revolutionary Renegades" (pp. 179–94) about "Red–Black Indian."

49. Thornton on Spanish obsession with interracial categories among *mestizo* offsprings of Spanish and Indian intermarriage and intermixing *(American Indian Holocaust Survival,* pp. 186–9). In addition, there is E. B. Reuter's dated but informative *Race Mixture: Studies in Intermarriage and Miscegenation* (New York: McGraw-Hill, 1931), which looks at "interracial" population groups.

50. Elliot on the Spanish notions of "Christian purity and race," which led to the ecclesiastical policy known as "limpiezas de sangre" (*Imperial Spain,* p. 107).

51. Thornton, *American Indian Holocaust Survival,* p. 55.

52. Harmon, "When an Indian is not an Indian?" pp. 108–11.

53. Vine Deloria, Jr., *A Better Day for Indians* (New York: Field Foundation, 1977), p. 20.

54. Vine Deloria, Jr., has commented on this phenomenon that he has run across in his examination of the older versions of some treaties between nations, which included sections about the "rights" of "mixed bloods" among tribal membership. This also seems to imply that the tribal leaders, as treaty delegates and negotiators, were using the language of the Europeans and American colonizers who were much more preoccupied with distinctions between "full bloods" and "half-breeds" among native groups.

55. Margaret Hacker, *Cynthia Ann Parker, the Life and Legend* (Austin: Texas Western Press, 1990).

56. Sandy Gonzales, "Intermarriage and Assimilation: The Beginning or the End?" *Wicazo Sa Review* 8, no. 2 (Fall 1992): 48–52. Her research includes a table that provides more specific differences in intermarriage and exogamy between the Indian population genders. Gonzales provides good data, but I find her work too narrow in scope, particularly the implications of a rather pessimistic outlook. Thornton *(American Indian Holocaust Survival,* p. 236): In 1980, over 50% of *all* American Indians were married to non-Indians, while only about one (%) of whites and two (%) blacks were married to someone of another race.

57. Jack D. Forbes, "Undercounting Native Americans: the 1980 Census and the Manipulation of Racial Identity in the U.S.," *Wicazo Sa Review* 6, no. 1 (Spring 1990): 2–26. Forbes also refers to how President Richard Nixon, before Watergate, designated the use of the term "Hispanic" to diffuse and deter the sociopolical issues of Spanish-speaking populations in the United States, who in census-taking, opted to identify with the Native roots among indigenous peoples.

58. A reform movement is challenging the race "classifiers" in the United States; among them is *Mestizaje,* representing Chicano and Native activists in the western states, who are redefining cultural identity for themselves. There are also other "interracial groups" among blacks, Indians, and Asians, who are countering with grievances of "ethnic sorting," as in the case of "affirmative action" profiling. For example, American Indians are usually classified by a race coding and "federally recognized" tribal affiliation, in contrast to the Eurocentric label

"Hispanics" imposed on all Spanish-speaking groups. The term Hispanic is supposed to be linked to Spanish culture, which denies many in this category their native heritage to the Americas. However, blacks and Asians are designated based on more distinct physical characteristics. These categories are inconsistent at best, and do not recognize the biological and cultural diversity among many, if not most, "mixed-blood identities" because of biological descendency and cultural heritage.

59. "Action Speaks Louder Than Words: Native Council of Canada Record on Native Women's Rights," *Native Women Journal* (Aug./Sept. 1992): 6–7. This record includes statements on "gender inequality in tribal governance and national recognition, among Métis Women's organizations with headquarters in Alberta.

60. Robert Stock, "The Settler State and the American Left," *New Studies on the Left* 14, no. 3 (Winter 1990–91): 72–78.

61. See W. Churchill and W. LaDuke on "radioactive colonization," in Jaimes, pp. 241–66.

62. M. A. Jaimes, "Native American Identity and Survival: Indigenism and Environmental Ethics" (forthcoming).

63. See Russell Thornton on Indian populations and demographics (*American Indian Holocaust Survival*); and 1980 census data and reports, Office of the U.S. Census, Washington, D.C.

64. John R. Wunder, *"Retained by the Peoples": A History of American Indians and the Bill of Rights* (New York: Oxford University Press, 1994).

65. H. K. Trask's presentation on "Native Hawaiian Sovereignty Rights."

66. Vine Deloria, Jr., "The Next Three Years: A Time for Change," *Indian Historian* 7, no. 2 (Spring 1974): 26.

67. Press release, March 28, 1994, from the International Confederation of Autonomous Chapters of the American Indian Movement, regarding summation of A.I.M, Tribunal held in San Francisco, March 26–28, 1994.

68. Al Gedicks, *The New Resource Wars: Native and Environmental Struggles Against Multinational Corporations* (Boston: South End Press, 1993).

PURITY, IMPURITY, AND SEPARATION

María Lugones

Note to the reader: This writing is done from within a hybrid imagination, within a recently articulate tradition of Latina writers who emphasize mestizaje *and multiplicity as tied to resistant and liberatory possibilities. All resemblance between this tradition and postmodern literature and philosophy is coincidental, though the conditions that underlie both may well be significantly tied. The implications of each are very different from one another.*

Voy a empezar en español y en la cocina. Two uses of the verb *separar. El primer sentido. Voy a separar la yema de la clara, separar un huevo.* I will *separate* the white from the yolk. I will *separate* an egg. I crack the egg and I now slide the white onto one half of the shell and place the egg white in a bowl. I repeat the operation until I have separated all of the egg white from the yolk. *Si la operación no ha sido exitosa, entonces queda un poquito de yema en la clara.* If the operation has not been successful, a bit of the yolk stains the white. I wish I could begin again with another egg, but that is a waste, as I was taught. So I must try to lift all the yolk from the white with a spoon, a process that is tedious and hardly ever entirely successful. The intention is to separate, first cleanly and then, in case of failure, a bit messily, the white from the yolk, to split the egg into two parts as cleanly as one can. This is an exercise in purity.

Part of my interest in this essay is to ask whether separation is always or necessarily an exercise in purity. I want to investigate the politics of purity and how they bear on the politics of separation. In the process, I will take neither the dominant nor the "standard" tongue as my anchor in playing with "separation," as those who separate may do so not in allegiance to but in defiance of the dominant intention. As I uncover a connection between impurity and resistance, my Latina imagination moves from resistance to *mestizaje.* I think of *mestizaje* as an example of and a metaphor for both impurity and resistance. I hold on to the metaphor and adopt *mestizaje* as a central name for impure resistance to interlocked, intermeshed oppressions.[1] Much of the time, my very use of the word "separate" exhibits a form of cultural *mestizaje.*[2]

> *If something or someone is neither/nor, but kind of*
> *both, not quite either,*
> *if something is in the middle of either/or,*
> *if it is ambiguous, given the available classification*
> *of things,*
> *if it is mestiza,*
> *if it threatens by its very ambiguity the orderliness*
> *of the system, of schematized reality,*
> *if given its ambiguity in the univocal ordering, it*
> *is anomalous, deviant, can it be tamed through*
> *separation? Should it separate so as to avoid*
> *taming? Should it resist separation? Should it*
> *resist through separation? Separate as in the*
> *separation of the white from the yolk?*

Segundo sentido. Estoy haciendo mayonesa. I am making mayonnaise. I place the yolk in a bowl, add a few drops of water, stir, and then add oil drop by drop, very slowly, as I continue stirring. If I add too much oil at once, the mixture *se separa,* it separates. I can remember doing the operation as an impatient child, stopping and saying to my mother *"Mamá, la mayonesa se separó."* In English, one might say that the mayonnaise curdled. Mayonnaise is an oil-in-water emulsion. As all emulsions, it is unstable. When an emulsion curdles, the ingredients become separate from each other. But that is not altogether an accurate description: rather, they coalesce toward oil or toward water, most of the water becomes separate from most of the oil—it is instead, a matter of different degrees of

coalescence.[3] The same with mayonnaise; when it separates, you are left with yolky oil and oily yolk.

> *Going back to mestizaje, in the middle of either/or,*
> *ambiguity, and thinking of acts that belong in lives*
> *lived in mestizo ways,*
> *thinking of all forms of mestizaje,*
> *thinking of breaching and abandoning dichotomies,*
> *thinking of being anomalous willfully or unwill-*
> *fully in a world of precise, hard-edged schema,*
> *thinking of resistance,*
> *resistance to a world of purity, of domination, of*
> *control over our possibilities,*
> *is separation not at the crux of mestizaje, ambigu-*
> *ity, resistance?*
> *Is it not at the crux both of its necessity and its pos-*
> *sibility? Separation as in the separation of the*
> *white from the yolk or separation as curdling?*

When I think of *mestizaje,* I think both of separation as curdling, an exercise in impurity, and of separation as splitting, an exercise in purity. I think of the attempt at control exercised by those who possess both power and the categorical eye and who attempt to split everything impure, breaking it down into pure elements (as in egg white and egg yolk) for the purposes of control. Control over creativity. And I think of something in the middle of either/or, something impure, something or someone mestizo, as both separated, curdled, and resisting in its curdled state. *Mestizaje* defies control through simultaneously asserting the impure, curdled multiple state and rejecting fragmentation into pure parts. In this play of assertion and rejection, the mestiza is unclassifiable, unmanageable. She has no pure parts to be "had," controlled.

Inside the world of the impure
There was a muchacha who lived near my house. La gente del pueblo *talked about her being una de las otras, "of the Others."* They said that for *six months she was a woman who had a vagina that bled once a month, and that for the other six months she was a man, had a penis and she peed standing up. They called her half and half, mita y mita, nei- ther one nor the other but a strange doubling, a*

deviation of nature that horrified, a work of nature inverted. [Anzaldúa 1987:19]

and Louie would come through—melodramatic music, like in the mono—tan tan taran!—Cruz Diablo, El Charro Negro! Bogart smile (his smile as deadly as his vaisas*!) He dug roles, man, and names—like "Blackie," "Little Louie . . ."*
Ese, Louie . . .

Chale, man, call me "Diamonds!" [Montoya 1972]

Now my mother, she doesn't go for cleanliness, orderliness, static have-come-from-nowhere objects for use. She shows you the production, her production. She is always in the middle of it and you will never see the end. You'll have to follow her through her path in the chaotic production, you'll have to know her comings and goings, her fluidity through the production. You'll have to, that is, if you want to use any of it. Because she points to what you need in her own way, her person is the "here" that ensures her subjectivity, she is the point of reference, and if you don't know her movements, her location, you can't get to the end of the puzzle. Unless she wants you to, and sometimes, she'll do that for you, because she hasn't stored that much resistance. She doesn't have names for things (oh, she has them somewhere, but uses them very little), as if she always saw them in the making, in process, in connection, not quite separable from the rest. She says "it," "under that," "next to me." "These go in the thing for things." And if you follow her movements up to the very present, you know just what she means, just what her hand is needing to hold and just where she left it and her words are very helpful in finding it. Now, clean, what you call clean, you will not see clean either. You'll see halfway. Kind of. In the middle of either/or. She doesn't see things as broken, finished, either. It's rather a very long process of deterioration. Not a now you see it, now you don't, gone forever. Just because it fell on the floor and broke in half and you glued it and you have to fill it half way, so stuff doesn't drip from the side, it doesn't stop being a tureen (or a flower pot for "centros de mesa," or maybe it'll be good as one of those thingamajigs to put things in). It's still good. And it hasn't changed its "nature" either. She has always had multiple functions for it, many possibilities. Its multiplicity has always been obvious to her.

Getting real close, like a confidence, you tell me, "Because certain individuals can get too accustomed to being helped." That snatch of mestizaje—"certain individuals"—the South American use of "individuos" chiseled into your English. Makes me feel good, in the know. I know what you mean mujer, South American style. Just like my "operation." Claro que se dice real close, it's not just for everyone's ears. You make me feel special. I know, I know about "certain individuals." Like the "apparatus" you borrow from me or I borrow from you.

"Culture is what happens to other people." I've heard something like that. I'm one of the other people, so I know there is something funny there. Renato Rosaldo helps me articulate what is peculiar, paradoxical. As he is critiquing classic norms in anthropology marking off those who are visible from those who are invisible in a culture, Rosaldo articulates the politics underlying them: "Full citizens lack culture, and those most culturally endowed lack full citizenship" (1989:198).

Part of what is funny here is that people with culture are people with a culture unknown by full citizens, not worth knowing. Only the culture of people who are culturally transparent is worth knowing, but it does not count as a culture. The people whose culture it is are postcultural. Their culture is invisible to them and thus nonexistent as such. But postcultural full citizens mandate that people with a culture give up theirs in favor of the nonexistent invisible culture. So, it's a peculiar status: I have "culture" because what I have exists in the eyes of those who declare what I have to be culture. But they declare it culture only to the extent that they know they don't know it except as an absence that they don't want to learn as a presence and they have the power not to know. Furthermore, they have the power to order me to cease to know. So, as I resist and know, I am both visible and invisible. Visible as other and invisible as myself, but these aren't separable bits. And I walk around as both other and myselves, resisting classification.

Rosaldo criticizes the "broad rule of thumb under classic anthropological norms . . . that if it's moving it isn't cultural" (1989:209). *"The blurred zones within a culture and the zones between cultures are endowed by the norms with a curious kind of hybrid invisibility"* (Rosaldo 1989:209). *Paradoxically "culture" needs to be both static, fixed and separate, different from the "post-cultural" (Rosaldo 1989:199) to be seen. So, if it's different but not static, it isn't "culture." But if it's different, if it's what "other people do," it's cultural. If the people who do it are other but what they do is not static, it is and it isn't culture. It's in the middle, anomalous, deviant, ambiguous, impure. It lacks the mark of separation as purity. If it's hybrid, it's in the middle of either/or twice.*

The play between feminine and masculine elements that we contain in heterosexist eyes;
the parody of masculine/feminine, the play with illusion that transgresses gender boundaries, the "now you see 'it' now you don't" magic tricks aimed at destroying the univocal character of the "it" that we disdain with playful intention;
the rejection of masculine/feminine in our self-understanding that some of us make our mark;
all contain a rejection of purity.

In every one of these examples there is curdling, *mestizaje,* lack of homogeneity. There is tension. The intentions are curdled, the language, the behavior, the people are mestizo.

I. CONTROL, UNITY, AND SEPARATION

Guide to the reader: I will presuppose that as I investigate the conceptual world of purity, you will keep the world of mestizaje, *of curdled beings, constantly superimposed onto it, even when that is made difficult by the writing's focus on the logic of purity. Sometimes the logic of purity dominates the text, sometimes the logic of curdling does. But at other points, both worlds become vivid as coexisting and the logic of what I say depends on the coexistence. The reader needs to see ambiguity, see that the split-separated are also and simultaneously curdled-separated. Otherwise, one is only seeing the success of oppression, seeing with the lover of purity's eyes. The reader also needs to, as it were, grant the assumptions of the lover of purity to understand his world. The fundamental assumption is that there is unity underlying multiplicity. The assumption is granted for the sake of entering the point of view and for the purposes of contestation. The questioning is done from within la realidad mestiza and*

the intent of the questioning is to clarify, intensify, aid the contestation between the two realities. As I enter the world of purity, I am interested in a cluster of concepts as clustered: control, purity, unity, categorizing. Control or categorizing in isolation from this network are not my concern.

My aim is to distinguish between multiplicity (mestizaje) and fragmentation and to explain connections that I see between the terms of this distinction and the logics of curdling (impurity) and of splitting (purity). Fragmentation follows the logic of purity. Multiplicity follows the logic of curdling. The distinction between fragmentation and multiplicity is central to this essay. I will exhibit it within individuals and within the social world.[4]

According to the logic of curdling, the social world is complex and heterogeneous and each person is multiple, nonfragmented, embodied. Fragmented: in fragments, pieces, and parts that do not fit well together; parts taken for wholes, composite, composed of the parts of other beings, composed of imagined parts, composed of parts produced by a splitting imagination, composed of parts produced by subordinates enacting their dominators' fantasies. According to the logic of purity, the social world is both unified and fragmented, homogenous, hierarchically ordered. Each person is either fragmented, composite, or abstract and unified—not exclusive alternatives. Unification and homogeneity are related principles of ordering the social world. Unification requires a fragmented and hierarchical ordering. Fragmentation is another guise of unity, both in the collectivity and the individual. I will connect mestizaje *in individuals to* mestizaje *in groups and thus in the social world, and I will connect fragmentation within individuals to the training of the multiple toward a homogeneous social world.*

I do not claim ontological originality for multiplicity here. Rather both the multiple-mestizo and the unified-fragmented coexist, each have their histories, are in contestation and in significant logical tension. I reveal the logics underlying the contestation. Sometimes my use of language strongly suggests a claim of originality for the multiple. I speak of the multiple as trained into unity and of its being conceived as internally separable. I could say that to split-separate the multiple is to exercise a split imagination. But if what is imagined is to gain a powerful degree of reality, unity must be more than a reading or interpretation. It must order people's lives and psyches. The becoming of the order is a historical process of domination in which power and ideology are at all times changing into each other.

Monophilia and purity are cut from the same cloth. The urge to control the multiplicity of people and things attains satisfaction through exercises in split separation. The urge to control multiplicity is expressed in modern political theory and ethics in an understanding of reason as reducing multiplicity to unity through abstraction and categorization, from a particular vantage point.[5] I consider this reduction expressive of the urge to control because of the logical fit between it and the creation of the fragmented individual. I understand fragmentation to be a form of domination.

I see this reduction of multiplicity to unity as being completed through a complex series of fictions. Once the assumption of unity underlying multiplicity is made, further fictions rationalize it as a discovery. The assumption makes these fictions possible, and they, in turn, transform it from a simple assumption into a fiction.

The assumption of unity is an act of split separation; as in conceiving of what is multiple as unified, what is multiple is understood as internally separable, divisible into what makes it one and the remainder. Or, to put it another way: to conceive of fragmentation rather than multiplicity is to exercise a split-separation imagination. This assumption generates and presupposes others. It generates the fictional construction of a vantage point from which unified wholes, totalities, can be captured. It generates the construction of a subject who can occupy such a vantage point. Both the vantage point and the subject are outside historicity and concreteness. They are both affected by and effect the reduction of multiplicity. The vantage point is privileged, simple, one-dimensional. The subject is fragmented, abstract, without particularity. The series of fictions hides the training of the multiple into unity as well as the survival of the multiple. It is only

from a historical enmeshing in the concrete that the training of the multiple into fragmented unities can be seen; that is, it can be seen from a different logic, one that rejects the assumption of unity. The ahistoricity of the logic of purity hides the construction of unity.

In understanding the fictitious character of the vantage point it is important that we recognize that its conception is itself derivative from the conception of reality as unified. If we assume that the world of people and things is unified, then we can conceive of a vantage point from which its unity can be grasped. The conception of the vantage point follows the urge to control; it is not antecedent to it, because unity is assumed. The vantage point is then itself beyond description, except as an absence: "outside of" is its central characteristic. The vantage point is not of this world, it is otherworldly, as ideal as its occupant, the ideal observer. It exists only as that from which unity can be perceived.

The subject who can occupy such a vantage point, the ideal observer, must himself be pure, unified, and simple so as to occupy the vantage point and perceive unity amid multiplicity.[6] He must not himself be pulled in all or several perceptual directions; he must not perceive richly. Reason, including its normative aspect, is the unified subject. It is what characterizes the subject as a unity. A subject who in its multiplicity perceives, understands, grasps its worlds as multiple sensuously, passionately as well as rationally without the splitting separation between sense/emotion/reason lacks the unidimensionality and the simplicity required to occupy the privileged vantage point. Such a subject occupies the vantage point of reason in a pragmatic contradiction, standing in a place where all of the subject's abilities cannot be exercised and where the exercise of its abilities invalidates the standpoint. So a passionate, needy, sensuous, and rational subject must be conceived as internally separable, as discretely divided into what makes it one—rationality—and into the confused, worthless remainder—passion, sensuality. Rationality is understood as this ability of a unified subject to abstract, categorize, train the multiple to the systematicity of norms, of rules that highlight, capture, and train its unity from the privileged vantage point.

The conception of this subject is derivative from the assumption of unity and separability. The very "construction" of the subject presupposes that assumption. So, though we are supposed to understand unity in multiplicity as that which is perceived by the rational subject occupying the vantage point of reason, we can see that the logic of the matter goes the other way around. Control cannot be rationally justified in this manner, as the urge to control antecedes this conception of reason. Part of my claim here is that the urge for control and the passion for purity are conceptually related.

If the modern subject is to go beyond conceptualizing the reduction to actually exercising control over people and things, then these fictions must be given some degree of reality. The modern subject must be dressed, costumed, masked so as to appear able to exercise this reduction of heterogeneity to homogeneity, of multiplicity to unity. The modern subject must be masked as standing separate from their own multiplicity and what commits him to multiplicity. So, his own purification into someone who can step squarely onto the vantage point of unity requires that his remainder become of no consequence to his own sense of himself as someone who justifiably exercises control over multiplicity. Thus his needs must be taken care of by others hidden in spaces relegated outside of public view, where he parades himself as pure. And it is important to his own sense of things and of himself that he pay little attention to the satisfaction of the requirements of his sensuality, affectivity, and embodiment.

Satisfying the modern subject's needs requires beings enmeshed in the multiple as the production of discrete units occurs amid multiplicity. Such production is importantly constrained by its invisibility and worthlessness in the eyes of those who attempt to control multiplicity. To the extent that the modern subject succeeds in this attempt to control multiplicity, the production is impelled by his needs. Those who produce it become producers of the structuring "perceived" by the lover of purity from the rational vantage point as well as its products. So in the logic of the lover of purity they exhibit a peculiar lack of agency, autonomy, self-regulating ability.[7]

As the lover of purity, the impartial reasoner is outside history, outside culture. He occupies the privileged vantage point with others like him, all characterized by the "possession" of reason. All occupants of this vantage point are homogeneous in their ability to comprehend and communicate. So "culture," which marks radical differences in conceptions of people and things, cannot be something they have. They are instead "postcultural" or "culturally transparent."[8]

Since his embodiment is irrelevant to his unity, he cannot have symbolic and institutionalized inscriptions in his body that mark him as someone who is "outside" his own production as the rational subject. To the extent that mastering institutional inscriptions is part of the program of unification, there cannot be such markings of his body. His difference cannot be thought of as "inscriptions" but only as coincidental, nonsymbolic marks. As his race and gender do not identify him in his own eyes, he is also race and gender transparent.

Paradoxically, the lover of purity is also constituted as incoherent, as contradictory in his attitude toward his own and others' gender, race, culture. He must at once emphasize them and ignore them. He must be radically self-deceiving in this respect. His production as pure, as the impartial reasoner, requires that others produce him. He is a fiction of his own imagination, but his imagination is mediated by the labor of others. He controls those who produce him, who to his eyes require his control because they are enmeshed in multiplicity and thus unable to occupy the vantage point of control. They are marked as other than himself, as lacking the relevant unity.

But the lack is not discovered, it couldn't be, since the unity is itself assumed. The lack is symbolically produced by marking the producers as gendered, racialized, and "cultured." The marking signifies that they are enmeshed in multiplicity and thus are different from the lover of purity. But he must deny the importance of the markings that separate them.

If women, the poor, the colored, the queer, the ones with cultures (whose cultures are denied and rendered invisible as they are seen as our mark) are deemed unfit for the public, it is because we are tainted by need, emotion, the body. This tainting is relative to the modern subject's urge for control through unity and the production and maintenance of himself as unified. To the extent that he is fictional, the tainting is fictional: seeing us as tainted depends on a need for purity that requires that we become "parts," "addenda" of the bodies of modern subjects— Christian white bourgeois men—and make their purity possible. We become sides of fictitious dichotomies. To the extent that we are ambiguous— nondichotomous—we threaten the fiction and can be rendered unfit only by decrying ambiguity as nonexistent—that is, by halving us, splitting us. Thus, we exist only as incomplete, unfit beings, and they exist as complete only to the extent that what we are, and what is absolutely necessary for them, is declared worthless.

The lover of purity is shot through and through with this paradoxical incoherence. When confronted with the sheer overabundance of the multiple, he ignores it by placing it outside value when it is his own substance and provides his sustenance. So, he is committed both to an overevaluation and a devaluation of himself, a torturing of himself, a disciplining or training of himself that puts him at the mercy of his own control. The incoherence is dispelled through separation, his own from himself. As he covets, possesses, destroys, pleases himself, he disowns his own urges and deeds. So, he is always rescued from his own incoherence by self-deception, weakness of the will, aggressive ignorance. After he

ignores the fundamental and unfounded presupposition of unity, all further ignoring becomes easier. He shuns impurity, ambiguity, multiplicity as they threaten his own fiction. The enormity of the threat keeps him from understanding it. So, the lover of purity remains ignorant of his own impurity, and thus the threat of all impurity remains significantly uncontaminated. The lover of purity cannot see, understand, and attempt to control the resistance contained in the impure. He can only attempt control indirectly, through the complex incoherence of affirming and denying impurity, training the impure into its "parts" and at the same time separating from it, erecting sturdy barriers both around himself and between the fictional "parts" of impure beings.

In *Purity and Danger,* Mary Douglas (1989) sees the impulse toward unity as characteristic of social structures, and she understands pollution behavior—behavior to control pollution, impurity—as a guarding of structure from the threat of impurity. According to Douglas, impurity, dirt, is what is "out of place" relative to some order. What is impure is anomalous and ambiguous because it is out of place. It threatens order because it is not definable, so separation from it is a manner of containing it. She also sees power in impurity. But it is not her purpose to distinguish between oppressive and nonoppressive structuring. Here, I want to precisely understand the particular oppressive character of the modern construction of social life and the power of impurity in resisting and threatening this oppressive structuring.

Part of what is interesting in Douglas is that she understands that what is impure is impure relative to some order and that the order is itself conventional. What is impure is anomalous. Douglas describes several ways of dealing with anomalies, but she does not emphasize that rendering something impure is a way of dealing with it. The ordering renders something out of place. Its complexity is altered by the ordering. The alteration is not only conceptual since its "life" develops in relation to this order. So, for example,

the multiplicitous beings required for the production of the unified subject are anomalous as
multiple. Unity renders them anomalous. So they
are altered to fit within the logic of unification.
They are split over and over in accordance with
the relevant dichotomies of the logic of unity. As
anomalous, they remain complex, defying the
logic of unity. That which is multiplicitous metamorphoses over and over in its history of resisting alteration and as the result of alteration. Both
the logic of control and unity and the logic of
resistance and complexity are at work in what is
impure. That is why I have and will continue to
use *impure* ambiguously both for something complex that is in process and thus cannot really be
split-separated and for that which is fragmented.

When seen as split, the impure/multiplicitous
are seen from the logic of unity, and thus their
multiplicity can neither be seen nor understood.
But splitting can itself be understood from the
logic of resistance and countered through curdling separation, a power of the impure. When
seen from the logic of curdling, the alteration of
the impure to unity is seen as fictitious and as an
exercise in domination: the impure are rendered
uncreative, ascetic, static, realizers of the contents
of the modern subject's imagination. Curdling, in
contrast, realizes their against-the-grain creativity, articulates their within-structure-inarticulate
powers.[9] As we come to understand curdling as
resisting domination, we also need to recognize
its potential to germinate a nonoppressive pattern, a mestiza consciousness, *una conciencia
mestiza.*[10]

Interrupción

*Oh, I would entertain the thought of separation
as really clean, the two components untouched by
each other, unmixed as they would be if I could go
away with my own people to our land to engage
in acts that were cleanly ours! But then I ask myself who my own people are. When I think of my
own people, the only people I can think of as my
own are transitionals, liminals, border-dwellers,*
*world-travelers, beings in the middle of either/
or. They are all people whose acts and thoughts
curdle-separate. So as soon as I entertain the
thought, I realize that separation into clean, tidy
things and beings is not possible for me because
it would be the death of myself as multiplicitous
and a death of community with my own. I understand my split or fragmented possibilities in
horror. I understand then that whenever I desire
separation, I risk survival by confusing split separation with separation from domination, that
is, separation among curdled beings who curdle
away their fragmentation, their subordination.
I can appreciate then that the logic of split-
separation and the logic of curdle-separation repel each other, that the curdled do not germinate
in split separation.*

II. SPLIT SELVES

Dual Personality

What Frank Chin calls a "dual personality" is
the production of a being who is simultaneously
different and the same as postcultural subjects, a
split and contradictory being who is a product of
the ethnocentric racist imagination (Chin 1991).
It is one way of dealing with the anomaly of being
cultured and culturally multiplicitous. The case I
know best is rural Chicanos. *Chicano* is the name
for the curdled or mestizo person. I will name
the dual personality *Mexican/American,* with no
hyphen in the name, to signify that if the split
were successful, there would be no possibility of
dwelling or living on the hyphen.[11]

The rural Mexican/American is a product of
the Anglo imagination, sometimes enacted by
persons who are the targets of ethnocentric racism in an unwillful parody of themselves. The
Anglo imagines each rural Mexican/American as
having a dual personality: the authentic Mexican
cultural self and the American self. In this notion, there is no hybrid self. The selves are conceptually different, apparently contradictory but
complementary; one cannot be found without

the other. The Anglo philosophy is that Mexican/ Americans should both keep their culture (so as to be different and not full citizens) and assimilate (so as to be exploitable), a position whose contradictoriness is obvious. But as a split dual personality, the authentic Mexican can assimilate without ceasing to be "cultured," the two selves complementary, the ornamental nature of the Mexican self resolving the contradiction.

The Mexican/American can assimilate because the *Mexican* in *Mexican/American* is understood to be a member of a superfluous culture, the culture an ornament rather than shaping or affecting American reality. A simple but stoic figure who will defend the land no matter what, the Mexican/American will never quite enter the twentieth century and will not make it in the twenty-first, given that in this scheme for the next century the land will no longer be used for farming but for the recreation of the Anglo upper class. The authentic Mexican is a romantic figure, an Anglo myth, alive in the pages of John Nichols's *Milagro Beanfield War* (1976): fiercely conservative and superexploitable.

As Americans, rural Mexican/Americans are not first-class citizens because the two sides of the split cannot be found without each other. The complementarity of the sides becomes clearer: the assimilated Mexican cannot lose culture as ornamental and as a mark of difference. So, a Mexican/American is not a postcultural American. The promise of postculturalism is part of what makes assimilation appealing, since the Mexican/American knows that only postculturals are full citizens. But assimilation does not make the Mexican/American postcultural. Making the Anglo ideals of progress and efficiency one's own only makes one exploitable but does not lead one to achieve full participation in Anglo life. Anglos declare Mexican/Americans unfit for control and portray them as men and women of simple minds, given to violence, drink, and hard work, accustomed to hardship and poverty, in particular.

The dual personality is part of the mythical portrait of the colonized (Memmi 1967).

The split renders the self into someone unable to be culturally creative in a live culture. Thus "authentic" Mexican craft shops exhibit *santos, trasteros, colchas, reredos.* Mexican artists cannot depart from the formulaic; they are supposed to be producing relics for the Anglo consumer of the picturesque. The mythical portrait, therefore, has acquired a degree of reality that both justifies and obscures Anglo dominance. The portrait does not lack in appeal. It makes one feel proud to be *Raza* because the portrait is heroic. It also makes one stilted, stiff, a cultural personage not quite sure of oneself, a pose, pure style, not quite at ease in one's own cultural skin, as if one did not quite know one's own culture, precisely because it is not one's own but a stereotype and because this authentic culture is not quite a live culture: it is conceived by the Anglo as both static and dying. As Rosaldo says, part of the myth is that "if it moves, it is not cultural" (1989:212). This authentic Mexican culture bears a relation to traditional culture. It is tradition filtered through Anglo eyes for the purposes of ornamentation. What is Anglo, authentically American, is also appealing: it represents progress, the future, efficiency, material well being. As American, one moves; as Mexican, one is static. As American, one is beyond culture; as Mexican, one is culture personified. The culturally split self is a character for the theatrics of racism.

The dual personality concept is a death-loving attempt to turn *Raza* into beautiful zombies: an attempt to eradicate the possibility of a mestizo—a consciousness, of our infusing every one of our possibilities with this consciousness and of our moving from traditional to hybrid ways of creation, including the production of material life.

As split, Mexican/Americans cannot participate in public life because of their difference, except ornamentally in the dramatization of equality. If we retreat and accept the "between *Raza*" nonpublic status of our concerns, to be resolved in the privacy of our communities, we participate in the logic of the split. Our communities are rendered private space in the public/private distinction. Crossing to the Anglo domain only in their terms is not an option either, as it follows the logic of the split without the terms ever becoming our own; that is the nature of this—if not of all—assimilation. So, the resistance and rejection of the culturally split self requires that we declare our communities public space and break the conceptual tie between public space and monoculturally conceived Anglo-only concerns: it requires that the language and conceptual framework of the public become hybrid.

Fragmentation

In *Justice and the Politics of Difference* (1990a) and "Polity and Difference" (in 1990b), Iris Young highlights the concept of a group as central to her understanding of the heterogeneous public, a conception of the civic public that does not ignore heterogeneity through reducing it to a fictitious unity. Instead of a unified public realm "in which citizens leave behind their particular group affiliations, histories, and needs to discuss a general interest or common good," she argues for "a group differentiated citizenship and a heterogeneous public" (Young 1990b:121).

Young understands a social group as "a collective of persons differentiated from at least one other group by cultural forms, practices, or way of life" (1990a:43). Groups become differentiated through the encounter and interaction between social collectivities that experience some differences in their way of life and forms of association as well as through social processes such as the sexual division of labor. Group members have "an affinity with other persons by which they identify with one another and by which other people identify them" (1990b:122). Group identity partly constitutes "a person's particular sense of history, understanding of social relations and personal possibilities, her or his mode of reasoning, values and expressive styles" (Young 1990b:122). Their similar way of life or experience prompts group members "to associate with each other more than with those not

identified with the group, or in a different way" (Young 1990a:43). A social group is not something one joins but, rather, "one finds oneself as a member of a group whose existence and relations one experiences as always already having been" (Young 1990b:122). But groups are fluid, "they come into being and may fade away" (Young 1990b:123). Though there is a lack of clarity in how Young identifies particular groups, as I understand her, African Americans, lesbians, differently abled women, Latinas, and Navajo are examples of social groups.

Young thinks that the "inclusion and participation of everyone in public discussion and decision making requires mechanisms of group representation" (Young 1990a:115). The "ideal of the public realm of citizenship as expressing a general will, a point of view and interest that citizens have in common and that transcends their differences . . . , leads to pressures for a homogeneous citizenry" (Young 1990a:116–17). In arguing for group representation as the key to safeguarding the inclusion and participation of everyone without falling into an egoistic, self-regarding view of the political process, Young tells us that "it is possible for persons to maintain their group identity and to be influenced by their perceptions of social events derived from their group specific experience and at the same time to be public spirited, in the sense of being open to listening to the claims of others and not being concerned for their own gain alone" (Young 1990a:120). She sees group representation as necessary because she thinks differences are irreducible: "People from one perspective can never completely understand and adopt the point of view of those with other group-based perspectives and histories" (Young 1990a:121). Though differences are irreducible, group representation affords a solution to the homogenization of the public because "commitment to the need and desire to decide together the society's policies fosters communication across those differences" (Young 1990a:121).

In Young's conception of the heterogeneous public, "each of the constituent groups affirms the presence of the others and affirms the specificity of its experience and perspective on social issues," arriving at "a political program not by voicing some 'principles of unity' that hide differences but rather by allowing each constituency to analyze economic and social issues from the perspective of its experience" (Young 1990a:123).

Young sees that each person has multiple group identifications and that groups are not homogeneous, but rather that each group has group differences cutting across it (Young, 1990a:123, 1990b:48). Social groups "mirror in their own differentiations many of the other groups in the wider society" (Young 1990b:48). There are important implications of group differences within social groups. Significantly, "individual persons, as constituted partly by their group affinities and relations, cannot be unified, themselves are heterogeneous and not necessarily coherent" (Young 1990a:48). Young sees a revolution in subjectivity as necessary. "Rather than seeking a wholeness of the self, we who are the subjects of this plural and complex society should affirm the otherness within ourselves, acknowledging that as subjects we are heterogeneous and multiple in our affiliations and desires" (Young 1990a:124).

Young thinks the women's movement offers some beginning models for the development of a heterogeneous public and for revolutionizing the subject through the practices it has instituted to deal with issues arising from group differences within social groups. From the discussion of racial and ethnic blindness and the importance of attending to group differences among women "emerged principled efforts to provide autonomously organized forums who see reason for claiming that they have as a group a distinctive voice that might be silenced in a general feminist discourse" (Young 1990a:162). Those discussions have been joined by "structured discussion among differently identifying groups of women" (Young 1990a: 162–163).

Young's complex account suggests the problem but not the solution to what I understand as the fragmentation of the subject, a consequence of group oppression where group oppression follows the logic of unity, of purity. I think we need a solution to the problem of walking from one of one's groups to another, being mistreated, misunderstood, engaging in self-abuse and self-betrayal for the sake of the group that only distorts our needs because they erase our complexity. Young lacks a conceptual basis for a solution because she lacks a conception of a multiple subject who is not fragmented. I think she does not see the need for such a conception because she fails to address the problem of the interlocking of oppressions. Fragmentation is conceptually at odds with seeing oppressions as interlocked.

I do not disagree with Young's rejection of the individualism that follows from thinking of social groups as "invidious fictions, essentializing arbitrary attributes" (Young 1990a:46), nor with her rejection of an ideal of interests as common, of the universal, homogeneous subject, and of assimilation. I do not disagree with her account of social groups either, nor with her account of the problematic nature of one's subjectivity when formed in affiliation with a multiplicity of groups. But her account leaves us with a self that is not just multiplicitous but fragmented, its multiplicity lying in its fragmentation. To explain this claim, I need to introduce the concepts of thickness and transparency.

Thickness and transparency are group relative. Individuals are transparent with respect to their group if they perceive their needs, interests, and ways as those of the group and if this perception becomes dominant or hegemonical in the group. Individuals are thick if they are aware of their otherness in the group, of their needs, interests, ways, being relegated to the margins in the politics of intragroup contestation. So, as transparent, one becomes unaware of one's own difference from other members of the group.

Fragmentation occurs because one's interests, needs, and ways of seeing and valuing things, persons, and relations are understood not as tied simply to group membership, but as the needs, interests, and ways of transparent members of the group. Thick members are erased. Thick members of several oppressed groups become composites of the transparent members of those groups. As thick, they are marginalized through erasure, their voices nonsensical. The interlocking of memberships in oppressed groups is not seen as changing one's needs, interests, and ways qualitatively in any group but, rather, one's needs, interests, and ways are understood as the addition of those of the transparent members. They are understood with a "pop-bead logic," to put it as Elizabeth Spelman does in *Inessential Woman* (1988). The title *All the Women Are White, All the Blacks Are Men, But Some of Us Are Brave* (Hull, Scott, and Smith 1982) captures and rejects this logic. White women are transparent as women; black men are transparent as black. Black women are erased and fighting against erasure. Black women are fighting for their understanding of social relations, their personal possibilities, their particular sense of history, their mode of reasoning and values and expressive styles being understood as neither reducible to anything else nor as outside the meaning of being black and of being women. Black and women are thus conceived as plural, multiplicitous, without fragmentation.

The politics of marginalization in oppressed groups is part of the politics of oppression, and the disconnection of oppressions is part of these politics. Avoiding recognition of the interlocking of oppressions serves many people well, but no one is served so well by it as the pure, rational, full-fledged citizen. So I see a cross-fertilization between the logic of purity used to exclude members of oppressed groups from the civic public and the separation and disconnection of oppressions. Liberatory work that makes vivid that oppressions must be fought as interlocked is consistently blocked in oppressed groups through the marginalization of thick members.

So unless one understands groups as explicitly rejecting the logic of fragmentation and

embracing a nonfragmented multiplicity that requires an understanding of oppressions as interlocked, group representation does most group members little good. It indeed fails at safeguarding the "inclusion and participation of everyone" in the shaping of public life. The logic of impurity, of *mestizaje*, provides us with a better understanding of multiplicity, one that fits the conception of oppressions as interlocked. I mean to offer a statement of the politics of heterogeneity that is not necessarily at odds with Young's, but its logic is different. Hers, though formulated in rejection of the logic of purity, is oddly consistent with though not necessarily tied to it. Mine is inconsistent with it. Communication across differences in her model may well fail to recognize that one is listening to voices representative only of transparents, voices that embody the marginalization of thick members and contain their fragmentation.

Social homogeneity, domination through unification, and hierarchical ordering of split social groups are connected tightly to fragmentation in the person. If the person is fragmented, it is because the society is itself fragmented into groups that are pure, homogeneous. Each group's structure of affiliation to and through transparent members produces a society of persons who are fragmented as they are affiliated to separate groups. As the parts of individuals are separate, the groups are separate, in an insidious dialectic.

Heterogeneity in the society is consistent with and may require the presence of groups. But groups in a genuinely heterogeneous society have complex, nonfragmented persons as members; that is, they are heterogeneous themselves. The affiliative histories include the formation of voices in contestation that reveal the enmeshing of race, gender, culture, class, and other differences that affect and constitute the identity of the group's members. This is a very significant difference in direction from the one suggested by the postmodern literature, which goes against a politics of identity and toward minimizing the political significance of groups.[12]

The position presented in this essay, a position that I also see in the literature on *mestizaje,* affirms a complex version of identity politics and a complex conception of groups.

Interrupción: Lesbian Separation

When I think of lesbian separation I think of curdle-separation. In this understanding of separation I am a lesbian separatist. We contain in our own and in the heterosexist construction of ourselves all sorts of ambiguities and tensions that are threatening to purity, to the construction of women as for use, for exploitation. We are outside the lover of purity's pale, outside his conceptual framework. Even the attempt to split ourselves into half man/half woman recognizes our impurity. In our own conception, we defy splitting separation by mocking the purity of the man/woman dichotomy or rejecting it.

But "Watchale esa!" doesn't resonate in its impurity implicitly in all lesbian ears, and not all lesbian hips move inspired by a Latin beat.

Lesbians are not the only transitionals, impure, ambiguous beings. And if we are to struggle against "our" oppression, Latina Lesbian cannot be the name for a fragmented being. Our style cannot be outside the meaning of Latina and cannot be outside the meaning of lesbian. So, our struggle, the struggle of lesbians, goes beyond lesbians as a group. If we understand our separation as curdle-separation, then we can rethink our relation to other curdled beings. Separation from domination is not split-separation.

III. IMPURITY AND RESISTANCE

People who curdle-separate are themselves people from whom others split-separate, dissociate, withdraw. Lovers of purity, controllers through split-separation not only attempt to split-separate us but also split-separate from us in ways I have discussed, such as ghettoization and conceptual exclusion. They also attempt to split-separate us from others who are themselves curdled

through the logic of marginalization, of transparency. The logic of transparency shines in the constructed lover of purity himself, the modern subject, the impartial reasoner. He is the measure of all things. He is transparent relative to his position in the hetero-relational patriarchy, to his culture, race, class, and gender. His sense is the only sense. So curdled thoughts are nonsensical. To the extent that his sense is the instrument of our communication, we become susceptible to the logic of transparency and see split-separation from other curdled beings as sensical in our resistance to oppression. We also become susceptible to being agents of the lovers of purity in carrying out the oppression of other curdled beings, in constructing his made-to-order orderly world. Thus, curdle-separation is blocked, barred, made into a hard to reach resistant and liberatory possibility. It is also dangerous because curdled beings may adopt the logic of transparency in self-contradiction and act as agents of the lover of purity in coercing us into fragmentation and oppression. I think this is a risk that we can minimize only by speaking the language of curdling among curdled beings in separation and living its logic and by listening for, responding to, evoking, sometimes demanding, such language and logic. I think this is a risk we must take because the logic of split-separation contains not resistance but co-optation. So we have to constantly consider and reconsider the question: Who are our own people?

I don't think we can consider "our own" only those who reject the same dichotomies we do. It is the impulse to reject dichotomies and to live and embody that rejection that gives us some hope of standing together as people who recognize each other in our complexity. The hope is based on the possibilities that the unsettling quality of being a stranger in our society reveals to us, the possibilities that purification by ordeal reveals to us. I think this is Anzaldúa's point in thinking of a borderland: "It is a constant state of transition. The prohibited and forbidden are its inhabitants those who cross over, pass over, or go through the confines of the 'normal.'. . . Ambivalence and unrest reside there and death is no stranger" (Anzaldúa 1987:3–4). For her, "To live in the Borderlands means you are neither *hispana india negra española ni gabacha, eres mestiza, mulata,* half-breed . . . half and half—both woman and man, neither—a new gender. . . . In the Borderlands you are the battleground where enemies are kin to each other" (Anzaldúa 1987:194).

But, of course, that is thin ground for thinking of others as "our own": that we might be revealed to each other as possible through the tramplings and denials and torturings of our ambiguity. A more solid ground because it is a more positive ground is the one that affirms the lack of constraint of our creativity that is at the center of curdling; that holds on to our own lack of script, to our being beings in the making; that might contain each other in the creative path, who don't discount but look forward to that possibility.

Ambiguous, neither this nor that, unrestrained by the logic of this and the logic of that, and thus its course not mapped, traced already in movements, words, relations, structures, institutions; not rehearsed over and over into submission, containment, subordination, asceticism—we can affirm the positive side of our being threatening as ambiguous. If it is ambiguous it is threatening because it is creative, changing, defiant of norms meant to subdue it. So we find our people as we make the threat good, day to day, attentive to our company in our groups, across groups. The model of curdling as a model for separation is a model for worldly separation—the separation of border-dwellers, of people who live in a crossroads, people who deny purity and are looking for each other for the possibility of going beyond resistance.

IV. THE ART OF CURDLING

Curdle-separation is not something that happens to us but something we do. As I have argued, it is something we do in resistance to the logic of control, to the logic of purity. Though transparents fail to see its sense, and thereby keep its

sense from structuring our social life, that we curdle testifies to our being active subjects, not consumed by the logic of control. Curdling may be a haphazard technique of survival as an active subject, or it can become an art of resistance, metamorphosis, transformation.

I recommend cultivating this art as a practice of resistance into transformation from oppressions as interlocked. It is a practice of festive resistance:

Bi- and multilingual experimentation;
code-switching;
categorial blurring and confusion;
caricaturing the selves we are in the worlds of our oppressors, infusing them with ambiguity;
practicing trickstery and foolery;
elaborate and explicitly marked gender transgression;
withdrawing our services from the pure or their agents
whenever possible and with panache;
drag;
announcing the impurity of the pure by ridiculing his inability at self-maintenance;
playful reinvention of our names for things and people, multiple naming;
caricaturing of the fragmented selves we are in our groups;
revealing the chaotic in production;
revealing the process of producing order if we cannot help producing it;
undermining the orderliness of the social ordering;
marking our cultural mixtures as we move;
emphasizing *mestizaje;*
crossing cultures;
etc.

We not only create ourselves and each other through curdling but also announce ourselves to each other through this art, our curdled expression. Thus, curdled behavior is not only creative but also constitutes itself as a social commentary. All curdled behavior, thought, and expression contain and express this second level of meaning, one of social commentary. When curdling becomes an art of resistance, the curdled presentation is highlighted. There is the distance of meta comment, auto-reflection, looking at oneself in someone else's mirror and back in one's own, of self-aware experimentation. Our commentary is not straightforward: the commentary underlines the curdling and constitutes it as an act of social creative defiance. We often intend and cultivate with style this social commentary, this meta meaning of our curdling. When confronted with our curdling or curdled expression or behavior, people often withdraw. Their withdrawal reveals the devaluation of ambiguity *as threatening* and is thus also a meta comment. It announces that, though we will not be acknowledged, we have been seen as threatening the univocity of life lived in a state of purity, their management of us, their power over us.

NOTES

1. I thank Marilyn Frye for her criticism of the choice of *interlocking in interlocking oppressions.* I agree with her claim to me that the image of interlocking is of two entirely discrete things, like two pieces of a jigsaw puzzle, that articulate with each other. I am not ready to give up the term because it is used by other women of color theorists who write in a liberatory vein about enmeshed oppressions. I think *interwoven* or *intermeshed* or *enmeshed* may provide better images. At the time of this writing, I had not drawn the distinction between intermeshed oppressions and the interlocking of oppressions. See both the Introduction and chapter 10, "Tactical Strategies of the Streetwalker" for the relation between the two terms of this distinction.

2. This is the same form found in my use of *operation, apparatus,* and *individual.* Providing linguistic puzzles is part of the art of curdling.

3. For this use of *emulsion,* see Vogt-Schild (1991).

4. It is important to problematize the singularity of "social world" and the distinction between social world and individual.

5. I have based this description of the connection between the urge to control and modern political theory and ethics on Iris Marion Young's "Impartiality and the Civic Public" (in Young 1990b). Much of what I say in section I is a restatement and elaboration on sections 1 and 2 of Young's

chapter. I have also benefited from Mangabeira Unger (1975) and Pateman (1988) in coming to this understanding.

6. The ideal observer, unified subject is male. This fictitious subject is not marked in terms of gender for reasons explained below.

7. See Smith (1974) and Hartsock (1988) for arguments backing this account.

8. See Rosaldo (1989:200, 203) for his use of *postcultural* and *culturally transparent.* I am using *postcultural* as he does. His use of *culturally transparent* was suggestive to me in reaching my own account.

9. See Douglas (1966): "In other words, where the social system is well-articulated, I look for articulate powers vested in the points of authority; where the social system is ill-articulated, I look for inarticulate powers vested in those who are a source of disorder" (Douglas 1966:99).

10. See Anzaldúa (1987, especially pp. 41–51, on the Coatlicue state, and pp. 77–91, on *la Conciencia de la Mestiza).*

11. Sonia Saldivar-Hull used the expression "living on the hyphen" in the panel discussion "Cultural Identity and the Academy," at the tenth annual Interdisciplinary Forum of the Western Humanities Conference on Cultures and Nationalisms, University of California, Los Angeles.

12. Two examples that come vividly to mind are the positions suggested in Butler (1990) and Haraway (1990).

REFERENCES

Anzaldúa, Gloria. 1987. *Borderlands/La Frontera: The New Mestiza.* San Francisco: Spinsters/Aunt Lute.

Butler, Judith. 1990. *Gender Trouble.* New York: Routledge.

Chin, Frank. 1991. Come All Ye Asian American Writers of the Real and the Fake. In *The Big Aiiieeeee!* CD. Ed. Jeffery Paul Chan, Frank Chin, Lawson Fusao Inada, and Shawn Wong. New York: Meridian.

Douglas, Mary. 1989. *Purity and Danger.* London: Ark Paperbacks.

Haraway, Donna. 1990. A Manifesto for Cyborgs. In *Feminism/Post Modernism,* edited by Linda J. Nicholson, 190–233. New York: Routledge.

Hartsock, Nancy C. M. 1988. The Feminist Standpoint: Developing the Ground for a Specifically Feminist Historical Materialism. In *Discovering Reality: Feminist Perspectives on Epistemology, Metaphysics, Methodology, and Philosophy of Science.* Ed. CD. Sandra Harding and Merrill Hintikka. Boston: Reidel.

Hull, Gloria T., Patricia Bell Scott, and Barbara Smith, eds. 1982. *All the Women Are White, All the Blacks Are Men, But Some of Us Are Brave.* New York: Feminist Press.

Mangabeira Unger, Roberto. 1975. *Knowledge and Politics.* New York: Free Press.

Memmi, Albert. 1967. *The Colonizer and the Colonized.* Boston: Beacon.

Montoya, José. 1972. El Louie. In *Literatura chicana, texto y contexto,* edited by Antonio Castaneda Shular, 173–76. Englewood Cliffs, N.J.: Prentice-Hall.

Nichols, John. 1976. *Milagro Beanfield War.* New York: Ballantine.

Pateman, Carole. 1988. *The Sexual Contract.* Stanford, Calif.: Stanford University Press.

Rosaldo, Renato. 1989. *Culture and Truth.* Boston: Beacon.

Smith, Dorothy. 1974. Women's Perspective as a Radical Critique of Sociology. *Sociological Enquiry* 44(1):7–14.

Spelman, Elizabeth. 1988. *Inessential Woman.* Boston: Beacon.

Vogt-Schild, A. G. 1991. Physical Parameters and Release Behaviors of W/O/W Multiple Emulsions Containing Cosurfactants and Different Specific Gravity of Oils. *Pharmaceutic Acta Helvetica* 66(12).

Young, Iris Marion. 1990a. *Justice and the Politics of Difference.* Princeton, N.J.: Princeton University Press.

———. 1990b. *Throwing Like a Girl and Other Essays in Feminist Philosophy and Social Theory.* Bloomington: Indiana University Press.

LOCATING TRAITOROUS IDENTITIES: TOWARD A VIEW OF PRIVILEGE-COGNIZANT WHITE CHARACTER

Alison Bailey

I had begun to feel pretty irregularly white. Klan folks had a word for it: *race traitor.* Driving in and out of counties with heavy Klan activity, I kept my eye on the rear-view mirror, and any time a truck with a confederate flag passed me, the hair on the back of my neck would rise. . . . I was in daily, intimate exposure to the cruel, killing effects of racism, which my Black friends spoke of in the same way that they commented on the weather, an equally constant factor in their lives. . . . I began to feel more uneasy around other whites and more at ease around people of color. . . . Maybe whiteness was more about consciousness than color? That scared me, too, the possibility of being caught between the worlds of race, white people kicking me out, people of color not letting me in. (Mab Segrest, *Memoir of a Race Traitor,* 1994, 80)

Recent scholarship in multicultural, postcolonial, and global feminisms has motivated a reanalysis of both feminist and mainstream philosophical texts, methodologies, concepts, and frameworks. One project springing from these new approaches is a literature critical of white identities. At present, white identity is constituted by and benefits from injustice. Transformative work demands that whites explore how to rearticulate our identities in ways that do not depend on the subordination of people of color.

This paper addresses a simple but troublesome puzzle: the problem of how to describe and understand the location of those who belong to dominant groups yet resist the usual assumptions and orientations of those groups. The discussion begins against the background of three archetypes of knowers: the disembodied spectator, the outsider within, and the traitor. It sets out Sandra Harding's (1991) account of traitorous identities. Then, it takes issue with her portrayal of traitors as insiders, who as a result of a shift in the way they understand the world, "become marginal." I argue that Harding's description is misleading and that it fails to capture her intended meaning. The paper offers an alternative characterization of traitors that is less prone to misinterpretation. Crafting a distinction between "privilege-cognizant" and "privilege-evasive" white scripts, I characterize race traitors as privilege-cognizant whites who refuse to animate the scripts whites are expected to perform, and who are unfaithful to worldviews whites are expected to hold. Finally, the paper develops the notion of traitorous scripts and explains how animating them helps to cultivate a traitorous character. Using Aristotle's view of character formation (1980) and María Lugones's (1987) concept of "world" traveling, I briefly sketch what it might mean to have a traitorous character.

DISEMBODIED SPECTATORS, OUTSIDERS WITHIN, AND TRAITORS

Feminist epistemologists have long been attentive to the relationship between knowing subjects' locations and their understandings of the world. Dissatisfaction with Enlightenment accounts of knowing subjects as faceless, disembodied spectators who hover over the Cartesian landscape has led feminist theorists to consider knowers as embodied subjects situated in politically identifiable social locations or contexts. Attention to knowers as socially situated creates a new angle of vision that allows us to consider the alternative epistemic resources these situated subjects offer. Patricia Hill Collins (1990) and Sandra Harding (1991), whose writings represent the variety of feminist standpoint theory I have in mind here, prefer this approach because it is attentive to the social and political structures, symbolic systems, and discourse that grant privilege to some groups at the expense of others.

If the archetypal knower in Cartesian epistemic dramas is the disembodied spectator, then the starring role in feminist standpoint theory is played by the outsider within. Collins's description of Black female domestics offers a clear illustration of this second archetype (Collins 1986, s14-s15; also 1990, 11–13). As outsiders within, Black women working as domestics have an unclouded view of the contradictions between the actions and ideologies of white families. This unique angle of vision is rooted in the contradictory location of the domestic, who is at once a worker, "privy to the most intimate secrets of white society," and a Black woman exploited by and excluded from privileges granted by white patriarchal rule. Her "Blackness makes her a perpetual outsider," but her work of caring for white women "allows her an insider's view of some of the contradictions between white women thinking that they are running their lives and the actual source of power in white patriarchal households" (Collins 1990, 11–12).

Outsiders within are thought to have an advantageous epistemic viewpoint that offers a more complete account of the world than insider or outsider perspectives alone. Their contradictory location gives rise to what W. E. B. DuBois refers to as a "double-consciousness," a sense of being able to see themselves through their own eyes and through the eyes of others (DuBois 1994, 2). Extending Collins's analysis, Harding argues that women scientists, African American women sociologists, or lesbian literary critics doing intellectual work in the predominantly white, heterosexual male academy also have "identities [that] appear to defy logic, for 'who we are' is in at least two places at once: outside and within, margin and center" (Harding 1991, 275). As strangers to the social order of the academy, they bring a unique combination of nearness and remoteness to their subject matter that helps to maximize objectivity (Harding 1991, 124).

Because insiders have few incentives or opportunities to cultivate a bifurcated consciousness, their identities are understood as obstacles to producing reliable accounts of the world. For example, class privilege makes it a challenge for those with money to understand why moving out of poverty is so difficult; the privilege afforded to white people by racism makes it hard for whites to grasp its pervasiveness. Similarly, heterosexuals are rarely in a position to analyze either heterosexual privilege or institutional and personal homophobia.[1]

For all of the social benefits afforded to insiders, some members of these dominant groups resist the assumptions most of their fellow insiders take for granted. Feminist standpoint theory has been less attentive to such subject positions than to disembodied spectators and outsiders within. However, in the final chapters of *Whose Science? Whose Knowledge?* (1991), Harding makes a compelling case for expanding the insights of standpoint theory to consider how traitorous identities might serve as sites for liberatory knowledge. Reaching deeper into the logic of standpoint theory she explains:

> One can begin to detect other identities for knowers . . . standing in the shadows behind the ones [identities] on which feminist and other liberatory thought has focused, identities that are struggling to emerge as respected and legitimate producers of illuminating analyses. From the perspective of the fiercely fought struggles to claim legitimacy for the marginalized identities, these identities appear to be monstrous: male feminists; whites against racism . . . heterosexuals against heterosexism; economically overadvantaged people against class exploitation. (Harding 1991, 274)

Harding's discovery suggests that insiders are not, by virtue of their social location, immune to understanding the viewpoints and experiences of marginalized groups. Anti-racist whites do criticize white privilege, and feminist men do resist gender roles that reinforce women's oppression. So, "People who do not have marginalized identities can nevertheless learn from and learn to use the knowledge generated from the perspective of outsiders within" (Harding 1991, 277). Those who do are said to have "traitorous identities" and to occupy "traitorous social locations" (Harding 1991, 288–96).

Harding observes a significant epistemic difference between how insiders who are "critically reflective" of their privilege, and insiders who are oblivious to privilege, understand the world. Traitors do not experience the world in the same way outsiders within experience it, but outsider-within political analyses do inform their politics. Outsider-within standpoints provide tools for members of dominant groups who may be unable to articulate or clarify the occluded nature of their privilege and its relation to the oppression experienced by outsiders. By learning about lives on the margins, members of dominant groups come to discover the nature of oppression, the extent of their privileges, and the relations between them. Making visible the nature of privilege, enables members of dominant groups to generate liberatory knowledge. Being white, male, wealthy, or heterosexual presents a challenge in generating this knowledge, but is not an insurmountable obstacle.

Knowledge emerging from outsider-within locations, then, is valuable on two counts. First, it calls attention to the experiences of marginalized groups overlooked by earlier epistemological projects. Second, those who occupy the center can learn from and learn to use the knowledge generated by the analyses of outsiders within to understand their relationships with marginalized persons from the standpoint of those persons' lives (Collins 1986, s29; Harding 1991, 277). Harding describes insiders who adopt a critically reflective stance toward privilege as "becoming marginal." But I think this phrase leads to a misunderstanding about what it means to be a traitor.

IN WHAT SENSE DO TRAITORS "BECOME MARGINAL"?

Describing subject identities in spatial terms initially offers a useful way of seeing social structures and imagining the power relations between knowers. In the margin-center cartography of feminist standpoint theory, traitors are described as people who "choose to become marginalized" (Harding 1991, 289, 295). But this description is misleading for several reasons. The problem with describing traitors as becoming marginal is more clearly understood if we keep an historical example in mind.

In 1954, Anne and Carl Braden purchased a home in a white section of Louisville, Kentucky, for the purpose of deeding it to Charlotte and Andrew Wade, a Black couple. Andrew Wade, a politically conscious member of the Progressive Party and a World War II veteran, was furious that, even with his service record, he could not purchase the home he wanted. The Bradens, a progressive couple who opposed segregation, agreed to buy the house and deed it to the Wades. Their choice to break with the unspoken practice that middle-class whites sell their homes only to other whites ostracized (marginalized?) them in a way that other white families, who followed expected house-selling practices, were not. After the transaction, Louisville's segregationists publicly denounced the Bradens as "traitors to [the] race." They argued that the Bradens ought to have known better than to transgress the unspoken rule that the races ought to live in separate communities (Braden 1958, 82). Within hours of the title transfer, the Bradens received threatening phone calls and bomb threats. Months later they were charged with attempting to overthrow the government of the Commonwealth of Kentucky. In what sense then, could the Bradens be said to have chosen to become marginal? In her memoir, Anne Braden explains how, in the events that followed the house purchase, "some of the protections that go with white skin in our society fell from Carl and me. To an extent, at least, we were thrown into the world of abuse where Negroes always live" (Braden 1958, 7).

Braden's choice of words here suggests that the couple's subject position changed in some sense, but it also presents two problems. First, at a glance, to describe the Bradens as having become marginal makes it sound as if the Bradens actually came to occupy outsider-within subject positions like those occupied by the Wades. Deeding the house to the Wades did cause the Bradens to

lose privilege in their community, so it might be said that they became marginal in the sense that they were ostracized from the white community because of their actions. But being cast out does not amount to the same thing as being situated as an outsider within. Given the wrath of segregationist whites, the Bradens' subject position might be said to have shifted in relation to white citizens who saw them as race traitors. However, because they were white in the eyes of those who did not know them, they did not completely lose their privilege. In spite of their actions, the Bradens continued to bear a socially privileged racial identity; the Wades never had this privilege. Whites who engage in traitorous challenges to segregation may undergo some shift in their subject position in the sense that they may be ostracized from certain communities, but they do not exchange their status as insiders for outsider-within status.

Harding anticipates this confusion and clarifies her position using the example of privilege-cognizant heterosexuals.

> Some people whose sexual identity was not "marginal" (in the sense that they were heterosexual) have "become marginal"—not by giving up their heterosexuality but by giving up the spontaneous consciousness created by their heterosexual experience in a heterosexist world. These people do not think "as lesbians," for they are not lesbian. But they do think as heterosexual persons who have learned from lesbian analyses. (Harding 1991, 289)

Although the Bradens did not live as Black families in segregated Louisville lived, they could understand, even if incompletely, what it might be like to live in Louisville as the Wades lived in it. It is precisely this understanding that Harding thinks the narratives and analyses generated by persons of color can foster.

Thus, Harding's intended meaning here is that it is possible for people like the Bradens to learn about the world of segregated Louisville as the Wades experienced it without actually coming to inhabit that world as do those who are marginal.

Describing the Bradens as "becoming marginal" best describes a shift in their way of seeing, understanding, and moving through the world. Part of the reason for this confusion is that the words "margin" and "center" are usually used in standpoint theory to describe subject locations, and here they are being used to describe an epistemic shift. "Becoming marginal" refers to the shift from a perspective to a standpoint. The first is the product of an unreflective account of one's subject location; the second, as the word "antiracist" indicates, is a political position achieved through collective struggle (Harding 1991, 123–27; Jaggar 1983, 317).

Harding's intended meaning of "becoming marginal" should now be clearer. However, even if we understand "becoming marginal" to refer to an epistemic shift, I would argue that this phrase does not really capture the meaning of the traitorous standpoint Harding finds so compelling. Describing traitors as "becoming marginal" encourages a blurring or conflating of the location of the outsiders within and the location of traitors. The description makes it sound as if traitors have a foot in each world and are caught equally between them, and this picture does not foreground white privilege. If, for the moment, we retain the language of standpoint theory, it is more accurate to describe the Bradens' actions as destabilizing the center. Race traitors are subjects who occupy the center but whose way of seeing (at least by insider standards) is *off-center*. That is, traitors destabilize their insider status by challenging and resisting the usual assumptions held by most white people (such as the belief that white privilege is earned, inevitable, or natural). Descriptions of traitors as decentering, subverting, or destabilizing the center arguably work better than "becoming marginal" because they do not encourage this conflation of the outsider within and the traitor. Decentering the center makes it clear that traitors and outsiders within have a common political interest in challenging white privilege, but that they do so from different social locations. Understanding traitors as destabilizers tidies up earlier misunderstandings, but I still think stand-

point theory's margin-center cartography tends to restrict Harding's description of these subjects. If this language encourages misperceptions about traitors, then we need to consider alternative descriptions of these disloyal subjects.

PRIVILEGE-COGNIZANT AND PRIVILEGE-EVASIVE WHITE SCRIPTS

Perhaps a clearer, more descriptive picture of traitors, one that focuses on their decentering projects, will emerge if we think of traitors as privileged subjects who animate privilege-cognizant white scripts. The distinction Harding observes between insiders who are critical of their position and insiders who are not is more accurately expressed as a distinction between "privilege-cognizant" and "privilege-evasive" white scripts (Frankenberg 1993, 137–91). Understanding traitors along these lines requires spelling out what is meant by a racial script and how privilege-cognizant and privilege-evasive white scripts differ.

Like sexism, racism is a social-political system of domination that comes with expected performances, attitudes, and behaviors, which reinforce and reinscribe unjust hierarchies. Feminists have long paid attention to the ways gender roles encourage habits and nurture systems that value men's ideas, activities, and achievements over those of women. The existence of sexism and racism as systems requires everyone's daily collaboration.

To understand the nature of this collaboration, it is helpful to think of the attitudes and behaviors expected of one's particular racial group as performances that follow historically preestablished scripts. Scripts differ with a subject's location within systems of domination. What it means to be a man or a woman is not exclusively defined by one's physical characteristics. Similarly, what it means to be Black, white, Comanche, Korean, or Latina is defined not only by a person's physical appearance (so-called "racial" markers such as skin color, hair, facial features, body shape), but also by that person's perform-ance—by the script that individual animates. When the concept of racial scripts is applied lo-cally, what it means to be a white woman in Lou-isville, or an African American man in Chicago includes a person's gestures, language, attitudes, concept of personal space, gut reactions to cer-tain phenomena, and body awareness. Attention to race as performative, or scripted, reveals the less visible, structural regulatory function of racial scripts that exclusive attention to appear-ance overlooks.

Marilyn Frye's (1992) discussion of "whitely" behavior and "whiteliness" offers a conceptual distinction that is instrumental in understanding the performative dimensions of race and the dis-tinction between privilege-evasive and privilege-cognizant scripts. Frye recognizes the need for a terminology that captures the contingency be-tween phenotype (racial appearance) and the value of whiteness. Paralleling the distinction feminists make between *maleness,* something persons are born with by virtue of their biological sex, and *masculinity,* something socially connected to maleness but largely the result of social training, Frye argues for an analogous pair of terms in racial discourse and coins "whitely" and "whiteliness" as the racial equivalents of maleness and masculin-ity, respectively. As Frye explains: "Being white skinned (like being male) is a matter of physical traits presumed to be physically determined: be-ing whitely (like being masculine) I conceive as a deeply ingrained way of being in the world" (Frye 1992, 150–51). The connection between "acting white" and "looking white" is contingent, so it is possible for persons who are not classified as white to perform in whitely ways and for persons who are white not to perform in whitely ways. Racial scripts are internalized at an early age to the point where they are embedded almost to invisibility in our language, bodily reactions, feelings, behaviors, and judgments. Whitely scripts are, no doubt, me-diated by a person's economic class, ethnicity, sex-uality, gender, religion, and geographical location, but privilege is granted on the basis of whitely per-

formances nevertheless (Davion 1995, 135–39). A few examples can highlight some facets of whitely, or privilege-evasive scripts.

Lillian Smith, a white woman growing up in Jim Crow Georgia, offers one illustration of a whitely script. She was taught to "[act] out a special private production of a little script that is written on the lives of most Southern children before they know words" (1949, 21).

> I do not remember how or when, but. . . . I knew that I was better than a Negro, that all black folks have their place and must be kept in it, that sex has its place and must be kept in it, that a terrifying disaster would befall the South if ever I treated a Negro as my social equal and as terrifying a dis-aster would befall my family if ever I were to have a baby outside of marriage. . . . I had learned that white southerners are hospitable, courteous, tact-ful people who treat those of their own group with consideration and who carefully segregate from all the richness of life "for their own good and wel-fare" thirteen million people whose skin is colored a little differently from my own. (Smith 1949, 18)

Smith describes this script as a "dance that crip-ples the human spirit." It was a dance she re-peated until the movements "were made for the rest of [her] life without thinking" (Smith 1949, 91). What I find remarkable about Smith's "lit-tle script" is the clarity with which she connects racial segregation and the control of white wom-en's sexuality.

Anne Braden recounts a similar script grow-ing up in Alabama and Mississippi in the 1930s. Braden's description is especially attentive to the spatial dimensions of racial scripts.

> Most of these things, it is true, were never said in words. They were impressed on the mind of the white child of the South's privileged class. . . .
>
> It was a chant of . . . we sit in the downstairs of the theater, Negroes sit upstairs in the balcony—you drink from this fountain, Negroes use that fountain—we eat in the dining room, Negroes eat in the kitchen—colored town, our streets—white schools, colored schools—be careful of Negro men on the streets—watch out—be careful—don't go

near colored town after dark—you sit on the front of the bus, they sit in the back—your place, their place—your world, their world. (Braden 1958, 21)

Braden also acknowledges an interesting linguistic facet of whitely scripts.

Sometimes the commandments became quite explicit. For example, I could not have been more than four or five years old when one day I happened to say something to my mother about a "colored lady." "You never call colored people ladies [her mother replied]. . . . You say colored woman and white lady—never a colored lady." (Braden 1958, 21)

Attentiveness to maintaining the boundaries of one's racial location, then, is a strong dimension of all racial scripts.

Racial scripts are not regulated only by attitudes and an awareness of people's appropriate place; scripts also have a strong corporeal element that emerges in gestures and reactions to persons who we think of as being unlike ourselves. We are all, on some level, attentive to the race of persons with whom we interact, and this shapes our encounters. Even privilege-cognizant whites who are consciously committed to combating racism may react with aversion and avoidance toward people of color. African Americans receiving these avoidance behaviors feel noticed—marked. In his essay "A Black Man Ponders His Power to Alter Public Space," Brent Staples (1986) offers the following account of a white woman who passes him on the street at night.

I often witness the "hunch posture," from women after dark on the warrenlike streets of Brooklyn, where I live. They seem to set their faces on neutral and, with their purse straps strung across their chests bandoleer style, they forge ahead as though bracing themselves against being tackled. I understand, of course, that. . . . women are particularly vulnerable to street violence, and young black males are drastically overrepresented among the perpetrators of violence. Yet these truths are no solace against the kind of alienation that comes of being ever the suspect, against being set apart, a fearsome entity with whom pedestrians avoid making eye contact. (Staples 1986, 54)

The majority of whitely scripts include being nervous around people of color, avoiding eye contact with them, or adopting closed, uncomfortable postures in their presence. The repeated animation of these scripts, however, reinscribes a racial order in which white lives, culture, and experiences are valued at the expense of the lives of persons of color, whose bodies are fearsome to whites and are who are cast as deviant, dirty, criminal, ugly, or degenerate.

These accounts of privilege-evasive scripts provide a contrast to my account of privilege-cognizant scripts; they also help to explain why privilege-cognizant scripts count as traitorous. What all racial scripts have in common is that in a white-centered culture, everyone is more or less expected to follow scripts that sustain white privilege. The whitely scripts described by Smith, Staples, and Braden are privilege-evasive: they do not challenge whites to think about privilege, and their reenactment reproduces white privilege. If scripts sustaining white privilege are required by members of all racial groups, then members of both privileged and oppressed groups can refuse to cooperate. What holds racism in place, metaphorically speaking, is not only that African Americans have sat in the back of the bus for so long, but also that whites have avoided the task of critically examining and giving up their seats in front. By refusing to examine privilege, whites uncritically resign themselves to whitely scripts—to having their identities shaped in ways they may not have chosen (Harding 1991, 294).

Recognizing that whites can use the analyses of outsiders within to forge traitorous scripts means we can learn to think and act not out of the "spontaneous consciousness" of the socially scripted locations that history has written for us, but out of the traitorous (privilege-cognizant) scripts we choose with the assistance of critical social theories generated by emancipatory movements (Harding 1991, 295). A key feature of privilege-cognizant standpoints is the choice to develop a critically reflective consciousness. As one participant in Ruth

Frankenberg's study of white women observes "coming from the white privileged class . . . means you don't have to look at anything else. You are never forced to until you choose to, because your life is so unaffected by anything like racism" (Frankenberg 1993, 161). Traitors *choose* to try to understand the price at which privileges are gained; they are critical of the unearned privileges granted to them by white patriarchal cultures, and they take responsibility for them.

Choosing to take responsibility for my interactions requires that I take responsibility for my "racial social location, by learning how I am connected to other whites and persons of color; by learning what the consequences of my beliefs and behaviors as a European American woman will be" (Harding 1991, 283). An integral moment in understanding my relation to people differently situated from me comes in learning to see how I am seen by outsiders. It requires a variation on DuBois's double consciousness.

Unlike whites who unreflectively animate whitely scripts, the traitor's task is to find ways to develop alternative scripts capable of disrupting the constant reinscription of whitely scripts. Privilege-cognizant whites actively examine their "seats in front" and find ways to be disloyal to systems that assign these seats. Some obvious examples include choosing to stop racist jokes, paying attention to body language and conversation patterns, and cultivating an awareness of how stereotypes shape perceptions of people of color. Telling, and permitting others to tell, racist jokes reinscribes images that are harmful. The traitor knows when it is appropriate to stop this reinscription. Similarly, the white woman who clutches her bags or steers her children away from African American youth, or the white man who acts uncomfortable or nervous in the presence of people of color, sends signals to those around him that members of these groups are to be feared. Whites who interrupt, ostracize, or dismiss the contributions of students of color in the classroom reproduce their invisibility by sending the message that these students' contributions

are unimportant. If traitors can rearticulate white scripts in ways that do not reinscribe these subordinating gestures, then we can begin to imagine ways of being, as Adrienne Rich (1979) says, "disloyal to civilization."

The language of racial scripts presents an account of traitors that avoids the misunderstandings generated by standpoint theory's margin-center cartography. It also offers a dynamic account of traitors that is consistent with the epistemic framework of standpoint theory. This distinction between privilege-cognizant and privilege-evasive scripts is another way of articulating the distinction standpoint theorists make between a standpoint and a perspective. Privilege-evasive white scripts might be said to have unreflective perspectives on race. For example, most liberal discourse on racism illustrates a form of linguistic privilege-evasiveness characteristic of the whitely scripts. Phrases such as "I don't see color, I just see people," or "We all belong to the same race—the human race" erase color, which also amounts to a failure to recognize whiteness (Frankenberg 1993, 149). Privilege-cognizant scripts rely on anti-racist standpoints because they come about through collective resistance to naturalized patterns of behavior and social actions that reproduce white privilege. Animating a privilege-cognizant script requires more than occasionally interrupting racist jokes, listening to people of color, or selling Black families real estate in white neighborhoods. An occasional traitorous act does not a traitor make. Truly animating a privilege-cognizant white script requires that traitors cultivate a character from which traitorous practices will flow.

CULTIVATING A TRAITOROUS CHARACTER

When traitors refuse to act out of the spontaneous whitely consciousness that history has bestowed on them, they shift more than just their way of seeing and understanding the world. To be a race traitor is to have a particular kind of character that predisposes a person to animate privilege-cognizant scripts. The shift from privilege-evasive to privilege-cognizant white scripts, then, can be understood as a shift in character. It is this change in character that causes whites to move "off-center," to reposition themselves with regard to privilege. This final section briefly explores what it might mean to cultivate a traitorous character and demonstrates why developing a traitorous character must include being a "world traveler."

The idea that animating privilege-cognizant scripts helps to cultivate a traitorous character, and that traitorous characters are more likely to animate these scripts is, at root, Aristotelian: becoming traitorous is a process similar to the acquisition of moral virtue (Aristotle 1980). For Aristotle, virtues arise through habit, not nature. Virtue is a disposition to choose according to a rule; namely, the rule by which a truly virtuous person possessed of moral insight would choose. All things that come to us by nature we first acquire potentially; it is only later that we exhibit the activity. We become virtuous by doing virtuous deeds. Although states of character arise from activity, Aristotle makes a distinction between two sorts of activities and their ends. There are activities such as shipbuilding, in which the product of one's activity (the ship) is an end distinct from the process of shipbuilding; and, there are activities such as getting in shape where the product (a healthy and fit body) is part of the activity of working out and not a distinct end. The activity of virtue resembles the workout example. Just as a person does not become fit by doing a series of situps and then declaring, "There, I am fit!" so a person does not become virtuous by doing a series of good deeds and then declaring, "Finally, I am virtuous!" Virtue and fitness arise in the process of continually working out or doing good deeds. We become virtuous when we have the practical wisdom, for example, to act courageously to the right degree, for the right reasons, and under the right circumstances.

When Harding describes standpoints as achievements, I think she means "achievement" in the sense in which having a virtuous character is an achievement (Harding 1991, 127). Achieving a traitorous standpoint, like cultivating virtue, is a process. When a person has the practical wisdom to know which lines in whitely scripts to change, when to change them, and when to leave them alone, then they can be said to possess the practical wisdom necessary for a traitorous character.[2] Having a traitorous character is not the same thing as possessing a particular trait. Just as there is no recipe for attaining a virtuous character, there is no one formula for becoming a race traitor. It is a mistake to think that becoming traitorous is tantamount to completely overcoming racism. There will be times when our traitorous practical wisdom will be a bit off and we will fall back into privilege-evasive scripts, often without being aware that we are doing so. An account of traitorous character recognizes this instability. Developing a traitorous character requires a political strategy. It is not enough, as Harding says, to repeat what African American thinkers say, and never to take responsibility for my own analyses of the world that I, a European American, can see through the lens of their insights. A "functioning anti-racist—one who can pass the 'competency test' as an anti-racist—must be an actively thinking anti-racist, not just a white robot programmed to repeat what Blacks say" (Harding 1991, 290–91).

Developing a traitorous character requires lots of legwork. Learning about the lives of those on the margins means understanding the material conditions that give rise to outsider-within analyses; and to gain such an understanding, traitors must be "world travelers." In her now-classic essay, "Playfulness, 'World'-Traveling, and Loving Perception" (1987), María Lugones offers an account of identity in which subjects are shifting and multiplicitous. Recognizing identities as plural takes place through a process she calls "world" traveling.[3] Lugones believes that women's failure to love one another stems from a failure to identify with women who inhabit worlds they do not share; it is a failure to see oneself in other women who are different. Lugones's work addresses this failure, which she attributes to seeing others, who occupy worlds outside the ones in which we feel comfortable, with "arrogant eyes." When white women perceive Asian women with "arrogant eyes," or when African American women view Jewish women with arrogant perception, they fail to interact and identify with one another lovingly. Because arrogance blocks coalition building, world traveling must be done with loving perception.

The notions of "world," "world-traveling," and "loving perception" help Lugones to explain why she is perceived as serious in Anglo, or white, worlds where she is not at ease, and as "playful" in Latina worlds where she is at home. The failure of white women to love women of color is implicit in whitely scripts in which Anglo women "ignore us, ostracize us, render us invisible, stereotype us, leave us completely alone, interpret us as crazy. All of this *while we are in their midst*" (Lugones 1987, 7).

The privilege-evasive scripts animated by white women are easily explained in the logic of world travel. The failure of whites to see race privilege is, in part, a function of a failure to world travel. In the United States, people of color world travel out of necessity, but white privilege ensures that most whites need to world travel only voluntarily. When Anglo women refuse to travel to worlds where they are ill at ease, they are animating privilege-evasive scripts. Most whites are at ease in white worlds where we are fluent speakers, where we know and can safely animate whitely scripts, where people of color are out of our line of vision, and where our racial identity is not at risk. When I restrict my movement to worlds in which I am comfortable, privilege is difficult to see, and whitely scripts are never challenged. Loving perception requires that white women world travel as a way of becoming aware of the privilege-evasive scripts we have learned.

World travel, then, is an indispensable strategy for cultivating a traitorous character. Traitors must get out of those locations and texts in which they feel at home. World travel forces us to put our privileged identities at risk by traveling to worlds where we often feel ill at ease or off-center. Like virtuousness, traitorousness requires developing new habits; and one crucial habit might be to resist the temptation to retreat back to those worlds where we feel at ease—whole. In the process of traveling, our identities fall apart, our privilege-evasive scripts no longer work, and the luxury of retreating to a safe space is temporarily removed. Travel makes privilege-evasive scripts visible and we get a glimpse of how we are seen through the eyes of those whom we have been taught to perceive arrogantly.

Mab Segrest's story is a moving illustration of how world travel is integral to coalition building across boundaries of race, gender, class, and sexual orientation. As a white lesbian doing civil rights work in North Carolina, Segrest explains how "with Reverend Lee and Christina in my first months at Statesville, I crossed and recrossed more racial boundaries than I had ever managed in the eighteen years I had lived in my similar Alabama hometown. With them, I had access to the Black community, and I saw white people through their eyes" (Segrest 1994, 17). Learning to see ourselves as others see us is a necessary starting point for learning to undo privilege-evasive scripts. Whites like Segrest, who, with "loving perception," travel to the worlds inhabited by African American civil rights activists in the South, put their identities at risk and, in so doing, realize the difficulties surrounding the process of unlearning privilege-evasive scripts.

The approach I have outlined here is not a radical break from Harding's original insight. What I have tried to do is to rearticulate her insights in a language that avoids some of the confusion I think the margin-center cartography of feminist standpoint theory encourages. I have also tried to explore what it might be like to cultivate a traitorous character in a way that focuses on traitorous performances, rather than on traitorous identities and locations. The idea that traitorousness requires developing a traitorous character that makes one more likely to animate a privilege-cognizant script is very much in the spirit of Harding's work. Although Harding's descriptions of traitors as "becoming marginal" through a process of "reinventing oneself as other" limits her descriptions of traitors, I think what she is after is an active account of traitorousness as more than just a political identity. Recall that "reinventing ourselves as other" refers to a shift in one's way of seeing, and Lugones's sense of world travel certainly does this. Harding hints at this when she says "intellectual and political *activity* are required in using another's insights to generate one's own analyses" (Harding 1991, 290). Harding's description of traitorousness as political activity is closer to the performative notion I have in mind, and I think it is one with which she would agree.

NOTES

This paper is the product of many conversations I had during a National Endowment for the Humanities summer seminar on feminist epistemologies, June-July 1996, Eugene, Oregon. I would like to thank Drue Barker, Lisa Heldke, Sarah Hoagland, Amber Katherine, Shelly Park, and Nancy Tuana for their thoughts on this topic during our time together. I would also like to thank the editors of this volume for their comments on earlier drafts of this essay.

1. As standpoint theory focuses on institutional systems, practices, and discourses that unequally distribute power, the word privilege is used to refer to systematically conferred advantages individuals enjoy by virtue of their membership in dominant groups with access to resources and institutional power that are beyond the common advantages of marginalized citizens (Bailey 1998).

2. Traitorous acts committed just for the sake of traitorousness can be dangerous. History and literature are filled with cases of well-meaning whites whose good intentions put the lives, jobs, or achievements of friends and acquaintances of color in jeopardy. See, e.g., the fictional case of Bigger Thomas in Richard Wright's novel *Native Son* (Wright 1940).

3. For those unfamiliar with Lugones's work, "worlds" are neither utopias nor constructions of whole societies. They may be small parts of a society (e.g., a barrio in Chicago, Chinatown, a lesbian bar, a women's studies class, or a farmworkers community). The shift from having one attribute, say playfulness, in a world where one is at ease, to having another attribute, say seriousness, in another world Lugones calls "travel" (Lugones 1987).

REFERENCES

Aristotle. 1980. *Nichomachean ethics.* Translated by W. D. Ross. New York: Oxford University Press.

Bailey, Alison. N.d. Privilege: Expanding on Marilyn Frye's "oppression." *Journal of Social Philosophy.*

Braden, Anne. 1958. *The wall between.* New York: Monthly Review Press.

Collins, Patricia Hill. 1986. Learning from the outsider within: The sociological significance of black feminist thought. *Social problems* 33(6): sl4–s32.

———. 1990. *Black feminist thought: Knowledge consciousness and the politics of empowerment.* New York: Routledge.

Davion, Victoria. 1995. Reflections on the meaning of white. In *Overcoming racism and sexism,* ed. Linda Bell and David Blumenfeld. Lanham, MD: Roman and Littlefield.

DuBois, W. E. B. 1994 [1903]. *The souls of black folk.* Mineloa, NY: Dover.

Frankenburg, Ruth. 1993. *White women, race matters: The social construction of whiteness.* Minneapolis: University of Minnesota Press.

Frye, Marilyn. 1992. White woman feminist. In *Willful virgin: Essays in feminist theory.* Freedom, CA: Crossing Press.

Harding, Sandra. 1991. *Whose science? whose knowledge?: Thinking from women's lives.* Ithaca: Cornell University Press.

Jaggar, Alison. 1983. *Feminist politics and human nature.* Totowa, NJ: Rowman and Allanheld.

Lugones, María. 1987. Playfulness, "world"-traveling, and loving perception. *Hypatia* 2(2): 3–21.

Rich, Adrienne. 1979. Disloyal to civilization: Feminism, racism, and gynophobia. In *On lies, secrets, and silences.* New York: W. W. Norton.

Segrest, Mab. 1994. *Memoir of a race traitor.* Boston: South End Press.

Smith, Lillian. 1949. *Killers of the dream*. New York: W. W. Norton.

Staples, Brent. 1986. Just walk on by: A black man ponders his power to alter public space. Ms. 15(3): 54, 86.

Wright, Richard. 1940. *Native son*. New York: Harper and Brothers.

TIDDAS SPEAKIN' STRONG: INDIGENOUS WOMEN'S SELF-PRESENTATION WITHIN WHITE AUSTRALIAN FEMINISM[1]

Aileen Moreton-Robinson

Feminism was presented initially to me as a political tool that addressed the oppression of Women. When I say I am a Black Feminist I mean I recognise that my primary oppression came as a result of my blackness, my Aboriginality, as well as my womanness and therefore my struggles on all these fronts are inseparable. A willingness and preparedness by white women to listen to Aboriginal women's experiences is not enough. Cultural and racial components of white femininity and histories have to be interrogated and dissected in a relational way, including the limitations of White Feminism, as we know it now (Johnson 1994:256).

As beneficiaries of colonisation, white feminists have challenged, gained concessions and remade themselves as middle-class white women through the state and other institutions in Australia. Although white feminists have theorised for, and about, the social location of Indigenous women and their experiences, they have not written from what hooks calls the "location of experience". She states that "when initiating theory from the location of experience, one can be less concerned with whether or not you will fall into the trap of separating feminist theory from concrete reality and practice" (hooks 1996:18). Due to the legacy

of colonisation it has only been since the second wave of feminism in Australia that Indigenous women have engaged with feminist theory and practice, but many remain sceptical of the offer of accommodating difference by allowing us voice and space within feminism. In Australia, white feminists' theory of accommodating difference has often required, in practice, the commitment of Indigenous women to the dominant framework of a democratic white feminism which affords us voice and space while imposing a duty of tolerance for and adherence to its own fundamental values and goals.

This essay argues that critiques of white feminism by black and Indigenous women challenge the universality of the subject position middle-class white woman in different but interconnected ways. These critiques are grounded in different experiences from those of white feminists, and they expose the reproduction of power relations between the white community and the Indigenous community within feminism. The priorities of Indigenous women are often in opposition to and are different from those of the white feminist movement and the nation state. Indigenous women's political activity and engagement with white feminists in text and practice reveal that, from the standpoint of the subject position "Indigenous woman", incommensurabilities and irreducible differences exist between us and white feminists—differences that are inextricably linked in different ways to the centring of the subject position middle-class white woman.

As knowing subjects, middle-class white feminists and Indigenous women speak from different cultural standpoints, histories and material conditions. These differences separate our politics and our analyses. Indigenous women do not want to be white women; we want to be Indigenous women who exercise and maintain our cultural integrity in our struggle for self-determination as Indigenous people. The essay begins with an overview of the history of Indigenous women's public political activity since the 1970s. This is followed by an analysis of Indigenous women's self-determination and cultural integrity as incommensurable experiences and irreducible differences. The sexual oppression of Indigenous women is then explored to illuminate the experience of not being located in a white female body. The centring of whiteness in feminism is then unmasked through an analysis of the textual engagement with white feminists by individual Indigenous women.

THE PUBLIC POLITICS OF INDIGENOUS WOMEN: AN OVERVIEW

Through our oral tradition, Indigenous women learn of other Indigenous women who have been, and are, involved in the political struggle of Indigenous people, whether as grandmothers, aunties, mothers, sisters and lovers or as activists in their own right. And in the documentary records of white people there is evidence of Indigenous women's political activity in the 1800s (Ryan 1986a). It is recorded, for instance, that young Indigenous women were sent by their elders to keep constant surveillance of explorers such as G. A. Robinson in Western Tasmania. Unfortunately, a comprehensive herstory of resistance by Indigenous women has not been researched and documented, unlike the frontier political activism of Indigenous men, which has been recorded in the works of historian Henry Reynolds (1981; 1987; 1989). In the 20th century, particularly in the 1920s, the political activism of William Ferguson and the Aborigines Protection Society is documented and recognised within academic political discourse (Stokes 1997:159–64). However, little is recorded of the Indigenous women who participated in and

organised food for political meetings addressed by Ferguson, which were held on reserves and missions in New South Wales. What we do know from the life writing of Indigenous woman Margaret Tucker is that she assisted regularly in setting up meetings in Sydney and relaying information to rural areas on Ferguson's activities. Other Indigenous women, such as Monica McGowan, became involved in Labor politics in the late 1940s, working for the then federal Labor politician Dan Curtin (Clare 1978: xii).

The 1960s and 1970s in Australia proved to be a time of change for Indigenous people. This was due to a number of factors, including white economic prosperity, the Declaration of Human Rights passed by the United Nations, the civil rights movement in the United States, organised Indigenous political action and a change in attitude by the Commonwealth government. Since the late 1950s, Indigenous women such as Oodgeroo Noonuccal (formerly Kath Walker) and Faith Bandler undertook political action to improve the living conditions and legal status of Indigenous people. These women and some Indigenous men were members of the white-majority Federal Council of Aborigines and Torres Strait Islanders (FCAATSI), the organisation that led the campaign to gain support for improving the impoverished conditions of Indigenous people. Roberta Sykes (1989) argues that a change in government attitude to the concerns of FCAATSI came after a meeting with the then prime minister, Sir Robert Menzies, who offered Kath Walker a drink. Sykes writes:

> And Kath Walker replied: "Mr. Prime Minister, if you were in Queensland and offered me a drink like that, you would be put in gaol." The Prime Minister was shocked. There is every likelihood that this small incident was a turning point in history—the highest "citizen" in the land caught out by his country's racist legislation. These laws denied Aboriginal people, including Kath Walker, a legitimate place in their own country, and made it a crime for any citizen to offer—or for an Aboriginal to accept—an alcoholic drink in any circumstances.

So it was that, shortly after Menzies' retirement, the government of his successor, Harold Holt, succumbed to growing pressure to place a referendum before the public on the question of rights for Aboriginal people. In May 1967, votes approved the proposal, giving the Federal government power to legislate on behalf of Aborigines, and to include them in the national census. Despite the popularity of the issue at the time, the vote was by no means unanimous (Sykes 1989:2).

However, the referendum did not automatically change the position of the majority of Indigenous women, who lived on missions, reserves and worked for payment in kind on cattle and sheep stations. Hope Neill, an Indigenous woman from Queensland, states that "other rules and regulations which governed our lives were still enforced. We were still given rations of meat, flour, treacle etc. There were still restrictions on our movements on or off the mission, and the managers still had total control over our property and money" (Neill 1989:69). White women had formal citizenship, the right to drink (but not in public bars), and were free to travel.

Major changes in government policy, and political commitment to the improvement of the conditions under which Indigenous people lived, did not occur until after the establishment of the Aboriginal Tent Embassy in Canberra in 1972. The Tent Embassy was set up in the grounds opposite what is now the old Parliament House, in protest at the apartheid conditions under which Indigenous people laboured and to draw attention to our claims to land rights and sovereignty (Sykes 1989:93). Indigenous women, including Cheryl Buchanan and Cilla Prior, were at the forefront of the tent embassy protest and were in the firing line the day the police came to remove the Embassy, as one woman recollects:

> I remember the day so clearly. We were all just standing around the tent and singing. Suddenly the air was charged. The squads of police were coming around the corner. They were marching, and we could hear their bloody big boots coming down on the road. Like that sound you hear in Nazi war films. We kept on singing. Men were on the inside, near the tent, protecting it. Women stood all the way around them. When we saw the police pause for a few seconds, you could tell they were going to attack us so we sent the children out of the way. And then it was on. I couldn't believe it. TV cameras from all the channels blazing, but still them [sic] kept on coming. They beat down all the women, walked over the top of them after they knocked them down, kicked them out of the way, and began slogging into the blokes. Some of the coppers had things held tightly in their hands to give extra weight, ballast, to their punches. They also had other things they hit us with. Some of our people were given electric shocks. It all happened so fast. We think they had electric pig prodders. But the main thing was that they were doing it in public. I don't think for one minute that—for any of the Blacks there it was their first beating from the coppers. But before that, it was all dark lane stuff. In cells. Or in paddy-wagons. No witnesses. If we didn't achieve anything else by that protest, we at least flushed out the truth about police bashing Blacks. The whole world saw it (Sykes 1989:95–96).

Kaplan (1996:143) asserts that a profound difference between white women and Indigenous women is revealed here. She argues that had the protesters been white we would expect the women to be in the middle of the circle surrounded by the men. She is correct to assume that a difference in gender relations is being performed. In Indigenous communities it is usual for women to place themselves between men in their disputes as a way of resolving or diminishing the incident. The Indigenous women at the Tent Embassy maintained their cultural integrity by performing the same cultural practice despite the history of violence suffered at the hands of the police.

After this incident, Labor Members of Parliament in opposition, who were acquainted with Indigenous protesters, capitalised on the event to call for the nation's support. As the future Labor prime minister Gough Whitlam, then stated, "Our treatment of the Aboriginal people of Australia is the litmus test of our dedication to justice, peace and equality in the world. By our conduct in this area, the world will judge us" (Sykes 1989:96). When Labor came to power in 1972 they created Aboriginal Affairs as a separate portfolio, and established the Department of Aboriginal Affairs and an elected National Aboriginal Consultative Committee to provide advice on matters and issues it wished to raise with government (Rowley 1986:30–42). When Labor lost office in 1975, the Liberal-National party coalition government changed the title of the NACC to the National Aboriginal Conference and restricted its role to advising only on matters referred by government.

The Tent Embassy protests in Canberra highlighted the struggle and impoverished conditions of Indigenous people. Some white feminists participated in protests and others wanted to hear more about Indigenous women: Indigenous women were invited to feminist conferences and rallies. The first recorded major conference in which Indigenous women participated was the Women and Politics conference in Canberra in 1975, at which Pat Eatock, an Indigenous woman, was an official rapporteur (Eatock 1987:28). At this conference Indigenous women called for an end to forced sterilisation, instead of supporting the white feminists' demand for the right to abortion (Burgmann 1993:41). White women were also seeking the right to say "yes" to their sexual freedom, whereas Indigenous women wanted the right to say "no" to sexual harassment. Differences such as these meant that Indigenous women had limited involvement in what were fundamentally white women's conferences; we were often positioned as tokens, assimilated or angry, by white participants (Eatock 1987:27; Huggins 1994:76). Such experiences reinforced the pattern of white women not respecting our differences as Indigenous women. It is a pattern repeated many times since the 1970s, for example in the Bell–Huggins debate. In practice, white feminist organisers failed to change the power relations between themselves and Indigenous participants, which in theory they were seeking to

overcome. At feminist conferences the agenda of white women remained centred.

Indigenous women were feeling alienated by the white women's movement. Our concerns were not being supported either within the movement or by the white males who controlled the Indigenous bureaucracy. In the late 1970s Indigenous women publicly sought recognition and implementation of our demands. In 1979 in Sydney, at a Teach-In on Land Rights, Indigenous women passed a resolution requesting the establishment of a Task Force on Indigenous women to evaluate our role and status in the Land Rights movement (Daylight & Johnstone 1986:85). This resolution was forwarded to and supported by the National Aboriginal Conference in June 1979. Indigenous women's issues were gaining momentum. In May 1980 at the Australian and New Zealand Association for the Advancement of Science (ANZAAS) conference, Indigenous women from around the country attended sessions set aside for their participation. They voiced their concerns through resolutions on income maintenance, employment, education, land rights and treaties, community services, health, housing, cultural traditions, child care and social problems (Fay-Gale 1983).[2]

In July 1981 Indigenous activist and lawyer Pat O'Shane was appointed to the Office of Women's Affairs (OWA), which in October 1982 was renamed the Office of the Status of Women. Her appointment, together with the political action taken by Indigenous women, led to the adoption of a more inclusive policy agenda by the OWA. On 27 July 1982 a working party of one member from the OWA, Mary Sexton, and a group of Indigenous women set out the aims for an Indigenous Women's Task Force. The women were Eleanor Bourke, Vera Budby, me (formerly Aileen Buckley), Pearl Duncan, Flo Grant, Marcia Langton and Patricia Williamson (Daylight & Johnstone 1986:86). Indigenous women were committed to the concept of a Task Force, but became frustrated by the lack of commitment by government. Indigenous women in Canberra secured funding to hold a national conference for Indigenous women, which was held in November 1982. This conference saw the establishment of the Federation of Aboriginal Women (FAW). The FAW voted on and established a national executive committee, of which I was a member, and produced 42 resolutions on political issues, some of which were forwarded to the National Aboriginal Conference (NAC) for action. These issues differed from those of the white women's movement. Indigenous women sought the protection and preservation of Indigenous cultural heritage and customary law; representation and advocacy at all levels of government and in our communities; national land rights legislation; Indigenous people's sovereignty and the adoption of self-determination as policy. Indigenous women also called for improvement in, and the development of, culturally appropriate service delivery in the areas of education and training, employment and income, alcohol and substance abuse, health, housing and legal aid. After its inaugural meeting, the FAW did not receive any further funding and was effectively erased from the political landscape. However, members did have input into the support group of the Task Force that was eventually established in the Office of the Status of Women in August 1983.

The Indigenous Women's Task Force consulted with Indigenous women nationally and provided a report to government in 1986. Since the tabling of the Report of the Task Force three Indigenous women's conferences have been held: the First International Indigenous Women's Conference in Adelaide, 7–18 July 1989; the Remote Area Aboriginal and Torres Strait Islander Women's Meeting in Laura, 1–4 July 1991; and the ATSIC National Women's Conference in Canberra, 6–10 April 1992. A major outcome of the Task Force's report was the establishment of the Aboriginal Women's Unit in the Department of Aboriginal Affairs. After a change of government which saw the Labor party return to power, the Department of Aboriginal Affairs was amalgamated with the Aboriginal Development Commission (ADC) in 1992 to become the Aboriginal and Torres Strait Islander Commission (ATSIC).[3] The Aboriginal Women's Unit became the Office of Indigenous Women, and is located in ATSIC's central office in Canberra. Although there has been a dialogue between the Office of Indigenous Women and the Office of the Status of Women, there has been virtually no policy development between the two offices, because their priorities and issues differ. As Huggins points out, "femocrats have not opened up areas where Indigenous demands are respected and the politics of difference is understood" (1994:75).

Statistically, on all social indicators, Indigenous women are socially separate from white feminists. Indigenous women's life expectancy is 20 years less than that for white women, and at any age we "are more than twice as likely to die as are non-Indigenous people. For those aged 25 to 44, the risk is five times greater than the national average" (Antonios 1997:24–28). Diabetes affects 30 per cent of the Indigenous population and Indigenous infant mortality is three to five times higher than for white Australia. Infectious diseases in our communities are 12 times higher than in the general population, and Indigenous women's chances of being admitted to hospital are 57 per cent higher than for white women. Indigenous people have the second highest leprosy rate in the world, and Indigenous families are 20 times more likely to be homeless than white families. Nationally, 32 per cent of Indigenous people do not drink alcohol and out of the 68 per cent who do drink, 22 per cent drink at harmful levels compared with 10 per cent of the non-indigenous drinking population in Australia. Only 33 per cent of Indigenous children will complete Year 12 of secondary school compared with 77 per cent of the rest of the population. In 1994 the unemployment rate for Indigenous people was 38 per cent compared with 8.7 per cent of the rest of the population; of the 62 per cent who were employed, 26 per cent work for their social security benefits under community development employment schemes.[4] In 1994 the mean individual income for Indigenous people was 65 per cent of that of the general population. Compared with 29 per cent of white women only 17 per cent of Indigenous women are employed in administrative, professional or para-professional positions. Labour markets for Indigenous women are either in government departments established to fund programs for Indigenous people or government-funded community based service delivery organisations. Few Indigenous women are employed in the private sector (Runciman 1994:47).

Indigenous children are over-represented in corrective institutions. They are more likely to appear before the children's court or panel and be placed in non-Indigenous substitute care as wards of the state. Indigenous imprisonment rates are up to 14.7 times higher than for other Australians (Antonios 1997:24–28). Indigenous women and men represent 40 per cent of the incarcerated population while representing only 2.5 per cent of the Australian population. In the Northern Territory Indigenous women die from homicide 28 times more often than the rest of the population (O'Donoghue 1992:19). A National Police Custody Survey in 1990 revealed that Indigenous people are underrepresented in the commission of major crimes such as homicide, theft and robbery, with the exception of assault, but are more likely to be incarcerated for offences such as disorderliness and drunkenness (Kaplan 1996:138).

These social indicators reveal that statistically and corporeally Indigenous women as a group constitute a resource-deprived and under-privileged minority in Australian society. White feminists have less power than white men, but they hold a higher socioeconomic position than Indigenous women (Kaplan 1996; Bulbeck 1997). Differences in socioeconomic positions mean that the life chances, opportunities and experiences of Indigenous women will differ from those of white middle-class feminists. Indigenous women are aware of the discrepancy in socioeconomic status and power between themselves and white feminists, which is why we expect white feminists, who advocate to improve the conditions of all women, to support our claims. The

Indigenous custom of sharing, which sets up relations of reciprocity and obligation, also informs Indigenous women's perceptions of being asked to participate in the women's movement. Indigenous women will lend support to white feminists in exchange for their support. However, Indigenous women believe that when white feminists advocate equality for all women, this should mean that the needs of those women who are in the most unequal position in society will be the first to be attended to within the women's movement. Indigenous women assert that by working to improve the conditions of impoverished women in Australia, the status of all women will be enhanced. This differs from the position of white feminists, who aspire to live under the same conditions and have the same opportunities and rights as white men.

INDIGENOUS WOMEN'S SELF-DETERMINATION AND CULTURAL INTEGRITY

The struggle for Indigenous rights, citizenship rights and justice means that the basis on which Indigenous women challenge the nation state is different from that used by white feminists. Feminists have not challenged the legitimacy of the nation state on the basis of the murder of Indigenous people or the theft of our lands under the legal fiction *terra nullius*. White feminists have challenged the nation state on the basis of, and about, their rights as white female citizens (Watson 1992; Grieve & Burns 1994). Indigenous women give priority to the collective rights of Indigenous people rather than the individual rights of citizenship. This does not mean that they are unconcerned with rights of citizenship or women's representation and advocacy in society. What Indigenous women embrace is a politics of Indigenous rights which encompasses the collective rights of Indigenous people and their individual rights as citizens, as the following resolutions reveal. In 1980 at the ANZAAS conference in Adelaide, Indigenous women resolved that:

The Australian Aborigines are the land owners of the country. The government needs to recognise this and meet the needs of the Aboriginal people by ensuring land rights, better education, employment and housing (Gale 1983:175).

And in 1989, at the first International Indigenous women's conference, it was recommended "that the State and Federal Governments recognise the right of Aboriginal people to maintain and foster our way of life and our own system of law and self government" (Huggins et al. 1989:8). The demand for the collective rights of sovereignty and rights of citizenship were echoed again in 1992 at the ATSIC National Women's conference, where it was resolved:

1. That we the Australian Aboriginal and Torres Strait Islander Indigenous women demand a commitment of:
   a. the recognition of sovereignty rights of Aboriginal and Torres Strait Islander people;
   b. increased socio economical and political status of Aboriginal and Torres Strait Islander people;
   c. the preservation of Aboriginal and Torres Strait Islander culture and customs;
   d. introduction of immediate strategies to combat racism;
   e. the immediate equitable delivery of quality federal social services to Aboriginal and Torres Strait Islander people (ATSIC 1992:7).

The collective rights of sovereignty are perceived by Indigenous women as being synonymous with the rights of self-determination, which in response to the effects of colonisation and decolonisation, particularly since the 1970s, has become locally and globally the objective of Indigenous peoples. The right to self-determination is embedded in a number of United Nation's conventions as part of the human rights discourse, and is accepted as a fundamental right of all peoples by the international community. Marcia Langton, who worked on developing the

United Nations draft universal declaration on the rights of Indigenous peoples, outlines the goals of Indigenous Australian self-determination, which include:

- the right to sovereignty and to self-determination as stated in the draft declaration of indigenous rights prepared in the United Nations;
- the right to self government currently being elaborated by the National Coalition of Aboriginal Organisations;
- land rights legislated at the federal level. The Federal Government should legislate for communal and inalienable land-rights for Aboriginal people throughout Australia which recognises Aboriginal sovereign rights and prior ownership of Australia, and which gives Aboriginal people the right to claim all unalienated land including public purpose land;
- the right to control access to Aboriginal land;
- the right to control access to rivers and waterways on or adjacent to Aboriginal land;
- the right to all minerals and resources on Aboriginal land;
- the right to marine resources of the sea and sea bed up to a limit of ten kilometres where the sea is adjacent to Aboriginal land;
- the right to refuse permission for mining and other developments on Aboriginal land;
- the right to negotiate terms and conditions under which developments take place, and the right to statutory and mining royalty equivalents;
- the right to compensation for land lost and for social and cultural disruption;
- the right to convert Aboriginal properties to inalienable freehold title;
- the right, guaranteed by legislation, to living areas or to decisions on pastoral leases, these areas to be of sufficient size to allow for the development of economic

activity and to be made available on the basis of need and/or on traditional or historical affiliations.

- All reserves currently occupied by Aboriginal people to be granted to Aboriginal people on the basis of occupation, needs and historical or traditional affiliation by way of direct executive action as for example has occurred in the reserves in the Northern Territory. In the case of the former Aboriginal reserves, which are currently vacant crown land, such land to be granted by way of direct executive action, to appropriate Aboriginal groups. Legislation for national compensation to be based on a formula as a percentage of the Gross National Product, to be agreed to by negotiations between Aboriginal people and the Australian government. These negotiations to be supervised by an internationally respected body acceptable to both parties (Langton 1988: 4–5).

Langton's summary of the goals of Indigenous self-determination are clearly not based on the same historical experiences, priorities and practice or theory of the subject position middle-class white woman as are embedded in Australian feminism. The goals of Indigenous women's and men's self-determination are underpinned and informed by the inter-substantiation of relations between Indigenous land, spirit, place, ancestors and bodies. The connection between self-determination and these relations is evident in the words of Barbara Flick, who states:

> I say that our struggle for independence is one that could be described as a marathon rather than a sprint—We hunger for the loss of our lands and we continue to struggle for repossession. We continue our demands for our birthrights. We struggle for the rights of our children to their own culture. They have the rights to learn about our religion and our struggle and they need to be instructed by us in the ways in which this world makes sense to us. We'll tell them the stories about our ancestor spirits,

their travels and their adventures. And about morality and the attitudes that we have towards all living things in our world. We can make them strong (Flick 1990:65).

The irreducible difference exemplified here, between white feminists and Indigenous women, is the embodied experience of Indigenous subjects, who have a connection to land that is not based on white conceptualisations of property. Indigenous self-determination thus encompasses our cultural sustenance and our political and economic empowerment; consequently, the nation state is positioned by Langton and other Indigenous women as a contractual partner in negotiations between a nation of Indigenous people and a nation of white people. Indigenous women are committed politically to achieving self-determination and maintaining their cultural integrity. Irene Watson, an Indigenous lawyer, asserts:

> It is vital for our survival as a people to assert the right to self-determination on all aspects of lives—our legal rights, health, housing, education, all functions of our existence must be determined by ourselves, from the perspective of positive Indigenous development and not welfare dependency (1992:180–81).

Indigenous people utilise the contradictory nature of power to position our politics on self-determination. We deploy a politics of embarrassment, which draws on the liberal democratic ideal of equal and human rights for all citizens in our struggle for self-determination, in order to expose the legacy of colonisation. In this struggle, Indigenous women are politically and culturally aligned with Indigenous men because, irrespective of gender, we are tied through obligations and reciprocity to our kin and country and we share a common history of colonisation (Behrendt 1993:32; Dudgeon et al. 1996:54). Individual accomplishment, ambition and rights are the essential values of the white feminist movement, whereas the family and kinship system in Indigenous communities means that Indigenous women's individual aims and objectives are often subordinated to those of family and community. Culturally and politically it is an irrelevant luxury for Indigenous women to prioritise white feminist issues over Indigenous issues for the sake of gender solidarity (Lucashenko 1994:22; Johnson 1994:256; Behrendt 1993:41).

The goals of self-determination in practice warrant the recognition, acceptance and accommodation of Indigenous cultural differences within Australian society on equal terms with the dominant values, beliefs and practices of white culture. Indigenous women seek to transform cultural and educational institutions so that our ways of knowing will be taught and respected, whereas white middle-class feminists seek to gender institutions from within the epistemological framework of the dominant white culture. Indigenous women's relations to country mean we have specific concerns about the lack of protection of our sacred sites and our lack of formal ownership. Under Australian law it is the Crown who owns our sacred sites not the custodians, Indigenous women. Moreover, "the culture and spirituality [of Indigenous women] is being destroyed at a faster rate than that of Indigenous men", because the patriarchal discipline of anthropology has fundamentally designated Indigenous men as the land owners (Behrendt 1993:28). Indigenous women continue to demand and struggle for the return of our lands, the right to our intellectual property, cultural heritage, religion and spirituality, and the right to learn and pass on our morality, attitudes and world view (Flick 1990:65; Jarro 1991:16; Smallwood 1992:75; Felton & Flanagan 1993:59).

Self-determination for Indigenous people involves cultural practices derived from knowledges that are outside the experiences and knowledges of the white feminist movement. Cultural oppression in the form of the erasure and denial of Indigenous cultural knowledges by white people is a part of our everyday existence; we must participate in a society not of our making under conditions not of our choosing. Ideologically and in practice, white feminists' complic-

ity in reproducing cultural oppression, which renders inferior such "differences", is part of the white patriarchal cultural hierarchy. Feminists exercise their white race privilege in the women's movement because "issues of importance to Indigenous women such as the preservation of culture are not part of the political agenda for white women" (Behrendt 1993:35). Even where white feminists have made Indigenous women's business a priority, as in the Hindmarsh Island issue, their capacity and ability to support Indigenous women is predicated on the use of their race and class privilege.

Unlike white middle-class feminists, when Indigenous women assert their rights of citizenship in relation to the provision of services from the state they do so on the basis that their cultural difference and integrity be maintained. In the resolutions from the six Indigenous women's conferences, service delivery was identified as inadequate in the areas of: child care; fostering and adoption; employment and income; education and training; family violence; alcohol, substance and sexual abuse; health; housing; law and legal aid; and sport and recreation. In these resolutions Indigenous women advocated that the development and provision of service delivery be culturally appropriate; that more Indigenous people be employed and trained in white departments providing services; that Indigenous people be consulted and provide advice on policy formulation and service delivery; that at the community level Indigenous people determine and have control over service provision; that culturally appropriate information be developed on service delivery for distribution to Indigenous communities; and that white service providers be taught about their racism and the cultures of Indigenous people (Fay-Gale 1983; Omand 1983; Daylight & Johnson 1986; Huggins et al. 1989; Renour 1991; ATSIC 1992). Indigenous women extend the politics of Indigenous rights to encompass self-determination and the rights of citizenship. However, rights of citizenship are not divorced from Indigenous rights. As Gracelyn

Smallwood argues, improvements in Indigenous health will be brought about only by Indigenous women and men's ownership of their country and control of its resources, in addition to improved health care provision (1992:73). White middle-class feminists are not by experience and descent situated within a politics of Indigenous rights, as they do not have the same relationship to the land as Indigenous women; it is outside their bodies, culture, memories and identity.

REPRESENTATIONS OF THE "INDIGENOUS WOMAN" AS SEXUAL OBJECT

From the time white men invaded our shores Indigenous women's sexuality was, and still is in some discourses, represented as something to be exploited and mythologised (Reynolds 1981). White men misunderstood and ignored the social and political ramifications of participating in the Indigenous protocol of exchanging sex as a means of binding white men into relations of reciprocity and obligation. Conflict usually followed such encounters, when white men did not behave like classificatory male kin who would have reciprocated with goods. White men positioned Indigenous protocol within the 18th century discourse of the sexually deviant native, which was used to justify the rape and sexual abuse of Indigenous women for over a century (Gilman 1992). Pat O'Shane argues that part of the destruction of Indigenous society can be attributed to miscegenation; Indigenous men's dignity and identity has suffered because of the sexual exploitation of Indigenous women (1976:32). Miscegenation impacted on both Indigenous men and Indigenous women. White middle-class feminists in the late 19th and early 20th centuries perceived miscegenation as being the result of Indigenous women's sexual promiscuity, lack of dignity and lack of self-respect.

Sexual relations between white men and Indigenous women were of concern to first-wave feminists up until World War II and were still of concern to governments in the 1960s:

> Of the five states and the Northern Territory, four authorities in 1961 exercised control of Aboriginal property; two required consent to marry; four exercised restrictions on freedom to move; two maintained special conditions of employment (and in two others there were *laissez-faire* conditions in the pastoral industry with the Aborigines excluded from the award); all but Victoria had laws against alcohol; four had laws to control cohabitation; three limited the franchise (Rowley 1972b:401).

Despite prohibitions on cohabitation, the Indigenous population continued to increase. However, the effects of miscegenation have been a burden carried predominantly by Indigenous women and their extended families. Indigenous women who had sexual relations with white men produced children who the men, more often than not, did not support in any way, shape or form. Indigenous women were then positioned in public discourse as being promiscuous. In the 1980s, after Indigenous women were entitled to receive single-parent support, they were labelled as "welfare bludgers" because it was perceived that they were breeding so they could receive welfare payments. Indigenous mothers, judged by the standards of white motherhood and deemed to be unfit, had their children removed from them, usually by white middle-class women who worked for welfare agencies. Huggins argues that

> . . . many Aboriginal children have suffered brutally at the hands of white women who have always known what is best for these children. White women were and still are a major force in the implementation of government policies of assimilation and cultural genocide. As welfare workers, institution staff, school teachers and adoptive and foster mothers, white women continue to play major oppressive roles in the lives of Aboriginal women and children. Racism in the welfare and education systems continues to be a major focus of Aboriginal women's political struggles today. These are the issues which Aboriginal women activists often see as priorities rather than those taken up by white feminists (Huggins 1994:75).

Unlike white feminists, Indigenous women are not concerned with child-minding centres for working women. Indigenous women want control of the fostering and welfare of Indigenous children to be placed in the hands of Indigenous people. From 1965 to 1980 approximately 2,000 Indigenous mothers had their children removed from them, some never to be returned (Gale 1983:170). The National Inquiry into the Separation of Aboriginal and Torres Strait Islander Children from Their Families found that from 1910 to 1970 "between one in three and one in ten Indigenous children were forcibly removed from their families and communities" (Wilson 1997:37). The Inquiry also found that Indigenous children who were removed have worse health and are incarcerated more often than the rest of the Indigenous population.

Indigenous women now have the legal right to take the fathers of their children to court for maintenance, but lack the financial support to take such action. Indigenous legal services are so overloaded with criminal work that family law cases do not take priority. Indigenous women called for an extension of Aboriginal Legal Service provision, as is evidenced in the resolution put forward in 1982 by the Federation of Aboriginal Women, which requested

> . . . that the Department of Aboriginal Affairs take the necessary action to amend the existing Charter of Aboriginal Legal Services, by the end of 1986, so that the Aboriginal Legal Services broaden their function beyond defending criminal matters to include legal work (Omond 1983:17).

In 1992, after reports from Indigenous women in various communities around Australia about the continued lack of access to legal services, Indigenous women at the ATSIC national conference put forward the following resolution:

> That the Office of Indigenous Women prepare a report to all commissioners, regional councillors and regional women's advisers on the Aboriginal Legal Service, including:

a) all expenditure that involve[s] representation of Aboriginal and Torres Strait Islander women by the legal service.

b) to determine the level and nature of services highlighting any special project involving Aboriginal and Torres Strait Islander women.

c) to ensure that the needs of Aboriginal and Torres Strait Islander women is further addressed with the new funds made available to Aboriginal Legal Service as a result of the Royal Commission into Aboriginal Deaths in Custody (ATSIC 1992:10–11)

Since this resolution ATSIC has implemented an Access and Equity plan designed to make its services, including legal services, more accessible to specific target groups within Indigenous communities (ATSIC 1993). In the past, Indigenous women had no legal avenue to take action against white men even though laws existed that made sexual intercourse between white men and Indigenous women illegal. Police who participated extensively in the same practices did not enforce these laws. Sexual intercourse was, and still is, an important social practice whereby heterosexual identities of masculinity and femininity are reinforced (Sullivan 1995:189). Sexual intercourse between Indigenous women and white men is a social practice which reinscribes white racial superiority into identities of white masculinity, because for over 200 years the Indigenous woman's body has been positioned within white society as being accessible, available, deviant and expendable.

The myth of the sexually promiscuous and deviant Indigenous woman meant that middle-class white women positioned her as competition (O'Shane 1976:33). First-wave feminists wanted Indigenous women removed from the approach of white men and remade in the image of their white sisters, who saw sexuality as inherently degrading (Saunders & Evans 1992; Lake 1996). The fathering of mixed descent children, while not condoned publicly, was and still is supported by cultural constructions of white masculinity which subscribe to the myth that male sexuality is an irrepressible force and male needs must be provided with an outlet. Indigenous women have been, and are, the object of white male sexual desires. Although there still is a stigma attached to such relationships, they are tolerated by white society on the basis that sex for men is impersonal and biologically driven and Indigenous women are sexually promiscuous and deviant. Middle-class white feminists have fought for sexual freedom outside marriage and the right to say "yes" without being positioned as whores (Summers 1975). Indigenous women, who have been positioned as sexually deviant whores, want the right to say "no".

This has led Roberta Sykes (1975:301–2) to argue that feminism has not understood who is the true victim of sexual oppression in this country. The sexualisation of Indigenous women has been and continues today to be one of the means by which white males exercise their control and reinforce their white privileged position in Australian society. The black female body has been represented in the West as an icon of sexual deviance since the 18th century. White men sexualised Australian society by inscribing onto Indigenous women's bodies a narrative of sexualisation separated from whiteness (hooks 1997:114). This distance is evident in the following conversation reported by Sykes. The white male owner of a cattle station was moving his Indigenous workers off the property when his brother asked, how could you do that when you sleep with the women? The white male owner replied that while he may have sex with black women he never gets intimate (Sykes 1975:302). Indigenous women were and are "considered easy game for the racist rapist" (O'Shane 1976:33). Daisy Corunna recalls her experiences of being a domestic servant in the early 1900s:

> We had no protection when we was in service. I know a lot of native servants had kids to white men because they were forced. Makes you want to cry

to think how black women have been treated in this country (Morgan 1987:329).

The rape and sexual abuse of Indigenous women by white men is tolerated in society because the imagined sexual promiscuity of Indigenous women is perceived to be biologically driven. Indigenous women are positioned as being either primitive or exotic sexual subjects. As primitive sexual subjects they are seen to be closer to animals than white women and therefore naturally predisposed to sex in any form, which is one reason why Indigenous women find it difficult to report rape.

Two reports on the rape of Indigenous women show that they are more susceptible than white women to rape by white strangers but will more than likely know their Indigenous attacker. The Human Rights Commission's Inquiry into Racist Violence found that it was common for white police to rape Indigenous women after taking them into custody (1991:88–89). Indigenous women's presence in predominantly white social domains is often consciously or unconsciously interpreted by white men as signalling sexual availability. Although white women may be propositioned in the same space, their whiteness means that they will not be approached as often and a rebuff is likely to be interpreted as an insult to the male's ego rather than as a challenge to the white patriarchal supremacy. A rebuff from an Indigenous woman can lead to retribution in the form of verbal or physical abuse or gang rape. Indigenous women have a fear of white social spaces inhabited by white males and will usually not enter them unless accompanied by several Indigenous people. Indigenous women are conscious of their personal safety because their positioning in white society as sexual deviants means that they are represented as being sexually available and easily accessed.

Rape of Indigenous women by Indigenous men occurs in our communities. Payne argues that, unlike white women, Indigenous women are subject to three types of law: "white man's law, traditional law and bullshit law, the latter being used to describe a distortion of traditional law used as a justification for assault and rape of women" (Payne 1990:10). In court Indigenous women who have been raped are subject to white male lawyers who argue what they claim to be the "traditional law" line. They also argue that rape by Indigenous men is part of "murri love-making" and is not as hurtful or serious for Indigenous women as it is for white women (Atkinson 1990:6). Such a positioning supports white ideological constructions of Indigenous women's sexuality as deviant; it is disconnected and different from white women's sexuality. Indigenous women believe that we must empower ourselves to find solutions to problems such as intra-racial rape and sexual abuse in order to be self determining as a people (Atkinson 1996:9). At the International Indigenous Women's conference held in Adelaide Indigenous women requested, to no avail, from government

> that funding be provided to train, and employ more Aboriginal people, to deal as a priority with the issue of child abuse and emotional abuse, rape, incest, sexual abuse, physical abuse, verbal abuse and emotional abuse (Huggins et al. 1989:15).

Whereas feminists demand legal abortions, Indigenous women want stricter controls over abortions and sterilisations because they have been practised on our bodies without our consent. In the 1970s Indigenous medical services were using Depo Provera as a form of cheap contraception: it did not work and many Indigenous women became pregnant and suffered spontaneous abortions. Depo Provera was banned as a form of contraception in the United States in the 1960s and it was not approved as contraception in Australia, yet Indigenous women were talking of its use when interviewed about contraception by members of the Indigenous Women's Taskforce in 1985 (Daylight & Johnson 1986:64). The Department of Aboriginal Affairs knew of its use and by omission endorsed its application to the bodies of Indigenous women, who experienced the drug's impact, but lacked the power to chal-

lenge its widespread use. The Department's sanctioning of such practices indirectly reinforced the racialised systemic oppression and mistreatment of Indigenous women who were denied subjectivity. As in the United States, the use of Depo Provera in Australia can be linked to "the culmination of decades of eugenically informed birth control—promoting white women's fertility while constricting that of black women" (Amos & Parmar 1984:13). When white feminists of the second wave fought to take control of their fertility and demanded contraception, they were not coerced into taking Depo Provera by the state.

INDIGENOUS WOMEN'S REPRESENTATIONS OF WHITENESS IN FEMINISM

Indigenous women such as Pat O'Shane (1976) and Jackie Huggins (1987) assert that Australia was colonised on a racially imperialistic basis, but such a statement does not assist us to understand the gendered nature of the racism. Both white women and white men benefited from and participated in the dispossession, massacre and incarceration of Indigenous men, women and children, but they did so to different degrees (Sykes 1984:68). White women civilised, while white men brutalised. Whiteness in its contemporary form in Australian society is culturally based. It controls institutions that are extensions of White Australian culture and is governed by the values, beliefs and assumptions of that culture. Whiteness confers both dominance and privilege; it is embedded in Australian institutions and in the social practices of everyday life. It is naturalised, unnamed and unmarked, and it is represented as the human condition that defines normality and inhabits it (Moreton-Robinson 1998:11). For Indigenous women whiteness represents dominance and privilege, which is why the concept "racism" features predominantly as the causal connection in analyses of power relations between Indigenous women and white feminists; the term "white" is used by Indigenous women as an adjective to identify feminism, racism and the beneficiaries of our oppression as well as Australian society (O'Shane 1976; Corbett 1994; Fesl 1984; Watson 1987; Huggins 1987, 1992, 1994; Huggins and Blake 1990; Huggins and Saunders 1993; Willets 1990; Andrews 1992; Liddy-Corpus 1992; Watson 1992; Johnson 1994; Behrendt 1993; Felton and Flanagan 1993; Lucashenko 1994; Wingfield 1994).

In their critiques of feminism, Indigenous and Black women have various positions on the extent and nature of white women's oppression. Some Indigenous women's critiques position whiteness as institutionalised racism in which the cultural pattern of the distribution of social goods and opportunities, including power, regularly and systematically privileges white women on the basis of their race. Roberta Sykes, a Black woman, argues that racism is institutionalised, and is a process that supports the dominant position of white women and white men. Both sexes have benefited from the dispossession and massacre of Indigenous people because they own land and stand to inherit it (Sykes 1984:68). White women have less economic, social and political power than white men but they have more than Indigenous women. Indigenous women such as Pat O'Shane argue that the social organisation of Australian society is based on white male supremacy and that white racism is embedded in the education, political, legal and economic institutions. White values, norms and beliefs permeate these institutions which confer dominance and privilege on both white women and white men. O'Shane identifies the women's movement as "white" because the norms, beliefs and values of the women's movement are those of white women. She states that white women want Indigenous women to be involved but only on the condition that they embrace feminist principles and support a white feminist agenda. O'Shane argues that racism, not sexism, is responsible for the dispossession and resulting disadvantaged position of Indigenous people in Australian society; therefore the women's movement should be

fighting racism if white women want sisterhood with Indigenous women (O'Shane 1976:33). Eve Fesl concurs with O'Shane. She argues that Indigenous women do not want to join the women's movement because we have a sisterhood of our own, and it is racism which is the primary form of oppression Indigenous women experience at the hands of white women and white men (Fesl 1984:109). Elizabeth Williams (1987) asserts that racism not sexism is the overwhelming concern of Indigenous people because the priorities of white women are at the expense of Indigenous people's self-determination.

Indigenous women use the concept "racism" to encompass white dominance, privilege, discrimination and Indigenous subordination. Helen Boyle argues that racism and class inequality have placed Indigenous women in the role of the submissive sex in the wider society and the dominant sex within the Indigenous community (Boyle 1983:47). Lila Watson states that she has listened to the voices of women's liberation but they speak only of white women's liberation. Watson argues that white women have not understood Indigenous society and values, so myths and misconceptions have developed over time (1987:7). Jackie Huggins argues that Australia was colonised on a white racially imperialistic basis which gave white women power over Indigenous men and women. White women have not chosen to examine the oppression of women by focusing on Indigenous women's experiences; instead they have been concerned with white middle-class women's oppression. Huggins further argues that white upper-class women are involved in the exploitation of other women through their alliances with their husbands and their economic, social and political commitment to private property, profiteering, militarism and racism (1987:78). She states that for these reasons Indigenous women have not joined the women's movement, which is fundamentally an argument between white women and white men. Huggins asserts that because of the white power structure in Australian society Indigenous women's alliances are with the Indigenous liberation movement (1987:79). She states that white feminists want to recruit into the women's movement Indigenous women who are compliant and uncritical of white experts who write and speak about them. She says there is little evidence of white feminists interrogating their racism and transforming their behaviour towards Indigenous women; instead, white feminists have sought to control and silence Indigenous women who speak for an anti-racist feminism (Huggins 1994: 75–76).

Whiteness as a hegemonic ideology centred in feminism is evident in the works of Behrendt (1993), Lucashenko (1994) and Felton and Flanagan (1993). In Behrendt's work the centring of whiteness in feminism is made visible through exposing the complicity of white women in Indigenous women's oppression. Behrendt (1993:29) argues that Indigenous women's herstory is "one of invasion, dispossession, destruction of culture, abduction, rape, exploitation of labour and murder". In white people's history white women are mythologised as the brave women who fought against the harsh climate, but no mention is made about how they lived and profited from the land stolen from Indigenous women. White women have privileges accorded them by their membership of the dominant group. They have access to more resources, enjoy a better standard of living, earn more money and are better educated than Indigenous women. Indigenous women's priorities are not the priorities of white women; if the specific needs of Indigenous women can be contained within a feminist framework, then resources do not have to be allocated to them and ideologies remain intact. Beherndt argues that white feminism is

> telling Aboriginal women not to see what they see: that their position in society is defined by their gender rather than their race, that the push for rights by white women will empower black women, that we are aligned with white women in the battle against oppression and that white women are as oppressed as we are. We do not believe any of these white lies. The experiences of black women are trivialised when viewed as merely an extension of the

experiences of white women—The failure of the feminist movement to meet the needs of minority women shows that just as men in our society will never know what it is like to be a woman, a white woman will never know the reality of living as a black woman (Behrendt 1993:37–43).

Melissa Lucashenko argues that white racism is the dominant form of oppression experienced by Indigenous women (1994:21). For Lucashenko, Indigenous women are not part of the feminist struggle because white hegemonic ideology is subscribed to by white women who rely on their race privilege to remain ignorant and avoid objecting to Indigenous women's oppression. Addressing white feminists, she states that Indigenous women are not a part of the white feminist struggle:

> . . . because in 1993 you have little or no understanding of your colonial presence; because you believe the media images of Indigenous women and Indigenous society; because you fail to recognise that Black Australia is as diverse as your Australia; because you think that "part-Aboriginal" is a meaningful concept; because Black Australian history to you is a void or an irrelevance; because no major women's body in Australia has come out publicly in favour of the High Court's native title finding; because women's services have few if any Black workers; because you insist on burying your own racism under an avalanche of pseudo-solidarity; because you do not know whose traditional land you stand on; because you are baffled by the idea that Black women are justified in fearing you; because you want to "help" Black women; because you presume that having attempted our genocide you can attempt our ideological resurrection; because you think that Indigenous culture survived for millennia in this country *without* Black feminists, and because of your imperialist attitude that you alone hold a meaningful concept of female strength and solidarity, for these and for many other reasons, we Black feminists are not a part of the Australian women's movement (Lucashenko 1994:24).

Felton and Flanagan argue that feminism is an ideology, which belongs to the dominant white culture. Feminism is perceived as a white middle-class movement where white feminist academics centre themselves as the norm (1993: 53–54). Felton and Flanagan argue that "white feminists possess an inability to look outside their own cultural perspective. Yet they constantly speak with some apparent legitimised authority about our experiences". White feminists have either positioned Indigenous women as anti-feminist or they attempt to include us by requiring us to assimilate white feminist thought. Felton and Flanagan assert that because white feminists have not challenged racism or placed colonisation on their agenda, Indigenous women perceive feminism as another white politically controlled institution. They argue that a new feminism needs to be constructed through a critique of white women's racism and Indigenous women's experiences of it. Felton and Flanagan conclude by stating that Indigenous women's fight for equality is not about being equal with Indigenous men, but rather having the same human rights as white men and white women. Whiteness is not invisible but is normalised, centred and imbued with power for Felton and Flanagan. White women are positioned as having the power and the belief that they think, feel and act like and for all women.

The identification of white racism as the dominant causal connection in power relations between white feminists and Indigenous women shows that the organisation of social relations and public life on the basis of whiteness plays an important role in the cultural formation of experiences of both Indigenous and white women. A covert subjective experience of white racism is demonstrated in the example given by Pat O'Shane (1976: 32–33). When O'Shane was admitted to the Bar, a number of members of the Women's Electoral Lobby in New South Wales would not support a resolution congratulating her on her admission because she did not look Indigenous enough. Through the actions of these white feminists Pat O'Shane was rendered invisible by the forced disappearance of her claim to be Indigenous. She was evaluated as being non-Indigenous on the basis of how whiteness represents Indigenousness.

How Indigenousness is defined is also central to the construction of the middle-class subject position white woman because it signifies difference and distance. For the possessors of the middle-class subject position white woman it remains invisible, unmarked and unnamed but centred as the norm in the Women's Electoral Lobby. For Pat O'Shane this subject position was visible and had the power to deny her reality by erasing her Indigenousness on the basis of its white representation. This is a quintessentially Indigenous experience because anthropological representations of the authentic "Indigenous woman" are a part of middle-class white feminist discourse. Therefore, it is not exceptional for an Indigenous woman within Australian feminism to feel that she is defined as a non-entity solely on the basis of being Indigenous (Gould 1992:84).

Indigenous women have been able to occupy a space to challenge the epistemic authority of white feminism through a counter hegemonic discourse. Indigenous women do not want to be white as Joan Wingfield's narrative illustrates:

> When I get together with other Aboriginal and Indigenous women it feels really close. We call ourselves "sisters". Because their society is much the same, they can understand a lot better than most Whites. It's just so much easier getting on with them, because you don't have to explain anything: they understand and accept. We're not all the same, we have differences but they can accept the differences without trying to change us to being the same as them, which is done by White society. Many Whites don't accept differences—they think they're better and that we should change to be like them (Wingfield 1994:154).

Indigenous women's politics are about sustaining and maintaining our cultural integrity and achieving self-determination. Indigenous women's critiques of feminism reveal that second-wave middle-class white feminists have the power to define and normalise themselves within feminist discourse through their centring as the all-knowing subject who constructs the "Other". The middle-class subject position white woman has been historically the symbol of true womanhood in Australian society. This subject position has socially supported race and class privileges and it is deployed in the everyday practices of white feminists and the setting and prioritising of white middle-class feminist goals. It is present by its absence in the sexualisation and racialisation of Indigenous women.

Indigenous women perceive that white women are overwhelmingly and disproportionately dominant, have the key and elaborated roles, and constitute the norm, the ordinary and the standard in Australian society. White women are represented everywhere in Australian feminism, but are not represented to themselves as "white"; instead they position themselves as variously classed, sexualised and abled. In other words, white women are not of a particular race; they are members of the human race (Dyer 1997:3). Felton and Flanagan argue that "white feminists possess an inability to look outside their own cultural perspective. Yet they constantly speak with some apparent legitimised authority about our experiences" (1993:54). For Indigenous women, white feminists centre their own experiences, ideologies and practices as part of their invisible race privilege.

What is evident from the positionings of middle-class white feminists and Indigenous women is that our respective subject positions speak out of different cultures, epistemologies, experiences, histories and material conditions which separate our politics and our analyses. White Australian feminism is incapable of theorising from the lived experience of Indigenous cultural worlds because white culture and history can not link feminists with the land as an Indigenous familial extension. Our claims to land invoke different sets of relations between land, place, people, spirits and history which form the basis of irreducible differences and incommensurabilities between white feminists and Indigenous women. These sets of relations are grounded in a different epistemology that privileges body, place, spirit and land through descent, experience and oral tradition.

NOTES

1. "Tiddas Speakin' Strong" in Australian Indigenous English means Indigenous women speaking powerfully.
2. Source: *Lousy Little Sixpence* 1982. Director Alec Morgan. Producers Alec Morgan and Gordon Bostock. 16 mm, 54 minutes. Sixpence Production, Chippendale, NSW.
3. The Aboriginal Development Commission was established in 1982 to provide enterprise and housing loans to Indigenous people.
4. It should be noted that the same scheme was not introduced for white people until 1997.

FOR FURTHER READING

Alcoff, Linda Martín. "Mestizo identity." In *The Idea of Race,* edited by Robert Bernasconi and Tommy Lott. Indianapolis, IN: Hackett Publishing Company, 2000.

Alcoff, Linda Martín. *Visible Identities: Race, Gender, and the Self.* Oxford University Press, 2006.

Anzaldúa, Gloria E. and Cherrie Moraga, eds. *This Bridge Called My Back: Writings by Radical Women of Color.* 2nd ed. Berkeley, CA: Third Woman Press, 2002.

Anzaldúa, Gloria E. and Analousie Keating, eds. *This Bridge We Call Home: Radical Visions for Transformation.* New York: Routledge, 1987/2002.

Babbit, Susan and Sue Campbell. *Racism and Philosophy.* Ithaca: Cornell University Press, 1999.

Cuomo, Chris J. and Kim Q. Hall. *Whiteness: Feminist Philosophical Narratives.* Totowa: Rowman and Littlefield, 1999.

Frankenburg, Ruth. *The Social Construction of Whiteness: White Women, Race Matters.* Minneapolis: University of Minneapolis Press, 1993.

Frye, Marilyn. "White woman feminist." In her *Willful Virgin: Essays in Feminist Theory*. Freedom, CA: The Crossing Press, 1992.

Gunn Allen, Paula. *Off the Reservation: Reflections on Boundary-Busting, Border Crossing, and Loose Cannons*. Boston: Beacon, 1999.

Guy-Sheftall, Beverly, ed. *Words of Fire: An Anthology of African-American Feminist Thought*. New York: The New Press, 1995.

Harding, Sandra, ed. *The Racial Economy of Science: Toward a Democratic Future*. Bloomington, IN: University of Indiana Press, 1993.

Haslanger, Sally. *"Future genders? Future races?"* In *Moral Issues in Global Perspective,* 2nd ed., edited by Christine M. Koggel. Orchard Park, NY: Broadview Press, 2005.

hooks, bell. *Feminist theory from margin to center*. 2nd ed. Boston: South End Press, 1984 [2000].

Hull, Gloria T., Patricia Bell Scott, and Barbara Smith. *All the Women Are White, All the Men Are Black, but Some of Us Are Brave*. New York: The Feminist Press, 1982.

James, Joy, and T. Denean Sharpley-Whiting. *The Black Feminist Reader*. London: Blackwell, 2000.

Lugones, María, and Elizabeth Spelman. "Have we got a theory for you!: Cultural imperialism and the demand for the woman's voice." In *Hypatia reborn: Essays in feminist philosophy,* edited by Asisah al-Hibri and Margaret A. Simons. Bloomington, IN: Indiana University, 1990.

Mills, Charles. *Blackness Visible: Essays on Philosophy and Race*. Ithaca: Cornell University Press, 1998.

Narayan, Uma, and Sandra Harding, eds. *Decentering the Center: Philosophy for a Multicultural, Postcolonial, and Feminist World*. Bloomington, IN: Indiana University Press, 2000.

Omi, Michael, and Howard Winant. *Racial Formation in the United States: From the 1960s to the 1990s*. 2nd ed. New York: Routledge, 1994.

Outlaw, Lucius. *Race and Philosophy*. New York: Routledge, 1996.

Robinson-Moreton, Aileen. *Talking Up to the White Woman: Aboriginal Women and Feminism*. St Lucia: University of Queensland Press, 2000.

Shah, Sonia. *Dragon Ladies: Asian American Feminists Breathe Fire*. Boston: South End Press, 1997.

Smith, Barbara, ed. *Home Girls: A Black Feminist Anthology*. New York: Kitchen Table Women of Color Press, 1983.

Williams, Patricia J. *The Alchemy of Race and Rights: Diary of a Law Professor*. Cambridge, MA: Harvard University Press, 1991.

Yancy, George. *What White Looks Like: African-American Philosophers on the Whiteness Question*. New York: Routledge, 2004.

Zack, Naomi. *Inclusive Feminism: A Third Wave Theory of Women's Commonality*. Lanham, MD: Rowman and Littlefield, 2005.

MEDIA RESOURCES

Race: The Power of Illusion. VHS or DVD (3 cassettes). Written, produced, and directed by Christine Herbes-Sommers, Llewellyn M. Smith, and Tracy Heather Strain (US, 2003). This series provides an excellent background to the essays in this chapter. It pairs nicely with the "AAA Statement on Race." Episode one explores how recent scientific discoveries have toppled the concept of biological race. Episode two questions the belief that race has always been with us. It traces the race concept to the European conquest of the Americas. Episode three focuses on how our institutions shape and create race. Available: California Newsreel, www.newsreel.org, or e-mail: contact@newsreel.org. California Newsreel, Order Department, P.O. Box 2284, South Burlington, VT 05407. Phone: 877–811–7495, fax: 802–846–1850.

The Color of Fear. VHS. Produced and directed by Lee Mun Wah; co-producer, Monty Hunter (US, 1994). This is a powerful conversation starter on race, but also works effectively as a conclusion to the chapter. Eight North American men of different races talk together about how racism affects them. Available: Stirfry Seminars and Consulting, http://www.stirfryseminars.com/pages/store.htm, 510–204–8840. Film orders: ext.100 or e-mail: sandye@stirfryseminars.com.

Black Is, Black Ain't. VHS and DVD. Director/producer, Marlon Riggs; co-producer, Nicole Atkinson; co-director/editor, Christiane Badgley; co-editor, Bob Paris (US, 1995). This is a wonderful film that gets at the heart of problems of essentialism and race. American culture has stereotyped black Americans for centuries. In this film, Riggs meets a cross-section of African Americans grappling with contradictory definitions of blackness. The film scrutinizes the identification of "blackness" with masculinity as well as sexism, patriarchy, and homophobia in black America. Available: http://www.newsreel. org/films/blackis.htm, or e-mail: contact@newsreel. org. California Newsreel, Order Department, P.O. Box 2284, South Burlington, VT 05407. Phone: 877–811–7495, fax: 802–846–1850.

In Whose Honor? VHS. Written and produced by Jay Rosenstein (US, 1997). A discussion of Chief Illiniwek as the University of Illinois mascot, and the effect this mascot has on Native peoples. Graduate student Charlene Teters shares the impact of the Chief Illiniwek mascot on her family. Interviewees include members of the Board of Trustees, students, alumni, current and former "Chiefs," and members of the community. Available: New Day Films, 22 D Hollywood Ave, Hohokus, NJ 07423. Phone: 888–367–9154, fax: 201–652–1973, e-mail: orders@newday.com.

Nice Colored Girls. VHS. Produced and directed by Tracey Moffatt (Australia, 1987). This stylistically daring film audaciously explores the history of exploitation between white men and Aboriginal women, juxtaposing the "first encounter" between colonizers and native women with the struggles of modern urban Aboriginal women to reverse their fortunes. Through counterpoint of sound, image, and printed text, the film conveys the perspective of Aboriginal women while acknowledging that oppression and enforced silence still shape their consciousness. Available: Women Make Movies, *www.wmm.com*, or 212–925–0606.

CHAPTER 6

POSTCOLONIAL AND TRANSNATIONAL FEMINISMS

The perspectives collected in this chapter focus on the legacies of colonialism and ongoing impacts of neocolonialism, in relation to interwoven local, national, and global realities. They also take contemporary capitalist globalization, described by Ophelia Schutte as "a process in Western capitalism that seeks to integrate as much of the world as possible into one giant market," to be a fundamental concern of contemporary feminist and democratic politics. Postcolonial and transnational approaches may be thought of as *critical* global feminisms. Rather than presenting a unified one-size-fits-all feminism for all the women of the world, they question "nation" as an axis of meaning and power that is dependent on and entwined with gender, race, and political economy in many complex ways. Postcolonial and transnational feminisms also respond to the hegemony of white Euro-American approaches that assert dreams of "global sisterhood," but inevitably propagate Western cultural imperialism by presuming to speak for other women, projecting universal theoretical models, and minimizing historical, economic, and cultural differences.

Instead of thinking in terms of a singular system such as patriarchy or the sex/gender system, critical global perspectives look at complex and interwoven relations of power and exchange in which sex and gender play a key but not exclusive role. Some of the methodological commitments of critical global feminisms are to "decolonize" feminist theory and practice, to refuse to speak for others, and to have the interests and perspectives of poor working women at the center of inquiry on their own terms. As Inderpal Grewal and Caren Kaplan explain, "Because transnational economic structures affect everyone in the global economy, we need categories of differentiation and analysis that acknowledge our structurally asymmetrical links and refuse to construct exotic authors and subjects" (Grewal and Kaplan, 15). Yet terms like "trans-" and "post-" can be misleading. Transnational feminist philosophies are not necessarily focused on the sort of international structures and relations that are discussed in male-stream political science, which presumes the legitimacy and primacy of nation-states and their political and military economies. Instead of taking national borders and relations for granted, transnational feminist perspectives are attentive to lines of connection and transfer above and below the level of nation-states, from international trade agreements to global media to everyday migrations and multicultural lives. They therefore focus on phenomena that flow through, disrupt, or transcend borders, such as patterns of sexual violence and exploitation, patterns of resistance to oppression, environmental injustices, and struggles for human rights and democratic reform. Such issues are addressed through analyses and politics that focus on local particularity and diversity, keeping the perspectives and interests of real communities at the center.

Similarly, postcolonial perspectives do not assume that history can be described as stages of development, from pre- to post-colonial, or that colonial relations are a thing of the past. As feminist literary scholar Anne McClintock writes,

> The term postcolonialism is, in many cases, prematurely celebratory. Ireland may, at a pinch, be postcolonial but for the inhabitants of British-occupied Northern Ireland, not to mention the Palestinian inhabitants of the Israeli Occupied Territories and the West Bank, there may be nothing 'post' about colonialism at all. Is South Africa postcolonial? East Timor? Australia? Hawaii? Puerto Rico? By what fiat of historical amnesia can the United States of America, in particular, qualify as postcolonial—a term that can only be a monumental affront to . . . Native American peoples? (McClintock, 13)

This is especially important to note in an era marked by the existence of fewer political colonies (in the sense of territories under the rule of distant governmental powers), but even more widespread "imperialism-without-colonies," especially in the form of U.S. economic, military, and cultural presence and influence worldwide. Postcolonial political theories are "post-" colonial because they criticize and speak back to colonial and imperial power and violence, from the perspectives of survivors rather than victims. Many postcolonial theorists identify as both the progeny of colonial subjects and the inheritors of

multiple intellectual traditions, including Western traditions and other "master" discourses. They use the tools of those traditions to develop revolutionary understandings of complex patterns of oppression and resistance, so as to promote global justice. Perhaps ironically, by also drawing on particular stories and case studies, postcolonial and transnational theorists construct more nuanced, politically useful, and broadly applicable feminist philosophies.

This chapter focuses on political theory drawn from such case studies. Chandra Mohanty's "Women Workers and Capitalist Scripts" begins with an acknowledgment that the "almost total saturation of the processes of capitalist domination makes it hard to envision forms of feminist resistance that would make a real difference in the daily lives of poor women workers." Yet, in her interviews with three different communities of Third World women workers, she is struck by their dignity in the face of overwhelming odds, and the potential for building "cross-border solidarities."[1] Mohanty compares the cases of lacemakers in India, computer industry line workers in Silicon Valley, California, and migrant women workers in Great Britain to illustrate the particular ways Third World women workers are exploited by global capitalism. In all three contexts Mohanty observes that women's work is constructed through existing hierarchies and ideologies, such as family norms, femininity, class, and ethnicity. Gender identity structures the ways working women are permitted or excluded from performing in their societies, and in turn, norms of gender, race, and other hierarchies are made to seem natural because they are propagated through the work women do. Yet, Mohanty argues, the structural and ideological commonalities among current forms of exploitative labor transnationally make possible a theory of Third

---

[1] In spite of its problems, Mohanty employs the term "Third World" because it names location, not only geographically, but in terms of peoples' shared relationships to histories of colonialism, and to ongoing neocolonical economic and geopolitical processes.

World women's common interests, grounded in shared critical positions and needs.

In "Feminism and Globalization Processes in Latin America," Ofelia Schutte also focuses on the ways neoliberalism (a specific ideology behind current globalization) reproduces and capitalizes on existing asymmetries of power, including those resulting from conquest and colonization. Deploying a critical standpoint she refers to as a "postcolonial feminist ethical perspective" to understand contemporary processes of capitalist globalization in Latin America, she shows how these dynamics create both increased pressures on women and new possibilities for organizing and resistance among women in the global workforce. For example, although global capital threatens to homogenize meaning, movements for women's human rights and equality also have expanded and grown through "globalized" discourses, technologies, and relationships. Among women activists in Latin America, this has led to "both a decentering of the feminist movement and a much more far reaching effect of feminist ideals."

A dominant theme in transnational feminism is the importance of uncovering the effects of global economic forces on local realities, as well as the impacts local realities can have on the global stage. In "The Prison Industrial Complex," Angela Davis discusses the development of contemporary systems of punishment in the United States as a major economic and political force within global capitalism. Transnational corporations rely on penal systems as sources of profit through the privatization of prisons, using inmates as a source of near-slave labor, broadening the reach of capital and exploitative labor into prisons, and exporting U.S.-based models of high-tech and particularly cruel forms of punishment all over the world. Like the military industrial complex, the global prison industrial complex generates huge profits through social destruction, and the impacts are especially harmful for African-Americans and other communities of color. In addition to suffering disturbing forms of violence in prisons, people of color "are considered dispensable within the 'free world' but as a major source of profit in the prison world."

Race- and gender-based violence has always been a primary tool of colonization. In "Sexual Violence as a Tool for Genocide," Andrea Smith examines America's role in perpetuating violence against Native American women and communities. Arguing that rape is not just an act perpetrated against individuals, she explains how sexual violence encompasses a wide range of strategies designed not only to devastate a people, but also to destroy their sense of being a people. Colonial sexual violence marks certain groups as rapeable. By extension, their cultures, lands, and spiritual ways of life are also seen by colonizers as violable. Examples include native children's forced removal from tribal lands to white boarding schools, violations of native land with nuclear testing, and the commodification of native spiritual practices, art, and cultural artifacts. As a consequence of genocide, forced removal, and ongoing abuse, Smith finds that many Indian people have internalized these violent policies by taking on self-destructive behaviors. Such deeply damaging behavior, which is particularly harmful to women, is a direct product of the colonial system. Smith's examination of how sexual violence serves the goals of patriarchy and colonialism together calls for reconsidering the strategies feminists employ to combat gender violence.

Aihwa Ong's essay, "Experiments with Freedom: Milieus of the Human," is also attentive to historical residues and their violent potential. Reflecting on international terrorism and other recent examples, Ong warns against optimism regarding the democratic potential of transnational relations. "It would appear that spatial freedom and movements we associate with diasporas and market-driven mobilities are no guarantees of the spread of human rights," she writes, because experiments with freedom include both collective drives that are antidemocratic, and violent movements for freedom from secular Western culture. Ong's analysis raises important questions about the extent to which feminist notions of "cosmopolitan citizenship" presuppose a mistaken universal notion of liberal democratic selves.

The final essay in this chapter is an excerpt from Gayatri Spivak's book, *A Critique of Postcolonial Reason*. Here, Spivak reads together several historical texts that question norms of gender while holding up and reproducing colonialist structures. She cautions against similar moves in academic feminism and literary studies. She describes Rudyard Kipling's short story, "William the Conquerer," as an example of "translation-as-violation," a depiction in which the inhabitants of a place have been replaced by the translator's fantasy of himself. Spivak argues that academic feminism risks a similar translation-as-violation when it conflates racism in the United States with exploitation in global capitalism, or assumes that marginal locations can be voluntarily inhabited or simply overcome. She recommends deconstruction as a strategy for avoiding or engaging those risks.

WOMEN WORKERS AND CAPITALIST SCRIPTS: IDEOLOGIES OF DOMINATION, COMMON INTERESTS, AND THE POLITICS OF SOLIDARITY

Chandra Talpade Mohanty

We dream that when we work hard, we'll be able to clothe our children decently, and still have a little time and money left for ourselves. And we dream that when we do as good as other people, we get treated the same, and that nobody puts us down because we are not like them. . . . Then we ask ourselves, "How could we make these things come true?" And so far we've come up with only two possible answers: win the lottery, or organize. What can I say, except I have never been lucky with numbers. So tell this in your book: tell them it may take time that people think they don't have, but they have to organize! . . . Because the only way to get a little measure of power over your own life is to do it collectively, with the support of other people who share your needs.

—Irma, a Filipina worker in the
Silicon Valley, California[1]

Irma's dreams of a decent life for her children and herself, her desire for equal treatment and dignity on the basis of the quality and merit of her work, her conviction that collective struggle is the means to "get a little measure of power over your own life," succinctly capture the struggles of poor women workers in the global capitalist arena. In this essay I want to focus on the exploitation of poor Third-World women, on their agency as workers, on the common interests of women workers based on an understanding of shared location and needs, and on the strategies/practices of organizing that are anchored in and lead to the transformation of the daily lives of women workers.

This has been an especially difficult essay to write—perhaps because the almost-total saturation of the processes of capitalist domination makes it hard to envision forms of feminist resistance which would make a real difference in the daily lives of poor women workers. However, as I began to sort through the actions, reflections, and analyses by and about women workers (or wage laborers) in the capitalist economy, I discovered the dignity of women workers' struggles in the face of overwhelming odds. From these struggles we can learn a great deal about processes of exploitation and domination as well as about autonomy and liberation.

A recent study tour to Tijuana, Mexico, organized by Mary Tong of the San Diego–based Support Committee for Maquiladora Workers, confirmed my belief in the radical possibilities of cross-border organizing, especially in the wake of NAFTA. Exchanging ideas, experiences, and strategies with Veronica Vasquez, a twenty-one-year-old Maquila worker fighting for her job, for better working conditions, and against sexual harassment, was as much of an inspiration as any in writing this essay. Veronica Vasquez, along with ninety-nine former employees of the Tijuana factory Exportadora Mano de Obra, S.A. de C.V., has filed an unprecedented lawsuit in Los Angeles, California, against the U.S. owner of Exportadora, National O-Ring of Downey, demanding that it be forced to follow Mexican labor laws and provide workers with three months' back pay after shutting down company operations in Tijuana in November 1994. The courage, determination, and analytical clarity of these young Mexican women workers in launching the first case to test the legality of NAFTA suggest that in spite of the global saturation of processes of capitalist domination, 1995 was a moment of great possibility for building cross-border feminist solidarity.[2]

Over the years, I have been preoccupied with the limits as well as the possibilities of constructing feminist solidarities across national, racial, sexual, and class divides. Women's lives as workers, consumers, and citizens have changed radically with the triumphal rise of capitalism in the global arena. The common interests of capital (e.g., profit, accumulation, exploitation, etc.) are somewhat clear at this point. But how do we talk about poor Third-World women workers' interests, their agency, and their (in)visibility in so-called democratic processes? What are the possibilities for democratic citizenship for Third-World women workers in the contemporary capitalist economy? These are some of the questions driving this essay. I hope to clarify and analyze the location of Third-World women workers and their collective struggles in an attempt to generate ways to think about mobilization, organizing, and conscientization transnationally.

This essay extends the arguments I have made elsewhere regarding the location of Third-World women as workers in a global economy.[3] I write now, as I did then, from my own discontinuous locations: as a South Asian anticapitalist feminist in the U.S. committed to working on a truly liberatory feminist practice which theorizes and enacts the potential for a cross-cultural, international politics of solidarity; as a Third-World feminist teacher and activist for whom the psychic economy of "home" and of "work" has always been the space of contradiction and struggle; and as a woman whose middle-class struggles for self-definition and autonomy outside the definitions of daughter, wife, and mother mark an intellectual and political genealogy that led me to this particular analysis of Third-World women's work.

Here, I want to examine the analytical category of "women's work," and to look at the historically specific *naturalization* of gender and race hierarchies through this category. An international division of labor is central to the establishment, consolidation, and maintenance of the current world order: global assembly lines are as much about the production of people as they are about "providing jobs" or making profit. Thus, naturalized assumptions about *work* and *the worker* are crucial to understanding the sexual politics of global capitalism. I believe that the relation of local to global processes of colonization and exploitation, and the specification of a process of cultural and ideological homogenization across national borders, in part through the creation of

the consumer as "the" citizen under advanced capitalism, must be crucial aspects of any comparative feminist project. This definition of the citizen-consumer depends to a large degree on the definition and disciplining of producers/workers on whose backs the citizen-consumer gains legitimacy. It is the worker/producer side of this equation that I will address. Who are the workers that make the citizen-consumer possible? What role do sexual politics play in the ideological creation of this worker? How does global capitalism, in search of ever-increasing profits, utilize gender and racialized ideologies in crafting forms of women's work? And, does the social location of particular women as workers suggest the basis for common interests and potential solidarities across national borders?

As global capitalism develops and wage labor becomes the hegemonic form of organizing production and reproduction, class relations within and across national borders have become more complex and less transparent.[4] Thus, issues of spatial economy—the manner by which capital utilizes particular spaces for differential production and the accumulation of capital and, in the process, transforms these spaces (and peoples)—gain fundamental importance for feminist analysis.[5] In the aftermath of feminist struggles around the right to work and the demand for equal pay, the boundaries between home/family and work are no longer seen as inviolable (of course these boundaries were always fluid for poor and working-class women). Women are (and have always been) in the workforce, and we are here to stay. In this essay, I offer an analysis of certain historical and ideological transformations of gender, capital, and work across the borders of nation-states,[6] and, in the process, develop a way of thinking about the common interests of Third-World women workers, and in particular about questions of agency and the transformation of consciousness.

Drawing specifically on case studies of the incorporation of Third-World women into a global division of labor at different geographical ends of the new world order, I argue for a historically delineated category of "women's work" as an example of a productive and necessary basis for feminist cross-cultural analysis.[7] The idea I am interested in invoking here is not "the work that women do" or even the occupations that they/we happen to be concentrated in, but rather the ideological construction of jobs and tasks in terms of notions of appropriate femininity, domesticity, (hetero)sexuality, and racial and cultural stereotypes. I am interested in mapping these operations of capitalism across different divides, in tracing the naturalization of capitalist processes, ideologies, and values through the way women's work is *constitutively* defined—in this case, in terms of gender and racial parameters. One of the questions I explore pertains to the way gender identity (defined in domestic, heterosexual, familial terms) structures the nature of the work women are allowed to perform or precludes women from being "workers" altogether.

While I base the details of my analysis in geographically anchored case studies, I am suggesting a comparative methodology which moves beyond the case-study approach and illuminates global processes which inflect and draw upon indigenous hierarchies, ideologies, and forms of exploitation to consolidate new modes of colonization (or referred to as "recolonization"). The local and the global are indeed connected through parallel, contradictory, and sometimes converging relations of rule which position women in different and similar locations as workers.[8] I agree with feminists who argue that class struggle, narrowly defined, can no longer be the only basis for solidarity among women workers. The fact of being women with particular racial, ethnic, cultural, sexual, and geographical histories has everything to do with our definitions and identities as workers. A number of feminists have analyzed the division between production and reproduction, and the construction of ideologies of womanhood in terms of public/private spheres. Here, I want to highlight a) the persistence of patriarchal definitions of womanhood in the arena of wage labor; b) the versatility and specificity of capitalist exploitative processes providing the basis for thinking about potential common interests and solidarity between Third-World women workers; and c) the challenges for collective organizing in a context where traditional union methods (based on the idea of the class interests of the male worker) are inadequate as strategies of empowerment.

If, as I suggest, the logic of a world order characterized by a transnational economy involves the active construction and dissemination of an image of the "Third World/racialized, or marginalized woman worker" that draws on indigenous histories of gender and race inequalities, and if this worker's identity is coded in patriarchal terms which define her in relation to men and the heterosexual, conjugal family unit, then the model of class conflict between capitalists and workers needs to be recrafted in terms of the interests (and perhaps identities) of Third-World women workers. Patriarchal ideologies, which sometimes pit women against men within and outside the home, infuse the material realities of the lives of Third-World women workers, making it imperative to reconceptualize the way we think about working-class interests and strategies for organizing. Thus, while this is not an argument for just recognizing the "common experiences" of Third-World women workers, it *is* an argument for recognizing (concrete, not abstract) "common interests" and the potential bases of cross-national solidarity—a common context of struggle. In addition, while I choose to focus on the "Third-World" woman worker, my argument holds for white women workers who are also racialized in similar ways. The argument then is about a *process* of gender and race domination, rather than about the *content* of "Third World." Making Third-World women workers visible in this gender, race, class formation involves engaging a capitalist script of subordination and exploitation. But it also leads to thinking about the possibilities of emancipatory action on the basis of the reconceptualization of Third-World women as agents rather than victims.

But why even use "Third World," a somewhat problematic term which many now consider outdated? And why make an argument which privileges the social location, experiences, and identities of Third-World women workers, as opposed to any other group of workers, male or female? Certainly, there are problems with the term "Third World." It is inadequate in comprehensively characterizing the economic, political, racial, and cultural differences *within* the borders of Third-World nations. But in comparison with other similar formulations like "North/South" and "advanced/underdeveloped nations," "Third World" retains a certain heuristic value and explanatory specificity in relation to the inheritance of colonialism and contemporary neocolonial economic and geopolitical processes that the other formulations lack.[9]

In response to the second question, I would argue that at this time in the development and operation of a "new" world order, Third-World women workers (defined in this context as both women from the geographical Third World and immigrant and indigenous women of color in the U.S. and Western Europe) occupy a specific social location in the international division of labor which *illuminates* and *explains* crucial features of the capitalist processes of exploitation and domination. These are features of the social world that are usually obfuscated or mystified in discourses about the "progress" and "development" (e.g., the creation of jobs for poor, Third-World women as the marker of economic and social advancement) that is assumed to "naturally" accompany the triumphal rise of global capitalism. I do not claim to explain *all* the relevant features of the social world or to offer a *comprehensive* analysis of capitalist processes of recolonization. However, I am suggesting that Third-World women workers have a potential identity in common, an identity as *workers* in a particular division of labor at this historical moment. And I believe that exploring and analyzing this potential commonality across

geographical and cultural divides provides both a way of reading and understanding the world and an explanation of the consolidation of inequities of gender, race, class, and (hetero)sexuality, which are necessary to envision and enact transnational feminist solidarity.[10]

The argument that multinationals position and exploit women workers in certain ways does not originate with me. I want to suggest, however, that in interconnecting and comparing some of these case studies, a larger theoretical argument can be made about the category of women's work, specifically about the Third-World woman as worker, at this particular historical moment. I think this intersection of gender and work, where the very definition of work draws upon and reconstructs notions of masculinity, femininity, and sexuality, offers a basis of cross-cultural comparison and analysis which is grounded in the concrete realities of women's lives. I am not suggesting that this basis for comparison exhausts the *totality* of women's experience cross-culturally. In other words, because similar ideological constructions of "women's work" make cross-cultural analysis possible, this does not automatically mean women's lives are the *same*, but rather that they are *comparable*. I argue for a notion of political solidarity and common interests, defined as a community or collectivity among women workers across class, race, and national boundaries which is based on shared material interests and identity and common ways of reading the world. This idea of political solidarity in the context of the incorporation of Third-World women into a global economy offers a basis for cross-cultural comparison and analysis which is grounded in history and social location rather than in an ahistorical notion of culture or experience. I am making a choice here to focus on and analyze the *continuities* in the experiences, histories, and strategies of survival of these particular workers. But this does not mean that differences and discontinuities in experience do not exist or that they are insignificant. The focus on continuities is a *strategic* one—it makes possible a way of reading the operation of capital from a location (that of Third-World women workers) which, while forming the bedrock of a certain kind of global exploitation of labor, remains somewhat invisible and undertheorized.

GENDER AND WORK: HISTORICAL AND IDEOLOGICAL TRANSFORMATIONS

"Work makes life sweet," says Lola Weixel, a working-class Jewish woman in Connie Field's film "The Life and Times of Rosie the Riveter." Weixel is reflecting on her experience of working in a welding factory during World War II, at a time when large numbers of U.S. women were incorporated into the labor force to replace men who were fighting the war. In one of the most moving moments in the film, she draws attention to what it meant to her and to other women to work side by side, to learn skills and craft products, and to be paid for the work they did, only to be told at the end of the war that they were no longer needed and should go back to being girlfriends, housewives, and mothers. While the U.S. state propaganda machine was especially explicit on matters of work for men and women, and the corresponding expectations of masculinity/femininity and domesticity in the late 1940s and 1950s, this is no longer the case in the 1990s. Shifting definitions of public and private, and of workers, consumers and citizens no longer define wage-work in visibly masculine terms. However, the dynamics of job competition, loss, and profit-making in the 1990s are still part of the dynamic process that spelled the decline of the mill towns of New England in the early 1900s and that now pits "American" against "immigrant" and "Third-World" workers along the U.S./Mexico border or in the Silicon Valley in California. Similarly, there are continuities between the women-led New York garment-workers strike of 1909, the Bread and Roses (Lawrence textile) strike of 1912, Lola Weixel's role in union organizing during WW II, and the frequent strikes in the 1980s and 1990s of Korean textile and electronic

workers, most of whom are young, single women.[11] While the global division of labor in 1995 looks quite different from what it was in the 1950s, ideologies of women's work, the meaning and value of work for women, and women workers' struggles against exploitation remain central issues for feminists around the world. After all, women's labor has always been central to the development, consolidation, and reproduction of capitalism in the U.S.A. and elsewhere.

In the United States, histories of slavery, indentured servitude, contract labor, self-employment, and wage-work are also simultaneously histories of gender, race, and (hetero)sexuality, nested within the context of the development of capitalism. Thus, women of different races, ethnicities, and social classes had profoundly different, though interconnected, experiences of work in the economic development from nineteenth-century economic and social practices (slave agriculture in the South, emergent industrial capitalism in the Northeast, the hacienda system in the Southwest, independent family farms in the rural Midwest, Native American hunting/gathering and agriculture) to wage-labor and self-employment (including family businesses) in the late-twentieth century. In 1995, almost a century after the Lowell girls lost their jobs when textile mills moved South to attract nonunionized labor, feminists are faced with a number of profound analytical and organizational challenges in different regions of the world. The material, cultural, and political effects of the processes of domination and exploitation which sustain what is called the New World Order(NWO)[12] are devastating for the vast majority of people in the world—and most especially for impoverished and Third-World women. Maria Mies argues that the increasing division of the world into consumers and producers has a profound effect on Third-World women workers, who are drawn into the international division of labor as workers in agriculture; in large-scale manufacturing industries like textiles, electronics, garments, and toys; in small-scale manufacturing of consumer goods like handicrafts and food processing (the informal sector); and as workers in the sex and tourist industries.[13]

The values, power, and meanings attached to being either a consumer or a producer/worker vary enormously depending on where and who we happen to be in an unequal global system. In the 1990s, it is, after all, multinational corporations that are the hallmark of global capitalism. In an analysis of the effects of these corporations on the new world order, Richard Barnet and John Cavanagh characterize the global commercial arena in terms of four intersecting webs: the Global Cultural Bazaar (which creates and disseminates images and dreams through films, television, radio, music, and other media), the Global Shopping Mall (a planetary supermarket which sells things to eat, drink, wear, and enjoy through advertising, distribution, and marketing networks), the Global Workplace (a network of factories and workplaces where goods are produced, information processed, and services rendered), and, finally, the Global Financial Network (the international traffic in currency transactions, global securities, etc.).[14] In each of these webs, racialized ideologies of masculinity, femininity, and sexuality play a role in constructing the legitimate consumer, worker, and manager. Meanwhile, the psychic and social disenfranchisement and impoverishment of women continues. Women's bodies and labor are used to consolidate global dreams, desires, and ideologies of success and the good life in unprecedented ways.

Feminists have responded directly to the challenges of globalization and capitalist modes of recolonization by addressing the sexual politics and effects on women of a) religious fundamentalist movements within and across the boundaries of the nation-state; b) structural adjustment policies (SAPs); c) militarism, demilitarization, and violence against women; d) environmental degradation and land/sovereignty struggles of indigenous and native peoples; and e) population control, health, and reproductive policies and practices.[15] In each of these cases, feminists have

analyzed the effects on women as workers, sexual partners, mothers and caretakers, consumers, and transmitters and transformers of culture and tradition. Analysis of the ideologies of masculinity and femininity, of motherhood and (hetero)sexuality and the understanding and mapping of agency, access, and choice are central to this analysis and organizing. Thus, while my characterization of capitalist processes of domination and recolonization may appear somewhat overwhelming, I want to draw attention to the numerous forms of resistance and struggle that have also always been constitutive of the script of colonialism/capitalism. Capitalist patriarchies and racialized, class/caste-specific hierarchies are a key part of the long history of domination and exploitation of women, but struggles against these practices and vibrant, creative, collective forms of mobilization and organizing have also always been a part of our histories. In fact, like Jacqui Alexander and a number of other authors, I attempt to articulate an emancipatory discourse and knowledge, one that furthers the cause of feminist liberatory practice. After all, part of what needs to change within racialized capitalist patriarchies is the very concept of work/labor, as well as the naturalization of heterosexual masculinity in the definition of "the worker."

Teresa Amott and Julie Matthaei, in analyzing the U.S. labor market, argue that the intersection of gender, class, and racial-ethnic hierarchies of power has had two major effects:

> First, disempowered groups have been concentrated in jobs with lower pay, less job security, and more difficult working conditions. Second, workplaces have been places of extreme segregation, in which workers have worked in jobs only with members of their same racial-ethnic, gender, and class group, even though the particular racial-ethnic group and gender assigned to a job may have varied across firms and regions.[16]

While Amott and Matthaei draw attention to the sex-and-race typing of jobs, they do not *theorize* the relationship between this job typing and the social identity of the workers concentrated in these low-paying, segregated, often unsafe sectors of the labor market. While the economic history they chart is crucial to any understanding of the race-and-gender basis of U.S. capitalist processes, their analysis begs the question of whether there is a connection (other than the common history of domination of people of color) between *how* these jobs are defined and *who* is sought after for the jobs.

By examining two instances of the incorporation of women into the global economy (women lacemakers in Narsapur, India, and women in the electronics industry in the Silicon Valley) I want to delineate the interconnections between gender, race, and ethnicity, and the ideologies of work which locate women in particular exploitative contexts. The contradictory positioning of women along class, race, and ethnic lines in these two cases suggests that, in spite of obvious geographical and sociocultural differences between the two contexts, the organization of the global economy by contemporary capital positions these workers in very similar ways, effectively reproducing and transforming locally specific hierarchies. There are also some significant continuities between homework and factory work in these contexts, in terms of both the inherent ideologies of work as well as the experiences and social identities of women as workers. This tendency can also be seen in the case studies of black women workers (of Afro-Caribbean, Asian, and African origin) in Britain, especially women engaged in homework, factory work, and family businesses.

HOUSEWIVES AND HOMEWORK: THE LACEMAKERS OF NARSAPUR

Maria Mies's 1982 study of the lacemakers of Narsapur, India, is a graphic illustration of how women bear the impact of development processes in countries where poor peasant and tribal societies are being "integrated" into an international division of labor under the dictates of capital accumulation. Mies's study illustrates how

capitalist production relations are built upon the backs of women workers defined as *housewives.* Ideologies of gender and work and their historical transformation provide the necessary ground for the exploitation of the lacemakers. But the definition of women as housewives also suggests the heterosexualization of women's work—women are always defined in relation to men and conjugal marriage. Mies's account of the development of the lace industry and the corresponding relations of production illustrates fundamental transformations of gender, caste, and ethnic relations. The original caste distinctions between the feudal warrior castes (the landowners) and the Narsapur (poor Christians) and Serepalam (poor Kapus/Hindu agriculturalists) women are totally transformed through the development of the lace industry, and a new caste hierarchy is effected.

At the time of Mies's study, there were sixty lace manufacturers, with some 200,000 women in Narsapur and Serepalam constituting the work force. Lacemaking women worked six to eight hours a day, and ranged in age from six to eighty. Mies argues that the expansion of the lace industry between 1970 and 1978 and its integration into the world market led to class/caste differentation within particular communities, with a masculinization of all nonproduction jobs (trade) and a total feminization of the production process. Thus, men sold women's products and lived on profits from women's labor. The polarization between men and women's work, where men actually defined themselves as exporters and businessmen who invested in women's labor, bolstered the social and ideological definition of women as housewives and their work as "leisure time activity." In other words, work, in this context, was grounded in sexual identity, in concrete definitions of femininity, masculinity, and heterosexuality.

Two particular indigenous hierarchies, those of caste and gender, interacted to produce normative definitions of "women's work." Where, at the onset of the lace industry, Kapu men and women were agricultural laborers and it was the lower-caste Harijan women who were lacemakers, with the development of capitalist relations of production and the possibility of caste/class mobility, it was the Harijan women who were agricultural laborers while the Kapu women undertook the "leisure time" activity of lacemaking. The caste-based ideology of seclusion and purdah was essential to the extraction of surplus value. Since purdah and the seclusion of women is a sign of higher caste status, the domestication of Kapu laborer women—where their (lacemaking) activity was tied to the concept of the "women sitting in the house" was entirely within the logic of capital accumulation and profit. Now, Kapu women, not just the women of feudal, landowning castes, are in purdah as housewives producing for the world market.

Ideologies of seclusion and the domestication of women are clearly sexual, drawing as they do on masculine and feminine notions of protectionism and property. They are also heterosexual ideologies, based on the normative definition of women as wives, sisters, and mothers—always in relation to conjugal marriage and the "family." Thus, the caste transformation and separation of women along lines of domestication and nondomestication (Kapu housewives vs. Harijan laborers) effectively links the work that women do with their sexual and caste/class identities. Domestication works, in this case, because of the persistence and legitimacy of the ideology of the housewife, which defines women in terms of their place within the home, conjugal marriage, and heterosexuality. The opposition between definitions of the "laborer" and of the "housewife" anchors the invisibility (and caste-related status) of work; in effect, it defines women as *non-workers*. By definition, housewives cannot be workers or laborers; housewives make male breadwinners and consumers possible. Clearly, ideologies of "women's place and work" have real material force in this instance, where spatial parameters construct and maintain gendered and caste-specific hierarchies. Thus, Mies's study illustrates the concrete effects of the social

definition of women as housewives. Not only are the lacemakers invisible in census figures (after all, their work is leisure), but their definition as housewives makes possible the definition of men as "breadwinners." Here, class and gender proletarianization through the development of capitalist relations of production, and the integration of women into the world market is possible because of the history and transformation of indigenous caste and sexual ideologies.

Reading the operation of capitalist process from the position of the housewife/worker who produces for the world market makes the specifically gendered and caste/class opposition between laborer and the nonworker (housewife) visible. Moreover, it makes it possible to acknowledge and account for the hidden costs of women's labor. And finally, it illuminates the fundamentally *masculine* definition of laborer/worker in a context where, as Mies says, men live off women who are the producers. Analyzing and transforming this masculine definition of labor, which is the mainstay of capitalist patriarchal cultures, is one of the most significant challenges we face. The effect of this definition of labor is not only that it makes women's labor and its costs invisible, but that it undercuts women's agency by defining them as victims of a process of pauperization or of "tradition" or "patriarchy," rather than as agents capable of making their own choices.

In fact, the contradictions raised by these choices are evident in the lacemakers' responses to characterizations of their own work as "leisure activity." While the fact that they did "work" was clear to them and while they had a sense of the history of their own pauperization (with a rise in prices for goods but no corresponding rise in wages), they were unable to explain how they came to be in the situation they found themselves. Thus, while some of the contradictions between their work and their roles as housewives and mothers were evident to them, they did not have access to an analysis of these contradictions which could lead to a) seeing the complete picture in terms of their exploitation; b) strategizing and organizing to transform their material situations; or c) recognizing their common interests as women workers across caste/class lines. As a matter of fact, the Serepelam women defined their lacemaking in terms of "housework" rather than wage-work, and women who had managed to establish themselves as petty commodity producers saw what they did as entrepreneurial: they saw themselves as selling *products* rather than *labor.* Thus, in both cases, women internalized the ideologies that defined them as nonworkers. The isolation of the work context (work done in the house rather than in a public setting) as well as the internalization of caste and patriarchal ideologies thus militated against organizing as *workers*, or as *women*. However, Mies suggests that there were cracks in this ideology: the women expressed some envy toward agricultural laborers, whom the lacemakers saw as enjoying working together in the fields. What seems necessary in such a context, in terms of feminist mobilization, is a recognition of the fact that the identity of the housewife needs to be transformed into the identity of a "woman worker or working woman." Recognition of common interests as housewives is very different from recognition of common interests as women and as workers.

IMMIGRANT WIVES, MOTHERS, AND FACTORY WORK: ELECTRONICS WORKERS IN THE SILICON VALLEY

My discussion of the U.S. end of the global assembly line is based on studies by Naomi Katz and David Kemnitzer (1983) and Karen Hossfeld (1990) of electronics workers in the so-called Silicon Valley in California. An analysis of production strategies and processes indicates a significant ideological redefinition of normative ideas of factory work in terms of the Third-World, immigrant women who constitute the primary workforce. While the lacemakers of Narsapur were located as *housewives* and their work defined as *leisure time activity* in a very complex international world market, Third-World women

in the electronics industry in the Silicon Valley are located as *mothers, wives,* and *supplementary* workers. Unlike the search for the "single" woman assembly worker in Third-World countries, it is in part the ideology of the "married woman" which defines job parameters in the Valley, according to Katz and Kemnitzer's data.

Hossfeld also documents how existing ideologies of femininity cement the exploitation of the immigrant women workers in the Valley, and how the women often use this patriarchal logic against management. Assumptions of "single" and "married" women as the ideal workforce at the two geographical ends of the electronics global assembly line (which includes South Korea, Hong Kong, China, Taiwan, Thailand, Malaysia, Japan, India, Pakistan, the Philippines, and the United States, Scotland, and Italy)[17] are anchored in normative understandings of femininity, womanhood, and sexual identity. The labels are predicated on sexual difference and the institution of heterosexual marriage and carry connotations of a "manageable" (docile?) labor force.[18]

Katz and Kemnitzer's data indicates a definition and transformation of women's work which relies on gender, race, and ethnic hierarchies already historically anchored in the U.S. Further, their data illustrates that the construction of "job labels" pertaining to Third-World women's work is closely allied with their sexual and racial identities. While Hossfeld's more recent study reinforces some of Katz and Kemnitzer's conclusions, she focuses more specifically on how "contradictory ideologies about sex, race, class, and nationality are used as forms of both labor control and labor resistance in the capitalist workplace today."[19] Her contribution lies in charting the operation of gendered ideologies in the structuring of the industry and in analyzing what she calls "refeminization strategies" in the workplace.

Although the primary workforce in the Valley consists of Third-World and newly immigrant women, substantial numbers of Third-World and immigrant men are also employed by the electronics industry. In the early 1980s, 70,000 women held 80 to 90 percent of the operative or laborer jobs on the shop floor. Of these, 45 to 50 percent were Third-World, especially Asian, immigrants. White men held either technican or supervisory jobs. Hossfeld's study was conducted between 1983 and 1986, at which time she estimates that up to 80 percent of the operative jobs were held by people of color, with women constituting up to 90 percent of the assembly workers. Katz and Kemnitzer maintain that the industry actively seeks sources of cheap labor by deskilling production and by using race, gender, and ethnic stereotypes to "attract" groups of workers who are "more suited" to perform tedious, unrewarding, poorly paid work. When interviewed, management personnel described the jobs as a) unskilled (as easy as a recipe); b) requiring tolerance for tedious work (Asian women are therefore more suited); and c) supplementary activity for women whose main tasks were mothering and housework.

It may be instructive to unpack these job labels in relation to the immigrant and Third-World (married) women who perform these jobs. The job labels recorded by Katz and Kemnitzer need to be analyzed as definitions of *women's work*, specifically as definitions of *Third-World/immigrant women's work*. First, the notion of "unskilled" as easy (like following a recipe) and the idea of tolerance for tedious work both have racial and gendered dimensions. Both draw upon stereotypes which infantalize Third-World women and initiate a nativist discourse of "tedium" and "tolerance" as characteristics of non-Western, primarily agricultural, premodern (Asian) cultures. Secondly, defining jobs as supplementary activity for *mothers* and *housewives* adds a further dimension: sexual identity and appropriate notions of heterosexual femininity as marital domesticity. These are not part-time jobs, but they are defined as supplementary. Thus, in this particular context, (Third-World) women's work needs are defined as temporary.

While Hossfeld's analysis of management logic follows similar lines, she offers a much more nuanced understanding of how the gender and racial

stereotypes prevalent in the larger culture infuse worker consciousness and resistance. For instance, she draws attention to the ways in which factory jobs are seen by the workers as "unfeminine" or not "ladylike." Management exploits and reinforces these ideologies by encouraging women to view femininity as contradictory to factory work, by defining their jobs as secondary and temporary, and by asking women to choose between defining themselves as women or as workers. Womanhood and femininity are thus defined along a domestic, familial model, with work seen as supplemental to this primary identity. Significantly, although 80 percent of the immigrant women in Hossfeld's study were the largest annual income producers in their families, they still considered men to be the breadwinners.

Thus, as with the exploitation of Indian lacemakers as "housewives," Third-World/immigrant women in the Silicon Valley are located as "mothers and homemakers" and only secondarily as workers. In both cases, men are seen as the real breadwinners. While (women's) work is usually defined as something that takes place in the "public" or production sphere, these ideologies clearly draw on stereotypes of women as homebound. In addition, the *invisibility* of work in the Indian context can be compared to the *temporary/secondary* nature of work in the Valley. Like the Mies study, the data compiled by Hossfeld and Katz and Kemnitzer indicate the presence of local ideologies and hierarchies of gender and race as the basis for the exploitation of the electronics workers. The question that arises is: How do women understand their own positions and construct meanings in an exploitative job situation?

Interviews with electronics workers indicate that, contrary to the views of management, women do not see their jobs as temporary but as part of a life-time strategy of upward mobility. Conscious of their racial, class, and gender status, they combat their devaluation as workers by increasing their income: by job-hopping, overtime, and moonlighting as pieceworkers. Note that, in effect, the "homework" that Silicon Valley workers do is performed under conditions very similar to the lacemaking of Narsapur women. Both kinds of work are done in the home, in isolation, with the worker paying her own overhead costs (like electricity and cleaning), with no legally mandated protections (such as a minimum wage, paid leave, health benefits, etc.). However, clearly the meanings attached to the work differ in both contexts, as does the way we understand them.

For Katz and Kemnitzer the commitment of electronics workers to class mobility is an important assertion of self. Thus, unlike in Narsapur, in the Silicon Valley, homework has an entrepreneurial aspect for the women themselves. In fact, in Narsapur, women's work turns the men into entrepreneurs! In the Valley, women take advantage of the contradictions of the situations they face as *individual workers*. While in Narsapur, it is purdah and caste/class mobility which provides the necessary self-definition required to anchor women's work in the home as leisure activity, in the Silicon Valley, it is a specifically *American* notion of individual ambition and entrepreneurship which provides the necessary ideological anchor for Third-World women.

Katz and Kemnitzer maintain that this underground economy produces an *ideological* redefinition of jobs, allowing them to be defined as *other than* the basis of support of the historically stable, "comfortable," white, metropolitan working class. In other words, there is a clear connection between low wages and the definition of the job as supplementary, and the fact that the lifestyles of people of color are defined as different and cheaper. Thus, according to Katz and Kemnitzer, *women* and *people of color* continue to be "defined out" of the old industrial system and become targets and/or instruments of the ideological shift away from class towards national/ethnic/gender lines.[20] In this context, ideology and popular culture emphasize the *individual maximization* of options for personal success. Individual success is thus severed from union activity, political struggle, and collective relations. Similarly, Hossfeld suggests that it is the racist and

sexist management logic of the needs of "immigrants" that allows the kind of exploitative labor processes that she documents.[21] However, in spite of Katz and Kemnitzer's complex analysis of the relationship of modes of production, social relations of production, culture, and ideology in the context of the Silicon Valley workers, they do not specify why it is *Third-World women* who constitute the primary labor force. Similarly, while Hossfeld provides a nuanced analysis of the gendering of the workplace and the use of racial and gendered logic to consolidate capitalist accumulation, she also sometimes separates "women" and "minority workers" (Hossfeld, p. 176), and does not specify why it is women of color who constitute the major labor force on the assembly lines in the Valley. In distinguishing between women and people of color, Katz and Kemnitzer tend to reproduce the old conceptual divisions of gender and race, where women are defined primarily in terms of their gender and people of color in terms of race. What is excluded is an *interactive* notion of gender and race, whereby women's gendered identity is grounded in race and people of color's racial identities are gendered.

I would argue that the data compiled by Katz and Kemnitzer and Hossfeld does, in fact, explain why Third-World women are targeted for jobs in electronics factories. The explanation lies in the redefinition of work as temporary, supplementary, and unskilled, in the construction of women as mothers and homemakers, and in the positioning of femininity as contradictory to factory work. In addition, the explanation also lies in the specific definition of Third-World, immigrant women as docile, tolerant, and satisfied with substandard wages. It is the ideological redefinition of women's work that provides the necessary understanding of this phenomenon. Hossfeld describes some strategies of resistance in which the workers utilize against management the very gendered and racialized logic that management uses against them. However, while these tactics may provide some temporary relief on the job, they build on racial and gender stereotypes which, in the long run, can be and are used against Third-World women.

DAUGHTERS, WIVES, AND MOTHERS: MIGRANT WOMEN WORKERS IN BRITAIN

Family businesses have been able to access minority women's labor power through mediations of kinship and an appeal to ideologies which emphasize the role of women in the home as wives and mothers and as keepers of family honor.[22]

In a collection of essays exploring the working lives of black and minority women inside and outside the home, Sallie Westwood and Parminder Bhachu focus on the benefits afforded the British capitalist state by the racial and gendered aspects of migrant women's labor. They point to the fact that what has been called the "ethnic economy" (the way migrants draw on resources to survive in situations where the combined effects of a hostile, racist environment and economic decline serve to oppress them) is also fundamentally a gendered economy. Statistics indicate that Afro-Caribbean and non-Muslim Asian women have a higher full-time labor participation rate than white women in the U.K. Thus, while the perception that black women (defined, in this case, as women of Afro-Caribbean, Asian, and African origin) are mostly concentrated in part-time jobs is untrue, the *forms* and *patterns* of their work lives within the context of homework and family firms, businesses where the entire family is involved in earning a living, either inside or outside the home bears examination. Work by British feminist scholars (Phizacklea 1983, Westwood 1984, 1988, Josephides 1988, and others) suggests that familial ideologies of domesticity and heterosexual marriage cement the economic and social exploitation of black women's labor within family firms. Repressive patriarchal ideologies, which fix the woman's role in the family are grounded in inherited systems of inequality and oppression in Black women's cultures of

origin. And these very ideologies are reproduced and consolidated in order to provide the glue for profit-making in the context of the racialized British capitalist state.

For instance, Annie Phizacklea's work on Bangladeshi homeworkers in the clothing industry in the English West Midlands illuminates the extent to which family and community ties, maintained by women, are crucial in allowing this domestic subcontracting in the clothing industry to undercut the competition in terms of wages and long work-days and its cost to women workers. In addition, Sallie Westwood's work on Gujarati women factory workers in the East Midlands hosiery industry suggests that the power and creativity of the shopfloor culture—which draws on cultural norms of femininity, masculinity and domesticity, while simultaneously generating resistance and solidarity among the Indian and white women workers—is, in fact, anchored in Gujarati cultural inheritances. Discussing the contradictions in the lives of Gujarati women within the home and the perception that male family members have of their work as an extension of their family roles (not as a path to financial independence), Westwood elaborates on the continuities between the ideologies of domesticity within the household, which are the result of (often repressive) indigenous cultural values and practices, and the culture of the shopfloor. Celebrating each other as daughters, wives, and mothers is one form of generating solidarity on the shopfloor—but it is also a powerful refeminization strategy, in Hossfeld's terms.

Finally, family businesses, which depend on the cultural and ideological resources and loyalties within the family to transform ethnic "minority" women into workers committed to common familial goals, are also anchored in women's roles as daughters, wives, mothers, and keepers of family honor (Josephides 1988, Bhachu 1998). Women's work in family business is unpaid and produces dependencies that are similar to those of homeworkers whose labor, although paid, is invisible. Both are predicated on ideologies of domesticity and womanhood which infuse the spheres of production and re-production. In discussing Cypriot women in family firms, Sasha Josephides cites the use of familial ideologies of "honor" and the construction of a "safe" environment outside the public sphere as the bases for a definition of femininity and womanhood (the perfect corollary to a paternal, protective definition of masculinity) that allows Cypriot women to see themselves as workers for their family, rather than as workers for themselves. All conflict around the question of work is thus accomodated within the context of the family. This is an important instance of the privatization of work, and of the redefinition of the identity of women workers in family firms as doing work that is a "natural extension" of their familial duties (not unlike the lacemakers). It is their identity as mothers, wives, and family members that stands in for their identity as workers. Parminder Bhachu's work with Punjabi Sikhs also illustrates this fact. Citing the growth of small-scale entrepreneurship among South Asians as a relatively new trend in the British economy, Bhachu states that women workers in family businesses often end up losing autonomy and reenter more traditional forms of patriarchal dominance where men control all or most of the economic resources within the family: "By giving up work, these women not only lose an independent source of income, and a large network of often female colleagues, but they also find themselves sucked back into the kinship system which emphasizes patrilaterality."[23] Women thus lose a "direct relationship with the productive process," thus raising the issue of the invisibility (even to themselves) of their identity as workers.

This analysis of migrant women's work in Britain illustrates the parallel trajectory of their exploitation as workers within a different metropolitan context than the U.S. To summarize, all these case studies indicate ways in which ideologies of domesticity, femininity, and race form the basis of the construction of the notion of "women's work" for Third-World women in the contemporary economy. In the case of the lacemakers, this is done through the definition of homework as leisure time activity and of the workers themselves as housewives. As discussed earlier, indigenous hierarchies of gender and caste/class make this definition possible. In the case of the electronics workers, women's work is defined as unskilled, tedious, and supplementary activity for mothers and homemakers. It is a specifically American ideology of individual success, as well as local histories of race and ethnicity that constitute this definition. We can thus contrast the *invisibility* of the lacemakers as workers to the *temporary* nature of the work of Third-World women in the Silicon Valley. In the case of migrant women workers in family firms in Britain, work becomes an extension of familial roles and loyalties, and draws upon cultural and ethnic/racial ideologies of womanhood, domesticity, and entrepreneurship to consolidate patriarchal dependencies. In all these cases, ideas of *flexibility, temporality, invisibility,* and *domesticity* in the naturalization of categories of work are crucial in the construction of Third-World women as an appropriate and cheap labor force. All of the above ideas rest on stereotypes about gender, race, and poverty, which, in turn, characterize Third-World women as workers in the contemporary global arena.

Eileen Boris and Cynthia Daniels claim that "homework belongs to the decentralization of production that seems to be a central strategy of some sectors and firms for coping with the international restructuring of production, consumption, and capital accumulation."[24] Homework assumes a significant role in the contemporary capitalist global economy. The discussion of homework performed by Third-World women in the three geographical spaces discussed above—India, U.S.A., and Britain—suggests something specific about capitalist strategies of recolonization at this historical juncture. Homework emerged at the same time as factory work in the early nineteenth century in the U.S., and, as a system, it has always reinforced the conjoining of capitalism and patriarchy. Analyzing the homeworker as a wage laborer (rather than an entrepreneur who controls both her labor and the market for it) dependent on the employer for work which is carried out usually in the "home" or domestic premises, makes it possible to understand the *systematic* invisibility of this form of work. What allows this work to be so fundamentally exploitative as to be invisible as a form of work are ideologies of domesticity, dependency, and (hetero)sexuality, which designate women— in this case, Third-World women—as primarily housewives/mothers and men as economic supporters/breadwinners. Homework capitalizes on the equation of home, family, and patriarchial and racial/cultural ideologies of femininity/masculinity with work. This is work done at home, in the midst of doing housework, childcare, and other tasks related to "homemaking," often work that never ceases. Characterizations of "housewives," mother," and "homemakers" make it impossible to see homeworkers as workers earning regular wages and entitled to the rights of workers. Thus, not just their *production,* but homeworkers' *exploitation* as workers, can, in fact, also remain invisible, contained within domestic, patriarchal relations in the family. This is a form of work that often falls outside accounts of wage labor, as well as accounts of household dynamics.[25]

Family firms in Britain represent a similar ideological pattern, within a different class dynamic. Black women imagine themselves as entrepreneurs (rather than as wage laborers) working for the prosperity of their families in a racist society. However, the work they do is still seen as an extension of their familial roles and often creates economic and social dependencies. This does not mean that women in family firms never attain a sense of autonomy, but that, as a system, the operation of family business exploits Third-World women's labor by drawing on and reinforcing indigenous hierarchies in the search for upward mobility in the (racist) British capitalist economy. What makes this form of work in the contemporary global capitalist arena so profoundly exploitative is that its invisibility

(both to the market, and sometimes to the workers themselves) is premised on deeply ingrained sexist and racist relationships within and outside heterosexual kinship systems. This is also the reason why changing the gendered relationships that anchor homework, and organizing homeworkers becomes such a challenge for feminists.

The analysis of factory work and family business in Britain and of homework in all three geographical locations raises the question of whether homework and factory work would be defined in these particular ways if the workers were single women. In this case, the construct of the *worker* is dependant on gender ideologies. In fact, the idea of work or labor as necessary for the psychic, material, and spiritual survival and development of women workers is absent. Instead, it is the identity of women as housewives, wives, and mothers (identities also defined outside the parameters of work) that is assumed to provide the basis for women's survival and growth. These Third-World women are defined out of the labor/ capital process as if work in their case isn't necessary for economic, social, psychic autonomy, independence, and self-determination–a nonalienated relation to work is a conceptual and practical impossibility in this situation.

COMMON INTERESTS/DIFFERENT NEEDS: COLLECTIVE STRUGGLES OF POOR WOMEN WORKERS

Thus far, this essay has charted the ideological commonalities of the exploitation of (mostly) poor Third-World women workers by global capitalist economic processes in different geographical locations. The analysis of the continuities between factory work and homework in objectifying and domesticating Third-World women workers such that their very identity as *workers* is secondary to familial roles and identities, and predicated on patriarchal and racial/ethnic hierarchies anchored in local/indigenous *and* transnational processes of exploitation exposes the profound challenges posed in organizing women workers on the basis of common interests. Clearly, these women are not merely victims of colonizing, exploitative processes—the analysis of the case studies indicates different levels of consciousness of their own exploitation, different modes of resistance, and different understandings of the contradictions they face, and of their own agency as workers. While the essay thus far lays the groundwork for conceptualizing the common interests of women workers based on an understanding of shared location and needs, the analysis foregrounds processes of *repression* rather than forms of *opposition*. How have poor Third-World women organized as workers? How do we conceptualize the question of "common interests" based in a "common context of struggle," such that women are agents who make choices and decisions that lead to the transformation of consciousness and of their daily lives as workers?

As discussed earlier, with the current domination in the global arena of the arbitary interests of the market and of transnational capital, older signposts and definitions of capital/labor or of "the worker" or even of "class struggle" are no longer totally accurate or viable conceptual or organizational categories. It is, in fact, the predicament of poor working women and their experiences of survival and resistance in the creation of new organizational forms to earn a living and improve their daily lives that offers new possibilities for struggle and action.[26] In this instance, then, the experiences of Third-World women workers are relevant for understanding and transforming the work experiences and daily lives of poor women everywhere. The rest of this essay explores these questions by suggesting a working definition of the question of the common interests of Third-World women workers in the contemporary global capitalist economy, drawing on the work of feminist political theorist Anna G. Jonasdottir.

Jonasdottir explores the concept of women's interests in participatory democratic political theory. She emphasizes both the formal and the content aspects of a theory of social and political interests that refers to "different layers of social existence: agency and the needs/desires that give strength and meaning to agency."[27] Adjudicating between political analysts who theorize common interests in formal terms (i.e., the claim to actively "be among," to choose to participate in defining the terms of one's own existence, or acquiring the conditions for choice), and those who reject the concept of interests in favor of the concept of (subjective) individualized, and group-based "needs and desires" (the consequences of choice), Jonasdottir formulates a concept of the common interests of women that emphasizes the former, but is a combination of both perspectives. She argues that the formal aspect of interest (an active "being among") is crucial: "Understood historically, and seen as emerging from people's lived experiences, interests about basic processes of social life are divided systematically between groups of people in so far as their living conditions are systematically different. Thus, historically and socially defined, interests can be characterized as 'objective.'"[28] In other words, there are systematic material and historical bases for claiming Third-World women workers have common interests. However, Jonasdottir suggests that the second aspect of theorizing interest, the satisfaction of needs and desires (she distinguishes between agency and the result of agency) remains a open question. Thus, the *content* of needs and desires from the point of view of interest remains open for subjective interpretation. According to Jonasdottir, feminists can acknowledge and fight on the basis of the (objective) common interests of women in terms of active representation and choices to participate in a democratic polity, while at the same time not reducing women's common interests (based on subjective needs and desires) to this formal "being among" aspect of the question of interest. This theorization allows us to acknowledge common interests and potential agency on the basis of systematic aspects of social location and experience, while keeping open what I see as the deeper, more fundamental question of understanding and organizing around the needs, desires, and choices (the question of critical, transformative consciousness) in order to transform the material and ideological conditions of daily life. The latter has a pedagogical and transformative dimension which the former does not.

How does this theorization relate to conceptualizations of the common interests of Third-World women workers? Jonasdottir's distinction between agency and the result of agency is a very useful one in this instance. The challenges for feminists in this arena are a) understanding Third-World women workers as having objective interests in common as workers (they are thus agents and make choices as workers); and b) recognizing the contradictions and dislocations in women's own consciousness of themselves as workers, and thus of their needs and desires—which sometimes militate *against* organizing on the basis of their common interests (the results of agency). Thus, work has to be done here in analyzing the links between the social location and the historical and current experiences of domination of Third-World women workers on the one hand, and in theorizing and enacting the common *social identity* of Third-World women workers on the other. Reviewing the forms of collective struggle of poor, Third-World women workers in relation to the above theorization of common interests provides a map of where we are in this project.

In the case of women workers in the free-trade zones in a number of countries, trade unions have been the most visible forum for expressing the needs and demands of poor women. The sexism of trade unions, however, has led women to recognize the need for alternative, more democratic organizational structures, and to form women's unions (as in Korea, China, Italy, and Malaysia)[29] or to turn to community groups, church committees, or feminist organizations. In the U.S., Third-World immigrant women in electronics factories have often been hostile to unions which they recognize as clearly modeled in the image of the white, male, working-class American worker. Thus, church involvement in immigrant women

workers struggles has been a important form of collective struggle in the U.S.[30]

Women workers have developed innovative strategies of struggle in women's unions. For instance, in 1989, the Korean Women Workers Association staged an occupation of the factory in Masan. They moved into the factory and lived there, cooked meals, guarded the machines and premises, and effectively stopped production.[31] In this form of occupation of the work premises, the processes of daily life become constitutive of resistance (also evident in the welfare rights struggles in the U.S.A.) and opposition is anchored in the systematic realities of the lives of poor women. It expresses not only their common interests as workers, but acknowledges their social circumstance as *women* for whom the artificial separation of work and home has little meaning. This "occupation" is a strategy of collective resistance that draws attention to poor women worker's *building community* as a form of survival.

Kumudhini Rosa makes a similar argument in her analysis of the "habits of resistance" of women workers in Free Trade Zones (FTZ) in Sri Lanka, Malaysia, and the Philippines.[32] The fact that women live and work together in these FTZs is crucial in analyzing the ways in which they build community life, share resources and dreams, provide mutual support and aid on the assembly line and in the street, and develop individual and collective habits of resistance. Rosa claims that these forms of resistance and mutual aid are anchored in a "culture of subversion" in which women living in patriarchal, authoritarian households where they are required to be obedient and disciplined, acquire practice in "concealed forms of rebelling" (86). Thus, women workers engage in "spontaneous" strikes in Sri Lanka, "wildcat" strikes in Malaysia, and "sympathy" strikes in the Philippines. They also support each other by systematically lowering the production target, or helping slow workers to meet the production targets on assembly lines. Rosa's analysis illustrates recognition of the common interests of women workers at a formal "being among" level. While women are conscious of the contradictions of their daily lives as women and as workers, and enact their resistance, they have not organized actively to identify their collective needs and to transform the conditions of their daily lives.

While the earlier section on the ideological construction of work in terms of gender and racial/ethnic hierarchies discussed homework as one of the most acute forms of exploitation of poor Third-World women, it is also the area in which some of the most creative and transformative collective organizing has occurred. The two most visibly successful organizational efforts in this arena are the Working Women's Forum (WWF) and SEWA (Self Employed Women's Association) in India, both registered as independent trade unions, and focusing on incorporating homeworkers, as well as petty traders, hawkers, and laborers in the informal economy into their membership.[33]

There has also been a long history of organizing homeworkers in Britain. Discussing the experience of the West Yorkshire Homeworking Group in the late 1980s, Jane Tate states that "a homework campaign has to work at a number of levels, in which the personal interconnects with the political, the family situation with work, lobbying Parliament with small local meetings. . . . In practical terms, the homeworking campaigns have adopted a way of organising that reflects the practice of many women's groups, as well as being influenced by the theory and practice of community work. It aims to bring out the strength of women, more often in small groups with a less formal structure and organization than in a body such as a union."[34] Issues of race, ethnicity, and class are central in this effort since most of the homeworkers are of Asian or Third-World origin. Tate identifies a number of simultaneous strategies used by the West Yorkshire Group to organize homeworkers: pinpointing and making visible the "real" employer (or the real enemy), rather than directing organizational efforts only against local subsidiaries; consumer education and pressure,

which links the buying of goods to homeworker struggles; fighting for a code of work practice for suppliers by forming alliances between trade unions, women's, and consumer groups; linking campaigns to the development of alternative trade organizations (for instance, SEWA); fighting for visibility in international bodies like the ILO; and, finally, developing transnational links between local grass-roots homeworker organizations—thus, sharing resources, strategies, and working toward empowerment. The common interests of homeworkers are acknowledged in terms of their daily lives as workers and as women—there is no artificial separation of the "worker" and the "homemaker" or the "housewife" in this context. While the West Yorkshire Homeworking Group has achieved some measure of success in organizing homeworkers, and there is a commitment to literacy, consciousness-raising, and empowerment of workers, this is still a feminist group that organizes women workers (rather than the impetus for organization emerging from the workers themselves—women workers organizing). It is in this regard that SEWA and WWF emerge as important models for poor women workers organizations.

Swasti Mitter discusses the success of SEWA and WWF in terms of: a) their representing the potential for organizing powerful women workers' organizations (the membership of WWF is 85,000 and that of SEWA is 46,000 workers) when effective strategies are used; and b) making these "hidden" workers visible as *workers* to national and international policy makers. Both WWF and SEWA address the demands of poor women workers, and both include a development plan for women which includes leadership training, child care, women's banks, and producer's cooperatives which offer alternative trading opportunities. Renana Jhabvala, SEWA's secretary, explains that, while SEWA was born in 1972 in the Indian labor movement and drew inspiration from the women's movement, it always saw itself as a part of the cooperative movement, as well. Thus, struggling for poor women workers' rights always went hand-in-hand with strategies to develop alternative economic systems. Jhabvala states, "SEWA accepts the co-operative principles and sees itself as part of the co-operative movement attempting to extend these principles to the poorest women. . . . SEWA sees the need to bring poor women into workers' co-operatives. The co-operative structure has to be revitalised if they are to become truely workers' organizations, and thereby mobilise the strength of the co-operative movement in the task of organising and strengthening poor women."[35] This emphasis on the extension of cooperative (or democratic) principles to poor women, the focus on political and legal literacy, education for critical and collective consciousness, and developing strategies for collective (and sometimes militant) struggle *and* for economic, social, and psychic development makes SEWA's project a deeply feminist, democratic, and transformative one. Self-employed women are some of the most disenfranchised in Indian society—they are vulnerable economically, in caste terms, physically, sexually, and in terms of their health, and, of course, they are socially and politically invisible. Thus, they are also one of the most difficult constituencies to organize. The simultaneous focus on collective struggle for equal rights and justice (struggle against) coupled with economic development on the basis of cooperative, democratic principles of sharing, education, self-reliance, and autonomy (struggle for) is what is responsible for SEWA's success at organizing poor, home-based, women workers. Jhabvala summarizes this when she says, "The combination of trade union and co-operative power makes it possible not only to defend members but to present an ideological alternative. Poor women's co-operatives are a new phenomenon. SEWA has a vision of the co-operative as a form of society which will bring about more equal relationships and lead to a new type of society."[36]

SEWA appears to come closest to articulating the common interests and needs of Third-World women workers in the terms that Jonasdottir elaborates. SEWA organizes on the basis of the objective interests of poor women workers—both the trade union and cooperative development aspect of the organizational strategies illustrate this. The status of poor women workers as workers and as citizens entitled to rights and justice is primary. But SEWA also approaches the deeper level of the articulation of needs and desires based on recognition of subjective, collective interests. As discussed earlier, it is this level of the recognition and articulation of common interest that is the challenge for women workers globally. While the common interests of women workers as *workers* have been variously articulated in the forms of struggles and organization reviewed above, the transition to identifying common needs and desires (the *content* aspect of interest) of Third-World women workers, which leads potentially to the construction of the *identity* of Third-World women workers, is what remains a challenge—a challenge that perhaps SEWA comes closest to identifying and addressing.

I have argued that the particular location of Third-World women workers at this moment in the development of global capitalism provides a vantage point from which to a) make particular practices of domination and recolonization visible and transparent, thus illuminating the minute and global processes of capitalist recolonization of women workers, and b) understand the commonalities of experiences, histories, and identity as the basis for solidarity and in organizing Third-World women workers transnationally. My claim, here, is that the definition of the social identity of women as workers is not only class-based, but, in fact, in this case, must be grounded in understandings of race, gender, and caste histories and experiences of work. In effect, I suggest that homework is one of the most significant, and repressive forms of "women's work" in contemporary global capitalism. In pointing to the ideology of the "Third-World woman worker" created in the context of a global division of labor, I am articulating differences located in specific histories of inequality, i.e., histories of gender and caste/class in the Narsapur context, and histories of gender, race, and liberal individualism in the Silicon Valley and in Britain.

However, my argument does not suggest that these are *discrete* and *separate* histories. In focusing on women's work as a particular form of Third-World women's exploitation in the contemporary economy, I also want to foreground a particular history that Third- and First-world women seem to have in common: the logic and operation of capital in the contemporary global arena. I maintain that the interests of contemporary transnational capital and the strategies employed enable it to draw upon indigenous social hierarchies and to construct, reproduce, and maintain ideologies of masculinity/femininity, technological superiority, appropriate development, skilled/unskilled labor, etc. Here I have argued this in terms of the category of "women's work," which I have shown to be grounded in an ideology of the Third-World woman worker. Thus, analysis of the location of Third-World women in the new international division of labor must draw upon the histories of colonialism and race, class and capitalism, gender and patriarchy, and sexual and familial figurations. The analysis of the ideological definition and redefinition of women's work thus indicates a political basis for common struggles and it is this particular forging of the political unity of Third-World women workers that I would like to endorse. This is in opposition to ahistorical notions of the common experience, exploitation, or strength of Third-World women or between third- and first-world women, which serve to naturalize normative Western feminist categories of self and other. If Third-World women are to be seen as the *subjects of theory and of struggle,* we must pay attention to the specificities of their/our common *and* different histories.

In summary, this essay highlights the following analytic and political issues pertaining to Third-World women workers in the global arena: 1) it writes a particular group of women workers into history and into the operation of contemporary capitalist hegemony; 2) it charts the links

and potential for solidarity between women workers across the borders of nation-states, based on demystifying the ideology of the masculinized worker; 3) it exposes a domesticated definition of Third-World women's work to be in actuality a strategy of global capitalist recolonization; 4) it suggests that women have common interests as workers, not just in transforming their work lives and environments, but in redefining home spaces so that homework is recognized as work to earn a living rather than as leisure or supplemental activity; 5) it foregrounds the need for feminist liberatory knowledge as the basis of feminist organizing and collective struggles for economic and political justice; 6) it provides a working definition of the common interests of Third-World women workers based on theorizing the common social identity of Third-World women as women/workers; and finally, 7) it reviews the habits of resistance, forms of collective struggle, and strategies of organizing of poor, Third-World women workers. Irma is right when she says that "the only way to get a little measure of power over your own life is to do it collectively, with the support of other people who share your needs." The question of defining common interests and needs such that the identity of Third-World women workers forms a potentially revolutionary basis for struggles against capitalist recolonization, and for feminist self-determination and autonomy, is a complex one. However, as maquiladora worker Veronica Vasquez and the women in SEWA demonstrate, women are already waging such struggles. The end of the twentieth century may be characterized by the exacerbation of the sexual politics of global capitalist domination and exploitation, but it is also suggestive of the dawning of a renewed politics of hope and solidarity.

NOTES

Even after a number of new beginnings and revisions, this essay remains a work in progress. I have come to the conclusion that this is indicative of both my own level of thinking about these issues as well as the current material and ideological conditions which position Third-World women wage-laborers in contradictory ways. I would like to thank Jacqui Alexander for careful, systematic, and patient feedback on this essay. The essay would not have been possible without Satya Mohanty's pertinent and incisive critique, and his unstinting emotional and intellectual support. My students at Hamilton College and colleagues at various institutions where I have presented sections of this argument are responsible for whatever clarity and lucidity the essay offers—thanks for keeping me on my toes. It is my involvement with the staff and board members of Grassroots Leadership of North Carolina that has sharpened my thinking about the struggles of poor and working people, and about the politics of solidarity and hope it engenders. Finally, it was Lisa Lowe, and then Mary Tong of the Support Committee for Maquiladora Workers, who brought the cross-border organizing of Veronica Vasquez and other workers to my attention. I thank all these organizers for teaching me and for the grassroots organizers work they continue to do in the face of great odds.

1. See Karen Hossfeld, "United States: Why Aren't High-Tech Workers Organised?" in Women Working Worldwide, eds., *Common Interests: Women Organising in Global Electronics* (London: Tavistock), pp. 33–52, esp. pp. 50–51.

2. See "Tijuanans Sue in L.A. after Their Maquiladora Is Closed," by Sandra Dribble, in *The San Diego Union-Tribune,* Friday, December 16, 1994. The Support Committee for Maquiladora Workers promotes cross-border organizing against corporate impunity. This is a San Diego–based volunteer effort of unionists, community activists, and others to assist workers in building autonomous organizations and facilitating ties between Mexican and U.S. workers. The Committee, which is coordinated by Mary Tong, also sees its task as educating U.S. citizens about the realities of life, work, and efforts for change among maquiladora workers. For more information write the Support Committee at 3909 Centre St., # 210, San Diego, CA 92103.

3. See my essay, "Cartographies of Struggle: Third World Women and the Politics of Feminism," in Mohanty, Russo, and Torres, eds. *Third World Women and The Politics of Feminism* (Bloomington: Indiana University Press,

1991), especially p. 39, where I identified five provisional historical, political, and discursive junctures for understanding Third-World feminist politics: "decolonization and national liberation movements in the third world, the consolidation of white, liberal capitalist patriarchies in Euro-America, the operation of multinational capital within a global economy, . . . anthropology as an example of a discourse of dominance and self-reflexivity, . . . (and) storytelling or autobiography (the practice of writing) as a discourse of oppositional consciousness and agency." This essay represents a continuation of one part of this project: the operation of multinational capital and the location of poor Third-World women workers.

4. See the excellent analysis in Teresa L. Amott and Julie A. Matthaei, *Race, Gender and Work: A Multicultural Economic History of Women in the United States* (Boston: South End Press, 1991), esp. pp. 22–23.

5. See Bagguley, Mark-Lawson, Shapiro, Urry, Walby, and Warde, *Restructuring: Place, Class and Gender* (London: Sage Publications, 1990).

6. Joan Smith has argued, in a similar vein, for the usefulness of a world-systems-theory approach (seeing the various economic and social hierarchies and national divisions around the globe as part of a singular systematic division of labor, with multiple parts, rather than as plural and autonomous national systems) which incorporates the notion of the "household" as integral to understanding the profoundly gendered character of this systemic division of labor. While her analysis is useful in historicizing and analyzing the idea of the household as the constellation of relationships that makes the transfer of wealth possible across age, gender, class, and national lines, the ideologies of masculinity, femininity, and heterosexuality that are internal to the concept of the household are left curiously intact in her analysis—as are differences in understandings of the household in different cultures. In addition, the impact of domesticating ideologies in the sphere of production, in constructions of "women's work" are also not addressed in Smith's analysis. While I find this version of the world-systems approach useful, my own analysis attempts a different series of connections and

theorizatons. See Joan Smith, "The Creation of the World We Know: The World-Economy and the Re-creation of Gendered Identities," in V. Moghadam, ed., *Identity Politics and Women: Cultural Reassertions in International Perspective* (Boulder: Westview Press, 1994), pp. 27–41.

7. The case studies I analyze are: Maria Mies, *The Lacemakers of Narsapur, Indian Housewives Produce for the World Market* (London: Zed Press, 1982); Naomi Katz and David Kemnitzer, "Fast Forward: the Internationalization of the Silicon Valley," in June Nash and M. P. Fernandez-Kelly, *Women, Men, and the International Division of Labor* (Albany: SUNY Press, 1983), pp. 273–331; Katz and Kemnitzer, "Women and Work in the Silicon Valley," in Karen Brodkin Sacks, *My Troubles Are Going to Have Trouble with Me: Everyday Trials and Triumphs of Women Workers* (New Brunswick, NJ: Rutgers University Press, 1984), pp. 193–208; and Karen J. Hossfeld, "Their Logic Against Them:" Contradictions in Sex, Race, and Class in the Silicon Valley," in Kathryn Ward, ed., *Women Workers and Global Restructuring* (Ithaca: Cornell University Press, 1990), pp. 149–178. I also draw on case studies of Black women workers in the British context in Sallie Westwood and Parminder Bhachu, eds., *Enterprising Women* (New York: Routledge, 1988).

8. There has been an immense amount of excellent feminist scholarship on women and work and women and multinationals in the last decade. In fact, it is this scholarship which makes my argument possible. Without the analytic and political insights and analyses of scholars like Aihwa Ong, Maria Patricia Fernandez-Kelly, Lourdes Beneria and Martha Roldan, Maria Mies, Swasti Mitter, and Sallie Westwood, among others, my attempt to understand and stitch together the lives and struggles of women workers in different geographical spaces would be sharply limited. This essay builds on arguments offered by some of these scholars, while attempting to move beyond particular cases to an integrated analysis which is not the same as the world-systems model. See especially Nash and Fernandez-Kelly, *Women, Men and the International Division of Labor*; Ward, ed., *Women Workers and Global Restructuring; Review of Radical Political*

Economics, vol. 23, no. 3–4 (Fall/Winter 1991), special issue on "Women in the International Economy"; Harriet Bradley, *Men's Work, Women's Work* (Minneapolis: University of Minnesota Press, 1989); Lynne Brydon and Sylvia Chant, *Women in the Third World, Gender Issues in Rural and Urban Areas* (New Brunswick, NJ: Rutgers University Press, 1989).

9. See Ella Shohat and Robert Stam, *Unthinking Eurocentrism: Multiculturalism and the Media* (London and New York: Routledge, 1994), esp. pp. 25–27. In a discussion of the analytic and political problems involved in using terms like "Third World," Shohat and Stam draw attention to the adoption of "third world" at the 1955 Bandung Conference of "nonaligned" African and Asian nations, an adoption which was premised on the solidarity of these nations around the anticolonial struggles in Vietnam and Algeria. This is the genealogy of the term that I choose to invoke here.

10. My understanding and appreciation of the links between location, experience, and social identity in political and intellectual matters grows out of numerous discussions with Satya Mohanty. See especially his essay, "Colonial Legacies, Multicultural Futures: Relativism, Objectivity, and the Challenge of Otherness," in *PMLA*, January 1995, pp. 108–117.

11. Karen Brodkin Sacks, "Introduction," in Karen Brodkin Sacks and D. Remy, eds., *My Troubles Are Going to Have Trouble with Me*, esp. pp. 10–11.

12. Jeremy Brecher, "The Hierarch's New World Order—and Ours," in Jeremy S. Brecher et al., eds., *Global Visions, Beyond the New World Order* (Boston: South End Press, 1993), pp. 3–12.

13. See Maria Mies, *Patriarchy and Accumulation on a World Scale: Women in the International Division of Labor* (London: Zed Press, 1986), pp. 114–15.

14. Richard J. Barnet and John Cavanagh, *Global Dreams: Imperial Corporations and the New World Order* (New York: Simon and Shuster, 1994), esp. pp. 25–41.

15. For examples of cross-national feminist organizing around these issues, see the following texts: Gita Sahgal and Nira Yuval Davis, eds., *Refusing Holy Orders, Women and*

Fundamentalism in Britain (London: Virago, 1992); Valentine M. Moghadam, *Identity Politics and Women, Cultural Reassertions and Feminisms in International Perspective* (Boulder: Westview Press, 1994); *Claiming Our Place, Working the Human Rights System to Women's Advantage* (Washington D.C.: Institute for Women, Law and Development, 1993); Sheila Rowbotham and Swasti Mitter, eds., *Dignity and Daily Bread: New Forms of Economic Organizing among Poor Women in the Third World and the First* (New York: Routledge, 1994); and Julie Peters and Andrea Wolper, eds., *Women's Rights, Human Rights: International Feminist Perspectives* (New York: Routledge, 1995).

16. Amott and Matthaei, eds., *Race, Gender and Work,* pp. 316–17.

17. Women Working Worldwide, *Common Interests,* ibid.

18. Aihwa Ong's discussion of the various modes of surveillance of young Malaysian factory women as a way of discursively producing and constructing notions of feminine sexuality is also applicable in this context, where "single" and "married" assume powerful connotations of sexual control. See Aihwa Ong, *Spirits of Resistance and Capitalist Discipline: Factory Women in Malaysia* (Albany: SUNY Press, 1987).

19. Hossfeld, "Their Logic Against Them," p. 149. Hossfeld states that she spoke to workers from at least thirty Third-World nations (including Mexico, Vietnam, the Philippines, Korea, China, Cambodia, Laos, Thailand, Malaysia, Indonesia, India, Pakistan, Iran, Ethiopia, Haiti, Cuba, El Salvador, Nicaragua, Guatemala, Venezuela, as well as southern Europe, especially Portugal and Greece). It may be instructive to pause and reflect on the implications of this level of racial and national diversity on the shopfloor in the Silicon Valley. While all these workers are defined as "immigrants," a number of them as recent immigrants, the racial, ethnic, and gender logic of capitalist strategies of recolonization in this situation locate all the workers in similar relationships to the management, as well as to the U.S. state.

20. Assembly lines in the Silicon Valley are often divided along race, ethnic, and gender lines, with workers competing against each other for greater productivity. Individual worker choices, however imaginative or ambitious, do not transform the system. Often they merely undercut the historically won benefits of the metropolitan working class. Thus, while moonlighting, overtime, and job-hopping are indications of individual modes of resistance, and of an overall strategy of class mobility, it is these very aspects of worker's choices which supports an underground domestic economy which evades or circumvents legal, institutionalized, or contractual arrangements that add to the indirect wages of workers.

21. Hossfeld, "Their Logic Against Them," p. 149: "You're paid less because women are different than men" or "Immigrants need less to get by."

22. Westwood and Bhachu, "Introduction," *Enterprising Women,* p. 5. See also, in the same collection, Annie Phizacklea, "Entrepreneurship, Ethnicity and Gender," pp. 20–33; Parminder Bhachu, "Apni Marzi Kardhi, Home and Work: Sikh Women in Britain, pp. 76–102; Sallie Westwood, "Workers and Wives: Continuities and Discontinuities in the Lives of Gujarati Women," pp. 103–31; and Sasha Josephides, "Honor, Family, and Work: Greek Cypriot Women Before and After Migration," pp. 34–57.

23. P. Bhachu, "Apni Marzi Kardhi, Home and Work," p. 85.

24. For a thorough discussion of the history and contemporary configurations of homework in the U.S., see Eileen Boris and Cynthia R. Daniels, eds., *Homework, Historical and Contemporary Perspectives on Paid Labor at Home* (Urbana: University of Illinois Press, 1989). See especially the "Introduction," pp. 1–12; M. Patricia Fernandez-Kelly and Anna García, "Hispanic Women and Homework: Women in the Informal Economy of Miami and Los Angeles," pp. 165–82; and Sheila Allen, "Locating Homework in an Analysis of the Ideological and Material Constraints on Women's Paid Work," pp. 272–91.

25. Allen, "Locating Homework."

26. See Rowbotham and Mitter, "Introduction," in Rowbotham and Mitter, eds., *Dignity and Daily Bread.*

27. Anna G. Jonasdottir, "On the Concept of Interest, Women's Interests, and the Limitations of Interest Theory," in Kathleen Jones and Anna G. Jonasdottir, eds., *The Political Interests of*

Gender (London: Sage Publications, 1988), pp. 33–65, esp. p. 57.

28. Ibid., p. 41.

29. See Women Working Worldwide, eds., *Common Interests.*

30. Ibid., p. 38.

31. Ibid., p. 31.

32. Kumudhini Rosa, "The Conditions and Organisational Activities of Women in Free Trade Zones: Malaysia, Philippines and Sri Lanka, 1970–1990," in Rowbotham and Mitter, eds., *Dignity and Daily Bread,* pp. 73–99, esp. p. 86.

33. Swasti Mitter, "On Organising Women in Causalized Work: A Global Overview," in Rowbotham and Mitter, eds., *Dignity and Daily Bread,* pp. 14–52, esp. p. 33.

34. Jane Tate, "Homework in West Yorkshire," in Rowbotham and Mitter, eds., *Dignity and Daily Bread,* pp. 193–217, esp. p. 203.

35. Renana Jhabvala, "Self-Employed Women's Association: Organising Women by Struggle and Development," in Rowbotham and Mitter, eds., *Dignity and Daily Bread,* pp. 114–38, esp. p. 116.

36. Ibid., p. 135.

FEMINISM AND GLOBALIZATION PROCESSES IN LATIN AMERICA

Ofelia Schutte

The aim of this essay is to describe contemporary processes of globalization as they take place in Latin America and to evaluate the effects of these processes especially on women, using a postcolonial feminist ethical perspective as a critical standpoint. Initially, I offer some reflections on the cultural location from which this chapter is written.[1] Intellectuals in the developed world occupy a position of privilege in relation to their counterparts in the developing world, regardless of one's personal desire for an equal reciprocal relationship. This historically determined inequality does not detract from the arguments or insights one may offer, but it does make me conscious of the fact that I do not write from a location experiencing the worst impact of globalization processes, a factor that may bias my outlook. Nevertheless, I offer a strong critique of globalization processes insofar as these are designed and implemented by neoliberal economic policy. In order to frame this critique, it is important

to distinguish between economic and political development. There is an evident tension in the West in the interaction of these two concepts. Concepts of political development (if informed by progressive social views) will clash with concepts of economic development (if informed by neoliberal views). The reason is that concepts of political development informed by progressive social views place a high priority on social justice, political equality, and (more recently) on environmental justice, whereas concepts of neoliberal economic development have as their single goal the strengthening of a global capitalist market. In contrast to modern concepts of political equality, neoliberalism requires and thrives on inequality.

Despite the evident clash between an economics that promotes inequality in the constant play of maximizing its self-interest and a politics that demands equality in the name of some common good owed to all citizens, I believe there is empirical room for modifying (neoliberal) economic policy through (progressive) political action. By means of a postcolonial feminist ethical perspective, I point both to the negative effects on women resulting from neoliberal globalization policies and to the constructive effects of feminist critiques of globalization and feminist political action. The critiques of globalization serve to demystify its aura of legitimacy, inevitability, and success. They point to the ethical void at the core of neoliberal globalization initiatives by showing the failure of these initiatives to take into account globalization's impact on ordinary people in the developing world, including women and girls, or the social costs, both short term and long term, of policy focused on trade and maximizing profits. The critiques I shall review also point to the limits a market-oriented, positivistic concept of growth places on human creativity, on transgressive art, and on cultural creation in general. My objective is to reaffirm here, as I have argued elsewhere, that a feminist ethics of development is needed from which to evaluate the merits and limitations of political and economic development.[2] This orientation builds on my previous work regarding the construction of identity in terms of socially oriented emancipatory projects.[3]

THE CRITIC'S LOCATION

A global feminist ethics (if there is to be such a thing) must first acknowledge the asymmetries of power between North and South marking women's lives.[4] For this reason, I prefer a use of the term "postcolonial" that acknowledges these asymmetries of power (not all uses of postcolonial do this) rather than "global" to situate such an ethical perspective. Indeed, global all too often connotes homogenization across places and cultures, which is the exact opposite of what a post-structuralist feminist perspective would want to invoke. The asymmetries of power marking North and South America have economic as well as historical components. The conquest and colonization of the Americas— with its array of racial, gendered, military, religious, and scientific hegemonies—is one such historical source; the advance of Western capitalism and its specific configuration of class society in developed and developing societies—as well as the relation between the two—is another. Cultural differences across the Americas point to incommeasurable worlds that may not be readily translatable to interlocutors

from asymmetrically constituted sites. Surely, when such incommeasurables are at stake, the elements that risk exclusion from representation in mainstream cultural transactions are those pertaining to the lifeworld of the less empowered parties.

My position does not entail that people across very different societies and cultures will be unable to agree on a certain set of values or mutual interests. On the contrary, reaching agreements across cultures is a valuable and, indeed, necessary aspect of social and political relations, particularly in this age of global technologies in which values are easily communicated across national borders. What I hold is that, given the asymmetrical conditions of power between dominant and subaltern parties (regardless of the public rhetoric that all parties to agreements are equal), the terms of such agreements and/or the languages in which global mainstream values are represented, even when well intended, embody the ideological presuppositions of the dominant parties and cultures. Discourses are effects of power, just as they are instrumental in generating new relations of power. As it pertains to feminism, the voices of women from developing countries that are most likely to be heard in the North are those that already speak within the discursive framework of the North's expectations. This means that to ensure the most open arena for discourse across cultures holding asymmetrical relations of power, the North's speakers must engage in a conscious practice of decentering their habitual standpoints. They must be prepared to accept suggestions that are not readily or always expected. I am convinced that of all the questions having to do with globalization, perhaps the most troubling is how globalization processes affect those persons, activities, and nonhuman entities excluded from its benefits. The reason is simple: globalization involves a process of integration or mainstreaming into a competitive transnational market economy. The failure to become integrated—or, at the extreme, the failure to obtain sufficient conditions for survival and growth under the terms of the neo-liberal global economy—therefore represents the ultimate penalty that globalization inflicts on its victims.

FEMINIST CRITIQUES OF GLOBALIZATION

Feminist critiques of globalization derive elements from feminist economics, political theory, and activism.[5] A sharper critique, whose theoretical base is broader than feminist, appears in literary criticism and cultural studies.[6] Feminist critiques, whether reformist or radical, are directed at globalization understood as a process in Western capitalism that seeks to integrate as much of the world as possible into one giant market. This sense of globalization refers, according to the neoliberal doctrine it implements, to the liberalization of markets, the privatization by capital of previously nonprivatized (often public or state-supported) programs, and the so-called flexibilization of the labor force. It also refers to the exclusive valuing of the monetized domain of the economy, with the result that voluntary or unpaid work is undercounted and/or devalued.[7] Because women's activities are overrepresented in the category of voluntary work and unpaid care work, feminists have a justified interest in analyzing why such work by women is invisible or undervalued by neoliberal policy.

Neoliberal globalization processes are enhanced and supported by technological advances and by conservative political measures. On the technological front, the extraordinary growth in technology and information sciences allows communication to flow almost instantaneously around the world, enabling large volumes of highly profitable long-distance and transnational financial and commercial transactions. On the political front, governments have been persuaded to enter into international trade agreements that supersede the national regulation of financial flows, trade, and commerce. Such agreements promote the flow of financial transactions, capital, and goods across national borders in ways that especially benefit transnational businesses and corporations. Because global commerce is aimed at extracting the highest possible profit for investors, with respect to the cost of human labor, the goal is to drive its cost down to the lowest possible denominator. Private companies (as well as governments) are led to downsize their labor force. This action is justified to the public as intended to relieve the alleged burden on taxpayers (in the case of governments) or to make products more competitive in price (in the case of the sale of commodities). Jobs that used to employ full-time workers are outsourced to lower paid, part-time, temporary and/or foreign labor. With trade barriers down as a result of international trade agreements, products can be manufactured or partially assembled virtually anywhere in the world as long as the price of labor is cost-effective.

The displacement of jobs created by profit-intensive capital flows also leads to the displacement of populations. Another aspect of the global economy is the steady migration of populations to sites they associate with improved subsistence or income. All aspects of these globalization processes affect women, whose lives are destabilized by economic hard times and by the increasing gap between the wealthy and the poor. Globalization offers some possibilities of economic improvement to skilled women who either are not involved in caring activities toward their family members or are able to benefit from substitute caregiving assistance. However, in ignoring or devaluing unpaid care work that on the whole is done primarily by women, globalization fails to create equitable conditions for women to be fully integrated into the neoliberal economy. It may be observed that globalization destroys good full-time jobs with benefits, replacing many of them with part-time jobs. At first glance, this appears to benefit women over men, since it was men who held the better jobs (now discarded), while women appear to be the primary targets for part-time labor (insofar as the rest of the time they are often occupied with unpaid care work).

Public relations campaigns in favor of neoliberal globalization therefore make it appear as if women as a group are among the main beneficiaries of the global economy. But this is misleading. Women in part-time jobs do not benefit when men lose full-time jobs. In cases in which they share a household with a male income earner, the loss of his job is a total loss for the household, regardless of whether the woman gains part-time employment. The benefit would be for both women and men to hold full-time, well-paying jobs. At present, more data are needed to track the actual effects on women and men of the "feminization of poverty."[8]

Other features of the neoliberal global economy lead to questionable results for women. For example, there are certain structural problems of trade liberalization as currently practiced that impact adversely on women's concerns for a decent quality of life. The World Trade Organization (WTO), founded in 1995, aims to reduce what it calls "obstacles to trade" on a worldwide basis. Among the things considered obstacles to trade are important elements of people's quality of life. For example, the WTO considers "regulations on foreign investment, environment protection, health and safety standards, laws on the ownership of natural resources and technology, and systems for placing government contracts and designing and operating social security systems" as barriers to trade.[9] The WTO acts on profit-oriented regulations that in turn suppress, delegitimate, or make obsolete various regulations a nation may have held regarding job security for workers, affirmative action for women and minorities, or environmental protection. These considerations and the laws based on them become invalidated by the WTO and its signatory countries whenever they are thought to interfere with the profit motive. The deregulation of quality-of-life issues occurs because short-term profit is placed ahead of long-term values. Against this view, there is a feminist consensus that "trade rules are . . . important but cannot take precedence over human rights and environmental sustainability."[10]

Feminist economists do not assume that globalization processes are inherently bad for women, but they point out that the effects on women's lives are uneven and that some women—particularly poor and rural women in developing countries—are hurt far more than others.[11] They argue, however, that even assuming that globalization offers uneven effects for women, "unless gender issues and concerns are widely understood, acknowledged, and addressed, globalization will only exacerbate the inequalities between men and women."[12] There are a number of structural reasons for this, although perhaps the easiest one to grasp is globalization's effect on maternity and women's work, which affects workingwomen of childbearing age. For example, recent studies in Argentina show that professional women are increasingly delaying their pregnancies—first from their twenties to their thirties, and now to a time closer to their forties—because of variable and insufficient labor rights regarding pregnancy and childbearing leave for working mothers.[13] With few reliable rights to protect them at work and in conditions of high unemployment and job scarcity, continued dependence on a wage-earning job takes precedence over personal lifestyle options. Moreover, neoliberal structural adjustment policies mandate state cuts for social assistance programs. As in the North, the burden of care shifts to the domestic sphere of the household, whose members must undertake the care of the young, the old, the sick, and the disabled.[14] Again, women are impacted disproportionately, since they are the principal caregivers. Seen from the angle of women's experiences and daily concerns to care for their loved ones, the profit drive of neoliberal globalization is blind to the concrete needs of ordinary people.

The term "social reproduction" is used by social scientists to refer to all the activities taking place in the home that guarantee the reproduction of the labor force from day to day and from generation to generation. Social reproduction includes caring for and raising children, cooking, cleaning, making sure the home environment is safe and healthy, fetching and preparing the meal ingredients, washing and ironing clothes, repairing torn clothes, caring for the sick and disabled, and providing emotional support for household members so that their sense of integrity, humanity, and dignity is promoted in the intimate home environment. The neoliberal economy tends to ignore all the preceding as economically irrelevant activities insofar as they are unpaid or do not register a cash flow in the monetized domain.[15] At the same time, the neoliberal economy reduces or shuts down assistance to citizens in the areas of health, education, and social services, arguing that the system would function better if part or all of these services were privatized. Unfortunately, privatizing health, for example, limits the access of the poorest people to services because of prohibitive costs. Alternatively, public facilities accessible to the poor are inadequately staffed because of the lack of public resources. Under neoliberal policies, there is no public structure, such as the state, that can serve as a supplier of jobs. Rather, the generation of new jobs and income must come from private enterprise or investments in a highly competitive market. Because markets are now open to global competition, affected companies that fail to cut down on costs, including labor costs, can easily go bankrupt. The purported benefits of such policies—lower consumer prices, lower inflation—only benefit a part of the public in the developing countries as long as severe poverty persists and the system continues to generate increased inequalities.

For those who lack accumulated capital or who may not have had sufficient access to education or training (categories in which many women and girls may be disadvantaged), it is not possible to benefit from this economic order. The road is difficult and uneven for many. It is not surprising that new forms of sex trade and even child prostitution are on the rise.

Globalization is also shaping sex commerce. Some developing countries are marketing sites for sex tourism, including interracial sex commerce.[16] A proportion of women will sell sex because there is demand for sex and, comparatively speaking, selling sex may be their best survival option. There is also a proliferation of women migrants or would-be migrants to the developed world who fill a market demand for domestic help[17] and for Internet-mediated mail-order brides. These are among the real effects of globalization and its impact on girls' and women's lives, contrary to the ubiquitous "benefit to consumers" claim one constantly hears about in the globalized media.

POLITICAL ORGANIZATION AND RESISTANCE TO GLOBAL EXPLOITATION

So far, I have mentioned some of the highlights of the neoliberal global economic program along with its negative or limiting impact on women. Women's response to facing the challenges of neoliberalism has been to insist that the gender impact of global economic policies be understood (so that damaging policies are identified and changed, if possible). Women have also organized politically to ensure a larger voice for women's issues and concerns both before the state and in civil society at large. In addition to grassroots mobilizations at the local level women have engaged in global organizing and transnational advocacy programs, including work conducted through, or in association with, the United Nations and with foreign-sponsored nongovernmental organizations (NGOs).

As is well known, in Latin America, the impact of neoliberal global economics coincided chronologically with a larger opening toward democracy in most of the region's countries. Politically, the democratic opening has provided a boon for the women's movement. It would not be farfetched to say that the women's movement has been one of the major players in the democratic transitions. The cause of modern democracy and the cause of women's equality are historically interrelated. As in North

America, the arguments for universal suffrage in Latin America mobilized women in the first wave of the movement to demand the right to vote and the right to equal political participation. In the 1970s the United Nations sponsored a Decade for the Advancement of Women (1975–1985), coinciding with the second wave. With its opening conference in Mexico City in 1975, the feminist agenda acquired significant international (as well as local and regional) visibility. One of the things the United Nations' decade achieved was to create an international network of activists that would articulate local and national activities with an international project for women's rights.

The three initial goals the United Nations identified for the Women's Decade were equality, development, and peace. Sharp economic and political antagonisms divided the (male-dominated) planet. It must be recalled that those were still the days of the Cold War. The Soviet-sponsored socialist bloc mobilized women for socialism, while the capitalist bloc mobilized women for Western values. Then, after the dissolution of the Soviet Union and the Eastern European socialist bloc, the advancement of capitalist neoliberal economic programs gained an increased impetus. At the same time, the new global linkages strengthened activists committed to human rights and equality internationally. In the early 1990s, what had been an international women's movement mediated by the concept of nationality was shaped and transformed into a global movement for women's rights in the context of the United Nations' ethical concept of human development. The United Nations Development Programme has documented these goals in a series of yearly reports. In addition, the United Nations Development Fund for Women (UNIFEM) articulated a global vision of women's leadership and what a just society must offer women and girls: an end to violence against women, a respect for women's rights as human rights, and a demand that women and girls be fully included in plans for economic and social development throughout the world. While it is true that this vision of women's emancipation was advocated in a dialogue with the world's national governments (given the United Nations' structure as a forum for nations' representation) and this did not allow for radicalism, nonetheless, the integration of a prowomen's agenda into the rest of the work of the United Nations has had a number of positive effects. By the mid-1990s and, specifically, the Beijing conference of 1995, a global gathering of official and unofficial delegates was celebrated in China. It is interesting to see how the Beijing experience, including the planning for it and its aftermath, affected the feminist and the women's political movement in Latin America.

In an exceptionally well-informed essay, Sonia Alvarez has shown the complexity of both the symbolism and the reality of the Beijing conference on the Latin American feminist movement.[18] She notes that over 1,800 participants from Latin America attended the NGO-sponsored unofficial conference in the "backwater town of Huairou, China," that met parallel to the official United Nations Conference on Women in Beijing.[19] The large size of the group reveals, according to Alvarez, an immense internal diversity currently characterizing the Latin American women's movement.[20] To use the term "feminist" here, though, would be a little misleading. Since the mid-1980s in Latin America, the boundaries between women who identify themselves as feminist and women who are active in the women's movement without using this label are rather fluid. The fluidity resulted partly because of the region's democratic opening throughout the 1980s. As Alvarez explains, this opening allowed many feminists whose consciousness had been forged in opposition to public power (during repressive regimes) to embrace electoral politics openly and even run for office as candidates for the opposition.[21] When running for and being elected to office, they had to move on to a range of projects other than feminism. It should also be noted, as Alvarez does in another section of the paper, that eventually friction and tension arose between feminists who joined public office and those who mistrusted the power of institutional agencies (including the United Nations).[22] A class division cut through the feminist movement, with some women privileged in positions of power and others, claiming a more authentic connection to their feminist roots, radically questioning the legitimacy of such power.

Nonetheless, the result by the 1990s (and beyond) is the presence of a broad spectrum of women in various institutions and public roles who also championed the cause of women's rights. The breadth of their activities, however, signifies a "*decentering* of contemporary Latin American feminist practices."[23] In other words, the political action of women who hold progressive views on gender issues is not confined to the feminist movement as such. Instead, such women occupy posts all across professional and political fields, integrating gender issues into whatever work they are doing. Alvarez points out that, at the same time, many self-identified feminists have accepted an expanded conception of feminism's goals. In particular, they see the goals of feminism as not limited to women's issues *per se,* but as offering an approach to issues spanning public policy as a whole.[24] If Alvarez's analysis is correct—and I see no reason to doubt it—we are witnessing both a decentering of the feminist movement and a much more far reaching effect of feminist ideals, as women influenced by feminist ideas but not totally defined by them increasingly occupy influential roles in society. This phenomenon creates difficulties for a researcher if she wants to trace a tidy map regarding feminism's range of operations and boundaries. What in fact has happened is that there are no such distinct boundaries. Boundaries are crossed back and forth enabling new alliances to be formed at the activist and political levels: "With the expansion of black feminism, lesbian feminism, popular feminism, ecofeminism, Christian feminism, and so on, the mid-1980s and 1990s witnessed

the proliferation of new actors whose political-personal trajectories often differed significantly from those of earlier feminists."[25] These data show that as women's experiences change, so does their appropriation of feminism.[26] To this I would add that some of the fundamental factors causing women's experiences to change are the globalization processes that redefine women's economic, social, and political participation in their respective communities.

Globalization processes have touched the lives of Latin American women in more than economic ways. For those who have access to the Internet, including activists for social and political change, it is now possible to link up with counterparts across the region or simply to learn of other groups' activities and successes. Examples of feminist organizations and collectives that have used the Web to disseminate views, to provide news or information about grassroots organizations and projects, or to post articles are Fempress,[27] La Morada,[28] and Creatividad Feminista.[29] An interesting feature of these grassroots women's collectives is that no overarching (masculine) entity controls them. In other words, no political party, no church, no nation, no global body, no economic conglomerate controls their multifaceted projects. Some of these Web sites offer information about female sexuality and women's life stages, as well as support groups for lesbian women, topics that move beyond the usual representations of gender found in the mainstream media. The dissemination of local activities and interests through information technologies not subject to the control of political parties and the proliferation of meanings with respect to feminism (so that only its plural form, "feminisms," makes sense anymore) are both structural features of postmodern times. Thus, the same global economy that displaces people, undermines their security, and generates unemployment by destroying large numbers of steady, long-term jobs, in so doing, creates discontent and mobilizes people to use the democratic instruments available to them in order to resist injustice and demand change. The significant amount of gender-related activism in Latin America demonstrates that women do not take the negative effects of globalization passively.

ACADEMIC STUDIES ON DEMOCRACY

For their part, Latin American intellectuals, sometimes in association with their Spanish counterparts, have also shown their commitment to the strengthening of democratic processes by writing on democracy and evaluating whether the global economy's performance in the region has benefited democratic institutions. So far, economic studies of neoliberal economics tend to show that neoliberalism and structural adjustment have increased, not diminished, existing inequalities both across and within countries. In an analysis of the impact of neoliberal structural reforms on the implementation of human rights policy in Latin America, the Brazilian scholar José Eduardo Faria concludes that the simultaneous weakening of the state and the rise in inequalities pose grave questions regarding the future of human rights in the region. He notes that the utopian character of human rights (if they are truly to be universalized and realized) leads to "a paradoxical situation: the more they are affirmed, the more it turns out that they are denied."[30] Clearly, society has not achieved the social or economic order that would guarantee human rights universally. How can a representative democracy prevail, he asks, without a sufficiently strong state "to correct, or at least, attenuate" the economic, regional, and ethnic inequalities marking various segments of the citizenry?[31] Or what does it mean to have a right to property when there are nonexistent conditions for vast numbers of people to become property owners?[32] Faria points to conditions of "social fragmentation" in which the concept of justice "tends to disappear from the collective consciousness," replaced by a forced obedience to those in power and a sense that society splits into those who are included and those who remain excluded from present economic and

political gains.[33] He argues that this fragmentation made visible by the poverty and misery of large sectors of the population represents a weakening of democracy (a democracy so many people fought so hard to obtain), since the poor have no effective representation in government. In such circumstances, appealing to human rights carries a utopian connotation and an implicit denunciation of the present state of affairs.[34] The ideal of human rights—extended to mean "the rights to life, to work, to health, to education, to nourishment and housing"—therefore becomes essential to the promise and implementation of a truly democratic agenda.[35] The sentiments and thoughts expressed by Faria are shared by many survivors of the repressive 1970s regimes in the southern cone, for whom the hope of the 1980s democratic opening was short lived, since it was accompanied on the economic front by the structural adjustment processes that left so many poor and disenfranchised people in the camp of the excluded.

The Argentine feminist philosopher María Luisa Femenías brings another voice to this debate by emphasizing informal channels of strengthening democracy at the popular level. She proposes the strengthening of social and political networks of solidarity as a way of reinforcing the effectiveness of an all-too-formal democracy. Femenías notes that even if the precepts of the law are formal and unpredictably implemented (as political observers concede), still "self-generated networks of solidarity constitute . . . a firm base from which to demand recognition [before the law]."[36] Femenías points to examples of women's political action taking unusual and nonhegemonic approaches, yet reaching some measure of political efficacy. A well-known example is the case of the Mothers of the Plaza de Mayo who defied the repressive government authority, and by the power of their moral appeal, they eventually brought down the legitimacy of authoritarian rule. But Femenías also mentions several other women's grassroots movements. These include women in farming, women in neighborhood associations, and women in community networks.[37] These groups used unconventional ways of mobilizing to achieve particular objectives and often dispersed once the objectives were achieved.[38] Nonetheless, these forms of association were empowering to those who participated in them and thereby helped to strengthen a participatory democratic agenda. Although it is a long struggle to change the system on behalf of full equality for women, Femenías points to the pervasive networking among women along different lines of the political process to promote progressive gender legislation reform.[39] In relation to grassroots efforts such as these, Alvarez pointed out that decentralizing the feminist movement has expanded its political effectiveness in helping women of different backgrounds and occupations unite for purposes of gender reform.[40] While it is true that the nation-state has been weakened significantly by neoliberal policies and that such economic policies have damaged labor rights, environmental protection, and many gender-related interests, the new political circumstances seem to offer women activists some opportunities to form influential coalitions on certain specific issues with respect to political development.

CULTURAL STUDIES CRITIQUES

Another important counterhegemonic critical sector comes from progressive thinkers in South America who insist, against trade liberalization and the flexibilization of the labor force, that human rights are nonnegotiable. The insistence not just on human rights as conservatively understood but understood generously as a base for the protection of multiple human needs and of yet-to-be unspecified differences is foremost in the democratic left's discourse. For example, the Argentine cultural critic Beatriz Sarlo states in a recent article that "the Left should maintain several completely nonnegotiable [principles] . . . the question of human rights as a perennial open question is one of them. . . . This question is nonnegotiable and spills over onto the expansion of rights, the emergence of new needs,

and the multiplication of differences."[41] Sarlo adds another very interesting point in the battle to unmask the dominant globalization ideology's claim of inevitability. She calls for a political left that is "antimimetic."[42] She characterizes the complacency of contemporary politics as incorporating a series of mimetic practices, among them: "surveys, the construction of a public opinion reflecting existing conditions, the conservative populist backing of all social fears, the automatic acquiescence before the established relations of power."[43] Sarlo's concerns are well taken. While the monitoring of public opinion is important in a democracy, the pressure on public opinion is to conform to the needs of the market. If public opinion, however, is shaped by the needs of the market, what is there left for democracy to do except to promote civil and political measures that continue to favor the market economy of liberalization, profit making, and the search for the cheapest labor and goods possible? The media's imparting of information to the public and its use of public opinion surveys constitute a vicious circle. Because large corporations often own the mainstream media, it stands to reason that they will promote the ideology of neoliberalism as the sure and reliable path to progress. Insofar as this is the case, we find ourselves in a revolving wheel where the needs of the market shape the popular mind, while everyone so (mis)informed will feel represented democratically the more that the government and public spheres are indeed controlled by the needs of the market. The global market's trajectory acts like a mirror before which the public checks to see if its political choices are satisfactory.

As evident in Sarlo's critique, the postmodern and post-structuralist critiques of representation are key avenues for a creative progressive approach to assessing the ideologies of globalization. Using a post-structuralist epistemology, the Chilean cultural critic Nelly Richard has called attention to the order of representation in the media and in human knowledge as a sociocultural construction—yet a construction so habitual that we consider it "natural."[44] More specifically, she considers the constructed order of the feminine and of the feminine writer as these images and meanings circulate in the literary market. "The 'gods of consumerism,'" Richard writes, "receive offerings as well from women writers whose works are successfully promoted by the international literary market that today converts the feminine and the Latin American into the double marginality illustrative of its offers of diversity, which translate center and margins into the same language of market pluralism."[45] Richard warns that "recognition and identification are the tranquilizing keys that link the reader to a matrix of meaning in which what is *legible* is born from the absolute and fixed identity between signifier and signified."[46] Richard is pointing here to the dangers of globalization as a technology that homogenizes meanings pretending at the same time to be an organ for maximizing pluralism as it incorporates those global others into the North's schemata of representations. It is sad to say that in the global market's reconceptualization of diversity, the truly diverse fails to qualify for representation because it is encoded differently from the signifying system that controls the global messages. Indeed, as anyone who has struggled with the meaning of "pluralism" and "diversity" in the United States will recognize, a certain canon of diversity that is extremely problematic is often constructed, framing the official meaning of "diversity." As this model attains popularity and becomes acceptable to the public, it acts as a cover-up for those transgressive alterities that social conventions find unmentionable.

This discussion leads us back to the problem many Latin American feminists have fought recurringly, namely, the suppression of *feminista* [feminist] by *femenina* [feminine][47] along with the latter references reassuring enactment of normative heterosexuality. Seen from this post-structuralist critical Latin American feminist perspective, the neoliberal market disciplines the conceptualization of the "global," the "plural," the "diverse," "the feminine," "the Latin

American," and so on, as it includes some players among its economic, social, and political beneficiaries, while excluding others. By the same token, what counts as "Latin American philosophy" and "thought" (*pensamiento*) according to the criteria of neoliberal globalization is subject to the same hegemonizing dichotomy. For this reason, it is important to remain politically alert to the seductions of the market and to insist on the value of progressive political alternatives whether we take a feminist route to the analysis of globalization or we adopt some other line of approach or methodology.

In the end, I hope this analysis has shed some light on the complexity of globalization processes and the importance of bringing gender and cultural location into a discussion of the direction and effects of these economic processes. Although I have not brought in other variables such as race, ethnicity, or class to the discussion, I believe these are equally important in providing a picture of those who are most vulnerable to the impact of globalization. The analysis I have given is meant to include the needs of the most marginal—hence the critique of neoliberalism and its exacerbation of economic inequalities. Through intellectual critique and analysis as well as political action, an ethical vision of human development can shed light on those aspects of globalization that fall far short of long-standing ideals of political equality, fairness, and social justice. The Latin American context in which these processes are played out and the alternative political options and criticisms suggested in response to them are truly enlightening as we face common challenges in today's global economy despite our multiple, nonhomogeneous locations.

NOTES

1. In this essay the English translations from Spanish language sources are my own.
2. Ofelia Schutte, "Political and Market Development: An Ethical Appraisal," *Journal of Social Philosophy* 31, no. 4 (2000): 453–64, 460–63.

3. Ofelia Schutte, *Cultural Identity and Social Liberation in Latin American Thought* (Albany: State University of New York Press, 1993), 1–8.

4. Ofelia Schutte, "Cultural Alterity: Cross-Cultural Communication and Feminist Thought in North-South Dialogue," *Hypatia: A Journal of Feminist Philosophy* (spec. issue on Global, Postcolonial, and Multicultural Feminisms, ed. Sandra Harding and Uma Narayan) 13, no. 2 (spring 1998): 53–72.

5. Lourdes Benería et al., "Introduction: Globalization and Gender," *Feminist Economics* (spec. issue on Globalization, ed. Lourdes Benería et al.) 6 (2000): vii–xviii; reviewed by Priti Ramamurthy, "Indexing Alternatives: Feminist Development Studies and Global Political Economy," *Feminist Theory* 1 (2000): 239–40, 240–56.

6. Gayatri Chakravorty Spivak, *A Critique of Postcolonial Reason: Toward a History of the Vanishing Present* (Cambridge, Mass.: Harvard University Press, 1999), 312–21; Nelly Richard, "Feminismo, Experiencia y Representación," *Crítica cultural y teoría literaria latinoamericanas* (spec. issue of *Revista Iberoamericana,* ed. Mabel Moraña) 62 (1996): 733–44.

7. Lorraine Corner, *Women, Men, and Economics: The Gender-Differentiated Impact of Macroeconomics* (New York: United Nations Development Fund for Women, 1996), 20–21.

8. UNIFEM Biennial Report, *Progress of the World's Women 2000* (New York: United Nations Development Fund for Women, 2000), 11–12.

9. UNIFEM Biennial Report, *Progress of the World's Women 2000,* 152.

10. UNIFEM Biennial Report, *Progress of the World's Women 2000,* 154.

11. Paloma de Villota, ed., *Globalización y género* (Madrid: Síntesis, 1999), 22–23.

12. Benería et al., "Introduction: Globalization and Gender," x.

13. Ana María Amado, "La Opción entre la Maternidad y el Trabajo," *Fempress: Agencia de Prensa Latinoamericana de la Mujer* 149, no. 1 at www.fempress.cl, Santiago de Chile, 13 December 2000 (accessed May 2, 2002).

14. For a groundbreaking book on the topic of the work involved in caring for dependents and the need for justice for caregivers, who are predominantly female, see Eva Kittay (1999). In an essay in progress, "Women, Dependency, and the Global Economy," I analyze the impact of the gender division of labor on unpaid care workers in light of the cutbacks on social assistance implemented by the neoliberal global economy.

15. Corner, *Women, Men, and Economics*, 30–31.

16. Laurie Shrage, *Moral Dilemmas in Feminism: Adultery, Abortion, and Prostitution* (New York: Routledge, 1994), 142–45.

17. Grace Chang, *Disposable Domestics: Immigrant Women Workers in the Global Economy* (Cambridge, Mass.: South End, 2000), 125.

18. Sonia E. Alvarez. "Latin American Feminisms 'Go Global': Trends of the 1990s and Challenges for the New Millennium," in *Cultures of Politics, Politics of Cultures,* ed. Sonia E. Alvarez, Evalina Dagnino, and Arturo Escobar (Boulder, Colo.: Westview, 1998), 293–324.

19. Alvarez, "Latin American Feminisms 'Go Global,'" 293.

20. Alvarez, "Latin American Feminisms 'Go Global,'" 293 ff.

21. Alvarez, "Latin American Feminisms 'Go Global,'" 298.

22. Alvarez, "Latin American Feminisms 'Go Global,'" 311–17.

23. Alvarez, "Latin American Feminisms 'Go Global,'" 299.

24. Alvarez, "Latin American Feminisms 'Go Global,'" 299.

25. Alvarez, "Latin American Feminisms 'Go Global,'" 301.

26. Alvarez, "Latin American Feminisms 'Go Global,'" 302.

27. Fempress at www.fempress.cl (accessed 13 March 2002).

28. La Morada at www.la-morada.com (accessed 13 March 2002).

29. Creatividad Feminista at creatividadfeminista.org (accessed 13 March 2002).

30. José Eduardo Faria, "Democracia y Gobernabilidad: Los Derechos Humanos a la Luz de la Globalización Económica," *Mundialización Económica y Crisis Político-Jurídica* (spec. issue of *Anales de la Cátedra Francisco Suárez*) 32 (1995): 73–100, 100.

31. Faria, "Democracia y Gobernabilidad," 76.

32. Faria, "Democracia y Gobernabilidad," 89.
33. Faria, "Democracia y Gobernabilidad," 89.
34. Faria, "Democracia y Gobernabilidad," 94–100.
35. Faria, "Democracia y Gobernabilidad," 78.
36. María Luisa Femenías, "Igualdad y Diferencia en Democracia: Una Síntesis Posible," *La Democracia en Latinoamérica* (spec. issue of *Anales de la Cátedra Francisco Suárez*) 33 (1999): 109–32, 127.
37. Femenías, "Igualdad y Diferencia en Democracia: Una Síntesis Posible," 126.
38. Femenías, "Igualdad y Diferencia en Democracia: Una Síntesis Posible," 126–27.
39. Femenías, "Igualdad y Diferencia en Democracia: Una Síntesis Posible," 131–32.
40. Alvarez, "Latin American Feminisms 'Go Global,'" 299–302.
41. Beatriz Sarlo, "Contra la Mímesis: Izquierda Cultural, Izquierda Política," *Revista de Crítica Cultural,* ed. Nelly Richard, 20 (June 2000): 22–23, 23.
42. Beatriz Sarlo, "Contra la Mímesis: Izquierda Cultural, Izquierda Política," 23.
43. Beatriz Sarlo, "Contra la Mímesis: Izquierda Cultural, Izquierda Política," 23.
44. Nelly Richard, "Feminismo, Experiencia y Representación," *Crítica Cultural y Teoría Literaria Latinoamericanas* (spec. issue of *Revista Iberoamericana,* ed. Mabel Moraña) 62 (1996): 733–44, 734.
45. Nelly Richard, "Feminismo, Experiencia y Representación," 742.
46. Nelly Richard, "Feminismo, Experiencia y Representación," 743.
47. Alvarez, "Latin American Feminisms 'Go Global,'" 297.

THE PRISON INDUSTRIAL COMPLEX

Angela Y. Davis

"For private business prison labor is like a pot of gold. No strikes. No union organizing. No health benefits, unemployment insurance, or workers' compensation to pay. No language barriers, as in foreign countries. New leviathan prisons are being built on thousands of eerie acres of factories inside the walls. Prisoners do data entry for Chevron, make telephone reservations for TWA, raise hogs, shovel manure, and make circuit boards, limousines, waterbeds, and lingerie for Victoria's Secret, all at a fraction of the cost of 'free labor.'"
—LINDA EVANS AND EVE GOLDBERG[1]

The exploitation of prison labor by private corporations is one aspect among an array of relationships linking corporations, government, correctional communities, and media. These relationships constitute what we now call a prison industrial complex. The term "prison industrial complex" was introduced by activists and scholars to contest prevailing beliefs that increased levels of crime were the root cause of mounting prison populations. Instead, they argued, prison construction and the attendant drive to fill these new structures with human bodies have been driven by ideologies of racism and the pursuit of profit. Social historian Mike Davis first used the term in relation to California's penal system, which, he observed, already had begun in the 1990s to rival agribusiness and land development as a major economic and political force.[2]

To understand the social meaning of the prison today within the context of a developing prison industrial complex means that punishment has to be conceptually severed from its seemingly indissoluble link with crime. How often do we encounter the phrase "crime and punishment"? To what extent has the perpetual repetition of the phrase "crime and punishment" in literature, as titles of television shows, both fictional and documentary, and in everyday conversation made it extremely difficult to think about punishment beyond this connection? How have these portrayals located the prison in a causal relation to crime as a natural, necessary, and permanent effect, thus inhibiting serious debates about the viability of the prison today?

The notion of a prison industrial complex insists on understandings of the punishment process that take into account economic and political structures and ideologies, rather than focusing myopically on individual criminal conduct and efforts to "curb crime." The fact, for example, that many corporations with global markets now rely on prisons as an important source of profit helps us to understand the rapidity with which prisons began to proliferate precisely at a time when official studies indicated that the crime rate was falling. The notion of a prison industrial complex also insists that the racialization of prison populations—and this is not only true of the United States, but of Europe, South America, and Australia as well—is not an incidental feature. Thus, critiques of the prison industrial complex undertaken by abolitionist activists and scholars are very much linked to critiques of the global persistence of racism. Antiracist and other social justice movements are incomplete with attention to the politics of imprisonment. At the 2001 United Nations World Conference Against Racism held in Durban, South Africa, a few individuals active in abolitionist campaigns in various countries attempted to bring this connection to the attention of the international community. They pointed out that the expanding system of prisons throughout the world both relies on and further promotes structures of racism even though its proponents may adamantly maintain that it is race-neutral.

Some critics of the prison system have employed the term "correctional industrial complex" and others "penal industrial complex." These and the term I have chosen to underscore, "prison industrial complex," all clearly resonate with the historical concept of a "military industrial complex," whose usage dates back to the presidency of Dwight Eisenhower. It may seem ironic that a Republican president was the first

to underscore a growing and dangerous alliance between the military and corporate worlds, but it clearly seemed right to antiwar activists and scholars during the era of the Vietnam War. Today, some activists mistakenly argue that the prison industrial complex is moving into the space vacated by the military industrial complex. However, the so-called War on Terrorism initiated by the Bush administration in the aftermath of the 2001 attacks on the World Trade Center has made it very clear that the links between the military, corporations, and government are growing stronger, not weaker.

A more cogent way to define the relationship between the military industrial complex and the prison industrial complex would be to call it symbiotic. These two complexes mutually support and promote each other and, in fact, often share technologies. During the early nineties, when defense production was temporarily on the decline, this connection between the military industry and the criminal justice/punishment industry was acknowledged in a 1994 *Wall Street Journal* article entitled "Making Crime Pay: The Cold War of the '90s":

> Parts of the defense establishment are cashing in, too, sensing a logical new line of business to help them offset military cutbacks. Westinghouse Electric Corp., Minnesota Mining and Manufacturing Co, GDE Systems (a division of the old General Dynamics) and Alliant Techsystems Inc., for instance, are pushing crime fighting equipment and have created special divisions to retool their defense technology for America's streets.[3]

The article describes a conference sponsored by the National Institute of Justice, the research arm of the Justice Department, entitled "Law Enforcement Technology in the 21st Century." The secretary of defense was a major presenter at this conference, which explored topics such as, "The role of the defense industry, particularly for dual use and conversion."

> Hot topics: defense-industry technology that could lower the level of violence involved in crime fighting. Sandia National Laboratories, for instance, is experimenting with a dense foam that

can be sprayed at suspects, temporarily blinding and deafening them under breathable bubbles. Stinger Corporation is working on "smart guns," which will fire only for the owner, and retractable spiked barrier strips to unfurl in front of fleeing vehicles. Westinghouse is promoting the "smart car," in which minicomputers could be linked up with big mainframes at the police department, allowing for speedy booking of prisoners, as well as quick exchanges of information . . .[4]

But an analysis of the relationship between the military and prison industrial complex is not only concerned with the transference of technologies from the military to the law enforcement industry. What may be even more important to our discussion is the extent to which both share important structural features. Both systems generate huge profits from processes of social destruction. Precisely that which is advantageous to those corporations, elected officials, and government agents who have obvious stakes in the expansion of these systems begets grief and devastation for poor and racially dominated communities in the United States and throughout the world. The transformation of imprisoned bodies—and they are in their majority bodies of color—into sources of profit who consume and also often produce all kinds of commodities, devours public funds, which might otherwise be available for social programs such as education, housing, childcare, recreation, and drug programs.

Punishment no longer constitutes a marginal area of the larger economy. Corporations producing all kinds of goods—from buildings to electronic devices and hygiene products—and providing all kinds of services—from meals to therapy and healthcare—are now directly involved in the punishment business. That is to say, companies that one would assume are far removed from the work of state punishment have developed major stakes in the perpetuation of a prison system whose historical obsolescence is therefore that much more difficult to recognize. It was during the decade of the 1980s that corporate ties to the punishment system became more

extensive and entrenched than ever before. But throughout the history of the U.S. prison system, prisoners have always constituted a potential source of profit. For example, they have served as valuable subjects in medical research, thus positioning the prison as a major link between universities and corporations.

During the post-World War II period, for example, medical experimentation on captive populations helped to hasten the development of the pharmaceutical industry. According to Allen Hornblum,

> [T]he number of American medical research programs that relied on prisoners as subjects rapidly expanded as zealous doctors and researchers, grantmaking universities, and a burgeoning pharmaceutical industry raced for greater market share. Society's marginal people were, as they had always been, the grist for the medical-pharmaceutical mill, and prison inmates in particular would become the raw materials for postwar profit-making and academic advancement.[5]

Hornblum's book, *Acres of Skin: Human Experiments at Holmesburg Prison,* highlights the career of research dermatologist Albert Kligman, who was a professor at the University of Pennsylvania. Kligman, the "Father of Retin-A,"[6] conducted hundreds of experiments on the men housed in Holmesburg Prison and, in the process, trained many researchers to use what were later recognized as unethical research methods.

> When Dr. Kligman entered the aging prison he was awed by the potential it held for his research. In 1966, he recalled in a newspaper interview: "All I saw before me were acres of skin. It was like a farmer seeing a fertile field for the first time." The hundreds of inmates walking aimlessly before him represented a unique opportunity for unlimited and undisturbed medical research. He described it in this interview as "an anthropoid colony, mainly healthy" under perfect control conditions.[7]

By the time the experimentation program was shut down in 1974 and new federal regulations prohibited the use of prisoners as subjects for academic and corporate research, numerous cosmetics and skin creams had already been tested. Some of them had caused great harm to these subjects and could not be marketed in their original form. Johnson and Johnson, Ortho Pharmaceutical, and Dow Chemical are only a few of the corporations that reaped great material benefits from these experiments.

The potential impact of corporate involvement in punishment could have been glimpsed in the Kligman experiments at Holmesburg Prison as early as the 1950s and 1960s. However, it was not until the 1980s and the increasing globalization of capitalism that the massive surge of capital into the punishment economy began. The deindustrialization processes that resulted in plant shutdowns throughout the country created a huge pool of vulnerable human beings, a pool of people for whom no further jobs were available. This also brought more people into contact with social services, such as AFDC (Aid to Families with Dependent Children) and other welfare agencies. It is not accidental that "welfare, as we have known it"—to use former President Clinton's words—came under severe attack and was eventually disestablished. This was known as "welfare reform." At the same time, we experienced the privatization and corporatization of services that were previously run by government. The most obvious example of this privatization process was the transformation of government-run hospitals and health services into a gigantic complex of what are euphemistically called health maintenance organizations. In this sense we might also speak of a "medical industrial complex."[8] In fact, there is a connection between one of the first private hospital companies, Hospital Corporation of America—known today as HCA—and Corrections Corporation of America (CCA). Board members of HCA, which today has two hundred hospitals and seventy outpatient surgery centers in twenty-four states, England, and Switzerland helped to start Correctional Corporations of America in 1983.

In the context of an economy that was driven by an unprecedented pursuit of profit, no matter what the human cost, and the concomitant dismantling of the welfare state, poor people's abilities to survive became increasingly constrained by the looming presence of the prison. The massive prison-building project that began in the 1980s created the means of concentrating and managing what the capitalist system had implicitly declared to be a human surplus. In the meantime, elected officials and the dominant media justified the new draconian sentencing practices, sending more and more people to prison in the frenzied drive to build more and more prisons by arguing that this was the only way to make our communities safe from murderers, rapists, and robbers.

> The media, especially television . . . have a vested interest in perpetuating the notion that crime is out of control. With new competition from cable networks and 24-hour news channels, TV news and programs about crime . . . have proliferated madly. According to the Center for Media and Public Affairs, crime coverage was the number-one topic on the nightly news over the past decade. From 1990 to 1998, homicide rates dropped by half nationwide, but homicide stories on the three major networks rose almost fourfold.[9]

During the same period when crime rates were declining, prison populations soared. According to a recent report by the U.S. Department of Justice, at the end of the year 2001, there were 2,100,146 people incarcerated in the United States.[10] The terms and numbers as they appear in this government report require some preliminary discussion. I hesitate to make unmediated use of such statistical evidence because it can discourage the very critical thinking that ought to be elicited by an understanding of the prison industrial complex. It is precisely the abstraction of numbers that plays such a central role in criminalizing those who experience the misfortune of imprisonment. There are many different kinds of men and women in the prisons, jails, and INS and military detention centers, whose lives are erased by the Bureau of Justice Statistics figures. The numbers recognize no distinction between the woman who is imprisoned on drug conspiracy and the man who is in prison for killing his wife, a man who might actually end up spending less time behind bars than the woman.

With this observation in mind, the statistical breakdown is as follows: There were 1,324,465 people in "federal and state prisons," 15,852 in "territorial prisons," 631,240 in "local jails," 8,761 in "Immigration and Naturalization Service detention facilities," 2,436 in "military facilities," 1,912 in "jails in Indian country," and 108,965 in "juvenile facilities." In the ten years between 1990 and 2000, 351 new places of confinement were opened by states and more than 528,000 beds were added, amounting to 1,320 state facilities, representing an eighty-one percent increase. Moreover, there are currently 84 federal facilities and 264 private facilities.[11]

The government reports, from which these figures are taken, emphasize the extent to which incarceration rates are slowing down. The Bureau of Justice Statistics report entitled "Prisoners in 2001" introduces the study by indicating that "the Nation's prison population grew 1.1%, which was less than the average annual growth of 3.8% since yearend 1995. During 2001 the prison population rose at the lowest rate since 1972 and had the smallest absolute increase since 1979."[12] However small the increase, these numbers themselves would defy the imagination were they not so neatly classified and rationally organized. To place these figures in historical perspective, try to imagine how people in the eighteenth and nineteenth centuries—and indeed for most of the twentieth century—who welcomed the new, and then quite extraordinary, system of punishment called the prison might have responded had they known that such a colossal number of lives would be eventually claimed permanently by this institution. I have already shared my own memories of a time three decades ago when the prison population was comprised of a tenth of the present numbers.

The prison industrial complex is fueled by privatization patterns that, it will be recalled, have also drastically transformed health care, education, and other areas of our lives. Moreover, the prison privatization trends—both the increasing presence of corporations in the prison economy and the establishment of private prisons—are reminiscent of the historical efforts to create a profitable punishment industry based on the new supply of "free" black male laborers in the aftermath of the Civil War. Steven Donziger, drawing from the work of Norwegian criminologist Nils Christie, argues:

> [C]ompanies that service the criminal justice system need sufficient quantities of raw materials to guarantee long-term growth. . . . In the criminal justice field, *the raw material is prisoners,* and industry will do what is necessary to guarantee a steady supply. For the supply of prisoners to grow, criminal justice policies must ensure a sufficient number of incarcerated Americans regardless of whether crime is rising or the incarceration is necessary.[13]

In the post–Civil War era, emancipated black men and women comprised an enormous reservoir of labor at a time when planters—and industrialists—could no longer rely on slavery, as they had done in the past. This labor became increasingly available for use by private agents precisely through the convict lease system, discussed earlier, and related systems such as debt peonage. Recall that in the aftermath of slavery, the penal population drastically shifted, so that in the South it rapidly became disproportionately black. This transition set the historical stage for the easy acceptance of disproportionately black prison populations today. According to 2002 Bureau of Justice Statistics, African-Americans as a whole now represent the majority of county, state, and federal prisoners, with a total of 803,400 black inmates—118,600 more than the total number of white inmates. If we include Latinos, we must add another 283,000 bodies of color.[14]

As the rate of increase in the incarceration of black prisoners continues to rise, the racial composition of the incarcerated population is approaching the proportion of black prisoners to white during the era of the southern convict lease and county chain gang systems. Whether this human raw material is used for purposes of labor or for the consumption of commodities provided by a rising number of corporations directly implicated in the prison industrial complex, it is clear that black bodies are considered dispensable within the "free world" but as a major source of profit in the prison world.

The privatization characteristic of convict leasing has its contemporary parallels, as companies such as CCA and Wackenhut literally run prisons for profit. At the beginning of the twenty-first century, the numerous private prison companies operating in the United States own and operate facilities that hold 91,828 federal and state prisoners.[15] Texas and Oklahoma can claim the largest number of people in private prisons. But New Mexico imprisons forty-four percent of its prison population in private facilities, and states such as Montana, Alaska, and Wyoming turned over more than twenty-five percent of their prison population to private companies.[16] In arrangements reminiscent of the convict lease system, federal, state, and county governments pay private companies a fee for each inmate, which means that private companies have a stake in retaining prisoners as long as possible, and in keeping their facilities filled.

In the state of Texas, there are thirty-four government-owned, privately run jails in which approximately 5,500 out-of-state prisoners are incarcerated. These facilities generate about eighty million dollars annually for Texas.[17] One dramatic example involves Capital Corrections Resources, Inc., which operates the Brazoria Detention Center, a government-owned facility located forty miles outside of Houston, Texas. Brazoria came to public attention in August 1997 when a videotape broadcast on national television showed prisoners there being bitten by police dogs and viciously kicked in the groin and stepped on by guards. The inmates, forced to crawl on the floor, also were being shocked with stun guns, while guards—who referred to one black prisoner as "boy"—shouted, "Crawl faster!"[18] In

the aftermath of the release of this tape, the state of Missouri withdrew the 415 prisoners it housed in the Brazoria Detention Center. Although few references were made in the accompanying news reports to the indisputably racialized character of the guards' outrageous behavior, in the section of the Brazoria videotape that was shown on national television, black male prisoners were seen to be the primary targets of the guards' attacks.

The thirty-two-minute Brazoria tape, represented by the jail authorities as a training tape—allegedly showing corrections officers "what *not* to do"—was made in September 1996, after a guard allegedly smelled marijuana in the jail. Important evidence of the abuse that takes place behind the walls and gates of private prisons, it came to light in connection with a lawsuit filed by one of the prisoners who was bitten by a dog; he was suing Brazoria County for a hundred thousand dollars in damage. The Brazoria jailors' actions—which, according to prisoners there, were far worse than depicted on the tape—are indicative not only of the ways in which many prisoners throughout the country are treated, but of generalized attitudes toward people locked up in jails and prisons.

According to an Associated Press news story, the Missouri inmates, once they had been transferred back to their home state from Brazoria, told the *Kansas City Star*:

> [G]uards at the Brazoria County Detention Center used cattle prods and other forms of intimidation to win respect and force prisoners to say, "I love Texas." "What you saw on tape wasn't a fraction of what happened that day," said inmate Louis Watkins, referring to the videotaped cellblock raid of September 18, 1996. "I've never seen anything like that in the movies.[19]

In 2000 there were twenty-six for-profit prison corporations in the United States that operated approximately 150 facilities in twenty-eight states.[20] The largest of these companies, CCA and Wackenhut, control 76.4 percent of the private prison market globally. CCA is headquartered in Nashville, Tennessee, and until 2001, its largest shareholder was the multinational headquartered in Paris, Sodexho Alliance, which, through its U.S. subsidiary, Sodexho Marriott, provides catering services at nine hundred U.S. colleges and universities. The Prison Moratorium Project, an organization promoting youth activism, led a protest campaign against Sodexho Marriott on campuses throughout the country. Among the campuses that dropped Sodexho were SUNY Albany, Goucher College, and James Madison University. Students had staged sit-ins and organized rallies on more than fifty campuses before Sodexho divested its holdings in CCA in fall 2001.[21]

Though private prisons represent a fairly small proportion of prisons in the United States, the privatization model is quickly becoming the primary mode of organizing punishment in many other countries.[22] These companies have tried to take advantage of the expanding population of women prisoners, both in the United States and globally. In 1996, the first private women's prison was established by CCA in Melbourne, Australia. The government of Victoria "adopted the U.S. model of privatization in which financing, design, construction, and ownership of the prison are awarded to one contractor and the government pays them back for construction over twenty years. This means that it is virtually impossible to remove the contractor because that contractor owns the prison."[23]

As a direct consequence of the campaign organized by prison activist groups in Melbourne, Victoria withdrew the contract from CCA in 2001. However, a significant portion of Australia's prison system remains privatized. In the fall of 2002, the government of Queensland renewed Wackenhut's contract to run a 710-bed prison in Brisbane. The value of the five-year contract is $66.5 million. In addition to the facility in Brisbane, Wackenhut manages eleven other prisons in Australia and New Zealand and furnishes health care services in eleven public prisons in the state of Victoria.[24] In the press release announcing this contract renewal, Wackenhut describes its global business activities as follows:

WCC, a world leader in the privatized corrections industry, has contracts/awards to manage 60 correctional/detention facilities in North America, Europe, Australia, South Africa and New Zealand with a total of approximately 43,000 beds. WCC also provides prisoner transportation services, electronic monitoring for home detainees, correctional health care and mental health services. WCC offers government agencies a turnkey approach to the development of new correctional and mental health institutions that includes design, construction, financing, and operations.[25]

But to understand the reach of the prison industrial complex, it is not enough to evoke the looming power of the private prison business. By definition, those companies court the state within and outside the United States for the purpose of obtaining prison contracts, bringing punishment and profit together in a menacing embrace. Still, this is only the most visible dimension of the prison industrial complex, and it should not lead us to ignore the more comprehensive corporatization that is a feature of contemporary punishment. As compared to earlier historical eras, the prison economy is no longer a small, identifiable, and containable set of markets. Many corporations, whose names are highly recognizable by "free world" consumers, have discovered new possibilities for expansion by selling their products to correctional facilities.

In the 1990s, the variety of corporations making money from prisons is truly dizzying, ranging from Dial Soap to Famous Amos cookies, from AT&T to health-care providers . . . In 1995 Dial Soap sold $100,000 worth of its product to the New York City jail system alone . . . When VitaPro Foods of Montreal, Canada, contracted to supply inmates in the state of Texas with its soy-based meat substitute, the contract was worth $34 million a year.[26]

Among the many businesses that advertise in the yellow pages on the corrections.com Web site are Archer Daniel Midlands, Nestle Food Service, Ace Hardware, Polaroid, Hewlett-Packard, RJ Reynolds, and the communications companies Sprint, AT&T, Verizon, and Ameritech. One conclusion to be drawn here is that even if private prison companies were prohibited—an unlikely prospect, indeed—the prison industrial complex and its many strategies for profit would remain relatively intact. Private prisons are direct sources of profit for the companies that run them, but public prisons have become so thoroughly saturated with the profit-producing products and services of private corporations that the distinction is not as meaningful as one might suspect. Campaigns against privatization that represent public prisons as an adequate alternative to private prisons can be misleading. It is true that a major reason for the profitability of private prisons consists in the nonunion labor they employ, and this important distinction should be highlighted. Nevertheless, public prisons are now equally tied to the corporate economy and constitute an ever-growing source of capitalist profit.

Extensive corporate investment in prisons has significantly raised the stakes for antiprison work. It means that serious antiprison activists must be willing to look much further in their analyses and organizing strategies than the actual institution of the prison. Prison reform rhetoric, which has always undergirded dominant critiques of the prison system, will not work in this new situation. If reform approaches have tended to bolster the permanence of the prison in the past, they certainly will not suffice to challenge the economic and political relationships that sustain the prison today. This means that in the era of the prison industrial complex, activists must pose hard questions about the relationship between global capitalism and the spread of U.S.-style prisons throughout the world.

The global prison economy is indisputably dominated by the United States. This economy not only consists of the products, services, and ideas that are directly marketed to other governments, but it also exercises an enormous influence over the development of the style of state punishment throughout the world. One dramatic example can be seen in the opposition to Turkey's attempts to transform its prisons. In October 2000, prisoners in Turkey, many of whom are associated with left

political movements, began a "death fast" as a way of dramatizing their opposition to the Turkish government's decision to introduce "F-Type," or U.S.-style, prisons. Compared to the traditional dormitory-style facilities, these new prisons consist of one- to three-person cells, which are opposed by the prisoners because of the regimes of isolation they facilitate and because mistreatment and torture are far more likely in isolation. In December 2000, thirty prisoners were killed in clashes with security forces in "twenty prisons.[27] As of September 2002, more than fifty prisoners have died of hunger, including two women, Gulnihal Yilmaz and Birsen Hosver, who were among the most recent prisoners to succumb to the death fast.

"F-Type" prisons in Turkey were inspired by the recent emergence of the super-maximum security—or supermax—prison in the United States, which presumes to control otherwise unmanageable prisoners by holding them in permanent solitary confinement and by subjecting them to varying degrees of sensory deprivation. In its *2002 World Report,* Human Rights Watch paid particular attention to the concerns raised by

> the spread of ultra-modern "super-maximum" security prisons. Originally prevalent in the United States . . . the supermax model was increasingly followed in other countries. Prisoners confined in such facilities spent an average of twenty-three hours a day in their cells, enduring extreme social isolation, enforced idleness, and extraordinarily limited recreational and educational opportunities. While prison authorities defended the use of supermaximum security facilities by asserting that they held only the most dangerous, disruptive, or escape-prone inmates, few safeguards existed to prevent other prisoners from being arbitrarily or discriminatorily transferred to such facilities. In Australia, the inspector of custodial services found that some prisoners were being held indefinitely in special high security units without knowing why or when their isolation would end.[28]

Among the many countries that have recently constructed super-maximum security prisons is

South Africa. Construction was completed on the supermax prison in Kokstad, KwaZulu-Natal in August 2000, but it was not officially opened until May 2002. Ironically, the reason given for the delay was the competition for water between the prison and a new low-cost housing development.[29] I am highlighting South Africa's embrace of the supermax because of the apparent ease with which this most repressive version of the U.S. prison has established itself in a country that has just recently initiated the project of building a democratic, nonracist, and nonsexist society. South Africa was the first country in the world to create constitutional assurances for gay rights, and it immediately abolished the death penalty after the dismantling of apartheid. Nevertheless, following the example of the United States, the South African prison system is expanding and becoming more oppressive. The U.S. private prison company Wackenhut has secured several contracts with the South African government and by constructing private prisons further legitimizes the trend toward privatization (which affects the availability of basic services from utilities to education) in the economy as a whole.

South Africa's participation in the prison industrial complex constitutes a major impediment to the creation of a democratic society. In the United States, we have already felt the insidious and socially damaging effects of prison expansion. The dominant social expectation is that young black, Latino, Native American, and Southeast Asian men—and increasingly women as well—will move naturally from the free world into prison, where, it is assumed, they belong. Despite the important gains of antiracist social movements over the last half century, racism hides from view within institutional structures, and its most reliable refuge is the prison system.

The racist arrests of vast numbers of immigrants from Middle Eastern countries in the aftermath of the attacks on September 11, 2001, and the subsequent withholding of information about the names of numbers of people held in INS detention centers, some of which are owned and operated by private corporations, do not augur a democratic future. The uncontested detention of increasing numbers of undocumented immigrants from the global South has been aided considerably by the structures and ideologies associated with the prison industrial complex. We can hardly move in the direction of justice and equality in the twenty-first century if we are unwilling to recognize the enormous role played by this system in extending the power of racism and xenophobia.

Radical opposition to the global prison industrial complex sees the antiprison movement as a vital means of expanding the terrain on which the quest for democracy will unfold. This movement is thus antiracist, anticapitalist, antisexist, and antihomophobic. It calls for the abolition of the prison as the dominant mode of punishment but at the same time recognizes the need for genuine solidarity with the millions of men, women, and children who are behind bars. A major challenge of this movement is to do the work that will create more humane, habitable environments for people in prison without bolstering the permanence of the prison system. How, then, do we accomplish this balancing act of passionately attending to the needs of prisoners—calling for less violent conditions, an end to state sexual assault, improved physical and mental health care, greater access to drug programs, better educational work opportunities, unionization of prison labor, more connections with families and communities, shorter or alternative sentencing—and at the same time call for alternatives to sentencing altogether, no more prison construction, and abolitionist strategies that question the place of the prison in our future?

NOTES

1. Linda Evans and Eve Goldberg, "The Prison Industrial Complex and the Global Economy" [pamphlet] (Berkeley, Calif: Prison Activist Resource Center, 1997).
2. See note 3.
3. *Wall Street Journal*, 12 May 1994.
4. Ibid.
5. Allen M. Hornblum, *Acres of Skin: Human Experiments at Holmesburg prison* (New York: Routledge, 1998), xvi.

6. Hornblum, 212.

7. Hornblum, 37.

8. See A S Relman, "The New Medical Industrial Complex," *New England Journal of Medicine* 30 (17) [23 October 1980]: 963–70.

9. Vince Beiser, "How We Got to Two Million: How Did the Land of the Free Become the World's Leading Jailer?" *Debt to Society*. MotherJones. com Special Report, 10 July 2001. Available at: www.mothe rjones.com/prisons/overview.html, 6.

10. Paige M. Harrison and Allen J. Beck, "Prisoners in 2001," Bureau of Justice Statistics Bulletin [Washington, D.C.: U.S. Department of Justice, Office of Justice Programs, July 2002, NCJ 195189], 1.

11. Allen Beck and Paige M. Harrison, "Prisoners in 2000," Bureau of Justice Statistics Bulletin [Washington, D.C.: U.S. Department of Justice, Office of Justice Programs, August 2001, NCJ 1888207], 1.

12. Harrison and Beck, "Prisoners in 2001."

13. Steve Donziger, *The Real War on Crime: Report of the National Criminal Justice Commission* [New York: Perennial Publishers, 1996], 87.

14. Allen J. Beck, Jennifer C. Karberg, and Paige M. Harrison. "Prison and Jail Inmates at Midyear 2001," Bureau of Justice Statistics Bulletin [Washington, D.C., U.S. Department of Justice, Office of Justice Programs, April 2002, NCJ 191702], 12.

15. Harrison and Beck, "Prisoners in 2001," 7.

16. Ibid.

17. Sue Anne Pressley, "Texas County Sued by Missouri Over Alleged Abuse of Inmates," *Washington Post,* 27 August 1997, A2.

18. Madeline Baro, "Video Prompts Prison Probe," *Philadelphia Daily News*, 20 August 1997.

19. "Beatings Worse Than Shown on Videotape, Missouri Inmates Say." The Associated Press, 27 August 1997, 7:40 P.M. EDT.

20. Joel Dyer, *The Perpetual Prison Machine: How America Profits from Crime* [Boulder, Col.: Westview Press, 2000].

21. Abby Ellin, "A Food Fight Over Private Prisons," *New York Times*. Education Life, Sunday, 8 April 2001.

22. See Julia Sudbury, "Mules and Other Hybrids: Incarcerated Women and the Limits of Diaspora," *Harvard Journal of African American Public Policy,* Fall 2002.

23. Amanda George, "The New Prison Culture: Making Millions from Misery," in Sandy Cook and Susanne Davies, *Harsh Punishment: International Experiences of Women's Imprisonment* by Sandy Cook and Susanne Davies [Boston: Northeastern Press, 1999], 190.

24. Press release issued by Wackenhut, 23 August 2002.

25. Ibid.

26. Dyer, 14.

27. See Amnesty International Press Release at www. geocities.com/turkishhungerstrike/amapril.html.

28. www.hrw.org/wr2k2/prisons.html

29. www.suntimes.co.za/20

SEXUAL VIOLENCE AS A TOOL OF GENOCIDE

Andrea Smith

[Rape] is nothing more or less than a conscious process of intimidation by which men keep all women in a state of fear.[1]

Rape as "nothing more or less" than a tool of patriarchal control undergirds the philosophy of the white-dominated women's antiviolence movement. This philosophy has been critiqued by many women of color, including critical race theorist Kimberle Crenshaw, for its lack of attention to racism and other forms of oppression. Crenshaw analyzes how male-dominated conceptions of race and white-dominated conceptions of gender stand in the way of a clear understanding of violence against women of color. It is inadequate, she argues, to investigate the oppression of women of color by examining race and gender oppressions separately and then putting the two analyses together, because the overlap between racism and sexism transforms the dynamics. Instead, Crenshaw advocates replacing the "additive" approach with an "intersectional" approach.

> The problem is not simply that both discourses fail women of color by not acknowledging the 'additional' issue of race or of patriarchy but, rather, that the discourses are often inadequate even to the discrete tasks of articulating the full dimensions of racism and sexism.[2]

Despite her intersectional approach, Crenshaw falls short of describing how a politics of intersectionality might fundamentally shift how we analyze sexual/domestic violence. If sexual violence is not simply a tool of patriarchy but also a tool of colonialism and racism, then entire communities of color are the victims of sexual violence. As Neferti Tadiar argues, *colonial relationships are themselves gendered and sexualized.*

> The economies and political relations of nations are libidinally configured, that is, they are grasped and effected in terms of sexuality. This global and regional fantasy is not, however, only metaphorical, but real insofar as it grasps a system of political and economic practices already at work among these nations.[3]

Within this context, according to Tadiar, "the question to be asked . . . is, Who is getting off on this? Who is getting screwed and by whom?"[4] Thus, while both Native men and women have been subjected to a reign of sexualized terror, sexual violence does not affect Indian men and women in the same way. When a Native woman suffers abuse, this abuse is an attack on her identity as a woman and an attack on her identity as Native. The issues of colonial, race, and gender oppression cannot be separated. This fact explains why in my experience as a rape crisis counselor, every Native survivor I ever counseled said to me at one point, "I wish I was no longer Indian." As I will discuss in this chapter, women of color do not just face quantitatively more issues when they suffer violence (e.g., less media attention,

language barriers, lack of support in the judicial system) but their experience is qualitatively different from that of white women.

Ann Stoler's analysis of racism sheds light on this relationship between sexual violence and colonialism. She argues that racism, far from being a reaction to crisis in which racial others are scapegoated for social ills, is a permanent part of the social fabric. "Racism is not an effect but a tactic in the internal fission of society into binary opposition, a means of creating 'biologized' internal enemies, against whom society must defend itself."[5] She notes that in the modern state, it is the constant purification and elimination of racialized enemies within the state that ensures the growth of the national body. "Racism does not merely arise in moments of crisis, in sporadic cleansings. It is internal to the biopolitical state, woven into the web of the social body, threaded through its fabric."[6]

Similarly, Kate Shanley notes that Native peoples are a permanent "present absence" in the U.S. colonial imagination, an "absence" that reinforces at every turn the conviction that Native peoples are indeed vanishing and that the conquest of Native lands is justified. Ella Shohat and Robert Stam describe this absence as,

> an ambivalently repressive mechanism [which] dispels the anxiety in the face of the Indian, whose very presence is a reminder of the initially precarious grounding of the American nation-state itself . . . In a temporal paradox, living Indians were induced to 'play dead,' as it were, in order to perform a narrative of manifest destiny in which their role, ultimately, was to disappear.[7]

This "absence" is effected through the metaphorical transformation of Native bodies into a pollution of which the colonial body must constantly purify itself. For instance, as white Californians described them in the 1860s, Native people were "the dirtiest lot of human beings on earth."[8] They wear "filthy rags, with their persons unwashed, hair uncombed and swarming with vermin."[9] The following 1885 Procter & Gamble ad for Ivory Soap also illustrates this equation between Indian bodies and dirt.

We were once factious, fierce and wild,
In peaceful arts unreconciled
Our blankets smeared with grease and stains
From buffalo meat and settlers' veins.
Through summer's dust and heat content
From moon to moon unwashed we went,
But IVORY SOAP came like a ray
Of light across our darkened way
And now we're civil, kind and good
And keep the laws as people should,
We wear our linen, lawn and lace
As well as folks with paler face
And now I take, where'er we go
This cake of IVORY SOAP to show
What civilized my squaw and me
And made us clean and fair to see.[10]

In the colonial imagination, Native bodies are also immanently polluted with sexual sin. Theorists Albert Cave, Robert Warrior, H. C. Porter, and others have demonstrated that Christian colonizers often likened Native peoples to the biblical Canaanites, both worthy of mass destruction.[11] What makes Canaanites supposedly worthy of destruction in the biblical narrative and Indian peoples supposedly worthy of destruction in the eyes of their colonizers is that they both personify sexual sin. In the Bible, Canaanites commit acts of sexual perversion in Sodom (Gen. 19:1–29), are the descendants of the unsavory relations between Lot and his daughters (Gen. 19:30–38), are the descendants of the sexually perverse Ham (Gen. 9:22–27), and prostitute themselves in service of their gods (Gen. 28:21–22, Deut. 28:18, 1 Kings 14:24, 2 Kings 23:7, Hosea 4:13, Amos 2:7).

Similarly, Native peoples, in the eyes of the colonizers, are marked by their sexual perversity. Alexander Whitaker, a minister in Virginia, wrote in 1613: "They live naked in bodie, as if their shame of their sinne deserved no covering: Their names are as naked as their bodie: They esteem it a virtue to lie, deceive and steale as their master the divell teacheth them."[12] Furthermore, according to Bernardino de Minaya, a Dominican cleric,

"Their marriages are not a sacrament but a sacrilege. They are idolatrous, libidinous, and commit sodomy. Their chief desire is to eat, drink, worship heathen idols, and commit bestial obscenities."[13]

Because Indian bodies are "dirty," they are considered sexually violable and "rapable," and the rape of bodies that are considered inherently impure or dirty simply does not count. For instance, prostitutes are almost never believed when they say they have been raped because the dominant society considers the bodies of sex workers undeserving of integrity and violable at all times. Similarly, the history of mutilation of Indian bodies, both living and dead, makes it clear that Indian people are not entitled to bodily integrity.

I saw the body of White Antelope with the privates cut off, and I heard a soldier say he was going to make a tobacco-pouch out of them.[14]

At night Dr. Rufus Choate [and] Lieutenant Wentz C. Miller . . . went up the ravine, decapitated the dead Qua-ha-das, and placing the heads in some gunny sacks, brought them back to be boiled out for future scientific knowledge.[15]

Each of the braves was shot down and scalped by the wild volunteers, who out with their knives and cutting two parallel gashes down their backs, would strip the skin from the quivering flesh to make razor straps of.[16]

Dr. Tuner, of Lexington, Iowa, visited this solitary grave [of Black Hawk] and robbed it of its tenant . . . and sent the body to Alton, Ill., where the skeleton was wired together. [It was later returned] but here it remained but a short time ere vandal hands again carried it away and placed it in the Burlington, Iowa Geographical and Historical Society, where it was consumed by fire in 1855.[17]

One more dexterous than the rest, proceeded to flay the chief's [Tecumseh's] body; then, cutting the skin in narrow strips . . . at once, a supply of razor-straps for the more "ferocious" of his brethren.[18]

Andrew Jackson . . . supervised the mutilation of 800 or so Creek Indian corpses—the bodies of men, women and children that he and his men massacred—cutting off their noses to count and preserve a record of the dead, slicing long strips of flesh from their bodies to tan and turn into bridle reins.[19]

A few nights after this, some soldiers dug Mangus' body out again and took his head and boiled it during the night, and prepared the skull to send to the museum in New York.[20]

In 1990, Illinois governor Jim Thompson echoed these sentiments when he refused to close down an open Indian burial mound in the town of Dixon. The State of Illinois had built a museum around this mound to publicly display Indian remains. Thompson argued that he was as much Indian as current Indians, and consequently, he had as much right as they to determine the fate of Indian remains.[21] The remains were "his." The Chicago press similarly attempted to challenge the identity of Indian people protesting his decision by asserting that they were either only "part" Indian, or merely claiming to be Indian.[22] In effect, the Illinois state government conveyed the message to Indians that being on constant display for white consumers, in life and in death, is acceptable. Furthermore, Indian identity itself is under the control of the colonizer, and subject to challenge or eradication at any time.

In 1992, Ontario finance minister Jim Flaherty argued that the Canadian government could boost health-care funding for "real people in real towns" by cutting the bureaucracy that serves *only* Native peoples.[23] The extent to which Native peoples are not seen as "real" people in the larger colonial discourse indicates the success of sexual violence, among other racist and colonialist forces, in destroying the perceived humanity of Native peoples. As Aime Cesaire puts it, colonization = thingification.[24] As Stoler explains this process of racialized colonization:

The more "degenerates" and "abnormals" [in this case Native peoples] are eliminated, the lives of those who speak will be stronger, more vigorous, and improved. The enemies are not political adversaries, but those identified as external and internal threats to the population. Racism is the condition that makes it acceptable to put [certain people] to death in a society of normalization.[25]

The project of colonial sexual violence establishes the ideology that Native bodies are inherently violable—and by extension, that Native lands are also inherently violable.

As a consequence of this colonization and abuse of their bodies, Indian people learn to internalize self-hatred, because body image is integrally related to self-esteem. When one's body is not respected, one begins to hate oneself.[26] Anne, a Native boarding school student, reflects on this process:

You better not touch yourself . . . If I looked at somebody . . . lust, sex, and I got scared of those sexual feelings. And I did not know how to handle them . . . What really confused me was if intercourse was sin, why are people born? . . . It took me a really long time to get over the fact that . . . I've sinned: I had a child.[27]

As her words indicate, when the bodies of Indian people are designated as inherently sinful and dirty, it becomes a sin just to be Indian. Native peoples internalize the genocidal project through self-destruction. As a rape crisis counselor, it was not a surprise to me that Indians who have survived sexual abuse would often say that they no longer wish to be Indian. Native peoples' individual experiences of sexual violation echo 500 years of sexual colonization in which Native peoples' bodies have been deemed-inherently impure. The Menominee poet Chrystos writes in such a voice in her poem "Old Indian Granny."

You told me about all the Indian women you counsel
who say they don't want to be Indian anymore
because a white man or an Indian one raped them
or killed their brother
or somebody tried to run them over in the street
or insulted them or all of it
our daily bread of hate
Sometimes I don't want to be an Indian either
but I've never said so out loud before . . .
Far more than being hungry
having no place to live or dance
no decent job no home to offer a Granny
It's knowing with each invisible breath
that if you don't make something pretty

they can hang on their walls or wear around
  their necks
you might as well be dead.[28]

Mending the Sacred Hoop Technical Assistance Project in Duluth, Minnesota, reports that a primary barrier antiviolence advocates face in addressing violence in Indian country is that community members will argue that sexual violence is "traditional." This phenomenon indicates the extent to which our communities have internalized self-hatred. Frantz Fanon argues, "In the colonial context, as we have already pointed out, the natives fight among themselves. They tend to use each other as a screen, and each hides from his neighbor the national enemy."[29] Then, as Michael Taussig notes, Native peoples are portrayed by the dominant culture as inherently violent, self-destructive, and dysfunctional.[30] For example, townsperson Mike Whelan made the following statement at a 1990 zoning hearing, calling for the denial of a permit for an Indian battered women's shelter in Lake Andes, South Dakota.

> Indian Culture as I view it, is presently so mongrelized as to be a mix of dependency on the Federal Government and a primitive society wholly on the outside of the mainstream of western civilization and thought. The Native American Culture as we know it now, not as it formerly existed, is a culture of hopelessness, godlessness, of joblessness, and lawlessness. . . . Alcoholism, social disease, child abuse, and poverty are the hallmarks of this so called culture that you seek to promote, and I would suggest to you that the brave men of the ghost dance would hang their heads in shame at what you now pass off as that culture. . . . I think that the Indian way of life as you call it, to me means cigarette burns in arms of children, double checking the locks on my cars, keeping a loaded shotgun by my door, and car bodies and beer cans on the front lawn. . . . This is not a matter of race, it is a matter of keeping our community and neighborhood away from that evil that you and your ideas promote.[31]

Similarly, in a recent case among the Aboriginal peoples of Australia, a judge ruled that a 50-year-old Aboriginal man's rape of a 15-year-old girl was not a serious crime, but an example of traditional culture. He ruled that the girl "knew what was expected of her" and "didn't need protection" when raped by a man who had been previously convicted of murdering his former wife. An "expert" anthropologist in the case testified that the rape was "traditional" and "morally correct."[32] According to Judy Atkinson, an Aboriginal professor, survivors have reported numerous incidents of law enforcement officials dismissing reports of violence because they consider such violence to be "cultural behavior." "We are living in a war zone in Aboriginal communities," states Atkinson. "Different behaviors come out of that," she says. "Yet the courts of law validate that behavior."[33]

Taussig comments on the irony of this logic: "Men are conquered not by invasion, but by themselves. It is a strange sentiment, is it not, when faced with so much brutal evidence of invasion."[34] But as Fanon notes, this destructive behavior is not "the consequence of the organization of his nervous system or of characterial originality, but the direct product of the colonial system."[35]

Tadiar's description of colonial relationships as an enactment of the "prevailing mode of heterosexual relations" is useful because it underscores the extent to which U.S. colonizers view the subjugation of women of the Native nations as critical to the success of the economic, cultural, and political colonization.[36] Stoler notes that the imperial discourses on sexuality "cast white women as the bearers of more racist imperial order."[37] By extension, Native women are bearers of a counter-imperial order and pose a supreme threat to the dominant culture. Symbolic and literal control over their bodies is important in the war against Native people, as these testimonies illustrate:

> When I was in the boat I captured a beautiful Carib woman . . . . I conceived desire to take pleasure. . . . I took a rope and thrashed her well, for which she raised such unheard screams that you would not have believed your ears. Finally we came to an agreement in such a manner that I can tell you that she seemed to have been brought up in a school of harlots.[38]

Two of the best looking of the squaws were lying in such a position, and from the appearance of the genital organs and of their wounds, there can be no doubt that they were first ravished and then shot dead. Nearly all of the dead were mutilated.[39]

One woman, big with child, rushed into the church, clasping the altar and crying for mercy for herself and unborn babe. She was followed, and fell pierced with a dozen lances. . . . The child was torn alive from the yet palpitating body of its mother, first plunged into the holy water to be baptized, and immediately its brains were dashed out against a wall.[40]

The Christians attacked them with buffets and beatings . . . Then they behaved with such temerity and shamelessness that the most powerful ruler of the island had to see his own wife raped by a Christian officer.[41]

I heard one man say that he had cut a woman's private parts out, and had them for exhibition on a stick. I heard another man say that he had cut the fingers off of an Indian, to get the rings off his hand. I also heard of numerous instances in which men had cut out the private parts of females, and stretched them over their saddle-bows and some of them over their hats.[42]

The history of sexual violence and genocide among Native women illustrates how gender violence functions as a tool for racism and colonialism among women of color in general. For example, African American women were also viewed as inherently rapable. Yet where colonizers used sexual violence to eliminate Native populations, slave owners used rape to reproduce an exploitable labor force. (The children of Black slave women inherited their slave status.) And because Black women were seen as the property of their slave owners, their rape at the hands of these men did not "count." As one southern politician declared in the early twentieth century, there was no such thing as a "virtuous colored girl" over the age of 14.[43] The testimonies from slave narratives and other sources reveal the systematic abuse of slave women by white slave owners.

For a period of four months, including the latter stages of pregnancy, delivery, and recent recovery therefrom . . . he beat her with clubs, iron chains and other deadly weapons time after time; burnt her; inflicted stripes over and often with scourges, which literally excoriated her whole body; forced her to work in inclement seasons, without being duty clad; provided for her insufficient food, exacted labor beyond her strength, and wantonly beat her because she could not comply with his requisitions. These enormities, besides others, too disgusting, particularly designated, the prisoner, without his heart once relenting, practiced . . . even up to the last hours of the victim's existence.

[A report of a North Carolina slaveowner's abuse and eventual murder of a slave woman.][44]

[My master] was a good man but he was pretty bad among the women. Married or not married, made no difference to him. Whoever he wanted among the slaves, he went and got her or had her meet him somewhere out in the bushes. I have known him to go to the shack and make the woman's husband sit outside while he went into his wife. . . . He wasn't no worse than none of the rest. They all used their women like they wanted to, and there wasn't nobody to say anything about it. Neither the woman nor the men could help themselves. They submitted to it but kept praying to God.

[Slave testimony from South Carolina.][45]

"Some of the troops," a white complained to their commander Rufus Saxton, "have forcibly entered the negro houses and after driving out the men (in one instance at the point of a bayonet) have attempted to ravish women." When the men protested and sought to protect "their wives and sisters," they "were cruelly beaten and threatened with instant death." "The morals of the old plantation" Saxton feared, "seem revived in the army of occupation."

[A report of the activities of Union soldiers during the Civil War.][46]

Immigrant women as well have endured a long history of sexual exploitation in the U.S. For instance, racially discriminatory employment laws forced thousands of Chinese immigrant women into prostitution. To supplement their meager incomes, impoverished Chinese families often sold their daughters into prostitution. Other women were lured to the U.S. with the promise of a stable marriage or job, only to find themselves trapped in the sex trade. By 1860, almost a quarter of the

Chinese in San Francisco (all female) were employed in prostitution.[47]

Karen Warren argues that patriarchal society is a dysfunctional system that mirrors the dysfunctional nuclear family. That is, severe abuse in the family continues because the family members learn to regard it as "normal." A victim of abuse may come to see that her abuse is not "normal" when she has contact with less abusive families. Similarly, Warren argues, patriarchal society is a dysfunctional system based on domination and violence. "Dysfunctional systems are often maintained through systematic denial, a failure or inability to see the reality of a situation. This denial need not be conscious, intentional, or malicious; it only needs to be pervasive to be effective."[48]

At the time of Columbus's exploits, European society was a dysfunctional system, racked by mass poverty, disease, religious oppression, war, and institutionalized violence. For example, in the Inquisition, hundreds of thousands of Jewish people were slaughtered and their confiscated property was used to fund Columbus's voyages. David Stannard writes,

> Violence, of course, was everywhere. . . . In Milan in 1476 a man was torn to pieces by an enraged mob and his dismembered limbs were eaten by his tormenters. In Paris and Lyon, Huguenots were killed and butchered, and their various body parts were sold openly in the streets. Other eruptions of bizarre torture, murder, and ritual cannibalism were not uncommon.[49]

Furthermore, European societies were thoroughly misogynistic. The Christian patriarchy which structured European society was inherently violent, as has been thoroughly documented.[50] For example, because English women were not allowed to express political opinions, a woman who spoke out against taxation in 1664 was condemned to having her tongue nailed to a tree near a highway, with a paper fastened to her back detailing her offense.[51] Hatred for women was most fully manifested in the witch hunts. In some English towns, as many as a third of the population were accused of witchcraft.[52] The

women targeted for destruction were those most independent from patriarchal authority: single women, widows, and healers.[53]

The more peaceful and egalitarian nature of Native societies did not escape the notice of the colonizers. In the "colonial" period, it was a scandal in the colonies that a number of white people chose to live among Indian people while virtually no Indians voluntarily chose to live among the colonists. According to J. Hector St. John de Crevecoeur, the eighteenth-century author of *Letters from an American Farmer,* "Thousands of Europeans are Indians, and we have no example of even one of these Aborigines having from choice become Europeans!"[54] Colonists also noted that Native peoples rarely committed sexual violence against white prisoners, unlike the colonists. Brigadier General James Clinton of the Continental Army said to his soldiers as they were sent off to destroy the Iroquois nation in 1779: "Bad as the savages are, they never violate the chastity of any women, their prisoners."[55] William Apess, a nineteenth century Pequot, asked, "Where, in the records of Indian barbarity, can we point to a violated female?"[56] Shohat and Stam argue, the real purpose behind colonial terror "was not to force the indigenes to become Europeans, but to keep Europeans from becoming indigenes."[57]

In contrast to the deeply patriarchal nature of European societies, prior to colonization, Indian societies for the most part were not male dominated. Women served as spiritual, political, and military leaders, and many societies were matrilineal. Although there existed a division of labor between women and men, women's labor and men's labor were accorded similar status.[58] As women and men lived in balance, Native societies were consequently much less authoritarian than their European counterparts. Paul LeJeune, a Jesuit priest, remarked in the seventeenth century:

> [Native peoples] imagine that they ought by right of birth, to enjoy the liberty of wild ass colts, rendering no homage to anyone whomsoever, except when they like . . . All the authority of their chief is in his tongue's end, for he is powerful insofar as he

is eloquent; and even if he kills himself talking and haranguing he will not be obeyed unless he pleases the savages.[59]

Furthermore, 70 percent of tribes did not practice war at all.[60] For those that did engage in war, the intent was generally not to annihilate the enemy, but to accrue honor through bravery. One accrued more honor by getting close enough to an enemy to touch him and leaving him alive than by killing him. Tom Holm writes:

> Traditional Indian warfare had much more in common with Euroamerican contact sports, like football, boxing, and hockey, than with wars fought in the European manner. This, of course, is not to say that nobody was ever killed . . . They were—just as they are in modern contact sports—but the point of the exercise was not as a rule purposefully lethal.[61]

Of course, in discussing these trends, it is important not to overgeneralize or give the impression that Native communities were utopian prior to colonization. Certainly gender violence occurred prior to colonization. Nevertheless, both oral and written records often note its relative rarity as well as the severity of the punishment for perpetrators of violence. This record of punishment for sexual assault among the Kiowa serves as an illustration:

> The Kiowas inflicted such embarrassment and ridicule on a criminal that he reportedly soon died. The man was a chronic rapist who was finally taught the error of his ways by the women; they laid an ambush and baited the trap with a beautiful young girl. When he took the bait, they suddenly appeared and overpowered him. As others held him helpless on the ground, each woman in turn raised her skirts and sat on his face. The experience was not in itself fatal, but the loss of status stemming from the derision it inspired was. The possibility of such drastic punishment was perhaps more chastening in its effect than the threat of the electric chair in more sophisticated societies.[62]

Similar practices existed among the Anishinabe:

> Wife battering, as we have seen, was neither accepted nor tolerated among the Anishinabe people until after the freedom to live Ojibwe was subdued.

Wife battering emerged simultaneously with the disintegration of Ojibwe ways of life and the beginning use of alcohol. The behavior of the Ojibwe people under the influence of alcohol is often totally contrary to Anishinabe values. It is especially contrary to the self discipline previously necessary to the development of Ojibwe character.

There is no single philosophy among the people in today's society regarding the social illness of wife battering. Many have forgotten or did not receive the teachings of the social laws surrounding it. In the old Ojibwe society, society itself was responsible for what took place within it; today that is not so. What is the evidence of that statement? The harmful, destructive, traumatic cycle of domestic violence that is befalling the Anishinabe Children of the Nation.

Today we have lost a lot of the traditions, values, ways of life, laws, language, teachings of the Elders, respect, humility as Anishinabe people because of the European mentality we have accepted. For the Anishinabe people to survive as a Nation, together we must turn back the pages of time. We must face reality, do an evaluation of ourselves as a people—why we were created to live in harmony with one another as Anishinabe people and to live in harmony with the Creator's creation.[63]

European women were often surprised to find that, even in war, they went unmolested by their Indian captors. Mary Rowlandson said of her experience: "I have been in the midst of roaring Lions, and Savage Bears, that feared neither God, nor Man, nor the Devil . . . and yet not one of them ever offered the least abuse of unchastity to me in word or action."[64] Between 1675 and 1763, almost 40 percent of women who were taken captive by Native people in New England chose to remain with their captors.[65] In 1899, an editorial signed by Mrs. Teall appeared in the *Syracuse Herald-Journal,* discussing the status of women in Iroquois society.

> They had one custom the white men are not ready, even yet, to accept. The women of the Iroquois had a public and influential position. They had a council of their own . . . which had the initiative in the discussion; subjects presented by them being settled in the councils of the chiefs and elders; in this

latter council the women had an orator of their own (often of their own sex) to present and speak for them. There are sometimes female chiefs . . . The wife owned all the property . . . The family was hers; descent was counted through the mother.[66]

In response to her editorial, a man who signed himself as "Student" replied:

> Women among the Iroquois, Mrs. Teall says . . . had a council of their own, and orators and chiefs. Why does she not add what follows in explanation of why such deference was paid to women, that "in the torture of prisoners women were thought more skillful and subtle than the men" and the men of the inquisition were outdone in the refinement of cruelty practiced upon their victims by these savages. It is true also that succession was through women, not the men, in Iroquois tribes, but the explanation is that it was generally a difficult guess to tell the fatherhood of children . . . The Indian maiden never learned to blush. The Indians, about whom so much rhetoric has been wasted, were a savage, merciless lot who would never have developed themselves nearer to civilization than they were found by missionaries and traders. . . . Their love was to butcher and burn, to roast their victims and eat them, to lie and rob, to live in filth, men, women, children, dogs and fleas crowded together.[67]

Thus, the demonization of Native women can be seen as a strategy of white men to maintain control over white women. This demonization was exemplified by the captivity narratives which became a popular genre in the U.S.[68] These narratives were supposedly first-person narratives of white women who were abducted by "savages" and forced to undergo untold savagery. Their tales, however, were usually written by white men who had their own agenda. For instance, in 1823 James Seaver of New York interviewed Mary Jemison, who was taken as captive by the Seneca. Jemison chose to remain among them when she was offered her freedom, but Seaver is convinced that she is protecting the Indian people by not describing their full savagery. "The vices of the Indians, she appeared disposed not to aggravate, and seemed to take pride in extolling their virtues. A kind of family pride induced her to withhold whatever would blot the character of her descendants, and perhaps induced her to keep back many things that would have been interesting."[69] Consequently, he supplements her narrative with material "from authentic sources" and Jemison's cousin, George.[70] Seaver, nevertheless, attributes these supplements to her voice in this supposed first-person narrative.

In these narratives, we can find what Carol Adams terms an "absent referent." Adams provides an example by noting how the term "battered woman" makes women the inherent victims of battering. The batterer is rendered invisible and is thus the absent referent.[71] Another example of an absent referent can be found in the Christian symbol of the crucifixion, in which Jesus is represented as one whose inherent nature and purpose is to be crucified. The individuals who put him on the cross, never depicted in representations of the cross, are erased as the perpetrators and they become the absent referent.

Andrea Dworkin argues that in a patriarchal system, "men are distinguished from women by their commitment to do violence rather than to be victimized by it. In adoring violence—from the crucifixion of Christ to the cinematic portrayal of General Patton—men seek to adore themselves."[72] June Namias argues that the point of these depictions is to instill the belief in white women that they need white men to protect them from savages.[73] Jane Caputi also suggests that in depictions of killings of women, the killer plays the alter ego to the male reader or viewer of the killing. "This convention allows the identifying viewer to gratifyingly fantasize himself in the two mutually reinforcing male roles at once. He is both . . . the protector and the menace."[74] According to Jane McCrea, the white man both symbolically kills the white woman through the Indians, which mirror his desires, and rushes to her rescue. The white male is absent when the violence occurs. Yet, he is the one who has created the image in which the white man is the absent referent. He glorifies his ability to brutalize white women through the Indian savage while denying his culpability.

Meanwhile, Native women are completely absent from this picture, and consequently, their actual sexual brutalization at the hands of white men escapes notice. The white man *literally* brutalizes her, while *symbolically* brutalizing the white woman through this representational practice. Native men are scapegoated for his actions so white women will see them as the enemy, while white men remain unaccountable.

Paula Gunn Allen argues that colonizers realized that in order to subjugate indigenous nations they would have to subjugate women within these nations. Native peoples needed to learn the value of hierarchy, the role of physical abuse in maintaining that hierarchy, and the importance of women remaining submissive to their men. They had to convince "both men and women that a woman's proper place was under the authority of her husband and that a man's proper place was under the authority of the priests."[75] She further argues:

> It was to the advantage of white men to mislead white women, and themselves, into believing that their treatment of women was superior to the treatment by the men of the group which they considered savage. Had white women discovered that all women were not mistreated, they might have been intolerant of their men's abusiveness.[76]

Thus in order to colonize a people whose society was not hierarchical, colonizers must first naturalize hierarchy through instituting patriarchy. Patriarchal gender violence is the process by which colonizers inscribe hierarchy and domination on the bodies of the colonized. Ironically, while enslaving women's bodies, colonizers argued that they were actually somehow freeing Native women from the "oppression" they supposedly faced in Native nations. Thomas Jefferson argued that Native women "are submitted to unjust drudgery. This I believe is the case with every barbarous people. It is civilization alone which replaces women in the enjoyment of their equality."[77] The *Mariposa Gazette* similarly noted that when Indian women were safely under the control of white men, they

are "neat, and tidy, and industrious, and soon learn to discharge domestic duties properly and creditably." In 1862, a Native man in Conrow Valley was killed and scalped with his head twisted off, his killers saying, "You will not kill any more women and children."[78] Apparently, Native women can only be free while under the dominion of white men, and both Native and white women have to be protected from Indian men, rather than from white men.

A 1985 Virginia Slims ad reflected a similar notion that white patriarchy saves Native women from oppression. On the left side of the ad was a totem pole of cartoonish figures of Indian women. Their names: Princess Wash and Scrub, Little Running Water Fetcher, Keeper of the Teepee, Princess Breakfast, Lunch and Dinner Preparer, Woman Who Gathers Firewood, Princess Buffalo Robe Sewer, Little Woman Who Weaves All Day, and Woman Who Plucks Feathers for Chief's Headdress. The caption on top of the totem pole reads: "Virginia Slims remembers one of many societies where the women stood head and shoulders above the men." On the right side of the ad is a model adorned with makeup and dressed in a tight skirt, nylons, and high heels, with the familiar caption: "You've come a long way, baby." The message is that Native women, oppressed in their tribal societies, need to be liberated into a patriarchal standard of beauty, where their true freedom lies. The historical record suggests, as Paula Gunn Allen argues, that the real roots of feminism should be found in Native societies. But in this Virginia Slims ad, feminism is tied to colonial conquest—(white) women's liberation is founded upon the destruction of supposedly patriarchal Native societies.

Today we see this discourse utilized in the "war on terror." To justify the bombing of Afghanistan, Laura Bush declared, "The fight against terrorism is also a fight for the rights and dignity of women."[79] These sentiments were shared by mainstream feminists. Eleanor Smeal, former president of the National Organization for Women (NOW) and founder and president of the Fund for a Feminist Majority said, "Without

9/11, we could not get the Afghanistan tragedy in focus enough for the world powers to stop the Taliban's atrocities or to remove the Taliban. Tragically, it took a disaster for them to act definitively enough."[80]

It seems the best way to liberate women is to bomb them. Meanwhile, the Revolutionary Association of Women of Afghanistan (RAWA), whose members were the very women who were to be liberated by this war, denounced it as an imperial venture.

> RAWA has in the past repeatedly warned that the U.S. government is no friend of the people of Afghanistan, primarily because during the past two decades she did not spare any effort or expense in training and arming the most sordid, the most treacherous, the most misogynic and anti-democratic indigenous Islamic fundamentalist gangs and innumerable crazed Arab fanatics in Afghanistan and in unleashing them upon our people. After the retreat of the Russian aggressors and the collapse of Najib's puppet regime in Afghanistan these fundamentalist entities became all the more wildly unbridled. They officially and wholeheartedly accepted the yoke of servitude to the interests of foreign governments, in which capacity they have perpetrated such crimes and atrocities against the people of Afghanistan that no parallel can be found in the history of any land on earth.
>
> RAWA roundly condemns the U.S. air strikes against Afghanistan because the impoverished masses of Afghanistan—already trapped in the dog-fighting between the US's Taliban and Jihadi flunkeys—are the ones who are most hurt in the attacks, and also because the US, like the arrogant superpower she is, has violated the sovereignty of the Afghan people and the territorial integrity of the Afghan homeland.
>
> The US is against fundamentalist terrorism to the extent and until such time as her proper interests are jeopardised; otherwise she is all too happy to be a friend and sponsor of any fundamentalist-terrorist criminal entity. If the US does not want her ridiculous bigotry to show and really wants to eliminate fundamentalist terrorism, she should draw lessons from her own past myopic policies and realise that the sources of fundamentalist terrorism are America's support to the most reactionary regimes

in Arab and non-Arab countries and her military and financial largesse to Afghan fundamentalist criminals. Terrorism will be uprooted only when these two sources are dried up.[81]

So why does a group like the Fund for a Feminist Majority ignore the voice of RAWA? Again, even within feminist circles, the colonial logic prevails that women of color, indigenous women, and women from Global South countries are only victims of oppression rather than organizers in their own right.

The "assimilation" into white society, however, only increased Native women's vulnerability to violence. For instance, when the Cherokee nation was forcibly relocated to Oklahoma during the Trail of Tears in the nineteenth century, soldiers targeted for sexual violence Cherokee women who spoke English and had attended mission schools instead of those who had not taken part in these assimilation efforts. They were routinely gang-raped, causing one missionary to the Cherokee, Daniel Butrick, to regret that any Cherokee had ever been taught English.[82] Homi Bhabha and Edward Said argue that part of the colonization process involves partially assimilating the colonized in order to establish colonial rule.[83] That is, if the colonized group seems completely different from the colonists, they implicitly challenge the supremacy of colonial rule because they are refusing to adapt the ways of the colonizers. Hence, the colonized must seem to partially resemble the colonists in order to reinforce the dominant ideology, and establish that the way colonizers live is the only good way to live. However, the colonized group can never be completely assimilated—otherwise, they would be equal to the colonists, and there would be no reason to colonize them. If we use Bhabha's and Said's analysis, we can see that while Cherokee women were promised that assimilation would provide them with the benefits of the dominant society, in fact assimilation efforts made them more easily subjugated by colonial rule.

Historically, white colonizers who raped Indian women claimed that the real rapists were Indian men.[84] Today, white men who rape and murder

Indian women often make this same claim. In the late 1980s, a white man, Jesse Coulter, raped, murdered, and mutilated several Indian women in Minneapolis. He claimed to be Indian, adopting the name Jesse Sittingcrow, and emblazoning an AIM tattoo on his arm.[85]

Roy Martin, a full-blooded Native man, was charged with sexual assault in Bemidji, Minnesota. The survivor identified the rapist as white, about 25 years old, with a shag haircut. Martin was 35 with hair past his shoulders.[86] In a search of major newspaper coverage of sexual assaults in Native communities from 1998 to 2004, I found coverage almost entirely limited to cases where Native man (or a white man who purports to be Native) was the suspected perpetrator and the victim was a white woman; there was virtually no coverage of Native women as victims of sexual assault. This absence is even more startling when one considers that Native women are more likely man other groups of women in the U.S. to be sexual assault victims.[87]

Similarly, after the Civil War, Black men in the U.S. were targeted for lynching for their supposed mass rapes of white women. The racist belief was that white women needed to be protected from predatory Black men, when in fact, Black women needed protection from white men. In her investigations of lynches that occurred between 1865 and 1895, anti-lynching crusader Ida B. Wells calculated that more than 10,000 Black people had been lynched. During that same period, not one white person was lynched for raping or killing a Black person.[88] In addition, while the ostensible reason for these lynches was to protect white women from Black rapists, Wells discovered that only a third of those lynched had even been accused of rape. And most of the Black men accused of rape had been involved in obviously consensual sexual relationships with white women.[89]

Of course, Indian men do commit acts of sexual violence. After years of colonialism and boarding school experience, violence has been internalized within Indian communities. However,

this view of the Indian man as the "true" rapist serves to obscure who has the real power in this racist and patriarchal society. Thus, the colonization of Native women (as well as other women of color) is part of the project of strengthening white male ownership of white women.

And while the era of Indian massacres in their more explicit form has ended in North America, the wholesale rape and mutilation of indigenous women's bodies continues. During the 1982 massacre of Mayan people in the Aldea Rio Negro (Guatemala), 177 women and children were killed. The young women were raped in front of their mothers, and the mothers were killed in front of their children. The younger children were then tied at the ankles and dashed against the rocks until their skulls were broken. This massacre, committed by the Guatemalan army, was funded by the U.S. government.[90]

In a 1997 massacre in Chiapas, Mexico, indigenous women were targeted by paramilitary forces for sexual mutilation, gang rape, and torture. Amnesty International reports that torture against indigenous peoples in Latin America is routine, including electric shocks, semi-asphyxiation with plastic bags or by submersion under water, death threats, mock executions, beatings using sharp objects, sticks, or rifle butts, rape, and sexual abuse.[91]

One wonders why the mass rapes in Guatemala, Chiapas, or elsewhere against indigenous people in Latin America does not spark the same outrage as the rapes in Bosnia in the 1990s. In fact, feminist legal scholar Catherine MacKinnon argues that in Bosnia, "The world has *never* seen sex used this consciously, this cynically, this elaborately, this openly, this systematically . . . as a means of destroying a whole people [emphasis mine]."[92] Here, MacKinnon seems to have forgotten that she lives on this land because millions of Native peoples were raped, sexually mutilated, and murdered. Is mass rape against European women genocide, while mass rape against indigenous women is business as usual?

The historical context of rape, racism, and colonialism continues to impact women in North America as well. This legacy is most evident in the rate of violence in American Indian communities—American Indian women are twice as likely to be victimized by violent crime as women or men of any other ethnic group. In addition, 60 percent of the perpetrators of violence against American Indian women are white.[93]

In times of crisis, sexual violence against Native women escalates. When I served as a nonviolent witness for the Chippewa spearfishers who were being harassed by white racist mobs in the 1980s, one white harasser carried a sign that read, "Save a fish; spear a pregnant squaw." During the 1990 Mohawk crisis in Quebec, Canada, a white mob surrounded an ambulance carrying a Native woman who was attempting to leave the Mohawk reservation because she was hemorrhaging after giving birth. She was forced to "spread her legs" to prove she had delivered a baby. The police at the scene refused to intervene. An Indian man was arrested for "wearing a disguise" (he was wearing jeans), and was brutally beaten at the scene, with his testicles crushed. Two women from Chicago Women of All Red Nations (WARN) went to Oka to videotape the crisis. They were arrested and held in custody for 11 hours without being charged, and were told that they could not go to the bathroom unless the male police officers could watch. The place they were held was covered with pornographic magazines.

This colonial desire to subjugate Indian women's bodies was quite apparent when, in 1982, Stuart Kasten marketed "Custer's Revenge," a videogame in which players got points each time they, in the form of Custer, raped an Indian woman. The slogan of the game is "When you score, you score." He describes the game as "a fun sequence where the woman is enjoying a sexual act willingly." According to the promotional material:

> You are General Custer. Your dander's up, your pistol's wavin'. You've hog-tied a ravishing Indian maiden and have a chance to rewrite history and even up an old score. Now, the Indian maiden's hands may be tied, but she's not about to take it lying down, by George! Help is on the way. If you're to get revenge you'll have to rise to the challenge, dodge a tribe of flying arrows and protect your flanks against some downright mean and prickly cactus. But if you can stand pat and last past the strings and arrows—You can stand last. Remember? Revenge is sweet.[94]

Sexual violence as a tool of racism also continues against other women of color. Trafficking in women from Asian and other Global South countries continues unabated in the U.S. According to the Central Intelligence Agency, 45,000 to 50,000 women are trafficked in the U.S. each year.[95] In addition, there are over 50,000 Filipina mail-order brides in the U.S. alone.[96] White men, desiring women they presume to be submissive, procure mail-order brides who, because of their precarious legal status, are vulnerable to domestic and sexual violence. As the promotional material for mail-order brides describes them, Filipinas have "exceptionally smooth skin and tight vaginas . . . [they are] low maintenance wives. [They] can always be returned and replaced by a younger model."[97]

Women of color are also targeted for sexual violence crossing the U.S. border. Blacks and Latinos comprise 43 percent of those searched through customs even though they comprise 24 percent of the population. The American Friends Service Committee documented over 346 reports of gender violence on the U.S.-Mexico border from 1993–1995 (and this is just the report of one agency, which does not account for the women who either do not report or report to another agency). This one case is emblematic of the kinds of abuse women face at the border: A Border Patrol agent, Larry Selders, raped several women over a period of time. Finally one of the rape victims in Nogales, Arizona had to sue the United States government for not taking action to investigate her rape. Selders demanded sex from the woman in return for her release. When she refused, Selders drove her out of town to an isolated area, raped her and threatened her not to say anything to anyone. Her defense describes in great detail the horrible trauma that she continued to suffer after the incident. Although the rape took place in 1993, it was only in October 1999 that the court finally arrived at a decision in favor of the victims. "The government guarded information about Selders' prior acts. It took more than three years of legal battles to uncover that at least three other victims were known to the government," declared the victim's attorney, Jesus Romo.[98]

SEXUAL VIOLENCE AND IMPUNITY

The ideology of Native women's bodies as rapable is evident in the hundreds of missing indigenous women in Mexico and Canada. Since 1993, over 500 women have been murdered in Juarez, Mexico. The majority have been sexually mutilated, raped, and tortured, including having had their nipples cut off. Poor and indigenous women have been particularly targeted. Not only have the local police made no effort to solve the cases, they appear to be complicit in the murders. Amnesty International and other human rights organizations and activists have noted their failure to seriously investigate the cases—the police have made several arrests and tortured those arrested to extract confessions, but the murders have continued unabated. Furthermore, the general response of the police to these murders is to blame the victims by arguing that they are sex workers or lesbians, and hence, inherently rapable.[99] For instance, one former state public prosecutor commented in 1999, "It's hard to go out on the street when it's raining and not get wet."[100]

Similarly, in Canada, over 500 First Nations women have gone missing or have been murdered in the past 15 years, with little police investigation. Again, it seems that their cases have been neglected because many of the women were homeless or sex workers. Ada Elaine Brown, the sister of Terri Brown, president of the Native Women's Association of Canada, was found dead in her bed in 2002. She was so badly beaten her family did

not recognize her. According to Terri Brown: "The autopsy report said it was a brain aneurysm. Yeah, because she was beaten to a pulp."[101]

Within the United States, because of complex jurisdictional issues, perpetrators of sexual violence can usually commit crimes against Native women with impunity. A review of U.S. criminal justice policy in Indian country helps to clarify the current situation. In *Ex Parte Crow Dog* (1883), the Supreme Court recognized the authority of Indian tribes over criminal jurisdiction on Indian lands. In response, the U.S. passed the Major Crimes Act (1885), which mandated that certain "major crimes" committed in Indian country must be adjudicated through the federal justice system. In 1883, the Bureau of Indian Affairs (BIA) created the Court of Indian Offenses, which appointed tribal officials to impose penalties based on Anglo-American standards of law. These courts were charged with enforcing the Code of Federal Regulations (CFR), the compilation of regulations issued by federal administrative agencies, which generally stressed laws intended to assimilate Native peoples, such as laws which prohibited the practice of Indian religions.

The 1950's ushered in what is called the "termination period" in U.S. Indian policy. The government began a policy of terminating tribal status for many Indian tribes and funded relocation programs to encourage Indian peoples to relocate to urban areas and assimilate into the dominant society. During this period, the U.S. government sharply defunded the justice systems in Indian country, leaving many tribes, who did not have their traditional systems intact, with no law enforcement at all.

After obliterating tribal justice systems, the U.S. government passed Public Law 280 (PL 280) in 1953, granting states criminal and limited civil jurisdiction over tribes covered in the Major Crimes Act, without tribal consent. PL 280 is a major infringement on Native sovereignty, since tribes have generally not come under state jurisdiction. That is, while the U.S. government policy has deemed tribes under the guardianship of the federal government, tribes are supposed to be recognized as sovereign to some degree and not under state government jurisdiction.

In 1968, the U.S. made provisions for tribes to retrocede from PL 280—however, retrocession can only be undertaken with the permission of the state. However, later court decisions have found that PL 280 provides for concurrent state jurisdict ion rather than state jurisdiction which supersedes tribal jurisdiction altogether. That is, while the state has the right to prosecute cases in PL 280 tribes, those tribes can prosecute the cases at the same time through tribal courts, if they have them.

However, with the advent of what is known as the period of "self-determination" in U.S. Indian policy beginning in 1968, many tribes, particularly non-PL 280 tribes, began to develop their own tribal governance. As a result, more than 140 tribes have their own court systems today. Of these, about 25 have retained CFR systems with BIA-appointed judges and others have their own tribal courts. Some tribes, operating under the radar of U.S. government surveillance, have never lost their traditional forms of governance and continue to practice them today.

But because rape falls under the Major Crimes Act, tribes are generally reliant upon the federal governments to prosecute sexual assault cases. Department of Justice representatives have informally reported that U.S. attorneys decline to prosecute about 75 percent of all cases involving any crime in Indian country. U.S. attorneys are particularly reluctant to prosecute rape cases; indeed, the Department of Justice reported in 1997 that only two U.S. attorneys regularly prosecute rape cases in Indian country.[102]

Because sexual assault is covered under the Major Crimes Act, many tribes have not developed codes to address the problem in those rape cases the federal government declines to prosecute. Those with codes are often hindered in their ability to investigate by a wait that may last more than a year before federal investigators

formally turn over cases. In addition, the Indian Civil Rights Act (ICRA) of 1968 limits the punishment tribal justice systems can enforce on perpetrators.[103] For instance, the maximum time someone may be sentenced to prison through tribal courts is one year.[104] Also, Native activist Sarah Deer (Muscogee) notes that the U.S. can prohibit remedies that do not follow the same penalties of the dominant system. Thus, sentencing someone to banishment or to another traditional form of punishment can be deemed a violation of ICRA.[105] In addition, U.S. courts have conflicting rulings on whether the Major Crimes Act even allows tribes to maintain concurrent jurisdiction over certain crimes, including sexual assault.[106]

To further complicate matters, tribes covered under PL 280, which gives states criminal jurisdiction, must work with state and county law enforcement officials who may have hostile relationships with the tribe. And because tribes are often geographically isolated—reservations are sometimes over 100 miles from the closest law enforcement agency, with many homes having no phone—local officials are unable to respond to an emergency situation. Racism on the part of local police officers in surrounding border towns also contributes to a lack of responsiveness in addressing rape cases. And since the federal government does not compensate state governments for law enforcement on reservations, and tribes generally do not pay local or federal taxes, states have little vested interest in providing "protection" for Indian tribes.

Finally, American Indian tribes do not have the right to prosecute non-Indians for crimes that occur on reservations. In *Oliphant v. Suquamish Indian Tribe* (1978), the Supreme Court held that Native American tribes do not have criminal jurisdiction over non-Native peoples on reservation lands. This precedent is particularly problematic for non-PL 280 tribes, because tribal police cannot arrest non-Indians who commit offenses. Furthermore, state law enforcement does not have jurisdiction on reservation lands.

So, unless state law enforcement is cross-deputized with tribal law enforcement, *no one* can arrest non-Native perpetrators of crimes on Native land.[107]

In response to these deplorable conditions, many Native peoples are calling for increased funding for criminal justice enforcement in tribal communities. It is undeniable that U.S. policy has codified the "rapability" of Native women. Indeed, the U.S. and other colonizing countries are engaged in a "permanent social war" against the bodies of women of color and indigenous women, which threaten their legitimacy.[108] Colonizers evidently recognize the wisdom of the Cheyenne saying "A nation is not conquered until the hearts of the women are on the ground."

NOTES

1. Susan Brownmiller, *Against Our Will* (Toronto: Bantam Books, 1986).
2. Kimberlé Crenshaw, "The Intersection of Race and Gender," in *Critical Race Theory,* ed. Kimberle Crenshaw, et. al. (New York: New Press, 1996).
3. Neferti Tadiar, "Sexual Economies of the Asia-Pacific," in *What's in a Rim? Critical Perspectives on the Pacific Region Idea,* ed. Arif Dirlik (Boulder: Westview Press, 1993).
4. Ibid.
5. Ann Stoler, *Race and the Education of Desire* (Chapel Hill: Duke University Press, 1997).
6. Ibid.
7. Ella Shohat and Robert Stam, *Unthinking Eurocentrism* (London: Routledge, 1994).
8. James Rawls, *Indians of California: The Changing Image* (Norman: University of Oklahoma, 1997).
9. Ibid.
10. Andre Lopez, *Pagans in Our Midst* (Mohawk Nation: Awkesasne Notes, n.d.).
11. Albert Cave, "Canaanites in a Promised Land," *American Indian Quarterly,* (Fall 1988); H.C. Porter, *The Inconstant Savage* (London: Gerald Duckworth & Co., 1979); Robert Warrior, "Canaanites, Cowboys, and Indians," in *Voices from the Margin,* ed. R.S. Sugirtharajah (Maryknoll: Orbis, 1991).
12. Robert Berkhofer, *The White Man's Indian* (New York: Vintage, 1978).
13. David Stannard, *American Holocaust* (Oxford: Oxford University Press, 1992).
14. David Wrone and Russell Nelson, eds., *Who's the Savage?* (Malabar: Robert Krieger Publishing, 1982).
15. Ibid.
16. Ibid.
17. Ibid.
18. Ibid.
19. Stannard, *American Holocaust.*
20. Wrone and Nelson, *Who's the Savage?*
21. Press conference, Chicago, Illinois, August 17, 1990.
22. Andrea Hermann and Maureen O'Donnell, "Indians Rap Thompson over Burial Site Display," *Chicago Sun Times,* August 17, 1990. As a result of the organizing efforts of Native people in Illinois, the site was eventually closed, but the remains were not reburied when the next governor took office.
23. Terry Pedwell, "Flaherty Slammed by Opposition over Native Health-Care Comments" (Canadian Press, January 21, 2002; available from http://www.bluecorncomics.com/stype215.htm.)
24. Aime Cesaire, *Discourse on Colonialism* (New York: Monthly Review Press, 1972).
25. Stoler, *Race and the Education of Desire.*
26. Ellen Bass and Laura Davis, *Courage to Heal* (Harper & Row: New York, 1988).
27. Celia Haig-Brown, *Resistance and Renewal* (Vancouver: Tilacrum, 1988).
28. Chrystos, *Fugitive Colors* (Vancouver: Press Gang, 1995).
29. Frantz Fanon, *Wretched of the Earth* (New York: Grove Press, 1963).
30. Michael Taussig, *Shamanism, Colonialism and the Wild Man* (Chicago: University of Chicago Press, 1991).
31. Native American Women's Health Education Resource Center, "Discrimination and the Double Whammy." (Lake Andes, South Dakota: 1990).
32. Sonia Shah, "Judge Rules Rape of Aboriginal Girl 'Traditional'" (Women's E-News, November 29, 2002; available from http://www.feminist.com/news/news126.html.)
33. Ibid.

34. Taussig, *Shamanism, Colonialism and the Wild Man.*

35. Fanon, *Wretched of the Earth.*

36. Tadiar, "Sexual Economies of the Asia-Pacific."

37. Stoler, *Race and the Education of Desire.*

38. Kirpatrick Sale, *The Conquest of Paradise* (New York: Plume, 1990).

39. Wrone and Nelson, *Who's the Savage?*

40. Ibid.

41. Bartolome de Las Casas, *Devastation of the Indies,* trans. Herma Briffault (Baltimore: John Hopkins University Press, 1992).

42. *Sand Creek Massacre: A Documentary History* (New York: Sol Lewis, 1973).

43. Angela Davis, *Woman, Race and Class* (New York: Vintage, 1981).

44. Eugene Genovese, *Roll, Jordan, Roll* (New York: Vintage, 1976).

45. Clifton Johnson, ed., *God Struck Me Dead* (Cleveland: Pilgrim Press, 1969).

46. Herbert Gutman, *Black Family in Slavery and Freedom* (Vintage: New York, 1976).

47. Thomas Almaguer, *Racial Faultlines* (Berkeley: University of California, 1994).

48. Karen Warren, "A Feminist Philosophical Perspective on Ecofeminist Spiritualities," in *Ecofeminism and the Sacred,* ed. Carol Adams (New York: Continuum, 1993).

49. Stannard, *American Holocaust.*

50. Mary Daly, *Gyn/Ecology* (Boston: Beacon Press, 1978); Andrea Dworkin, *Woman Hating* (New York: E.P. Dutton, 1974); Anne Barstow, *Witchcraze* (New York: Dover, 1994); Barbara Ehrenreich and Deirdre English, *For Her Own Good* (Garden City: Anchor, 1979); Rosemary Radford Ruether, ed., *Religion and Sexism* (New York: Simon & Schuster, 1974); Rosemary Radford Ruether, *New Woman, New Earth* (Minneapolis: Seabury Press, 1975); Stannard, *American Holocaust.*

51. Matilda Joslyn Gage, *Women, Church and State* (Watertown, MA: Persephone Press, 1980).

52. Stannard, *American Holocaust.*

53. Ehrenreich and English, *For Her Own Good.*

54. Stannard, *American Holocaust.*

55. Wrone and Nelson, *Who's the Savage?*

56. Barry O'Connell, ed., *On Our Own Ground: The Complete Writings of William Apess, a Pequot* (Amherst: University of Massachusetts, 1992).

57. Shohat and Stam, *Unthinking Eurocentrism.*

58. M. Annette Jaimes and Theresa Halsey, "American Indian Women: At the Center of Indigenous Resistance in North America," in *State of Native America,* ed. M. Annette Jaimes (Boston: South End Press, 1992).

59. Paula Gunn Allen, *The Sacred Hoop* (Boston: Beacon, 1986).

60. Jaimes and Halsey, "American Indian Women."

61. Tom Holm, "Patriots and Pawns," in *State of Native America,* ed. M. Annette Jaimes (Boston: South End Press, 1992).

62. Jane Richardson, *Law and Status among the Kiowa Indians* (New York: JJ Augustin, 1940).

63. "Anishinabe Values/Social Law Regarding Wife Battering," *Indigenous Woman* 1, no. 3 (n.d.). See similar viewpoints in Charon Asetoyer, "Health and Reproductive Rights," in *Indigenous Women Address the World,* ed. Indigenous Women's Network (Austin: Indigenous Women's Network, 1995); Division of Indian Work Sexual Assault Project, "Sexual Assault Is Not an Indian Tradition," (Minneapolis: n.d.).

64. Mary Rowlandson, *A Narrative of the Captivity and Removes of Mrs. Mary Rowlandson* (Fairfield: Ye Talleon Press, 1974).

65. June Namias, *White Captives* (Chapel Hill: University of North Carolina Press, 1993). I am not arguing that the nonpatriarchal nature of Native societies is the only reason white women may have chosen to live with their captors, but that it is a possible explanation for why many chose to stay.

66. Lopez, *Pagans in Our Midst.*

67. Ibid.

68. It is difficult to ascertain the true nature of Indian captivity of white people based on these narratives because of their anti-Indian bias. For instance, *A Narrative of the Horrid Massacre by the Indians of the Wife and Children of the Christian Hermit* sets out to prove that Indians are so biologically cruel that there is nothing else for whites to do than exterminate them. However, even the narrator admits that Indians killed his family because he "destroyed their village." He further states that Natives "are kind and hospitable, but toward those who *intentionally* [italics mine] offend them, the western savage [sic] is implacable. *A Narrative of the Horrid*

Massacre by the Indians of the Wife and Children of the Christian Hermit (St. Louis: Leander W. Whiteney and Co., 1833). June Namias suggests that captivity of white people became more brutal as the conquest drove Native people to the point of desperation. She also says that since captivity narratives by Jesuits seem to be the most graphic in nature, it is possible that they embellished their stories to enhance their status as martyrs and encourage greater funding for their missions. Namias, *White Captives*. Francis Jennings argues also that there were some practices of torture among the Iroquois, though not other northeastern tribes, and that it became more pronounced as the conquest against them became more brutal. He states, however, that Native people never molested women or girls. Francis Jennings, *Invasion of the Americas* (New York: Norton, 1975). Richard Drinnon believes that most male captives were killed, except that some might have been adopted into the tribe to replace those that had been killed in battle. Women and children were not killed. Richard Drinnon, *Facing West* (New York: Schocken Books, 1980). All of these discussions are based on Native practices after colonization and the infusion of violence into their societies.

69. James Seaver, *Narrative of the Life of Mrs. Mary Jemison* (New York: Corinth Books, 1975).

70. Ibid.

71. Carol Adams, *Neither Man nor Beast* (New York: Continuum, 1994).

72. Andrea Dworkin, *Pornography* (New York: Periree, 1981).

73. Namias, *White Captives*.

74. Jane Caputi, *Age of Sex Crime* (Bowling Green, OH: Popular Press, 1987).

75. Allen, *The Sacred Hoop*.

76. Paula Gunn Allen, "Violence and the American Indian Woman," in *The Speaking Profits Us,* ed. Maryviolet Burns (Seattle: Center for the Prevention of Sexual and Domestic Violence, 1986).

77. Roy Harvey Pearce, *Savagism and Civilization* (Baltimore: John Hopkins Press, 1965).

78. Rawls, *Indians of California*.

79. Laura Flanders, "What Has George W. Ever Done for Women?" *The Guardian*, March 26, 2004.

80. Ellie Smeal, Fund For a Feminist Majority, 2001.

81. RAWA, "The U.S. Bares Its Fangs to Its Flunkeys," http://rawa.fancymarketing.net/attacke.htm, August 21, 1998.

82. E. Raymond Evans, "Fort Marr Blackhouse," *Journal of Cherokee Studies* 2, no. 2 (1977).

83. Homi Bhabha, "Of Mimicry and Men," in *Tensions of Empire,* ed. Frederick Cooper and Ann Laura Stoler (Berkeley: University of California Press, 1997); Edward Said, *Orientalism* (New York: Vintage, 1994).

84. Wrone and Nelson, *Who's the Savage?*

85. Mark Brunswick and Paul Klauda, "Possible Suspect in Serial Killings Jailed in New Mexico," *Minneapolis Star and Tribune,* May 28, 1987.

86. "Indian Being Tried for Rape with No Evidence," *Fargo Forum,* January 9, 1995.

87. Lawrence Greenfield and Steven Smith, "American Indians and Crime," (Washington, D.C.: Bureau of Justice Statistics: U.S. Department of Justice, 1999).

88. Davis, *Women, Race and Class*.

89. Paula Giddings, *Where and When I Enter* (New York: Bantam Books, 1984).

90. Dona Antonia, lecture, University of California-Davis, 1996.

91. Amnesty International, "Mexico: Under the Shadow of Impunity," March 9, 1999, http://web.amnesty.org/library/index/eng AMR410021999?open&of=eng-2am

92. Catherine MacKinnon, "Postmodern Genocide," *Ms.,* July/August 1993.

93. Greenfield and Smith, *American Indians and Crime.* Native youth are also 49% more likely to be victimized by violent crime than the next highest ethnic group—African Americans. National Center for Victims of Crime, http://www.ncvc.org.

94. Promotional material from Public Relations: Mahoney/Wasserman & Associates, Los Angeles, CA, n.d.

95. Joe Brinkley, "CIA Reports Widespread Immigrant Sexual Slavery," *San Francisco Examiner,* April 2, 2000.

96. Neferti Tadiar, "Colonization and Violence Against Women of Color," lecture, The Color of Violence: Violence Against Women of Color Conference, University of California-Santa Cruz, April, 2000.

97. Ibid.

98. Anannya Bhattacharjee, In *Whose Safety? Women of Color and the Violence of Law Enforcement* (Philadelphia: American Friends Service Committee, 2001).

99. Bill Hewitt, "A Wave of Murders Terrorizes the Women of Ciudad Juarez," *People,* August 25, 2003; Evelyn Nieves, "To Work and Die in Juarez," *Mother Jones,* May/June, 2002.

100. Amnesty International, Mexico, "Intolerable Killings: Ten years of abductions and murders in Ciudad Juarez and Chihuahua," August 11, 2003.

101. Linda Diebel, "500 Missing: Aboriginal Canadians Take Fight for Justice for Invisible Victims to U.N.," *Toronto Star*, November 30, 2002.

102. This information was conveyed by Department of Justice representatives at the Strategic Planning Meeting on Crime and Justice Research in Indian Country (Portland, Oregon), October 14–15, 1998 and the Mending the Sacred Hoop Faculty Development Session (Memphis, Tennessee) May 21–23, 1998.

103. The Indian Civil Rights Act was passed ostensibly to protect the civil rights of Indian peoples, but the effect of this act was to limit tribal sovereignty over tribal members if tribal acts infringed on the "civil rights" of its members, as understood by the U.S. government. Consequently, tribes are limited in the types of strategies and punishments they can use to address sexual violence to the types of strategies and punishments that are seen as acceptable by the U.S. government.

104. For history of Indian policy, see Sharon O'Brien, *American Indian Tribal Governments* (Norman: University of Oklahoma, 1989); Luana Ross, *Inventing the Savage: The Social Construction of Native American Criminality* (Austin: University of Texas Press, 1998); Carole Goldberg, *Planting Tail Feathers* (Los Angeles: American Indian Studies Center, UCLA, 1997). For more resources on current criminal justice policy, see the website of the Tribal Law and Policy Institute, Los Angeles, CA, <www.tribal-institute.org.>

105. Sarah Deer, "Expanding the Network of Safety: Tribal Protection Orders and Victims of Sexual Assault," unpublished paper.

106. Ibid.

107. Ibid.

108. Stoler, *Race and the Education of Desire.*

EXPERIMENTS WITH FREEDOM: MILIEUS OF THE HUMAN

Aihwa Ong

1. INTRODUCTION: EFFERVESCENT FREEDOMS

Over 150 years ago, Karl Marx proclaimed that capitalism had opened up fractures and fissures in the solid crust of European society. "Beneath the apparently solid surface, they betray oceans of liquid matter, only needing expansion to rend into fragments continents of hard rock" (577). Marx and Friedrich Engels's famous phrase, "all that is solid melts into air" (Berman 5), captures the constant political and cultural upheavals that characterize global modernity. Today, the ruptures and revolutions are associated with contradictory globalizing phenomena. The interplay between a capricious world and experiments with freedoms threatens to render modern norms of citizenship and human rights "antiquated before they can ossify" (Marx and Engels 70).

The explosive growth and destruction of global markets is associated with various kinds of freedoms: freedom from old traditions, old obligations, spatial confinements, and political arrangements. Experimentations with freedoms—at the political, social, and individual levels—have historically accompanied capitalist expansion. The rise of nation-states in a global order has paralleled the growth of a world economy. These parallel developments have greatly complicated the meaning of freedom and obscured our understanding of the various forms it can take. What is citizenship if not the institutionalization of human rights as political membership in a nation-state? What are human rights if not the freedom from basic human want promised by a global community? Indeed, citizenship concepts that appear to us as enduring global norms of human existence are in constant flux, mirroring the constant upheavals of society and the eternal restlessness of capitalism.

Contemporary globalization once again opens up questions about the nature of human freedom and claims in environments of uncertainties and risks. Insecurities linked to mass displacements, economic downturns, and market exclusions highlight the protective limits of citizenship and human rights against a variety of adversities. Here, I distinguish between two categories of individual freedoms. First, positive freedom refers to the rights and claims on the government to provide fundamental means of subsistence such as food, shelter, jobs, and so on. Positive liberty also includes individual rights to equal treatment and protection by the state. Second, negative freedom refers to freedom from state interference in speech, behavior, and movement, that is, the rights to human agency. This freedom is liberty from state encroachment and limitation on individual liberty. Negative liberty can include the exercise of autonomous neoliberal practices across national boundaries, or even freedom to reject democracy. These two understandings of freedoms—individual rights protection in the democratic nation-state, and negative rights to exercise human agency unrestrained by state power—are in constant articulation in transnational movements around the world.[1]

Economic globalization is viewed by humanists as an opportunity for transforming citizenship and respatializing claims and entitlements in transnational networks. The claim is that the intensification of interconnectedness associated with capitalism has created opportunities for the rise of feelings and institutions of global solidarity (cosmopolitanism). The proliferation of multilateral agencies such as the United Nations and non-governmental organizations (NGOS), it has been claimed, is interweaving political communities in complex constellations for realizing global common good.

There is the claim that "cosmopolitan citizenship" is developing from the norms of exchange, dialogue, mediation, and mutual understanding that link different sites as "overlapping communities of fate" (Held et al. 445). Other views also claim that spatial freedoms linked to markets and mobilities are key to the formation of liberatory "postnational" identities. Missing from such discussions are the kinds of negative freedoms—freedom from state controls—unleashed in globalized environments.

Experiments with individual freedom do not always result in the realization of Enlightenment ideals of cosmopolitanism or the expansion of human rights. One can say that the ease of crossing borders is associated not primarily with goals of realizing the common global good but with specific individual goals or with political agendas that seek non-democratic visions. This article will discuss these two models of negative freedom—spatially driven affiliations and market-driven autonomous action—that are remaking the meaning of citizenship. These parallel processes of freedom from the nation-states are disembedding elements of citizenship from the territoriality of the nation-state. Emergent forms and norms of transnational ties and claims tend to be contingent and shifting and to respond to various political and ethical goals, not just human rights.

A neoliberal ethos is now transforming citizens into self-governing subjects whose human capital becomes a passport toward realizing individual freedom in diverse transnational realms. Extremist notions of individual freedom ("citizenship")—to be forged by the autonomous action of free individuals—can be a threat to democracy. Meanwhile, other kinds of border-runners are engaged in clandestine, terrorist activities in the name of liberation from Western-imposed values and practices. These two kinds of transborder activities—free economic agency in borderless markets and terrorist networking to create alternative polities—are currently among the most powerful forms of transnational citizenship and yet also among the least addressed by humanists. In short, emerging norms and practices of freedom are diverse, less inevitable precursors to universal human rights than situated, fraught, and contingent solutions to the problems of contemporary living that are not inevitable precursors to universal human rights.

2. DIASPORA: COSMOPOLITANISM

Diasporas and contingent transnational ties are assumed to have normative goals of bringing about global solidarity, a kind of nascent transnational citizenship, or Cosmopolitanism with a big "C."[2] Scholars have looked to the mass migrations spawned by global capitalism as the bearers of cosmopolitan ideals, expressed in antistate or anticapitalist sentiments. Stuart Hall and Paul Gilroy, among others, have attributed a humanistic, liberatory dimension to border-crossings, especially by subaltern groups but also middle-class migrants to Western metropolitan sites. The tendency has been to project onto "actually existing cosmopolitanisms" (Malcomson 238) political features that subvert the agendas of global capitalism and/or struggle against oppressive practices of the nation-state. One perspective explores how subaltern cultures of colonization, displacement, or resistance are endowed with normative ideals of feelings of solidarity beyond the particularistic ties of localized cultures. For instance, James Clifford argues that among "dispersed and connected" (482) Pacific islanders, diasporism is intertwined with indigenism. Their lateral relations of exchanges and alliances engage in "subaltern region-making" (475) outside capitalist circulations. Ongoing migrations are linked to the preservation and/or the recovery of indigenous traditions, as for instance, among "fourth world peoples" such as in the Canadian Northwest, and the Maoris in New Zealand.

Other perspectives seem influenced by the example of Salman Rushdie, who became a heroic diasporic figure after an Iranian cleric issued a fatwa or religious edict calling for his death for blaspheming Islam in one of his novels. Rushdie was given extensive security protection in England and the US and became celebrated as a wonderful diasporic figure of freedom from ancient tyranny in the Old World. South Asian diasporic subjects in advanced capitalist societies are widely constructed as liberatory figures who subvert oppressive national cultures and even the capitalism that sustains their elite status. These approaches find in diasporism and cross-border identities the normative beginnings of postnational citizenship.

Popular academic constructions of diaspora tend to romanticize global movements, presenting transnational communities as invariably opportunities for the transborder actualization of human freedom. The valorization of diasporas has focused on the quest by oppressed peoples for positive freedoms in democratic metropolitan sites. But the question is what kinds of freedoms are being pursued, since there are different visions and practices of freedom that may not be liberatory in the democratic sense. There are expatriate and refugee streams that seek other visions of freedom, that is, negative freedoms from Western political institutions and values and positive freedoms to found alternative identities and nations. Running alongside transnational cosmopolitan trends are powerful diaspora reimaginings that interact with but reject the universality of Enlightenment ideals.

3. DIASPORA: DETERRITORIALIZED NATION

If nations are imaginary constructs, they can always be reimagined in ways that depart from the present order of modern nation-states and in favor of separatist politics. Benedict Anderson, who coined the concept of imagined communities in his 1983 book of the same name, is skeptical about the liberatory promise of expatriate cultures and claims. He warns that "long-distance nationalism" (73) by overseas compatriots can be dangerous because it lacks accountability institutionalized by the international system. Indeed, the accelerated flows of the rich and the poor, of professional elites and low-skill migrants, of investors and refugees have engendered a variety of imagined solidarities based on a kind of political freedom that comes with deterritorialization. Scott Malcomson has reluctantly conceded limits to the universalization of this aspect of Western culture. "As for the extension of cosmopolitan ethical practice, I tend to think that will come from the non-Western world, which is today the more natural forcing ground of cosmopolitanism. Among other things, those outside the West have a far greater self-interest in true—that is, non-imperial (and non-"rational")—cosmopolitanism" (241–42).

Broadly speaking, non-Western transnational groups are organized according to highly particularistic attachments of ethnicity, nation, religion, or culture, but which now freely stretch across conventional borders. Transnational claims of citizenship may very well be precursors to new (or very old) forms of alternative nation building. Among contemporary migrants, worldly experience can engender not only a consciousness about the differences between the New World and the Old[3] but also a desire to recover the glories of ancient cultures. In an age of Asian economic emergence, precolonial hauntings about the greatness of Chinese civilization, the glories of Hindustan, or the might of the Ottoman empire have become intensified, especially among elite emigrants relocated to Western metropolitan sites. Some transnational groups have developed chauvinist agendas to act on behalf of their "own people," a grouping no longer circumscribed by the borders of a single nation-state.[4] The universal serialization of ethnic, racial, and cultural categories by the global mass media and popular culture has provided

the institutional grammar for mobilizing scattered populations on a global scale.[5] Cyber-driven nationalism combined with print capitalism is creating opportunities to construct borderless ethnicities and deterritorialized nations.

For instance, in the aftermath of the Asian financial crisis, some overseas Chinese professionals based in the West set up a Global Huaren (Chinese) website to intervene on behalf of Chinese Indonesians who were attacked. Drawn from different countries to Western metropolitan centers, these professionals imagine themselves as belonging to the same ethnic series, and by invoking "diaspora," they stretch the Chinese category to incorporate diverse populations into a global ethnic network. The cyber interventions in the Indonesian situation, while casting a welcome light on the atrocities of state-instigated attacks, also threatened to derail Indonesian attempts to rebuild community belonging following the event.[6] This would-be global ethnicity, based on networks of ethnic wealth and education acquired in global sites, shows that there is nothing "natural" about "diasporic groups." They have to be constructed by actors invoking an ethnic grammar and connected through techno-material forms that enable a global reach.

The most vivid examples of transnational identities are promoted by radical networks that seek to remake existing nation-states and establish new nations.[7] Despite Anderson's wariness of expatriates' "unaccountable politics," one need not view all forms of long-distance nationalism as a "menacing potent for the future" (Anderson 72). Some expatriate movements can install, and have installed, democratic reforms in their homeland. Nevertheless, some radical militant networks have other goals of universalisim. Only a tiny fraction of Muslims in diaspora are involved in violent jidahist politics, but their transnational activities represent a kind of alternative political globalization.

The radical Islamic Al Qaeda network may be said, with some simplification, to have a dual jihadist goal: to be rid of an American presence in the Middle East and to eventually found "purer" forms of Islamic polities free of Western secularist influence. Such groups have a religio-military vision of borderless identity inspired by both a geographical and a spiritual diaspora. Radical Islamic networks mobilize Muslim adherents from diverse countries to a goal that is both broad and simple and thus easily translatable across cultures. On the one hand, militants capitalize on the deeplyfelt sense of Islamic brotherhood and, on the other, they tap the belief among some Muslims that they are dutybound to respond to the call of the jihad and to die for the cause (*istimata*). Al Qaeda and its affiliated groupings have recruited disaffected Muslims living in Europe and North America. In another case, diasporic Muslims originating from Morocco, Egypt, Syria, Palestine, and Algeria and living in Spain, France, England, and the Netherlands were linked by an ultraorthodox sect founded by Takir wal Hijra in Egypt in the 1960s. Members of this network carried out the Madrid bombings early in 2003 and the recent murder of a Dutchman who made a film crudely satirizing Muslims.[8] Besides terrorist attacks in Western milieus, militants associated with Al Qaeda seek to recreate the Arab caliphate in the Middle East as a defense against Western domination.

Diasporic jihadist unity is expressed by providing teaching, military training, and resources to like-minded groups and their varied regional agendas. Al-Qaeda is loosely connected to Jemaah Islamiyah ("Muslim Nation"), a radical network based in Java, Indonesia. Besides Osama bin Laden, the paradigmatic diasporic militant figure was Hambali, or Riduan Isamuddin, an Indonesian member of Jemaah Islamiyah who was operations chief for Al Qaeda in Southeast Asia. Hambali was suspected of masterminding a series of attacks, including the October 2002 Bali bombings, in order to chase Westerners from the region. The purported goals of Jemaah Islamiyah are to attack secular states and to eventually realize the goal of "restoring" a caliphate state in Southeast Asia. The power of terrorist networks suggests a vision of transnational citizenship that

rejects modern nation-states, that seeks to reterritorialize nation-states currently divided by political borders as a transnational community rooted in a great religion.

Jihadist solidarity stretching across far-flung sites is frequently aided by local women. Media attention has focused on female suicide bombers and militants in Israel, Chechnya, and South Asia. But I am referring to ordinary women in various locations who give less spectacular but ultimately more practical support to transborder militant operations. Precolonial trade between the Arab world, South Asia, and Southeast Asia traditionally relied on marriage to local women to forge economic links, incorporate migrants, and spread Islam. This practice has been used by radical networks like Al-Qaeda as a consistent strategy to bond with local groups, gain resources, and influence political action. Some foreign operatives marry the kinswomen of local leaders, thus acquiring legitimacy, residency permits, translation services, new identities, and cover to carry out covert action in foreign sites. Other overseas militants marry unknowing young women in Southeast Asia. For instance, Indonesian Mira Agustina was introduced by matchmakers to an Al-Qaeda operative Omar Al-Faruq, a Kuwaiti who was later arrested in Thailand and turned over to American custody. When Mira learned that her husband had planned to bomb the US in September, 2002, she exclaimed, "My husband can't be a terrorist!" ("Married" 3). Unbeknownst to her, her father's villa was used to plot attacks around the region.[9] The most notorious Al-Qaeda terrorist in Southeast Asia was Indonesian Riduan Isamuddin who married a Malaysian-Chinese Muslim although he already had wives in Cambodia and Pakistan, who were all apparently unaware of his activities. The Islamic focus on the sacredness of family, culture, and sacrifice is a powerful draw on female support everywhere. Thus, marriage and kinship practices embed foreign operatives in sympathetic environments, providing cultural translation and social cohesion that integrate long-distance diaspora politics. Religion and marriage, more than jet planes and the Internet, are the vital elements in forging links in the diasporic chain, enabling the spatial freedom for diverse and shifting forms of coalitions that seek, through secrecy and violence, to found deterritorialized nations. The popular view of diaspora as ethnicity has elided the fact that diaspora is really a political formation seeking its own nation.

Diasporic yearnings are deeply anchored in political desires for return to a spiritual home that can be realized in this worldly culture and geography. As scholars, we have focused on those diasporic communities that are purportedly invested with Western "rational" universals, and in whose border crossings we can see a glimmer of a cosmopolitan future. But the postcolonial hauntings intensified by cultural and transnational displacements can also inspire antihumanistic, antirationalist goals. Other ethical considerations come into play, in the form of the desire not for solidarity as world citizens but for the kind of ethnoracial or religious segregations that threaten the global community. One need not subscribe to Samuel Huntington's "clash of civilizations," as his 1996 book is titled, to observe that actual existing aspirations to transnational citizenship are not always framed in cosmopolitan terms but seek rather to politically consolidate transnational ethnic and religious powers of freedom. Clearly, not only diverse militant but also fundamentalist and moderate transnational Muslim movements are responding to deep yearnings for a resurgent Islamic sociality—an Umma—that ignores the man-made borders of nation-states. The new "Islamic world" is not a geographical space but a metarealm, a "satwhal" or emerging reality based on the aspirations of many Muslims in the global South to be merged as an international community.[10]

It seems wise to consider diaspora not as a pregiven instrument of cosmopolitan politics but as a contingent strategy of power that pursues different kinds of freedom, including freedom from secular Western culture. Some diasporic communities may seek subaltern emancipation outside the nation-state in the transnational spaces already shaped by capitalist forces. But more powerful migrant groups build on the mobilization of transnational resources to construct alternative ways of global belonging based on exclusive categories of ethnicity, race, and religion. Thus the goals of diasporic nations can also threaten Western values of freedom, democracy, and human rights that underpin the contemporary global system of nation-states. Emergent cross-border identities, affiliations, and nationalisms actually attest to the limits rather than the universality of cosmopolitan ideals. Meanwhile, Western notions about individual freedoms have not remained unchanged, going through permutations linked to global market forces.

4. INDIVIDUAL FREEDOM AS NEOLIBERAL LOGIC

While the above approaches focus on migrant populations generating new notions of citizenship, I consider the migration of social technologies as an equally important contributor to mutations in citizenship. By "human" or "social technology," I mean rational means-ends procedures designed to produce desired outcomes in human conduct. Nikolas Rose has argued in *Powers of Freedom* (1999) that in advanced liberal democracies such as the United Kingdom, market-driven logics have infiltrated the thinking and practice of governing. The post-World War II welfare state is withering, withdrawing, nominally, from caring for all citizens, but now wants them to act as free subjects who self-actualize and act on their own behalf. "Government at a distance" (Rose 49) is a decentralized mode of power that depends on a loose network of social agencies and actors to disseminate key values and norms of self-governing conduct. An ensemble of institutions—schools, museums, corporations, NGOs—diffuse ideas and techniques for acting on the self and for reforming/reengineering the self in order to confront globalized insecurities and challenges.

There is thus a fundamental shift in the ethics of subject formation, or the ethics of citizenship, as governing becomes concerned less with the social and collective management of the population (biopolitics) and more with instilling behavior of individual self-management (ethico-politics). Ethics is used here not in the sense of the moral guidelines but as the practice of self-care that determines how the individual constitutes herself as a moral subject in a political community. An ethical regime can therefore be construed as a style of living guided by given values for constituting oneself in line with a particular moral code.[11] The neoliberal ethical regime requires citizens to be self-responsible, self-enterprising subjects. Such ethics are framed as an animation of various capacities of individual freedom, expressed both in freedom from state protection and guidance and in freedom to make calculated choices as a rational response to globalized uncertainties.[12] These ideas were first promoted by Frederic von Hayek, centering on the figure of the *homo economicus,* a self-maximizing figure forged in the effervescent conditions of market competition.[13] The ethics of individual economic action as an efficient way to distribute public resources ("neoconservatism") were gradually implemented under Reaganite economics in the US and the Thatcherite regime in England. But while Rose and others such as Urlich Beck in *Risk Society* (1992) attribute these new ethics of compulsory individual freedom to advanced capitalist societies, I maintain that such rationalities of governing and ethics of citizen-formation are not confined to the West but have migrated to emerging sites of hypergrowth.

I call such ethico-politics technologies of neoliberalism with a small "n," and its adoption is changing the ethical basis of citizenship in politically diverse locations. The universalizing, mobile figure of neoliberalism interacts with diverse political regimes—capitalist, authoritarian, and postsocialist, among others.[14] The new logics of market-driven individualism subvert the freedoms enshrined in citizenship by stripping away the old guarantees of citizenship protections. In the US, more people, along with welfare recipients, are actually losing entitlements as citizens. Middle-class lives are in jeopardy as college-educated individuals become unprotected from corporate decisions to outsource well-paying jobs. In socialist China, the authorities no longer provide subsidies for housing, food, and health, causing millions of peasants to migrate to cities to seek jobs in the private sector. In authoritarian Singapore, extensive social services are now conditional upon high individual achievements in education and entrepreneurial skills. Increasingly, citizens in diverse political milieus are obliged to become free of state supports and to develop skills as free agents of their own lives.

In diverse Asian growth zones, citizenship values are now pegged to the demands and dynamism of markets. Whether we are talking about Singapore, an emerging hub of biotechnology, the megacities on China's coast, or cyber centers in India, the ideal "citizens" are "global talent," or locals and foreigners who have acquired globally marketable knowledge and skills to contribute to the growth of particular sites. Singapore has constituted such specialized zones by mobilizing foreign technology and actors to help create an environment for the accumulation of intellectual capital in science and technology. In China, the new stress is also on developing "human talent" (*ren cai*) and on concentrating professionals and experts in a few centers of growth in information technology industries. For instance, Shenzhen, across the border from Hong Kong, is drawing technical experts from all over the country to build a global media industry. Shanghai, the Manhattan of China, will be the site of a world fair to showcase its international professional standards in many fields. Hyderabad and Bangalore in India are zones for software engineering that have attracted skilled jobs from the US. In these milieus, "global" refers not so much to foreigners as to globally relevant knowledge and skills that can be acquired by the self-enterprising subject. Neoliberal calculations now directly engage the problems of managing labor and life in these disparate centers with different political traditions. Thus, this globalism as market-relevant knowledge is in itself a cosmopolitan (universalizing) force, without necessarily bearing or proliferating democratic values.

The new norm of belonging to "Asian world cities" is not as a citizen who makes demands on the government but as individuals who take the initiative as mobile, flexible, and reflexive actors responding autonomously to market forces. There is thus a shift in the ethics of citizenship, from a stress on equal access to rights and claims on the state to a focus on individual obligation to maximize self-interest in turbulent economic conditions. Responsible citizenship is to be enacted in autonomous actions of individual self-enterprise and risk taking, without state support. In addition, there is the requirement of self-enterprising citizens to interact with technological systems and to remake themselves as reflexive knowledge workers.

In East and South Asian environments, neoliberal ethics of self-responsible citizenship are linked to social obligations to build the nation. In India and Malaysia, discourses about "knowledge workers" and "knowledge society" urge citizens to self-improve in order to develop high-tech industries.[15] The accumulation of intellectual capital as an obligation of citizenship is most extreme in Singapore. Ordinary citizens are expected to develop new mindsets and build digital capabilities, while professionals are urged to achieve norms of "techno-preneurial citizenship" or lose out to more skilled and entrepreneurial expatriates and be reduced to a second-class citizenry. A journalist told me that Singaporeans are accustomed to being told that they are to compete with foreigners on their own home turf. It's a matter of merit, not race or ethnicity, she claims: "If you're no good, you're no good. The job goes to better educated people," no matter where they are from.

Despite having a population of four million that is already one-quarter expatriate, Singapore has an aggressive headhunting program that recruits

experts in all fields in order to make it "a fertile ground for breeding creativity" ("Contact"). There is the construction of the island as a globalized nursery for growing intellectual capital. Nonbreeding subjects are rendered nonworthy subjects. Talented expatriates enjoy better salaries, housing allowances, and preferential tax breaks than run-of-the-mill citizens. Consequently, the problems of living, working, and productivity increasingly pivot around individual self-actualizing talent rather than conventional citizenship claims. The influx of exciting, risk-taking, and creative foreigners, it is hoped, will shake up narrowly trained, security-conscious citizens constrained by Confucian norms and group thinking. Neoliberal ethics trump Confucian ethics as governing technologies seek to animate self-governing subjects who can make calculated investments in their lives for uncertain times. The moral measures of citizens, expatriates, and habitués of globalized sites are now set spinning by the gyrations in global markets. Residents in such globalized sites are valued and protected not because of their citizenship status but for their powers of self-management and cutting-edge skills that sustain the competitiveness of growth zones.

In short, this form of "transnational citizenship" is rooted in an instrumentalist definition of individual freedom as economic optimization in the realm of borderless markets. These "global citizens" do not, practically speaking, rely on a specific citizenship status to make a living but travel the world to perform globalized functions in the nodes of a far-flung archipelago. They are substitutable for one another in any given site, members of a circulating intellectual "labor aristocracy" (including writers and professors) who serve the contemporary demands of global capital. In Asian growth zones, the discourse of constant self-improvements is directed at contributions to "civic society," in political solidarity with the national community. The common feature is that regardless of settings, the stakes of citizenship are raised for the majority. Especially in places like Singapore, those who cannot scale the skills ladder and measure up to neoliberal ethics of citizenship are increasingly marginalized as deviant, even risky subjects who threaten the new normativity. The adoption of neoliberal criteria systematically undercuts juridical principles of citizenship that promise universal rights to all.

5. MILIEUS OF THE HUMAN

But what about "cosmopolitan citizenship," the kind of "good" global solidarity that is linked to human rights? Briefly, there are two aspects of this discussion. First, in Western democracies, the discourse of cosmopolitanism has been about ways of incorporating noncitizens. In the European Union, where the federalization of nation-states has created social conditions of a broadened civil society, debates over the integration of diverse communities with non-European origin have focused on balancing an imaginary of European civilization and the need to give migrant communities some legal protection. There is a process of "disaggregating" citizenship into different bundles of rights and benefits, so that migrant workers can experience a limited measure of political representation. In *Limits of Citizenship* (1994), Yasmin Soysal maintains that human rights discourses have influenced European states to differently incorporate migrants and noncitizens. Such bundles of limited benefits and civil rights constitute a form of partial citizenship, or "postnational" political membership. But clearly, a stronger version of cosmopolitan citizenship that would offer permanent asylum to refugees is yet to be realized or perhaps not realizable in countries feeling overwhelmed by immigrants from outside Europe.

Cosmopolitanism as intra-European solidarity based on liberal democracy and civil rights is easier to countenance. Jurgen Habermas notes that the divisive onslaught of deregulated markets has threatened the democratic achievements of European societies, thereby creating a "democratic deficit" in public life (14). He argues that distinctive European rights—inclusive systems of social security, social norms regarding class

and gender, investment in public social services, rejection of the death penalty, and so on—constitutes a substantive conception of citizenship that must be protected. He invokes the image of a transnational public sphere and an EU constitution that can give symbolic weight to a shared political culture. But despite the proliferation of transnational connections, cosmopolitanism in the sense of transnational solidarity to protect European cultural distinctiveness may be more easily agreed upon than a true cosmopolitanism that absorbs illegal migrants and asylum-seekers from outside the continent. Observers such as Douglas Holmes in *Integral Europe* (2000) have noted the rise of subnationalist identities in the wake of demands for European integration.

Second, cosmopolitanism as the universalization of the human rights regime is represented in an array of United Nations (UN) conventions in defense of the tortured and the displaced, exploited children, trafficked women, and migrant workers, among other globally disadvantaged groups. But the ideals of basic human rights are only enforceable (short of occupation by another sovereign power) by nation-states within their own territories. In practice, the assemblage of UN bodies and NGOs that seek to spread rights mainly do two things: apply pressure on errant governments to stem abuses against their own citizens (using aid as a carrot) or intervene in humanitarian crises by providing relief funds. Thus, despite the UN legitimation and coordination, NGO practices tend to be specific, strategic, temporary stop-gap measures. Private NGOs such as Greenpeace, Doctors Without Borders, and Oxfam International are also said to constitute the ligaments of an emergent global civil society. The global NGO response to the 2004 Asian tsunami calamities is a heartwarming and striking example of how NGOs coming together in a particular crisis create a sense of the world not as divided nations, but as a series of overlapping "communities of fate" (Held et al. 445). The media glare on victims in ten countries and global competition in donor generosity create a picture of intense feelings of global solidarity. But nevertheless, despite claims about emerging "transnational civil society" (452), NGO interventions tend to be sporadic, uneven, and shifting, driven more by particular crises than a sustained commitment to implementing values or rights of social equality. Transnational NGOs, numerous though they are, do not coalesce into a system of global governance that can actually safeguard the human rights of the globe's inhabitants, as many European theorists tend to claim. The discourse says that human rights should be protected, but the NGOs cannot actually deliver human rights.

I tend to view NGO interventions in contingent and limited terms, as situated and strategic interventions into the problems of diverse milieus of living. NGOs are practitioners of humanity, and, in an everyday sense, they wrestle continually with the ethical implications of particular situations of life and labor. Ethically speaking, citizenship is about resolving problems of life and labor in particular milieus, creating solutions that are contingent, provisional, and varied, in connection with political and economic uncertainties.[16] In ordinary but especially emergency situations, NGOs sort out different categories of human beings, determining who should be aided, live, or die. The triage system in desperate humanitarian interventions unavoidably grades humanity into different categories of biological worth. For instance, local NGOs who fight on behalf of foreign domestic workers in Southeast Asia—many treated like slaves—do not invoke human rights. Rather, NGOs seek to secure minimalist conditions for sheer survival. Malaysian NGOs do this by appealing to the moral economies of the host societies and noting that the biological welfare of migrant workers will yield higher labor productivity. There is thus a convergence between appeals for the moral protection of migrants' rights to biological survival on the one hand and a concern to link their welfare to the economic interests of affluent households that hire them.[17] These NGOs are not making absolute judgments about equal

access to human rights nor demanding that these contract migrant workers be given citizenship in nation-states that refuse to absorb low-skill workers as permanent citizens. As mentioned above, even in Europe there is extreme resistance to granting citizenship to migrants from the South. Promigrant NGOs in France have been able to claim the biolegitimacy of HIV-positive migrants as legitimate grounds for claiming citizenship. But again, this is by no means an established institutional practice.[18] Gradations of the "biopolitical backwardness" of migrants and the relative wealth of the host society affect the capacity of NGOs in Southeast Asia to make effective claims on behalf of poor migrants. In short, NGO interventions make only on-the-ground decisions about who can or should survive, how this can be done, and how and when to make claims, depending on situated constellations of political and ethical forces.

Humanists continue to uphold human rights as a global ideal, but they should not thereby develop willful blindspots to actually existing transnational politics. Experiments in freedom in the transnational realm include the pursuit of individual freedom as well as the violent realization of particularistic and exclusivist identities. Transnational human rights regimes can only spread a thin and fragile cover over bare life. Meanwhile, the numbers of globally excluded populations daily crowd the planet and our conscience.

Fast-changing markets, knowledge, and human practices have intensified volatilities surrounding citizenship and what it means to be human. Advances in biotechnology are creating "posthuman" beings and a variety of living forms that challenge the concept of individualism, individual subjectivity, and the nature of the human.[19] These new animations and articulations are happening in particular laboratories and at the truly planetary scale by putting at stake our existence as humans. It appears that we are at the dawn of a discussion of the complex, contingent, and tenuous links between individual humans and individual rights. Human and nonhuman life forms are in flux.

Given our acute sense of the unknown emerging in the horizon, claims about universal human equality can only be made with a great deal less certainty than in the heyday of the post-World War II human rights declaration. The conversion of claims of sheer survival into political rights, from alien status to legitimate citizenship, is more contingent than ever. It would appear that spatial freedom and movements we associate with diasporas and market-driven mobilities are no guarantees of the spread of human rights; on the contrary, these border-crossing movements often attest to the rise of nondemocratic forms of negative freedom. Transnational NGOs can only intervene in specific milieus, tinkering at the edge of sheer life, falling far short of claims about "a single normative rights standard" (Ignatieff 318).

NOTES

1. For consideration of "negative" and "positive" freedoms in a human rights regime, see Amy Gutmann's Introduction to *Human Rights as Politics and Idolatry/Michael Ignatieff,* ed. Amy Gutmann (2001) vii–xxvii, esp. ix.

2. See Immanuel Kant, "Perpetual Peace: A Philosophical Sketch," *Political Writings,* ed. Hans Reiss (1991).

3. The concept of double consciousness popularized by Benedict Anderson and Paul Gilroy must be broadened to include adherents beyond trafficked slaves in early modernity, anticolonial leaders, and diasporic peoples. Indeed, other migrant populations may experience multiple consciousness, depending on specific itineraries and peregrinations through centuries of travel, as exemplified by the experiences of overseas Chinese. See Donald Nonini and Aihwa Ong, "Introduction: Chinese Transnationationalism as an Alternative Modernity," *Ungrounded Empires,* ed. Aihwa Ong and Donald Nonini (1997) 3–36.

4. Israel is the preeminent example of a nation-state founded through the diasporic longings of "a people," but some contemporary diasporic groups seek to "recover" polities that straddled contemporary national divisions.

5. See Anderson's *The Spectre of Comparison.*

6. See Aihwa Ong, "Cyberpublics and Diaspora Politics among Transnational Chinese," *Interventions* 5.1 (2003): 82–100.

7. One may point to Israel as a nation-state founded by diasporic groups, and the existence of which depends on endemic violence against other inhabitants of the land.

8. See, e.g., "New Terror Threat in EU: Extremists with Passports," *The Wall Street Journal,* 27 Dec. 2004: A1, 5.

9. See also Zuraidah Ibrahim, *Jemaah Islamiyah Wives: Supportive Bystanders or Ignorant Partners?* MA thesis in Asian Studies, University of California, Berkeley, Fall 2005.

10. See Yasushi Kosugi, "Islamic Regionalism," presented at the "Regions in Globalization" conference, Kyoto University, 25–27 Oct. 2002.

11. See Michel Foucault, "The Ethics of the Concern for Self as a Practice of Freedom," *Ethics, Vol. 1, Essential Works of Foucault, 1954–1984,* trans. Robert Hurley et al., ed. Paul Rabinow (1994): 281–302.

12. See Rose 188.

13. See *The Essence of Hayek,* ed.Chiaki Nishiyama and Kurt R. Leube (1984).

14. See Aihwa Ong, "Neoliberalism as Exception, Exception to Neoliberalism," *Neoliberalism as Exception: Mutations in Citizenship and Sovereignty* (2006).

15. See Aihwa Ong, "Ecologies of Expertise: Assembling Flows, Managing Citizenship," *Global Assemblages: Technology, Politics, and Ethics as Anthropological Problems,* ed. Aihwa Ong and Stephen J. Collier (2005): 337–53.

16. See Stephen Collier and Andrew Lakoff, "Regimes of Living," *Global Assemblages: Technology, Politics, and Ethics as Anthropological Problems,* ed. Aihwa Ong and Stephen J. Collier (2005): 29–30.

17. See Aihwa Ong, "A Bio-Cartography: Maids, Neo-Slavery, and NGOs," *Neoliberalism as Exception.*

18. See Didier Fassin, "The Biopolitics of Otherness," *Anthropology Today* 17.1 (2001): 277–82.

19. See, e.g., Sarah Franklin, "Stems R Us: Emergent Life Forms and the Global Biological," *Global Assemblages,* ed. Ong and Collier: 59–78.

WORKS CITED

Anderson, Benedict. *The Spectre of Comparison.* London: Verso, 2002.

Berman, Marshall. *All That Is Solid Melts Into Air: The Experience of Modernity.* New York: Penguin Books, 1988.

Clifford, James. "Indigenous Articulations." *The Contemporary Pacific* 13.2 (2001): 468–90.

"Contact Singapore." Advertisement. <www.contactsingapore.org.sg/time>.

Habermas, Jurgen. "Why Europe Needs a Constitution." *New Left Review* 11 (Sept.–Oct. 2001): 5–26.

Held, David, et al. *Global Transformations: Politics, Economics and Culture.* Stanford: Stanford UP, 1999.

Ignatieff, Michael. "Human Rights." *Human Rights in Political Transition: Gettysburg to Bosnia.* Ed.

Carla Hesse and Robert Post. New York: Zone Books, 1999. 313–324.

Malcomson, Scott L. "The Varieties of Cosmopolitan Experience," *Cosmopolitics.* Ed. Pheng Cheah and Bruce Robbins. Minneapolis: U of Minnesota P, 1998. 233–45.

"Married to Al-Qaeda," *The Straits Times* (Sunday), 17 Nov. 2002: 3

Marx, Karl. "Speech at the Anniversary of the People's Paper," *The Marx-Engels Reader.* Ed. Robert C. Tucker. New York: Norton, 1978. 577–78.

Marx, Karl, and Friedrich Engels. *Manifesto of the Communist Party: The Revolution of 1848.* Ed. and intro., David Fernbach. Harmondsworth: Penguin, 1973.

Rose, Nikolas. *Powers of Freedom: Reframing Political Thought.* Cambridge: Cambridge UP, 1999.

FROM *A CRITIQUE OF POSTCOLONIAL REASON*

Gayatri Chakravorty Spivak

Writing in the 1880s, Kipling is attempting to create a species of New Woman in his short story "William the Conqueror"; and, in the attempt, he reveals most of the shortcomings of a benevolent masculism.[1] William is the name of the female protagonist. By implying archly that her conquest of the heart of the male protagonist is to be compared to the Norman Conquest of England, is Kipling producing a proleptic parody of "the personal is political"? We cannot know. If, however, in pondering this question we overlook the fact that, under cover of the romance, the conquest of India is being effaced and reinscribed as a historically appropriate event rather than anything that could in fact be called a "conquest," we are, once again, applying the dark double standard.

Kipling's New Woman is distinctly unbeautiful. "Her face was white as bone, and in the centre of her forehead was a big silvery scar the size of a shilling—the mark of a Delhi sore."[2] She does that most unfeminine thing: travel by dreadful train across horrid India in the company of men to tend the poor bestial Indians in the throes of the Madras famine of 1876–1878. Kipling is no doubt ironic (again, somewhat archly, but that is his habitual tone) about the traffic of British girls

---

[1] I hope the reader will tolerate this word. I like the faint echo of "muscling" in there. "Masculinism" seems to be about being masculine; the corresponding word, relating to being feminine, would be "femininism."

[2] Rudyard Kipling, *The Writings in Prose and Verse* (New York: Scribner's, 1913), vol. 31, no. 1, p. 227. Hereafter cited in text as *WC*. "It was a story about 'a new sort of woman,' wrote Carrie [Rudyard's wife], and 'she turned out stunningly'... She is presented in the round, as no earlier of Kipling's heroines had been" (Charles Carrington, *Rudyard Kipling: His Life and Work* [London: Macmillan, 1955], pp. 276, 277). But even such a temperate "feminist" gesture was quickly misunderstood. The protagonist has been described as "a hard-riding young lady with a preference for men of action" (Stephen Lucius Gwynn, "The Madness of Mr. Kipling," in *Kipling: The Critical Heritage,* ed. Roger Lancelot Green [London: Routledge, 1971], p. 213).

in the colonies. In recompense, to treat "William" differently, he makes her almost a man. She "look[s] more like a boy than ever" *(WC* 229); and her brother admits that "she's as clever as a man, confound her" *(WC* 235). In the end, however, Kipling shows that a woman's a woman for all that, and she conquers, as women will, through love. "Life with men who had a great deal of work to do, and very little time to do it in, had taught her the wisdom of effacing as well as of fending for herself" *(WC* 236). And she nurtures sentiments appropriate to a true "man's woman": "That[to make fun of a girl]'s different. . . . She was only a girl, and she hadn't done anything except walk like a quail, and she *does.* But it isn't fair to make fun of a man" *(WC* 257).

Kipling does not write about sexual difference subtly. I will point at one more detail to indicate the kind of function it performs in his text. In the interest of creating a "different" kind of romance, Kipling gives to his hero some soft and "feminine" qualities. The protagonists come together in love when he teaches her how to milk goats to feed starving Indian babies. But this possible effeminacy is forestalled by a proper objective correlative from classical pastoral with Biblical overtones: "One waiting at the tent door beheld with new eyes a young man, beautiful as Paris, a god in a halo of golden dust, walking slowly at the head of his flocks, while at his knee ran small naked Cupids" *(WC* 249).[3] Before we dismiss this as Victorian kitsch—some critics find this passage admirable—we should note that this is the story's icon for imperialism *in loco*

parentis.[4] It is made painfully clear a few pages later: "She dreamed for the twentieth time of the god in the golden dust, and woke refreshed to feed loathsome black children" *(WC* 261; "Kipling's attitude to children, with its special tenderness and understanding").[5] At any rate, love flourishes and, at the end of the story, at the festival of Christmas, "drawing closer to Scott . . . it was William who wiped her eyes," even as some men of the Club sang "Glad tidings of great joy I bring/ To you and all mankind" *(WC* 274). It is one of the clichés of imperialism that the settlement of the colonies—the liberation of Kuwait?—is part of these glad tidings.

There is a lot of self-conscious "local color" in the story. At first glance, then, it might seem as if the complaint about Baudelaire, that he denies the negress her proper and specific space, cannot be entertained here. And it is of course correct that Kipling is a chronicler of "Indian life." Let us therefore pause a moment on Kipling's technique of specifying India.

"Is it officially declared yet?" are the first words of the text. Narrative logic throws a good deal of weight on the answer to this question. Indeed, the first movement of narrative energy in "William the Conqueror" seems to be a demonstration of how an affirmative answer to this question might be shaped. Slowly the reader comes to sense that the "it" in question is the precise descriptive substantive "Famine," and that the affirmative answer to the initial question is coded in benevolent imperialism: "the operation of the Famine Code" *(WC* 223)—the exasperated yet heroic British tending the incompetent, unreasonable, and childish South Indians. The panoramic heterogeneity of the people and landscape of southern India is offered in declaration of and apposition to the monolithic rubric: Famine.

The narrative purpose of "Famine"—the container of the specificity of South India—is

---

[3] I cannot resist the temptation to include here a comparable bit of Orientalism, transforming the actual Indian scene into a biblical Orient to be found in J. W. Kaye's contemporary *History of the Sepoy War in India, 1857–58* (London: W. H. Allen, 1880–88). Kaye is describing British women taken out to grind corn by insurgent Indian soldiers during the so-called Indian Mutiny: "As they sat there on the ground, these Christian captives must have had some glimmering recollection of their biblical studies, and remembered how in *the East* the grinding of corn was ever regarded as a symbol of subjection." (Kaye, *History,* 2:355, emphasis mine; cited in Rudrangshu Mukherjee, "'Satan Let Loose upon Earth': The Massacres in Kanpur in the Revolt of 1847 in India," paper delivered at Subaltern Studies Conference, Calcutta, Dec. 23, 1989).

[4] For favorable assessments of this passage, see Green, *Kipling,* p. 213 and Carrington, *Rudyard Kipling,* p. 224.
[5] Kingsley Amis, *Rudyard Kipling and His World* (New York: Scribner's, 1975), p. 25.

instrumental. When it has served to promote love between the two human (that is, British) actors, the rubric is dissolved, the declaration undone: "And so Love ran about the camp unrebuked in broad daylight, while men picked up the pieces and put them neatly away of the Famine in the Eight Districts"(*WC* 204).[6]

The action moves back to Northwest India, where it began. Here is an account of that move: "The large open names of the home towns were good to listen to. Umballa, Ludhiana, Phillour, Jullundur, they rang like marriage-bells in her ears, and William felt deeply and truly sorry for all strangers and outsiders—visitors, tourists, and those fresh caught for the service of the country" (*WC* 273).

These sonorous place-names are in Punjab. We have left Madras behind as we have left "Famine" behind. The mention of "home" and "outside" is not a specification of India at all, but rather the disappearance of India if defined as the habitation of Indians. The description of William and Scott's "homecoming" to the North leaves the distinct impression that the North is more British—India has receded here. This is how the roll of names I quote above is introduced:

> The South of Pagodas and palm-trees, the over-populated Hindu South, was done with. Here was the land she knew, and before her lay the good life

she understood, among folk of her own caste and mind. They were picking them up at almost every station now—men and women coming in for the Christmas Week, with racquets, with fox-terriers and saddles. . . . Scott would stroll up to William's window, and murmur: "Good enough, isn't it?" and William would answer with sighs of pure delight: "Good enough, indeed." *(WC* 272)

Thus the incantation of the names, far from being a composition of place, is precisely the combination of effacement of specificity and appropriation that one might call violation. It starts early on in a benign way, as we encounter the hero putting on evening clothes: "Scott moved leisurely to his room, and changed into *the evening-dress of the season and the country;* spotless white linen from head to foot, with a broad silk cummerbund" (*WC* 225; emphasis mine). "The dress of the season and country" sutures nature and culture and inscribes nature appropriately. Thus "home" and "outside" become terms of a distinction between the old and the new British in India. The words "Punjabi" and "Madrassi" are consistently used for the British who "serve" in those parts of India. The word "native," which is supposed to mean "autocthonous," is paradoxically recoded as an unindividuated para-humanity that cannot aspire to a proper habitation.[7]

Kipling uses many Hindusthani words in his text—pidgin Hindusthani, barbaric to the native speaker, devoid of syntactic connections, always infelicitous, almost always incorrect. The narrative practice sanctions this usage and establishes it as "correct," without, of course, any translation. This is British pidgin, originating in a decision

---

[6] I am not considering the contentious question of Kipling's "imperialism" here. I am looking rather at the fact that sexual difference becomes relevant in this text only in terms of the colonizer. It is, however, worth pointing at a poignant piece of evidence of the effects of imperialism. Almost all the Western critics I have read, many of them (such as T. S. Eliot, George Orwell, Lionel Trilling, Randall Jarrell) conveniently collected in Green, *Kipling,* and Eliot L. Gilbert, ed., *Kipling and the Critics* (New York: New York Univ. Press, 1965), speak of the formative impact of Kipling's stories and novels upon their boyhood. Compare the following remark by a Bengali writer to that collective testimony: "I read Kipling's *Jungle Book* first at the age of ten in an East Bengal village, but never read anything else by him for fear of being hurt by his racial arrogance" (Nirad C. Chaudhuri, "The Wolf without a Pack," *TLS* [Oct. 6, 1978]); the above is a memory; it is followed in Chaudhuri's piece by a judgment, reflecting so-called decolonization and the disavowal of the economic, with which I cannot agree.

[7] This appropriation of the place-name is much more striking in the American case. For the "failed parallel" between India and the United States, see Spivak, "Scattered Speculations on the Question of Cultural Studies," *Outside,* p. 262. When epistemic violation succeeds, these re-codings are internalized. This need not necessarily be a dead end. Such internalizations can be de-hegemonized, the oppressor's name charged with a resistant meaning, conducive to strategic unification. For comments on such a move in the Indian tribal context, see Spivak, "Woman in Difference: Mahasweta Devi's 'Douloti the Bountiful,'" in *Outside,* pp. 77–95.

that Hindusthani is a language of servants not worth mastering "correctly"; this is the version of the language that is established textually as "correct."[8] By contrast, the Hindusthani speech of the Indian servants is painstakingly translated into archaic and awkward English. The servants' occasional forays into English are mocked in phonetic transcription. Let us call this set of moves—in effect a mark of perceiving a language as subordinate—translation-as-violation. And let us contrast this to a high European moment in the discussion of translation as such.

Walter Benjamin wrote as follows on the topic of translation from classical Greek into German: "Instead of making itself similar to the meaning . . . the translation must rather, lovingly and in detail, in its own language, form itself according to the manner of meaning in the original, to make both recognizable as broken parts of the greater language." This passage quite logically assumes that the language one translates from is structurally the language of authority rather than subordination. Commenting on this passage de Man writes, "The faithful translation, which is always literal, how can it also be free? It can only be free if it reveals the instability of the original, and if it reveals that instability as the linguistic tension between trope and meaning. Pure language is perhaps more present in the translation than in the original, but in the mode of trope."[9]

The distant model of this high discourse on translation is the European Renaissance, when a tremendous activity of translation from texts of classical antiquity helped shape hegemonic Europe's cultural self-representation. (German cultural self-representation, in the eighteenth and nineteenth centuries, of non-participation

in the Renaissance gives the specifically German speculations on the problem of translation a particular character.) When, however, the violence of imperialism straddles a subjected language, translation can become a species of violation as well. Freedom-in-troping arguments from the European Renaissance do not apply directly to the translation-as-violation in Kipling's text.[10]

Just as they do not deny the irreducible hybridity of all language. When Mahasweta constructs a unique underclass hybrid language of Eastern India and uses it skillfully to contrast passages in Sanskritized Bengali, the politics of her technique is quite different from Kipling's.

I have been arguing that the tropological deconstruction of masculism does not exempt us from performing the lie of imperialism. Let us consider David Arnold's essay on the Madras famine in that frame. (Some of the documentation provided by Arnold puts the noble-whites-helping-imcompetent-blacks scenario into question.)[11] In my experience, most classroom discussions of Kipling's story are taken up by the analysis of the taming-of-the-tomboy routine between the two white protagonists. Toward the end of such a class hour I deflected the discussion to a quotation in Arnold's essay of a Tamil sexual-rôle-reversal doggerel sung by peasant women in order to make the drought end: "A wonder has taken place, O Lord! The male is grinding millet and the female is ploughing fields./Is not your heart moved with pity, O God! / The widow Brahmani is ploughing the field." In order to think this folk-ritual as potentially efficacious by way of a reminder of chaos in a universe that should be divinely ordered, the women must take seriously a patriarchal division of sexual labor. What little

---

[8] I am not speaking, of course, of British scholarship in Indian languages, generally in grammar-establishment and philology. That specialized work takes its place in the history of the constitution of disciplines and as such in the epistemic project of imperialism. I have commented on it briefly in the next chapter.
[9] De Man, "'Conclusions': Walter Benjamin's 'The Task of the Translator,'" in *The Resistance to Theory* (Minneapolis: Univ. of Minnesota Press, 1986), pp. 91–92.

[10] I have developed this argument at greater length in "The Politics of Translation," in *Outside,* pp. 179–200.
[11] David Arnold, "Famine in Peasant Consciousness and Peasant Action: Madras 1876–78," in Ranajit Guha, ed., *Subaltern Studies: Writings on South Asian History and Society,* vol. 3 (Delhi: Oxford Univ. Press, 1984), pp. 62–115. The passage quoted is from p. 73.

time was left in the class was taken up with a young woman's insistence that the peasant women must have been singing the doggerel ironically. This is of course one possibility among many. But when we are ignorant of the historical frame, of the *pouvoir-savoir* mechanisms by which a subject is constituted and interpellated within that frame, insistence on this sort of pop-psych irony most often springs from the imposition of our own historical and voluntarist constitution within the second wave of U.S. academic feminism as a "universal" model of the "natural" reactions of the female mind.[12] This may also be called an example of translation-as-violation.

The structure of translation-as-violation describes certain tendencies within third-worldist literary pedagogy more directly. It is of course part of my general argument that, unless third-worldist feminism develops a vigilance against such tendencies, it cannot help but participate in them. Our own mania for "third world literature" anthologies, when the teacher or critic often has no sense of the original languages, or of the subject-constitution of the social and gendered agents in question (and when therefore the student cannot sense this as a loss), participates more in the logic of translation-as-violation than in the ideal of translation as freedom-in-troping. What is at play there is a phenomenon that can be called "sanctioned ignorance," now sanctioned more than ever by an invocation of "globality"— a word serving to hide the financialization of the globe, or "hybridity"—a word serving to obliterate the irreducible hybridity of all language.

Let us look briefly at the document from the East India Company. (Although a commercial company, between the end of the eighteenth and the middle of the nineteenth centuries the East India Company governed its possessions in India. This is referred to in greater detail in the next chapter. Here suffice it to remind ourselves that we are reading about the employment of Indians in their own governance.) The language here is so explicit that not much analytical effort is required. Let me tabulate the points I would emphasize. This document reflects an attempt, in the interests of efficiency, to revise racial discrimination based on chromatism, the visible difference in skin color. (Chromatism seems to have something like a hold on the official philosophy of U.S. anti-racist feminism. When it is not "third world women," the buzzword is "women of color." This leads to absurdities. Japanese women, for instance, have to be coded as "third world women!" Hispanics must be seen as "women of color," and postcolonial female subjects, even when they are women of the indigenous elite of Asia and Africa, obvious examples of the production of Ariel's mate, are invited to masquerade as Caliban in the margins. This nomenclature is based on the implicit acceptance of "white" as "transparent" or "no-color," and is therefore reactive upon the self-representation of the white.)

The standards being applied in the document to legitimate racial discrimination show that both the native male and the native female are clearly inferior to the European female. Indeed, as in "William the Conqueror" and the classroom reaction to it, sexual difference comes into play only in the white arena. The concept of legitimacy in the union of the sexes only comes into being with the introduction of the European. And, even as Caliban is defined out, it is only the produced Ariel who is allowed into the arena; the final requirement for the acceptable half-caste is a "European liberal education."[13] Here, then, are extracts from the document itself:

> The chairman laid before [a Secret Court of the Directors of the Hon'ble Company Held on 6th March, 1822] a Paper signed by Himself and the Deputy Chairman submitting several suggestions

---

[12] The last chapter of Carolyn G. Heilbrun's moving book *Writing a Woman's Life* (New York: Norton, 1988), pp. 124–131, is also an example of this.

[13] For a comparable screening and a selective Christianization of slaves in South Africa, see Robert Shell, *Children of Bondage: A Social History of the Slave Society at the Cape of Good Hope, 1652–1838* (Hanover, N. H.: Univ. Press of New England, 1994).

in view to an exposition and practical illustration of the Standing Order of 1791 which provides "That no person the son of a Native Indian shall be appointed to employment in the Civil, Military, or Marine Service of the Company."[14]

Here are the passages on chromatism and the acceptability of the European female:

> It may be *fairly* deduced, that the *complexion* of those Persons was in view of the Court a serious objection to their admission. . . . The next object of consideration is the offspring of a connection between a European and a half-caste; and *it appears a matter of indifference whether the European blood be on the Male or the Female side.* The Candidates for admission to the company's service, who have been of this class of persons, have since 1791 been subjected to the examination of one of the Committees of the Direction; and if they have exhibited signs of native origin in their colour or otherwise, have been accepted or rejected by the Committee according to the degree in which their hue appeared objectionable or unobjectionable. These rejections . . . have produced some anomalies. One Brother has been accepted, another rejected. Europeans whose parents were both European, have been on the brink of Rejection for their dark complexion. . . . Discrepancies have arisen from the different views entertained by the Committee. (emphasis mine.)

In the interest of the efficient management of these anomalies and absurdities, the following criteria are offered. Here we will encounter native intercourse implicitly placed outside of legitimacy as such; and the clinching requirement of a "European liberal education."

> It is submitted
> That the Sons of aboriginal Natives of India and of the Countries to the Eastward of Native Portugese Indians, of Native West Indians, and of Africans of either sex, who are the Offspring of a connection of such Natives with Europeans, be invariably held ineligible. . . . That the Descendants from aboriginal Native Indians in the second and succeeding

generations shall be held eligible . . . on production of certain Certificates . . . that the grandfather or grandmother of the Candidate . . . was bona fide an European . . . that the father or mother of the Candidate was bona fide an European. A Certificate of Marriage of the father and mother of the candidate. The Baptismal Certificate of the Candidate. A certificate from the Master or Masters of some reputable seminary or seminaries in the United Kingdom of Great Britain and Ireland that the Candidate has had the benefit of a liberal Education under his or her tuition for a period of six years. . . . The inconveniences which might arise from the indiscriminate or unconditional admission into the Company's service of the Descendants of aboriginal Native Indians in the second or succeeding generations will be obviated . . . by the stipulated qualification of *legitimate birth* and liberal European education. (emphasis mine.)

To repeat, this document describes the efficient articulation of the right of access to a white world administering the black.[15] Because I think that this point cannot be too strongly made, I have put it forth as Exhibit C in my argument that much so-called cross-cultural disciplinary practice, even when "feminist," reproduces and forecloses colonialist structures: sanctioned ignorance, and a refusal of subject-status and therefore human-ness; that an unexamined chromatism is not only no solution but belongs to the repertory of colonialist axiomatics. On the face of it, the document seems infinitely more brutal than anything that might happen in the house of feminist criticism.[16]

---

[15] "Aboriginal" is being used here to mean full-blooded subcontinentals.
[16] More than a decade after first writing. I take comfort in the fact that Colette Guillaumin was already speaking of this in 1977. Guillaumin, *Racism, Sexism, Power and Ideology*, tr. Robert Miles (London: Routledge, 1995), pp.141–142 and *passim.* How is one to read religiosity and nationalism in the production of U.S. protest? Consider "grave suspicions concerning the prominence of regressive tendencies in the political culture of the Federal Republic" (Richard Wolin, "Introduction," in Jürgen Habermas, *The New Conservatism: Cultural Criticism and the Historians' Detace,* tr. Shierty Weber Nicholsen [Cambridge: MIT Press, 1989], p. xxxi). Consider World War II, and you have John Okada's *No-No Boys* (Seattle: Univ. of Washington Press, 1957), see Sanda Lwin, Columbia

---

[14] L/P & S/l/2, Minutes of the Secret Court of Directors, 1784–1858.

(continued on next page)

But mere benevolent intentions will not remove the possibility that the *structural* effect of limited access to the norm can be shared by two such disparate phenomena.

When versions of this general argument are presented to academic women's resource groups and the like, sympathy seems instantaneous. Yet, because of the presence of the double standard, the difference in the quality or level of generosity of discourse and allocation for the matter of the first and third worlds remains striking. This discrepancy is also to be observed within curricular planning. In the distribution of resources, feminist literary criticism celebrates the heroines of the North Atlantic tradition in a singular and individualist way, and the collective presence of women elsewhere in a pluralized and inchoate fashion. These tendencies are not covered over by our campus battles for affirmative action on behalf of "women of color," or by "international conferences" using non-repeatable funds (soft money) as substitutes for curricular change. Such battles should of course be fought with our full participation, such conferences arranged when they replace white boys talking postcoloniality. But they are ad hoc anti-sexist and anti-racist activities that should be distinguished from a specifically feminist revolution in habits of thought and intervention through a persistently critical classroom presence. In the absence of persistent vigilance, there is no guarantee that an upwardly mobile woman of color in the U.S. academy would not participate in the structure I have outlined—at least to the extent of conflating the problems of ethnic domination in the United States with the problems of exploitation across the international division of labor; just as many in Britain tend to confuse it with problems of Immigration Law. It may be painful to reckon that this, too, is a case of the certified half-caste's limited access to the norm. It is almost as if the problem of racism within feminism can qualify as such only when resident or aspiring to be resident in the North.

Indeed, those of us who ask for these standards are becoming marginalized within mainstream feminism. We are deeply interested in the tropological deconstruction of masculist universalism. But when questions of the inscription of feminine subject effects arise, we do not want to be caught within the institutional performance of the imperialist lie. We know the "correction" of a performative deconstruction is to point at another troping, and thus to another errant performance, that the critique must be persistent. We want the chance of an entry into that vertiginous process. And this can perhaps begin to happen if, in terms of disciplinary standards, you grant the thoroughly stratified larger theatre of the South, the stage of so-called de-colonization, equal rights of historical, geographical, linguistic specificity and theoretical agency. If Feminism takes its place with ethnic studies as American studies, or postcolonialism as migrant hybridism, the South is once again in shadow, the diasporic stands in for the native informant.

Univ. dissertation in progress. Consider globalization, and you come to realize that what Guillaumin calls "the *idea of* race" is in the domain of sex, not the "idea of sex," but gender; and it can be "transformed" that much more easily at the end "of the present century into a means for [global capital; she is, as a European and in the middle of the Cold War, still talking 'state'] to achieve their goals of domination, exploitation and extermination. This is a matter of simple fact" (p. 99). Population control policy as gynoride is part of Malini Karkal's thesis. The transformation of "Women in Development" to "Gender and Development" (acknowledged World Bank/UN policy) for achieving the financialization of the globe is part of that current work of cuine that constantly threatens to unhinge this book.

III

It is well to remember this when we quite correctly congratulate ourselves on today's literary criticism in the United States, attentive to the representation and self-representation of margins. So much so, indeed, that the President's Forum at the Modern Language Association annual convention almost routinely addresses questions of marginality. The American Comparative Literature Association took note of multiculturalism in a recent autocritical document.[17] Such congratulations are altogether appropriate because it is also true that, perhaps as a result of these efforts, a strong demand to keep U.S. culture purely "Western" has also been consolidated.[18] But this confrontation, important as it is, does

not amount to granting equal representation to the South; it testifies to the internal transformation of the North in response to global trends. Under pressure of this internal debate, we often conflate the two; and we tend to monumentalize something we call "margins," where the distinction between North and South is domesticated. Yet, for the sake of the daily work at the ground level, we must still raise the persistent voice of autocritique, lest we unwittingly fill the now unrecognizably displaced subject-position of the native informant.

As we try to shore up our defenses, we tend to leave untouched the politics of the specialists of the margin—area studies, anthropology, and the like. Third World studies, including Third World feminist studies in English, become so diluted that all linguistic specificity or scholarly depth in the study of culture is often ignored. Indeed, works in often indifferent English translation or works written in English or the European languages in the recently decolonized areas of the globe or written by people of so-called ethnic origin in First World space are beginning to constitute something called "Third World literature." Within this arena of tertiary education in literature, the upwardly mobile exmarginal, *justifiably* searching for validation, can help commodify marginality. Sometimes, with the best of intentions and in the name of convenience, an institutionalized double standard tends to get established: one standard of preparation and testing for our own kind and quite another for the rest of the world. Even as we join in the struggle to establish the institutional study of marginality we must still go on saying "And yet . . ."

Consider Sartre, speaking his commitment just after World War II:

> And, diverse though man's projects [*projets*—this word has the general existentialist sense of undertaking to construct a life] may be, at least none of them is wholly foreign to me. . . . Every project, even that of a Chinese, an Indian or a Negro, can be understood by a European. . . . The European of 1945 can throw himself [pro-ject] out of a situation

---

[17] The results have since been collected in Charles Bernheimer, ed., *Comparative Literature in the Age of Multiculturalism* (Baltimore: Johns Hopkins Univ. Press, 1995).

[18] Some of the initial texts were Allan Bloom, *The Closing of the American Mind: How Higher Education Has Failed Democracy and Impoverished the Souls of Today's Students* (New York: Simon and Schuster, 1987); and E. D. Hirsch, *Cultural Literacy: What Every American Needs to Know* (New York: Vintage, 1988). It is interesting to compare these with, say, Nathan Glazer, *Beyond the Melting Pot: The Negroes, Puerto Ricans, Jews, Italians, and Irish of New York City* (Cambridge: MIT Press, 1963). So far at first writing. But the field shifts fast here. At the time of revision, the plot has thickened. Arthur Schlesinger, Jr., *The Disuniting of America* (New York: Norton, 1992), exhorts the new multiculturalism to embrace the pluralist American dream in the approved American way. Daniel Patrick Moynihan, *Pandaemonium: Ethnicity in International Politics* (New York: Oxford Univ. Press, 1993) and Zbigniew K. Brzezinski, *Out of Control: Global Turmoil on the Eve of the Twenty-First Century* (New York: Scribner, 1993) appropriate some of the slogans of the other side. Charles Taylor, *Multiculturalism and "The Politics of Recognition"* (Princeton: Princeton Univ. Press, 1992), Bruce Ackerman, *The Future of Liberal Revolution* (New Haven: Yale Univ. Press, 1992), and John Rawls, *Political Liberalism* (New York: Columbia Univ. Press, 1993) come to terms with multiculturalism in the post-Soviet conjuncture in more sophisticated ways. Their treatment signals toward my work in progress. I return now to the original footnote. I have not updated the original in collecting ugly arguments for reverse discrimination: "Leftist teachers have created an atmosphere in which those who question the value of women's studies and ethnic studies are labelled sexist, racist or 'cold warriors'" (Lawrence W. Hyman, "The Culture Battle," *On Campus* 8 (Apr. 1989): 5; see also Lee Dembert, "Left Censorship at Stanford," *New York Times* 5 May 1989, p. A35. Roger Kimball, *Tenured Radicals: How Politics Has Corrupted Our Higher Education* (New York: Harper, 1990) remains a dubious classic. I cannot resist the temptation of marking two recent skirmishes: Governor Pete Wilson, in his capacity as trustee of the University of California, obliges that system to drop affirmative action; Yale University returns $20 million—donated for teaching "Western Civilization" courses—to alumnus Lee Bass. This note could easily invaginate this book, for here the native informant changes as fast as the national debt. "My Teaching for the Times," in Jan Nederveen Pieterse and Bhikhu Parekh, eds., *The Decolonizing of the Imagination* (London: Zed, 1995), pp. 177–202, is still pertinent, I think. But one must reconcile oneself to writing for an anthropology of the future.

which he conceives towards his limits *[se jeter à partir d'une situation qu'il conçoit vers ses limites]* in the same way, and . . . he may redo [*refaire*] in himself the project of the Chinese, of the Indian or the African. . . . There is always some way of understanding an idiot, a child, a primitive man or a foreigner *if one has sufficient information.*[19]

Sartre's personal and political good faith cannot be doubted. Yet, commenting on Sartre's anthropologizing of Heidegger, Derrida wrote in 1968: "Everything occurs as if the sign 'man' had no origin, no historical, cultural, or linguistic limit."[20] Indeed, if one looks at the rhetorical trace of Rome in "none of [man's projects] is wholly alien to me" *[humani nil a me alienum puto* (Terence via the *philosophes*)]*, one realizes that the history obliterated here is that of the arrogance of the radical European humanist conscience, which will consolidate it*self* by imagining the other, or, as Sartre puts it, "redo in himself the other's project," through the collection of information. Much of our literary critical globalism or Third Worldism cannot even qualify to the conscientiousness of this arrogance.

The opposite point of view, although its political importance cannot be denied, that only the marginal can speak for the margin, can, in its institutional consequences, legitimize such an arrogance of conscience. Faced with this double bind, let us consider a few methodological suggestions:

1. Let us learn to distinguish between "internal colonization"—the patterns of exploitation and domination of disenfranchised groups within a metropolitan country like the United States or Britain—and the colonization of other spaces, of which Robinson Crusoe's island is a "pure" example.[21]

2. Let us learn to discriminate the terms *colonialism*—in the European formation stretching from the mid-eighteenth to the mid-twentieth centuries—*neocolonialism*—dominant economic, political, and culturalist maneuvers emerging in our century after the uneven dissolution of the territorial empires—and *postcoloniality*—the contemporary global condition, since the first term is supposed to have passed or be passing into the second.

3. Let us take seriously the possibility that systems of representation come to hand when we secure our *own* culture—our own cultural explanations. Consider the following set:

   a. The making of an American is defined by at least a desire to enter the "We the People" of the Constitution. One cannot dismiss this as mere "essentialism" and take a position against civil rights, the Equal Rights Amendment, or the transformative opinions in favor of women's reproductive rights. We in the United States cannot not want to inhabit this rational abstraction.

   b. Traditionally, this desire for the abstract collective American "We the People" has been recoded by the fabrication of ethnic enclaves, affectively bonded subcultures, simulacra for survival that, claiming to preserve the ethnos of origin, move further and further away from the vicissitudes and transformations of the nation or group of origin. "How seriously can we[Africans] take . . . [Alice Walker's] Africa, which reads like an overlay of South Africa over a vaguely realized Nigeria?"[22]

---

[19] Sartre, *Existentialism and Humanism,* tr. Philip Mairet (New York: Haskell House, 1948), pp. 46–47. Translation modified.
[20] Derrida, "The Ends of Man," in *Margins,* p. 116. He has since written on Heidegger's philosophical complicity with Nazism in *Of Spirit.*

[21] For internal colonization, see Amin, *Unequal Development,* p. 369; Philip S. Foner and George E. Walker, *Proceedings of the Black National and State Conventions, 1865–1900* (Philadelphia: Temple Univ. Press, 1986); Cherríe Moraga, *The Last Generation* (Boston: South End Press, 1993).
[22] J. M. Coetzee, "The Beginnings of (Wo)man in Africa," *New York Times Book Review,* 30 Apr. 1989.

c. Our current tendency to obliterate the difference between U.S. internal colonization and the transformations and vicissitudes in decolonized space in the name of the pure native invests this already established ethnocultural agenda. At worst, it secures the "They" of development or aggression against the Constitutional "We." At best, it suits our institutional convenience, bringing the Third World home. The double standard can then begin to operate.[23]

In the face of the double bind of Eurocentric arrogance or unexamined nativism, the suggestions above are substantive. Deconstructive cautions would put a critical frame almost around them (we can never be fully critical) and in between them, so that we do not compound the problem by imagining the double bind too easily resolved. In fact, and in the most practical way, double binds are less dangerously enabling than the unilaterality of dilemmas solved. Thus, if we keep in mind only the substantive suggestions, we might want to help ourselves by a greater effort at historical contextualization. Yet this too, if unaccompanied by the habit of critical reading, may feed the Eurocentric arrogance in Sartre's declaration: "there is always some way of understanding [the other] if one has sufficient information." The necessarily open critical frame reminds us that the institutional organization of historical context is no more than *our* unavoidable starting point. The question remains: With this necessary preparation, to quote Sartre again, *how* does "the European"—or, in the neocolonial context, the U.S. critic and teacher of the humanities—"redo *in himself* [or herself] the project of the Chinese, of the Indian or the African?"

In the face of *this* question, deconstruction might propose a double gesture: Begin where you are; but, when in search of absolute justifications, remember that the margin as such is the impossible boundary marking off the wholly other, and the encounter with the wholly other, as it may be figured, has an unpredictable relationship to our ethical rules. The named marginal is as much a concealment as a disclosure of the margin, and where s/he discloses, s/he is singular. This double gesture informs the remark made in 1968 at a philosophical colloquium: "I was thinking, first of all, of all those places—cultural, linguistic, political, etc.—where the organization of a philosophical colloquium simply would have no meaning, where it would be no more meaningful to instigate it than to prohibit it."[24]

If we want to start something, we must ignore that our starting point is, *all efforts taken,* shaky. If we want to get something done, we must ignore that, *all provisions made,* the end will be inconclusive. This ignoring is not an active forgetfulness; it is, rather, an active *marginalizing* of the marshiness, the swampiness, the lack of firm grounding in the margins, at beginning and end. Those of us who "know" this also know that it is in those margins that philosophy philosophizes. These necessarily and actively marginalized margins haunt what we start and get done, as curious guardians. Paradoxically, if we do not marginalize them but make them the center of our attention, they slip away and nothing gets done. Perhaps *some* of the problems with *some* of what is recognizably deconstructive has been a seeming fixation with the stalled origin and the stalled end; many names for *différance* and *aporia.* Derrida's work on the ethical, on justice and the gift, faces those problem.[25] Here let me say a cruder thing: if we forget the productive unease that what we do with the utmost care is judged in the margins, in the political field one gets the liberal pluralism of repressive tolerance and sanctioned ignorance, and varieties of fundamentalism, totaliarianism, and cultural revolution; and in the field of writing about and teaching literature, one gets the benign or resentful conservatism of the

---

[23] The last few paragraphs are a self-citation from "Scattered Speculations on the Question of Cultural Studies," in Spivak, *Outside,* pp. 278–279.

[24] Derrida, "Ends of Man," pp. 112–113.

[25] In "Force of Law," *Given Time, Gift of Death, Aporias* and *passim* (as they say).

establishment *and* the multiculturalist masquerade of the privileged as the disenfranchised, or their liberator, both anchored in a lack of respect for the singularity and unverifiability of "literature as such."

This is marginal in the general sense, no more and no less than a formula for doing things: the active and necessary marginalization of the strange guardians in the margin who keep us from vanguardism. The marginal in the narrow sense are the victims of the best-known history of centralization: the emergence of the straight white Christian man of property as the ethical subject. Because there is something like a relationship between the general and the narrow sense, the problem of making a margin in the house of feminism can be stated in another way. In her influential and by now classic essay "The Laugh of the Medusa," Hélène Cixous writes: "As subject *for* history, woman occurs simultaneously in several places.[26] This can be taken to mean that, in a historical narrative in which single male figures or groups of men are definitive, woman or women as such cannot fit neatly into the established periodizing rubrics or categories. Maximally, as Cixous goes on to point out, this might

also mean that the feminist woman becomes part of every struggle, *in a certain way.*

Academic U.S. feminism has not really been part of every struggle. But today's increasing interest in multiculturalist or postcolonial marginality, in marginality in the narrow sense, is a straw in the globalizing wind within feminism in the academy. The exuberance of this interest sometimes overlooks a problem: that a concern with women, *and* men, who have not been written in the *same* cultural inscription (a working hypothesis that works well in colonial situations), cannot be mobilized *in the same way* as the investigation of gendering in one's own. It is not impossible, but new ways have to be learned and taught, and attention to the margin in general must be persistently renewed. We understand it more easily when folks of the other *gender* inscription wish to join in our struggle. For example, given the history of centuries of patriarchal privilege—including malevolence *and* benevolence toward women—I confess to a certain unease—not prohibitive obviously—celebrating a man's text about a woman.[27] Yet, when we want to intervene in the heritage of colonialism or the practice of neocolonialism, we take our goodwill for our guarantee.

---

[26] Hélène Cixous, "The Laugh of the Medusa," in Elaine Marks and Isabelle de Courtivron, eds., *New French Feminisms: An Anthology* (Amherst: Univ. of Massachusetts Press, 1980), p. 252.

[27] Editor's note: Spivak refers here to her reading of the novel *Foe,* by J. M. Coetzee, elsewhere in *A Critique of Postcolonial Reason.*

FOR FURTHER READING

Alexander, M. Jacqui, and Chandra Talpade Mohanty, eds. *Feminist Genealogies, Colonial Legacies, Democratic Futures.* New York: Routledge, 1997.

Alexander, M. Jacqui. "Erotic autonomy as a politics of decolonization: An anatomy of feminist and state practice in the Bahamas tourist economy." In *Feminist Genealogies, Colonial Legacies," Democratic Futures,* edited by M. Jacqui Alexander and Chandra Talpade Mohanty. New York: Routledge, 1997.

Basch, Linda G., Nina Glick Schiller, and Cristina Szanton Blanc, eds. *Nations Unbound: Transnational Projects, Postcolonial Predicaments, and Deterritorialized Nation-States.* New York: Gordon and Breach, 1994.

Basu, Amrita, ed. *The Challenge of Local Feminisms: Women's Movements on Global Perspective.* Boulder, CO: Westview Press, 1995.

Bhaskaran, Suparna. *Made in India: Decolonizations, Queer Sexualities, Trans/national Projects.* New York: Palgrave Macmillan, 2004.

Chowdhry, Geeta, and Sheila Nair, eds. *Power, Postcolonialism, and International Relations: Reading Race, Gender and Class*. New York: Routledge, 2002.

Dhruvarajan, Vanaja, and Jill Vickers ed. *Gender, Race, and Nation: A Global Perspective*. Toronto: University of Toronto Press, 2002.

Fuentes, Annette, and Barbara Ehrenreich. *Women in the Global Factory*. Reprint edition. Boston: South End Press, 1983.

Grewal, Inderpal, and Caren Kaplan, eds. *Scattered Hegemonies: Postmodernity and Transnational Feminist Practices*. Minneapolis: University of Minnesota Press, 1994.

Grewal, Inderpal. *Transnational America: Feminisms, Diasporas, and Neoliberalisms*. Durham: Duke University Press, 2005.

Hawkesworth, Mary E. *Globalization and Feminist Activism*. Lanham, MD: Rowman and Littlefield, 2006.

Heldke, Lisa. *Exotic Appetites: Ruminations of a Food Adventurer*. New York: Routledge, 2003.

Kaplan, Caren, Norma Alarcón, and Minoo Moallem, eds. *Between Woman and Nation: Nationalisms, Transnational Feminisms, and the State*. Durham, NC: Duke University Press, 1999.

————. *Questions of Travel: Postmodern Discourses of Displacement*. Durham, NC: Duke University Press, 1996.

Keating, Ana Louise, and Gloria Anzaldúa, eds. *This Bridge We Call Home: Radical Visions for Transformation*. New York: Routledge, 2002.

McClintock, Anne, Aamir Mufti, and Ella Shohat, eds. *Dangerous Liaisons: Gender, Nation, and Postcolonial Perspectives*. Minneapolis: University of Minnesota Press, 1997.

McClintock, Anne. *Imperial Leather: Race, Gender, and Sexuality in the Colonial Conquest*. New York: Routledge, 1995.

Mies, Maria. *Patriarchy and Accumulation on a World Scale: Women in the International Division of Labour*. 2nd ed. London: Zed Books, 1999.

Mohanty, Chandra Talpade. *Feminism Without Borders: Decolonizing Theory, Practicing Solidarity*. Durham, NC: Duke University Press, 2003.

————. "Under Western Eyes." In *Colonial Discourse and Postcolonial Theory: A Reader*, edited by Patrick Williams and Laura Chrisman. New York: Columbia University Press, 1994.

Morgan, Robin. *Sisterhood Is Global*. New York: The Feminist Press, 1996.

Narayan, Uma, and Sandra Harding, eds. *Decentering the Center: Philosophy for a Multicultural, Postcolonial, and Feminist World*. Bloomington: Indiana University Press, 2000.

Narayan, Uma. *Dislocating Cultures: Identities, Traditions, and Third-World Feminism*. New York: Routledge, 1997.

Ruether, Rosemary Radford. *Integrating Ecofeminism, Globalization, and World Religions*. Lanham, MD: Rowman and Littlefield, 2005.

Scott, Joan W., Debra Keates, and Cora Kaplan, eds. *Transitions, Environments, Translations: Feminisms in International Politics*. New York: Routledge, 1997.

Shohat, Ella, ed. *Talking Visions: Multicultural Feminism in a Transitional Age*. Cambridge, MA: MIT Press, 1999.

Spivak, Gayatri Chakravorty. "Can the Subaltern Speak? Speculations on Widow Sacrifice." *Wedge* 7/8 (1985): 120–130.

Stoler, Ann Laura. *Carnal Knowledge and Imperial Power: Race and the Intimate in Colonial Rule*. Berkeley: University of California Press, 2002.

Trinh, T. Minh-Ha. *Woman Native Other: Writing Postcoloniality and Feminism*. Bloomington, IN: Indiana University Press, 1989.

Visvanathan, Nalini, Lynn Duggan, Laurie Nisonoff, and Nan Wiegersma, eds. *Women, Gender, and Development Reader*. Atlantic Highlands, NJ: Zed Books, 1997.

MEDIA RESOURCES

Behind the Labels: Garment Workers on U.S. Saipan. VHS. Produced by Tia Lessin and Oxygen (US, 2001). Lured by false promises and driven by desperation, thousands of Chinese and Filipina women pay high fees to work in garment factories on the Pacific island of Saipan—the only U.S. territory exempt from labor and immigration laws. The clothing they sew, bearing the "Made in the USA" label, is shipped duty and quota-free to the United States for sale by The GAP, J. Crew, Polo, and other retailers. Powerful hidden-camera footage and garment workers' personal stories offer an unforgettable glimpse into indentured labor and the workings of the global sweatshop—where

14-hour shifts, payless paydays, and lock-downs are routine. Available: Witness Video, http://www.witness.org/, or 718–783–1593.

Books Not Bars. VHS. Directed by Mark Landsman (US, 2001). This video documents the inspiring youth-led movement against the massive prison industry in the United States. It illustrates the negative impact of this for-profit prison industry on youth—particularly those from communities of color. The video provides inspiring examples of peer activism, youth organizing, and mobilization around prison issues, providing youth with tangible ways to get involved with the movement to reform the U.S. prison system. A nice follow-up to Angela Davis's essay. Available: Witness Video, http://www.witness.org/, or 718–783–1593.

Homeland: Four Portraits of Native Action. DVD/VHS. Directed by Roberta Grossman. Produced by The Katahdin Foundation (US, 2005). Having brutally occupied the homeland of Native Americans, the invading Europeans forced the indigenous population onto reservations—land that was specifically selected because of its apparent worthlessness. To add salt to wounds, multinational energy companies are coming back to extract the hidden mineral wealth of the reservations, and are leaving a trail of toxins that, if unchecked, will make the land unlivable for centuries to come. A wonderful illustration of Andrea Smith's account of conquest. Available: Bullfrog Films, www.bullfrogfilms.com, or 800–543–3764.

Life and Debt. VHS. Produced by Stephanie Black (US, 2001). Jamaica is a prime example of the impact economic globalization can have on a developing country. This film dissects the "mechanism of debt" that is destroying local agriculture and industry while substituting sweatshops and cheap imports. An unapologetic look at the "new world order," from the point of view of Jamaican workers, farmers, and government and policy officials who see the reality of globalization from the ground up. Available: Public Broadcasting Service, http://www.pbs.org/.

Not for Sale. DVD/VHS. Produced by Moving Images. Directed by Mark Dworkin and Melissa Young (US, 2002). An engaging documentary that explores the biocolonial aspects of global trade agreements like the WTO. Patents and other intellectual property rights have expanded to include ownership of knowledge and living creatures. What does this mean for the environment, our food supply, and human rights? This film looks at farmers, indigenous people, and antiglobalization activists who oppose patents on life and advocate for a world where life is not a commodity but something to be treasured. Available: Bullfrog Films, www.bullfrogfilms.com, or 800–543–3764.

This Black Soil: A Story of Resistance and Rebirth. DVD. Directed by Teresa Konechne. Produced by Working Hands Productions (US, 2004). This inspiring film chronicles the successful struggle of an impoverished rural African-American community to pursue a new vision of prosperity. Catalyzed by the defeat of a state plan to build a maximum-security prison in their backyard, residents secure grants, create a non-profit organization, purchase the proposed prison site land, and begin building a new community with affordable housing, sustainable wages, a daycare center, and a community farm. The film provides a vision beyond the horrors of the prison industrial complex outlined by Angela Davis. Available: Bullfrog Films, www.bullfrogfilms.com, or 800–543–3764.

CHAPTER 7

FEMINIST ETHICAL THEORY

Feminism is based on the foundational claim that men's subordination of women is a fundamental moral wrong, and so feminists everywhere have long brought serious attention to ethical matters and methods, and to exhibiting the wrongs of sexism. Many have argued that women's experiences and perspectives offer ethical insights that are different or superior to those emphasized in male-centered traditions, but oppression prevents women's full exercise of moral agency. A classic example, Mary Wollstonecraft's *A Vindication of the Rights of Woman* explained that women's tendencies to exhibit exemplary care and compassion flow from reproductive roles, but also suggested that cultural conceptions of virtue harm women by upholding damaging social norms. In the twentieth century, even before feminism hit the academic scene, the work of quite a few women philosophers and intellectuals (such as Jane Addams, Anna Julia Cooper, Simone Weil, Simone de Beauvoir, Iris Murdoch, and Hannah Arendt) focused on both the pressing moral issues of their times, and the more abstract questions about the relationships between ethics, politics, and agency.

Ethical and moral questions are fundamental to Western philosophy, and moral rules can be a great tool of oppression, so it is not surprising that ethics has become such a rich and influential field in feminist philosophy. Moral judgments can prevent the subordinated from exercising freedom or questioning authority, or rationalize punishment for transgressions. And the sexism in canonical moral philosophy is rather overt. Western philosophy typically takes privileged masculine (and often white or bourgeois) ideals to represent human goodness, virtue, and ethical decision making, and promotes approaches that value distanced reason and autonomy over female-associated traits such as emotional complexity and interdependence. They also usually ignore intimate and "private sphere" concerns, or misrepresent female agency as irrational or overly emotional. Confronting those shortcomings head-on, some of the first explicitly feminist works published in academic philosophy aimed to serve feminist activist and political efforts by bringing sharp analytical attention to practical issues of particular interest to women, such as affirmative action, equal pay, abortion rights, rape, and sexual divisions of labor. Scholars also began to uncover and analyze the gender biases of canonical figures in Western ethics, and to explore the deep philosophical implications of beginning investigations about ethics from female perspectives, with women's interests in mind, and with a rock-bottom commitment to understanding and eliminating oppression. Feminist ethics became a field of moral theory particularly attentive to ethical dimensions of dominance and subordination, the gendered dimensions of moral agency, and the cross-pollinations of public and private realms and realities.

Work in feminist ethics was heavily influenced by the publication of psychologist Carol Gilligan's *In A Different Voice: Psychological Theory and Women's Development* in 1982, which brought questions about gender and moral development to the fore. Gilligan was deeply critical of the work of Lawrence Kohlberg, who previously described a general picture of healthy moral development as a progression through various levels, from immature dependence, to conformity with convention, to mature independent thought in relation to universal principles (such as utilitarianism or the Kantian categorical imperative). Kohlberg's scale was developed through interviews with boys and men, but when female subjects were evaluated in relation to his scale, they seemed rarely to progress beyond his "conventional" level, and therefore appeared morally deficient or immature. Gilligan's own subsequent studies asked whether Kohlberg's schema distorted women's moral experience, and if girls and women actually have a distinct and effective pattern of moral development—a "care perspective," in contrast with a "justice perspective." As the selections in this chapter make clear, her work ignited interesting, important, and long-standing debates about gender difference, ethics, and the legitimacy of stereotypically feminine virtues.

In the first selection, "Moral Orientation and Moral Development," Carol Gilligan describes care and justice perspectives as analogous to the black and white figure in Gestalt psychology that

may be seen as either a vase or as two female profiles. Similarly, subjects frame moral situations in terms of either justice or care, but not both simultaneously. The two moral orientations cannot be integrated, and they also are not complete opposites. Philosophically, their distinctness makes it all the more obvious that the care perspective ought to be fully explored and elaborated by ethical theory. Gilligan concludes that by making the care perspective more coherent and its terms more explicit, ethical theory can increase women's abilities to articulate their experiences and perceptions. It may also foster the ability of others to hear them.

Seyla Benhabib shows in more detail how the Gilligan-Kohlberg controversy illustrates central issues in ethical theory of particular importance to feminists. Benhabib sketches feminist theory's tasks as including social scientific research, which provides analyses of the ways in which sex/gender systems continually reinscribe oppression, and normative reflection on these findings, so as to identify liberatory options. Identifying a split that must be challenged both experimentally and theoretically, she shows that the justice perspective is culturally associated with the public, historical, and moral, and therefore confines the moral point of view to the perspective of a bodiless, amorphous, and "generalized" other. In contrast, views about the good life are culturally associated with the private, natural, and nonmoral, and so their roles in ethical deliberation are ignored. Benhabib suggests the need to recognize "situated concrete others" as a way to undo the binary between justice and the good life, and indicates how communicative ethics and a relational view of the self are useful for developing critical and emancipatory alternatives to justice traditions.

Returning to specific questions about caring, in "Taking Care: Care as Practice and Value," Virginia Held provides a critical overview of feminist perspectives on ethics of care that have developed since Gilligan's studies, tracing the various meanings and senses of caring offered by a range of authors. She describes work in feminist philosophy as aiming to "understand, evaluate, and guide the relatedness of human beings, built and rebuilt," a central task for ethical theory. After reviewing the theories of Nel Noddings, Joan Tronto, Annette Baier, and other leading thinkers in the field, Held concludes that we need to understand care as both a value and a practice. As a practice, care is a way of being in the world, not reducible to individual acts. Understanding the value of care includes recognizing its role in social and political life beyond the family and household. Because of its fundamental role in human moral life, we ought to consider care a value worthy of the sort of theoretical elaboration justice has received.

Kelly Oliver's "Conflicted Love" explores the influence of stereotypic representations of maternity and paternity on the potential for loving relationships. Despite the fact that there are many family forms, the myth of the natural nuclear heterosexual two-parent unit continues to drive theoretical conceptions of the family, and psychoanalytic understandings of the conflicts at the heart of selfhood. But those models present an image of a father as an absent, disembodied authority incapable of love, and an embodied mother who fulfills animal needs but who cannot love as a social or ethical being. How could ethical agency be enabled by such distorting ideas about social bodies and their capacities? To answer this, Oliver rethinks gendered bodies, thus opening up possibilities for the transformation of familial relationships and the ethical possibilities fostered there.

Alongside efforts to reform or revise existing moral models, some feminist philosophers have pressed a more foundational rejection of traditional and male-defined ideas about ethics. Sarah Hoagland's essay "Separating from Heterosexualism" characterizes traditional ethics as a closed system of social control that inculcates antagonistic values of dominance and subordination, and undermines individual moral agency. She argues that heterosexualism, colonialism,

and racism normalize dominant and subordinate relationships and thus undermine the agency of oppressed/resisting subjects, and that reformative strategies fail to deeply challenge the institutional power that limits and distorts agency. For example, ideals of femininity normalize male domination by painting a picture of women content with their subordination, so from a conceptual system that upholds such ideals, women's resistance can only be seen as irrational or insane. To see and understand women's moral agency as resistance requires a revolution in value. Hoagland believes that lesbian agency and communities are built on such revolutionary value, providing excellent grounding for female moral agency.

Feminist ethical theory continues to engage practical ethical matters, including racial privilege, LGBT rights, sex work, reproductive technologies, violence, militarism, and environmental issues. Taking such a political approach to be paradigmatic of feminist ethics, in "Seeing Power in Morality," Margaret Urban Walker finds morality to be an important tool for those with less power to gain understanding and challenge inequalities. Western moral theory has often described moral rationality in ideal or transcendent terms, as if ethical deliberations ought to be independent of material realities, social histories, and human contingencies. Such a view considers attention to political and other life conditions as antithetical to understanding ethics. But Walker shows that we can be sensitive to the presence of power of social practices without reducing ethics to raw power, by joining feminist insights with naturalist attention to the ways power can be morally exercised through arrangements of responsibilities.

In contrast with ethical theories that conceive of agency as mostly about choices, in "The Moral Powers of Victims," Claudia Card points out that living with moral atrocities, or evils, and their legacies is seldom a moral choice. In addition to the direct harms they cause, the evils of genocide, slavery, mass rape, and torture change moral relationships dramatically by creating obligations in perpetrators and bystanders who benefit from those crimes, and moral powers in victims who survive. Card elucidates the negative and positive moral powers that survivors use to move toward healing and rectification. As many other philosophers have shown, blame and its related attitudes of condemnation and resentment are negative powers that can identify and trigger guilt and obligation. But Card is particularly interested in the positive power of forgiveness, which can relieve victims' burdens that may not be morally discharged in any other way. Her discussion of the dilemmas of forgiveness addresses questions at the heart of ethical life in a world filled with violent abuses of power, where we still strive for hope and flourishing.

MORAL ORIENTATION AND MORAL DEVELOPMENT

Carol Gilligan

When one looks at an ambiguous figure like the drawing that can be seen as a young or old woman, or the image of the vase and the faces, one initially sees it in only one way. Yet even after seeing it in both ways, one way often seems more compelling. This phenomenon reflects the laws of perceptual organization that favor certain modes of visual grouping. But it also suggests a tendency to view reality as unequivocal and thus to argue that there is one right or better way of seeing.

The experiments of the Gestalt psychologists on perceptual organization provide a series of demonstrations that the same proximal pattern can be organized in different ways so that, for example, the same figure can be seen as a square or a diamond, depending on its orientation in relation to a surrounding frame. Subsequent studies show that the context influencing which of two possible organizations will be chosen may depend not only on the features of the array presented but also on the perceiver's past experience or expectation. Thus, a birdwatcher and a rabbit-keeper are likely to see the duck-rabbit figure in different ways; yet this difference does not imply that one way is better or a higher form of perceptual organization. It does, however, call attention to the fact that the rabbit-keeper, perceiving the rabbit, may not see the ambiguity of the figure until someone points out that it can also be seen as a duck.

This essay presents a similar phenomenon with respect to moral judgment, describing two moral perspectives that organize thinking in different ways. The analogy to ambiguous figure perception arises from the observation that although people are aware of both perspectives, they tend to adopt one or the other in defining and resolving moral conflict. Since moral judgments organize thinking about choice in difficult situations, the adoption of a single perspective may facilitate clarity of decision. But the wish for clarity may also imply a compelling human need for resolution or closure, especially in the face of decisions that give rise to discomfort or unease. Thus, the search for clarity in seeing may blend with a search for justification, encouraging the position that there is one right or better way to think about moral problems. This question, which has been the subject of intense theological and philosophical debate, becomes of interest to the psychologist not only because of its psychological dimensions—the tendency to focus on one perspective and the wish for justification—but also because one moral perspective currently dominates psychological thinking and is embedded in the most widely used measure for assessing the maturity of moral reasoning.

In describing an alternative standpoint, I will reconstruct the account of moral development around two moral perspectives, grounded in different dimensions of relationship that give rise to moral concern. The justice perspective, often equated with moral reasoning, is recast as one way of seeing moral problems and a care perspective is brought forward as an alternate vision or frame. The distinction between justice and care as alternative perspectives or moral orientations is based empirically on the observation that a shift in the focus of attention from concerns about justice to concerns about care changes the definition of what constitutes a moral problem, and leads the same situation to be seen in different ways. Theoretically, the distinction between justice and care cuts across the familiar divisions between thinking and feeling, egoism and altruism, theoretical and practical reasoning. It calls attention to the fact that all human relationships, public and private, can be characterized *both* in terms of equality and in terms of attachment, and that both inequality and detachment constitute grounds for moral concern. Since everyone is vulnerable both to oppression and to abandonment, two moral visions—one of justice and one of care—recur in human experience. The moral injunctions not to act unfairly toward others, and not to turn away from someone in need, capture these different concerns.

The conception of the moral domain as [comprising] at least two moral orientations raises new questions about observed differences in moral judgment and the disagreements to which they give rise. Key to this revision is the distinction between differences in developmental stage (more or less adequate positions within a single orientation) and differences in orientation (alternative perspectives or frameworks). The findings reported in this paper of an association between moral orientation and gender speak directly to the continuing controversy over sex differences in moral reasoning. In doing so, however, they also offer an empirical explanation for why previous thinking about moral development has been organized largely within the justice framework.

My research on moral orientation derives from an observation made in the course of studying the relationship between moral judgment and action. Two studies, one of college students describing their experiences of moral conflict and choice, and one of pregnant women who were considering abortion, shifted the focus of attention from the ways people reason about hypothetical dilemmas to the ways people construct moral conflicts and choices in their lives. This change in approach made it possible to see what experiences people define in moral terms, and to explore the relationship between the understanding of moral problems and the reasoning strategies used and the actions taken in attempting to resolve them. In this context, I observed that women, especially when speaking about their own experiences of moral conflict and choice, often define moral problems in a way that eludes the categories of moral theory and is at odds with the assumptions that shape psychological thinking about morality and about the self.[1] This discovery, that a different voice often guides the moral judgments and

the actions of women, called attention to a major design problem in previous moral judgment research: namely, the use of all-male samples as the empirical basis for theory construction.

The selection of an all-male sample as the basis for generalizations that are applied to both males and females is logically inconsistent. As a research strategy, the decision to begin with a single-sex sample is inherently problematic, since the categories of analysis will tend to be defined on the basis of the initial data gathered and subsequent studies will tend to be restricted to these categories. Piaget's work on the moral judgment of the child illustrates these problems since he defined the evolution of children's consciousness and practice of rules on the basis of his study of boys playing marbles, and then undertook a study of girls to assess the generality of his findings. Observing a series of differences both in the structure of girls' games and "in the actual mentality of little girls," he deemed these differences not of interest because "it was not this contrast which we proposed to study." Girls, Piaget found, "rather complicated our interrogatory in relation to what we know about boys," since the changes in their conception of rules, although following the same sequence observed in boys, did not stand in the same relation to social experience. Nevertheless, he concluded that "in spite of these differences in the structure of the game and apparently in the players' mentality, we find the same process at work as in the evolution of the game of marbles."[2]

Thus, girls were of interest insofar as they were similar to boys and confirmed the generality of Piaget's findings. The differences noted, which included a greater tolerance, a greater tendency toward innovation in solving conflicts, a greater willingness to make exceptions to rules, and a lesser concern with legal elaboration, were not seen as germane to "the psychology of rules," and therefore were regarded as insignificant for the study of children's moral judgment. Given the confusion that currently surrounds the discussion of sex differences in moral judgment, it is important to emphasize that the differences observed by Piaget did not pertain to girls' understanding of rules *per se* or to the development of the idea of justice in their thinking, but rather to the way girls structured their games and their approach to conflict resolution—that is, to their use rather than their understanding of the logic of rules and justice.

Kohlberg, in his research on moral development, did not encounter these problems since he equated moral development with the development of justice reasoning and initially used an all-male sample as the basis for theory and test construction. In response to his critics, Kohlberg has recently modified his claims, renaming his test a measure of "justice reasoning" rather than of "moral maturity" and acknowledging the presence of a care perspective in people's moral thinking.[3] But the widespread use of Kohlberg's measure as a measure of moral development together with his own continuing tendency to equate justice reasoning with moral judgment leaves the problem of orientation differences unsolved. More specifically, Kohlberg's efforts to assimilate thinking about care to the six-stage developmental sequence he derived and refined by analyzing changes in justice reasoning (relying centrally on his all-male longitudinal sample), underscores the continuing importance of the points raised in this paper concerning (1) the distinction between differences in developmental stage within a single orientation and differences in orientation, and (2) the fact that the moral thinking of girls and women was not examined in establishing either the meaning or the measurement of moral judgment within contemporary psychology.

An analysis of the language and logic of men's and women's moral reasoning about a range of hypothetical and real dilemmas underlies the distinction elaborated in this paper between a justice and a care perspective. The empirical association of care reasoning with women suggests that discrepancies observed between moral theory and the moral judgments of girls and women may reflect a shift in perspective, a change in moral orientation. Like the figure-ground shift in ambiguous figure perception, justice and care as moral perspectives are not opposites or mirror-images of one another, with justice uncaring and care unjust. Instead, these perspectives denote different ways of organizing the basic elements of moral judgment: self, others, and the relationship between them. With the shift in perspective from justice to care, the organizing dimension of relationship changes from inequality/equality to attachment/detachment, reorganizing thoughts, feelings, and language so that words connoting relationship like "dependence" or "responsibility" or even moral terms such as "fairness" and "care" take on different meanings. To organize relationships in terms of attachment rather than in terms of equality changes the way human connection is imagined, so that the images or metaphors of relationship shift from hierarchy or balance to network or web. In addition, each organizing framework leads to a different way of imagining the self as a moral agent.

From a justice perspective, the self as moral agent stands as the figure against a ground of social relationships, judging the conflicting claims of self and others against a standard of equality or equal respect (the Categorical Imperative, the Golden Rule). From a care perspective, the relationship becomes the figure, defining self and others. Within the context of relationship, the self as a moral agent perceives and responds to the perception of need. The shift in moral perspective is manifest by a change in the moral question from "What is just?" to "How to respond?"

For example, adolescents asked to describe a moral dilemma often speak about peer or family pressure in which case the moral question becomes how to maintain moral principles or standards and resist the influence of one's parents or friends. "I have a right to my religious opinions," one teenager explains, referring to a religious difference with his parents. Yet, he adds, "I respect their views." The same dilemma, however, is also construed by adolescents as a problem of attachment, in which case the moral question becomes: how to respond both to oneself and to one's friends or one's parents, how to maintain or strengthen connection in the face of differences in belief. "I understand their fear of my new religious ideas," one teenager explains, referring to her religious disagreement with her parents, "but they really ought to listen to me and try to understand my beliefs."

One can see these two statements as two versions of essentially the same thing. Both teenagers present self-justifying arguments about religious disagreement; both address the claims of self and of others in a way that honors both. Yet each frames the problem in different terms, and the use of moral language points to different concerns. The first speaker casts the problem in terms of individual rights that must be respected within the relationship. In other words, the figure of the considering is the self looking on the disagreeing selves in relationship, and the aim is to get the other selves to acknowledge the right to disagree. In the case of the second speaker, figure and ground shift. The relationship becomes the figure of the considering, and relationships are seen to require listening and efforts at understanding differences in belief. Rather than the right to disagree, the speaker focuses on caring to hear and to be heard. Attention shifts from the grounds for agreement (rights and respect) to the grounds for understanding (listening and speaking, hearing and being heard). This shift is marked by a change in moral language from the stating of separate claims to rights and respect ("I have a right . . . I respect their views.") to the activities of relationship—the injunction to listen and try to understand ("I understand . . . they ought to listen . . . and try to understand."). The metaphor of moral voice itself carries the terms of the care perspective and reveals how the language chosen for moral theory is not orientation neutral.

The language of the public abortion debate, for example, reveals a justice perspective. Whether the abortion dilemma is cast as a conflict of rights or in terms of respect for human life, the claims of the fetus and of the pregnant woman are balanced or placed in opposition. The morality of abortion decisions thus construed hinges on the scholastic or metaphysical question as to whether the fetus is a life or a person, and whether its claims take precedence over those of the pregnant woman. Framed as a problem of care, the dilemma posed by abortion shifts. The connection between the fetus and the pregnant woman becomes the focus of attention and the question becomes whether it is responsible or irresponsible, caring or careless, to extend or to end this connection. In this construction, the abortion dilemma arises because there is no way not to act, and no way of acting that does not alter the connection between self and others. To ask what actions constitute care or are more caring directs attention to the parameters of connection and the costs of detachment, which become subjects of moral concern.

Finally, two medical students, each reporting a decision not to turn in someone who has violated the school rules against drinking, cast their decision in different terms. One student constructs the decision as an act of mercy, a decision to override justice in light of the fact that the violator has shown "the proper degrees of contrition." In addition, this student raises the question as to whether or not the alcohol policy is just, i.e., whether the school has the right to prohibit drinking. The other student explains the decision not to turn in a proctor who was drinking on the basis that turning him in is not a good way to respond to this problem, since it would dissolve the relationship between them and thus cut off an avenue for help. In addition, this student raises the question as to whether the proctor sees his drinking as a problem.

This example points to an important distinction, between care as understood or construed within a justice framework and care as a framework or a perspective on moral decision. Within a justice construction, care becomes the mercy that tempers justice; or connotes the special obligations or supererogatory duties that arise in personal relationships; or signifies altruism freely chosen—a decision to modulate the strict demands of justice by considering equity or showing forgiveness; or characterizes a choice to sacrifice the claims of the self. All of these interpretations of care leave the basic assumptions of a justice framework intact: the division between the self and others, the logic of reciprocity or equal respect.

As a moral perspective, care is less well elaborated, and there is no ready vocabulary in moral theory to describe its terms. As a framework for moral decision, care is grounded in the assumption that self and other are interdependent, an assumption reflected in a view of action as responsive and, therefore, as arising in relationship rather than the view of action as emanating from within the self and, therefore, "self governed." Seen as responsive, the self is by definition connected to others, responding to perceptions, interpreting events, and governed by the organizing tendencies of human interaction and human language. Within this framework, detachment, whether from self or from others, is morally problematic, since it breeds moral blindness or indifference—a failure to discern or respond to need. The question of what responses constitute care and what responses lead to hurt draws attention to the fact that one's own terms may differ from those of others. Justice in this context becomes understood as respect for people in their own terms.

The medical student's decision not to turn in the proctor for drinking reflects a judgment that turning him in is not the best way to respond to the drinking problem, itself seen as a sign of detachment or lack of concern. Caring for the proctor thus raises the question of what actions are most likely to ameliorate this problem, a decision that leads to the question of what are the proctor's terms.

The shift in organizing perspective here is marked by the fact that the first student does not consider the terms of the other as potentially different but instead assumes one set of terms. Thus the student alone becomes the arbiter of what is *the* proper degree of contrition. The second student, in turn, does not attend to the question of whether the alcohol policy itself is just or fair. Thus each student discusses an aspect of the problem that the other does not mention.

These examples are intended to illustrate two cross-cutting perspectives that do not negate one another but focus attention on different dimensions of the situation, creating a sense of ambiguity around the question of what is the problem to be solved. Systematic research on moral orientation as a dimension of moral judgment and action initially addressed three questions: (1) Do people articulate concerns about justice and concerns about care in discussing a moral dilemma? (2) Do people tend to focus their attention on one set of concerns and minimally represent the other? and (3) Is there an association between moral orientation and gender? Evidence from studies that included a common set of questions about actual experiences of moral conflict and matched samples of males and females provides affirmative answers to all three questions.

When asked to describe a moral conflict they had faced, 55 out of 80 (69 percent) educationally advantaged North American adolescents and adults raised considerations of both justice and care. Two-thirds (54 out of 80) however, focused their attention on one set of concerns, with focus defined as 75 percent or more of the considerations raised pertaining either to justice or to care. Thus the person who presented, say, two care considerations in discussing a moral conflict was more likely to give a third, fourth, and fifth than to balance care and justice concerns—a finding consonant with the assumption that justice and care constitute organizing frameworks for moral decision. The men and the women involved in this study (high school students, college students, medical students, and adult professionals) were equally likely to demonstrate the focus phenomenon (two-thirds of both sexes fell into the outlying focus categories). There were, however, sex differences in the direction of focus. With one exception, all of the men who focused, focused on justice. The women divided, with roughly one third focusing on justice and one third on care.[4]

These findings clarify the different voice phenomenon and its implications for moral theory and for women. First, it is notable that if women were eliminated from the research sample, care focus in moral reasoning would virtually disappear. Although care focus was by no means characteristic of all women, it was almost exclusively a female phenomenon in this sample of educationally advantaged North Americans. Second, the fact that the women were advantaged means that the focus on care cannot readily be attributed to educational deficit or occupational disadvantage—the explanation Kohlberg and others have given for findings of lower levels of justice reasoning in women.[5] Instead, the focus on care in women's moral reasoning draws attention to the limitations of a justice-focused moral theory and highlights the presence of care concerns in the moral thinking of both women and men. In this light, the Care/Justice group composed of one third of the women and one third of the men becomes of particular interest, pointing to the need for further research that attends to the way people organize justice and care in relation to one another—whether, for example, people alternate perspectives, like seeing the rabbit and the duck in the rabbit-duck figure, or integrate the two perspectives in a way that resolves or sustains ambiguity.

Third, if the moral domain is [composed] of at least two moral orientations, the focus phenomenon suggests that people have a tendency to lose sight of one moral perspective in arriving at a moral decision—a liability equally shared by both sexes. The present findings further suggest that men and women tend to lose sight of different perspectives. The most striking result is the virtual absence of care-focus reasoning among the men. Since the men raised concerns about care in discussing moral conflicts and thus presented care concerns as morally relevant, a question is why they did not elaborate these concerns to a greater extent.

In summary, it becomes clear why attention to women's moral thinking led to the identification of a different voice and raised questions about the place of justice and care within a comprehensive moral theory. It also is clear how the selection of an all-male sample for research on moral judgment fosters an equation of morality with justice, providing little data discrepant with this view. In the present study, data discrepant with a justice-focused moral theory comes from a third of the women. Previously, such women were seen as having a problem understanding "morality." Yet these women may also be seen as exposing the problem in a justice-focused moral theory. This may explain the decision of researchers to exclude girls and women at the initial stage of moral judgment research. If one begins with the premise that "all morality consists in respect for rules,"[6] or "virtue is one and its name is justice,"[7] then women are likely to appear problematic within moral theory. If one begins with women's moral judgments, the problem becomes how to construct a theory that encompasses care as a focus of moral attention rather than as a subsidiary moral concern.

The implications of moral orientation for moral theory and for research on moral development are extended by a study designed and conducted by Kay Johnston.[8] Johnston set out to explore the relationship between moral orientation and problem-solving strategies, creating a standard method using fables for assessing spontaneous moral orientation and orientation preference. She asked 60 eleven- and fifteen-year-olds to state and to solve the moral problem posed by the fable. Then she asked: "Is there another way to solve this problem?" Most of the children initially constructed the fable problems either in terms of justice or in terms of care; either they stood back from the situation and appealed to a rule or principle for adjudicating the conflicting claims or they entered the situation in an effort to discover or create a way of responding to all of the needs. About half of the children, slightly more fifteen- than eleven-year-olds, spontaneously switched moral orientation when asked whether there was another way to solve the problem. Others did so following an interviewer's cue as to the form such a switch might take. Finally, the children were asked which of the solutions they described was the best solution. Most of the children answered the question and explained why one way was preferable.

Johnston found gender differences parallel to those previously reported, with boys more often spontaneously using and preferring justice solutions and girls more often spontaneously using and preferring care solutions. In addition, she found differences between the two fables she used, confirming Langdale's finding that moral orientation is associated both with the gender of the reasoner and with the dilemma considered.[9] Finally, the fact that children, at least by the age of eleven, are able to shift moral orientation and can explain the logic of two moral perspectives, each associated with a different problem-solving strategy, heightens the analogy to ambiguous figure perception and further supports the conception of justice and care as organizing frameworks for moral decision.

The demonstration that children know both orientations and can frame and solve moral problems in at least two different ways means that the choice of moral standpoint is an element of moral decision. The role of the self in moral judgment thus includes the choice of moral standpoint, and this decision, whether implicit or explicit, may become linked with self-respect and self-definition. Especially in adolescence, when choice becomes more self-conscious and self-reflective, moral standpoint may become entwined with identity and self-esteem. Johnston's finding that spontaneous moral orientation and preferred orientation are not always the same raises a number of questions as to why and under what conditions a person may adopt a problem-solving strategy that he or she sees as not the best way to solve the problem.

The way people choose to frame or solve a moral problem is clearly not the only way in which they can think about the problem, and is not necessarily the way they deem preferable. Moral judgments thus do not reveal *the* structure of moral thinking, since there are at least two ways in which people can structure moral problems. Johnston's demonstration of orientation-switch poses a serious challenge to the methods that have been used in moral judgment and moral development research, introducing a major interpretive caution. The fact that boys and girls at eleven and fifteen understand and distinguish the logics of justice and care reasoning directs attention to the origins and the development of both ways of thinking. In addition, the tendency for boys and girls to use and prefer different orientations when solving the same problem raises a number of questions about the relationship between these orientations and the factors influencing their representation. The different patterns of orientation use and preference, as well as the different conceptions of justice and of care implied or elaborated in the fable judgments, suggest that moral development cannot be mapped along a single linear stage sequence.

One way of explaining these findings, suggested by Johnston, joins Vygotsky's theory of cognitive development with Chodorow's analysis of sex differences in early childhood experiences of relationship.[10] Vygotsky posits that all of the higher cognitive functions originate as actual relations between individuals. Justice and care as moral ideas and as reasoning strategies thus would originate as relationships with others—an idea consonant with the derivation of justice and care reasoning from experiences of inequality and attachment in early childhood. All children are born into a situation of inequality in that they are less capable than the adults and older children around them and, in this sense, more helpless and less powerful. In addition, no child survives in the absence of some kind of adult attachment—or care, and through this experience of relationship children discover the responsiveness of human connection including their ability to move and affect one another.

Through the experience of inequality, of being in the less powerful position, children learn what it means to depend on the authority and the good will of others. As a result, they tend to strive for equality of greater power, and for freedom. Through the experience of attachment, children discover the ways in which people are able to care for and to hurt one another. The child's vulnerability to oppression and to abandonment thus can be seen to lay the groundwork for the moral visions of justice and care, conceived as ideals of human relationship and defining the ways in which people "should" act toward one another.

Chodorow's work then provides a way of explaining why care concerns tend to be minimally represented by men and why such concerns are less frequently elaborated in moral theory. Chodorow joins the dynamics of gender identity formation (the identification of oneself as male or female) to an analysis of early childhood relationships and examines the effects of maternal child care on the inner structuring of self in relation to others. Further, she differentiates a positional sense of self from a personal sense of self, contrasting a self defined in terms of role or position from a self known through the experience of connection. Her point is that maternal child care fosters the continuation of a relational sense of self in girls, since female gender identity is consonant with feeling connected with one's mother. For boys, gender identity is in tension with mother-child connection, unless that connection is structured in terms of sexual opposition (e.g., as an Oedipal drama). Thus, although boys experience responsiveness or care in relationships, knowledge of care or the need for care, when associated with mothers, pose a threat to masculine identity.[11]

Chodorow's work is limited by her reliance on object relations theory and problematic on that count. Object relations theory ties the formation of the self to the experience of separation, joining separation with individuation and thus counterposing the experience of self to the experience of connection with others. This is the line that

Chodorow traces in explicating male development. Within this framework, girls' connections with their mothers can only be seen as problematic. Connection with others or the capacity to feel and think *with* others is, by definition, in tension with self-development when self-development or individuation is linked to separation. Thus, object-relations theory sustains a series of oppositions that have been central in Western thought and moral theory, including the opposition between thought and feelings, self and relationship, reason and compassion, justice and love. Object relations theory also continues the conventional division of psychological labor between women and men. Since the idea of a self, experienced in the context of attachment with others, is theoretically impossible, mothers, described as objects, are viewed as selfless, without a self. This view is essentially problematic for women, divorcing the activity of mothering from desire, knowledge, and agency, and implying that insofar as a mother experiences herself as a subject rather than as an object (a mirror reflecting her child), she is "selfish" and not a good mother. Winnicott's phrase "good-enough mother" represents an effort to temper this judgment.

Thus, psychologists and philosophers, aligning the self and morality with separation and autonomy—the ability to be self-governing—have associated care with self-sacrifice, or with feelings—a view at odds with the current position that care represents a way of knowing and a coherent moral perspective. This position, however, is well represented in literature written by women. For example the short story "A Jury of Her Peers," written by Susan Glaspell in 1917, a time when women ordinarily did not serve on juries, contrasts two ways of knowing that underlie two ways of interpreting and solving a crime.[12] The story centers on a murder; Minnie Foster is suspected of killing her husband.

A neighbor woman and the sheriff's wife accompany the sheriff and the prosecutor to the house of the accused woman. The men, representing the law, seek evidence that will convince a jury to convict the suspect. The women, collecting things to bring Minnie Foster in jail, enter in this way into the lives lived in the house. Taking in rather than taking apart, they begin to assemble observations and impressions, connecting them to past experience and observations until suddenly they compose a familiar pattern, like the log-cabin pattern they recognize in the quilt Minnie Foster was making. "Why do we *know*—what we know this minute?" one woman asks the other, but she also offers the following explanation:

> We live close together, and we live far apart. We all go through the same things—it's all just a different kind of the same thing! If it weren't—why do you and I *understand*.[13]

The activity of quilt-making—collecting odd scraps and piecing them together until they form a pattern—becomes the metaphor for this way of knowing. Discovering a strangled canary buried under pieces of quilting, the women make a series of connections that lead them to understand what happened.

The logic that says you don't kill a man because he has killed a bird, the judgment that finds these acts wildly incommensurate, is counterposed to the logic that sees both events as part of a larger pattern—a pattern of detachment and abandonment that led finally to the strangling. "I *wish* I'd come over here once in a while," Mrs. Hale, the neighbor, exclaims. "That was a crime! Who's going to punish that?" Mrs. Peters, the sheriff's wife, recalls that when she was a girl and a boy killed her cat, "If they hadn't held me back I would have—" and realizes that there had been no one to restrain Minnie Foster. John Foster was known as "a good man . . . He didn't drink, and he kept his word as well as most, I guess, and paid his debts." But he also was "a hard man," Mrs. Hale explains, "like a raw wind that gets to the bone."

Seeing detachment as the crime with murder as its ultimate extension, implicating themselves and also seeing the connection between their own and Minnie Foster's actions, the women solve the crime by attachment—by joining together, like the "knotting" that joins pieces of a quilt. In the decision to remove rather than to reveal the evidence, they separate themselves from a legal system in which they have no voice but also no way of voicing what they have come to understand. In choosing to connect themselves with one another and with Minnie, they separate themselves from the law that would use their understanding and their knowledge as grounds for further separation and killing.

In a law school class where a film-version of this story was shown, the students were divided in their assessment of the moral problem and in their evaluation of the various characters and actions. Some focused on the murder, the strangling of the husband. Some focused on the evidence of abandonment or indifference to others. Responses to a questionnaire showed a bi-modal distribution, indicating two ways of viewing the film. These different perspectives led to different ways of evaluating both the act of murder and the women's decision to remove the evidence. Responses to the film were not aligned with the sex of the viewer in an absolute way, thus dispelling any implication of biological determinism or of a stark division between the way women and men know or judge events. The knowledge gained inductively by the women in the film, however, was also gained more readily by women watching the film, who came in this way to see a logic in the women's actions and to articulate a rationale for their silence.

The analogy to ambiguous figure perception is useful here in several ways. First, it suggests that people can see a situation in more than one way, and even alternate ways of seeing, combining them without reducing them—like designating the rabbit-duck figure as both duck and rabbit. Second, the analogy argues against the tendency to construe justice and care as opposites or mirror-images and also against the implication that these two perspectives are readily integrated or fused. The ambiguous figure directs attention to the way in which a change in perspective can reorganize perception and change understanding, without implying an underlying reality or pure form. What makes seeing both moral perspectives so difficult is precisely that the orientations are not opposites or mirror images or better and worse representations of a single moral truth. The terms of one perspective do not contain the terms of the other. Instead, a shift in orientation denotes a restructuring of moral perception, changing the meaning of moral language and thus the definition of moral conflict and moral action. For example, detachment is considered the hallmark of mature moral thinking within a justice perspective, signifying the ability to judge dispassionately, to weigh evidence in an even-handed manner, balancing the claims of others and self. From a care perspective, detachment is *the* moral problem.

> "I could've come," retorted Mrs. Hale . . . "I wish I had come over to see Minnie Foster sometimes. I can see now . . . If there had been years and years of—nothing, then a bird to sing to you, it would be awful—still—after the bird was still. . . . I know what stillness is."

The difference between agreement and understanding captures the different logics of justice and care reasoning, one seeking grounds for agreement, one seeking grounds for understanding, one assuming separation and thus the need for some external structure of connection, one assuming connection and thus the potential for understanding. These assumptions run deep, generating and reflecting different views of human nature and the human condition. They also point to different vulnerabilities and different sources of error. The potential error in justice reasoning lies in its latent egocentrism, the tendency to confuse one's perspective with an objective standpoint or truth, the temptation to define others in one's own terms by putting oneself in their place. The potential error in care reasoning lies in the tendency to forget that one has terms, creating a tendency to enter into another's perspective and to see oneself as "selfless"

by defining oneself in other's terms. These two types of error underlie two common equations that signify distortions or deformations of justice and care: the equation of human with male, unjust in its omission of women; and the equation of care with self-sacrifice, uncaring in its failure to represent the activity and the agency of care.

The equation of human with male was assumed in the Platonic and in the Enlightenment tradition as well as by psychologists who saw all-male samples as "representative" of human experience. The equation of care with self-sacrifice is in some ways more complex. The premise of self-interest assumes a conflict of interest between self and other manifest in the opposition of egoism and altruism. Together, the equations of male with human and of care with self-sacrifice form a circle that has had a powerful hold on moral philosophy and psychology. The conjunction of women and moral theory thus challenges the traditional definition of human and calls for a reconsideration of what is meant by both justice and care.

To trace moral development along two distinct although intersecting dimensions of relationship suggests the possibility of different permutations of justice and care reasoning, different ways these two moral perspectives can be understood and represented in relation to one another. For example, one perspective may overshadow or eclipse the other, so that one is brightly illuminated while the other is dimly remembered, familiar but for the most part forgotten. The way in which one story about relationship obscures another was evident in high school girls' definitions of dependence. These definitions highlighted two meanings—one arising from the opposition between dependence and independence, and one from the opposition of dependence to isolation ("No woman," one student observed, "is an island.") As the word "dependence" connotes the experience of relationship, this shift in the implied opposite of dependence indicates how the valence of relationship changes, when connection with others is experienced as an impediment to autonomy or independence, and when it is experienced as a source of comfort and pleasure, and as a protection against isolation. This essential ambivalence of human connection provides a powerful emotional grounding for two moral perspectives, and also may indicate what is at stake in the effort to reduce morality to a single perspective.

It is easy to understand the ascendance of justice reasoning and of justice-focused moral theories in a society where care is associated with personal vulnerability in the form of economic disadvantage. But another way of thinking about the ascendance of justice reasoning and also about sex differences in moral development is suggested in the novel *Masks,* written by Fumiko Enchi, a Japanese woman.[14] The subject is spirit possession, and the novel dramatizes what it means to be possessed by the spirits of others. Writing about the Rokujo lady in *Tales of Genji,* Enchi's central character notes that

> her soul alternates uncertainly between lyricism and spirit possession, making no philosophical distinction between the self alone and in relation to others, and is unable to achieve the solace of a religious indifference.[15]

The option of transcendence, of a religious indifference or a philosophical detachment, may be less available to women because women are more likely to be possessed by the spirits and the stories of others. The strength of women's moral perceptions lies in the refusal of detachment and depersonalization, and insistence on making connections that can lead to seeing the person killed in war or living in poverty as someone's son or father or brother or sister, or mother, or daughter, or friend. But the liability of women's development is also underscored by Enchi's novel in that women, possessed by the spirits of others, also are more likely to be caught in a chain of false attachments. If women are at the present time the custodians of a story about human attachment and interdependence, not only within the family but also in the world at large,

then questions arise as to how this story can be kept alive and how moral theory can sustain this story. In this sense, the relationship between women and moral theory itself becomes one of interdependence.

By rendering a care perspective more coherent and making its terms explicit, moral theory may facilitate women's ability to speak about their experiences and perceptions and may foster the ability of others to listen and to understand. At the same time, the evidence of care focus in women's moral thinking suggests that the study of women's development may provide a natural history of moral development in which care is ascendant, revealing the ways in which creating and sustaining responsive connection with others becomes or remains a central moral concern. The promise in joining women and moral theory lies in the fact that human survival, in the late twentieth century, may depend less on formal agreement than on human connection.

NOTES

1. Gilligan, C. (1977). "In a Different Voice: Women's Conceptions of Self and of Morality." *Harvard Educational Review* 47 (1982):481–517; *In a Different Voice: Psychological Theory and Women's Development.* Cambridge, Mass.: Harvard University Press.
2. Piaget, J. (1965). *The Moral Judgment of the Child.* New York: N.Y.: The Free Press Paperback Edition, pp. 76–84.
3. Kohlberg, L. (1984). *The Psychology of Moral Development.* San Francisco, Calif.: Harper & Row Publishers, Inc.
4. Gilligan, C. and J. Attanucci. (1986). *Two Moral Orientations.* Harvard University, unpublished manuscript.
5. See Kohlberg, L. *op. cit.,* also Walker, L. (1984). "Sex Differences in the Development of Moral Reasoning: A Critical Review of the Literature." *Child Development* 55 (3):677–91.
6. Piaget, J., *op. cit.*
7. "Kohlberg, L., *op. cit.*

8. Johnston, K. (1985). *Two Moral Orientations—Two Problem-solving Strategies: Adolescents' Solutions to Dilemmas in Fables.* Harvard University, unpublished doctoral dissertation.

9. Langdale, C. (1983). *Moral Orientation and Moral Development: The Analysis of Care and Justice Reasoning Across Different Dilemmas in Females and Males from Childhood through Adulthood.* Harvard University, unpublished doctoral dissertation.

10. Johnston, K., *op. cit.;* Vygotsky, L. (1978). *Mind in Society.* Cambridge, Mass.: Harvard University Press; Chodorow, N. (1974). "Family Structure and Feminine Personality" in *Women, Culture and Society,* L. M. Rosaldo and L. Lamphere, eds., Stanford, Calif.: Stanford University Press; see also Chodorow, N. (1978). *The Reproduction of Mothering: Psychoanalysis and the Sociology of Gender,* Berkeley, Calif.: University of California Press.

11. Chodorow, N., *op. cit.*

12. Glaspell, S. (1927). *A Jury of Her Peers,* London: E. Benn.

13. *Ibid.*

14. Fumiko, E. (1983). *Masks.* New York: Random House.

15. Ibid. p. 54.

THE GENERALIZED AND THE CONCRETE OTHER: THE KOHLBERG-GILLIGAN CONTROVERSY AND MORAL THEORY

Seyla Benhabib

Can there be a feminist contribution to moral philosophy? Can those men and women who view the gender-sex system of our societies as oppressive, and who regard women's emancipation as essential to human liberation, criticize, analyze, and when necessary, replace the traditional categories of moral philosophy so as to contribute to women's emancipation and human liberation? By focusing on the controversy generated by Carol Gilligan's work, this essay seeks to outline such a feminist contribution to moral philosophy.

I. THE KOHLBERG-GILLIGAN CONTROVERSY

Carol Gilligan's research in cognitive, developmental moral psychology recapitulates a pattern made familiar to us by Thomas Kuhn.[1] Noting a discrepancy between the claims of the original research paradigm and the data, Gilligan and her co-workers first extend this paradigm to accommodate anomalous results. This extension then allows them to see some other problems in a new light; subsequently, the basic paradigm of the study of the development of moral judgment, according to Lawrence Kohlberg's model, is fundamentally revised. Gilligan and her co-workers now maintain that Kohlbergian theory is valid only for measuring the development of one aspect of moral orientation that focuses on the ethics of justice and rights.

In the 1980 article "Moral Development in Late Adolescence and Adulthood: A Critique and Reconstruction of Kohlberg's Theory," Murphy and Gilligan note that moral judgment data from a longitudinal study of twenty-six undergraduates scored by Kohlberg's revised manual replicate his original findings that a significant percentage of subjects appear to regress from adolescence to adulthood.[2] The persistence of this relativistic regression suggests a need to revise the theory. In this paper, they propose a distinction between "post-conventional formalism" and "post-conventional contextualism." While the post-conventional type of reasoning solves the problem of relativism by constructing a system that derives a solution to all moral problems from concepts like social contract or natural rights, the second approach finds the solution in the following way: "While no answer may be objectively right in the sense of being context-free, some answers and some ways of thinking are better than others." (Murphy and Gilligan 1980: 83) The extension of the original paradigm from post-conventional formalist to post-conventional contextual then leads Gilligan to see some other discrepancies in the theory in a new light, especially women's persistently low score when compared to their male peers. Distinguishing between the ethics of justice and rights, and the ethics of care and responsibility allows her to account for women's moral development and the cognitive skills they show in a new way. Women's moral judgment is more contextual, more immersed in the details of relationships and narratives. Women show a greater propensity to take the standpoint of the "particular other," and appear more adept at revealing feelings of empathy and sympathy required by this. Once these cognitive characteristics are seen not as deficiencies, but as essential components of adult moral reasoning at the post-conventional stage, then women's apparent moral confusion of judgment becomes a sign of their strength. Agreeing with Piaget that a developmental theory hangs from its vertex of maturity, "the point towards which progress is traced," a change in "the definition of maturity," writes Gilligan, "does not simply alter the description of the highest stage but recasts the understanding of development, changing the entire account."[3] The contextuality, narrativity, and the specificity of women's moral judgment is not a sign of weakness or deficiency, but a manifestation of a vision of moral maturity that views the self as a being immersed in a network of relationships with others. According to this vision, the respect for each others' needs and the mutuality of effort to satisfy them sustain moral growth and development.

When confronted with such a challenge, it is common for adherents of an old research paradigm to respond by arguing (a) that the data base

does not support the conclusions drawn by revisionists, (b) that some of the new conclusions can be accommodated by the old theory, and (c) that the new and old paradigms have different object domains and are not concerned with explaining the same phenomena at all. In his response to Gilligan, Kohlberg has followed all three alternatives.

A. The Data Base

In his 1984 "Synopses and Detailed Replies to Critics," Kohlberg argues that available data on cognitive moral development do not report differences among children and adolescents of both sexes with respect to justice reasoning.[4] "The only studies," he writes, "showing fairly frequent sex differences are those of adults, usually of spouse housewives. Many of the studies comparing adult males and females without controlling for education and job differences ... do report sex differences in favor of males." (Kohlberg 1984: 347) Kohlberg maintains that these latter findings are not incompatible with his theory.[5] For, according to this theory, the attainment of stages four and five depends upon experiences of participation, responsibility, and role taking in the secondary institutions of society such as the workplace and government, from which women have been and still are, to a large extent, excluded. The data, he concludes, does not damage the validity of his theory, but shows the necessity for controlling for such factors as education and employment when assessing sex differences in adult moral reasoning.

B. Accommodation Within the Old Theory

Kohlberg now agrees with Gilligan that "the acknowledgement of an orientation of care and response usefully enlarges the moral domain." (Kohlberg 1984: 340) In his view, though, justice and rights, care and responsibility, are not two *tracks* of moral development, but two moral *orientations*. The rights orientation and the care orientation are not bipolar or dichotomous. Rather, the care-and-response orientation is directed primarily to relations of special obligation to family, friends, and group members, "relations which often include or presuppose general obligations of respect, fairness, and contract." (Kohlberg 1984: 349) Kohlberg resists the conclusion that these differences are strongly "sex related"; instead, he views the choice of orientation "to be primarily a function of setting and dilemma, not sex." (Kohlberg 1984: 350)

C. Object Domain of the
Two Theories

In an earlier response to Gilligan, Kohlberg had argued as follows:

> Carol Gilligan's ideas, while interesting, were not really welcome to us, for two reasons . . . The latter, we thought, was grist for Jane Loewinger's mill in studying stages of ego development, but not for studying the specifically moral dimension in reasoning . . . Following Piaget, my colleagues and I have had the greatest confidence that reasoning about justice would lend itself to a formal structuralist or rationalist analysis . . . whereas questions about the nature of the "good life" have not been as amenable to this type of statement.[6]

In his 1984 reply to his critics, this distinction between moral and ego development is further refined. Kohlberg divides the ego domain into the cognitive, interpersonal, and moral functions. (Kohlberg 1984: 398) Since, however, ego development is a necessary but not sufficient condition for moral development, in his view, the latter can be studied independently of the former. In light of this clarification, Kohlberg regards Murphy's and Gilligan's stage of "post-conventional contextualism" as being more concerned with questions of ego as opposed to moral development. While not wanting to maintain that the acquisition of moral competencies ends with reaching adulthood, Kohlberg nevertheless insists that adult moral and ego

development studies only reveal the presence of "soft" as opposed to "hard" stages. The latter are irreversible in sequence and integrally related to one another in the sense that a subsequent stage grows out of and presents a better solution to problems confronted at an earlier stage.[7]

It will be up to latter-day historians of science to decide whether, with these admissions and qualifications, Kohlbergian theory has entered the phase of "ad-hocism," in Imre Lakatos's words,[8] or whether Gilligan's challenge, as well as that of other critics, has moved this research paradigm to a new phase, in which new problems and conceptualizations will lead to more fruitful results.

What concerns me in this paper is the question, what can feminist theory contribute to this debate? Since Kohlberg himself regards an interaction between moral philosophy and the empirical study of moral development as essential to his theory, the insights of contemporary feminist philosophy can be brought to bear upon some aspects of his theory. I want to define two premises as constituents of feminist theorizing. First, for feminist theory, the gender-sex system is not a contingent but an essential way in which social reality is organized, symbolically divided, and experienced. By the "gender-sex" system, I mean the social-historical, symbolic constitution, and interpretation of the differences of the sexes. The gender-sex system is the context in which the self develops an *embodied* identity, a certain mode of being in one's body and of living the body. The self becomes an *I* in that it appropriates from the human community a mode of psychically, socially, and symbolically experiencing its bodily identity. Societies and cultures reproduce embodied individuals through the gender-sex system.[9]

Second, the historically known gender-sex systems have contributed to the oppression and exploitation of women. The task of feminist critical theory is to uncover where and how this occurs and to develop an emancipatory and reflective analysis that aids women in their struggles to overcome oppression and exploitation. Feminist theory can contribute to this task in two ways: by developing an *explanatory-diagnostic analysis* of women's oppression across history, cultures, and societies, and by articulating an *anticipatory-utopian critique* of the norms and values of our current society and culture, which projects new modes of togetherness and of relating to ourselves and to nature in the future. Whereas the first aspect of feminist theory requires critical, social-scientific research, the second is primarily normative and philosophical: it involves the clarification of moral and political principles, both at the meta-ethical level with respect to the *logic of justification* and at the substantive, normative level with reference to their concrete content.[10]

In this essay, I shall try to articulate such an anticipatory-utopian critique of universalistic moral theories from a feminist perspective. I want to argue that the *definition* of the moral domain, as well as of the ideal of *moral autonomy*, not only in Kohlberg's theory but in universalistic, contractarian theories from Hobbes to Rawls, lead to a *privatization* of women's experience and to the exclusion of its consideration from a moral point of view. In this tradition, the moral self is viewed as a *disembedded* and *disembodied* being. This conception of the self reflects aspects of male experience; the "relevant other" in this theory is never the sister but always the brother. This vision of the self is incompatible with the very criteria of reversibility and universalizability advocated by defenders of universalism. A universalistic moral theory restricted to the standpoint of the "generalized other" falls into epistemic incoherencies that jeopardize its claim to adequately fulfill reversibility and universalizability.

Universalistic moral theories in the western tradition from Hobbes to Rawls are *substitutionalist,* in the sense that the universalism they defend is defined surreptitiously by identifying the experiences of a specific group of subjects as the paradigmatic case of all humans. These subjects are invariably white, male adults who are propertied or professional. I want to distinguish *substitutionalist* from *interactive* universalism.

Interactive universalism acknowledges the plurality of modes of being human, and differences among humans, without endorsing all these pluralities and differences as morally and politically valid. While agreeing that normative disputes can be rationally settled, and that fairness, reciprocity, and some procedure of universalizability are constituents, that is, necessary conditions of the moral standpoint, interactive universalism regards difference as a starting point for reflection and action. In this sense, "universality" is a regulative ideal that does not deny our embodied and embedded identity, but aims at developing moral attitudes and encouraging political transformations that can yield a point of view acceptable to all. Universality is not the ideal consensus of fictitiously defined selves, but the concrete process, in politics and morals, of the struggle of concrete, embodied selves, striving for autonomy.

II. JUSTICE AND THE AUTONOMOUS SELF IN SOCIAL CONTRACT THEORIES

Kohlberg defines the privileged object domain of moral philosophy and psychology as follows:

> We say that *moral* judgments or principles have the central function of resolving interpersonal or social conflicts, that is, conflicts of claims or rights. . . . Thus moral judgments and principles imply a notion of equilibrium, or reversibility of claims. In this sense they ultimately involve some reference to justice, at least insofar as they define "hard" structural stages. (Kohlberg 1984: 216)

Kohlberg's conception of the moral domain is based upon a strong differentiation between justice and the good life.[11] This is also one of the cornerstones of his critique of Gilligan. Although acknowledging that Gilligan's elucidation of a care-and-responsibility orientation "usefully enlarges the moral domain" (Kohlberg 1984: 340), Kohlberg defines the domain of *special relationships of obligation* to which care and responsibility are oriented as follows: "the spheres of kinship, love, friendship, and sex that elicit considerations of care are usually understood to be spheres of personal decision-making, as are, for instance, the problems of marriage and divorce:" (Kohlberg 1984: 229–30) The care orientation is said thus to concern domains that are more "personal" than "moral in the sense of the formal point of view." (Kohlberg 1984: 360) Questions of the good life, pertaining to the nature of our relationships of kinship, love, friendship, and sex, on the one hand, are included in the moral domain but, on the other hand, are named "personal" as opposed to "moral" issues.

Kohlberg proceeds from a definition of morality that begins with Hobbes, in the wake of the dissolution of the Aristotelian-Christian world view. Ancient and medieval moral systems, by contrast, show the following structure: a definition of man-as-he-ought-to-be, a definition of man-as-he-is, and the articulation of a set of rules or precepts that can lead man-as-he-is into man-as-he-ought-to-be.[12] In such moral systems, the rules that govern just relations within the human community are embedded in a more encompassing concept of the good life. This good life, the *telos* of man, is defined ontologically with reference to man's place in the cosmos at large.

The destruction of the ancient and medieval teleological concept of nature through the attack of medieval nominalism and modern science, the emergence of capitalist exchange relations, and the subsequent division of the social structure into the economy, the polity, civil associations, and the domestic-intimate sphere, radically alter moral theory. Modern theorists claim that the ultimate purposes of nature are unknown. Morality is thus emancipated from cosmology and from an all encompassing world view that normatively limits man's relation to nature. The distinction between justice and the good life, as it is formulated by early contract theorists, aims at defending this privacy and autonomy of the self, first in the religious sphere, and then in the scientific and philosophical spheres of "free thought" as well.

Justice alone becomes the center of moral theory when bourgeois individuals in a disenchanted universe face the task of creating the legitimate basis of the social order for themselves. What "ought" to be is now defined as what all would have rationally to agree to in order to ensure civil peace and prosperity (Hobbes, Locke); or the "ought" is derived from the rational form of the moral law alone (Rousseau, Kant). As long as the social bases of cooperation and the rights-claims of individuals are respected, the autonomous bourgeois subject can define the good life as his mind and conscience dictate.

The transition to modernity does not only privatize the self's relation to the cosmos and to ultimate questions of religion and being. First, with western modernity the concept of privacy is so enlarged that an intimate domestic-familial sphere is subsumed under it. Relations of "kinship, friendship, love, and sex," indeed, as Kohlberg takes them to be, come to be viewed as spheres of "personal decision-making." At the beginning of modern moral and political theory, however, the "personal" nature of these spheres does not mean the recognition of equal, female autonomy, but rather the removal of gender relations from the sphere of justice. While the bourgeois male celebrates his transition from conventional to post-conventional morality, from socially accepted rules of justice to their generation in light of the principles of a social contract, the domestic sphere remains at the conventional level. The sphere of justice, from Hobbes through Locke and Kant, is regarded as the domain wherein independent, male heads-of-household transact with one another, while the domestic-intimate sphere is put beyond the pale of justice and restricted to the reproductive and affective needs of the bourgeois *pater familias*. Agnes Heller has named this domain the "household of the emotions."[13] An entire domain of human activity, namely, nurture, reproduction, love, and care, which becomes the woman's lot in the course of the development of modern, bourgeois society, is excluded from moral and political considerations, and confined to the realm of "nature."

Through a brief historical genealogy of social contract theories, I want to examine the distinction between justice and the good life as it is translated into the split between the public and the domestic. This analysis will also allow us to see the implicit ideal of autonomy cherished by this tradition.

At the beginning of modern moral and political philosophy stands a powerful metaphor: the "state of nature." At times this metaphor is said to be fact. Thus, in his *Second Treatise of Civil Government,* John Locke reminds us of "the two men in the desert island, mentioned by Garcilasso de la Vega . . . or a Swiss and an Indian, in the woods of America."[14] At other times it is acknowledged as fiction. Thus, Kant dismisses the colorful reveries of his predecessors and transforms the "state of nature" from an empirical fact into a transcendental concept. The state of nature comes to represent the idea of *Privatrecht,* under which is subsumed the right of property and "thinglike rights of a personal nature" (*auf dingliche Natur persönliche Rechte*), which the male head of household exercises over his wife, children, and servants.[15] Only Thomas Hobbes compounds fact and fiction, and against those who consider it strange "that Nature should thus dissociate, and render men apt to invade, and destroy one another,"[16] he asks each man who does not trust "this Inference, made from the passions," to reflect why "when taking a journey, he arms himself, and seeks to go well accompanied; when going to sleep, he locks his dores; when even in his house he locks his chests. . . . Does he not there as much accuse mankind by his actions, as I do by my words?" (Hobbes, *Leviathan,* 187) The state of nature is the looking glass of these early bourgeois thinkers in which they and their societies are magnified, purified, and reflected in their original, naked verity. The state of nature is both nightmare (Hobbes) and utopia (Rousseau). In it, the bourgeois male recognizes his flaws, fears, and anxieties, as well as his dreams.

The varying content of this metaphor is less significant than its simple and profound message: in the beginning man was alone. Again, it is Hobbes who gives this thought its clearest formulation. "Let us consider men . . . as if but even now sprung out of the earth, and suddenly, like mushrooms, come to full maturity, without all kind of engagement to each other."[17] This vision of men as mushrooms is an ultimate picture of autonomy. The female, the mother of whom every individual is born, is now replaced by the earth. The denial of being born of woman frees the male ego from the most natural and basic bond of dependence. Nor is the picture very different for Rousseau's noble savage who, wandering wantonly through the woods, occasionally mates with a female and then seeks rest.[18]

The state-of-nature metaphor provides a vision of the autonomous self: this is a narcissist who sees the world in his own image; who has no awareness of the limits of his own desires and passions; and who cannot see himself through the eyes of another. The narcissism of this sovereign self is destroyed by the presence of the other. As Hegel expresses it:

> "Self-consciousness is faced by another self-consciousness; it has come *out of itself.* This has a twofold significance: first, it has *lost* itself, for it finds itself as an *other* being; secondly, in doing so it has superseded the other, for it does not see the other as an essential being, but in the other sees its own self.[19]

The story of the autonomous male ego is the saga of this initial sense of *loss* in confrontation with the other, and the gradual recovery from this original narcissistic wound through the sobering experience of war, fear, domination, anxiety, and death. The last installment in this drama is the social contract: the establishment of the law to govern all. Having been thrust out of their narcissistic universe into a world of insecurity by their sibling brothers, these individuals have to reestablish the authority of the father in the image of the law. The early bourgeois individual not only has no mother but no father as well; rather, he strives to reconstitute the father in his own self-image. What is usually celebrated in the annals of modern moral and political theory as the dawn of liberty is precisely this destruction of political patriarchy in bourgeois society.

The constitution of political authority civilizes sibling rivalry by turning their attention from war to property, from vanity to science, from conquest to luxury. The original narcissism is not transformed; only now ego boundaries are clearly defined. The law reduces insecurity, the fear of being engulfed by the other, by defining mine and thine. Jealousy is not eliminated but tamed; as long as each can keep what is his and attain more by fair rules of the game, he is entitled to it. Competition is domesticized and channeled towards acquisition. The law contains anxiety by defining rigidly the boundaries between self and other, but the law does not cure anxiety. The anxiety that the other is always on the look to interfere in your space and appropriate what is yours; the anxiety that you will be subordinated to his will; the anxiety that a group of brothers will usurp the law in the name of the "will of all" and destroy "the general will," the will of the absent father, remains. The law teaches how to repress anxiety and to sober narcissism, but the constitution of the self is not altered. The establishment of private rights and duties does not overcome the inner wounds of the self; it only forces them to become less destructive.

This imaginary universe of early moral and political theory has had an amazing hold upon the modern consciousness. From Freud to Piaget, the relationship to the brother is viewed as the humanizing experience that teaches us to become social, responsible adults.[20] As a result of the hold of this metaphor upon our imagination, we have also come to inherit a number, of philosophical prejudices. For Rawls and Kohlberg, as well, the autonomous self is disembedded and disembodied; moral impartiality is learning to recognize the claims of the other who is just like oneself; fairness is public justice; a public system of rights and duties is the best way to arbitrate conflict, to distribute rewards and to establish claims.

Yet this is a strange world: it is one in which individuals are grown up before they have been born; in which boys are men before they have been children; a world where neither mother, nor sister, nor wife exist. The question is less what Hobbes says about men and women, or what Rousseau sees the role of Sophie to be in Émile's education. The point is that in this universe, the experience of the early modern female has no place. Women are simply what men are not. Women are not autonomous, independent, and aggressive but nurturant, not competitive but giving, not public but private. The world of the female is constituted by a series of negations. *She* is simply what *he* happens not to be. Her identity becomes defined by a lack—the lack of autonomy, the lack of independence, the lack of the phallus. The narcissistic male takes her to be just like himself, only his opposite.

It is not the misogynist prejudices of early modern moral and political theory alone that lead to women's exclusion. It is the very constitution of a sphere of discourse that bans the female from history to the realm of nature, from public light to the interior of the household, from the civilizing effect of culture to the repetitious burden of nurture and reproduction. The public sphere, the sphere of justice, moves in historicity, whereas the private sphere, the sphere of care and intimacy, is unchanging and timeless. It pulls us toward the earth even when we, as Habbesian mushrooms, strive to pull away from it. The dehistoricization of the private realm signifies that, as the male ego celebrates his passage from nature to culture, from conflict to consensus, women remain in a timeless universe, condemned to repeat the cycles of life.

This split between the public sphere of justice, in which history is made, and the atemporal realm of the household, in which like is reproduced, is internalized by the male ego. The dichotomies are not only without but within. He himself is divided into the public persona and the private individual. Within his chest clash the law of reason and the inclination of nature, the brilliance of cognition and the obscurity of emotion. Caught between the moral law and the starry heaven above and the earthly body below,[21] the autonomous self strives for unity. But the antagonism—between autonomy and nurturance, independence and bonding, sovereignty of the self and relations to others—remains. In the discourse of modern moral and political theory, these dichotomies are reified as being essential to the constitution of the self. While men humanize outer nature through labor, inner nature remains ahistorical, dark, and obscure. I want to suggest that contemporary universalist moral theory has inherited this dichotomy between autonomy and nurturance, independence and bonding, the sphere of justice and the domestic, personal realm. This becomes most visible in its attempt to restrict the moral point of view to the perspective of the "generalized other."

III. THE GENERALIZED VERSUS THE CONCRETE OTHER

Let me describe two concepts of self-other relations that delineate both moral perspectives and interactional structures. I shall name the first the standpoint of the "generalized"[22] and the second that of the "concrete" other. In contemporary moral theory, these concepts are viewed as incompatible, even as antagonistic. These two perspectives reflect the dichotomies and splits of early modern moral and political theory between autonomy and nurturance, independence and bonding, the public and the domestic, and more broadly, between justice and the good life. The content of the generalized as well as the concrete other is shaped by the dichotomous characterization, which we have inherited from the modern tradition.

The standpoint of the generalized other requires us to view each and every individual as a rational being entitled to the same rights and duties we would want to ascribe to ourselves. In assuming this standpoint, we abstract from the individuality and concrete identity of the other. We assume that the other, like ourselves, is a

being who has concrete needs, desires, and affects, but what constitutes moral dignity is not what differentiates us from each other, but rather what we, as speaking and acting rational agents, have in common. Our relation to the other is governed by the norms of *formal equality* and *reciprocity:* each is entitled to expect and to assume from us what we can expect and assume from him or her. The norms of our interactions are primarily public and institutional ones. If I have a right to x, then you have the duty not to hinder me from enjoying x and conversely. In treating you in accordance with these norms, I confirm in your person the rights of humanity and I have a legitimate right to expect that you will do the same in relation to me. The moral categories that accompany such interactions are those of right, obligation, and entitlement; the corresponding moral feelings are those of respect, duty, worthiness, and dignity.

The standpoint of the concrete other, by contrast, requires us to view each and every rational being as an individual with a concrete history, identity, and affective-emotional constitution. In assuming this standpoint, we abstract from what constitutes our commonality. We seek to comprehend the needs of the other, his or her motivations, what he or she searches for and desires. Our relation to the other is governed by the norms of *equity* and *complementary reciprocity:* each is entitled to expect and to assume from the other forms of behavior through which the other feels recognized and confirmed as a concrete, individual being with specific needs, talents, and capacities. Our differences in this case complement rather than exclude one another. The norms of our interaction are usually private, noninstitutional ones. They are norms of friendship, love, and care. These norms require in various ways that I exhibit more than the simple assertion of my rights and duties in the face of your needs. In treating you in accordance with the norms of friendship, love, and care, I confirm not only your *humanity* but your human *individuality.* The moral categories that accompany such interactions are those of responsibility, bonding, and sharing. The corresponding moral feelings are those of love, care, sympathy, and solidarity.

In contemporary universalist moral psychology and moral theory, it is the viewpoint of the "generalized other" that predominates. In his article on "Justice as Reversibility: The Claim to Moral Adequacy of a Highest Stage of Moral Development," for example, Kohlberg argues that

> moral judgments involve role-taking, taking the viewpoint of the others conceived as *subjects* and coordinating these viewpoints . . . Second, equilibriated moral judgments, involve principles of justice or fairness. A moral situation in disequilibrium is one in which there are unresolved, conflicting claims. A resolution of the situation is one in which each is "given his due" according to some principle of justice that can be recognized as fair by all the conflicting parties involved.[23]

Kohlberg regards Rawls's concept of "reflective equilibrium" as a parallel formulation of the basic idea of reciprocity, equality, and fairness intrinsic to all moral judgments. The Rawlsian "veil of ignorance," in Kohlberg's judgment, not only exemplifies the formalist idea of universalizability but that of perfect *reversibility* as well.[24] The idea behind the veil of ignorance is described as follows:

> The decider is to initially decide from a point of view *that ignores his identity* (veil of ignorance) under the assumption that decisions are governed by maximizing values from a viewpoint of rational egoism in considering each party's interest. [Kohlberg 1981: 200; my emphasis]

What I would like to question is the assumption that "taking the viewpoint of others" is truly compatible with this notion of fairness as reasoning behind a "veil of ignorance."[25] The problem is that the defensible kernel of the ideas of reciprocity and fairness are thereby identified with the perspective of the disembedded and disembodied generalized other. Now since Kohlberg presents his research subjects with

hypothetically constructed moral dilemmas, it may be thought that his conception of "taking the standpoint of the other" is not subject to the epistemic restrictions that apply to the Rawlsian original position. Subjects in Kohlbergian interviews do not stand behind a veil of ignorance. However, the very *language* in which Kohlbergian dilemmas are presented incorporate these epistemic restrictions. For example, in the famous Heinz dilemma, as in others, the motivations of the druggist as a concrete individual, as well as the history of the individuals involved, are excluded as irrelevant to the definition of the moral problem at hand. In these dilemmas, individuals and their moral positions are represented by abstracting from the narrative history of the self and its motivations. Gilligan also notes that the implicit moral epistemology of Kohlbergian dilemma frustrates women, who want to phrase these hypothetical dilemmas in a more contextual voice, attuned to the standpoint of the concrete other. The result is that

> though several of the women in the abortion study clearly articulate a post-conventional meta-ethical position, none of them are considered principled in their normative moral judgments of Kohlberg's hypothetical dilemmas. Instead, the women's judgments point toward an identification of the violence inherent in the dilemma itself, which is seen to compromise the justice of any of its possible resolutions. [Gilligan 1982: 101]

Through an immanent critique of the theories of Kohlberg and Rawls, I want to show that ignoring the standpoint of the concrete other leads to epistemic incoherence in universalistic moral theories. The problem can be stated as follows: according to Kohlberg and Rawls, moral reciprocity involves the capacity to take the standpoint of the other, to put oneself imaginatively in the place of the other, but under conditions of the "veil of ignorance," the *other as different from the self* disappears. Unlike in previous contract theories, in this case the other is not constituted through projection, but as a consequence of total abstraction from his or her identity. Differences are not denied; they become irrelevant. The Rawlsian self does not know:

> his place in society, his class position or status; nor does he know his fortune in the distribution of natural assets and abilities, his intelligence and strength, and the like. Nor, again, does anyone know his conception of the good, the particulars of his rational plan of life, or even the special features of his psychology such as his aversion to risk or liability to optimism or pessimism.[26]

Let us ignore for a moment whether such selves who also do not know "the particular circumstances of their own society" can know anything at all that is relevant to the human condition, and ask instead, are these individuals *human selves* at all? In his attempt to do justice to Kant's conception of noumenal agency, Rawls recapitulates a basic problem with the Kantian conception of the self, namely, that noumenal selves cannot be *individuated*. If all that belongs to them as embodied, affective, suffering creatures, their memory and history, their ties and relations to others, are to be subsumed under the phenomenal realm, then what we are left with is an empty mask that is everyone and no one. Michael Sandel points out that the difficulty in Rawls's conception derives from his attempt to be consistent with the Kantian concept of the autonomous self, as a being freely choosing his or her own ends in life.[27] However, this moral and political concept of autonomy slips into a metaphysics according to which it is meaningful to define a self independently of *all* the ends it may choose and all and any conceptions of the good it may hold. (Sandel 1984: 47ff.) At this point we must ask whether the *identity* of any human self can be defined with reference to its capacity for agency alone. Identity does not refer to my potential for choice alone, but to the actuality of my choices, namely, to how I, as a finite, concrete, embodied individual, shape and fashion the circumstances of my birth and family, linguistic, cultural, and gender identity into a coherent narrative that stands as my life's story. Indeed, if we recall that every autonomous being is one born of others and not, as Rawls, following

Hobbes, assumes, a being "not bound by prior moral ties to another,"[28] the question becomes: how does this finite, embodied creature constitute into a coherent narrative those episodes of choice and limit, agency and suffering, initiative and dependence? The self is not a thing, a substrate, but the protagonist of a life's tale. The conception of selves who can be individuated prior to their moral ends is incoherent.

If this concept of the self as a mushroom, behind a veil of ignorance, is incoherent, then it follows that there is no real *plurality* of perspectives in the Rawlsian original position, but only a *definitional identity*. For Rawls, as Sandel observes, "our individuating characterisitics are given empirically, by the distinctive concatenation of wants and desires, aims and attributes, purposes and ends that come to characterize human beings in the particularity." (Sandel 1984: 51) But how are we supposed to know what these wants and desires are independently of knowing something about the person who holds these wants, desires, aims and attributes? Is there perhaps an "essence" of anger that is the same for each angry individual; an essence of ambition that is distinct from ambitious selves? I fail to see how individuating characteristics can be ascribed to a transcendental self who can have any and none of these, who can be all or none of them.

If selves who are epistemologically and metaphysically prior to their individuating characteristics, as Rawls takes them to be, cannot be human selves at all; if, therefore, there is no human *plurality* behind the veil of ignorance but only *definitional identity* then this has consequences for criteria of reversibility and universalizability said to be a constituent of the moral point of view. Definitional identity leads to *incomplete reversibility,* for the primary requisite of reversibility, namely, a coherent distinction between me and you, the self and the other, cannot be sustained under these circumstances. Under conditions of the veil of ignorance, the other disappears.

It is no longer plausible to maintain that such a standpoint can universalize adequately. Kohlberg views the veil of ignorance not only as exemplifying reversibility but universalizability as well. This is the idea that "we must be willing to live with our judgment or decision when we trade places with others in the situation being judged." (Kohlberg 1981: 197) But the question is, *which* situation? Can moral situations be individuated independently of our knowledge of the agents involved in these situations, of their histories, attitudes, characters, and desires? Can I describe a situation as one of arrogance or hurt pride without knowing something about you as a concrete other? Can I know how to distinguish between a breach of confidence and a harmless slip of the tongue, without knowing your history and your character? Moral situations, like moral emotions and attitudes, can only be individuated if they are evaluated in light of our knowledge of the history of the agents involved in them.

While every procedure of universalizability presupposes that "like cases ought to be treated alike" or that I should act in such a way that I should also be willing that all others in a like situation act like me, the most difficult aspect of any such procedure is to know what constitutes a "like" situation or what it would mean for another to be exactly in a situation like mine. Such a process of reasoning, to be at all viable, must involve the viewpoint of the concrete other, for situations, to paraphrase Stanley Cavell, do not come like "envelopes and golden finches," ready for definition and description, "nor like apples ripe for grading."[29] When we morally disagree, for example, we do not only disagree about the principles involved; very often we disagree because what I see as a lack of generosity on your part, you construe as your legitimate right not to do something; we disagree because what you see as jealousy on my part, I view as my desire to have more of your attention. Universalistic moral theory neglects such everyday, interactional morality and assumes that the public standpoint of justice, and our quasi-public personalities as right-bearing individuals, are the center of moral theory.[30]

Kohlberg emphasizes the dimension of ideal role-taking or taking the viewpoint of the other

in moral judgment. Because he defines the other as the generalized other, however, he perpetrates one of the fundamental errors of Kantian moral theory. Kant's error was to assume that I, as a pure rational agent reasoning for myself, could reach a conclusion that would be acceptable for all at all times and places.[31] In Kantian moral theory, moral agents are like geometricians in different rooms who, reasoning alone for themselves, all arrive at the same solution to a problem. Following Habermas, I want to name this the "monological" model of moral reasoning. Insofar as he interprets ideal role-taking in the light of Rawls's concept of a "veil of ignorance," Kohlberg as well sees the silent thought process of a single self who imaginatively puts himself in the position of the other as the most adequate form of moral judgment.

I conclude that a definition of the self that is restricted to the standpoint of the generalized other becomes incoherent and cannot individuate among selves. Without assuming the standpoint of the concrete other, no coherent universalizability test can be carried out, for we lack the necessary epistemic information to judge my moral situation to be "like" or "unlike" yours.

IV. A COMMUNICATIVE ETHIC OF NEED INTERPRETATIONS AND THE RELATIONAL SELF

In the preceding sections of this essay, I have argued that the distinction between justice and the good life, the restriction of the moral domain to questions of justice, as well as the ideal of moral autonomy in universalist theories, result in the privatization of women's experience and lead to epistemological blindness toward the concrete other. The consequence of such epistemological blindness is an internal inconsistency in universalistic moral theories, insofar as these define "taking the standpoint of the other" as essential to the moral point of view. My aim has been to take universalistic moral theories at their word and to show through an immanent critique, first of the "state of nature" metaphor and then of the "original position," that the concept of the autonomous self implied by these thought experiments is restricted to the "generalized other."

This distinction between the generalized and the concrete other raises questions in moral and political theory. It may be asked whether, without the standpoint of the generalized other, it would be possible to define a moral point of view at all.[32] Since our identities as concrete others are what distinguish us from each other according to gender, race, class, cultural differentials, as well as psychic and natural abilities, would a moral theory restricted to the standpoint of the concrete other not be a racist, sexist, cultural relativist, discriminatory one? Furthermore, without the standpoint of the generalized other, it may be argued, a political theory of justice suited for modern, complex societies is unthinkable. Certainly rights must be an essential component in any such theory. Finally, the perspective of the "concrete other" defines our relations as private, noninstitutional ones, concerned with love, care, friendship, and intimacy. Are these activities so gender-specific? Are we not all "concrete others"?

The distinction between the "generalized" and the "concrete other," as drawn in this essay so far, is not a *prescriptive* but a *critical* one. My goal is not to prescribe a moral and political theory consonant with the concept of the "concrete other." For, indeed, the recognition of the dignity and worthiness of the generalized other is a *necessary,* albeit *insufficient,* condition to define the moral standpoint in modern societies. In this sense, the concrete other is a critical concept that designates the *ideological* limits of universalistic discourse. It signifies the *unthought*, the *unseen,* and the *unheard* in such theories. This is evidenced by Kohlberg's effort, on the one hand, to enlarge the domain of moral theory to include in it relations to the concrete other and, on the other hand, to characterize such special relations of obligation as "private, personal" matters of evaluative life choices alone. Urging an examination

of this unthought is necessary to prevent the preemption of the discourse of universality by an unexamined particularity. Substitutionalist universalism dismisses the concrete other, while interactive universalism acknowledges that every generalized other is also a concrete other.

From a meta-ethical and normative standpoint, I would argue, therefore, for the validity of a moral theory that allows us to recognize the dignity of the generalized other through an acknowledgment of the moral identity of the concrete other. The point is not to juxtapose the generalized to the concrete other or to seek normative validity in one or another standpoint. The point is to think through the ideological limitations and biases that arise in the discourse of universalist morality through this unexamined opposition. I doubt that an easy, integration of both points of view, of justice and of care, is possible, without first clarifying the moral framework that would allow us to question both standpoints and their implicit gender presuppositions.

For this task a model of communicative need interpretations suggests itself.[33] Not only is such an ethic, as I interpret it, compatible with the dialogic, interactive generation of universality, but most significant, such an ethic provides the suitable framework within which moral and political agents can define their own concrete identities on the basis of recognizing each other's dignity as generalized others. Questions of the most desirable and just political organization, as well as the distinction between justice and the good life, the public and the domestic, can be analyzed, renegotiated, and redefined in such a process. Since, however, all those affected are participants in this process, the presumption is that these distinctions cannot be drawn in such a way as to privatize, hide, and repress the experiences of those who have suffered under them, for only what all could consensually agree to be in the best interest of each could be accepted as the outcome of this dialogic process.

One consequence of this communicative ethic of need interpretations is that the object domain of moral theory is so enlarged that not only rights but needs, not only justice but possible modes of the good life, are moved into an anticipatory-utopian perspective. What such discourses can generate are not only universalistically prescribable norms, but also intimations of otherness in the present that can lead to the future.

In his current formulation of his theory, Kohlberg accepts this extension of his Stage 6 perspective into an ethic of need interpretations, as suggested first by Habermas.[34] However, he does not see the incompatibility between the communicative ethics model and the Rawlsian "original position."[35] In defining reversibility of perspectives, he still considers the Rawlsian position to be paradigmatic. (Kohlberg 1984: 272, 310) Despite certain shared assumptions, the communicative model of need interpretations and the justice model of the original position need to be distinguished from each other.

First, in communicative ethics, the condition of ideal role-taking is not to be construed as a *hypothetical* thought process, carried out singly by the moral agent or the moral philosopher, but as an *actual* dialogue situation in which moral agents communicate with one another. Second, it is not necessary to place any epistemic constraints upon such an actual process of moral reasoning and disputation, for the more knowledge is available to moral agents about each other, their history, the particulars of their society, its structure and future, the more rational will be the outcome of their deliberations. Practical rationality entails epistemic rationality as well, and more knowledge rather than less contributes to a more rational and informed judgment. To judge rationally is not to judge as if one did not know what one could know, but to judge in light of all available and relevant information. Third, if there are no knowledge restrictions upon such a discursive situation, then it also follows that there is no privileged subject matter of moral disputation. Moral agents are not only limited to reasoning about primary goods, which they are assumed to want no matter what else they want. Instead, both the *goods* they desire and their *desires* themselves become legitimate topics of moral disputation. Finally, in such moral discourses, agents can also change levels of reflexivity, that is, they can introduce meta-considerations about the very conditions and constraints under which such dialogue takes place and evaluate their fairness. There is no closure of reflexivity in this model as there is, for example, in the Rawlsian one, which enjoins agents to accept certain rules of the bargaining game prior to the very choice of principles of justice.[36] With regard to the Kohlbergian paradigm, this would mean that moral agents can challenge the relevant *definition* of a moral situation, and urge that this very definition itself become the subject matter of moral reasoning and dispute.

A consequence of this model of communicative ethics would be that the language of rights and duties can now be challenged in light of our need interpretations. Following the tradition of modern social contract theories, Rawls and Kohlberg assume that our affective-emotional constitution, the needs and desires in light of which we formulate our rights and claims, are private matters alone. Their theory of the self, and, in particular, the Rawlsian metaphysics of the moral agent, does not allow them to view the constitution of our inner nature in *relational* terms.

A relational-interactive theory of identity assumes that inner nature, while being unique, is not an immutable given.[37] Individual need interpretations and motives carry within them the traces of those early childhood experiences, fantasies, wishes, and desires as well as the self-conscious goals of the person. The grammatical logic of the word "I" reveals the unique structure of ego identity: every subject who uses this concept in relation to herself knows that all other subjects are likewise "I"s. In this respect, the self only becomes an "I" in a community of other selves who are also "I"s. Every act of self-reference expresses simultaneously the uniqueness and difference of the self as well as the commonality among selves. Discourses about needs and motives unfold in this space created by commonality and uniqueness, generally shared socialization, and the contingency of individual life-histories.

The nonrelational theory of the self, which is privileged in contemporary universalist moral theory, by contrast, removes such need interpretations from the domain of moral discourse. They become "private," nonformalizable, nonanalyzable, and amorphous aspects of our conceptions of the good life. I am not suggesting that such concept of the good life either *can* or *should* be universalized, but only that our affective-emotional constitution, as well as our concrete history as moral agents, ought to be considered accessible to moral communication, reflection, and transformation. Inner nature, no less than the public sphere of justice, has a historical dimension. In it are intertwined the history of the self and the history of the collective. To condemn it to silence is, as Gilligan has suggested, not to hear that other voice in moral theory. I would say more strongly that such discourse continues woman's oppression by privatizing their lot and by excluding a central sphere of their activities from moral theory.

As the second wave of the women's movement, both in Europe and the United States has argued, to understand and to combat woman's oppression, it is no longer sufficient to demand woman's political and economic emancipation alone; it is also necessary to question those psychosexual relations in the domestic and private spheres within which women's lives unfold, and through which gender identity is reproduced. To explicate woman's oppression, it is necessary to uncover the power of those symbols, myths, and fantasies that entrap both sexes in the unquestioned world of gender roles. Perhaps one of the most fundamental of these myths and symbols has been the ideal of autonomy conceived in the image of a disembedded and disembodied male ego. This vision of autonomy was and continues to be based upon an implicit politics which defines the domestic, intimate sphere as ahistorical,

unchanging, and immutable, thereby removing it from reflection and discussion.[38] Needs, as well as emotions and affects, become mere given properties of individuals, which moral philosophy recoils from examining, on the grounds that it may interfere with the autonomy of the sovereign self. Women, because they have been made the "housekeeper of the emotions" in the modern, bourgeois world, and because they have suffered from the uncomprehended needs and phantasies of the male imagination, which has made them at once into Mother Earth and nagging bitch, the Virgin Mary and the whore, cannot condemn this sphere to silence. What Carol Gilligan has heard are those mutterings, protestations, and objections which women, confronted with ways of posing moral dilemmas that seemed alien to them, have voiced. Only if we can understand why their voices have been silenced, and how the dominant ideals of moral autonomy in our culture, as well as the privileged definition of the moral sphere, continue to silence women's voices, do we have a hope of moving to a more integrated vision of ourselves and of our fellow humans as generalized as well as "concrete" others.

NOTES

1. Thomas Kuhn, *The Structure of Scientific Revolutions,* vol. 2., no. 2 of *International Encyclopedia of Unified Science* (Chicago: University of Chicago Press, 1970, second edition), pp. 52ff.

2. John Michael Murphy and Carol Gilligan, "Moral Development in Late Adolescence and Adulthood: A Critique and Reconstruction of Kohlberg's Theory," *Human Development* 23 (1980), pp. 77–104; cited in the text as Murphy and Gilligan, 1980.

3. Carol Gilligan, *In a Different Voice: Psychological Theory and Women's Development* (Cambridge: Harvard University Press, 1982), pp. 18–19; cited in the text as Gilligan 1982.

4. Lawrence Kohlberg, "Synopses and Detailed Replies to Critics," with Charles Levine and Alexandra Hewer, in L. Kohlberg, *Essays on Moral Development,* vol. II, *The Psychology of*

Moral Development (San Francisco: Harper & Row, 1984), p. 341. This volume is cited in the text as Kohlberg 1984.

5. There still seems to be some question as to how the data on women's moral development is to be interpreted. Studies that focus on late adolescents and adult males and that show sex differences, include J. Fishkin, K. Keniston, and C. MacKinnon, "Moral Reasoning and Political Ideology," *Journal of Personality and Social Psychology* 27 (1973), pp. 109–19; N. Haan, J. Block, and M.B. Smith, "Moral Reasoning of Young Adults: Political-Social Behavior, Family Background, and Personality Correlates," *Journal of Personality and Social Psychology* 10 (1968), pp. 184–201; C. Holstein, "Irreversible, Stepwise Sequence in the Development of Moral Judgment: A Longitudinal Study of Males and Females," *Child Development* 47(1976), pp. 51–61. While it is clear that the available evidence does not throw the model of stage-sequence development into question, the prevalent presence of sex differences in moral reasoning does raise questions about *what* exactly this model might be measuring. Norma Haan sums up this objection to the Kohlbergian paradigm as follows: "Thus the moral reasoning of males who live in technical, rationalized societies, who reason at the level of formal operations and who *defensively intellectualize and deny interpersonal and situational detail,* is especially favored in the Kohlbergian scoring system," in "Two Moralities in Action Contexts: Relationships to Thought, Ego Regulation, and Development" (*Journal of Personality and Social Psychology* 36 (1978), p. 287; emphasis mine). I think Gilligan's studies also support the finding that inappropriate "intellectualization and denial of interpersonal, situational detail" constitutes one of the major differences in male and female approaches to moral problems. This is why, as I argue in the text, the separation between ego and moral development, as drawn by Kohlberg and others, seems inadequate to deal with the problem, since formalist ethical theories do seem to favor certain ego attitudes like defensiveness, rigidity, inability to empathize, and lack of flexibility over others like a nonrepressive attitude toward emotions, flexibility, and presence of empathy.

6. L. Kohlberg, "A Reply to Owen Flanagan and Some Comments on the Puka-Goodpaster Exchange," in *Ethics* 92 (April 1982), p. 316. Cf. also Gertrud Nunner-Winkler, "Two Moralities? A Critical Discussion of an Ethic of Care and Responsibility Versus an Ethics of Rights and Justice," in *Morality, Moral Behavior and Moral Development,* edited by W. M. Kurtines and J. L. Gewirtz (New York: John Wiley and Sons, 1984), p. 355. It is unclear whether the issue is, as Kohlberg and Nunner-Winkler suggest, one of distinguishing between "moral" and "ego" development or whether cognitive-developmental moral theory does not presuppose a model of ego development that clashes with more psychoanalytically oriented variants. In fact, to combat the charge of "maturationism" or "nativism" in his theory, which would imply that moral stages are a priori givens of the mind unfolding according to their own logic, regardless of the influence of society or environment upon them, Kohlberg argues as follows: "Stages," he writes, "'are equilibriations arising from interaction between the organism (with its structuring tendencies) and the structure of the environment (physical or social). Universal moral stages are as much a function of universal features of social structure (such as institutions of law, family, property) and social interactions in various cultures, as they are products of the general structuring tendencies of the knowing organism." (Kohlberg, "A Reply to Owen Flanagan," p. 521) If this is so, then cognitive-developmental moral theory must also presuppose that there is a *dynamic* between self and social structure whereby the individual learns, acquires or internalizes the perspectives and sanctions of the social world. But the mechanism of this dynamic may involve learning as well as resistance, internalization as well as projection and fantasy. The issue is less whether moral development and ego development are distinct—they may be conceptually distinguished and yet in the history of the self they are related—but whether the model of ego development presupposed by Kohlberg's theory is not distortingly *cognitivistic* in that it ignores the role of affects, resistance, projection, phantasy, and defense mechanisms in socialization processes.

7. For this formulation, see J. Habermas, "Interpretive Social Science vs. Hermeneuticism," in *Social Science as Moral Inquiry*, edited by N. Haan, R. Bellah, P. Rabinow, and W. Sullivan (New York: Columbia University Press, 1983), p. 262.

8. Imre Lakatos, "Falsification and the Methodology of Scientific Research Programs," in *Criticism and the Growth of Knowledge*, edited by I. Lakatos and A. Musgrave (Cambridge: Cambridge University Press, 1970), pp. 117ff.

9. Let me explain the status of this premise. I would characterize it as a "second-order research hypothesis" that both guides concrete research in the social sciences and that can, in turn, be falsified by them. It is not a statement of faith about the way the world is: the cross-cultural and transhistorical universality of the sex-gender system is an empirical fact. It is also most definitely not a normative proposition about the way the world *ought* to be. To the contrary, feminism radically challenges the validity of the sex-gender system in organizing societies and cultures, and advocates the emancipation of men and women from the unexamined and oppressive grids of this framework.

10. For further clarification of these two aspects of critical theory, see my *Critique, Norm, and Utopia: A Study of the Foundations of Critical Theory* (New York: Columbia University Press, 1986), Part Two, "The Transformation of Critique."

11. Although frequently invoked by Kohlberg, Nunner-Winkler, and also Habermas, it is still unclear *how* this distinction is drawn and how it is justified. For example, does the justice/good life distinction correspond to sociological definitions of the public vs. the private? If so, what is meant by the "private"? Is women-battering a "private" or a "public" matter? Another way of drawing this distinction is to separate what is universalizable from what is culturally contingent, dependent upon the specifics of concrete life-forms, individual histories, and the like. Habermas, in particular, relegates questions of the good life to the aesthetic-expressive sphere; cf. "A Reply to My Critics," in *Habermas: Critical Debates*, ed. by John B. Thompson and David Held (Cambridge: MIT Press, 1982), p. 262; "Moralbewusstsein und kommunikatives Handeln," in *Moralbewusstsein und kommunikatives Handeln* (Frankfurt: Suhrkamp, 1983), pp. 190ff. Again, if privacy in the sense of intimacy is included in the "aesthetic expressive" sphere, we are forced to silence and privatize most of the issues raised by the women's movement, which concern precisely the quality and nature of our "intimate" relations, fantasies, and hopes. A traditional response to this is to argue that in wanting to draw this aspect of our lives into the light of the public, the women's movement runs the risk of authoritarianism because it questions the limits of individual "liberty." In response to this legitimate political concern, I would argue that one must distinguish two issues: on the one hand, questioning life-forms and values that have been oppressive for women, and making them "public" in the sense of making them accessible to reflection, action, and transformation by revealing their *socially constituted* character; and on the other hand, making them "public" in the sense that these areas become subject to legislative and administrative state-action. The second may, but need not, follow from the first. Because feminists focus on pornography as an "aesthetic-expressive" mode of denigrating women, it does not thereby follow that their critique should result in public legislation against pornography. Whether there ought to be this kind of legislation needs to be examined in the light of relevant legal, political, or constitutional arguments. Questions of political authoritarianism arise at this level, but not at the level of a critical-philosophical examination of traditional distinctions that have privatized and silenced women's concerns.

12. Alasdair MacIntyre, *After Virtue* (Notre Dame: University of Notre Dame Press, 1981), pp. 50–51.

13. Agnes Heller, *A Theory of Feelings* (Holland: Van Gorcum, 1979), pp. 184ff.

14. John Locke, *The Second Treatise of Civil Government* in *Two Treatises of Government,* edited and with an introduction by Thomas I. Cook (New York: Haffner Press, 1947), p. 128.

15. Immanuel Kant, *The Metaphysical Elements of Justice,* translated by John Ladd (New York: Liberal Arts Press, 1965), p. 55.

16. Thomas Hobbes, *Leviathan* (1651), edited and with an introduction by C. B. Macpherson (Middlesex: Penguin Books, 1980), p. 186. All future citations in the text are to this edition.

17. Thomas Hobbes, "Philosophical Rudiments Concerning Government and Society," in *The English Works of Thomas Hobbes,* edited by Sir W. Molesworth, vol. II (Darmstadt, 1966), p. 109.

18. J. J. Rousseau, "On The Origin and Foundations of Inequality Among Men," in J. J. Rousseau, *The First and Second Discourses,* edited by R. D. Masters, translated by Roger D. and Judith R. Masters (New York: St. Martin's Press, 1964), p. 116.

19. G. W. F. Hegel, *Phänomenologie des Geistes,* edited by Johannes Hoffmeister (Hamburg: Felix Meiner, 1952), 6th ed., p. 141, (Philosophische Bibliothek, Bd. 114), translation used here by A. V. Miller, *Phenomenology of Spirit* (Oxford: Clarendon Press, 1977), p. 111.

20. Sigmund Freud, *Moses and Monotheism,* translated by Katharine Jones (New York: Vintage, Random House, 1967), pp. 103ff.; Jean Piaget, *The Moral Judgment of the Child,* translated by Marjorie Gabain (New York: Free Press, 1965), pp. 65ff. Cf. the following comment on boys' and girls' games: "The most superficial observation is sufficient to show that in the main the legal sense is far less developed in little girls than in boys. We did not succeed in finding a single collective game played by girls in which there were as many rules and, above all, as fine and consistent an organization and codification of these rules as in the game of marbles examined above." (p. 77)

21. Kant, "Critique of Practical Reason" in *Critique of Practical Reason and Other Writings in Moral Philosophy,* translated and edited with an introduction by Louis White Beck (Chicago: University of Chicago Press, 1949), p. 258.

22. Although the term "generalized other" is borrowed from George Herbert Mead, my definition of it differs from his. Mead defines the "generalized other" as follows: "The organized community or social group which gives the individual his unity of self may be called the 'generalized other.' The attitude of the generalized other is the attitude of the whole community." George Herbert Mead, *Mind, Self and Society: From the Standpoint of a Social Behaviorist,* edited with introduction by Charles W. Morris (Chicago: University of Chicago Press, 1955), tenth printing, p. 154. Among such communities, Mead includes a ball team as well as political clubs, corporations, and other more abstract social classes or subgroups such as the class of debtors and the class of creditors (*ibid,* p. 157). Mead himself does not limit the concept of the "generalized other" to what is described in the text. In identifying the "generalized other" with the abstractly defined, legal and juridical subject, contract theorists and Kohlberg depart from Mead. Mead criticizes the social contract tradition precisely for distorting the psycho-social genesis of the individual subject, cf. *ibid.,* p. 233.

23. Kohlberg, "Justice as Reversibility: The Claim to Moral Adequacy of a Highest Stage of Moral Judgment," in *Essays on Moral Development,* vol. I, *The Philosophy of Moral Development* (San Francisco: Harper & Row, 1981), p. 194, cited in the text as Kohlberg 1981.

24. Whereas all forms of reciprocity involve some concept of reversibility, these vary in degree: reciprocity can be restricted to the reversibility of actions but not of moral perspectives, to behavioral role models but not to the principles which underlie the generation of such behavioral expectations. For Kohlberg, the "veil of ignorance" is a model of perfect reversibility, for it elaborates the procedure of "ideal role-taking" or "moral musical chairs" where the decider "is to successively put himself imaginatively in the place of each other actor and consider the claims each would make from his point of view." (Kohlberg 1981, p. 199) My question is: are there any real "others" behind the "veil of ignorance" or are they indistinguishable from the self?

25. I find Kohlberg's general claim that the moral point of view entails reciprocity, equality, and fairness unproblematic. Reciprocity is not only a fundamental *moral* principle, but defines, as Alvin Gouldner has argued, a fundamental *social norm,* perhaps, in fact, the very concept of a social norm ("The Norm of Reciprocity: A Preliminary Statement," *American Sociological Review,* vol. 25 (April 1960), pp. 161–78). The existence of ongoing social relations in a human community entails some definition of reciprocity in the actions, expectations, and claims of the group. The fulfillment of such reciprocity, according to whatever interpretation is given to it, would then be considered fairness by members of the group.

Likewise, members of a group bound by relations of reciprocity and fairness are considered equal. What changes through history and culture are not these formal structures implicit in the very logic of social relations (we can even call them social universals), but the criteria of inclusion and exclusion. Who constitutes the *relevant* human groups: masters vs. slaves, men vs. women, Gentiles vs. Jews? Similarly, *which* aspects of human behavior and objects of the world are to be regulated by norms of reciprocity: in the societies studied by Levi-Strauss, some tribes exchange sea shells for women. Finally, *in terms* of what is the equality among members of a group established: would this be gender, race, merit, virtue, or entitlement? Clearly Kohlberg presupposes a *universalist-egalitarian* interpretation of reciprocity, fairness, and equality, according to which all humans, in virtue of their mere humanity, are to be considered beings entitled to reciprocal rights and duties.

26. John Rawls, *A Theory of Justice* (Cambridge: Harvard University Press, 1971; second printing, 1972), p. 137.

27. Michael J. Sandel, *Liberalism and the Limits of Justice* (Cambridge: Harvard University Press, 1982; reprinted 1984), p. 9; cited in the text as Sandel 1984.

28. Rawls, *A Theory of Justice,* p. 128.

29. Stanley Cavell, *The Claims of Reason* (Oxford: Oxford University Press, 1982), p. 265.

30. A most suggestive critique of Kohlberg's neglect of interpersonal morality has been developed by Norma Haan in "Two Moralities in Action Contexts: Relationships to Thought, Ego Regulation, and Development," pp. 286–305. Haan reports that "the formulation of formal morality appears to apply best to special kinds of hypothetical, rule-governed dilemmas, the paradigmatic situation in the minds of philosophers over the centuries." (p. 302) Interpersonal reasoning, by contrast, "arises within the context of moral dialogues between agents who strive to achieve balanced agreement, based on compromises they reach or on their joint discovery of interests they hold in common." (p. 303) For a more extensive statement see also Norma Haan, "An Interactional Morality of Everday Life," in *Social Science as Moral Inquiry,* pp. 218–51. The conception of "communicative need interpretations," which I

argue for below, is also such a model of interactional morality which, nonetheless, has implications for *institutionalized* relations of justice or for public morality as well, cf. note 37.

31. Cf. E. Tugendhat, "Zur Entwicklung von moralischen Begründungs-strukturen im modernen Recht," *Archiv für Recht und Sozialphilosophie,* vol. LXVIII (1980), pp. 1–20.

32. Thus a Rawlsian might object that while the epistemic information pertaining to the standpoint of the concrete other may be relevant in the application and contextualizing of general moral and political principles, it is unclear why such information need also be taken into account in the original choice or justification of such principles. For the moral point of view only concerns the constituents of our common humanity, not those differences which separate us from each other. I would like to distinguish here between the normative standpoint of *universalism,* which I share with Rawls and Kohlberg, and the methodological problem of formalism. Although the two have often gone together in the history of moral and political thought they need not do so. A formalist method, which also proceeds via an idealized thought-experiment, is subject to certain epistemic difficulties which are well known in the literature critical of social contract theories. And as Rawls himself has had to admit in his later writings, the device of the "original position" does not justify the concept of the person from which he proceeds, rather it presupposes it (cf. "Kantian Constructivism in Moral Theory"). Once this admission is made, however, and the device of the "original position" with its "veil of ignorance" is said to presuppose a concept of the person rather than justify it, then the kinds of criticisms raised in my paper that concern moral identity and epistemology must also be taken into account. Rawls's concepts of the moral person and autonomy remain restricted to the discourse of the "generalized other." I would like to thank Diane T. Meyers for bringing this objection to my attention.

33. Although I follow the general outline of Habermas' conception of communicative ethics, I differ from him insofar as he distinguishes sharply between questions of justice and the good life (see note 11 above), and insofar as in his description of the

"seventh stage," he equivocates between concepts of the "generalized" and the "concrete other"; cf. J. Habermas, "Moral Development and Ego Identity," in *Communication and the Evolution of Society,* translated by T. McCarthy (Boston: Beacon Press, 1979), pp. 69–95. The "concrete other" is introduced in his theory through the back door, as an aspect of ego autonomy, and as an aspect of our relation to inner nature. I find this implausible for reasons discussed above.

34. See Habermas, *ibid.,* p. 90, and Kohlberg's discussion in Kohlberg 1984: 35–86.

35. In an earlier piece, I have dealt with the strong parallelism between the two conceptions of the "veil of ignorance" and the "ideal speech situation"; see my "The Methodological Illusions of Modern Political Theory: The Case of Rawls and Habermas," *Neue Hefte für Philosophie* (Spring 1982), no. 21. pp. 47–74. With the publication of *The Theory of Communicative Active,* Habermas himself has substantially modified various assumptions in his original formulation of communicative ethics, and the rendition given here follows these modifications; for further discussion see my "Toward a Communicative Ethics," in *Critique, Norm, and Utopia,* chap. 8.

36. Cf. Rawls, *A Theory of Justice,* pp. 118ff.

37. For recent feminist perspectives on the development of the self, cf. Dorothy Dinnerstein, "*The Mermaid and the Minotaur: Sexual Arrangements and Human Malaise* (New York: Harper, 1976); Jean Baker Miller, "The Development of Women's Sense of Self," work-in-progress paper published by the Stone Center for Developmental Services and Studies at Wellesley College, 1984; Nancy Chodorow, *The Reproduction of Mothering* (Berkeley: University of California Press, 1978); Jessica Benjamin, "Authority and the Family Revisited: Or, A World Without Fathers?" in *New German Critique* 13 (1978), pp. 35–58; Jane Flax, "The Conflict Between Nurturance and Autonomy in Mother-Daughter Relationships and Within Feminism," in *Feminist Studies,* vol. 4, no. 2 (June 1981), pp. 171–92; and I. Balbus, *Marxism and Domination* (Princeton: Princeton University Press, 1982).

38. The distinction between the public and the private spheres is undergoing a tremendous realignment in late-capitalist societies as a result of a complicated series of factors, the chief of which may be the changing role of the state in such societies in assuming more and more tasks that were previously more or less restricted to the family and reproductive spheres, e.g., education, early child care, health care, care for the elderly, and the like. Also, recent legislation concerning abortion, wife battering, and child abuse, suggests that the accepted legal definitions of these spheres have begun to shift as well. These new sociological and legislative developments point to the need to fundamentally rethink our concepts of moral, psychological, and legal autonomy, a task hitherto neglected by formal-universalist moral theory. I do not want to imply, by any means that the philosophical critique voiced in this paper leads to a wholly positive evaluation of these developments or to the neglect of their contradictory and ambivalent character for women. My analysis would need to be complemented by a critical social theory of the changing definition and function of the private sphere in late-capitalist societies. As I have argued elsewhere, these social and legal developments not only lead to an extension of the perspective of the "generalized other," by subjecting more and more spheres of life to legal norms, but create the potential for the growth of the perspective of the "concrete other," that is, an association of friendship and solidarity in which need interpretations are discussed and new needs created. I see these associations as being created by new social movements like ecology and feminism, in the interstices of our societies, partly in response to and partly in consequence of, the activism of the welfare state in late-capitalist societies; cf. *Critique, Norm, and Utopia,* pp. 343–353. I am much indebted to Nancy Fraser for her elaboration of the political consequences of my distinction between the "generalized" and the "concrete" other in the context of the paradoxes of the modern welfare state in her "Feminism and the Social State." (*Salmagundi,* April 1986) An extensive historical and philosophical analysis of the changing relation between the private and the public is provided by Linda Nicholson in her book, *Gender and History: The Limits of Social Theory in the Age of the Family.* (New York: Columbia University Press, 1986).

TAKING CARE: CARE AS PRACTICE AND VALUE

Virginia Held

The last words I spoke to my older brother after a brief visit and with special feeling were "take care." He had not been taking good care of himself, and I hoped he would do better; not many days later he died, of problems quite possibly unrelated to those to which I had been referring.

We often say "take care" as routinely as "goodbye" or some abbreviation and with as little emotion. But even then it does convey some sense of connectedness. More often, when said with some feeling, it means something like "take care of yourself because I care about you." Sometimes we say it, especially to children or to someone embarking on a trip or an endeavor, meaning "I care what happens to you so please don't do anything dangerous or foolish." Or, if we know the danger is inevitable and inescapable, it may be more like a wish that the elements will let the person take care so the worst can be evaded. And sometimes we mean it as a plea: "Be careful not to harm yourself or others because our connection will make us feel with and for you." We may be harmed ourselves or partly responsible, or if you do something you will regret we will share that regret.

One way or another this expression, like many others, illustrates human relatedness and the daily reaffirmations of connection. It is the relatedness of human beings, built and rebuilt, that the ethics of care is being developed to try to understand, to evaluate, and to guide.

For a little over two decades now, the concept of care as it figures in the ethics of care has been assumed, explored, elaborated, and employed in the development of theory. But definitions have often been imprecise, or trying to arrive at them has simply been postponed, as in my own case, in the growing discourse. Perhaps this is entirely appropriate for new explorations, but the time may have come to seek greater clarity. Of course, to a considerable extent, we know what we are talking about when we speak of taking care of a child or providing care for the ill. But care has many, many forms, and as the ethics of care evolves, so should our understanding of what care is.

A seemingly easy distinction to make is between care as the activity of caring for someone and the mere "caring about" of how we feel about certain issues.[1] But the distinction may not be as clear as it appears since when we care for a child, for instance, we certainly also care about her. And if we really do care about world hunger, we will probably be doing something about it—such as, at least, giving money to alleviate it or to change the conditions that bring it about—and thus establishing some connection between ourselves and the hungry we say we care about.[2] And if we really do care about global climate change and the harm it will bring to future generations, we imagine a connection between ourselves and those future people who will judge our irresponsibility, and we change our consumption practices or political activities to decrease the likely harm.

Many of those writing about care agree that the care that is relevant to an ethics of care must at least be able to refer to an activity, as in taking care of someone. Most, though not all, of those writing on care do not lose sight of how care involves work and the expenditure of energy on the part of the person doing the caring. But it is often thought to be more than this.

There can, of course, be different emphases in how we think of care. I will be trying to clarify the meaning of care in contexts for which taking care of children or those who are ill are in some ways paradigmatic. But the caring relations I will be thinking about will go far beyond such contexts.

It is fairly clear that engaging in the work of taking care of someone is not the same as caring for them in the sense of having warm feelings for them. But whether certain feelings must accompany the labor of care is more in doubt.

Nel Noddings focuses especially on the attitudes of caring that typically accompany the activity of care. Close attention to the feelings, needs, desires, and thoughts of those cared for and a skill in understanding a situation from that person's point of view are central to caring for someone.[3] Carers act in behalf of others' interests, but they also care for themselves since without the maintenance of their own capabilities, they will not be able to continue to engage in care. To Noddings, the cognitive aspect of the carer's attitude is "receptive-intuitive" rather than "objective-analytic," and understanding the needs of those cared for depends more on feeling with them than on rational cognition. In the activity of care, abstract rules are of limited use. There can be a natural impulse to care for others, but to sustain it persons need to make a moral commitment to the ideal of caring.[4] For Noddings, care is an attitude and an ideal manifest in activities of care in concrete situations. In her recent book, *Starting at Home,* she explores what a caring society would be like. She seeks a broad, near universal description of "what we are like" when we engage in caring encounters, and she explores "what characterizes consciousness in such relations."[5]

Care is much more explicitly labor in Joan Tronto's view. She and Berenice Fisher have defined it as activity that includes "everything that we do to maintain, continue, and repair our 'world' so that we can live in it as well as possible," and care can be for objects and for the environment, as well as for other persons.[6] This definition almost surely seems too broad: vast amounts of economic activity could be included, like house construction and commercial dry cleaning, and the distinctive features of caring labor would be lost. It does not include the sensitivity to the needs of the cared for that others often recognize in care, nor what Noddings calls the needed "engrossment" with the other. And, Tronto explains, it excludes production, play, and creative activity, whereas a great deal of care, for instance, child care, can be playful and is certainly creative.

If one accepts Marx's distinction between productive and reproductive labor and then sees caring as reproductive labor, as some propose, one misses the way caring, especially for children, can be transformative rather than merely reproductive and repetitive. Although this has not been acknowledged in traditional views of the household, the potential for creative transformation in the nurturing that occurs there, and in child care and education generally, is enormous. Care has the capacity to shape new *persons* with ever more advanced understandings of culture and society and morality.[7] Only a biased and damaging misconception holds that caring merely reproduces our material and biological realities, and what is new and creative and distinctively human must occur elsewhere.

Diemut Bubeck offers one of the most precise definitions of care in the literature: "Caring for is the meeting of the needs of one person by another person, where face-to-face interaction between carer and cared for is a crucial element of the overall activity and where the need is of such a nature that it cannot possibly be met by the person in need herself."[8] She distinguishes between caring for someone and providing a service; on her definition, to cook a meal for a small child is caring, but a wife who cooks for her husband when he could perfectly well cook for himself is not engaging in care but rather providing a service to him. Care, Bubeck asserts, is "a response to a particular subset of basic human needs, i.e. those which make us dependent on others."[9]

In Bubeck's view, care does not require any particular emotional bond between carer and cared for, and it is important to her general view that care can and often should be publicly provided, as in public health care. She seems to think that care is almost entirely constituted by the objective fact of needs being met, rather than by the attitude or ideal with which the carer is acting. Her conception is then open to the objection that, as long as the deception is successful, someone going through the motions of caring for a child while wishing the child dead is engaged in care of as much moral worth as that of a carer who intentionally and with affection seeks what is best for the child. For me this objection is fatal. I suppose a strict utilitarian might say that if the child is fed and clothed and hugged, the emotional tone with which these are done is of no moral significance. But to me it is clear that in the wider moral scheme of things, though I cannot argue it here, it is significant. A world in which the motive of care is good will rather than ill will (plus any self-interest that may additionally be needed to motivate the care giver to do the work) is a better world. Even if the child remains unaware of the ill will, an unlikely though possible circumstance, and even if the child grows up with the admirable sensitivity to the feelings of others that would constitute a better outcome, even on a utilitarian scale, than if she doesn't, the motive would still matter. An important aspect of care is how it *expresses* our attitudes and relationships.

Sara Ruddick sees care as work but also as more than this. She says that "as much as care is labor, it is also relationship . . . caring labor is intrinsically relational. The work is constituted in and through the relation of those who give and receive care. . . . More critically, some caring relationships seem to have a significance in 'excess' of the labor they enable."[10] She compares the work of a father who is bringing a small child to a day-care center and that of the day-care worker who is receiving the child. Both can perform the same work of reassuring the child, hugging him, transferring him from father to worker, and so on. But the character and meaning of the father's care may be in excess of the work itself. For the father, the work is a response to the relationship, whereas for the day-care worker, the relationship is probably a response to the work. So we may want to reject a view that equates care entirely with the labor involved.

To Bubeck, to Noddings in her early work, and to a number of others who are writing on care, its face-to-face aspect is central. This has been thought to make it difficult to think of our concern for more distant others in terms of caring. Bubeck, however, does not see her view as leading to the conclusion that care is limited to the context of the relatively personal, as Noddings's view suggested, because Bubeck includes the activities of the welfare state in the purview of the ethics of care. She thinks the care to be engaged in, as in child-care centers and centers for the elderly, will indeed be face-to-face, but she advocates widespread and adequate public funding for such activity.

Bubeck rejects the particularistic aspects of the ethics of care. She advocates generalizing the moral principle of meeting needs, and thus the way in which an ethic of care can provide for just political and social programs becomes evident. But this comes too close, in my view, to collapsing the ethics of care into utilitarianism. In addition to being the meeting of objective needs, care seems to be at least partly an attitude and motive, as well as a value. Bubeck builds the requirements of justice into the ethics of care. But this may still not allow care to be the primary moral consideration of a person, say, in a rich country, who is engaging in empowering someone in a poor country, if there will never be in this engagement any face-to-face aspect. And this is troubling to many who see care as a fundamental value, with as much potential for moral elaboration as justice, but doubt that justice can itself be adequately located entirely within care or that care should be limited to relatively personal interactive work.

Peta Bowden has a different view than Bubeck of what caring relations are like. She starts with what she calls an intuition: that caring is ethically important. Caring, she says, "expresses ethically significant ways in which we matter to each other, transforming interpersonal relatedness into something beyond ontological necessity or brute survival."[11] Adopting a Wittgensteinian approach to understanding and explicitly renouncing any attempt to provide a definition of care, she carefully examines various examples of caring practices: mothering, friendship, nursing, and citizenship. In including citizenship, she illustrates how face-to-face interaction is not a necessary feature of all caring relations, though it characterizes many.

In his detailed discussion of caring as a virtue, Michael Slote thinks it entirely suitable that our benevolent feelings for distant others be conceptualized as caring. "An ethic of caring," in his view, "can take the well-being of all humanity into consideration."[12] Where Bubeck rejects the view of caring as motive, he embraces it. To him, caring just is a "motivational attitude."[13] And in the recent volume *Feminists Doing Ethics,* several contributors see care as a virtue.[14]

I think feminists should object to making care entirely a matter of motive or of virtue since this runs such a risk of losing sight of it as work. Encouragement should not be given to the tendency to overlook the question of who does most of this work. But that caring is not only work is also persuasive, so we might conclude that care must be able to refer to work, to motive, to value, and perhaps to more than these.

In her influential book *Love's Labor,* Eva Kittay examines what she calls "dependency work," which overlaps with care but is not the same. She defines dependency work as "the work of caring for those who are inevitably dependent," for example, infants and the severely disabled.[15] When not done well, such work can be done without an affective dimension, though it typically includes it.[16] Kittay well understands how dependency work is relational and how the dependency relation "at its very crux, is a moral one arising out of a claim of vulnerability on the part of the dependent, on the one hand, and of the special positioning of the dependency worker to meet the need, on the other."[17] The relation is importantly one of trust. And since dependency work is so often unpaid, when dependency workers use their time to provide care instead of working at paid employment, they themselves become dependent on others for the means with which to do so and for their own maintenance.

Ann Ferguson and Nancy Folbre's conception of "sex-affective production" has much to recommend it in understanding the concept of care. They characterize sex-affective production as "childbearing, childrearing, and the provision of nurturance, affection, and sexual satisfaction."[18] It is not limited to the labor involved in caring for the dependent but also includes the provision of affection and the nurture of relationships. Ferguson and Folbre are especially concerned with analyzing how providing this kind of care leads to the oppression of women. But one can imagine such care as nonoppressive, for both the carers and the cared for. Bubeck and Kittay focus especially on the necessary care that the dependent cannot do without. But when we also understand how increasing levels of affection, mutual concern, and emotional satisfaction are valuable, we can aim at promoting care far beyond the levels of necessity. So understanding care as including rather than excluding the sharing of time and attention and services, even when the recipients are not dependent on them, seems appropriate.

Sara Ruddick usefully notes that "three distinct though overlapping meanings of 'care' have emerged in recent decades. 'Care' is an ethics defined in opposition to 'justice'; a kind of labor; a particular relationship."[19] She herself argues for a view of care as a kind of labor, but not only that, and advocates "attending steadily to the relationships of care."[20] Ruddick doubts that we ought to define an ethics of care in opposition to an ethics of justice since we ought to see how justice is needed in caring well and in family life. But then she wonders how, if care is seen as a kind of labor rather than an already normative concept contrasted with justice, it can give rise to an ethics. Her answer follows, and these passages are worth quoting extensively:

> The "ethics" of care is provoked by the habits and challenges of the work, makes sense of its aims, and spurs and reflects upon the self-understanding of workers. The ethics also extends beyond the activities from which it arises, generating a stance (or standpoint) toward "nature," human relationships, and social institutions. . . . First memories of caring and being cared for inspire a sense of obligation. . . . [And] a person normatively identifies with a

conception of herself as someone who enters into and values caring relationships, exercising particular human capacities as well. Neither memory nor identity "gives rise" to an "ethics" that then leaves them behind. Rather there is an interplay in which each recreates the other.[21]

I think care is surely a form of labor, but it is much more. The labor of care is already relational and can for the most part not be replaced by machines in the way so much other labor can. Ruddick agrees that "caring labor is intrinsically relational,"[22] but she thinks the relationship is something assumed rather than necessarily focused on. I think that as we clarify care, we need to see it in terms of *caring relations.*

I doubt that we ought to accept the contrast between justice as normative and care as nonnormative, as the latter would be if it were simply labor. I think it is better to think of contrasting practices and the values they embody and should be guided by. An activity must be purposive to count as work or labor, but it need not incorporate any values, even efficiency, in the doing of it. Chopping at a tree, however clumsily, in order to fell it, could be work. But when it does incorporate such values as doing so effectively, it becomes the practice of woodcutting. So we do better to focus on practices of care rather than merely on the work involved.

Practices of justice such as primitive revenge and an eye for an eye have from earliest times been engaged in and gradually reformed and refined. By now we have legal, judicial, and penal practices that only dimly resemble their ancient forerunners, and we have very developed theories of justice and of different kinds of justice with which to evaluate such practices. Practices of care, from mothering to medical care to teaching children to cultivating professional relations, have also changed a great deal from their earliest forms, but to a significant extent without the appropriate moral theorizing. That, I think, is what the ethics of care should be trying to fill in. The practices themselves already incorporate various values, often unrecognized, especially by the philosophers engaged in moral theorizing, who ought to be attending to them. And the practices themselves as they exist are often riddled with the gender injustices that pervade societies in most ways but that especially characterize most practices of care. So, moral theorizing is needed to understand the practices and to reform them.

Consider, for instance, mothering, in the sense of caring for children. It had long been imagined in the modern era, after the establishment of the public-private distinction, to be "outside morality." Feminist critique has been needed to show how profoundly mistaken such a view is. Moral issues are confronted constantly in the practice of mothering, and there is constant need for the cultivation of the virtues appropriate to this practice. To get a hint of how profoundly injustice is embedded in the practice of mothering, one can compare the meaning of "mothering" with that of "fathering," which historically has meant no more than impregnating a woman and being the genetic father of a child. "Mothering" suggests that this activity must or should be done by women, whereas, except for lactation, there is no part of it that cannot be done by men as well. Many feminists argue that for actual practices of child care to be morally acceptable, they will have to be radically transformed to accord with principles of equality, though existing conceptions of equality should probably not be the primary moral focus of practices of care. And this is only the beginning of the moral scrutiny to which they should be subject.

This holds also for other practices that can be thought of as practices of care. We need, then, not only to examine the practices and discern with new sensitivities the values already embedded or missing within them but also to construct the appropriate normative theory with which to evaluate them, reform them, and shape them anew. This, I think, involves understanding care as a value worthy of the kind of theoretical elaboration justice has received. And understanding the value of care involves understanding how it should not be limited to the household or family;

care should be recognized as a political and social value also.

We all agree that justice is a value. There are also practices of justice: law enforcement, court proceedings, and so on. Practices incorporate values but also need to be evaluated by the normative standards values provide. A given actual practice of justice may only very inadequately incorporate within it the value of justice, and we need justice as a value to evaluate such a practice. The value of justice picks out certain aspects of the overall moral spectrum, those having to do with fairness, equality, and so on, and it would not be satisfactory to have only the most general value terms, such as "good" and "right," "bad" and "wrong," with which to do the evaluating of a practice of justice. Analogously, for actual practices of care we need care, as a value to pick out the appropriate cluster of moral considerations, such as sensitivity, trust, and mutual concern, with which to evaluate such practices. It is not enough to think of care as simply work, describable empirically, with "good" and "right" providing all the normative evaluation of actual practices of care. Such practices are often morally deficient in ways specific to care, as well as to justice.

If we say of someone that "he is a caring person," this includes an evaluation that he has a characteristic that, other things being equal, is morally admirable. Attributing a virtue to someone, as when we say that she is generous or trustworthy, describes a disposition but also makes a normative judgment. And it is highly useful to be able to characterize people and societies in specific and subtle ways, recognizing the elements of our claims that are empirically descriptive and those that are normative. The subtlety needs to be available not only at the level of the descriptive but also within out moral evaluations. "Caring," thus, picks out a more specific value to be found in persons' and societies' characteristics than merely finding them to be good or bad or morally admirable or not on the whole. But we may resist reducing care to a virtue if by that we refer only

to the dispositions of individual persons since caring is so much a matter of the relations between them.

Diana Meyers examines the entrenched cultural imagery that can help explain the hostility often encountered by advocates of the ethics of care who seek to expand its applicability beyond the household and to increase care in public life:

> Oscillating sentimentality and contempt with regard to motherhood and childhood fuel this problem. If motherhood and childhood are conditions of imperfect personhood, as they are traditionally thought to be, no one would want to be figured as a mother or as a child in relations with other persons. This perverse constellation of attitudes is enshrined in and transmitted through a cultural stock of familiar figures of speech, stories, and pictorial imagery.[23]

As she explores various illustrative tropes, she shows that the myth of the "independent man" as model, with mothers and children seen as deficient, though lovable, is part of what needs to be overcome in understanding the value of care.

The concept of care should not in my view be a naturalized concept, and the ethics of care should not be a naturalized ethics.[24] Care is not reducible to the behavior that has evolved and that can be adequately captured in empirical descriptions, as when an account may be given of the child care that could have been practiced by our hunter-gatherer ancestors, and its contemporary analogues may be considered. Care as relevant to an ethics of care incorporates the values we decide as feminists to find acceptable in it. And the ethics of care does not accept and describe the practices of care as they have evolved under actual historical conditions of patriarchal and other domination; it evaluates such practices and recommends what they morally ought to be like.

I think, then, of care as practice and value. The practices of care are, of course, multiple, and some seem very different from others. Taking care of a toddler so that he does not hurt himself but is not unduly fearful is not much like patching up the mistrust between colleagues that will enable them to work together. Dressing a wound so that it will not become infected is not much like putting up curtains to make a room attractive and private. And neither is much like arranging for food to be delivered to families who need it half a world away. Yet all care involves attentiveness, sensitivity, and responding to needs. It is helpful to clarify this, as it is to clarify how justice in all its forms requires impartiality, treating persons as equals, and recognizing their rights. This is not at all to say that a given practice should involve a single value only. On the contrary, as we clarify the values of care, we can better advocate their relevance for many practices from which they have been largely excluded.

Consider police work. Organizationally a part of the "justice system," it must have the enforcement of the requirements of justice high among its priorities. But as it better understands the relevance of care to its practices, as it becomes more caring, it can often accomplish more through educating and responding to needs, building trust between police and policed, and thus preventing violations of law than it can through traditional "law enforcement" after prevention has failed. Sometimes the exclusion of the values of care is more in theory than in practice. An ideal market that treats all exchanges as impersonal and all participants as replaceable has no room for caring. But actual markets often include significant kinds of care and concern, of employers for employees, of employees for customers, and so on. As care is better understood, the appropriate places for caring relations in economic activity may be better appreciated.[25]

At the same time, practices of care are not devoted solely to the values of care. They often need justice also. Consider mothering, fathering in the sense of caring for a child, or "parenting" if one prefers this term. This is probably the most caring of the caring practices since the emotional tie between carer and cared for is characteristically so strong. This practice has caring well for the child as its primary value. But as understanding

of what this involves becomes more adequate, it should include normative guidance on how to avoid such tendencies as mothers may have to unduly interfere and control, and it can include the aspect well delineated by Sara Ruddick: "respect for 'embodied willfulness.'"[26] Moreover, practices of parenting must include justice in requiring the fair treatment of multiple children in a family and in fairly distributing the burdens of parenting.

Ruddick worries that if we think of justice and care as separate ethics, this will lead to the problem that, for instance, responding to needs, as economic and social rights do, cannot be part of the concerns of justice. To hold this position would be especially unfortunate just as the economic and social rights of meeting basic needs are gaining acceptance as human rights at the global level (even if not in the United States, where having such needs met is not recognized as a right). I believe Ruddick's concern is not a problem and that the difference here is one of motive. The motive for including economic and social rights among the human rights on the grounds of justice is that it would be unfair and a failure of equality, especially of rights to equal freedom, not to do so.[27] When meeting needs is motivated by care, on the other hand, it is the needs themselves that are responded to and the persons themselves with these needs that are cared for. This contrast is especially helpful in evaluating social policies, for instance, welfare policies. Even if the requirements of justice and equality would be met by a certain program, of payments let's say, we could still find the program callous and uncaring if it did not concern itself with the actual well-being, or lack of it brought about by the program. One can imagine such payments being provided very grudgingly and the recipients of them largely disdained by the taxpayers called on to fund them. And one can imagine the shame and undermining of self-respect that would be felt by the recipients of these payments. Except that the amounts of the payments and the range of recipients of them never came close to what justice would require, the rest of this description is fairly accurate about welfare programs in the United States. One can compare this with what a caring program would be like. In addition to meeting the bare requirements of justice, it would foster concern for the actual needs of recipients, offer the needed services to meet them, and express the morally recommended care and concern of the society for its less fortunate and more dependent members.

It seems to me that justice and care, as values, each invoke associated clusters of moral considerations and that these considerations are different. Actual practices should usually incorporate both care and justice, but with appropriately different priorities. For instance, the practice of child care by employees in a childcare center should have as its highest priority the safeguarding and appropriate development of children, including meeting their emotional, as well as physical and educational, needs. Justice should not be absent: the children should be treated fairly and with respect, and violations of justice such as would be constituted by racial or ethnic discrimination against some of the children should not be tolerated. But providing care rather than exemplifying justice would be the primary aim of the activity. In contrast, a practice of legislative decision making on the funding to be supplied to localities to underwrite their efforts to improve law enforcement should have justice as its primary aim. Localities where crime is a greater threat should receive more of such funding so that equality of personal security is more nearly achieved. Care should not be absent: concern for victims of crime and for victims of police brutality should be part of what is considered in such efforts. But providing greater justice and equality rather than caring for victims would be the primary aim of such legislative decision making.

Sara Ruddick does not consider justice inherently tied to a devaluation of relationships. I think justice and its associated values are more committed to individualism than she seems to think. It seems to me that it is on grounds of care rather than justice that we can identify with

others enough to form a political entity and to develop civil society.[28] Moreover, relations of care seem to me to be wider and deeper than relations of justice. Within relations of care, we can treat people justly, as if we were liberal individuals agreeing on mutual respect. This can be done in more personal contexts, as when friends compete fairly in a game they seek to win or when parents treat their children equally. Or it can be done in public, political, and social contexts, as when people recognize each other as fellow members of a group that is forming a political entity that accepts a legal system. When justice is the guiding value, it requires that individual rights be respected. But when we are concerned with the relatedness that constitutes a social group and is needed to hold it together, we should look, I think, to care.

My own view, then, is that care is both a practice and a value. As a practice, it shows us how to respond to needs and why we should. It builds trust and mutual concern and connectedness between persons. It is not a series of individual actions but a practice that develops, along with its appropriate attitudes. It has attributes and standards that can be described, but more important, that can be recommended and that should be continually improved as adequate care comes closer to being good care. Practices of care should express the caring relations that bring persons together, and they should do so in ways that are progressively more morally satisfactory. Caring practices should gradually transform children and others into human beings who are increasingly more morally admirable.

Consider how trust is built, bit by bit, largely by practices of caring. Trust is fragile and can be shattered in a single event; to rebuild it may take a long time and many expressions of care, or the rebuilding may be impossible. Relations of trust are among the most important personal and social assets. To develop well and to flourish, children need to trust those who care for them, and the providers of such care need to trust the fellow members of their communities that the trust of their children will not be misplaced. For peace to be possible, antagonistic groups need to learn to be able to trust each other enough so that misplaced trust is not even more costly than mistrust. To work well, societies need to cultivate trust between citizens and between citizens and governments; to achieve whatever improvements of which societies are capable, the cooperation that trust makes possible is needed. Care is not the same thing as trust, but caring relations should be characterized by trust, and caring is the leading contributor to trust.

In addition to being a practice, care is also a value. Caring persons and caring attitudes are valued, and we can organize many evaluations of how persons are interrelated around a constellation of moral considerations associated with care or its absence. For instance, we can ask of a relation whether it is trusting and mutually considerate or hostile and vindictive. I disagree with the view that care is the same as benevolence because I think it is more the characterization of a social relation than the description of an individual disposition, and social relations are not reducible to individual states. It is caring relations that ought to be cultivated between persons in their personal lives and between the members of caring societies. Such relations are often reciprocal over time if not at given times. The values of caring are especially exemplified in caring relations, rather than in persons as individuals. Caring relations form the small societies of family and friendship on which larger societies depend. And caring relations of a weaker but still evident kind between more distant persons allow them to trust one another enough to live in peace and to respect each others' rights. For progress to be made, persons need to care together as a group for the well-being of their members and of their environment.

The ethics of care builds relations of care and concern and mutual responsiveness to need on both the personal and wider social levels. Within social relations in which we care enough about one another to form a social entity, we may agree on various ways to deal with one another. For instance, for limited purposes we may imagine each other as liberal individuals, independent, autonomous, and rational, and we may adopt liberal schemes of law and governance and policies to maximize individual benefits. But we should not lose sight of the deeper reality of human interdependency and of the need for caring relations to undergird or surround such constructions. The artificial abstraction of the model of the liberal individual is at best suitable for a restricted and limited part of human life rather than for the whole of it. The ethics of care provides a way of thinking about and evaluating both the more immediate and the more distant human relations with which to develop morally acceptable societies.

NOTES

I wish to thank especially Sara Ruddick and Hilde Nelson for helpful comments and the American Society for Value Inquiry for the occasion to present this essay at its session at the meeting of the Central Division of the American Philosophical Association in Chicago in April 2002. I am also grateful to the Philosophy Department at Vanderbilt University where the essay was presented and discussed in April 2003.

1. Jeffrey Blustein, *Care and Commitment* (New York: Oxford University Press, 1991); and Harry G. Frankfurt, *The Importance of What We Care About* (Cambridge: Cambridge University Press, 1988).
2. Joan C. Tronto, *Moral Boundaries: A Political Argument for an Ethic of Care* (New York: Routledge, 1993).
3. Nel Noddings, *Caring: A Feminine Approach to Ethics and Moral Education* (Berkeley: University of California Press, 1986), esp. 14–19.
4. Ibid., 42, 80.
5. Nel Noddings, *Starting at Home: Caring and Social Policy* (Berkeley: University of California Press, 2002), 13.
6. Tronto, *Moral Boundaries,* 103; and Berenice Fisher and Joan Tronto, "Toward a Feminist Theory of Caring," in *Circles of Care,* ed. E. Abel and M. Nelson (Albany: SUNY Press, 1990), 40.

7. Virginia Held, *Feminist Morality: Transforming Culture, Society, and Politics* (Chicago: University of Chicago Press, 1993).

8. Diemut Bubeck, *Care, Gender, and Justice* (Oxford: Oxford University Press, 1995), 129.

9. Ibid., 133.

10. Sara Ruddick, "Care as Labor and Relationship," in *Norms and Values: Essays on the Work of Virginia Held,* ed. Joram C. Haber and Mark S. Halfon (Lanham, Md.: Rowman & Littlefield, 1998), 13–14.

11. Peta Bowden, *Caring* (London: Routledge, 1997), 1.

12. Michael Slote, *Morals from Motives* (New York: Oxford University Press, 2001), ix.

13. Ibid., 30.

14. See chapters by Lisa Tessman, Margaret McLaren, and Barbara Andrew in *Feminists Doing Ethics,* ed. Peggy DesAutels and Joanne Waugh (Lanham, Md.: Rowman & Littlefield, 2001).

15. Eva Feder Kittay, *Love's Labor: Essays on Women, Equality, and Dependency* (New York: Routledge, 1999), ix.

16. Ibid., 30.

17. Ibid., 35.

18. Ann Ferguson and Nancy Folbre, "The Unhappy Marriage of Patriarchy and Capitalism," in *Women and Revolution,* ed. Lydia Sargent (Boston: South End Press, 1981), 314.

19. Ruddick, "Care as Labor and Relationship," 4.

20. Ibid.

21. Ibid., 20–21.

22. Ibid., 14.

23. Diana Tietjens Meyers, *Gender in the Mirror: Cultural Imagery and Women's Agency* (New York: Oxford University Press, 2002), 65.

24. Virginia Held, "Moral Subjects: The Natural and the Normative," Presidential Address, American Philosophical Association, Eastern Division, *Proceedings and Addresses of the American Philosophical Association* (Newark, Del.: APA, November 2002).

25. Virginia Held, "Care and the Extension of Markets," *Hypatia* 17, no. 2 (Spring 2002): 19–33.

26. Sara Ruddick, "Injustice in Families: Assault and Domination," in *Justice and Care: Essential Readings in Feminist Ethics,* ed. Virginia Held (Boulder, Col.: Westview, 1995).

27. Virginia Held, *Rights and Goods: Justifying Social Action* (Chicago: University of Chicago Press, 1989), esp. chap. 8.

28. Virginia Held, "Rights and the Presumption of Care," in *Rights and Reason: Essays in Honor of Carl Wellman,* ed. Marilyn Friedman, Larry May, Kate Parsons, and Jennifer Stiff (Dordrecht: Kluwer, 2000).

CONFLICTED LOVE

Kelly Oliver

CONFLICTED LOVE

The popularity of self-help programs, various forms of therapy and counseling, antidepressant drugs, and new age religions suggests a wide-spread search for meaning, acceptance, self-esteem, and ultimately, love.[1] Bookstores across the Western World have self-help sections filled with books discussing how to find love, how to maintain love, how to rekindle love, how to feel lovable, how to love yourself.[2] Why, as a society, are we haunted with feelings that we are unloved or unlovable? While the prevalence of domestic violence, neglect, and children living in poverty may contribute to the impossibility of imagining love in contemporary culture, these traumas do not explain why so many children who have so-called normal childhoods and normal relations with their parents grow up to suffer from depression, melancholy, or anxiety. If depression is becoming the norm, perhaps it is time to investigate our fantasies of normality.

In spite of the realities of multiple family forms—single-parent families, blended families, adopted children, lesbian parents, gay parents, communal families—and the fact that the nuclear family with father as breadwinner and mother as homemaker is the minority, our cultural imaginary still revolves around the heterosexual two-parent family. That is still considered the norm in our culture. My purpose in this essay is to investigate some of the conflicting presuppositions upon which the normalcy of the nuclear family is supposed. By pointing to conflicts at the heart of our stereotypes of maternity and paternity, I hope to challenge normal conceptions of the family. In addition, I argue that these norms actually undermine the possibility of imagining loving relationships.

While theories in psychology and psychoanalysis may actually perpetuate the fantasies that give rise to emotional suffering, they do not cause them. Still, examining psychoanalytic theories may help identify some of the problems. If we read psychoanalysis not as the study of the structure and dynamics of the *universal* human psyche, but as the study of the psychic manifestations of *particular aspects* of human cultures—which can be described according to structures, systems, and dynamics—then psychoanalysis might become a useful diagnostic indicator for various changes in symptomology across or within cultures. As an indicator of cultural symptoms, psychoanalysis is not limited to diagnosing individuals in relation to norms, but is useful in diagnosing those cultural norms themselves.

Conflicts at the heart of Freudian psychoanalytic theory reflect cultural stereotypes. Two sets of conflicts fundamental to both psychoanalytic theory and cultural stereotypes are: 1. The conflicting beliefs that an infant's primary relationships become models for her subsequent social relationships and that the infant's relationship with her mother is antisocial and must be broken off; 2. the conflicting beliefs that the father represents the authority of culture against nature and that the father's authority comes from nature. Analysis of these conflicts can indicate why our stereotypes about mothers and fathers make it difficult to imagine loving relationships. If all of our relationships are formed on the basis of our primary relationships, then in order to imagine loving relationships we need to imagine those primary relationships as loving. But, if our stereotypes of mothers and fathers figure them as something other than embodied human beings, then love relationships with embodied human beings become difficult. If our stereotypes of mothers and of fathers render these figures incapable of love, then it becomes difficult to imagine being loved in any relationship.

Given the assumption that all of our relations are modeled on our primary relations, our relations should be modeled on our first relation, the relation to the maternal body. Yet the way in which the maternal body is conceived within psychoanalytic theory, philosophy, and our culture in general prevents this relation from serving as a model for any subsequent social relation. The relation with the maternal body is imagined as antisocial, a nonrelation which, if anything, threatens the social. If infants don't separate from their mothers' bodies, then there can be no society. The first relationship with the maternal body, then, is in the paradoxical position of both providing the prototype for all subsequent relations and threatening the very possibility of any social relation.

The paradoxical position of the mother is the result of the imagined opposition between nature and culture. Western philosophy as we know it began with the birth of the soul. Plato proposed a dramatic and antagonistic relationship between body and soul. Aristotle followed by insisting that it is man's capacity for reason that separates him from the animals. Bodies and animals are governed by the laws of the natural world, but the mind and human beings are governed by the higher principles of reason. With its emphasis on reason against body, philosophy has insisted on a sharp distinction between nature and culture. Only human beings are properly social; only human beings have culture; only human beings love. The legacy of this mind/body dualism has been fraught with problems, not the least of which is the paradox of love. If the mother's love is made paradoxical by the identification of mother and antisocial body, the father's love is made abstract or impossible by the identification of father and anti-body culture. Within Freud's account, the relationship between father and son is one of rivalry and guilt, while the relationship between father and daughter is one of envy and frustration; the father is the representative of threats and power. Within Lacan's account, the father is associated with the Name or No; that is to say, the father brings language and law to break up the primary dyad. The father's body doesn't matter (Lacan 1977, 199). Why is the father's body irrelevant to procreation? How can paternity just as well be attributed to a spirit? What does this tell us about our cultural images of paternity in an age when so many fathers are absent from the lives of their children?

The absent father is fundamental to our image of fatherhood and paternity. In important ways the necessity of the father's absence is embedded in recent rhetoric of family values and manly responsibility. The association between the father and the law, name, or authority makes the father an abstract disembodied principle. Patriarchy is founded on the father's authority. Paternal authority is associated with culture against maternal nature. But, in both philosophy and psychoanalytic theory, its turns out that the paternal authority that legitimates culture and breaks with antisocial nature is founded on the father's *natural* authority because of his *natural* strength or aggressive impulses. The paternal authority of culture is founded on the father's *naturally* stronger body; might makes right. After grounding the father's authority in nature, our philosophers and psychoanalytic theorists have disassociated the father from nature by disembodying him. The father is physically absent from the family scene because he is part of culture.

Even when he is present in the lives of his children, the father is present as an abstraction; his body is merely the representative of abstract authority or law. The association between father and culture, and the opposition between nature and culture or body and mind, disembodies the father. His body must be evacuated to maintain images of his association with culture against nature; his body threatens a fall back into nature. Just as the stereotype of the mother-infant relationship as an antisocial natural relationship does not permit love because love is social, the stereotype of the disembodied abstract father who represents the authority of culture cannot provide love because love is concrete and embodied. Western images of conception, birth, and parental relationships leave us with a father who is not embodied, who cannot love but only legislates from some abstract position, and a mother who is nothing but body, who can fulfill animal needs but cannot love as a social human being.

My purpose in this essay is to exploit the conflicts in psychoanalytic theory and philosophy in order to suggest that the maternal body itself is social and law-making and that the paternal function is embodied. I argue that love requires both embodiment and sociality. If, on the level of our cultural imaginary, the maternal body is not social, then it cannot be an adequate model for subsequent love relations. If, on the level of our cultural imaginary, the paternal function is not embodied, then it cannot be an adequate model for subsequent love relations. The conflicts in our stereotypes of maternity and paternity as they are manifest in the history of philosophy and psychoanalysis point to more complex images of maternity and paternity, our primary relationships, and the possibility of love.

ANIMAL BODY MOTHER

In philosophy, psychoanalytic theory, and other disciplines, women have been reduced to their reproductive function, which is seen as a natural animal function. Men, on the other hand, can escape or sublimate their nature in order to perform higher functions. Freud, for example, defines civilization as the sublimation or repression of drives that women, because of their anatomy, cannot fully experience and therefore cannot sublimate. In addition, he argues that civilization is the result of the repression or sublimation of aggressive drives, drives which are primarily related to the infant's relationship with the maternal body.

Although Freud's attention to sexuality, sexual difference, and cultural influences on the body continues to make his work useful for feminists, his descriptions of female sexuality, maternity, and the connections between the two are themselves a product of the sexism of his time. Even as Freud's writings are among the first to blur the distinctions between mind and body, soma and psyche, nature and culture, science and literature, when it comes to his speculations about women he often falls back into a rigid nature-culture binary in which women represent passive nature and men represent active culture. Freud's association between women and nature is apparent both in his social theories of the development of civilization in works such as *Totem and Taboo* (1953e) and *Civilization and Its Discontents* (1961), and in his psychological theories of individual development in works such as "The Dissolution of the Oedipus Complex" (1953a), "Some Psychical Consequences of the Anatomical Distinction between the Sexes" (1953d) "Female Sexuality" (1953b), and "On Feminine Sexuality" (1953c). In the next section, on paternity, I will draw on the works on the development of civilization, and in this section, on maternity, I will draw on the works on individual sexual development.

For Freud, the infant can leave its dyadic dependence on the maternal body only through the agency of the father. The father threatens the child with castration if it does not leave its mother. The male child takes these threats seriously and sublimates his desires for his mother. But he must also give up his identification with his mother; it is this identification that threatens his ability to become social. He is coaxed into

identifying with his father by the promise of a future satisfaction of his incestuous desire for his mother with a mother substitute. He identifies with his father's virility, his ability to satisfy his desire and his woman. The male child must give up his primary identification with his mother because she is stuck in nature and he will be too if he doesn't leave her. More than this, she is feminine and he cannot be masculine unless he gives up his identification with her. Freud ties himself into knots trying to explain the relationship between femininity and masculinity and transitions from one to the other with his bisexuality thesis. Elsewhere, I have argued that Freud's bisexuality thesis and his theories of feminine sexuality manifest a fear of the femininity in men, and ultimately a fear of birth, the fear that men were once part of a female body.[3]

For Freud, the female child must separate from her mother in order to become autonomous and social, and yet in order to become feminine she must continue her identification with her mother. Because she continues her identification with her mother, and because she cannot completely fear the threat of castration from the father since she is already castrated, the female child does not become fully social. She has an inferior sense of justice since she doesn't have a fully developed super-ego because she doesn't fear castration. She gains what autonomy she has by resenting her mother for not having a penis and envying her father for having one. Her only satisfaction comes from having a baby, which operates as a penis substitute. For Freud, it seems that maternity is the goal of female sexuality. The female child, along with the mother, is stuck in nature because her anatomy prevents her from feeling the father's threats. For Freud, in men and women, femininity becomes associated with passivity and masculinity becomes associated with activity.

The move from nature to culture is a move from the mother to the father. It is motivated by the father's threats, which are effective only if one has a penis. In Freud's account, culture is necessarily and by nature patriarchal. Yet, it is nature that culture leaves behind. Because she is associated with nature, the mother must be left behind in order for the child to become social. As Kristeva points out, for Freud the mother is so unimportant to culture and the development of the psyche that Freud hardly mentions her. His theory also leaves the mother behind. By now, Freud's theory of the Oedipus complex is a familiar story; it is a story of active men fighting over passive women.

In the twentieth century, in more subtle ways, Jacques Lacan promotes theories that oppose the mother to culture and associate the father with culture (see Lacan 1977, 200). Entering language and the symbolic require leaving the mother behind. For Lacan, the mother is associated with a realm of need associated with what he calls "the real." The real operates in his theory as something like nature from which we are estranged by our position in culture. For linguistic, symbolic, or cultural beings, nature is always perceived from the vantage point of culture. This is why Lacan claims that we are cut off from the real. Our reality has little to do with the real, which breaks into reality only rarely, in extreme moments of trauma or *jouissance*. This maternal realm of "nature," needs, and the real is "left behind" when the paternal agent intervenes and introduces the infant to language. To say, however, that this maternal realm of plenitude and satisfaction is left behind is complicated for Lacan because he insists that it is imaginary in the first place.

For Lacan the realm of maternity is more nuanced than for Freud. Not only is the maternal body associated with bodily need and its satisfaction and thereby with the real, but also the maternal body is associated with what Lacan calls the *imaginary*. The infant already inhabits an imaginary world in which it imagines that its needs are met automatically because it imagines itself at one with the maternal body in a dyadic relationship. This imaginary unity with the maternal body is the illusion of plenitude and satisfaction for which we are left forever longing. On Lacan's

account, the paternal function necessarily breaks off this mother-infant dyad so that the child can become social. In this sense, the primary relationship with the mother is antisocial and must be abandoned through the agency of the paternal function.

For the infant the mother is not an object or a person; she is nothing more than the satisfaction of natural needs like food, the first bearer of what Lacan calls *objet petit a, object small a,* named for the first letter of the French word for *other, l'autrui*. The *object small a* is connected with the real and is therefore inaccessible. It operates as something even more rudimentary than partial objects and becomes the foundation of both trauma and *jouissance,* or what we could call sexual chemistry, that unknown something that attracts us to someone (1981, 62–64). When the infant begins to experience a lack of satisfaction, when its needs are not met automatically, then it begins to sense that its mother is distinct. Under threats of castration, translated by Lacan into threats of the lack of satisfaction, the infant substitutes demands, or words, for its natural longings or needs. But there is always a gap between the need and the demand that expressed that need (Lacan 1977, 286–87). Ultimately, what the infant needs is to have its needs met automatically without having to ask; it needs to feel at one with the satisfaction of its needs; it needs to be one with its mother, its satisfaction. So, with the onset of language and culture, the infant can no longer get what it needs. Lacan calls this gap between need and demand, desire. Desire is unfulfillable. As with Freud's scenario, with Lacan the infant is forced into a painful world of unfulfillable desires through threats and prohibitions instituted by the father.

In spite of their attempts to theorize between nature and culture, both Freud and Lacan oppose the maternal body to culture and place the father and his law and language on the side of culture. Both leave it to the paternal function or agency to break up the antisocial mother-child dyad so that the infant can enter culture. Even while Freud disconnects sexuality from nature, blurs the distinction between normal sexuality and perversion, and suggests that the drives move between soma and psyche, at the same time he abandons the maternal body to the realm of nature. The remnants of lingering biologism are most apparent in Freud's treatment of feminine sexuality and his statements on maternity. And even while Lacan attempts to exorcise the remnants of biologism in Freud's theory by turning to linguistics, draws on Freud's more progressive suggestions on the ideational component of our relations to our bodies, and insists that phallocentrism is the product of culture and not nature, his diagnosis of culture does little to challenge the association of the maternal body with an antisocial realm and the paternal function with culture. Although Lacan moves us from the realm of biology to the realm of semiotics and linguistics, he still associates antisocial need and an imaginary antisocial dyad with the maternal body and socialized desire with the paternal function. Within his theory it seems that language is always at odds with the needs associated with the maternal body; language is always nothing more than a frustrated attempt to articulate need, ultimately what he calls an impossible demand for love.

But what if we need to commune with other people? What if we need to be social? Then, perhaps, language does more than fail to articulate bodily drives or needs. Even assuming that it fails to communicate needs, perhaps language succeeds in forming communion between bodies. Language brings us together because it is an activity that we engage in with each other and not because it does or does not succeed in capturing or communicating something in particular. We keep talking not just because we can never say what we are trying to say—that is, what we need—but also because we need to be together through words. For Lacan, demands are always demands for love, and as demands, they can never succeed in getting us what we want. This view of the relationship between love and demand seems to presuppose that language is merely a feeble container for

something else. Yet, words are not just symbols that contain various conscious and unconscious significations; they are also part of a process of communicating, in the sense of communing, with each other. Language is not just something we use or something that uses us; rather, it is something we do, something that we do together.

The body and needs are not antithetical to culture; the body, the maternal body in particular, does not have to be sacrificed to culture. Needs, associated with the maternal body, are not left behind once the child can make demands and acquires language. Lacan's notion that language leaves us lacking satisfaction or that it is a necessary but poor substitute for the maternal body, needs, or drives, assumes that drives and needs are antithetical to language (or in Lacanian parlance, that the real is cut off from the symbolic).[4] Although Lacan insists that the unconscious is structured like a language, so presumably Freudian drives operate according to the logic of language, it is unclear on Lacan's account how drives could be expressed in language. If drives or needs make their way into language, then the maternal realm that Freud and Lacan identify as a hindrance to the properly social realm not only gives birth to the social but also is necessary for the continued operation of the social. We need to be social. Moreover, drives are what motivate language. Culture grows organically out of the body.

Combining Freud's theory of the drives with Lacan's turn to linguistics, Julia Kristeva goes further than either Freud or Lacan when she suggests that drives are discharged in language and that the structure of language is operating within the material of the body. There is no impasse between the body and language. Rather, the body is in language and language is in the body. Kristeva takes up Freud's theory of drives as instinctual energies that operate between biology and culture. Drives have their source in organic tissue and aim at psychological satisfaction. In *Revolution*, Kristeva describes drives as "material, but they are not solely biological since they both connect and differentiate the biological and symbolic within the dialectic of the signifying body invested in practice" (1984b, 167). Over a decade later, Kristeva emphasizes the same dialectical relationship between the two spheres—biological and social—across which the drives operate. In *New Maladies of the Soul,* she describes the drives as "a pivot between 'soma' and 'psyche', between biology and representation" (1995, 30).[5] Drives can be reduced neither to the biological nor to the social; they operate in between these two realms and bring one realm into the other. Drives are energies or forces that move between the body and representation.

Instead of lamenting what is lost, absent, or impossible in language, Kristeva marvels at this bodily realm that makes its way into language. The force of language is living drive force transferred into language. Signification is like a transfusion of the living body into language. This is why psychoanalysis can be effective; the analyst can diagnose the active drive force as it is manifest in the analysand's language. In *Time and Sense,* Kristeva suggests that transference in the psychoanalytic session inscribes flesh in words (1996). Psychoanalysts "transform the patient's flesh, which [they] have shared with [their] own, into word-presentations" (1997, 126). In this way, psychoanalysis can treat somatic symptoms by transforming the body through words. And while, for Kristeva, bodily drives involve a type of violence, negation, or force, this process does not merely necessitate sacrifice and loss. The drives are not sacrificed to signification; rather, bodily drives are an essential semiotic element of signification.

In addition to proposing that bodily drives make their way into language, Kristeva maintains that the logic of signification is already present in the material of the body. In *Revolution in Poetic Language,* she proposes that the processes of identification or incorporation and differentiation or rejection that make language use possible are operating within the material of the body. She maintains that before the infant passes through what Freud calls the Oedipal situation,

or what Lacan calls the Mirror Stage, the patterns and logic of language are already operating in a preoedipal situation. In *Revolution in Poetic Language,* she focuses on differentiation or rejection and the oscillation between identification and differentiation. She analyzes how material rejection (for example the expulsion of waste from the body) is part of the process that sets up the possibility of signification.[6]

For Kristeva the body, like signification, operates according to an oscillation between instability and stability, or negativity and stasis. For example, the process of metabolization is a process that oscillates between instability and stability: food is taken into the body and metabolized and expelled from the body. Because the structure of separation is bodily, these bodily, operations prepare us for our entrance into language.

At bottom, Kristeva criticizes the traditional account because it cannot adequately explain the child's move to signification. If what motivates the move to signification are threats and the pain of separation, then why would anyone make this move? Why not remain in the safe haven of the maternal body and refuse the social and signification with its threats? Kristeva suggests that if the accounts of Freud and Lacan were correct, then more people would be psychotic (see 1984b, 132; 1987, 30, 31, 125). The logic of signification is already operating in the body and therefore the transition to language is not as dramatic and mysterious as traditional psychoanalytic theory makes it out to be.

Kristeva tries to rescue the mother from the crypt of nature by separating the maternal body as a container that meets the infant's needs from the maternal function that sets up the possibility of language and law. The maternal body as the satisfier of needs must be abjected; "matricide," says Kristeva, is "our vital necessity" (1989, 27). But the mother is more than a container; she is a desiring subject and as such she is social. Moreover, in her relations with her infant she provides regulation, what Kristeva calls the maternal law before the law, that sets up paternal law. So, although Kristeva insists that the maternal body must be abjected, she describes the maternal body as proto-social. Maternity is between nature and culture and the maternal body can never be left behind by culture. In Kristeva's texts, the maternal body challenges the opposition between nature and culture. If the mother is not reducible to her body and if her body encourages rather than threatens the social, then we might go one step further than Kristeva and imagine a loving mother. If the maternal body cannot be reduced to antisocial nature, we might go two steps further than Kristeva and suggest that matricide is necessary only to maintain patriarchy.

If the logic and structure of bodily drives is the same as the logic and structure of language, then the primary relation between the bodies of mother and child does not have to be antisocial or threatening. In addition, the drives themselves can be seen as social. The drives themselves are also proto-social in that they are not contained within one body or psyche; rather, as Teresa Brennan argues in *The Interpretation of the Flesh,* drives move between bodies; they are exchanged (1992). Affective energy is transferred between people. For example, a person can walk into a room and her mood can affect everyone in the room; it is as if her mood radiates throughout the room. Emotions and affects migrate or radiate between human beings.

Affective energy transfers take place in all interpersonal interactions. The idea that we can transfer affects through contact and conversation resonates with most people who have had the experience of a conversation with a loved one in which s/he is upset during the conversation: after the conversation s/he feels much better, but now the other party to the conversation is upset. This kind of situation suggests a transfer of affect. Even our language in such interpersonal situations suggests an exchange of affect: "I won't take it any more"; "Don't give me that." This intersubjective theory of drives points to the sociality of the body. If bodily drives are not contained within the boundaries of one body or subject but are interpsychic, then

bodily drives are always a matter of social exchanges. These exchanges are *protodialogues* that take place between bodies, bodies that are social even if they are not properly subjects.

Language has its source in the body, and not just because it takes a mouth to speak and a hand to write. Language speaks and writes bodily affects and bodily drives, without which there would be no motivation for language. We use language not only to communicate information but also to make psychophysical connections to others. Lacan might be right that every demand is a demand for love. But he is wrong that these demands are doomed to failure. If we need to speak, if we need to make demands just as we need food, then demands are not cut off from our basic need for the satisfaction from our mothers that Lacan associates with love. Also, if drives and bodily needs are discharged in language, then they are not lost and we need not mourn the loss in order to enter culture; the maternal body is not killed and we need not mourn her death. Law and regulation implicit in language are already operating within the body. Law is not antithetical to the maternal body. It is not necessary to reject the maternal body in order to enter the realm of law and society. Rather, the maternal body as social and lawful sets up the possibility of sociality, relationship, and love.

NOBODY FATHER

It is commonplace that our traditions associate the father with authority. From John Locke and Jean-Jacques Rousseau to Jacques Lacan, father knows best. Liberal theorists try to distinguish between legitimate and illegitimate authority by insisting that might does not make right. Yet, there are conflicts in the beginnings of liberal theory between the might of the father and his legitimate authority and the authority of the government. Both Locke and Rousseau present contradictory accounts of the relationship between the family and the state. Locke attempts to distinguish the "master of the family" from the leaders of political society by delineating the limitations of the paternal authority and appealing to a more democratic form of government than that of the patriarchal family. At the same time, he identifies the father as the *natural* ruler of the family "as the abler and the stronger" (Locke 1980, 44). Moreover, he describes the evolution to political society from patriarchal families as the evolution of the paternal authority which nourishes political society: "without such nursing father tender and careful of the public weal, all governments would have sunk under the weakness and infirmities of their infancy, and the prince and the people had soon perished together" (1980, 60). Paternal authority, founded in might, takes on the tender maternal role of nourishing and nursing political society.

Rousseau is also concerned that political society be based on legitimate authority and not just the brute strength of natural authority. "The more these natural forces are dead and obliterated, and the greater and more durable are the acquired forces, the more too is the institution solid and perfect" (Rousseau 1987, 163). The father is by nature the authority in the family: "For several reasons derived from the nature of things, in the family it is the father who should command. . . . [a] husband should oversee his wife's conduct, for it is important to him to be assured that the children he is forced to recognize and nurture belong to no one but himself" (Rousseau 1987, 112). Yet, while nature governs the family through the father, the state can only exist against nature. The laws of society are at odds with the laws of nature. "In effect, though nature's voice is the best advice a good father could listen to in the fulfillment of his duty, for the magistrate it is merely a false guide which works constantly to divert him from his duties which sooner or later leads to his downfall or to that of the state unless he is restrained by the most sublime virtue" (Rousseau 1987, 113).

Still, in *On the Social Contract,* Rousseau maintains that "the most ancient of all societies

and the only natural one, is that of the family. . . . The family therefore is, so to speak, the prototype of political societies; the leader is the image of the father, the populace is the image of the children. . . . The entire difference consists in the fact that in the family the love of the father for his children repays him for the care he takes for them, while in the state, where the leader does not have love for his people, the pleasure of commanding takes the place of this feeling" (1987, 142). In the very next section, he goes on to insist that might does not make right and that physical power has nothing to do with moral or civil duty.

Implicit in the theories of both Locke and Rousseau are the contradictory claims that the authority of political society is based on right and not might, that only in nature does might constitute authority, that civil society supersedes nature, that the father's authority is based on natural physical strength, that political society is based on the father's authority. The father's authority is based in nature and physical strength, and yet it becomes the basis for a legitimate patriarchal government that is based in right and not might. How does the father's natural strength come to represent right and not might? How does the father transcend his natural authority based solely in his physical strength in order to take up his civil authority based in his moral and intellectual strength?

This question is answered by Hegel, who moves man into the social at the expense of woman. Man can enter culture because woman never leaves nature. In *Philosophy of Right,* Hegel says that man has his "actual substantive life in the state" and woman has her "substantive destiny in the family" (Hegel 1952, 114). Whereas men are capable of higher intellectual life, women inhabit a realm of feelings; "women correspond to plants because their development is more placid and the principle that underlies it is the rather vague unity of feeling" (Hegel 1952, 263). Women are "educated" into this natural realm of feeling "who knows how?—as it were by breathing in ideas, by living rather than by acquiring knowledge. The status of manhood, on the other hand, is attained only by the stress of thought and much technical exertion" (Hegel 1952, 264). Whereas love governs the domain of the family, law governs the state; love, a feeling, is subjective and contingent and therefore the unity of the family can dissolve, whereas law is objective and necessary and therefore the unity of the state is stronger than the unity of the family (Hegel 1952, 265). In *Phenomenology of Spirit,* Hegel describes how man leaves the world of the family and feelings and enters the world of the state and laws through the recognition of the women in his family who provide the support against which he can pull himself up to a higher level of consciousness. For Hegel, man's nature seems to be paradoxical in itself insofar as man's nature is to go beyond nature. Woman's nature is to love while man's nature is to lay down the law.

We might think that the association between woman and love and man and law was an eighteenth- or nineteenth-century idea that we have outgrown. But these associations have only been fortified in the twentieth century by psychoanalysis. With psychoanalysis, might makes right in that the father's threats set up and fortify the child's superego or moral sense. The authority of the father, based in his physical strength and virility, is internalized to form the moral conscience. While Locke and Rousseau covertly appeal to the father's might in their explanations of the formation of civil society and moral right, in *Civilization and its Discontents,* Freud openly identifies moral right and civil law with paternal authority, based as it is in the father's bullying castration threats which lead the son to wish to kill the father and the inevitable guilt associated with that wish. "What began in relation to the father is completed in relation to the group" (Freud 1961, 80).

Freud continues the argument that men are naturally more civilized than women, who belong at home with the children: "[W]omen soon come into opposition to civilization and display their retarding and restraining influence—those very

women who, in the beginning, laid the foundations of civilization by the claims of their love. Women represent the interests of the family and sexual life. The work of civilization has become increasingly the business of men, it confronts them with ever more difficult tasks and compels them to carry out instinctual sublimations of which women are little capable" (Freud 1961, 50). Women are not capable of instinctual sublimations because their anatomy does not permit them to act on those very instincts that must be sublimated in order to become civilized—namely, urinating on fire and presumably incest with their mothers.

Freud identifies control over fire as one of the primary achievements of primitive man that allowed him to become civilized. In a footnote in *Civilization and its Discontents,* he hazards a conjecture on the origins of civilization as the origins of control over fire:

> The legends that we possess leave no doubt about the originally phallic view taken of tongues of flame as they shoot upwards. Putting out fire by micturating . . . was therefore a kind of sexual act with a male, an enjoyment of sexual potency in a homosexual competition. The first person to renounce this desire and spare the fire was able to carry it off with him and subdue it to his own use. By damping down the fire of his own sexual excitation, he had tamed the natural force of fire. This great cultural conquest was thus the reward for his renunciation of instinct. Further, it is as though woman had been appointed guardian of the fire which was held captive on the domestic hearth, because her anatomy made it impossible for her to yield to the temptation of this desire. (Freud 1961, 37)

Civilization begins when man curbs his desire to display his virility by urinating on phallic flames. Woman cannot sublimate the desire to pee on the fire because she cannot first act on the desire. We might wonder why Freud doesn't conclude that woman necessarily sublimates this desire since she can't act on it; that her anatomy demands sublimation whereas the male's does not; that in woman, nature has insured sublimation of aggressive instincts and therefore the advancement of the species. Instead, Freud identifies civilization, law, and morality with man's virility and its sublimation, where this sublimation is also described as man's virile act of control over himself.

Like Locke, Rousseau, and Hegel before him, Freud identifies the father as the first authority upon which the authority of all subsequent government develops. "A Prince is known as the father of his country; the father is the oldest, first, and for children the only authority; and from his autocratic power the other social authorities have developed in the course of the history of human civilization" (Freud 1967, 251). For Freud, the father and his threats of castration intervene in the mother-child relationship to break the son out of this natural bond and propel him into culture. The daughter never fully enters culture since, already castrated, she does not feel the same effects of the castration threat and cannot internalize the paternal authority to the same degree. The internalization of the father's authority marks the child's proper entrance into the social.

Following Freud, Jacques Lacan describes the child's acquisition of language and socialization in terms of the father's authority. The father's "no," or prohibition, along with his name, or symbols, move the child away from the natural relationship with the mother to a social relationship. Lacan reiterates the association between father and culture and mother and nature: "the father is the representative, the incarnation, of a symbolic function which concentrates in itself those things most essential in other cultural structures: namely, the tranquil, or rather, symbolic, enjoyment, culturally determined and established, of the mother's love, that is to say, of the pole to which the subject is linked by a bond that is irrefutably natural" (Lacan 1979, 422–23). Here Lacan explicitly associates the mother with nature and the father with culture. Once again the father's threats and prohibitions propel the child into culture and away from its relationship with its mother. The child's identification with the desire of the mother, its image of itself as

her fulfillment, must be replaced by the father's name, words, and symbols. The father's name is a symbol that also designates ownership; the children, marked by his name, belong to the father.

For Lacan the father represents law and language while the mother represents love and need. Her body, the imaginary satisfaction of needs, is lost to culture. What of the father's body? As far as Lacan is concerned, the father has no body; his body is irrelevant: "For, if the symbolic context requires it, paternity will nonetheless be attributed to the fact that the woman met a spirit at some fountain or some rock in which he is supposed to live. . . . It is certainly this that demonstrates that the attribution of procreation to the father can only be the effect of a pure signifier, of a recognition, not of a real father, but of what religion had taught us to refer to as the Name-of-the-Father" (Lacan 1977, 199). Procreation is attributed to the father through his name; his name is the guarantee that the child belongs to him. And, if the real father plays a role in the child's development, that role is dwarfed by the ever present ideal of fatherhood. The greater the discrepancy between the role of the real father and the ideal father, the more powerful the ideal father becomes in psychic development.[7]

It is the power associated with traditional paternal authority that makes the father's body and his phallus/penis represent power and authority. For Freud (and arguably for Lacan) this power is explicitly associated with the phallus/penis. Paradoxically, the ultimate virility of this masculine power is the sublimation of aggressive sex drives into productive and reproductive social economy. Aggressive instincts turn inward to aggress the self; this becomes self-control. Within this economy the penis takes on tremendous exchange value insofar as it, and control over it, is what makes society possible—recall Freud's account of control over fire. Freud's penis becomes Lacan's phallus, a transcendental signifier that makes economy and exchange possible. In the words of Alphonso Lingis, "the paternal body presents itself as the supreme value in human commerce, the incarnation of law, reason, and ideals, in the measure that it incarnates the renunciation of the productive libido—infantile, insignificant, and uneconomical—the libido without character—disordered, contaminating, squandering. It governs a domestic economy in which commodities are accumulated as accouterments of the phallic order" (Lingis 1994, 128). The paternal body, then, is the supreme value in human commerce insofar as it represents the repudiation of the body.

Yet, the paternal repudiation of the body in favor of law and reason is *based* on the body. For Freud it is the anatomy of the male body that makes the repudiation and sublimation of the aggressive sexual instincts possible. The male body is powerful only because it can act on its aggressive instincts in ways that the female body cannot. Paradoxically, for Freud it is not these acts that make men dominant, but the control over and repudiation of these acts. Men can control the body but only because their bodies are so hard to control. The force of the control required to subdue the body is proportionate to the strength of the body.

In philosophy and in psychoanalysis the father's authority as representative of law and culture has been based on his physical strength. Whereas the mother's relationship to the family is natural, the father transcends this natural relationship and engenders society. But it turns out that the father's authority can be justified only by appeals to the very nature that he is said to transcend. From Locke to Lacan, the authority of culture is legitimated in its opposition to the brute force of nature. But, insofar as the authority of culture, ultimately of patriarchy, is justified by appealing to the father's natural authority in the family, culture collapses back into nature. The authority of culture comes from the brute force of nature. Might does make right. And culture is not the antithesis of nature after all. On the other hand, if the law takes us beyond nature's triumph of the strongest, then patriarchy has no justification and there is no necessary connection between law and paternity.

CONCLUSION

It seems that whereas the female body has been reduced to the maternal body and relegated to nature, the male body has been a ghostly absent paternal body that safeguards culture. Whereas the female/maternal has been reduced to body, the male/paternal has been dissociated from body. The disassociation of the father from the body suggests that all fathers are absent fathers. The reduction of the mother to the body suggests that relations between children and mothers are antisocial.

I have pointed to conflicts and inconsistencies at the core of these traditional images of antisocial natural mothers and anti-body cultural fathers. I have argued that rather than threatening the social relationship and cultural law, the maternal body sets up the possibility of the social, law, and therefore love. The body is not opposed to culture and the maternal body need not be sacrificed to culture. If the body is not opposed to culture, then the father's body need not be sacrificed either. The father can be social or part of culture and embodied at the same time, which makes paternal love possible. Traditional theories of paternal authority which seem to exempt all bodies, including the male body, from culture ultimately base paternal authority and patriarchy itself on the authority and strength of the male body. By challenging the opposition between nature and culture, between the body and the social, we can challenge stereotypes that associate the maternal with nature and the paternal with culture. Conversely, by calling into question the associations of maternal and nature and paternal and culture, we can call into question the opposition between nature and culture. By bringing nature and culture together in our primary relationships, we can imagine subsequent relationships that are both embodied and social, prerequisites for human love.

Without prominent images of an embodied father and a social mother, the images of maternity and paternity in western culture leave us with melancholy images of isolation and unlovability. If we are to recreate images of ourselves as lovable and social, then we have to recreate love. And to recreate love, we have to recreate ourselves out of the possibility of loving mothers and loving fathers, mothers who are social and fathers who are embodied. Only then can we feel lovable and love each other. Changing the stereotypes and images that populate our cultural imaginary is an important step in changing our social situations. Our relationships, family structures, and family dynamics change when we can imagine them differently; and as we recreate our families outside the restrictive and unrealistic ideal of the nuclear family, we transform our images of ourselves, our relations to others, and the possibility of love.

NOTES

1. The attempt to find meaning through new age religions is particularly interesting. Before the scientific revolution, religion with its sacred mysteries provided meaning for people's lives. After the scientific revolution, science replaced religion and demystified religion. Recently, science has lost the ability to explain our world. The experts present such conflicting data on everything from oat bran to ozone that people have lost faith in science. New age religion is a synthesis of sorts of science and religion. It uses the rhetoric of science, with talk of harnessing energies and forces, in order to promote self esteem and a better future.

   While Nancy Reagan consulted an astrologer, Hillary Clinton consults a new age psychologist, a "global midwife," as reported in *The New York Times,* 24 June 1996.

2. Veroff et al. indicate that the number of people going to therapy has dramatically increased since World War II (1981, 166–67, 176–77). Robert Bellah et al. suggest that people go to therapy looking for love (1985).

3. See chapter one of my *Womanizing Nietzsche: Philosophy's Relation to the "Feminine"* (1995).

4. For Freud, drives make their way into language only by tricking the ego and superego.

5. For a more developed account of Kristeva's theory of drives, see my introduction to *The Portable Kristeva* (1997).

6. Kristeva's writings themselves can be read as an oscillation between an emphasis on separation and rejection and an emphasis on identification and incorporation. In *Revolution in Poetic Language* (1984b) and *Powers of Horror* (1982), she focuses on separation and rejection; in *Tales of Love (1987)* and *Black Sun* (1993), she focuses on identification and incorporation. In *Strangers to Ourselves* (1995), she again analyzes separation and rejection. And in *New Maladies of the Soul* (1996), she again analyzes identification and incorporation. In an interview with Rosalind Coward in 1984 at the Institute of Contemporary Arts, Kristeva claims that for this reason, *Powers of Horror* and *Tales of Love* should be read together; alone, each provides only half of the story (1984a).

7. John Brenkman makes this argument in *Straight Male Modern* (1993).

REFERENCES

Bellah, Robert, et al. 1985. *Habits of the heart,* Berkeley; University of California Press.

Brenkman, John, 1993. *Straight male modern,* New York: Routledge Press.

Brennan, Teresa, 1992. *The interpretation of the flesh*, New York: Routledge Press.

Freud, Sigmund, 1953a. The dissolution of the oedipus complex. In *The standard edition of the complete psychological works of Sigmund Freud,* vol. 19, ed. and trans. James Strachey. London: Hogarth.

———. 1953b. Female sexuality. In *The standard edition of the complete psychological works of Sigmund Freud,* vol. 21, ed. and trans. James Strachey. London: Hogarth.

———. 1953c. On feminine sexuality. In *The standard edition of the complete psychological works of Sigmund Freud,* ed. and trans. James Strachey. London: Hogarth.

———. 1953d. Some psychical consequences of the anatomical distinction between the sexes. In *The standard edition of the complete psychological works of Sigmund Freud*, vol. 19, ed. and trans. James Strachey. London: Hogarth.

———. 1953e. Totem and taboo. In *The standard edition of the complete psychological works of Sigmund Freud,* vol. 13, ed. and trans. James Strachey. London: Hogarth.

———. 1961. *Civilization and it discontents*. Trans. James Strachey. New York: Norton Publishers.

———. 1967. *The interpretation of dreams*. Trans. James Strachey. New York: Avon Books.

Hegel, G. W. F. 1952. *Philosophy of right*. Trans. T. M. Knox. London: Oxford University Press.

———. 1977. *Phenomenology of spirit*. Trans. A.V. Miller. Oxford: Clarendon Press.

Kristeva, Julia. 1984a. *Desire*. Julia Kristeva in conversation with Rosalind Coward. *Institute of Contemporary Arts Documents:* 22–27.

———. 1984b. *Revolution in poetic language*. Trans. Margaret Waller. New York: Columbia University Press.

———. 1987. *Tales of love*. Trans. Leon Roudiez. New York: Columbia University Press.

———. 1989. *Black sun*. Trans. Leon Roudiez. New York: Columbia University Press.

———. 1995. *New maladies of the soul*. Trans. Ross Guberman. New York: Columbia University Press.

———. 1996. *Time and sense*. Trans. Ross Guberman. New York: Columbia University Press.

———. 1997. *The portable Kristeva*. Ed. Kelly Oliver. New York: Columbia University Press.

Lacan, Jacques. 1977. *Ecrits*. Trans. Alan Sheridan. New York: Norton.

———. 1979. The neurotic's individual myth. *The Psychoanalytic Quarterly* 48 (3): 422–23.

———. 1981. *The four fundamental concepts of psychoanalysis,* Trans. Alan Sheridan. New York: Norton.

Lingis, Alphonso: 1994. *Foreign bodies*. New York: Routledge Press.

Locke, John. 1980. *Second treatise on government*. Ed. C.B. MacPherson. Cambridge: Hackett Publishing.

Oliver, Kelly. 1995. *Womanizing Nietzsche: Philosophy's relation to the "feminine."* New York: Routledge Press.

———. 1997. *Family values: Subjects between nature and culture.* New York: Routledge Press.

Rousseau, Jean Jacques. 1987. On social contract, and Discourse on political economy. In *The basic political writing,* ed. and trans. Donald Cress. Cambridge: Hackett Publishing.

Veroff, Joseph. et al. 1981. *Mental health in America*. New York: Basic Books.

SEPARATING FROM HETEROSEXUALISM

Sarah Hoagland

In writing about Lesbian Ethics, I am concerned with moral change. And given that lesbians are oppressed within the existing social framework, I am concerned with questioning the values of such a framework as well as with considering different values around which we can weave a new framework. In other words, I am interested in moral revolution. Significantly, however, within traditional ethics the only type of moral change we tend to acknowledge is moral reform.

Moral reform is the attempt to bring human action into greater conformity with existing ethical principles and thereby alleviate any injustice which results from the breach of those principles. In addressing the question of moral change, Kathryn Pyne Addelson argues:

> The main body of tradition in ethics has occupied itself with the notions of obligation, moral principle, justification of acts under principle, justification of principle by argument. When moral change was considered at all, it was seen as change to bring our activities into conformity with our principles, as change to dispel injustice, as change to alleviate suffering.[1]

She goes on to suggest:

> But moral reform is not the only type of moral change. There is also moral revolution. Moral revolution has not to do with making our principles consistent, not to do with greater application of what we *now* conceive as justice. That is the task of moral reform, because its aim is the preservation of values. But the aim of moral revolution is the creation of values.[2]

In recognizing only moral reform, traditional ethics discourages us from radically examining the values around which existing principles revolve, or the context in which we are to act on those principles (such as oppression), or the structure which gives life to just those values. Traditional ethics concerns itself almost exclusively with questions of obligation, justification, and principle, and does not leave room for us to examine underlying value or create new value. As a result, Kathryn Pyne Addelson argues, "the narrow focus of traditional ethics makes it impossible to account for the behavior of the moral revolutionary *as* moral behavior."[3]

For example, someone engaged in moral reform might question the use of the concept of 'evil': she might question the concept of 'woman' as evil (the myth of eve) or the concept of 'jew' as evil (the jewish blood libel[a]), or she might question the concepts of 'black' and 'darkness' as sinister and evil, suggesting that these are all inappropriate applications of 'evil'. Nevertheless, she would not question the concept of 'evil' itself; her concern would be with its application.

On the other hand, someone engaged in moral revolution might question the concept of 'evil', arguing that 'evil' is a necessary foil for 'good'— that there must be something designated as evil to function as a scapegoat for the shortcomings or failures of that which is designated as good. She might point out that 'good' requires 'evil' and therefore that evil can never be eradicated if good is to prevail. She might suggest that we could create a moral value in which we had no need of the concepts of 'good' or 'evil'.

I want a moral revolution. I don't want greater or better conformity to existing values. I want change in value. Our attempts to reform existing institutions merely result in reinforcing the existing social order.

For example, a woman may elect to teach a women's studies course using writings on women's rights. She may present classic arguments in favor of women's rights: exposing the contradiction of denying women's rights while affirming democratic ideals, or exposing the hypocrisy in recruiting women during times of need and yet espousing an ideology, which negates women's competence. And she could include absurd anti-feminist documents, such as material by a woman doctor denying that women should be professional, or a piece which argues that a woman should stand by her man—no matter what—for the "good" of "society." To give the illusion of objectivity, she might even invite speakers to present arguments against equal rights for women, thereby airing "both sides" of the issue.

However, in addressing and defending women's rights, she is implicitly acknowledging that women's rights are debatable. She is, by that very act, affirming that there is a legitimate question concerning women's rights, even if she is quite clear about the answer she espouses. And she is agreeing that society has a "right" to determine women's place.

Significantly, however, she cannot broach or even formulate a question about men's rights or men's competence without appearing radical beyond reason. That is, men's rights are not debatable.[b] Thus, in agreeing to defend women's

---

[a] This is the myth that jews slaughter christian children on easter and use their blood during passover, for example, in baking matzoh. It is the myth which justified the christian slaughter of jews during easter which dates back to the middle ages. Similar muslim persecutions of jews date back to the fifteenth century, and there are references to use of the libel by muslims as late as the nineteenth century.[4]

[b] Of course, men do engage in questions about other men's rights. But there is no general idea that perhaps men as a group ought to be written out of the u.s. constitution.

rights, she is solidifying status quo values which make women's but not men's rights debatable in a democracy.

A feminist challenging sexist values by defending women's rights is actually coerced into agreeing with the sexist structure of society at a more basic level. And insofar as her challenge appeals to ethical questions of justice, it is subject to consideration of whether such rights are consistent with the existing social order.

I want a moral revolution.

HETEROSEXUALISM

In her 1949 ground-breaking work *The Second Sex,* Simone de Beauvoir asked, "Why is it that women do not dispute male sovereignty?"[5] Her question presupposes a particular philosophical theory about human nature and interaction developed by Hegel. This theory is that each consciousness (person) holds a fundamental hostility toward every other consciousness and that each subject (person) sets himself up as essential by opposing himself to all others. That is, human relations are fundamentally antagonistic, and the hostility is reciprocal. One who does not succeed in opposing another finds himself having to accept the other's values and so becomes submissive to him.[6] Now, in asking why women do not dispute male sovereignty, Simone de Beauvoir is asking why women have not antagonistically opposed men as men have opposed women and each other. In asking this question, she is suggesting (1) that women have never opposed men and so are submissive, not from having lost to men, but from having accepted a position of subordination, and (2) that to achieve the status of subject, to resist male domination, among other things, women must oppose men as men have opposed women and other men.[c]

In discussing women's subordination, Simone de Beauvoir argues that "the couple is a funda-

mental unity with its two halves riveted together." The basic trait of woman is to be fundamentally the other. Thus, women have gained only what men have been willing to grant, and have taken nothing.[9]

Simone de Beauvoir suggests several reasons for this: women lack the concrete means of organizing; women have no past or history of their own; women have lived dispersed among men; and women feel solidarity with the men of their class and race. She points out, for example, that white women hold allegiance to white men, not to black women.[10] She adds that to renounce the status of other is to renounce the privileges conferred through alliance with a superior caste.[11] She concludes:

> Thus woman may fail to lay claim to the status of subject because she lacks definite resources, she feels the necessary bond that ties her to man regardless of reciprocity, and because she is often very well pleased with her role as *Other.*[12]

In other words, according to Simone de Beauvoir, yet another reason women have not disputed male sovereignty and laid claim to their own existence is that women are not fully displeased with being defined as other.

Simone de Beauvoir then discusses how all this came to be, because, as she announces:

> One is not born, but rather becomes a woman.[13]

One is not born a woman because 'woman' is a constructed category. And it is intimately connected to the category 'man'.

While I disagree that women always have been under men and also I disagree that to resist male sovereignty women must become like men, nevertheless a basic relationship of dominance and subordination appears to exist between men and women, and it is not clear, with a few

---

[c] Indeed, Simone de Beauvoir argues that in giving life, women are merely ensuring repetition and are no different

than other animals. However man, in risking his life (by becoming a warrior and attempting to take life), is transcending it and is thereby creating value.[7] As Nancy Hartsock notes, "Thus, it is woman's failure to engage in combat that defines her static and repetitive existence, her maternity that condemns her to give life without risking her life."[8]

notable exceptions since the onset of patriarchy, that women have resisted that relationship.[d] In my opinion, to fully evaluate the relationship of dominance and subordination we need concern ourselves not only with addressing sexism, or even homophobia or heterosexism, but more substantially, with the actual relationship of heterosexualism.

Understanding sexism involves analyzing how institutional power is in the hands of men, how men discriminate against women, how society classifies men as the norm and women as passive and inferior, how male institutions objectify women, how society excludes women from participation as full human beings, and how what has been perceived as normal male behavior is also violence against women. In other words, to analyze sexism is to understand primarily how women are victims of institutional and ordinary male behavior.

Understanding heterosexism, as well as homophobia,[e] involves analyzing, not just women's victimization, but also how women are defined in terms of men or not at all, how lesbians and gay men are treated—indeed scapegoated—as deviants, how choices of intimate partners for both women and men are restricted or denied through taboos to maintain a certain social order. (For example, if sexual relations between men were openly allowed, then men could do to men what men do to women[16] and, further, (some) men could become what women are. This is verboten. In addition, if love between women were openly explored, women might simply walk away from men, becoming 'not-women'. This, too, is verboten.) Focusing on heterosexism challenges heterosexuality as an institution, but it can also

lead lesbians to regard as a political goal our acceptance, even assimilation, into heterosexual society: we try to assure heterosexuals we are normal people (that is, just like them), that they are being unjust in stigmatizing us, that ours is a mere sexual preference.

Understanding heterosexualism involves analyzing the relationship between men and women in which both men and women have a part. Heterosexualism is men dominating and de-skilling women in any of a number of forms, from outright attack to paternalistic care, and women devaluing (of necessity) female bonding as well as finding inherent conflicts between commitment and autonomy and consequently valuing an ethics of dependence. Heterosexualism is a way of living (which actual practitioners exhibit to a greater or lesser degree) that normalizes the dominance of one person in a relationship and the subordination of another. As a result, it undermines female agency.

What I am calling 'heterosexualism' is not simply a matter of males having procreative sex with females.[17] It is an entire way of living which involves a delicate, though at times indelicate, balance between masculine predation upon and masculine protection of a feminine object of masculine attention.[f] Heterosexualism is a particular economic, political, and emotional relationship between men and women: men must dominate women and women must subordinate themselves to men in any of a number of ways.[g] As a result,

---

[d] Two notable recent exceptions are the european beguines and the chinese marriage resisters.[14]

[e] Sheila Kitzinger suggests we stop using 'homophobia' altogether. She argues that the term did not emerge from within the women's liberation movement but rather from the academic discipline of psychology. She questions characterizing heteropatriarchal fear of lesbians as irrational, she challenges the psychological (rather than political) orientation of 'phobia', and she notes that within psychology, the only alternative to 'homophobia' is liberal humanism.[15]

[f] I think the main model for personal interaction for women and lesbians has been heterosexual. However, for men in the anglo-european tradition there has also been a model of male homosexual interaction—a form of male bonding, even though sex between men has come to be persecuted. And while it is not my intention here to analyze the model, I will suggest that it revolves around an axis of dominance and submission, and that heterosexualism is basically a refined male homosexual model.[18]

[g] Julien S. Murphy writes: "Heterosexuality is better termed heteroeconomics, for it pertains to the language of barter, exchange, bargain, auction, buy and sell. . . . Heterosexuality is the economics of exchange in which a gender-based power structure continually reinstates itself through the appropriation of the devalued party in a duo-gendered system. Such reinstatement happens through each instance of 'striking a deal' in the market of sex."[19]

men presume access to women while women remain riveted on men and are unable to sustain a community of women.

In the u.s., women cannot appear publicly without some men advancing on them, presuming access to them. In fact, many women will think something is wrong if this doesn't happen. A woman simply is someone toward whom such behavior is appropriate. When a woman is accompanied by a man, however, she is usually no longer considered fair game. As a result, men close to individual women—fathers, boyfriends, husbands, brothers, escorts, colleagues—become protectors (theoretically), staving off advances from other men.

The value of special protection for women is prevalent in this society. Protectors interact with women in ways that promote the image of women as helpless: men open doors, pull out chairs, expect women to dress in ways that interfere with their own self-protection.[20] And women accept this as attentive, complimentary behavior and perceive themselves as persons who need special attention and protection.[h]

What a woman faces in a man is either a protector or a predator, and men gain identity through one or another of these roles.[21] This has at least five consequences. First, there can be no protectors unless there is a danger. A man cannot identify himself in the role of protector unless there is something which needs protection. So it is in the interest of protectors that there be predators. Secondly, to be protected, women must be in danger. In portraying women as helpless and defenseless, men portray women as victims . . . and therefore as targets.

Thirdly, a woman (or girl) is viewed as the object of male passion and thereby its cause. This is most obvious in the case of rape: she must have done something to tempt him—helpless hormonal bundle that he is. Thus if women are beings who by nature are endangered, then, obviously, they are thereby beings who by nature are seductive—they actively attract predators. Fourthly, to be protected, women must agree to act as men say women should: to appear feminine, prove they are not threatening, stay at home, remain only with the protector, devalue their connections with other women, and so on.

Finally, when women step out of the feminine role, thereby becoming active and "guilty,"[i] it is a mere matter of logic that men will depict women as evil and step up overt physical violence against them in order to reaffirm women's victim status. For example, as the demand for women's rights in the u.s. became publicly perceptible, the depiction of lone women as "sluts" inviting attack also became prevalent. A lone female hitchhiker was perceived, not as someone to protect, but as someone who had given up her right to protection and thus as someone who was a target for attack. The rampant increase in pornography—entertainment by and for men about women—is men's general response to the u.s. women's liberation movement's demand of integrity, autonomy, and dignity for women.

What radical feminists have exposed through all the work on incest (daughter rape) and wife-beating is that protectors are also predators. Of course, not all men are wife- or girlfriend-beaters, but over half who live with women are. And a significant number of u.s. family homes shelter an "incestuous" male.[23]

Although men may exhibit concern over woman-abuse, they have a different relationship to it

---

[h] In questioning the value of special protection for women, I am not saying that women should never ask for help. That's just foolish. I am talking about the ideal of women as needing sheltering. The concept of children needing special protection is prevalent and I challenge that concept when it is used to abrogate their integrity "for their own good." But at least protection for children theoretically involves ensuring that (male) children can grow up and learn to take care of themselves. That is, (male) children are protected until they have grown and developed skills and abilities they need to get on in this world. No such expectation is included in the ideal of special protection for women: the ideal of special protection of women does not include the expectation that women will ever be in a position to take care of themselves (grow up).

[i] In her analysis of fairy tales, Andrea Dworkin points out that an active woman is portrayed as evil (the stepmother) and a good woman is generally asleep or dead (snow white, sleeping beauty).[22]

than women; their concerns are not women's concerns. For example, very often men become irate at the fact that a woman has been raped or beaten by another man. But this is either a man warming to his role of protector—it rarely, if ever, occurs to him to teach her self-defense—or a man deeply affected by damage done to his "property" by another man. And while some men feel contempt for men who batter or rape, Marilyn Frye suggests it is quite possible their contempt arises, not from the fact that womanabuse is happening, but from the fact that the batterer or rapist must accomplish by force what they themselves can accomplish more subtly by arrogance.[24]

The current willingness of men in power to pass laws restricting pornography is a matter of men trying to reestablish the asexual, virginal image of (some) women whom they can then protect in their homes. And they are using as their excuse right-wing women as well as feminists who appear to be asking for protection, like proper women, rather than demanding liberation. Men use violence when women don't pay attention to them. Then, when women ask for protection, men can find meaning by turning on the predators—particularly ones of a different race or class.

In other words, the logic of protection is essentially the same as the logic of predation. Through predation, men do things to women and against women all of which violate women and undermine women's integrity. Yet protection objectifies just as much as predation. To protect women, men do things to women and against women; acting "for a woman's own good," they violate her integrity and undermine her agency.

Protection and predation emerge from the same ideology of male dominance, and it is a matter of indifference to the successful maintenance of male domination which of the two conditions women accept. Thus Sonia Johnson writes:

> Our conviction that if we stop studying and monitoring men and their latest craziness, that if we abandon our terrified clawing and kicking inter-spersed with sniveling and clutching—our whole sick sadomasochistic relationship with the masters—they will go berserk and kill us, is the purest superstition. With our eyes fully upon them they kill us daily; with our eyes riveted upon them they have gone berserk.[25]

Early radical feminists claimed that women are colonized.[26] It is worth reconsidering this claim. Those who wish to dominate a group, and who are successful, gain control through violence. This show of force, however, requires tremendous effort and resources; so colonizers introduce values portraying the relationship of dominant colonizer to subordinate colonized as natural and normal.

One of the first acts of colonizers after conquest is to control the language, work often accomplished by christian missionaries. Their mission is to give the language written form and then set up schools where it is taught to those native to the land. Here new values are introduced: for example, concepts of 'light' and 'dark' as connoting good and evil respectively. Words for superiors and deities then begin to carry a 'light' connotation as well as appear in the masculine gender. Further, values are embedded which support colonial appropriation of natural resources, and which disavow the colonized's ancestral ways and economic independence. As the colonized are forced to use the colonizers' language and conceptual schema, they can begin to internalize these values. This is "salvation," and colonizers pursue what they have called manifest destiny or "the white man's burden."

The theory of manifest destiny implies that colonizers are bringing civilization (the secular version of salvation) to "barbarians" ("heathens"). Colonizers depict the colonized as passive, as wanting and needing protection (domination), as being taken care of "for their own good." Anyone who resists domination will be sorted out as abnormal and attacked as a danger to society ("civilization") or called insane and put away in the name of protection (their own or society's).

Thus colonizers move from predation—attack and conquest—to benevolent protection. Those who have been colonized are portrayed as helpless, childlike, passive, and feminine; and the colonizers become benevolent rulers, accepting the burden of the civilized management of resources (exploitation).

After the social order has been established, should the colonized begin to resist protection and benevolence, insisting that they would rather do it themselves regardless of immediate consequences, the colonizers will once again turn predators, stepping up violence to convince the colonized that they need protection and that they cannot survive without the colonizers. One of the lines attributed to Mahatma Gandhi in the movie *Gandhi* is significant to this point: "To maintain the benevolence and dominate us, you must humiliate us." When all else fails, men will engage in war to affirm their "manhood"; their "right" to conquer and protect women and other "feminine" beings (i.e., anyone else they can dominate).

The purpose of colonization is to appropriate foreign resources. It functions by de-skilling a people and rendering them economically dependent. In his book on colonialism, *How Europe Underdeveloped Africa,* Walter Rodney argues that african societies would not have become capitalist without white colonialism.[27] His thesis is that africa was proceeding economically in a manner distinct from precapitalist development until europeans arrived to colonize africa and underdevelop it. Aborting the african economy and making it over to meet their own needs, europeans robbed africans of their land and resources. Further, europeans robbed africans of their autonomous economic skills, primarily by means of transforming the education system and teaching african peoples to disavow the knowledge of their ancestors. This de-skilling of conquered peoples is crucial to domination because it means that the colonized become dependent on the colonizers for survival. Actually, however, it is the colonizers who cannot survive—as colonizers—without the colonized.

Bette S. Tallen suggests that, in like fashion, women have been de-skilled under heterosexualism, becoming economically dependent on men, while men appropriate women's resources.[28] As Sonia Johnson notes:

> According to United Nations statistics, though women do two-thirds of the world's work, we make only one-tenth of the world's money and own only one-hundredth of the world's property.[29]

The de-skilling of women differs depending on specific historical and material conditions. For example, in her analysis of pre-industrial, seventeenth-century britain, Ann Oakley notes that women engaged in many trades separate from their husbands, or as widows. The industrial revolution changed all that and deprived many women of their skills.[30] Prior to this, during the burning times, european men appropriated women's healing skills, birthing skills, and teaching skills, and attempted to destroy women's psychic skills.[j] As Alice Molloy writes, "the so-called history of witchcraft is simply the process by which women were separated from each other and from their potential to synthesize information."[32] In general, many women no longer have their own programs, they've lost access to their own tools. As a result, they are coerced into embracing an ideology of dependence on men.

Heterosexualism has certain similarities to colonialism, particularly in its maintenance through force when paternalism is rejected (that is, the stepping up of male predation when women reject male protection) and in its portrayal of domination as natural (men are to dominate women as naturally as colonizers are to dominate the colonized, and without any sense of themselves as oppressing those they dominate except during

---

[j] Currently, men are attempting to control woman's procreative abilities altogether by controlling female generative organs and processes.[31]

times of overt aggression) and in the de-skilling of women. And just as it is colonizers who cannot survive as colonizers without the colonized, so it is men who cannot survive as men (protectors or predators) without women.

I want a moral revolution.

The primary concept used to interpret and evaluate individual women's choices and actions is 'femininity'. 'Femininity' normalizes male domination and paints a portrait of women as subordinate and naively content with being controlled. Thus patrihistorians claim that women have remained content with their lot, accepting male domination throughout time, with the exception of a few suffragists and now a few aberrant feminists.

Yet if we stop to reflect, it becomes clear that within the confines of the feminine stereotype no behavior *counts* as resistance to male domination. And if nothing we can point to or even imagine counts as proof against the claim that all (normal) women are feminine and accept male domination, then we are working within a closed, coercive conceptual system.

For example, some acts which men claim support the feminine stereotype of white middle-class women indicate, instead, resistance. Alix Kates Shulman in *Memoirs of an Ex-Prom Queen* portrays a "fluffy-headed" housewife who regularly burns the dinner when her husband brings his boss home unexpectedly, and who periodically packs raw eggs in his lunch box.[33] Such acts are used by those in power as proof that women have lesser rational ability, but actually they indicate resistance—sabotage. Such acts may or may not be openly called sabotage by the saboteurs, but women engage in them as an affirmation of existence in a society which denies a woman recognition independently of a man.

Donna Deitch's documentary *Woman to Woman* offers a classic example of what I am calling sabotage.[34] Four females—two housewives, a daughter, and the interviewer—sit around a kitchen table. One housewife protests that she is not a housewife, she is not married to the house. The inter-

viewer asks her to describe what she does all day. The woman relates something like the following: she gets up, feeds her husband, feeds her children, drives them to the school bus, drives her husband to work, returns to do the dishes, makes the beds, goes out to do the shopping, returns to do a wash. The woman continues listing her activities, then stops, shocked, and says: "Wait a minute, I *am* married to the house." She complains of difficulty in getting her husband to give her enough money for the household, of frustration because he nevertheless holds her responsible for running the house, and of degradation because she must go to him, apologetically, at the end of each budget period to ask for extra money to cover expenses when he could have provided her with sufficient funds from the beginning.

Suddenly she gets a gleam in her eye, lowers her voice, and leans forward, saying: "Have you ever bought something you don't need?" She explains that she buys cans of beans and hoards them. Then she says: "You have to know you're alive; you have to make sure you exist."[35] She has separated herself from her husband's perceptions of her: she is not simply an extension of his will, she is reclaiming (some) agency—sabotage. Yet under the feminine stereotype, we are unable to perceive her as in any way resisting her husband's domination.[k]

Significantly, 'femininity' is a concept used to characterize any group which men in power wish to portray as requiring domination. Kate Millett points out that 'femininity' characterizes traits those in power cherish in subordinates.[38] And Naomi Weisstein notes that feminine characteristics add up to characteristics stereotypically attributed to minority groups.[39] The literature indicates that nazis characterized jews as feminine, using the ideology in justification of their massacre.

---

[k] There have been many unacknowledged forms of resistance to male domination, for example, the use of purity to control male sexual aggressions[36] as well as the use of piety to challenge a husband's authority. Further, many women entered convents to avoid marriage.[37] Typically, patrihistorians describe such strategies in ways that make it impossible to perceive them as resistance.

Men accused at the salem witch trials were characterized as feminine.[40] Mary Daly notes that the iroquois were "cast into a feminine role by the Jesuits."[41] An investigation of anthropological literature from the first part of this century reveals that white british anthropologists described the physiological characteristics of black africans—men and women—in a bestially feminine manner. And as Kate Millett points out, Jean Genet's definition of 'femininity' in male homosexuality is "submission to the imperious male."[42]

The concept of 'femininity' provides a basic model for oppression in anglo-european thinking.[1] A feminine being is by nature passive and dependent. It follows that those to whom the label is applied must by their very nature seek protection (domination) and should be subjected to authority "for their own good." 'Femininity' portrays those not in power as needing and wanting to be controlled. It is a matter of logic, then, that those who refuse to be controlled are abnormal.

Consider the fact that white history depicts black slaves (though not white indentured servants) as lazy, docile, and clumsy on grounds such as that slaves frequently broke tools. Yet a rational woman under slavery, comprehending that her situation is less than human, that she functions as an extension of the will of the master, will not run to pick up tools. She acts instead to differentiate herself from the will of her master: she breaks tools, carries on subversive activities—sabotage.

Her master, in turn, perceiving her as subhuman and subrational, names her "clumsy," "childlike," "foolish" perhaps, but not a saboteur. Some sabotage was detected and punished, for example, when slave women poisoned masters or committed arson. However records of such events were often buried,[44] and the stereotype of slaves as incompetent persists. Perhaps most powerful was the use of spirituals to keep present the idea of escape, songs such as "Swing Low, Sweet Chariot" or songs about Moses and the promised land. They also announced particular escape plans such as the departure of Harriet Tubman on yet another trip to the north. Whites perceived the happy song of simple-minded folk.[45]

If officially slaves are subhuman and content with their lot and masters are acting in slaves' best interests, then it follows that any resistance to the system is an abnormality or an indication of madness. Indeed, in recollecting the stories of her grandmother's slave days, Annie Mae Hunt tells us that "if you run off, you was considered sick."[46] That is to say, slaves existed in a conceptual framework where running away from slavery was generally perceived by masters and even at times by slaves as an indication, not of (healthy) resistance, but of mental imbalance.

Such was the extent of the coercion of the masters' framework. However, creating a different value framework, we can understand the behaviors of slaves, out of which the masters constructed and fed the slave stereotypes, as providing ample evidence of resistance and sabotage.[47]

During the holocaust and, more significantly, after it, in the telling of the stories, patrihistorians have depicted jews under nazi domination as cooperative and willing (feminine) victims. This stereotype—as is true of the slave stereotype—is still alive today. Yet again, we can ask: What would *count* as resistance? For example, jews at auschwitz who committed suicide by hurling themselves against an electric fence have been depicted as willing victims. But the nazis did not leave their bodies for all to see, they quickly took them away. In determining the time of their own deaths, those

---

[1] In pointing out how the concept of 'femininity' applies to various oppressed peoples, I do not mean to suggest that the *experience* of oppression is the same. The experience of black men or the *experience* of jewish men has not been the same as that of poor white gentile women or black women or jewish women or wives of southern plantation owners. Black male slaves were depicted as strong, virile beasts. If wives of southern plantation owners were also perceived as animals (pets), still there were crucial differences. And black slave women were treated as the opposite of the white southern belle. As Angela Davis points out, black women slaves were treated essentially as beasts of burden. Most worked in the fields, and some worked as coalminers or lumberjacks or ditchdiggers. And while white masters raped them in a show of economic and sexual mastery, black women were compelled to work while pregnant and nursing, and their children were treated like the offspring of animals—to be sold off.[38]

who committed suicide were resisting nazi domination by exercising choice, interrupting the plans of the masters, and thus differentiating their selves from the will of their masters.

Many, many types of resistance occurred. From Simone Wallace, Ellen Ledley, and Paula Tobin:

> Each act of staying alive when the enemy has decided you must die is an act of resistance. The fight against a helplessness and apathy which aids the enemy is resistance. [Other acts include]: sabotage in the factories, encouraging others to live who are ready to give in and die, smuggling food and messages, breaking prison rules whenever possible, simply keeping themselves alive. Other forms of resistance, even more readily recognizable as such, took place from the killing of guards, bombing of factories, stealing guns, Warsaw uprisings, etc.[48]

Literature about the holocaust is full of jewish resistance, of sabotage; yet for the most part, short of armed uprisings such as happened in the warsaw ghetto, that resistance is not recognized or not acknowledged, and the stereotype of the willing (feminine) victim persists.

If we operate in a conceptual framework which depicts humans as inherently dominant or subordinate, then we will not perceive resistance or include it in our descriptions of the world unless those who resist overthrow those who dominate and begin to dominate them (i.e., when there is essentially no revolution in value). For example, the strategies of the women at greenham common, in resisting the deployment of u.s. cruise missiles, involve innovative means of thwarting the dominant/subordinate relationship—the women simply don't play by the rules and instead do the unexpected. Their strategies are characterized by spontaneity, flexibility, decentralization, and they work creatively with the situations that present themselves.[49] When we recognize as resistance only those acts which overthrow the dominators, we miss a great deal of information.

Consider the white upper-class victorian lady. In *The Yellow Wallpaper,* Charlotte Perkins Gilman portrays conditions faced by such women in the 1880s.[50] These conditions included a prescription of total female passivity by mind gynecologists such as S. Weir Mitchell,[51] prescriptions resulting from male scientists' sudden interest in women as the first wave of feminism attracted their attention, prescriptions enforced by those in control. The heroine is taken by her husband to a summer home for rest. He locks her in a nursery with bars on the windows, a bed bolted to the floor, and hideous wallpaper, shredded in spots. He rebuts her despair with the rhetoric of protection, refusing to indulge her "whims" when she protests the room's atrocity. He also stifles all her attempts at creativity, flying into a rage when he discovers that she has been writing in her diary. In the end she manages to crawl behind the wallpaper, escaping into "madness." Charlotte Perkins Gilman shows us a woman with every avenue of creativity and integrity patronizingly and paternalistically cut off "for her own good"; and we watch her slowly construct her resistance. Not surprisingly, male scientists and doctors of the day perceived nothing more in the story than a testament of feminine insanity.[52]

Resistance, in other words, may even take the form of insanity when someone is isolated within the confines of domination and all means of maintaining integrity have been systematically cut off. Mary's journey into oblivion with morphine in *Long Day's Journey into Night* is another example of resistance to domination, to the fatuous demands of loved ones, of husband and adult male children.[53] But the framework of "femininity" dictates that such behavior be perceived as part of the "mysterious" nature of woman rather than recognized as resistance.

Significantly, one and the same word names 'insanity' and 'anger': 'mad'. As Phyllis Chesler documents, gynecologists call women "mad" whose behavior they can no longer understand as functioning in relation to men.[54] On the other hand, 'madness' in relation to 'anger' is defined as "ungovernable rage or fury."[55] We can ask, ungovernable by whom? Madness in anger and madness in insanity indicate that men have lost control.[m] When women are labeled "mad," they have become useless to men, a threat to male supremacy.

Thus, to maintain the feminine stereotype, men will characterize overt, clear-cut, obvious forms of resistance as insanity when women engage in them.[n] Just as slaves who ran away from masters were perceived as insane, so are women who fight back against battering husbands. Women who kill long-term battering husbands are, for the most part, forced to use the plea of insanity rather than the plea of self-defense: lawyers advise clients to plead insanity, and juries convict those who instead plead self-defense. As a result, the judicial system promotes the idea that the woman who effectively resists aggressive acts of male domination is insane. Insanity, thus, becomes part of women's nature, and resistance to domination becomes institutionally nonexistent.

However, institutionally characterizing women who fight back as insane is still not enough for men in power. Perceiving the plea of insanity as a license to kill, even though it means incarceration for an unspecified amount of time, media men began a campaign against women who fought back against husbands and boyfriends who beat them—depicting these women as "getting away with" murder.[57] Our governing fathers have reduced or,

in some places, completely withdrawn funding of shelters for women, especially if there is lesbian presence, on the grounds that these shelters break up the family. And agencies on "domestic violence" work to keep the family intact, burying the conditions of oppression women face within the nuclear and extended family by obliterating the distinction between aggressor and victim.[58] The concept of 'femininity' not only blocks social perception of female resistance. When female resistance threatens to break through the stereotype and become socially perceptible, the conceptual framework comes full circle: authorities deny that the "problem" is the result of male domination.

Finally, many social scientists regard female competence itself in women as threatening to men, as subversive to the nuclear or extended family, and as going against the grain of civilization, hence as socially undesirable. For example, the moynihan report yielded a resurgence of white as well as black men espousing the theory of the black matriarch who "castrates" black men—implying that for black men to claim their manhood, or masculinity, black women must step behind and become subordinate to them.[59]

'Femininity' functions as a standard of heterosexualism. Standards or measures determine fact and are used to create (and later discover) fact; they themselves, however, are not discovered. An inch, for example, was not discovered. It was created and is used to determine boundaries. No amount of investigation into surfaces will ever confirm or disprove that inches exist or that inches accurately reflect the world. A standard is a way of measuring the world, of categorizing it, of determining its boundaries so men can act upon it. 'Femininity' is such a standard: it is a way of categorizing the world so that men can act upon it, and women can respond.

'Femininity' is a label whereby one group of people are defined in relation to another in such a way that the values of dominance and subordination are embedded in perceptual judgment of reality as if they were the essence of those involved. Under the feminine characterization, women

---

[m] When reading between the lines and reclaiming women from the past, we can examine the alternatives available to them and in that context understand their behavior. Thus, insanity itself can be a form of resistance, as can suicide. On the other hand, behavior that is not insanity may nevertheless be depicted as insane. As a result, there is a fine line, which can fade at times, between insanity as resistance and the behavior of the resistor who has not gone insane—who has maintained the confidence of her perceptions.

[n] In 1916, a play by Susan Glaspell was first performed about a nebraska woman who strangled her husband in his sleep. The (male) authorities arrive on the scene all officious and yet cannot discover the motive—without which they cannot convict her. Their wives, having come along to get some clothes for the woman in jail, discover a number of things, including the body of a canary whose neck had been wrung. Joking about women's work, the men ignore the women, thinking them dealing with "trifles." Comprehending what had happened, the women hide the evidence; the woman who killed her husband is found innocent by a "jury of her peers."[56]

appear naively content with being controlled to such an extent that resistance to domination ceases to exist—that is, goes undetected. Female resistance is rendered imperceptible or perceived as abnormal, mad, or of no significance by both women and men.

Now, some might object that (some of) the choices I've described as resistance or sabotage are self-defeating. For example, the housewife who spends money on items she does not need is limiting her ability to obtain things she does need. Thus, through this act of defiance she is really hurting herself. Or, the woman who burns dinners when her husband brings his boss home unexpectedly is still dependent on her husband having a job and would benefit from any promotion he might receive. If she fails to present herself as a competent hostess, the boss may decide against promoting her husband, noting that her husband does not have the trappings necessary for the social atmosphere within which business deals are made—namely, a charming wife and competent hostess. Thus, in sabotaging her husband's plans when he is inconsiderate, she appears to be acting against her own best interests.

Or, again, the slave who breaks her master's tools could find herself in even more dire circumstances. Although she is slowing the master's work, she will likely be punished for it. And should she appear too incompetent (unruly), she could be sold to someone perhaps more physically brutal, separated from those who know and care about her. Her sabotage seems to do more damage to herself than to anyone else. Someone might object that a woman making these choices may be resisting, but ultimately she is "cutting off her nose to spite her face." The woman who becomes an addict or an alcoholic or the woman who chooses suicide . . . surely their acts are self-defeating, for the women lose themselves.

In a certain respect such acts of sabotage are self-defeating, but in other respects this is inaccurate. I have suggested that in situations in which a woman makes such choices, often she acts to differentiate herself from the will of the one who

dominates. The one who dominates may be able to severely restrict the range of her choices, he may physically threaten her, he may have legal power of life and death over her. But it is yet another matter for him to totally control her, to make her believe she is nothing but an extension of his will.

My thesis is that when someone is in danger of losing any sense that she has a self about whom she can make decisions, she will in some way resist. When a man regards a woman as a being whose will should effectively be merged with his such that she is a mere extension of it, she will act in basic ways to block that merger and separate herself from his will. In such circumstances sabotage cannot logically be self-defeating because, simply, the situation allows for no self to begin with.

Acts of sabotage can function to establish that self, to affirm a woman's separateness in her own mind. It may be more important to the woman who burns dinners to remind her self (and maybe her husband) that he cannot take her for granted than it is for her to rise socially and economically if that means that in doing so she will be taken for granted to an even greater extent. And it may be more important to the slave that she affirm her existence by thwarting the master's plan in some way than it is to try to secure safety in a situation in which believing she is safe is dangerously foolish. Even when a woman withdraws herself through alcohol or takes herself out still further through suicide, she may be establishing, rather than defeating, the self as a separate and distinct entity.° If a woman establishes her self as separate (at least in her own awareness) from the will of him who dominates by making certain decisions and carrying them out, then those choices are not self-defeating, since without them there would be no self to defeat.

In other respects, however, such actions *are* self-defeating. In the first place, to be successful, acts of sabotage cannot be detected as sabotage in a system where there is no hope of redress. While they

---

° Thus alcoholism among lesbians has been a way of pursuing lesbian choices while rejecting the coercion of heterosexuality and the concept of 'woman'.

may function to differentiate one's self from those who dominate, they do not challenge the feminine stereotype, rather they presuppose it. Even when engaged in by a majority of women, isolated and individual acts of sabotage do not change the conceptual or material conditions which lead a woman to engage in such acts. Instead, those in power will use such actions to bolster the idea that dominated beings require domination (protection) "for their own good." In this respect, then, acts of sabotage could be said to be self-defeating. But then the same could be said of any act a woman engages in. This is the trap of oppression,[60] the double bind of heterosexualism.

More significantly, acts of sabotage become self-defeating if the one who engages in them begins to internalize the feminine stereotype. For example, the woman who hoards beans may be resisting her husband's tyranny over the family budget, resisting his perception of her as merely existing to carry out his plans. But if he regards control of her budget as part of his god-given right—no, duty—as a man, then any resistance from her will have to be nipped in the bud, and if it recurs, severely dealt with. Now, in wasting household money, she may be affirming her self while not wishing to openly challenge his perceptions and bring his wrath upon her. But if she must attend too closely to his perceptions and encourage them, she may cross over and come to believe she is incompetent. And at this point her acts become self-defeating.

Or, the woman who "accidentally" burns dinners when her husband's boss comes in unexpectedly may be resisting her husband's vacuous perception of her. If his taking her for granted is a result of his sense of order in the universe such that she is simply not the sort of being who could have any say in things, then trying to prove otherwise may be fruitless. Instead, her goal may be to resist his psychological coercion by playing with his mind, acting the fluffy-headed housewife in order to thwart his expectations of her.

In this case the woman is using the traditional feminine stereotype to her (momentary) advantage. But in so doing, she may undermine her sense of self (unless she has an extremely strong capacity to maintain the sense of what she is doing in direct opposition to the entire set of values within which she must function). The stakes involved here are high—just as when a woman uses stereotypic feminine behaviors to get what she wants and make herself feel superior to the men she manipulates. She is in serious danger of internalizing the social perception of her self as 'feminine'. And should she internalize that value, her acts do become self-defeating.

A woman acting in isolation to maintain a sense of self under heterosexualism faces significant obstacles, for her choices have repercussions beyond an individual level. Again, while such acts of sabotage may be resistance, they don't effect change. For resistance to effect change, there must be a movement afoot, a conspiracy, a breathing together. And this brings up a third way acts of sabotage can be self-defeating. Since successful acts of sabotage cannot be detected as sabotage by those who dominate, then when there is a movement afoot, the choice to commit acts of sabotage becomes no different than the choice to participate in the dominance/subordination relationship of heterosexualism by embracing and developing feminine wiles.

That is, during times when a movement is afoot, when there is a conspiracy of voices, those women who choose to remain isolated from other women and yet engage in acts of sabotage when necessary may well be engaging in truly self-defeating behavior. They are bypassing a chance for more effective resistance and are in even greater danger of internalizing the values of heterosexualism. In this way, isolated acts of resistance can be self-defeating.

'Femininity' is a concept which goes a long way in the social construction of heterosexual reality. A movement of women could withdraw from that framework and begin to revalue that reality and women's choices within it. A movement of women can challenge the feminine stereotype, dis-cover women's resistance, and provide a base for more effective resistance. A movement of women can challenge the consensus that made the individual act of sabotage plausible.

Yet if that movement does not challenge the concept of 'femininity', ultimately it will not challenge the consensus, it will not challenge the dominance and subordination of heterosexualism. For example, radical feminists and revolutionary feminists in england criticize the women's work at greenham common for appealing too much to traditional feminine stereotypes, including woman as nurturer and peacemaker as well as sacrificer for her children. As a result, they argue, the peace movement coopts feminism.[61]

Further, feminism itself is in danger of perpetuating the value of 'femininity' in interpreting and evaluating individual women's choices. Feminists continue to note how women are victims of institutional and ordinary behavior, but many have ceased to challenge the concept of 'woman' and the role men and male institutions play as "protectors" of women. And feminism is susceptible to what Kathleen Barry calls 'victimism', which in effect portrays women as helpless and in need of protection.[62]

BLAMING THE VICTIM

So much of our moral and political judgment involves either blaming the victim[63] or victimism. Victimism is the perception of victims of acknowledged social injustice, not as real persons making choices, but instead as passive objects of injustice. Kathleen Barry explains that in order to call attention to male violence and to prove that women are harmed by rape, feminists have portrayed women who have been raped by men as victims pure and simple—an understandable development. The problem is that

> the status of "victim" creates a mind set eliciting pity and sorrow. Victimism denies the woman the integrity of her humanity through the whole experience, and it creates a framework for others to know her not as a person but as a victim, someone to whom violence was done. . . . Victimism is an

objectification which establishes new standards for defining experience; those standards dismiss any question of will, and deny that the woman even while enduring sexual violence is a living, changing, growing, interactive person.[64]

For my purposes, blaming the victim involves holding a person accountable not only for her choice in a situation but for the situation itself, as if she agreed to it. Thus in masculinist thought, a woman will be judged responsible for her own rape. Victimism, on the other hand, completely ignores a woman's choices. In other words, victimism denies a woman's moral agency. Under victimism, women are still passive, helpless, and in need of special protection—still feminine.

A movement which challenges the dominant valuation of women will focus on women as agents in a relationship rather than as a type. A woman is not a passive being to whom things unfortunately or intentionally happen. She is a breathing, judging being, acting in coerced and oppressive circumstances. Her judgments and choices may be ineffective on any given occasion, or wrong, but they are decisions nevertheless. She is an agent and she is making choices. More than a victim, Kathleen Barry suggests, a woman caught in female sexual slavery is a survivor, making crucial decisions about what to do in order to survive. She is a moral agent who makes judgments within a context of oppression in consideration of her own needs and abilities.

By perceiving women's behavior, not through the value of 'femininity', but rather as actions of moral agents making judgments about their own needs and abilities in coerced and oppressive circumstances, we can begin to conceive of ourselves and each other as agents of our actions (though not creators of the circumstances we face under oppression). And this is a step toward realizing an ethical existence under oppression, one not caught up with the values of dominance and subordination.

Further, we can also begin to understand women's choices which actually embrace the feminine stereotype. Some women embrace 'femininity' outright, man-made though it is, or embrace particular aspects of it which involve some form of ritual or actual subordination to men, in the pursuit of what these women judge to be their own best interests. Some women embrace 'femininity' in a desperate attempt to find safety and to give some meaning to their existence.

In the first chapter of *Right-Wing Women,* Andrea Dworkin analyzes the choices of some white christian women, arguing that "from father's house to husband's house to a grave that still might not be her own, a woman acquiesces to male authority in order to gain some protection from male violence.[65] She argues that such acquiescence results from the treatment girls and women receive as part of their socialization:

> Rebellion can rarely survive the aversion therapy that passes for being brought up female. Male violence acts directly on the girl through her father or brother or uncle or any number of male professionals or strangers, as it did and does on her mother, and she too is forced to learn to conform in order to survive. A girl may, as she enters adulthood, repudiate the particular set of males with whom her mother is allied, run with a different pack as it were, but she will replicate her mother's patterns in acquiescing to male authority within her own chosen set. Using both force and threat, men in all camps demand that women accept abuse in silence and shame, tie themselves to hearth and home with rope made of self-blame, unspoken rage, grief, and resentment.[66]

Andrea Dworkin also argues that some women continue to submit to male authority because they finally believe it is the only way they can make sense of and give meaning to their otherwise apparently meaningless existence as women.[67] They find meaning through being bound to their protectors and having a common enemy. Their anger is thus given form and a safety valve, and is thereby deflected from its logical target. They become antisemites, queer-haters, and racists, and so create purpose in their existence.

Andrea Dworkin's analysis highlights two points of interest here. First, these women have

the same information that radical feminists have (they know what men do), yet they are making different choices. Secondly, their choices stem from judgments they make about their own best interests. That is, they are choosing what they consider their best option from among those available. These are survival choices made in circumstances with restricted options.

Another group of women embrace 'femininity' from a different direction. In discussing why more black women are not involved in activist women's groups, instead considering themselves "Black first, female second" and embracing a version of the feminine ideal, Brunetta R. Wolfman presents a number of factors. She points to the traditionally greater independence black women enjoy from black men in the united states, since the legal end of slavery, than white women have enjoyed from white men. And she points to the commitment of women to the black church, in terms of time and loyalty, whereby a "scrub woman or maid could aspire to be the head of the usher board and a valuable, respected member of the congregation."[68]

However, she notes that the pattern in the black church here as well as in civil rights groups such as the n.a.a.c.p. or the urban league, has been one of women assuming secondary roles in deference to male leadership. She also points to the romantic sense of nobility, purity, and race pride personified in the stereotype of 'the black woman' and promulgated by nationalistic ideologies such as that of Marcus Garvey or the black muslims:

> The Muslims have taken the idealized Euro-American image of the middle-class wife and mother and made it the norm for the sect so that the women members must reject the traditional independence of black women, adopting another style in the name of a separatist religious ideology. In return, Muslim men must respect and protect their women, a necessary complement to demands placed on females.[69]

This point is reiterated by Jacquelyn Grant as she argues:

> It is often said that women are the "backbone" of the church. . . . It has become apparent to me that most of the ministers who use this term are referring to location rather than function. What they really mean is that women are in the background and should be kept there: they are merely support workers.[70]

Brunetta R. Wolfman goes on to discuss demands placed on black women by the black community as well as community expectation of a subordinate position for women. For example, she points out that women in the movement '60s were expected to keep black men from involving themselves with white women. She argues that this "duty is in keeping with a traditional feminine role, that of modifying or being responsible for the behavior of the group in general and the males in particular."[71] Further, she points out how feminist values such as control of one's own body were undermined as black (and white) men told black women there was no choice but to bear children in order to counterattack the white racist plan of black genocide being carried out through birth control programs.

While noting that the women's liberation movement included many demands that would help the social and economic position of black women, Brunetta R. Wolfman suggests that (many) black women have not responded to it, instead becoming a conservative force in the black community, partly because they have a strong sense of self as contributor to the survival of the black community and partly because they have been identified by american society as the polar opposite of the feminine ideal.[72] That is, since they have been excluded from the feminine ideal, they now embrace it.[p]

---

[p] Other women have not involved themselves in the women's movement or have withdrawn from it because of racism among white women. My focus here is on women who embrace an ideal of feminine behavior in lieu of resistance to male domination.

The jeopardy of racial genocide stemming from an external enemy and used to justify the ideology of male domination is real for u.s. black and other women of color in a way that it is not for u.s. right-wing christian white women. Nevertheless, the choice of embracing 'femininity' and male authority is similar in both cases, as is the threat members of each group face from men.

Further, such choices are not qualitatively different from choices made by feminists to defer to men and men's agendas and to soothe male egos in the pursuit of women's rights. (And such choices do not preclude acts of sabotage of the sort I've discussed when male domination encroaches too far upon a woman's sense of self.) They are survival choices. And what we can consider from outside the feminine valuation is whether such choices in the long run are self-enhancing or self-defeating.

The answers are varied and complex. But insofar as they lean toward the idea that embracing 'femininity' is not self-defeating, they also perpetuate what it means to be a 'woman': to be a 'woman' is to be subject to male domination and hence to be someone who enacts her agency through manipulation—exercising (some modicum of) control from a position of subordination. Should she act in any other way, she is, under heterosexualism, not only unnatural but also unethical.

Thus, while promoting an ethic for females, heterosexualism is a set of values which undermines female agency outside the master/slave values. Women hang on to those values out of fear, out of a choice to focus on men while taking women for granted, and out of a lack of perception of any other choices. As a result, although many women individually have resisted male domination—in particular, men's attempts to make women mere extensions of men's will—it is less clear that (with a few notable exceptions), as Simone de Beauvoir suggested, women as a group dispute male sovereignty. However, in claiming this, I am not suggesting that disputing male sovereignty means attempting to oppose men as men have opposed women.[q] Rather, I am suggesting that it seems, for the most part, that women, whether as saboteurs or acceptors of male domination, have not disputed the entire dominance/subordination game of heterosexualism.

I want a moral revolution.

CONCLUSION

Through all of this, I am not trying to argue that heterosexualism is the "cause" of oppression. I do mean to suggest, however, that any revolution which does not challenge it will be incomplete and will eventually revert to the values of oppression. Heterosexualism is the form of social organization through which other forms of oppression, at times more vicious forms, become credible, palatable, even desirable. Heterosexualism—that is, the balance between masculine predation upon and masculine protection of a feminine object of masculine attention—de-skills a woman, makes her emotionally, socially, and economically dependent, and allows another to dominate her "for her own good" all in the name of "love." In no other situation[r] are people expected to love, identify with, and become other to those who dominate them to the extent that women are supposed to love, identify with, and become other to men.

It is heterosexualism which makes us feel that it is possible to dominate another for her own good, that one who resists such domination is abnormal or doesn't understand what is good for her, and that one who refuses to participate in dominant/subordinate relationships doesn't exist. And once we accept all this, imperialism, colonialism, and ethnocentrism, for example, while existing all along, become more socially tolerable in liberal thought. They become less a matter of exercising overt force and more a matter of the natural function of (a) social order.

Heterosexualism is a conceptual framework within which the concept of 'moral agency' independent of the master/slave virtues cannot find fertile ground. And it combines with ethical judgments to create a value whose primary function is not the moral development of individuals but rather the preservation of a patriarchal social control. Thus I want to challenge our acceptance and use of that ethics.

In discussing what I call Lesbian Ethics, I do not claim that lesbians haven't made many of the choices (heterosexual) women have made or that lesbians haven't participated in the consensus of straight thinking or that lesbians have withdrawn from the value of dominance and subordination and the security of established meaning we can find therein. I am not claiming that lesbians have lived under different conceptual or material conditions. I am claiming, however, that lesbian choice holds certain possibilities. It is a matter of further choice whether we go on to develop these possibilities or whether instead we try to fit into the existing heterosexual framework in any one of a number of ways.

Thus I am claiming that the conceptual category 'lesbian'–unlike the category 'woman'—is not irretrievably tied up with dominance and subordination as norms of behavior. And I am claiming that by attending each other, we may find the possibility of ethical values appropriate to lesbian existence, values we can choose as moral agents to give meaning to our lives as lesbians. In calling for withdrawal from the existing heterosexual value system, I am calling for a moral revolution, a revolution of lesbianism.

---

[q] Even what the amazons from between the black and caspian seas are reputed to have done was not a matter of opposing men as men have opposed women. At various times, some worry that women or lesbians or separatists want to do to men what men have done to women. Yet nowhere have I found any indication of women or lesbians wanting to subject men the way men have subjected women: have men de-skilled and dependent on women, have men find their identity through their relationships with women, have men isolated in women's houses waiting to care-take women, and so on. Mostly, I suspect, women and lesbians don't want the burden. Women's resistance to male domination has taken many forms. But in my understanding, it has never, even in fantasy, been a reversal of men's efforts.

[r] The situation of the mammy is similar. Racism and the politics of property intervened, however, to keep her from being quite so close to the master or mistress as woman is to man. Nevertheless, this did not make her situation any more palatable, and in many respects, it was worse.

NOTES

1. Kathryn Pyne Parsons [Addelson], "Nietzsche and Moral Change," in *Woman in Western Thought,* ed. Martha Lee Osborne (New York: Random House, 1979), p. 235.

2. Ibid.

3. Ibid.

4. Note David K. Shipler, *Arab and Jew: Wounded Spirits in a Promised Land* (New York: Random House/Times Books, 1986). Bette S. Tallen brought this to my attention.

5. Simone de Beauvoir, *The Second Sex,* trans. H. M. Parshley (New York: Bantam Books, 1970), p. xvii.

6. Ibid., pp. xvii–xviii.

7. Ibid., pp. 58–9.

8. Nancy C.M. Hartsock, *Money, Sex, and Power* (Boston: Northeastern University Press, 1985), p. 288.

9. Simone de Beauvoir, *Second Sex,* p. xix.

10. Ibid.

11. Ibid., p. xx.

12. Ibid., p. xxi.

13. Ibid., p. 249.

14. Janice G. Raymond, *A Passion for Friends: Toward a Philosophy of Female Affection* (Boston: Beacon Press, 1986), chapters 2 and 3, pp. 71–147; note also Marjorie Topky, "Marriage Resistance in Rural Kwangtung," in *Women in Chinese Society,* ed. Margery Wolf and Roxane Witke (Stanford, Calif.: Stanford University Press, 1975), pp. 67–88.

15. Sheila Kitzinger, "Heteropatriarchal Language: the Case Against "Homophobia'," *Gossip* 5, pp. 15–20.

16. Conversation, Marilyn Frye. Note Andrea Dworkin, *Pornography: Men Possessing Women* (New York: G.P. Putnam's Sons, 1979), p. 61.

17. Conversation, Ariane Brunet.

18. Note, e.g., Andrea Dworkin, *Pornography,* pp. 61–2.

19. Julien S. Murphy, "Silence and Speech in Lesbian Space," paper presented at Mountain Moving Coffeehouse, Chicago, Ill., 1984.

20. For further development of this point, note Marilyn Frye, "Oppression," in *The Politics of Reality: Essays in Feminist Theory* (Trumansburg, N. Y.: The Crossing Press, 1983, now in Freedom, Calif.), pp. 5–6.

21. Note Susan Griffin, "Rape: The All-American Crime," in *Feminism and Philosophy,* ed. Mary Vetterling-Braggin, Frederick A. Elliston, & Jane English (Totowa, N.J.: Littlefield, Adams & Co., 1977), especially p. 320.

22. Andrea Dworkin, *Woman Hating* (New York: E.P. Dutton & Co., 1974), pp. 29–49.

23. Sonia Johnson, presidential campaign speech, Chicago, Ill., 1984; conversation, Pauline Bart. The figure on wife-beating comes from the "Uniform Crime Reports of 1982," federal reports on incidences of domestic crime. According to a fact sheet from the Illinois Coalition on Domestic Violence, "National Domestic Violence Statistics, 1/84," ten to twenty percent of American children are abused. Another fact sheet, "Verified Domestic Statistics," researched and compiled by the Western Center on Domestic Violence (San Francisco, Calif.), cites estimates of Maria Roy, *The Abusive Partner* (New York: Van Nostrand Reinhold, 1982) as indicating that violence against wives will occur at least once in two-thirds of all marriages. Another fact sheet, "Wife Abuse: The Facts" (Center for Woman Policy Studies, 2000 P. Street N.W., Washington, D.C. 20036), cites Murray Straus, Richard Gelles and Suzanne Steinmetz, *Beyond Closed Doors: Violence in the American Family* (Garden City, N.Y.: Doubleday, 1980) as saying that twenty-five percent of wives are severely beaten during their marriage. There are many more statistics . . . you get the idea. Bette S. Tallen was extremely helpful in obtaining some of this information. Note also Del Martin, *Battered Wives,* revised and updated (Volcano Press, Inc., 330 Ellis St., #518, Dept. B, San Francisco, CA 94102, 1976, 1981); Leonore Walker, *The Battered Woman* (New York: Harper & Row, 1979), Florence Rush, *The Best Kept Secret: The Sexual Abuse of Children* (Englewood Cliffs, N.J.: Prentice-Hall, Inc., 1980); Diana E. H. Russell, *Sexual Exploitation: Rape, Child Sexual Abuse, and Workplace Harassment* (Beverly Hills, Calif.: Sage Publications, 1984); and Elizabeth A. Stanko *Intimate Intrusions: Women's Experience of*

Male Violence (Boston, Mass.: Routledge & Kegan Paul, 1985) among others.

24. Marilyn Frye, "In and Out of Harm's Way: Arrogance and Love," *Politics of Reality,* p. 72.

25. Sonia Johnson, "Excerpts from the last chapter of *Going Out Of Our Minds and Other Revolutionary Acts of the Spirit,*" *Mama Bears News & Notes* 3, no. 2 (April/May 1986): 15; also in *Going Out of Our Minds: The Metaphysics of Liberation* (Freedom, Calif.: The Crossing Press, 1987), p. 336.

26. Note, for example, Barbara Burris, "The Fourth World Manifesto," *Notes from the Third Year,* 1971, revised and reprinted in *Radical Feminism,* ed. Anne Koedt, Ellen Levine, and Anita Rapone (New York: New York Times Book Co., 1973), pp. 322–57; Margaret Small, "Lesbians and the Class Position of Women," in *Lesbianism and the Women's Movement,* ed. Nancy Myron and Charlotte Bunch (Baltimore: Diana Press, 1975), pp. 49–61; Robin Morgan, "On Women as a Colonized People," in *Going Too Far: The Personal Chronicle of a Feminist* (New York: Random House, 1977); Anne Summers, *Damned Whores and God's Police: The Colonization of Women in Australia* (Ringwood, Victoria, Australia: Penguin, 1975); and Kathleen Barry, "Sex Colonization," in *Female Sexual Slavery* (Englewood Cliffs, N.J.: Prentice-Hall, 1979), pp. 163–204.

27. Walter Rodney, *How Europe Underdeveloped Africa* (Washington, D.C.: Howard University Press, 1982).

28. Conversation, Bette S. Tallen.

29. Sonia Johnson, "Telling the Truth." *Trivia* 9 (Fall 1986): 21; also in *Going Out of Our Minds,* p. 249.

30. Ann Oakley, *Women's Work: The Housewife, Past and Present* (New York: Vintage Books/Random House, 1974), p. 19.

31. Gena Corea, *The Mother Machine: Reproductive Technologies from Artificial Insemination to Artificial Wombs* (New York: Harper & Row, 1985), p. 303.

32. Alice Molloy, *In Other Words: Notes on the Politics and Morale of Survival* (Oakland, Calif.: Women's Press Collective, n.d., write Alice Molloy, Mama Bears, 6536 Telegraph Ave., Oakland, CA 94609).

33. Alix Kates Shulman, *Memoirs of an Ex-Protes Queen* (New York: Bantam Books, 1973).

34. Information on this film can be obtained from the American Film & Video Network, 1723 Howard, Evanston, Ill.

35. This monologue is based on my memory and possibly inaccurate in detail. I believe, however, that I have invoked the general idea the woman was expressing.

36. Sheila Jeffries, *The Spinster and Her Enemies: Feminism and Sexuality, 1880–1930* (Boston: Pandora Press, 1985); Andrea Dworkin, *Pornography.*

37. This is one of the themes in *Lesbian Nuns: Breaking the Silence* (Tallahassee, Fla: The Naiad Press, 1985).

38. Kate Millett, *Sexual Politics* (New York: Doubleday, 1969), p. 26.

39. Naomi Weisstein, *Psychology Constructs the Female, or: The Fantasy Life of the Male Psychologist,* reprint (Boston: New England Free Press, 1968); reprinted in *Sisterhood Is Powerful: An Anthology of Writings from the Women's Liberation Movement,* ed. Robin Morgan (New York: Random House, 1970), pp. 205–20; and in *Women in Sexist Society,* ed. Vivian Gornick and Barbara K. Moran (New York: Signet, 1971), pp. 207–24; also in *Radical Feminism,* ed. Anne Koedt, Ellen Levine, and Anita Rapone, pp. 178–97.

40. Research of Betty Carpenter, personal communication.

41. Mary Daly, *Pure Lust: Elemental Feminist Philosophy* (Boston: Beacon Press, 1984), p. 38.

42. Kate Millett, *Sexual Politics,* p. 347.

43. Angela Davis, *Women, Race and Class* (New York: Vintage Books/Random House, 1983), chapter 1, pp. 3–29.

44. Angela Davis, "Reflections on the Black Woman's Role in the Community of Slaves," in *Contemporary Black Thought: Best From The Black Scholar,* ed. Robert Chrisman and Nathan Hare (Indianapolis: Bobbs-Merrill, 1973), p. 148; note also Herbert Aptheker, *American Negro Slave Revolts* (New York: International Publishers, 1970) (1st. ed., 1943), as cited by Angela Davis.

45. Note, for example, Earl Conrad, *Harriet Tubman* (New York: Paul S. Eriksson, Inc., 1969).

46. Ruthe Winegarten, "I Am Annie Mae: The Personal Story of a Black Texas Woman," *Chrysalis* 10 (Spring 1980): 15; later published: *I Am Annie Mae: An Extraordinary Woman in Her Own Words: The Personal Story of a Black Texas Woman,* ed. Ruthe Winegarten (Austin, Tex.: Rosegarden Press, 1983).

47. After formulating this thesis, I came across documented evidence of it. Note Gilbert Osofsky, ed., *Puttin' On Ole Massa* (New York: Harper & Row, 1969); Aran Bontemps, ed., *Great Slave Narratives* (Boston: Beacon Press, 1969); and Willie Lee Rose, ed., *A Documentary History of Slavery in North America* (New York: Oxford University Press, 1976). Unfortunately, these collections almost exclusively address the lives of men. For a ground-breaking work on women slaves, note Erlene Stetson, "Studying Slavery: Some Literary and Pedagogical Considerations on the Black Female Slave," in *All the Women Are White, All the Blacks Are Men, But Some of Us Are Brave: Black Women's Studies,* ed. Gloria T. Hull, Patricia Bell Scott, and Barbara Smith (Old Westbury, N.Y.: Feminist Press, 1982), pp. 61–84; note also, Angela Davis, "Reflections on the Black Woman's Role in the Community of Slaves."

48. Simone Wallace, Ellen Ledley, Paula Tobin, letter to *off our backs,* December 1979, p. 28.

49. Note, for example, Barbara Harford and Sarah Hopkins, eds., *Greenham Common: Women at the Wire* (London: Women's Press, 1984); also Alice Cook & Gwyn Kirk, *Greenham Women Everywhere: Dreams, Ideas and Actions From the Women's Peace Movement* (Boston: South End Press, 1984).

50. Charlotte Perkins Gilman, *The Yellow Wallpaper* (Old Westbury, N.Y.: Feminist Press, 1973).

51. For information on S. Weir Mitchell, note G. J. Barker-Benfield, *The Horrors of the Half-Known Life: Male Attitudes Toward Women and Sexuality in Nineteenth Century America* (New York: Harper & Row, 1976).

52. Elaine R. Hedges, "Afterword," in *The Yellow Wallpaper,* Charlotte Perkins Gilman.

53. Eugene O'Neill, *Long Day's Journey into Night* (New Haven, Conn.: Yale University Press, 1955).

54. Phyllis Chesler, *Women and Madness* (Garden City, N.Y.: Doubleday, 1972).

55. *The Compact Edition of the Oxford English Dictionary,* 1971.

56. Susan Glaspell, "Trifles: A Play in One Act," in *Plays* (Boston: Small Maynard & Co., 1920, an authorized facsimile of the original book was produced by Xerox University Microfilms, Ann Arbor, Michigan, 1976). Blanche Hersh brought this play to my attention.

57. Ann Jones, *Women Who Kill* (New York: Holt, Rinehart, and Winston, 1980), p. 291.

58. Kathleen Barry, *Female Sexual Slavery,* pp. 142–4.

59. For some discussion of this, note Jean Carey Bond and Pat Peery, "Is the Black Male Castrated?" in *Black Woman,* ed. Toni Cade, pp. 113–9; Patricia Bell Scott, "Debunking Sapphire: Toward a Non-Racist and Non-Sexist Social Science," in *But Some of Us Are Brave,* pp. 85–92; Bonnie Thornton Dill, "The Dialectics of Black Womanhood," in *Feminism & Methodology,* ed. Sandra Harding (Bloomington: Indiana University Press, 1987), pp. 98–9; and Angela Davis, "Reflections on the Black Woman's Role in the Community of Slaves"; note also Erlene Stetson, "Studying Slavery."

60. Note Marilyn Frye, "Oppression," in *The Politics of Reality,* pp. 1–16.

61. Note, for example, *Breaching the Peace: A Collection of Radical Feminist Papers* (London: Onlywomen Press, 1983).

62. Kathleen Barry, *Female Sexual Slavery,* pp. 43–6.

63. William Ryan, *Blaming the Victim* (New York: Vintage Books, 1976).

64. Kathleen Barry, *Female Sexual Slavery,* p. 45.

65. Andrea Dworkin, *Right-Wing Women* (New York: G. P. Putnam's Sons/Perigee, 1983), p. 14.

66. Ibid., p. 15.

67. Ibid., pp. 17, 21.

68. Brunetta R. Wolfman, "Black First, Female Second," in *Black Separatism and Social Reality: Rhetoric and Reason,* ed. Raymond L. Hall (New York: Pergamon Press, 1977), p. 228.

69. Ibid., p. 229.

70. Jacquelyn Grant, "Black Women and the Black Church," in *But Some of Us Are Brave,* p. 141.

71. Brunetta R. Wolfman, "Black First, Female Second," p. 230.

72. Ibid., p. 231.

SEEING POWER IN MORALITY: A PROPOSAL FOR FEMINIST NATURALISM IN ETHICS

Margaret Urban Walker

It is often said that the opposition of morality to power is virtually coextensive with canonical Western moral thought. It is supposedly installed as a founding distinction in the dialogues of Plato, where Socrates more than once defeats the view that justice is the advantage of the stronger. But this is not quite right. Socrates opposes not "power" but brute force and the unbridled exercise of rapacious desire on or in spite of others. Indeed, in Plato's *Republic* the ideal state Socrates envisions can only achieve a true moral order in this world through detailed and extensive coordination of coercive, controlling, and productive powers of several types.

The Platonic root of canonical Western moral theory is really something else: the conviction that morality "itself" is something ideal. Plato's Socrates sees any imperfect, power-dependent worldly realization of moral order as an unstable and shadowy semblance of something itself fully real, true, perfect, and unchanging, not within the plane of ordinary human existence or within the range of those cognitive powers through which we know things of the ordinary world. This Platonic legacy of the *ideality* or *transcendent nature* of morality still reigns. Through most of the canonized Western tradition moral theory has consistently been done as if morality were ideal, and most philosophers today continue to make theory about morality as if it were effectively ideal, even if they do not literally believe that—that is, they treat it is a subject matter largely independent of empirical information about the real histories and contingencies of human relations in society. This legacy underlies many philosophers' boredom with or contempt for too much interest in how human beings actually live and what it has been or is like for them—each of them—to live that way. They think that there is little to be learned from what is about what ought to be.

The ideality of morality has enjoyed many formulations: a vision of The Good, a divine command, an unchanging natural moral law; an intuition of nonnatural properties, the transcendental logic of pure practical reason, the logic of moral language, the necessary conditions of agency as such, the pragmatic transcendental presuppositions of the ideal speech situation, or what certain imagined beings would have to endorse in certain imagined situations in which they mostly cannot know things about actual human beings in actual situations. I do not see strong prospects for any longer defending the view of morality as truly ideal or transcendent. Yet many feminist philosophers, too, share in the tradition that sees the ideality of morality as both inspiring and protective.

A continuing fear is that if morality is too much a matter of what is, and of who has the power to make it so, then those without or with less power are left without moral appeal. This fear has real basis: Power unconstrained by moral compunction and unanswerable in fact to standards with moral authority is always something to be feared—and not only by the weakest. But it is a mistake to think that a naturalistic and power-sensitive view of morality itself must "reduce" morality to power or make morality disappear in favor of power. Instead, it should be an instrument for testing the legitimacy of powers that claim moral justification. Still, there is the philosopher's wish, in feminist philosophy serving a political vision, to stand on moral ground that cannot shift. I do not believe that the desire for apodictically secured foundations for morality can be satisfied. That is not, however, some problem about the infirmity of morality. In a postfoundationalist era, it is only to say that our moral grounds cannot be better, epistemically, than the others that anchor out understanding of the world.

There is an alternative to the idealism of a transcendent view, on the one hand, and, on the other, the normative emptiness of a view that rejects morality wholesale in favor of "amoral contests about the just and the good in which truth is always grasped as coterminous with power, always already power, as the voice of power."[1] I cannot defend an entire view of morality here, but I make a proposal for an empirically obligated and politically emancipatory naturalism in ethics that sees the ineliminable roles of power in morality "itself."[2]

MORALITY OF POWER, MORALITY IN POWER

Feminist ethics is inevitably, and fundamentally, a discourse about morality and power. The most obvious way feminist ethics and politics connect morality and power is in examining the morality of specific distributions and exercises of power. Feminism's traditional critique challenges morally the coercive, arbitrary, cruel, and oppressive powers of men over women in many systems of gender. Feminism claims for women on moral grounds economic, political, social, sexual, epistemic, discursive, and symbolic powers denied them by individual, institutional, and cultural male dominance. Feminism must also oppose domination structured by hierarchies or exclusions of class, race, sexuality, age, and ability, for these always partly organize gender even as they are themselves realized in part through specific organizations of gender. To acknowledge this obligation is not, however, to have in hand either the theoretical or the political strategies necessary to fulfill it.

Feminist moral theory also continues to produce unprecedented theoretical understandings of the moral meaning of relations of unequal power, especially asymmetric relations of dependency as well as interdependencies that do not even approximate reciprocal exchanges. This theorization of the morality of unequal power, of "power-over," "responsibility-for," "depending-on," and "trusting-to," reaches to the roots of our conceptualization of human beings as moral beings and requires us to see our moral being in terms of varied relations, both symmetrical and asymmetrical, immediate and highly mediated, to others. The full impact of this reconception on ethical theory and practice is still at the edge of imagination; it remains unclear whether or in what versions some familiar moral and political conceptions can meet the realities of human society as a scene of inescapable connection, dependence, vulnerability, and entrustment.

Feminism's insistent reexaminations of morality and power on these fronts are connected by the need to explore likenesses and differences among legitimate and illegitimate powers, their conditions, and their effects in relations of many kinds. Socially enforced dominance must do quite a lot of things to and with people to make coerced vulnerabilities appear as inevitable ones. Feminist, race, culture, and postcolonial theory continue to reveal this. We cannot distinguish inevitable vulnerabilities and dependencies from manipulated ones until we understand both the manipulated ones in all their subtle and overt varieties and the inevitable ones from the viewpoints of both those who are vulnerable *and* those who respond to them, as care, ageism, and disability theories show. Works of lesbians, gay men, transsexuals, and sex workers on constructions of sexuality and their implications for identity, citizenship, and family dissect the powers of modern institutions and expert discourses to naturalize norms and to moralize what is natural only for some.

To understand the moral necessity, arbitrariness, or catastrophe of giving some people powers over others or of reserving certain powers for some people rather than others, it seems we need the whole manifold of objects of comparison: people in relations of reciprocal risk and trust; people positioned higher or lower by socially enforced hierarchies of power and privilege, whether legitimately or not; those variously less physically able than most others; the immature and the less mature; the cognitively or socially limited or incompetent; those inescapably or radically dependent. Ours then becomes a question of moral terms for the equivalent political and social membership, the essential material and personal support, and the dignifying care, participation, governance, and representation *of all of us.* It is not clear to me that this question has ever really been set before in the 2,500-year history of the canonical, and usually ostensibly "universalist," Western tradition. Feminist thought has played a crucial role in formulating and pressing this question, showing how tirelessly one must think through ethical problems posed by many relationships and exercises of power.

I suggest now that these mutually deepening insights about the morality of power be joined to another kind of view about the powers of and for morality. This is a naturalist view in which morality "itself" is *a disposition of powers through an arrangement of responsibilities.* In this view the very existence of morality requires many social powers. Powers to control, educate, and influence are required to cultivate and foster senses of responsibility. Powers to govern, persuade, inspire, reward, recruit, and punish are necessary to impose and enforce distributions of responsibility, norms for who may do what to whom, who must do what for whom, and whose business anyone's welfare or behavior is. Powers to give or pay, to speak, silence, or credit speaking, to rule and punish, to represent, ritualize, and memorialize are needed to nourish relations of responsibility materially, discursively, legally, and symbolically.

But social orders require as well the sustenance of distinctively moral powers: the powers of morality when embodied in the self-understandings of agents and in the structure of discourses and institutions. Even as moral understandings are carried by social arrangements, they imbue these arrangements with (ideally) mutually understood importance and depth. Moral understandings thus create meaning for us in reproducing our social arrangements and sustain pride, gratitude, and trust among us in

doing so. They mobilize resentment toward, and shame in, those who deny or undermine them. Where moral understandings command our confidence, they move us in trust and hope to continue or adopt a certain way of living, and we invoke them to move others to do so with us. Social arrangements, limited and enabled by many powers, give body to morality in the world. Morality in turn disciplines many natural human powers of self-direction, expression, attention, reason, feeling, imagination, and mutual responsiveness—in service of a shared way of life whose authority inheres in being understood always as more than *simply* that.

The central point of this view is that morality is *not socially modular.* Morality is neither a dimension of reality beyond or separate from shared life nor a distinct and detachable set of understandings within it. Our moral practices are not extricable from other social ones. Moral practices in particular lifeways are entirely enmeshed with other social practices; and moral identities, with social roles and positions. Moral understandings are effected through social arrangements, while all important social arrangements include moral practices as working parts. Moral concepts and judgments are an integral part, but only one part, of practices that attempt to organize feelings, behavior, and judgment in ways that keep people's expectations in rough equilibrium.

This has implications for moral philosophy. In moral theory we abstract moral ideas from social practice, imaginatively varying, simplifying, or idealizing them. This is unavoidable but leaves questions about how the social provenance of ideas shapes what they can mean, whether novel applications we imagine for them can be achieved, and at what costs. None of us can access by pure reflection necessary moral precepts or pure moral concepts that are not in fact derived from our socially situated experiences of actual forms of social life or our socially constrained imagination of others. If there were a fund of purely moral knowledge accessible to some kind of purely reflective inquiry, then we could do this. But there could be such a fund of purely moral knowledge only if morality completely transcended history and culture, if it were, once again, something *ideal or transcendent.* To speak of morality as a disposition of powers through an arrangement of responsibilities is to say that morality is not like this. Morality is not a norm that either exists independently of human activity and judgment or remains invariant because it is in no way a function of changes in the course of the histories of human beings in societies. This means that philosophers must ask themselves on what socially cultured experience of morality they draw in making claims about "morality itself"; about the presuppositions of being a "person" or an "agent"; or about the intuitions, sense of justice, or concept of responsibility they claim is "ours." It also means that philosophers need to investigate whether and how moral views can be seated in and sustained by actual social arrangements. What disposition of powers do moral views assume and effect, at whose service or expense, with what methods of recruitment and enforcement, and through what ecologies of feeling and attitude? Finally, philosophers will have to acknowledge that many types of empirical information are necessary in investigating the possibility and justifiability of forms of moral life.

No other kind of moral philosophy has explored these issues as persistently and with as profound results as has feminist ethics. A lot of moral philosophy does not explore them at all. My proposal is that feminist and other politically emancipatory ethics adopt the methodological framework that makes sense of this theoretical practice, what I am calling a "naturalistic" one.

WHAT KIND OF NATURALISM?

Naturalism is a protean and loaded term that sparks suspicions and resistance of several kinds. *Naturalism* may suggest a commitment to natural kinds or natural essences, a presumption in favor of scientific knowledge or a scientific basis for morality, or an essentially descriptive and explanatory enterprise that will miss the "normative" character of morality and the critical character of moral philosophy. None of this is what I mean by "naturalism."

I mean by it that morality is a naturally occurring structure of all human social groups. It recruits and produces many powers to shape interpersonal response and self-direction around shared understandings that guide judgment, action, and expectation. Moral theory needs to study this structure in its various forms but also to grasp the characteristic way that this kind of structure presents itself to its participants. To investigate how the patterning that constitutes moral relations has the kinds of force and meaning that it does is to ask, What are some distinctive aspects of people's grasp of their social relations that make those relations *moral* ones, that give them the kinds of *authority* that we associate with morality? Moral theory has to use this descriptive and explanatory understanding of the specifically *moral authority of morality* in turn to take up its normative critical task: to investigate whether specific moral arrangements are what they must present themselves to be to have this force and meaning. The descriptive and analytical work constructs a working model of what moral relations are like that can guide the normative inquiry. The normative inquiry, testing how supposedly moral arrangements may or may not turn out to be what their authority requires, in turn refines the model: It reveals more about the ways the various working parts of social arrangements and self-understandings must either pull together or be kept safely apart for a social-moral order to roll (or lurch) on.

My own analytical model of morality is that moral structure shows itself in practices of responsibility. The practices implement and enforce understandings of who may do what to whom, who must do what for whom, and to whom various ones of us have to account. This model directs us to look very closely at how these practices construct and circulate understandings of people's identities, their relations to others (or lack thereof), and commonly intelligible values that sustain a given distribution of responsibilities. Actual attention to our own and others' moral cultures reveals that typically there are different responsibilities assigned to or withheld from different groups of people within the same society. In fact, the differences between groups are defined in important part by the forms and limits of agency these distributions of responsibility impute to them. Practices of responsibility show what is valued (at least by those with most power to define the practices) as well as who is valued by whom for what.

But moral practices are ways of going on together that claim something more for themselves than the inertia of habit and tradition, which are already crumbling as soon as their adherents see them as exactly and *only* that. And moral practices claim something quite other for their specific kind of power over us than main force, coercive threat, or manipulation. At the core of any moral-social order there must be trust that certain basic understandings are common, that the common understandings are the operative ones shaping shared life, and that these operative understandings constitute a way of life that is not only "how we live" but also "how to live," a way worthy of people's allegiance, effort, restraint, or sacrifice. Without this, there really are just ways some people can make others behave.

The "normativity" of morality—the specifically moral authority of morality, whatever powers hold its practices in place—does not descend from someplace outside all human judgment; it inheres in the durability of our understandings and the trust they support under the right kind of tests. The relevant tests are those that reassure us that we do understand how we live and that how we live is indeed worthy, considered in its own conditions and effects or considered in comparison to some other way. So, the tests must tap the experiences and understandings of those who live the lifeway under test. If our way of life in reality betrays our shared understandings, or if these understandings turn out to be driven by deception, manipulation, coercion, or violence directed at some of us by others, where all are nonetheless supposed to "share" in this purported vision of the good, then our trust is not sustained and our practices lose their *moral* authority, whatever other powers continue to hold them in place. They become then nothing more than habits or customs, ways we live that are no longer credible or trustworthy as "how to live." Substantial parts of moral-social orders commonly fail to be credible to, or trustworthy for, many participants who are less valued, protected, or rewarded than others in their orders' differential distributions of responsibility.

This "transparency testing" is both a tool of normative philosophical critique and an actual social process that may be relatively inchoate and undirected or politically accentuated and mobilized.[3] Yet moral understandings in life or philosophy are only ever tested for their worthiness in light of some moral standards or other. We always stand on some moral values as we consider the authority of others; sometimes we stand on certain applications of a moral standard to contest other applications of the same one. This only means that, with respect to moral beliefs, we are not in a different situation than is now widely acknowledged for other empirical beliefs: We are always in the position of using some of what we know to discover whether, and how, we know anything else. So it is for moral knowledge: We never get completely behind or beneath all moral beliefs. And any moral standards we apply in testing others are realized in or abstracted from human practices, discourses, and institutions that are themselves configured and reproduced by power. We cannot get behind or under the powers for and of morality, either.

In this view there is no standpoint completely transcendent to and neutral among all forms of social practice and the conceptions of value and responsibilities they implement. But this does not mean that we "lose" the essential dimension of normativity. It means that we never get outside of it, but are never done with reconfirming it, by testing the actual social conditions and effects of the moral practices that claim our trust. Testing the moral authority of our practices means discovering how they actually go, what they actually mean, and what it is actually like to live them from particular places within them. It means examining the power-bound social arrangements that necessarily embody morality. The moral authority of these arrangements, however, is in no way reducible to the fact of their existence.

Scientific knowledge enjoys no hegemony or even privilege in this critical project. It is one source of our understanding of some features of how we live, but it does not trump historical, ethnographic, hermeneutic, cultural, political, and critical studies of lived experience and its meanings; nor can it replace the mutually situating testimonies of all those whose experience of a way of life bears on its claims to authority. Attention to variety in moral practices and appreciation of how they work for people placed variously within them tend to undermine rather than support essentialist generalizations about *how* beings must live to *be* human ones. These studies lead us to explore instead the intricate social architectures that produce specific understandings of ourselves as human beings. This naturalism installs precisely an open-ended and open-minded need to *look and see* how moral ideas materialize in social practices that then constrain at a given time what these moral ideas mean.

A feminist naturalism finds it both too soon and too late for ideal theory. It is too late to turn back from some things we know. We know that past and existing practices of responsibility have encoded oppressive and demeaning social hierarchies covered by deceptively inclusive-sounding ideas like "the good life for man," or "the kingdom of ends," or "our sense of justice." Yet it is too soon to rest confident in what little we know. We may not fully grasp the material conditions

and practical constraints under which moral theories and ideals can achieve the emancipatory applications *for all of us* that many of us desire.

RECONSIDERING MODERN UNIVERSALISM

I want to use an example, very briefly, of one such uncertain place to which we are delivered by the parallel efforts of feminist theory and critical race theory. Insistently tracking the real intrication of morality and power, feminist and race theory have established a deeply unsettling assessment of one of the most powerful paradigms of modern liberal moral and political theory: the social contract. This conceptual model is still central to moral philosophy today and remains for many feminists a best hope as a model for moral egalitarianism.

Feminist deconstructions of the social contract have uncovered the inescapably gendered conceptual and practical foundations of early modern and contemporary contractarian thinking.[4] The mutually accepted equality of certain Anglo-European men made them free by their own agreement to view *each other* that way. They agreed among themselves to positions for certain women that were defined by their relations to those women—specifically, relations of power over, or access to, them. That is, mutual recognition of these men's rights over certain women is one of the significant respects in which the men define themselves as equal. Furthermore, the hierarchical sexual division of labor is a material condition for men to be free to engage in the economic competition, social participation, and political contests that both express and measure their equality in society's public sphere. This pattern continued well into the twentieth century with assumptions that the discourse of justice and equality defines statuses within the "public" lives of household "heads."

Race theorists have excavated the historical foundations of modern Europe's self-definition as the universe of civilized men. Enlightenment ideals of reason and personhood played central roles in constituting—again deliberately, consciously, and violently—a raced equality that defined white men as moral subjects and political peers in important part by entitling them to power over or access to nonwhite people and what nonwhite people have. As Charles Mills puts it, a "racial contract" has always underwritten the still-invoked social one.[5] Mills, along with other race theorists, makes a compelling case from textual and historical evidence that the equality of Anglo-European men was imagined from the outset in terms of who these men were not, and were not like. More tellingly, separate moral and juridical statuses were explicitly elaborated for nonwhite others in the course of, and for the purpose of, explicitly elaborating and justifying white men's entitlements to work, rule, displace, civilize, own, or kill them.[6] Now the pattern continues in the form of widespread denial by whites of pervasive racism and persisting disadvantage, strategic exclusion, and raced violence in a society organized, politically and epistemically, to sustain this deniability.

Neither of these compelling bodies of critique has yet been joined to the other in a unifying, or at least mutually clarifying, analysis of the contractarian constructions of equality as both Whiteness and Maleness (and perhaps of each in terms of the other). Each of these inquiries, however, powerfully confronts the unsavory historical amnesia and institutional legitimation that allow us to keep thinking about, and circulating, and teaching these views "as if" they "really" proclaimed the universally inclusive freedom and equality, or equal moral worth, of all human beings. In demonstrable and demonstrated fact, they did not. Nor did they intend to. They intended and did the reverse, intentionally erecting the ideal of *equality for equals* to assure mutually the rights of certain people in part by defining them as rights over other people. In all versions of this contract equality was seen as conferred by a restricted class of men on its members, and among the things conferred was the right of those equal to each other to distinguish themselves from the rest, particularly by specific powers *over* those not equal to them.

These historically informed analyses exhibit a central feature of the modern liberal idea of equality *in the context of the actual social arrangements that made sense of it.* This construction of equality requires there to be something *other* than equality. What is other is not merely different but must define and support the equality of equals. Despite claims for its revolutionary nature, the ostensible universalism of modern equality repeats the subsumptive universalism of classical thought. In this conceptual structure, some nature or possible perfection of humanity (usually "Man") was to be realized in the persons of a few human beings suited to it. But the many others are not left out; they occupy *indispensable* roles in relation to the few. Legitimized asymmetrical exercises of power over the many lesser others distinguish the few who enjoy these powers over the many, and not over each other, *as equals.* Concretely, those who are able but not equal supply the wherewithal of common life that is necessary to sustain the "achievement" of equality by some.[7]

This persistent logic of equality (as we have always known it and as it has in fact evolved in tandem with the practices that make sense of it) is that it qualifies some by subsuming or subjecting others. The fundamental problem with the status of women and nonwhite men in the social contract (and the actual society it images) is *not* capricious and arbitrary exclusion from a status they might just as well have occupied alongside white men if the qualifications were fair, although efforts to "correct" contractarian thought tend to "add in" or "add on" some of those historically excluded. The problem is instead a kind of pointed and invidious *inclusion* in subordinate or diminished statuses that serve to define entitlements of the equals and the nature of equality itself. Equals do not just have different and greater powers and entitlements *relative* to those below; they are defined *as equal* to one another by their shared entitlements *to* and powers *over* those below. The former aspect of unequal status, "distributive" inequality, can be remedied by equalizing "shares" in available goods or access to them. But there is a real puzzle in fixing the latter key feature of equality: If powers *over* others are what defines the equals, then when equality is extended to those below, over whom are they entitled to rule? In other words, the part of the equality status that is defined structurally by "power over Xs" cannot be reduced to any version of "difference from Xs." Yet what we have learned from studies of race and gender oppression shows that it is "power over" that is fundamental; distributive inequality and the social marking of "differences" are *effects* of systemic powers of some over others.

For me, this persistently subsuming and subjecting logic of consensual equality poses the question of whether an "association of equals" can in fact be rendered universal. One profound contribution of feminist ethics has been its insistence that moral theory address immaturity, vulnerability, disability, dependency, and incapacity as inevitable, central, and normal in human life. The model of an association of equals does not seem capable of including all of us and will not give the needed guidance, as Eva Kittay puts it, "on our unequal vulnerability in dependency, on our moral power to respond to others in need, and on the primacy of human relations to happiness and well-being."[8] In pursuing an encompassing moral universalism—this time, *for the first time*—we cannot ignore theoretically what we cannot dispense with humanly: many "powers over" are indispensable "powers for," that is, on behalf of, the infant, the immature, the frail, the ill; the occasionally, developmentally, or permanently dependent; the mildly or severely incapacitated. These are not different (kinds of) people. *They are all of us at some times—and necessarily.* It remains unclear to me whether there really can be a single universal and substantive moral status; if there is, I doubt that it can be the status of

equality. I do not yet see the deeper logic of moral equality, or a fully inclusive logic beyond equality, that is universal in its moral embrace while it differentiates not only among persons but fluidly within the lives of persons, over times and contexts, in its assignments of responsibility.

MORALITY, NOT IDEOLOGY

A moral inquiry that reflects on practices of responsibility for an actual social life will not talk about morality instead of power but, rather, will explore the moral authority of some powers and the arbitrariness, cruelty, or wastefulness of others. It is a heavy irony that interrogating the ways that power (inevitably) constructs morality so often prompts the charge that one is "reducing morality to ideology." In fact, exactly the reverse is true. In one useful characterization of ideology, it is a practice of presenting claims as existing "above the fray of power and politics," for instance, as being "theoretical, rational, or spiritual and, on that basis, justified in acting as the final arbiter over others,"[9] thus "hiding the social histories and circumstances from which ideas . . . derive their logics."[10] Claims about or within morality are used ideologically when they pretend to operate beyond or above all social powers, rather than as a means of distributing and authorizing social powers and so needing justification as such. The alternative, I have argued, is always to see the power in morality—and to "see through" it to its conditions and costs. This is what I am calling naturalism in moral philosophy. It is something feminist moral philosophers are usually already very good at doing.

NOTES

1. Wendy Brown, *States of Injury: Power and Freedom in Late Modernity* (Princeton, N.J.: Princeton University Press, 1995), 45. Brown argues that "surrendering epistemological foundations means giving up the ground of specifically *moral*

claims against domination" (45), but this is true only if moral claims cannot receive an alternative epistemological account, just as other knowledge claims now usually do. Brown repeats the view that the discursive roots of a morality-power antagonism go back to Plato.

2. This is the view I defend at length in *Moral Understandings: A Feminist Study in Ethics* (New York: Routledge, 1998).

3. See *Moral Understandings,* chapters 3 and 9, for fuller discussion of transparency as a moral and epistemic ideal and of transparency testing as an aspect of actual social processes in real times and spaces.

4. Many people have contributed to this analysis. Some examples of sustained discussions of the historical realities include Carol Pateman, *The Sexual Contract* (Stanford: Stanford University Press, 1988); Linda Nicholson, *Gender and History: The Limits of Social Theory in the Age of the Family* (New York: Columbia University Press, 1986); Patricia S. Mann, *Micro-Politics: Agency in a Postfeminist Era* (Minneapolis: University of Minnesota Press, 1994); and Brown, *States of Injury.* Exposures of the continuing occlusion and exclusion of women in Rawls's thought include Susan Moller Okin, *Justice, Gender, and the Family* (New York: Basic Books, 1989), and Eva Feder Kittay, *Love's Labor: Essays on Women, Equality, and Dependency* (New York: Routledge, 1999).

5. Charles W. Mills, *Racial Contract* (Ithaca, N.Y.: Cornell University Press, 1997), 93.

6. Two incisive accounts are those of Mills, *The Racial Contract,* especially chapters 1 and 2, and Lucius T. Outlaw Jr., *On Race and Philosophy* (New York: Routledge, 1996), especially chapter 3. A provocative collection of classical modern philosophical texts that construct race distinctions is Emmanual Chukwudi Eze, *Race and the Enlightenment: A Reader* (Cambridge, Mass.: Blackwell Publishers, 1997). On the specifically American construction of black/white distinction in the context of Anglo-European philosophy and culture, see Winthrop D. Jordan's massive study, *White over Black: American Attitudes toward the Negro, 1550–1812* (Chapel Hill: University of North Carolina Press, 1968). Richard H. Popkin provides an interesting account of the intertwining histories of biblical and philosophical thinking about race in "The Philosophical Bases of Modern Racism," in *Philosophy and the Civilizing Arts,* ed. Craig Walton and John P. Austen (Athens: Ohio University Press, 1974), 126–53.

7. In *Doctrine of Right* Kant distinguishes "passive citizens" who do not have the same schedule of rights as "active" ones. As Tamar Shapiro explains, passive citizens include not only the "natural" ones, women and children, but also those economically dependent, including apprentices, domestic servants, domestic laborers, private tutors, and tenant farmers. Shapiro explains that Kant distinguishes this restricted citizenship from the "freedom and equality *as human beings*" shared by all and disallows the treatment of passive citizens as things or as members of a permanent underclass, although the possibilities for women to work their way up remains doubtful. See Tamar Shapiro, "What Is a Child?" *Ethics* 109 (1999): 715–38. Shapiro's discussion illustrates how the category of those subsumed as "dependent" has encompassed all those whose labor materially supported the "independence" that qualifies relatively few as equals. This "independence" is an amalgam of entitlement to, power over, and exemption from the labors of others. It also dramatizes the question of what moral conceptions like "freedom and equality" mean divorced from actual social implementation of these statuses. In one straightforward sense, they *do not* mean "freedom and equality." Tellingly, Shapiro reconstructs childhood as a "moral predicament," an unfortunate situation to be overcome.

8. Kittay, *Love's Labor,* 113.

9. E. Doyle McCarthy, *Knowledge as Culture: The New Sociology of Knowledge* (New York: Routledge, 1996), 31.

10. McCarthy, *Knowledge as Culture,* 7.

THE MORAL POWERS OF VICTIMS

Claudia Card

LIVING WITH EVILS

Lesbian, gay, and transgender people in the United States live surrounded by the hatred of people who would eliminate us if they could.[1] Girls learn early that the world is dangerous for unprotected females and that female competence is more often punished than rewarded. Racial minorities are grossly overrepresented in U.S. prisons. Jewish and Gypsy histories are to a great extent histories of the survival of evils that were fatal for many. The world's poor, its vast majority, suffer daily living conditions conducive to high infant mortality, lifelong poor health, and early death for survivors of childhood.[2] The United States, justly proud of its early history as a haven for refugees, was nevertheless founded on a bedrock of slavery and mass murder. As John Stuart Mill observed, with characteristic understatement, "Unquestionably it is possible to do without happiness; it is done involuntarily by nineteen-twentieths of mankind."[3] Whether to live with evils and their legacies is seldom a choice. The questions are about how to do it well, especially, how to interrupt cycles of hostility generated by past evils and replace mutual ill will with good.

In *Living with One's Past,* Norman Care reflects on issues presented by problematic aspects of one's own moral history, choices that implicated one in the genesis of potentially serious harms to others.[4] His work is exceptional in contemporary ethics in addressing how to live with profound regrets, how to respond to wrongs done, rather than simply how to prevent future ones. Similarly, the concerns of this essay are about living with evils, ongoing and past, and their aftermaths. I approach them from the positions of victims.

I begin with a discussion of rectifications and remainders, core concepts for responding to evils, and briefly consider limits of punishment as rectification for atrocities. I then take up moral powers of victims, negative and positive, that tend toward rectification. The negative power is blame (and related attitudes of condemnation and resentment), which can evoke guilt and associated senses of obligation in those blamed. The positive power, treated at greater length, is forgiveness, which can relieve burdens that may not be morally relievable in other ways. When gratitude and guilt are experienced as unpayable debts, both might be regarded as what Bernard Williams has called "remainders."[5]

Legacies of evil are receiving international attention as nations address histories of apartheid, genocide, mass rape, disappearances, and torture. Martha Minow and Carlos Santiago Nino write thoughtfully and informatively about social, political, and legal responses to atrocities, exploring alternatives to the opposite extremes of vengeance and amnesty. They discuss truth commissions, monument building, barring former collaborators from positions of social responsibility, and payments, trials, apologies, and other reparations.[6] These measures are undertaken by states and nongovernmental organizations with the pragmatic aim of ending cycles of atrocity in such countries as South Africa, Chile, or the former Yugoslavia. My concerns here are more with responses by individuals who do not hold positions of political influence but must find ways to go on feeling, thinking, and acting in the face of histories and legacies of evil, both interpersonal and institutional. To the extent that Nino is right that at the level of governmental action, "silence and impunity have been the norm rather than the exception" and that "the few investigations that have been undertaken often targeted the wrong actions and the wrong people," ordinary citizens often cannot take satisfaction in state action but must make their own peace.[7]

John Kekes writes insightfully on how to live with the knowledge that evils continue to be a significant part of the human condition. He evaluates attitudes philosophers have advocated toward life and toward humanity in general in light of this appreciation.[8] My concerns here are with attitudes not toward life or humanity as such but toward individuals—victims, perpetrators, bystanders, and beneficiaries (ourselves included)—who are connected with particular evils.

Evils change moral relationships among those who become perpetrators, bystanders, beneficiaries, or victims. They create moral powers in survivors, obligations in perpetrators, beneficiaries, and bystanders, and new options for many. Like benefactors, who can call upon the gratitude or indebtedness of beneficiaries, victims have moral powers: to blame or resent, to forgive, and, if politically empowered, to punish or retaliate, exact reparations and apologies, and to pardon or show mercy. Like creditors and benefactors who can forgive or exact debts, voluntarily releasing others or holding them to obligation, victims have moral powers to release or hold perpetrators to obligation. Beneficiaries can do little to change their own ethical status in relation to benefactors. Regardless of whether they meet their obligations, they remain indebted unless benefactors release them. Similarly, perpetrators can do little to change their own ethical status in relation to victims but remain morally dependent on them (or their representatives) for release. Yet benefactors and victims can forfeit moral powers through misconduct. Just as unscrupulous or abusive benefactors can cease to deserve gratitude, thereby involuntarily releasing beneficiaries from obligation, unscrupulous or abusive victims can cease to deserve apologies or reparations, involuntarily releasing perpetrators from obligation.

How one exercises moral powers or responds to obligations created by evildoing is important to one's character and relationships with others, even apart from deterrent or preventive effects of one's responses. Often perpetrators cannot repair harm or adequately compensate victims. Yet perpetrators and victims can communicate how they feel about what was done in ways that matter to those involved. Apologies, forgiveness or pardon

(or the choice not to), and such responses as guilt, shame, gratitude, and resentment indicate how perpetrators and victims value what was done and what was suffered. These responses reveal how the parties see themselves in relation to each other and to the deed, showing something of who they are and thereby something of their worthiness to associate with each other.

The shift from a focus on escape, avoidance, and prevention to a focus on living with and responding to evils is found in Schopenhauer's masterpiece *The World as Will and Representation* and his essay *On the Basis of Morality* as well as in many of Nietzsche's writings, from *The Birth of Tragedy* to *On the Genealogy of Morality*.[9] For Schopenhauer, salvation comes with a quieting of the will, the stoicism of ceasing to value what inevitably brings suffering. His solution is an escape after all, not from suffering or harm but from experiencing it as intolerable, an ingenious escape through a revaluation of suffering. For Schopenhauer, salvation lies not only beyond ethics but beyond the phenomenal world.

Nietzsche rejected Schopenhauer's nihilism regarding the world of sense but stole his ideas of revaluation and moving beyond evil. Like Schopenhauer he abandoned traditional Western religious hopes of an afterlife with its promised rewards and compensations. Although he also abandoned moral categories, especially that of evil, he departed from Schopenhauer by embracing finite embodiment, with its vulnerabilities. Retaining Schopenhauer's pessimism regarding the prevalence of pain and suffering, Nietzsche found that to sustain an optimistic attitude of affirming life, he had to reconceive and revalue pain and suffering as concomitants of the will to power and reconceive morality as rooted in a dangerous attempt at domination by those who were lacking in vitality.[10]

But what if life as such is not worthy of affirmation? A more moderate view than either Schopenhauer's or Nietzsche's is that some lives are worthy of affirmation, whereas others truly are not. Moral concepts may be necessary or at least helpful to ultimately sustainable affirmations of particular lives. If Schopenhauer and Nietzsche are right about the prevalence of suffering and harm, as compared with joy and happiness, then in order to find many of our lives worthy of affirmation, we may need or be greatly helped by moral rectifications. And we may want or need to be able to acknowledge moral remainders—imbalances, debts, or unexpiated wrongs that remain even after we have done what can be done to put things right.

RECTIFICATIONS, REMAINDERS, AND PUNISHMENT

Punishment, mercy, forgiveness, and sometimes paying or acknowledging debts of gratitude are common attempts at rectification. Rectifications aim to correct imbalances, redress wrongs, settle scores, put things right between us. In addition to punishment, resentment, praise, and blame, on which there is a large literature, the rectifications most explored by philosophers are forgiveness, mercy, and gratitude.[11] Other rectifications, such as amnesty, apology, compensation, pardon, repentance, restitution, and reward, can be considered in terms of their relationships to these.

Certain emotional residues have been referred to as "moral remainders" ever since Bernard Williams observed that "moral conflicts are neither systematically avoidable, nor all soluble without remainder."[12] Remainders are rectificatory feelings regarding what otherwise proves unrectifiable by our actions. Guilt, shame, remorse, regret, and often gratitude are remainders. These emotional residues acknowledge an unexpiated wrong, an unrectified shortcoming, or an unpaid debt. Remainders offer us a limited redemption in that they reveal our appreciation that all has not been made right, or that not all is as it should be (or would be, ideally) between us.

My use of the term "remainder" extends that of Williams in two ways. First, for Williams re-

mainders are negative, produced by wrongdoing. And yet moral transactions also leave positive remainders when not everything good can be reciprocated. We acknowledge positive remainders in unpayable debts of gratitude. Second, for Williams remainders are not our lingering emotional responses but unexpiated wrongs themselves, the things inevitably not made right. I find it natural, however, to think of emotional and attitudinal responses to such moral facts as also remainders. Thus, regret, remorse, and sometimes shame and guilt are moral remainders. Like the insoluble parts of moral conflicts, these responses remain, even after we have done what we can to set matters right. They are rectificatory responses of feeling rather than action. They reveal important values of an agent who has acted wrongly or is identified with a bad action or bad state of affairs, or those of a beneficiary unable to reciprocate benefits. Remainders can survive both rectificatory action and hard choices in complex situations where inevitably some are wronged or receive less than their due and the best one can do is seek the least undesirable outcome.

Aristotle said of shame, in explaining its status as a "quasi-virtue," that ideally occasions for it will not arise but that if they do, it is better to have shame than to be shameless.[13] He appears to have had no conception of guilt as distinct from shame. Today shame, remorse, and regret are most discussed in terms of their relationships to guilt, a paradigmatic emotional remainder. According to Nietzsche's genealogy of morality, guilt was not always a remainder but was originally an economic debt or, rather, a substitute for it in those who could not or would not pay the original debt.[14] Guilt today is ambiguous between a verdict (which can lead to imposition of a "debt" to be paid others in the form of punishment) and emotional self-devaluation or self-punishment. Self-devaluation or punishment can linger sometimes as long as the verdict, which is not canceled by paying the debt. This lingering guilt is a moral remainder.

Punishment is held by most theorists to presuppose, as a matter of definition, a finding of guilt (the verdict). It is also commonly thought to expiate guilt (the debt), to enable the offender to atone for the offense. As a response to evils, punishment is truly a mixed bag. Only partially rectificatory, it takes on the project of prevention as well. Commonly defended as retribution and ideally enabling offenders to pay their debts as well as enabling victims to let go of the past, punishment is also defended by appeal to deterrent effects. Contemporary philosophers endorse compromise theories of punishment that treat both retribution and deterrence as principles limiting the justifiable infliction and severity of penalties. According to compromise theories, providing a certain range of penalties for a kind of offense is not justifiable unless the penalties are neither more severe than needed for adequate deterrence nor more severe than would be proportionate to the harm of the offense or the offender's culpability or both.[15] Both preventive and rectificatory aims are compromised in attempts to reach a set of penalties acceptable from both points of view.

For domestic violence and atrocities involving mass murder, penalties satisfying the compromise theories tend to fall dramatically short of what offenders deserve. As I write, the federal government is getting ready to execute Timothy McVeigh for the 1996 Oklahoma City bombing and to show the execution to the families of survivors on closed-circuit television. How could viewing that execution possibly compare with having seen or heard the building blow up, without warning, with all the children in daycare and workers just settling in to begin their day? It is also unclear what, if any, deterrent effect punishment can have regarding these crimes, as the causes of such behavior are poorly understood. Domestic violence often appears motivated by rage; mass murder, by ideology. In neither case is a prudential appeal to self-interest likely to obtain much purchase. Yet in calculating deterrence, rational self-interest on the part of potential offenders is assumed. The upshot is a paradoxical state of affairs in which deeds seemingly deserving of the worst punishments are frequently not punished at all or are punished more lightly than other, less harmful crimes. Torture, for example, is seldom punished, and when it is, the penalties tend not to be commensurate with the offense and are usually inflicted on lesser ranking perpetrators rather than on those responsible for the orders. Nino observes that the same is true of war crimes generally. He discusses at length the case of Argentina, which eventually pardoned or issued amnesties to perpetrators of its "dirty war," including those who dropped many "disappeared" victims into the ocean from airplanes.[16] Blanket amnesties and pardons unaccompanied by other measures designed to acknowledge injustices and prevent perpetrators from profiting leave victims' needs and resentments unaddressed.

If resentment is, as Rawls argues, a natural response to others' unjustly being enriched at one's expense, punishment goes some way toward neutralizing resentment by acknowledging the injustice and removing at least some of the offender's profit from it.[17] Yet punishment does not go the whole distance required to neutralize resentment. For in removing or counterbalancing the offender's profit, punishment need not do anything to alleviate harm suffered by victims of the offense. Victims are sometimes surprised at how unsatisfying it can be simply to see the offender brought low, especially if the crime was atrocious and its harm enduring.

Historically, shunning and ostracism were alternatives to punishment. In ancient times, ostracism was practically a death sentence. Unlike shunning, punishment permits wrongdoers to pay for what are judged to be their wrongs and renew relationships or be readmitted to society without having to agree that they did what they were accused of, that they were to blame for it, or that it was wrong. Acknowledging fallibility in trials and judges, the practice of punishment allows the wrongfully convicted to maintain a certain integrity. To be consistent, punishment ought not to include penalties, such as death, that are entirely irreversible in cases of wrongful convictions.

The practice of shunning, in contrast to punishment, requires repentance as the price of reacceptance. It has the disadvantage of insufficiently acknowledging fallibility in accusers and judges. But in theory at least, shunning has the advantage of acknowledging the moral powers of victims, their powers to blame and forgive, as well as some obligations of perpetrators, such as the obligation to apologize. Punishment, in contrast, offers little room for the exercise of the moral powers of victims and inadequately acknowledges the obligations of perpetrators, such as the obligation to repair damage.

Yet considering how imprisonment and parole have (often not) worked in practice, the difference in real life between shunning and punishment is far from sharp. Former prisoners are often not regarded as having paid adequately for their offenses, and paroles may be contingent on prisoners' contrition, which presupposes admission of guilt. Both shunning and punishment with possible parole thereby encourage dishonesty in the wrongly accused or convicted, and both practices founder on major atrocities. No payment is adequate to mass murder, and mere contrition should not be sufficient for reacceptance while reparable damage remains. As a response to atrocities, legal punishment is highly incomplete. Yet monetary payments to victims of war rape notoriously risk adding insult to injury.

Increasingly, many find punishment insufficient to enable victims and perpetrators to move on, even when the offense is not an atrocity and when moving on is the outcome ultimately desired by all. Prisons tend to make prisoners worse.[18] They do not fit felons well for readmission to society. Only a fraction of the guilty are apprehended and convicted. There is unjust arbitrariness in who that fraction is. Many innocents are convicted. The death penalty becomes an atrocity itself when the innocent poor are foreseeably more likely to suffer it than the guilty rich.[19]

Even if penalties could be devised more nearly commensurate with evil deeds than convention

currently allows, as in the case of the fantasized penalties for war rape, many scruples would argue against their infliction. Minow notes that the adversarial trial system prioritizes winning cases rather than getting at truth.[20] This fact makes it even more important that punishments be revocable in cases of wrongful conviction. But revocable penalties tend to be less commensurate with evil deeds, the harm of which is commonly irrevocable, and so they tend to leave aspects of the evil unaddressed.

But even when there is no question of adequate retribution, compensation, or restitution, trials can still be held to get at the truth. Past deeds can be verified and publicized by truth commissions. Offenders can publicly apologize and reveal what they know. Their labors or assets can provide surviving victims with benefits to relieve health care costs incurred as a result of injury or trauma. Victims and rescuers can be memorialized in monuments and museums. Perpetrators and collaborators can be barred from future positions of social trust and honor. But there remain questions of individual response. How are perpetrators and victims to think, feel, and act in relation to one another after an atrocity, even if such measures are taken?

When a punishment is neither death nor life imprisonment without parole, criminal offenders, some guilty of evil deeds, are eventually released into society. Critics who would lengthen sentences and abolish parole to avoid or postpone this event do well to recall that most criminal offenders are never caught and that of those caught, only a fraction are convicted or plea-bargained into penalties. Most perpetrators remain free, publicly unidentified. Many evils are not criminal. Some that are exist in law enforcement, hidden for decades, as revealed by Conroy's inquiries into the practice in Chicago of police torture of those suspected of killing police.[21] We live already in a society in which victims and perpetrators share common spaces. The problem of paroling convicted offenders is probably not the risk of increasing crime but, rather, what sorts of accountability should be expected of freed felons. If living with ordinary freed felons is a challenge, how are victims to live with war criminals who have escaped, received amnesty, served limited sentences, or even been elected or appointed to influential social or political positions?

These questions can be heard to ask whether or how to exercise the moral powers of victims, if victims include all whose security is endangered by evil deeds. When blame evokes guilt and a sense of obligation, it further empowers victims, morally, who can then draw on that sense of obligation in the interests of rectification. If Joel Feinberg is right, however, that punishment has the expressive function of condemnation (a form of blame), Nietzsche also seems right that punishment (alone) does not make those who suffer it "better," but, rather, tames them, makes them more prudent, calculating, secretive, dishonest.[22] Punishment is, fortunately, not the only vehicle for expressing blame. Blame can be expressed also or instead in demands or requests for such things as confessions, apologies, restitution, and reparations.

The reciprocal goodwill that can be initiated by forgiveness and mercy—when they are perceived as issuing from strength rather than weakness—and by seeking accountability in the form of confessions, apologies, and reparations, rather than in the form of punishment, appears a promising substitute for the cycles of hostility that punishment alone seems unable to terminate. There is good reason to explore these responses as supplements, if not alternatives, to punishment for atrocities. The rest of this essay explores the ethics of forgiveness, treating forgiveness as a complex moral power of victims that can release perpetrators from troubling remainders.

FORGIVING EVILDOERS

Forgiveness is a liberal response to wrongdoers, as mercy is a liberal response to those whom we have the power or authority to harm or make suffer. There is no consensus among philosophers regarding the value of forgiveness or even the conditions of its possibility. Questions asked include when, what, and whom we can forgive (can we forgive the dead?), who "we" are (who is in a position to forgive?), what forgiveness does (for the forgiven, for the forgiver), what it implies (must punishment be remitted? must the parties reconcile?), when one ought to forgive, when forgiveness is deserved, optional, or, if ever, wrong (Is it wrong to forgive the unrepentant?). These questions become more difficult and more important when the wrong is an evil.

Paradigm forgiveness is interpersonal (forgiver and forgiven are different persons). It has several characteristic features, which may be broken down as follows. In ideal interpersonal forgiveness there is a change of heart in the offended party regarding the offender, which consists of (1) a renunciation of hostility out of (2) a charitable or compassionate concern for the (perceived) offender; (3) an acceptance of the offender's apology and contrition; (4) a remission of punishment, if any, over which the forgiver has authority or control; and (5) an offer to renew relationship (to "start over") or accept the other as a (possible) friend or associate. Offered as a gift, forgiveness may be accepted or rejected. If accepted, it may evoke gratitude and place the recipient under new obligations. Offenders who do not acknowledge wrongdoing, however, may perceive offers of forgiveness as arrogant and offensive.

For the offender who accepts it, forgiveness lifts or eases the burden of guilt, much as forgiving a debt relieves the debtor of an obligation to repay. This relief often seems to be its major point. Relief is apt to be especially valued by debtors who could never fully repay anyway, and for offenses for which reparations are inevitably inadequate. Forgiveness is thus a way of addressing negative remainders that perpetrators are unable to address adequately themselves. For the forgiver, forgiveness involves a renunciation of feelings of injury and hostility, although not of the judgment of having been wronged. To blame is to hold the offense against the offender, to hold the offender still accountable. The forgiver ceases to hold it against the offender but does not cease to regard it as an offense (or there is nothing to forgive). Thus, forgiveness frees both parties to move on. It is, as Hannah Arendt put it, one of our remedies for the irreversibility of the past.[23]

Although forgiveness cannot be compelled, one can be at fault in failing to offer it to those who deserve it or refusing to grant it when asked by those who have done all they can to atone. But one can also be at fault in offering it too freely or quickly. Because it is a power, those who are in other ways disempowered may be tempted to exercise it too freely. Victims of exploitation may be further exploited by oppressors who take advantage of this vulnerability by encouraging feelings of virtue for the readiness to forgive. Women often find themselves in this position in sexist relationships, where there is often much to forgive and women are praised for being "understanding." It may be more difficult to imagine being tempted to accept forgiveness when one ought not, when, for example, one has done no wrong to be forgiven (or is not sorry). Yet women also find themselves in this position, as when Helmer decides to forgive Nora in Ibsen's play "A Doll's House."[24] Inappropriately accepting forgiveness can appear to be (or be) the easiest way to move past conflicts in sexist relationships, although in Ibsen's play, Nora refuses Helmer's "forgiveness."

Some features of the paradigm case of forgiveness are not naturally or unproblematically present in less central instances of forgiveness. Nonparadigmatic cases include those in which the offender does not admit wrongdoing, or is no longer living, or in which the offender is living but not sorry, or is unwilling or unable to express contrition, or the offense is especially heinous, or the victim is no longer living, or both offender and forgiver are oneself, or both are groups (such as nations), rather than individual persons. Some evils, such as genocide, are perpetrated not just by individuals but by groups or corporate bodies—nations, governments, armies, political parties. Victims of genocide are also not just individuals but groups—national, religious, ethnic, or racial.[25] But what can it mean for a group to forgive a group?[26] A group does not literally have a heart to change, neither feelings of hostility toward nor the capacity for compassion for perpetrators. What can it mean for even an individual to forgive a group? Groups lack feelings of contrition, although they can apologize and make amends. Group forgiveness is not simply reducible to members of one group forgiving members of another. Often, members of the respective groups are strangers to one another. Often, those who apologize or accept an apology are not those who did or suffered the wrong but belong to a later generation.

Questions of the possibility and value of forgiving evildoers become more tractable when we return to the several features of the paradigm case and make the questions more specific. Some features of the paradigm are possible and appropriate in nonstandard cases when others are not. Regarding unrepentant offenders, for example, there comes a time when it is good for victims to let go of resentment, even if there is no basis for compassion for the offender. When the victim has no authority to punish, the victim's forgiveness may be irrelevant to the wisdom of punishment. When one or both parties are groups, one can apologize and the other accept the apology and reduce penalties or press for smaller reparations, even though groups lack feelings. Groups can be harmed, and they can act. They can hold (or cease to hold) a perpetrator accountable and in that way hold an injury against the perpetrator. This opens a space for the possibility of forgiveness between groups, although such forgiveness is not a paradigm case.

People can forgive at least what they can resent. We can resent agents and deeds, as well as the results of wrongful deeds, such as the unearned wealth of others or undeserved poverty. We can forgive agents for wrongful deeds or for unearned privileges. In an eighteenth century sermon on the topic, still widely cited, Bishop Joseph Butler presented the Christian duty to forgive as a duty simply to avoid excess resentment.[27] It is true that ordinary wrongs are resented by those wronged. But "resentful," "angry," and even "indignant" grossly underdescribe characteristic moral responses to atrocities. We resent insults, cheating, and unfairness. But evils leave us speechless, appalled, horrified, nauseated. When we do find speech, atrocities evoke rage and condemnation. Like resentment, condemnation is a form of blame. It holds perpetrators' deeds against them. Forgiveness is no antidote to speechlessness, horror, nausea, and the like. But it is a possible antidote to blame and thus to condemnation.

Arendt wrote that people "are unable to forgive what they cannot punish" and that "they are unable to punish what has turned out to be unforgivable."[28] It is plausible that one would not wish to punish what is unforgivable, if punishing allows the offender to pay for the crime and thereafter be done with it. But is it true that we cannot forgive what cannot be paid for? If, because atrocities are not adequately punishable, they are also unforgivable, then it appears that we can forgive only ordinary wrongs, not extraordinary ones. Yet it is for extraordinary wrongs that forgiveness seems most needed and valued. Here the burdens of guilt can weigh heaviest and threaten to spiral into future hostilities. Perhaps it is not that we *cannot* forgive extraordinary wrongs but that often we ought not, that forgiveness should be granted only slowly and with caution, depending on what else the perpetrator does (by way of confession, apology, reparation, regeneration), that conditions that make it morally an option are difficult to satisfy, often unlikely. Even if atrocity victims eventually forgive evildoers, perhaps perpetrators should be slow to forgive themselves. But this thought supposes that forgiving oneself makes sense.

Arendt said we are unable to forgive ourselves, that only others can forgive us.[29] Butler's view of forgiveness as a renunciation of resentment explains Arendt's observations. For we resent only others, not ourselves. Yet we blame, even condemn, ourselves. Self-forgiveness makes sense as a renunciation of self-condemnation or self-blame. Self-forgiveness may be hasty when others who could forgive us have not done so or have not had the opportunity. Still, when others' forgiveness is not enough, or if they are unable or unlikely to forgive us, perhaps we should sometimes forgive ourselves. Based on our having owned up, apologized, undertaken reparations, and so forth, we might cease to regard ourselves negatively. Conversely, some willingness to forgive oneself, even for evil deeds, may be needed to sustain motivation to fulfill our obligations and avoid repeating wrongs. Perpetrators need the sense that they are worth the effort that self-improvement will require. Some self-forgiveness may be requisite to that sense of self-worth.

Perhaps the truth behind Arendt's claim that we are unable to forgive ourselves is that forgiving oneself and being forgiven by another have different aims and accomplish different things. Another's forgiveness is a gift, which we can accept or reject. Self-forgiveness is an achievement (as is forgiving another). One has to overcome hostility toward and develop a certain compassion for oneself. Forgiveness by another may be requisite to a renewal of relationship. But some measure of self-forgiveness may be requisite to one's own self-respect.

Although, like Butler, Arendt emphasizes the liberality of forgiveness, presenting it as letting go of the deed, she also presents it as charitable, claiming that we forgive the offense for the sake of the offender.[30] That idea suggests an explanation for why some evil organizations, such as the National Socialist Party or the Ku Klux Klan, are unforgivable. Unlike people who create and belong to them, organizations as such need have no dignity or inherent worth. The worth of an organization is a function of the principles and procedures that define it. If it is defined by evil principles and inadequate procedures for change and evolves no better ones, there is nothing to redeem it. (Nations often do evolve. The principles and values at their core change as generations and regimes succeed one another.) Unlike the worth of organizations, that of individuals is not determined simply by principles they happen to espouse but is a function also of traits and capacities that preexist and outlast particular endorsements. These traits and capacities can form a basis for a charitable response, even toward those who espouse evil principles.

Forgiveness, as a move from defensive hostility to a more compassionate, pacific attitude, is a natural response to an offender's apology. And yet, when former perpetrators are rendered powerless or at least no longer dangerous, the victim's need for hostile defensiveness can disappear even without any apology or amends. A more limited change of heart or attitude in the victim may then be possible and desirable, based not on charity for the offender but on the victim's own needs or desires to move on. This limited change of heart may be better regarded as forgiveness of the offense than as forgiveness of the offender. It consists of renouncing the sense of injury and concomitant hostilities and redirecting one's emotional energies in other, more constructive ways that need have nothing to do with the offender. Thus, Howard McGary argues that rational self-interest offers African Americans powerful reason to move beyond resentment regarding histories of slavery. He advocates such forgiveness (letting go) for the sake of the forgiver rather than for the sake of the forgiven.[31] A reason to agree with him in considering this letting go to be genuinely forgiveness is that it truly is a change of heart, not just (or even) forgetting. It includes a renunciation of something that underlies blaming, namely, the sense of injury and the hostilities that go with it. Unlike paradigm forgiveness, it need not be offered or granted to the offender, and it is not undertaken for the offender's sake. But forgiveness need not be "all or nothing" with respect to the five features of the paradigm case. Renouncing hostilities and feelings of injury can leave open the question of whether reparations should be sought. For the harm remains, even if one ceases to resent it.[32]

Ought one to forgive an unrepentant evildoer?[33] Ordinarily, a truly repentant offender deserves forgiveness. Paradigmatically, either a repentant offender apologizes and asks forgiveness, which is then granted, or else a victim offers forgiveness, which is accepted and then followed by repentance. Yet some find that they can forgive the dead who never asked for it when they were alive and never even admitted wrongdoing. Although here we can no longer offer forgiveness to the offender, we can cease to resent the dead and choose to remember them for their good qualities. In part 2 of *The Metaphysics of Morals,* Kant wrote that we ought to defend the ancients "from all attacks, accusations, and disdain, insofar as this is possible," out of gratitude to them as our teachers, although he also cautioned against romantically attributing to them superiority of goodwill over that of our contemporaries.[34] One might also think a charitable attitude warranted toward the dead on the ground that they can no longer defend themselves. It might be replied that if the dead cannot defend themselves, they cannot be further hurt, either. Their reputations, however, can suffer. But unrepentant perpetrators' inability to defend themselves or their reputations may not be a sufficiently good reason to forgive them, if their deeds were atrocious and they subsequently took no responsibility when they could have. Forgiving the unrepentant, dead or alive, is probably best decided by the interests of the forgiver.

Yet the question is often raised how we can forgive the unrepentant without condoning their offenses, tacitly approving them, and thereby tacitly encouraging their emulation. The question is also raised what remains to be forgiven when an offender does repent and regenerate? Aurel Kolnai presented these two questions as a paradox of forgiveness.[35] Together they suggest that forgiveness is either inappropriate or else redundant. Without repentance, it seems inappropriate. With repentance, it seems redundant.

For criminal evils, condonation can be avoided by combining the change of heart with such other measures as supporting punishment, or punishment together with responses that Minow presents as lying "between vengeance and forgiveness": reparations, commemorative monuments to victims and rescuers or resistors, investigations into the truth, publicity of facts, support services for victims, and refusals to place offenders in positions of honor or social trust.[36] Insofar as these activities do not imply emotional hostility toward offenders, they are compatible with some measure of forgiveness of even the unregenerate. They offer public evidence that the offender is held responsible and the offense not condoned. As to Kolnai's second question, what remains to be forgiven even in a transformed offender is the offense, for which the offender, however changed, remains responsible. A transformed offender does not cease to be guilty of or accountable for past deeds. A transformed offender is apt to feel more guilty than before and be in greater need of forgiveness. Forgiving does not dissolve responsibility, even though it conveys a sympathetic response to the offender, which can alleviate guilt.

Does forgiveness imply a willingness to renew relations? Must forgiver and forgiven reconcile? Must friendship now be possible between them? The thought that willingness to reconcile is implied by forgiveness might explain some inclinations to find atrocities unforgivable. In their jointly authored collection of essays, *Mercy and Forgiveness,* Jean Hampton suggests that normally forgiveness does imply a willingness to renew relationship, whereas Jeffrie Murphy regards renewal as an open question that depends on many factors.[37] Hampton finds the strongest case for reconciliation in repentant offenders. But she admits that renewal may be a bad idea with offenders who remain dangerous, as in the case of battered intimates who rightly believe their abusers unregenerate. Her thought appears to be that reconciliation may simply provide the offender easy opportunities to repeat the offense. Yet there are more factors to consider. Did the forgiveness leave open questions of reparation?

Sometimes it is wise to reconcile only conditionally on the offender's living up to obligations of reparation or restitution. If an offender who is capable of restitution is unwilling, that unwillingness provides a reason not to reconcile. Like a failure to repent, it evidences lack of goodwill.

The wisdom of reconciliation depends partly on the reliability of the offender, not simply on the renunciation of hostilities by the forgiver. Repentance by itself is often insufficient to indicate reliability. Hampton's view seems to imply that renewal of relationships would be a normal course of events even with perpetrators of atrocities, provided that they were repentant and rightly judged no longer dangerous. And yet, for mass murder, repentance is grossly insufficient in that it neither addresses the harm to survivors, who may require continuing medical and psychological care, nor by itself does it imply regeneration. Repentance is a first step toward regeneration. But character change requires not just good intentions but time for the development of new habits of thought, feeling, and action. The offender can develop those new habits by interacting with others, not necessarily former victims. It is not as though the offender is prevented from regenerating if the forgiver chooses not to be a part of that process. Further, some perpetrators are no longer dangerous only because their circumstances have changed, not because they have changed. Reestablishment of some relations may be prudent or politic independently of forgiveness, to keep lines of communication open for one's own protection or the protection of others. But one can renounce hostility without becoming open to renewal of relations or friendly association. Even if ordinarily forgiveness does enable a renewal of relationships, some elements of forgiveness still free us to move on when we choose not to reconcile.

When punishment is at issue, the question often arises of whether forgiveness implies pardon or a penalty reduction or remission. Arendt called forgiveness and punishment alternative ways of trying to put an end to what is past.

But she also noted that they are not opposites.[38] Hastings Rashdall found forgiveness and punishment to be in tension, especially in the case of a divine punisher.[39] Others, including Murphy, take human forgiveness of criminal offenders as their paradigm and find no incompatibility between punishment and forgiveness, arguing that legal punishment need not manifest resentment but may be required out of social justice in the distribution of power or advantage and for deterrence to protect the innocent. In his famous 1939 essay "Punishment," J. D. Mabbott argued that legal punishment and forgiveness are tasks that fall to different parties and hence that there is no incompatibility.[40] Murphy's and Mabbott's arguments support the conclusion that forgiveness need not imply total absolution. It frees one only from the forgiver's resentment or blame, not from that of others or even from the guilt that justifies punishment. It is at most a limited redemption of the past's irreversibility.

Still, when we ought to support the punishment of forgiven evildoers, just as when we are wise not to reconcile with those we forgive, we may at the same time rightly regret the fact. Such regret is a "moral remainder." This example shows, incidentally, that regret does not presuppose that the regretter acted wrongly or was even responsible for what is regretted. Such regret is primarily a sense of loss. Here it is the loss of a permissible opportunity to engage in such otherwise natural manifestations of a forgiving attitude as remitting or not supporting punishment.

A difficult and interesting question is whether some deeds truly are unforgivably heinous, however deeply repented. This question seems multiply ambiguous. First, does "unforgivable" mean *"incapable* of being forgiven"? Or *"unworthy* of being forgiven"? If it means "incapable," the question of whether some deeds are unforgivably heinous is either the logical question of whether forgiveness is incoherent as a response to some offenses or else an empirical, psychological question about whether survivors of some evils are simply not able to renounce hostility

or offer others release. Of course, some victims die and others are so badly injured that they are physically unable to communicate. The empirical question of interest is about an otherwise competent survivor's ability or inability to undergo the requisite change of heart.

I find no logical incoherence in the idea of forgiving extremely heinous offenses, although the wisdom of doing so is a further question. And perhaps the harms suffered by some victims do in fact render them incapable of renouncing hostility, or of taking a charitable attitude toward the perpetrator, and so on. The ethically interesting question is, of course, whether some offenses are so heinous that they are unforgivable in the sense that they ought not to be forgiven. Again, the question becomes more manageable if we look individually at the elements of forgiveness in a paradigm case and consider which, if any, are unwise in the case of especially heinous offenses.

Are some offenses so heinous that victims and their sympathizers should never renounce hostility? That they should not take a charitable or compassionate attitude toward the perpetrator? That they should reject the perpetrator's contrition, apologies, repentance, reparations? That they should support no mitigation of punishment? That they should refuse ever to renew relations? Some of these questions seem answerable independently of others. Even if the offender is unworthy of compassion and deserves to be regarded ever after with distrust, it may still be advisable for victims to let go, eventually, of hostility. And as Mabbott and Murphy saw, the advisability of victims' letting go does not imply the advisability of the state's remitting punishment. Nor, for reasons just given, does it imply the advisability of reconciliation.

Still, some elements of paradigmatic forgiveness are interconnected with others. Accepting reparations, for example, is a way of renewing relations. If a renewal of relations is permanently unacceptable, victims may be justified in refusing to accept perpetrators' attempts at reparation. Such a refusal, however, would not commit them to never renouncing hostilities or never taking a charitable or compassionate attitude toward the perpetrators. Thus, there may be no simple answer to whether some atrocities are unforgivably heinous. It may be that some breaches of trust or goodwill can never be mended, that nothing the offender could do would be sufficient to provide others with good evidence of adequate reliability. If so, some atrocities are so heinous that some elements of forgiveness are wisely withheld permanently from some of its perpetrators.

The atrocities of slavery and genocide are popular candidates for unforgivable evils. Yet both slavery and genocide are practices that involve many individual perpetrators, corporate bodies, and organizations acting in a variety of circumstances, playing different roles, doing things at different times, some things much more serious than others, some deeds far more pivotal than others. Neither slavery nor genocide is itself one deed. Neither is perpetrated by one agent or even by one body of agents. Not surprisingly, survivors and their descendants find the issues complex. Some, such as Simon Wiesenthal, have published their reflections on specific episodes.

WIESENTHAL'S DILEMMAS

In his memoir *The Sunflower* Simon Wiesenthal reflects upon a dilemma of forgiveness that he confronted as a concentration camp prisoner during the Holocaust.[41] He was asked for forgiveness by a youthful dying Nazi soldier, who identified himself simply as Karl and who confessed to having taken part in a merciless mass slaughter of Jews. Karl explained that shortly after this atrocity, he incurred his current fatal wounds in battle when he flashed back to the deed and was unable to fire his rifle in self-defense. That was a year before. He was near the end.

Wiesenthal had been on work detail and had no idea what he was about to confront when a nurse (at Karl's request) had brought him, a randomly chosen Jew, to hear Karl's confession and receive his deathbed plea for forgiveness. It was

dangerous to leave the work detail and follow the nurse, as she had no authority over him, and if he were caught, not only would his own life be jeopardized but the lives of his fellow prisoners could be jeopardized as well. Still, there was the possibility that she might be leading him to hidden food, which could save lives. So he followed.

The nurse led Wiesenthal to a room where Karl was lying on a table, bandaged head to foot, with holes for mouth and nostrils. As Karl began to speak, Wiesenthal listened. He retrieved a letter from Karl's mother when it fell to the floor and brushed a fly from Karl's head. He silently heard Karl's anguish and repentance but also asked himself why a Jew should have to listen to this, as he was reminded vividly of atrocities he had witnessed and of what his family had suffered. Yet he did not withdraw his hand when Karl took it at one point to stay him from leaving. But finally, when Karl had finished, Wiesenthal got up and left without having spoken a word.

Karl died the next day, and Wiesenthal refused the package of his belongings which the nurse said Karl left him. After the war, remembering the address on the fallen letter, he visited Karl's widowed mother and gained an audience with her by pretending to have been Karl's friend. Her reminiscences confirmed Karl's account of his early years, which was evidence of his truthfulness. Wiesenthal then decided not to reveal Karl's murderous deed. He thereby granted one of Karl's dying wishes—that his mother be spared disillusionment about her son's honor.

The decision not to disillusion Karl's mother, like Wiesenthal's demeanor during the confession, appears compassionate. It appears to reciprocate Karl's final efforts at good will. Yet this reciprocity was not offered to Karl but at most to his memory. It preserved Karl's good image with his mother. All that remained of Karl at that point was his image, the memories. Karl himself was forever unaware of Wiesenthal's feelings and of most of Wiesenthal's actions.

Did Wiesenthal's compassionate conduct really demonstrate forgiveness? Perhaps no simple yes or no answer quite does justice to the case. Drawing on elements of paradigm forgiveness, we might say that Wiesenthal's conduct both at the confession and over the years demonstrates at most a very limited forgiveness. It exhibits some elements: compassion, a willingness to listen to apology and contrition, a granting of one of Karl's dying wishes. Yet other elements are unclear or absent. It is not clear that Wiesenthal accepted the apology he heard, although he may have done so eventually, during the visit to Karl's mother. Nor is it clear that he sympathized with Karl's remorse during the confession, although he was compassionate, at least decent, about Karl's helplessness. Most readers take Wiesenthal's silence at Karl's bedside as a refusal of forgiveness. Wiesenthal himself seems to take it that way. By not speaking, he did not offer Karl the gift of forgiveness. But what complex feelings lay in Wiesenthal's heart? Would he have been wrong to forgive a deed done to others? Readers of the memoir raised these questions.

Wiesenthal circulated his memoir to philosophers, rabbis, priests, ministers, novelists, and other prominent thinkers, soliciting their reflections about what he did, what they might have done in his place, what it would or would not have been right to do. Two overlapping sets of responses have been published as symposia, in two editions, with Wiesenthal's memoir.[42] Together, the memoir and symposia touch on most of the ethical and philosophical questions that have been asked about forgiveness.

Many of Wiesenthal's symposiasts thought he would have been wrong to forgive. They argued that it would be presumptuous to forgive in the name of those murdered or to forgive an offense done an entire group to which one belongs, that doing so would usurp others' prerogatives, even though the others did not survive to exercise those prerogatives. A few thought he should have spoken some comforting words or even words of forgiveness in response to Karl's dying wish. A few others thought that if they had been in Wiesenthal's place, they would have strangled Karl in his bed. Some thought that although Wiesenthal would not have been wrong to forgive, neither was he wrong not to.

We can never know how Karl's character would have developed had he miraculously survived. Would he have publicly renounced or denounced Nazism? Joined a resistance movement? Continued to risk his life for what he thought was right? Would he have become more concerned about others' suffering and less absorbed in his own needs for absolution? Or would he have become hardened to atrocities? Would he have rationalized that he had no power to change things and eventually refused to continue reflecting on the moral questions? Answers to such questions are relevant to the moral value of offering him whatever forgiveness was possible. They become especially important given that he was only twenty-one and had fallen under the spell of Nazism as a child in the Hitler Youth. Deathbed confessions are a pale substitute for character change, which requires continuing activity and development, not just insight or right intentions. But, of course, all that Karl was able to offer, given his previous inexperienced and disastrous choices, was that pale substitute.

Returning to the analysis of paradigm forgiveness, we may be able to clarify what was possible and what was at stake in the dilemmas confronting Wiesenthal. That analysis suggests that he confronted not one question but several. To review, in paradigm forgiveness, there is a change of heart based on (1) a renunciation of hostility and (2) undertaken out of compassion for the offender, which involves (3) an acceptance of the offender's apology and contrition, (4) remission of punishment, if any, over which the forgiver has control, and (5) a willingness to reconcile or be open to establishing friendly relations. Wiesenthal's conduct suggests that he chose compassion over hostility. But that does not imply acceptance of the apology and contrition. Remission of punishment and reconciliation may at first seem inapplicable in this case. Yet the facts are not so simple.

Regarding the arrogance of forgiving offenses committed against others, three kinds of observations seem in order. The first is that one need not be a victim in order to blame or condemn. If one element of forgiveness is renunciation of not only resentment but also blame or condemnation, there seems no logical reason why that element should be available only to victims. Second, in renouncing one's own blaming or condemning attitudes, one need not presume to speak for or in the name of others. One person's forgiveness is compatible with others' refusals. Insofar as forgiveness releases the forgiven from obligations, it releases only from obligations to the forgiver, not from obligations to others. But third, and perhaps more important, it is not clear that Wiesenthal was not a victim. Atrocities done to Jews simply because they are Jews endanger all Jews. Karl had the nurse bring him specifically "a Jew," not any particular Jew—apparently any Jew would do. The atrocity in which Karl participated was inflicted on its victims simply because they were Jews, not because of anything they had done or even might do in the future. And so it seems inaccurate to regard the offense as having been done only to third parties. Karl himself appears not to have regarded it that way. Nor does Wiesenthal.

Officially no punishment was in question. And yet what Karl suffered from his mortal injuries, in consequence of his remorse, could be regarded as something like a substitute for punishment, a piece of poetic justice in which the crime backfires. Wiesenthal could offer no relief from the injuries, nor was he asked to do so. He might have offered Karl a certain peace of mind by speaking words of comfort, and that he refused to do. But that refusal was not tantamount to imposing punishment. It did nothing to worsen Karl's injuries. It was simply a refusal to alleviate completely Karl's burdens of guilt. Still, just by listening to Karl's confession and contrition, Wiesenthal did relieve some of that burden. He offered Karl some relief just by staying, even though he wanted to leave.

The reconciliation element of forgiveness may appear moot in this case, as Karl did not live. Yet in refusing the package of Karl's belongings, Wiesenthal does appear to have refused reconciliation, or to have come as close as one could come to doing so under the circumstances. That package would have been a connection to Karl, and he refused that connection. He did not permanently reject all connections, however, because he followed up later by visiting Karl's mother to check out Karl's history. That visit was a voluntarily renewed connection with what remained of Karl, namely the memories that his mother was able to share, although it was not obviously undertaken for Karl's sake.

Did Wiesenthal make wise choices? It seems to me that he was appropriately cautious and that he was respectful, even generous. He did not rush to judgment either for or against, and in his conduct toward Karl, his demeanor was and continues to be exemplary. The only real point at which I could wish he had chosen differently—as he himself also seemed to wish, by the conclusion of his memoir—is the point at which he decided not to tell the mother the truth about how he met Karl, including the atrocity confession. The most charitable reading of that decision is that it was undertaken out of respect for Karl's dying wish that his mother never know of his participation in an atrocity. Wiesenthal realized, from listening to the mother, that Karl had been honest with him, and he apparently concluded that Karl's remorse was genuine. He may have excused or forgiven Karl's preoccupation, as a result of youthful naivete, with his own moral neediness, which led him to inflict his conscience on a concentration camp victim and further risk the life of that prisoner as well as those of other prisoners in order to do so.

But Karl's mother said to Wiesenthal, upon realizing that her visitor was Jewish, that she and her non-Jewish neighbors were not responsible for what was done to the Jews during the war and that her son was such a good person that he would never have participated in such things. She deserved to be disillusioned about those beliefs, regardless of what Karl deserved. Since she was alive, whereas he was not, I would weight this point more heavily. If, as it appears, one element of Wiesenthal's decision not to tell was a compassionate desire to spare the mother the pain of a spoiled memory of her son, since the good memory of her son seemed the most precious thing she had left after the war, it is difficult not to regard that aspect of his choice as misguided generosity. Women can survive the pain of knowing what their children have done and can sometimes grow from it. Those who said "we were not responsible" because "we didn't know," when they ignored what was happening around them and did not try to find out, had some moral growing to do. Wiesenthal might have taken Karl's mother more seriously by challenging her image of her son, and thereby her image of what "good" people are capable of doing, rather than leaving her with her comforting illusions and self-deceptions.

The point is not that Karl's mother's moral growth was Wiesenthal's responsibility. He had no obligation to visit her in the first place. But, paradoxically, he seemed almost more ready to forgive the mother, who apparently had no remorse, than the son who had. For in the former case, keeping silent is what forgiveness seemed to require, whereas in the latter, it would have been speaking up. Yet Wiesenthal seems uneasy about the element of silence in both instances.

The Sunflower is not just about forgiveness. It is at the same time about silence and witnessing. The sunflowers of the title were planted each on a soldier's grave in a cemetery that Wiesenthal and other prisoners passed on their way to work. They struck him as like silent periscopes, continuing vital connections of the dead to the world of the living. There were no markers for Jews cremated or buried in mass graves. Wiesenthal's memoir itself is like a sunflower for Jews who did not survive, a vital connection between the dead and the living from one who miraculously survived to bear witness, to be a periscope for those who

cannot bear witness themselves. But unlike the sunflowers, the memoir speaks.

During an early flashback in the memoir, Wiesenthal recalls the "day without Jews" at his high school, when hooligans physically assaulted Jewish students to prevent them from taking their examinations. Only about 20 percent of students, he estimated, actually participated in the violence. But they could not have gotten away with it so handily if the rest of the non-Jewish students had not been silent.

When *Die Sonnenblume* was first published in 1969 in France, there had already been popular calls for letting bygones be bygones, with respect to World War II, when not that much had yet been done in the way of public rememberings of atrocities. Wiesenthal's memoir helped to break silence regarding the Holocaust. The question of whether and when to speak, whether and when to say anything at all, is as much at issue as the question of forgiveness in Wiesenthal's concluding questions about what he should have done. Throughout his encounter with Karl, he spoke not a word, although readers might not catch that immediately, since he carried on a busy interior monologue the whole time. But he writes in conclusion:

> Well, I kept silent when a young Nazi on his deathbed begged me to be his confessor. And later when I met his mother I again kept silent rather than shatter her illusions about her dead son's inherent goodness. And how many bystanders kept silent as they watched Jewish men, women, and children being led to the slaughterhouses of Europe? There are many kinds of silence, Indeed it can be more eloquent than words. . . . Was my silence at the bedside of the dying Nazi right or wrong? This is a profound moral question.[43]

Forgiveness breaks silence when it is offered to another, as does the refusal of forgiveness when that is given voice. Unexpressed questioning or changes of heart, like unexpressed dissent from evil, risks nothing and achieves nothing. It allows others to do as they will. What is difficult but has the potential to bring change is reaching out, taking risks, making explicit the complexities in one's heart. Karl was one German citizen who finally broke silence, in however limited a way, regarding major atrocities of his day and his role in them. Karl must have had a sunflower on his German soldier's grave. But Wiesenthal's memoir bears witness to Karl's truth also. It is at the same time Wiesenthal's own personal confession, reaching out to many hearts by breaking silence about the complexities in his own.

NOTES

1. See *Hate Crimes: Confronting Violence Against Lesbians and Gay Men,* ed. Gregory M. Herek and Kevin T. Berrill (Newbury Park, Calif.: Sage, 1992), and the film *Boys Don't Cry.*

2. For a graphic contemporary account of surviving poverty that rivals those of Charles Dickens, see Frank McCourt, *Angela's Ashes* (New York: Scribner, 1996). For tables on life expectancy and other interesting statistics in developing countries, see Martha Nussbaum's introduction to *Women, Culture, and Development: A Study of Human Capabilities,* ed. Nussbaum and Jonathan Glover (Oxford: Clarendon Press, 1995), pp. 16–34.

3. John Stuart Mill, *The Philosophy of John Stuart Mill: Ethical, Political and Religious,* ed. Marshall Cohen (New York: Modern Library, 1961), p. 340.

4. Norman S. Care, *Living with One's Past: Personal Fates and Moral Pain* (Philadelphia: Temple University Press, 1996).

5. Bernard Williams, "Ethical Consistency," in Williams, *Problems of the Self: Philosophical Papers, 1956–72* (Cambridge: Cambridge University Press, 1973), pp. 166–86.

6. Martha Minow, *Between Vengeance and Forgiveness: Facing History After Genocide and Mass Violence* (Boston: Beacon, 1998); Carlos Santiago Nino, *Radical Evil on Trial* (New Haven: Yale University Press, 1996).

7. Nino, *Radical Evil,* p. 3.

8. John Kekes, *Facing Evil* (Princeton: Princeton University Press, 1990), esp. pp. 182–237.

9 Arthur Schopenhauer, *The World as Will and Representation,* 2 vols., trans. E. F. J. Payne

(New York: Dover, 1969), and *On the Basis of Morality,* trans. E. F. J. Payne (Indianapolis: Bobbs-Merrill, 1965). Most of Nietzsche's best-known books are collected in two volumes, both translated and edited by Walter Kaufmann: *The Portable Nietzsche* (New York: Penguin, 1976) and *Basic Writings of Nietzsche* (New York: Modern Library, 1992). For his *On the Genealogy of Morality: A Polemic,* I prefer the translation of Maudemarie Clark and Alan J. Swenson (Indianapolis: Hackett, 1998).

10. For more on the theme of Nietzsche's revaluation of suffering, see Ivan Soll, "Nietzsche on Cruelty, Asceticism, and the Failure of Hedonism" in *Nietzsche, Genealogy, Morality: Essays on Nietzsche's On the Genealogy of Morals,* ed. Richard Schacht (Berkeley: University of California Press, 1994), pp. 168–92.

11. On punishment, see Gertrude Ezorsky, ed., *Philosophical Perspectives on Punishment* (Albany: State University of New York Press, 1972): H. D. Acton, ed., *The Philosophy of Punishment* (New York: St. Martin's, 1969); and A. C. Ewing, *The Morality of Punishment with Suggestions for a General Theory of Ethics* (London: 1929; reprint Montclair, N.J.: Patterson Smith, 1970). On resentment, in addition to Nietzsche, *On the Genealogy of Morality,* see Max Scheler, *Ressentiment,* trans. William W. Holdheim (New York: Schocken, 1972), and P. F. Strawson, "Freedom and Resentment," in Strawson, *Freedom and Resentment and Other Essays* (London: Methuen and Co., 1974), pp. 1–25. On praise and blame, see Joel Feinberg, "Justice and Personal Desert," in Feinberg, *Doing and Deserving* (Princeton: Princeton University Press, 1970), and Richard B. Brandt, *Ethical Theory: Problems of Normative and Critical Ethics* (Englewood Cliffs, N.J.: Prentice-Hall, 1959), or William K. Frankena, *Ethics,* 2d ed. (Englewood Cliffs, N.J.: Prentice-Hall, 1973), pp. 62–78. On forgiveness, see Simon Wiesenthal, *The Sunflower: On the Possibilities and Limits of Forgiveness,* rev. and exp., with symposium ed. Harry James Cargas and Bonny V. Fetterman (New York: Schocken, 1997); Joram Graf Haber, *Forgiveness* (Savage, Md.: Rowman and Littlefield, 1991); Aurel Kolnai, "Forgiveness," in Kolnai, *Ethics, Value, and Reality: Selected Papers of*

Aurel Kolnai (Indianapolis: Hackett, 1978), pp. 210–24; and Cheshire Calhoun, "Changing One's Heart," *Ethics* 103 (Oct. 1992): 76–96. On mercy, see Alwynne Smart, "Mercy," in Acton, *The Philosophy of Punishment;* Claudia Card, "On Mercy," *Philosophical Review* 81, 2 (April 1972): 182–207; and Martha Nussbaum, "Equity and Mercy," *Philosophy and Public Affairs* 22, 2 (Spring 1993): 83–125. On gratitude, see Terrence McConnell, *Gratitude* (Philadelphia: Temple University Press, 1993), and Card, "Gratitude and Obligation," *American Philosophical Quarterly* 25, 2 (April 1988): 25–37.

12. Williams, "Ethical Consistency," p. 179.

13. Aristotle, *The Nicomachean Ethics,* trans. David Ross (New York: Oxford University Press, 1925), pp. 104–105 (4:9; 1126b12–35).

14. Nietzsche, *On the Genealogy of Morality,* p. 39. Norman O. Brown argues that Nietzsche got it backward, that economic debts are a form taken by guilt. See Brown, *Life Against Death: The Psychoanalytic Meaning of History* (New York: Vintage, 1959), p. 268.

15. See, e.g., Claudia Card, "Retributive Penal Liability," *American Philosophical Quarterly Monograph 7: Studies in Ethics* (Oxford: Blackwell, 1973), pp. 17–35; also, H. L. A. Hart, "Prolegomena to the Principles of Punishment," in Hart, *Punishment and Responsibility: Essays in the Philosophy of Law* (Oxford: Clarendon Press, 1968), pp. 1–27, and Kurt Baier, "Is Punishment Retributive?" *Analysis* 4 (1952): 25–32.

16. Nino, *Radical Evil,* pp. 45–104.

17. John Rawls, "The Sense of Justice," *Philosophical Review 72* (1963): 281–305.

18. Prisons tend to make guards worse, too. See Ted Conover, *Newjack: Guarding Sing Sing* (New York: Random House, 2000). Conover, an investigative journalist, trained and served for a year as a guard in Sing Sing in order to be able to write about conditions there.

19. See Barry Scheck, Peter Neufeld, and Jim Dwyer, *Actual Innocence: Five Days to Execution, and Other Dispatches from the Wrongly Convicted* (New York: Doubleday, 2000), and Edwin M. Borchard, *Convicting the Innocent: Errors of Criminal Justice* (New Haven: Yale University Press, 1932).

20. Minow, *Between Vengeance and Forgiveness,* pp. 25–90.

21. John Conroy, *Unspeakable Acts, Ordinary People: The Dynamics of Torture* (New York: Knopf, 2000), pp. 225–41.

22. Joel Feinberg, "The Expressive Function of Punishment," in Feinberg, *Doing and Deserving,* pp. 95–118; Nietzsche, *On the Genealogy of Morality,* p. 56.

23. Hannah Arendt, *The Human Condition* (Chicago: University of Chicago Press, 1958), pp. 236–43.

24. Henrik Ibsen, *Eleven Plays of Henrik Ibsen* (New York: Modern Library, 1935), p. 83. Introduction by H. L. Mencken.

25. How to define "genocide" is a matter of controversy, and one of the chief subjects of controversy is which groups to include. See *Genocide: Analyses and Case Studies,* ed. Frank Chalk and Kurt Jonassohn (New Haven: Yale University Press, 1990).

26. On the status of groups as ethical agents and bearers of interests and rights, see Larry May, *The Morality of Groups: Collective Responsibility, Group-Based Harm, and Corporate Rights* (Notre Dame, Ind.: University of Notre Dame, 1987).

27. Bishop Joseph Butler, *Fifteen Sermons Preached at Rolls Chapel* (2d. ed. 1729; reprint, London: G. Belland Sons, 1967). See Sermons 8–9 on resentment and forgiveness of injuries.

28. Arendt, *The Human Condition,* p. 241.

29. Ibid., p. 243.

30. Ibid., p. 241.

31. Howard McGary, "Forgiveness and Slavery," in McGary and Bill Lawson, *Between Slavery and Freedom: Philosophy and American Slavery* (Bloomington: Indiana University Press, 1992), pp. 90–112.

32. For an interesting discussion of the reparations issue for African Americans in relation to slavery, see Randall Robinson, *The Debt: What America Owes to Blacks* (New York: Dutton, 2000).

33. In *Forgiveness: A Philosophical Study* (Lanham, Md.: Rowman and Littlefield, 1991), Joram Graf Haber defends the view that "the only acceptable reason to forgive a wrongdoer is that the wrongdoer has repented the wrong she did—has had a change of heart," p. 90.

34. Immanuel Kant, *Practical Philosophy,* trans. Mary Gregor (Cambridge: Cambridge University Press, 1996), p. 574.
35. Aurel Kolnai, "Forgiveness," 215–17.
36. See Minow, *Between Vengeance and Forgiveness,* p. 23 for a similar list of responses to atrocities that fall between vengeance and forgiveness.
37. Jeffrie G. Murphy and Jean Hampton. *Mercy and Forgiveness* (Cambridge: Cambridge University Press, 1988).

38. Arendt, *The Human Condition,* p. 241.
39. Hastings Rashdall, *Theory of Good and Evil: A Treatise* on *Moral Philosophy,* 2d ed. (London: Humphrey Milford, 1924) 1: 306–12.
40. J. D. Mabbott, "Punishment," *Mind* n. s. 48 (1939): 152–67.
41. Wiesenthal, *The Sunflower,* pp. 3–98.
42. The first symposium appeared in the 1976 edition published by Schocken; the second in the 1997 edition.
43. Wiesenthal, *The Sunflower,* p. 97.

FOR FURTHER READING

Baier, Annette C. *Moral Prejudices: Essays on Ethics.* Cambridge, MA: Harvard University Press, 1994.

Bell, Linda. *Rethinking Ethics in the Midst of Violence: A Feminist Approach to Freedom.* Landham, MD: Roman and Littlefield, 1993.

Benhabib, Seyla. *Situating the Self: Gender, Community, and Postmodernism in Contemporary Ethics.* New York: Routledge, 1992.

Calhoun, Chesire. "Justice, Care, Gender Bias. *Journal of Philosophy* 85 (September 1988): 451–63.

Card, Claudia, ed. *Feminist Ethics.* Lawrence: University of Kansas, 1991.

Card, Claudia. *The Atrocity Paradigm: A Theory of Evil.* New York: Oxford University Press, 2002.

Cuomo, Chris. *Feminism and Ecological Communities: An Ethic of Flourishing.* New York: Routledge Press, 1998.

Daly, Mary. *Gyn/Ecology: The Metaethics of Radical Feminism.* Boston: Beacon, 1978.

Friedman, Marilyn. "Feminism and Modern Friendship: Dislocating Communities." *Ethics* 99 (1989): 275–90.

Gilligan, Carol. *In a Different Voice: Psychological Theory and Women's Development.* Cambridge, MA: Harvard University Press, 1982.

Held, Virginia. *Feminist Morality: Transforming Culture, Society, and Politics.* Chicago: The University of Chicago Press, 1993.

Held, Virginia, ed. *Justice and Care: Essential Readings in Feminist Ethics.* Boulder: Westview Press, 1995.

Hoagland, Sarah Lucia. *Lesbian Ethics: Toward New Value.* Palo Alto, CA: Institute of Lesbian Studies, 1988.

Kittay, E., and D. Meyers, eds. *Women and Moral Theory.* Savage, MD: Rowman and Littlefield, 1987.

May, Larry. *Masculinity and Morality.* Ithaca, NY: Cornell University Press, 1998.

Morgan, Kathryn Pauly. "Women and Moral Madness." *Canadian Journal of Philosophy* 13 (1987): 201–26.

Noddings, Nel. *Caring: A Feminine Approach to Ethics and Moral Education.* Berkeley: University of California Press, 1984.

Oliver, Kelly, ed. *Ethics, Politics, and Difference in Julia Kristeva's Writings.* New York: Routledge, 1993.

Ruddick, Sarah. *Maternal Thinking: Toward a Politics of Peace.* New York: Ballantine Books, 1989.

Tessman, Lisa. *Burdened Virtues: Virtue Ethics for Liberatory Struggles.* New York: Oxford University Press, 2005.

Tong, Rosemarie. *Feminine and Feminist Ethics.* Belmont, CA: Wadsworth, 1993.

Toronto, Joan. "Beyond Gender Difference to a Theory of Care." *Signs* 12 (1987): 644–63.

Walker, Margaret Urban. *Moral Understandings: A Feminist Study in Ethics.* New York: Routledge, 1998.

Wollstonecraft, Mary. *A Vindication of the Rights of Woman.* New York: Dover, 1792/1988.

MEDIA RESOURCES

A Jury of Her Peers. VHS. Produced by Sally Heckel (US, 1980). A powerful adaptation of Susan Glaspell's 1917 short story "A Jury of Her Peers." On a desolate American farm in the early 1900s, a farmer is found murdered in his sleep and his wife is jailed as the prime suspect. Glaspell presents a riveting tale of revenge, justice, and women's shared experience. The film illustrates Gilligan's claim that men and women appear to experience, know, and conceptualize the world differently. A good film to watch before reading the Gilligan essay. Available: Women Make Movies, http://www.wmm.com/, or 1–800–343–5540.

Beyond Good & Evil: Children, Media & Violent Times. VHS/DVD. Co-produced and written by Chyng Sun, co-produced and directed by Miguel Picker (US, 2003). The belief that "good triumphs over evil" resonates deeply in our psyche through religious, cultural, and political discourses. This video examines how the "good and evil" rhetoric, in both the entertainment and the news media, has helped children to dehumanize enemies, justify their killing, and treat the suffering of innocent civilians as necessary sacrifice. An interesting follow-up to Claudia Card's piece in this section. Available through the Media Education Foundation: 1–800–897–0089 or http://www.mediaed.org/index_html.

Carol Gilligan "Voice and Relationship: Rethinking the Foundation of Ethics." Ethics across the Curriculum, University of San Diego, 30 January, 1997. Real Time video clip. Available: http://ethics.sandiego.edu/video/Gilligan/Lecture/Voice_and_Relationship.html.

Crash. DVD. Story by Paul Haggis, screenplay by Paul Haggis and Bobby Moresco, directed by Paul Haggis (US, 2004). A car accident brings together a group of strangers in Los Angeles. This feature film takes a provocative, unflinching look at the complexities of racial tolerance and ethical life in contemporary America. Available: http://www.lgf.com/video/index.php.

CHAPTER 8

FEMINIST POLITICAL PHILOSOPHIES

Political philosophy seeks to apply moral concepts to the social sphere to articulate a vision of the good society. The normative approach of the discipline is uncontroversial: It explores questions about how people *should* govern themselves, how political systems *ought* to work, and offers standards by which to analyze and judge these institutions and organizations. Although the two are sometimes used interchangeably, most scholars distinguish between "political philosophy" and the broader, more descriptive, empirical field of "political science," which investigates how political systems actually work. Sometimes the more ambiguous term "political theory" is used to encompass both aspects. Since a great deal of feminist work emphasizes women's lived experiences and the documentation of inequalities, feminist political philosophy can have a distinctly applied bent.

Women have been historically excluded from politics, so it is not surprising that feminist philosophers have made considerable effort to argue for women's political enfranchisement and offer alternative starting points for political inquiry. Mary Wollstonecraft's *Vindication of the Rights of Woman* (1795), John Stuart Mill and Harriet Taylor's *The Subjection of Women* (1869), Carol Pateman's *The Sexual Contract* (1988), Susan Moller Okin's *Justice, Gender and the Family* (1989), and Catherine MacKinnon's *Toward a Feminist Theory of the State* (1989) are a few examples of works written in response to women's exclusion from politics. Feminist critical projects like these work to address the political dimensions of family, sex, marriage, housework, and childrearing in light of traditional approaches to political philosophy.

"The personal is political," a rallying cry of second wave feminists, pushed political thinkers to challenge the private/public distinction, which defined politics in terms of civic life. That idea taught many to see politics (power) in everyday acts such as housework, sexual expression, reproductive choices, caring labor, and the family. Women rapidly began to understand that what they thought were their own individual problems were really shared artifacts and expressions of structural inequalities. The challenge to the traditional public/private dichotomy showed how private spheres are saturated with public meaning, and how gender-role expectations are reinscribed in public policies.

The readings in this section move in emphasis from private to public. Many, but certainly not all, feminist approaches to politics begin with lines of inquiry that politicize the private sphere by either challenging what have been called "male-stream" concepts and values (e.g., autonomy) or by turning a political lens on experiences that traditional approaches have largely ignored (e.g., marriage and the family wage). Attention to the ways women's experiences have challenged basic political concepts (e.g., fairness) raise further questions about whether differences of race, ability, sexual orientation, or ethnicity might be used as political resources for generating unique approaches to particular political topics such as democracy, equality, and war.

Autonomy is a primary value in liberal political theory. Yet feminists have suggested that personal autonomy, represented by a masculine-style preoccupation with self-sufficiency and self-realization, is inhospitable to women. Traditional liberal accounts of autonomy downplay the social relationships and personal connections upon which women have historically depended for the survival of themselves and their dependents. In "Autonomy, Social Disruption, and Women," Marilyn Friedman argues that the Western cultural understanding of autonomy, as something to be achieved by erecting a wall of rights and privileges between yourself and those around you, is distorted and needs to be redefined if it is to be relevant to women. She suggests that new paradigms of autonomy should involve female protagonists, avoid glorified, so-called "masculine traits" (i.e., reason, independence, and outspokenness) and foreground the importance of social relationships. Feminists ought to cautiously embrace a relational approach to autonomy that understands persons as fundamentally social beings who develop autonomy through social interactions.

All autonomous persons are ultimately dependent persons who require care. Women's increased participation in paid employment has generated a crisis in providing adequate care for children, the elderly, and ill family members. Enacting legisla-

tion such as the 1993 Family Medical Leave Act (FMLA) is one response to this crisis. In "Taking Dependency Seriously," Eva Feder Kittay observes that, despite Western democracies' recent attention to gender equality, the liberal egalitarian tradition (e.g., John Rawls) leaves no room for dependency concerns. Kittay offers what she calls a "dependency critique," which holds social cooperation as key component of human life. On her account, the Rawlsian picture of society as "a fair system of social cooperation" among similarly situated free and equal individuals who come together to improve their life choices leaves no room for dependency concerns. The liberal picture presupposes a mutual reciprocity that is impossible in some dependent-caregiver relations. To overcome this, Kittay offers the *doula* as an alternative model of social cooperation. The FMLA recognizes this alternative and makes provisions for dependency work; however, its scope and benefits make only limited contributions to fairness and equality.

When relationships are unequal, dependency may create vulnerability. Yet outside of feminist scholarship few social justice theorists have paid much attention to the inequalities in marriage and families. Theories of justice rarely equate injustice with intimate relations. In "Vulnerability by Marriage," Susan Moller Okin argues that the typical gender-structured practices in family life that make women and children dependent and vulnerable are unjust. She begins with a basic account of the moral status of vulnerability and how asymmetrical vulnerabilities create social obligations, which must be fulfilled if we are to avoid charges of exploitation. Applying these observations to marriage, she offers evidence on how the social conditioning of women for marriage, their primary roles as caregivers, sex inequality in the workplace, housework, and the distribution of burdens and benefits in divorce collectively create social vulnerability. Until there is justice within the family, women will be unable to gain equality in politics, at work, or in any other sphere.

If women's dependency in marriage is primarily economic, then questions of autonomy and dependency structure contemporary discussions of gender and the welfare state. The rise of industrial capitalism brought with it the creation of "the family wage" whereby entire families were dependent almost exclusively upon the male household head's wage earnings. The current crisis of the welfare state is bound up in both the world collapse of the family wage and the outdated assumptions and gendered economic roles it presupposes. In "After the Family Wage: Gender Equity and the Welfare State," Nancy Fraser examines two feminist alternatives to the welfare state: the "universal breadwinner model" and the "caregiver parity model." Her argument presupposes a complex conception of gender equity grounded in five distinct normative principles. She applies these standards to the universal breadwinner and caregiver parity models, respectively. Although both models are improvements over the modern welfare state, she argues that neither approach, even in its idealized forms, can deliver full gender equity. She concludes that a new vision of the postindustrial society is only achievable by effectively deconstructing gender difference as we know it.

Critical application of traditional political values to the family and private spheres provide one route into political issues. But, naturally, feminists also have been attentive to issues of sinequality and discrimination in social policy. Prior to the Enlightenment, many traditions dictated that each group had its place: some were born to rule and others to serve. This view was replaced with the liberal humanist view that human norms and attributes exist to which everyone can aspire, and they can be used to judge the merit of individuals equally. Iris Young's "Difference and Social Policy: Reflections in the Context of Social Movements," challenges the liberal humanist principle that equates fairness with sameness. Although these standards appear neutral, they all too often favor some groups and disadvantage others by forcing them to deny aspects of their identity or culture. Over the last forty years, movements started by black nationalists, native peoples, gays and lesbians, people with disabilities, and

feminists have challenged the universal liberal humanist ideals that define liberation in terms of assimilation and transcending group difference, and have asserted the virtues of using difference as a political resource. The politics of difference seeks to override the principle of equal treatment with the principle that group differences should be acknowledged in order to reduce actual oppression. Young illustrates this in her discussions of the right to pregnancy and maternity leave, mandatory retirement, and questions about cultural integrity and invisibility. She concludes that there are a vast number of issues such as comparable worth, affirmative action, and bilingual/bicultural education, where fairness involves attention to differences and their effects.

Attention to the private sphere and the realities of women's lives also helps us to see the unofficial centers of "empire making." What role might gender play in empire building? Empires are built not only on the battlefield, in houses of government, or though economic treaties behind closed doors, they are also built in brothels, parlors, factories, and other "private" spaces. In "Updating the Gendered Empire," Cynthia Enloe argues that if we are to make sense of American empire building, we need to become more curious about the lives and feelings of women in empires. Empire-building strategies rely on and exploit particular ideas about the kinds of women there are, where those women should be, and what they should be doing. She asks readers to imagine the multiple ways women's lives support and subvert imperial enterprises. Using this approach, she asks three Afghan and three Iraqi women to "step up" and tell their stories. These women's observations illustrate the complex and subtle ways that shared masculinity sustains alliances, and how making sense of masculinized political cultures cannot be accomplished by focusing exclusively on the varieties of men. Instead paying serious attention to "women's experiences, actions, and ideas is the only way to understand how masculinity as an ideology can be seen with political clarity" (Enloe 2004, 305).

AUTONOMY, SOCIAL DISRUPTION, AND WOMEN[1]

Marilyn Friedman

OF AUTONOMY AND MEN

Are women in Western societies alienated by the ideal of autonomy? Many feminist philosophers have recently suggested that women find autonomy to be a notion inhospitable to women, one that represents a masculine-style preoccupation with self-sufficiency and self-realization at the expense of human connection.

Paul Gauguin's life epitomizes what many feminists take to be the masculine ideal of autonomy. Gauguin abandoned his family and middle-class life as a banker in Denmark to travel to Mediterranean France, Tahiti, and Martinique in search of artistic subjects and inspiration. He deserted his wife and five children, one might say, to paint pictures in sunny locales. Biographies of Gauguin's life reveal that he agonized for some time over the decision to leave his family. He once wrote: "One man's faculties can't cope with two things at once, and I for one can do *one thing only:* paint. Everything else leaves me stupefied."[2] Gauguin's self-reflective agonies, I believe, would qualify as autonomous, according to many contemporary definitions.

How has Western culture assessed Gauguin's life and work? Gauguin was *canonized* by Western art history. Of course, he had the moral good luck to have painted important pictures, something that Bernard Williams might call a "good for the world."[3] Whereas his fame is certainly based on his paintings and not on his familial desertion, nevertheless, the fact of his having left behind a wife and five children for sunnier prospects has done nothing to tarnish his stature. If anything, it has added a romantic allure to his biography.

Narratives of this sort suggest that autonomy in practice is antithetical to women's interests

because it prompts men to desert the social relationships on which many women depend for the survival and well-being of themselves and their children. In the past, because of women's restricted opportunities, the loss of support suffered by abandoned women has often been worse than the heterosexual relationships on which they depended.

Men are supposed to "stand up like a man" for what they believe or value, including the simple assertion of their self-interests. Women are instead supposed to "*stand by* your man." The maxim "stand up like a *woman*!" has no serious meaning. It conjures up imagery that is, at best, merely humorous. There is no doubt which model of behavior as exhibited by which gender receives the highest honors in Western public culture.

Still today, women in general define themselves more readily than men in terms of personal relationships. In addition, women's moral concerns tend to focus more intensely than those of men on sustaining and enhancing personal ties.[4] Also, popular culture still presumes that women are more concerned than men to create and preserve just the sorts of relationships, such as marriage, that autonomy-seeking men sometimes want to abandon.[5] Feminist analysis has uncovered ways in which close personal involvement and identification with others have been culturally devalued, in tandem with the devaluation of women, by comparison with the public world of impersonal relationships that men have traditionally monopolized.[6] Focusing on the importance of the social is one feminist strategy for combating these traditions of thought and for elevating social esteem for women. Many feminist philosophers have thus emerged as champions of social relationships and of relational approaches to diverse philosophical concepts.[7]

The cultural understanding of autonomy needs to change if the concept is to be relevant for women. I discuss three such changes: new paradigms of autonomy that involve female protagonists, redefinitions of autonomy that avoid stereotypically masculine traits, and redefinitions of autonomy that somehow involve social relationships or are at least not antithetical to them. Indeed such an account has been under development for some time in philosophical literature, and my suggestions on these points are not new. Of course, nothing guarantees a priori that we will find an account of autonomy that synthesizes these elements consistently with the core notion of self-determination that sets limits to our understanding of autonomy. I am optimistic, however, that a female-friendly account of autonomy can be, and has in part already been, developed.

At any rate, I mention these points merely to set the stage for my fourth, and primary, thesis: at the same time that we embrace relational accounts of autonomy, we should also be cautious about them. Autonomy increases the risk of disruption in interpersonal relationships. Although this is an empirical and not a conceptual claim about autonomy, nevertheless, the risk is significant. It makes a difference in whether the ideal of autonomy is genuinely hospitable to women.

After providing a capsule characterization of autonomy that is typical of accounts in the contemporary philosophical literature, I address each of the preceding points in turn.

PERSONAL AUTONOMY: A CAPSULE ACCOUNT

Autonomy involves choosing and living according to standards or values that are, in some plausible sense, one's "own." A plausible sense of "ownness" involves at least two dimensions. First, someone must reflect in an autonomy-conferring manner on the particular choices she makes and the standards or values by which she will be guided. Autonomy-conferring reflection, in my view, is not confined to rational reflection. Such terms as "critical," "reflection," "consideration," "evaluation," "scrutiny," and "choice," as I use them, encompass emotional as well as strictly rational or narrowly cognitive dimensions of personal processes.[8]

Second, the reflection itself must be relatively free of those varieties of interference that impede the achievement of autonomy. What varieties these are I do not specify except to say that socialization does not as such impede autonomy, whereas coercion as such does do so.[9] These circular terms ("autonomy-conferring reflection" and "autonomy-impeding interference") are not meant to articulate the notions in question but merely to serve as placeholders for a fully fleshed account of the nature of autonomy, which is not my present concern.

For the most part, my discussion focuses on personal autonomy, something best defined by reference to moral autonomy. Moral autonomy has to do with what one regards either as morally required or as morally permissible. It involves choosing and living according to rules that one considers to be morally binding. Personal autonomy involves acting and living according to one's own choices, values, and identity within the constraints of what one regards as morally permissible.[10]

OF AUTONOMY AND WOMEN

First, I consider the historic association of autonomy with men. Autonomy, its constituent traits, and the actions and lives that seem to manifest it are publicly esteemed much more often in men than in women. As noted earlier, the preponderance of men in narratives of autonomy could easily cast a masculine shadow over the concept.

Does a concept become irrevocably shaped by the paradigms that initially configure its usage? I believe that it does not and that autonomy can accordingly be freed of its historically near exclusive association with male biographies and male-identified traits. Doing so will require systematic rethinking. In part, we need new paradigms of autonomy that feature female protagonists.[11]

A particularly *feminist* appropriation of the concept of autonomy requires narratives of women who strive in paradigmatically or distinctively female situations against patriarchal constraints to express and refashion their deepest commitments and senses of self. Such narratives are already widely available. Susan Brison, for example, writes of regaining autonomous control over her life after she was tragically raped and almost murdered.[12] Patricia Hill Collins explains the power and importance of self-definition to African-American women, who are fighting the dominating cultural images of themselves as mammies, matriarchs, and welfare mothers.[13] Minnie Bruce Pratt tells of how she struggled to live as a lesbian while at the same time renouncing the racism and antisemitism that she had derived from her family and community of origin.[14]

In addition, there are women's autonomy narratives that are not particularly about overcoming patriarchal constraints. Sara Ruddick's account of maternal thinking, for example, draws heavily on stories of women who reflected deeply on how to care well for their children, an otherwise conventional female task.[15] In short, there is already available a large variety of narratives that exemplify women's autonomous struggles, both feminist and nonfeminist.

It is, in addition, helpful to remember that autonomy is not always valued in men. Whole groups of minority men have had their autonomous aspirations crushed by white Western societies. Moreover, white men do not always tolerate autonomy from one another. In traditional, patriarchal hierarchies, such as military or corporate structures, even many *white* men are routinely punished for being autonomous, for challenging accepted norms and authoritative dictates, for not being a "team player."[16]

Some male philosophers, in addition, criticize the ideal of autonomy in at least some of its versions. Male communitarians challenge what they take to be the overly individualistic and ungrounded autonomy of the liberal tradition.[17] Sounding a different note, Loren Lomasky regards autonomy as a source of "massive dislocation" and "widespread human misery." He criticizes autonomy as a rallying cry of the "Red Guards" and of proponents of the welfare state who reject the "traditional ways" of family life.[18]

Thus, the historical link between autonomy and men is not uniform. It is being further challenged today by the growing diversity of women's lives. Autonomy is now available to, and sometimes celebrated in, women, and it is not always celebrated in men. The gender paradigms of autonomy are shifting. On the basis of paradigms alone, autonomy is no longer straightforwardly male-oriented or alien to women.

AUTONOMY AND GENDER STEREOTYPES

My second point is that we should seek redefinitions of autonomy that avoid stereotypically masculine traits. Autonomy has often been conceptualized in terms of traits that suggest an antifemale bias. Traditional ideals of autonomy, for example, have been grounded in reason. Genevieve Lloyd and others have argued that traditional conceptions of reason have excluded anything deemed "feminine," such as emotion.[19] The exclusion of emotion from the concept of reason, however, is less prominent a view today than it once was. Some recent accounts of rationality by both feminists and mainstream philosophers blur the boundary between reason and emotion and thus promise to undermine this traditional dichotomy.[20] In case those accounts prove to be well grounded, this particular philosophical basis for thinking that autonomy is an antifemale ideal would have been eliminated.[21]

Besides connecting autonomy to reason, popular Western culture has also associated autonomy with other masculine-defined traits, for example, independence and outspokenness.[22] Traits popularly regarded as feminine, by contrast, have no distinctive connection to autonomy—social interactiveness, for example.[23] Thus popular gender stereotypes have associated autonomy with men but not with women; these stereotypes might invidiously infect philosophical thinking about autonomy.

To be sure, because of gender differences in socialization, autonomy might actually occur less often in women than in men. As Diana Meyers has documented, male socialization still promotes autonomy competency more effectively than does female socialization.[24] Overall, men have had far greater opportunities than women to act and live autonomously.[25] Such modes of action and living have in the past been closed to most women because they required unavailable (to women) resources such as political power, financial independence, or the freedom to travel unmolested in public space—to jog safely, for example, through New York City's Central Park.

The more frequent appearance of autonomy in men than in women, combined with the association of stereotypically masculine but not feminine traits with autonomy, might unwittingly bias philosophical investigations of autonomy. Together with their nonphilosophical peers, philosophers might fail to recognize manifestations of autonomy by women. Philosophers who try to conceptualize autonomy might do so with autonomous males in mind as paradigm cases. They might go on to mistake what are merely masculine traits for the traits that make up autonomy competency as such. Thus contemporary philosophical accounts of autonomy should be scrutinized particularly with a view to eliminating any covert masculine paradigms that might lie behind them.

In addition to creating a male bias that might influence philosophical reflections on autonomy, male stereotypes are also easy to exaggerate in ways that could further distort the conception of autonomy. The male-stereotyped traits of independence and self-sufficiency have often been interpreted, both in general culture and in philosophical traditions, in asocial, atomistic terms that seem to sanction detachment from close personal relationships with others.[26] Many feminists have argued that this illusory goal of atomistic self-sufficiency has indeed structured male development and male perspectives in those cultures that require men to repudiate the feminine

to consolidate their own masculine gender identity.[27] Some feminists worry that the very concept of autonomy has been irremediably contaminated by this atomistic approach, which neglects the social relationships that are vital for developing the character traits required for mature autonomy competency.[28] Much of that socialization consists of women's traditional child-care labor.

Philosophical accounts might err in this regard more by omission than by commission. Some contemporary accounts, for example, fail to mention how the human capacity for autonomy develops in the course of socialization.[29] By neglecting to mention the role of socialization in the development of mature autonomy competency, traditional accounts of autonomy ignore one crucial way in which autonomous persons are ultimately dependent persons after all, and in particular, dependent on women's nurturing. This philosophical omission does nothing to undermine the conceited cultural illusion of the "self-made man" as a paradigm of autonomy.

To be sure, no respectable philosopher today would *explicitly* deny that a social upbringing and ongoing personal interaction are necessary to become autonomous. These conditions impart the self-concept and resources for critical reflection that autonomy requires. Also, no respectable philosopher would deny that women's labors still make up the lion's share of child care, especially in the crucial years of early formative socialization. Careful philosophical thought on these issues should correct the pop-cultural view of some men as impossibly "self-made," a view that denies women their proper share of credit for nurturing or supporting the autonomy competency found in those men. The point is that philosophers must actively take pains to weed out inappropriate male paradigms that might contaminate their own or a wider cultural understanding of key philosophical notions.

In virtue of disregarding the fundamentally social nature of autonomy and autonomous persons, the myth of the self-made man rests on a mistake. The fact that mistaken conceptions of autonomy are male-biased, however, does not show that autonomy *properly understood* is male-biased or antifemale.

SOCIAL RECONCEPTUALIZATIONS OF AUTONOMY

My third point is that we need an account of autonomy that brings out its relational character. Fortunately, a relational approach to autonomy has been emerging for some time. Two developments are relevant to this issue: a procedural conception of autonomy and a relational or intersubjective conception of autonomy.[30]

According to a procedural account, personal autonomy is realized by the right sort of reflective self-understanding or internal coherence along with an absence of undue coercion or manipulation by others. Autonomy, in this sort of view, is not a matter of living substantively in any particular way.[31] My own capsule account of autonomy in the previous section is a procedural account. Although this sort of account can be debated,[32] it is nevertheless common in philosophy today. In a procedural conception, avoiding or abandoning close personal relationships is in no sense required by autonomy. Nor is it for any reason inherently a better way for any individual to strive for autonomy.

Although the language of autonomy in popular culture might still suggest asocial atomistic images of the self-made man, academic philosophers now seldom share this view. The atomistic "self-made" conception of autonomy is a substantive conception of a particular sort of life or mode of behaving that someone must choose in order to realize autonomy. Such an ideal falls outside the bounds of procedural accounts of autonomy. It is not a proper part of them.

In addition to focusing mainly on procedural matters, many contemporary philosophers of autonomy have also tended to gravitate toward relational or intersubjective accounts of autonomy. This is true of both feminist and mainstream philosophers. At present, both construe autonomy in social, relational, interpersonal, or intersubjective terms.[33]

According to the relational approach, persons are fundamentally social beings who develop the competency for autonomy through social interaction with other persons. These developments take place in a context of values, meanings, and modes of self-reflection that cannot exist except as constituted by social practices. Also, according to some theorists, autonomy is itself the capacity for a distinctive form of social and, in particular, dialogical engagement.[34]

Autonomy is no longer thought to require someone to be a social atom, that is, radically socially unencumbered, defined merely by the capacity to choose, or to be able to exercise reason prior to any of her contingent ends or social engagements.[35] It is now well recognized that our reflective capacities and our very identities are always partly constituted by communal traditions and norms that we cannot put entirely into question without at the same time voiding our very capacities to reflect.

We are each reared in a social context of some sort, typically although not always that of a family, itself located in wider social networks such as community and nation. Nearly all of us remain, throughout our lives, involved in social relationships and communities, at least some of which partly define our identities and ground our highest values. These relationships and communities are fostered and sustained by varied sorts of ties that we share with others, such as languages, activities, practices, projects, traditions, histories, goals, views, values, and mutual attractions—not to mention common enemies and shared injustices and disasters.

Someone who becomes more autonomous concerning some tradition, authority, view, or value in her life does not stop depending on other persons or relationships, nor does she evade her own necessarily social history of personal development. Her initial detached questioning does not arise in a social vacuum but is likely to be prompted by commitments reflecting still other relationships that for the present time remain unquestioned and perhaps heteronomous. A shift in social relationships or commitments is not equivalent to, nor need it betoken, wholesale social detachment.

Autonomy does not require self-creation or the creation of law ex nihilo, a limitation that we need not join Richard Rorty in lamenting.[36] Becoming more procedurally autonomous concerning particular standards, norms, or dictates involves reflecting on them in a language that one did not create—according to further norms and standards that one has almost surely taken over from others—in light of what is most central to that product of social development that is oneself.[37] Also, autonomy is always a matter of degree, of more or less. Reflective consideration still counts as a gain in autonomy even if done in the light of other standards and relationships not simultaneously subjected to the same scrutiny.

HOW AUTONOMY DISRUPTS PERSONAL RELATIONSHIPS

Feminists have sought a relational account of autonomy to render it relevant to women. Philosophers in general have sought such an account to make good on a widely shared intuition that autonomy is not antithetical to other social values and virtues that concern us all, such as love, friendship, care, loyalty, and devotion.[38] Many philosophers seem to expect that most of what we want or value in interpersonal relationships will prove to be consistent with the ideal of autonomy, once we develop an appropriately social conception of it.

That conviction, however, may be unfounded. It underestimates, I believe, the disruption that autonomy can promote in close personal relationships and in communities. Although autonomy is not inherently antithetical to social relationships, nevertheless, in practice autonomy often contingently disrupts particular social bonds. How it sometimes interferes with social relationships and what this implies about its value for women

make up the fourth and primary theme of this article.

Human relationships and communities, as noted, are held together by a variety of ties that persons share, including languages, practices, traditions, histories, goals, views, and values. Any of these elements in someone's life can become the focus of her critical scrutiny. Whenever someone questions or evaluates any tie or commitment that binds her to others, the possibility arises that she may find that bond unwarranted and begin to reject it. Rejecting values that tie someone to others may lead her to try to change the relationships in question or simply to detach herself from them. Someone might also reflect on the very nature of her relationships to particular others and come to believe that those ties are neglecting or smothering important dimensions of herself. To liberate those aspects of herself, she might have to distance herself from the problematic relationships.

Most personal and communal relationships are multifaceted and based on more than one sort of tie. Kinship, for example, keeps many people in contact with relatives whose values would otherwise repel them. Childhood friends who travel disparate paths in life may retain shared memories that keep them ever fondly in touch with each other. A shared ethnic identity may link economically diverse people in the pursuit of collective political ends or cultural self-affirmation. Thus, friends, relatives, or other associates who diverge over important values may still remain related to each other in virtue of other shared ties.

The resilience of social relationships is, of course, not always a blessing. Relationships in which one partner exploits or abuses the other can also, and regrettably, last for years.[39] Sometimes, however, a person becomes so disenchanted with her relationships or their underlying values that they become, to her, unbearable. At that level of discontent, and assuming viable alternatives, she may begin to withdraw from the relationships. In so doing, she displays just the sort of relational disconnection that can stem from a person's autonomous reflections on (and growing dissatisfaction with) her prior commitments.

Alternatively, someone's increasing autonomy might result in the breakup of a relationship not because she rejects it but rather because other parties to the relationship reject her. They might despise the changes in her behavior that they are witnessing. Some parents, for example, disown children who rebel too strongly against deeply held parental values. Peer groups often ostracize their members for disregarding important norms that prevail in their own subcultures.

Strictly speaking, to say that autonomy unqualified (sometimes) disrupts social relationships is misleading. The mere capacity for autonomy is not intrinsically socially disruptive. What disrupts a social relationship in a particular case is the actual exercise of the capacity. More strictly still, the differences that arise between people as a result of one party's autonomous rejection of values or commitments that the other party still holds may lead one party to draw away from or reject the other. Thus, to borrow a rhetorical turn of phrase from the U.S. lobbying group the National Rifle Association (!), it is not *autonomy* (as a dispositional capacity) that disrupts social relationships; it is *people* who disrupt social relationships.

The exercise of autonomy, it should be emphasized, is not sufficient as such to disrupt particular relationships. The connection between autonomy and social disruption is merely contingent. Someone's autonomous reflections increase the chances of disruption in her social relationships but do not make it a necessary consequence. In certain sorts of circumstances, autonomy may not even make social disruption more likely than it already is. Someone's reflective consideration might lead her to appreciate in a new light the worth of her relationships or the people to whom she is socially attached and to enrich her commitment to them. In such cases, autonomy would strengthen rather than weaken relational ties. Even if someone began to disagree with significant others about important matters, their relationship might still not suffer. People use many

interpersonal strategies to keep differing commitments from disrupting social harmony—"never discuss religion or politics," for example.[40]

Thus, someone's autonomy is not a *sufficient* condition for the disruption of her social relationships. Nor is it a *necessary* condition. A person might end a relationship because of new commitments that she has reached heteronomously. Peer pressure, for example, can promote knee-jerk rebelliousness that disrupts personal relationships as much as the greatest soul searching and critical self-reflection. Someone's attitudes can also change as the result of traumatic experiences over which she had no control. These changes may occasion deep rifts in her relationships with close others.[41] Someone's increasing autonomy is thus neither a sufficient nor a necessary cause of disruption in social relationships.

Nevertheless, the contingently possible connection between autonomy and social disruption is of noteworthy importance. When a culture places great value on autonomy, members of that culture are thereby encouraged to question their prior allegiances and the standards that impinge on them. Autonomy as a cultural ideal creates a supportive climate for personal scrutiny of traditions, standards, and authoritative commands.[42] Public discourse in such a culture will tend to promote open dialogue and debate over values and traditions. Autonomy-idealizing societies may protect such discourse, and the normative critiques it can foster, with a legal right to a substantial degree of freedom of expression.

Thus, other things being equal, in a culture that prizes autonomy, all traditions, authorities, norms, views, and values become more vulnerable to rejection by at least some members of the society than they would be in a society that devalued autonomy. No commitment in such a culture remains entirely immune to critical scrutiny, whether the commitment concerns religion, sex, family, government, economy, art, education, race, ethnicity, gender, or anything else.

Once such scrutiny takes place, the likelihood increases that people who are socially linked to each other will begin to diverge over views or values they previously shared, including the value of their social ties. Once people begin to diverge over important matters, they are more likely than they were before to disagree and quarrel with each other or to lose mutual interest and drift apart. In this way (other things being equal), an autonomy-idealizing culture increases the risk of (though it certainly does not guarantee) ruptures in social relationships.

To be sure, cultures that idealize autonomy do not always extend this ideal to all social groups. Sometimes certain sorts of people, white men, for example, receive the lion's share of the social protections and rewards for being autonomous. Also, even an autonomy-idealizing culture may shield certain norms or values from critical scrutiny. In such a society, values that protect dominant social groups, those privileged to enjoy the value of autonomy, might not get as much critical attention as they deserve. Whereas limitations on rampant autonomy might be necessary to prevent wholesale social breakdown, they can also create bastions of unquestioned autonomous privilege. In such a culture, autonomy might well be a restricted, domesticated, socially nonthreatening luxury.

Nevertheless, as long as autonomy is culturally valued even for only some groups and for only certain issues, its very cultural availability opens up the possibility for wide social transformation. Even if idealized for only a privileged few, it can always fall into the "wrong" hands. New groups might coincidentally acquire autonomy competency in virtue of social changes, such as the spread of literacy and formal education. They might then go on to contest norms and values previously left unscrutinized. This possibility has been historically crucial for women and other subordinated groups. The ideal of autonomy is thus always a potential catalyst for social disruption in interpersonal relationships.

Notice also that the rupture that autonomy can promote in any one particular social relationship does not necessarily amount to an overall decline in the societal quantity of relationality, to put the point inelegantly. Typically, when someone questions some prior commitment, such as a religious commitment, which cemented certain relationships in her life, she is probably doing so in company with other skeptics whose reflections prompt and reinforce her own rising doubts. When she turns away from her prior religious community, she is likely to be turning toward a different community, perhaps a religiously neutral secular community or a new religious group. Those with whom someone shares her new commitments may have given her a vocabulary or perspective for reflecting on her central concerns. Without any empirical backing for this claim, I nevertheless estimate that in most cases in which autonomous reflection does lead people to reject the commitments that bound them to particular others, they are at the same time taking up new commitments that link them through newly shared conviction to *different* particular others. This is one important reason for thinking of autonomy as social in character.

Although people in an autonomy-valuing society might have as many interpersonal relationships as those in a society that devalued autonomy, it is reasonable to speculate that the nature of people's relationships would differ in the two cases. Where people are permitted with relative ease to leave relationships that have become dissatisfying to them, we should expect attachments to be less stable, to shift and change with greater frequency, than in societies in which personal autonomy (or relational mobility) is discouraged. The types and qualities of relationships in an autonomy-promoting culture would also probably differ from those of an autonomy-discouraging culture. Relationships into which people are born and in which they are first socialized—those of family, church, neighborhood, friendship, and local communities—would probably be disrupted first, if any, by widespread individually autonomous reflections on basic values and commitments. In a culture that values autonomy, it is likely that more people than otherwise would gravitate toward voluntary relationships formed in adult life around shared values and attitudes.[43]

WOMEN AND THE SOCIAL DISRUPTIONS OF AUTONOMY

What difference should it make to our theory of autonomy that autonomy, however social its nature or origin, might promote the disruption of social relationships? More precisely in the present context, what difference does this possibility make to *women?* If autonomy is sometimes socially disruptive, does that make it inimical to the relational orientation that many feminists celebrate in women and display in their own moral concerns?

Some people exhibit what I call autonomophobia, or fear of autonomy. What they usually fear is not their own autonomy; it is the autonomy of *others* that scares them. Their concern is that autonomous people will disrupt or desert valuable, *shared* relationships. Which relationships are thought to be valuable will be specified differently from distinct critical perspectives. Feminists, and many women in general, often worry about the relationships on which many women depend for material and emotional sustenance.

Whether or not any particular woman benefits or suffers in virtue of the exercise of autonomy depends on how she is positioned in relation to it. When a woman is connected to someone else whose autonomous pursuits disrupt their relationship, the immediate effect on her is likely to be simply a loss—of whatever benefits she derived from their relationship. Autonomophobia is thus a legitimate concern. It arises from the ways in which our lives are intertwined with those of other persons. When others who are close to us reflect on their own deepest commitments, they might well find grounds for challenging or abandoning the relationships and communities that we share with them. We might find ourselves helpless as a result. Social relationships and communities are collective projects. They function best when sustained jointly by people with important values or norms in common. In a culture that idealizes autonomy, each individual faces the

insecurity of investing herself in relationships and communities that the other participants might, on critical reflection, come to reject.

Historically, the disruption of personal relationships has had a different impact on men than on women. Because women were usually limited to dependence on men for financial support, whereas men had no comparable limitation, women doubtless suffered more than they benefited from the cultural idealization of autonomy. Men have been historically better situated than women to forsake personal relationships that came to seem dissatisfying to them. Unlike most women, many men have had the material and cultural resources with which to support themselves, as well as greater opportunities to seek more satisfying relationships elsewhere. Men were able to abandon their responsibilities to women and children to pursue forms of personal fulfillment unavailable to women.

Men who, like Gauguin, produced good enough subsequent works have been celebrated for autonomous pursuits that involved neglecting or abandoning relationships that supported women and children. Dependent women and children have suffered greatly from these male desertions. Women's own autonomous living, by contrast, brought them much more censure and hardship than praise.[44] Since women tend to be more financially dependent on men than men are on women even today, autonomophobia is understandably still more often a female than a male concern. Thus, men's autonomy would have done women little direct good and could have imposed serious harm.

On the other hand, many social relationships constrain and oppress women, indeed the very women who work to sustain them. Apart from whether or not women *want* to devote their lives to maintaining close personal ties, gender norms have required it of them. Women have been expected to make the preservation of certain interpersonal relationships such as those of family their highest concern regardless of the costs to themselves. Women who have had important commitments other than those of taking care of family members were nevertheless supposed to subordinate such commitments to the task of caring for loved ones. Many men, by contrast, have been free to choose or affirm their highest commitments from among a wide panorama of alternatives. Indeed, men are sometimes lauded for just the sort of single-minded pursuit of an ideal that imposes sacrifices on all the people close to them.

Traditionally, the majority of women derived their primary adult identities from their marriages and families. For at least some groups of women, however, social and economic opportunities have broadened in the late twentieth century. Because of expanding financial opportunities in the West, many women no longer need to accommodate themselves *uncritically* to traditional marriages or other relational ties to sustain themselves. As many feminists have well recognized, there is no reason to defend social relationships without qualification. There is nothing intrinsic to each and every social relationship that merits female or feminist allegiance.[45] The traditional relational work of women has included sublime joy and fulfillment but also abuse, exploitation, and subordination. There are some, perhaps many, relationships that women, too, should want to end.

Thus, the disruption of social relationships that can follow someone's growing autonomy is not itself inherently alien to women, nor is it a dimension of the ideal of autonomy that women today should automatically reject. What should matter to any particular woman in any given case is the worth of the relationship in question and how its disruption would bear on herself and on innocent others. The old question, "can this marriage be saved?" should be revised to, "can this marriage be saved from *oppressiveness?*" Some relationships should be preserved and others should be abolished. Even relationships that should be preserved can always be improved. Sometimes what disrupts social relationships is good for particular women. Since the socially disruptive potential of autonomy can at least sometimes be good for women, it does not constitute a reason for women to repudiate the ideal of autonomy.

Indeed, reflecting on one's relationships or the norms or values that underlie them might be the *only* way someone can determine for herself the moral quality of those relationships. A woman who does not reflect on her relationships, communities, norms, or values is incapable of recognizing for herself where they go wrong or of aiming on her own to improve them. Her well-being depends on those who control her life and on their wisdom and benevolence—regrettably, not the most reliable of human traits. Autonomy is thus crucial for women in patriarchal conditions, in part *because* of its potential to disrupt social bonds. That autonomy is sometimes antithetical to social relationships is oftimes a good for women. With all due respect to Audre Lorde, the "master's tools" *can* "dismantle the master's house."[46]

Thus, although women still have occasion to fear *men's* autonomy, it seems that many women have good reason to welcome our *own*. When a woman is the one who is exercising autonomy, even if its exercise disrupts relationships in her life the value of her gain in autonomous living might well make the costs to her worth her while. She may plausibly fear what increasingly autonomous others might do to the relationships between herself and them, but it would not make sense for her to reject autonomy for herself. A woman might choose not to *exercise* autonomy under certain conditions. She might, for example, devote herself loyally to an ideal that she can only serve by working with a group of persons who sometimes take specific actions she does not understand or endorse. She can hardly want to give up, however, the very option of so devoting herself. To reflect on the standards or values according to which one will behave or live one's life, as one does when resolving to dedicate oneself to a particular ideal, is already to exercise a degree of autonomy. It would be self-defeating, at the same time, to reject autonomy altogether as a value for oneself.

Once women admit that autonomy might be a value for us, it would be difficult to deny its value for persons in general. The capacity for autonomy seems instrumentally valuable as a means for resisting oppression and intrinsically valuable as part of the fullest humanly possible development of moral personality. In these respects it seems valuable for anyone. The problem arises with the need for reciprocity. We cannot esteem autonomy in women while deprecating it in men. Yet men's autonomy and the social disruption it can promote does sometimes threaten women's well-being. I have argued that when women have access to means for their own material support, this risk is lessened.[47] Women can then gain at least as much from a generalized cultural idealization of autonomy as they risk by it.

There are, as well, certain mitigating possibilities that reduce, even though they do not eliminate, the likelihood that autonomy might cause social disruption. Autonomy does not necessarily lead someone to reject her prior commitments. Someone else's increasing autonomy might instead enhance her appreciation of her close relationships. Even if she comes to regard a relationship as seriously flawed, she might work to improve it rather than abandoning it.

These possibilities suggest that alongside autonomy as a cultural ideal, we should also idealize the values and responsibilities that make relationships and communities worthwhile.[48] We can emphasize, for example, the ways in which close relationships are vital sources of care for the most vulnerable members of our society.[49] We should articulate these values in public dialogues in which all can participate, including those who might become autonomously skeptical about those social ties.

This balanced pursuit of the values of community along with the ideal of autonomy is a partial response to the concern that the empirical social disruptiveness of autonomy lessens the value of autonomy for women. There is no way, however, to alleviate this concern fully. The possibility of social disruptiveness is one risk that must be faced by persons and cultures who would idealize personal autonomy.[50] I have argued that social disruptiveness is, at least, a mixed curse, one that harbors the potential for good, as well as bad, consequences.

In addition, the mantra of "family values" that is invoked uncritically in so much public debate in the United States should remind us as feminists of the hazards of allowing any relationships, including those we most cherish, to be entirely insulated from the critical reflection of all their participants. Even care for the most vulnerable can usually be improved. It is a form of respect toward those with whom we most want affiliation to want *them* to find forms of commitment to us that reflect *their* most cherished values.

NOTES

1. I am grateful to Natalie Stoljar and Catriona Mackenzie for helpful editorial suggestions on an earlier draft of this article.
2. Yann le Pichon, *Gauguin: Life, Art, Inspiration* (New York: Abrams, 1987), p. 26.
3. Bernard Williams's discussion of moral luck deploys the hypothetical biography of an artist whose life resembles that of the historic Gauguin; see Williams, "Moral Luck," in *Moral Luck* (Cambridge: Cambridge University Press, 1981), p. 37. See my discussion of Williams on the Gauguin-like example in my *What Are Friends For? Feminist Perspectives on Personal Relationships and Moral Theory* (Ithaca, N. Y.: Cornell University Press, 1993), pp. 163–170.
4. See the germinal work on this topic by Carol Gilligan, *In a Different Voice* (Cambridge, Mass.: Harvard University Press, 1982), and Nel Noddings, *Caring: A Feminine Approach to Ethics and Moral Education* (Berkeley: University of California Press, 1984).
5. See Susan Faludi's discussion of the popularization of research results alleging that women's chances of marrying fall precipitously after age forty, in *Backlash: The Undeclared War against American Women* (New York: Crown Publishers, 1991), chap. 1. Faludi argues persuasively that the conclusions were misrepresented in the mass media. My point is a different one: these research results would not have received popular attention if it hadn't been for the presumption that people, including women, would want to know about them.
6. See Gilligan, *In a Different Voice,* chap.1.

7. See, for example, Helen Longino, *Science as Social Knowledge* (Princeton, N.J.: Princeton University Press, 1990).

8. For an account of emotion as a source of autonomy, see Bennett W. Helm, "Freedom of the Heart," *Pacific Philosophical Quarterly* 77 (1996): 71–87. Harry Frankfurt discusses caring and love as sources of autonomy but uses those terms to refer to states of will rather than of emotion; see, for example, *The Importance of What We Care About* (Cambridge: Cambridge University Press, 1988), and "Autonomy, Necessity, and Love," in *Vernunftbegriffe in der Moderne: Stuttgarter Hegel-Kongress 1993,* ed. Hans Friedrich Fulda and Rolf-Peter Horstmann (Stuttgart: Klett-Cotta, 1994), pp. 433–447.

9. Of course, socialization might itself be coercive. See John Christman's approach to this problem in "Autonomy and Personal History," *Canadian Journal of Philosophy* 20 (1991): 1–24.

10. Diana T. Meyers, *Self, Society, and Personal Choice* (New York: Columbia University Press, 1989), pp. 13–17.

11. Morwenna Griffiths explores the importance of narratives in the cultural understanding of autonomy in *Feminisms and the Self: The Web of Identity* (London: Routledge, 1995).

12. Susan Brison, "Surviving Sexual Violence," *Journal of Social Philosophy* 24, no.1 (Spring 1993): 5–22.

13. Patricia Hill Collins, *Black Feminist Thought: Knowledge, Consciousness, and the Politics of Empowerment* (New York: Routledge, 1991), especially chaps. 4 and 5.

14. Minnie Bruce Pratt, "Identity: Skin Blood Heart," in *Yours in Struggle: Three Feminist Perspectives on Anti-Semitism and Racism,* ed. Elly Bulkin, Minnie Bruce Pratt, and Barbara Smith (Brooklyn, N.Y.: Long Haul Press, 1984), pp. 9–63.

15. Sara Ruddick, *Maternal Thinking: Toward a Politics of Peace* (New York: Ballantine, 1989).

16. The chancellor at a university near my own, for example, was recently fired by his university's governing board. The faculty members who supported him thought the problem was, as one of them put it, that the chancellor was "too autonomous, too independent." Faculty supporters described the governing board as wanting a "team player" instead. See Susan C. Thomson and Kim Bell, "Mizzou Chancellor Wants Buyout," *St. Louis Post-Dispatch,* June 14, 1996, C7. Note that the figure of a "team player" is a historically masculine metaphor for a cooperative social agent. The differences between women's and men's paradigm images of social cooperation deserve some study.

17. Michael J. Sandel, *Liberalism and the Limits of Justice* (Cambridge: Cambridge University Press, 1982), and Alasdair MacIntyre, *After Virtue,* 2nd ed. (Notre Dame, Ind.: University of Notre Dame Press, 1984).

18. Loren E. Lomasky, *Persons, Rights, and the Moral Community* (New York: Oxford University Press, 1987), p. 249. In the now common procedural account of autonomy, a view that I share (see the section on social reconceptualizations), no particular choices are intrinsic to autonomy. An autonomous person might embrace traditional relationships, reject traditional relationships, welcome the Red Guards, or abhor the Red Guards. What matters is how she arrived at her political views and whether those views reflect her own considered convictions. Lomasky construes autonomy as a failing only of those who make political choices he rejects, but this is just as mistaken as assuming that autonomy is a virtue only of those who make what one considers to be the right political choices.

19. Genevieve Lloyd, *The Man of Reason: "Male" and "Female" in Western Philosophy* (Minneapolis: University of Minnesota Press, 1984). See also Lorraine Code, *Rhetorical Spaces: Essays on Gendered Locations* (New York: Routledge, 1995), especially chap. 10, "Critiques of Pure Reason."

20. Feminist sources include Code, *Rhetorical Spaces,* and Alison M. Jaggar, "Love and Knowledge: Emotion in Feminist Epistemology," in *Gender/Body/Knowledge,* ed. Alison M. Jaggar and Susan R. Bordo (New Brunswick, N.J.: Rutgers University Press, 1989), pp. 145–171. Nonfeminist sources include Allan Gibbard, *Wise Choices, Apt Feelings: A Theory of Normative Judgment* (Cambridge, Mass.: Harvard University Press, 1990).

21. A different approach would be to argue that the stereotypic association of women with emotion was always groundless and that women are as

able as men to exercise a narrowly cognitive mode of reason. Sec Louise M. Antony and Charlotte Witt, eds., *A Mind of One's Own: Feminist Essays on Reason and Objectivity* (Boulder, Colo.: Westview Press, 1993), especially the essays by Margaret Atherton and Louise Antony. See the discussion of these essays by Code, *Rhetorical Spaces,* pp. 217–223.

22. See Susan Golombok and Robyn Fivush, *Gender Development* (Cambridge: Cambridge University Press, 1994), pp. 7–8.

23. Ibid., p. 18. A social or relational account of autonomy, such as that presented here, is one that construes social relationships as necessary for autonomy but not sufficient for it. There is nothing about social interconnection as such that entails, causes, or suggests autonomy.

24. Meyers, *Self, Society and Personal Choice,* especially part 3.

25. This point is, of course, not universal throughout Western cultures. Men of oppressed groups, such as racial minorities, may not have had significantly greater opportunities than the women of their own groups to act and live autonomously.

26. Many feminists have charged the traditional philosophical ideal of autonomy with excessive individualism; see, for example, Lorraine Code, "Second Persons," in *What Can She Know?: Feminist Theory and the Construction of Knowledge* (Ithaca, N.Y.: Cornell University Press, 1991). pp. 76–79.

27. See, for example, Evelyn Fox Keller, *Reflections on Gender and Science* (New Haven, Conn.: Yale University Press, 1985); Nancy Chodorow, *The Reproduction of Mothering: Psychoanalysis and the Sociology of Gender* (Berkeley: University of California Press, 1978); and Jessica Benjamin, *The Bonds of Love: Psychoanalysis, Feminism, and the Problem of Domination* (New York: Pantheon, 1988).

28. Annette Baier, "Cartesian Persons," in *Postures of the Mind: Essays on Mind and Morals* (Minneapolis: University of Minnesota Press, 1985). See also the discussion of this notion in Code, "Second Persons."

29. One prominent philosopher who neglects socialization, and, indeed, social relationships generally, in his account of autonomy is Frankfurt, *Importance of What We Care About.*

30. See the discussion of both of these points by John Christman, "Feminism and Autonomy," in *"Nagging" Questions: Feminist Ethics in Everyday Life,* ed. Dana E. Bushnell (Lanham, Md.: Rowman & Littlefield, 1995), pp. 17–39.

31. Gerald Dworkin provides one example of a procedural account of autonomy; see his *The Theory and Practice of Autonomy* (Cambridge: Cambridge University Press, 1988), pp. 18, 21–33.

32. See Marina Oshana, "Personal Autonomy and Society," *Journal of Social Philosophy* 29, no. 1 (Spring 1998): 81–102.

33. Feminist theorists who have developed this view include Keller, *Reflections on Gender and Science;* Jennifer Nedelsky, "Reconceiving Autonomy: Sources, Thoughts, and Possibilities," *Yale Journal of Law and Feminism* 1, no. 1 (Spring 1989): 7–36; Meyers, *Self, Society, and Personal Choice;* and Code, "Second Persons." Mainstream theorists who have developed this view include Joseph Raz, *The Morality of Freedom* (Oxford: Clarendon Press, 1986); Dworkin, *Theory and Practice of Autonomy;* and Joel Feinberg, "Autonomy," in *The Inner Citadel,* ed. John Christman (New York: Oxford University Press, 1989), pp. 27–53. For a discussion of the convergence of these two groups around a social conception of autonomy, see Christman, "Feminism and Autonomy," and my "Autonomy and Social Relationships: Rethinking the Feminist Critique," in *Feminists Rethink the Self,* ed. Diana T. Meyers (Boulder, Colo.: Westview Press, 1997), pp. 40–61. Some mainstream philosophers deny that the traditional notion of autonomy, even in its rigorous Kantian formulation, ever really excluded or ignored the importance of interpersonal relationships; see J. B. Schneewind, "The Use of Autonomy in Ethical Theory," in *Reconstructing Individualism: Autonomy, Individuality, and the Self in Western Theory,* ed. Thomas C. Heller, Morton Sosna, and David E. Wellbery (Stanford, Cal.: Stanford University Press, 1986), and Thomas E. Hill, Jr., "The Importance of Autonomy," in *Autonomy and Self-Respect* (Cambridge: Cambridge University Press, 1991).

34. See, for example, Jurgen Habermas, *Moral Consciousness and Communicative Action,* trans. Christian Lenhardt and Shierry Weber Nicholsen

(Cambridge, Mass.: MIT Press, 1990), and Joel Anderson, "A Social Conception of Personal Autonomy: Volitional Identity, Strong Evaluation, and Intersubjective Accountability," Ph.D. dissertation, Northwestern University, Evanston, Ill, 1996.

35. See, for example, Sandel, *Liberalism and the Limits of Justice,* p. 19.

36. Richard Rorty, *Contingency, Irony, and Solidarity* (Cambridge: Cambridge University Press, 1989).

37. Gerald Dworkin notes the impossibility of creating our own moral principles. Such a requirement "denies our history. . . . We . . . are deeply influenced by parents, siblings, peers, culture, class, climate, schools, accident, genes, and the accumulated history of the species. It makes no more sense to suppose we invent the moral law for ourselves than to suppose that we invent the language we speak for ourselves" (*The Theory and Practice of Autonomy,* p. 36).

38. Ibid., p. 21.

39. If abusive relationships persist for long periods of time, it is usually because the abused partner has, or thinks she has, no other viable options or because she sacrifices her own well-being to that of her abuser. For a survey of why long-time battered women finally seek court orders of protection against abusive male partners, see Karla Fischer and Mary Rose, "When 'Enough is Enough': Battered Women's Decision Making around Court Orders of Protection," *Crime and Delinquency* 41, no. 4 (October 1995): 414–429.

40. I do not endorse this maxim; I merely cite it as an example of the strategies that people use to keep disagreements from disrupting social relationships.

41. See Brison's discussion in "Surviving Sexual Violence," of the difficulties that arose in her relationships with family, friends, and others after she was violently raped.

42. As Dworkin notes, "Those who practice in their daily life a critical reflection on their own value structure will tend to be suspicious of modes of thought that rely on the uncritical acceptance of authority, tradition, and custom" (*The Theory and Practice of Autonomy,* p. 29).

43. For further discussion of this theme, see my *What Are Friends For?* chap. 9.

44. See Alison MacKinnon, *Love and Freedom: Professional Women and the Reshaping of Personal Life* (Cambridge: Cambridge University Press, 1997), on the hurdles faced by women in Australia at the end of the nineteenth and beginning of the twentieth century who sought higher education and careers outside the home.

45. There are many feminist discussions of problems that women face in social relationships; see, for example, Susan Moller Okin, *Justice, Gender, and the Family* (New York: Basic Books, 1989).

46. See Audre Lorde, "The Master's Tools Will Never Dismantle the Master's House," *Sister Outsider* (Freedom, Cal.: Crossing Press, 1984), pp. 110–113.

47. On this topic, see the essays in Martha Nussbaum and Jonathan Glover, eds., *Women, Culture and Development: A Study of Human Capabilities* (Oxford: Clarendon Press, 1995).

48. See the essays in *Feminism and Community,* eds. Penny Weiss and Marilyn Friedman (Philadelphia: Temple University Press, 1995).

49. See, for example, Robert E. Goodin, *Protecting the Vulnerable: A Reanalysis of Our Social Responsibilities* (Chicago: University of Chicago Press, 1985); Neera Kapur Badhwar, ed., *Friendship: A Philosophical Reader* (Ithaca, N.Y.: Cornell University Press, 1993); Joan C. Tronto, *Moral Boundaries: A Political Argument for an Ethic of Care* (New York: Routledge, 1994).

50. Should we devalue autonomy for individuals, perhaps recasting it as an ideal for groups only? The notion of group autonomy is extremely important, especially for oppressed groups; see, for example, Laurence Mordekhai Thomas, *Vessels of Evil: American Slavery and the Holocaust* (Philadelphia: Temple University Press, 1993), pp. 182–189. Group autonomy, however, does not necessarily help individuals when they face oppressive conditions in isolation. It complements but does not replace individual autonomy. In addition, group autonomy promotes its own risk of social disruption in the relationships between groups. The possible advantages, as well as the possible costs, of autonomy's socially disruptive potential simply reappear at a more encompassing level of social integration.

TAKING DEPENDENCY SERIOUSLY: THE FAMILY AND MEDICAL LEAVE ACT, DEPENDENCY WORK, AND GENDER EQUALITY

Eva Feder Kittay

Contemporary industrialized societies have been confronted with the fact and consequences of women's increased participation in paid employment. Whether this increase has resulted from women's desire for equality or from changing economic circumstances, women and men have been faced with a crisis in the organization of work that concerns dependents, that is, those unable to care for themselves. This is labor that has been largely unpaid, often unrecognized, and yet is indispensable to human society.

Dependents require care. They are unable either to survive or to thrive without attention to basic needs. Dependency needs range from the utter helplessness of a newborn infant to the incapacity of illness or frail old age. Dependency can be protracted (e.g., the extended dependency of early childhood) or brief (e.g., a temporary illness). An individual who is dependent may be able to function otherwise independently if only she is given needed assistance in limited areas, or she may be dependent in every aspect of her being, that is, utterly dependent. At some stage in the lives of each of us we face at least one period of utter dependency; and, with accident and disease forever a danger to the most independent of us, we are all, at least potentially, dependents. In our dependency, we not only require care, but require a sustaining relation with a care-giver who provides this care—for *who* does the caring is often as important as the care itself. These dependencies may be alleviated or aggravated by cultural practices and prejudices, but given the immutable facts of human development, disease,

and decline, no culture that endures beyond one generation can secure itself against the claims of human dependency. While we are all dependent on some form of care or support, at least minimally, and although dependencies vary in degree, those that involve the survival or thriving of a person cut most deeply through the fiction of a social order presumably constituted by independent equal persons.

For the past two decades, feminists have argued that this fiction is parasitic on a tradition in which women attend to those dependencies. The labor has been seen as part of their familial obligations, obligations that trump all other obligations. Women who have been sufficiently wealthy or of sufficiently high status have sometimes had the option to confer the daily labor of dependency care to others—generally other women, mostly poor and ill-situated. Poor women who have had dependency responsibilities along with paid employment have often relied on female familial help. The gendered and privatized nature of dependency work has meant, first, that men have rarely shared these responsibilities—at least with the women of their own class—and, second, that the equitable distribution of dependency work, both among genders and among classes, has rarely been considered in the discussions of political and social justice which take as their starting point the public lives of men.

As women from many different classes increasingly participate in paid employment, adequate provisions for dependency care—child daycare, care for the elderly, time for family members to care for ill children, and so on—have surfaced as a major social concern. One response has been various kinds of social legislation that provide for leaves for parents with newborn children and for workers with family members who are ill or temporarily disabled. It is no secret that among industrialized nations, the United States, in spite of its early history of equal opportunity employment legislation, is especially primitive in its response to the concerns of dependency work. At long last, in 1993, a national piece of legislation,

The Family and Medical Leave Act (FMLA) (Public Law 103-3, February 5, 1993, 107 Stat., 6-29) provides for some parental leave and some leave time to take care of ailing family members. The act is a rare piece of social policy insofar as it recognizes a public responsibility for dependency care.

The standard liberal tradition that policymakers appeal to, most especially in the United States, but to varying degrees in other Western democracies as well, does not acknowledge the claims of dependency. The liberal political philosophy that supplies the idealizations and the utopian visions of which contemporary society is an (albeit poor) approximation have as little to say about dependency as do the policymakers. The result is particularly detrimental to women's aspirations to empowerment and equality. And this despite the pretensions to a gender egalitarianism in the rhetoric of Western democracies and in the presumed gender-blindness of liberal political philosophy.

This neglect suggests that the ability to incorporate dependency concerns serves as a criterion of adequacy for any theory of a just social order that purports to advocate gender equality. John Rawls's egalitarianism will serve as the case study for the adequacy of liberal philosophy in recognizing dependency concerns. Elsewhere I discuss the adequacy of Rawlsian contractual liberalism to dependency concerns in detail (Kittay, N.d.). Here I focus on the notion of social cooperation as a keystone of that theory. The egalitarian ideal informing and informed by the idea of social cooperation leaves no space for dependency concerns because it requires the idea of mutual reciprocity by cooperating members. But such reciprocity cannot always pertain to persons in a relation of dependency, that is, between dependent and care-giver. In order to include the fact of dependency and its impact on those who do dependency work, we are compelled to enlarge the concept of social cooperation to consider a form of social interaction that, without being exploitative or neglectful of the concerns of any party, does not presume equality in power

and situation of all parties. In the FMLA, we find elements of the expanded notion of social cooperation I advocate. But it falls short of what the crisis requires, and its limitations can be attributed to its fundamental adherence to the liberal model that is being criticized. The inadequacy of the FMLA reveals the failure of liberal theories to conceptualize social cooperation in such a way that provides women with the gender equality they purport to endorse.

THE DEPENDENCY CRITIQUE OF LIBERAL EGALITARIANISM

Contemporary liberal egalitarians tend to regard gender as a morally irrelevant category and endorse the ideal of sexual equality. Feminists, however, have asked not only what it will take for women to achieve equality but have interrogated liberal understandings of the ideal itself. Some feminists have evoked both women's difference from men and women's differences among themselves.[1] Their *difference critiques* of equality have pointed to the implicit use of men—*more specifically white middle-class men*—as *the* standard against which equality is assessed. These feminists have argued that this norm is unfit for incorporating all whose identity is marked by their gender, race, class, and other socially salient difference.[2] Other feminists, elaborating a *dominance critique*, have underscored the power difference between men and women. Men's entrenched dominance over women means that gender-neutral, equality-based policies either fail to address issues that specifically affect women or merely preserve the relations of dominance that are already in effect.[3] The considerations to which I have alluded in the introductory paragraphs of this essay form still another critique of dominant views of equality. This I call the *dependency* critique.[4] The dependency critique maintains that by construing society as an association of equals, conceived as individuals with equal powers, equally situated in the competition for the benefits of social cooperation, one disregards the inevitable dependencies of the human condition, thereby neglecting the condition both of dependents and those who care for dependents (see Kittay, N.d.).

The dependency critique looks beyond women's socially prescribed differences from and subordination to men by considering the difficulties in assimilating women to the liberal ideal of equality. Its focus is on the circumstances under which the ideal was conceived and, more specifically, on the presumption that inevitable human dependencies and the consequences of such dependency for social organization are outside the political sphere for which the ideal of equality was articulated. Traditional formulations of liberal equality which originated as a challenge to feudalism posited an ideal for male heads of household. The feudalistic dependencies inherent in political hierarchy were targets of liberal thinkers such as Locke and Rousseau. Yet by positing equality for the male heads of households the dependencies of human development and frailty can remain unaddressed, at least as long as the household can accommodate these needs—an accommodation made possible by the privatized labor of women. The dependencies that cannot be banished by fiat are sustained by a social organization that creates a secondary dependence in those who care for dependents. They remain outside the society of equals insofar as they cannot function as the independent and autonomous agents of liberal theory who are presumed to be equally empowered and equally situated to engage in a fair competition for the benefits of social cooperation. For the woman who cares for dependents, the *dependency worker,* is not so situated—not as long as her responsibilities lie with another who cannot survive or thrive without her ministrations. Her attention is directed to another's needs; even her understanding of her own needs are enmeshed with the needs of a vulnerable other whose fundamental well-being is entrusted to her. And yet, within a liberal doctrine of society as a contractual agreement between equals, she should

be an autonomous and independent individual. Liberalism constructed an equality for heads of households (wherein dependencies exist within the household and are attended to by women), and then counted the head of household as an *individual* who is independent and who can act on his own behalf. The equality for individuals overlays the equality for household heads, creating the illusion that dependencies do not exist and that the extension of equality to all, not only heads of households, is easily accomplished.

The illusion sustains a fiction that society is composed only of independent individuals who come together to form associations of social cooperation[5] and that an egalitarian notion of justice is served by considering those individuals to be free and equal (that is, self-originating sources of claims) who are equally situated and equally empowered. But social cooperation is required not only by autonomous and independently functioning individuals for the purposes of mutually improving life chances, but first and foremost for the purpose of sustaining those who are not independently functioning, those who are not equally situated, and those who are unable to benefit from an equal empowerment. They are persons who are too young, too ill, too disabled, or too enfeebled by old age to care for themselves and to speak for themselves. These persons are our children, our parents, our siblings, our companions, and, at some points in life, ourselves. In states of dependency, we are unable to discharge the responsibilities and carry the burdens of the *equal* citizen; we have to rely on our caretaker to fulfill our basic needs; and we have no public or political voice except the voice of the dependency worker charged with articulating as well as meeting our needs. These dependencies are part of a network of interdependencies that form the central bonds of human social life. The care and attention to the vulnerabilities of dependent persons on the part of the dependency worker and the trust invested by the dependent in the dependency worker are among the most essential of social interactions.

When the fact of dependency and its social dimensions within the political conception of society is omitted, the secondary dependence of the dependency worker and the contribution of even the most dependent to the fabric of human relations is missed. The dependency worker acquires a dependence on others to supply the resources needed to sustain herself and the dependents who are in her charge. The dependency relation is a cooperative arrangement sustained by these resources, the labor of the dependency worker, and the responsiveness to care on the part of the cared-for.[6] The dependency worker may be unpaid, caring for familial dependents, or paid, caring for dependents in an institutional or home setting. Whether her work is done for pay or as a familial obligation,[7] the dependency worker attends to and voices the needs and desires of her charge in addition to, and sometimes at the expense of, her own; she assumes the same responsibilities other citizens have to each other and to themselves and assumes the added responsibility on behalf of one who cannot meet these responsibilities alone. In the distribution of burdens and benefits, most liberal egalitarian theories count each person as one. The incapacity of the dependent—to sustain her share of burdens and claim her share of benefits—and the obligation of the dependency worker—to assume the burdens of more than one and, at times, to put the benefits to her charge ahead of her own—ill-suits an economy of social cooperation presumed for an association of equals: that each will equally assume a share of the burdens and each will claim her own share of benefits. That women historically and customarily assume the role of dependency worker means that such an account of equality leaves out many women who retain their role and status as dependency workers. Because a redistribution of dependency work has too often exploited the situation of poor women, the dependency critique provides a framework for investigating theories and policies of equality across race and class as well as gender, and looks toward a more adequate understanding of gender equality.

PRESUPPOSITIONS OF RAWLSIAN EQUALITY

Rawls identifies society "as a fair system of social cooperation" and looks for "principles specifying the basic rights and liberties and the forms of equality most appropriate to those cooperating, once they are regarded as citizens, as free and equal persons" (Rawls 1993, 27).

Free and equal persons come together in the initial situation to choose principles of justice they can accept when they do not know their own status in life, their own conception of the good, their own particular dispositions and psychological propensities, and to what generation they belong. In *Political Liberalism* Rawls again characterizes the modeling of the equality of citizens: "To model this equality in the original position we say that the parties, as representatives of those who meet the condition, are symmetrically situated. This requirement is fair because in establishing fair terms of social cooperation (in the case of the basic structure) the only relevant feature of persons is their possessing the moral powers . . . and their having the normal capacities to be a cooperating member of society over the course of a lifetime" (Rawls 1993, 79). He speaks of the "representation for equality" as "an easy matter" of situating the parties to the original position symmetrically to one another and describing them identically. And yet in this easy and seemingly transparent move, so much is presumed.

First, *all* citizens are idealized as "fully cooperating members of society *over the course of a complete life*" (Rawls 1980, 546; emphasis mine). Rawls continues, "The idealization means that everyone has sufficient intellectual powers to play a *normal* part in society, and no one suffers from *unusual* needs that are *especially difficult* to fulfill, for example *unusual and costly medical requirements*" (1980, 546; emphasis mine).[8] The theory is constructed for the "normal" situation and only afterwards made to accommodate *unusual* circumstances. But if the normal situation is not that of a fully functioning person who is a co-operating member throughout his or her lifetime, if we are instead all potential dependents and the "unusual" needs are an inevitable feature of any human community, and if these needs demand dependency workers constrained in the degree of their full cooperation as *independent* citizens, then the idealization does not merely grease the wheels of the Rawlsian construction but renders it of questionable value in providing a theory that will deliver justice for dependents and dependency workers.

Second, the symmetry that Rawls posits for the representatives in original position is bound to a notion of persons as *free* and equal. For a person to be free means here, in part, to view oneself as a "self-originating" or "self-authenticating source of valid claims." But can the dependency worker be seen as "a self-originating source of valid claims"? She is as likely to put forward the claims of her charge as she is to put forward her own. Furthermore, there is often no clear separation between claims that she makes on her own behalf and those that originate with the charge— even though the conflict between these sets of claims can sometimes be palpable. If there is an important notion of freedom for the dependency worker, it is often one that recognizes the bond she shares with her dependent, even as it recognizes her own independent personhood.

Third, equality requires a measure. In Rawls's theory the comparative measure of interpersonal well-being is the index of primary goods, a list of goods that all persons require if they are to be able to realize their own conception of the good, given the moral powers that we have as free and equal persons. Rawls's moral powers do not include the responsiveness to vulnerability needed for care; nor do they include the good of being cared for when we become dependent or having the support we require to care for another if another becomes dependent on us. Consequently, the centrality of dependency in human life, and the concomitant value of human relationship and care in a relationship are absent from the list of primary goods.

Fourth, Rawls, building on Hume, identifies the "circumstances of justice." These are the circumstances under which the constitution of a society of free and equal persons who cooperate in the benefit and the burdens of social organization takes place. Missing from these is the circumstance of human development that incurs a period of dependency for each of us, a period during which we are unequally situated relative to those who are independent.[9]

Last, a sense of justice depends on an acceptance of a conception of social cooperation. Rawls writes of "the equally sufficient capacity (which I assume to be realized) to understand and to act from *the public conception of social cooperation*" (Rawls 1980, 546; emphasis mine). It is this notion of social cooperation that I explore here.

THE RAWLSIAN CONCEPTION OF SOCIAL COOPERATION

Social cooperation, writes Rawls, involves "fair terms of cooperation," not "simply . . . coordinated social activity efficiently organized and guided by publicly recognized rules to achieve some overall end" (1993, 300). That is, along with coordinated self-interested activity—what Rawls calls the *rational*—social cooperation demands a sense of what is fair—what Rawls calls the *reasonable*.

If they are both rational and reasonable, dependency concerns ought to be included within the features of a well-ordered society reflected in the public conception of social cooperation. To insist that it is reasonable to expect that the social order consider the care of dependents follows directly from the observation that any society into which we are born and expect to live out our lives contains those who are dependent and thus unable to realize any of their moral capacities—much less survive or thrive—independently. Only if a human society exists under especially hard conditions would we exempt its members from the moral responsibility to care for its dependents. Thus it is reasonable to expect that a well-ordered society is one that attends to the needs of dependents and whatever else that necessitates.

Furthermore, we can argue for the rationality of each individual—acting in their own self-interest—to choose principles that would include such concerns among the terms of social cooperation, for given the developmental nature and the fragility of human life, it is likely that dependency will touch each of our lives in some form. Whether we find ourselves dependent or needing to care for a dependent, it is rational to suppose that we would wish to be cared for or to be provided the resources by which we can provide care.

Although the inclusion of dependency concerns within a conception of social cooperation is both reasonable and rational, the mention of such are not to be found. The acknowledgment of "*normal health care*" (1993, 21; emphasis mine), covers some dependency concerns, but leaves out the daily care of infants and young children—which are not *health* care—and prolonged illness or states of diminished independence (e.g., a handicapping condition), which arguably are not conventionally understood as "normal" health care.

Rawls has many times acknowledged limits to his theory and expressed hopes that the theory could be extended, but the omission of dependency concerns is a result of the characterization of social cooperation—a characterization which it is the goal of this essay to identify and dispute. "Fair terms of cooperation," according to this view, articulates "an idea of reciprocity and mutuality: all who cooperate must benefit, or share in common burdens, in some appropriate fashion judged by a suitable benchmark of comparison" (Rawls 1993, 300). The point is made still sharper when Rawls writes, "Those who can take part in social cooperation over a complete life, and who are willing to honor the appropriate fair terms of agreement are regarded as equal citizens" (1993, 302).

But this understanding of social cooperation leaves out many persons. The second quotation cited in the preceding paragraph even suggests that Rawls does not extend *citizenship* to those who are permanently and so sufficiently inca-

pacitated that they cannot be expected to restrict their freedoms in relevant ways[10] or to participate and so reciprocate in relevant ways. But why should the contingent fact that someone is born, let us say, sufficiently mentally disabled necessitate his or her exclusion from citizenship? There are some political activities the mentally disabled may not be able to engage in—for example, they may be incapable of enough political understanding to vote—but surely they need to receive the protections of political justice all the same.[11] The temporarily dependent can defer reciprocating until the individual regains full capability. But during our period of dependency we cannot reciprocate. Those who restrict their liberty, or use their labor, resources, or energy on our behalf cannot be repaid by us as long as we remain dependent. We may or may not be able to reciprocate at some time, but the labor expended on our behalf cannot be so expended on the condition that we will reciprocate: a child may not reach maturity; an ill person may die; a now needy and elderly parent may not have been an adequate provider or nurturer. Who then is to reciprocate the efforts of the caretaker?[12] Unless the needs of their caretakers are to be met in some other form of reciprocity, the only available moral characterizations of the caretaker's function is as exploitation or supererogation. When we consider relations of dependency, we see that they are not characterized as social cooperation according to fair terms of cooperation, and those whose social relations are defined by the dependency relation then fall outside the bounds of social cooperation as understood by Rawls's characterization.

Relations of dependency may be excluded from the discussion either because (1) they are not appropriately characterized as pertaining to *political* justice or (2) they pertain to political justice but not to a theory that holds that justice is fairness.[13] Is it then appropriate to exclude the dependent and the dependency worker from a fully adequate conception of social cooperation? First, if political justice is to express the principles of a well-ordered society, then it seems that dependency concerns do fall within the scope of political justice. A society that does not care for its dependents or that cares for them only by unfairly exploiting the labor of some cannot be said to be well-ordered any more than a society that enslaves part of its population. I cannot see how any thoughtful reflection would yield an opposing insight. Second, if the "fair terms of cooperation" are identified as the reasonable and the rational, then I have already shown that it is both reasonable and rational to consider dependency matters in formulating principles of justice for a well-ordered society. Furthermore, if we reorient our political insights so that we see the centrality of human relationship to our happiness and well-being, and we recognize dependency relations as foundational human relations, then it becomes obvious that such concerns are among the basic motivations for creating a social order, and that a just social order must concern itself with what fairness requires for both dependents—who, even in their neediness, contribute to the ongoing nature of human relationships—and the one who cares for dependents—whose social contribution is invisible when dependency is thought to be outside the social order. If our reflective judgments confirm that those who are dependent (whether temporarily or permanently) ought to be appropriately cared for, and if those reflections focus on the importance of the central human bonds that form around dependency needs, then a society is well-ordered only if it offers adequate support to dependents and those who care for them in relations of dependency.[14]

SOCIAL COOPERATION AS *DOULIA*

If fairness obtains only for those who are themselves fully functioning, have normal capacities, and are in social interactions with others who are similarly endowed, then even if we insist that dependency concerns have a political dimension, justice as fairness will not pertain to dependency concerns. This idea of fairness and social cooperation is grounded on a notion of reciprocity alien to those in dependency relations. But if social cooperation can be seen to involve a second sort of interaction (similar to, but distinct from, the reciprocal interaction among those equally situated and equally empowered), then there is a way we can expand the conception of justice as fairness. Cooperation between persons where intergenerational needs are to be met will illustrate the point. When we consider the Family and Medical Leave Act, we see how it incorporates, to a limited degree, an expanded notion of reciprocity and social cooperation.

Families in modern industrial and urbanized societies are often not grounded in a community and often live far from other family members. Periods in which some family members are stressed by special dependency cares are particularly difficult. These are the stressful times that the FMLA is meant to alleviate. The situation of the postpartum mother who is caring for her newborn is especially interesting. Her need is most acute directly after childbirth when her infant is utterly dependent and her own body requires healing and rest—even for the production of her infant's food. Traditional societies sometimes mark this period as a time when the mother is entitled to special privileges and care. Contemporary mothers in the United States have had to make do with very inadequate provisions. At least until the enactment of FMLA (which as we will see only applies to some, not all, workers), the father (if present) has rarely been released from his employment, regardless of employment status; the mother is often pressured to return to paid employment as soon as possible, a situation alleviated but not fully remedied by FMLA; friends and relatives, whose assistance is not an option in FMLA, since it defines family narrowly, are rarely available to help and less so since so many women are now in the paid work force; and paid help, for those who can afford help, is the "baby nurse." Generally, however, it is not the baby who needs a nurse; the recuperating mother is normally capable of caring for the baby only if someone helps her take care of herself and her other duties. Adapting a strategy found in a number of traditional cultures, some have instituted a form of caretaking whereby the postpartum mother is assigned a postpartum care-giver, a *doula,* who assists the mother, and at times relieves her.[15] *Doula* originally meant slave or servant in Greek, but it is appropriated here to mean a person who renders a service to another who renders service to a dependent. A doula is not provided for in the FMLA, nor am I arguing here that it be provided. But I want to reflect on the principle embodied in the person of the doula and in the practice which we will call *doulia.*[16]

Let us extend the idea of a doula beyond one who provides a service to the postpartum mother, so that it describes those who attend to the needs of those who attend to another who is utterly dependent upon them (whether temporarily or permanently). In so doing we displace both the relation of servant and served and the traditional relation of reciprocity among equals as models of cooperative activity and put at the center a relation of *nested dependencies.* These nested dependencies link those who help and those who require help to give aid to ones who cannot help themselves. Extending the notion of the service performed by the doula, let us speak of "doulia" to indicate a concept by which service is tendered to those who become needy by virtue of attending to those in need, so that all can be well cared for.[17] The form of social cooperation that emerges from the relation between the doula, the mother, and the infant is captured by the colloquial phrase "What goes round comes round" when it is used to describe a form of cooperation often engaged in by members of poorer communities:[18] I, as a member of the community, help another who requires my help, with the expectation that someone in the community, not necessarily the individual whom I helped, will come to my aid if and when that is required.

This notion of social cooperation is not as far from the Rawlsian project as it may at first seem.

Rawls understands that society is an association that persists through generations and that our efforts to pass the world on to the next generation without depleting its resources—a responsibility entailed by the "just savings principle"—is not reciprocated to us by those we benefit. The "chronological unfairness" to which Rawls refers resembles the cooperative idea embodied in doulia. And indeed, both the savings principle and doulia are consequences of the facts of human development and generation: as the benefit of the previous generation passes through us to the next and so on, the care a mother bestows on her child calls not only for reciprocation from the adult child but also for the grown children to care appropriately for a future generation.[19]

But how, one might ask, does this private interaction of mother, infant, and doula translate into a public conception of social cooperation? For this we need a public conception of doulia. To urge that the well-being of dependents *and* their caretakers *and* the relation itself between caretaker and dependent must be seen as requirements of public understanding of social cooperation, I invoke the fact that dependency is inherent to the human condition, that it often marks our most profound attachments, that care of a dependent morally obliges the dependency worker to give a certain priority to the welfare of her charge, and that the constitution of dependency relations is such that the parties are of necessity unequal. That is, it is the responsibility of the public order to ensure that a dependent has a caretaker, that the dependency relation is respected, and that the caretaker is adequately provided for so that her dependency work does not in turn deplete her. Without a broadened conception of reciprocity and a suitably modified sense of fairness, the dependency worker and dependent cannot be embraced within the bonds of social cooperation and accorded their full moral worth as equals in a well-ordered society.

In the next section, I argue that to the extent that the FMLA recognizes the dependency responsibilities of those engaged in paid employment and accepts a public responsibility to assure that those in a relation of dependency have adequate care and can give adequate care, it identifies social cooperation in the enlarged sense of doulia. Where it restricts leave time and opportunities, and where it limits resources allocated to those in relations of dependency, it reverts to the traditional liberal model.

READING THE FAMILY AND MEDICAL LEAVE ACT OF 1993

The FMLA is, in many ways, emblematic of the sort of legislation and social policy that is required to meet dependency needs of paid workers. It permits up to twelve workweeks of unpaid leave within any twelve-month period for one or more of the following reasons:

(A) Because of the birth of a son or daughter of the employee and in order to care for such son or daughter.
(B) Because of the placement of a son or daughter with the employee for adoption or foster care.
(C) In order to care for the spouse, or son, daughter, or parent of the employee, if such spouse, son, daughter, or parent has a serious health condition.
(D) Because of a serious health condition that makes the employee unable to perform the functions of the position of such employee. (Public Law 103-3—Feb. 5, 1993, 107 Stat. 9)

This law expressly recognizes the dependency relations that I have argued are so grievously ignored in much political theory. And it recognizes the importance of acknowledging some of the demands of dependency not only of the employee herself, but those of the individuals who depend on her. Given that the United States has had no provisions set by law to address the needs of paid employees with such concerns, the Family and Medical Leave Act is an immensely important piece of legislation.

But the law is relatively limited in its scope and in the real benefits it provides, and so its contribution to fair equality for all is circumscribed. I suggest that the limitations are traceable to an ideology of reciprocity and equality that continues to push dependency concerns back into the domain of the private, that is, to a conception of dependency concerns which still fails to recognize the extent to which addressing these needs is a matter of the social cooperation required for a well-ordered and just society.

Among the limitations of the act are the following: leave is unpaid; employers with less than fifty employees are exempt from the FMLA; and the FMLA construes family in relatively traditional terms. Let us look at the "Findings and Purposes" of the FMLA, and then return to consider if these bear on the limitations of the act.
(a) FINDINGS.—Congress finds that—

(1) the number of single-parent households and two-parent households in which the single parent or both parents work is increasing significantly;
(2) it is important for the development of children and the family unit that fathers and mothers be able to participate in early child-rearing and the care of family members who have serious health conditions;
(3) the lack of employment policies to accommodate working parents can force individuals to choose between job security and parenting;
(4) there is inadequate job security for employees who have serious health conditions that prevent them from working for temporary periods;
(5) due to the nature of the roles of men and women in our society, the primary responsibility for family caretaking often falls on women, and such responsibility affects the working lives of women more than it affects the working lives of men; and
(6) employment standards that apply to one gender only have serious potential for encouraging employers to discriminate against

employees and applicants for employment who are that gender. (Public Law 103-3, 107 Stat. 6-7)

First among the findings is that the number of single-parent households and two-parent households in which the parent(s) all work has significantly increased. The fact that this counts as a finding for a bill such as the FMLA is indicative of the way in which the breakdown of the sexual division of labor on the male side of the divide—expanding the paid labor force to include more women—is putting pressure on degenderizing the female side of the divide—the largely private and unpaid care for dependents. This is the first significant step in understanding that dependency concerns need to be a part of the public understanding of social cooperation: that decisions to undertake dependency care cannot remain matters of private decision making with only private consequences, but belong within the public arena.

The second finding serves to recognize the nonfungibility of many dependency relations—e.g., the need of a sick child to have a parent attending her—but also moves retrogressively in the direction of the privatization of dependency care by suggesting that the importance of early child rearing and care of family members who have serious health conditions is for "the development of children and the family unit" rather than for the general welfare of the nation and so a public feature of social cooperation.

The third finding points to the need for policies that avoid pitting job security against parenting demands. Both job security and parenting are regarded as matters that are important for the well-being of individuals. The law recognizes the importance of the state in assuring both goods to those individuals who may be torn between competing concerns, and so it establishes a responsibility of public institutions to assure that individuals can fulfill dependency responsibilities as well as job-related duties, and that the burden of dependency work must sit not solely on the

shoulders of those who undertake these obligations.[20] But how far does it go? Not very far. The leave is unpaid and the exemption for employers of fewer than fifty persons is not insignificant. There is no acknowledgment of public responsibility to assure job security, given parental responsibility for children. Why should parenting responsibilities be privileged with respect to job security? The basis for securing such a privileged relation is tenuous indeed, as the law's limited scope indicates.

It is here that a public conception of doulia needs to be brought into play—the reciprocity of doulia. More than "accommodation" is required. Accommodation presumes the situation of employment as it is now; accommodation neither challenges concepts of what counts as part of the economy nor employment conditions that presume privatized dependency arrangements. To acknowledge the contribution of those engaged in dependency work to the larger society—the contribution to the continuity, stability, and resources of society—means that the larger society has an obligation to support dependency work. Supporting dependency work means relieving the dependency worker of some of the costs and burdens of responsibility for the care of dependents. The argument from a public conception of doulia is that *fairness* demands that business or government—whatever public institutions are appropriate—carry some of the costs of dependency work so that dependents within our society can be properly cared for without exploiting dependency workers.

The fourth finding, which addresses the inadequate job security for workers with serious or prolonged health conditions, is an acknowledgment of the vulnerability to dependency that is shared by all employees.

The fifth and sixth findings are of special interest, for they acknowledge the inequity that results from the gender-specific nature of much dependency work. That work has occupied the female side of the sexual division of labor. The fifth and sixth findings call our attention to the failure of efforts to bring about gender equality on the side of the sexual division of labor traditionally occupied by men when the labor on the other side of the divide—the side traditionally occupied by women (see Hadfield 1993) remains the sole, and unsupported, responsibility of women. The justification for the bill that can be garnered from findings five and six is an equality argument, an inference sustained by the fourth and fifth stated purposes of the bill (see below). But until we reconstrue equality and political conceptions such as justice and social cooperation, and until it becomes a public priority to refashion sensibilities accordingly, the FMLA cannot alter the gender-structured nature of dependency concerns nor can it move us sufficiently in the direction of understanding that dependency work cannot be privatized and genderized without violating justice and equality.

Now let us now look at the "Purposes" of the act. I reproduce these in full: (b) PURPOSES.—It is the purpose of this Act—

(1) to balance the demands of the workplace with the needs of families, to promote the stability and economic security of families, and to promote national interests in preserving family integrity;

(2) to entitle employees to take reasonable leave for medical reasons, for the birth or adoption of a child, and for the care of a child, spouse, or parent who has a serious health condition;

(3) to accomplish the purposes described in paragraphs (1) and (2) in a manner that accommodates the legitimate interests of employers;

(4) to accomplish the purposes described in paragraphs (1) and (2) in a manner that, consistent with the Equal Protection Clause of the Fourteenth Amendment, minimizes the potential for employment discrimination on the basis of sex by ensuring generally that leave is available for eligible medical reasons (including maternity-related disability) and for compelling family reasons, on a gender-neutral basis; and

(5) to promote the goal of equal employment opportunity for women and men, pursuant to such clause. (Public Law 103-3, 107 Stat. 6-7)

The purposes of this act recognize "national interests in preserving family integrity." But the act does not identify what about family integrity is important for the national interest, and so it cannot count anything but a limited set of traditional structures as family. The purpose stated in (3) is to "accomplish the purposes described in (1) and (2) in a manner that accommodates the legitimate interests of employers." But if there are national interests in preserving family integrity, why should (1) and (2) not trump the interests of employers? And if they don't, what are the consequences?

In the light of the reading of the "Findings and Purposes," let us consider what I have listed as the limitations of the act. First, the leave is unpaid—all twelve weeks of permissible leave time are unpaid. To take off from work to attend a sick child then remains a luxury, or a factor moving one closer to impoverishment. Not only is the United States one of the last industrialized countries to have a family leave policy, it is also the only one in which the leave is entirely unpaid.[21] One of the purported findings to which the act is addressed is the increase in the number of single-parent households. But how many single-parent employees can afford to be without pay for three months of the year? How are they supposed to put food on the table of a sick and needy person? One need not argue that the full twelve weeks ought to be paid, but surely some of that time needs to be paid leave—by law, not merely by the goodwill of some employers who provide paid leave—if it is to have a substantial impact on the practices of single-parent households—which now constitute one-fourth of all households.[22]

Second, employers with fewer than fifty employees are exempt from the family leave policy. But employees in companies with fewer than fifty employees make up a very large portion of the American work force. In fact, they make up the *majority* of the work force.[23] That means that a majority of paid employees in this country are not covered under the FMLA! What is clear, again, is that heeding dependency concerns is not viewed as a general responsibility. These can be trumped by the employers' needs—benefits for whom are not only thought to be personal but also to be part of the economic well-being of the wider public—and nothing is put in place to meet the putatively *personal* demands of the employee, even when family integrity is identified as a "national interest." Dependency care is not counted as part of the economic structure; it does not figure into the Gross National Product.

Third, the FMLA construes family in relatively traditional terms. Although *parent* includes not only biological parents but also any individuals who have stood in *loco parentis,* and the term *son or daughter* is defined as "a biological, adopted, or foster child, a stepchild, a legal ward, or a child of a parent standing in loco parentis," the term "spouse" is restricted to husband or wife, leaving out nonmarried adults who are cohabitating, gay and lesbian families, extended families, and so forth. Contrast this with the "nurturance leave" proposed by feminist legal theorist Nadine Taub (1984, 85), which argues for nurturance leaves for any adult members of a household. If the stress in our policies is to support dependency relations because the fabric of social structure is founded on the maintenance of such relations, then the relations themselves and not the social institutions in which they have traditionally been lodged ought to become the focus of our concern.

The decisions or situations from which these dependency relations result may appear to be private decisions between the parties involved—decisions between parties which do not devolve obligations on third parties. But there are some social institutions which appear to be formed by private decisions between the parties involved and which nonetheless induce obligations in third parties.[24] Marriage is such an institution. The private decision another and I make to be a married cou-

ple means that socially and legally certain actions are binding on my employer, my landlord, hospitals, insurance agencies, the IRS, and so on. In an analogous fashion, the private decision to take on the work of dependency and to form a dependency relation with a charge ought to induce third party obligations to support the dependency worker in his or her care for the charge. In the case of marriage, the binding obligations are part of a larger societal interest in maintaining the institution of marriage. Recognition of its legal and social status means that the existence of a connection between two individuals is acknowledged.

A major reason, however, to recognize such institutions is that they are the loci of the care and sustenance of dependents. The relation of dependency is morally and socially still more salient and fundamental than marriage, and so forms the very ground of this feature of the marriage relation. But the social technology of traditional marriage and family makes the dependency worker and charge within the nuclear family vulnerable to the vicissitudes of the marriage arrangement and vulnerable in a relation of (to use Amartya Sen's term) "cooperative conflict."[25] The claim on third parties to support and help sustain the dependency relation, independent of a particular arrangement such as marriage, has morally the stronger claim. This claim is realized in the public obligation of social cooperation I have called *doulia.* The argument for such doulia transcends the institution of marriage as traditionally understood and family arrangements sanctioned by traditional marriage and biological relation. Its basis is the undertaking of care, and responsibility for care, and the dependency to which the caretaker then becomes vulnerable.

The FMLA is an example of the legislative and policy directions in which the dependency critique urges us, but it remains still all too firmly grounded in a conception of society primarily constituted by those who are healthy, autonomous adults, who, as Rawls would have it, are "fully functioning" and for whom justice requires the reciprocity of those equally situated. We need to shift our vision and see society as constituted by the nested dependencies that require a concept of justice between persons who are equal in their connectedness but unequal in their vulnerability and for whom a notion of doulia—of caring for those who care—is central.

The arguments in this essay have been directed at demonstrating that the Rawlsian and the liberal account of social cooperation is at best incomplete and at worst inadequate, and that legislation such as the FMLA falls short of meeting the needs of dependency demands as long as it remains within a framework which is represented in the Rawlsian account. The claim here is that a society cannot be well-ordered, that is, it cannot be one in which all its members are sustained and included within the ideal of equality, if it fails to be a society characterized by care. For a society to be characterized by care, we need something other than the affirmation of the importance of family integrity. We need structures that will assure that dependency work, whether done in families or other social institutions, can be carried out under nonexploitative conditions. What is required is that the public understanding of social cooperation include respect for the importance of caring for one another and the value of receiving care and giving care. It then becomes a matter of political justice for basic institutions to *make provisions for and facilitate satisfactory dependency relations*. The only assurance that both dependents and dependency workers are well cared for and can benefit from an egalitarian ideal is the inclusion of enabling conditions and resources for care through the social institutions that reflect the public understanding of social cooperation. For a well-ordered society, therefore, to instill in its citizens a sense of justice and a sense of what is right, it must also be sensitive to our vulnerability to dependency and to the vulnerability of those who attend to dependents.[26] Rawls speaks of the need to give priority to the basic liberties

and points out that even when the political will does not yet exist to do what is required (as it does not in the society in which we live), "part of the political task is to help fashion it" (1993, 297). The possibilities of the FMLA and its shortcomings indicate that it is no less the case that since the political will to imbue citizens with such a sensitivity and sense of priority for care does not yet exist, "part of the political task is to help fashion it."

NOTES

I thank the editors of this special issue and the anonymous reviewers for their suggestions. I also thank Lisa Conradi for her comments at the Conference on Feminism and Social Policy, the audience at the session for their remarks, and members of the New York City Society for Women in Philosophy Research Group in Ethical, Social and Political Philosophy for their helpful discussion of an earlier draft.

1. The literature is extensive. I mention but a few discussions of difference feminists. See Allen (1987); hooks (1987); Kay (1985); Littleton (1987); Minow (1990); Scales-Trent (1989); West (1987); Williams (1982, 1985); Wolgast (1980).

2. bell hooks (1987) asks, "Since men are not equals in white supremacist, capitalist, patriarchical class structure, which men do women want to be equal to?" The point stressed by a number of feminists and captured by hooks is that the striving for equality on the part of the largely white and middle-class women's movement presumes an egalitarianism into which women can integrate themselves. In Kittay (N.d.), I call this the "heterogeneity critique." It speaks to a heterogeneity among women not acknowledged in demands for sexual equality. Because the heterogeneity critique is aimed less at any particular formulation of equality than at a prevailing formulation of sex equality which masks intragender inequalities, inequalities that result from race, class, sexual orientation, age, and disabilities, as well cross-gender inequalities, it is orthogonal to the other critiques. The

force of the heterogeneity critiques emerges with special poignancy when one looks at the racial complexion of dependency workers in countries blighted by racial inequity.

3. Catharine MacKinnon is the main exponent of this view (1987, 1989).

4. Several feminist theorists have regarded the work of liberal political philosophers with an eye toward issues of dependency without articulating the dependency critique. Those who have done so have spoken of "the need for more than justice," as Baier (1987) entitles one work expounding this theme (see also Baier 1985, 1986). Others, such as Patemen (1988) and Held (1987a, 1987b) have shed light on the unacknowledged gender considerations that undergird a social contract engaged in by men. The work of Okin (1979, 1989a, 1989b) brings the historical and contemporary neglect of women's involvement in dependency to the forefront of her political considerations. Okin has been the most articulate, yet sympathetic critic of the influential political theory of John Rawls on matters that concern familial dependency relations. Tronto's (1993) work bringing the notion of care into the arena of political theory may also be seen to be a contribution to the dependency critique.

5. See Young (N.d.) for an interesting discussion of a false ideal of independence in understanding citizenship.

6. Tronto (1993) points out that caring is an activity that requires several stages for its completion: caring about, caring for, response to care. We may note that the person cared for need be only potentially responsive in order for her to be a part of a dependency relation.

7. I thank John Baker for suggesting that I make explicit my view that the dependency critique is meant to hold for dependency workers whether they voluntarily take on that task or whether they are perforce burdened with it.

8. Rawls repeats a similar statement in *Political Liberalism*: "The normal range is specified as follows: since the fundamental problem of justice concerns the relations among those who are full and active participants in society, and directly or indirectly associated together over the course of a whole life, it is reasonable to *assume that*

everyone has physical needs and psychological capacities within some normal range. Thus the problem of special health care and how to treat mentally defective are set. If we can work out a viable theory for the normal range, we can attempt to handle these other cases later" (Rawls 1993, 272 n. 10; emphasis is mine).

9. Each of the above points, as well as a discussion of social cooperation are elaborated in Kittay (unpublished).

10. In *A Theory of Justice*, Rawls writes: "The main idea is that when a number of persons engage in a mutually advantageous cooperative venture according to rules, and thus restrict their liberty in ways necessary to yield advantages for all, those who have submitted to the restrictions have a right to a similar acquiescence on the part of those who have benefitted from their submission" (Rawls 1971, 112).

11. I thank Susan Okin for valuable discussion on this point.

12. It needs to be pointed out that the paid dependency worker is often paid not by the dependent, but by someone who stands in a relation of guardianship or stewardship to the dependent.

13. "How deep a fault this is must wait until the case itself can be examined," says Rawls and reminds us that political justice needs to be complemented by additional virtues (1993, 21).

14. When we look back to *A Theory of Justice,* we see that for Rawls the problem appears to be how to have strangers cooperate. Friends and intimate associates, so the supposition goes, cooperate because they have ties of sentiment. But consider, when a mother acts toward a child through ties of sentiment, many of her own needs—often including the need to earn an income—go unattended unless she has intimate ties to someone who is willing to cooperate and attend her needs. That is, her ties of sentiment provide little in the way of societal cooperative efforts that suffice to sustain her and her children. (Furthermore, the assumption that the mother's cooperative behavior toward her children is motivated by parental ties of sentiment makes a puzzle of the apparent frequency with which men so often feel less obligated by ties of sentiment to provide for their children when no longer involved with the mother—U.S.

fathers currently owe mothers $24 billion in unpaid child support, according to the *Report of the Federal Office of Child Support Enforcement [1990]*). It is just such a precarious dependence on ties of sentiment on the part of those (women mostly) who do dependency work, especially when it is unpaid—that leave them (again, women for the most part) so vulnerable to exploitation, (male) domination, and poverty. It is such precariousness that makes her inclusion in the political sphere so tentative.

15. See Aronow (1993). One of the doulas "recalls arriving at home late morning to find mothers who haven't eaten or dressed. 'They are so concerned that the baby is O.K., they forget to take care of themselves'" (Aronow 1993, 8).

16. I wish to thank Elfie Raymond for helping me search for a term to capture the concept articulated here.

17. See Stacks (1974) for a discussion of this ethic in the African American community. What Stacks describes as "swapping" is more like a one-to-one reciprocal arrangement than what I am trying to characterize by *doulia*. However, it resembles *doulia* insofar as reciprocity is deferred and is geared to the meeting of needs as they arise rather than as payment qua tit-for-tat exchanges.

18. This is a phrase Rawls borrows from Alexander Herzen. See Rawls (1971, 291).

19. I do not mean to suggest that we have a duty to *have* children because we have been cared for, but that we owe to any children we may have a quality of care at least as high as the care we received. And furthermore that the care bestowed on us is, in fact *reciprocated,* through care to the next generation.

20. That burden can be measured, in part, in economic terms. Estimates of the costs to workers of not having a parental leave only are $607 million versus approximately $110 million as based on the more generous leave policies of earlier versions of the act (Spalter-Roth and Hartmann 1990, 42). The cost is greatest to those least able to bear these costs, namely workers with the lowest incomes, with African American men doing worse than white men, white women doing worse than white men, and African American women doing worse than white women

(Spalter-Roth and Hartmann 1990, 2833). See Spalter-Roth and Hartmann (1990) for a detailed analysis. It is curious that in speaking of the cost of meeting dependency needs, the cost to businesses is a seen as a public concern, while the cost to the workers who bear the major burden is regarded a private concern.

21. Ellen Gilensky, Families and Work Institute, personal communication with author, New York City, 1 August 1994.

22. On the morning of the day I was to read this paper at the Feminist Theory and Social Policy Conference held at the University of Pittsburgh, the public radio station announced on its news program that in Pittsburgh the figure was one-third of all households.

23. Only 44 percent of women workers and 52 percent of men workers are covered by the current act which exempts employers with fewer than fifty employees (see Spalter-Roth and Hartmann 1990, 44).

24. This idea can be found in Kaplan (1993).

25. Sen (1990) has argued this point with respect to certain third world countries. Borrowing from the work of Okin (1989) and others, I extend Sen's argument to apply to traditional marriage within the industrialized world as well (Kittay N.d.).

26. See Goodin (1985) for a very useful discussion of our obligations to protect those who are vulnerable.

REFERENCES

Allen, Anita L. 1987. Taking Liberties: Privacy, Private Choice, and Social Contract Theory. *University of Cincinnati Law Review* 56(1–2).

Aronow, Ina. 1993. Doulas Step in when Mothers Need a Hand. *New York Times,* 1 August, 1, 8, Westchester Weekly.

Baier, Annette. 1985. Caring about Caring. In *Postures of the Mind: Essays on Mind and Morals.* Minneapolis: University of Minnesota Press.

———. 1986. Trust and Antitrust. *Ethics* 96: 231–60.

———. 1987. The Need for More than Justice. In *Science, Morality and Feminist Theory,* ed. Marsha Hanen and Kai Nielsen. Calgary: University of Calgary Press.

Daniels, Norman. 1990. Equality of What: Welfare, Resources, or Capabilities? *Philosophy and Phenomenological Research Supplement* 50: 273–96.

Goodin, Robert. 1985. *Protecting the Vulnerable.* Chicago: University of Chicago Press.

Hadfield, Gillian K. 1993. Households at Work: Beyond Labor Market Policies to Remedy the Gender Gap. *Georgetown Law Journal* 82: 89.

Held, Virginia. 1978. Men, Women, and Equal Liberty. In *Equality and Social Policy,* ed. Walter Feinberg. Urbana: University of Illinois Press.

———. 1987a. Non-contractual Society: A Feminist View. *Canadian Journal of Philosophy* 13: 111–37.

———. 1987b. Feminism and Moral Theory. In *Women and Moral Theory.* See Kittay and Meyers 1987.

hooks, bell. 1987. Feminism: A Movement to End Sexist Oppression. In *Equality and Feminism,* ed. Anne Phillips. New York: New York University Press.

Jaggar, Alison M. 1985. Women: Different but Equal? Douglass College, Rutgers University.

Kaplan, Morris. 1993. Intimacy and Equality: The Question of Lesbian and Gay Marriage. Paper delivered at the Stony Brook Philosophy Colloquium Series, 4 March.

Kay, Herma Hill. 1985. Equality and Difference: The Case of Pregnancy. *Berkeley Women's Law Journal* 1.

Kittay, Eva Feder. N.d. *Equality and the Inclusion of Women.* New York: Routledge. Forthcoming.

———. Unpublished. Equality, Rawls and the Dependency Critique.

Kittay, Eva F. and Diana T. Meyers. 1987. *Women and Moral Theory.* Totowa, NJ: Rowman and Littlefield.

Littleton, Christine A. 1987. Equality Across Difference: A Place for Rights Discourse? *Wisconsin Women's Law Journal* 3: 189–212.

MacKinnon, Catharine A. 1987. *Feminism Unmodified: Discourses on Life and Law.* Cambridge: Harvard University Press.

———. 1989. *Toward a Feminist Theory of the State.* Cambridge: Harvard University Press.

Minow, Martha. 1990. *Making All the Difference: Inclusion, Exclusion and the American Law.* Ithaca: Cornell University Press.

Okin, Susan. 1979. *Women in Western Political Thought.* Princeton: Princeton University Press.

———. 1989a. *Justice, Gender, and the Family.* New York: Basic Books.

———. 1989b. Humanist Liberalism. In *Liberalism and the Moral Life,* ed. Nancy L. Rosenbaum. Cambridge: Harvard University Press.

Pateman, Carol. 1988. *The Sexual Contract.* Stanford: Stanford University Press.

Public Law 103–3, 5 February 1993, 107 Stat., pp. 6–29.

Rawls, John. 1971. *A Theory of Justice.* Cambridge: Harvard University Press.

———. 1980. Kantian Constructivism in Moral Theory: The Dewey Lectures. *The Journal of Philosophy* 77(9): 515–72.

———. 1993. *Political Liberalism.* New York: Columbia University Press.

Scales-Trent, Judy. 1989. Black Women and the Constitution: Finding Our Place, Asserting Our Rights. *Harvard Civil Rights-Civil Liberties Law Review* 24: 9–44.

Sen, Amartya. 1990. Gender and Cooperative Conflict. In *Persistent Inequalities,* ed. Irene Tinker. Oxford: Oxford University Press.

Spalter-Roth, Roberta M. and Heidi I. Hartmann. 1990. Unnecessary Losses: Cost to Americans of the Lack of a Family and Medical Leave. Washington, DC: Institute for Women's Policy Research.

Stacks, Carol B. 1974. *All Our Kin: Strategies for Survival in a Black Community,* New York: Harper and Row.

Taub, Nadine. 1984–85. From Parental Leaves to Nurturing Leaves. *Review of Law and Social Change,* 13.

Tronto, Joan C. 1993. *Moral Boundaries: A Political Argument for an Ethic of Care.* New York: Routledge.

West, Robin L. 1987. The Difference in Women's Hedonic lives: A pheno-meno-logical Critique of Feminist legal theory. *Wisconsin Women's Law Journal* 3: 81–145.

Williams, Wendy W. 1982. The Equality Crisis: Some Reflections on Culture, Courts, and Feminism. *Women's Rights Law Reporter* 7: 175–200.

———. 1985. Equality's Riddle: Pregnancy and the Equal Treatment/Special Treatment Debate. *New York University Review of Law and Social Change,* 13.

Wolgast, Elizabeth, 1980. *Equality and the Rights of Women.* Ithaca: Cornell University Press.

Young, Iris Marion. N.d. Mothers, Citizenship and Independence: A Critique of Pure Family Values. *Ethics.* Forthcoming.

VULNERABILITY BY MARRIAGE

Susan Okin

Major contemporary theories of social justice pay little or no attention to the multiple inequalities between the sexes that exist in our society, or to the social construct of gender that gives rise to them. Neither mainstream theorists of social justice nor their critics (with rare exceptions) have paid much attention to the internal inequalities of the family. They have considered the family relevant for one or more of only three reasons. Some have seen the family as an impediment to equal opportunity. But the focus of such discussion has been on class differentials among families, not on sex differentials within them. While the concern that the family limits equality of opportunity is legitimate and serious, theorists who raise it have neglected the issue of gender and therefore ignored important aspects of the problem. Those who discuss the family without paying attention to the inequalities between the sexes are blind to the fact that the gendered family radically limits the equality of opportunity of women and girls of all classes—as well as that of poor and working-class children of both sexes. Nor do they see that the vulnerability of women that results from the patriarchal structure and practices of the family *exacerbates* the problem that the inequality of families poses for children's equality of opportunity. As I shall argue, with the increasing prevalence of families headed by a single female, children suffer more and more from the economic vulnerability of women.

Second and third, theorists of justice and their critics have tended either to idealize the family as a social institution for which justice is not an appropriate virtue, or, more rarely, to see it as an important locus for the development of a sense of justice. I have disagreed strongly with those who, focusing on an idealized vision of the family, perceive it as governed by virtues nobler than justice and therefore not needing to be subjected to the tests of justice to which we subject other fundamental social institutions. While I strongly support the *hope* that families will live up to nobler virtues, such as generosity, I contend that in the real world, justice is a virtue of fundamental importance for families, as for other basic social institutions. An important sphere of distribution of many social goods, from the material to the intangible, the family has a history of distributing these goods in far from just ways. It is also, as some who have overlooked its internal justice have acknowledged, a sphere of life that is absolutely crucial to moral development. If justice cannot at least begin to be learned from our day-to-day experience within the family, it seems futile to expect that it can be developed anywhere else. Without just families, how can we expect to have a just society? In particular, if the relationship between a child's parents does not conform to basic standards of justice, how can we expect that child to grow up with a sense of justice?

It is not easy to think about marriage and the family in terms of justice. For one thing, we do not readily associate justice with intimacy, which is one reason some theorists idealize the family. For another, some of the issues that theories of justice are most concerned with, such as differences in standards of living, do not obviously apply among members of a family. Though it is certainly not the case in some countries, in the United States the members of a family, so long as they live together, usually share the same standard of living. As we shall see, however, the question of who earns the family's income, or how the earning of this income is shared, has a great deal to do with the distribution of power and influence within the family, including decisions on how to spend this income. It also affects the distribution of other benefits, including basic security. Here, I present and analyze the facts of contemporary gender-structured marriage in the light of theories about power and vulnerability and the issues of justice they inevitably raise. I argue that marriage and the family, as currently practiced in our society, are unjust institutions. They constitute the pivot of a societal system of gender that renders women vulnerable to dependency, exploitation, and abuse. When we look seriously at the distribution between husbands and wives of such critical social goods as work (paid and unpaid), power, prestige, self-esteem, opportunities for self-development, and both physical and economic security, we find socially constructed inequalities between them, right down the list.

The argument I shall make depends to a large extent on contemporary empirical data, but also reflects the insights of two theorists, moral philosopher Robert Goodin and economist Albert O. Hirschman. Neither has used his argument to make a case about the injustice of the gender-structured family, but both establish convincing arguments about power and vulnerability that will be invaluable as we look at the data about contemporary marriage.

Goodin's recent book *Protecting the Vulnerable* discusses the significance of socially caused vulnerability for issues of justice. He argues that, over and above the general moral obligations that we owe to persons in general, "we bear special responsibilities for protecting those who are particularly vulnerable to us."[1] His major aim is to justify the obligations that welfare states place on citizens to contribute to the welfare of their more vulnerable fellow citizens. But his arguments can be employed to shed light on a number of other important social issues and institutions, including marriage and the family. Goodin's theory is particularly applicable to marriage because of its concern not only with the protection of the vulnerable but also with the moral status of vulnerability itself. Obviously, as he acknowledges, some cases of vulnerability have a large natural component—the vulnerability of infants, for example, although societies differ in how they allocate responsibility for protecting infants. Some instances of vulnerability that may at first appear "natural," such as those caused by illness, are in fact to a greater or lesser extent due to existing social arrangements.[2] And "some of the most

important dependencies and vulnerabilities seem to be *almost wholly social in character*" (emphasis added).[3] Because asymmetric vulnerabilities create social obligations, which may fail to be fulfilled, and because they open up opportunities for exploitation, Goodin argues that insofar as they are alterable they are morally unacceptable and should be minimized. In this, he cites and follows the example of John Stuart Mill, who complained about the "great error of reformers and philanthropists [who] . . . nibble at the consequences of unjust power, instead of redressing the injustice itself."[4] As Goodin concludes, in the case of those vulnerabilities that are "created, shaped, or sustained by current social arrangements . . . [w]hile we should always strive to protect the vulnerable, we should also strive to reduce the latter sort of vulnerabilities insofar as they render the vulnerable liable to exploitation."[5]

One of the tests Goodin employs to distinguish such unacceptable relations of asymmetrical vulnerability from acceptable relations of mutual vulnerability or interdependence is to examine the respective capacities of the two parties to withdraw from the relationship. Even if there is some degree of inequality in a relationship, Goodin says, "as long as the subordinate party can withdraw without severe cost, the superordinate cannot exploit him."[6] As I shall argue, the differing respective potentials for satisfactory withdrawal from the relationship is one of the major elements making marriage, in its typical contemporary manifestations in the United States, a morally unacceptable relationship of vulnerability.

The idea that the mutuality or asymmetry of a relationship can be measured by the relative capacities of the parties to withdraw from it has been developed extensively by Albert O. Hirschman, in two books written many years apart. In his 1970 book entitled *Exit, Voice and Loyalty*, Hirschman makes a convincing connection between the influence of voice by members within groups or institutions and the feasibility of their exit from them. There is a complex relation, he argues, between voice and exit. On the one hand, if the exit option is readily available, this will "tend to *atrophy the development of the art of voice.*" Thus, for example, dissatisfied customers who can easily purchase equivalent goods from another firm are unlikely to expend their energies voicing complaints. On the other hand, the nonexistence or low feasibility of the exit option can impede the effectiveness of voice, since the *threat* of exit, whether explicit or implicit, is an important means of making one's voice influential. Thus "voice is not only handicapped when exit is possible, but also, though in a quite different way, when it is not." Because of this, for members' influence to be most effective, "there should be the possibility of exit, but exit should not be too easy or too attractive."[7] Hirschman concludes that institutions that deter exit by exacting a very high price for it, thereby rendering implausible the threat of exit, also repress the use and effectiveness of voice. Thus both potential modes of influence for combating deterioration are rendered ineffective.

Because the subjects of Hirschman's attention in *Exit, Voice and Loyalty* are groups with many members, his concern is with the power of the members vis-à-vis the institution, rather than with the power of the members relative to one another. But in the case of a two-member institution, such as marriage, special dynamics result from the fact that exit by one partner does not just weaken the institution, but rather results in its dissolution. Whether or not the other party wishes to exit, he or she is effectively expelled by the decision of the other to exit. Because of this, the *relative* potential of the exit option for the two parties is crucial for the relationship's power structure. Hirschman had made this argument, in the context of international relations, in a book published twenty-five years earlier, *National Power and the Structure of Foreign Trade.*[8] There he showed how state A can increase its power and influence by developing trading relations with state B, which is more dependent on the continuance of the trading relationship than A is.

While both states gain something from the trade, the gain is far more significant in the one case than in the other. Thus the less dependent state's greater potential for exiting unharmed from the relationship gives it power or influence that can be used (through explicit or implicit threat of withdrawal) to make the more dependent state comply with its wishes. In addition, because of the extent of its dependence on trade with A, state B may alter its economic behavior in such a way that it becomes even more dependent on its trade with A.[9] Power (which may or may not remain latent) is likely to result from dependencies that are entered into voluntarily by parties whose initial resources and options differ, and in such circumstances the asymmetric dependency may well increase in the course of the relationship.

How do these principles apply to marriage? Few people would disagree with the statement that marriage involves, in some respects, especially emotionally, *mutual* vulnerability and dependence. It is, clearly, also a relationship in which some aspects of unequal vulnerability are not determined along sex lines. For example, spouses may vary in the extent of their love for and emotional dependence on each other; it is certainly not the case that wives always love their husbands more than they are loved by them, or vice versa. Nevertheless, as we shall see, in crucial respects gender-structured marriage *involves women in a cycle of socially caused and distinctly asymmetric vulnerability.* The division of labor within marriage (except in rare cases) makes wives far more likely than husbands to be exploited both within the marital relationship and in the world of work outside the home. To a great extent and in numerous ways, contemporary women in our society are *made* vulnerable by marriage itself. They are first set up for vulnerability during their developing years by their personal (and socially reinforced) expectations that they will be the primary caretakers of children, and that in fulfilling this role they will need to try to attract and to keep the economic support of a man, to whose work life they will be expected to give priority. They are rendered vulnerable by the actual division of labor within almost all current marriages. They are disadvantaged at work by the fact that the world of wage work, including the professions, is still largely structured around the assumption that "workers" have wives at home. They are rendered far more vulnerable if they become the primary caretakers of children, and their vulnerability peaks if their marriages dissolve and they become single parents.

Marriage has a long history, and we live in its shadow. It is a clear case of Marx's notion that we make our history "under circumstances directly encountered, given and transmitted from the past."[10] Certainly, gender is central to the way most people think about marriage. A recent, detailed study of thousands of couples, of different types—married and unmarried, heterosexual, gay and lesbian—confirms the importance of gender to our concept of marriage. Philip Blumstein and Pepper Schwartz's findings in *American Couples* demonstrate how not only current family law but the traditional expectations of marriage influence the attitudes, expectations, and behavior of married couples. By contrast, the lack of expectations about gender, and the lack of history of the institution of marriage, allow gay and lesbian couples more freedom in ordering their lives together and more chance to do so in an egalitarian manner. As the study concludes: "First, while the heterosexual model offers more stability and certainty, it inhibits change, innovation, and *choice* regarding roles and tasks. Second, the heterosexual model, which provides so much efficiency, is predicated on the man's being the dominant partner." The unmarried couples interviewed did not, in general, assume so readily that one partner would be the primary economic provider or that they would pool their income and assets. Homosexual couples, because of the absence of both marriage and the "gender factor," made even fewer such assumptions than did cohabiting heterosexual couples. They were almost unanimous, for example, in refusing to assign to either partner the role of homemaker. By contrast, many of the

married respondents still enthusiastically subscribed to the traditional female/male separation of household work from wage work. While the authors also found the more egalitarian, two-paycheck marriage "emerging," they conclude that "the force of the previous tradition still guides the behavior of most modern marriages."[11]

It is important to recollect, in this context, how recently white married women in the United States have begun to work outside the home in significant numbers. Black women have always worked, first as slaves, then mostly—until very recently—as domestic servants. But in 1860, only 15 percent of all women were in the paid labor force and, right up to World War II, wage work for married women was strongly disapproved of. In 1890, only 5 percent of married women were in the labor force, and by 1960 the rate of married women's labor force participation had still reached only 30 percent. Moreover, wage work has a history of extreme segregation by sex that is closely related to the traditional female role within marriage. The largest category of women workers were domestic servants as late as 1950, since which time clerical workers have outnumbered them. Service (mostly no longer domestic) is still very predominantly female work. Even the female-dominated professions, such as nursing, grade-school teaching, and library work, have been "pink-collar labor ghettos [which] have historically discouraged high work ambitions that might detract from the pull of home and children." Like saleswomen and clerical workers, these female professionals "tend to arrive early in their 'careers' at a point above which they cannot expect to rise."[12] In sum, married women's wage work has a history of being exceptional, and women's wage work in general has been—as much of it still is—highly segregated and badly paid.

VULNERABILITY BY ANTICIPATION OF MARRIAGE

In many respects, marriage is an institution whose tradition weighs upon those who enter into it. The cycle of women's vulnerability begins early, with their anticipation of marriage. Almost all women and men marry, but marriage has earlier and far greater impact on the lives and life choices of women than on those of men.[13] Socialization and the culture in general place more emphasis on marriage for girls than for boys and, although people have recently become less negative about remaining single, young women are more likely than young men to regard "having a good marriage and family life" as extremely important to them.[14] This fact, together with their expectation of being the parent primarily responsible for children, clearly affects women's decisions about the extent and field of education and training they will pursue, and their degree of purposiveness about careers. It is important to note that vulnerability by anticipation of marriage affects at least as adversely the futures of many women who do *not* marry as it affects those who do. This is particularly significant among disadvantaged groups, particularly poor urban black women, whose actual chances of marrying and being economically supported by a man are small (largely because of the high unemployment rate among the available men), but who are further burdened by growing up surrounded by a culture that still identifies femininity with this expectation.

Even though the proportion of young women who plan to be housewives exclusively has declined considerably,[15] women's choices about work are significantly affected from an early age by their expectations about the effects of family life on their work and of work on their family life. As is well known, the participation of women in the labor force, especially women with small children, has continued to rise.[16] But, although a small minority of women are rapidly increasing the previously tiny percentages of women in the elite professions, the vast majority of women who work outside the home are still in low-paying jobs with little or no prospect of advancement. This fact is clearly related to girls' awareness of the complexity they are likely to face in combining work with family life.[17] As the authors of one study conclude: "the occupational aspirations

and expectations of adolescents are highly differentiated by sex . . . [and this] differentiation follows the pattern of sexual segregation which exists in the occupational structure." They found not only that the high school girls in their large-scale study were much less likely than the boys to aspire to the most prestigious occupations, but that the girls who had such aspirations displayed a much lower degree of confidence than the boys about being able to attain their goal.[18]

As the women Kathleen Gerson recently studied looked back on their girlhood considerations about the future, virtually all of them saw themselves as confronting a choice: *either* domesticity and motherhood *or* career.[19] Given the pervasiveness of sex-role socialization (including the mixed or negative messages that girls are often given about their future work lives), the actual obstacles that our social structures place in the way of working mothers, and the far greater responsibility, both psychological and practical, that is placed on mothers than on fathers for their children's welfare, it is not surprising that these women perceived a conflict between their own work interests and the interests of any children they might have.[20] While many reacted against their own mothers' domestic lives, very few were able to imagine successfully combining motherhood with a career. And those who did generally avoided confronting the dilemmas they would have to face.[21] But most grew up with the belief that "a woman can have either a career or children, but not both.[22] Not surprisingly, many of them, assuming that they would want to have children, followed educational and work paths that would readily accommodate the demands of being a primary parent. The only way that those who were career-oriented came to believe that they might avoid the difficult choice, and even attempt to combine their work with mothering, was by deciding to be trailblazers, rejecting strongly ingrained beliefs about the incompatibility of the two.

Needless to say, such a choice does not confront boys in their formative years. *They* assume—

reasonably enough, given our traditions and present conditions and beliefs—that what is expected of them as husbands and fathers is that, by developing a solid work life, they will provide the primary financial support of the family. Men's situation can have its own strains, since those who feel trapped at work cannot opt for domesticity and gain as much support for this choice as a woman can.[23] For those who become unemployed, the conflict of their experience with society's view of the male as provider can be particularly stressful. But boys do not experience the dilemma about work and family that girls do as they confront the choices that are crucial to their educations, future work lives and opportunities, and economic security.

It is no wonder, then, that most women are, even before marriage, in an economic position that sets them up to become more vulnerable during marriage, and most vulnerable of all if their marriage ends and—unprepared as they are—they find themselves in the position of having to provide for themselves and their children.

VULNERABILITY WITHIN MARRIAGE

Marriage continues the cycle of inequality set in motion by the anticipation of marriage and the related sex segregation of the workplace. Partly because of society's assumptions about gender, but also because women, on entering marriage, tend already to be disadvantaged members of the work force, married women are likely to start out with less leverage in the relationship than their husbands. As I shall show, answers to questions such as whose work life and work needs take priority, and how the unpaid work of the family will be allocated—if they are not simply assumed to be decided along the lines of sex difference, but are live issues in the marriage—are likely to be strongly influenced by the differences in earning power between husbands and wives. In many marriages, partly because of discrimination at work and the wage gap between the sexes, wives (despite initial personal ambitions and even when they are full-time wage workers) come to perceive themselves as benefiting from giving priority to their husbands' careers. Hence they have little incentive to question the traditional division of labor in the household. This in turn limits their own commitment to wage work and their incentive and leverage to challenge the gender structure of the workplace. Experiencing frustration and lack of control at work, those who thus turn toward domesticity, while often resenting the lack of respect our society gives to full-time mothers, may see the benefits of domestic life as greater than the costs.[24]

Thus, the inequalities between the sexes in the workplace and at home reinforce and exacerbate each other. It is not necessary to choose between two alternative, competing explanations of the inequalities between men and women in the workplace—the "human capital" approach, which argues that, because of expectations about their family lives, women *choose* to enter lower-paid and more dead-end occupations and specific jobs,[25] and the workplace discrimination explanation, which blames factors largely outside the control of female employees. When the pivotal importance of gender-structured marriage and the expectation of it are acknowledged, these explanations can be seen, rather, as complementary reasons for women's inequality. *A cycle of power relations and decisions pervades both family and workplace, and the inequalities of each reinforce those that already exist in the other.* Only with the recognition of this truth will we be able to begin to confront the changes that need to occur if women are to have a real opportunity to be equal participants in either sphere.[26]

Human capital theorists, in perceiving women's job market attachment as a matter of voluntary choice, appear to miss or virtually to ignore the fact of unequal power within the family. Like normative theorists who idealize the family, they ignore potential conflicts of interest, and consequently issues of justice and power differentials, *within* families. This means that they view the question of whether a wife works solely in terms of the total aggregate costs and benefits for the family unit as a whole.[27] They assume that if a wife's paid work benefits the family more (in terms, say, of aggregate income and leisure) than her working exclusively within the household, her rational choice, and that of her husband, will be that she should get a job; if the reverse is true, she should not. But this simplistic attention to the family's "aggregate good" ignores the fact that a wife, like a husband, may have an independent interest in her own career advancement or desire for human contact, for example, that may give her an incentive to work even if the family as a whole may on that account find its life more difficult. Further, the human capital approach overlooks the fact that such goods as leisure and influence over the expenditure of income are by no means always equally shared within families. It also fails to recognize that the considerable influence that husbands often exert over their wives' decisions on whether to take paid work may be motivated not by a concern for the aggregate welfare of the household but, at least in part, by their desire to retain the authority and privilege that accrues to them by virtue of being the family's breadwinner.[28] Thus the decisions of married women about their participation in the job market, even when they *are* choices, may not be such simple or voluntary choices as human capital theory seems to imply.

In addition, those who seek to explain women's comparative disadvantage in the labor market by their preference for domestic commitments do not consider whether at least some of the causality may run in the opposite direction. But there is considerable evidence that women's "choices" to become domestically oriented, and even whether to have children, may result at least in part from their frequently blocked situations at work. Kathleen Gerson's study shows that, though they usually did not notice the connection, many of the women in her sample decided to leave wage work and turn to childbearing and domesticity coincidentally with becoming frustrated with the dead-end nature of their jobs. Conversely, she found that some women who had initially thought of themselves as domestically oriented, and who had in many cases chosen traditionally female occupations, reversed

these orientations when unusual and unexpected opportunities for work advancement opened up to them.[29]

Even if these problems with the human capital approach did not exist, we would still be faced with the fact that the theory can explain, at most, half of the wage differential between the sexes. In the case of the differential between white men and black women, 70 percent of it is unexplained. At *any* given level of skill, experience, and education, men earn considerably more than women. The basic problem with the human capital approach is that, like much of neoclassical economic theory, it pays too little attention to the multiple constraints placed on people's choices. It pays too little attention to differentials of power between the sexes both in the workplace and in the family. It thus ignores the fact that women's commitment and attachment to the workplace are strongly influenced by a number of factors that are largely beyond their control. As we have seen, a woman's typically less advantaged position in the work force and lower pay may lead her to choices about full-time motherhood and domesticity that she would have been less likely to make had her work life been less dead-ended. They also give her less power in relation to her husband should she want to resist the traditional division of labor in her household and to insist on a more equal sharing of child care and other domestic responsibilities. Those who stress the extent to which both husbands and wives cling to the "male provider/female nurturer" roles as unobjectionable because efficient and economically rational for the family unit need to take a step back and consider the extent to which the continued sex segregation of the work force serves to perpetuate the traditional division of labor within the household, even in the face of women's rising employment.

Housework and the Cycle of Vulnerability

It is no secret that in almost all families women do far more housework and child care than men do. But the distribution of paid and unpaid work within the family has rarely—outside of feminist circles—been considered a significant issue by theorists of justice. Why should it be? If two friends divide a task so that each takes primary responsibility for a different aspect of it, we would be loath to cry "injustice" unless one were obviously coercing the other. But at least three factors make the division of labor within the household a very different situation, and a clear question of justice. First, the uneven distribution of labor within the family is strongly correlated with an innate characteristic, which appears to make it the kind of issue with which theorists of justice have been most concerned. The virtually automatic allocation to one person of more of the paid labor and to the other of more of the unpaid labor would be regarded as decidedly odd in any relationship other than that of a married or cohabiting heterosexual couple.[30] One reason for this is that, as we shall see, it has distinct effects on the distribution of power. While the unequal distribution of paid and unpaid work has different repercussions in different types of marriages, it is always of significance. Second, though it is by no means always absolute, the division of labor in a traditional or quasi-traditional marriage is often quite complete and usually long-standing. It lasts in many cases at least through the lengthy years of child rearing, and is by no means confined to the preschool years. Third, partly as a result of this, and of the structure and demands of most paid work, the household division of labor has a lasting impact on the lives of married women, especially those who become mothers. It affects every sphere of their lives, from the dynamics of their marital relationship to their opportunities in the many spheres of life outside the household. The distribution of labor within the family by sex has deep ramifications for its respective members' material, psychological, physical, and intellectual well-being. One cannot even begin to address the issue of why so many women and children live in poverty in our society, or why women are inadequately represented in the higher echelons

of our political and economic institutions, without confronting the division of labor between the sexes within the family. Thus it is not only itself an issue of justice but it is also at the very root of other significant concerns of justice, including equality of opportunity for children of both sexes, but especially for girls, and political justice in the broadest sense.

The justice issues surrounding housework are not simply issues about who does *more* work. However, on average, wives living with their husbands *do* now work slightly more total hours than their husbands do.[31] In addition, this averaging obscures a great variety of distributions of both quantity and type of work within marriages. For the purposes of this discussion, it will be helpful to separate couples into two major categories: those in which the wife is "predominantly houseworking" (either a full-time housewife or employed part-time) and those in which the wife is "predominantly wage-working" (employed full-time or virtually full-time).[32] Within each category, I shall look at issues such as the distribution of work (paid and unpaid), income, power, opportunity to choose one's occupation, self-respect and esteem, and availability of exit. As we shall see, wives in each category experience a somewhat different pattern of injustice and vulnerability. But, except in the case of some of the small number of elite couples who make considerable use of paid help, the typical divisions of labor in the family cannot be regarded as just.

Predominantly Houseworking Wives When a woman is a full-time housewife—as are about two-fifths of married women in the United States who live with their husbands—she does less total work, on average, than her employed husband: 49.3 hours per week, compared with his 63.2. This is also true of couples in which the wife works part-time (defined as fewer than thirty hours per week, including commuting time), though the average difference per week is reduced to eight hours in this case.[33] This is, of course, partly because housework is less burdensome than it was before the days of labor-saving devices and declining fertility. Not surprisingly, however, during the early years of child rearing, a nonemployed wife (or part-time employed wife) is likely to work about the same total number of hours as her employed husband. But the *quantity* of work performed is only one of a number of important variables that must be considered in order for us to assess the justice or injustice of the division of labor in the family, particularly in relation to the issue of the cycle of women's vulnerability.

In terms of the quality of work, there are considerable disadvantages to the role of housewife.[34] One is that much of the work is boring and/or unpleasant. Surveys indicate that most people of both sexes do not like to clean, shop for food, or do laundry, which constitute a high proportion of housework. Cooking rates higher and child care even higher, with both sexes, than other domestic work.[35] In reality, this separation of tasks is strictly hypothetical, at least for mothers, who are usually cleaning, shopping, doing laundry, and cooking at the same time as taking care of children. Many wage workers, too, do largely tedious and repetitive work. But the housewife-mother's work has additional disadvantages. One is that her hours of work are highly unscheduled; unlike virtually any other worker except the holder of a high political office, she can be called on at any time of the day or night, seven days a week. Another is that she cannot, nearly as easily as most other workers, change jobs. Her family comes to depend on *her* to do all the things she does. Finding substitutes is difficult and expensive, even if the housewife is not discouraged or forbidden by her husband to seek paid work. The skills and experience she has gained are not valued by prospective employers. Also, once a woman has taken on the role of housewife, she finds it extremely difficult, for reasons that will be explored, to shift part of this burden back onto her husband. Being a housewife thus both impairs a woman's ability to support herself and constrains her future choices in life.[36]

Many of the disadvantages of being a housewife spring directly or indirectly from the fact that all her work is unpaid work, whereas more than four-fifths of her husband's total work is paid work. This may at first seem a matter of little importance. If wives, so long as they stay married, usually share their husbands' standards of living for the most part, why should it matter who earns the income? It matters a great deal, for many reasons. In the highly money-oriented society we live in, the housewife's work is devalued. In fact, in spite of the fact that a major part of it consists of the nurturance and socialization of the next generation of citizens, it is frequently not even acknowledged as work or as productive, either at the personal or at the policy level. This both affects the predominantly houseworking wife's power and influence within the family and means that her social status depends largely upon her husband's, a situation that she may not consider objectionable so long as the marriage lasts, but that is likely to be very painful for her if it does not.[37]

Also, although married couples usually share material well-being, a housewife's or even a part-time working wife's lack of access to much money of her own can create difficulties that range from the mildly irritating through the humiliating to the devastating, especially if she does not enjoy a good relationship with her husband. Money is the subject of most conflict for married couples, although the issue of housework may be overtaking it.[38] Bergmann reports that in an informal survey, she discovered that about 20 percent of the housewife-mothers of her students were in the position of continually having to appeal to their husbands for money. The psychological effects on an adult of economic dependence can be great. As Virginia Woolf pointed out fifty years ago, any man who has difficulty estimating them should simply imagine himself depending on his wife's income.[39] The dark side of economic dependence is also indicated by the fact that, in the serious predivorce situation of having to fight for their future economic well-being, many wives even of well-to-do men do not have access to enough cash to pay for the uncovering and documentation of their husband's assets.

At its (not so uncommon) worst, the economic dependence of wives can seriously affect their day-to-day physical security. As Linda Gordon has recently concluded: "The basis of wife-beating is male dominance—not superior physical strength or violent temperament . . . but social, economic, political, and psychological power. . . . Wife-beating is the chronic battering of a person of inferior power who for that reason cannot effectively resist."[40] Both wife abuse and child abuse are clearly exacerbated by the economic dependence of women on their husbands or cohabiting male partners. Many women, especially full-time housewives with dependent children, have no way of adequately supporting themselves, and are often in practice unable to leave a situation in which they and/or their children are being seriously abused. In addition to increasing the likelihood of the more obvious forms of abuse—physical and sexual assault— the fear of being abandoned, with its economic and other dire consequences, can lead a housewife to tolerate infidelity, to submit to sexual acts she does not enjoy, or experience psychological abuse including virtual desertion.[41] The fact that a predominantly houseworking wife has no money of her own or a small paycheck is not necessarily significant, but it can be very significant, especially at crucial junctures in the marriage.

Finally, as I shall discuss, the earnings differential between husband and housewife can become devastating in its significance for her and for any dependent children in the event of divorce (which in most states can now occur without her consent). This fact, which significantly affects the relative potential of wives and husbands for exit from the marriage, is likely to influence the distribution of power, and in turn paid and unpaid work, *during* the marriage as well.

Predominantly Wage-Working Wives and Housework   Despite the increasing labor force participation of married women, including mothers,

"working wives still bear almost all the responsibility for housework." They do less of it than housewives, but "they still do the vast bulk of what needs to be done," and the difference is largely to be accounted for not by the increased participation of men, but by lowered standards, the participation of children, purchased services such as restaurant or frozen meals, and, in elite groups, paid household help. Thus, while the distribution of paid labor between the sexes is shifting quite considerably onto women, that of unpaid labor is not shifting much at all, and "the couple that shares household tasks equally remains rare."[42] The differences in total time spent in all "family work" (housework and child care plus yard work, repairs, and so on) vary considerably from one study to another, but it seems that fully employed husbands do, *at most,* approximately half as much as their fully employed wives, and some studies show a much greater discrepancy.

Bergmann reports that "husbands of wives with full-time jobs averaged about two minutes more housework per day than did husbands in housewife-maintaining families, hardly enough additional time to prepare a soft-boiled egg."[43] Even unemployed husbands do much less housework than wives who work a forty-hour week. Working-class husbands are particularly vocal about not being equal partners in the home, and do little housework. In general, however, a husband's income and job prestige are *inversely* related to his involvement in household chores, unless his wife is employed in a similarly high-paid and prestigious job. Many husbands who profess belief in sharing household tasks equally actually do far less than their wives, when time spent and chores done are assessed. In many cases, egalitarian attitudes make little or no difference to who actually does the work, and often "the idea of shared responsibility turn[s] out to be a myth."[44]

Some scholars are disinclined to perceive these facts as indicating unequal power or exploitation. They prefer to view them as merely embodying adherence to traditional patterns, or to justify them as efficient in terms of the total welfare of the family (the husband's time being too valuable to spend doing housework).[45] There are clear indications, however, that the major reason that husbands and other heterosexual men living with wage-working women are not doing more housework is that *they do not want to, and are able, to a very large extent, to enforce their wills.* How do we know that the unequal allocation of housework is not equally women's choice? First, because most people do not like doing many of the major household chores. Second, because almost half of wage-working wives who do more than 60 percent of the housework say that they would prefer their husbands to do more of it.[46] Third, because husbands with higher salaries and more prestigious jobs than their wives (the vast majority of two-job couples) are in a powerful position to resist their wives' appeal to them to do more at home, and it is husbands with the highest prestige who do the least housework of all. Even when there is little conflict, and husbands and wives seem to agree that the woman should do more of the housework, they are often influenced by the prevailing idea that whoever earns less or has the less prestigious job should do more unpaid labor at home. But since the maldistribution of wages and jobs between the sexes in our society is largely out of women's control, even *seemingly nonconflictual* decisions made on this basis cannot really be considered fully voluntary on the part of wives.[47] Finally, the resistance of most husbands to housework is well documented, as is the fact that the more housework men do, the *more* it becomes a cause of fighting within couples. Examining factors that caused the breakup of some of the couples in their sample, Blumstein and Schwartz say:

> Among both married and cohabiting couples, housework is a source of conflict. . . . [A] *woman cannot be perceived as doing less housework than her partner wants her to do without jeopardizing the relationship.* However, a man, who is unlikely to be doing even half the work, can be perceived as doing less than his fair share without affecting the couple's durability. *It is difficult for women to*

> *achieve an equal division of housework and still preserve the relationship*[48] [emphasis added].

As a result, in many of the households in which men and women both work full-time—those for which much paid household help or reliance on other purchased services is not a practical option—the unequal distribution of housework between husbands and wives leads to gross inequities in the amount and type of work done by each.

Power in the Family

There are very few studies of power within marriage. Of those few, the one most frequently cited until recently—Robert O. Blood, Jr., and Donald M. Wolfe's 1960 *Husbands and Wives*—though informative is now outdated and unreliable in the way it interprets its own findings.[49]

Only recently, with the publication of Blumstein and Schwartz's *American Couples,* have we had a large-scale and more neutral account of the power picture behind decision making by couples. They asked thousands of couples to respond on a scale of 1 to 9 (with 5 defined as "both equally") to the question: "In general, who has more say about important decisions affecting your relationship, you or your partner?" Clearly, what this new study reveals about married couples confirms the major findings that Blood and Wolfe's earlier study discovered but obscured. First, though the number of marriages in which spouses consider that they share decision-making power relatively equally has increased considerably, the tendency in others is still distinctly toward male rather than female dominance.[50] Second, it is still clearly the case that the possession by each spouse of resources valued by the *outside* world, especially income and work status, rather than resources valuable primarily within the family, has a significant effect on the distribution of power in the relationship.

Blumstein and Schwartz preface their findings about couples, money, and power by noting that they are not likely to accord with "cherished

American beliefs about fairness and how people acquire influence in romantic relationships." Perhaps this is why, as they point out, although "economic factors tend to be involved in every aspect of a couple's life," standard textbooks on marriage and the family are unlikely to devote more than five pages to this subject. Just as political and moral theorists have been extremely reluctant to admit that questions of justice pertain to family life, a similar tendency to idealize—and to conceal dominance—has apparently characterized sociologists of the family until recently, too. But Blumstein and Schwartz's study establishes quite decisively that "in three out of four of the types of couples . . . studied [all types except lesbian couples], . . . the amount of money a person earns—in comparison with a partner's income—establishes relative power."[51] Given that even the 26 percent of all wives who work full-time earn, on average, only 63 percent as much as the average full-time working husband, and the average wife who works for pay (full- or part-time) earns only 42 percent as much, it is therefore not at all surprising that male dominance is far more common than female dominance in couples who deviate from a relatively egalitarian distribution of power.[52] When women are employed, and especially when their earnings approach those of their husbands, they are more likely to share decision-making power equally with their husbands and to have greater financial autonomy. In marriages in which the husband earned over $8,000 more than the wife (more than half the marriages in the Blumstein and Schwartz sample), the husband was rated as more powerful (as opposed to an equal sharing of power or to the wife's being more powerful) in 33 percent of cases. In marriages in which the incomes of husband and wife were approximately equal, only 18 percent of the husbands were rated as more powerful. The workplace success of wives, then, helps considerably to equalize the balance of power within their marriages and gains them greater respect from their husbands, who often have little respect for housework. Success at

work, moreover, can reduce the expectation that a wife will do the vast bulk of family work.[53] Nevertheless, the full-time employment, and even the equal or greater earnings, of wives do not guarantee them equal power in the family, for the male-provider *ideology* is sometimes powerful enough to counteract these factors.[54]

Given these facts about the way power is distributed in the family, and the facts brought out earlier about the typical contentiousness of the issue of housework, it is not difficult to see how the vulnerability of married women in relation to the world of work and their inequality within the family tend to form part of a vicious cycle. Wives are likely to start out at a disadvantage, because of both the force of the traditions of gender and the fact that they are likely to be already earning less than their husbands at the time of marriage. In many cases, the question of who is responsible for the bulk of the unpaid labor of the household is probably not raised at all, but *assumed*, on the basis of these two factors alone. Because of this "nondecision" factor, studies of marital power that ask only about the respective influence of the partners over *decisions* are necessarily incomplete, since they ignore distributions of burdens and benefits that may not be perceived as arising from decisions at all.[55]

VULNERABILITY BY SEPARATION OR DIVORCE

The impact of the unequal distribution of benefits and burdens between husbands and wives is hardest and most directly felt by the increasing numbers of women and children whose families are no longer intact. In 1985, 28 percent of ever-married white women and 49 percent of ever-married black women in the United States were separated, divorced, or widowed.[56] Marital disruption through the death of a spouse, divorce, or separation is consistently rated as the most psychologically stressful life event for men and women alike.[57] But in women's lives, the personal disruption caused by these events is frequently exacerbated by the serious social and economic dislocation that accompanies them.

Not only has the rate of divorce increased rapidly but the differential in the economic impact of divorce on men and women has also grown. Divorce and its economic effects contribute significantly to the fact that nearly one-quarter of all children now live in single-parent households, more than half of them, even after transfer payments, below the poverty level. Moreover, partly because of the increased labor force participation of married women, there has been a growing divergence between female-maintained families and two-parent families.[58] These dramatic shifts, with their vast impact on the lives of women and children, must be addressed by any theory of justice that can claim to be about all of us, rather than simply about the male "heads of households" on which theories of justice in the past have focused.

There is now little doubt that, while no-fault divorce does not appear to have caused the increasing rate of divorce, it has considerably affected the economic outcome of divorce for both parties.[59] Many studies have shown that whereas the average economic status of men improves after divorce, that of women and children deteriorates seriously. Nationwide, the per-capita income of divorced women, which was only 62 percent that of divorced men in 1960, decreased to 56 percent by 1980.[60] The most illuminating explanation of this is Lenore Weitzman's recent pathbreaking study, *The Divorce Revolution*. Based on a study of 2,500 randomly selected California court dockets between 1968 and 1977 and lengthy interviews with many lawyers, judges, legal experts, and 228 divorced men and women, the book both documents and explains the differential social and economic impact of current divorce law on men, women, and children. Weitzman presents the striking finding that in the first year after divorce, the average standard of living of divorced men, adjusted for household size, increases by 42 percent while that of divorced women falls by 73 percent. "For most women and children," Weitzman concludes:

divorce means precipitous downward mobility—both economically and socially. The reduction in income brings residential moves and inferior housing, drastically diminished or nonexistent funds for recreation and leisure, and intense pressures due to inadequate time and money. Financial hardships in turn cause social dislocation and a loss of familiar networks for emotional support and social services, and intensify the psychological stress for women and children alike. On a societal level, divorce increases female and child poverty and creates an ever-widening gap between the economic well-being of divorced men, on the one hand, and their children and former wives on the other.[61]

Weitzman's findings have been treated with disbelief by some, who claim, for example, that California, being a community property state, is atypical, and that these figures could not be projected nationwide without distortion. However, studies done in other states (including common law states and both urban and rural areas) have corroborated Weitzman's central conclusion: that the economic situation of men and that of women and children typically diverge after divorce.[62]

The basic reason for this is that the courts are now treating divorcing men and women more or less as equals. Divorcing men and women are not, of course, equal, both because the two sexes are not treated equally in society and, as we have seen, because typical, gender-structured marriage makes women socially and economically vulnerable. The treatment of unequals as if they were equals has long been recognized as an obvious instance of injustice. In this case, the injustice is particularly egregious because the inequality is to such a large extent the result of the marital relationship itself. Nonetheless, that divorce as it is currently practiced in the United States involves such injustice took years to be revealed. There are various discrete parts of this unjust treatment of unequals as if they were equals, and we must briefly examine each of them.

The first way in which women are unequally situated after divorce is that they almost always continue to take day-to-day responsibility for the children. The increased rate of divorce has especially affected couples between the ages of twenty-five and thirty-nine—those most likely to have dependent children. And in approximately 90 percent of cases, children live with mothers rather than fathers after divorce. This is usually the outcome preferred by both parents. Relatively few fathers seek or are awarded sole custody, and in cases of joint custody, which are increasing in frequency, children still tend to live mainly with their mothers. Thus women's postdivorce households tend to be larger than those of men, with correspondingly larger economic needs, and their work lives are much more limited by the needs of their children.[63]

Second, as Weitzman demonstrates, no-fault divorce laws, by depriving women of power they often exerted as the "innocent" and less willing party to the divorce, have greatly reduced their capacity to achieve an equitable division of the couple's tangible assets. Whereas the wife (and children) typically used to be awarded the family home, or more than half of the total tangible assets of the marriage, they are now doing much worse in this respect. In California, the percentage of cases in which the court explicitly ordered that the family home be sold and the proceeds divided rose from about one-tenth of divorces in 1968 to about one-third in 1977. Of this one-third, 66 percent had minor children, who were likely on this account to suffer significantly more than the usual dislocations of divorce. James McLindon's study of divorcing couples in New Haven, Connecticut, confirms this effect of no-fault divorce. In the case of an older housewife, forced sale of the family home can mean the loss of not only her marriage, occupation, and social status, but also her home of many years, all in one blow.[64] Whether what is supposed to be happening is the "equal" division of property, as in the community property states, or the "equitable" division, as in the common law states, what is in fact happening is neither equal nor equitable. This is partly because even when the division of *tangible* property is fairly equal, what is in fact most families' principal asset is largely or

entirely left out of the equation. This leads us to the third component of injustice in the current practice of divorce.[65]

As we have seen, most married couples give priority to the husband's work life, and wives, when they work for wages, earn on average only a small fraction of the family income, and perform the great bulk of the family's unpaid labor. The most valuable economic asset of a typical marriage is not any tangible piece of property, such as a house (since, if there is one, it is usually heavily mortgaged). By far the most important property acquired in the average marriage is its career assets, or human capital, the vast majority of which is likely to be invested in the husband. As Weitzman reports, it takes the average divorced man only about *ten months* to earn as much as the couple's entire net worth.[66] The importance of this marital asset is hard to overestimate, yet it has only recently begun to be treated in some states as marital property for the purposes of divorce settlements.[67] Even if "marital property" as traditionally understood is divided evenly, there can be no equity so long as this crucial piece is left in the hands of the husband alone. Except for the wealthy few who have significant material assets, "support awards that divide income, especially future income, are the most valuable entitlements awarded at divorce.[68] Largely because of the division of labor within marriage, to the extent that divorced women have to fall back on their own earnings, they are much worse off than they were when married, and than their ex-husbands are after divorce. In many cases, full-time work at or around the minimum wage, which may be the best a woman without much job training or experience can earn, is insufficient to pull the household out of poverty. As Bianchi and Spain state, "women's labor market adjustments to accommodate children, which are often made within a two-parent family context and seem economically rational at the time, cause difficulty later when these same women find themselves divorced and in great need of supporting themselves and their children.[69]

For reasons that seem to have been exacerbated by no-fault divorce laws, most separated or divorced women *do* have to fall back on their own earnings. These earnings—as opposed to spousal support payments or public transfer payments—make up the major portion of the income of female-maintained families. In 1980, they constituted the entire income of almost half such households.[70] The major reason for this is that, loath to recognize that the husband's earning power, and therefore his continuing income, is the most important asset of a marriage, judges have not been dividing it fairly at the time of divorce. As Weitzman summarizes the situation, "Under the new divorce laws, . . . a woman is now expected to become self-sufficient (and, in many cases, to support her children as well).[71] Alimony and child support are either not awarded, not adequate, or not paid, in the great majority of cases. For many separated or divorced women, as for most single mothers, the idea of the male provider is nothing but a misleading myth that has negatively affected their own work lives while providing them with nothing at all.

In many divorces, there is inadequate income to support two households, with the paradoxical result that poor women with dependent children are even less likely than others to be awarded child support. But even in the case of families who were comfortably off, judges frequently consider what proportion of his income the husband will need to maintain his own standard of living (and even that of his hypothetical future family) before considering the needs of his wife and children. Instead of thinking in terms of compensating wives for all the unpaid effort that most have expended on the home and children, judges are thinking in terms of "what she can earn, and what he can pay."[72]

The inadequate levels of child support ordered are only part of the problem. A nationwide survey showed that, in 1981, the ordered amounts were paid in full in less than one-half of cases. Approximately one-quarter of mothers awarded support received partial payment, and one-quarter received no payment at all.[73] In general, except in the case of fathers earning more than $50,000, who comply in more than 90 percent of cases, nonpayment of child support bears little relation to the father's income. One of the major problems appears to be the ineffectiveness or lack of enforcement procedures.[74] With the Child Support Enforcement Amendments of 1984, the problem has now been addressed by federal legislation mandating the withholding of payments from the father's paycheck. Even when paid in full, however, the amounts of alimony and child support that are being awarded are grossly unfair, given the unequal situations in which marriage leaves men and women. The effect of judges' tendency to regard the husband's post-divorce income as first and foremost *his* is that they "rarely require him to help [his former wife and children] sustain a standard of living *half as good at his own*"[75] (emphasis added).

Another reason that divorced women are likely to have to rely on their own, often inadequate earnings is that they are much less likely than their ex-husbands to remarry. The reasons for this are almost all socially created and therefore alterable. In the vast majority of cases, a divorced mother continues to take primary responsibility for the children, but she has lost to a very large extent the financial resources she had within marriage, making her a less attractive marital partner than the typical divorced man. Custody of children is known to be a factor that discourages remarriage. Men who divorce in their thirties and forties are typically noncustodial parents, and are often at the height of their earning power—not an insignificant factor in attracting a subsequent, sometimes much younger wife. Such a couple will not be affected by the social disapproval attached to a woman who marries a much younger man, in the rare case that she does so. Whereas increasing age is not much of an impediment for a man seeking to remarry, it seriously affects a woman's chances, which decrease from 56 percent in her thirties to less than 12 percent if she is in her fifties or older when divorced. This is largely, of course, because so much more emphasis is placed on youth and good looks as constituting attractiveness in women than in men. And ironically, success at work, highly correlated with remarriage for men, is inversely correlated for women.[76]

By attempting to treat men and women as equals at the end of marriage, current divorce law neglects not only the obvious fact that women are *not* the socioeconomic equals of men in our society, but also the highly relevant fact that the experience of gendered marriage and primary parenting greatly exacerbates the inequality that women already bring with them into marriage. To divide the property equally and leave each partner to support himself or herself and to share support of the children might be fair in the case of a marriage in which the paid and unpaid labor had been shared equally, and in which neither spouse's work life had taken priority over that of the other. However, as we have seen, such marriages are exceedingly rare.

This implies, of course, that social reform could significantly alter the negative impact of divorce on those who suffer most from it. The important lesson is that women's vulnerability within marriage and their disadvantaged position in the case of marital breakdown are intimately linked. Women are made vulnerable by anticipation of gendered marriage, and are made more vulnerable by entering into and living within such marriage. But they are *most* vulnerable if they marry and have children, but then the marriage fails. Surely women's awareness of this situation has some effects on their behavior and on the distribution of power within marriage itself.

EXIT, THREAT OF EXIT, AND POWER IN THE FAMILY

At the beginning of this essay, I summarized Goodin's argument that socially created asymmetric vulnerability is morally unacceptable, and should be minimized. I also referred to Hirschman's arguments about the effects of persons' relative potentials for exit on their power or influence within relationships or groups. Neither of these theorists considers the institution of contemporary marriage an example of such power imbalance.[77] But the evidence presented here suggests that typical, contemporary, gender-structured marriage is an excellent example of socially created vulnerability, partly because the asymmetric dependency of wives on husbands affects their potential for satisfactory exit, and thereby influences the effectiveness of their voice within the marriage.

If we are to aim at making the family, our most fundamental social grouping, more just, we must work toward eradicating the socially created vulnerabilities of women that stem from the division of labor and the resultant division of power within it. In order to do anything effective about the cycle of women's socially created vulnerability, we must take into account the current lack of clarity in law, public policy, and public opinion about *what marriage is.* Since evidently we do not all agree about what it is or should be, we must think in terms of building family and work institutions that enable people to structure their personal lives in different ways. If they are to avoid injustice to women and children, these institutions must encourage the avoidance of socially created vulnerabilities by facilitating and reinforcing the equal sharing of paid and unpaid work between men and women, and consequently the equalizing of their opportunities and obligations in general. They must also ensure that those who enter into relationships in which there is a division of labor that might render them vulnerable are fully protected against such vulnerability, both within the context of the ongoing relationship and in the event of its dissolution.

NOTES

1. Robert E. Goodin, *Protecting the Vulnerable: A Reanalysis of Our Social Responsibilities* (Chicago: University of Chicago Press, 1985), p. 109. He specifies, further: "Vulnerability amounts to one person's having the capacity to produce

consequences that matter to another. Responsibility amounts to his being accountable for those consequences of his actions and choices" (p. 114).

2. Ibid., p. 190. This is so in at least two respects: *who* becomes disabled by illness or accident is affected by social inequalities and working conditions, and the extent to which physical or mental disabilities render one vulnerable is partly a factor of social provisions (for example, wheelchair ramps) for the less able.

3. Ibid., p. 191.

4. John Stuart Mill, *Principles of Political Economy* (London: Parker and Son, 1848), bk. 5, chap. 11, sec. 9; cited by Goodin, *Protecting the Vulnerable,* p. 189.

5. Goodin, *Protecting the Vulnerable,* p. xi. This succinct statement of the position (argued in his chap. 7) is quoted from Goodin's synopsis.

6. Ibid., *Protecting the Vulnerable,* p. 197.

7. Albert O. Hirschman, *Exit, Voice and Loyalty: Responses to Decline in Firms, Organizations, and States* (Cambridge: Harvard University Press, 1970), pp. 43, 55, 83.

8. Albert O. Hirschman, *National Power and the Structure of Foreign Trade* (Berkeley: University of California Press, 1945; expanded ed. 1980). See pp. vi–viii of the expanded edition for a summary of the original argument, as well as some later reservations of the author about his failure to try to find a remedy for the asymmetrical dependency he had uncovered.

9. Ibid., *National Power,* p. 31.

10. Karl Marx, *The Eighteenth Brumaire of Louis Bonaparte,* in *Selected Works* (Moscow: Progress Publishers, 1969), vol. 2, p. 378.

11. Philip Blumstein and Pepper Schwartz, *American Couples* (New York: Morrow, 1983), pp. 324, 115.

12. Quotations are from Kathleen Gerson, *Hard Choices: How Women Decide About Work, Career, and Motherhood* (Berkeley: University of California Press, 1985), p. 209. For sources of this data, see also Jacob Mincer, "Labor Force Participation of Married Women: A Study of Labor Supply," in *Aspects of Labor Economics: A Conference of the Universities—National Bureau Committee for Economic Research* (Princeton: Princeton University Press, 1962), p. 64; Ruth Sidel, *Women and Children Last: The Plight of Poor Women in Affluent America* (New York:

Viking, 1986), esp. pp. 50–56, 60; Suzanne M. Bianchi and Daphne Spain, *American Women in Transition* (New York: Russell Sage, 1986), p. 196. Gerson places "careers" in quotation marks here because she and her respondents understand the word to mean "not mere labor force participation, but rather long-term, full-time attachment to paid work with the expectation, or at least the hope, of advancement over time" (p. 126*n* l). It does not imply any differentiation between manual and intellectual, or professional and nonprofessional work. I shall use *career* in this nonelitist sense.

13. For the past century, nearly 90 percent of women have married by the age of thirty and between 80 percent and 90 percent have become mothers by the age of forty. In 1986, only 4.7 percent of women and 5.7 percent of men aged 45–54 in the U.S. had never married.

14. Bianchi and Spain, *American Women,* p. 9, quoting Arland Thornton and Deborah Freedman, "Changing Attitudes Toward Marriage and Single Life," *Family Planning Perspectives* 14 (November–December, 1982): 297–303.

15. Bianchi and Spain report that between 1969 and 1975, the proportion of women in their early twenties who planned to be housewives (versus working outside the home) declined from about half to one-quarter among whites and from about half to one-fifth among blacks. This decline was especially marked among those with the most education. *American Women,* p. 18.

16. The labor force participation rate of U.S. women has risen steadily for three decades, from 35 percent (of those aged sixteen or more) in 1960 to 57 percent in 1986. Roughly 70 percent of women between the ages of twenty and thirty-four were employed in 1983, including (in 1983 and 1986) more than 50 percent of married women with children under the age of six.

17. Gerson, *Hard Choices.* Other studies of the cross-pressures relating to sex roles that many women experience when planning their educations and work lives include: Bernard C. Rosen and Carol S. Aneshensel, "Sex Differences in the Educational-Occupational Expectation Process," *Social Forces* 57, no. 1 (1978); Nira Danziger, "Sex-Related Differences in the Aspirations of High School Students," *Sex Roles* 9, no. 6 (1983); Larry C. Jensen, Robert Christensen, and Diana

J. Wilson, "Predicting Young Women's Role Preference for Parenting and Work," *Sex Roles* 13, nos. 9–10 (1985); and Margaret Mooney Marini and Ellen Greenberger, "Sex Differences in Occupational Aspirations and Expectations," *Sociology of Work and Occupations* 5, no. 2 (1978).

18. Marini and Greenberger, "Sex Differences," 147–48, 157. Only 47 percent of the girls but 75 percent of the boys with the highest aspirations expected to reach them. The girls' levels of ambition were less affected than the boys' by either socioeconomic background or academic achievement. See also "In Career Goals, Female Valedictorians Fall Behind," *New York Times,* November 8, 1987, sec. 12, p. 7.

19. Gerson, *Hard Choices,* esp. pp. 136–38. Though Gerson's sample includes no women of color, it represents in other respects a wide range of class backgrounds and present situations. Gerson presents a number of surprising findings. One is that more of the women in her sample *changed* their orientation—from domestic to nondomestic or vice versa—than maintained their original orientation.

20. On female socialization, see Nancy Chodorow, *The Reproduction of Mothering* (Berkeley: University of California Press, 1978); Lenore J. Weitzman, "Sex-Role Socialization," in *Women: A Feminist Perspective,* 2nd ed., ed. Jo Freeman (Palo Alto: Mayfield, 1979). On the practical conflicts faced by wage-working mothers, see, for example, Linda J. Beckman, "The Relative Rewards and Costs of Parenthood and Employment for Employed Women," *Psychology of Women Quarterly* 2, no. 3 (1978); Mary Jo Frug, "Securing Job Equality for Women: Labor Market Hostility to Working Mothers," *Boston University Law Review* 59, no. 1 (1979).

21. In Gerson's sample, only 14 percent of the respondents' own mothers had worked during their preschool years, and 46 percent had mothers who had never worked outside the home until their children left (p. 45). On avoidance of the conflict between wage work and motherhood, see Gerson, *Hard Choices,* pp. 64–65.

22. Ibid., p. 137.

23. Moreover, the support that *women* can expect for this choice is now waning. See, for example, Gerson, *Hard Choices,* pp. 77–80, 212.

24. Gerson, *Hard Choices,* chap. 5 and pp. 130–31.

25. Key articles contributing to this argument are Jacob Mincer, "Labor Force Participation of Married Women"; Jacob Mincer and Solomon Polachek, "Family Investment in Human Capital: Earnings of Women," in *Marriage, Family Human Capital, and Fertility,* ed. Theodore W. Schulz (Chicago: University of Chicago Press, 1974); Jacob Mincer and Haim Ofek, "Interrupted Work Careers: Depreciation and Restoration of Human Capital," *Journal of Human Resources* 17 (Winter 1982); Solomon Polachek, "Occupational Self-Selection: A Human Capital Approach to Sex Differences in Occupational Structure," *Review of Economics and Statistics* 63 (February 1981). Gary Becker's *A Treatise on the Family* (Cambridge: Harvard University Press, 1981) also belongs within this general mode of thinking.

26. Works in which these interconnections are best recognized and analyzed include Bianchi and Spain, *American Women,* pp. 188–95; Bergmann, *Economic Emergence;* Fuchs, *Women's Quest;* Gerson, *Hard Choices;* Heidi Hartmann, "Capitalism, Patriarchy, and Job Segregation by Sex," *Signs I,* no. 3 (1976); and Sylvia Walby, *Patriarchy at Work: Patriarchal and Capitalist Relations in Employment* (Minneapolis: University of Minnesota Press, 1986), pp. 71–74. Fuchs concludes: "There is prejudice, and there is exploitation [in the workplace], but the enormous amount of sex segregation by occupation and industry, the huge gap in wages, and the unequal burdens in the home are mostly attributable to other factors…. [W]omen's weaker economic position results primarily from conflicts between career and family, conflicts that are stronger for women than for men" (*Women's Quest,* pp. 4–5).

27. See, for example, Becker, *A Treatise on the Family.*

28. See Walby, *Patriarchy at Work,* p. 73, and Blumstein and Schwartz, *American Couples,* pp. 131–35, for examples of this influence.

29. Gerson, *Hard Choices,* chaps. 5 and 6. Of those who found themselves trapped in female labor market ghettos, she says: "Previous ambivalences toward motherhood subsided, and domesticity became more attractive than it had earlier appeared. … [T]he decision to have a child typically coincided with mounting frustration at work. … The experience of blocked work mobility, although

not the only factor, was a major contributing factor in this group's decision to become mothers" (pp. 107–8). "Blocked mobility triggered a downward spiral of aspirations and gave childbearing a liberating aura by comparison.... In important respects, women's work is organized to promote this turn toward a home-centered life" (p. 110).

30. Blumstein and Schwartz's comparisons of homosexual couples (male and female) with heterosexual couples (cohabiting and married) demonstrate vividly the extent to which the division of labor in the household is affected by sex difference. In all but about 1 percent of contemporary homosexual households, they found that the homemaker/provider division of roles is avoided. Even when one partner is not working, and is in fact doing more of the housework, the tendency is to think of him or her as "temporarily unemployed" or "a student." Lesbians take particular care to distribute household duties equitably. And yet, contrary to what one might expect on the basis of some arguments (including that of economist Gary Becker), such households seem to be managed with considerable efficiency. Blumstein and Schwartz, *American Couples,* pp. 116, 127–31, 148–51.

31. Victor Fuchs, *Women's Quest,* pp. 77–78. This represents a change from previous findings, and is due to women's increased hours of paid work. Between 1960 and 1986, Fuchs reports, "on average, wives increased their total work load by four hours per week while husbands decreased theirs by two and a half hours" (p.78). Cf. Barbara Bergmann, *Economic Emergence,* p. 263, who reports (based on 1975–76 data) husbands' averaging approximately one hour per day more of total work time than wives.

32. Since it is the most recently completed large-scale study of housework available, I use the 1975–76 Michigan Survey Research Center's statistics as analyzed by Bergmann (pp. 261–66). However, I conflate some of her many categories into fewer categories, for the sake of clarity and brevity. My reason for combining part-time employed wives with housewives rather than with fully employed wives is that part-time work is usually badly paid, insecure, dead-ended, and undervalued.

33. Bergmann, *Economic Emergence,* p. 263, table 11–2, using University of Michigan 1975–76 data.

Note that, given Fuch's findings, these figures may well have changed, since women working part-time are likely to be working longer hours.

34. See Bergmann, *Economic Emergence,* chap. 9, "The Job of Housewife." One indicator that the homemaker role involves considerable disadvantages is the extremely small number of men who choose it. Blumstein and Schwartz say that despite recent media interest in househusbands, "try as we might, . . . we could not find a significant number" of them. "Only 4 of 3,632 husbands describe their work as taking care of the house full-time" (*American Couples,* pp. 146, 561*n,* 11). Bergmann reports: "In January 1986, 468,000 men were estimated to be out of the workforce because they were 'keeping house,' 22 percent more than in 1980" (*Economic Emergence,* p. 259, citing U.S. Bureau of Labor Statistics, *Employment and Earnings* (February 1986), p. 15. Another factor influencing this, however, as both Blumstein and Schwartz and Gerson note, may be the fact that few married women wish to undertake the full provider role.

35. Bergmann, *Economic Emergence,* p. 267.

36. See Weitzman, *The Divorce Revolution,* esp. pp. xi, 35.

37. See Gerson, *Hard Choices,* pp. 211–12, for a good summary of how "work associated with child rearing and the private sphere has been systematically devalued," and the current effects of this on domestically oriented women. See also Polatnick, "Why Men Don't Rear Children." Studies such as Blumstein and Schwartz's cite examples of husbands using in arguments the fact that their wives do not earn money: "If you're so smart, how come you don't earn anything?" (*American Couples,* pp. 58–59). See Weitzman, *The Divorce Revolution,* pp. 315–16, on divorcing housewives' devaluing of their work, and pp. 334–36, on how their identification by their husbands' social status can lead to a loss of sense of identity by wives after divorce. At the public policy level, the lack of recognition of the economic value of housewives' work is indicated by the fact that housework is included in the GNP only if it is paid work done by a housekeeper. The old story about the parson who lowers the GNP by marrying his housekeeper still holds true, in spite of the fact that it has

been estimated that, if it *were* included, unpaid housework done in the industrialized countries would constitute between 25 and 40 percent of the GNP. Debbie Taylor et al., *Women: A World Report* (Oxford: Oxford University Press, 1985).

38. Blumstein and Schwartz say: "Money matters are the most commonly discussed issues among married couples. In study after study, going back several decades, between one quarter and one third of all married couples ranked money as their primary problem" *(American Couples,* p. 52). Fuchs reports that, according to Morton H. Shaevitz, an expert on gender relations, "Arguments about housework are the leading cause of domestic violence in the United States" *(Women's Quest,* p. 74, citing *Healthcare Forum* 1987, p. 27).

39. Bergmann, *Economic Emergence,* pp. 211–12; Virginia Woolf, *Three Guineas* (London: Harcourt Brace, 1938), p. 110; see also pp. 54–57.

40. Linda Gordon, *Heroes of Their Own Lives* (New York: Viking, 1988), p. 251.

41. Bergmann, *Economic Emergence,* pp. 205–6; Sidel, *Women and Children,* pp. 40–46. See also Lenore Walker, *The Battered Woman* (New York: Harper & Row, 1979). Fears stemming from economic dependence seem to be just beneath the surface, with many housewives, and ready to emerge at the hint of a sympathetic ear. Gerson occasionally reports this (e.g., p. 115), and I have heard the same fears of being left, expressed by acquaintances who are economically dependent wives, since I told them of my work on this book. Chapter 8 of Lillian Rubin's *Worlds of Pain* (New York: Basic Books, 1976) is an excellent source on the effects of the relative powerlessness and dependence of working-class housewives on their unwilling compliance with their husbands' sexual demands. Blumstein and Schwartz discuss at some length the relationship between power and sexual initiation, refusal, consideration of each partner's needs, and satisfaction *(American Couples,* pp. 206–306 passim).

42. See Bergmann, *Economic Emergence,* chap. 11; Bianchi and Spain, *American Women,* pp. 231–40; Blumstein and Schwartz, *American Couples,* pp. 144–48; Gerson, *Hard Choices,* p. 170. Quotations are from Blumstein and Schwartz, p. 144, and Gerson, p. 170. There is broad agreement on this issue, though some studies find that, in very

recent years, male participation in housework and child care appears to be slightly on the rise. Bergmann reports that when some of the couples who participated in the 1975–76 University of Michigan Study were resurveyed in 1981–82, it appeared that "these husbands had increased their contributions by about an hour per week over the six-year interval" (p. 266). On the other hand, she finds that "younger husbands appear to do even less housework than their older counterparts, although neither group of men averages as much as half an hour per day" (p. 264).

43. Bergmann, *Economic Emergence,* p. 263. She defines as "housewife-maintaining" "those families in which the wives devoted five or fewer hours a week to paid employment" (p. 62n). Sharon Y. Nickols and Edward Metzen, in "Impact of Wife's Employment upon Husband's Housework," *Journal of Family Issues 3* (June 1982), found on the basis of a time-allocation study from 1968 to 1973 that when wives became employed their average hours per week spent in housework dropped from thirty-five to twenty-three, but that their husbands' average contribution stayed at two hours per week.

44. Blumstein and Schwartz, *American Couples,* p. 145. They find that, among full-time employed married couples who profess strongly egalitarian attitudes about housework, 44 percent of wives compared with 28 percent of husbands do more than ten hours of housework per week. Also, some of the examples they cite suggest that the "egalitarianism" of these professed attitudes may be rather superficial; as one wife says of her husband's cleaning the floors and oven: "He takes care of that *for me*" (p. 142, emphasis added). See also Shelley Coverman, "Explaining Husbands' Participation in Domestic Labor," *The Sociological Quarterly* 26, no. 1 (1985); Bianchi and Spain, *American Women,* p. 233.

45. For recent examples, see Becker, *A Treatise on the Family;* and Jonathan Gershuny, *Social Innovation and the Division of Labour* (Oxford: Oxford University Press, 1983), p. 156.

46. Bergmann, *Economic Emergence,* pp. 267–68 and refs., p. 350n9.

47. Blumstein and Schwartz, *American Couples,* pp. 139–54, esp. 151–54. See below on the importance of "nondecisions" in studying power.

48. Blumstein and Schwartz, *American Couples,* p. 312. They also say: "It seems to be a cultural given in America that growing up female makes housework something women do . . . [whereas] growing up male in this country causes even liberal men to reject household tasks" (p. 148). On the issue of income differential and housework, Bianchi and Spain conclude: "In two-parent families, until such time as wives command salaries equal to their husbands' salaries, on average, it is unlikely that men will devote as much time and energy to the nurturance of the family" (*American Women,* p. 243). On conflict, Blumstein and Schwartz report that, in their large sample, the amount of fighting that took place about housework increased with the amount of housework the husband did (*American Couples,* pp. 146, 562n32).

49. Blood and Wolfe, *Husbands and Wives.* For critiques of this study, see David M. Heer, "The Measurement and Bases of Family Power: An Overview," *Marriage and Family Living* 25, no. 2 (1963); Constantia Safilios-Rothschild, "Family Sociology or Wives' Family Sociology? A Cross-Cultural Study of Decision Making," *Journal of Marriage and the Family* 31, no. 2 (1969); and Dair Gillespie, "Who Has the Power? The Marital Struggle," *Journal of Marriage and the Family* 33, no. 3 (1971).

50. Blumstein and Schwartz, *American Couples,* figs. 1 and 2 and text, pp. 54, 57. The most male-dominant category of marriage that they identify is that in which husbands and wives believe in the male provider role. Of these, about 40 percent consider their relationship to be male-dominated, five times more than consider it female-dominated. But even among these couples, slightly more than half believe that their relationships are equal in terms of power.

51. Blumstein and Schwartz, *American Couples,* pp. 53, 52.

52. Bianchi and Spain, *American Women,* p. 202. In 1986, working wives contributed about 28 percent to family income. Congressional Caucus for Women's Issues: *Selected Statistics on Women,* July 1988, p. 3.

53. Blumstein and Schwartz, *American Couples,* pp. 53–93 passim and 139–44. See also Polatnick, "Why Men Don't Rear Children," esp. pp. 23–25.

54. Blumstein and Schwartz, *American Couples,* pp. 56–57.

55. See Peter Bachrach and Morton S. Baratz, "The Two Faces of Power," *American Political Science Review* 56 (1962): 947–52, on the importance of taking account of "nondecisions" when studying the distribution of power. Unfortunately, the phrasing of the question about power that Blumstein and Schwartz posed to their respondents does not allow us to look at nondecisions. It seems very likely, given the strongly gendered traditions of marriage, that many married couples would not have regarded "Who will be the primary parent?" or "Who will do the housework?" as "important decision[s] affecting [the] relationship," since they would not have regarded them as things to be decided at all. An ongoing study includes a question that addresses this issue: *Study of First Years of Marriage* (Survey Research Center, Institute for Social Research, University of Michigan, Ann Arbor, 1986), question D6, p. 28.

56. U.S. Bureau of the Census, Current Population Reports: *Marital Status and Living Arrangements,* March 1985 (Washington, D.C.: Government Printing Office).

57. Weitzman, *The Divorce Revolution,* p. 349 and refs.

58. Ellwood, *Poor Support,* chap. 5; Sidel, *Women and Children,* p. xvi. For female-headed households in 1984, the poverty rate was 34.5 percent. Of children in female-maintained households, 53.9 percent were poor. The poverty line income for a family of four in 1984 was $10,609, which allows $2.43 per person per day for food, and leaves $589.40 per month for all the family's other needs. See Bianchi and Spain, *American Women,* p. 207, on the growing economic discrepancy between two-parent families and female-maintained families, and p. 211 on the chronicity of poverty of the latter.

59. Bianchi and Spain, *American Women,* p. 26, citing numerous studies. See also James B. McLindon, "Separate But Unequal: The Economic Disaster of Divorce for Women and Children," *Family Law Quarterly* 21, no. 3 (1987). However, cf. Herbert Jacob's dissenting argument in "Another Look at No-Fault Divorce and the Post-Divorce Finances of Women," *Law and Society Review* 23, no. 1 (1989). Beginning

with California in 1970, all states except South Dakota now have some form of no-fault divorce law. Twenty-two states still have fault-based divorce as well as no-fault. Most of the pure no-fault states allow unilateral divorce by one party without the consent of the other. Weitzman, *The Divorce Revolution,* pp. 41–43, 417–19.

60. Bianchi and Spain, *American Women,* pp. 30–32 and refs., 205–7, 216–18; Gerson, *Hard Choices,* pp. 221–22 and refs. As Bianchi and Spain comment, "although female-maintained families have become more middle class—at least as indexed by the educational attainment of the householder—their income situation relative to husband-wife households has deteriorated" (p. 207).

61. Weitzman, *The Divorce Revolution,* p. 323. See esp. introduction and chaps. 2 and 10. See also Saul Hoffman and John Holmes, "Husbands, Wives, and Divorce," in *Five Thousand American Families—Patterns of Economic Progress,* ed. Greg J. Duncan and James N. Morgan (Ann Arbor, Mich.: Institute for Social Research, 1976); and Judith Wallerstein and Joan Kelly, *Surviving the Breakup: How Children and Parents Cope with Divorce* (New York: Basic Books, 1980). This last study, of the effects of divorce in an affluent community (Marin County, California), reports that three-quarters of the divorced women experienced a significant decline in their standard of living, and for one-third this change was sudden and severe. As Weitzman points out, census figures corroborate the findings of these researchers: "In 1979, the median per capita income of divorced women who had not remarried was $4,152, just over half of the $7,886 income of divorced men who had not remarried" (p. 343).

62. A study of all the divorce cases that closed in a five-month period (1982–83) in four counties in Vermont shows a 120 percent gain in postdivorce *per capita* income for men, a 25 percent drop for children, and a 33 percent drop for women (assuming that all support ordered is paid). Heather Ruth Wishik, "Economics of Divorce: An Exploratory Study," *Family Law Quarterly* 20, no. 1 (1986). A study of divorce in New Haven, Connecticut, comparing a sample of 102 cases from the fault-based period (1970–71)

with a sample of 100 from the no-fault period (1982–83) shows that the frequency, amount, and duration of alimony awarded has decreased, and that women are now less likely to be awarded the family home and much more likely to work for wages. Although 61 percent of the 1980s divorced women worked full-time and another 17 percent worked part-time, "the husband's average postdivorce per capita income surpassed that of his wife and children overall and in every income group . . . [averaging] $333 to [his wife's and each child's] $122 per week." McLindon, "Separate But Unequal," p. 391. See also Rosalyn B. Bell, "Alimony and the Financially Dependent Spouse in Montgomery County, Maryland," *Family Law Quarterly* 22, no. 3 (1988), esp. 279–84; and the excellent discussions in Mary Ann Glendon, *Abortion and Divorce in Western Law* (Cambridge: Harvard University Press, 1987), chap. 2; and Herma Hill Kay, "Equality and Difference: A Perspective on No-Fault Divorce and Its Aftermath," *University of Cincinnati Law Review* 56, no. 1 (1987).

63. Weitzman, *The Divorce Revolution,* pp. xiii–xiv and chaps. 8, 9; Blumstein and Schwartz, *American Couples,* pp. 33–34. Gerson says: "Although joint custody arrangements are on the rise, Hacker (1982) reports that the number of divorced fathers with sole custody of their children has actually decreased in the last decade" (*Hard Choices,* p. 221). See also Clair Vickery, "The Time-Poor: A New Look at Poverty," *Journal of Human Resources* 12 (Winter 1977), on the extra time demands on custodial mothers.

64. Weitzman, *The Divorce Revolution,* pp. 78–96; McLindon, "Separate But Unequal," pp. 375–78. It is no wonder that, as Weitzman reports, "many women who have lived through and for their husbands say that the loss of the role of wife is tantamount to 'losing a part of myself' " (p. 335).

65. Weitzman, *The Divorce Revolution,* chap. 4.

66. Ibid., pp. 53, 60.

67. Some changes have been occurring; most states now regard pensions and other retirement benefits as marital assets, but far fewer are viewing other career assets, such as professional degrees, training, or goodwill, this way. Weitzman, *The Divorce Revolution,* p. 47 and chap. 5. See also Doris Jonas Freed and Timothy B. Walker, "Family Law

in the Fifty States: An Overview," *Family Law Quarterly* 28, no. 4 (1985): 411–26.

68. Weitzman, *The Divorce Revolution,* p. 61; see also pp. 68–69.

69. Bianchi and Spain, *American Women,* p. 243; see also pp. 207–11.

70. Ibid., p. 206. See also McLindon, "Separate But Unequal." Weitzman reports that about 14 percent of the women in her weighted sample resorted to welfare in the first year after divorce (*The Divorce Revolution,* p. 204); and that the structure of the job market is such that only half of all full-time female workers earn enough to support two children above the poverty line without supplemental income from either their father or the government (p. 351).

71. Weitzman, *The Divorce Revolution,* p. 143.

72. Ibid., p. x.

73. Bianchi and Spain, *American Women,* pp. 212–14; Sidel, *Women and Children,* p. 103. The level of noncompliance among Weitzman's California interviewees was even higher. She reports that only one-third of the wives awarded child support said they received the full amounts during the first year after divorce, and that 43 percent received little or nothing (*The Divorce Revolution,* p. 283).

74. Weitzman, *The Divorce Revolution,* pp. 295–300, esp. table 25, p. 296.

75. Ibid., p. 183. See also Ellwood, *Poor Support,* pp. 158–60. Glendon and Weitzman are hopeful that the new enforcement measures will help alleviate custodial mothers' poverty. Glendon, *Abortion and Divorce,* pp. 88–89, 110–11; Weitzman, *The Divorce Revolution,* pp. 307–9.

76. On custody as a factor affecting remarriage, see, for example, Becker, *A Treatise on the Family,* p. 225. On women's work success, see Blumstein and Schwartz, *American Couples,* pp. 32–33.

77. Goodin refers to marriage in the past as an institution of exploitation and domination but, because he thinks that "the traditional division of marital labor . . . is surely dead or dying," he concludes that "modern marriage relations . . . embody . . . a morally desirable sort of 'symmetry and complementarity' " (*Protecting the Vulnerable,* pp. 72–79, 196). When Hirschman rarely and briefly refers to the family in the course of his arguments about the effect of exit potential on influence, what he says indicates that he is thinking almost entirely about families of origin, rather than families created by marriage (*Exit, Voice and Loyalty,* pp. 33, 76). In the only place in the book where he exhibits any interest in the applicability of his argument to families by marriage, he briefly comments that the high costs (in energy and emotional expenditure as well as money) of obtaining a divorce may act as an incentive to the use of the voice option in resolving marital disputes (p. 79). However, in a recent paper, Hirschman argues that no-fault divorce law "undercuts the recourse to voice" in resolving marital difficulties. He suggests that those who framed the new laws "probably did not realize the extent to which the earlier obstacles to divorce indirectly encouraged attempts at mending the so easily frayed marital relationship and how much the new freedom to exit would torpedo such attempts." Citing Weitzman's work, he also makes brief reference to the differential impact of divorce on the two parties. "Exit and Voice: An Expanding Sphere of Influence," in A. O. Hirschman, ed., *Rival Views of Market Society and Other Recent Essays,* (New York: Viking, 1986), pp. 96–98.

AFTER THE FAMILY WAGE: GENDER EQUITY AND THE WELFARE STATE

Nancy Fraser

The current crisis of the welfare state has many roots—global economic trends, massive movements of refugees and immigrants, popular hostility to taxes, the weakening of trade unions and labor parties, the rise of national and "racial"-ethnic antagonisms, the decline of solidaristic ideologies, and the collapse of state socialism. One absolutely crucial factor, however, is the crumbling of the old gender order. Existing welfare states are premised on assumptions about gender that are increasingly out of phase with many people's lives and self-understandings. They therefore do not provide adequate social protections, especially for women and children.

The gender order that is now disappearing descends from the industrial era of capitalism and reflects the social world of its origin. It was centered on the ideal of the family wage. In this world, people were supposed to be organized into heterosexual, male-headed nuclear families, which lived principally from the man's labor market earnings. The male head of the household would be paid a family wage, sufficient to support children and a wife and mother, who performed domestic labor without pay. Of course, countless lives never fit this pattern. Still, it provided the normative picture of a proper family.

Today, however, the family-wage assumption is no longer tenable—either empirically or normatively. We are currently experiencing the death throes of the old, industrial gender order with the transition to new, postindustrial phase of capitalism. The crisis of the welfare state is bound up with these epochal changes. It is rooted in part in the collapse of the world of the family wage, and of its central assumptions about labor markets and families.

In the labor markets of postindustrial capitalism, few jobs pay wages sufficient to support a family single-handedly; many, in fact, are temporary or part-time and do not carry standard benefits.[1] Women's employment is increasingly common, moreover—although far less well-paid than men's.[2] Postindustrial families, meanwhile, are less conventional and more diverse.[3] Heterosexuals are marrying less and later, and divorcing more and sooner. And gays and lesbians are pioneering new kinds of domestic arrangements.[4] Gender norms and family forms are highly contested, finally. Thanks in part to the feminist and gay and lesbian liberation movements, many people no longer prefer the male breadwinner/ female homemaker model. As a result of these trends, growing numbers of women, both divorced and never married, are struggling to support themselves and their families without access to a male breadwinner's wage.[5]

In short, a new world of economic production and social reproduction is emerging—a world of less stable employment and more diverse families. Although no one can be certain about its ultimate shape, this much seems clear: the emerging world, no less than the world of the family wage, will require a welfare state that effectively insures people against uncertainties. If anything, the need for such protection is increased. It is clear, too, that the old forms of welfare state, built on assumptions of male-headed families and relatively stable jobs, are no longer suited to providing this protection. We need something new, a postindustrial welfare state suited to radically new conditions of employment and reproduction.

What then should a postindustrial welfare state look like? Conservatives have lately had a lot to say about "restructuring the welfare state," but their vision is counterhistorical and contradictory; they seek to reinstate the male breadwinner/ female homemaker family for the middle class, while demanding that poor single mothers work. Neoliberal proposals have recently emerged in the United States, but they too are inadequate in the current context. Punitive, androcentric, and obsessed with employment despite the absence of good jobs, they are unable to provide security in a postindustrial world.[6]

Both of these approaches ignore one crucial thing: a postindustrial welfare state, like its industrial predecessor, must support a gender order. But the only kind of gender order that can be acceptable today is one premised on gender equity.

Feminists, therefore, are in a good position to generate an emancipatory vision for the coming period. They, more than anyone, appreciate the importance of gender relations to the current crisis of the industrial welfare state and the centrality of gender equity to any satisfactory resolution. Feminists also appreciate the importance of care work for human well-being and the effects of its social organization on women's standing. They are attuned, finally, to potential conflicts of interest within families and to the inadequacy of androcentric definitions of work.

To date, however, feminists have tended to shy away from systematic reconstructive thinking about the welfare state. Nor have we yet developed a satisfactory account of gender equity that can inform an emancipatory vision. We need now to undertake such thinking. We should ask: What new, postindustrial gender order should replace the family wage? And what sort of welfare state can best support such a new gender order? What account of gender equity best captures our highest aspirations? And what vision of social welfare comes closest to embodying it?

Two different kinds of answers are presently conceivable, I think, both of which qualify as feminist. The first I call the universal breadwinner model. It is the vision implicit in the current political practice of most U.S. feminists and liberals. It aims to foster gender equity by promoting women's employment; the centerpiece of this model is state provision of employment-enabling services such as day care. The second possible answer I call the caregiver parity model. It is the vision implicit in the current political practice of most Western European feminists and social democrats. It aims to promote gender equity chiefly by supporting informal care work; the centerpiece of this model is state provision of caregiver allowances.

Which of these two approaches should command our loyalties in the coming period? Which expresses the most attractive vision of a postindustrial gender order? Which best embodies the ideal of gender equity?

In this essay, I outline a framework for thinking systematically about these questions. I analyze highly idealized versions of universal breadwinner and caregiver parity in the manner of a thought experiment. I postulate, contrary to fact, a world in which both of these models are feasible in that their economic and political preconditions are in place. Assuming very favorable conditions then, I assess the respective strengths and weaknesses of each.

My discussion proceeds in four parts. In the first section, I propose an analysis of gender equity that generates a set of evaluative standards. Then, in the second and third sections, I apply those standards to universal breadwinner and caregiver parity, respectively. I conclude, in the fourth section, that neither of those approaches, even in an idealized form, can deliver full gender equity. To have a shot at that, I contend, we must develop a new vision of a postindustrial welfare state, which effectively deconstructs gender difference as we know it.

I. GENDER EQUITY: A COMPLEX CONCEPTION

To evaluate alternative visions of a postindustrial welfare state, we need some normative criteria. Gender equity, I have said, is one indispensable standard. But of what precisely does it consist?

Feminists have so far associated gender equity with either equality or difference, where equality means treating women exactly like men, and where difference means treating women differently insofar as they differ from men. Theorists have debated the relative merits of these two approaches as if they represented two antithetical poles of an absolute dichotomy.[7] These arguments have generally ended in stalemate. Proponents of difference have successfully shown that equality strategies typically presuppose "the male as norm," thereby disadvantaging women and imposing a distorted standard on everyone. Egalitarians have argued just as cogently, however, that difference approaches typically rely on essentialist notions of femininity, thereby reinforcing existing stereotypes and confining women within existing gender divisions. Neither equality nor difference, then, is a workable conception of gender equity.

We need a vision or picture of where we are trying to go, and a set of standards for evaluating various proposals as to how we might get there. The equality/difference theoretical impasse is real, moreover; it cannot be simply sidestepped or embraced. Nor is there any "wholly other" third term that can magically catapult us beyond it. What then should feminist theorists do?

I propose that we reconceptualize gender equity as a complex, not a simple, idea. This means breaking with the assumption that gender equity can be identified with any single value or norm, whether it be equality, difference, or something else. Instead we should treat it as a complex notion comprising a plurality of distinct normative principles. The plurality will include some notions associated with the equality side of the debate, as well as some associated with the difference side. It will also encompass still other normative ideas that neither side has accorded due weight.

In what follows, I assume that gender equity is complex, and I propose an account of it that is designed for the specific purpose of evaluating alternative pictures of a postindustrial welfare state. This account might not be perfectly suited to handling issues other than welfare. Nevertheless, I believe that the general idea of treating gender equity as a complex conception is widely applicable. The analysts here may serve as a paradigm case demonstrating the usefulness of this approach.

For this particular thought experiment, in any case, I unpack the idea of gender equity as a compound of five distinct normative principles. Let me enumerate them one by one.

Antipoverty Principle

The first and most obvious objective of social-welfare provision is to prevent poverty. Preventing poverty is crucial to achieving gender equity now, after the family wage, given the high rates of poverty in solo-mother families and the vastly increased likelihood that U.S. women and children will live in such families.[8] If it accomplishes nothing else, a welfare state should at least relieve suffering by meeting otherwise unmet basic needs. Arrangements, such as those in the United States, that leave women, children,

and men in poverty, are unacceptable according to this criterion. Any postindustrial welfare state that prevented such poverty would constitute a major advance. So far, however, this does not say enough. The antipoverty principle might be satisfied in a variety of different ways, not all of which are acceptable. Some ways, such as the provision of targeted, isolating and stigmatized poor relief for solo-mother families, fail to respect several of the following normative principles, which are also essential to gender equity in social welfare.

Antiexploitation Principle

Antipoverty measures are important not only in themselves, but also as a means to another basic objective: preventing exploitation of vulnerable people.[9] This principle, too, is central to achieving gender equity after the family wage. Needy women with no other way to feed themselves and their children, for example, are liable to exploitation—by abusive husbands, by sweatshop foremen, and by pimps. In guaranteeing relief of poverty then, welfare provision should also aim to mitigate exploitable dependency.[10] The availability of an alternative source of income enhances the bargaining position of subordinates in unequal relationships. The nonemployed wife who knows she can support herself and her children outside of her marriage has more leverage within it; her "voice" is enhanced as her possibilities of "exit" increase.[11] The same holds for the low-paid nursing home attendant in relation to her boss.[12] For welfare measures to have this effect, however, support must be provided as a matter of right. When receipt of aid is highly stigmatized or discretionary, the antiexploitation principle is not satisfied.[13] At best, the claimant would trade exploitable dependence on a husband or a boss for exploitable dependence on a caseworker's whim.[14] The goal should be to prevent at least three kinds of exploitable dependencies: exploitable dependence on an individual family member, such as a husband or an adult child; exploitable dependence on employers and supervisors; and exploitable dependence on the personal whims of state officials. Rather than shuttle people back and forth among these exploitable dependencies, an adequate approach must prevent all three simultaneously.[15] This principle rules out arrangements that channel a homemaker's benefits through her husband. It is likewise incompatible with arrangements that provide essential goods, such as health insurance, only in forms linked conditionally to scarce employment. Any postindustrial welfare state that satisfied the antiexploitation principle would represent a major improvement over current U.S. arrangements. But even it might not be satisfactory. Some ways of satisfying this principle would fail to respect several of the following normative principles, which are also essential to gender equity in social welfare.

Equality Principles

A postindustrial welfare state could prevent women's poverty and exploitation and yet still tolerate severe gender inequality. Such a welfare state is not satisfactory. A further dimension of gender equity in social provision is redistribution, reducing inequality between women and men. Equality, as we saw, has been criticized by some feminists. They have argued that it entails treating women exactly like men according to male-defined standards, and that this necessarily disadvantages women. That argument expresses a legitimate worry, which I will address under another rubric below. But it does not undermine the ideal of equality per se. The worry pertains only to certain inadequate ways of conceiving equality, which I do not presuppose here. At least three distinct conceptions of equality escape the objection. These three are essential to gender equity in social welfare.

Income Equality   One form of equality that is crucial to gender equity concerns the distribution of real per capita income. This kind of

equality is highly pressing now, after the family wage, when U.S. women's earnings are less than 70% of men's, when much of women's labor is not compensated at all, and when many women suffer from "hidden poverty" due to unequal distribution within families.[16] As I interpret it, the principle of income equality does not require absolute leveling, but it does rule out arrangements that reduce women's incomes after divorce by nearly half, whereas men's incomes nearly double.[17] It likewise rules out unequal pay for equal work and the wholesale undervaluation of women's labor and skills. The income equality principle requires a substantial reduction in the vast discrepancy between men's and women's incomes. In so doing, it tends, as well, to help equalize the life-chances of children, because a majority of U.S. children are currently likely to live at some point in solo-mother families.[18]

Leisure-Time Equality   A second kind of equality that is crucial to gender equity concerns the distribution of leisure time. This sort of equality is highly pressing now, after the family wage, when many women, but only a few men, do both paid work and unpaid primary care work, and when women suffer disproportionately from "time poverty."[19] One recent British study found that 52% of women surveyed, compared to 21% of men, said they "felt tired most of the time.[20] The leisure-time equality principle rules out welfare arrangements that would equalize incomes while requiring a double shift of work from women, but only a single shift from men. It likewise rules out arrangements that would require women, but not men, to do either the "work of claiming" or the time-consuming "patchwork" of piecing together income from several sources and of coordinating services from different agencies and associations.[21]

Equality of Respect   A third kind of equality that is crucial to gender equity pertains to status and respect. This kind of equality is especially pressing now, after the family wage, when post-industrial culture routinely represents women as sexual objects for the pleasure of male subjects. The principle of equal respect rules out social arrangements that objectify and denigrate women—even if those arrangements prevent poverty and exploitation, and even if, in addition, they equalize income and leisure time. It is incompatible with welfare programs that trivialize women's activities and ignore women's contributions—hence with welfare reforms in the United States that assume AFDC claimants do not "work." Equality of respect requires recognition of women's personhood and recognition of women's work.

A postindustrial welfare state should promote all three of these conceptions of equality. Such a state would constitute an enormous advance over present arrangements, but even it might not go far enough. Some ways of satisfying the equality principles would fail to respect the following principle, which is also essential to gender equity in social welfare.

Antimarginalization Principle

A welfare state could satisfy all the preceding principles and still function to marginalize women. By limiting support to generous mothers' pensions, for example, it could render women independent, well provided for, well rested, and respected, but enclaved in a separate domestic sphere, removed from the life of the larger society. Such a welfare state would be unacceptable. Social policy should promote women's full participation on a par with men in all areas of social life—in employment, in politics, in the associational life of civil society. The antimarginalization principle requires provision of the necessary conditions for women's participation, including day care, elder care, and provision for breast-feeding in public. It also requires the dismantling of masculinist work cultures and woman-hostile political environments. Any postindustrial welfare state that provided these

things would represent a great improvement over current arrangements.

Antiandrocentrism Principle

A welfare state that satisfied many of the foregoing principles could still entrench some obnoxious gender norms. It could assume the androcentric view that men's current life patterns represent the human norm and that women ought to assimilate to them. (This is the real issue behind the previously noted worry about equality.) Such a welfare state is unacceptable. Social policy should not require women to become like men, nor to fit into institutions designed for men, to enjoy comparable levels of well-being. Policy should aim instead to restructure androcentric institutions so as to welcome human beings who can give birth and who often care for relatives and friends, treating them not as exceptions, but as ideal-typical participants. The antiandrocentrism principle requires decentering masculinist norms—in part by revaluing practices and traits that are currently undervalued because they are associated with women. It entails changing men as well as changing women.

Here then is an account of gender equity in social welfare. On this account, gender equity is a complex idea comprising five distinct normative principles, one of which—equality—is internally complex and encompasses three distinct subprinciples. Each of the principles is essential to gender equity. Thus no postindustrial welfare state can realize gender equity unless it satisfies them all.

How then do the principles interrelate? Some of the five tend usually to support one another; others could well work at cross-purposes. Everything, in fact, depends on context. Some institutional arrangements permit simultaneous satisfaction of several principles with a minimum of mutual interference; other arrangements, in contrast, set up zero-sum situations, in which attempts to satisfy one principle interfere with attempts to satisfy another. Promoting gender equity after the family wage, therefore, means attending to multiple aims that are potentially in conflict. The goal should be to find approaches that avoid trade-offs and maximize prospects for satisfying all—or at least most—of the five principles.

In the next sections, I use this approach to assess two alternative models of a postindustrial welfare state. First, however, I want to flag three sets of relevant issues. One concerns the social organization of care work. Precisely how this work is organized is crucial to human well-being in general and to the social standing of women in particular. In the era of the family wage, care work was treated as the private responsibility of individual women. Today, however, it can no longer be treated in that way. Some other way of organizing it is required, but a number of different scenarios are conceivable. In evaluating postindustrial welfare state models then, we must ask: how is responsibility for care work allocated between such institutions as the family, the market, civil society, and the state? And how is responsibility for this work assigned within such institutions: by gender? by class? by "race"-ethnicity? by age?

A second set of issues concerns differences among women. Gender is the principal focus of this essay, to be sure, but it cannot be treated en bloc. The lives of women and men are cross-cut by several other salient social divisions, including class, race-ethnicity, sexuality, and age. Models of postindustrial welfare states, then, will not affect all women—nor all men—in the same way; they will generate different outcomes for differently situated people. For example, some policies will affect women who have children differently from those who do not; some, likewise, will affect women who have access to a second income differently from those who do not; and some, finally, will affect women employed full-time differently from those employed part-time, and differently yet again from those who are not employed. For each model then, we must ask: which groups of women would be advantaged and which groups disadvantaged?

A third set of issues concerns desiderata for postindustrial welfare states other than gender equity. Gender equity, after all, is not the only goal of social welfare. Also important are non-equity goals, such as efficiency, community, and individual liberty. In addition, there remain other equity goals, such as racial-ethnic equity, generational equity, class equity, and equity among nations. All of these issues are necessarily backgrounded here.

With these considerations in mind, let us now examine two strikingly different feminist visions of a postindustrial welfare state, and let us ask: which comes closest to achieving gender equity in the sense I have elaborated here?

II. UNIVERSAL BREADWINNER MODEL

In one vision of postindustrial society, the age of the family wage would give way to the age of the universal breadwinner. This is the vision implicit in the current political practice of most U.S. feminists and liberals. (It was also assumed in the former state-socialist countries!) It aims to achieve gender equity principally by promoting women's employment. The point is to enable women to support themselves and their families through their own wage earning. The breadwinner role is to be universalized, in sum, so that women too can be citizen-workers.

Universal breadwinner is a very ambitious postindustrial scenario, requiring major new programs and policies. One crucial element is a set of employment-enabling services, such as day care and elder care, aimed at freeing women from unpaid responsibilities so that they can take full-time employment on terms comparable to men. Another essential element is a set of workplace reforms aimed at removing equal-opportunity obstacles, such as sex discrimination and sexual harassment. Reforming the workplace requires reforming the culture however—eliminating sexist stereotypes and breaking the cultural association of breadwinning with masculinity. Also required are policies to help change socialization, so as first, to reorient women's aspirations toward employment and away from domesticity, and second, to reorient men's expectations toward acceptance of women's new role. None of this would work, however, without one additional ingredient: macroeconomic policies to create full-time, high paying, permanent jobs for women. These would have to be true breadwinner jobs in the primary labor force, carrying full, first-class social-insurance entitlements. Social insurance, finally, is central to universal breadwinner. The aim here is to bring women up to parity with men in an institution that has traditionally disadvantaged them.

How would this model organize care work? The bulk of such work would be shifted from the family to the market and the state, where it would be performed by employees for pay.[22] Who then are these employees likely to be? In the United States today, paid institutional care work is poorly remunerated, largely feminized, and largely racialized,[23] but such arrangements are precluded in this model. If the model is to succeed in enabling all women to be breadwinners, it must upgrade the status and pay attached to care work employment, making it too into primary labor force work. Universal breadwinner, then, is necessarily committed to a policy of "comparable worth"; it must redress the widespread undervaluation of skills and jobs currently coded as feminine and/or "non-White," and it must remunerate such jobs with breadwinner-level pay.

Universal breadwinner would link many benefits to employment and distribute them through social insurance. In some cases, such as pensions, benefit levels would vary with earnings. In this respect, the model resembles the industrial era welfare state. The difference is that many more women would be covered on the basis of their own employment records, and many more women's employment records would look considerably more like men's.

Universal breadwinner is far removed from present realities. It requires massive creation of primary labor force jobs—jobs sufficient to support a family single-handedly. That, of course, is wildly askew of current postindustrial trends, which generate jobs not for breadwinners, but for "disposable workers."[24] Let us assume for the sake of the thought experiment, however, that its conditions of possibility could be met, and let us consider whether the resulting postindustrial welfare state could claim title to gender equity.

Antipoverty

We can acknowledge straight off that universal breadwinner would do a good job of preventing poverty. A policy that created secure breadwinner-quality jobs for all employable women and men—while providing the services that would enable women to take such jobs—would keep most families out of poverty, and generous levels of residual support would keep the rest out of poverty through transfers. Failing that, however, several groups are especially vulnerable to poverty in this model: those who cannot work, those who cannot get secure, permanent, full-time, good-paying jobs—disproportionately women and/or people of color; and those with heavy, hard-to-shift, unpaid care work responsibilities—disproportionately women.

Antiexploitation

The model should also succeed in preventing exploitable dependency for most women. Women with secure breadwinner jobs are able to exit unsatisfactory relations with men, and those who do not have such jobs but know they can get them will also be less vulnerable to exploitation. Failing that, the residual system of income support provides backup protection against exploitable dependency—assuming that it is generous, nondiscretionary, and honorable. Failing that, however, the groups mentioned above remain especially vulnerable to exploitation—by abusive men, by unfair or predatory employers, by capricious state officials.

Equality

Income Equality   Universal breadwinner is only fair, however, at achieving income equality. Granted, secure breadwinner jobs for women—plus the services that would enable women to take them—would narrow the gender wage gap.[25] Reduced inequality in earnings, moreover, translates into reduced inequality in social-insurance benefits, and the availability of exit options from marriage should encourage a more equitable distribution of resources within it. But the model is not otherwise egalitarian. It contains a basic social fault line dividing breadwinners from others, to the considerable disadvantage of the others—most of whom would be women. Apart from comparable worth, moreover, it does not reduce pay inequality among breadwinner jobs. To be sure, the model reduces the weight of gender in assigning individuals to unequally compensated breadwinner jobs, but it thereby increases the weight of other variables, presumably class, education, race-ethnicity, and age. Women—and men—who are disadvantaged in relation to those variables will earn less than those who are not.

Leisure-Time Equality   The model is poor, moreover, with respect to equality of leisure time, although it improves on current arrangements. It assumes that all of women's current domestic and care work responsibilities can be shifted to the market and/or the state. But that assumption is patently unrealistic. Some things, such as childbearing, attending to family emergencies, and much parenting work, cannot be shifted—short of universal surrogacy and other presumably undesirable arrangements. Other things, such as cooking and (some) housekeeping, could be shifted—provided we were prepared to accept collective living arrangements or high levels of commodification. Even those tasks that are shifted, finally, do not disappear without a trace, but give rise to burdensome new tasks of coordination. Women's chances for equal leisure, then, depend on whether men can be induced

to do their fair share of this work. On this, the model does not inspire confidence. Not only does it offer no disincentives to free riding, but in valorizing paid work, it implicitly denigrates unpaid work, thereby fueling the motivation to shirk.[26] Women without partners would, in any case, be on their own. And those in lower-income households would be less able to purchase replacement services. Employed women would have a second shift on this model then, albeit a less burdensome one than some have now; and there would be many more women employed full-time. Universal breadwinner, in sum, is not likely to deliver equal leisure. Anyone who does not free ride in this possible postindustrial world is likely to be harried and tired.

Equality of Respect   The model is only fair, moreover, at delivering equality of respect. Because it holds men and women to the single standard of the citizen-worker, its only chance of eliminating the gender respect gap is to admit women to that status on the same terms as men. This, however, is unlikely to occur. A more likely outcome is that women would retain more connection to reproduction and domesticity than men, thus appearing as breadwinners manqué. In addition, the model is likely to generate another kind of respect gap. By putting a high premium on breadwinner status, it invites disrespect for others. Participants in the means-tested residual system will be liable to stigmatization, and most of these will be women. Any employment-centered model, even a feminist one, has a hard time constructing an honorable status for those it defines as nonworkers.

Antimarginalization

This model is also only fair at combating women's marginalization. Granted, it promotes women's participation in employment, but its definition of participation is narrow. Expecting full-time employment of all who are able, the model may actually impede participation in politics and civil

	Universal Breadwinner
Antipoverty	Good
Antiexploitation	Good
Income equality	Fair
Leisure-time equality	Poor
Equality of respect	Fair
Antimarginalization	Fair
Antiandrocentrism	Poor

Figure 1

society. Certainly it does nothing to promote women's participation in those arenas. It fights women's marginalization, then, in a one-sided, "workerist" way.

Antiandrocentrism

Finally, the model performs poorly in overcoming androcentrism. It valorizes men's traditional sphere—employment—and simply tries to help women fit in. Traditionally, female care work, in contrast, is treated instrumentally; it is what must be sloughed off to become a breadwinner. It is not itself accorded social value. The ideal typical citizen here is the breadwinner, now nominally gender neutral. But the content of the status is implicitly masculine; it is the male half of the old breadwinner/homemaker couple, now universalized and required of everyone. The female half of the couple has simply disappeared. None of her distinctive virtues and capacities has been preserved for women, let alone universalized to men. The model is androcentric.

We can summarize the merits of universal breadwinner in Figure 1. Not surprisingly, universal breadwinner delivers the best outcomes to women whose lives most closely resemble the male half of the old family-wage ideal couple. It is especially good to childless women and to women without other major domestic responsibilities that cannot easily be shifted to social services. But for those women, as well as for others, it falls short of full gender equity.

III. CAREGIVER PARITY MODEL

In a second vision of postindustrial society, the era of the family wage would give way to the era of caregiver parity. This is the picture implicit in the political practice of most Western European feminists and social democrats. It aims to promote gender equity principally by supporting informal care work. The point is to enable women with significant domestic responsibilities to support themselves and their families, either through care work alone or through care work plus part-time employment. (Women without significant domestic responsibilities would presumably support themselves through employment.) The aim is not to make women's lives the same as men's, but rather to "make difference costless."[27] Thus childbearing, childrearing, and informal domestic labor are to be elevated to parity with formal paid labor. The caregiver role is to be put on a par with the breadwinner role—so that women and men can enjoy equivalent levels of dignity and well-being.

Caregiver parity is also extremely ambitious. On this model, many (although not all) women will follow the current U.S. female practice of alternating spells of full-time employment, spells of full-time care work, and spells that combine part-time care work with part-time employment. The aim is to make such a life pattern costless. To this end, several major new programs are necessary. One is a program of caregiver allowances to compensate childbearing, childraising, housework, and other forms of socially necessary domestic labor; the allowances must be sufficiently generous at the full-time rate to support a family—hence equivalent to a breadwinner wage.[28] Also required is a program of workplace reforms. These must facilitate the possibility of combining supported care work with part-time employment and of transitioning between different life states. The key here is flexibility. One obvious necessity is a generous program of mandated pregnancy and family leave so that caregivers can exit and enter employment without losing security or seniority. Another is a program of retraining and job search for those not returning to old jobs. Also essential is mandated flextime so that caregivers can shift their hours to accommodate their care work responsibilities, including shifts between full- and part-time employment. Finally, in the wake of all this flexibility, there must be programs to ensure continuity of all the basic social-welfare benefits, including health, unemployment, disability, and retirement insurance.

This model organizes care work very differently from universal breadwinner. Whereas that approach shifted care work to the market and the state, this one keeps the bulk of such work in the household and supports it with public funds.[29] Caregiver parity's social-insurance system also differs sharply. To assure continuous coverage for people alternating between care work and employment, benefits attached to both must be integrated in a single desert-based system. In this system, part-time jobs and supported care work must be covered on the same basis as full-time jobs. Thus a woman finishing a spell of supported care work would be eligible for unemployment insurance benefits on the same basis as a recently laid off employee in the event she could not find a suitable job, and a supported care worker who became disabled would receive disability payments on the same basis as a disabled employee. Years of supported care work would count on a par with years of employment toward eligibility for retirement pensions. Benefit levels would be fixed in ways that treat care work and employment equivalently.

Caregiver parity, too, is far removed from current U.S. arrangements. It requires large outlays of public funds to pay caregiver allowances, hence major structural tax reform and a sea change in political culture. Let us assume for the sake of the thought experiment, however, that

its conditions of possibility could be met. And let us consider whether the resulting postindustrial welfare state could claim title to gender equity.

Antipoverty

Caregiver parity would do a good job of preventing poverty—including for those women and children who are currently most vulnerable. Sufficiently generous allowances would keep solo-mother families out of poverty during spells of full-time care work, and a combination of allowances and wages would do the same during spells of part-time supported care work and part-time employment. (Wages from full-time employment must also be sufficient to support a family with dignity.) Because each of these options would carry the basic social-insurance package, moreover, women with feminine work patterns would have considerable security. Adults with neither care work nor employment records would be most vulnerable to poverty in this model; most of these would be men. Children, in contrast, would be well protected.

Antiexploitation

Caregiver parity should also succeed in preventing exploitation for most women, including those who are most vulnerable today. By providing income directly to nonemployed wives, it reduces their economic dependence on husbands. It also provides economic security to single women with children, reducing their liability to exploitation by employers. Insofar as caregiver allowances are desert based and nondiscretionary, finally, recipients are not subject to caseworkers' whims. Once again, it is adults with neither care work nor employment records who are most vulnerable to exploitation in this model, and the majority of them would be men.

Income Equality   Caregiver parity performs quite poorly, however, with respect to income equality. Although the system of allowances plus wages provides the equivalent of a basic minimum breadwinner wage, it also institutes a "mommy track" in employment—a market in flexible, non-continuous full- and/or part-time jobs. Most of these jobs will pay considerably less even at the full-time rate than comparable breadwinner-track jobs. Two-partner families will have an economic incentive to keep one partner on the breadwinner track rather than to share spells of care work between them; given current labor markets, making the breadwinner the man will be most advantageous for heterosexual couples. Given current culture and socialization, moreover, men are generally unlikely to choose the mommy track in the same proportions as women. So the two employment tracks will carry traditional gender associations. Those associations are likely in turn to produce discrimination against women in the breadwinner track. Caregiver parity may make difference cost less then, but it will not make difference costless.

Leisure-Time Equality Caregiver parity does somewhat better, however, with respect to equality of leisure time. It makes it possible for all women to avoid the double shift if they choose, by opting for full- or part-time supported care work at various stages in their lives. (Currently, this choice is available only to a small percentage of privileged U.S. women.) We just saw, however, that this choice is not truly costless. Some women with families will not want to forego the benefits of breadwinner-track employment and will try to combine it with care work. Those not partnered with someone on the caregiver track will be significantly disadvantaged with respect to leisure time, and probably in their employment as well. Men, in contrast, will largely be insulated from this dilemma. On leisure time, then, the model is only fair.

Equality of Respect Caregiver parity is also only fair at promoting equality of respect. Unlike universal breadwinner, it offers two different routes to that end. Theoretically, citizen-workers and citizen-caregivers are statuses of equivalent dignity. But are they really on a par with one another? Caregiving is certainly treated more respectfully in this

model than in current U.S. society, but it remains associated with femininity. Breadwinning likewise remains associated with masculinity. Given those traditional gender associations, plus the economic differential between the two lifestyles, caregiving is unlikely to attain true parity with breadwinning. In general, it is hard to imagine how "separate but equal" gender roles could provide genuine equality of respect today.

Antimarginalization

Caregiver parity performs poorly, moreover, in preventing women's marginalization. By supporting women's informal care work, it reinforces the view of such work as women's work and consolidates the gender division of domestic labor. By consolidating dual labor markets for breadwinners and caregivers, moreover, the model marginalizes women within the employment sector. By reinforcing the association of caregiving with femininity, finally, it may also impede women's participation in other spheres of life, such as politics and civil society.

Antiandrocentrism

Yet caregiver parity is better than universal breadwinner at combating androcentrism. It treats caregiving as intrinsically valuable, not as a mere obstacle to employment, thus challenging the view that only men's traditional activities are fully human. It also accommodates feminine life patterns, thereby rejecting the demand that women assimilate to masculine patterns. But the model still leaves something to be desired. Caregiver parity stops short of affirming the universal value of activities and life patterns associated with women. It does not value caregiving enough to demand that men do it too; it does not ask men to change. Thus caregiver parity represents only one-half of a full-scale challenge to androcentrism. Here, too, its performance is only fair.

Caregiver parity's strengths and weaknesses are summarized in Figure 2. In general, caregiver

	Caregiver Parity
Antipoverty	Good
Antiexploitation	Good
Income equality	Poor
Leisure-time equality	Fair
Equality of respect	Fair
Antimarginalization	Poor
Antiandrocentrism	Fair

Figure 2

parity performs best for women with significant care work responsibilities. But for those women, as well as for others, it fails to deliver full gender equity.

IV. CONCLUSION: GENDER EQUITY IN A POSTINDUSTRIAL WELFARE STATE REQUIRES DECONSTRUCTING GENDER

Both universal breadwinner and caregiver parity are highly utopian visions of a postindustrial welfare state. Either one of them would represent a major improvement over current U.S. arrangements. Yet neither is likely to be realized soon. Both models assume background preconditions that are strikingly absent today. Both presuppose major political-economic restructuring, including significant public control over corporations, the capacity to direct investment to create high-quality permanent jobs, and the ability to tax profits and wealth at rates sufficient to fund expanded high-quality social programs. Both models also assume broad popular support for a postindustrial welfare state that is committed to gender equity.

If both models are utopian in this sense, neither is utopian enough. Neither universal breadwinner nor caregiver parity can actually make good on its promise of gender equity—even under very favorable conditions. Although both are good at preventing women's poverty and exploitation, both are only fair at redressing inequality

of respect: Universal breadwinner holds women to the same standard as men while constructing arrangements that prevent them from meeting it fully; caregiver parity, in contrast, sets up a double standard to accommodate gender difference while institutionalizing policies that fail to assure equivalent respect for feminine activities and life patterns. When we turn to the remaining components of gender equity, moreover, the two models' strengths and weaknesses diverge. Whereas universal breadwinner is better at preventing women's marginalization and at reducing income inequality between men and women, caregiver parity is better at redressing inequality of leisure time and at combating androcentrism. Neither model, however, promotes women's full participation on a par with men in politics and civil society. And neither values female-associated practices enough to ask men to do them, too; neither asks men to change. (The relative merits of universal breadwinner and caregiver parity are summarized in Figure 3.) Neither model, in sum, provides everything that feminists want. Even in a highly idealized form, neither delivers full gender equity.

If these were the only possibilities, we would face a very difficult set of trade-offs. Suppose, however, we reject this Hobson's choice and try to develop a third alternative. The trick is to envision a postindustrial welfare state that combines the best of universal breadwinner with the best of caregiver parity, while jettisoning the worst features of each. What third alternative is possible?

So far, we have examined—and found wanting—two initially plausible approaches: one aiming to make women more like men are now, and the other leaving men and women pretty much unchanged, while aiming to make women's difference costless. A third possibility is to induce men to become more like most women are now—that is, people who do primary care work.

Consider the effects of this one change on the models we have just examined. If men were to do their fair share of care work, universal breadwinner would come much closer to equalizing

	Universal Breadwinner	Caregiver Parity
Antipoverty	Good	Good
Antiexploitation	Good	Good
Income equality	Fair	Poor
Leisure-time equality	Poor	Fair
Equality of respect	Fair	Fair
Antimarginalization	Fair	Poor
Antiandrocentrism	Poor	Fair

Figure 3

leisure time and eliminating androcentrism, whereas caregiver parity would do a much better job of equalizing income and reducing women's marginalization. Both models, in addition, would tend to promote equality of respect. If men were to become more like women are now, in sum, both models would begin to approach gender equity.

The key to achieving gender equity in a postindustrial welfare state, then, is to make women's current life patterns the norm. Women today often combine breadwinning and caregiving, albeit with great difficulty and strain. A postindustrial welfare state must ensure that men do the same, while redesigning institutions so as to eliminate the difficulty and strain. Such a welfare state would promote gender equity by dismantling the gendered opposition between breadwinning and caregiving. It would integrate activities that are currently separated from one another, eliminate their gender coding, and encourage men to perform them too.

This, however, is tantamount to a wholesale restructuring of the institution of gender. The construction of breadwinning and caregiving as separate roles, coded masculine and feminine respectively, is a principal undergirding of the current gender order. To dismantle those roles and their cultural coding is in effect to overturn that order. It means subverting the existing gender division of labor and reducing the salience of gender as a structural principle of social organization.[30] At the limit, it suggests deconstructing gender.[31]

Only by embracing the aim of deconstructing gender can we mitigate potential conflicts among our five component principles of gender equity, thereby minimizing the necessity of trade-offs. Rejecting that aim, in contrast, makes such conflicts, and hence trade-offs, more likely. Achieving gender equity in a postindustrial welfare state, then, requires deconstructing gender.

A thought experiment, I noted at the outset, is not a policy analysis. But it can nevertheless have political implications. By clarifying that gender equity requires deconstructing gender, the reasoning here suggests a strategy of radical reform. This means building movements whose demands for equity cannot be satisfied within the present gender order. It means organizing for reforms that "advance toward a radical transformation of society."[32]

Crucial to such a strategy is a third—deconstructive—vision of a postindustrial welfare state. What then might such a welfare state look like? Unlike caregiver parity, its employment sector would not be divided into two different tracks; all jobs would assume workers who are caregivers, too; all would have a shorter work week than full-time jobs have now; and all would have employment-enabling services. Unlike universal breadwinner, however, employees would not be assumed to shift all care work to social services. Some informal care work would be publicly supported and integrated on a par with paid work in a single social-insurance system. Some would be performed in households by relatives and friends, but such households would not necessarily be heterosexual nuclear families. Other supported care work would be located outside of households altogether—in civil society. In state-funded but locally organized institutions, childless adults, older people, and others without kin-based responsibilities would join parents and others in democratic, self-managed care work activities. This approach would not only deconstruct the opposition between breadwinning and caregiving; it would also deconstruct the associated opposition between bureaucratized public institutional settings and intimate private domestic settings. Treating civil society as a site for care work offers a wide range of new possibilities for promoting equal participation in social life, now no longer restricted to formal employment.

Much more work needs to be done to develop this third—deconstructive—vision of a postindustrial welfare state. A key is to develop policies that discourage free riding. Contra conservatives, the real free riders in the current system are not poor solo mothers who shirk employment. Instead, they are men of all classes who shirk care work and domestic labor, and especially corporations who free ride on the labor of working people, both underpaid and unpaid.

A good statement of the deconstructive vision comes from the Swedish Ministry of Labor: "To make it possible for both men and women to combine parenthood and gainful employment, a new view of the male role and a radical change in the organization of working life are required."[33] The trick is to imagine a social world in which citizens' lives integrate wage earning, caregiving, community activism, political participation, and involvement in the associational life of civil society—while also leaving time for some fun. This world is not likely to come into being in the immediate future. But it is the only imaginable postindustrial world that promises true gender equity, and unless we are guided by this vision now, we will never get any closer to achieving it.

NOTES

1. See Harvey (1989), Lash and Urry (1987), and Reich (1991).
2. Smith (1984).
3. Stacey (1987).
4. Weston (1991).
5. Ellwood (1988).
6. Fraser (1993).
7. Bartlett and Kennedy (1991).
8. Ellwood (1988).
9. Goodin (1988).
10. Not all dependencies are exploitable. Goodin (1988, 175–6) specifies the following four conditions that must be met if a dependency is to be exploitable: (1) the relationship must be asymmetrical; (2) the subordinate party must need the resource that the superordinate supplies; (3) the subordinate must depend on some particular superordinate for the supply of needed resources; and (4) the superordinate must enjoy discretionary control over the resources that the subordinate needs from him or her.
11. See Hirschman (1970), Okin (1989), and Hobson (1990).
12. Piven and Cloward (1971), Esping-Andersen (1990).
13. Goodin (1988).
14. Sparer (1970).
15. See Orloff (1993). The antiexploitation objective should not be confused with current U.S. attacks on welfare dependency, which are highly ideological. These attacks define dependency exclusively as receipt of public assistance. They ignore the ways in which such receipt can promote claimants' independence by preventing exploitable dependence on husbands and employers (Fraser and Gordon 1994).
16. Lister (1990), Sen (1990).
17. Weitzman (1985).
18. Ellwood (1988, 45).
19. Hochschild (1989), Schor (1991).
20. Bradshaw and Holmes (1989, as cited by Lister, 1990).
21. Balbo (1987).
22. This could be done in several different ways. Government could itself provide day care, and so on, in the form of public goods, or it could fund marketized provision through a system of vouchers. Alternatively, employers could be mandated to provide employment-enabling services for their employees, either through vouchers or in-house arrangements. The state option means higher taxes, of course, but it may be preferable nevertheless. Mandating employer responsibility creates a disincentive to hire workers with dependents, to the likely disadvantage of women.
23. Glenn (1992).
24. Kilborn (1993).

25. Exactly how much depends on the government's success in eliminating discrimination and in implementing comparable worth.
26. Universal breadwinner apparently relies on persuasion to induce men to do their fair share of unpaid work. The chances of that working would be improved if the model succeeded in promoting cultural change and in enhancing women's voice within marriage. But it is doubtful that this would suffice.
27. Littleton (1991).
28. On what principle(s) would these benefits be distributed? Caregiver allowances could in theory be distributed on the basis of need, as a means-tested benefit for the poor—as they have always been in the United States. But that would contravene the spirit of caregiver parity. One cannot consistently claim that the caregiver life is equivalent in dignity to the breadwinner life, while supporting it only as a last-resort stopgap against poverty.
29. Susan Okin (1989) has proposed an alternative way to fund care work. In her scheme the funds would come from what are now considered to be the earnings of the caregiver's partner. A man with a nonemployed wife, for example, would receive a paycheck for one half of his salary; his employer would cut a second check in the same amount payable directly to the wife. Intriguing as this idea is, one may wonder whether it is really the best way to promote wives' independence from husbands, because it ties her income so directly to his.
30. Okin (1989).
31. J. Williams (1991).
32. Gorz (1967, 6).
33. As quoted in Lister (1990, 463).

REFERENCES

Abramowitz, Mimi. 1988. *Regulating the Lives of Women: Social Welfare Policy from Colonial Times to the Present.* Boston: South End.

Balbo, Laura. 1987. "Crazy Quilt." In *Women and the State,* edited by Ann Showstack Sassoon. London: Hutchinson.

Bartlett, Katharine T., and Rosanne Kennedy, eds. 1991. *Feminist Legal Theory: Readings in Law and Gender* Boulder, CO: Westview.

Ellwood, David T. 1988. *Poor Support: Poverty in the American Family.* New York: Basic Books.

Esping-Andersen, Gosta. 1990. *The Three Worlds of Welfare Capitalism.* Princeton, NJ: Princeton University Press.

Fraser, Nancy. 1987 "Women, Welfare, and the Politics of Need Interpretation." *Hypatia: A Journal of Feminist Philosophy* 2, no. 1: 103–21. (Reprinted in Fraser, *Unruly Practices: Power, Discourse, and Gender in Contemporary Social Theory.* Minneapolis: University of Minnesota Press, 1989.)

——— 1993. "Clintonism, Welfare, and the Antisocial Wage: The Emergence of a Neoliberal Political Imaginary." *Rethinking Marxism* 6, no. 1: 9–23.

Fraser, Nancy, and Linda Gordon. 1992. "Contract versus Charity: Why Is There No Social Citizenship in the United States?" *Socialist Review* 22, no. 3: 45–68.

——— 1994. "A Genealogy of 'Dependency': Tracing a Keyword of the U.S. Welfare State." *Signs: Journal of Women in Culture and Society* 19, no. 2: 309–36.

Glenn, Evelyn Nakano. 1992. "From Servitude to Service Work: Historical Continuities in the Racial Division of Paid Reproductive Labor." *Signs: Journal of Women in Culture and Society* 18, no. 1: 1–43.

Goodin, Robert. 1988. *Reasons for Welfare: The Political Theory of the Welfare State.* Princeton, NJ: Princeton University Press.

Gordon, Linda. 1988. "What Does Welfare Regulate?" *Social Research* 55, no. 4: 609–30.

Gorz, Andre. 1967. *Strategy for Labor: A Radical Proposal.* Translated by Martin A. Nicolaus and Victoria Ortiz. Boston: Beacon.

Harvey, David. 1989. *The Condition of Postmodernity: An Inquiry into the Origins of Cultural Change.* Oxford: Basil Blackwell.

Hirschman, Albert O. 1970. *Exit, Voice, and Loyalty: Responses to Decline in Firms. Organizations, and States.* Cambridge, MA. Harvard University Press.

Hobson, Barbara. 1990. "No Exit, No Voice: Women's Economic Dependency and the Welfare State." *Acta Sociologica* 33, no. 3: 235–50.

——— 1993. "Economic Dependency and Women's Social Citizenship: Some Thoughts on Esping-Andersen's Welfare State Regimes." Unpublished typescript.

Hochschild, Arlie. 1989. *The Second Shift: Working Parents and the Revolution at Home.* New York: Viking.

Jenson, Jane. 1990. "Representations of Gender: Policies to 'Protect' Women Workers and Infants in France and the United States before 1914." In *Women, the State, and Welfare,* edited by Linda Gordon, 152–77. Madison: University of Wisconsin Press.

Kilborn, Peter. 1993. March 15. "New Jobs Lack the Old Security in Time of 'Disposable Workers.'" *The New York Times,* pp. A1, A6.

Land, Hilary. 1978. "Who Cares for the Family?" *Journal of Social Policy* 7, no. 3: 257–84.

Lash, Scott, and John Urry. 1987. *The End of Organized Capitalism.* Cambridge: Polity.

Lister, Ruth. 1990. "Women, Economic Dependency, and Citizenship." *Journal of Social Policy* 19, no. 4: 445–67.

Littleton, Christine A. 1991. "Reconstructing Sexual Equality." In *Feminist Legal Theory: Readings in Law and Gender,* edited by Katharine T. Bartlett and Rosanne Kennedy, 35–56. Boulder, CO: Westview.

Nelson, Barbara. 1984. "Women's Poverty and Women's Citizenship: Some Political Consequences of Economic Marginality." *Signs: Journal of Women in Culture and Society* 10, no. 2: 209–31.

——— 1990. "The Origins of the Two-Channel Welfare State: Workmen's Compensation and Mothers' Aid." In *Women, the State, and Welfare,* edited by Linda Gordon, 123–51. Madison: University of Wisconsin Press.

Okin, Susan Moller. 1989. *Justice, Gender, and the Family.* New York: Basic Books.

Orloff, Ann Shola. 1993. "Gender and the Social Rights of Citizenship: The Comparative Analysis of Gender Relations and Welfare States." *American Sociological Review* 58, no. 3: 303–28.

Piven, Frances Fox, and Richard A. Cloward. 1971. *Regulating the Poor.* New York: Random House.

Reich, Robert. 1991. *The Work of Nations: Preparing Ourselves for 21st Century Capitalism.* New York: Alfred A. Knopf.

Schor, Juliet. 1991. *The Overworked American: The Unexpected Decline of Leisure.* New York: Basic Books.

Sen, Amartya. 1990. "More Than 100 Million Women Are Missing." *The New York Review of Books* 37, no. 20: 61–6.

Smith, Joan. 1984. "The Paradox of Women's Poverty: Wage-Earning Women and Economic Transformation." *Signs: Journal of Women in Culture and Society* 9, no. 2: 291–310.

Sparer, Edward V. 1970. "The Right to Welfare." In *The Rights of Americans: What They Are—What They Should Be,* edited by Norman Dorsen, 65–93. New York: Pantheon.

Stacey, Judith. 1987. "Sexism By a Subtler Name? Postindustrial Conditions and Postfeminist Consciousness in the Silicon Valley." *Socialist Review* 96: 7–28.

Taylor-Gooby, Peter. 1993. "Scrounging, Moral Hazard, and Unwaged Work: Citizenship and Human Need." Unpublished typescript.

Weitzman, Lenore. 1985. *The Divorce Revolution: The Unexpected Social Consequences for Women and Children in America.* New York: Free Press.

Weston, Kath. 1991. *Families We Choose: Lesbians, Gays, Kinship.* New York: Columbia University Press.

Williams, Joan. 1991. "Deconstructing Gender." In *Feminist Legal Theory: Readings in Law and Gender,* edited by Katharine T. Bartlett and Rosanne Kennedy, 95–123. Boulder, CO: Westview.

DIFFERENCE AND SOCIAL POLICY: REFLECTIONS IN THE CONTEXT OF SOCIAL MOVEMENTS

Iris Marion Young

Legal theory, policy discussion, and political philosophy have recently been much occupied with the issue of equal treatment versus special treatment for oppressed and disadvantaged groups. The debate is abstract, but I suggest that it loses some of this abstractness if we focus on the wider context of movements of oppressed groups that question the liberal humanist ideal of liberation as transcending group difference. Since the 1960s women, Blacks, American Indians, gay men and lesbians, old people, the disabled, and other oppressed groups have asserted a politics that reclaims a positivity and specificity to group difference. By asserting this politics these groups redefine the meaning of difference so that it no longer means exclusive opposition and deviation from a norm, and reveal that the liberal humanist ideal of universal standards according to which everyone should be measured tends to perpetuate disadvantage and silence the specific culture and experience of some groups. This politics of difference seeks to sever the association of equality with sameness, and focuses on equality as participation and inclusion. Where group differences continue to exist and some groups have greater power and privilege, promoting the participation and inclusion of currently disadvantaged groups often requires recognizing the specificity of their situation and culture, rather than being blind to difference.

Debate about sameness versus difference has raged particularly strongly in recent years among feminist theorists. Focusing on difference by feminist theorists seems particularly risky because "natural" differences have been used in so many ways to justify excluding women from meaningful participation in society; but by recognizing that feminism is simply one of the several movements of the oppressed and disadvantaged that challenge the assumption that social equality entails that everyone conform to common standards and is treated in the same way, this risk is reduced. Treatment of pregnant and birthing women in relation to the workplace is neither the only nor the primary context in which the issue of same treatment versus different treatment arises. Thus, situated in this larger context feminists are better able to defend different treatment without restricting this defense to gender contexts or only on biological grounds.

I. LIMITS OF THE LIBERAL HUMANIST IDEAL

There was once a time of caste and class, when tradition decreed that each group had its place, and that some are born to rule while others to serve. Law and social norms defined rights, privileges, and obligations differently for different groups, distinguished by characteristics of sex, race, religion, class or occupation. Social in-

equality was justified by church and state on the grounds that people have different natures, and some natures are better than others.

Then one day Enlightenment dawned, heralding a revolutionary conception of humanity and society. All people are equal, these upstart men declared, inasmuch as all have a capacity for reason and moral sense. Law and politics should therefore grant to everyone equality of political and civil rights. With these bold ideas the battle lines of modern political struggle were drawn.

For over 200 years since first rang out those voices of Reason, the forces of light have struggled for liberty and political equality against the dark forces of irrational prejudice, arbitrary metaphysics, and the crumbling towers of patriarchal church, state and family. In the New World we had a head start in this fight, since, the American war of Independence was fought on these enlightenment principles, and our Constitution stood for liberty and equality. So we did not have to throw off the yokes of class and religious privilege, as did our Old World comrades. Yet the United States had its own aristocratic horrors in the form of slavery and the exclusion of women from public life. In protracted and bitter struggles these bastions of privilege based on group difference began to give way finally to topple in the 1960's.

Today a few vestiges of prejudice and discrimination remain, but we are working on them, and have just about realized the dream those Enlightenment fathers dared to have. The state and law should express rights only in universal terms that apply to all in the same way, and differences among persons and groups should be a purely accidental and private matter. Today we are seeking a society where differences in race, sex, religion, and ethnicity make no more difference in people's rights and opportunities than do difference of hair color. We believe that people should be treated as individuals, not as members of groups; their life options and rewards should be based solely on their individual achievement. We tell each other this story and make our children perform it for our sacred holidays—Thanksgiving Day, Fourth of July, Lincoln's Birthday. We have constructed Martin Luther King Day to fit the narrative so well that we have already forgotten that it took a fight to get it included in the canon year.

There is much truth to this story. The liberal humanist ideal of liberation as transcending group differences did and does inspire movements against oppression and domination, and the successes of these movements have created social values and institutions we would not want to lose. The liberal humanist ideal has been crucial in denying essential differences among groups that previously were invoked to justify privileges for some and exclusion for others. The struggles inspired by this ideal resulted in legal recognition that all United States citizens are entitled to equal protection under the law and cannot be excluded from public institutions or employment solely on grounds of group membership. A people could do worse than to tell this story after big meals and occasionally call upon one another to live up to it.

Still, the story has its limits. Though legal equality has been largely achieved for all groups, with the shameful exception of gay men and lesbians, by any measure of equality some groups continue to be disadvantaged and oppressed, while others continue to have power and privilege. Because legally sanctioned impediments to the inclusion of women, Blacks and other racialized groups, and disabled people have been removed, some individuals from these groups have been able to attain positions they otherwise could not have achieved, and a few have even gained positions of high prestige and power. As groups, however, segregation, disadvantage and exclusion continues, and there is little sign of a breakdown of these inequalities.

Though in many respects the law is now blind to group differences, not all members of society are, and therefore some groups continue to be marked as deviant or the "Other." In daily interactions assumptions continue to be made about certain groups that justify exclusion, avoidance, paternalism, and authoritarian treatment. Continued racist, sexist, homophobic, ageist, and ableist behavior and institutions create particular circumstances for the members of these groups, usually by disadvantaging them in their opportunity to develop their capacities and by giving them particular experiences. In part because these groups have been segregated and excluded from one another and in part because they have particular histories and traditions, there are cultural differences among them, differences including language, style of living, body comportment and gesture, values, and perspectives on society. Thus, the differences that continue to exist among groups are partly imposed by the effects of discrimination and partly chosen voluntarily by the members of the group.

The liberal humanist ideal presumes that there are norms and attributes of humanity in general to which everyone can aspire and which can be used to judge the merit and capacities of people as individuals, rather than as members of groups. Once the impediments of discrimination and stereotyping are removed, then inequalities will reflect tastes, capacities, and efforts, rather than any group attributes.

Measuring all according to the same standards and treating everyone in the same way often contributes to perpetuating disadvantage and oppression where the commitment to the equal moral worth of all persons has been achieved, but where group differences and group inequalities remain. The ideal of a common humanity in which all can participate without regard for race, gender, religion or sexuality poses as neutral and universal—speaking correctly, being rational, professional, decent, intelligent, and so on. These supposedly neutral attributes of assessing merit, however, require substantive behaviors to be judged, and insofar as the ideals are substantive they must be particular. Oppressed groups find that rationality, intelligence, correct speech, proper body comportment, and the like, reflect the experience and way of life of the dominant white middle class men. Because women or Blacks, for example, often have not been socialized in the same way as those white middle class men, they are less able to conform to these allegedly neutral standards of competence. They then are at a disadvantage in a merit competition under rules of equal treatment.

Even though these standards claim to be neutral, they tend to be biased in favor of the privileged groups, thus disadvantaging some persons, and forcing them to deny aspects of their identity or culture if they are to properly measure up to the standards. To the degree that members of oppressed groups conform to dominant standards and achieve by those mainstream criteria, they find that they must invalidate aspects of their experience and identity. When we use an ideal of general human standards, then we make Puerto Ricans, or Chinese Americans ashamed of their accents or their parents, Black children despise the female dominated kin networks of their neighborhoods, and women root out their tendency to cry. Therefore, even when formerly excluded groups succeed in conforming to the standards they do not experience as neutral, they often do so at the expense of splitting or denying their identities as feminine, Black, Indian, and so on.

II. THE POLITICS OF DIFFERENCE

As a result of such experiences, some social movements of the oppressed have challenged the ideal of liberation as transcending group difference and have asserted instead the positivity of group-based experience. In the late 1960s, for example, Black Power and Black Nationalism advocates criticized the assimilationist goal that characterized the civil rights movement, and asserted instead a positivity and specificity to Afro-American culture, and the need for separate political organization.[1] Many Black liberation theorists continue to argue that the Afro-American experience gives to black people distinctive cultural forms and ways of understanding society that make assimilation to white-dominated culture both difficult and undesirable.[2]

Recent movements for American Indian rights provide an even more telling example of the assertion of positive group difference. Indians have sought to recover and preserve their languages, rituals and crafts, and this renewal of pride in traditional culture also fostered a separatist political movement. The desire to pursue land rights claims and to fight for control over resources on reservations arises from what has become a fierce commitment to tribal self-determination, that is, the desire to develop and maintain political and economic bases in, but not of, white society. Indians demand that rights to jobs, health care, and social services be recognized at the same time as their right to group-based political and cultural self-determination.[3]

These are but two examples of a widespread tendency in the politics of the 1970s and 80s for oppressed, disadvantaged or specially-marked groups to organize autonomously and positively assert their cultural and experiential specificity. In the last twenty years movements of Spanish-speaking Americans, Jewish Americans, gay men and lesbians, and old people, have all asserted a positive group difference against the universalist and assimilationist principles of liberal humanism. Paradoxical as it sounds, such

---

[1] *See, e.g.,* S. Carmichael & C. Hamilton, *Black Power* (1967); *see also* J. Bayes, *Minority Politics and Ideologies in the United States,* ch. 3 (1982); L. Lader, *Power on the Left,* ch. 5 (1979).

[2] *See, e.g.,* Sheila Collins' discussion of the "melting pot" myth. S. Collins in *The Rainbow Challenge: The Jackson Campaign and the Future of U.S. Politics* (1986); *see also* H. Cruse, *Plural but Equal: Black and Minorities in America's Plural Society* (1987). Many black theorists couch this discussion specifically in terms of a confrontation with typical Marxian assumptions of a unified proletariat. *See* Harris, *Historical Subjects and Interests: Race, Class and Conflict,* in *The Year Left: An American Socialist Yearbook.* (J. Brenner, et al. eds. 1987); Outlaw, *On Race and Class, Or, On the Prospects of "Rainbow" Socialism,* in The Year Left, *supra,* at 106.

[3] *See* V. Deloria & C. Lytle, *The Nations Within,* chs. 15–17 (1984); R. Ortiz, *Indians of the Americas,* pt. III (1984).

challenges to the ideal have become possible only once that ideal has received wide recognition in the society. Only when the principle that persons should not be inhibited from institutional participation because of group membership has been widely affirmed, can oppressed groups discover the mechanisms that perpetuate exclusion and disadvantage even when there is formal equality.

The women's movement has also generated its own versions of a politics of difference. Humanist feminism, which predominated in nineteenth century feminism and in the contemporary women's movement until the late 1970s, finds in any assertion of difference between women and men only a legacy of female oppression and an ideology to legitimate continued exclusion of women from socially valued human activity. Thus it is analogous to an ideal of assimilation in identifying sexual equality with gender blindness, measuring women and men according to the same standards and treating them in the same way. Indeed, for many feminists, androgyny named the ideal of sexual liberation—a society in which gender difference itself would be eliminated. Given the strength and plausibility of this vision of sexual equality, how confusing it was when feminists also began taking the turn to difference, asserting the positivity and specificity of female experience and values.[4]

In practice, female assimilation has meant that women should aspire to enter male dominated realms of business and politics and compete in those realms on a par with men. Women who seek equality must be strong, rational, competitive and independent, and leave behind the traditionally feminine sphere in which they learned

to be emotionally caring, nurturing, and cooperative. Some feminists who assert the positivity of female difference, on the other hand, seek to revalue activities and relations traditionally labeled as feminine.[5] Others look to the sexual division of labor and find in women's laboring activities the bases of specific positive values and approaches to the world.[6] Under these versions of feminism women should not seek to be like men, but rather, should press for a social restructuring that will recognize and promote the values and forms of human relationship typical of "private" institutions of mothering, sistering, and domestic caretaking.

While the women's movement has tended to discuss and theorize women's specific experience and culture, at the same time there has been increasing discussion among feminists in recent years about the oppressive implication of any assumption that there is a single female experience. Feminist conferences and publications have generated particularly fruitful, though often emotionally-wrenching discussions of the oppression of racial and ethnic blindness and the importance of attending to group differences among women.[7] From such discussions principled efforts have emerged to provide autonomously organized forums for Black women, Latinas, Jewish women, lesbians, differently-abled women, old women, and any other women who see reason for claiming they have, as a

---

[4] I have developed an account of this contrast between humanist feminism and a feminism that affirms rather than denies female difference at greater length elsewhere. Young, *Humanism, Gynocentrism and Feminist Politics,* 8 *Women's Stud. Intl Q* 173 (1985) (special issue entitled "Hypatia: A Journal of Feminist Philosophy"); *see also* Miles, *Feminist Radicalism in the 1980's,* in Feminism Now: Theory and Practice (M. Kroker, A. Kroker, P. McCollum, & M. Verthuy eds. 1985).

[5] The theory of gender psychology developed by Nancy Chodorow that women's identities are defined more in relation to other people's than men's, N. Chodorow, *The Reproduction of Mothering* (1978), has inspired some feminists to find gender-specific approaches to morality, science, and other human activities. *See* C. Gilligan, *In a Different Voice* (1982); *see also Women and Moral Theory* (E. Kittay ed. 1986); J. Grimshaw, *Philosophy and Feminist Thinking* (1986) (particularly chs. 7, 8); E. Keller, *Reflections on Gender and Science* (1985).

[6] L. Leghorn & K. Parker, *Women's Worth* (1981); N. Hartsock, *Money, Sex and Power,* ch. 10 (1983); Ruddick, *Maternal Thinking,* in *Mothering: Essays in Feminist Theory,* 213 (J. Trebilcot ed. 1984).

[7] *See, e.g.,* E. Bulkin, M. Pratt, & B. Smith, *Yours in Struggle* (1984).

group, a distinctive voice that might be silenced in a general feminist discourse. These discussions of difference within the women's movement mirror the puzzles generated by assertions of difference in all oppressed social movements. The practices feminists have instituted to structure discussion and interaction among differently identifying groups of women offer beginning models for how to institute a politics that attends to difference.

The politics of difference asserted by all these diverse social movements is more liberating than liberal humanism in three ways. First, asserting the value and specificity of the culture and attributes of oppressed groups relativizes the dominant culture. That is, when feminists assert the validity of feminine sensitivity and the positive value of nurturing behavior; when gays describe the prejudice of heterosexuals as homophobic and their own sexuality as positive and self developing; and when blacks affirm a distinct Afro-American tradition, then the dominant culture is forced to discover itself for the first time as specific: as Anglo, European, Protestant, masculine, straight. If whites, men, professionals, and other dominant groups come to notice that their experiences and ways of understanding social relations are particular, they can perhaps become more aware of how their standards of authority, intelligence, reasonableness, creativity, and the like are colored by that experience. It then becomes increasingly difficult for dominant groups to maintain their norms as neutral and universal, and to construct the values and behavior of the oppressed as deviant, perverted, or inferior.

Second, the politics of difference promotes a notion of group solidarity against the individualism of liberal humanism. Liberal humanism values treating and evaluating each person as an individual, ignoring differences of race, sex, religion, and ethnicity. With the institutionalization of formal equality, some members of the formerly excluded groups have indeed succeeded by mainstream standards, but structural patterns of group privilege and oppression remain nonetheless. The politics of difference stands for a group solidarity that measures liberation according to how far women, blacks, Latinos, and so on as groups have come toward equality with other groups.

Third, the assertion of positive group difference provides a standpoint from which to criticize prevailing institutions and norms. Black Americans find in their traditional communities, which refer to their members as "brother" and "sister," a sense of solidarity absent from the calculating individualism of white professional capitalist society. Feminists find in the traditional female values of nurturing a challenge to a militarist worldview, and lesbians find in their relationships a confrontation with the assumption of complementary gender roles in sexual relationships. From their experience of a culture tied to the land, Native Americans formulate a critique of the instrumental rationality of European culture that results in pollution and ecological destruction. The relativizing of the dominant culture, then, does more than reveal the specificity of the dominant norms that claim universality and neutrality. It also provides access to questioning which of those norms are indeed humanly valuable, and which reinforce the power and privilege of the groups whose experience they reflect.

III. RECLAIMING THE MEANING OF DIFFERENCE

Since proponents of asserting group specificity certainly wish to affirm the liberal humanist claim that all persons are of equal worth, they appear to be faced with a dilemma. How can a group both claim a right to inclusion in all human activities and at the same time assert and celebrate its specificity? Analyzing W. E. B. Dubois's arguments for cultural pluralism, Bernard Boxill poses the dilemma this way: "On the one hand, we must overcome segregation because it denies the idea of human brotherhood; on the other hand, to overcome segregation we must self-segregate and therefore also deny the idea of human brotherhood."[8] Martha Minow poses a similar dilemma. "Are the stigma and unequal treatment encountered by minority groups better remedied by separation or by integration of such groups with others? Either remedy risks reinforcing the stigma associated with assigned difference by either ignoring it or focusing on it."[9]

Many people both inside and outside of the movements find the rejection of the liberal humanist ideal and the assertion of a positive group difference both confusing and controversial. They fear that any admission by oppressed groups that they are different from the dominant groups risks justifying anew the subordination, special marking, and exclusion of those groups along pre-modern lines. Since calls for a return of women to the kitchen, blacks to servant roles and separate schools, disabled people to nursing homes, are not absent from contemporary politics, the sort of dilemma that Boxill and Minow highlight takes on particular poignancy. It may be true that the liberal humanist ideal that treats everyone the same and applies the same standards to all perpetuates disadvantage because real group differences remain that make it unfair to compare the unequals. The assimilationist ideal of liberal humanism, however, is far preferable to a reestablishment of separate and unequal spheres for different groups justified because the groups are different.

This dilemma of difference appears, however, only if equality implies sameness and difference implies deviance, exclusion, and inequality. The social movements asserting positive group difference directly challenge these meanings of equality and difference themselves. They engage the meaning of difference itself as a terrain of political struggle, rather than leaving it to be monopolized by those who seek to use difference to justify exclusion and subordination.

In the ideologies of racism, sexism, anti-Semitism and homophobia, some groups are marked with an essence. The ideology alleges that group members have specific dispositions that suit them for some activities and not others by virtue of characteristics the group is alleged to have by nature, and hence out of its control. "Difference" in these ideologies always means exclusionary opposition to a standard of true universal humanity. There are rational men, and there are women, there are civilized men, and there are wild and savage peoples. The marking of difference always carries a good/bad opposition, it is always devaluation, the naming of an inferiority in relation of a superior standard of humanity. "Difference" here always means absolute otherness; the group marked as different has no common nature with the normal or neutral ones.

This attempt to measure all against some universal standard generates dichotomies—masculine/feminine, civilized/savage, etc.[10] The second term is defined negatively as the lack of the truly human qualities; at the same time it is defined as complement to the valued term, as what brings it to completion. By loving and affirming him, a woman serves as a mirror to a man, holding up

---

[8] B. Boxill, *Blacks and Social Justice,* 174 (1984).

[9] Minow, *Learning to Live with the Dilemma of Difference: Bilingual and Special Education,* 48 *Law & Contemp. Probs.* 157 (1985). While Minow's reference is specifically to the situation of how children who do not speak English well or children with special needs should be treated by the educational system, the dilemma she articulates applies to the broad situation of any groups traditionally stigmatized as different, and who have in the past found such labeling used to justify their exclusion from valued social activities.

[10] I believe that post-modernist critiques of the logic of Western metaphysics uncover much about how this process of attempting to bring particulars under a single category or standard generates exclusive dichotomies. While there are important differences between Theodore Adorno's critique of what he calls a logic of identity in Western thought, and Jacques Derrida's critique of a metaphysics of presence, they both describe this process of totalization that expels what does not fit the unity to a category completely outside. Both provide some indication of what a positive understanding of difference as particularity without exclusivity might mean. *See* T. Adorno, *Negative Dialectics* (1973); J. Derrida, *Of Grammatology* (1976). I have developed a more extended account of how their philosophies can apply to social theory elsewhere. Young, *The Ideal of Community and the Politics of Difference,* 12 *Soc. Theory & Prac.* 1 (1986); *see also* F. Dallmayr, *Twilight of Subjectivity: Contributions to a Post-Structuralist Theory of Politics* (1981).

his virtues for him to see.[11] By carrying the white man's burden, the civilized will realize universal humanity by taming and educating the savage peoples. In no case is the group defined as different recognized and affirmed in its own specificity from its own point of view. Thus, this assertion of difference as exclusive opposition actually denies difference because it universalizes the perspective of particular groups into a common measure of persons, and never affirms group identity in its incommensurable specificity.

By asserting a positive meaning for their own identity, oppressed groups seek to seize power over the defining difference itself and to eliminate the presumption of difference as deviance in relation to a norm. By puncturing the universalist claim to unity that expels some groups and turns them into the Other, the assertion of positive group specificity opens the possibility for understanding the relationship of one group to another merely as difference, instead of exclusion, opposition, or dominance. What can such a positive conception of group difference mean? Group identity should be understood in relational terms.[12] Social processes generate relational differentiations, situations of clustering and affective bonding in which persons feel affinity for particular other people. My "affinity group" in a given social situation are those people with whom I feel the most comfortable. Such affinity differentiates groups, but not according to a substantive identity: there is no common nature that members of the group have.[13]

The politics of difference promotes a conception in which groups do not stand in a relation of inside and outside. That groups define themselves as different does not mean that they have nothing in common. Groups themselves, moreover, are not unities; every group has group differences cutting across it. Difference here does not mean opposition and exclusivity, but particularity, specificity, and the impossibility of reducing either social process or individual subjectivity to unity.

IV. DIFFERENCE AND SOCIAL POLICY

The issue of the right to pregnancy and maternity leave, and the right to special treatment for nursing mothers, is highly controversial among feminists today.[14] I do not intend here to wind through the intricacies of what has become a conceptually challenging and interesting debate in legal theory. As Linda Krieger argues, the issue of rights for pregnant and birthing mothers in relation to the workplace has created a paradigm crisis for our understanding of sexual equality because the application of a principle of equal treatment on this issue has yielded results whose effects on women are at best ambiguous and at worst detrimental.[15]

In my view an equal treatment approach on this issue is inadequate because it either implies that women do not receive any right to leave and then return to a secure job when having babies, or

---

[11] L. Irigaray, *Speculum of the Other Woman* (G. Gill trans. 1985). Irigaray applies the critique of the metaphysics of presence to sex and gender, suggesting that gender opposition between the masculine and the feminine is founded on a denial and repression of sexual difference.

[12] *See* Minow, *supra* note 11, at 204–06.

[13] I take the term "affinity" from Donna Haraway's use of it in *A Manifesto for Cyborgs: Science, Technology, and Socialist Feminism in the 1980's, Socialist Rev.,* Mar.–Apr. 1985, at 65. The term connotes for her the effort in contemporary anti-racist movements and the women's movement "to craft a poetic/political unity without relying on a logic of appropriation, incorporation, and taxonomic identification." *Id.,* at 74.

[14] Throughout this section I will use the term "special rights" to designate the differential treatment I am arguing particular groups should receive. I use the term in much the same way that Elizabeth Wolgast develops it. E. Wolgast, *Equality and the Rights of Women* (1980). Like Wolgast, I would wish to distinguish a class of rights that all persons should have, general rights, and a class of rights that categories of persons have by virtue of particular circumstances. That is, the distinction should refer only to different levels of generality, where "special" means only "specific." Unfortunately, "special rights" tends to carry a connotation of *exceptional,* that is, specially marked and deviating from the norm. As I assert below, however, the goal is not to compensate for deficiencies in order to help people be "normal," but to denormalize, so that in certain contexts and at certain levels of abstraction everyone has "special" rights.

[15] Krieger, "Through a Glass Darkly: Paradigms of Equality and the Search for a Women's Jurisprudence," 2 *Hypatia* 45 (1987). Deborah Rhode provides an excellent synopsis of the dilemmas involved in this crisis in "Justice and Gender" (unpublished manuscript) (chapter 9).

it assimilates such guarantees under a supposedly gender neutral category of "disability." Such assimilation is unacceptable because pregnancy and childbirth are normal conditions of normal women, that are socially necessary work and that have unique and variable characteristics and needs.[16]

Assimilating pregnancy into disability gives a negative meaning to these processes as "unhealthy." It suggests, moreover, that the primary or only reason that a woman has a right to leave and return to a secure job is that she is physically unable to work at her job, or that doing so would be more difficult than when she is not pregnant and recovering from childbirth. While these are important reasons, depending on the individual woman, another reason is that she ought to have the time to establish breastfeeding and to develop a relationship and routine with her child, if she chooses.[17]

The pregnancy leave debate has been so heated and extensive because both feminists and non-feminists tend to think of biological sex difference as the most fundamental and eradicable difference. When difference means deviance, stigma and disadvantage, this impression can engender the fear that sexual equality is not attainable. I think it is important to emphasize that reproduction is by no means the only context in which issues of same versus different treatment arises. It is not even the only context where it

arises for issues involving bodily difference. The last twenty years have seen significant success in winning special rights for persons with physical and mental disabilities. These are clear cases where promoting equality in participation and inclusion requires attending to the particular needs of different groups.

Another bodily difference that has not been as widely discussed in law and policy literature, but should be, is age. With increasing numbers of willing and able old people marginalized in our society, the issue of mandatory retirement has been increasingly discussed. This discussion has not exploded because serious consideration of working rights for all people able and willing to work implies major restructuring of the allocation of labor in an economy with already socially volatile levels of unemployment. Forcing people out of their workplaces solely on account of their age is arbitrary and unjust. Yet I think it is also unjust to require old people to work on the same terms as younger people. Old people should have different working rights. When they reach a certain age they should be allowed to retire and receive income benefits. If they wish to continue working they should be allowed more flexible and part-time schedules than most workers currently have.

Each of these cases of special rights in the workplace—pregnancy and birthing, physical disability, and being old—has its own purposes and structures. They all challenge, however, the same paradigm of the "normal, healthy" worker. In each case the circumstance that calls for different treatment should not be understood as lodged in the differently treated workers, per se, but in their interaction with the structure and norms of the workplace.[18] Even in cases such as these, difference does not have its source in natural, unalterable, biological attributes, but in

---

[16] *See* Scales, *Towards a Feminist Jurisprudence,* 56 *Ind. L.J.* 375 (1981). Christine Littleton provides a very good analysis of the feminist debate about equal versus different treatment regarding pregnancy and childbirth, among other legal issues for women. Littleton, *Reconstructing Sexual Equality,* 75 *Calif. L. Rev.* 000 (1987). Littleton suggests, as I have stated above, that only the dominant male conception of work keeps pregnancy and birthing from being conceived of as work.

[17] Fathers also should have the right to establish relationship[s] with their babies without suffering disadvantage in the workplace. I support the concept of parental leave, which should be formulated in gender[-]neutral terms. Unless men are encouraged to take parental leaves the gender division of labor in child rearing cannot be undermined. Women's special rights for pregnancy, childbirth and lactation, should not be assimilated into parental leave in general, however. They are two different rights.

[18] Littleton suggests that difference should be understood not as a characteristic of particular sorts of people, but of the interaction of particular sorts of people with specific workplace structures. Littleton, *supra* note 16, at 546.

the relationship of bodies to rules and practices. In each case the political claim for special rights emerges not from a need to compensate for an inferiority, as some would interprete it, but a positive assertion of specificity in different forms of life.

Issues of difference arise for law and policy, moreover, not only regarding bodily being, but just as importantly for cultural integrity and invisibility. By culture I mean group specific phenomena of behavior, temperament, or meaning. Cultural differences include phenomena of language, speaking style or dialect, body comportment, gesture, social practices, values, group specific socialization, and so on. The politics of difference suggests that the social groups in our society that suffer oppression and disadvantage have culturally specific forms of life produced both by the self-segregated affinity of the group members and by their history of exclusion and disadvantage. Since difference does not imply exclusive opposition, saying that social groups are culturally different does not imply that they do not also have elements of shared culture with other groups. To the degree that groups are culturally different, however, equal treatment in many issues of social policy is unjust because it denies these cultural differences at the same time that it makes them a liability. There are a vast number of issues where fairness involves attention to cultural differences and their effects, but I shall briefly discuss three: affirmative action, comparable worth, and bilingual bicultural education and service.

Whether they involve quotas or not, affirmative action programs violate a principle of equal treatment because they are race or gender conscious in setting criteria for school admissions, jobs, or promotions. These policies are usually justified in one of two ways. Giving preference to race or gender is either understood as just compensation for groups that have suffered discrimination in the past, or it is understood as compensation for the present disadvantage these groups suffer because of that history of discrimination and exclusion.[19] I do not wish to quarrel with either of these justifications for the differential treatment based on race or gender implied by affirmative action policies, but only to suggest a third possible interpretation of these policies. Affirmative action policies can be understood as compensating for the cultural biases of standards and evaluators used by the schools or employers. If these standards and evaluators are assumed to reflect at least to some degree the specific life and cultural experience of dominant groups—whites, Anglos, or men—and that the development of truly neutral standards and evaluations is difficult or impossible because female, black, or Latino, cultural experience and the dominant cultures are in many respects not reducible to a common measure, then affirmative action policies compensate for the dominance of one set of cultural attributes. Such an interpretation of affirmative action has the advantage of locating the "problem" that affirmative action solves at least partly in the evaluators and their standards, rather than only in the disadvantaged group.

While not a matter of different treatment as such, comparable worth policies similarly claim to challenge cultural biases in traditional evaluation in the worth of female-dominated occupations, and in doing so require attending to differences. Schemes of equal pay for work of comparable worth require that predominantly-male and predominantly-female jobs have similar wage structures if they involve similar degrees of skill, difficulty, stress, and so on. The problem in implementing these policies, of course, lies in designing methods of comparing the jobs, which are often very different. Most schemes of comparison choose to minimize these differences by using supposedly gender neutral criteria, such as educational attainment, speed of work, manipulation of symbols, decision making, and so on. Some writers have suggested, however, that standard classifications of job traits may be systematically

---

[19] For one among many discussions of such "backward looking" and "forward looking" arguments, see B. Boxill, *supra* note 10, ch. 7.

biased to keep specific kinds of tasks involved in many female dominated occupations hidden.[20] Many female-dominated occupations involve gender specific kinds of labor—such as nurturing, smoothing over social relations, or the exhibition of sexuality—that most task observation ignores.[21] A fair assessment of the skills and complexity of many female-dominated jobs may therefore involve paying explicit attention to gender differences in kinds of jobs rather than applying gender blind categories of comparison.

Finally, linguistic and cultural minorities should have the right to maintain their languages and cultures and at the same time be entitled to all the benefits of citizenship, as well as valuable education and career opportunities. This right implies a positive obligation on the part of governments and other public bodies to print documents and to provide services in the native language of recognized linguistic minorities, and to provide bilingual instruction in schools. Cultural assimilation should not be a condition of full social participation, because it requires a person to transform his or her sense of identity, and when realized on a group level means altering or annihilating the group's identity. This principle does not apply to any persons who do not identify with majority language or culture within a society, but only to sizeable linguistic or cultural minorities living in distinct though not necessarily segregated communities. In the United States,

then, special rights for cultural minorities apply at least to Spanish-speaking Americans and Indians.

At stake in all these policy issues, as many writers have pointed out, is the meaning of social equality, and indeed, whether equality remains a useful concept for promoting social justice. The politics of difference denies that equality implies sameness, and instead interprets the goal of equality as the full participation and inclusion of currently oppressed and disadvantaged groups in all of society's institutions and social positions, and especially those most highly valued.[22]

The universalist claims that there is a contradiction in asserting that formerly segregated groups have a right to inclusion, and at the same time that these groups have a right to different treatment. There is no contradiction here, however, if attending to difference is necessary in order to make participation and inclusion possible. Groups with different circumstances or forms of life should be able to participate together in public institutions without shedding their distinct identities or suffering disadvantage because of them. The goal is not to give special compensation to the deviant until they achieve normality, but rather to de-normalize the way institutions formulate their rules by revealing the plural circumstances and needs that exist, or ought to exist, within them.

---

[20] *See* Beatty & Beatty, "Some Problems with Contemporary Job Evaluation Systems," in *Comparable Worth and Wage Discrimination: Technical Possibilities and Political Realities* 59 (H. Remick ed. 1981); Steinberg, "A Want of Harmony: Perspectives on Wage Discrimination and Comparable Worth," in *Comparable Worth and Wage Discrimination, supra,* at 23; *Women, Work and Wages* 81 (D. Treiman & H. Hartmann eds. 1981).

[21] D. Alexander, *Gendered Job Traits and Women's Occupations* (Ph.D. diss., Economics, Univ. of Massachusetts, 1987).

[22] I do not take it that a conception of equality as participation and inclusion need be interpreted as an "equality of results," where that implies a strict proportional representation of formerly excluded groups in institutions and kinds of positions or occupations. Too many writers pose the alternatives in a dichotomous fashion that suggests that if equality does not mean being blind to difference, then it must mean equal results in this sense. *See, e.g.,* Reynolds, "Stotts: Equal Opportunity, Not Equal Results, in The Moral Foundations of Civil Rights" 39 (R. Fullinwider & C. Mills eds. 1986).

UPDATING THE GENDERED EMPIRE: WHERE ARE THE WOMEN IN OCCUPIED AFGHANISTAN AND IRAQ?

Cynthia Enloe

Empire. Until not long ago the study of empires was the purview of academic historians. Some historians, though, especially male historians, recently managed to draw considerable attention from thoughtful magazines and television's serious talk shows for their hefty new or reissued books on empire.[1] Sales figures began to rise and media invitations rolled in. Readers and viewers were beginning to look for parallels to contemporary international affairs. We often try to sort out puzzles by thinking through analogies. Analogies are powerful. If we get our analogies wrong, our explanations are likely to be askew. In the wake of the U.S. military invasions of Afghanistan in 2001 and Iraq in 2003, those experts invited to speak in the public arena began to summon British and even Roman history in order to ask: Are we today seeing the emergence of a new empire?

As the U.S.-led wars in Afghanistan and Iraq dragged on, there were good reasons not only for media commentators and political decision-makers, but also for ordinary citizens to become curious about past experiences of empire. History teachers began to feel vindicated. Victorian wasn't just stuffy furniture. Caesar wasn't just a salad dressing.

Does the global reach of the present United States military, political, cultural, and economic influence have the cohesiveness, the expansiveness, and the sustainability to amount to an "empire"? Or, to put it more concretely: If we compare the U.S. role in the world today—its invasions and political occupations of Afghanistan and Iraq; its diplomatic roles in the former Yugoslavia and Liberia; its global network of military bases stretching from North Carolina and San Diego to Guam, South Korea, Okinawa, Uzbekistan, Kuwait, Iraq, Turkey, Bosnia, Germany, and Britain; its refusal to ratify a host of new international treaties; its manufacturing, trading, and banking practices from Poland to Indonesia—with those military, cultural, economic, and diplomatic practices of earlier Roman, Persian, Hapsburg, Ottoman, British, Belgian, Russian, Chinese, Japanese, U.S., French, Spanish, and Dutch empires, do we risk comparing an orange with apples? *Or* are we perhaps on firmer ground, comparing a new apple with a host of earlier apples?

Despite their remarkable absence from interview shows and op-ed pages, scores of feminist historians have given us fresh, detailed accounts of how both women and notions of femininity were pressed into service by earlier empire-builders.

Where were the women? Thanks to three decades of sleuthing by feminist historians, we now know where to point our analytical binoculars. We know not to look just at the gilded diplomatic halls, the bloody battlefields, and the floors of stock exchanges. We have been taught by these pioneering feminist historians to point our glasses farther afield. If groundbreaking feminist historians—Philippa Levine, Piya Chatterjee, Kumari Jayawaradena, and others—were invited to submit feature articles and to give mainstream media interviews, they would urge us instead to look inside brothels, to peer into respectable parlors, to press our noses against the sooty windows of factories, to keep an eye on sexual relations on tea plantations.[2] All of these sites, it turns out, though far from the official centers of imperial power, have been sites of empire-making. That is, empires are built in parlors. Empires are built in brothels. Empires are built in allegedly "private" places. Given that, we need to examine the current possibility of a U.S. imperial enterprise from the vantage points of parlors and brothels. To make sense of putative American empire-building, we have to become much more curious—curious about the marriage aspirations of factory women, about the gender dynamics

inside soldiers' families, about sexual policies of the U.S. military forces in Afghanistan,
Uzbekistan, Iraq, and Kuwait. And that is just the
beginning. Reports now labeled "human interest
stories" have to be considered as serious com-
mentaries on foreign policy.

These thoughtful, worldly feminist investigators also have shown us how diverse and complex
women's actions and feelings have been within
empires. Women as tea pickers, women as nan-
nies, women as teachers, women as wives, women
as explorers, women as missionaries, women as
activist reformers, women as mothers, women as
educators, women as mistresses, women as prostitutes, women as textile factory workers, women
as writers, women as overseas settlers, women as
anticolonial nationalists—each in their own way
played crucial, yet overlooked, roles in greasing (or
clogging) the wheels of an imperial enterprise. The
roles each group played were "crucial" because
so many empire-builders designed international
power-extension strategies that relied on particular ideas about where different sorts of women
"naturally" were meant to be. The imperial strategists may have been men, but they were men who
thought (and worried) a lot about women. The imperial strategists—and their male opponents too—
may constantly have weighed varieties of masculinity, but they could do so only by trying to rank
and manipulate the varieties of femininity.[3] By not
asking about women in this current, possibly imperial enterprise—except, that is, for the Western
media's seeming addiction to the visual image of
the veiled Muslim woman—the commentators
now capturing the public limelight are making
both themselves as men inside empires and other
men and masculinities in empires virtually invisible. Feminists all over the world have learned how
risky *those* sins of omission can be.

WILL THE WOMEN STAND UP?

In the 1980s, at a meeting in Happy Valley, Labrador, a group of Native Canadian women of the
Innu community brought together several dozen

women, mostly from other parts of Canada, to
discuss the effects that a NATO air force base was
having on their lives. The term "empire" was not
used. Yet fueling this collective conversation was
a shared feminist curiosity about how unequal international power relations between allied masculinized governments depend not only on certain relationships between men and women but
also on global presumptions about where women
will be—and where they should stay. The Innu
women were helping us to "unpack" NATO.

One morning the Innu organizers cleared the
meeting hall of chairs and asked each of us to
imagine ourselves to be a particular woman who
was playing a role, maybe even unconsciously, in
sustaining, questioning, or resisting this NATO
air force base. As each of us thought of a woman,
we took on her persona, spoke to the group in the
first person as that woman, and joined others sitting on the floor. The floor soon became a complex world of militarized relationships among
diverse women. Within an hour that late-winter
morning—it was April, but the ice was just re-
ceding on the nearby lake—we had populated
the wooden floor with women from Canada, the
United States, Britain, and Germany, with women
married to air force officers, local Innu girls dating young fliers, other Innu women camping on
the NATO runways to protest low-flying training
flights, Canadian feminists in Toronto unaware
of the Canadian government's alliance policies in
"remote" Labrador, women from the Philippines
eager to share their own experiences of foreign
military bases, and more.

More recently, in Tokyo and Okinawa, groups
of us tried a similar feminist exercise, inspired by
the Innu activists' innovation. Our aim also was
to make women visible in international power
politics. We sought to piece together a map of
where women are in sustaining, questioning,
and resisting the unequal U.S.-Japan military
alliance. Any assessment of American empire-
building today must look closely at the dynamics
sustaining this unequal alliance. This time we
couldn't move the furniture, so we stood up.

Women and men in the audience, one by one, imagined themselves a particular woman living her life inside this alliance. As we took on the persona of a particular woman, we got onto our feet and spoke out:

> I am a young African American woman proud to be serving in the U.S. Marines stationed in Okinawa; thank God, I didn't take that job at Wal-Mart.

> I am an Okinawan woman, and I think I'm becoming what you might call an Okinawan nationalist because I'm growing more resentful of officials in the Tokyo government who routinely override our Okinawan concerns when they agree to allow so many U.S. bases to operate here on our land.

> I am a young Japanese mainland college graduate. As a woman, I've decided that enlisting in the Japanese Self-Defense Force will offer me more career opportunities than a dead-end job working as a corporate "office lady."

As some people stood up, others in the audience began to think of more women whose feelings, ideas, and actions were shaping—though scarcely controlling—the current U.S.-Japanese military alliance, a government-to-government agreement that was projecting American military dominance throughout Asia and the Pacific and as far away as Afghanistan. Our "map" was becoming bigger and more complicated with every person who stood up:

> I am a Yokohama high school student; my friends and I are dating American sailors to improve our English.

> I am a dairy farmer in Kyushu. I care personally about Article Nine, the peace article of the Japanese Constitution, so, in between my daily milkings and stall muckings, I write a small newsletter to tell other Japanese people what it means to live next to a fighter air base. One Friday a month I go and sit outside the gates of the Self-Defense Force fighter plane base; sometimes a dozen people come to join me; other times I'm sitting there all alone.

Over on the other side of the hall another Japanese young woman then stood up:

> I am an American white woman married to a U.S. Navy officer. I'm surprised that the navy's family housing here in Japan is so much nicer than what I have to endure at the base back in the U.S. Maybe I'll urge my husband to reenlist after all.

Then another:

> I'm one of those guides you see up in the front of tourist buses all over Okinawa; but recently I've retrained myself to become what's called a "peace guide." Now as my tourist bus travels around the countryside, I point out to visitors all the good farmland and beautiful coastal beaches that have been taken over by American military bases.

Way in the back a young man stood up:

> I'm just a housewife. My husband runs a small construction company, which makes me feel so nervous because the Japanese economy has been in recession now for over a decade. I don't like our government offering to send Japanese soldiers to help the Americans occupy Iraq, but I feel relieved that my husband's company just won a government contract to build a new road leading to a U.S. base. How should I reconcile my mixed feelings?

A graduate student at a Tokyo university was sitting toward the front of the room. She waited until the end and then stood up. She turned around to look at others in the large lecture hall:

> I'm just starting my doctoral dissertation in political science. There aren't many Japanese women teaching international relations, so to get a university job, I'll need to have the full support of my dissertation supervisor. He's quite well known in the field. Listening to everyone talk here tonight, I now want to change my dissertation research focus so I can look at the lives of Japanese girls and women living near a military base. I want to find out how they relate to the base and what that means for how they imagine themselves in Japanese political life. But my faculty supervisor won't think that asking these questions amounts to doing "real" international politics. How can I persuade him?

These collective acts of Innu, Okinawan, and Tokyo feminist imaginations revealed to all of us several important political realities. Each revelation is relevant to our current thinking about where women are in pursuing—or subverting—any imperial enterprise. *First,* women are intimately engaged in the little-noticed daily workings of those unequal international military alliances that are the backbone of nascent or mature empire-building. *Second,* women's roles in these large structures of international power are far from uniform. In fact, some of these women might view some of the other women who are engaged in the same global structure as too remote or too unsympathetic to become potential partners because of their class, ethnicity, nationality, ideological location, or even just their job. This, despite the fact that some of these women live their daily lives within just a mile of each other.

Third, every one of these women, nonetheless, is where she is on the globalized political map because of dominant notions about femininity and ideas about how she, as a woman or a girl, should relate to men and to masculinized foreign policies. *Fourth,* many women are privately ambivalent about the complicit roles they play in these unequal international power structures; some of them are actively self-conscious about their ambivalence. *Fifth,* while most of these women never make the headlines, they are counted upon by foreign policy-makers to keep playing their supportive, or at least passive, roles. Today's unequal international alliances depend on that.

AFGHAN WOMEN STAND UP

While spending several months in Tokyo's Ochanomizu University in early 2003, as the Bush administration mobilized to invade Iraq, I had the good fortune to meet and listen to one of the handful of Afghan women who had been appointed to senior posts in the interim government created in the wake of the U.S.-led military invasion of Afghanistan. She herself was not a cabinet minister. Only two of the twenty-seven members chosen for cabinet posts in the interim administration of President Hamid Karzai were women. But she was a deputy minister, with considerable responsibility for shaping the policies and institutions of the post-Taliban state. She was now in her fifties and had been a professional woman before the Taliban's ascendancy. Before that she had fought with the insurgent Afghan *mujahideen* forces against the occupying Soviet army.

As this story will suggest, it seems wise even today not to mention her name or even her precise post. She was in Tokyo at the invitation of the Japanese government, specifically of Japanese women working inside the government's overseas aid program, a program coordinated with the United Nations relief efforts in postinvasion, post-Taliban Afghanistan.

While passionate about the need to invest in girls' and women's training and empowerment, this Afghan woman official did not see herself as a natural ally of the Afghan women's organization best known outside of the country, the Revolutionary Association of the Women of Afghanistan, or RAWA.[4] Afghans (like the Vietnamese, Filipinos, and Tanzanians) have experienced not just one, but several waves of imperialist occupation: Persian, British, Russian, and now American. Creating a sense of national identity in countries such as Afghanistan has meant for many women advocates crafting comparative judgments about both past and present foreign rulers and about rival male-led local parties, each claiming to represent the nation, each claiming to know what is best for the nation's women.

One activist local woman's savvy use of openings created by the latest occupying power looks to another activist local woman like collaboration with the enemy, betrayal of the nation. Neither woman controls the masculinized political contest. Having to make such choices, often in the midst of war, displacement, and confusion, does not breed trust among women.

Thus this woman as a deputy minister, so eager for support in her efforts on behalf of girls' and women's empowerment in the midst of the U.S.-led occupation, voiced distrust of the women active in RAWA. She distrusted their local and international politics, even though RAWA's women activists had taken risks to do this work, as she also had, both inside Afghanistan during the Taliban's rule and in the increasingly politicized male-run refugee camps over the border in Pakistan.[5] She imagined, nevertheless, that the women active in RAWA had been too sympathetic to Kabul's 1980s Soviet-backed secular regime. So now, during the current U.S.-backed regime, this woman was not only seething with frustration at the patriarchal resistance she encountered daily from the men at the top of the Karzai regime, she was simultaneously keeping an arm's length distance from the activist women of RAWA.

Imperialism does this. It can send out fissures among the advocates of women's rights.

During one of these Tokyo discussions, the Japanese woman who hosted this Afghan deputy minister whispered, "In all the times I have met with her in Kabul, I have never seen her smile." Now, after two weeks in secure Tokyo, enjoying daily conversations with Japanese specialists on women's and girls' health, economy, politics, and education, she seemed to be letting down her guard. She dared to smile. She even made a joke. She had good reason, though, to maintain her deadpan "game face" when she was doing her risky work in Kabul. Not long before, her son had been beaten severely on a street in Kabul by a group of unidentified men. Before he lost consciousness, he heard his assailants warn him, "Tell your mother to get out of the place where she doesn't belong." The message was clear: a year and a half after the U.S. military and their Northern Alliance partners toppled the Taliban regime, any woman who dared to take on a modicum of political authority was still endangering not only herself, but members of her family. This woman was not easily cowed. Following her son's beating, she became angrier

and more committed. But smiling was a luxury that an activist woman still could ill afford in Kabul.

Listening between-the-lines to the conversations between this Afghan deputy minister and the Japanese aid officials hosting her prompted one to ask more questions about the genderings of militarized occupation.

Security—how to measure it, who gets to define it? These issues became contested during the U.S.-led occupation of Afghanistan. It was in the name of what it called the pursuit of "national security" that the Bush administration mounted its invasion of Afghanistan in 2001. In the months following the invasion, now in the name of concentrating its own military forces on combat missions to eliminate the remnants of both Taliban and Al Qaeda armed forces, the U.S. government rejected repeated requests by the UN secretary general, international relief agencies, the Karzai administration, and local Afghan women's groups to extend the reach of the international peace-keeping force—a NATO force, though nominally operating under a UN mandate—beyond the city limits of Kabul. The woman deputy minister told her Japanese hosts that one reason it was proving so difficult to achieve genuine parity between newly recruited male and female teachers was that many men in government claimed that the school districts outside the capital remained too dangerous for women teachers and principals to be appointed.

Danger—when governments claim danger, does the deepening of masculinized authority follow?

Combat—why has a "combat mission" repeatedly trumped peacekeeping and policing in the hierarchical game of competing masculinities? For the first two years of the U.S. military operation in Afghanistan it appeared as though the American military's civilian superiors in Washington wanted to ensure that American soldiers in Afghanistan stayed firmly in control of the hallowed "combat" mission. The supposedly "softer" masculinized missions of policing and peacekeeping seemingly were best left as the responsibility of German, Canadian, and Dutch men.

This story of the rarely smiling Afghan woman official might be taken by some Americans as a vindication of the Bush administration's militarized, expansionist foreign policy: that is, the violence perpetrated against women by the Taliban regime in the late 1990s was so extreme that only a foreign-led militarized response and foreign occupation were appropriate. In fact, many Americans had only the vaguest notion of where Afghanistan was, or what the longtime U.S. government involvement in its twenty-year civil war had been, or how its Taliban-controlled government was related to the clandestine operations of the insurgent movement led by Osama bin Laden. Consequently, for these American voters, forging a link between the geopolitics of counterterrorism and the liberation of benighted women proved especially helpful in constructing their own informal narratives of the causes for the 2001 U.S. invasion of Afghanistan. The fact that there were *any* women in the postinvasion Karzai interim government and that those women remained under threat only served to entrench many Americans' justifying narrative.

But there is an alternative interpretation. To explore this alternative, we need to ask another Afghan woman to "stand up." This is a young woman living in the Afghanistan province of Herat. Her mother is literate, having attended school in the 1970s, a time when the Afghan regime then in power cited the education of girls as a primary strategy for national modernization. Thus she is eager for her daughter to attend school. But mother and daughter remain subject to public intimidation in Herat if they voice such aspirations. This young woman's life two years after the U.S. invasion is not governed by the American, UN, and Afghan officials working in Kabul. Her life—her sense of security, physical mobility, personal identity, public identity, educational and economic opportunities—is governed by the self-proclaimed provincial governor of Herat, Ismail Khan.

English-language commentators have called Ismail Khan a "warlord." The label makes Khan sound archaic. It is a label that dampens our political curiosity. In reality, the power Khan and other Afghan regional "warlords" wield in postinvasion Afghanistan derives from two very modern resources: first, Ismail Khan commands a sizable army of his own, equipped with modern weaponry; second, he is deemed an "ally" by the U.S. military.[6]

Herat's Ismail Khan had contributed his troops to a loose amalgam of militarized Afghan opponents, first of the Soviet army in the 1980s and then of the Taliban regime. His forces and those of the other "warlords" are now called the Northern Alliance. The name makes them sound akin to NATO. These Afghan regional commanders were useful to the U.S. government during its own rivalry with the Soviet Union during the Cold War, and they became useful again when the United States decided to wage war against the Taliban and Al Qaeda. In October 2001 the Northern Alliance's commanders and all-male militias—despite their interethnic tensions, they share a history of opposition to the modernizing, secularizing reforms of the 1970s Kabul government—were selected by Washington's war-planners to be their most trusted, effective military allies on the ground when they devised their invasion of Afghanistan in the aftermath of the attacks on New York's World Trade Towers and the Pentagon.

Which men the expansionist foreign elite chooses to become their trusted local allies will almost certainly have repercussions for local women. Moreover, which men an invading force selects as its local allies will either enhance or, more commonly, undermine the viability of those foreign expansionists' use of "women's emancipation" as a moral justification for their expansionist enterprise. When U.S. policy-makers in Washington selected Ismail Khan and his fellow Northern Alliance antimodernist regional commanders as their most promising allies, they did not employ "the empowerment of Afghan women" as their chief criterion. Instead, the Washington strategists used "ground-level military capability" and "previous experience of cooperation with us" as their principal criteria for choosing their Afghan allies.

The criteria that any expansionist government uses when it chooses its local allies are much better predictors of the expansionists' postinvasion commitment to women's advancement than is any *post hoc* discourse of moral justification.

Furthermore, which men the invading force chooses as its primary local allies will also privilege certain forms of local masculinity. This was true in earlier imperial enterprises, and it is true in any putative imperial enterprises today. Internationally ambitious governments typically have sought local allies as they expanded the reach of their power and authority. Stories of the Spanish expansion into Mexico; the Dutch expansion into what is now Indonesia; the British expansions into Malaya, India, and Egypt; the U.S. expansion into the Philippines; the French expansion into Vietnam—each testifies to this common expansionist strategy of forging unequal local alliances-of-convenience. Empires, that is, are crafted out of unequal alliances between the ambitious imperialists and those local actors who calculate, often mistakenly, that they will be able to extract strategic gains for themselves even out of a clearly imbalanced alliance. Bedfellows are not all equal. All masculinities are not equal.

Virtually every one of these imperializing alliances was between men. This fact is not trivial.

In postinvasion Afghanistan, the likelihood of the young Herat woman experiencing meaningful liberation, of the sort wishfully imagined by so many Americans who lent their moral support for the U.S. invasion of Afghanistan, has been *made* dependent on a deeply masculinized local provincial regime whose power is ensured by a deeply masculinized foreign institution, the U.S. military.

Several independent human rights researchers investigated what happened to Afghan girls and women between 2001 and 2003. What these

researchers discovered, not only in Ismail Khan's Herat, but in many other provinces outside of Kabul where Northern Alliance commanders have used their militias and their intimate ties with American soldiers on the ground to consolidate their grasp on the levers of local power (and money), is that the military strategy that the Bush administration adopted to conduct its invasion has hobbled, not facilitated, the genuine liberation of most of Afghanistan's women and girls. These observers noted the apparently easy rapport that had developed between the male American Special Forces soldiers—the Special Forces being perhaps the most masculinized of all U.S. military units—and the local governor's militiamen, perhaps due to their shared identity as "combat-tested men." The investigators also noted that, despite their opposition to the Taliban regime, Ismail Khan and the Northern Alliance commanders were committed to a very patriarchal form of post-Taliban social order. Ismail Khan thus shared with the Taliban's and Al Qaeda's male leaders a belief that controlling women's marital and sexual relations was important for sustaining a hold on power.[7]

The Northern Alliance and its relationships with the U.S. military warrant feminist-informed investigations for several reasons. We need to know in precisely which ways shared masculinity has facilitated the sustaining of this alliance between Herat's "warlord" Ismail Khan and the U.S. field commanders. We also need to know in exactly which ways, other differences notwithstanding, shared masculinities created easy rapport between the American and Afghan Northern Alliance commanders' rank-and-file men, assisting both in consolidating their authority in their respective daily operations. In addition, we need to explore the ways in which this two-layered masculinization served to entrench the Northern Alliance regional commanders' own notions of subordinate femininity.

Further, in our investigation of contemporary American expansionism, we need to pay serious attention to the rivalry between the Northern

Alliance commanders' model of masculinity and the models of masculinity being projected by the Kabul-based senior civilian officials in Hamid Karzai's cabinet. Some Afghans declared this to be a contest between the "warlords" and the "neckties." Men such as Ismail Khan could claim that the "neckties" sitting in Kabul had become the "lackeys" of the U.S. and other foreign donors (the UN, the European Union, and Japan). Khan and the other warlords—despite their intense ethnicized distrust of each other—on the other hand, could claim to be combat-tested veterans, commanders of men, men who had wielded manly violence and risked their lives to defend the nation. The warlords thus could drape over their patriarchal shoulders the mantle of masculinized nationalism. Their ability to control the women in their provinces and to act as the guardians of "true" Afghan femininity had become a crucial component of their ability to mobilize their own male armies and to collect their own tax revenues.

On the other hand, the "neckties"—represented especially in President Karzai's minister of finance—could claim to be Men of Reason. "Reason" and "combat"—both have been used repeatedly by men of myriad cultures to compete with other men for the political brass ring: being recognized as the most manly of public men. The Afghan men in neckties could thus see themselves as builders of a new centralized constitutional state, a political order based on laws and budgets, not on artillery and armed road blocks. The necktie wearers could portray themselves as being able to represent the nation's interests where it counted, not on some desolate battlefield, but in the corridors of the most important masculinized international arenas, the United Nations Security Council, the U.S. State Department, the World Bank, the European Commission.[8]

One might think that any form of dominant masculinity might be better for most women than the warlord variety is. In practice, however, Afghan women hoping for the access to education, public voice, and economic opportunities that U.S. officials promised for women commonly have found that there is little space left for autonomous women in such a warlords vs. neckties masculinized contest. In such a contest, women are deemed crucial by the rivals, but merely as symbols, subordinates, admirers, or spectators. Men rivaling each other in the arena of politicized masculinity always have needed to ensure that "their" women will play those politically salient feminized roles. That is not liberation. That is not authentic citizenship.

Wait. Now another Afghan woman is standing up. She is Suraya Parlika. Trained as a lawyer, she has led the Afghan women's lawyers association based in Kabul, one of several nongovernmental organizations founded by women in the wake of the fall of the Taliban regime. In late 2003 Suraya Parlika decided to monitor the commission assigned to draft Afghanistan's new constitution.[9] She and her colleagues were thus prepared not only to read the fine print of the newly drafted Afghan constitution; but also to write constitutional proposals of their own. Coming to the meeting, Suraya Parlika and her colleagues each chose to defy intimidating personal threats against Afghans daring to introduce the discourse of human rights into local politics.[10]

Suraya Parlika and her co-organizers took the unusual step of inviting—and persuading the Karzai government to temporarily release just for this purpose—three women prisoners: Eqlima, who had been jailed on charges of running away from an abusive uncle's home; Mina, who had been arrested for running away from a "husband" to whom she had been sold; Rosia, who had been imprisoned for fleeing her father-in-law's house after being forced to marry her brother-in-law after her own husband's death. Parlika and the other activist women invited these three imprisoned women to their conference because they believed that a country's constitution could not be fairly and realistically drafted *unless* its provisions flowed from an understanding of the experiences of debilitating gender power imbalance that actually shaped the daily lives of women and girls.

With her co-organizers, Suraya Parlika was going far beyond Abigail Adams's much-quoted eighteenth-century modest admonition to John, her constitution-drafting husband: "Remember the ladies." These Afghan women activists were drawing lessons from their own twentieth-century Afghan experiences of living with constitutions written, constitutions amended, constitutions partially implemented, constitutions left unimplemented. Like women activists recently in South Africa, Cambodia, Palestine, Rwanda, and East Timor, and like feminists active in UN peace-keeping operations around the world, these Afghan women meeting in postinvasion Kandahar had become convinced that the writing of a new constitution must become women's business. Any constitution, after all, is a blueprint for a state's power and authority, a design for distributing powers and responsibilities within the state's institutions, and a map of citizens' limitations, rights, and responsibilities.

Since every stroke of the constitutional pen can either empower women as full citizens or turn them into marginalized dependents of male citizens and a patriarchal state, drafting and ratifying a constitution must be processes that include politically conscious women, preferably in equal numbers with men around the drafting table and in the ratifying assembly. If that fair representation proved impossible to achieve, then, these women had concluded, women had to be on the alert, mobilized right outside the drafting room door. In fact, the 2003 Afghanistan constitution-drafting commission did include seven women among its thirty-five appointed members—a significant presence, though men remained a decisive majority. Thus Suraya Parlika and her colleagues used their four days to listen to the stories of Eqlima, Rosia, and Mina and then to draw up their own constitutional proposals.

Here are the provisions Parlika and her colleagues concluded had to be explicitly included in the new Afghanistan constitution if it were to ensure Afghan women's participation in public life as fully autonomous and effective citizens:

(1) mandatory education for girls through secondary school, (2) guaranteed freedom of speech for women, (3) insurance that every woman would be free to cast her own ballot and to run for elected office, (4) insurance that women would have equal representation with men in the government's new legislature, (5) the appointment of an equal number of women and men to judgeships, (6) entitlement of women to pay rates equal to those of men, and (7) a guarantee that women would have the right to exert control over their own finances and to inherit property.[11]

All of these provisions, individually and taken together, would not only upset political convention, but fundamentally rearrange the relationships between women and men in the sphere commonly imagined to be "private." Yet the women conferees weren't finished. After listening carefully to the stories of Rosia, Eqlima, and Mina, Parlika and the other activists pressed for additional provisions in the new Afghanistan constitution: (8) permission for women to bring criminal charges against men for domestic violence and sexual harassment, whether those violations occurred in a public place or inside a home, (9) a ban on the common practice of family members handing over girls and women to another family as compensation for crimes committed by the former against the latter, (10) raising the legal age of marriage from sixteen years to eighteen years, (11) the right of women to marry and divorce "in accordance with Islam," and (12) a reduction of the time that women would have to wait to remarry if their husbands abandoned them or disappeared.[12]

These twelve provisions did not add up to the vision of a post-Taliban "good society" for which most Northern Alliance male commanders had been waging their wars. Those Northern Alliance commanders, several of whom had served as governors and cabinet ministers in the interim government, were among the influential men who tried to wield influence over the large national council, the *loya jirga,* that convened in Kabul in December 2003. This was the national assembly designated to consider—and amend—the draft constitution. The success of Parlika Suraya and her allies in pressing for a new constitutional state that was structurally and ideologically designed to fulfill the promise of women's liberation depended in large part on whether the U.S. government still imagined the Northern Alliance commanders to be its chief partners in expanding the American security net's global reach. It remained unclear who American officials would choose as their best allies to achieve American and global "security": the warlords, the neckties, or the women activists.

In January 2004 the *loya jirga's* delegates, after heated debate, passed a draft constitution. At the heart is ambiguity. On the one hand is the guarantee of women's and men's equality. On the other hand is the pledge that Afghanistan's future law-making will be "informed by" the principles of Islam, which when interpreted by conservatives, treat such gendered equality as anathema. Who will support Afghan women activists when they press the new government to enforce the constitution's first guarantee?[13]

WHERE ARE THE WOMEN IN THE U.S.-DOMINATED OCCUPATION OF IRAQ?

Three women who might help us better understand the U.S.-British military invasion of Iraq and its drawn-out militarized occupation are Raja Habib Khuzai, one of three Iraqi women members of the U.S.-anointed Governing Council; Nimo Din'Kha Skander, a woman who operates a small hair salon in Baghdad, and Kawkab Jalil, one of the women activists who have begun organizing independently to advocate for women's participation in the U.S. occupation era's emerging political system.

These three women do not represent all of the women in Iraq, nor would they make such a claim. But if we start to take seriously at least these three distinct, complex, thinking women, we are likely to make visible where women are and where femininities are in the consolidation or, alternatively, the subversion of the U.S. expansionist enterprise. That, in turn, should shine a bright light on where the men are and where rival masculinities are in Iraqis' U.S.-dominated postinvasion lives.

Raja Habib Khuzai takes the floor. She is a medical doctor and maternity hospital director, a skilled professional. Until September 2003 Khuzai was one of three women on the twenty-five-member Iraqi Governing Council. After September she was one of only two. On September 20, 2003, her colleague, Akila al-Hashimi, was gunned down by unknown assailants in broad daylight as she was leaving her Baghdad home.[14] Akila al-Hashimi, then fifty, had been a career Iraqi diplomat. She was described by journalists as a "member of a prominent family of Shiite clerics" and a "force for peace and tolerance."[15]

Both Akila al-Hashimi and Raja Habib Khuzai had been selected to serve on the U.S.-approved Governing Council in early July 2003 as a result of what was reportedly intense behind-the-scenes bargaining, bargaining not unlike the sort that had produced the interim cabinet of Afghanistan president Hamid Karzai a year earlier. The need to use the maddening passive tense—"had been selected"—in the previous sentence is telling. To date, we do not know precisely what dynamics shaped this Baghdad bargaining and its eventual outcome. But in virtually every political system we know about, the less transparent any process of political bargaining is, the more likely it is to be governed by presumptions of masculinized politics.

The cause for this masculinization is this: closed-door bargaining is less vulnerable to popular pressure and popular scrutiny. Those who wield the most influence in such backroom political transactions are those who come into the process with resources that can be converted into political currency. First are those who have organized public support—based on religion, ethnicity, or political party affiliation. In Afghanistan rivalries between self-declared male leaders of the Pashtun majority and the Uzbek and Tajik minorities became central in the bargaining. Similarly, in Iraq the ethnicized and sectarian male-led organizations of Shiite and Sunni Muslims, Kurdish ethnic communities, and Kurdish rival political parties were seen as the salient divisions that required juggling on the Governing Council. That is, organized ethnic, religious, and ideological divisions were thought by the crafters of the new Afghan and Iraqi governments to be the salient bases for representation. Gender was deemed by these same men to be simply symbolic, a step above trivial. Second among the individuals enjoying an advantage in closed-door bargaining sessions are those who have ready access to weapons and to armed men. Third are those with economic resources—companies of their own, trading connections, open lines to donors, bank accounts abroad. And fourth among the advantaged bargainers are those people who have earned credibility in the eyes of those foreign men orchestrating the bargaining. In the case of the formation of the postinvasion Iraqi Governing Council, that meant credibility in the eyes of the American occupation officials and their superiors in Washington. Some players in any backroom bargaining possess all four convertible resources. In most political systems all of these bargaining chips are kept out of the hands of all but a very few women.

The bargaining process that produced the 2003 Iraqi Governing Council had been going on among a virtually all-male cast of characters in various forums since December 2002, months before the Bush administration and its British allies launched their military invasion. At the December 2002 London meeting convened by the Bush administration, sixty Iraqis were invited. They were deemed by Washington strategists to be key players in the opposition to the Saddam Hussein regime. Of the sixty, three were women. In May 2003, with the Americans now in military control of Baghdad (though scarcely having a firm grasp on the country's postwar politics), the Bush administration called a second meeting

to map out a post-Saddam political system. This time American officials invited three hundred Iraqis. Now the number of women included rose to five.[16]

What was notable about the three women eventually selected for membership in the Iraqi Governing Council was that they did not have access to the four bargaining chips crucial to effective political influence. That is, Raja Habib Khuzai and the other two women each entered the Governing Council without their own political parties, without their own militias, without their own treasuries, and without their own direct lines of communication to Washington.

Looking down the list of the twenty-five members of the Governing Council, what stood out was how their twenty-two male colleagues were identified. These men were identified not as individuals with their own professional credentials, but instead as leaders of this or that political party or public organization. Perhaps the three women were selected by the bargainers precisely because they could make the Council look minimally legitimate to the world, while not possessing the political resources needed to shape the Council's agenda. Maybe the three women would not even make common cause with each other. Masculinizing the internal culture of the new Governing Council thus could proceed undisturbed. Maybe.

It likely became difficult for any of the three women (or later two) on the Council to wield effective influence with either their fellow Council members or with the U.S. occupation authorities. Thus when the question arose about what steps should be taken to draft a new constitution for Iraq and reporters tried to figure out who among the Governing Council's members seemed to be wielding the most influence in that debate, the names of the "power brokers" mentioned were all male.[17]

Now an Iraqi beautician stands up. Dressed in snug-fitting pants and a flower-patterned top, she is Nimo Din'Kha Skander.[18] She describes her small business, the Nimo Beauty Salon, as a lively place. Just a single room in the busy Karrada neighborhood of Baghdad, the salon attracts women of several generations for haircuts, facials, and hair dyeing. Some of her customers wear head scarves, but many do not. The Nimo Beauty Salon is also a place where political affairs are regularly analyzed. Nimo Din'Kha Skander could be seen as presiding over a political forum.

While choosing hair colors, she and her customers talk about where the country is heading, whether male clerics could ever win a majority of Iraqis' votes, what the American occupiers ultimately intend. Like other Iraqi women and girls, they have heard harrowing stories of abductions and rapes of women since the lawlessness escalated after the collapse of Saddam Hussein's regime. They talk about the rapes in whispers. Stories of sexual assaults make many of them afraid to travel about the city. They know of some women and girls who have become afraid to leave their homes at all. There is no sign that the new U.S.-recruited-and-trained police force is being taught to take violence against women seriously. The police recruits selected by the U.S. occupation officials, furthermore, appear to be only men. The militias still controlled by some clerics and certain political parties also seem to be exclusively male.[19] This combination of masculinized security forces and a lack of gender-security-planning consciousness deprives Iraqi women of opportunities to be effective participants in the emerging new political system. It is no wonder that only men appear at street demonstrations.[20]

Despite the political character of their conversations at the Nimo Beauty Salon, these women see "politics" as happening somewhere else, somewhere they are not. In this perception, Nimo Din'Kha Skander and her customers share a view commonly held by more influential political commentators. Everyone imagines a beauty parlor to be a feminized space, a private place. Politics couldn't, therefore, be going on here. It takes a feminist curiosity to see a beauty salon as

a political forum—and to pay attention. Here is where the relationship between public and private power is being sorted out. Here the nature of the past's influence on the present is being weighed. Here the implications of sexual violence for enacting effective citizenship are being exposed. A feminized space is not the opposite of a political place. For many women, especially in a time of foreign military occupation, governmental flux, masculinized rivalries, and increasing sexualized violence, a feminized space may be the most secure political place for them to trade analyses and strategies.

Baghdad in the 1990s was not Kabul in the 1990s. The Nimo Beauty Salon was never shut down by the regime of Saddam Hussein. In fact, Nimo Din'Kha Skander takes pride in having had Saddam Hussein's second wife as a customer. Yet, over the past decade, there have been changes in the constrictions faced by women, which many women have internalized.

The regime headed by Saddam Hussein was built on the strength of the Baathist party, a political party despised by both the young Afghan men who joined the Taliban and the Arab men who became followers of Osama bin Laden. The Baathist party was a secular, nationalist political party. Iraqi women first voted in 1980. Women's education, women's paid work, women's votes, all were encouraged by the Baathist-run government, not for the sake of democratization but for the sake of economic growth, to earn Iraq the status of being a "modern" nation and to maximize the regime's wartime mobilization. By 2000, 78 percent of school-age Iraqi girls were enrolled in primary schools.[21] However, after its 1991 defeat in the first Gulf War and during the subsequent decade of international economic sanctions, Saddam Hussein's regime sought to garner more regional aid by diluting its secular ideology and vaguely courting Islamic support. During the 1980s war with Iran, the Iraqi regime sought to attract more women into paid civil service jobs in order to replace the thousands of men it was drafting into its army. By contrast, during the 1990s, the regime, worried about dents in Iraqi men's sense of manly esteem after two devastating wartime defeats, promoted a more conservative brand of femininity. At the same time, many younger Iraqi women—now enduring postwar hardships and cut off from the outside world, not free to travel as their mothers and aunts had before them—began to adopt a more literal interpretation of Islamic femininity. To the dismay of many older urban Iraqi women, who had fought in earlier decades for women's right to live their lives as autonomous individuals, it became more common for young Iraqi women to adopt head scarves.[22]

Women's liberation in any country rarely follows a simple path "onward and upward." Women's status and political participation can vary surprisingly from one decade to another, from one generation to another. One's feminist curiosity, consequently, needs to have staying power. One cannot afford the luxury of turning away to follow the "next new thing" as soon as women in a country have won the vote, or as soon as a handful of women have been awarded cabinet portfolios, or even when many women have gained access to reproductive rights.

Progress in rolling back patriarchy can prove stunningly ephemeral. Older women are sometimes more literate, more worldly, more economically autonomous than their daughters and nieces. With some wars and postwartimes women's sphere of economic, social, and even political influence widens. With other wars and postwartimes those spheres dramatically shrink. The key causal factor here is whether the war-waging and postwar government is masculinist. If the government continues to privilege masculinity, then even those policies it may enact to widen women's spheres of activity can be reversed as soon as it decides such a reversal is politically convenient. This is a lesson that both Afghan and Iraqi women have learned. The broadening of women's autonomy is secure only when that broadening actually rolls back the masculinization of both local and foreign interventionist political cultures and government power.

Kawkab Jalil now rises to her feet. She is dressed in a fashionably tailored long black dress.[23] Her fingernails are hennaed. Her dark hair is uncovered. Kawkab Jalil, who is forty-six, explains that she only donned the scarf a year earlier due to social pressure, but recently put it aside when she decided that she did not have to prove her feminine respectability to strangers. She did not remove her head scarf to make Americans feel satisfied in their roles as "liberators." Jalil had stayed in Iraq during the eight-year war with Iran, the years of international sanctions, the era of increasing intimidation by the Baathist regime. She stayed even after being forced out of her long-standing job at the state electrical company when she refused to join the ruling party. In the wake of the fall of the Baathist regime and the confusion set off by the U.S. military conquest, Jalil says, "We need more courage, further boldness. We must reflect a bright future of Iraqi women. Not be oppressed, weak people who have no power."[24]

Kawkab Jalil was not a participant in the backroom bargaining sessions that produced the U.S.-appointed Governing Council. She instead joined a small number of Iraqi women in activating independent women's advocacy organizations designed to put pressure on both the Governing Council and the U.S. occupation authorities. Jalil herself has become a member of the Iraqi Women's League leadership committee. The League was founded in the 1950s but was forced underground during the Saddam Hussein era. By August 2003, five months after the American and British invasion, the League membership had risen to five hundred women, though Jalil and other women of the older generation noticed that many of the younger women who were now becoming active remained tentative. It was not a matter of their age, but rather of their historical generation. These younger Iraqi women had grown up with little chance to speak out or to learn organizational skills.[25]

Among the conditions that Jalil and other Iraqi activist women have tried to transform into political issues is the escalating violence against women. In August 2003 another women's group, the Organization of Women's Freedom in Iraq (OWFI), led a public demonstration in Baghdad to call for official action to stop the abduction of and assaults on women. Sixty people came out to demonstrate. One middle-aged woman who attended said, "This is my first demonstration for thirty-five years. . . . I came out here all by myself today to raise my voice, but where are all the women?"[26] A majority of the demonstrators, even on this issue so crucial to women, were men. The attendance gender profile says less about women's political consciousness than it does about how far—in any society—the threat of violence suppresses women's capacity to behave as fully participant political actors.

Insofar as the American occupation officials and their hand-picked Iraqi male advisors treated violence against women as a secondary matter, as something that could be dealt with later, the emerging Iraqi political system would become masculinized. Violence against women, as so many feminists—from the Congo to Kosovo to East Timor—have taught us, must be accorded urgent political attention if women are to gain the status of genuinely autonomous citizens.[27]

About the three women chosen behind closed doors to serve on the twenty-five-member Iraqi Governing Council, activist women such as Kawkab Jalil have expressed skepticism. At one strategy meeting, women kept telling an American reporter, "We do not know them . . . who are they?"[28] They noted that not one of the then-three women on the Council seemed to have an influential organizational support base of her own and thus would be unlikely to carry much political weight in either the Council's own deliberations or lobbying the American authorities. Warned a schoolteacher, "And if they're going to fail, that's it. They won't give this chance to women again."[29]

Then there is the serious matter of drafting Iraq's new constitution. Iraqi women activists, just like Afghanistan's women's rights advocates, decided that those chosen to draft, amend, and ratify the new constitution would shape women's lives for years to come. Thus women activists were dismayed at the composition of the committee chosen to draft the new constitution: of twenty-five members, all were men.[30] It appeared that the U.S. occupation authorities, their superiors in Washington, and the members of the Iraqi Governing Council all deemed women's future relationships to the state, to the law, and to male citizens well cared for in the hands of a small group of ethnically, religiously, and ideologically competitive men. But, these Iraqi activist women argued, this was a highly questionable supposition.

To bolster their political position, some Iraqi activist women therefore began to foster alliances with women activists outside Iraq. A group of exiled Iraqi women in Britain created the Iraqi Women's Rights Coalition (IWRC), which began to publish its own newsletter, *Equality Rights Now!* These British-based Iraqi women lent support to the women who, in June 2003, founded the Organization of Women's Freedom in Iraq.[31] One of the group's first efforts was to establish a shelter in Baghdad for Iraqi women suffering from domestic violence, including threats of "honor killings" by their own brothers, fathers, and uncles.[32] In August 2003 OWFI members wrote a formal letter to Paul Bremer, the chief U.S. occupation administrator in Baghdad, calling on him to use his authority to address the "unprecedented violence against women." He did not reply.[33]

In October 2000 the U.S. government voted, along with a majority of the UN Security Council, in favor of Security Council Resolution 1325. This groundbreaking resolution committed all agencies of the UN and every UN member state to ensuring that both women and women's concerns become integral to every new security institution and every decision-making stage in peacekeeping and national reconstruction in any area of armed conflict. Despite its vote for the historic SCR 1325, the U.S. government felt free to appoint an all-male constitution-drafting committee in occupied Iraq and to create newly re-masculinized Iraqi police and security forces.[34]

CONCLUSION

In October 2003, one of the founders of OWFI, Yanar Mohammed, sought to raise the consciousness of Americans by traveling to New York. Yanar Mohammed, once active in Iraq's Communist party, a group banned by the Baathist regime, had spent her exile years in Canada. She returned to Iraq in the wake of the invasion to contribute to the new mobilization of women. Sponsoring her visit was a group of New York women who had created the Working Committee in Support of Iraq's Women.[35]

Women in colonized countries, women in militarily occupied countries, and women under local authoritarian rulers all have a long history of seeking alliances with those women abroad who seem sympathetic to their causes. The internationalization of women-to-women political alliances is not new. It began in the mid-1800s. There is plenty of evidence, garnered by feminist historians, to suggest that sustaining such alliances is hard political work.[36] There are the pulls and pushes of local women's own non-feminist male potential allies. Men who oppose foreign occupation or foreign domination are not necessarily men who see the "sovereign nation" as composed of women and men living as equals in the family, the market, the courts, the universities, and the state's policy-making circles. Yet it is precisely those nonfeminist, even outrightly patriarchal, men with whom some women may believe they must make common cause, at least tactically. This can prove hard to explain to overseas feminist partners. Then there are the pitfalls of miscommunication. Mail now travels in a cybernetic flash, rather than via weeks of ocean voyage, but speed does not assure shared understanding of the terms and phrases. In fact, today any miscommunication can be spread far and wide with alarming quickness and so prove harder to undo. And there is burnout. Doing alliance-building among women, none of whom control abundant resources of time or money, can tax the most dedicated of internationally minded feminists.

In addition, as we have painfully learned, there is the perpetual temptation for women residing outside the war-torn or imperially occupied country to imagine that, by dint of their access to media and financial resources, those women residing in the affluent country also may have a superior understanding of what should be prioritized in the local women's struggle. And there is local women activists' complementary temptation to tailor their strategies and their discourses to reassure the seemingly well-endowed overseas supporters.

On the other hand, the step-by-step building of such dynamic cross-national alliances among women holds out the possibility that women in the imperially minded country will themselves gain a new understanding of their own government's policies and actions overseas, and this will prompt them to publicly question their government's official justifications for expansionist maneuvers carried out in their names. Moreover, if women pursue a genuine cross-national alliance of equals, it will involve a lot of intense listening, questioning, and rethinking. Such efforts, in turn, can sharpen activists' feminist understandings of what causes the perpetuation of masculinization in public life, not only "over there" but "here at home."

The intensity and variety of cross-national feminist interactions today are beyond anything seen before in the history of empires or international politics. These feminist interactions are producing fresh analyses of what is causing and perpetuating unequal international power and offering strategies to expose those causes and subvert them. Thus it would be a mistake, I think, to imagine that the latest version of empire-building in the name of "world order" or "global security" or "civilization" is an unstoppable steamroller.

Crafting a system of expansive, cohesive political influence—an empire—has always been a tricky enterprise. Only in retrospect do the earlier British, Ottoman, or Spanish empires look deceptively unavoidable. In practice, there were doubters and critics whom imperialists had to try to persuade or silence at home; there were rebels and recalcitrants they needed to co-opt or suppress in the occupied society. Silencing, suppressing, persuading, co-opting—these imperial activities have not guaranteed success over the long term. In large part, each is dependent on certain gender ideologies. And these ideologies, we have seen, are vulnerable to contradiction and challenge.

Masculinity has always been an essential tool wielded in this many-pronged process of empire-building. At home it has been necessary to convince both men and women that a militarized manliness (especially one allied with a manly sort of reason and a manly brand of commercial competitiveness) was a superior form of humanity. Both men and women have had to be persuaded that this construction of privileged masculinity endowed those actors who claimed to possess it with unique capacities to bring security and a sense of moral well-being to citizens at home, while it simultaneously conferred enlightenment, progress, and "civilization" on those abroad over whom they held sway. Security, moral satisfaction, progress, civilization—all are gendered. Subtract the politics of masculinity and the politics of femininity from one's investigation, and one is likely to produce an unreliable explanation of how empire-building proceeds—or falters.

For such militarized expansionism does falter, does lose its protective glow at home and among the co-opted and daunted abroad. It falters if the "civilizing" rewards promised turn out to fuel not the blessings of technocracy, order, and peace, but instead violence, corruption, and demoralization. Ambitious expansionism also stumbles if the performers of privileged masculinity appear self-serving or naive—or both.

The privileging of masculinity in general and certain forms of masculinity in particular thus need to be investigated. Making sense of the masculinized political cultures and masculinized political processes that legitimize and energize global expansionism, however, cannot be accomplished just by paying attention to varieties of men. Paying serious attention to women—to their experiences, their actions, and their ideas, in all their diversity; that is, wielding a feminist curiosity—is the only way to ensure that men-as-men and masculinity as an ideology can be seen with political clarity.

But what if we don't? No sustained curiosity about women means no discussion of the politics of femininity. No serious analysis of the politics of women and femininity converts into no concentrated public thinking about men and masculinities. No focused investigation of men and masculinities means no understanding of the genderings of international affairs. No curiosity about how and why international affairs have become reliant on particular ideas about femininity and masculinity produces little chance to make the global workings of unequal power fully visible. No visible rendering of internationalized gender means no possibility of instituting genuine and lasting change in those unequal power arrangements at home and abroad.

NOTES

1. Among the most talked about have been Niall Ferguson, *Empire* (New York: Basic Books, 2003); Paul Kennedy, *The Rise and Fall of Great Powers* (New York: Vintage, 1989); Eric Hobsbawm, *The Age of Empire, 1875–1914* (New York: Vintage, 1987); and Simon Schama, *The Embarrassment of Riches* (New York: Vintage, 1987).

2. Philippa Levine, *Prostitution, Race and Politics: Policing Venereal Disease in the British Empire* (New York: Routledge, 2003); Piya Chatterjee, *A Time for Tea: Women, Labor, and Post/Colonial Politics on an Indian Plantation* (Durham: Duke

University Press, 2001); Kumari Jayawardena, *The White Women's Other Burden: Western Women and South Asia during British Rule* (New York: Routledge, 1995).

3. See Insook Kwon, "'The New Women's Movement' in 1920s Korea: Rethinking the Relationship between Imperialism and Women," *Gender and History* 10, no. 3 (November 1998): 358–80; Vron Ware, *Beyond the Pale: White Women, Racism and History* (London: Verso, 1991); Laura Wexler, *Tender Violence: Domestic Visions in an Age of U.S. Imperialism* (Chapel Hill: University of North Carolina Press, 2000); Amy Kaplan and Donald E. Pease, eds., *Cultures of United States Imperialism* (Durham: Duke University Press, 1993); Lora Wildenthal, *German Women for Empire, 1884–1945* (Durham: Duke University Press, 2001); Kristin L. Hoganson, *Fighting for American Manhood: How Gender Politics Provoked the Spanish-American and Philippine-American Wars* (New Haven: Yale University Press, 1998); Nupur Chaudhuri and Margaret Strobel, eds., *Western Women and Imperialism: Complicity and Resistance* (Bloomington: Indiana University Press, 1992); Louise Young, *Japan's Total Empire* (Berkeley: University of California Press, 1998); Mona Etienne and Eleanor Leacock, eds., *Women and Colonization* (New York: Praeger, 1980); Clare Midgley, ed., *Gender and Imperialism* (New York: Manchester University Press, 1998). See also two critically insightful novels by the pre–World War II Dutch writer Madelon H. Lulofs, set in 1930s colonial Indonesia: *Rubber* (New York: Oxford University Press, 1987) and *Coolie* (New York: Oxford University Press, 1987).

4. Anne E. Brodsky, *With All Our Strength: The Revolutionary Association of the Women of Afghanistan* (New York: Routledge, 2003).

5. For a feminist analysis of how Pakistani government officials, Afghan male party leaders in exile, and complying international agencies and donors together have colluded to deepen the masculinization of the political, economic, and cultural power inside the refugee camps during the period from 1990 to 2003, despite women and children comprising a majority of the camps' residents, see Saba Gul Khattak, "In/Security: Afghan Refugees and Politics in Pakistan," *Critical Asian Studies* 35, no. 2 (June 2003): 195–208.

6. A detailed account of Ismail Khan's mode of provincial rule is contained in Barry Bearak, "Unreconstructed," *New York Times Magazine,* June 1, 2003, 40–47, 62–101.

7. For information on the abuse of women and girls in Herat, see "We Want to Live as Humans: Repression of Women and Girls in Western Afghanistan," report by Human Rights Watch, New York, December 2002; "Afghanistan Report," by Amnesty International, Washington, D.C., October 5, 2003. For a detailed journalistic account of the Taliban's and Al Qaeda's marriage politics, see Amy Waldman, "Kabul Brides Married Taliban for Better, Then for Worse," *New York Times,* December 31, 2001.

8. Bearak, "Unreconstructed," 62.

9. This account is derived from Carlotta Gall's article "Women Gather in Afghanistan to Compose a Bill of Rights," *New York Times,* September 28, 2003. In September 2003 she attended a small, unofficial conference in the southern city of Kandahar along with other women—lawyers, human rights specialists, and civil society leaders. They represented groups such as Women for Afghan Women and the Afghan women lawyers' association, groups of Afghan women who were literate. By contrast, according to feminist geographer Joni Seager, an estimated 80 percent of Afghan women (compared to 53 percent of men) were still unable to gain access to the tools that would allow them to learn how to read and write (Joni Seager, *The Penguin Atlas of Women in the World* [New York: Penguin Books, 2003], 113).

10. Preeta D. Bansal and Felice D. Gaer, "Silenced Again in Kabul," *New York Times,* October 1, 2003.

11. Gall, "Women Gather in Afghanistan."

12. Ibid.

13. Sonali Kolhatkar describes the Afghan *loya jirga's* constitutional debates and its gendered dynamics and outcome in her article "Afghan Women Continue to Fend for Themselves," *Foreign Policy in Action,* March 2004, 1–9.

14. Patrick E. Tyler, "Attackers Wound an Iraqi Official in a Baghdad Raid," *New York Times*, September 21, 2003. Akila al-Hashimi died of her wounds.

15. Alex Berenson, "U.N. Chief Orders Further Reduction of Staff in Baghdad," *New York Times,* September 26, 2003. Just two months before being assassinated and shortly after being appointed to the Governing Council, Akila al-Hashimi had been one of three Council members to represent the interim government on a trip to New York to lobby members of the United Nations (Felicity Barringer, "U.N. Gives Iraqi Governing Council Qualified Welcome," *New York Times,* July 23, 2003).

16. Zainab Al-Suwaij, "Iraq's Silenced Majority," *New York Times,* May 23, 2003.

17. Patrick Tyler, "Iraqi Groups Badly Divided over How to Draft a Charter," *New York Times,* September 30, 2003.

18. Much of the following derives from Sabrina Tavernise, "Iraqi Women Wary of New Upheavals," *New York Times,* May 5, 2003.

19. Amy Waldman, "U.S. Struggles to Transform a Tainted Iraqi Police Force," *New York Times,* June 30, 2003.

20. Human Rights Watch, *Report on Women's Rights in Iraq* (New York: Human Rights Watch, July 2003); Neela Banerjee, "Rape (and Silence about It) Haunts Baghdad," *New York Times,* July 16, 2003.

21. Seager, *Penguin Atlas of Women,* 114–15.

22. Tavernise, "Iraqi Women Wary of New Upheavals."

23. Most of the following is derived from Sharon Waxman, "Facing the Future," *Washington Post,* June 17, 2003.

24. Ibid.

25. Lauren Sandler, "Veiled Interests," *Boston Globe,* August 31, 2003.

26. Ibid.

27. The women inside the United Nations and their allies in feminist nongovernmental organizations have been most influential in pressing all international agencies and donor countries to take seriously the political implications of violence against women in war zones and in postwar reconstruction efforts. One of the closest monitors of these efforts is *PeaceWomen,* an electronically distributed newsletter published by the Women's International League for Peace and Freedom (www.peacewomen.org). See also UNIFEM's report on the chief conditions and official attitudes that obstruct women's effective participation in postconflict political life: Elisabeth Rehnand and Ellen Johnson Sirleaf, *World Progress of Women 2002,* vol. 1, *Women, War, and Peace* (Bloomfield, Conn.: Kumarian Press, 2003).

28. Sandler, "Veiled Interests."

29. Ibid.

30. Ibid.

31. See www.peacewomen.org, September 12, 2003.

32. E-mail announcement circulated by the New York–headquartered National Council for Research on Women (www.ncrw.org), October 10, 2003.

33. Lauren Sandler, "Veiled and Worried in Baghdad," *New York Times,* September 16, 2003.

34. For a feminist discussion of the strengths and weaknesses of UN Security Council Resolution 1325, see Carol Cohn, Helen Kinsella, and Sheri Gibbings, "Women, Peace and Security: Resolution 1325," *International Feminist Journal of Politics* 6, no. 1 (March 2004): 130–40.

35. E-mail from National Council for Research on Women.

36. See, for example, Claire Midgley, *Women against Slavery: The British Campaigns 1780–1870* (New York: Routledge, 1992); Lila Rupp, *Worlds of Women: The Making of an International Women's Movement* (Princeton, N.J.: Princeton University Press, 1997); Margot Badran, *Feminists, Islam, and Nation: Gender and the Making of Modern Egypt* (Princeton, N.J.: Princeton University Press, 1995). For case studies of contemporary efforts at creating genuine alliances of women across national boundaries, see Felicity Hill, Mikele Abotiz, and Sara Poehlman-Doumbouya, "Non-governmental Organizations' Role in the Buildup and Implementation of Security Council Resolution 1325," *Signs* 28, no. 4 (Summer 2003): 1255–70; Pam Spees, "Women's Advocacy in the Creation of the International Criminal Court," *Signs* 28, no. 4 (Summer 2003): 1233–54; Sherrill Whittington, "Gender and Peacekeeping: The United Nations Transitional Administration in East Timor," *Signs* 28, no. 4 (Summer 2003): 1283–88; Mrinalini Sinha, Donna J. Guy, and Angela Woolacott, eds., "Feminisms and Internationalism" (special issue), *Gender and History* 10, no. 3 (November 1998).

FOR FURTHER READING

Brown, Wendy. *States of Injury: Power and Freedom in Late Modernity*. Princeton: Princeton University Press, 1995.

Bryson, Valerie. *Feminist Political Theory: An Introduction*. New York: Paragon House, 1992.

Butler, Judith, and Joan W. Scott, eds. *Feminists Theorize the Political*. New York: Routledge, 1992.

DiStephano, Christine. *Configurations of Masculinity: A Feminist Perspective on Modern Political Theory*. Ithaca, NY: Cornell University Press, 1991.

Elshtain, Jean Bethke. *Public Man, Private Woman*. Princeton: Princeton University Press, 1981.

Enloe, Cynthia. *The Curious Feminist: Searching for Women in a New Age of Empire*. Berkeley: University of California Press, 2004.

Enloe, Cynthia. *Maneuvers: The International Politics of Militarizing Women's Lives*. Berkeley: University of California Press, 2000.

Enloe, Cynthia. *Bananas, Beaches and Bases: Making Feminist Sense of International Politics*. Berkeley, CA: University of California Press, 1989.

Fraser, Nancy. "After the Family Wage: Gender Equity and the Welfare State." *Political Theory* 22(4) (1994): 591–618.

Fraser, Nancy. *Justice Interruptus: Critical Reflections on the "Postsocialist" Condition*. New York: Routledge, 1997.

Friedman, Marilyn. "Autonomy, Social Disruption and Women." In *Relational Autonomy: Feminist Perspectives on Autonomy, Agency and the Social Self*, edited by Catriona Mackenzie and Natalie Stoljar. New York: Oxford, 2000.

Hartman, Heidi I. "The Unhappy Marriage of Marxism and Feminism: Toward a More Progressive Union." In *Women and Revolution: A Discussion of the Unhappy Marriage of Marxism and Feminism*, edited by Lydia Sargent. Boston: South End Press, 1981.

Hirschmann, Nancy J., and Christine DiStefano, eds. *Revisioning the Political: Feminist Reconstructions of Traditional Concepts in Western Political Theory*. Boulder, CO: Westview Press, 1996.

Jaggar, Alison, ed. *Feminist Politics and Human Nature*. Totowa, NJ: Rowman and Littlefield, 1983.

Kittay, Eva. "Taking Dependency Seriously: The Family Medical Leave Act Considered in Light of the Social Organization of Dependency Work

and Gender Equality." *Hypatia* 10(1) (1995): 8–29.

MacKinnon, Catherine. *Toward a Feminist Theory of the State*. Cambridge, MA: Harvard University Press, 1989.

Mansbridge, Jane J., and Susan Moller Okin. "Feminism." In *A Companion to Contemporary Political Philosophy*, edited by Robert E. Goodin and Philip Petit. Oxford: Blackwell, 1993, pp. 269–91.

Meyers, Diana Tietjens, ed. *Feminist Social Thought: A Reader*. New York: Routledge, 1997.

Mohanty, Chandra, Ann Russo, and Lourdes Torres, eds. *Third World Women and the Politics of Feminism*. Bloomington, IN: Indiana University Press, 1991.

Nussbaum, Martha. *Women and Development: The Capabilities Approach*. Cambridge: Cambridge University Press, 2001.

Okin, Susan. "Vulnerability by Marriage." In her *Justice, Gender and the Family*. New York: Basic Books, Inc., 1991.

Pateman, Carol, *The Sexual Contract*. Cambridge: Polity Press, 1989.

Pateman, Carol, and Elizabeth Gross, eds. *Feminist Challenges: Social and Political Theory*. Lebanon, NH: Northeastern University Press, 1988.

Ruddick, Sarah. *Maternal Thinking: Towards a Feminist Politics of Peace*. Boston: Beacon, 1989.

Scott, Joan W., Cora Kaplan, and Debra Keates, eds. *Transitions Environments Translations: Feminisms in International Politics*. New York: Routledge, 1997.

Shanley, Mary Lundon, and Carole Pateman, eds. *Feminist Interpretations of Political Theory*. University Park, PA: Penn State University Press, 1991.

Shanley, Mary Lundon, and Uma Narayan, eds. *Reconstructing Political Theory: Feminist Perspectives*. Cambridge: Polity Press, 1997.

Tong, Rosemarie Putnam. *Feminist Thought: A More Comprehensive Introduction*. 2nd ed. Boulder, CO: Westview Press, 1998.

Weiss, Penny A. *Conversations with Feminism: Political Theory and Practice*. Totowa, NJ: Rowman and Littlefield, 1998.

Young, Iris Marion. "Difference and Social Policy: Reflections in the Context of Social Movements." *University of Cincinnati Law Review* 56(2) (1987): 535–50.

Young, Iris Marion. *Justice and the Politics of Difference*. Princeton, NJ: Princeton University Press, 1998.

MEDIA RESOURCES

Afghanistan Unveiled. VHS/DVD. A film by Brigitte Brault and Alna Women Filming Group (Afghanistan, 2003). Filmed by the first ever team of women video journalists trained in Afghanistan, this rare film explores the effects of the Taliban's rule and the U.S.-sponsored bombing campaign on Afghani women. A nice prelude to Enloe's essay on empire. Available: Women Make Movies, www. wmm.com, or 212–925–0606.

Dispatches: Iraq, The Woman's Story. VHS/DVD. A film by an anonymous Iraqi woman. A compelling account of the life inside Iraq that is rarely seen on the news (Iraq, 2006). The stories of ordinary women whose struggle to survive has only worsened since the war began. Two women risk their lives traveling for three months all over the country to talk to women about their lives in the midst of war. Available as a download from: http://video.google.com/videoplay?docid=891513925297288257.

Women: The New Poor. VHS. A film by Bea Milwe (U.S. 1990). Detailing effects of job discrimination and personal misfortune, this informative documentary focuses on four women: Bernice, an unemployed African American single mother; Dody, a displaced homemaker with a Connecticut home beyond her means; Paula, a young divorcee with three part-time jobs; and Alexis, a Latina who moved into a shelter with her teenage daughter after a fire destroyed their home. Stressing the need for education, job training and support, this film illustrates commonalities among poor women of different backgrounds and their attempts to defy the statistics of poverty. Available: Women Make Movies, www.wmm.com, or 212-925-0606.

Sentenced to Marriage. VHS/DVD. A film by Anat Zuria, produced by Amit Breuer (Israel, 2004). This documentary exposes the process of divorce for women in Israel where secular law does not exist, and divorce is dealt with according to archaic and fundamentalist orthodox Jewish law. Zuria gains rare access to the rabbinical courts to follow two women caught in the demoralizing legal labyrinth. Though husbands can live with other women and even withhold child support, wives are forbidden contact with other men. This film adds an interesting addition to some of the observations made in Susan Okin's piece. Available: Women Make Movies, www.wmm.com, or 212–925–0606.

CHAPTER 9

FEMINIST EPISTEMOLOGIES

Epistemology, or theories of knowledge, names the branch of philosophy concerned with the nature, scope, sources, structures, and limits of human knowledge. Western philosophy has been particularly fixated on questions about truth and belief, the nature of the mind, the role reason plays in knowing, and the supremacy of scientific knowledge. These inquiries usually have presupposed that the "perfect knower" is a universal ideal, that all knowing is cognitive, that scientific knowledge is paradigmatic, and that the production of knowledge is politically neutral. Feminist theorists challenge these assumptions by demonstrating how sexism and other harmful biases have shaped presuppositions about the nature of knowing. Feminist epistemology begins with a critique of western scientific and philosophical traditions, and continues with projects that reframe our understandings of what it means to know something, and that reconstruct these understandings on "newer more self-conscious ground" (Alcoff and Potter 1987, 3). Feminists working in epistemology have broadened the field of inquiry by acknowledging the ways knowledge is embodied, emotional, socially situated, and informed by specific experiences and

goals. While the principle task of most Anglo-American epistemology has been to refute the skeptic and to determine the conditions for objective knowledge, feminist epistemologies focus on the social and historical circumstances that determine knowledge in particular contexts, and on the relationships between knowledge production and forms of power. So, feminist epistemology does not merely add details to existing accounts of knowledge—it shifts the epistemic framework and raises new questions about agency, cognitive authority, objectivity, and rationality.

In the 1980s, several key critical examinations of traditional theories of science and rationality, and their relationships to canonical views on sex and gender, initiated a terrific wave of feminist work on epistemology. Genevieve Lloyd's *The Man of Reason* (1984), Evelyn Fox Keller's *Reflections on Gender and Science* (1985), and Susan Bordo's *The Flight to Objectivity* (1987) drew clear connections between Enlightenment ideals of rationality, objectivity, and detachment, and the masculine ideals organizing scientific inquiry. In "Purification and Transcendence," Bordo offers a detailed analysis of the work of René Descartes, and especially his canonical *Meditations on First Philosophy* (1641). Bordo argues that the Cartesian epistemic project of seeking god-like certainty and objectivity is grounded in an intellectual "flight" from the (feminine) body, toward a masculine stance that pursues knowledge as pure thought and perception, and that takes knowers to be transcendent and disembodied subjects. The anxieties regarding emotion and the uncontrollable body that ground Descartes' projects create a notion of the body as completely separate and separable from the mind, a fiction that persists in contemporary epistemology and philosophy of mind.

The philosophical ideal of a "disembodied subject" engaging in "pure thought" shows how thoroughly emotions and other feelings have been ignored or dismissed by many influential theories of knowledge. Indeed, in "Love and Knowledge," Alison Jaggar argues that western philosophy, with some exceptions, understands reason in opposition to emotion. Reason, the faculty that supposedly generates knowledge, is associated with male competence and emotion, which allegedly distracts from knowledge, is linked to uncontrollable feminine appetites. The reason/emotion dichotomy is not only misogynist, but also relies on a rather naïve view even of what emotions are. Anticipating some of the key questions in contemporary philosophical writings on mind and emotion, Jaggar develops an alternative account, arguing that emotions are vital for reason, perception, and systematic knowledge.

Another feminist project calls attention to the unseen political dimensions of epistemological endeavors. In "How Is Epistemology Political?," Linda Martín Alcoff clarifies and examines the relation between epistemology and power. As a discipline, epistemology is a social practice engaged in primarily by elite professionals in academic settings where authority is almost always aligned with race, gender, and class privilege. It follows that history, identity, culture, and context often determine methods of hypothesis formation, ideas about what counts as evidence, and beliefs about what is reasonable or justified. In cultures of dominance and subordination, oppressive power

relations may be reinforced by epistemological theories and methods. It is therefore crucial to identify the relations between particular theories and the forms of social power they propagate. As Alcoff argues, attention to those dimensions will inevitably strengthen epistemology as a practice that aims to better understand knowledge.

The problematic ideals and assumptions criticized by Bordo, Jaggar, and Alcoff are not passing fads in the history of philosophy: they ground "S-knows-that-*p*" approaches to questions of knowledge that are standard in contemporary analytic philosophy.[1] In "Taking Subjectivity into Account," Lorraine Code criticizes the propositional focus of epistemology by arguing that it is inattentive to the identities of knowing subjects. The assumptions that ways of knowing are universal and knowers are interchangeable are easy to maintain if we consider only how one comes to know about everyday medium-sized objects like coffee cups and patches of color. But there is no reason that "perception at a distance" should be the template for all knowing practices. For example, knowing other people in personal relationships is at least as important as knowledge of objects. And the "S-knows-that-*p*" template can be harmful to members of groups who are often treated as objects of study and not knowers in their own right. Code proposes that we approach epistemic projects with a "qualified relativism" that will remap the epistemic terrain in ways that are attentive not only to physical geography, but also to subject positions and the sociopolitical structures.

Other approaches consider and construct distinctly feminist theories of knowledge by taking up questions about the relations between bias, truth, and objectivity. They demonstrate the

---

[1] A great deal of standard twentieth-century philosophy took as its leading challenge to discover necessary and sufficient conditions for the truth of sentences of the form "S-knows-that-*p*," where 'S' refers to some subject—a knower—and '*p*' refers to some proposition that is known by the subject. For example, "Sally knows that the glass is on the table." It was then asked, what are the necessary and sufficient conditions for the truth of the assertion "S knows that *p*?"

ubiquity of political biases in these discussions and go on to argue that "objectivity" can best be served by adding marginalized voices, making the politics behind epistemic and scientific projects visible, or using methodologies that are transparent and self-reflexive. Sandra Harding takes up in "'Strong Objectivity' and Socially Situated Knowledge," arguing that so-called "value-neutral" accounts of objectivity ignore the powerful cultural background beliefs shaping inquiry. In response to this observation she proposes a version of feminist standpoint theory[2] that not only admits to the importance of certain aspects of modern scientific commitment to objectivity, but also acknowledges that deeply stratified societies cannot produce value-free knowledge. Nonetheless, Harding thinks that members of oppressed communities can generate uniquely important knowledge. She argues for "strong objectivity," which includes multiple standpoints, fosters a stronger empiricism, generates a more rigorous objectivity, and produces a more accurate picture of how we know the world.

Certainly it would be a mistake to assume that women everywhere share the same concerns or priorities around questions of knowledge production. So, we might ask, how do different cultural priorities shape the questions that feminist epistemological projects choose to address? In "The Project of Feminist Epistemology: Perspectives from a Nonwestern Feminist," Uma Narayan examines the dangers of theorizing knowledge and

values in ways that ignore nonwestern women's experiences and present western theoretical insights too dogmatically. Her essay outlines several concerns for nonwestern feminists involved in epistemological projects. For example, Narayan notes that westerners' primary critical focus on positivism ignores the fact that religious values, which often shape strongly nonwestern cultural views of gender, are not positivist; and that the political liberalism associated with positivism sometimes offers concepts that are useful for fighting oppression. She also questions the popular idea that members of oppressed groups are epistemically privileged, and that privileged groups can learn to see privilege more clearly by paying attention to the critical insights of the oppressed. In the end, she advocates a more complex theory of epistemic advantage: one that does not romanticize the "double consciousness" of marginalized groups, but instead recognizes the high emotional price many people pay for living the multiple realities that give rise to their unique ways of knowing.

Philosophers have had plenty to say about knowledge, but relatively very little to say about ignorance. Ignorance is not a simple lack of knowing: it is often a social production that is actively fostered and preserved. It is therefore crucial for feminist epistemologies to focus not only on what is known, but also on the practices that systematically erase some forms of knowledge, produce ignorance, and prevent resistance. In "Coming to Understand: Orgasm and the Epistemology of Ignorance," Nancy Tuana examines scientific, feminist, and common-knowledge constructions of female sexual pleasure in order to track the production of knowledge and ignorance about female orgasm. She investigates what we do and do not know about female genitalia and orgasm, and why geographies of the female body have largely excluded or misrepresented the clitoris and other organs of female pleasure. There is the strong correlation between pleasure and knowledge. For this reason questions about whose pleasures are enhanced and whose are suppressed by ignorance must be addressed in any study of the science of sexuality.

---

[2] Feminist standpoint theory is rooted in the Marxist observation that socially oppressed classes can access knowledge unavailable to the socially privileged—particularly knowledge of power relations. It argues that the epistemic locations of marginalized groups (e.g., women or the proletariat) can yield more comprehensive and accurate questions, observations, and analyses of the world than those of dominant groups. Standpoint theorists make an important distinction between a *woman's perspective* and a *feminist standpoint*. A "standpoint" is a form of understanding that results from political struggle: it is not a form of understanding that one has simply by virtue of having a particular gender identity or body. A feminist standpoint is crafted through gender-sensitive political engagement with the world, and women's perspective is something women are imagined to have by virtue of living their lives as women.

PURIFICATION AND TRANSCENDENCE IN DESCARTES'S MEDITATIONS

Susan Bordo

Me-thinks, I see how all the old Rubbish must be thrown away, and the rotten Buildings be overthrown, and carried away with so powerful an Inundation. These are the days that must lay a new foundation of a more magnificent Philosophy, never to be overthrown . . . a true and permanent Philosophy.
—HENRY POWER, *EXPERIMENTAL PHILOSOPHY*

CARTESIANISM AND THE QUEST FOR PURITY

Where there is anxiety, there will almost certainly be found a mechanism of defense against that anxiety. In *Pensées*, VI, 113, Pascal expresses, in one line, what might be seen as the *modus operandi* for the modern struggle for control over the sense of arbitrary allotment of time and place within an indifferent, alien universe. *"Through space,"* he says, *"the universe grasps me and swallows me up like a speck; through thought I grasp it."* If the impersonal, arbitrary universe of the early modern era is capable of physically "swallowing" him, like a random bit of ontological debris, *he* is nonetheless capable of containing and subduing it—through comprehension, through the "grasp" of the mind. As in much of early modern science and philosophy—in Bacon, most dramatically—the dream of knowledge is here imagined as an explicit revenge fantasy, an attempt to wrest back control from nature.

The fantasy of absolute understanding, of course, motivated Descartes much more than Pascal. But the thought through which Descartes conquered the indifferent, infinite universe was a thought very different from that imagined in Pascal's *Pensées*. To *comprehend*—to contain the

whole within the grasp of the mind—is simply not possible for a finite intelligence, as Descartes makes clear.[1] Rather, what seizes the Cartesian imagination is the possibility of *pure* thought, of *pure* perception. Such perception, far from embracing the whole, demands the disentangling of the various objects of knowledge *from* the whole of things, and beaming a light on the essential separateness of each—its own pure and discrete nature, revealed as *it* is, free of the "distortions" of subjectivity. Arithmetic and geometry are natural models for the science that will result; for, as Descartes says, they "alone deal with an object so pure and uncomplicated, that they need make no assumptions at all which experience renders uncertain" (*Regulae,* HR, I, 5). The "intuitions" of the *Regulae,* the "simples" of the *Discourse,* and the clear and distinct perceptions of the *Meditations* are attempts to describe the possibility of such objects for philosophy, a class of "privileged representations," as Rorty puts it, "so compelling that their accuracy cannot be doubted." Much of Meditation IV, I will argue, turns on the delineation of such a class of ideas.

For these "privileged representations" to reveal themselves, the knower must be purified, too—of all bias, all "perspective," all emotional attachment. And for Descartes, this necessarily involves the transcendence of the body, not only of the "prejudices" acquired through the body-rule of infancy but of all the bodily distractions and passions that obscure our thinking. The *Meditations,* I propose, should be read as providing a guide and exemplar of such bodily transcendence.

The result for Descartes is a new model of knowledge, grounded in *objectivity,* and capable of providing a new epistemological security to replace that which was lost in the dissolution of the medieval world-view. It is a model that, although under attack, is still largely with analytic philosophy today, and that still revolves around the imagery of *purity.* Locke spoke of philosophy as removing the "rubbish lying in the way of knowledge." Three centuries later, Quine wrote that the task of the philosopher was "clearing the ontological slums" (p. 275). The image of the philosopher as tidying the mess left by others is more subtly presented by Arthur Danto, who views the philosopher as "executing the tasks of conceptual housekeeping [the sciences and other disciplines] are too robustly busy to tend to themselves" (p. 10).

The creation of a "pure" realm, untouched by uncertainty and risk, always necessitates, as Dewey points out (p. 8), the designation of a contrastingly "impure" realm to absorb or take responsibility for the messy aspects of experience. In the history of philosophy, the role of the unclean and the impure has been played, variously, by material reality, practical activity, change, the emotions, "subjectivity," and most often—as for Descartes—by the *body*. In Locke and Danto's conception of philosophy, the other disciplines play this role: They are the earth to philosophy's spirit, the "matter" to philosophy's "form", providing the "stuff" to be analyzed, organized and corrected by philosophy's purifying scrutiny.[2]

What makes such conceptions peculiarly Cartesian is not just their implicit assumption that the philosopher is in possession of some neutral "matrix" (as Rorty calls it) with which to perform an ultimate critical or conceptual cleansing, but their passion for intellectual separation, demarcation, and *order*. The other disciplines, as Feyerabend says, must be "tamed [and put] in their place" (p. 21); their "robust" effort is fine, so long as there is someone specifically charged to clean up the conceptual debris left in its wake.

Rorty is critical of this conception of the role of the philosopher, according to which the philosopher occupies a space, not within the cultural conversation, but removed, at a distance, linguistically interpreting, logically overseeing, and epistemologically scrutinizing the proceedings. The pretension to do so is not only professionally hubristic, insisting as it does that the philosopher's voice "always has an overriding claim on the attention of other participants in the conversation" (p. 392), but is based on a profound self-deception.

For Rorty, the belief that one may lay claim to an ultimate critical framework of any sort is illusory, an attempt to "escape from history," context, and human finitude (p. 9). Rorty here places himself firmly within the Nietzschean and Deweyan "therapeutic" traditions in philosophy, for whom the intellectual hunger for purity, clarity, and order is revealed to have an "underside"—in the desire for control over the more unruly, "cthonic" dimensions of experience. The sociologist Richard Sennett, too, has described what he calls the "purification urge"—toward ordering the world according to firm, clearly articulated categories permitting of no ambiguity and dissonance—as "the desire to be all-powerful, to control the meanings of experience before encounter so as not to be overwhelmed" (p. 116). Against any possible threat to that organization, strict rules against mixing categories or blurring boundaries must be maintained. The ontological order must be clear and distinct. The anthropologist Mary Douglas has argued that maintaining such pristine ontological integrity—"keeping distinct the categories of creation . . . [through] correct definition, discrimination and order"—animates religious conceptions of purity (1966, p. 53). For the Cartesian, too, ambiguity and contradiction are the worst transgressions. That which cannot be categorized cleanly deserves no place in the universe.

For Descartes, the quest for purity of thought serves more historically specific mechanisms, as well. For, the alien, impersonal nature of the infinite universe—that wasteland of meaninglessness, that terrifying, cold expanse—is precisely what allows it to be known with precision, clarity, and detachment. In a universe in which the spiritual and the physical merge, where body and mind participate in knowledge, objectivity is impossible. (And, in such a world, objectivity is not an ideal.) The quest for objectivity, on the other hand, is capable of transforming the barren landscape of the modern universe into a paradise for analysis, dissection, and "controlled" experimentation. Its barrenness, which filled

Pascal with such existential dread, is, of course, precisely what makes it capable of being "read" mathematically and taken apart with philosophical accuracy—and moral impunity.

THE PURIFICATION OF THE UNDERSTANDING

At the start of the fourth Meditation, Descartes finds himself on the horns of the dilemma. The proof of the existence of a veracious God has insured him that he is not the victim of a systematic deception and—what amounts to the same thing—that his own capacity for judgment, "doubtless received from God," will not "lead me to err if I use it aright" (HR, I, 172). Yet, of course, we *do* err. How to reconcile this fallibility with his newly established faith in the veracity of God and the fitness of his own faculties?

Descartes, to begin with, considers several solutions of a traditional nature. He first considers that his own nature, not being God-like, but rather somewhere "between the supreme Being and non-being," must "in some degree participate . . . in nought or in non-being." He should not be surprised therefore to find in himself, in addition to the positive faculties given to him by God, *defects* in those faculties. Error need not be attributed to "a special faculty given me by God"; rather, "I fall into error from the fact that the power given me by God for the purpose of distinguishing truth from error is not infinite" (HR, I, 172–3).

But this answer does not satisfy Descartes, "for error is not a pure negation [i.e., is not the simple defect or want of some perfection which ought not to be mine], but it is a lack of some knowledge which it seems I ought to possess" (HR, I, 173). And the seeming failure of God to bestow on me an understanding that would be without such a lack requires explanation.

Perhaps, however, my intellectual defects serve higher ends. It is not, after all, within my capacity to understand all of God's design; for all I know, my own imperfections when consid-

ered as "part of the whole universe" are "very perfect." (HR, I, 173). This explanation is not rejected by Descartes, but he does not go any further with it. It appears to function, rather, as a "traditionalist" prelude to what will turn out to be a decidedly innovative approach to the problem of error.

The form of that new approach, like many of Descartes's most radical departures from scholasticism, is itself traditional—an epistemological variant of the Augustinian "solution" to the problem of evil. For Augustine, "God made man but not the sin in him": Human evil is the result of our capacity for free will—given to us by God, and itself good—but meaningless unless the choice of evil is a real possibility. Freedom is not freedom if it is determined to choose the good; in "allowing" us to sin, God is not responsible for evil but for giving us the capacity to behave as moral agents. The will alone is responsible for sin.

Descartes's strategy for dealing with the "problem of error" corresponds to Augustine's approach to the problem of evil. As, for Augustine, God is absolved and the human being charged with sole responsibility for moral fallenness, so, for Descartes, the human being is charged with all responsibility for *epistemological* "fallenness":

> . . . it is not an imperfection in God that He has given me the liberty to give or withhold my assent from certain things as to which He has not placed a clear and distinct knowledge in my understanding: but it is without doubt an imperfection in me not to make good use of my freedom, and to give my judgment readily on matters which I only understand obscurely (HR, I, 177).

It is important to note that judgment here is conceived as an act distinct from the act of understanding. For, "by the understanding alone I [neither assert nor deny anything, but] apprehend the ideas of things as to which I can form a judgement" (HR, I, 174). Judgment is rather an act of the will, as Descartes makes clear in the *Notes*

Directed Against a Certain Programme:

> . . . I saw that, over and above perception, which is required as a basis for judgment, there must needs be affirmation, or negation, to constitute the form of the judgment, and that it is frequently open to us to withhold our assent, even if we perceive a thing. I referred the act of judging, which consists in nothing but *assent,* i.e., affirmation or negation, not to the perception of the understanding, but to the determination of the will (HR, I, 446).

Errors, therefore, are acts of the will, or, more precisely, acts of misuse of the will. The way they occur is the following: Although the faculty of will, like the understanding, is "perfect of its kind," being "much wider in its range and compass than the understanding," it sometimes gives its assent to "things which I do not understand" (HR, I, 175). This assent to the obscure or confused represents a misuse of the will, for "the light of nature teaches us that the knowledge of the understanding should always precede the determination of the will" (HR, I, 177; see also *Principle* XLIII, I, 236).

The conception of judgment as an act of will rather than intellect (a radical departure from scholastic tradition), is essential to Descartes's epistemological program in several ways:

1. It is essential to the comprehensibility of Cartesian doubt. For, the methodical "absten[ion] from giving assent to dubious things" that is Cartesian doubt *is* an act of will rather than intellect. It is an attitude chosen prior to any particular intellectual act, and (even though undertaken to confront a *real* skeptical threat, as I have suggested previously) is deliberately chosen as a route to that goal.

2. As suggested earlier, it exonerates God from the responsibility for error, just as, for Augustine, the attribution of sin to human will exonerates God from the responsibility of having created evil. As such, it is actually the final (though not explicitly presented as such) stage in the full proof of the existence of a veracious God. For, how can I reconcile the veracity of God with the fact of human error? Unless the responsibility for error can be shown to lie elsewhere, the image, if not of an evil genius, then at least of a less than totally veracious God, again could undercut our newly won confidence in our facilities. But since error is the result, instead, of the *wrong use* which we make of the humanly *perfect* faculties given to us by God, the responsibility for it is all ours—and within our control.

3. It serves as an argument for the purity of the understanding. The above correspondence between Descartes's treatment of error and the traditional handling of the "problem of evil" was first described by Etienne Gilson[3] and is ascribed to, in passing, by J. L. Evans (p. 137), Bernard Williams (p. 169), and Hiram Caton (p. 90). The way this correspondence has been formulated, however, has missed something whose significance is crucial to understanding the fourth Meditation. All emphasis, in Gilson's account, has been placed on the exoneration of *God* from the charge of responsibility for error—which indeed is stressed by Descartes, and which is the obvious keynote comparsion to be made *if* the "problem of error" is taken to be *symmetrically* correspondent with the solution to the problem of evil. But it is not symmetrically correspondent. In the context of the problem of evil, the traditional arguments exonerate God alone, not also the will. Whereas, in the context of the problem of intellectual error, on the other hand, in exonerating God, Descartes also exonerated the intellect itself, and not incidentally.[4] In relocating error "outside" the understanding, Descartes is not only placing it in the province of the will, but purging the understanding of what stands in the way of *its* perfection. It therefore counts as an argument for the purity of the understanding as much as an argument for the goodness of God.

The difference is crucial, not only to clarification of the arguments which follow in the

Meditations, and to our understanding of the overall project of the *Meditations,* but to our understanding of the philosophical and cultural reconstruction within which Descartes plays such a central role. What we are enabled to see, *in process* as it were, is a historical movement away from a transcendent God as the only legitimate object of worship to the establishing of the *human intellect* as godly, and as appropriately to be revered and submitted to—once "purified" of all that stands in the way of its godliness. Shortly, for modern science, God will indeed become downright superfluous. In the *Meditations,* God most certainly is not. But God's role in that work nonetheless almost approaches the metaphorical: Just as the Evil Genius functions as a personification of the possibility of radical defect in the human faculties of knowing, so a veracious God seems a personification of faith in those faculties. That Descartes's strategy for exonerating God for error is *simultaneously* a strategy for purifying the understanding is suggestive of a merging of foci here. The godly intellect is on the way to becoming the true deity of the modern era.

That Descartes employs an epistemological variant of a traditional solution to the "problem of evil" suggests that *purification* is not too strong a term to describe his project for certifying the perfection of the intellect. The project to conceptually purify one realm, as noted earlier, necessitates a "relocation" of all threatening elements "outside." They become *alien.* This is the strategy employed by Augustine in his answer to the problem of evil, as William James points out in *The Varieties of Religious Experience.* There, James argues that the construal of evil as a "problem" for which God must be absolved of responsibility necessitates transforming "an essential part of our being" into "a waste element, to be sloughed off . . . diseased, inferior, excrementitious stuff" (p. 129).

The strategy, as Mary Douglas points out, is the same, in form and function, as that of social rituals of purification, in which a society establishes some substance or group as impure and "taboo," thus "defining" it as outside the social body. Insuring

that the tabooed thing or group remains separate and does not contaminate the social body sometimes requires violent expulsions, as in witch hunting (1982, pp. 107–124). But usually the taboo functions through the establishment of separate metaphysical "realms"—a good "inside" and a bad "outside"—as, pursuing this analogy, it does for Descartes. Error is not extinguished, but excluded; it is conceptualized as belonging outside an inner circle of purity, in this case, the godly intellect.

Douglas suggests the term "dirt-rejecting" for those philosophers who pursue such purification strategies (1966, p. 164).[5] In terms of such a category, Descartes is an epistemological "dirt-rejecter." Not that he doesn't see confusion and obscurity everywhere ("smudges on the mirror of nature," as a colleague has described it)—for he does. But his entire system is devoted to circumscribing an intellectual arena which is pristinely immune to contamination, a mirror which is impossible to smudge. Here, we should recall the Cartesian imagery of mistaken ideas as spoiled and rotting fruit, capable of corrupting everything that comes into contact with them. Error can no longer be conceptualized as a negation by Descartes (as the medievals had been able to do). For the culture he lived in, unlike the medieval world, uncertainty and confusion seemed so ubiquitous as to suggest that human nature may have been malevolently (or at least mischievously) *designed* to err. But error can be reconceptualized as "belonging" to a faculty other than the intellect (just as evil had been conceived as belonging to *us,* rather than God). In this way the first step is made toward preparing the intellect to enter into a pure, "godly" relation with its objects of knowledge.

PASSIVITY AND TRUTH

Descartes's initial "purification of the understanding" is, however, *only* a first step. For, the intellect has not quite been purged of all the elements lying in the way of its purity. Denial, assertion, desiring, aversion, and doubting have all become the province of the will. Only the "acts of understanding"—perceiving, imagining, conceiving—remain the province of the understanding. In Meditation III, Descartes had described these as the only forms to which the title "idea" should be properly applied, because they alone do not "add something else to the idea which I have of the thing" (HR, I, 159). They are, in other words, *representations*. And, as such, they may of course *mis*represent. Therein lies the problem. If the faculty of judgment is free (as at this point it seems to be) to accept or reject the claims of the ideas that it surveys that they represent the state of things, what is to prevent us from constantly falling into error? The ideas that "pass in review" (to borrow Rorty's phrase) before the "inner eye" of judgment are, after all, a motley array. They include both perceptions that are the result of the acts of volition (imaginatively constructed entities, intelligible objects) and "passive" perceptions, "receive[d] from the things represented by them" (*Passions of the Soul*, HR, I, 340). The latter include the perceptions that occur within dreams and daydreams, bodily perceptions such as pain, heat and cold, the emotions ("the passions of the soul"), and the perceptions of external objects. This is a diverse assemblage, a real democracy of inner representations, united by their common relation to the "inner arena"—the soul—which Descartes likens to the relation between the shapes a piece of wax may take and the wax itself.

> It receives its ideas partly from objects in contact with the senses, partly from impressions in the brain, and partly from precedent dispositions in the soul and motions of the will. Similarly, a piece of wax owes its shapes partly to the pressure of other bodies, partly to its own earlier shape or other qualities such as heaviness and softness, and partly also to its own movement, when, having been pushed it has in itself the power to continue moving (to Mesland, May 2, 1644; PL, 148).

In this analogy, the suggestion is that all our ideas have equal power to impress themselves on the intellect. But for Descartes, the intellect is not quite the democracy of ideas suggested by the analogy with wax. For some ideas are aristocrats and have the power to compel the assent of the will.

> For example, when I lately examined whether anything existed in the world, and found that from the very fact that I considered this question it followed very clearly that I myself existed, I could not prevent myself from believing that a thing I so clearly conceived was true: not that I found myself compelled to do so by some external cause, but simply because from great clearness in my mind there followed a great inclination of my will . . . (Meditation IV, HR, I, 176).
>
> The will of a thinking thing is borne, willingly indeed and freely (for that is the essense of the will), but none the less infallibly, toward the good that it clearly knows (Reply II, HR, II, 56).
>
> For it seems to me certain that *a great light in the intellect is followed by a strong inclination in the will;* so that if we see very clearly that a thing is good for us it is very difficult—and, on my view, impossible, as long as one continues in the same thought—to stop the course of our desire (to Mesland, May 2, 1644; PL, 149).

We are free, to be sure, to cease to *attend* to our clear and distinct perceptions (from this comes the fact that we "earn merit" for the good acts that follow "infallibly" from those perceptions), but to choose to attend is to immediately "ensure that our will follows so promptly the light of our understanding that there is no longer in any way indifference" (to Mesland, PL, 150).[6]

On closer inspection, indeed, it turns out that there is, in fact, only *one* way in which the judgment can *err:* by giving assent to the obscure and confused. This limitation on error runs throughout the Cartesian corpus, from the *Regulae,* which instructs us "never to assume what is false is true" (HR, I, 9), but does not mention the converse, to the *Principles:* "We deceive ourselves *only* when we form judgments about anything insufficiently known to us" (HR, I, 232). And, of course, in the *Meditations:*

> Whence then come my errors? They come from the sole fact that . . . I do not restrain [the will] within [the bounds of the understanding], but extend it

also to things which I do not understand: and as the will is of itself indifferent to these, it easily falls into error and sin, and chooses the evil for the good, or the false for the true (HR, I, Meditation IV, 175–176).

In the above quotation, what Descartes calls the "understanding" is *identified* with the capacity to *correctly* (i.e., clearly and distinctly) understand, rather than with the general faculty of receiving, recalling, or combining ideas. His inconsistency is not my focus here, however. What is important is that a new mental arena has been designated, one which is normatively delineated—by the qualities of clearness and distinctness. And the capacity to fall into error has been circumscribed as well. It is connected, not with the freedom of the will but with the *indifference* of the will. These, for Descartes, are two very different things. To explain this will require some sorting out of the Cartesian doctrine of the will: the faculty of will itself is simply

> the power of choosing to do a thing or not to do it (that is, to affirm or deny, to pursue or to shun it), or rather it consists alone in the fact that in order to affirm or deny, pursue or shun those things placed before us by the understanding, we act so that we are unconscious that any outside force constrains us in doing so (Meditation IV, HR, I, 175).

It is important to note that for Descartes the power of the will to choose a course of action is not simply "negative" freedom—is not simply the absence of force or constraint on our actions—a "freedom" shared by animals, who do not *will* their activities, and who cannot therefore be said to be truly "free" (to Mesland, PL, 150). Rather, the power of the will is the "positive faculty of determining oneself to one or other of two contraries" (to Mesland, February 9, 1645; PL, 161), the power, in other words, of acting *voluntarily* (and not merely automatically or instinctually).

Within this general freedom, Descartes notes, there are different grades of freedom. The highest—the "greater liberty," as Descartes calls it—consists in one of two things: *either* "a great

faculty in determining oneself" through "follow[ing] the course which appears to have the most reasons in its favor" *or* "a greater use of the positive power which we have of following the worse, although we see the better" (to Mesland, PL, 160). The latter refers to those special cases when we "hold back from pursuing a clearly known good, or from admitting a clearly perceived truth [because] we consider it a good thing to demonstrate the freedom of our will by doing so" (to Mesland, PL, 160). The former reconciles the *freedom* of the will with the will's assent to the clear and distinct perception. Indeed, Descartes affirms that the "greater the inclination of the will" that follows from the "clearness of the mind," the "greater [the] freedom or spontaneity" of the act (Meditation IV, HR, I, 176).

This reconciliation is similar to the reconciliation of determinism and freedom offered by so-called "soft determinists," who replace the traditional opposition between these two with an opposition between freedom and external compulsion. For the soft determinist, I am free, not insofar as my actions are *undetermined,* but insofar as they are determined by my *own* inclinations rather than an external force. And for Descartes, indeed, the "lowest degree of liberty" is *indifference:* the state in which nothing in the self determines us to any direction, when the will "is not impelled one way rather than another by any perception of truth or goodness" (to Mesland, PL, 159).

The capacity to err derives, as we have seen, from this state of indifference. Correspondingly, when we *cannot* maintain indifference—when we are irresistibly drawn to one side rather than another—we can be assured that we are in the presence of truth.

The Cartesian clear and distinct perception is very like an emotion (as emotions are conceived by Descartes) in its capacity to *overtake* us, to absorb us, to render us passive in the face of its strength. But while the emotions may overtake us in ways that obscure our intellectual vision (that is, in the traditional picture that comes down to us from Descartes), the clear and distinct idea overtakes the propensity to error itself. *Our* very passivity in the face of a clear and distinct idea is the mark of *its* truth.

Passivity in the face of an idea—the inability to say "no" to an idea—is a hallmark of epistemological reassurance to one degree or another throughout the *Meditations.* We encounter it first in the fleeting moments of the first and second Meditations when the pull of the clear and distinct perception temporarily subdues doubt. Even *before* it is demonstrated that "all that I know clearly is true," "my mind is such that I could not prevent myself from holding [my perception] to be true so long as I conceive them clearly" (HR, I, 180). This passivity, however, is not to be trusted, for my mind may be such, too, that it is fundamentally flawed, and responds to the false as though it were true (HR, I, 184). I need to be assured that I may trust my own responses (that God has not created me such that I am systematically deceived) before I can take them as guides to the truth of things.

The *cogito,* too, is a case—though a special one—of an idea that compels assent. It is special, as I have argued previously, because it is one of a very small class of ideas whose denial, paradoxically, involves assent. It is more resilient to doubt, therefore, than other clear and distinct perceptions, since even if I am sure that my mind is fundamentally flawed, I am still "sure," that is, *thinking* something. But the compelling nature of the *cogito,* in any case, does not assure me that the compelling nature of all other clear and distinct ideas will "as a general rule" insure me of their truth.

For that assurance Descartes needs God. And he needs, in addition (and what amounts to the same thing, but in an "epistemological" form that is a working model of *knowing*), to be assured that we will not be drawn to error in submitting to the force of the intellect. This is what the fourth Meditation accomplishes: *first,* by identifying (if somewhat inconsistently) the intellect with the arena of the clear and distinct, and *second,* by attributing error, not just to the will, but to the *indifferent* will. The will that is compelled by the intellect can never err.

Now the passivity of the soul can be more fully trusted, and we may let our ideas "speak to us," attending to those we can answer and those we cannot. In Meditation IV, for example, the following argument occurs, in which the fact that our perceptions of external objects are not subject to voluntary control turns out to be a strong reason for believing that they proceed from the things they seem to represent.

> There is certainly further in me a certain passive faculty of perception, that is, of receiving and recognizing the ideas of sensible things, but this would be useless to me . . . if there were not either in me or in some other thing another active faculty capable of forming and producing these ideas. But this active faculty cannot exist in me . . . seeing that it does not presuppose thought, and also that those ideas are often produced in me without my contributing in any way to the same, and often even against my will; it is thus necessarily the case that the faculty resides in some substance different from me in which all the reality which is objectively in the ideas that are produced by this faculty is formally or eminently contained, as I remarked before (HR, I, 191).

This argument does not differ significantly from the argument that Descartes recalls from his naïve, pre-doubting days:

> . . . It was not without reason that I believed myself to perceive objects quite different from my thought, to wit, bodies from which those ideas proceeded; for I found by experience that these ideas presented themselves to me without my consent being requisite, so that I could not perceive any object, however desirous I might be, unless it were present to the organs of sense; and it was not in my power not to perceive it, when it was present. (HR, I, 187–188).

The difference is not a difference in argument, but a difference in self-trust. Prior to the proofs of God and the account of error, even the strongest natural inclination may be looked on as suspect, once the immediacy of the moment has passed.

> For since nature *seemed* to cause me to lean towards many things from which reason repelled me, I did

not believe that I should trust much to the teachings of nature. And although the ideas which I receive by the senses do not depend on my will, I did not think that one should for that reason conclude that they proceeded from things different from myself, since possibly some faculty might be discovered in me—though hitherto unknown to me—which produced them (HR, I, 189; emphasis added).

The qualification "seemed to" is important, for the fourth Meditation has established that this "seeming" was an illusion—that error is always the result of indifference (allowed for only by the obscure and confused perception) and not of real inclination. It is significant, too, that Descartes says that his new-found self-trust is the result, not just of knowing "more clearly the author of my being," but of "know[ing] myself better" (HR, I, 189). The latter was the point of the fourth Meditation—to translate my knowledge that this is God's world into a new model of the human intellect. This new model is one in which indifference rather than inclination is the hallmark of error, and in which, therefore, a class of "godly" ideas—"king," as Dewey puts it, "to any beholding mind that may gaze upon it" (p. 23)—could reign supreme. Having attributed judgment to the will, for Descartes it is doubly imperative to circumscribe a set of realities within the intellect that are capable of bending judgment to their authority. The very last thing that Descartes would want is a Jamesian "will to believe," in which the belief in truth itself is "but a passionate affirmation of desire," and behind every particular intellectual position lies "fear and hope, prejudice and passion" (1897, p. 9). Objective evidence and certainty may be "fine ideals to play with," says James, "but where on this moon-lit and dream-visited planet are they found?" (p. 14); "Pretend as we may, the whole man within us is at work when we form our philosophical opinions" (p. 92). The clear and distinct idea, on the contrary, assures us that it is precisely when we form our philosophical opinions that the "whole man" may be *passified*—quite literally—by the purity and authority of the object.

This is, of course, no new theme in the history of philosophy, which is studded with metaphors suggesting spectatorship rather than participation, the "known" specifically conceived as that realm in which the distorting effects of human interest and activity are eliminated, and in which fixity and purity thus rule. But before the sixteenth and seventeenth centuries, such conceptions had been reserved for the sort of knowing that has formal, immutable, or immaterial "reality" as its object. It is only with Descartes that fixity and purity—"the immutable state of mind"—began to be demanded of the knowledge necessary to certify concrete perceptions of the self (that I have hands, eyes, senses, etc.), of particular "corporeal things" (other animals, inanimate things) and, indeed, of *anything* external to consciousness. And it is only in the sixteenth and seventeenth centuries that earthly science, insofar as it is trustworthy, is equated with "spectatorship" and the passive reception of ideas.[7] It is in the work of Descartes that we find the official philosophical birth of the notion of mind as "mirror of nature."

THE TRANSCENDENCE OF THE BODY

The Cartesian purification of the understanding, at this point, is still abstract and conceptual—not methodological. How does one do it? Some *method* of purification must be supplied, some rules to direct the understanding. On this score, of course, Descartes is emphatic: We must learn *how* to achieve the proper sort of receptivity to ideas. And although all persons are capable of learning this, "there are very few who rightly distinguish between what is really perceived and what they fancy they perceive, because but few are accustomed to clear and distinct perceptions" (Reply VII, HR, II, 307).

Descartes recognizes that people may be wrong about what they take to be the clearness and distinctness of ideas. He has even proven himself guilty of it at various points in the progress of the *Meditations*. He agrees with Gassendi that without a method "which will direct and show us when we are in error and when not, so often as we think we clearly and distinctly perceive anything" (HR, II, 152), we are thrown back on each individual's sense of conviction, a psychological datum that cannot be trustworthy in all cases. But, then, in which cases, and for what reasons is testimony to personal conviction trustworthy? The problem is further compounded by the similarities between the workings of the clear and distinct perceptions, which irresistibly dispose the will through the power of intellectual insight, and the emotions, which irresistibly dispose the will through the force of the bodily—the attendant "commotion" in the heart, blood and "animal spirits" which "prevents the soul from being able at one to change or arrest its passions" (HR, I, 352).[8] To be sure, the clear and distinct perception is "seen" with the mind, whereas the emotions are felt by the body. But the issue at stake here is not how to distinguish between the two; rather, what is at issue is the epistemological trustworthiness of the "irresistible" *qua* irresistible: If the will can be overtaken and bent in directions that oppose reason (as it is often by the body [I, 353]), then how can the will's passivity itself serve as a mark that reason has conducted itself to the truth (as it is supposed to via the clear and distinct perception)?

We need to recall now that what principally stands in the way of the "habit" of clear and distinct perception (taken as an activity now, rather than a content or object) is what Descartes generally calls "prejudice," but which, on closer inspection, turns out to be a specific sort of prejudice—that of "seeing" with one's *body* rather than one's *mind*. This, as we have seen, is the original, and most formidable legacy of infancy, a time in which the mind, "newly united" to the body, was "wholly occupied in perceiving or feeling the ideas of pain, pleasure, heat, cold and other similar ideas which arise from its union and intermingling with the body" (to Hyperaspistes, August 1641, PL, 111). "The body is

always a hindrance to the mind in its thinking," he tells Burman, "and this was especially true in youth" (B, 8).

That Descartes views the "prison of the body" as the chief, if not sole, source of our inability to perceive clearly and distinctly is evidenced by a remarkable passage in the letter to Hyperaspistes, in which Descartes maintains that the infant "has in itself the ideas of God, itself, and all such truths as are called self-evident . . . if it were taken out of the prison of the body it would find [those ideas] within itself" (PL, 111). That this "prison" can, in fact, be transcended in adulthood is no less in doubt for Descartes.

> Nothing in metaphysics causes more trouble than the making the perception of its primary notions clear and distinct. For, though in their own nature they are as intelligible as, or even more intelligible than those the geometricians study, yet being contradicted by the many preconceptions of our senses to which we have since our earliest years been accustomed, they cannot be perfectly apprehended *except by those who give strenuous attention and study to them, and withdraw their minds as far as possible from matters corporeal* (Reply II, HR, II, 49–50; emphasis added).

In *The Passions of the Soul,* Descartes explicitly opposes his own view—that the body is the source of all in us that is "opposed to reason"—to the traditional view that it is the inferior, appetitive, or sensuous part of the soul itself that wars with the rational (HR, I, 353). He is thus able, given the "real distinction between soul and body" (see *Principle* LX, HR, I, 243; Meditation VI, HR, I, 190; *Discourse,* HR, I, 101; to Reneri, April 1638, PL, 52) to conceptualize the possibility of complete intellectual transcendence of the appetitive and sensuous. Although the soul "can have its operations disturbed by the bad disposition of the bodily organs" (PL, 52) or the passions, "even those who have the feeblest souls can acquire a very absolute dominion over all their passions if sufficient industry is applied in training and guiding them" (*Passions,* HR, I, 356).

Such "training" is largely a matter of accumulating, in the moments when the soul's operations are undisturbed, a strong arsenal of rational truth to rely on when agitation threatens. The resolution to carry out what reason recommends, at such time, is the essence of human happiness, as Descartes tells Elizabeth (August 4, 1645, PL, 165). When Elizabeth (quite understandably) expressed skepticism over this, pointing out that there are diseases that overpower the faculty of reason "and with it the satisfaction proper to a rational mind," Descartes confidently replied that repetition is the key: ". . . if one often has a certain thought while one's body was at liberty, it returns again no matter how indisposed the body may be." He himself, he assured her, had in this way completely eliminated bad dreams from his sleep (PL, 168). He presumably did not notice that they return in the first Meditation.

Not only, however, may the properly trained mind overcome the passions. In certain mental acts, as Margaret Wilson points out (in Hooker, 99), it actually does "think without the body," as Descartes claims it can in the letter to Reneri (PL, 52) and in Meditation VI (HR, I, 193). These are the acts of "pure intellection" or "pure understanding," which not only have no "imagic" content (e.g., the chiliagon, the idea of God, the idea of a thinking thing), but no corporeal correlates at all. Unlike sensation, imagery and memory, acts of "pure understanding" (and the memory of them) are not only "phenomenologically" independent of the body, but independent of all physical processes whatever. In a letter to Mesland, for example (PL, 148), Descartes argues that the memory of intellectual things, unlike those of material things, depends on "traces" left in thought itself, not in the brain. And in the Gassendi Replies he states quite emphatically that "I have often also shown distinctly that mind can act independently of the brain; for certainly the brain can be of no use in pure thought: its only use is for imagining and perceiving" (HR, I, 212).[9]

To achieve this autonomy, the mind must be gradually liberated from the body: it must *become*

a "pure mind." First, constant vigilance must be maintained against the distractions of the body. Throughout the *Meditations,* emphasis is placed on training oneself in nonreliance on the body and practice in the art of "pure understanding." It is virtually a kind of mechanistic yoga.

> I shall now close my eyes, I shall stop my ears, I shall call away all my senses, I shall efface even from my thoughts all the images of corporeal things, or at least (for that is hardly possible) I shall esteem them as vain and false; and thus holding converse only with myself and considering my own nature, I shall try little by little to reach a better knowledge of and a more familiar acquaintanceship with myself (Meditation III, HR, I, 157).

Indeed, much of the *Meditations* may be read as prescribing rules for the liberation of mind from the various seductions of the body, in order to cleanse and prepare it for the reception of clear and distinct ideas. The initial requirement is to "deliver [the] mind from every care . . . and agitat[ion from the] passions" (HR, I, 145). Since, as we have seen, our passionate inclinations can bend the will in directions which oppose reason, it is essential that we not be susceptible to their coercive power while we are pursuing truth. The field must be cleared of such influence, so we will be receptive to the coerciveness exercised by ideas alone.

The next step is to topple the "prejudices" acquired through the body-rule of infancy and childhood. These prejudices have their origin in a hyperabsorption in the senses. But their precise form, as we have seen, is the inability to properly distinguish what is happening solely "inside" the subject from what has an external existence—e.g., the attribution of heat, cold, etc., to the object, of greater "reality" to rocks than water because of their greater heaviness, and so on. As an infant "swamped" inside the body, one simply did not have a perspective from which to discriminate, to judge. In Meditation I, Descartes re-creates that state of utter entrapment, by luring the reader, first, through the continuities between madness and dreaming—that state each night when all of us lose our adult clarity and detachment—and then to the possibility that the whole of our existence may be like a dream, a grand illusion so encompassing that there is no conceivable perspective from which to judge its correspondence with reality. The difference, of course, is that in childhood, we *assumed* that what we felt was a measure of external reality; now, as mature Cartesian doubters, we reverse that prejudice. We assume nothing. We refuse to let our bodies mystify us. And we begin afresh, as pure minds.

This reading of the *Meditations* suggests that a long-standing issue for Cartesian scholars may be founded on a mistake about the nature of Descartes's epistemological program. From Gassendi and Leibniz to Prichard, Ashworth, and Gewirth, commentators have criticized and wrestled with the seeming lack of "objective" criteria for the clearness and distinctness of ideas; with the seeming need for a method, as Gassendi put it, "which will direct and show us when we are in error and when not, so often as we think that we clearly and distinctly perceive anything" (HR, II, 152). Gassendi was struck, as Montaigne had been before him, by the vicissitudes of human certainty and the tenacity with which people may cling to their ever-shifting convictions. He was impressed with, and reminded Descartes of, the number of people willing to die for false beliefs, beliefs that those people presumably perceived as true. Descartes's answer—that he has *supplied* the needed method of discrimination in the procedure of the *Meditations,* "where I first laid aside all prejudices, and afterward enumerated all the chief ideas, distinguishing the clear from the obscure and confused" (HR, II, 214)—did not satisfy Gassendi. It seemed to him to beg the question, like many of Descartes's replies to his critics. Descartes, for his part, was unimpressed with Gassendi's example of those who face death for the sake of (possibly false) opinions, because "it can never be proved that they clearly and distinctly perceive what they pertinaciously affirm" (HR, II, 214). Is Descartes's reasoning hopelessly circular, as Ashworth, following Gassendi, claims (p. 102)?

I would suggest that when Descartes tells Gassendi that he has "attended" to the problem of "finding a method for deciding whether we err or not when we think that we perceive something clearly" (HR, II, 214), he does *not* mean that he believes himself to have supplied criteria for the clearness and distinctness of ideas. He has "attended" to the problem, rather, by supplying "rules for the direction of the mind" (read: rules for the transcendence of the body) that will prepare the mind to be swayed by nothing but the peculiar coerciveness of ideas, that will methodically eliminate all seductions except for the purely intellectual. Once that state of mental readiness has been achieved (something one can only know for oneself. Descartes would insist), the mind's *subjective* responses—its convictions—can be trusted. While Gassendi and other critics have complained of the lack of an "objective" test of ideas, Descartes, I propose, was up to something entirely different: He was offering a program of purification and training—for the liberation of *res cogitans* from the confusion and obscurity of its bodily swamp.

THE CARTESIAN WAY WITH DUALISM

Disdain for the body, the conception of it as an alien force and an impediment to the soul, is, of course, very old in our Greco-Christian traditions. Descartes was not the first philosopher to charge the body with responsibility for obscurity and confusion in our thinking. Rather, as Plato says in the *Phaedo,* ". . . it is characteristic of the philosopher to despise the body" (65). And, according to Plato, this disdain is well-founded: "A source of countless distractions by reason of the mere requirement of food, liable also to diseases which overtake and impede us in the pursuit of truth: [the body] fills us full of loves, and lusts, and fears, and fancies of all kinds, and endless foolery, and in very truth, as men say, takes away from us the power of thinking at all" (66c).

Descartes, then, was not the first philosopher to view the body with disdain. Platonic and neo-Platonic thought, and the Christian traditions that grew out of them, all exhibit such a strain. Nor was Descartes the first to view human existence as bifurcated into the realms of the physical and the spiritual, with the physical cast in the role of the alien and impure. For Plato, the body is often described via the imagery of separateness from the self: It is "fastened and glued" to me, "nailed" and "riveted" to me (83d). Images of the body-as-confinement from which the soul struggles to escape—"prison," "cage"—abound in Plato, as they do in Descartes. For Plato, as for Augustine later, the body is the locus of all that which threatens our attempts at control. It overtakes, it overwhelms, it erupts and disrupts. This situation becomes an incitement to battle the unruly forces of the body. Although less methodically than Descartes, Plato provides instruction on how to gain control over the body, how to achieve intellectual independence from the lure of its illusions and become impervious to its distractions. A central theme of the *Phaedo,* in fact, is the philosopher's training in developing such independence from the body.

But while dualism runs deep in our traditions, it is only with Descartes that body and mind are *defined* in terms of mutual exclusivity. For Plato (and Aristotle), the living body is permeated with soul, which can only depart the body at death. For Descartes, on the other hand, soul and body become two distinct substances. The body is pure *res extensa*—unconscious, extended stuff, brute materiality. "Every kind of thought which exists in us," he says in the *Passions of the Soul,* "belongs to the soul" (HR, I, 332). The soul, on the other hand, is pure *res cogitans*—mental, incorporeal, without location, *bodyless:* ". . . in its nature entirely independent of body, and not in any way derived from the power of matter" *(Discourse,* HR, I, 118).

The mutual exclusivity of mind and body has important consequences. Plato's and Aristotle's view that "soul" is a principle of life is one which

Descartes takes great pains to refute in the *Passions of the Soul.* For Descartes, rather, the "life" of the body is a matter of purely mechanical functioning.

> [W]e may judge that the body of a living man differs from that of a dead man just as does a watch or other automaton (i.e., a machine that moves of itself), when it is wound up and contains in itself the corporeal principle of those movements for which it is designated along with all that is requisite for its action, from the same watch or other machine when it is broken and when the principle of its movement ceases to act (HR, I, 333).

While the body is thus likened to a machine, the mind (having been conceptually purified of all material "contamination") is defined by precisely and only those qualities which the human being shares with God: freedom, will, consciousness. For Descartes there is no ambiguity or complexity here. The body is excluded from all participation, all connection with God; the soul alone represents the godliness and the goodness of the human being.

In Plato and Aristotle, the lines simply cannot be drawn in so stark a fashion. In the *Symposium,* we should remember, the love of the body is the first, and necessary, step on the spiritual ladder which leads to the glimpsing of the eternal form of beauty. For the Greek philosophers, the body is not simply an impediment to knowledge; it may also function as a spur to spiritual growth. Its passions may motivate the quest for knowledge and beauty. Moreover, since soul is inseparable from body except at death, any human aspirations to intellectual "purity" during one's lifetime are merely wishful fantasy. "While in company with the body the soul cannot have pure knowledge," Plato unequivocally declares in the *Phaedo.*

For the Greeks, then, there are definite limits to the human intellect. For Descartes, on the other hand, epistemological hubris knows few bounds.[10] The dream of purity is realizable during one's lifetime. For, given the right method, one can transcend the body. This is, of course, what Descartes believed himself to have accomplished in the *Meditations.* Addressing Gassendi as "O flesh!" he describes himself as "a mind so far withdrawn from corporeal things that it does not even know that anyone has existed before it" (HR, II, 214).

That such a radical program of mental purification is so central to the Cartesian epistemological program is not surprising. For, the body is not only the organ of the deceptive senses, and the site of disruption and "commotion" in the heart, blood, and animal spirits. It is also the most brute, pressing and ubiquitous reminder of how *located* and perspectival our experience and thought is, how bounded in time and space. "Birth, the past, contingency, the necessity of a point of view . . . such is the body," says Sartre. The Cartesian knower, on the other hand, being without a body, not only has "no need of any place" (*Discourse,* HR, I, p. 101) but actually is "no place." He[11] therefore cannot "grasp" the universe—which would demand a place "outside" the whole. But, assured of his own transparency, he can relate with absolute neutrality to the objects he surveys, unfettered by the perspectival nature of embodied vision. He has become, quite literally, *"objective."*

Not only, in this way, is the spectre of "subjectivity" laid to rest, but the very impersonality of the post-Copernican universe is turned to human advantage. For impersonality has become the mark of the truth of the known. Resistant to human will, immune to every effort of the knower to make it what *he* would have it be rather than what it "is," purified of all "inessential" spiritual associations and connections with the rest of the universe, the clear and distinct idea is both compensation for and conqueror of the cold, new world.

NOTES

1. Even to assert the fact of infinity, for Descartes, is to transcend the bounds of human knowledge. For, although it "is impossible to prove or even to conceive that there are bounds to the matter of which the world is made," there may nonetheless

be limits "which are known to God though inconceivable to me" (PL, 221). The most we can say about the extent of the universe is that it is "from [our] own point of view . . . indefinite"; only God can be "positively conceive[d] as infinite" (PL, 242), since this infinity is necessarily contained in his essence. And even the "positive" knowledge that God is infinite does not entail the ability to "grasp" the infinite. For, although we are certain that God, unlike the universe, can have no limits (*Principle* XXVII, HR, I, 230):

> . . . our soul, being finite, cannot comprehend or conceive Him. In the same way we can touch a mountain with our hands but we cannot put our arms around it as we could put them around a tree or something else not too large for them. To comprehend something is to embrace it in one's thought; to know something it is sufficient to touch it with one's thought (To Mersenne, May 27, 1630, PL, 15. See also Reply, I, II, 18).

By virtue of our finitude, then—although we can "touch" the infinite with our thought—we can neither completely comprehend the scope of the universe nor can we comprehend the infinite *qua* infinite. Neither of these limitations disturbs Descartes; indeed, they are essential to his system: If the human being's comprehension were *not* limited, neither of the third Meditation's proofs of the existence of God could gain a foothold. For, the proof from the idea of God depends upon my recognition that I lack the formal reality (infinite goodness, wisdom, and power) required for *me* to be the cause of the idea of a being with such qualities. And the "causal" argument depends upon the same recognition, but as entailing the necessity of postulating something other than *me* as the cause of myself (for if it had been me, why would I have created myself so imperfect?) (HR, I, 168).

2. Mary Douglas (1966, 1982) has written of the frequency with which social orders are demarcated into a pure "us" and a taboo "them" group. The strategy not only allows the projection of responsibility for disorder onto the outsider group, it also, as Richard Sennet has emphasized, confers the illusion of stable identity and

solidarity on the insider group—"the pleasure in recognizing 'us' and 'who we are' " (p. 31). Bruce Wilshire, in a profound and insightful study of the development of professionalism in academia, has explored how these dynamics function, albeit in disguised and mystified form, in the extreme insularity of professional academic disciplines (*Professionalism and the Eclipse of University Teaching: Dynamics of Purification and Exclusion,* manuscript in progress).

3. *The Cartesian Doctrine of Freedom.* See Kenny, 1972, p.8.

4. To exonerate God from responsibility for error, as Kenny points out, it would have been sufficient for Descartes to have made judgment a *voluntary* act of the intellect (as walking is a voluntary act of the body). He needn't have gone so far as to make it an act of the *will.* Imagining and conceiving, for example, appear to be such voluntary acts of the intellect for Descartes. They require the participation of the will (see *Passions of the Soul,* HR, I, 340; PL, 177–78), but are not themselves *acts* of the will. Judgment is, and Kenny puzzles over this, suggesting that it may have something to do with Descartes's desire to preserve a continuity between error and moral fault (1972, p. 8). Without disagreeing with this, I want to note that if the exoneration of the *intellect* is an aim of the fourth Meditation, this could *not* be accomplished by making judgment a voluntary act of the intellect. It requires a "relocation" of the sources of error to an arena distinct from the intellect.

5. "Dirt-affirming" philosophies, by contrast, are those within whose system everything actual has a function. For James, Hegel is the paradigm example of this (Douglas, 1982, p. 164).

6. There has been a scholarly debate about whether this capacity of clear and distinct ideas to "determine" the will is in tension with the Cartesian doctrine of the will as infinite. Kenny (1972, p. 8) and Williams (p. 180) see this as a genuine tension. Hiram Caton, on the other hand, resolves the apparent contradiction by noting that for Descartes, truth and falsity are not "symmetrical values in a binary matrix" (p. 92). Rather, he maintains, Descartes holds to a *rationalist* theory of truth, in which "judgement plays no role" and "clear ideas are known to be true *per se,*" and a *voluntarist* theory of error, in which judgment is required for the commission of error (p. 93). Although I do not wish to comment on this debate as such, my own reading of the fourth Meditation, as presented in this essay, can be seen to have a greater affinity with Caton's views on the matter.

7. These function in the context of epistemological "purification rituals" for authors other than Descartes, too. Evelyn Fox Keller, in her inspired and fascinating reading of Bacon's *Masculine Birth of Time,* attempts to correct the popular misconception that seventeenth-century science is *only* about aggression and control of nature, by focusing on Bacon's model of mind, which, like Descartes's, emphasizes the ideals of *submissiveness* and *receptivity* to the "true native rays" of things. To achieve this receptivity, however, requires that the mind first purify and cleanse *itself* of "idols" and "false preconceptions." As Keller describes Bacon's project:

> To receive God's truth, the mind must be pure and clean, submissive and open. Only then can it give birth to a masculine and virile science. That is, if the mind is pure, receptive, and submissive in its relation with God, it can be transformed by God into a forceful, potent, and virile agent in its relation to nature. Cleansed of contamination, the mind can be impregnated by God and, in that act, virilized: made potent and capable of generating virile offspring in its union with Nature (p. 38).

8. Although Descartes maintains that the emotions can "indirectly" be governed by the will (e.g., through the decision to try to "reason through" or talk oneself out of a particular fear [I, 352]), we can never simply will ourselves *not* to be afraid, or depressed, or jealous. Once an emotion is experienced, "the most that the will can do . . . is not to yield to its effects and to restrain many of the movements to which it disposes the body" (I, 252).

9. Phenomenologically, the distinguishing feature of acts of the pure intellect is, besides their lack of imagic content (PL, 107), that they formed through *reflection of the mind on itself* (see to Mersenne, October 16, 1639, PL, 66). This is not to say that they are formed through reflection on *thinking.* Rather, the exercise of pure intellect

is an inquiry into the *ideas* of the mind (e.g., of the idea of the wax, of the self, of God, of mind, of body). It is an investigation which sets as its goal what the mind *cannot conceive* the object in question as being without, lest the object cease to be what it is (Gewirth, 1955, pp. 271–273). This, determined through a rigorous series of "reductions," as Gewirth calls them, in which the mind has "reduced [ideas] to their elements and tried to separate and combine them in various ways" will be the essence of the object, its "true and immutable nature" (in Doney, 276). (Thus, God cannot be conceived without existence, nor wax without extension, nor myself without thought, etc.)

This operation, if performed successfully, will result in the conviction that the mind has reached the limits of its freedom of imagination and will: It will find itself coerced and compelled "by the internal meaning of ideas" (Gewirth, 1955, p. 274). But it is important to note that the culminating compulsion is reached as a result of an arduous and deliberately undertaken process; the mind must *subject* itself to the coerciveness exercised by the internal meanings of ideas. To do this it has to learn to "see" with *its* eye and not that of the body.

10. See endnote #1 for a discussion of the Cartesian limits to human understanding.
11. The male pronoun is the appropriate one here.

LOVE AND KNOWLEDGE: EMOTION IN FEMINIST EPISTEMOLOGY

Alison M. Jaggar

INTRODUCTION: EMOTION IN WESTERN EPISTEMOLOGY

Within the western philosophical tradition, emotions usually have been considered as potentially or actually subversive of knowledge.[1] From Plato until the present, with a few notable exceptions, reason rather than emotion has been regarded as the indispensable faculty for acquiring knowledge.[2]

Typically, although again not invariably, the rational has been contrasted with the emotional, and this contrasted pair then often has been linked with other dichotomies. Not only has reason been contrasted with emotion, but it has also been associated with the mental, the cultural, the universal, the public and the male, whereas emotion has been associated with the irrational, the physical, the natural, the particular, the private, and of course, the female.

Although western epistemology has tended to give pride of place to reason rather than emotion, it has not always excluded emotion completely from the realm of reason. In the *Phaedrus*, Plato portrayed emotions, such as anger or curiosity, as irrational urges (horses) that must always be controlled by reason (the charioteer). On this model, the emotions did not need to be totally suppressed, but rather needed to be directed by reason: for example, in a genuinely threatening situation, it was thought not irrational but foolhardy not to be afraid.[3] The split between reason and emotion was not absolute, therefore, for the Greeks. Instead, the emotions were thought to provide indispensable motive power that needed to be channeled appropriately. Without horses, after all, the skill of the charioteer would be worthless.

The contrast between reason and emotion was sharpened in the seventeenth century by redefining reason as a purely instrumental faculty. For both the Greeks and the medieval philosophers, reason had been linked with value insofar as reason provided access to the objective structure or order of reality, seen as simultaneously natural and morally justified. With the rise of modern science, however, the realms of nature and value were separated: nature was stripped of value and reconceptualized as an inanimate mechanism of no intrinsic worth. Values were relocated in human beings, rooted in human preferences and emotional responses. The separation of supposedly natural fact from human value meant that reason, if it were to provide trustworthy insight into reality, had to be uncontaminated by or abstracted from value. Increasingly, therefore, though never universally,[4] reason was reconceptualized as the ability to make valid inferences from premises established elsewhere, the ability to calculate means but not to determine ends. The validity of logical inferences was thought independent of human attitudes and preferences; this was now the sense in which reason was taken to be objective and universal.[5]

The modern redefinition of rationality required a corresponding reconceptualization of emotion. This was achieved by portraying emotions as nonrational and often irrational urges that regularly swept the body, rather as a storm sweeps over the land. The common way of referring to the emotions as the "passions" emphasized that emotions happened to or were imposed upon an individual, something she suffered rather than something she did.

The epistemology associated with this new ontology rehabilitated sensory perception that, like emotion, typically had been suspected or even discounted by the western tradition as a reliable source of knowledge. British empiricism, succeeded in the nineteenth century by positivism, took its epistemological task to be the formulation of rules of inference that would guarantee the derivation of certain knowledge from the "raw data" supposedly given directly to the senses. Empirical testability became accepted as the hallmark of natural science; this, in turn, was viewed as the paradigm of genuine knowledge. Epistemology often was equated

with the philosophy of science, and the dominant methodology of positivism prescribed that truly scientific knowledge must be capable of intersubjective verification. Because values and emotions had been defined as variable and idiosyncratic, positivism stipulated that trustworthy knowledge could be established only by methods that neutralized the values and emotions of individual scientists.

Recent approaches to epistemology have challenged some fundamental assumptions of the positivist epistemological model. Contemporary theorists of knowledge have undermined once-rigid distinctions between analytic and synthetic statements, between theories and observations and even between facts and values. Thus far, however, few challenged the purported gap between emotion and knowledge. In this essay, I wish to begin bridging this gap through the suggestion that emotions may be helpful and even necessary rather than inimical to the construction of knowledge. My account is exploratory in nature and leaves many questions unanswered. It is not supported by irrefutable arguments or conclusive proofs; instead, it should be viewed as a preliminary sketch for an epistemological model that will require much further development before its workability can be established.

EMOTION

What Are Emotions?

The philosophical question, "What are emotions?" requires both explicating the ways in which people ordinarily speak about emotion and evaluating the adequacy of those ways for expressing and illuminating experience and activity. Several problems confront someone trying to answer this deceptively simple question. One set of difficulties results from the variety, complexity, and even inconsistency of the ways in which emotions are viewed, both in daily life and in scientific contexts. It is in part this variety that makes emotions into a "question" and at the same time precludes answering that question by simple appeal to ordinary usage. A second difficulty is the wide range of phenomena covered by the term "emotion": these extend from apparently instantaneous "knee-jerk" responses of fright to lifelong dedication to an individual or a cause; from highly civilized aesthetic responses to undifferentiated feelings of hunger and thirst,[6] from background moods such as contentment or depression to intense and focused involvement in an immediate situation. It may well be impossible to construct a manageable account of emotion to cover such apparently diverse phenomena.

A further problem concerns the criteria for preferring one account of emotion to another. The more one learns about the ways in which other cultures conceptualize human faculties, the less plausible it becomes that emotions constitute what philosophers call a "natural kind." Not only do some cultures identify emotions unrecognized in the west, but there is reason to believe that the concept of emotion itself is a historical invention, like the concept of intelligence (Lewontin 1982) or even the concept of mind (Rorty 1979). For instance, anthropologist Catherine Lutz argues that the "dichotomous categories of 'cognition' and 'affect' are themselves Euroamerican cultural constructions, master symbols that participate in the fundamental organization of our ways of looking at ourselves and others, both in and outside of social science" (Lutz 1987: 308, citing Lutz 1985, 1986). If this is true, then we have even more reason to wonder about the adequacy of ordinary western ways of talking about emotion. Yet we have no access either to our own emotions or to those of others independent of or unmediated by the discourse of our culture.

In the face of these difficulties, I shall sketch an account of emotion with the following limitations. First, it will operate within the context of western discussions of emotion: I shall not question, for instance, whether it would be possible or desirable to dispense entirely with anything

resembling our concept of emotion. Second, although this account attempts to be consistent with as much as possible of western understandings of emotion, it is intended to cover only a limited domain, not every phenomenon that may be called an emotion. On the contrary, it excludes as genuine emotions both automatic physical responses and nonintentional sensations, such as hunger pangs. Third, I do not pretend to offer a complete theory of emotion; instead, I focus on a few specific aspects of emotion that I take to have been neglected or misrepresented, especially in positivist and neopositivist accounts. Finally, I would defend my approach not only on the ground that it illuminates aspects of our experience and activity that are obscured by positivist and neopositivist construals but also on the ground that it is less open than these to ideological abuse. In particular, I believe that recognizing certain neglected aspects of emotion makes possible a better and less ideologically biased account of how knowledge is, and so ought to be, constructed.

Emotions as Intentional

Early positivist approaches to understanding emotion assumed that an adequate account required analytically separating emotion from other human faculties. Just as positivist accounts of sense perception attempted to distinguish the supposedly raw data of sensation from their cognitive interpretations, so positivist accounts of emotion tried to separate emotion conceptually from both reason and sense perception. As one way of sharpening these distinctions, positivist construals of emotion tended to identify emotions with the physical feelings or involuntary bodily movements that typically accompany them, such as pangs or qualms, flushes or tremors; emotions were also assimilated to the subduing of physiological function or movement, as in the case of sadness, depression, or boredom. The continuing influence of such supposedly scientific conceptions of emotion can be seen in the fact that "feeling" is often used colloquially as a synonym for emotion, even though the more central meaning of "feeling" is physiological sensation. On such accounts, emotions were not seen as being *about* anything; instead, they were contrasted with and seen as potential disruptions of other phenomena that *are* about some thing, phenomena such as rational judgments, thoughts, and observations. The positivist approach to understanding emotion has been called the Native View (Spelman 1982).

The Native View of emotion is quite untenable. For one thing, the same feeling or physiological response is likely to be interpreted as various emotions, depending on the context of experience. This point often is illustrated by reference to the famous Schachter and Singer experiment; excited feelings were induced in research subjects by the injection of adrenalin, and the subjects then attributed to themselves appropriate emotions depending on their context (Schachter and Singer 1969). Another problem with the Native View is that identifying emotions with feelings would make it impossible to postulate that a person might not be aware of her emotional state, because feelings by definition are a matter of conscious awareness. Finally, emotions differ from feelings, sensations, or physiological responses in that they are dispositional rather than episodic. For instance, we may assert truthfully that we are outraged by, proud of, or saddened by certain events, even if at that moment we are neither agitated nor tearful.

In recent years, contemporary philosophers have tended to reject the Native View of emotion and have substituted more intentional or cognitivist understandings. These newer conceptions emphasize that intentional judgments as well as physiological disturbances are integral elements in emotion.[7] They define or identify emotions not by the quality or character of the physiological sensation that may be associated with them but rather by their intentional aspect, the associated judgment. Thus, it is the content of my associated thought or judgment that determines whether my

physical agitation and restlessness are defined as "anxiety about my daughter's lateness" rather than as "anticipation of tonight's performance."

Cognitivist accounts of emotion have been criticized as overly rationalist and inapplicable to allegedly spontaneous, automatic, or global emotions, such as general feelings of nervousness, contentedness, angst, ecstasy, or terror. Certainly, these accounts entail that infants and animals experience emotions, if at all, in only a primitive, rudimentary form. Far from being unacceptable, however, this entailment is desirable because it suggests that humans develop and mature in emotions as well as in other dimensions, increasing the range, variety and subtlety of their emotional responses in accordance with their life experiences and their reflections on these.

Cognitivist accounts of emotion are not without their own problems. A serious difficulty with many is that they end up replicating within the structure of emotion the very problem they are trying to solve—namely, that of an artificial split between emotion and thought—because most cognitivist accounts explain emotion as having two "components": an affective or feeling component and a cognition that supposedly interprets or identifies the feelings. Such accounts, therefore, unwittingly perpetuate the positivist distinction between the shared, public, objective world of verifiable calculations, observations, and facts, and the individual, private, subjective world of idiosyncratic feelings and sensations. This sharp distinction breaks any conceptual links between our feelings and the "external" world: if feelings still are conceived as blind or raw or undifferentiated, then we can give no sense to the notion of feelings fitting or failing to fit our perceptual judgments, that is, being appropriate or inappropriate. When intentionality is viewed as intellectual cognition and moved to the center of our picture of emotion, the affective elements are pushed to the periphery and become shadowy conceptual danglers whose relevance to emotion is obscure or even negligible. An adequate cognitive account of emotion must overcome this problem.

Most cognitivist accounts of emotion thus remain problematic insofar as they fail to explain the relation between the cognitive and the affective aspects of emotion. Moreover, insofar as they prioritize the intellectual aspect over feelings, they reinforce the traditional western preference for mind over body.[8] Nevertheless, they do identify a vital feature of emotion overlooked by the Native View—namely, its intentionality.

Emotions as Social Constructs

We tend to experience our emotions as involuntary individual responses to situations, responses that are often (though, significantly, not always) private in the sense that they are not perceived as directly and immediately by other people as they are by the subject of the experience. The apparently individual and involuntary character of our emotional experience often is taken as evidence that emotions are presocial, instinctive responses, determined by our biological constitution. This inference, however, is quite mistaken. Although it is probably true that the physiological disturbances characterizing emotions (facial grimaces, changes in the metabolic rate, sweating, trembling, tears and so on) are continuous with the instinctive responses of our prehuman ancestors, and also that the ontogeny of emotions to some extent recapitulates their phylogeny, mature human emotions are neither instinctive nor biologically determined. Instead, they are socially constructed on several levels.

The most obvious way in which emotions are socially constructed is that children are taught deliberately what their culture defines as appropriate responses to certain situations: to fear strangers, to enjoy spicy food, or to like swimming in cold water. On a less conscious level, children also learn what their culture defines as the appropriate ways to express the emotions that it recognizes. Although there may be cross-cultural similarities in the expression of some apparently universal emotions, there are also wide divergences in what are recognized as expressions of grief, respect, contempt, or anger. On an even deeper level, cultures construct divergent understandings of what emotions are. For instance, English metaphors and metonymies are said to reveal a "folk" theory of anger as a hot fluid contained in a private space within an individual and liable to dangerous public explosion (Lakoff and Kovecses 1987). By contrast, the Ilongot, a people of the Philippines, apparently do not understand the self in terms of a public/private distinction and consequently do not experience anger as an explosive internal force: for them, rather, it is an interpersonal phenomenon for which an individual may, for instance, be paid (Rosaldo 1984).

Further aspects of the social construction of emotion are revealed through reflection on emotion's intentional structure. If emotions necessarily involve judgments, then obviously they require concepts, which may be seen as socially constructed ways of organizing and making sense of the world. For this reason, emotions simultaneously are made possible and limited by the conceptual and linguistic resources of a society. This philosophical claim is borne out by empirical observation of the cultural variability of emotion. Although there is considerable overlap in the emotions identified by many cultures (Wierzbicka 1986), at least some emotions are historically or culturally specific, including perhaps *ennui, angst,* the Japanese *amai* (in which one clings to another, affiliative love) and the response of "being a wild pig," which occurs among the Gururumba, a horticultural people living in the New Guinea Highlands (Averell 1980: 158). Even apparently universal emotions, such as anger or love, may vary crossculturally. We have just seen that the Ilongot experience of anger apparently is quite different from the contemporary western experience. Romantic love was invented in the Middle Ages in Europe and since that time has been modified considerably; for instance, it is no longer confined to the nobility, and it no longer needs to be extramarital or unconsummated. In some cultures, romantic love does not exist at all.[9]

Thus there are complex linguistic and other social preconditions for the experience, that is, for the existence of human emotions. The emotions that we experience reflect prevailing forms of social life. For instance, one could not feel or even be betrayed in the absence of social norms about fidelity: it is inconceivable that betrayal or indeed any distinctively human emotion could be experienced by a solitary individual in some hypothetical presocial state of nature. There is a sense in which any individual's guilt or anger, joy or triumph, presupposes the existence of a social group capable of feeling guilt, anger, joy, or triumph. This is not to say that group emotions historically precede or are logically prior to the emotions of individuals; it is to say that individual experience is simultaneously social experience.[10] In later sections, I shall explore the epistemological and political implications of this social rather than individual understanding of emotion.

Emotions as Active Engagements

We often interpret our emotions as experiences that overwhelm us rather than as responses we consciously choose: that emotions are to some extent involuntary is part of the ordinary meaning of the term "emotion." Even in daily life, however, we recognize that emotions are not entirely involuntary and we try to gain control over them in various ways, ranging from mechanistic behavior modification techniques designed to sensitize or desensitize our feeling responses to various situations to cognitive techniques designed to help us think differently about situations. For instance, we might try to change our response to an upsetting situation by thinking about it in a way that will either divert our attention from its more painful aspects or present it as necessary for some larger good.

Some psychological theories interpret emotions as chosen on an even deeper level, interpreting them as actions for which the agent disclaims responsibility. For instance, the psychologist

Averell likens the experience of emotion to playing a culturally recognized role: we ordinarily perform so smoothly and automatically that we do not realize we are giving a performance. He provides many examples demonstrating that even extreme and apparently totally involving displays of emotion in fact are functional for the individual and/or the society.[11] For example, when students were asked to record their experiences of anger or annoyance over a two-week period, they came to realize that their anger was not as uncontrollable and irrational as they had assumed previously, and they noted the usefulness and effectiveness of anger in achieving various social goods. Averell, notes, however, that emotions often are useful in attaining their goals only if they are interpreted as passions rather than as actions. He cites the case of one subject led to reflect on her anger, who later wrote that it was less useful as a defense mechanism when she became conscious of its function.

The action/passion dichotomy is too simple for understanding emotion, as it is for other aspects of our lives. Perhaps it is more helpful to think of emotions as habitual responses that we may have more or less difficulty in breaking. We claim or disclaim responsibility for these responses depending on our purposes in a particular context. We could never experience our emotions entirely as deliberate actions, for then they would appear nongenuine and inauthentic, but neither should emotions be seen as nonintentional, primal, or physical forces with which our rational selves are forever at war. As they have been socially constructed, so may they be reconstructed, although describing how this might happen would require a long and complicated story.

Emotions, then, are wrongly seen as necessarily passive or involuntary responses to the world. Rather, they are ways in which we engage actively and even construct the world. They have both "mental" and "physical" aspects, each of which conditions the other; in some respects, they are chosen, but in others they are involuntary; they presuppose language and a social order. Thus, they can be attributed only to what are sometimes called "whole persons," engaged in the ongoing activity of social life.

Emotion, Evaluation and Observation

Emotions and values are closely related. The relation is so close, indeed, that some philosophical accounts of what it is to hold or express certain values reduce these phenomena to nothing more than holding or expressing certain emotional attitudes. When the relevant conception of emotion is the Native View, then simple emotivism certainly is too crude an account of what it is to hold a value; on this account, the intentionality of value judgments vanishes and value judgments become nothing more than sophisticated grunts and groans. Nevertheless, the grain of important truth in emotivism is its recognition that values presuppose emotions to the extent that emotions provide the experiential basis for values. If we had no emotional responses to the world, it is inconceivable that we should ever come to value one state of affairs more highly than another.

Just as values presuppose emotions, so emotions presuppose values. The object of an emotion—that is, the object of fear, grief, pride, and so on—is a complex state of affairs that is appraised or evaluated by the individual. For instance, my pride in a friend's achievement necessarily incorporates the value judgment that my friend has done something worthy of admiration.

Emotions and evaluations, then, are logically or conceptually connected. Indeed, many evaluative terms derive directly from words for emotions: "desirable," "admirable," "contemptible," "despicable," "respectable," and so on. Certainly it is true (pace J. S. Mill) that the evaluation of a situation as desirable or dangerous does not entail it is universally desired or feared but it does entail that desire (or fear) is viewed generally as an appropriate response to the situation. If someone is unafraid in a situation generally perceived as dangerous, her lack of fear requires further explanation; conversely, if someone is afraid without evident danger, then her fear is denounced as irrational or pathological. Thus, every emotion presupposes an evaluation of some aspect of the environment while, conversely, every evaluation or appraisal of the situation implies that those who share that evaluation will share, *ceteris paribus,* a predictable emotional response to the situation.

The rejection of the Native View and the recognition of intentional elements in emotion already incorporate a realization that observation influences and indeed partially constitutes emotion. We have seen already that distinctively human emotions are not simple instinctive responses to situations or events; instead, they depend essentially on the ways that we perceive those situations and events, as well on the ways that we have learned or decided to respond to them. Without characteristically human perceptions of and engagements in the world, there would be no characteristically human emotions.

Just as observation directs, shapes, and partially defines emotion, so too emotion directs, shapes, and even partially defines observation. Observation is not simply a passive process of absorbing impressions or recording stimuli; instead, it is an activity of selection and interpretation. What is selected and how it is interpreted are influenced by emotional attitudes. On the level of individual observation, this influence always has been apparent to common sense, which notes that we remark very different features of the world when we are happy, depressed, fearful, or confident. Social scientists are now exploring this influence of emotion on perception. One example is the so-called Honi phenomenon, named after the subject Honi who, under identical experimental conditions, perceived strangers' heads as changing in size but saw her husband's head as remaining the same.[12]

The most obvious significance of this sort of example is to illustrate how the individual experience of emotion focuses our attention selectively, directing, shaping and even partially defining our observations, just as our observations direct, shape and partially define our emotions. In addition, the example argues for the social construction of what are taken in any situation to be undisputed facts. It shows how these facts rest on intersubjective agreements that consist partly in shared assumptions about "normal" or appropriate emotional responses to situations (McLaughlin 1985). Thus these examples suggest that certain emotional attitudes are involved on a deep level in all observation, in the intersubjectively verified and so supposedly dispassionate observations of science as well as in the common perceptions of daily life. In the next section, I shall elaborate this claim.

EPISTEMOLOGY

The Myth of Dispassionate Investigation

As we have seen already, western epistemology has tended to view emotion with suspicion and even hostility.[13] This derogatory western attitude towards emotion, like the earlier western contempt for sensory observation, fails to recognize that emotion, like sensory perception, is necessary to human survival. Emotions prompt us to act appropriately, to approach some people and situations and to avoid others, to caress or cuddle, fight or flee. Without emotion, human life would be unthinkable. Moreover, emotions have an intrinsic as well as an instrumental value. Although not all emotions are enjoyable or even justifiable, as we shall see, life without any emotion would be life without any meaning.

Within the context of western culture, however, people often have been encouraged to control or even suppress their emotions. Consequently, it is not unusual for people to be unaware of their emotional state or to deny it to themselves and others. This lack of awareness, especially combined with a neopositivist understanding of emotion that construes it just as a feeling of which one is aware, lends plausibility to the myth of dispassionate investigation. But lack of awareness of emotions certainly does not mean

that emotions are not present subconsciously or unconsciously, or that subterranean emotions do not exert a continuing influence on people's articulated values and observations, thoughts and actions.[14]

Within the positivist tradition, the influence of emotion usually is seen only as distorting or impeding observation or knowledge. Certainly it is true that contempt, disgust, shame, revulsion, or fear may inhibit investigation of certain situations or phenomena. Furiously angry or extremely sad people often seem quite unaware of their surroundings or even their own conditions; they may fail to hear or may systematically misinterpret what other people say. People in love are notoriously oblivious to many aspects of the situation around them.

In spite of these examples, however, positivist epistemology recognizes that the role of emotion in the construction of knowledge is not invariably deleterious and that emotions may make a valuable contribution to knowledge. But the positivist tradition will allow emotion to play only the role of suggesting hypotheses for emotion. Emotions are allowed this because the so-called logic of discovery sets no limits on the idiosyncratic methods that investigators may use for generating hypotheses.

When hypotheses are to be tested, however, positivist epistemology imposes the much stricter logic of justification. The core of this logic is replicability, a criterion believed capable of eliminating or cancelling out what are conceptualized as emotional as well as evaluative biases on the part of individual investigators. The conclusions of western science thus are presumed "objective," precisely in the sense that they are uncontaminated by the supposedly "subjective" values and emotions that might bias individual investigators (Nagel 1968: 33–4).

But if, as has been argued, the positivist distinction between discovery and justification is not viable, then such a distinction is incapable of filtering out values in science. For example, although such a split, when built into the western scientific method, generally is successful in neutralizing the idiosyncratic or unconventional values of individual investigators, it has been argued that it does not, indeed cannot, eliminate generally accepted social values. These values are implicit in the identification of the problems that are considered worthy of investigation, in the selection of the hypotheses that are considered worthy of testing, and in the solutions to the problems that are considered worthy of acceptance. The science of past centuries provides ample evidence of the influence of prevailing social values, whether seventeenth century atomistic physics (Merchant 1980) or nineteenth century competitive interpretations of natural selection (Young 1985).

Of course, only hindsight allows us to identify clearly the values that shaped the science of the past and thus to reveal the formative influence on science of pervasive emotional attitudes, attitudes that typically went unremarked at the time because they were shared so generally. For instance, it is now glaringly evident that contempt for (and perhaps fear of) people of color is implicit in nineteenth century anthropology's interpretations and even constructions of anthropological facts. Because we are closer to them, however, it is harder for us to see how certain emotions, such as sexual possessiveness or the need to dominate others, currently are accepted as guiding principles in twentieth century sociobiology or even defined as part of reason within political theory and economics (Quinby 1986).

Values and emotions enter into the science of the past and the present not only on the level of scientific practice but also on the metascientific level, as answers to various questions: What is science? How should it be practiced? And what is the status of scientific investigation versus nonscientific modes of enquiry? For instance, it is claimed with increasing frequency that the modern western conception of science, which identifies knowledge with power and views it as a weapon for dominating nature, reflects the imperialism, racism and misogyny of the societies that created it. Several feminist theorists have argued that modern epistemology itself may be viewed as an expression of certain emotions alleged to be especially characteristic of males in certain periods, such as separation anxiety and paranoia (Flax 1983; Bordo 1987) or an obsession with control and fear of contamination (Scheman 1985; Schott 1988).

Positivism views values and emotions as alien invaders that must be repelled by a stricter application of the scientific method. If the forgoing claims are correct, however, the scientific method and even its positivist construals themselves incorporate values and emotions. Moreover, such an incorporation seems a necessary feature of all knowledge and conceptions of knowledge. Therefore, rather than repressing emotion in epistemology it is necessary to rethink the relation between knowledge and emotion and construct a conceptual model that demonstrates the mutually constitutive rather than oppositional relation between reason and emotion. Far from precluding the possibility of reliable knowledge, emotion as well as value must be shown as necessary to such knowledge. Despite its classical antecedents and like the ideal of disinterested enquiry, the ideal of dispassionate enquiry is an impossible dream, but a dream nonetheless, or perhaps a myth that has exerted enormous influence on western epistemology. Like all myths, it is a form of ideology that fulfills certain social and political functions.

The Ideological Function of the Myth

So far, I have spoken very generally of people and their emotions, as though everyone experienced similar emotions and dealt with them in similar ways. It is an axiom of feminist theory, however, that all generalizations about "people" are suspect. The divisions in our society are so deep, particularly the divisions of race, class, and gender, that many feminist theorists would claim that talk about people in general is ideologically dangerous because such talk obscures the fact that no one is simply a person but instead is constituted fundamentally by race, class and gender.

Race, class, and gender shape every aspect of our lives, and our emotional constitution is not excluded. Recognizing this helps us to see more clearly the political functions of the myth of the dispassionate investigator.

Feminist theorists have pointed out that the western tradition has not seen everyone as equally emotional. Instead, reason has been associated with members of dominant political, social, and cultural groups and emotion with members of subordinate groups. Prominent among those subordinate groups in our society are people of color, except for supposedly "inscrutable orientals," and women.[15]

Although the emotionality of women is a familiar cultural stereotype, its grounding is quite shaky. Women appear to be more emotional than men because they, along with some groups of people of color, are permitted and even required to express emotion more openly. In contemporary western culture, emotionally inexpressive women are suspect as not being real women,[16] whereas men who express their emotions freely are suspected of being homosexual or in some other way deviant from the masculine ideal. Modern western men, in contrast with Shakespeare's heroes, for instance, are required to present a facade of coolness, lack of excitement, even boredom, to express emotion only rarely and then for relatively trivial events, such as sporting occasions, where the emotions expressed are acknowledged to be dramatized and so are not taken entirely seriously. Thus, women in our society form the main group allowed or even expected to feel emotion. A woman may cry in the face of disaster, and a man of color may gesticulate, but a white man merely sets his jaw.[17]

White men's control of their emotional expression may go to the extremes of repressing their emotions, failing to develop emotionally, or even losing the capacity to experience many emotions. Not uncommonly, these men are unable to identify what they are feeling, and even they may be surprised, on occasion, by their own apparent lack of emotional response to a situation, such as a death, where emotional reaction is perceived as appropriate. In some married couples, the wife implicitly is assigned the job of feeling emotion for both of them. White, college-educated men increasingly enter therapy in order to learn how to "get in touch with" their emotions, a project other men may ridicule as weakness. In therapeutic situations, men may learn that they are just as emotional as women but less adept at identifying their own or others' emotions. In consequence, their emotional development may be relatively rudimentary; this may lead to moral rigidity or insensitivity. Paradoxically, men's lacking awareness of their own emotional responses frequently results in their being more influenced by emotion rather than less.

Although there is no reason to suppose that the thoughts and actions of women are any more influenced by emotion than the thoughts and actions of men, the stereotypes of cool men and emotional women continue to flourish because they are confirmed by an uncritical daily experience. In these circumstances, where there is a differential assignment of reason and emotion, it is easy to see the ideological function of the myth of the dispassionate investigator. It functions, obviously, to bolster the epistemic authority of the currently dominant groups, composed largely of white men, and to discredit the observations and claims of the currently subordinate groups including, of course, the observations and claims of many people of color and women. The more forcefully and vehemently the latter groups express their observations and claims, the more emotional they appear and so the more easily they are discredited. The alleged epistemic authority of the dominant groups then justifies their political authority.

The previous section of this essay argued that dispassionate inquiry was a myth. This section has shown that the myth promotes a conception of epistemological justification vindicating the silencing of those, especially women, who are defined culturally as the bearers of emotion and so are perceived as more "subjective," biased, and irrational. In our present social context, therefore, the ideal of the dispassionate investigator is a classist, racist, and especially masculinist myth.[18]

Emotional Hegemony and Emotional Subversion

As we have seen already, mature human emotions are neither instinctive nor biologically determined, although they may have developed out of presocial, instinctive responses. Like everything else that is human, emotions in part are socially constructed; like all social constructs, they are historical products, bearing the marks of the society that constructed them. Within the very language of emotion, in our basic definitions and explanations of what it is to feel pride or embarrassment, resentment or contempt, cultural norms and expectations are embedded. Simply describing ourselves as angry, for instance, presupposes that we view ourselves as having been wronged, victimized by the violation of some social norm. Thus, we absorb the standards and values of our society in the very process of learning the language of emotion, and those standards and values are built into the foundation of our emotional constitution.

Within a hierarchical society, the norms and values that predominate tend to serve the interest of the dominant groups. Within a capitalist, white supremacist, and male-dominant society, the predominant values will tend to be those that serve the interests of rich white men. Consequently, we are all likely to develop an emotional constitution that is quite inappropriate for feminism. Whatever our color, we are likely to feel what Irving Thalberg has called "visceral racism"; whatever our sexual orientation, we are likely to be homophobic; whatever our class, we are likely to be at least somewhat ambitious and competitive; whatever our sex, we are likely to feel contempt for women. The emotional responses may be rooted in us so deeply that they are relatively impervious to intellectual argument and may recur even when we pay lip service to changed intellectual convictions.[19]

By forming our emotional constitution in particular ways, our society helps to ensure its own perpetuation. The dominant values are implicit in responses taken to be precultural or acultural, our so-called gut responses. Not only do these conservative responses hamper and disrupt our attempts to live in or prefigure alternative social forms but also, and insofar as we take them to be natural responses, they limit our vision theoretically. For instance, they limit our capacity for outrage; they either prevent us from despising or encourage us to despise; they lend plausibility to the belief that greed and domination are inevitable human motivations; in sum, they blind us to the possibility of alternative ways of living.

This picture may seem at first to support the positivist claim that the intrusion of emotion only disrupts the process of seeking knowledge and distorts the results of that process. The picture, however, is not complete; it ignores the fact that people do not always experience the conventionally acceptable emotions. They may feel satisfaction rather than embarrassment when their leaders make fools of themselves. They may feel resentment rather than gratitude for welfare payments and hand-me-downs. They may be attracted to forbidden modes of sexual expression. They may feel revulsion for socially sanctioned ways of treating children or animals. In other words, the hegemony that our society exercises over people's emotional constitution is not total.

People who experience conventionally unacceptable, or what I call "outlaw," emotions often are subordinated individuals who pay a disproportionately high price for maintaining the status quo. The social situation of such people makes them unable to experience the conventionally prescribed emotions: for instance, people of color are more likely to experience anger than amusement when a racist joke is recounted, and women subjected to male sexual banter are less likely to be flattered than uncomfortable or even afraid.

When unconventional emotional responses are experienced by isolated individuals, those concerned may be confused, unable to name their experience; they may even doubt their own sanity. Women may come to believe that they are "emotionally disturbed" and that the embarrassment or fear aroused in them by male sexual innuendo is prudery or paranoia. When certain emotions are shared or validated by others, however, the basis exists for forming a subculture defined by perceptions, norms, and values that systematically oppose the prevailing perceptions, norms, and values. By constituting the basis for such a subculture, outlaw emotions may be politically (because epistemologically) subversive.

Outlaw emotions are distinguished by their incompatibility with the dominant perceptions and values, and some, though certainly not all, of these outlaw emotions are potentially or actually feminist emotions. Emotions become feminist when they incorporate feminist perceptions and values, just as emotions are sexist or racist when they incorporate sexist or racist perceptions and values. For example, anger becomes feminist anger when it involves the perception that the persistent importuning endured by one woman is a single instance of a widespread pattern of sexual harassment, and pride becomes feminist pride when it is evoked by realizing that a certain person's achievement was possible only because that individual overcame specifically gendered obstacles to success.[20]

Outlaw emotions stand in a dialectical relation to critical social theory: at least some are necessary to developing a critical perspective on the world, but they also presuppose at least the beginnings of such a perspective. Feminists need to be aware of how we can draw on some of our outlaw emotions in constructing feminist theory and also of how the increasing sophistication of feminist theory can contribute to the reeducation, refinement, and eventual reconstruction of our emotional constitution.

Outlaw Emotions and Feminist Theory

The most obvious way in which feminist and other outlaw emotions can help in developing alternatives to prevailing conceptions of reality is by motivating new investigations. This is possible because, as we saw earlier, emotions may be long-term as well as momentary; it makes sense to say that someone continues to be shocked or saddened by a situation, even if she is at the moment laughing heartily. As we have seen already, theoretical investigation is always purposeful, and observation is always selective. Feminist emotions provide a political motivation for investigation and so help to determine the selection of problems as well as the method by which they are investigated. Susan Griffin makes the same point when she characterizes feminist theory as following "a direction determined by pain, and trauma, and compassion and outrage" (Griffin 1979:31).

As well as motivating critical research, outlaw emotions may also enable us to perceive the world differently than we would from its portrayal in conventional descriptions. They may provide the first indications that something is wrong with the way alleged facts have been constructed, with accepted understandings of how things are. Conventionally unexpected or inappropriate emotions may precede our conscious recognition that accepted descriptions and justifications often conceal as much as reveal the prevailing state of affairs. Only when we reflect on our initially puzzling irritability, revulsion, anger, or fear, may we bring to consciousness our "gut-level" awareness that we are in a situation of coercion, cruelty, injustice, or danger. Thus, conventionally inexplicable emotions, particularly, though not exclusively, those experienced by women, may lead us to make subversive observations that challenge dominant conceptions of the status quo. They may help us to realize that what are taken generally to be facts have been constructed in a way that obscures the reality of subordinated people, especially women's reality.

But why should we trust the emotional responses of women and other subordinated groups? How can we determine which outlaw emotions we should endorse or encourage and which reject? In what sense can we say that some emotional responses are more appropriate than others? What reason is there for supposing that certain alternative perceptions of the world, perceptions informed by outlaw emotions, are to be preferred to perceptions informed by conventional emotions? Here I can indicate only the general direction of an answer, whose full elaboration must await another occasion.[21]

I suggest that emotions are appropriate if they are characteristic of a society in which all humans (and perhaps some nonhuman life too) thrive, or if they are conducive to establishing such a society. For instance, it is appropriate to feel joy when we are developing or exercising our creative powers, and it is appropriate to feel anger and perhaps disgust in those situations where humans are denied their full creativity or freedom. Similarly, it is appropriate to feel fear if those capacities are threatened in us.

This suggestion obviously is extremely vague and may even verge on the tautological. How can we apply it in situations where there is disagreement over what is or is not disgusting or exhilarating or unjust? Here I appeal to a claim for which I have argued elsewhere: the perspective on reality that is available from the standpoint of the oppressed, which in part at least is the standpoint of women, is a perspective that offers a less partial and distorted and therefore more reliable view (Jaggar 1983: chap. 11). Oppressed people have a kind of epistemological privilege insofar as they have easier access to this standpoint and therefore a better chance of ascertaining the possible beginnings of a society in which all could thrive. For this reason, I would claim that the emotional responses of oppressed people in general, and often of women in particular, are more likely to be appropriate than the emotional responses of the dominant class. That is, they are more likely to incorporate reliable appraisals of situations.

Even in contemporary science, where the ideology of dispassionate inquiry is almost overwhelming, it is possible to discover a few examples that seem to support the claim that certain emotions are more appropriate than others in both a moral and epistemological sense. For instance, Hilary Rose claims that women's practice of caring, even though warped by its containment in the alienated context of a coercive sexual division of labor, nevertheless has generated more accurate and less oppressive understandings of women's bodily functions, such as menstruation (Rose 1983). Certain emotions may be both morally appropriate and epistemologically advantageous in approaching the nonhuman and even the inanimate world. Jane Goodall's scientific contribution to our understanding of chimpanzee behavior seems to have been made possible only by her amazing empathy with or even love for these animals (Goodall 1987). In her study of Barbara McClintock, Evelyn Fox Keller describes McClintock's relation to the objects of her research—grains of maize and their genetic properties—as a relation of affection, empathy and "the highest form of love: love that allows for intimacy without the annihilation of difference." She notes that McClintock's "vocabulary is consistently a vocabulary of affection, of kinship, of empathy" (Keller 1984:164). Examples like these prompt Hilary Rose to assert that a feminist science of nature needs to draw on heart as well as hand and brain.

Some Implications of Recognizing the Epistemic Potential of Emotion

Accepting that appropriate emotions are indispensable to reliable knowledge does not mean, of course, that uncritical feeling may be substituted for supposedly dispassionate investigation. Nor does it mean that the emotional responses of women and other members of the underclass are to be trusted without question. Although our emotions are epistemologically indispensable, they are not epistemologically indisputable. Like all our faculties, they may be misleading, and their data, like all data, are always subject to reinterpretation and revision. Because emotions are not presocial, physiological responses to unequivocal situations, they are open to challenge on various grounds. They may be dishonest or self-deceptive, they may incorporate inaccurate or partial perceptions, or they may be constituted by oppressive values. Accepting the indispensability of appropriate emotions to knowledge means no more (and no less) than that discordant emotions should be attended to seriously and respectfully rather than condemned, ignored, discounted, or suppressed.

Just as appropriate emotions may contribute to the development of knowledge so the growth of knowledge may contribute to the development of appropriate emotions. For instance, the powerful insights of feminist theory often stimulate new emotional responses to past and present situations. Inevitably, our emotions are affected by the knowledge that the women on our faculty are paid systematically less than the men, that one girl in four is subjected to sexual abuse from heterosexual men in her own family, and that few women reach orgasm in heterosexual intercourse. We are likely to feel different emotions towards older women or people of color as we reevaluate our standards of sexual attractiveness or acknowledge that Black is beautiful. The new emotions evoked by feminist insights are likely in turn to stimulate further feminist observations and insights, and these may generate new directions in both theory and political practice. There is a continuous feedback loop between our emotional constitution and our theorizing such that each continually modifies the other and is in principle inseparable from it.

The ease and speed with which we can reeducate our emotions unfortunately is not great. Emotions are only partially within our control as individuals. Although affected by new information, they are habitual responses not quickly unlearned. Even when we come to believe consciously that our fear or shame or revulsion is unwarranted, we may still continue to experience emotions inconsistent with our conscious politics. We may still continue to be anxious for male approval, competitive with our comrades

and sisters and possessive with our lovers. These unwelcome, because apparently inappropriate, emotions should not be suppressed or denied; instead, they should be acknowledged and subjected to critical scrutiny. The persistence of such recalcitrant emotions probably demonstrates how fundamentally we have been constituted by the dominant world view, but it may also indicate superficiality or other inadequacy in our emerging theory and politics.[22] We can only start from where we are—beings who have been created in a cruelly racist, capitalist, and male-dominated society that has shaped our bodies and our minds, our perceptions, our values and our emotions, our language and our systems of knowledge.

The alternative epistemological model that I suggest displays the continuous interaction between how we understand the world and who we are as people. It shows how our emotional responses to the world change as we conceptualize it differently and how our changing emotional responses then stimulate us to new insights. The model demonstrates the need for theory to be self-reflexive, to focus not only on the outer world but also on ourselves and our relation to that world, to examine critically our social location, our actions, our values, our perceptions and our emotions. The model also shows how feminist and other critical social theories are indispensable psychotherapeutic tools because they provide some insights necessary to a full understanding of our emotional constitution. Thus, the model explains how the reconstruction of knowledge is inseparable from the reconstruction of ourselves.

A corollary of the reflexivity of feminist and other critical theory is that it requires a much broader construal than positivism accepts of the process of theoretical investigation. In particular, it requires acknowledging that a necessary part of theoretical process is critical self-examination. Time spent in analyzing emotions and uncovering their sources should be viewed, therefore, neither as irrelevant to theoretical investigation nor even as a prerequisite for it; it is not a kind of clearing of the emotional decks, "dealing with" our emotions so that they will not influence our thinking. Instead, we must recognize that our efforts to reinterpret and refine our emotions are necessary to our theoretical investigation, just as our efforts to reeducate our emotions are necessary to our political activity. Critical reflection on emotion it not a self-indulgent substitute for political analysis and political action. It is itself a kind of political theory and political practice, indispensable for an adequate social theory and social transformation.

Finally, the recognition that emotions play a vital part in developing knowledge enlarges our understanding of women's claimed epistemic advantage. We can now see that women's subversive insights owe much to women's outlaw emotions, themselves appropriate responses to the situations of women's subordination. In addition to their propensity to experience outlaw emotions, at least on some level, women are relatively adept at identifying such emotions, in themselves and others, in part because of their social responsibility for caretaking, including emotional nurturance. It is true that women (like all subordinated peoples, especially those who must live in close proximity with their masters) often engage in emotional deception and even self-deception as the price of their survival. Even so, women may be less likely than other subordinated groups to engage in denial or suppression of outlaw emotions. Women's work of emotional nurturance has required them to develop a special acuity in recognizing hidden emotions and in understanding the genesis of those emotions. This emotional acumen can now be recognized as a skill in political analysts and validated as giving women a special advantage both in understanding the mechanisms of domination and in envisioning freer ways to live.

CONCLUSION

The claim that emotion is vital to systematic knowledge is only the most obvious contrast between the conception of theoretical investigation that I have sketched here and the conception provided by positivism. For instance, the alternative approach emphasizes that what we identify as emotion is a conceptual abstraction from a complex process of human activity that also involves acting, sensing, and evaluating. This proposed account of theoretical construction demonstrates the simultaneous necessity for and interdependence of faculties that our culture has abstracted and separated from each other: emotion and reason, evaluation and perception, observation and action. The model of knowing suggested here is nonhierarchical and antifoundationalist; instead, it is appropriately symbolized by the radical feminist metaphor of the upward spiral. Emotions are neither more basic than observation, reason, or action in building theory, nor secondary to them. Each of these human faculties reflects an aspect of human knowing inseparable from the other aspects. Thus, to borrow a famous phrase from a Marxian context, the development of each of these faculties is a necessary condition for the development of all.

In conclusion, it is interesting to note that acknowledging the importance of emotion for knowledge is not an entirely novel suggestion within the western epistemological tradition. The archrationalist, Plato himself, came to accept in the end that knowledge required (a very purified form of) love. It may be no accident that in the *Symposium* Socrates learns this lesson from Diotima, the wise woman!

NOTES

I wish to thank the following individuals who commented helpfully on earlier drafts of this paper or made me aware of further resources: Lynne Arnault, Susan Bordo, Martha Bolton, Cheshire Calhoun, Randy Cornelius, Shelagh Crooks, Ronald De Sousa, Tim Diamond, Dick Foley, Ann Garry, Judy Gerson, Mary Gibson, Sherry Gorelick, Marcia Lind, Helen Longino, Catherine Lutz, Andy McLaughlin, Uma Narayan, Linda Nicholson, Bob Richardson, Sally Ruddick, Laurie Shrage, Alan Soble, Vicky Spelman, Karsten

Struhl, Joan Tronto, Daisy Quarm, Naomi Quinn and Alison Wylie. I am also grateful to my colleagues in the fall of 1985 Women's Studies Chair Seminar at Douglass College, Rutgers University, and to audiences at Duke University, Georgia University Centre, Hobart and William Smith Colleges, Northeastern University, the University of North Carolina at Chapel Hill and Princeton University, for their responses to earlier versions of this paper. In addition, I received many helpful comments from members of the Canadian Society for Women in Philosophy and from students in Lisa Heldke's classes in feminist epistemology at Carleton College and Northwestern University. Thanks, too, to Delia Cushway, who provided a comfortable environment in which I wrote the first draft.

1. Philosophers who do not conform to this generalization and constitute part of what Susan Bordo calls a "recessive" tradition in western philosophy include Hume and Nietzsche, Dewey and James (Bordo 1987:114–118).

2. The western tradition as a whole has been profoundly rationalist, and much of its history may be viewed as a continuous redrawing of the boundaries of the rational. For a survey of this history from a feminist perspective, see Lloyd 1984.

3. Thus, fear and other emotions were seen as rational in some circumstances. To illustrate this point, E. V. Spelman quotes Aristotle as saying (in the *Nicomachean Ethics,* Bk. IV, ch. 5): "[Anyone] who does not get angry when there is reason to be angry, or who does not get angry in the right way at the right time and with the right people, is a dolt" (Spelman 1982:1).

4. Descartes, Leibnitz, and Kant are among the prominent philosophers who did not endorse a wholly stripped-down, instrumentalist conception of reason.

5. The relocation of values in human attitudes and preferences in itself was not grounds for denying their universality, because they could have been conceived as grounded in a common or universal human nature. In fact, however, the variability, rather than the commonality, of human preferences and responses was emphasized; values gradually came to be viewed as individual, particular, and even idiosyncratic rather than as universal and objective. The only exception to the variability of human desires was the supposedly universal urge to egoism and the motive to maximize one's own utility, whatever that consisted of. The value of autonomy and liberty, consequently, was seen as perhaps the only value capable of being justified objectively because it was a precondition for satisfying other desires.

6. For instance, Julius Moravcsik has characterized as emotions what I would call "plain" hunger and thirst, appetites that are not desires for any particular food or drink (Moravcsik 1982: 207–224). I myself think that such states, which Moravcsik also calls instincts or appetites, are understood better as sensations than emotions. In other words, I would view so-called instinctive, nonintentional feelings as the biological raw material from which full-fledged human emotions develop.

7. Even adherents of the Native View recognize, of course, that emotions are not entirely random or unrelated to an individual's judgments and beliefs; in other words, they note that people are angry or excited *about* something, afraid or proud *of* something. On the Native View, however, the judgments or beliefs associated with an emotion are seen as its causes and thus as related to it only externally.

8. Cheshire Calhoun pointed this out to me in private correspondence.

9. Recognition of the many levels on which emotions are socially constructed raises the question whether it makes sense even to speak of the possibility of universal emotions. Although a full answer to this question is methodologically problematic, one might speculate that many of what we westerners identify as emotions have functional analogues in other cultures. In other words, it may be that people in every culture behave in ways that fulfill at least some social functions of our angry or fearful behavior.

10. The relationship between the emotional experience of an individual and the emotional experience of the group to which the individual belongs may perhaps be clarified by analogy to the relation between a word and the language of which it is a part. That a word has meaning presupposes that it is part of a linguistic system without which it has no meaning; yet the language itself has no meaning over and above

the meaning of the words of which it is composed, together with their grammatical ordering. Words and language presuppose and mutually constitute each other. Similarly, both individual and group emotion presuppose and mutually constitute each other.

11. Averell cites dissociative reactions by military personnel at Wright Paterson Air Force Base and shows how these were effective in mustering help to deal with difficult situations while simultaneously relieving the individual of responsibility or blame (Averell 1980:157).

12. These and similar experiments are described in Kilpatrick 1961: ch.10, cited by McLaughlin 1985:296.

13. The positivist attitude toward emotion, which requires that ideal investigators be both disinterested and dispassionate, may be a modern variant of older traditions in western philosophy that recommended that people seek to minimize their emotional responses to the world and develop instead their powers of rationality and pure contemplation.

14. It is now widely accepted that the suppression and repression of emotion has damaging if not explosive consequences. There is general acknowledgement that no one can avoid at some time experiencing emotions she or he finds unpleasant, and there is also increasing recognition that the denial of such emotions is likely to result in hysterical disorders of thought and behavior, in projecting one's own emotions on to others, in displacing them to inappropriate situations, or in psychosomatic ailments. Psychotherapy, which purports to help individuals recognize and "deal with" their emotions, has become an enormous industry, especially in the U.S. In much conventional psychotherapy, however, emotions still are conceived as feelings or passions, "subjective" disturbances that afflict individuals or interfere with their capacity for rational thought and action. Different therapies, therefore, have developed a wide variety of techniques for encouraging people to "discharge" or "vent" their emotions, just as they would drain an abscess. Once emotions have been discharged or vented they are supposed to be experienced less intensely, or even to vanish entirely, and consequently to exert less

influence on individuals' thoughts and actions. This approach to psychotherapy clearly demonstrates its kinship with the "folk" theory of anger mentioned earlier, and it equally clearly retains the traditional western assumption that emotion is inimical to rational thought and action. Thus, such approaches fail to challenge and indeed provide covert support for the view that "objective" knowers are not only disinterested but also dispassionate.

15. E.V. Spelman (1982) illustrates this point with a quotation from the well known contemporary philosopher, R. S. Peters, who wrote "we speak of emotional outbursts, reactions, upheavals and women" (*Proceedings of the Aristotelian Society,* New Series, vol. 62).

16. It seems likely that the conspicuous absence of emotion shown by Mrs Thatcher is a deliberate strategy she finds necessary to counter the public perception of women as too emotional for political leadership. The strategy results in her being perceived as a formidable leader, but as an Iron Lady rather than a real woman. Ironically, Neil Kinnock, leader of the British Labor Party and Thatcher's main opponent in the 1987 General Election, was able to muster considerable public support through television commercials portraying him in the stereotypically feminine role of caring about the unfortunate victims of Thatcher economics. Ultimately, however, this support was not sufficient to destroy public confidence in Mrs Thatcher's "masculine" competence and gain Kinnock the election.

17. On the rare occasions when a white man cries, he is embarrassed and feels constrained to apologize. The one exception to the rule that men should be emotionless is that they are allowed and often even expected to experience anger. Spelman (1982) points out that men's cultural permission to be angry bolsters their claim to authority.

18. Someone might argue that the viciousness of this myth was not a logical necessity. In the egalitarian society, where the concepts of reason and emotion were not gender-bound in the way they still are today, it might be argued that the ideal of the dispassionate investigator could be epistemologically beneficial. Is it possible that, in such socially and conceptually egalitarian

circumstances, the myth of the dispassionate investigator could serve as a heuristic device, an ideal never to be realized in practice but nevertheless helping to minimize "subjectivity" and bias? My own view is that counterfactual myths rarely bring the benefits advertised and that this one is no exception. This myth fosters an equally mythical conception of pure truth and objectivity, quite independent of human interests or desires, and in this way it functions to disguise the inseparability of theory and practice, science and politics. Thus, it is part of an antidemocratic world view that mystifies the political dimension of knowledge and unwarrantedly circumscribes the arena of political debate.

19. Of course, the similarities in our emotional constitutions should not blind us to systematic differences. For instance, girls rather than boys are taught fear and disgust for spiders and snakes, affection for fluffy animals, and shame for their naked bodies. It is primarily, though not exclusively, men rather than women whose sexual responses are shaped by exposure to visual and sometimes violent pornography. Girls and women are taught to cultivate sympathy for others; boys and men are taught to separate themselves emotionally from others. As I have noted already, more emotional expression is permitted for lower-class and some nonwhite men than for ruling-class men, perhaps because the expression of emotion is thought to expose vulnerability. Men of the upper classes learn to cultivate an attitude of condescension, boredom, or detached amusement. As we shall see shortly, differences in the emotional constitution of various groups may be epistemologically significant in so far as they both presuppose and facilitate different ways of perceiving the world.

20. A necessary condition for experiencing feminist emotions is that one already be a feminist in some sense, even if one does not consciously wear that label. But many women and some men, even those who would deny that they are feminist, still experience emotions compatible with feminist values. For instance, they may be angered by the perception that someone is being mistreated just because she is a woman, or they may take special pride in the achievement of a woman. If those who experience such emotions

are unwilling to recognize them as feminist, their emotions are probably better described as potentially feminist or prefeminist emotions.

21. I owe this suggestion to Marcia Lind.

22. Within a feminist context, Berenice Fisher suggests that we focus particular attention on our emotions of guilt and shame as part of a critical reevaluation of our political ideals and our political practice (Fisher 1964).

REFERENCES

Averell, James R. 1980. "The Emotions." In *Personality: Basic Aspects and Current Research,* ed. Ervin Staub. Englewood Cliffs, N.J.: Prentice Hall.

Bordo, Susan R. 1987. *The Flight to Objectivity: Essays on Cartesianism and Culture.* Albany, N.Y.: SUNY Press.

Fisher, Berenice. 1984. "Guilt and Shame in the Women's Movement: The Radical Ideal of Action and its Meaning for Feminist Intellectuals." *Feminist Studies* 10:185–212.

Flax, Jane. 1983. "Political Philosophy and the Patriarchal Unconscious: A Psychoanalytic Perspective on Epistemology and Metaphysics." In *Discovering Reality: Feminist Perspectives on Epistemology, Metaphysics, Methodology and Philosophy of Science,* ed. Sandra Harding and Merrill Hintikka. Dordrecht, Holland: D. Reidel Publishing.

Goodall, Jane. 1986. *The Chimpanzees of Bombe: Patterns of Behavior.* Cambridge, Mass.: Harvard University Press.

Griffin, Susan. 1979. *Rape: The Power of Consciousness.* San Francisco: Harper & Row.

Hinman, Lawrence. 1986. "Emotion, Morality and Understanding." Paper presented at Annual Meeting of the Central Division of the American Philosophical Association, St. Louis, Missouri, May 1986.

Jaggar, Alison M. 1983. *Feminist Politics and Human Nature.* Totowa, N.J.: Rowman and Allanheld; Brighton, UK: Harvester Press.

Keller, Evelyn Fox. 1984. *Gender and Science.* New Haven, Conn.: Yale University Press.

Kilpatrick, Franklin P., ed. 1961. *Explorations in Transactional Psychology.* New York: New York University Press.

Lakoff, George and Zoltan Kovecses. 1987. "The Cognitive Model of Anger Inherent in American English." In *Cultural Models in Language and*

Thought, ed. N. Quinn and D. Holland. New York: Cambridge University Press.

Lewontin, R. C. 1982. "Letter to the Editor." *New York Review of Books,* 4 (February): 40–1. This letter was drawn to my attention by Alan Soble.

Lloyd, Genevieve. 1984. *The Man of Reason: 'Male' and 'Female' in Western Philosophy*. Minneapolis: University of Minnesota Press.

Lutz, Catherine. 1985. "Depression and the Translation of Emotional Worlds." In *Culture and Depression: Studies in the Anthropology and Cross-cultural Psychiatry of Affect and Disorder,* ed. A. Kleinman and B. Good. Berkeley, Calif: University of California Press, 63–100.

Lutz, Catherine. 1986. "Emotion, Thought, and Estrangement: Emotion as a Cultural Category." *Cultural Anthropology* 1:287–309.

Lutz, Catherine. 1987. "Goals, Events and Understanding in Ifaluck and Emotion Theory." In *Cultural Models in Language and Thought,* ed. N. Quinn and D. Holland. New York: Cambridge University Press.

McLaughlin, Andrew. 1985. "Images and Ethics of Nature." *Environmental Ethics* 7:293–319.

Merchant, Carolyn M. 1980. *The Death of Nature: Women, Ecology and the Scientific Revolution*. New York: Harper & Row.

Moravcsik, J. M. E. 1982. "Understanding and the Emotions." *Dialectics* 36, 2–3:207–224.

Nagel, Ernest. 1968. "The Subjective Nature of Social Subject Matter." In *Readings in the Philosophy of the Social Sciences,* ed. May Brodbeck. New York: Macmillan.

Quinby, Lee. 1986. Discussion following talk at Hobart and William Smith Colleges, April 1986.

Rorty, Richard. 1979. *Philosophy and the Mirror of Nature*. Princeton: Princeton University Press.

Rosaldo, Michelle Z. 1984. "Toward an Anthropology of Self and Feeling." In *Culture Theory,* ed. Richard A. Shweder and Robert A. LeVine. New York: Cambridge University Press.

Rose, Hilary. 1983. "Hand, Brain, and Heart: A Feminist Epistemology for the Natural Sciences." *Signs: Journal of Women in Culture and Society* 9, 1:73–90.

Schachter, Stanley and Jerome B. Singer. 1969. "Cognitive, Social and Psychological Determinants of Emotional State." *Psychological Review* 69:379–399.

Scheman, Naomi. "Women in the Philosophy Curriculum." Paper presented at the Annual Meeting of the Central Division of the American Philosophical Association, Chicago, April 1985.

Schott, Robin M. 1988. *Cognition and Eros: A Critique of the Kantian Paradigm*. Boston, Mass: Beacon Press.

Spelman, Elizabeth V. 1982. "Anger and Insubordination." Manuscript; early version read to Midwest chapter of the Society for Women in Philosophy, Spring 1982.

Wierzbicka, Anna. 1986. "Human Emotions: Universal or Culture-Specific?" *American Anthropologist* 88:584–594.

Young, Robert M. 1985. *Darwin's Metaphor: Nature's Place in Victorian Culture*. Cambridge: Cambridge University Press.

HOW IS EPISTEMOLOGY POLITICAL?

Linda Martín Alcoff

Epistemology is typically understood as that branch of philosophy which seeks to have knowledge about knowledge itself. Though this was once considered to be above the fray of politics, increasingly epistemology is charged with having a politics, usually an oppressive one. From some Continental philosophers comes the charge that epistemology seeks a totalizing standard of justification that would narrow the scope of debate and authorize only certain privileged speakers, thus supporting current structures of social domination and even totalitarianism.[1] From radical philosophers of various types we hear that epistemology frames its inquiry in such a way as to exclude the possibility of interrogating the social and political identities of knowing subjects or the impact of these identities on the knowledge produced, thus rendering epistemology's political biases immune from criticism.[2] And from an increasing number of philosophers of science we hear that epistemology rarely takes into account the fact that scientific knowledge emerges from a social praxis that occurs in the interface between scientific and political/economic institutions, and that the latter have determinate effects not only on the priorities of research but on which hypotheses are considered plausible.[3]

If these charges are mostly right, as I think they are, the problems that they identify must result from a more general but unacknowledged relationship between epistemology and politics, a relationship that is necessary rather than contingent. In this essay my principal aim is to elucidate this more general relationship and to clarify the ways in which it might be said that epistemology is political or has a necessary relationship to politics or political phenomena. But this thesis immediately raises further questions that need to be explored, such as: If epistemology is indeed political, can a self-consciousness of that fact peacefully coexist with the tradition itself? Or, as some have argued, should epistemology be replaced with the sociology of knowledge or with hermeneutics? If the answer to that question is no, then what are the implications of the political character of epistemology for it as a philosophical practice and a program of inquiry? And finally, are the politics of epistemology necessarily conservative or oppressive, as some critics have maintained?

Before we can consider answers to these questions, however, we need to clarify the sense in which it can plausibly be maintained that epistemology is political. It strikes me that there are three principal ways in which it might be argued that a significant relationship between epistemology and politics obtains. First, it could be argued that the conditions for the production of epistemologies are political in the sense that these

conditions reflect social hierarchies of power and privilege to determine who can participate in epistemological discussions and whose views on epistemology have the potential to gain wide influence. Thus, on this view, epistemology is political in its conditions of production. Second, it could be argued that specific theories of knowledge produced by epistemologists reflect the social locatedness of the particular theorist(s). Thus, the social and political identity of theorists will have a substantive effect on the epistemology they devise. This argument implies a rejection of the view that theories and minds can be separated from theorists and bodies, where bodies are understood to have social location and meaning. Third, it could be argued that epistemologies have political effects insofar as they are discursive interventions in specific discursive and political spaces. Thus, certain theories of justification will have the effect of authorizing or disauthorizing certain kinds of voices and may legitimate or delegitimate given discursive hierarchies and arrangements of speaking.

These three possibilities can mutually coexist, in any given combination. Let us look at each in turn.

THE CONDITIONS OF PRODUCTION

The first option highlights the fact that epistemology is not simply a collection of texts but a social practice engaged in by specific kinds of participants in prescribed situations. For the most part, thinking about thinking itself goes on among professional philosophers, at least in its formalized and published manifestations.[4] And it goes on in academic institutions that are themselves constrained and determined by their embeddedness within larger socioeconomic institutions. The result of this process is that epistemology is primarily a conversation between relatively privileged males; indeed, if one looks at the *Philosophers' Index* for recent articles in epistemology or attends the epistemology sessions at the American Philosophical Association, epistemology is striking among all the various branches of philosophy for its gender and race exclusivity.

It could be argued that this exclusivity results from a meritocracy in academic institutions, such that only those most gifted at epistemology are able to participate in it. Such a position would then have to maintain that those most gifted are generally middle- and upper-class white males.[5] This argument is obviously politically offensive, but it can be countered on other grounds as well. The high cost of tuition, the hierarchical differences between the higher education available to the rich and poor, and the class divisions exacerbated by racism and sexism in U.S. society could all be pointed out to show that who gets to do philosophy is not determined solely or primarily by merit, if we assume for the moment that the characterization of merit itself can be made without political considerations.[6] We might also point to the fact that first-generation college students—the group most likely to include larger numbers of people of color and working-class students—generally tend away from the humanities and more toward programs that can guarantee well-paying jobs. They also sometimes gravitate toward careers that can contribute more directly to their communities.

It could be countered that merit is not so much at play here as interest and that the segment of the population that engages in epistemology is that segment most interested in pursuing it. But the factors listed above that contraindicate merit as the determining factor also contraindicate interest as a primary cause. Interest and merit may play a determining role within that group of students that has reasonable access to philosophy, to determine who among this group become epistemologists; but this group is just the group of (primarily) upper- and middle-class white males. The conclusion to which we are thus compelled is that the political relationships of power and privilege in any given society have determinate effects on the conditions in which epistemology is practiced. This fact does not obtain merely when the society is not egalitarian, but would

also obtain in an egalitarian society, since there too relations of power and privilege (in this case, fair ones) would determine the possibility of merit and interest becoming primary causal factors in delimiting the class of epistemologists.

The sense in which it is true that the conditions of the production of epistemology are political can be broadened beyond consideration of who ends up in humanities programs to a consideration of the informal but no less powerful systems of discursive hierarchy and authority. In our society processes of socialization produce a situation in which there exists a presumption in favor of the views and arguments advanced by certain kinds of people over others. Thus men's views tend to be given more weight than women's, white's over nonwhite's, and persons of a professional-managerial class over persons of the working class. It is true that the subject matter under discussion can have a legitimate effect on who is accorded discursive authority, such that those with direct experience are more credible than those without it, but there are so many systematic divergences from this general rule that it seems ineffectual. For example, in terms of general and universal claims, which philosophy understands itself most often to be making, although one might guess that the logic of the situation would dictate that anyone at all could have the right to make such claims, in fact discursive authority is accorded by class, race, sexuality, and gender. African Americans may be considered experts on African Americans but rarely will an African American political candidate be seen by whites as capable of understanding the situation of the whole community, whereas whites more often assume that white candidates can achieve this universal point of view. In the analogous arena of literary theory, bell hooks has argued that Black writers are too often read by whites as writing about "blackness," whereas white writers are assumed to write about "life."[7]

There are many more such instances where the hierarchy of discursive authority goes against apparent logic or the basic rules of empiricism in order to maintain systems of privilege. Thus, for example, children who have been victimized by sexual abuse are less likely to be believed by adult jurors than the accused adults.[8] Midwives with extensive experience attending to women in labor as well as their own personal experience of childbirth are less likely to be believed than male obstetricians fresh out of medical school. Assembly-line workers with decades of experience are routinely ignored in decisions about how to increase efficiency on the line, and deference is instead given to college-trained efficiency "experts." Because these instances contradict basic empiricist rules or what passes for "common sense" so sharply, they reveal that there are political forces at work in determining who gets discursive credibility. And this suggests that many if not most discursive situations are political in the sense that who is allowed to speak, who is listened to with attention, who has the presumption of credibility in their favor, and who is likely to be ignored or disbelieved is partly a function of the hierarchy of political status existent in the society.[9] Given that epistemology is similarly produced in discursive situations, whether written or spoken, the conditions of its production will be affected by these social conventions of discursive hierarchy, consciously or unconsciously, thus influencing whose arguments are considered plausible enough to be given consideration.

Of course, some might concede that for the reasons described above, epistemology has a necessary relationship to politics, but then argue that this relationship remains at the extrinsic level and has no substantive bearing on the content or character of epistemological work itself. If we turn here, however, to the second form of the relationship between epistemology and politics, we find arguments that show why it is of substantive epistemic concern who the people doing epistemology are.

THE IDENTITY OF THEORISTS

The majority of the work showing that the identity of epistemic theorists is epistemologically relevant has been done by feminist philosophers.

Naomi Scheman, for example, has argued that the predominance of skepticism as the determining problem for epistemology is correlated with common features of socialized masculine identity formation.[10] Susan Bordo has shown correlations between such features as a fear of the feminine and the dominant Cartesian paradigm of disembodied objective knowing.[11] Elizabeth Potter has demonstrated a connection between Robert Boyle's articulation of experimental methods and his preoccupation with gender dimorphism.[12] Andrea Nye has argued that Western formulations of logic from Parmenides through Frege exemplify the desire of aristocratic males to maintain their own authority and control over the behavior of all social subjects, and thus to maintain a system of strictly controlled hierarchical relations that benefit them.[13] Genevieve Lloyd has shown that the ideals of reason developed throughout the history of Western philosophy are integrally connected to ideals of masculinity.[14] For a more contemporary case, Lorraine Code has argued that Richard Foley's epistemology commits the error of assuming that he can generalize from his own experience to the experience of all other human beings, an assumption usually found (and sometimes accorded to) dominant groups but less commonly found in subordinate groups. Her argument suggests not only that Foley's assumption is mistaken, but that there is a noncoincidental connection between Foley's epistemic conclusions and the fact that he is a male.[15] None of the works I have cited argues for a gender reductionism, or what might be called "vulgar feminism," in the sense that the evaluation of epistemology and philosophy could be *reduced* to an issue of gender identity. Such a reductionism, which is a caricature of existing feminist philosophy, is a straw position put forward only (so far as I know) by the detractors of this work.

It is also important to note that the work outlined above is not suggesting a causal relationship between epistemology and morphology or certain metaphysical entities such as sex. Within feminist philosophy, in general, the term "maleness" does not merely or primarily connote a physiological condition as it connotes a social and political one. That is, maleness, like femaleness and whiteness and so forth, is a socially constructed identity with specified attributes of privilege and authority, a range of possible freedoms, and a designated hierarchical relationship to other possible identities. If we think of it as a social location in this way, it is easier to understand that maleness brings a particular perspective, shared assumptions and values, and social meanings.

But if the connection posited by this growing body of work is not arguing for a gender reductionism or a morphological determinism, what is it arguing for? It argues that there exists a relationship of partial determination between theories and the social identity of theorists, in general, which applies to epistemology as well. Helen Longino has provided a conception of theory-choice that can help us to make sense of this phenomenon without positing all epistemologists as intentionally promoting their own privilege or as uniformly unwilling to use available unbiased methods of argument. Longino argues that no such "pure" methods are available, since background assumptions which contain metaphysical commitments as well as contextual values enter necessarily into the process of knowing.[16] The influence of these assumptions and values cannot be restricted to the so-called "context of discovery" because they have an important impact on the formulation of hypotheses, which hypotheses are taken to be plausible, the kinds of analogies and models that get seriously entertained, and the determination of the kind of evidence considered sufficient to justify theories. After all these factors are set in place, the process of theory-choice may indeed conform to a paradigm of objectivity since, as Longino and others have pointed out, once you determine the scale that will be used to assess temperature, the determination of the temperature is really an objective matter. But the realm of objectivity in this traditional sense does not extend very far. The models of justification that are considered plausible and

thus are up for debate and consideration, the goals of epistemology itself, its unexamined assumptions about the locus and contours of knowing that set up the problematic of epistemological research—all these elements are significantly influenced by contextual values that are themselves a function in part of who the epistemologist is.

To give just one example, traditional epistemology has most often assumed that knowing occurs between an individual and an object or world.[17] This typically Western assumption of individualism (which operates as both an ontological assumption and a value) dictates the kinds of problems and hurdles epistemologists set themselves to overcome: how can I (by myself) justify my beliefs; how can the massive number of beliefs I hold be justified on the basis of my own narrow observational input; and, for naturalized epistemology, how can we describe the complex brain states involved in various epistemic functions. But little knowledge is actually achieved individually—most knowledge is produced through collective endeavor and is largely dependent on the knowledge produced by others. If epistemology were to dispense with its individualist assumption and begin with a conception of knowing as collective, a different agenda of issues would suggest itself. For example, we would need a more complicated understanding of the epistemic interrelationships of a knowing community; we would want to understand the relation between modes of social organization and the types of beliefs that appear reasonable; and we would need to explore the influence of the political relationship between individuals on their epistemic relationships.

This analysis indicates that the formative assumptions and values of any group of epistemologists, whether privileged European American males or a national minority, can have a significant impact on the epistemological theories thus produced. This need not devolve into a dysfunctional, absolute relativism, especially if we begin to acknowledge such influences so that they can be identified as far as possible and raised for debate and discussion. To assume that the interdiction of political issues entails a radical relativism is to assume that political debate is doomed to irrationality. But political issues are no less susceptible to rational consideration and discussion than epistemological ones.

DISCURSIVE EFFECTS

This brings us to the third possible formulation of the relationship between politics and epistemology. It should be clear by this point that I am defining politics as anything having to do with relationships of power and privilege between persons, and the way in which these relationships are maintained and reproduced or contested and transformed. It should also be clear that given this definition, politics is ubiquitous in the social landscape. To the extent that discourse is produced and circulated through social practices, all discourse has political involvements. The analysis thus far given could be applied to any social knowledge or project of inquiry. Epistemology cannot be singled out as having a connection to political relations and structures, and therefore it may seem as if the targeting of epistemology as a special case is unnecessary and even unfair.

Although it is true that the general features of epistemology's relationship to and involvement with politics are not unique, it is also true that there are specificities to this relationship that bear exploration. For one thing, it is an important task to identify the connections between particular and influential epistemological theories and traditions and the political identities or social locatedness of epistemological theorists, a task that the feminist work cited above has initiated. And moreover, there are reasons why such a critique of epistemology has a unique importance. As many have pointed out, philosophy is not just one discourse among many discourses of knowledge; it is, rather, the discourse that sets out the structures of legitimation for all other discourses. This is particularly true of epistemology, which takes as its objective the delineation

of a conceptual apparatus by which all knowledge claims can be judged. Like Marx, I reject the view that philosophy, as a body of texts and ideas, actually is the causal mechanism making possible the emergence of other discourses; like Hegel, I hold, rather, that philosophy comes usually afterward and in the midst of emerging dominant discourses and provides the arguments and theories that then "justify" these discourses' dominance. Even without absolute causal power, however, philosophy and epistemology are critical discursive sites because they are influential in the crafting of what Lyotard calls narratives of legitimation or delegitimation for essentially all other discourses that claim knowledge.

Epistemology thus has a particularly strong relationship to other discourses, a relationship that is thematized in epistemology's own self-definition. Epistemology presents itself as the theory of knowledge, and thus presents itself as the arbiter of all claims to know. It is in this light that the third possible way to formulate the relationship between epistemology and politics as listed above has a particular importance. This possibility, it will be recalled, held that epistemology is political in the sense that epistemologies have political effects as discursive interventions in specific spaces, for example, to authorize or disauthorize certain kinds of voices, certain kinds of discourses, and certain hierarchical structures between discourses.

There is again a wealth of work that has explored such political effects. One of Marx's most important philosophical contributions was to begin this materialist critique of philosophy itself. On his view, the tendency under conditions of commodity production to develop positivist conceptions of knowledge, to conceal or deny the influence of social and political factors on the development of conceptual frameworks, and to remove theories from their historical embeddedness produces a reification of knowledge as absolute, uncontestable, and unchanging—just as capitalist ideology promotes the idea that capitalism as an economic system is absolute, uncontestable, and unchangeable. Thus, the de-historicized view of knowledge dominant in "bourgeois" philosophy has the political effect of producing a fatalism about the status quo. When such an epistemology is taken up within the social sciences, theoretical descriptions of a reified, unchangeable human nature are produced.

Adorno and Horkheimer further argued that the ontology of nature as an inert object and the privileging of "prediction and control" as the goal of scientific inquiry are noncoincidentally functional for the capitalist project of maximizing the exploitation of resources and the domination of nature without constraint. This mechanistic conceptualization of nature as inert is correlated with the ontology of truth that involves a detached thing-in-itself, without subjectivity, and thus unresistant to human manipulation. The need to demythologize and desubjectify nature led to a conception of inquiry as involving an active knower and an inert, passive thing-in-itself. And this conception had the political effect of making it easier to exploit natural resources by making the nonreciprocal relationship of unchecked exploitation between "Man" and nature appear to be a natural one. Moreover, when the object of inquiry is not nature but other human beings, the result of this ontology becomes not only the exploitation of nature but the domination and oppression of large sectors of humanity.

More recently, feminist philosophers have argued that dominant epistemological frameworks and theories have had the political effect of (unjustifiably) excluding women's voices and disauthorizing women's claims to know. For example, Elizabeth Potter has argued that Locke's development of an empiricist epistemology in the seventeenth century had the political effect of silencing the emerging voices of lower-class sectarian women and thus altering the progress of women's liberation.[18] With Vrinda Dalmiya, I have argued that the requirement for justification that a knowledge claim be capable of being rendered into propositional form has had the political effect of helping to disauthorize much of

women's traditional knowledge, including the wealth of knowledge of midwifery.[19] Much of the feminist work cited in the previous section also shows that the mind–body dualism and disembodied conceptions of objectivity found in the Cartesian tradition of epistemology work to undermine women's ability to claim knowledge given their socially constructed association with the body, emotion, and nature—elements that are considered more of a hindrance than a help in the achievement of epistemic justification. The tyranny of this subject-less, value-less conception of objectivity has had the effect of authorizing those scientific voices that have universalist pretensions and disauthorizing personalized voices that argue with emotion, passion, and open political commitment. Most recently, this struggle has been framed as a conflict between the (correctly) apolitical and the "politically correct." Only the latter group, which includes disproportionate numbers of scholars who are working-class, white women, and/or persons of color, is said to have a politics, which is then said to disqualify them from the academy. This notion of objective inquiry, then, continues to have significant political effects in censoring certain kinds of voices and obscuring the real political content of others.

These examples establish that epistemologies have political effects on the development and contestation of discourses, though these effects will be determined as much by the specific political struggles and the array of forces that exist in particular social contexts where the epistemologies emerge as by the content of the epistemologies themselves.[20]

BUT WHAT ABOUT TRUTH?

But, one might ask here, what about truth? The preceding discussion may appear to have conveniently left out the fact that epistemology is most fundamentally a project in the pursuit of truth. And if truth has a relationship to politics, then it may appear that there is no possibility of achieving "real" truth, epistemology must dissolve in the face of skepticism, and the whole project of this essay dissolves into incoherence as well to the extent that it is making truth claims.

In response to this point, it can first be noted that it is not necessary to hold that truth has a relationship to politics in order to hold that epistemology does. Epistemology is concerned not only with truth but also with belief and standards of justification, and we can show that there is a connection between politics and the latter two without any danger of incoherence.

Second, truth, it needs to be remembered, is also a human idea with a genealogy, historical location, and variability in the way it is conceptualized and defined. The metaphors and models by which we characterize the nature of truth are likely to contain both metaphysical and political background assumptions. The belief that truth is outside history, above politics, and that therefore science and philosophy are likewise immune from political evaluation and historical analysis is a belief that both can and has served a variety of political ends, arguably both positive and negative ones.

Finally, we need to remember that truth can be given a variety of definitions. Truth has been defined as correspondence to an independent reality, as coherence between beliefs or between theories and models of reality, as instrumental success, and as a state of subjective certainty. Which alternative is chosen may have political ramifications, and certain definitions may have clear political connections, such as the definition of truth as instrumental success arising in a capitalist era in which all value is put on the "bottom line" and practical, usable results.

To acknowledge these points does not require that we collapse truth into an issue of political debate or replace epistemic considerations with political ones. Both epistemic and political considerations need to be taken into account in the work that goes on within epistemology, given that it cannot "transcend" its political involvements or social and historical embeddedness. But how should epistemic and political considerations be combined? Or should the political considerations be included in sociologies of knowledge rather than epistemology?

Given the depth and degree of the relationship between epistemology and politics, it seems obvious that such a segregation will only weaken epistemology by keeping it blind to its own political assumptions and involvements. If there is danger in a total replacement of epistemic with political considerations in theory-choice within epistemology, there is also danger in continuing to ignore the political elements at work within the discipline. Thus, acknowledging and exploring the political content of epistemology is a necessity for epistemic reasons, so that this content can no longer operate as a silent, unanalyzed influence. And it is also our political responsibility to acknowledge and explore the political effects of our program of work and the ways in which it may be enhancing or undermining current struggles for political progress. In the concluding section, then, I explore what kinds of concrete and specific changes should be made in the practice of epistemology itself once we acknowledge its connections to politics.

AN EPISTEMOLOGY WITHOUT BAD FAITH

It is not possible to disinvest epistemology of its relationship to politics. To the extent that epistemology is done by people, debated between people, and engaged in through the use of discourse in a Foucauldian sense, epistemology will be of necessity political, since all persons, their interrelationships, and their discourses have political identities and associations, power differentials, and political assumptions, goals, and effects. But this need not lead to a quietism or despair that our enterprise is unalterably mired in irrational power struggles. It is more likely that the acknowledgment and exploration of the relationship of epistemology to politics will improve epistemology rather than sound its death knell, since such an exploration will increase the accuracy of epistemology's self-understanding and enhance its ability for self-critique. For this to occur, the internal methods of theory-development and debate will need to be transformed. There needs to be a change in the conditions of the production of epistemology, in its procedures of criticism and debate, and in the bases on which critiques can be made. Such transformations will not eradicate the influence of politics on epistemology but will alter the form and nature of that influence.

In regard to the first type of relationship between epistemology and politics—the fact that the conditions of epistemology's production involve political relationships of subordination and domination—it seems obvious that our goal should be to make it possible for the group of epistemologists to be chosen or selected not by unfair privilege and prejudice or by economic and discursive advantage, but by merit, or aptitude, and interest. This can be accomplished only through a social transformation sufficiently radical to eliminate the major structures of domination in our society, certainly a utopian goal but one worthy of pursuit. It should be noted, however, that the achievement of such a goal would not eliminate political influence over the conditions of epistemology's production, but would rather transform the political relationships that determine those conditions.

This project, difficult as it is, is further complicated by the fact that the determination of what counts as having a merit for or aptitude in epistemology is itself political as well. Merit is presumably judged on the basis of the ability to produce "good" epistemological work, but what counts as "good" work is subject to variable judgment, itself affected by background assumptions and contextual values. Given this, we need to find alternatives to a scenario in which the current group of epistemologists, a group that was not created primarily by merit and interest, is judging the merit of all the new candidates to the profession. We need, in other words, a form of affirmative action for the judgment and development

of new work in epistemology, not because the new works may not yet have sufficient quality, but because the determination of quality itself is subject to group-related assumptions and values. Like affirmative action programs in general, such an affirmative action would be based not on the argument that work of an inferior quality should be accepted in order to increase inclusiveness, but on the idea that quality itself is in part a political determination.

The practical implications of the second claim—that is, that there are determinate relations between the epistemologies produced and the theorists of those epistemologies—are simply that we need to do genealogies of these relationships. This is simply to continue the project begun by some feminist epistemologists. Such genealogies will be informative and enlightening for their own sake, but they will also shed light on how to incorporate the fact of the social embeddedness of epistemological theories within the process of critique and the methods of analysis that theories are subjected to within epistemology. This will most likely entail that the informal fallacy known as the "genetic fallacy" will be transformed or abolished, since it stipulates that issues involving the genesis of theories are not germane to philosophical criticism. Thus, in general, such genealogies will be able to specify further ways in which the discipline needs to be transformed.

The third way in which epistemology is connected to politics—in that epistemologies have political effects as discursive interventions in specific contexts—suggests similarly that an analysis of those effects, or the projected effects, of given theories should become a standard feature of the analysis and evaluation of epistemological alternatives. Such an analysis of effects has an impetus in both epistemic and political considerations. On political grounds, if, for example, one has a commitment to maximize discursive democracy as far as possible, or the ability and right of as many people to speak and be given credibility as possible, then one will want to know how a given theory of epistemic justification will contribute to that project. On epistemic grounds, it seems likely that if a given theory of epistemic justification has the effect of authorizing only privileged voices, helping to legitimate an oppressive status quo or buttressing colonialist and racist conceptions about which cultures are "advanced" and which are "backward," this is a good indication that extraepistemic and spurious assumptions or commitments are involved in the development and influence of such a theory of justification. What epistemically reputable reasons might be given for maintaining a system of discursive privilege so suspiciously parallel to current social hierarchies? Given that a positive answer to this question is implausible, then, if such effects obtain or are likely to obtain, the epistemic reasons given for the theory and its framing within epistemic debates should be carefully interrogated. In other words, undemocratic political effects provide a presumption against a theory's epistemic credibility.

Moreover, Hilary Putnam has recently argued, à la Dewey, that the full development of science and the most adequate interpretations of its maxims will be maximized in some proportion to the degree of democratic inclusiveness of the enterprise.[21] This conclusion follows once we acknowledge that science rarely involves deductive deliberation and more often involves processes of interpretation of data and application of maxims that admit of variability. Such processes of *decision making* will be epistemically more adequate when all the viable alternatives are available for consideration. A lone scientist or a small, homogeneous research team is less likely to be able to produce or imagine all the viable alternatives than a more heterogeneous group. On this view, science has an intrinsic reason to pursue social democracy.

This argument can be used to support the claim that epistemologies need to have a liberatory agenda for epistemic reasons. Given that the primary political effects of epistemologies are effects on the ability of certain groups of people to speak and be accorded credibility, I define a liberatory agenda in epistemology as one that seeks to maximize both the number and the diversity of persons who have such discursive possibilities. Conversely, an oppressive agenda is one that would minimize discursive access and in particular restrict it to those groups in power. We do not need to uphold the relativist notion that everyone's view has an equal claim to truth in order to hold that truth is more likely to be obtained through a process that includes the articulation and examination of all possible views. The artificial exclusion of views, or their exclusion from the realm of debate on the basis of non-epistemic reasons such as racism or sexism, is a matter of epistemic concern since it will have a deleterious effect on the strength and comprehensiveness of the view(s) that win dominance. And this means that it is not the influence of politics per se we need to eliminate from epistemology; it is the influence of oppressive politics.[22]

Despite the radical nature of the transformations thus far suggested (a radicalness that is simply a testimony to the stubborn persistence of epistemology's political blind spot), these suggestions indicate that epistemology itself as a project of inquiry about knowledge need not be eradicated. It is not epistemology itself but particular epistemological theories that have oppressive political effects, contra Heidegger and Derrida. Richard Rorty too makes the conflation between epistemology as a project of inquiry about the nature and conditions of knowledge and as a specific and substantive epistemological tradition that has been dominant in Western philosophy since Descartes or, on some readings, since Plato. This tradition—which has encompassed Cartesianism, mind–body dualism, a mirror theory of representation, scientism, and certain incarnations of positivism—has had significant oppressive effects. Moreover, this tradition, given its reliance on a de-contextualized conception of knowledge, will not be able to coexist peacefully with a developed awareness of epistemology's political connections. Though

I cannot develop the argument here, I hold that other epistemological traditions, such as pragmatism, coherentism, and naturalized epistemology, are more flexible or accommodating.

My conclusion, then, is that epistemology, as a project of inquiry into knowledge, can survive the development of its own self-consciousness, so to speak, or an awareness of its own political character. Moreover, such a redescription and transformation of epistemology will provide a new counter-argument to those who would dismiss it on the grounds that it is a sterile, irrelevant discussion without connection to social life.

FINAL OBSTACLES

There remain two further obstacles that a revisionist epistemology must overcome.

First, an argument fashioned from Foucault's writings could be developed along the lines of the following: "Epistemology is necessarily reactionary because it presumes to sit in judgment on all other discourses. Thus it seeks discursive hegemony, creates hierarchies between discourses, and then helps to oppress and subjugate subordinate discourses." The fact that epistemology presumes to sit in judgment on all other discourses, however, does not guarantee its active or actual hegemony, as Foucault would be the first to admit. No discourse has absolute power over the discursive field. And epistemology is itself a discursive field that is internally contested and heterogeneous. Moreover, the existence of hierarchical relations between discourses is inevitable—an absolute proliferation of discourses without distinction is neither possible nor desirable. Structured frameworks are required to create discourses, and, in whatever way knowledge is defined, the identification of knowledge necessitates the ability to identify that which is not knowledge. Thomas Kuhn argues this in connection to the work of "normal" science, and Donald Davidson makes this argument in connection to meaning and errors in understanding.

Even Foucault makes a similar claim in connection to the manner in which power operates: according to him, it is implausible to understand power as operating merely on the basis of repression and constraint. Its influence, persistence, and ubiquitousness require that we understand power as also creating and producing pleasures, discourses, and possibilities for action and experience. On Foucault's view, discourses are created through the structured relations among meaning, power/knowledge, and desire, and power should be generally understood not as a system for constraint and oppression but simply as a field of structured possibilities. Foucault found all such structures to be "dangerous," and he therefore advocated a kind of cognitive skepticism (or the epistemic equivalent of a permanent revolution) characterized by a constant vigilance and critique. But Foucault was not so unrealistic as to argue that all such structured relations can be dispensed with, and he even asserted that power exists everywhere. Therefore, notwithstanding his own rejection of (analytic) epistemology, these views suggest that a wholesale repudiation of epistemology on the grounds that it attempts to create structured relationships between discourses is naive. The point of critique should concern the form and nature of the structure, or its range and degree of effective hegemony, not its very existence.

A second objection to my thesis might go like this: "Epistemology is indelibly tainted by its absolutist, ahistorical orientation. Therefore, it would be wiser to replace it than to try and reform it. And besides, we need an altogether new project that refuses the separation between sociology and epistemology, as well as other disciplines. Our new understanding of knowledge shows precisely that it cannot be adequately theorized within the field of philosophy as traditionally understood."

Of course, it is relatively trivial which particular name is given to the project of inquiry that I have been discussing. The more important issue is the nature of the project. Nonetheless, I argue that because epistemology has always included heterogeneous orientations and been a contested field, it is not monolithically incapable of transforming in the ways I have suggested. Retaining the name does imply a continuation of that which has gone before, but there are some elements in the history of epistemological work with which it will be useful to maintain a continuity. Moreover, retaining the name might reflect more accurately epistemology's heterogeneous past and counteract the distorted histories that homogenize the field and erase the existence of discontinuities and radical oppositions.

This raises the philosophical issue of how philosophy is itself understood. Some see it as the exploration of a closed set of "fundamental" questions, and when a thinker is not grappling with a question within that set, then she or he is said to be doing something other than philosophy. Such a view is ahistorical and dogmatic. It understands philosophy in terms of a dogma that in this case is a set of questions, and it rejects the view that this set exists within history and is subject to historical change. But historical changes in philosophy can mean and often have meant that the questions themselves are altered, in their framing and their assumptions, and also that new questions replace old ones. And these changes have also affected the way in which the various branches of philosophy are defined and demarcated.

A nondogmatic, historically conscious view of philosophy would therefore understand philosophy's set of questions, the tasks that it sets for itself, as open-ended rather than closed. What is attractive to many students about philosophy, I wager, is the feeling that here, ultimately, everything is open for discussion. No question can be regarded as nonsensical and out of bounds for all time, though philosophy like every other discipline needs its period of "normal" science. Because of its emphasis on reflection and the criticism of thinking itself, the project of philosophy seems uniquely situated to engage in transformative critiques. But if this commitment to reflection is to avoid dogmatism, it must include the

possibility of the transformation of philosophy itself up to and including its own eradication.

At this historical juncture, philosophy in general and epistemology in particular need a major overhaul. We must become more self-conscious of the machinations of power and desire in our own field, in both our theories and our research agenda. At the same time, like the theorists of the Frankfurt School, I believe that the present era needs reflective thinking more than ever, and needs a space where thinking can occur outside the dynamics of commodity production and the demand for instrumental usefulness toward the maintenance of this system (or as much outside as possible), and outside a closed set of prescribed questions deemed fruitful for social maintenance. And one of the most critical areas of work in which reflection is needed is in the area of knowledge. It has been said that a defining feature of postmodern society is its crisis and confusion in regard to what can count as knowledge, even while there are more and conflicting knowledge claims bombarding the consumer every day. This crisis of knowledge is positive only to the extent that it can lead to a critique of authoritarian epistemologies and the development of better, more self-aware, and liberatory ones. We need the project of epistemology to continue in such a way that it can contribute to this important work.

Given the connections between epistemology and politics, and a clearer understanding of the nature of belief-formation and justification, however, it is also the case that an exploration of knowledge necessitates the combining of traditional philosophical methods and concerns with sociological, psychological, and historical ones. This move, which was called for over a century ago in the writings of Marx, is finally occurring under the banner of naturalized epistemology, though psychology and cognitive science are more often brought into play than history and sociology.[23] But what this move already implies is that the traditional way in which the academic disciplines have been divided and categorized needs radical transformation. An orientation toward border control between disciplines serves no legitimate intellectual purpose and is usually promoted out of institutional conservatism and narrow career pragmatism.

Thus I agree that the project of inquiry into knowledge, as I have understood epistemology to be, requires a new configuration of disciplinary identities. The contours of such a configuration are beyond my ability to determine, but I am certain that ongoing work in the interface between politics and epistemology can begin to reveal the future path our project should take.

NOTES

1. See, e.g., Jean-François Lyotard, *The Postmodern Condition: A Report on Knowledge,* trans. G. Bennington and B. Massumi (Minneapolis: University of Minnesota Press, 1984); and Michel Foucault, *Power/Knowledge: Selected Interviews and Other Writings,* ed. Colin Gordon, trans. Colin Gordon et al. (New York: Pantheon Books, 1980).

2. See, e.g., Sandra Harding, *The Science Question in Feminism* (Ithaca, N.Y.: Cornell University Press, 1986); Lorraine Code, *What Can She Know? Feminist Theory and the Construction of Knowledge* (Ithaca, N.Y.: Cornell University Press, 1991); Andrea Nye, *Words of Power: A Feminist Reading of the History of Logic* (New York: Routledge, 1990); Stephen A. Resnick and Richard D. Woolf, *Knowledge and Class: A Marxian Critique of Political Economy* (Chicago: University of Chicago Press, 1987).

3. See, e.g., Helen Longino, *Science as Social Knowledge: Values and Objectivity in Scientific Inquiry* (Princeton: Princeton University Press, 1990); Joseph Rouse, *Knowledge and Power: Toward a Political Philosophy of Science* (Ithaca, N.Y.: Cornell University Press, 1987); Lynn Hankinson Nelson, *Who Knows: From Quine to a Feminist Empiricism* (Philadelphia: Temple University Press, 1990); *Ideology of/in the Natural Sciences,* ed. Hilary Rose and Steven Rose (Cambridge, Mass.: Schenkman, 1976).

4. Here and throughout this chapter my frame of reference is Western Europe, the United States, and Australia.

5. Such an argument is not unheard-of among philosophers. See Michael Levin's apologia for the white domination in philosophy in his letter to the *Proceedings and Addresses of the APA,* 63, 5 (Jan. 1990): 62–63.

6. For an excellent history of racism in the history of U.S. education, see Meyer Weinberg, *A Chance to Learn: A History of Race and Education in the United States* (Cambridge: Cambridge University Press, 1977).

7. bell hooks, *Yearning: Race, Gender, and Cultural Politics* (Boston: South End Press, 1990).

8. In this scenario, where it is a child's word against an adult's, one might think that neither should get presumptive credibility. Or one might argue that the child should, on the grounds that it is extremely difficult and costly to any child to report such a crime, whereas adult denials are in line with their own interest. And the notion that children tend to lie about such things has been adequately disproved. See Florence Rush, *The Best Kept Secret: Sexual Abuse of Children* (New York: McGraw-Hill, 1980), pp. 155–57.

9. Such discursive hierarchies are also a function of the dominant conception of objectivity, of mind–body dualism, and of the fact that natural science is most often taken to be the paradigm of knowledge, but whether these conceptual commitments are causes or effects of systems of discursive hierarchy should not be assumed without argument. This is discussed further on.

10. Scheman, "Othello's Doubt/Desdemona's Death: The Engendering of Skepticism," in *Power, Gender, Values,* ed. Judith Genova (Edmonton, Canada: Academic Printing and Publishing, 1987), pp. 113–34.

11. Bordo, *The Flight to Objectivity: Essays on Cartesianism and Culture* (Albany: SUNY Press, 1987).

12. Potter, "Making Gender/Making Science: Gender Ideology and Boyle's Experimental Philosophy," forthcoming in her book *Gender Politics in Seventeenth-Century Science.*

13. Nye, *Words of Power.*

14. Lloyd, *The Man of Reason: "Male" and "Female" in Western Philosophy* (Minneapolis: University of Minnesota Press, 1984).

15. Code, *What Can She Know?* pp. 8, 302, 310. See also her "Taking Subjectivity into Account," in *Feminist Epistemologies,* ed. Linda Alcoff and Elizabeth Potter (New York: Routledge, 1993). Code points out that Foley's assumption is not at all uncharacteristic of work in analytic epistemology, and she uses him as an example only because of the specific clarity his work affords her case.

16. This analysis is taken from her *Science as Social Knowledge,* which, although primarily directed at knowing within science, can be applied to epistemology as well.

17. This example is discussed in Nelson, *Who Knows* (sec esp. chap. 6).

18. Potter, "Locke's Epistemology and Women's Struggles," forthcoming in *Critical Feminist Essays in the History of Western Philosophy,* ed. Bat-Ami Bar On.

19. Alcoff and Dalmiya, "Are Old Wives' Tales Justified?" in *Feminist Epistemologies,* ed. Alcoff and Potter (New York: Routledge, 1993).

20. These effects do not imply the existence of intentions of any type on the part of epistemologists: the effects are not dependent on the existence of intentions and may very well counter the political intentions of the theorist. This is also true of the two other types of relationships between epistemology and politics which we have discussed; neither of

them entails or requires an ascription of political intentions on the part of the epistemologist.

21. Putnam, "Moral Objectivism and Pragmatism," presented at the World Institute for Development Economics Research conference "Human Capabilities: Women, Men, and Equality," Helsinki, August 1991.

22. It could be argued here that assessing epistemologies in terms of their effects runs into incoherence given the fact that the determination of effects will, of course, require that we be able to make truth claims and thus have an epistemology already in place. This sort of difficulty faces every epistemology and is sometimes referred to as the problem of the criterion. One solution to this problem is to provide a coherentist account that would require coherence between levels, such that the criteria of adequacy we impose on an epistemology should be consistent with that epistemology itself. In this way, an epistemology can give an account of itself, or account for its legitimation on its own terms.

23. Incorrectly, in my view. This focus is due to the fact that those epistemologists continue to see knowing as fundamentally an individual enterprise, such that the facts about individual psychological development and brain behavior are regarded as more important than group dynamics or social phenomena. See Nelson's alternative orientation to naturalized epistemology in her *Who Knows.*

TAKING SUBJECTIVITY INTO ACCOUNT

Lorraine Code

1. THE PROBLEM

Suppose epistemologists should succeed in determining a set of necessary and sufficient conditions for justifying claims that "*S* knows that *p*" across a range of "typical" instances.

Furthermore, suppose that these conditions could silence the skeptic who denies that human beings can have certain knowledge of the world. Would the epistemological project then be completed? I maintain that it would not.

There is no doubt that a discovery of necessary and sufficient conditions that offered a response to the skeptic would count as a major epistemological breakthrough. But once one seriously entertains the hypothesis that knowledge is a *construct* produced by cognitive agents within social practices and acknowledges the variability of agents and practices across social groups, the possible scope even of "definitive" justificatory strategies for S-knows-that-p claims reveals itself to be very narrow indeed. My argument here is directed, in part, against the breadth of scope that many epistemologists accord to such claims. I am suggesting that necessary and sufficient conditions in the "received" sense—by which I mean conditions that hold for any knower, regardless of her or his identity, interests, and circumstances (i.e., her or his subjectivity)—could conceivably be discovered only for a narrow range of artificially isolated and purified empirical knowledge claims, which might be paradigmatic by fiat but are unlikely to be so 'in fact.'

In this essay I focus on S-knows-that-p claims and refer to S-knows-that-p epistemologies because of the emblematic nature of such claims in the Anglo-American epistemology. My suggestion is not that discerning necessary and sufficient conditions for the justification of such claims is the sole, or even the central, epistemological preoccupation. Rather, I use this label, S-knows-that-p, for three principal reasons as a trope that permits easy reference to the epistemologies of the mainstream. First, I want to mark the positivist-empiricist orientation of these epistemologies, which is both generated and enforced by appeals to such paradigms. Second, I want to show that these paradigms prompt and sustain a belief that universally necessary and sufficient conditions can indeed be found. Finally—and perhaps most importantly—I want to distance my discussion from analyses that privilege scientific knowledge, as do S-knows-that-p epistemologies implicitly and often explicitly, and hence to locate it within an "epistemology of everyday lives."

Coincidentally—but only, I think, coincidentally—the dominant epistemologies of modernity with their Enlightenment legacy and later infusion with positivist-empiricist principles, have defined themselves around ideals of pure objectivity and value-neutrality. These ideals are best suited to govern evaluations of the knowledge of knowers who can be considered capable of achieving a "view from nowhere"[1] that allows them, through the autonomous exercise of their reason, to transcend particularity and contingency. The ideals presuppose a universal, homogeneous, and essential "human nature" that allows knowers to be substitutable for one another. Indeed, for S-knows-that-p epistemologies, knowers worthy of that title can act as "surrogate knowers," who are able to put themselves in anyone else's place and know his or her circumstances and interests in just the same way as she or he would know them.[2] Hence those circumstances and interests are deemed epistemologically irrelevant. Moreover, by virtue of their detachment, these ideals erase the possibility of analyzing the interplay between emotion and reason and obscure connections between knowledge and power. They lend support to the conviction that cognitive products are as neutral—as politically innocent—as the processes that allegedly produce them. Such epistemologies implicitly assert that if one cannot see "from nowhere" (or equivalently, from an ideal observation position that could be anywhere and everywhere)—if one cannot take up an epistemological position that mirrors the "original position" of "the moral point of view"—then one cannot *know* anything at all. If one cannot transcend subjectivity and the particularities of its "location," then there is no knowledge worth analyzing.

The strong prescriptions and proscriptions that I have highlighted reveal that S-knows-that-p epistemologies work with a closely specified kind of knowing. That knowledge is by no means representative of "human knowledge" or "knowledge in general" (if such terms retain a legitimate reference in these postmodern times), either diachronically (across recorded history) or synchronically (across the late twentieth-century epistemic terrain). Nor have *theories* of knowledge throughout the history of philosophy developed uniformly around these same exclusions and inclusions. Neither Plato, Spinoza, nor Hume, for example, would have denied that there are interconnections between reason and "the passions"; neither Stoics, Marxists, phenomenologists, pragmatists, nor followers of the later Wittgenstein would represent knowledge seeking as a disinterested pursuit, disconnected from everyday concerns. And these are but a few exceptions to the "rule" that has come to govern the epistemology of the Anglo-American mainstream.

The *positivism* of positivist-empiricist epistemologies has been instrumental in ensuring the paradigmatic status of *S*-knows-that-*p* claims and all that is believed to follow from them.[3] For positivist epistemologists, sensory observation in ideal observation conditions is the privileged source of knowledge, offering the best promise of certainty. Knowers are detached, neutral spectators, and the objects of knowledge are separate from them; they are inert items in the observational knowledge-gathering process. Findings are presented in *propositions* (e.g., *S*-knows-that-*p*), which are verifiable by appeals to the observational data. Each individual knowledge-seeker is singly and separately accountable to the evidence; however, the belief is that *his* cognitive efforts are replicable by any other individual knower in the same circumstances. The aim of knowledge seeking is to achieve the capacity to predict, manipulate, and control the behavior of the objects known.

The fact/value distinction that informs present-day epistemology owes its strictest formulation to the positivist legacy. For positivists, value statements are not verifiable and hence are meaningless; they must not be permitted to distort the facts. And it is in the writings of the logical positivists and their heirs that one finds the most definitive modern articulations of the supremacy of scientific knowledge (for which read "the knowledge attainable in physics"). Hence, for example, Karl Popper writes: "Epistemology I take to be the theory of *scientific knowledge*."[4]

From a positivistically derived conception of scientific knowledge comes the ideal objectivity that is alleged to be achievable by any knower who deserves the label. Physical science is represented as the site of ideal, controlled, and objective knowing at its best; its practitioners are held to be knowers *par excellence*. The

positivistic separation of the contexts of discovery and justification produces the conclusion that even though information gathering (discovery) may sometimes be contaminated by the circumstantial peculiarities of everyday life, justificatory procedures can effectively purify the final cognitive product—knowledge—from any such taint. Under the aegis of positivism, attempts to give epistemological weight to the provenance of knowledge claims—to grant justificatory or explanatory significance to social- or personal-historical situations, for example—risk committing the "genetic fallacy." More specifically, claims that epistemological insight can be gained from understanding the psychology of knowers or analyzing their socio-cultural locations invite dismissal either as "psychologism" or as projects belonging to the sociology of knowledge. For epistemological purists, many of these pursuits can provide anecdotal information, but none contributes to the real business of epistemology.

In this sketch I have represented the positivist credo at its starkest because it is these stringent aspects of its program that have trickled down not just to produce the tacit ideals of the epistemological orthodoxy but to inform even well-educated laypersons' conceptions of what it means to be objective and of the authoritative status of modern science.[5] Given the spectacular successes of science and technology, it is no wonder that the scientific method should appear to offer the best available route to reliable, objective knowledge not just of matters scientific but of everything one could want to know, from what makes a car run to what makes a person happy. It is no wonder that reports to the effect that "Science has proved . . . " carry an immediate presumption of truth. Furthermore, the positivist program offered a methodology that would extend not just across the natural sciences, but to the human/social sciences as well. All scientific inquiry—including inquiry in the human sciences—was to be conducted on the model of natural scientific inquiry, especially as practiced in physics.[6] Knowledge of people could be scientific to the extent that it could be based on empirical observations of predictable, manipulable patterns of behavior.

I have focused on features of mainstream epistemology that tend to sustain the belief that a discovery of necessary and sufficient conditions for justifying S-knows-that-p claims could count as the last milestone on the epistemological journey. Such claims are distilled, simplified observational knowledge claims that are objectively derived, propositionally formulable, and empirically testable. The detail of the role they play varies according to whether the position they figure in is foundational or coherentist, externalist or internalist. My intent is not to suggest that S-knows-that-p formulations capture the essence of these disparate epistemic orientations or to reduce them to one common principle. Rather, I am contending that certain reasonably constant features of their diverse functions across a range of inquiries—features that derive at least indirectly from the residual prestige of positivism and its veneration of an idealized scientific methodology—produce epistemologies for which the places S and p can be indiscriminately filled across an inexhaustible range of subject matters. The legislated (not "found") context-independence of the model generates the conclusion that knowledge worthy of the name must transcend the particularities of experience to achieve objective purity and value neutrality. This is a model within which the issue of taking subjectivity into account simply does not arise.

Yet despite the disclaimers, hidden subjectivities produce these epistemologies and sustain their hegemony in a curiously circular process. It is true that, in selecting examples, the context in which S knows or p occurs is rarely considered relevant, for the assumption is that only in abstraction from contextual confusion can clear, unequivocal knowledge claims be submitted for analysis. Yet those examples tend to be selected—whether by chance or by design—from the experiences of a privileged group of people and to be presented as paradigmatic for all knowledge. Hence a certain range of contexts is,

in effect, presupposed. Historically, the philosopher arrogated that privilege to himself, maintaining that an investigation of his mental processes could reveal the workings of human thought. In Baconian and later positivist-empiricist thought, as I have suggested, paradigmatic privilege belongs more specifically to standardized, faceless observers or to scientists. (The latter, at least, have usually been white and male.) Their ordinary observational experiences provide the "simples" of which knowledge is comprised: observational simples caused, almost invariably, by medium-sized physical objects such as apples, envelopes, coins, sticks, and colored patches. The tacit assumptions are that such objects are part of the basic experiences of every putative knower and that more complex knowledge—or scientific knowledge—consists in elaborated or scientifically controlled versions of such experiences. Rarely in the literature, either historical or modern, is there more than a passing reference to knowing other people, except occasionally to a recognition (i.e., observational information) that this is a man—whereas that is a door or a robot. Neither with respect to material objects nor to other people is there any sense of how these "knowns" figure in a person's life.

Not only do these epistemic restrictions suppress the context in which objects are known, they also account for the fact that, apart from simple objects—and even there it is questionable—one cannot, on this model, know anything well enough to do very much with it. One can only *perceive* it, usually at a distance. In consequence, most of the more complex, contentious, and locationally variable aspects of cognitive practice are excluded from epistemological analysis. Hence the knowledge that epistemologists analyze is not of concrete or unique aspects of the physical/social world. It is of *instances* rather than particulars; the norms of formal sameness obscure practical and experiential differences to produce a picture of a homogeneous epistemic community, comprised of discrete individuals with uniform access to the stuff of which knowledge is made.

The project of remapping the epistemic terrain that I envisage is subversive, even anarchistic, in challenging and seeking to displace some of the most sacred principles of standard Anglo-American epistemologies. It abandons the search for and denies the possibility of the disinterested and dislocated view from nowhere. More subversively, it asserts the political investedness of most knowledge-producing activity and insists upon the accountability—the epistemic responsibilities— of knowing subjects to the community, not just to the evidence.[7]

Because my engagement in the project is specifically prompted by a conviction that *gender* must be put in place as a primary analytic category, I start by assuming that it is impossible to sustain the presumption of gender-neutrality that is central to standard epistemologies: the presumption that gender has nothing to do with knowledge, that the mind has no sex, that reason is alike in all men, and man "embraces" woman.[8] But gender is not an enclosed category, for it is always interwoven with such other sociopolitical-historical locations as class, race, and ethnicity, to mention only a few. It is experienced differently, and it plays differently into structures of power and dominance at its diverse intersections with other specificities. From these multiply describable locations, the world looks quite different from the way it might look from nowhere. Homogenizing those differences under a range of standard or typical instances always invites the question, "standard or typical for whom?"[9] Answers to that question must necessarily take subjectivity into account.

My thesis, then, is that a "variable construction" hypothesis[10] requires epistemologists to pay as much attention to the nature and situation— the location—of S as they commonly pay to the content of p; I maintain that a constructivist reorientation requires epistemologists to take subjective factors—factors that pertain to the circumstances of the subject, S—centrally into account in evaluative and justificatory procedures. Yet the socially located, critically dialogical nature of the reoriented epistemological project preserves a realist orientation, ensuring that it will not slide into subjectivism. This caveat is vitally important. Although I shall conclude this essay with a plea for a hybrid breed of relativism, my contention will be that realism and relativism are by no means incompatible. Although I argue the need to excise the positivist side of the positivist-empiricist couple, I retain a modified commitment to the empiricist side for several reasons.

I have suggested that the stark conception of objectivity that characterizes much contemporary epistemology derives from the infusion of empiricism with positivistic values. Jettison those values, and an empiricist core remains that urges both the survival significance and emancipatory significance of achieving reliable knowledge of the physical and social world.[11] People need to be able to explain the world and to explain their circumstances as part of it; hence they need to be able to assume its 'reality' in some minimal sense. The fact of the world's intractability to intervention and wishful thinking is the strongest evidence of its independence from human knowers. Earthquakes, trees, disease, attitudes, and social arrangements are *there* requiring different kinds of reaction and (sometimes) intervention. People cannot hope to transform their circumstances and hence to realize emancipatory goals if their explanations cannot at once account for the intractable dimensions of the world and engage appropriately with its patently malleable features. Therefore it is necessary to achieve some match between knowledge and "reality," even when the reality at issue consists, primarily in social productions such as racism or tolerance, oppression or equality of opportunity. A reconstructed epistemological project has to retain an empirical-realist core that can negotiate the fixities and less stable constructs of the physical-social world, while refusing to endorse the objectivism of the positivist legacy or the subjectivism of radical relativism.

2. AUTONOMOUS SOLIDARITY

Feminist critiques of epistemology and philosophy of science/social science have demonstrated that the ideals of the autonomous reasoner—the dislocated, disinterested observer—and the epistemologies they inform are the artifacts of a small, privileged group of educated, usually prosperous, white men.[12] Their circumstances enable them to believe that they are materially and even affectively autonomous and to imagine that they are nowhere or everywhere, even as they occupy an unmarked position of privilege. Moreover, the ideals of rationality and objectivity that have guided and inspired theorists of knowledge throughout the history of western philosophy have been constructed through processes of excluding the attributes and experiences commonly associated with femaleness and underclass social status: emotion, connection, practicality, sensitivity, and idiosyncrasy.[13] These systematic excisions of "otherness" attest to a presumed—and willed—belief in the stability of a social order that the presumers have good reasons to believe that they can ensure, because they occupy the positions that determine the norms of conduct and enquiry. Yet all that these convictions demonstrate is that ideal objectivity is a generalization from the *subjectivity* of quite a small social group, albeit a group that has the power, security, and prestige to believe that it can generalise its experiences and normative ideals across the social order, thus producing a group of like-minded practitioners ("we") and dismissing "others" as deviant, aberrant ("they").

Richard Foley's book *The Theory of Epistemic Rationality* illustrates my point. Foley bases his theory on a criterion of first-person persuasiveness, which he calls a "subjective foundationalism." He presents exemplary knowledge claims in the standard *S*-knows-that-*p* rubric. Whether or not a propositional knowledge claim turns out to be warranted for any putative knower/believer will depend upon its being "uncontroversial," "argument-proof" *for that individual,* "in the sense

that all possible arguments against it are implausible."[14] Foley is not concerned that his "subjective" appeal could force him into subjectivism or solipsism. His unconcern, I suggest, is precisely a product of the confidence with which he expands his references to *S* into "we." Foley's appeals to *S*'s normality—to his being "one of us" "just like the rest of us"—to his not having "crazy, bizarre [or] outlandish beliefs,"[15] "weird goals," or "weird perceptions,"[16] underpin his assumption that in speaking for *S* he is speaking for everyone—or at least for "all of *us*." Hence he refers to what "any normal individual on reflection would be likely to think,"[17] without pausing to consider the presumptuousness of the terminology. There are no problems, no politics of "we-saying" visible here; this is an epistemology oblivious to its experiential and political specificity. Yet its appeals to a taken-for-granted normality, achieved through commonality, align it with all of the positions of power and privilege that unthinkingly consign to epistemic limbo people who profess "crazy, bizarre, or outlandish" beliefs and negate their claims to the authority that knowledge confers. In its assumed political innocence, it prepares the ground for the practices that make 'knowledge' an honorific and ultimately exclusionary label, restricting it to the products of a narrow subset of the cognitive activities of a closely specified group. The histories of women and other "others" attempting to count as members of that group are justifiably bitter. In short, the assumptions that accord *S*-knows-that-*p* propositions a paradigmatic place generate epistemologies that derive from a privileged subjective specificity to inform sociopolitical structures of dominance and submission. Such epistemologies—and Foley's is just one example—mask the specificity of their origins beneath the putative neutrality of the rubric.

Therefore, although subjectivity does not figure in any explicit sense in the formulaic, purely place-holder status of *S* in Foley's theory, there is no doubt that the assumptions that allow him to presume *S*'s normality—and apolitical status—in effect work to install a very specific conception of subjectivity in the *S*-place: a conception that demands analysis if the full significance of the inclusions and exclusions it produces are to be understood. These "subjects" are interchangeable only across a narrow range of implicit group membership. And the group in question is the dominant social group in western capitalist societies: propertied, educated, white men. Its presumed political innocence needs to be challenged. Critics must ask for whom this epistemology exists; whose interests it serves; and whose it neglects or suppresses in the process.[18]

I am not suggesting that *S*-knows-that-*p* epistemologies are the only ones that rely on silent assumptions of solidarity. Issues about the implicit politics of "we-saying" infect even the work of such an antifoundationalist, anti-objectivist, anti-individualist as Richard Rorty, whom many feminists are tempted to see as an ally in their successor epistemology projects. Again, the manner in which these issues arise is instructive.

In that part of his work with which feminist and other revisionary epistemologists rightly find an affinity,[19] Rorty develops a sustained argument to the effect that the "foundational" (for which read "empiricist-positivist and rationalist") projects of western philosophy have been unable to fulfill their promise. That is to say, they have not been successful in establishing their claims that knowledge must—and can—be grounded in absolute truth and that necessary and sufficient conditions can be ascertained. Rorty turns his back on the (in his view) ill-conceived project of seeking absolute epistemic foundations to advocate a process of "continuing conversation rather than discovering truth."[20] The conversation will be informed and inspired by the work of such "edifying philosophers" as Dewey, Wittgenstein, Heidegger, and (latterly) Gadamer. It will move away from the search for foundations to look within communally created and communably available history, tradition, and culture for the only possible bases for truth claims. Relocating questions about knowledge and truth to positions within the conversations of humankind does

seem to break the thrall of objectivist detachment and to create a forum for dialogic, cooperative debate of the epistemological issues of everyday, practical life. Yet the question is how open that forum would—or could—be; who would have a voice in Rorty's conversations? They are not likely, I suspect, to be those who fall under Foley's exclusions.

In his paper "Solidarity or Objectivity?", Rorty reaffirms his repudiation of objectivist epistemologies to argue that "for the pragmatist [i.e., for him, as pragmatist] . . . knowledge is, like 'truth,' simply a compliment paid to the beliefs which *we* think so well justified that, for the moment, further justification is not needed."[21] He eschews epistemological analysis of truth, rationality, and knowledge to concentrate on questions about "what self-image our society should have of itself."[22] Contending that philosophy is a frankly ethnocentric project and affirming that "'there is only the dialogue,' only *us*," he advocates throwing out "the last residue of transcultural rationality."[23] It is evidently his belief that communal solidarity, guided by principles of liberal tolerance—and of Nietzschean irony—will both provide solace in this foundationless world *and* check the tendencies of ethnocentricity to oppress, marginalize, or colonize.

Yet as Nancy Fraser aptly observes: "Rorty homogenizes social space, assuming tendentiously that there are no deep social cleavages capable of generating conflicting solidarities and opposing 'we's.'"[24] Hence he can presume that there will be no disagreement about the best self-image of "our" society; he can fail to note—or at least to take seriously—the androcentricity, class-centricity, and all of the other centricities that his solidarity claims produce. The very goal of achieving "as much intersubjective agreement as possible," of extending "the reference of 'us' as far as we can,"[25] with the belief that tolerance will do the job when conflicts arise, is unlikely to convince members of groups who have never felt solidarity with the representers of the self-image of the society. The very promise of inclusion in the extension of that "we" is as likely to occasion anxiety as it is to offer hope. Naming ourselves as "we" empowers us, but it always risks disempowering others. The we-saying, then, of assumed or negotiated solidarity must always be submitted to critical analysis.

Now it is neither surprising nor outrageous that epistemologies should derive out of specific human interests. Indeed, it is much less plausible to contend that they do not; human cognitive agents, after all, have made them. Why would they not bear the marks of their makers? Nor does the implication of human interests in theories of knowledge, prima facie, invite censure. It does alert epistemologists to the need for case-by-case analysis and critique of the sources out of which claims to objectivity and neutrality are made.[26] More pointedly, it forces the conclusion that if the ideal of objectivity cannot pretend to have been established in accordance with its own demands, then it has no right to the theoretical hegemony to which it lays claim.

Central to the program of taking subjectivity into account that feminist epistemological inquiry demands, then, is a critical analysis of that very politics of "we-saying" that objectivist epistemologies conceal from view. Whenever an *S*-knows-that-*p* claim is declared paradigmatic, the first task is to analyze the constitution of the group(s) by whom and for whom it is accorded that status.

3. SUBJECTS AND OBJECTS

I have noted that the positivist-empiricist influence on the principal epistemologies of the mainstream manifests itself in assumptions that verifiable knowledge—knowledge worthy of the name—can be analyzed into observational simples; that the methodology of the natural sciences, and especially physics, is a model for productive enquiry; and that the goal of developing a "unified science" translates into a "unity of knowledge" project in which all knowledge—including everyday and social-scientific knowledge about people—would be modeled on the knowledge ideally obtainable in physics. Reliance upon *S*-knows-that-*p* paradigms sustain these convictions. In the preceding section I have shown that these paradigms, in practice, are problematic with respect to the subjects (knowers) who occupy the *S* position, whose subjectivity and accountability are effaced in the formal structure. In this section I shall show that they are ultimately oppressive for subjects who come to occupy the *p* position—who become objects of knowledge—because their subjectivity and specificity are reduced to interchangeable, observable variables. When more elaborated knowledge claims are at issue—theories and interpretations of human behaviors and institutions are the salient examples here—these paradigms generate a presumption in favor of apolitical epistemic postures that is at best deceptive and at worst dangerous, both politically and epistemologically.

This last claim requires some explanation. The purpose of singling out *paradigmatic* knowledge claims is to establish exemplary instances that will map, feature by feature, onto knowledge that differs from the paradigm in content across a wide range of possibilities. Strictly speaking, paradigms are meant to capture just the formal, structural character of legitimate (appropriately verifiable) knowledge. But their paradigmatic status generates presumptions in favor of much wider resemblances across the epistemic terrain than the strictest reading of the model would permit. Hence it looks as if it is not just the paradigm's purely formal features that are generalizable to knowledge that differs not just in complexity but in kind from the simplified, paradigmatic example. Of particular interest in the present context is the fact that paradigms are commonly selected from mundane experiences of virtually indubitable facticity ("Susan knows that the door is open"); they are distilled from simple objects in the world that seem to be just neutrally *there*. There appear to be no political stakes in knowing such a fact. Moreover, it looks (at least from the vantage point of the epistemologist) as though the poorest, most "weird," and most marginalized of knowers would have access to and know about these things in exactly the same way. Hence the substitutionalist assumption that the paradigm relies on points to the conclusion that *all* knowing—knowing theories, institutions, practices, life forms, *and* forms of life—is just as objective, transparent, and apolitical an exercise.

My contention that subjectivity has to be taken into account takes issue with the belief that epistemologists need only to understand the conditions for propositional, observationally derived knowledge, and all the rest will follow. It challenges the concommitant belief that epistemologists need only to understand how such knowledge claims are made and justified by individual, autonomous, self-reliant reasoners to understand all the rest. Such beliefs derive from conceptions of detached and faceless cognitive agency that mask the variability of the experiences and practices from which knowledge is constructed.

Even if necessary and sufficient conditions cannot yet be established, say in the form of unassailable foundations or seamless coherence, there are urgent questions for epistemologists to address. They bear not primarily upon criteria of evidence, justification, and warrantability but upon the "nature" of inquirers: upon their interests in the inquiry, their emotional involvement and background assumptions, and their character; upon their material, historical, and cultural circumstances. Answers to such questions will rarely offer definitive assessments of knowledge claims and hence are not ordinarily open to the charge that they commit the genetic fallacy; but they can be instructive in debates about the worth of such claims. I am thinking of questions about how credibility is established, about connections between knowledge and power, about political agendas and epistemic responsibilities, and about the place of knowledge in ethical and aesthetic judgments. These questions are less concerned with individual, monologic cognitive projects than with the workings of epistemic communities as they are manifested in structures of authority and expertise and in the processes through which knowledge comes to inform public opinion. Such issues will occupy a central place in reconstructed epistemological projects that eschew formalism in order to engage with cognitive practices and to promote emancipatory goals.

The epistemic and moral/political ideals that govern inquiry in technologically advanced, capitalist, free-enterprise western societies are an amalgam of liberal-utilitarian moral values and the empiricist-positivist intellectual values that I have been discussing in this essay. These ideals and values shape both the intellectual enterprises that the society legitimates and the language of liberal individualism that maps out the rhetorical spaces where those enterprises are carried out. The ideal of tolerance and openness is believed to be the right attitude from which, initially, to approach truth claims. It combines with the assumptions that objectivity and value-neutrality govern the rational conduct of scientific and social-scientific research to produce the philosophical commonplaces of late twentieth-century anglo-American societies, not just in "the academy" but in the public perception—the "common sense," in Gramsci's terms—that prevails about the academy and the scientific community.[27] (Recall that for Rorty, tolerance is to ensure that postepistemological societies will sustain productive conversations.) I have noted that a conversational item introduced with the phrase "Science has proved . . ." carries a presumption in favor of its reliability *because of* its objectivity and value-neutrality—a presumption that these facts can stand up to scrutiny *because* they are products of an objective, disinterested process of inquiry. (It is ironic that this patently "genetic" appeal—that is, to the genesis of cognitive products in a certain kind of process—is normally cited to discredit other genetic accounts!) Open and fair-minded consumers of science will recognize its claims to disinterested, tolerant consideration.

I want to suggest that these ideals are inadequate to guide epistemological debates about contentious issues and hence that it is deceptive and dangerous to ignore questions about subjectivity in the name of objectivity and value-neutrality. (Again, this is why simple observational paradigms are so misleading.) To do so, I turn to an example that is now notorious, at least in Canada.

Psychologist Philippe Rushton claims to have demonstrated that "Orientals as a group are more intelligent, more family-oriented, more law-abiding and less sexually promiscuous than whites, and that whites are superior to blacks in all the same respects."[28] Presented as "facts" that "science [i.e., an allegedly scientific psychology] has proved . . ." by using an objective statistical methodology, Rushton's findings carry a presumption in favor of their reliability *because* they are products of objective research.[29] The "Science has proved . . ." rhetoric creates a public presumption in favor of taking them at face value, believing them true until they are proven false. It erects a screen, a blind, behind which the researcher, like any other occupant of the *S* place, can abdicate accountability to anything but "the facts" and can present himself as a neutral, infinitely replicable vehicle through which data passes en route to becoming knowledge. He can claim to have fulfilled his epistemic obligations if, "withdraw[ing] to his professional self,"[30] he can argue that he has been "objective," detached and disinterested in his research. The rhetoric of objectivity and value-neutrality places the burden of proof on the challenger rather than the fact-finder and judges her guilty of intolerance, dogmatism, or ideological excess if she cannot make her challenge good. That same rhetoric generates a conception of knowledge for its own sake that at once effaces accountability requirements and threatens the dissolution of viable intellectual and moral community.

I have noted that the "Science has proved . . ." rhetoric derives from the sociopolitical influence of the philosophies of science that incorporate and are underwritten by *S*-knows-that-*p* epistemologies. Presented as the findings of a purely neutral observer who "discovered" facts about racial inferiority and superiority in controlled observation conditions so that he could not rationally withhold assent, Rushton's results ask the community to be equally objective and neutral in assessing them. These requirements are at once reasonable and troubling. They are reasonable because the empiricist-realist component that I maintain is vital to any emancipatory epistemology makes it a mark of competent, reasonable inquiry to approach even the most unsavory truth claims seriously, albeit critically. But the requirements are troubling in their implicit appeal to a doxastic involuntarism that becomes an escape hatch from the demands of subjective accountability. The implicit claim is that empirical inquiry is not only a neutral and impersonal process but also an inexorable one; it is compelling, even coercive, in what it turns up to the extent that a rational inquirer *cannot* withhold assent. He has no choice but to believe that *p,* however unpalatable the findings may be. The individualism and presumed disinterestedness of the paradigm reinforces this claim.

It is difficult, however, to believe in the coincidence of Rushton's discoveries; they could only be compelling in that strong sense if they could be shown to be purely coincidental—brute fact—something he came upon as he might bump into a wall. Talk about his impartial reading of the data assumes such hard facticity: the facticity of a blizzard or a hot sunny day. "Data" is the problematic term here, suggesting that facts presented themselves neutrally to Rushton's observing eye as though they were literally given, not sought or made. Yet it is not easy to conceive of Rushton's "data" in perfect independence from ongoing debates about race, sex, and class.

These difficulties are compounded when Rushton's research is juxtaposed against analogous projects in other places and times. In her book, *Sexual Science.*[31] Cynthia Russett documents the intellectual climate of the nineteenth century, when claims for racial and sexual equality were threatening upheavals in the social order. She notes that there was a concerted effort just at that time among scientists to produce studies that would demonstrate the "natural" sources of racial and sexual *in*equality. Given its aptness to the climate of the times, it is hard to believe that this research was "dislocated," prompted by a disinterested spirit of objective, neutral fact-finding. It is equally implausible, at a time when racial and sexual unrest is again threatening the complacency of the liberal dream—and meeting with strong conservative efforts to contain it—that it could be purely by coincidence that Rushton reaches the conclusion he does. Consider Rushton's contention that the brain has increased in size and the genitals have shrunk correspondingly over the course of human evolution; blacks have larger genitals, ergo. . . . Leaving elementary logical fallacies aside, it is impossible not to hear echoes of nineteenth-century medical science's "proofs" that excessive mental activity in women interferes with the proper functioning of the uterus; hence, permitting women to engage in higher intellectual activity impedes performance of their proper reproductive roles.

The connections Rushton draws between genital and brain size, and conformity to idealized patterns of good liberal democratic citizenship, trade upon analogous normative assumptions. The rhetoric of stable, conformist family structure as the site of controlled, utilitarian sexual expression is commonly enlisted to sort the "normal" from the "deviant" and to promote conservative conceptions of the self-image a society should have of itself.[32] The idea that the dissolution of "the family" (the nuclear, two-parent, patriarchal family) threatens the destruction of civilized society has been deployed to perpetuate white male privilege and compulsory heterosexuality, especially for women. It has been invoked to preserve homogeneous WASP values from disruption by "unruly" (not law-abiding, sexually promiscuous) elements. Rushton's contention that "naturally occurring" correlations can explain the demographic distribution of tendencies to unruliness leaves scant room for doubt about what he believes a society concerned about

its self-image should do: suppress unruliness. As Julian Henriques puts a similar point, by a neat reversal, the "black person becomes the cause of racism whereas the white person's prejudice is seen as a natural effect of the information-processing mechanisms."[33] The "facts" that Rushton produces are simply presented to the scholarly and lay communities so that they allegedly "speak for themselves" on two levels: both roughly as data and in more formal garb as research findings. What urgently demands analysis is the process by which these "facts" are inserted into a public arena that is prepared to receive them, with the result that inquiry stops right where it should begin.[34]

My point is that it is not enough just to be more rigorously empirical in adjudicating such controversial knowledge claims with the expectation that biases that may have infected the "context of discovery" will be eradicated in the purifying process of justification. Rather, the scope of epistemological investigation has to expand to merge with moral-political inquiry, acknowledging that "facts" are always infused with values and that both facts and values are open to ongoing critical debate. It would be necessary to demonstrate the innocence of descriptions (their derivation from pure data) and to show the perfect congruence of descriptions with "the described" in order to argue that descriptive theories have no normative force. Their assumed innocence licenses an evasion of the accountability that socially concerned communities have to demand of their producers of knowledge. Only the most starkly positivistic epistemology merged with the instrumental rationality it presupposes could presume that inquirers are accountable only to the evidence. Evidence is *selected,* not found, and selection procedures are open to scrutiny. Nor can critical analysis stop there, for the funding and institutions that enable inquirers to pursue certain projects and not others explicitly legitimize the work.[35] So the lines of accountability are long and interwoven; only a genealogy of their multiple strands can begin to unravel the issues.

What, then, should occur within epistemic communities to ensure that scientists and other knowers cannot conceal bias and prejudice or claim *a right not to know* about their background assumptions and the significance of their locations?

The crux of my argument is that the phenomenon of the disinterested inquirer is the exception rather than the rule; there are no dislocated truths, and some facts about the locations and interests at the source of inquiry are always pertinent to questions about freedom and accountability. Hence I am arguing, with Naomi Scheman, that

> Feminist epistemologists and philosophers of science [who] *along with others who have been the objects of knowledge-as-control* [have to] understand and . . . pose alternatives to the epistemology of modernity. As it has been central to this epistemology to guard its products from contamination by connection to the particularities of its producers, it must be central to the work of its critics and to those who would create genuine alternatives to remember those connections . . .[36]

There can be no doubt that research is—often imperceptibly—shaped by presuppositions and interests external to the inquiry itself, which cannot be filtered out by standard, objective, disinterested epistemological techniques.[37]

In seeking to explain what makes Rushton possible,[38] the point cannot be to exonerate him as a mere product of his circumstances and times. Rushton accepts grants and academic honors in his own name, speaks "for himself" in interviews with the press, and claims credit where credit is to be had. He upholds the validity of his findings. Moreover, he participates fully in the rhetoric of the autonomous, objective inquirer. Yet although Rushton is plainly accountable for the sources and motivations of his projects, he is not singly responsible. Such research is legitimized by the community and speaks in a discursive space that is available and prepared for it. So scrutinizing Rushton's "scientific" knowledge claims demands an examination of the moral and intellectual health of

a community that is infected by racial and sexual injustices at every level. Rushton may have had reasons to believe that his results would be welcome.

Equally central, then, to a feminist epistemological program of taking subjectivity into account are case-by-case analyses of the political and other structural circumstances that generate projects and lines of inquiry. Feminist critique—with critiques that center on other marginalizing structures—needs to act as an "experimental control" in epistemic practice so that every inquiry, assumption, and discovery is analyzed for its place in and implications for the prevailing sex/gender system, in its intersections with the systems that sustain racism, homophobia, and ethnocentrism.[39] The burden of proof falls upon inquirers who claim neutrality. In all "objective" inquiry, the positions and power relations of *gendered* and otherwise located subjectivity have to be submitted to piece-by-piece scrutiny that will vary according to the field of research. The task is intricate, because the subjectivity of the inquirer is always also implicated and has to be taken into account. Hence, the inquiry is at once critical and self-critical. But this is no monologic, self-sufficient enterprise. Conclusions are reached and immoderate subjective omissions and commissions become visible in dialogic processes among inquirers and—in social science—between inquirers and the subjects of their research.

It emerges from this analysis that although the ideal objectivity of the universal knower is neither possible nor desirable, a realistic commitment to achieving empirical adequacy that engages in situated analyses of the subjectivities of both the knower and (where appropriate) the known is both desirable and possible. This exercise in supposing that the places in the *S*-knows-that-*p* formula could be filled by asserting "Rushton knows that blacks are inferior" shows that simple, propositional knowledge claims that represent inquirers as purely neutral observers of unignorable data cannot be permitted to count as paradigms of knowledge. Objectivity *requires* taking subjectivity into account.

4. KNOWING SUBJECTS

Women—and other "others"—are *produced* as "objects of knowledge-as-control" by *S*-knows-that-*p* epistemologies and the philosophies of science/social science that they inform. When subjects become objects of knowledge, reliance upon simple observational paradigms has the consequence of assimilating those subjects to physical objects, reducing their subjectivity and specificity to interchangeable, observable features.

S-knows-that-*p* epistemologies take for granted that observational knowledge of everyday objects forms the basis from which all knowledge is constructed. Prima facie, this is a persuasive belief. Observations of childhood development (at least in materially advantaged, "normal" western families) suggest that simple observational truths are the first bits of knowledge an infant acquires in learning to recognize and manipulate everyday objects. Infants seem to be objective in this early knowing: they *come across* objects and learn to deal with them; apparently without preconceptions and without altering the properties of the objects. Objects ordinarily remain independent of a child's knowing; these same objects—cups, spoons, chairs, trees, and flowers—seem to be the simplest and surest things that every adult knows. They are *there* to be known and are reasonably constant through change. In the search for examples of what standard knowers know "for sure," such knowledge claims are obvious candidates. So it is not surprising that they have counted as paradigmatic.

I want to suggest, however, that when one considers how basic and crucial *knowing other people* is in the production of human subjectivity, paradigms and objectivity take on a different aspect.[40] If epistemologists require paradigms or other less formal exemplary knowledge claims, knowing other people in personal relationships is at least as worthy a contender as knowledge of everyday objects. Developmentally, learning what she or he can expect of other people is one of the first and most essential kinds of knowledge a child acquires. She or he learns to respond *cognitively* to the people who are a vital part of and provide access to her or his environment *long before* she or he can recognize the simplest physical objects. Other people are the point of origin of a child's entry into the material/physical environment both in providing or inhibiting access to that environment—in *making* it—and in fostering entry into the language with which children learn to name. Their initial induction into language generates a framework of presuppositions that prompts children, from the earliest stages, to construct their environments variously, according to the quality of their affective, intersubjective locations. Evidence about the effects of sensory and emotional deprivation on the development of cognitive agency shows that a child's capacity to make sense of the world (and the manner of engaging in that process) is intricately linked with her or his caregivers' construction of the environment.

Traditionally, theories of knowledge tend to be derived from the experiences of uniformly educated, articulate, epistemically "positioned" adults who introspect retrospectively to review what they must once have known most simply and clearly. Locke's *tabula rasa* is one model; Descartes's radical doubt is another. Yet this introspective process consistently bypasses the epistemic significance of early experiences with other people, with whom the relations of these philosophers must surely have been different from their relations to objects in their environment. As Seyla Benhabib wryly notes, it is a strange world from which this picture of knowledge is derived: a world in which "individuals are grown up before they have been born; in which boys are men before they have been children; a world where neither mother, nor sister, nor wife exist."[41] Whatever the historical variations in childraising practices, evidence implicit in (similarly evolving) theories of knowledge points to a noteworthy constancy. In separated adulthood, the knowledge that enables a knower to give or withhold trust as a child—and hence to survive—is passed over as unworthy of philosophical notice. It is tempting to conclude that theorists of knowledge must either be childless or so disengaged from the rearing of children as to have minimal developmental awareness. Participators in childraising could not easily ignore the primacy of knowing and being known by other people in cognitive development, nor could they denigrate the role such knowledge plays throughout an epistemic history. In view of the fact that disengagement throughout a changing history and across a range of class and racial boundaries has been possible primarily for *men* in western societies, this aspect of the androcentricity of objectivist epistemologies is not surprising.

Knowing other people in relationships requires constant learning: how to be with them, respond to them, and act toward them. In this respect it contrasts markedly with the immediacy of common, sense-perceptual paradigms. In fact, if exemplary "bits" of knowledge were drawn from situations where people have to *learn* to know, rather than from taken-for-granted adult expectations, the complexity of knowing even the simplest things would not so readily be masked, and the fact that knowledge is *qualitatively* variable would be more readily apparent. Consider the strangeness of traveling in a country and culture where one has to suspend judgment about how to identify and deal with things like simple artifacts, flora and fauna, customs and cultural phenomena. These experiences remind epistemologists of how tentative the process of making everyday observations and judgments really is.

Knowledge of other people develops, operates, and is open to interpretation at various levels; it admits of degree in ways that knowing that a book is red does not. Such knowledge is not primarily propositional; I can know that Alice is clever and not *know* her very well at all in a "thicker" sense. Knowing "facts" (the standard *S*-knows-that-*p* substitutions) is part of such knowing, but the knowledge involved is more than and different from its propositional parts. Nor is this knowledge reducible to the simple observational knowledge of the traditional paradigms. The fact that it is acquired differently, interactively, and relationally differentiates it both as process and as product from standard propositional knowledge. Yet its status as knowledge disturbs the smooth surface of the paradigm's structure. The contrast between its multidimensional, multiperspectival character and the stark simplicity of standard paradigms requires philosophers to reexamine the practice of granting exemplary status to those paradigms. "Knowing how" and "knowing that" are implicated, but they do not begin to tell the whole story.

The contention that people are *knowable* may sit uneasily with psychoanalytic decenterings of conscious subjectivity and postmodern critiques of the unified subject of Enlightenment humanism. But I think this is a tension that has to be acknowledged and maintained. In practice, people often know one another well enough to make good decisions about who can be counted on and who cannot, who makes a good ally and who does not. Yet precisely because of the fluctuations and contradictions of subjectivity, this process is ongoing, communicative, and interpretive. It is never fixed or complete; any fixity claimed for "the self" will be a fixity in flux. Nonetheless, I argue that something must be fixed to "contain" the flux even enough to permit references to and ongoing relationships with "this person." Knowing people always occurs within the terms of this tension.

Problems about determining criteria for justifying claims to know another person—the utter availability of necessary and sufficient conditions, the complete inadequacy of *S*-knows-that-*p* paradigms—must account for philosophical reluctance to count this as knowledge that bears epistemological investigation. Yet my suggestion that such knowledge is a model for a wide range of knowledge and is not merely inchoate and unmanageable recommends itself the more strongly in view of the extent to which cognitive practice is grounded upon such knowledge. I am thinking not just of everyday interactions with other people, but of the specialized knowledge—such as Rushton's—that claims institutional authority. Educational theory and practice, psychology, sociology, anthropology, law, some aspects of medicine and philosophy, politics, history, and economics all depend for their credibility upon knowing people. Hence it is all the more curious that observation-based knowledge of material objects and the methodology of the physical sciences hold such relatively unchallenged sway as the paradigm—and paragon—of intellectual achievement. The results of according continued veneration to observational paradigms are evident in the reductive approaches of behaviorist psychology. They are apparent in parochial impositions of meaning upon the practices of other cultures which is still characteristic of some areas of anthropology, and in the simple translation of present-day descriptions into past cultural contexts that characterizes some historical and archaeological practice. But feminist, hermeneutic, and postmodern critiques are slowly succeeding in requiring objectivist social scientists to reexamine their presuppositions and practices. In fact, it is methodological disputes within the social sciences—and the consequent unsettling of positivistic hegemony—that, according to Susan Hekman, have set the stage for the development of a productive, postmodern approach to epistemology for contemporary feminists.[42]

I am not proposing that knowing other people should become *the* new epistemological paradigm but rather that it has a strong claim to exemplary status in the epistemologies that feminist and other case-by-case analyses will produce. I am proposing further that if epistemologists require a model drawn from "scientific" inquiry, then a reconstructed, interpretive social science, liberated from positivistic constraints, will be a better resource than natural science—or physics—for knowledge as such.

Social science of whatever stripe is constrained by the factual-informational details that constrain all attempts to know people; physical, historical, biographical, environmental, social-structural, and other *facts* constitute its "objects" of study. These facts are available for objective analysis, yet they also lend themselves to varying degrees of interpretation and ideological construction. Social science often focuses upon meanings, upon purposeful and learned behavior, preferences, and intentions, with the aim of explaining what Sandra Harding calls "the origins, forms and prevalence of apparently irrational but culturewide patterns of human belief and action."[43] Such phenomena cannot be measured and quantified to provide results comparable to the results of a controlled physics experiment. Yet this constraint neither precludes social-scientific objectivity nor reclaims the methodology of physics as paradigmatic. Harding is right to maintain that "the totally reasonable exclusion of intentional and learned behavior from the subject matter of physics is a good reason to regard enquiry in physics as atypical of scientific knowledge-seeking."[44] I am arguing that it is equally atypical of everyday knowledge-seeking. Interpretations of intentional and learned behavior are indeed subjectively variable; taking subjectivity into account does not *entail* abandoning objectivity. Rabinow and Sullivan put the point well: "Discourse being about something, one must understand the world in order to interpret it . . . Human action and interpretation are subject to many *but not infinitely many* constructions."[45] When theorists acknowledge the oddity and peculiar insularity of physics-derived paradigms with their suppression of subjectivity, it is clear that their application to areas of inquiry in which subjectivities are the "objects" of study has to be contested.

The problem about claiming an exemplary role for personal-knowledge paradigms is to show how the kinds of knowledge integral to human relationships could work in situations where the object of knowledge is inanimate. The case has to be made by analogy and not by requiring knowers to convert from being objective observers to being friends with tables and chairs, chemicals, particles, cells, planets, rocks, trees, and insects. There are obvious points of disanalogy, not the least of which derives from the fact that chairs and plants and rocks cannot reciprocate in the ways that people can. There will be none of the mutual recognition and affirmation between observer and observed that there is between people. But Heisenberg's "uncertainty principle" suggests that not even physical objects are inert in and untouched by observational processes. If there is any validity to this suggestion, then it is not so easy to draw rigid lines separating responsive from unresponsive objects. Taking knowledge of other people as a model does not, *per impossibile,* require scientists to begin talking to their rocks and cells or to admit that the process is not working when the rocks fail to respond. It calls, rather, for a recognition that rocks, cells, and scientists are located in multiple relations to one another, all of which are open to analysis and critique. Singling out and privileging the asymmetrical observer–observed relation is but one possibility.

A more stubborn point of disanalogy may appear to attach to the belief that it is *possible* to know physical objects, whereas it is never possible really to know other people. But this apparent disanalogy appears to prevent the analogy from going through because of another feature of the core presupposition of empiricist-objectivist theories.

According to the standard paradigms, empirical observation can produce knowledge that is universally and uncontrovertibly established for all time. Whether or not such perfect knowledge has ever been achieved is an open question; a belief in its possibility guides and regulates mainstream epistemologies and theories of science. The presumption that knowing other people is difficult to the point of near impossibility is declared by contrast with those paradigms, whose realization may only be possible in contrived, attenuated instances. By *that* standard, knowing other people, however well, does look like as pale an approximation as it was for Descartes,

by contrast with the "clear and distinct ideas" he was otherwise able to achieve. The question, again, is why *that* standard, which governs so minuscule a part of the epistemic lives even of members of the privileged professional class and gender, should regulate legitimate uses of the label "knowledge."

If the empiricist-positivist standard were displaced by more complex analyses in which knowledge claims are provisional and approximate, knowing other people might not seem to be so different. Current upheavals in epistemology point to the productivity of hermeneutic, interpretive, literary methods of analysis and explanation in the social sciences. The skills these approaches require are not so different from the interpretive skills that human relationships require. The extent of their usefulness for the natural sciences is not yet clear. But one point of the challenge is to argue that natural-scientific enquiry has to be located differently, where it can be recognized as a sociopolitical-historical activity in which knowing who the scientist is can reveal important epistemological dimensions of her or his inquiry.

A recognition of the space that needs to be kept open for reinterpretation of the contextualizing that adequate knowledge requires becomes clearer in the light of the "personal" analogy. Though the analogy is not perfect, it is certainly no more preposterous to argue that people should try to know physical objects in the nuanced way that they know their friends than it is to argue that they should try to know people in the unsubtle way that they often claim to know physical objects.

Drawing upon such an interpretive approach across the epistemic terrain would guard against reductivism and rigidity. Knowing other people occurs in a persistent interplay between opacity and transparency, between attitudes and postures that elude a knower's grasp and patterns that are clear and relatively constant. Hence knowers are kept on their cognitive toes. In its need to accommodate change and growth, this knowledge contrasts further with traditional paradigms that deal, on the whole, with objects that can be treated as permanent. In knowing other people, a knower's subjectivity is implicated from its earliest developmental stages; in such knowing, her or his subjectivity is produced and reproduced. Analogous reconstructions often occur in the subjectivity of the person(s) she or he knows. Hence such knowledge works from a conception of subject–object relations different from that implicit in simple empirical paradigms. Claims to know a person are open to negotiation between knower and "known," where the "subject" and "object" positions are always, in principle, interchangeable. In the process, it is important to watch for discrepancies between a person's sense of her or his own subjectivity and a would-be knower's conception of how things are for her or him; neither the self-conception nor the knower-conception can claim absolute authority, because the limits of self-consciousness constrain the process as closely as the interiority of mental processes and experiential constructs and their unavailability to observation.

That an agent's subjectivity is so clearly implicated may create the impression that this knowledge is, indeed, purely subjective. But such a conclusion would be unwarranted. There *are* facts that have to be respected: facts that constitute "the person one is" at any historical moment.[46] Only certain stories can accurately be told; others simply cannot. "External" facts are obvious constraints: facts about age, sex, place and date of birth, height, weight, and hair color—the information that appears on a passport. They would count as objective even on a fairly traditional understanding of the term. Other information is reasonably objective as well: facts about marriage or divorce, childbirth, siblings, skills, education, employment, abode, and travel. But the intriguing point about knowing people—and another reason why it is epistemologically instructive— is that even knowing all the *facts* about someone does not count as knowing her as the person she is. No more can knowing all the facts about oneself, past and present, guarantee self-knowledge.

Yet none of these problems raise doubts that there is such a creature as the person I am or the person anyone else is now. Nor do they indicate the impossibility of knowing other people. If the limitations of these accumulated factual claims were taken seriously with respect to empirical knowledge more generally, the limitations of an epistemology built from *S*-knows-that-*p* claims would be more clearly apparent.

That perfect, objective knowledge of other people is not possible gives no support to a contention *either* that "other minds" are radically unknowable *or* that people's claims to know one another never merit the label "knowledge." Residual assumptions to the effect that people are opaque to one another may explain why this knowledge has had minimal epistemological attention. Knowledge, as the tradition defines it, is *of* objects; only by assimilating people to objects can one hope to know them. This long-standing assumption is challenged by my claims that knowing other people is an exemplary kind of knowing and that subjectivity has always to be taken into account in making and assessing knowledge claims of any complexity.

5. RELATIVISM AFTER ALL?

The project I am proposing, then, requires a new *geography* of the epistemic terrain: one that is no longer primarily a physical geography, but a population geography that develops qualitative analyses of subjective positions and identities and the sociopolitical structures that produce them. Because differing social positions generate variable constructions of reality and afford different perspectives on the world, the revisionary stages of this project will consist of case-by-case analyses of the knowledge produced in specific social positions. These analyses derive from a recognition that knowers are always *somewhere*— and at once limited and enabled by the specificities of their locations.[47] It is an interpretive project, alert to the possibility of finding generalities and commonalities within particulars and hence of the explanatory potential that opens up when such commonalities can be delineated. But it is wary of the reductivism that results when commonalities are presupposed or forced. It has no ultimate foundation, but neither does it float free, because it is grounded in experiences and practices, in the efficacy of dialogic negotiation and of action.

All of this having been said, my argument in this essay points to the conclusion that necessary and sufficient conditions for establishing empirical knowledge claims cannot be found, at least where experientially significant knowledge is at issue. Hence it poses the question whether feminist epistemologists must, after all, "come out" as relativists. In view of what I have been arguing, the answer to that question will have to be a qualified "yes." Yet the relativism that my argument generates is sufficiently nuanced and sophisticated to escape the scorn—and the anxiety—that "relativism, after all" usually occasions. To begin with, it refuses to occupy the negative side of the traditional absolutism/relativism dichotomy. It is at once realist, rational, and significantly objective; hence it is not forced to define itself within or against the oppositions between realism and relativism, rationality and relativism, or objectivism and relativism.[48] Moreover, it takes as its starting point a recognition that the "positive" sides of these dichotomies have been caricatured to affirm a certainty that was never rightfully theirs.

The opponents of relativism have been so hostile, so thoroughly scornful in their dismissals, that it is no wonder that feminists, well aware of the folk-historical identification of women with the forces of unreason, should resist the very thought that the logic of feminist emancipatory analyses points in that direction.[49] Feminists know, if they know anything at all, that they have to develop the best possible explanations—the "truest" explanations—of how things are if they are to intervene effectively in social structures and institutions. The intransigence of material circumstances constantly reminds them

that their world-making possibilities are neither unconstrained nor infinite; they have to be able to produce accurate, transformative analyses of things as they *are*. In fact, many feminists are vehement in their resistance to relativism precisely because they suspect—not without reason—that only the supremely powerful and privileged, the self-proclaimed sons of God, could believe that they can make the world up as they will and practice that supreme tolerance in whose terms all possible constructions of reality are equally worthy. Their fears are persuasive. Yet even at the risk of speaking within the oppositional mode, it is worth thinking seriously about the alternative. For there is no doubt that only the supremely powerful and privileged could believe, in the face of all the evidence to the contrary, that there is only one true view, and it is theirs; that they alone have the resources to establish universal, incontrovertible, and absolute Truth. Donna Haraway aptly notes that: "Relativism is a way of being nowhere and claiming to be everywhere"[50] but absolutism is a way of being everywhere while pretending to be nowhere—and neither one, in its starkest articulation, will do. For this reason alone, it is clear that the absolutism/relativism dichotomy needs to be displaced because it does not, as a true dichotomy must, use up all of the alternatives.[51]

The position I am advocating is one for which knowledge is always *relative to* (i.e., a perspective *on,* a standpoint *in*) specifiable circumstances. Hence it is constrained by a realist, empiricist commitment according to which getting those circumstances right is vital to effective action. It may appear to be a question-begging position, for it does assume that the circumstances can be known, and it relies heavily upon pragmatic criteria to make good that assumption. It can usually avoid regress, for although the circumstances in question may have to be specified *relative to* other circumstances, prejudgments, and theories, it is never (as with Neurath's raft) necessary to take away all of the pieces—all of the props—at once. Inquiry grows out of and turns back to practice, to action; inquirers are always *in media res,* and the *res* are both identifiable and constitutive of perspectives and possibilities for action. Practice will show, not once and for all but case by case, whether conclusions are reasonable and workable. Hence the position at once allows for the development of practical projects and for their corrigibility.

This "mitigated relativism" has a skeptical component: a consequence many feminists will resist even more vigorously than they will resist my claim for relativism. Western philosophy is still in thrall to an Enlightenment legacy that equates skepticism with nihilism: the belief that if no absolute foundations—no necessary and sufficient conditions—can be established, then there can be no knowledge.[52] Nothing is any more reasonable or rational than anything else; there is nothing to believe in. This is the skepticism that necessary and sufficient conditions are meant to forestall.

But there are other skepticisms which are resourceful, not defeatist. The ancient skepticisms of Pyrrho and Sextus Empiricus were declarations not of nihilism but of the impossibility of certainty, of the need to withhold definitive judgment. They advocated continual searching in order to prevent error by suspending judgment. They valued a readiness to reconsider and warned against hasty conclusions. These were skepticisms about the possibility of definitive knowledge but not about the existence of a (knowable?) reality. For Pyrrhonists, skepticism was a moral stance that was meant to ensure the inner quietude (*ataraxia*) that was essential to happiness.[53]

My suggestion that feminist epistemologists can find a resource in such skepticisms cannot be pushed to the point of urging that they take on the whole package. There is no question that the quietude of *ataraxia* could be the achievement that feminists are after. Nor could they take on a skepticism that would immobilize them by negating all possibilities for action: a quietism born of a theorized incapacity to choose or take a stand. So the skepticism that flavors the position I am advocating is better characterized as a common-sense, practical skepticism of everyday life than as a technical, philosophers' skepticism. It resembles the "healthy skepticism" that parents teach their children about media advertising and the skepticism that marks cautiously informed attitudes to politicians' promises.

Above all, feminists cannot opt for a skepticism that would make it impossible to know that certain practices and institutions are *wrong* and likely to remain so. The political ineffectiveness of universal tolerance no longer needs demonstrating: sexism is only the most obvious example of an undoubted intolerable. (Seyla Benhabib notes that Rorty's "admirable demand to 'let a hundred flowers bloom' is motivated by a desire to depoliticize philosophy."[54]) So even the skepticism that I am advocating is problematic in the sense that it has to be carefully measured and articulated if it is not to amount merely to "an apology for the existing order."[55] Its heuristic, productive dimensions are best captured by Denise Riley's observation that "an active skepticism about the integrity of the sacred category 'women' would be no merely philosophical doubt to be stifled in the name of effective political action in the world. On the contrary, it would be a condition *for* the latter."[56] It is in "making strange," loosening the hold of taken-for-granted values, ideals, categories, and theories, that skepticism demonstrates its promise.

Michel Foucault is one of the most articulate late twentieth-century successors of the ancient skeptics. A skeptic in his refusal of dogmatic unities, essences, and labels, Foucault examines changing practices of knowledge rather than taking the standard epistemological route of assuming a unified rationality or science. He eschews totalizing, universalist assumptions in his search for what John Rajchman calls the "invention of specific forms of experience which are taken up and transformed again and again."[57] His is a skepticism about the certainty and stability of systems of representation. Like the ancient skeptics, Foucault can be cast as a realist. He never doubts that there *are* things, institutions, and practices whose genealogies and archaeologies can be written. His position recommends itself for the freedom that its skeptical component offers. Hence he claims

> All my analyses are against the idea of universal necessities in human existence. They show the arbitrariness of institutions and show which space of freedom we can still enjoy and how many changes can still be made.[58]

Yet this is by no means an absolute freedom, for Foucault also observes

> My point is not that everything is bad, but that everything is dangerous, which is not exactly the same as bad. If everything is dangerous, then we always have something to do. So my position leads not to apathy but to a hyper- and pessimistic activism. . . . [T]he ethico-political choice we have to make . . . is to determine which is the main danger.[59]

One of the most urgent tasks that Foucault has left undone is that of showing how we can *know* what is dangerous.

There are many tensions within the strands that my skeptical-relativist recommendations try to weave together. For these I do not apologize. At this critical juncture in the articulation of emancipatory epistemological projects it is impossible to have all of the answers, to resolve all of the tensions and paradoxes. I have exposed some ways in which *S*-knows-that-*p* epistemologies are dangerous and have proposed one route toward facing and disarming those dangers: taking subjectivity into account. The solutions that route affords and the further dangers it reveals will indicate the directions that the next stages of this enquiry must take.[60]

NOTES

1. I allude here to the title of Thomas Nagel's book, *A View From Nowhere* (Oxford: Oxford University Press, 1986).
2. I owe the phrase *surrogate knower* to Naomi Scheman, which she coined in her paper "Descartes and Gender," presented to the conference "Reason, Gender, and the Moderns," University of Toronto, February 1990. I draw on this idea to make a set of points rather different from these in my "Who Cares? The Poverty of Objectivism for Moral Epistemology," in Alan Megill, ed., *Rethinking Objectivity Annals of Scholarship* 9 (1992).
3. For an account of the central tenets of logical positivism, a representative selection of articles, and an extensive bibliography, see A. J. Ayer, ed., *Logical Positivism* (New York: The Free Press, 1959).
4. Karl Popper, *Objective Knowledge* (Oxford: Clarendon Press, 1972), 108; emphasis in original.
5. Mary Hesse advisedly notes that philosophers of science would now more readily assert than they would have done in the heyday of positivism that facts in both the natural and social sciences are "value-laden." [See Mary Hesse, *Revolutions and Reconstructions in the Philosophy of Science* (Bloomington: Indiana University Press, 1980), 172–73.] I am claiming, however, that everyday conceptions of scientific authority are still significantly informed by a residual positivistic faith.
6. For classic statements of this aspect of the positivistic program see, for example, Rudolf Carnap, "Psychology in Physical Language"; and Otto Neurath, "Sociology and Physicalism," in Ayer, ed., *Logical Positivism.*
7. I discuss such responsibilities in my *Epistemic Responsibility* (Hanover, N.H.: University Press of New England, 1987).
8. See, for example, Joan Wallach Scott, "Is Gender a Useful Category of Historical Analysis?" in her book *Gender and the Politics of History* (New York: Columbia University Press, 1989).
9. Paul Moser, for example, in reviewing my *Epistemic Responsibility,* takes me to task for not announcing "the necessary and sufficient conditions for one's being epistemically responsible." He argues that even if, as I claim throughout the book, epistemic responsibility does not lend itself to analysis in those terms, "we could still provide necessary and sufficient conditions for the wide range of typical instances, and then

handle the wayward cases independently" [Paul Moser, review of *Epistemic Responsibility,* in *Philosophical Books* 29 (1988): 154–56]. Yet it is precisely their "typicality" that I contest. Moser's review is a salient example of the tendency of dominant epistemologies to claim as their own even those positions that reject their central premises.

10. See p. 1 of this essay for a formulation of this thesis.

11. These aims are continuous with some of the aims of recent projects to naturalize epistemology by drawing on the resources of cognitive psychology. See especially W. V. Quine, "Epistemology Naturalized," in *Ontological Relativity and Other Essays* (New York: Columbia University Press, 1969), Hilary Kornblith, ed. *Naturalizing Epistemology* (Cambridge, Mass.: MIT Press, 1985); and his paper "The Naturalistic Project in Epistemology: A Progress Report," presented to the American Philosophical Association, Los Angeles, April 1990; and Alvin I. Goldman, *Epistemology and Cognition* (Cambridge, Mass.: Harvard University Press, 1986). Feminist epistemologists who are developing this line of inquiry are Jane Duran, *Toward a Feminist Epistemology* (Savage, MD: Rowman and Littlefield, 1991); and Lynn Hankinson Nelson, *Who Knows: From Quine to a Feminist Empiricism* (Philadelphia: Temple University Press, 1990). Feminists who find a resource in this work have to contend with the fact that the cognitive psychology that informs it presupposes a constancy in "human nature," exemplified in "representative selves" who have commonly been white, male, and middle class. They have also to remember the extent to which appeals to "nature" have oppressed women and other marginal groups.

12. For an extensive bibliography of such critiques up to 1989, see Alison Wylie, Kathleen Okruhlik, Sandra Morton, and Leslie Thielen-Wilson, "Philosophical Feminism: A Bibliographic Guide to Critiques of Science," *Resources for Feminist Research/Documentation sur la Recherche Feministe* 19, 2 (June 1990): 2–36.

13. For an analysis of the androcentricity—the 'masculinity' of these ideals—and their 'feminine' exclusions in theories of knowledge see Genevieve Lloyd, *The Man of Reason* (Minneapolis: University of Minnesota Press, 1984); and Susan Bordo, *The Flight to Objectivity* (Albany: State University of New York Press, 1987). For discussions of the scientific context, see Evelyn Fox Keller, *Reflections on Gender and Science* (New Haven: Yale University Press, 1985); Sandra Harding, *The Science Question in Feminism* (Ithaca: Cornell University Press, 1986); and Nancy Tuana, ed., *Feminism and Science* (Bloomington: Indiana University Press, 1989).

14. Richard Foley, *The Theory of Epistemic Rationality* (Cambridge, Mass.: Harvard University Press, 1987), 48.

15. Ibid., 114.

16. Ibid., 140.

17. Ibid., 54.

18. I have singled out Foley's book because it is such a good example of the issues I am addressing. But he is by no means atypical. Space does not permit a catalogue of similar positions, but Lynn Hankinson Nelson notes that "Quine apparently assumes that at a given time "we" will agree about the question worth asking and the standards by which potential answers are to be judged, so he does not consider social arrangements as epistemological factors" (*Who Knows,* 170). Quine assumes, further, that "in the relevant community . . . we will all . . . see the same thing" (p. 184).

19. Here I am thinking of Richard Rorty, *Philosophy and the Mirror of Nature,* (Princeton: Princeton University Press, 1979); and *Consequences of Pragmatism* (Minneapolis: University of Minnesota Press, 1982).

20. *Philosophy and the Mirror of Nature,* 373.

21. Richard Rorty, "Solidarity or Objectivity?" in John Rajchman and Cornel West, eds., *Post-Analytic Philosophy* (New York: Columbia University Press, 1985), 7; emphasis added.

22. Ibid., 11.

23. Ibid., 15.

24. Nancy Fraser, "Solidarity or Singularity? Richard Rorty between Romanticism and Technocracy," in Nancy Fraser, *Unruly Practices: Power, Discourse and Gender in Contemporary Social Theory* (Minneapolis: University of Minnesota Press, 1989), 104.

25. Rorty, "Solidarity or Objectivity?," 5.

26. I borrow the idea, if not the detail, of the potential of case-by-case analysis from Roger A. Shiner, "From Epistemology to Romance Via Wisdom," in Ilham Dilman, ed., *Philosophy and Life: Essays on John Wisdom* (The Hague: Martinus Nijhoff, 1984), 291–314.

27. See Antonio Gramsci, *Selections from the Prison Notebooks,* trans. and ed. Quintin Hoare and Geoffrey Nowell Smith (New York: International Publishers, 1971).

28. Rudy Platiel and Stephen Strauss, *The Globe and Mail,* 4 February 1989. I cite the newspaper report because the media produce the public impact that concerns me here. I discuss neither the quality of Rushton's research practice nor the questions his theories and pedagogical practice pose about academic freedom. My concern is with how structures of knowledge, power, and prejudice grant him an epistemic place.

29. Commenting on the psychology of occupational assessment, Wendy Hollway observes: "That psychology is a science and that psychological assessment is therefore objective is a belief which continues to be fostered in organizations." She further notes: "The legacy of psychology as science is the belief that the individual can be understood through measurement" [Wendy Hollway, "Fitting work: psychological assessment in organizations," in Julian Henriques, Wendy Hollway, Cathy Urwin, Couze Venn, and Valerie Walkerdine, *Changing the Subject: Psychology, social regulation and subjectivity* (London: Methuen, 1984), 35, 55].

30. The phrase is Richard Schmitt's, from "Murderous Objectivity: Reflections on Marxism and the Holocaust," in Roger S. Gottlieb, ed., *Thinking the Unthinkable: Meanings of the Holocaust* (New York: Paulist Press, 1990), 71. I am grateful to Richard Schmitt for helping me to think about the issues I discuss in this section.

31. Cynthia Eagle Russett, *Sexual Science: The Victorian Construction of Womanhood* (Cambridge, Mass.: Harvard University Press, 1989). In this connection, see also Lynda Birke, *Women, Feminism, and Biology* (Brighton: Harvester Press, 1986); and Janet Sayers, *Biological Politics* (London: Tavistock Publications, 1982).

32. The best-known contemporary discussion of utilitarian, controlled sexuality is Michel Foucault, *The History of Sexuality Volume I: An Introduction,* trans. Robert Hurley (New York: Vintage Books, 1980). In Foucault's analysis, sexuality is utilitarian both in reproducing the population and in cementing the family bond.

33. Julian Henriques, "Social psychology and the politics of racism," in Henriques et al., *Changing the Subject,* 74.

34. Clifford Geertz comments: "It is not . . . the validity of the sciences, real or would-be, that is at issue. What concerns me, and should concern us all, are the axes that, with an increasing determination bordering on the evangelical, are being busily ground with their assistance" ["Anti Anti-Relativism," in Michael Krausz, ed., *Relativism: Interpretation and Confrontation* (Notre Dame: University of Notre Dame Press, 1989), 20].

35. Philippe Rushton has received funding from the Social Sciences and Humanities Research Council of Canada and the Guggenheim Foundation in the USA, agencies whose status in the North American intellectual community confers authority and credibility. He has also received funding from the Pioneer Fund, an organization with explicit white supremacist commitments.

36. Naomi Scheman, "Commentary," in the Symposium on Sandra Harding's 'The Method Question' *APA Feminism and Philosophy Newsletter* 88.3 (1989): 42.

37. Helen Longino observes: ". . . How one determines evidential relevance, why one takes some state of affairs as evidence for one hypothesis rather than for another, depends on one's other beliefs, which we can call background beliefs or assumptions" (p. 43). And "When, for instance, background assumptions are shared by all members of a community, they acquire an invisibility that renders them unavailable for criticism" (p. 80). In *Science as Social Knowledge: Values and Objectivity in Scientific Inquiry* (Princeton: Princeton University Press, 1990).

38. Here I am borrowing a turn of phrase from Michel Foucault, when he writes in quite a different context: "And it was this network that made possible the individuals we term Hobbes, Berkeley,

Hume, or Condillac" [Michel Foucault, *The Order of Things: An Archaeology of the Human Sciences* (New York: Random House, 1971), 63].

39. I owe this point to the Biology and Gender Study Group, in "The Importance of Feminist Critique for Contemporary Cell Biology," in Nancy Tuana, ed., *Feminism and Science* (Bloomington: Indiana University Press, 1989), 173.

40. The argument about the primacy of knowing other people is central to the position I develop in my *What Can She Know? Feminist Theory and the Construction of Knowledge* (Ithaca: Cornell University Press, 1991). Portions of this section of this essay are drawn, with modifications, from the book.

41. Seyla Benhabib, "The Generalized and the Concrete Other," in Seyla Benhabib and Drucilla Cornell, eds., *Feminism As Critique* (Minneapolis: University of Minnesota Press, 1987), 85.

42. See Susan Hekman, *Gender and Knowledge: Elements of a Postmodern Feminism* (Boston: Northeastern University Press, 1990), especially p. 3. For an introduction to these disputes, see Paul Rabinow and William M. Sullivan, eds., *Interpretive Social Science: A Second Look* (Berkeley: University of California Press, 1987).

43. Sandra Harding, *The Science Question in Feminism*. (Ithaca: Cornell University Press, 1986), 47. Harding contends that "a critical and self-reflective social science should be the model for all science, and . . . if there are any special requirements for adequate explanations in physics, they are just that—special" (Ibid., 44).

44. Ibid., 46.

45. Introduction, "The Interpretive Turn," in Rabinow and Sullivan, *Interpretive Social Science,* 13; emphasis added.

46. The phrase is Elizabeth V. Spelman's, in "On Treating Persons as Persons," *Ethics* 88 (1978): 151.

47. Here I borrow a phrase from Susan Bordo, "Feminism, Postmodernism, and Gender-Scepticism," in Linda Nicholson, ed., *Feminism/Postmodernism* (New York: Routledge, 1990), 145.

48. I allude here to three now-classic treatments of the relativism question: Anne Seller, "Realism versus Relativism: Toward a Politically Adequate Epistemology," in Morwenna Griffiths and Margaret Whitford, eds., *Feminist Perspectives in Philosophy* (Bloomington: Indiana University Press, 1988); Martin Hollis and Steven Lukes, eds., *Rationality and Relativism* (Cambridge, Mass.: MIT Press, 1982), and Richard Bernstein, *Beyond Objectivism and Relativism* (Philadelphia: University of Pennsylvania Press, 1983).

49. Sandra Harding resists endorsing relativism even in her discussions of standpoint and postmodern epistemologies. In a recent piece she introduces the neologism "interpretationism" as a solution, noting that "relativism is a consequence, but not always the intent, of interpretationism." (See her "Feminism, Science, and the Anti-Enlightenment Critiques," in Linda Nicholson, ed., *Feminism/Postmodernism,* 102, n. 5.) By contrast, I am uring the value of endorsing a reconstructed relativism, shorn of its enfeebling implications.

50. Donna Haraway, "Situated Knowledges: The Science Question in Feminism and the Privilege of Partial Perspective," *Feminist Studies* 14, 3 (Fall 1988).

51. See Nancy Jay, "Gender and Dichotomy," *Feminist Studies* 7 (1981) for a discussion of the exclusiveness of dichotomies.

52. Peter Unger, in *Ignorance: A Case for Skepticism* (Oxford: Clarendon Press, 1975), argues that because no knowledge claim can meet the exacting standards of formulation in absolute terms, there is only conjecture, opinion, and fantasy. People are doomed to ignorance and should simply avow their skepticism.

53. In thinking about Pyrrhonian skepticism I am indebted to David R. Hiley, "The Deep Challenge of Pyrrhonian Skepticism," *Journal of the History of Philosophy* 25, 2 (April 1987): 185–213.

54. Seyla Benhabib, "Epistemologies of Postmodernism: A Rejoinder to Jean-Francois Lyotard," in Linda Nicholson, ed., *Feminism/Postmodernism,* 124.

55. The phrase is Hiley's, p. 213.

56. Denise Riley, *"Am I That Name?" Feminism and the Category of Women in History* (Minneapolis: University of Minnesota Press, 1988), 113.

57. John Rajchman, *Michel Foucault: The Freedom of Philosophy* (New York: Columbia University Press, 1985), 3.

58. Rux Martin, "Truth, Power, Self: An Interview with Michel Foucault, October 25, 1982," in Luther H. Martin, Huck Gutman and Patrick H.

Hutton, eds., *Technologies of the Self: A Seminar with Michel Foucault* (Amherst: University of Massachusetts Press, 1988), 11.

59. Michel Foucault, "On the Genealogy of Ethics: An Overview of Work in Progress." Afterword, in Hubert L. Dreyfus and Paul Rabinow, *Michel Foucault: Beyond Structuralism and Hermeneutics,* 2nd ed. (Chicago: University of Chicago Press, 1983), 231.

60. Earlier versions of this paper were presented at the American Philosophical Association conference at Los Angeles and to the Departments of Philosophy at McMaster University and McGill University. I am grateful to participants in those discussions—especially to Susan Dwyer, Hilary Kornblith, and Doug Odegard—for their comments and to Linda Alcoff and Libby Potter for their valuable editorial suggestions.

"STRONG OBJECTIVITY" AND SOCIALLY SITUATED KNOWLEDGE

Sandra Harding

I argued that a feminist standpoint theory can direct the production of less partial and less distorted beliefs. This kind of scientific process will not merely acknowledge the social-situatedness—the historicity—of the very best beliefs any culture has arrived at or could in principle "discover" but will use this fact as a resource for generating those beliefs.[1] Nevertheless, it still might be thought that this association of objectivity with socially situated knowledge is an impossible combination. Has feminist standpoint theory really abandoned objectivity and embraced relativism? Or, alternatively, has it remained too firmly entrenched in a destructive objectivism that increasingly is criticized from many quarters?

THE DECLINING STATUS OF "OBJECTIVISM"

Scientists and science theorists working in many different disciplinary and policy projects have objected to the conventional notion of a value-free, impartial, dispassionate objectivity that is supposed to guide scientific research and without which, according to conventional thought one cannot separate justified belief from mere opinion, or real knowledge from mere claims to knowledge. From the perspective of this conventional notion of objectivity—sometimes referred to as "objectivism"—it has appeared that if one gives up this concept, the only alternative is not just a cultural relativism (the sociological assertion that what is thought to be a reasonable claim in one society or subculture is not thought to be so in another) but, worse, a judgmental or epistemological relativism that denies the possibility of any reasonable standards for adjudicating between competing claims. Some fear that to give up the possibility of one universally and eternally valid standard of judgment is perhaps even to be left with no way to argue rationally against the possibility that *each person's* judgment about the regularities of nature and their underlying causal tendencies must be regarded as equally valid. The reduction of the critic's position to such an absurdity provides a powerful incentive to question no further the conventional idea that objectivity requires value-neutrality. From the perspective of objectivism, judgmental relativism appears to be the only alternative.

Insistence on this division of epistemological stances between those that firmly support value-free objectivity and those that support judgmental

[1] See Donna Haraway, "Situated Knowledges: *The Science Question in Feminism* and the Privilege of Partial Perspective," *Feminist Studies* 14:3 (1988).

relativism—a dichotomy that unfortunately has gained the consent of many critics of objectivism as well as its defenders—has succeeded in making value-free objectivity look much more attractive to natural and social scientists than it should. It also makes judgmental relativism appear far more progressive than it is. Some critics of the conventional notion of objectivity have openly welcomed judgmental relativism.[2] Others have been willing to tolerate it as the cost they think they must pay for admitting the practical ineffectualness, the proliferation of confusing conceptual contradictions, and the political regressiveness that follow from trying to achieve an objectivity that has been defined in terms of value-neutrality. But even if embracing judgmental relativism could make sense in anthropology and other social sciences, it appears absurd as an epistemological stance in physics or biology. What would it mean to assert that no reasonable standards can or could in principle be found for adjudicating between one culture's claim that the earth is flat and another culture's claim that the earth is round?

The literature on these topics from the 1970s and 1980s alone is huge and located in many disciplines. Prior to the 1960s the issue was primarily one of ethical and cultural absolutism versus relativism. It was the concern primarily of philosophers and anthropologists and was considered relevant only to the social sciences, not the natural sciences. But since then, the recognition has emerged that cognitive, scientific, and epistemic absolutism are both implicated in ethical and cultural issues and are also independently problematic. One incentive to the expansion was Thomas Kuhn's account of how the natural sciences have developed in response to what scientists have found "interesting," together with the subsequent post-Kuhnian philosophy and social studies of the natural sciences.[3] Another has been the widely recognized failure of the social

sciences to ground themselves in methods and theoretical commitments that can share in the scientificity of the natural sciences. Paradoxically, the more "scientific" social research becomes, the less objective it becomes.[4]

Further incentives have been such political tendencies as the U.S. civil rights movement, the rise of the women's movement, the decentering of the West and criticisms of Eurocentrism in international circles, and the increasing prominence within U.S. political and intellectual life of the voices of women and of African Americans and other people of Third World descent. From these perspectives, it appears increasingly arrogant for defenders of the West's intellectual traditions to continue to dismiss the scientific and epistemological stances of Others as caused mainly by biological inferiority, ignorance, underdevelopment, primitiveness, and the like. On the other hand, although diversity, pluralism, relativism, and difference have their valuable political and intellectual uses, embracing them resolves the political-scientific-epistemological conflict to almost no one's satisfaction.

I make no attempt here to summarize the arguments of these numerous and diverse writings.[5]

---

[2] See, e.g., David Bloor, *Knowledge and Social Imagery* (London: Routledge & Kegan Paul, 1977); and many of the papers in *Knowledge and Reflexivity,* ed. Steve Woolgar (Beverly Hills, Calif.: Sage, 1988).

[3] Thomas Kuhn, *The Structure of Scientific Revolutions* (Chicago: University of Chicago Press, 1962).

[4] This is an important theme in Richard Bernstein, *Beyond Objectivism and Relativism* (Philadelphia: University of Pennsylvania Press, 1983). Similar doubts about the ability of legal notions of objectivity to advance justice appear in many of the essays in "Women in Legal Education: Pedagogy, Law, Theory, and Practice," *Journal of Legal Education* 38 (1988), special issue, ed. Carrie Menkel-Meadow, Martha Minow, and David Vernon.

[5] Discussions on one or more of these focuses can be found in Martin Hollis and Steven Lukes, eds., *Rationality and Relativism* (Cambridge, Mass: Harvard University Press, 1982); Michael Krausz and Jack Meiland, eds., *Relativism: Cognitive and Moral* (Notre Dame, Ind.: University of Notre Dame Press, 1982); Richard Bernstein, *Beyond Objectivism;* and S. P. Mohanty, "Us and Them: On the Philosophical Bases of Political Criticism," *Yale Journal of Criticism* 2:2 (1989). A good brief bibliographic essay on the recent philosophy of science within and against which the particular discussion of this essay is located is Steve Fuller, "The Philosophy of Science since Kuhn: Readings on the Revolution That Has Yet to Come," *Choice,* December 1989. For more extended studies that are not incompatible with my arguments here, see Steve Fuller, *Social Epistemology* (Bloomington: Indiana University Press, 1988); and Joseph Rouse, *Knowledge and Power: Toward a Political Philosophy of Science* (Ithaca: Cornell University Press, 1987).

My concern is more narrowly focused: to state as clearly as possible how issues of objectivity and relativism appear from the perspective of a feminist standpoint theory.

Feminist critics of science and the standpoint theorists especially have been interpreted as supporting either an excessive commitment to value-free objectivity or, alternatively, the abandonment of objectivity in favor of relativism. Because there are clear commitments within feminism to tell less partial and distorted stories about women, men, nature, and social relations, some critics have assumed that feminism must be committed to value-neutral objectivity. Like other feminists, however, the standpoint theorists have also criticized conventional sciences for their arrogance in assuming that they could tell one true story about a world that is out there, ready-made for their reporting, without listening to women's accounts or being aware that accounts of nature and social relations have been constructed within men's control of gender relations. Moreover, feminist thought and politics as a whole are continually revising the ways they bring women's voices and the perspectives from women's lives to knowledge-seeking, and they are full of conflicts between the claims made by different groups of feminists. How could feminists in good conscience do anything but abandon any agenda to legitimate one over another of these perspectives? Many feminists in literature, the arts, and the humanities are even more resistant than those in the natural and social sciences to claims that feminist images or representations of the world hold any special epistemological or scientific status. Such policing of thought is exactly what they have objected to in criticizing the authority of their disciplinary canons on the grounds that such authority has had the effect of stifling the voices of marginalized groups. In ignoring these views, feminist epistemologists who are concerned with natural or social science agendas appear to support an epistemological divide between the sciences and humanities, a divide that feminism has elsewhere criticized.

The arguments of this essay move away from the fruitless and depressing choice between value-neutral objectivity and judgmental relativism. This essay draws on some assumptions underlying the analyses of earlier chapters in order to argue that the conventional notion of objectivity against which feminist criticisms have been raised should be regarded as excessively weak. A feminist standpoint epistemology requires strengthened standards of objectivity. The standpoint epistemologies call for recognition of a historical or sociological or cultural relativism—but not for a judgmental or epistemological relativism. They call for the acknowledgment that all human beliefs—including our best scientific beliefs—are socially situated, but they also require a critical evaluation to determine which social situations tend to generate the most objective knowledge claims. They require, as judgmental relativism does not, a scientific account of the relationships between historically located belief and maximally objective belief. So they demand what I shall call *strong objectivity* in contrast to the weak objectivity of objectivism and its mirror-linked twin, judgmental relativism. This may appear to be circular reasoning—to call for scientifically examining the social location of scientific claims—but if so, it is at least not viciously circular.[6]

---

[6] Additional writings informing this essay include esp. Haraway, "Situated Knowledges"; Donna Haraway, *Primate Visions: Gender, Race, and Nature in the World of Modern Science* (New York: Routledge, 1989); Jane Flax, *Thinking Fragments: Psychoanalysis, Feminism, and Postmodernism in the Contemporary West* (Berkeley: University of California Press, 1990); and the writings of standpoint theorists themselves, esp. Nancy Hartsock, "The Feminist Standpoint: Developing the Ground for a Specifically Feminist Historical Materialism," in *Discovering Reality: Feminist Perspectives on Epistemology, Metaphysics, Methodology, and Philosophy of Science,* ed. Sandra Harding and Merrill Hintikka (Dordrecht: Reidel, 1983); Dorothy Smith, *The Everyday World as Problematic: A Feminist Sociology* (Boston: Northeastern University Press, 1987); Hilary Rose, "Hand, Brain, and Heart: A Feminist Epistemology for the Natural Sciences," *Signs* 9:1 (1983); Patricia Hill Collins, "Learning from the Outsider Within: The Sociological Significance of Black Feminist Thought," *Social Problems* 33(1986)—though each of these theorists would no doubt disagree with various aspects of my argument.

This essay also considers two possible objections to the argument presented, one that may arise from scientists and philosophers of science, and another that may arise among feminist themselves.

OBJECTIVISM'S WEAK CONCEPTION OF OBJECTIVITY

The term "objectivism" is useful for the purposes of my argument because its echoes of "scientism" draw attention to ways in which the research prescriptions called for by a value-free objectivity only mimic the purported style of the most successful scientific practices without managing to produce their effects. Objectivism results only in semiscience when it turns away from the task of critically identifying all those broad, historical social desires, interests, and values that have shaped the agendas, contents, and results of the sciences much as they shape the rest of human affairs. Objectivism encourages only a partial and distorted explanation of why the great moments in the history of the natural and social sciences have occurred.

Let me be more precise in identifying the weaknesses of this notion. It has been conceptualized both too narrowly and too broadly to be able to accomplish the goals that its defenders claim it is intended to satisfy. Taken at face value it is ineffectively conceptualized, but this is what makes the sciences that adopt weak standards of objectivity so effective socially: objectivist justifications of science are useful to dominant groups that, consciously or not, do not really intend to "play fair" anyway. Its internally contradictory character gives it a kind of flexibility and adaptability that would be unavailable to a coherently characterized notion.

Consider, first, how objectivism operationalizes too narrowly the notion of maximizing objectivity. The conception of value-free, impartial, dispassionate research is supposed to direct the identification of all social values and their elimination from the results of research, yet it has been operationalized to identify and eliminate *only* those social values and interests that differ among the researchers and critics who are regarded by the scientific community as competent to make such judgments. If the community of "qualified" researchers and critics systematically excludes, for example, all African Americans and women of all races, and if the larger culture is stratified by race and gender and lacks powerful critiques of this stratification, it is not plausible to imagine that racist and sexist interests and values would be identified within a community of scientists composed entirely of people who benefit—intentionally or not—from institutional racism and sexism.

This kind of blindness is advanced by the conventional belief that the truly scientific part of knowledge-seeking—the part controlled by methods of research—is only in the context of justification. The context of discovery, where problems are identified as appropriate for scientific investigation, hypotheses are formulated, key concepts are defined—this part of the scientific process is thought to be unexaminable within science by rational methods. Thus "real science" is restricted to those processes controllable by methodological rules. The methods of science—or, rather, of the special sciences—are restricted to procedures for the testing of already formulated hypotheses. Untouched by these careful methods are those values and interests entrenched in the very statement of what problem is to be researched and in the concepts favored in the hypotheses that are to be tested. Recent histories of science are full of cases in which broad social assumptions stood little chance of identification or elimination through the very best research procedures of the day.[7]

---

[7] This is the theme of many feminist, left, and antiracist analyses of biology and social sciences. See, e.g., Anne Fausto-Sterling, *Myths of Gender: Biological Theories about Women and Men* (New York: Basic Books, 1985); Stephen Jay Gould, *The Mismeasure of Man* (New York: Norton, 1981); Robert V. Guthrie, *Even the Rat Was White: A Historical View of Psychology* (New York: Harper & Row, 1976); Haraway, *Primate Visions;* Sandra Harding, ed., *Feminism and Methodology: Social Science Issues* (Bloomington: Indiana University Press, 1987); Joyce Ladner, ed., *The Death* of *White Sociology* (New York: Random House, 1973); Hilary Rose and Steven Rose, eds., *Ideology of/in the Natural Sciences* (Cambridge, Mass.: Schenkman, 1979); Londa Schiebinger, *The Mind Has No Sex: Women in the Origins of Modern Science* (Cambridge, Mass.: Harvard University Press, 1989).

Thus objectivism operationalizes the notion of objectivity in much too narrow a way to permit the achievement of the value-free research that is supposed to be its outcome.

But objectivism also conceptualizes the desired value-neutrality of objectivity too broadly. Objectivists claim that objectivity requires the elimination of *all* social values and interests from the research process and the results of research. It is clear, however, that not all social values and interests have the same bad effects upon the results of research. Some have systematically generated less partial and distorted beliefs than others—or than purportedly value-free research—as has earlier been argued.

Nor is this so outlandish an understanding of the history of science as objectivists frequently intimate. Setting the scene for his study of nineteenth-century biological determinism, Stephen Jay Gould says:

> I do not intend to contrast evil determinists who stray from the path of scientific objectivity with enlightened antideterminists who approach data with an open mind and therefore see truth. Rather, I criticize the myth that science itself is an objective enterprise, done properly only when scientists can shuck the constraints of their culture and view the world as it really is. . . . Science, since people must do it, is a socially embedded activity. It progresses by hunch, vision, and intuition. Much of its change through time does not record a closer approach to absolute truth, but the alteration of cultural contexts that influence it so strongly.[8]

Other historians agree with Gould.[9] Modern science has again and again been reconstructed by a set of interests and values—distinctively Western, bourgeois, and patriarchal—which

were originally formulated by a new social group that intentionally used the new sciences in their struggles against the Catholic Church and feudal state. These interests and values had both positive and negative consequences for the development of the sciences. Political and social interests are not "add-ons" to an otherwise transcendental science that is inherently indifferent to human society; scientific beliefs, practices, institutions, histories, and problematics are constituted in and through contemporary political and social projects, and always have been. It would be far more startling to discover a kind of human knowledge-seeking whose products could—alone among all human products—defy historical "gravity" and fly off the earth, escaping entirely their historical location. Such a cultural phenomenon would be cause for scientific alarm; it would appear to defy principles of "material" causality upon which the possibility of scientific activity itself is based.[10]

Of course, people in different societies arrive at many of the same empirical claims. Farmers, toolmakers, and child tenders in every culture must arrive at similar "facts" about nature and social relations if their work is to succeed. Many of the observations collected by medieval European astronomers are preserved in the data used by astronomers today. But what "facts" these data refer to, what further research they point to, what theoretical statements they support and how such theories are to be applied, what such data signify in terms of human social relations and relations to nature—all these parts of the sciences can differ wildly, as the contrast between medieval and contemporary astronomy illustrates.

There are yet deeper ways in which political values permeate modern science. For even relatively conservative tendencies in the

---

[8] Gould, *Mismeasure of Man,* 21–22.

[9] E.g., William Leiss, *The Domination of Nature* (Boston: Beacon Press, 1972); Carolyn Merchant, *The Death of Nature: Women, Ecology, and the Scientific Revolution* (New York: Harper & Row, 1980); Wolfgang Van den Daele, "The Social Construction of Science," in *The Social Production of Scientific Knowledge,* ed. Everett Mendelsohn, Peter Weingart, and Richard Whitley (Dordrecht: Reidel, 1977).

[10] Rouse, *Knowledge and Power,* provides a good analysis of the implications for science of Foucauldian notions of politics and power.

post-Kuhnian philosophies of science, the sciences' power to manipulate the world is considered the mark of their success. The "new empiricism" contrasts in this respect with conventional empiricism. As Joseph Rouse puts the point:

> If we take the new empiricism seriously, it forces us to reappraise the relation between power and knowledge in a more radical way. The central issue is no longer how scientific claims can be distorted or suppressed by polemic, propaganda, or ideology. Rather, we must look at what was earlier described as the achievement of power through the application of knowledge. But the new empiricism also challenges the adequacy of this description in terms of "application." The received view distinguishes the achievement of knowledge from its subsequent application, from which this kind of power is supposed to derive. New empiricist accounts of science make this distinction less tenable by shifting the locus of knowledge from accurate representation to successful manipulation and control of events. Power is no longer external to knowledge or opposed to it: power itself becomes the mark of knowledge.[11]

The best as well as the worst of the history of the natural sciences has been shaped by— or, more accurately, constructed through and within—political desires, interests, and values. Consequently, there appear to be no grounds left from which to defend the claim that the objectivity of research is advanced by the elimination of all political values and interests from the research process. Instead, the sciences need to legitimate *within scientific research,* as part of practicing science, critical examination of historical values and interests that may be so shared within the scientific community, so invested in by the very constitution of this or that field of study, that they will not show up as a cultural bias between experimenters or between research communities. What objectivism cannot conceptualize is the need for critical examination of the "intentionality of nature"—meaning not that nature is no different from humans (in having intentions, desires, interests, and values or in constructing its own meaningful "way of life," and so on) but that nature as-the-object-of-human-knowledge never comes to us "naked"; it comes only as already constituted in social thought.[12] Nature-as-object-of-study simulates in this respect an intentional being. This idea helps counter the intuitively seductive idea that scientific claims are and should be an epiphenomenon of nature. It is the development of strategies to generate just such critical examination that the notion of strong objectivity calls for.

Not everyone will welcome such a project; even those who share these criticisms of objectivism may think the call for strong objectivity too idealistic, too utopian, not realistic enough. But is it more unrealistic than trying to explain the regularities of nature and their underlying causal tendencies scientifically but refusing to examine *all* their causes? And even if the ideal of identifying all the causes of human beliefs is rarely if ever achievable, why not hold it as a desirable standard? Anti-litter laws improve social life even if they are not always obeyed.[13]

Weak objectivity, then, is a contradictory notion, and its contradictory character is largely responsible for its usefulness and its widespread appeal to dominant groups. It offers hope that scientists and science institutions, themselves admittedly historically located, can produce claims that will be regarded as objectively valid without their having to examine critically their

---

[11] Rouse, *Knowledge and Power,* 19. Among the "new empiricist" works that Rouse has in mind are Larry Laudan, *Progress and Its Problems: Toward a Theory of Scientific Growth* (Berkeley: University of California Press, 1977); Mary Hesse, *Revolutions and Reconstructions in the Philosophy of Science* (Bloomington: University of Indiana Press, 1980); Nancy Cartwright, *How the Laws of Physics Lie* (Oxford: Oxford University Press, 1983).

[12] See Haraway, *Primate Visions,* esp. chap. 10, for analysis of differences between the Anglo-American, Japanese, and Indian constructions of "nature" which shape the objects of study in primatology.

[13] Fuller uses the anti-litter law example in another context in *Social Epistemology.*

own historical commitments, from which—intentionally or not—they actively construct their scientific research. It permits scientists and science institutions to be unconcerned with the origins or consequences of their problematics and practices, or with the social values and interests that these problematics and practices support. It offers the possibility of enacting what Francis Bacon promised: "The course I propose for the discovery of sciences is such as leaves but little to the acuteness and strength of wits, but places all wits and understandings nearly on a level." His "way of discovering sciences goes far to level men's wits, and leaves but little to individual excellence; because it performs everything by surest rules and demonstrations."[14]

For those powerful forces in society that want to appropriate science and knowledge for their own purposes, it is extremely valuable to be able to support the idea that ignoring the constitution of science within political desires, values, and interests will somehow increase the reliability of accounts of nature and social life. The ideal of the disinterested rational scientist advances the self-interest of both social elites and, ironically, scientists who seek status and power. Reporting on various field studies of scientific work, Steve Fuller points out that Machiavellian judgments

> simulate those of the fabled "rational" scientist, since in order for the Machiavellian to maximize his advantage he must be ready to switch research programs when he detects a change in the balance of credibility—which is, after all, what philosophers of science would typically have the rational scientist do. To put the point more strikingly, it would seem that as the scientist's motivation approximates total *self-interestedness* (such that he is always able to distance his own interests from those of any social group which supports what may turn out to be a research program with diminishing credibility), his behavior approximates total

disinterestedness. And so we can imagine the ultimate Machiavellian scientist pursuing a line of research frowned upon by most groups in the society—perhaps determining the racial component in intelligence is an example—simply because he knows of its potential for influencing the course of future research and hence for enhancing his credibility as a scientist.[15]

The history of science shows that research directed by maximally liberatory social interests and values tends to be better equipped to identify partial claims and distorting assumptions, even though the credibility of the scientists who do it may not be enhanced during the short run. After all, antiliberatory interests and values are invested in the natural inferiority of just the groups of humans who, if given real equal access (not just the formally equal access that is liberalism's goal) to public voice, would most strongly contest claims about their purported natural inferiority. Antiliberatory interests and values silence and destroy the most likely sources of evidence against their own claims. That is what makes them rational for elites.

STRONG OBJECTIVITY: A COMPETENCY CONCEPT

At this point, what I mean by a concept of strong objectivity should be clear. In an important sense, our cultures have agendas and make assumptions that we as individuals cannot easily detect. Theoretically unmediated experience, that aspect of a group's or an individual's experience in which cultural influences cannot be detected, functions as part of the evidence for scientific claims. Cultural agendas and assumptions are part of the background assumptions and auxiliary hypotheses that philosophers have identified. If the goal is to make available for critical scrutiny *all* the evidence marshaled for or against a scientific hypothesis, then this evidence too requires critical examination *within* scientific research processes.

---

[14] Quoted in Van den Daele, "Social Construction of Science," 34.

[15] Fuller, *Social Epistemology,* 267.

In other words, we can think of strong objectivity as extending the notion of scientific research to include systematic examination of such powerful background beliefs. It must do so in order to be competent at maximizing objectivity.

The strong objectivity that standpoint theory requires is like the "strong programme" in the sociology of knowledge in that it directs us to provide symmetrical accounts of both "good" and "bad" belief formation and legitimation.[16] We must be able to identify the social causes of good beliefs, not just of the bad ones to which the conventional "sociology of error" and objectivism restrict causal accounts. However, in contrast to the "strong programme," standpoint theory requires causal analyses not just of the micro processes in the laboratory but also of the macro tendencies in the social order, which shape scientific practices. Moreover, a concern with macro tendencies permits a more robust notion of reflexivity than is currently available in the sociology of knowledge or the philosophy of science. In trying to identify the social causes of good beliefs, we will be led also to examine critically the kinds of bad beliefs that shape our own thought and behaviors, not just the thought and behavior of others.

To summarize the argument of the last chapter, in a society structured by gender hierarchy, "starting thought from women's lives" increases the objectivity of the results of research by bringing scientific observation and the perception of the need for explanation to bear on assumptions and practices that appear natural or unremarkable from the perspective of the lives of men in the dominant groups. Thinking from the perspective of women's lives makes strange what had appeared familiar, which is the beginning of any scientific inquiry.[17]

Why is this gender difference a scientific resource? It leads us to ask questions about nature and social relations from the perspective of devalued and neglected lives. Doing so begins research in the perspective from the lives of "strangers" who have been excluded from the culture's ways of socializing the "natives," who are at home in its institutions and who are full-fledged citizens. It starts research in the perspective from the lives of the systematically oppressed, exploited, and dominated, those who have fewer interests in ignorance about how the social order actually works. It begins research in the perspective from the lives of people on the "other side" of gender battles, offering a view different from the "winner's stories" about nature and social life which men's interpretations of men's lives tend to produce. It starts thought in everyday life, for which women are assigned primary responsibility and in which appear consequences of dominant group activities—consequences that are invisible from the perspective of those activities. It starts thought in the lives of those people to whom is assigned the work of mediating many of the culture's ideological dualisms—especially the gap between nature and culture. It starts research in the lives not just of strangers or outsiders but of "outsiders within," from which the relationship between outside and inside, margin and center, can more easily be detected. It starts thought in the perspective from the life of the Other, allowing the Other to gaze back "shamelessly" at the self who had reserved for himself the right to gaze "anonymously" at whomsoever he chooses. It starts thought in the lives of people who are unlikely to permit the denial of the interpretive core of all knowledge claims. It starts thought in the perspective from lives that at this moment in history are especially revealing of broad social contradictions. And no doubt there are additional ways in which thinking from the perspective of women's lives is especially revealing of regularities in nature and social relations and their underlying causal tendencies.

It is important to remember that in a certain sense there are no "women" or "men" in the

---

[16] I use "good" and "bad" here to stand for "true" and "false," "better confirmed" and "less well confirmed," "plausible" and "implausible," and so on.

[17] Starting thought from women's lives is something that both men and women must *learn* to do. Women's telling their experiences is not the same thing as thinking from the perspective of women's lives.

world—there is no "gender"—but only women, men, and gender constructed through particular historical struggles over just which races, classes, sexualities, cultures, religious groups, and so forth, will have access to resources and power. Moreover, standpoint theories of knowledge, whether or not they are articulated as such, have been advanced by thinkers concerned not only with gender and class hierarchy (recollect that standpoint theory originated in class analyses) but also with other "Others."[18] To make sense of any actual woman's life or the gender relations in any culture, analyses must begin in real, historic women's lives, and these will be women of particular races, classes, cultures, and sexualities. The historical particularity of women's lives is a problem for narcissistic or arrogant accounts that attempt, consciously or not, to conduct a cultural monologue. But it is a resource for those who think that our understandings and explanations are improved by what we could call an intellectual participatory democracy.

The notion of strong objectivity welds together the strengths of weak objectivity and those of the "weak subjectivity" that is its correlate, but excludes the features that make them only weak. To enact or operationalize the directive of strong objectivity is to value the Other's perspective and to pass over in thought into the social condition that creates it—not in order to stay there, to "go native" or merge the self with the Other, but in order to look back at the self in all its cultural particularity from a more distant, critical, objectifying location. One can think of

the subjectivism that objectivism conceptualizes as its sole alternative as only a "premodern" alternative to objectivism; it provides only a premodern solution to the problem *we* have here and now at the moment of postmodern criticisms of modernity's objectivism. Strong objectivity rejects attempts to resuscitate those organic, occult, "participating consciousness" relationships between self and Other which are characteristic of the premodern world.[19] Strong objectivity requires that we investigate the relation between subject and object rather than deny the existence of, or seek unilateral control over, this relation.

HISTORICAL RELATIVISM VERSUS JUDGMENTAL RELATIVISM

It is not that historical relativism is in itself a bad thing. A respect for historical (or sociological or cultural) relativism is always useful in starting one's thinking. Different social groups tend to have different patterns of practice and belief and different standards for judging them; these practices, beliefs, and standards can be explained by different historical interests, values, and agendas. Appreciation of these empirical regularities are especially important at this moment of unusually deep and extensive social change, when even preconceived schemes used in liberatory projects are likely to exclude less-well-positioned voices and to distort emerging ways of thinking that do not fit easily into older schemes. Listening carefully to different voices and attending thoughtfully to others' values and interests can enlarge our vision and begin to correct for inevitable enthnocentrisms. (The dominant values, interests, and voices are not among these "different" ones; they are the

---

[18] See, e.g., Samir Amin, *Eurocentrism* (New York: Monthly Review Press, 1989); Bettina Aptheker, *Tapestries of Life: Women's Work, Women's Consciousness, and the Meaning of Daily Life* (Amherst: University of Massachusetts Press, 1989); Collins, "Learning from the Outsider Within"; Walter Rodney, *How Europe Underdeveloped Africa* (Washington, D.C.: Howard University Press, 1982); Edward Said, *Orientalism* (New York: Pantheon Books, 1978); Edward Said, Foreword to *Selected Subaltern Studies,* ed. Ranajit Guha and Gayatri Chakravorty Spivak (New York: Oxford University Press, 1988), viii.

[19] See Morris Berman, *The Reenchantment of the World* (Ithaca: Cornell University Press, 1981), for an analysis of the world that modernity lost, and lost for good. Some feminists have tried to dismantle modernist projects with premodernist tools.

powerful tide against which "difference" must swim.)

To acknowledge this historical or sociological fact, as I have already argued, does not commit one to the further epistemological claim that there are therefore no rational or scientific grounds for making judgments between various patterns of belief and their originating social practices, values, and consequences. Many thinkers have pointed out that judgmental relativism is internally related to objectivism. For example, science historian Donna Haraway argues that judgmental relativism is the other side of the very same coin from "the God trick" required by what I have called weak objectivity. To insist that no judgments at all of cognitive adequacy can legitimately be made amounts to the same thing as to insist that knowledge can be produced only from "no place at all": that is, by someone who can be every place at once.[20] Critical preoccupation with judgmental relativism is the logical complement to the judgmental absolutism characteristic of Eurocentrism. Economist Samir Amin criticizes the preoccupation with relativism in some Western intellectual circles as a kind of "inverted Eurocentrism":

> The view that any person has the right—and even the power—to judge others is replaced by attention to the relativity of those judgments. Without a doubt, such judgments can be erroneous, superficial, hasty, or relative. No case is ever definitely closed; debate always continues. But that is precisely the point. It is necessary to pursue debate and not to avoid it on the grounds that the views that anyone forms about others are and always will be false: that the French will never understand the Chinese (and vice versa), that men will never understand women, etc; or, in other words, that there is no human species, but only "people." Instead, the claim is made that only Europeans can truly understand Europe, Chinese China, Christians

Christianity, and Moslems Islam; the Eurocentrism of one group is completed by the inverted Eurocentrism of others.[21]

Historically, relativism appears as a problematic intellectual possibility only for dominating groups at the point where the hegemony of their views is being challenged. Though the recognition that other cultures do, in fact, hold different beliefs, values, and standards of judgment is as old as human history, judgmental relativism emerged as an urgent intellectual issue only in nineteenth-century Europe, with the belated recognition that the apparently bizarre beliefs and behaviors of Others had a rationality and logic of their own. Judgmental relativism is not a problem originating in or justifiable in terms of the lives of marginalized groups. It did not arise in misogynous thought about women; it does not arise from the contrast feminism makes between women's lives and men's. Women do not have the problem of how to accommodate intellectually both the sexist claim that women are inferior in some way or another and the feminist claim that they are not. Here relativism arises as a problem only from the perspective of men's lives. Some men want to appear to acknowledge and accept feminist arguments without actually giving up any of their conventional androcentric beliefs and the practices that seem to follow so reasonably from such beliefs. "It's all relative, my dear," is a convenient way to try to accomplish these two goals.

We feminists in higher education may have appeared to invite charges of relativism in our language about disseminating the results of feminist research and scholarship beyond women's studies programs into the entire curriculum and canon. We speak of "mainstreaming"

---

[20] Haraway, "Situated Knowledges" makes these points and uses the phrase "the God trick."

[21] Amin, *Eurocentrism,* 146–47. Amin further makes clear that it takes more than *mere* debate—i.e., only intellectual work—to come to understand the lives or point of view of "people" who are on trajectories that oppose one's own in political struggles. The following paragraph draws on "Introduction: Is There a Feminist Method?" in *Feminism and Methodology,* p. 10.

and "integrating" the research, scholarship, and curriculum of Other programs and of encouraging "inclusiveness" in scholarship and the curriculum. We enroll our women's studies courses in campuswide projects to promote "cultural diversity" and "multiculturalism," and we accept students into such courses on these terms. Do these projects conflict with the standpoint logic? Yes and no. They conflict because the notions involved are perfectly coherent with the maintenance of elitist knowledge production and systems. Let me make the point in terms of my racial identity as white. "They (those people of color at the margins of the social order) are to be integrated with us (whites at the center), leaving us unchanged and the rightful heirs of the center of the culture. They are to give up their agendas and interests that conflict with ours in order to insert their contributions into the research, scholarship, or curriculum that has been structured to accommodate our agendas and interests." This is just as arrogant a posture as the older cultural absolutism. From the perspective of racial minorities, integration has never worked as a solution to ethnic or race relations in the United States. Why is there reason to think it will work any better for the marginalized projects in intellectual circles?

Should we therefore give up attempts at an "inclusive curriculum" and "cultural diversity" because of their possible complicity with sexism, racism, Eurocentrism, heterosexism, and class oppression? Of course the answer must be no. It is true that this kind of language appears to betray the compelling insights of the standpoint epistemology and to leave feminist programs in the compromised position of supporting the continued centering of white, Western, patriarchal visions. But many feminist projects—including women's studies programs themselves—are forced to occupy whatever niches they can find within institutional structures that are fundamentally opposed to them or, at least, "prefeminist." An implicit acceptance of pluralism, if not judgmental relativism—at least at the institutional level—appears to be the

only condition under which women's voices and feminist voices, male and female, can be heard at all.

After all, isn't feminism just one "equal voice" among many competing for everyone's attention? The nineteenth-century "natives" whose beliefs and behaviors Europeans found bizarre were not in any real sense competing for an equal voice within European thought and politics. They were safely off in Africa, the Orient, and other faraway places. The chances were low that aborigines would arrive in Paris, London, and Berlin to study and report back to their own cultures the bizarre beliefs and behaviors that constituted the "tribal life" of European anthropologists and *their* culture. More important, there was no risk at all that they could have used such knowledge to assist in imposing their rule on Europeans in Europe. Women's voices, while certainly far from silent, were far more effectively contained and muted than is possible today. As a value, a moral prescription, relativism was a safe stance for Europeans to choose; the reciprocity of respect it appeared to support had little chance of having to be enacted. Today, women and feminists are not safely off and out of sight at all. They are present, speaking, within the very social order that still treats women's beliefs and behaviors as bizarre. Moreover, their speech competes for attention and status as most plausible not only with that of misogynists but also with the speech of other Others: African Americans, other peoples of color, gay rights activists, pacifists, ecologists, members of new formations of the left, and so on. Isn't feminism forced to embrace relativism by its condition of being just one among many countercultural voices?

This description of the terrain in which feminists struggle to advance their claims, however, assumes that people must either choose only one among these countercultures as providing an absolute standard for sorting knowledge claims, or else regard all of them as competing and assign them equal cognitive status. Actually, it is a different scenario that the countercultures can envision and even occasionally already enact: the fundamental tendencies of each must permeate each of the others in order for each movement to succeed. Feminism should center the concerns of each of these movements, and each of them must move feminist concerns to its center.

To summarize, then, a strong notion of objectivity requires a commitment to acknowledge the historical character of every belief or set of beliefs—a commitment to cultural, sociological, historical relativism. But it also requires that judgmental or epistemological relativism be rejected. Weak objectivity is located in a conceptual interdependency that includes (weak) subjectivity and judgmental relativism. One cannot simply give up weak objectivity without making adjustments throughout the rest of this epistemological system.

RESPONDING TO OBJECTIONS

Two possible objections to the recommendation of a stronger standard for objectivity must be considered here. First, some scientists and philosophers of science may protest that I am attempting to specify standards of objectivity for all the sciences. What could it mean to attempt to specify *general* standards for increasing the objectivity of research? Shouldn't the task of determining what counts as adequate research be settled within each science by its own practitioners? Why should practicing scientists revise their research practices because of what is thought by a philosopher or anyone else who is not an expert in a particular science?

But the issue of this essay is an epistemological issue—a metascientific one—rather than an issue within any single science. It is more like a directive to operationalize theoretical concepts than like a directive to operationalize in a certain way some particular theoretical notion within physics or biology. The recommended combination of strong objectivity with the acknowledgment of historical relativism would, if adopted, create a

culturewide shift in the kind of epistemology regarded as desirable. Certainly, strategies for enacting commitments to strong objectivity and the acknowledgment of historical relativism would have to be developed within each particular research program; plenty of examples already exist in biology and the social sciences. My position is that the natural sciences are backward in this respect; they are not immune from the reasonableness of these directives, as conventionalists have assumed.

The notion of strong objectivity developed here represents insights that have been emerging from thinkers in a number of disciplines for some decades—not just "wishful thinking" based on no empirical sciences at all. Criticisms of the dominant thought of the West from both inside and outside the West argue that its partiality and distortions are the consequence in large part of starting that thought only from the lives of the dominant groups in the West. Less partiality and less distortion result when thought starts from peasant life, not just aristocratic life; from slaves' lives, not just slaveowners' lives; from the lives of factory workers, not just those of their bosses and managers; from the lives of people who work for wages and have also been assigned responsibility for husband and child care, not just those of persons who are expected to have little such responsibility. This directive leaves open to be determined within each discipline or research area what a researcher must do to start thought from women's lives or the lives of people in other marginalized groups, and it will be easier—though still difficult—to provide reasonable responses to such a request in history or sociology than in physics or chemistry. But the difficulty of providing an analysis in physics or chemistry does not signify that the question is an absurd one for knowledge-seeking in general, or that there are no reasonable answers for those sciences too.

The second objection may come from feminists themselves. Many would say that the notion of objectivity is so hopelessly tainted by its historical complicity in justifying the service of science to the dominant groups that trying to make it function effectively and progressively in alternative agendas only confuses the matter. If feminists want to breathe new life into such a bedraggled notion as objectivity, why not at least invent an alternative term that does not call up the offenses associated with the idea of value-neutrality, that is not intimately tied to a faulty theory of representation, to a faulty psychic construction of the ideal agent of knowledge, and to regressive political tendencies.

Let us reorganize some points made earlier in order to get the full force of this objection. The goal of producing results of research that are value-free is part of the notion of the ideal mind as a mirror that can reflect a world that is "out there," ready-made. In this view, value-free objectivity can locate an Archimedean perspective from which the events and processes of the natural world appear in their proper places. Only false beliefs have social causes—human values and interests that blind us to the real regularities and underlying causal tendencies in the world, generating biased results of research. True beliefs have only natural causes: those regularities and underlying causal tendencies that are *there,* plus the power of the eyes to see them and of the mind to reason about them. This theory of representation is a historically situated one: it is characteristic only of certain groups in the modern West. Can the notion of objectivity really be separated from this implausible theory of representation?

Value-free objectivity requires also a faulty theory of the ideal agent—the subject—of science, knowledge, and history. It requires a notion of the self as a fortress that must be defended against polluting influences from its social surroundings. The self whose mind would perfectly reflect the world must create and constantly police the borders of a gulf, a no-man's-land, between himself as the subject and the object of his research, knowledge, or action. Feminists have been among the most pointed critics of this self-versus-Other construct,[22] referring to it as "abstract masculinity."[23] Moreover, its implication in Western constructions of the racial Other against which the "white" West would define its admirable projects is also obvious.[24] Can the notion of objectivity be useful in efforts to oppose such sexism and racism?

Equally important, the notion of value-free objectivity is morally and politically regressive for reasons additional to those already mentioned. It justifies the construction of science institutions and individual scientists as "fast guns for hire." It has been used to legitimate and hold up as the highest ideal institutions and individuals that are, insofar as they are scientific, to be studiously unconcerned with the origins or consequences of their activities or with the values and interests that these activities advance. This nonaccidental, determined, energetic lack of concern is supported by science education that excludes training in critical thought and that treats all expressions of social and political concern—the concerns of the torturer and the concerns of the tortured—as being on the same low level of scientific "rationality." Scandalous examples of the institutional impotence of the sciences as sciences to speak to the moral and political issues that shape their problematics, consequences, values, and interests have been identified for decades. The construction of a border between scientific method and violations of human and, increasingly, animal

---

[22] See, e.g., Nancy Chodorow, *The Reproduction of Mothering* (Berkeley: University of California Press, 1978); Dorothy Dinnerstein, *The Mermaid and the Minotaur: Sexual Arrangements and Human Malaise* (New York: Harper & Row, 1976); Carol Gilligan, *In a Different Voice: Psychological Theory and Women's Development* (Cambridge, Mass.: Harvard University Press, 1982); Evelyn Fox Keller, *Reflections on Gender and Science* (New Haven, Conn.: Yale University Press, 1984).

[23] Hartsock, "The Feminist Standpoint."

[24] See, e.g., Sander Gilman, *Difference and Pathology: Stereotypes of Sexuality, Race, and Madness* (Ithaca: Cornell University Press, 1985); V. Y. Mudimbe, *The Invention of Africa: Gnosis, Philosophy, and the Order of Knowledge* (Bloomington: Indiana University Press, 1988); Said, *Orientalism,* and Foreword to Guha and Spivak. *Subaltern Studies.*

rights must be conducted "outside" that method, by government statements about what constitutes acceptable methods of research on human and animal subjects, what constitutes consent to experimentation, the subsequent formation of "ethics committees," and so on. Can the notion of objectivity be extracted from the morals and politics of "objective science" as a "fast gun for hire"?

These are formidable objections. Nevertheless, the argument of this book is that the notion of objectivity not only can but should be separated from its shameful and damaging history. Research is socially situated, and it can be more objectively conducted without aiming for or claiming to be value-free. The requirements for achieving strong objectivity permit one to abandon notions of perfect, mirrorlike representations of the world, the self as a defended fortress, and the "truly scientific" as disinterested with regard to morals and politics, yet still apply rational standards to sorting less from more partial and distorted belief. Indeed, my argument is that these standards are more rational and more effective at producing maximally objective results than the ones associated with what I have called weak objectivity.

As I have been arguing, objectivity is one of a complex of inextricably linked notions. Science and rationality are two other terms in this network. But it is not necessary to accept the idea that there is only one correct or reasonable way to think about these terms, let alone that the correct way is the one used by dominant groups in the modern West. Not all reason is white, masculinist, modern, heterosexual, Western reason. Not all modes of rigorous empirical knowledge-seeking are what the dominant groups think of as science—to understate the point. The procedures institutionalized in conventional science for distinguishing between how we want the world to be and how it is are not the only or best ways to go about maximizing objectivity. It is important to work and think outside the dominant modes, as the minority movements

have done. But it is important, also, to bring the insights developed there into the heart of conventional institutions, to disrupt the dominant practices from within by appropriating notions such as objectivity, reason, and science in ways that stand a chance of compelling reasoned assent while simultaneously shifting and displacing the meanings and referents of the discussion in ways that improve it. It is by thinking and acting as "outsiders within" that feminists and others can transform science and its social relations for those who remain only insiders or outsiders.

One cannot afford to "just say no" to objectivity. I think there are three additional good reasons to retain the notion of objectivity for future knowledge-seeking projects but to work at separating it from its damaging historical associations with value-neutrality.

First, it has a valuable political history. There have to be standards for distinguishing between how I want the world to be and how, in empirical fact, it is. Otherwise, might makes right in knowledge-seeking just as it tends to do in morals and politics. The notion of objectivity is useful because its meaning and history support such standards. Today, as in the past, there are powerful interests ranged against attempts to find out the regularities and underlying causal tendencies in the natural and social worlds. Some groups do not want exposed to public scrutiny the effect on the environment of agribusiness or of pesticide use in domestic gardening. Some do not want discussed the consequences for Third World peasants, for the black underclass in the United States, and especially for women in both groups of the insistence on economic production that generates profit for elites in the West. The notion of achieving greater objectivity has been useful in the past and can be today in struggles over holding people and institutions responsible for the fit between their behavior and the claims they make.

Second, objectivity also can claim a glorious intellectual history. The argument of this essay has emphasized its service to elites, but it also has been invoked to justify unpopular criticisms of partisan but entrenched beliefs. Standpoint theory can rightfully claim that history as its legacy.

Finally, the appeal to objectivity is an issue not only between feminist and prefeminist sciences but within each feminist and other emancipatory movement. There are many feminisms, some of which result in claims that distort the racial, class, sexuality, and gender relationships in society. Which ones generate less and which more partial and distorted accounts of nature and social life? The notion of objectivity is useful in providing a way to think about the gap we want between how any individual or group wants the world to be and how in fact it is.

The notion of objectivity—like such ideas as science and rationality, democracy and feminism—contains progressive as well as regressive tendencies. In each case, it is important to develop the progressive and to block the regressive ones.

REFLEXIVITY REVISITED

The notion of "strong objectivity" conceptualizes the value of putting the subject or agent of knowledge in the same critical, causal plane as the object of her or his inquiry. It permits us to see the scientific as well as the moral and political advantages of this way of trying to achieve a reciprocal relationship between the agent and object of knowledge. The contrast developed here between weak and strong notions of objectivity permits the parallel construction of weak versus strong notions of reflexivity.

Reflexivity has tended to be seen as a problem in the social sciences—and only there. Observation cannot be as separated from its social consequences as the directives of "weak objectivity," originating in the natural sciences, have assumed. In social inquiry, observation changes the field observed. Having recognized his complicity in the lives of his objects of study, the researcher is then supposed to devise various strategies to try

to democratize the situation, to inform the "natives" of their options, to make them participants in the account of their activities, and so forth.[25]

Less commonly, reflexivity has been seen as a problem because if the researcher is under the obligation to identify the social causes of the "best" as well as the "worst" beliefs and behaviors of those he studies, then he must also analyze his own beliefs and behaviors in conducting his research project—which have been shaped by the same kinds of social relations that he is interested to identify as causes of the beliefs and behaviors of others. (Here, reflexivity can begin to be conceptualized as a "problem" for the natural sciences, too.) Sociologists of knowledge in the recent "strong programme" school and related tendencies, who emphasize the importance of identifying the social causes of "best belief," have been aware of this problem from the very beginning but have devised no plausible way of resolving it—primarily because their conception of the social causes of belief in the natural sciences (the subject matter of their analyses) is artificially restricted to the micro processes of the laboratory and research community, explicitly excluding race, gender, and class relations. This restricted notion of what constitutes appropriate subject matter for analyses of the social relations of the sciences is carried into their understanding of their own work. It generates ethnographies of their own and the natural science communities

---

[25] A fine account of the travails of such a project reports Robert Blauner and David Wellman's dawning recognition that nothing they did could eliminate the colonial relationship between themselves and their black informants in the community surrounding Berkeley: see their "Toward the Decolonization of Social Research," in Ladner, *The Death of White Sociology.* Economist Vernon Dixon argues that from the perspective of an African or African American world view, the idea that observation would not change the thing observed appears ridiculous; see his "World Views and Research Methodology," in *African Philosophy: Assumptions and Paradigms for Research on Black Persons,* ed. L. M. King, Vernon Dixon, and W. W. Nobles (Los Angeles: Fanon Center, Charles R. Drew Postgraduate Medical School, 1976), and my discussion of the congruence between African and feminine world views in *The Science Question in Feminism* (Ithaca: Cornell University Press, 1986), chap. 7.

which are complicitous with positivist tendencies in insisting on the isolation of research communities from the larger social, economic, and political currents in their societies. (These accounts are also flawed by their positivist conceptions of the object of natural science study).[26]

These "weak" notions of reflexivity are disabled by their lack of any mechanism for identifying the cultural values and interests of the researchers, which form part of the evidence for the results of research in both the natural and social sciences. Anthropologists, sociologists, and the like, who work within social communities, frequently appear to desire such a mechanism or standard; but the methodological assumptions of their disciplines, which direct them to embrace either weak objectivity or judgmental relativism, have not permitted them to develop one. That is, individuals express "heartfelt desire" not to harm the subjects they observe, to become aware of their own cultural biases, and so on, but such reflexive goals remain at the level of desire rather

than competent enactment. In short, such weak reflexivity has no possible operationalization, or no competency standard, for success.

A notion of strong reflexivity would require that the objects of inquiry be conceptualized as gazing back in all their cultural particularity and that the researcher, through theory and methods, stand behind them, gazing back at his own socially situated research project in all its cultural particularity and its relationships to other projects of his culture—many of which (policy development in international relations, for example, or industrial expansion) can be seen only from locations far away from the scientist's actual daily work. "Strong reflexivity" requires the development of oppositional theory from the perspective of the lives of those Others ("nature" as already socially constructed, as well as other peoples), since intuitive experience, for reasons discussed earlier, is frequently not a reliable guide to the regularities of nature and social life and their underlying causal tendencies.

Standpoint theory opens the way to stronger standards of both objectivity and reflexivity. These standards require that research projects use their historical location as a resource for obtaining greater objectivity.

---

[26] See, e.g., Bloor, *Knowledge and Social Imagery;* and Steve Woolgar's nevertheless interesting paper, "Reflexivity Is the Ethnographer of the Text," as well as other (somewhat bizarre) discussions of reflexivity in Woolgar, *Knowledge and Reflexivity.*

THE PROJECT OF FEMINIST EPISTEMOLOGY: PERSPECTIVES FROM A NONWESTERN FEMINIST

Uma Narayan

A fundamental thesis of feminist epistemology is that our location in the world as women makes it possible for us to perceive and understand different aspects of both the world and human activities in ways that challenge the male bias of existing perspectives. Feminist epistemology is a particular manifestation of the general insight that the nature of women's experiences as individuals and as social beings, our contributions to work, culture, knowledge, and our history and political interests have been systematically ignored or misrepresented by mainstream discourses in different areas.

Women have been often excluded from prestigious areas of human activity (for example, politics or science) and this has often made these activities seem clearly "male." In areas where women were not excluded (for example, subsistence work), their contribution has been misrepresented as secondary and inferior to that of men. Feminist epistemology sees mainstream theories about various human enterprises, including mainstream theories about human knowledge, as one-dimensional and deeply flawed because of the exclusion and misrepresentation of women's contributions.

Feminist epistemology suggests that integrating women's contribution into the domain of science and knowledge will not constitute a mere adding of details; it will not merely widen the canvas but result in a shift of perspective enabling us to see a very different picture. The inclusion of women's perspective will not merely amount to women participating in greater numbers in the existing practice of science and knowledge, but it will change the very nature of these activities and their self-understanding.

It would be misleading to suggest that feminist epistemology is a homogenous and cohesive enterprise. Its practitioners differ both philosophically and politically in a number of significant ways (Harding 1986). But an important theme on its agenda has been to undermine the abstract, rationalistic, and universal image of the scientific enterprise by using several different strategies. It has studied, for instance, how contingent historical factors have colored both scientific theories and practices and provided the (often sexist) metaphors in which scientists have conceptualized their activity (Bordo 1986; Keller 1985; Harding and O'Barr 1987). It has tried to reintegrate values and emotions into our account of our cognitive activities, arguing for both the inevitability of their presence and the importance of the contributions they are capable of making to our knowledge (Gilligan 1982). It has also attacked various sets of dualisms characteristic of western philosophical thinking—reason versus emotion, culture versus nature, universal versus particular—in which the first of each set is identified with science, rationality, and the masculine and the second is relegated to the nonscientific, the nonrational, and the feminine (Harding and Hintikka 1983; Lloyd 1984; Wilshire essay in this volume).

At the most general level, feminist epistemology resembles the efforts of many oppressed groups to reclaim for themselves the value of their own experience. The writing of novels that focused on working-class life in England or the lives of black people in the United States shares a motivation similar to that of feminist epistemology—to depict an experience different from the norm and to assert the value of this difference.

In a similar manner, feminist epistemology also resembles attempts by third-world writers and historians to document the wealth and complexity of local economic and social structures that existed prior to colonialism. These attempts are useful for their ability to restore to colonized peoples a sense of the richness of their own history and culture. These projects also mitigate the tendency of intellectuals in former colonies who are westernized through their education to think that anything western is necessarily better and more "progressive." In some cases, such studies help to preserve the knowledge of many local arts, crafts, lore, and techniques that were part of the former way of life before they are lost not only to practice but even to memory.

These enterprises are analogous to feminist epistemology's project of restoring to women a sense of the richness of their history, to mitigate our tendency to see the stereotypically "masculine" as better or more progressive, and to preserve for posterity the contents of "feminine" areas of knowledge and expertise—medical lore, knowledge associated with the practices of childbirth and child rearing, traditionally feminine crafts, and so on. Feminist epistemology, like these other enterprises, must attempt to balance the assertion of the value of a different culture or experience against the dangers of romanticizing it to the extent that the limitations and oppressions it confers on its subjects are ignored.

My essay will attempt to examine some dangers of approaching feminist theorizing and epistemological values in a noncontextual and nonpragmatic way, which could convert important feminist insights and theses into feminist epistemological dogmas. I will use my perspective as a nonwestern, Indian feminist to examine critically the predominantly Anglo-American project of feminist epistemology and to reflect on what such a project might signify for women in nonwestern cultures in general and for nonwestern feminists in particular. I will suggest that different cultural contexts and political agendas may cast a very different light on both the "idols" and the "enemies" of knowledge as they have characteristically been typed in western feminist epistemology.

In keeping with my respect for contexts, I would like to stress that I do not see nonwestern feminists as a homogenous group and that none of the concerns I express as a nonwestern feminist may be pertinent to or shared by *all* nonwestern feminists, although I do think they will make sense to many.

In the first section, I will show that the enterprise of feminist epistemology poses some political problems for nonwestern feminists that it does not pose, in the same way, for western feminists. In the second section, I will explore some problems that nonwestern feminists may have with feminist epistemology's critical focus on positivism. In the third section, I will examine some political implications of feminist epistemology's thesis of the "epistemic privilege" of oppressed groups for nonwestern feminists. And in the last section, I will discuss the claim that oppressed groups gain epistemic advantages by inhabiting a larger number of contexts, arguing that such situations may not always confer advantages and may sometimes create painful problems.

NONWESTERN FEMINIST POLITICS AND FEMINIST EPISTEMOLOGY

Some themes of feminist epistemology may be problematic for nonwestern feminists in ways that they are not problematic for western feminists. Feminism has a much narrower base in most nonwestern countries. It is primarily of significance to some urban, educated, middle-class, and hence relatively westernized women, like myself. Although feminist groups in these countries do try to extend the scope of feminist concerns to other groups (for example, by fighting for childcare, women's health issues, and equal wages issues through trade union structures), some major preoccupations of western feminism—its critique of marriage, the family, compulsory heterosexuality—presently engage the attention of mainly small groups of middle-class feminists.

These feminists must think and function within the context of a powerful tradition that, although it systematically oppresses women, also contains within itself a discourse that confers a high value on women's place in the general scheme of things. Not only are the roles of wife and mother highly praised, but women also are seen as the cornerstones of the spiritual well-being of their husbands and children, admired for their supposedly higher moral, religious, and spiritual qualities, and so on. In cultures that have a pervasive religious component, like the Hindu culture with which I am familiar, everything seems assigned a place and value as long as it keeps to its place. Confronted with a powerful traditional discourse that values woman's place as long as she keeps to the place prescribed, it may be politically counterproductive for nonwestern feminists to echo uncritically the themes of western feminist epistemology that seek to restore the value, cognitive and otherwise, of "women's experience."

The danger is that, even if the nonwestern feminist talks about the value of women's experience in terms totally different from those of the traditional discourse, the difference is likely to be drowned out by the louder and more powerful voice of the traditional discourse, which will then claim that "what those feminists say" vindicates its view that the roles and experiences it assigns to women have value and that women should stick to those roles.

I do not intend to suggest that this is not a danger for western feminism or to imply that there is no tension for western feminists between being critical of the experiences that their societies have provided for women and finding things to value in them nevertheless. But I am suggesting that perhaps there is less at risk for western feminists in trying to strike this balance. I am inclined to think that in nonwestern countries feminists must still stress the negative sides of the female experience within that culture and that the time for a more sympathetic evaluation is not quite ripe.

But the issue is not simple and seems even less so when another point is considered. The imperative we experience as feminists to be critical of how our culture and traditions oppress women conflicts with our desire as members of once colonized cultures to affirm the value of the same culture and traditions.

There are seldom any easy resolutions to these sorts of tensions. As an Indian feminist currently living in the United States, I often find myself torn between the desire to communicate with honesty the miseries and oppressions that I think my own culture confers on its women and the fear that this communication is going to reinforce, however unconsciously, western prejudices about the "superiority" of western culture. I have often felt compelled to interrupt my communication, say on the problems of the Indian system of arranged marriages, to remind my western friends that the experiences of women under their system of "romantic love" seem no more enviable. Perhaps we should all attempt to cultivate the methodological habit of trying to understand the complexities of the oppression involved in different historical and cultural settings while eschewing, at least for now, the temptation to make comparisons across such settings, given the dangers of attempting to compare what may well be incommensurable in any neat terms.

THE NONPRIMACY OF POSITIVISM AS A PROBLEMATIC PERSPECTIVE

As a nonwestern feminist, I also have some reservations about the way in which feminist epistemology seems to have picked positivism as its main target of attack. The choice of positivism as the main target is reasonable because it has been a dominant and influential western position and it most clearly embodies some flaws that feminist epistemology seeks to remedy.

But this focus on positivism should not blind us to the facts that it is not our only enemy and that nonpositivist frameworks are not, by virtue of that bare qualification, any more worthy of our tolerance. Most traditional frameworks that nonwestern feminists regard as oppressive to women are not positivist, and it would be wrong to see feminist epistemology's critique of positivism given the same political importance for nonwestern feminists that it has for western feminists. Traditions like my own, where the influence of religion is pervasive, are suffused through and through with values. We must fight not frameworks that assert the separation of fact and value but frameworks that are pervaded by values to which we, as feminists, find ourselves opposed. Positivism in epistemology flourished at the same time as liberalism in western political theory. Positivism's view of values as individual and subjective related to liberalism's political emphasis on individual rights that were supposed to protect an individual's freedom to live according to the values she espoused.

Nonwestern feminists may find themselves in a curious bind when confronting the interrelations between positivism and political liberalism. As colonized people, we are well aware of the facts that many political concepts of liberalism are both suspicious and confused and that the practice of liberalism in the colonies was marked by brutalities unaccounted for by its theory. However, as feminists, we often find some of its concepts, such as individual rights, very useful in our attempts to fight problems rooted in our traditional cultures.

Nonwestern feminists will no doubt be sensitive to the fact that positivism is not our only enemy. Western feminists too must learn not to uncritically claim any nonpositivist framework as an ally; despite commonalities, there are apt to be many differences. A temperate look at positions we espouse as allies is necessary since "the enemy of my enemy is my friend" is a principle likely to be as misleading in epistemology as it is in the domain of Realpolitik.

The critical theorists of the Frankfurt School will serve well to illustrate this point. Begun as a group of young intellectuals in the post-World War I Weimar Republic, the members were significantly influenced by Marxism, and their interests ranged from aesthetics to political theory to epistemology. Jürgen Habermas, the most eminent critical theorist today, has in his works attacked positivism and the claim of scientific theories to be value neutral or "disinterested." He has attempted to show the constitutive role played by human interests in different domains of human knowledge. He is interested, as are feminists, in the role that knowledge plays in the reproduction of social relations of domination. But, as feminist epistemology is critical of all perspectives that place a lopsided stress on reason, it must also necessarily be critical of the rationalist underpinnings of critical theory.

Such rationalist foundations are visible, for example, in Habermas's "rational reconstruction" of what he calls "an ideal speech situation," supposedly characterized by "pure intersubjectivity," that is, by the absence of any barriers to communication. That Habermas's "ideal speech situation" is a creature of reason is clear from its admitted character as a "rationally reconstructed ideal" and its symmetrical distribution of chances for all of its participants to choose and apply speech acts.

This seems to involve a stress on formal and procedural equality among speakers that ignores substantive differences imposed by class, race, or gender that may affect a speaker's knowledge of the facts or the capacity to assert herself or command the attention of others. Women in academia often can testify to the fact that, despite not being forcibly restrained from speaking in public forums, they have to overcome much conditioning in order to learn to assert themselves. They can also testify as to how, especially in male-dominated disciplines,

their speech is often ignored or treated with condescension by male colleagues.

Habermas either ignores the existence of such substantive differences among speakers or else assumes they do not exist. In the latter case, if one assumes that the speakers in the ideal speech situation are not significantly different from each other, then there may not be much of significance for them to speak about. Often it is precisely our differences that make dialogue imperative. If the ideal speakers of the ideal speech situation are unmarked by differences, there may be nothing for them to surmount on their way to a "rational consensus." If there are such differences between the speakers, then Habermas provides nothing that will rule out the sorts of problems I have mentioned.

Another rationalist facet of critical theory is revealed in Habermas's assumption that justifiable agreement and genuine knowledge arise only out of "rational consensus." This seems to overlook the possibility of agreement and knowledge based on sympathy or solidarity. Sympathy or solidarity may very well promote the uncovering of truth, especially in situations when people who divulge information are rendering themselves vulnerable in the process. For instance, women are more likely to talk about experiences of sexual harassment to other women because they would expect similar experiences to have made them more sympathetic and understanding. Therefore, feminists should be cautious about assuming that they necessarily have much in common with a framework simply because it is nonpositivist. Nonwestern feminists may be more alert to this error because many problems they confront arise in nonpositivist contexts.

THE POLITICAL USES OF "EPISTEMIC PRIVILEGE"

Important strands in feminist epistemology hold the view that our concrete embodiments as members of a specific class, race, and gender as well as our concrete historical situations necessarily play significant roles in our perspective on the world; moreover, no point of view is "neutral" because no one exists unembedded in the world. Knowledge is seen as gained not by solitary individuals but by socially constituted members of groups that emerge and change through history.

Feminists have also argued that groups living under various forms of oppression are more likely to have a critical perspective on their situation and that this critical view is both generated and partly constituted by critical emotional responses that subjects experience vis-à-vis their life situations. This perspective in feminist epistemology rejects the "Native View" of emotions and favors an intentional conception that emphasizes the cognitive aspect of emotions. It is critical of the traditional view of the emotions as wholly and always impediments to knowledge and argues that many emotions often help rather than hinder our understanding of a person or situation.

Bringing together these views on the role of the emotions in knowledge, the possibility of critical insights being generated by oppression, and the contextual nature of knowledge may suggest some answers to serious and interesting political questions. I will consider what these epistemic positions entail regarding the possibility of understanding and political cooperation between oppressed groups and sympathetic members of a dominant group—say, between white people and people of color over issues of race or between men and women over issues of gender.

These considerations are also relevant to questions of understanding and cooperation between western and nonwestern feminists. Western feminists, despite their critical understanding of their own culture, often tend to be more a part of it than they realize. If they fail to see the contexts of their theories and assume that their perspective has universal validity for all feminists, they tend to participate in the dominance that western culture has exercised over nonwestern cultures.

Our position must explain and justify our dual need to criticize members of a dominant group (say men or white people or western feminists) for their lack of attention to or concern with problems that affect an oppressed group (say, women or people of color or nonwestern feminists, respectively), as well as for our frequent hostility toward those who express interest, even sympathetic interest, in issues that concern groups of which they are not a part.

Both attitudes are often warranted. On the one hand, one cannot but be angry at those who minimize, ignore, or dismiss the pain and conflict that racism and sexism inflict on their victims. On the other hand, living in a state of siege also necessarily makes us suspicious of expressions of concern and support from those who do not live these oppressions. We are suspicious of the motives of our sympathizers or the extent of their sincerity, and we worry, often with good reason, that they may claim that their interest provides a warrant for them to speak for us, as dominant groups throughout history have spoken for the dominated.

This is all the more threatening to groups aware of how recently they have acquired the power to articulate their own points of view. Nonwestern feminists are especially aware of this because they have a double struggle in trying to find their own voice: they have to learn to articulate their differences, not only from their own traditional contexts but also from western feminism.

Politically, we face interesting questions whose answers hinge on the nature and extent of the communication that we think possible between different groups. Should we try to share our perspectives and insights with those who have not lived our oppressions and accept that they may fully come to share them? Or should we seek only the affirmation of those like ourselves, who share common features of oppression, and rule out the possibility of those who have not lived these oppressions ever acquiring a genuine understanding of them?

I argue that it would be a mistake to move from the thesis that knowledge is constructed by human subjects who are socially constituted to the conclusion that those who are differently located socially can never attain *some* understanding of our experience or *some* sympathy with our cause. In that case, we would be committed to not just a perspectival view of knowledge but a relativistic one. Relativism, as I am using it, implies that a person could have knowledge of only the sorts of things she had experienced personally and that she would be totally unable to communicate any of the contents of her knowledge to someone who did not have the same sorts of experiences. Not only does this seem clearly false and perhaps even absurd, but it is probably a good idea not to have any a priori views that would imply either that all our knowledge is always capable of being communicated to every other person or that would imply that some of our knowledge is necessarily incapable of being communicated to some class of persons.

"Nonanalytic" and "nonrational" forms of discourse, like fiction or poetry, may be better able than other forms to convey the complex life experiences of one group to members of another. One can also hope that being part of one oppressed group may enable an individual to have a more sympathetic understanding of issues relating to another kind of oppression—that, for instance, being a woman may sensitize one to issues of race and class even if one is a woman privileged in those respects.

Again, this should not be reduced to some kind of metaphysical presumption. Historical circumstances have sometimes conspired, say, to making working-class men more chauvinistic in some of their attitudes than other men. Sometimes one sort of suffering may simply harden individuals to other sorts or leave them without energy to take any interest in the problems of other groups. But we can at least try to foster such sensitivity by focusing on parallels, not identities, between different sorts of oppressions.

Our commitment to the contextual nature of knowledge does not require us to claim that those who do not inhabit these contexts can never have any knowledge of them. But this commitment does permit us to argue that it is *easier* and *more likely* for the oppressed to have critical insights into the conditions of their own oppression than it is for those who live outside these structures. Those who actually *live* the oppressions of class, race, or gender have faced the issues that such oppressions generate in a variety of different situations. The insights and emotional responses engendered by these situations are a legacy with which they confront any new issue or situation.

Those who display sympathy as outsiders often fail both to understand fully the emotional complexities of living as a member of an oppressed group and to carry what they have learned and understood about one situation to the way they perceive another. It is a commonplace that even sympathetic men will often fail to perceive subtle instances of sexist behavior or discourse.

Sympathetic individuals who are not members of an oppressed group should keep in mind the possibility of this sort of failure regarding their understanding of issues relating to an oppression they do not share. They should realize that nothing they may do, from participating in demonstrations to changing their lifestyles, can make them one of the oppressed. For instance, men who share household and child-rearing responsibilities with women are mistaken if they think that this act of choice, often buttressed by the gratitude and admiration of others, is anything like the woman's experience of being forcibly socialized into these tasks and of having others perceive this as her natural function in the scheme of things.

The view that we can understand much about the perspectives of those whose oppression we do not share allows us the space to criticize dominant groups for their blindness to the facts of oppression. The view that such an understanding, despite great effort and interest, is likely to be incomplete or limited, provides us with the ground for denying total parity to members of a dominant group in their ability to understand our situation.

Sympathetic members of a dominant group need not necessarily defer to our views on any particular issue because that may reduce itself to another subtle form of condescension, but at least they must keep in mind the very real difficulties and possibility of failure to fully understand our concerns. This and the very important need for dominated groups to control the means of discourse about their own situations are important reasons for taking seriously the claim that oppressed groups have an "epistemic advantage."

THE DARK SIDE OF "DOUBLE VISION"

I think that one of the most interesting insights of feminist epistemology is the view that oppressed groups, whether women, the poor, or racial minorities, may derive an "epistemic advantage" from having knowledge of the practices of both their own contexts and those of their oppressors. The practices of the dominant groups (for instance, men) govern a society; the dominated group (for instance, women) must acquire some fluency with these practices in order to survive in that society.

There is no similar pressure on members of the dominant group to acquire knowledge of the practices of the dominated groups. For instance, colonized people had to learn the language and culture of their colonizers. The colonizers seldom found it necessary to have more than a sketchy acquaintance with the language and culture of the "natives." Thus, the oppressed are seen as having an "epistemic advantage" because they can operate with two sets of practices and in two different contexts. This advantage is thought to lead to critical insights because each framework provides a critical perspective on the other.

I would like to balance this account with a few comments about the "dark side," the disadvantages, of being able to or of having to inhabit two mutually incompatible frameworks that provide differing perspectives on social reality. I suspect that nonwestern feminists, given the often complex and troublesome interrelationships between the contexts they must inhabit, are less likely to express unqualified enthusiasm about the benefits of straddling a multiplicity of contexts. Mere access to two different and incompatible contexts is not a guarantee that a critical stance on the part of an individual will result. There are many ways in which she may deal with the situation.

First, the person may be tempted to dichotomize her life and reserve the framework of a different context for each part. The middle class of nonwestern countries supplies numerous examples of people who are very westernized in public life but who return to a very traditional lifestyle in the realm of the family. Women may choose to live their public lives in a "male" mode, displaying characteristics of aggressiveness, competition, and so on, while continuing to play dependent and compliant roles in their private lives. The pressures of jumping between two different lifestyles may be mitigated by justifications of how each pattern of behavior is appropriate to its particular context and of how it enables them to "get the best of both worlds."

Second, the individual may try to reject the practices of her own context and try to be as much as possible like members of the dominant group. Westernized intellectuals in the nonwestern world often may almost lose knowledge of their own cultures and practices and be ashamed of the little that they do still know. Women may try both to acquire stereotypically male characteristics, like aggressiveness, and to expunge stereotypically female characteristics, like emotionality. Or the individual could try to reject entirely the framework of the dominant group and assert the virtues of her own despite the risks of being marginalized from the power structures of the society; consider, for example, women who seek a certain sort of security in traditionally defined roles.

The choice to inhabit two contexts critically is an alternative to these choices and, I would argue, a more useful one. But the presence of alternative contexts does not by itself guarantee that one of the other choices will not be made. Moreover, the decision to inhabit two contexts critically, although it may lead to an "epistemic advantage," is likely to exact a certain price. It may lead to a sense of totally lacking roots or any space where one is at home in a relaxed manner.

This sense of alienation may be minimized if the critical straddling of two contexts is part of an ongoing critical politics, due to the support of others and a deeper understanding of what is going on. When it is not so rooted, it may generate ambivalence, uncertainty, despair, and even madness, rather than more positive critical emotions and attitudes. However such a person determines her locus, there may be a sense of being an outsider in both contexts and a sense of clumsiness or lack of fluency in both sets of practices. Consider this simple linguistic example: most people who learn two different languages that are associated with two very different cultures seldom acquire both with equal fluency; they may find themselves devoid of vocabulary in one language for certain contexts of life or be unable to match real objects with terms they have acquired in their vocabulary. For instance, people from my sort of background would know words in Indian languages for some spices, fruits, and vegetables that they do not know in English. Similarly, they might be unable to discuss "technical" subjects like economics or biology in their own languages because they learned about these subjects and acquired their technical vocabularies only in English.

The relation between the two contexts the individual inhabits may not be simple or straightforward. The individual subject is seldom in a position to carry out a perfect "dialectical synthesis" that preserves all the advantages of both contexts and transcends all their problems. There may be a number of different "syntheses," each of which avoids a different subset of the problems and preserves a different subset of the benefits.

No solution may be perfect or even palatable to the agent confronted with a choice. For example, some Indian feminists may find some western modes of dress (say trousers) either more comfortable or more their "style" than some local modes of dress. However, they may find that wearing the local mode of dress is less socially troublesome, alienates them less from more traditional people they want to work with, and so on. Either choice is bound to leave them partly frustrated in their desires.

Feminist theory must be temperate in the use it makes of this doctrine of "double vision"—the claim that oppressed groups have an epistemic advantage and access to greater critical conceptual space. Certain types and contexts of oppression certainly may bear out the truth of this claim. Others certainly do not seem to do so; and even if they do provide space for critical insights, they may also rule out the possibility of actions subversive of the oppressive state of affairs.

Certain kinds of oppressive contexts, such as the contexts in which women of my grandmother's background lived, rendered their subjects entirely devoid of skills required to function as independent entities in the culture. Girls were married off barely past puberty, trained for nothing beyond household tasks and the rearing of children, and passed from economic dependency on their fathers to economic dependency on their husbands to economic dependency on their sons in old age. Their criticisms of their lot were articulated, if at all, in terms that precluded a desire for any radical change. They saw themselves sometimes as personally unfortunate, but they did not locate the causes of their misery in larger social arrangements.

I conclude by stressing that the important insight incorporated in the doctrine of "double vision" should not be reified into a metaphysics that serves as a substitute for concrete social analysis. Furthermore, the alternative to "buying" into an oppressive social system need not be a celebration of exclusion and the mechanisms of marginalization. The thesis that oppression may bestow an epistemic advantage should not tempt us in the direction of idealizing or romanticizing oppression and blind us to its real material and psychic deprivations.

REFERENCES

Bordo, S. 1986. "The Cartesian Masculinization of Thought." *Signs* 11:439–456.

Gilligan, C. 1982. *In A Different Voice: Psychological Theory and Women's Development.* Cambridge, Mass.: Harvard University Press.

Harding, S. 1986. *The Science Question in Feminism.* Ithaca, N.Y.: Cornell University Press.

Harding, S., and M. Hintikka. 1983. *Discovering Reality: Feminist Perspectives on Epistemology, Metaphysics, Methodology, and Philosophy of Science.* Dordrecht: Reidel.

Harding, S., and J. O'Barr, eds. 1987. *Sex and Scientific Inquiry.* Chicago: University of Chicago Press.

Keller, E. F. 1985. *Reflections on Gender and Science.* New Haven, Conn.: Yale University Press.

Lloyd, G. 1984. *The Man of Reason.* Minneapolis: University of Minnesota Press.

COMING TO UNDERSTAND: ORGASM AND THE EPISTEMOLOGY OF IGNORANCE

Nancy Tuana

Lay understanding and scientific accounts of female sexuality and orgasm provide a fertile site for demonstrating the importance of including epistemologies of ignorance within feminist epistemologies. Ignorance is not a simple lack. It is often constructed, maintained, and disseminated and is linked to issues of cognitive authority, doubt, trust, silencing, and uncertainty. Studying both feminist and nonfeminist understandings of female orgasm reveals practices that suppress or erase bodies of knowledge concerning women's sexual pleasures.

It is a common tenet of theorists working in the sociology of scientific knowledge (SSK) that an account of the conditions that result in scientists accepting apparently true beliefs and theories is as crucial as an analysis of those that result in their holding to apparently false theories and beliefs. In outlining the Strong Programme in SSK studies, David Bloor (1976) argues against the asymmetry position common to philosophies of science. On such a position, only false beliefs that have had a history of influence upon science, such as views about ether, humors, or phlogiston, are in need of a sociological account. True beliefs or theories, however, are viewed as in need of no such explanation in that their acceptance can be accounted for simply by their truth. Bloor and other SSK theorists argue that such appeals to truth are inadequate, insisting that the acceptance of a belief as true, even in science, involves social factors. The appeal to reality thus does not suffice in explaining why a belief has come to be accepted by scientists.

In a similar fashion it is important that our epistemologies not limit attention simply to what is known or believed to be known. If we are to fully understand the complex practices of knowledge production and the variety of features that account for why something is known, we must also understand the practices that account for *not* knowing, that is, for our *lack* of knowledge about a phenomenon or, in some cases, an account of the practices that resulted in a group *unlearning* what was once a realm of knowledge. In other words, those who would strive to understand how we know must also develop epistemologies of ignorance.[1]

Ignorance, far from being a simple lack of knowledge that good science aims to banish, is better understood as a practice with supporting social causes as complex as those involved in knowledge practices. As Robert Proctor argued in his study of the politics of cancer research and dissemination, *Cancer Wars,* we must "study the social construction of ignorance. The persistence of controversy is often not a natural consequence of imperfect knowledge but a political consequence of conflicting interests and structural apathies. Controversy can be engineered: ignorance and uncertainty can be manufactured, maintained, and disseminated" (1995, 8).

An important aspect of an epistemology of ignorance is the realization that ignorance should not be theorized as a simple omission or gap but is, in many cases, an active production. Ignorance is frequently constructed and actively preserved, and is linked to issues of cognitive authority, doubt, trust, silencing, and uncertainty. Charles Mills, for example, argues that matters related to race in Europe and the United States involve an active production and preservation of ignorance: "On matters related to race, the Racial Contract prescribes for its signatories an inverted epistemology, an epistemology of ignorance, a particular pattern of localized and global cognitive dysfunctions (which are psychologically and socially functional), producing the ironic outcome that whites will in general be unable to understand the world they themselves have made" (1997, 18).

Although such productions are not always linked to systems of oppression, it is important to be aware of how often oppression works through and is shadowed by ignorance. As Eve Kosofsky Sedgwick argues in her *Epistemology of the Closet,* "ignorance effects can be harnessed, licensed, and regulated on a mass scale for striking

enforcements" (1990, 5). Indeed, tracing what is not known and the politics of such ignorance should be a key element of epistemological *and* social/political analyses, for it has the potential to reveal the role of power in the construction of what is known and to provide a lens for the political values at work in our knowledge practices.

Epistemologies that view ignorance as an arena of not-yet-knowing will also overlook those instances where knowledge once had has been lost. What was once common knowledge or even common scientific knowledge can be transferred to the realm of ignorance not because it is refuted and seen as false, but because such knowledge is no longer seen as valuable, important, or functional. Obstetricians in the United States, for example, no longer know how to turn a breech, not because such knowledge, in this case a knowing-how, is seen as false, but because medical practices, which are in large part fueled by business and malpractice concerns, have shifted knowledge practices in cases of breech births to Caesareans. Midwives in most settings and physicians in many other countries still possess this knowledge and employ it regularly. Epistemologies of ignorance must focus not only on cases where bodies of knowledge have been completely erased, or where a realm has never been subject to knowledge production, but also on these in-between cases where what was once common knowledge has been actively "disappeared" amongst certain groups. We must also ask the question now common to feminist and postcolonialist science studies of who benefits and who is disadvantaged by such ignorance (see, for example, Harding 1998; Tuana 1996b).

While we must abandon the assumption that ignorance is a passive gap in what we know, awaiting scientific progress and discovery, it would be premature to seek out a theory of ignorance with the expectation of finding some universal calculus of the "justified true belief" model. Why we do not know something, whether it has remained or been made unknown, who knows and who is ignorant, and how each of these shift historically or from realm to realm, are all open to question. Furthermore, while the movements and productions of ignorance often parallel and track particular knowledge practices, we cannot assume that their logic is similar to the knowledge that they shadow. The question of how ignorance is sustained, cultivated, or allowed is one that must be asked explicitly and without assuming that the epistemic tools cultivated for understanding knowledge will be sufficient to understanding ignorance. The general point, however, still holds that we cannot fully account for what we know without also offering an account of what we do not know and who is privileged and disadvantaged by such knowledge/ignorance.

Female sexuality is a particularly fertile area for tracking the intersections of power/knowledge-ignorance.[2] Scientific and common-sense knowledge of female orgasm has a history that provides a rich lens for understanding the importance of explicitly including epistemologies of ignorance alongside our theories of knowledge. And so it is women's bodies and pleasures that I embrace.

EPISTEMOLOGIES OF ORGASM

Following in the footsteps of foremothers as interestingly diverse as Mary Daly (1978) and Donna Haraway (2000), I adopt the habit of invoking a material-semiotic presence. I write under the sign of Inanna, the Sumerian Queen of Heaven and Earth.[3] Let her be a reminder that sign and flesh are profoundly interconnected.[4]

What I tell you
Let the singer weave into song.
What I tell you,

Let it flow from ear to mouth,
Let it pass from old to young:

My vulva, the horn,
The Boat of Heaven,
Is full of eagerness like the young moon.
My untilled land lies fallow.

As for me, Inanna,
Who will plow my vulva?
Who will plow my high field?
Who will plow my wet ground?
(*—Inanna* 1983, 36–37)

No doubt it sounds strange to ears schooled by a Foucaultian sensitivity to things sexual for me to frame an epistemology of ignorance around women's sexuality in general, and their orgasms in particular. Indeed, it was Michel Foucault who warned that the disciplining practices of the nineteenth century had constructed sex as "a problem of truth": "[T]he truth of sex became something fundamental, useful, or dangerous, precious or formidable; in short, that sex was constituted as a problem of truth" (1990, 56). Can my investigations of the power dimensions of ignorance concerning women's orgasms not fall prey to a constructed desire for the "truth of sex?"

One might suggest that I follow Foucault's admonition to attend to bodies and pleasures rather than sexual desire to avoid this epistemic trap. And indeed, I do desire to trace bodies and pleasures as a source of subversion. The bodies of my attention are those of women, the pleasures those of orgasm. But bodies and pleasures are not outside the history and deployment of sex-desire. Bodies and pleasures will not remove me, the epistemic subject, from the practice of desiring truth. Bodies and pleasures, as Foucault well knew, have histories. Indeed the bodies that I trace are material-semiotic interactions of organisms/environments/cultures.[5] Bodies and their pleasures are not natural givens, not even deep down. Nor do I believe in a true female sexuality hidden deep beneath the layers of oppressive socialization. But women's bodies and pleasures provide a fertile lens for understanding the workings of power/knowledge-ignorance in which we can trace who desires what knowledge; that is, we can glimpse the construction of desire (or lack thereof) for knowledge of women's sexuality. I also believe that women's bodies and pleasures can, at this historical moment, be a wellspring for resisting sexual normalization.[6] Although my focus in this essay will be on the former concern, I hope to provide sufficient development of the latter to tantalize.

I have no desire in this essay to trace the normalizing and pathologizing of sexual subjectivities. My goal is to understand what "we" do and do not know about women's orgasms, and why. My "we"s include scientific communities, both feminist and nonfeminist, and the common knowledges of everyday folk, both feminist and nonfeminist. Of course I cannot divorce normalizing sexualities from such a study of women's orgasms, for, as we will see, what we do and do not know of women's bodies and pleasures interact with these practices. Although part of my goal is to trace an epistemology of orgasm, I do so because of a firm belief that as we come to understand our orgasms, we will find a site of pleasure that serves as a resource for resisting sexual normalization through the practices of becoming sexual.

In coming to understand, I suggest that we begin at the site of the clitoris.

UNVEILING THE CLITORIS

Inanna placed the shugurra, *the crown of the steppe, on her head.*
She went to the sheepfold, to the shepherd.
She leaned back against the apple tree.
When she leaned against the apple tree,
    her vulva was wondrous to behold.
Rejoicing at her wondrous vulva,
    the young woman Inanna applauded
    herself.

        —Inanna: Queen of Heaven and Earth:
        Her Stories and Hymms from Sumer

What we do and do not know about women's genitalia is a case study of the politics of ignorance. The "we"s I speak of here are both the "we"s of the general population in the United States[7] and the "we"s of scientists. Let me begin with the former. I teach a popular, large lecture course on sexuality. I have discovered that the students in the class know far more about male genitals than they

do about female genitals. Take, for example, the clitoris. The vast majority of my female students have no idea how big their clitoris is, or how big the average clitoris is, or what types of variations exist among women. Compare to this the fact that most of my male students can tell you the length *and* diameter of their penis both flaccid and erect, though their information about the average size of erect penises is sometimes shockingly inflated—a consequence, I suspect, of the size of male erections in porn movies. An analogous pattern of knowledge-ignorance also holds across the sexes. That is, both women and men alike typically know far more about the structures of the penis than they do about those of the clitoris.

This is not to say that women do not know anything about their genitalia. But what they, and the typical male student, know consists primarily in a more or less detailed knowledge of the menstrual cycle and the reproductive organs. Women and men can typically draw a relatively accurate rendition of the vagina, uterus, fallopian tubes, and ovaries, but when asked to provide me with a drawing (from memory) of an external and an internal view of female sexual organs, they often do not include a sketch of the clitoris; and when they do, it is seldom detailed.

This pattern of knowledge-ignorance mirrors a similar pattern in scientific representations of female and male genitalia. Although the role of the clitoris in female sexual satisfaction is scientifically acknowledged, and well known by most of us, the anatomy and physiology of the clitoris, particularly its beginnings and ends, is still a contested terrain. A brief history of representations of the clitoris provides an interesting initial entry into this epistemology of ignorance. Let me begin with the "facts."

As I and many other theorists have argued, until the nineteenth century, men's bodies were believed to be the true form of human biology and the standard against which female structures—bones, brains, and genitalia alike—were to be compared (see Laqueur 1990; Gallagher and Laqueur 1987; Schiebinger 1989; and Tuana 1993). The clitoris fared no differently. Medical science held the male

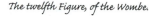
The twelfth Figure, of the Wombe.

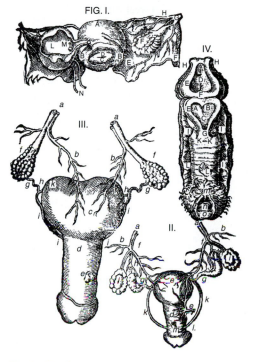

Illustration 1
The workes of that famous chirurgion Ambrose Pare, translated out of Latine and compared with the French by Thomas Johnson. London, Printed by T. Cotes and R. Young, Anno 1634. Page 127.

genitals to be the true form, of which women's genitals were a colder, interior version (see Illustration 1). As Luce Irigaray (1985) would say, through this speculum women's genitals were simply those of a man turned inside out and upside down. It thus comes as no surprise that the clitoris would be depicted as, at best, a diminutive homologue to the penis. A history of medical views of the clitoris is not a simple tale. It includes those of Ambroise Paré, the sixteenth-century biologist, who, while quite content to chronicle and describe the various parts and functions of women's reproductive organs, refused to discuss what he called this "obscene part," and admonished "those which desire to know more of it" to read the work of anatomists such as Renaldus Columbus and Gabriello Fallopius (Paré 1968, 130). A history of the clitoris

must also include the subject, well dissected by Thomas Laqueur (1989, 1986), whether, despite the proliferation of terms such as *kleitoris, columnella, virga* (rod), and *nympha* in texts from Hippocrates to the sixteenth century, these meant anything quite like what "clitoris" meant after the sixteenth century when the link between it and pleasure was bridged.

What was so "discovered" was, of course, complex. Renaldus Columbus, self-heralded as he who discovered the clitoris, refers us to "protuberances, emerging from the uterus near that opening which is called the mouth of the womb" (1559, 11.16.447; Laqueur 1989, 103). He described the function of these protuberances as "the seat of women's delight" which "while women are eager for sex and very excited as if in a frenzy and aroused to lust . . . you will find it a little harder and oblong to such a degree that it shows itself a sort of male member," and when rubbed or touched "semen swifter than air flows this way and that on account of the pleasure even with them unwilling" (1559, 11.16.447–8; Laqueur 1989, 103). Though a different clitoris than we are used to, I will later argue that Columbus provides an interesting rendition of this emerging flesh relevant to an epistemology of knowledge-ignorance.

While much pleasure can result from a thorough history of the clitoris, let me forebear and leap ahead to more contemporary renditions of this seat of pleasure. Even after the "two-sex" model became dominant in the nineteenth century, with its view of the female not as an underdeveloped male but as a second gender with distinctive gender differences, the clitoris got short shrift. It was often rendered a simple nub, which though carefully labeled, was seldom fleshed out or made a focus of attention (see Illustration 2). Even more striking is the emerging practice from the 1940s to the 1970s of simply omitting even the nub of this seat of pleasure when offering a cross-sectional image of female genitalia (see Illustrations 3 and 4). It is important to remember that this display, or lack thereof, is happening at a time when displays of the penis are becoming ever more complex (see Illustration 5).

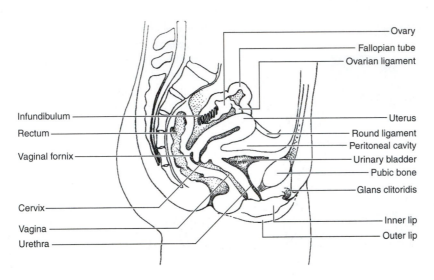

Illustration 2
Figure 4.3, Sagittal section of female internal anatomy (Rosen and Rosen 1981, 138).

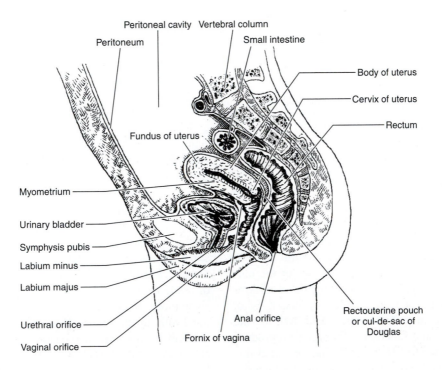

Illustration 3
Figure 24–6, Median sagittal section of female pelvis (Kimber, Gray, Stackpole, Leavell, and Miller 1966, 712).

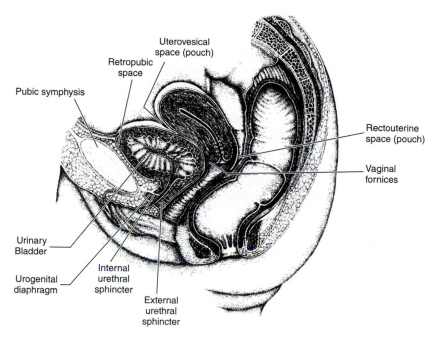

Illustration 4
Figure 5–13, Female pelvic organs (Christensen and Telford 1978, 182).

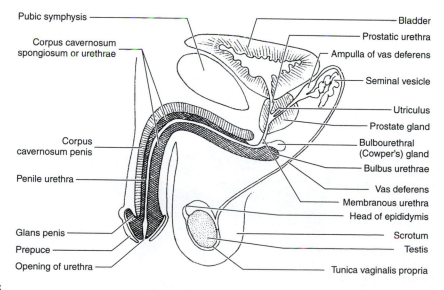

Illustration 5
Figure 24–3, Diagram of midsagittal section of male reproductive organs (Kimber, Gray, Stackpole, Leavell, and Miller 1966, 708).

Enter the women's health movement, and illustrations of women's genitals shift yet again, at least in some locations. Participants in the self-help women's movement, ever believers in taking matters into our own hands, not only took up the speculum as an instrument of knowledge and liberation but questioned standard representations of our anatomy. The nub that tended to disappear in standard anatomical texts took on complexity and structure in the hands of these feminists. In the 1984 edition of the Boston Women Health Collective's book, *Our Bodies, Ourselves,* the clitoris expanded in size and configuration to include three structures: the shaft, the glans, and the crura. This new model received its most loving rendition thanks to the leadership of the Federation of Feminist Women's Health Centers and the illustrative hands of Suzann Gage (1981) in *A New View of Woman's Body* (see Illustration 6).

On such accounts, the lower two-thirds of the clitoris is hidden beneath the skin of the vulva. The clitoral glans surmounts the shaft, or body of the clitoris, which is partly visible, and then extends under the muscle tissue of the vulva (see Illustration 7). To this is attached the crura, two stems of tissue, the corpora cavernosa, which arc out toward the thighs and obliquely toward the vagina. The glans of the clitoris, they explain, is a bundle of nerves containing 8,000 nerve fibers, twice the number in the penis, and which, as you know, respond to pressure, temperature, and touch. The "new view" presented to us provides not only far more detail about the clitoral structures, but also depicts the clitoris as large and largely internal. Unlike typical nonfeminist depictions of the clitoris as largely an external genitalia (see Illustration 8), the new view rendered visible the divide between external and internal (see Illustration 9).

Now to be fair, some very recent nonfeminist anatomical texts have included this trinity of shaft, glans, and crura.[8] But none of these texts focus attention on coming to understand the sexual response patterns of these and other bits.[9]

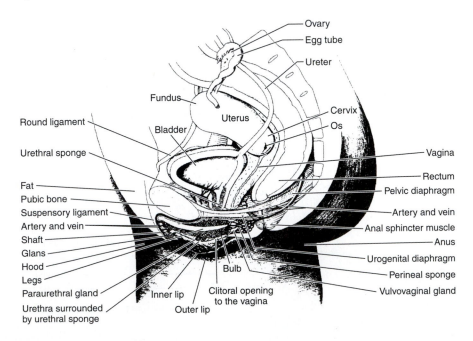

Illustration 6

Figure 3.9, A cross section of the clitoris (Federation of Feminist Women's Health Centers 1981, 41).

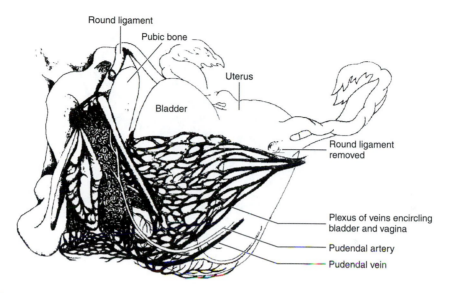

Illustration 7
Figure 3.10, How the clitoris is situated in the pelvis (Federation of Feminist Women's Health Centers 1981, 42).

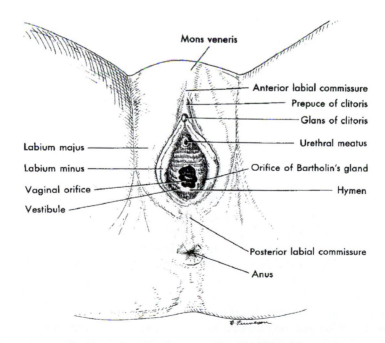

Illustration 8
Figure 24–8, External female genitalia (Kimber, Gray, Stackpole, Leavell, and Miller 1966, 717).

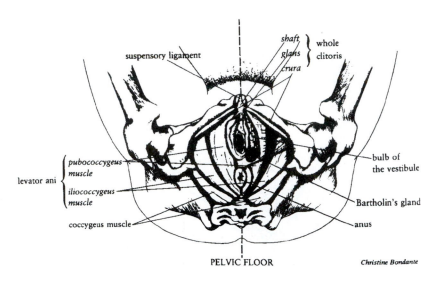

PELVIC FLOOR

Christine Bondante

Illustration 9
Figure of the pelvic floor, clitoris, etc. (Boston Women's Health Book Collective 1984, 206).

Feminist imagery diverges significantly from non-feminist in providing us far more detailed views of the impact of sexual stimulation on the glans and crura of the clitoris, as well as the labia majora and the bulbs of the vestibule, the latter of which possess a very extensive blood vessel system that becomes very engorged during arousal, doubling, even tripling in size, we are told, during sexual arousal (see Illustration 10). The always-found illustrations of male erections (see Illustration 11), are now accompanied by an illustration of female erections (see Illustration 12), something absent in nonfeminist texts. Feminist texts also lovingly detail the other bits that are part of our seat of delight. Reminding us that the clitoris, impressive though it be, is not our only sensitive bit, feminists also provide us with images of the urethral sponge that lies between the front wall of the vagina and the urethra, which expands with blood during sexual arousal (see Illustration 13). It was this structure that was allegedly "discovered" with Columbus-like gusto (Christopher, this time, not Renaldus) by Ernst Grafenburg (1950) and popularized as the "G-spot." Although a few nonfeminist anatomical illustrators, post-Grafenburg, provide us

glimpses of this pleasurable sponge (see Illustration 14), apparently neither they nor Grafenburg have gotten the hang of the feminist speculum, for they continue to overlook feminist presentations of the other sponge, the perineal sponge located between the vagina and the rectum, which also engorges when a woman is sexually aroused (see Illustration 15). Pressure on any of these engorged structures can result in pleasure and orgasm.

We have a classic case of separate and unequal when it comes to contemporary nonfeminist depictions of female and male genitals. All the abovementioned contemporary anatomy textbooks include detailed renditions of the structures of the penis, with the *corpus cavernosum* and the *corpus spongiosum,* important sites of male engorgement, carefully drawn and labeled, while offering only the merest bit of a nub as a sufficient representation of the clitoris.[10]

FINGERING TRUTH

So how do we put our finger on the truth of women's clitoral structures? Whose cartographies do we believe? For those of us who follow

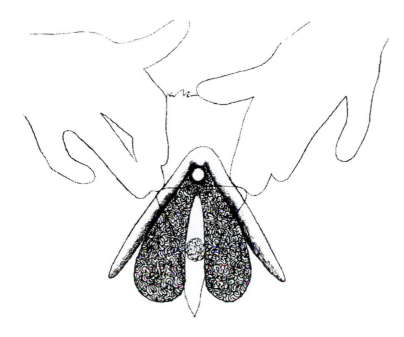

Illustration 10
Figure 3.23, An inner view of the clitoris during the plateau phase (Federation of Feminist Women's Health Centers 1981, 51).

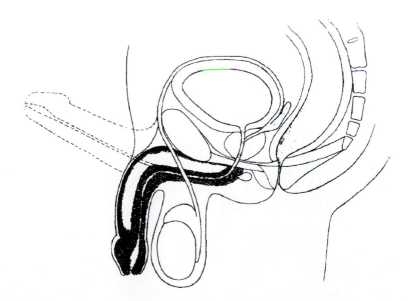

Illustration 11
Figure 3.17, Side view of the penis (Federation of Feminist Women's Health Centers 1981, 49).

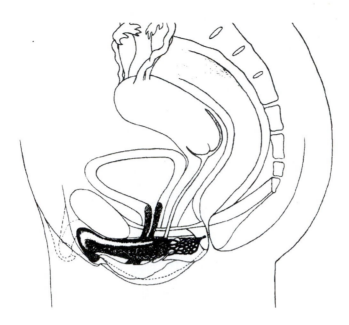

Illustration 12
Figure 3–16, Side view of the clitoris (Federation of Feminist Women's Health Centers 1981, 48).

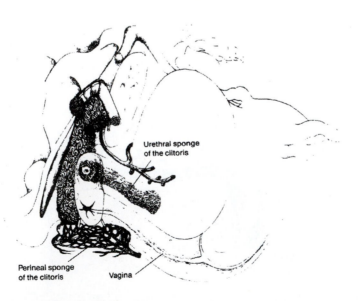

Illustration 13
Figure 3.12, Urethral sponge (Federation of Feminist Women's Health Centers 1981, 43).

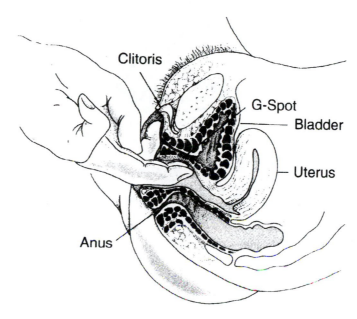

Illustration 14
Figure 5.7, The Grafenberg spot (Rathus, Nevid, and Fichner-Rathus 2002, 167).

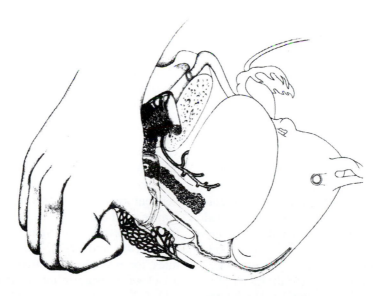

Illustration 15
Figure 3.14, Self-examination of the perineal sponge (Federation of Feminist Women's Health Centers 1981, 45).

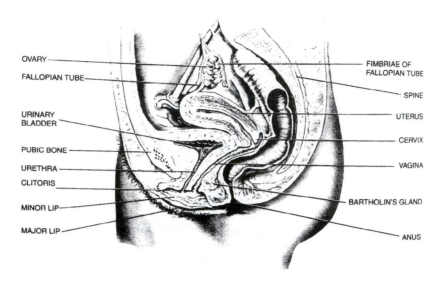

Illustration 16
Figure 2.4, Female sexual and reproductive organs (Kelly 1994, 44).

the speculum, the feminist influenced model of the three-fold clitoral structures have become scripture, with each detail ever more lovingly drawn. But rather than follow desire and insist that the feminist depictions of the clitoris are the truth, let me rather trace the ebbs and flows of this knowledge/ignorance.

Despite fifteen years of clear illustrations of this new view of clitoral structures, our impact has been surprisingly minimal, at least so far. A review of anatomical illustrations in standard college human sexuality textbooks reveals a surprising lack of attention to the functions and structures of the clitoris (see Illustration 16).[11] No surprise, then, that my students have, at best, a passing knowledge of the depths and complexity of its structures. These are the very same students, I remind you, who have relatively detailed knowledge of the structures of female reproductive organs and of the structures of male genitalia, though the terminology they use to label those parts often turns to street talk rather than the high Latin of medical textbooks. The human sexuality textbook writers have clearly bought the line that "size doesn't matter," and continue to depict the clitoris as a modest, undifferentiated nub of flesh.

A politics of ignorance is at work here, one linked to the politics of sex and reproduction. Whether female and male genitalia are seen as homologous or analogous (or somewhere in between), centuries of scientific theories and lay beliefs have treated their pleasures differently. The importance of male pleasure and ejaculation for conception has been little disputed from the Greeks to the present. In contrast, the question of female seed and the link between it and female pleasure was always a point of controversy. Many scientists from the Greeks and well into the sixteenth century disputed the very existence of female seed or semen, though those in the earlier centuries who did ascribe to the existence of female seed often argued for the importance of female pleasure as the vehicle for its release (see Tuana 1988 and 1993). The infertility of prostitutes, for example, was often explained as due to a lack of pleasure in intercourse (Cadden 1993, 142–43). But by the thirteenth century and onward, the link between conception and female pleasure in sex was typically denied even by those who allowed for the existence of female seed. Women's sexual pleasure came to be seen as inessential to reproduction, although many scholars admitted that it might be useful in promoting the desire for intercourse.

Now to this view of the function (or lack thereof) of female erotic pleasure add the politics of sex, namely the view that the only or at least the main function of sex is reproduction. To this add the politics of female sexuality, namely the tenet common in scientific and popular accounts well into the nineteenth century that women were more lustful than men and that their sexuality was a danger to men,[12] and a path is cleared to an understanding of why clitoral structures get lost in the process. The logic becomes quite clear: A) There is no good reason to pay attention to the clitoris, given that it allegedly plays no role in reproduction and that sex is to be studied (only) in order to understand reproduction. B) Worse, there is good reason to not pay attention to the clitoris lest we stir up a hornet's nest of stinging desire.[13] From Pandora on, and well into the nineteenth century, women's stinging desire and limb-gnawing passion had been branded the cause of the fall of mankind. What better reason to construct and maintain an epistemology of ignorance? What better way to disqualify and perhaps even control women's sexual satisfaction.[14]

But I simplify here to make my point. It is not true that history records no moments in the contemporary period when scientists focused their speculums on clitoral structures. Leaving Sigmund Freud aside for the moment, genitals came under scrutiny during the end of the nineteenth century as science constructed the category of the "invert," namely, those who mixed with members of their own sex. Evolutionary theory linked the newly "uncovered" sexual identity of the homosexual to degeneracy, and widespread societal fears of the degeneration of the race (that is, the white race), led to broadened support for eugenics movements. Scientists, now more intent than ever before on social control, began to examine bodies for signs of degeneration to provide

support for proper "matings" and to discourage the dangerous mixing of people across racial or sexual boundaries. Belief in the degeneration of the race led many to believe that so-called "inverts" were proliferating. Anxiety led to a desire to be able to track such undesirables and an equally strong desire to believe that their perversity and devolution would be clearly marked on their bodies. Given the desire for such knowledge, it did not take long before genitals, or at least deviant genitals, would become a focus of the scientific gaze, hornet's nest or not. Although through images to be kept only for the eyes of professionals, whose objectivity and dispassionate nature would protect them from corruption, science began to turn its gaze on the structures of the clitoris to seek out and control deviancy.

The Sex Variant study, conducted in New York City from 1935–1941, was one example of scientific investigations launched to interrogate the marks of deviance that had been imprinted onto the structures of the body. The professed goal of the study was to identify inverts so that physicians could then try to stop them from reproducing and further contaminating the race. Gynecologist Robert Latou Dickinson, the principle investigator of the Sex Variant study, believed that deviance and degeneration would be mapped on women's genitals. Clitorises were examined, measured, and sketched, along with the various contours of vulva, breast, and nipple sizes. Dickinson concluded that, indeed, the genitals of inverts were a symbol of their deviance, arguing that their genitals were different from those of "normal" women—their vulvae, larger; their clitorises, notably erectile; their labium, longer and more protruding; their vaginas, distensible; their hymens, insensitive; and their uteruses, smaller (see Illustration 17). As an aside, it should be noted here that Dickinson's gynecological studies included *only* so-called inverts (the "normal" vulva, he apparently drew from memory.) This was also a period when the genitals of "inferior" races, particularly those of African descent, were examined and measured,

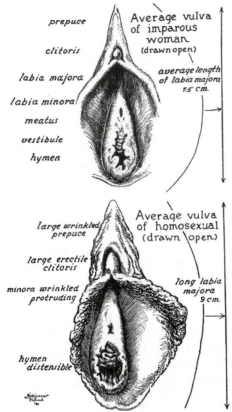

Typical sex variant vulva and average

Illustration 17
Figure 3, Typical sex variant vulva and average (Dickinson 1941, 1102).

with investigators once again believing that proof of inferiority would be marked on their genitals.[15]

The point here is that this epistemology is not about truth. I am not arguing that the feminist model of the three-fold structures of the clitoris finally uncovered the long submerged truth of the clitoris. Nor am I arguing that feminists were, finally, practicing good science and being objective. These cartographies were and are fueled by our desire to transform normative heterosexuality's vagina-only attention to pleasure. Nor am I claiming that there were no discourses on the clitoris as a source

of sexual pleasure in medical and popular literature until feminists and their speculums entered the scene. Indeed, one can find dozens, if not hundreds, of accounts of female orgasm resulting from this feminine seat of pleasure in texts as disparate as those written by midwives and penned by pornographers. Nor am I arguing that the speculum was never focused on the female vulva. However, a complex absence exists, a gap that I find important, one often repeated today. What is missing or only sketchily attended to in nonfeminist anatomies, at least when the focus is on the "normal" rather than the "deviant," is the desire to map the geographies and functions of the clitoris and our other pleasurable bits. What nonfeminist anatomists sketch seldom goes beyond the identification of this pleasurable (or dangerous) lump of flesh. What I am arguing is that the history of our knowledges-ignorances of the clitoris—indeed, our lived experiences of its beginnings and ends—is part of an embodied discourse and history of bodies and pleasures. It is a chapter in the tale of power/knowledge-ignorance.

THE ISSUE OF PLEASURE

Who would want a shotgun when you can have a semiautomatic?
—NATALIE ANGIER
WOMAN: AN INTIMATE GEOGRAPHY

Let me remain a moment at this site of pleasure. Remember with me that until the nineteenth century not only women's desire for sex but the very pleasures they received from it were seen as far greater than those of men. In the words of Tiresias, he who had lived both as a woman and as a man, when it comes to the issue of pleasure:

If the parts of love's pleasures be divided by ten, Thrice three go to women, one only to men. (Apollodorus 3.6.7)

This image of women's sexuality shifts, at least for certain women, as we move into the nineteenth century, and with this move, we can locate a shift of knowledge-ignorance.

> *My lord Dumuzi is ready for the holy loins.*
> *The plants and herbs in his field are ripe.*
> *"O Dumuzi! Your fullness is my delight."*

> *. . . . He shaped my loins with his fair hands,*
> *The shepherd Dumuzi filled my lap with cream*
>   *and milk,*
> *He stroked my pubic hair,*
> *He watered my womb.*
> *He laid his hands on my holy vulva,*
> *He smoothed my black boat with cream,*
> *He quickened my narrow boat with milk.*
>   *(Inanna 1983, 41, 43)*

Many of our sociological surveys of sexuality, though not all, figure sex as it is figured in the story of Inanna, between a woman and a man. Although this is far too narrow a story to tell if what we want is an account of bodies and pleasures, let me focus on the differences between this ancient account and contemporary embodiments of heterosexual female sexuality.

A 1994 survey of heterosexual women and men in the United States between the ages of 18 and 59 reveals that one out of every three women surveyed reported that they were uninterested in sex and one out of every five women reported that sex provided little pleasure, in both cases double the number of men reporting a lack of interest or pleasure in sex (Laumann, Gagnon, Michael, and Michaels 1994). Add to this the fact that almost 25 percent of the women surveyed reported being unable to reach orgasm, in comparison with 8 percent of men, and we begin to see an impact of knowledge-ignorance on bodies and pleasures. The pleasure gap surrounding heterosexual women's and men's first coital experiences is even more startling: 79 percent of men reported that they were certain they had an orgasm during their first sexual experience, while only 7 percent

of the women could so report (Sprecher, Barbee, and Schwartz 2001).

These are astonishing figures in themselves, but they become all the more startling when set alongside of women's multi-orgasmic capacities. Women's capacity for multiple orgasm, though taken to be a revelation by contemporary scientists, was a commonplace in many scientific and popular circles in the past.

> *He caressed me on the . . . fragrant honey-bed.*
> *My sweet love, lying by my heart,*
> *Tongue-playing, one by one,*
> *My fair Dumuzi did so fifty times.*

> *Now my sweet love is sated. (Inanna 1983, 48)*

What was once taken to be ordinary knowledge of women's more robust sexuality and her greater orgasmic capacity submerged into the mire of ignorance sometime during the turn of the last century, where it went dormant (or perhaps just pornographic) for about fifty years and then resurfaced in the new science of sexuality.

Woman's multi-orgasmic capacity became a subject for contemporary scientific study when Kinsey's 1953 study, *Sexual Behavior in the Human Female,* revealed that almost half of the women studied reported the ability to experience multiple orgasms. Shere Hite's 1976 report on female sexuality confirmed Kinsey's results. 48 percent of the women in Hite's survey reported that they often required more than one orgasm to be sexually satisfied (1976, 602–603). William H. Masters and Virginia G. Johnson (1966) similarly documented women's ability to have more than one orgasm without a significant break. They noted that if proper stimulation continues after a woman's first climax, she will in most cases be capable of having additional orgasms—they report between five and six—within a matter of minutes. Masters and Johnson also report that with direct clitoral stimulation, such as an electric vibrator, many women have from twenty to fifty orgasms.

Despite having science and all those measuring tools on our side, efforts continue to suppress this bit of knowledge. As just one example, Donald Symons in *The Evolution of Human Sexuality* (1979), strikes a typical pose when he assures his readers that the multiply orgasmic woman "… is to be found primarily, if not exclusively, in the ideology of feminism, the hopes of boys, and the fears of men" (1979, 92).

Foucault warned us away from desire as a category implicated in the construction of human identities and cultures, but urged a greater attention to pleasure. His *History of Sexuality* (1990) documents the uses of pleasure in the practices of normalizing power and includes pleasure, not just desire, as fundamental to understanding the genealogy of sexuality. But Foucault's account also includes a creative, indeed resistant, aspect of pleasure, in which pleasure could be a site for resisting sexual normalization and a wellspring for enriching the art of living.[16]

At a time when popular culture and science alike are convinced of men's greater sexual drives, when a long entrenched fear of the power of women's sexuality is still in the background, when a clear double standard of sexuality disciplines women and men alike, and when heterosexuality remains the normalized sexuality, it is perhaps no surprise that far more women than men are dissatisfied when it comes to the issue of pleasure. But I desire to flesh out pleasure in ways that have the potential to resist this type of normalization. As a first step, I stand Inanna and Tiresias alongside the nineteenth century's passionless woman and the twentieth century's preorgasmic but sexually active woman, and by coming to understand the politics of knowledge-ignorance behind their presence, invoke the female orgasm.

THE EITHER/OR OF WOMEN'S ORGASMS

Let me return to my history of the clitoris. In this section I will complicate this study of the epistemology of ignorance-knowledge regarding female sexuality by bringing function to form, turning my attention to accounts of the role of the clitoris in female orgasm. To understand the almost complete circumcision of female orgasmic potentiality affected by labeling practically any clitoral "excitability" deviant during the first half of the twentieth century, we must turn to Freud. The longest playing of the orgasm debates in the twentieth century began with Freud's declaration of not one but two types of orgasm: the vaginally adult kind and her immature kid sister, the clitoral orgasm (1962, 124). From this one little act of counting to two erupted a huge, now almost centuries-long debate.

Let me begin my account by returning to Columbus. While Columbus's clitoris and mine are not located in the same place, the link he makes between it and sexual pleasure marks a movement I would like us to remember. His account bears repeating. He tells us that he discovered "protuberances, emerging from the uterus near that opening which is called the mouth of the womb" that were, in his words, "the seat of women's delight," which when rubbed or touched "semen swifter than air flows this way and that on account of the pleasure even with them unwilling" (1559, 11.16.447–48; Laqueur 1989, 103). Columbus functions according to an older economy in which women's pleasure in sex mattered because it was needed for conception.

While still marked by a male economy—both in representation ("it shows itself a sort of male member") and in function ("even with them unwilling")—Columbus's depiction of the clitoris evinces another economy that dissolves the boundary between inside and out, between the so-called "external" and the "internal" genitalia. It also provides an interesting example of how knowledge once found can be lost. Columbus, a man of his time, viewed female genitalia as homologous to male genitalia but marked by a lack of heat that resulted in them remaining, for the most part, inside the body. In identifying a "protuberance" that emerges from the uterus, Columbus acknowledged that it, like the penis, grew in size when aroused, but he did not limit female pleasure to it. He acknowledged other sites of pleasure, such as the circular folds of the cervix that cause a friction from which lovers experience wonderful pleasure and the various bits of flesh closer to the vulva by which "pleasure or delight in intercourse is not a little increased" (1559, 11.16.445; Laqueur 1989, 105). Columbus's geography described various linked structures as contributing to woman's pleasure, but he had no desire to determine where one part or orgasm stops and another begins. Nor was there a desire to locate pleasure in a clearly defined site. Protuberances, folds, and bits of flesh alike are, for Columbus, that from which pleasure flows.

What Columbus had put together, Freud would cast asunder. While Freud retained a remnant of the one-sex model, arguing that "portions of the male sexual apparatus also appear in women's bodies, though in an atrophied state" (1964, 114), he argues for an important psychical difference between the pleasures of men and those of women. In boys there is a relatively unproblematic "accession of libido" during puberty. In girls, however, he tells us that there is "a fresh wave of repression in which it is precisely clitoroidal sexuality that is effected" (1962, 123). That is, to become a woman the girl must abandon the pleasures of the clitoris and discover those of the vagina. "When erotogenic susceptibility to stimulation has been successfully transferred by a woman from the clitoris to the vaginal orifice, it implies that she has adopted a new leading zone for the purposes of her later sexual activity" (1962, 124). This is an economy that requires a level of differentiation not found in Columbus. Freud's is a map of the female genitals that requires that we can, and do, distinguish between the clitoris and all its bits, on the one hand, and the vagina and its bits of flesh on the other. And it is here, despite the trace of the one-sex model, that Freud imposes a two-sex economy that divides the clitoris from the other bits. But he does so to perpetuate an even older economy that perceives the purpose of female

pleasure, when properly channeled, to be heterosexual reproduction. Indeed, "the intensification of the brake upon sexuality brought about by pubertal repression in women serves as a stimulus to the libido of men and causes an increase in its activity" (1962, 123). In other words, repressed female sexuality increases male desire—quite a modern trope.

The story, of course, shifts in the 1960s with the tools of Masters and Johnson and the politics of feminism. Masters and Johnson (1966) rejected the purported distinction between clitoral and vaginal orgasm, arguing physiologically speaking for only one kind of orgasm. Peering through their speculums, they concluded that allegedly vaginal orgasms, which they revealingly identified as those experienced during intercourse (notice the functionality of the definition), were no different than allegedly clitoral orgasms, for both resulted from the same phenomena, namely clitoral stimulation. We are told that penile coital thrusting draws the clitoral hood back and forth against the clitoris and vaginal pressure heightens blood flow in the clitoris, further setting the stage for orgasm.

These findings were, and still are, met with skepticism in the scientific community, but not in the feminist community. Following closely on the heels of Masters and Johnson's pronouncements and the second wave of feminism that hit in the late 1960s, feminist theorists such as Ann Koedt (1970) and Alix Shulman (1971) insisted that we women should all "think clitoris" and reject the myth of the vaginal orgasm. Their concern was to discredit the vaginal orgasm and the years of pressure placed on women who did not have the "right kind." But to make the case, a frustrating reversal occurred where *only* the clitoris was *the* source of sensation—and remember we do not yet have the enlarged *Our Bodies, Ourselves* (1984) conception of the clitoris to turn to. Shulman tells us that the vagina has so little sensation that "women commonly wear a diaphragm or tampon in it, and even undergo surgery on it, without feeling any sensation at all" (1971, 294).

And although Shulman does not deny that some women might sometimes experience orgasm through intercourse, for after all some women, she tells us, sometimes experience orgasm through breast stimulation or mental stimulation or even through dreams, she does disparage the level of pleasure intercourse can provide: "Masters and Johnson observe that the clitoris is automatically 'stimulated' in intercourse since the hood covering the clitoris is pulled over the clitoris with each thrust of the penis in the vagina—much, I suppose, as a penis is automatically 'stimulated' by a man's underwear whenever he takes a step. I wonder, however, if either is erotically stimulating by itself" (1971, 296).

Despite Masters and Johnson and feminist slogans, the days of vaginal orgasm are not (yet) numbered. Josephine Singer and Irving Singer (1972), for example, argue still for two types of orgasms, the vulval and the uterine. They contend that what Masters and Johnson observed were vulval orgasms, which remain the same despite the source of stimulation, clitoral or vaginal. But they argue that the uterine orgasm occurs only in response to deep thrusting against the cervix that slightly displaces the uterus and stimulates the tissues that cover the abdominal organs. This view of two types of orgasm has received additional support from scientists who argue that orgasms that result from deep cervical or uterine stimulation are controlled by a different neural pathway and produce different subjective experiences than do those generated through clitoral stimulation (for example, see Alzate 1985; Perry and Whipple 1981; and Whipple 1995).

One response to the orgasm debates is to ask what keeps them so entrenched? As breasts and other non-genital bits attest to, the origins of orgasms are a complex matter. Why the persistence in counting even when we are reassured (repeatedly) that they are all equally "good" (see McAnulty and Burnette 2001, 119)? Though I have no doubt that the answer to this question is complex, let me explore two of its components: the geography of the genitals, and the persistence of the belief that the function of sex is reproduction.

Those who sketch anatomical renditions of male and female genitals insist on making a distinction between internal and external genitalia. A factor of arbitrariness is clearly marked on this distinction. For males the penis is wholly an external genital, but testicles get divided in two, with the scrotum being listed as an external sex organ and the testes as internal. Since lots of bits of the penis are internal, one wonders why we even bother to make this distinction. But when it comes to the analogous division of female genitals, more than arbitrariness is at play. The politics of reproduction gets written explicitly into this division, for in the female another descriptive phrase for the internal female sex organs is "the female reproductive system" (Rathus 2002, 106). This division reinforces the orgasm debates and provides a way to "make sense" of the claim for different kinds of orgasms, those that originate from outside and those from inside.

What we have here is an instance of the politics of knowledge-ignorance. This division of female genitals evinces the persistence of a politics of viewing reproduction as central to sexuality, so that it becomes a defining element in the demarcation of female genitalia. If you set sail by Columbus's map, you would not arrive at the planned destination. Still, like his earlier navigator namesake, where you do arrive is interesting too. Seeing orgasm and reproduction as a piece of a whole cloth, Columbus had no desire to demarcate the clitoris as "external" and hence not part of the female reproductive system. But once the clitoris and its orgasmic pleasures were seen as inessential to reproduction, few anatomists saw any value in charting its contours and it was relegated into that little undifferentiated nub that could easily be deemed "external" and "nonreproductive," with the "true" genitals, those that matter, being the internal genitalia.[17]

This politics of knowledge-ignorance is in turn marked by a persistent refusal to admit that the new feminist-inspired view of female genitals dissolves the basis for the internal/external divide, for, on its view, the clitoris is always already both. And once one has this richer understanding of all the bits involved in female orgasm, and little political commitment to retaining a teleology of reproduction in accounts of pleasure, then nothing turns on demarcating types of orgasm based on physiological location. In *Women's Experience of Sex,* Sheila Kitzinger sums up this view thusly: "Asking whether orgasm is in the clitoris or in the vagina is really the wrong question" (1985, 76). But here, despite feminist insistence that their accounts were about truth—"I think that we were revealing the truth. And how can you argue with anatomy?"[18]— we find ourselves in that complex intersection between knowledge-ignorance and power-politics. The desire to "cut nature at its joints" often requires value-laden, strategic decisions. Feminists cut nature at different joints than do others who represent the clitoris because their values concerning the politics of sex differ from the values of non-feminist anatomists. Perhaps the body speaks, but understanding what it says requires interpretation.

What we learn from feminist explorations of our genital geography is twofold. First, if you view the clitoris as an important knowledge project, whether because you are convinced that orgasm is primarily clitoral and your geographies aim to understand pleasure or because, like Columbus, you think orgasm is central to reproduction and you aim to understand reproduction, then you will focus far more attention on the structures of the clitoris than if you see it as an uninteresting though pleasant nub. What we attend to and what we ignore are often complexly interwoven with values and politics. Second, if you discover new knowledge about something others do not take seriously, do not expect your knowledge projects to have much effect. The veil of ignorance is not so easily lifted.

BODIES AND PLEASURES

I return to my tropes, Inanna and Tiresias, and add a third to this gathering, Annie Sprinkle, porn-star-turned-performance-artist/sex educator.

If bodies and pleasures are to be seen as a resource, it is important not to think that our goal is to find those pleasures free from sexual normalization, free from disciplinary practices. Here I follow LaDelle McWhorter, who claims that "instead of refusing normalization outright, we need to learn ways to use the power of its disciplines to propel us in new directions" (1999, 181). Though we cannot simply remove ourselves from disciplinary practices, she argues that it is possible to affirm "development without affirming docility, [through] affirming the free, open playfulness of human possibility within regimes of sexuality without getting stuck in or succumbing to any one sexual discourse or formation" (1999, 181). McWhorter, following Foucault, suggests that one path to this playfulness is to deliberately separate practice from goal and simply engage in disciplinary practices for their own sake, for the pleasures they bring, rather than for some purpose beyond them. "What if we used our capacities for temporal development not for preparation for some task beyond that development but for the purpose of development itself, including the development of our capacities for pleasure? What if we used pleasure rather than pain as our primary disciplinary tool?" (1999, 182). Following Foucault, what we must work on ". . . is not so much to liberate our desires but to make ourselves infinitely more susceptible to pleasure" (Foucault 1989, 310).

Annie Sprinkle, in her one-woman show, "Herstory of Porn: Reel to Real," describes the new direction her work took in the mid-1980s when she devoted her talents to displaying the beauty of sex and the undiscovered power of orgasms. "Some people discover Jesus and want to spread the word. I discovered orgasms and want to spread the word" (Sprinkle 1999). Sprinkle's new productions attempt to refocus attention from power to pleasure. "There's a lot of people who talk about violence, rape, and abuse. But, there's not a lot of people that talk about pleasure, bliss, orgasm, and ecstasy" (Sprinkle 1999). Sprinkle's work has transformed over time. At one point her performances focused attention on female orgasmic ejaculations, providing audiences with sights seldom before seen on stage and ones that were, as the title of her performance explains, real, not reel. She has also advocated and really performed the nongenital breath or energy orgasm in which one "can simply lie down, take a few breaths, and go into an orgasmic state."

Sprinkle is not advocating a new homologous model of female orgasm—women ejaculate too—or an ultimate radical feminist rejection of penetrative sex. Rather than setting up new disciplinary practices with clearly defined markers between "good" feminist sex and "bad" nonfeminist sex, Sprinkle explores pleasure and refers to herself as a "metamorphosexual." I am not here claiming that Sprinkle's pleasures are outside sexual normalization, but I do think she stands before us as one who explores pleasure for its own sake. I offer her pleasures as an example of how we might, in McWhorter's words, "live our bodies as who we are, to intensify our experiences of bodiliness and to think from our bodies, if we are going to push back against the narrow confines of the normalizing powers that constrict our freedom" (1999, 185).

Sprinkle's pleasures are themselves part of disciplinary practices. It is important if we go the way of pleasure that we not desire pleasures that escape power. For Sprinkle's body and pleasures are situated in economies partially shaped by the feminist speculum. A more complete story would situate Sprinkle in the decades of practices of the feminist health movement and feminist efforts to take back our bodies and our sexualities. This pleasurable account I must leave for another time. Here I will simply tantalize by repeating Sprinkle's gospel that we return to our bodies and to our orgasms, and spread the word.

CONCLUSION

It comes as no surprise that a correlation often exists between ignorance and pleasure. The feminist quest to enhance knowledge about women's bodies and their sexual experiences had as its goal the enhancement of women's pleasures. As should now be clear, knowledge and pleasures are complexly interrelated. Indeed the old adage that "ignorance is bliss" takes on new meanings when read through the lens of an epistemology attentive to both knowledge and ignorance. Whose pleasures were enhanced by ignorance and whose were suppressed by knowledge are complex questions that must be asked repeatedly in any study of the science of sexuality.

My goal in this essay was twofold. First, I wanted to share a genuine fascination with the study of the science of sexuality, particularly in relation to female sexuality. While much effort has gone into studying the formation of sexual *identities,* far less has been devoted to the science of sexuality. While I do not want to suggest that this aspect of sexual science or our sexual experiences are divorced from the constructions of sexual identities, I do believe that a fascination with the latter has deferred full attention from the former. While sexual identity issues will always be an aspect of any study of the science of sexuality, it is my conviction that an inclusion of sexuality will highlight other axes of power.

My second goal in writing this essay was to begin to outline the importance and power of attending to what we do not know and the power/politics of such ignorances. Although my account is preliminary and suggestive, I have presented the following claims:

- Any complete epistemology must include a study of ignorance, not just knowledge.
- Ignorance—far from being a simple, innocent lack of knowledge—is a complex phenomenon that like knowledge, is interrelated with power; for example, ignorance is frequently constructed, and it is linked to issues of cognitive authority, trust, doubt, silencing, etc.
- While many feminist science studies theorists have embraced the interrelationship of knowledge and values, we must also see the ways in which ignorance, too, is so interrelated.

- The study of ignorance can provide a lens for the values at work in our knowledge practices.
- We should not assume that the epistemic tools we have developed for the study of knowledge or the theories we have developed concerning knowledge practices will transfer to the study of ignorance.

"IN CONCLUSION"

Inanna went to visit Enki, the god of wisdom, who possessed the holy laws of heaven and earth. She drank beer with him. They drank beer together. They drank more and more beer together, until Enki, god of wisdom, agreed to give Inanna all the holy laws. She accepted the holy laws, gathered them together, placed them in the Boat of Heaven, and sailed back across the water. [My vulva, the horn, the Boat of Heaven, is full of eagerness like the young moon.] Upon reaching land and unloading the holy laws, Inanna discovered that she returned with more holy laws than had been given her by Enki.
—Inanna: Queen of Heaven and Earth:
Her Stories and Hymms from Sumer

I hope by now you are laughing softly with me. Lean back against the apple tree. Feel the delicate fire running under your skin. Our vulvae are wondrous to behold. Rejoice at your wondrous vulva and applaud yourself.

NOTES

My thanks to Lynn Hankinson Nelson, Alison Wylie, and the anonymous reviewers for their very helpful editorial suggestions.

1. I choose to employ the phrase "epistemologies of ignorance" despite its potential awkwardness (theories of knowledge of ignorance) for a number of reasons. The alternative term, agnoiology, has histories I have no desire to invoke. First employed by James Frederick Ferrier (1854) to refute William Hamilton's (1858–60) thesis of the unknowableness of the Absolute Reality, Ferrier posits ignorance as properly attributable only to an *absence or lack* of knowledge of that which it is possible for us to know and precludes the term "ignorance" from being applied to anything that is unintelligible or self-contradictory. Ferrier used the term agnoiology to distinguish what was truly knowable—and thus the proper subject matter of epistemology—from that which was unknowable (1854, 536). The term agnoiology has been resuscitated by Keith Lehrer (1990) as part of an argument demonstrating that skepticism has not been philosophically refuted; he argues that the possible truth of the skeptical hypothesis entails that we can never achieve completely justified true belief. Hence, Lehrer concludes that we do not know anything, even that we do not know anything. His point is that rational belief and action do not require refuting the skeptical hypothesis, nor do they need the validating stamp of "knowledge."

2. Perhaps more important, I wish to retain the rhetorical strength of "epistemology" when investigating ignorance. Too often, as evidenced by both Ferrier and Lehrer, ignorance is only a vehicle to reveal the proper workings of knowledge or, in the case of Lehrer, rational belief and action. Ignorance itself is not interrogated but is set up as the background against which one unfurls enriched knowledge. It is my desire to retain a focus on ignorance, to foreground ignorance as a location for understanding the workings of power. Just as we have epistemology/ies of science, of religion, and so on, I wish to argue for an epistemology of the complex phenomenon of ignorance as well as to suggest that no theory of knowledge is complete that ignores ignorance.

3. I will use this particular rhetorical form to both visually remind readers of Foucault's notion of power/knowledge (1980) and to add to it my emphasis on ignorance. I am not here claiming that Foucault did not understand how the workings of power/knowledge served to suppress knowledge practices, but with our contemporary philosophical emphasis on what we do know, I think the constant reminder to attend to what we do not know is crucial. Without the reminder, the politics of ignorance are too often erased.

4. The story of Inanna and the translations that I quote are part of a large body of Sumerian tales, legends, and poems about the Queen of Heaven and Earth inscribed on various clay tablets dating back to 2000 B.C.E.

5. For an interesting discussion of Haraway's use of such rhetorical signs, see her *How Like a Leaf* (2000).

6. This conception of bodily being is developed extensively in Tuana 1996a and 2001.

7. McWhorter, in her recent *Bodies & Pleasures* (1999), convincingly (and pleasurably) argues that a neglected aspect of Foucault's philosophy is his account of pleasure as creative and as a resource for political resistance. My use of Foucault in this essay owes much to her reading.

8. It is important to emphasize that what we do and do not know is often "local" to a particular group or a particular culture. I locate my "we" in this section as the common knowledge of laypeople in the United States both because the studies and surveys that I will employ were limited to this group and in recognition of the fact that knowledge-ignorance about women's sexuality varies tremendously from one culture/country to another.

9. Richard D. McAnulty and M. Michele Burnette (2001, 67) describe the clitoris as composed of shaft and glans, but make no effort to provide an illustration. Spencer A. Rathus, Nevid, and Fichner-Rathus (2002) is the first textbook designed for college human sexuality classrooms that includes an illustration of what they label the "whole clitoris," namely, the shaft, glans, and crura.

10. McAnulty and Burnette, for example, while admitting a more complex structure for the clitoris, simply indicate that "the glans of the clitoris has a high concentration of touch and temperature receptors and should be the primary center of sexual stimulation and sensation in the female" (2001, 67). Later, when discussing the female sexual response cycle, they simply note that the diameter of the clitoral shaft increases (2001, 114).

11. For an interesting discussion of anatomical conventions in depicting female genitalia see Moore and Clarke 1995.

12. I've examined the various editions of Albert Richard Allgeier and Elizabeth Rice Allgeier (1984,

1988, 1998), Curtis O. Byer and Louis W. Shainberg (1985, 1988, 1991, 1998, 2001), Gary Kelly (1988, 1994, 1998, 2001), McAnulty and Burnette (2001), and Rathus, Nevin, and Fichner-Rathus (1993, 2000, 2002). Only Rathus, Nevin, and Fichner-Rathus include this expanded model of the clitoris. But while they provide the most detailed discussion of women's multi-orgasmic capacity, their images and discussion of the female response phases are surprisingly traditional, with the clitoris once again relegated to a mere nub.

13. I support these claims in my book, *The Less Noble Sex* (1993).

14. The reference here is to Hesiod's depiction of the creation of the first woman, Pandora. After she was molded in the shape of a goddess by Hephaistos, Zeus ordered Aphrodite to bequeath to her "stinging desire and limb-gnawing passion" (Hesiod 1983, line 66–67).

15. As just one of literally thousands of examples of the view that women's greater susceptibility to sexual temptation required control, I refer the reader to David Hume's (1978) discussion of chastity and modesty. Hume argues that women have such a strong temptation to infidelity that the only way to reassure men that the children their wives bear are their own biological offspring is for society to "attach a peculiar degree of shame to their infidelity, above what arises merely from its injustice"; also, because women are particularly apt to overlook remote motives in favor of present temptations, he argues "'tis necessary, therefore, that, beside the infamy attending such licenses, there should be some preceding backwardness or dread, which may prevent their first approaches, and may give the female sex a repugnance to all expressions, and postures, and liberties, that have an immediate relation to that enjoyment" (1978, Bk. 3, Pt. 2, Sec. 12, Para. 6/9, 571–72).

16. Scientists believed that enlarged clitorises were both a result of and a reason for hypersexuality, and both sex deviants and racially "inferior" women were viewed as sexually deviant because of heightened sexual "excitability." For further discussion of these themes see Fausto-Sterling 1995 and Terry 1995 and 1999.

17. See McWhorter 1999 for an insightful analysis of the difference between desire and pleasure.

"The art of living" is, of course, Beauvoir's phrase.

18. This view of female genitals is surprisingly resilient. A recent story in my local State College, Pennsylvania newspaper, *The Center Daily Times,* reported that two women who were running nude were acquitted of charges of streaking. The story explains that the streaking law requires that the genitalia be exposed, something that the judge in this case decided is nearly impossible for women, since, in the judge's view, female genitalia are all internal! My thanks to David O'Hara for calling this story to my attention.

REFERENCES

Allgeier, Albert Richard, and Elizabeth Rice Allgeier. 1984, 1988, 1998. *Sexual Interactions.* Lexington, Mass.: D. C. Heath and Co.

Alzate, Heli. 1985. "Vaginal Eroticism: A Replication study." *Archives of Sexual Behavior* 14 (6): 529–37.

Annie Sprinkle's Herstory of Porn. 1999. Produced and directed by Annie Sprinkle and Carol Leigh (Scarlot Harlot). 69 min. Hardcore Documentary. Videocassette.

Apollodorus. 1976. *The Gods and Heroes of the Greeks: The Library of Apollodorus.* Trans. Michael Simpson. Amherst: University of Massachusetts Press.

Baker, R. Robin, and Mark A. Bellis. 1995. *Human Sperm Competition: Copulation, Masturbation, and Infidelity.* London: Chapman and Hall.

Barash, David. 1977. *Sociobiology and Behavior.* New York: Elsevier North-Holland.

Bloor, David. 1976. *Knowledge and Social Imagery.* London: Routledge and Kegan Paul.

Boston Woman's Health Book Collective. 1984. *The New Our Bodies, Ourselves: A Book by and for Women.* New York: Simon and Schuster.

Byer, Curtis O., and Louis W. Shainberg. 1985, 1988, 1991, 1998, 2001. *Dimensions of Human Sexuality.* Boston: McGraw Hill.

Cadden, Joan. 1993. *Meanings of Sex Difference in the Middle Ages: Medicine, Science and Culture.* Cambridge: Cambridge University Press.

Christensen, John B., and Ira Telford. 1978. *Synopsis of Gross Anatomy 3rd ed.* New York: Harper and Row.

Columbus, Renaldus. 1559. *De re anatomica.* Venice.

Daly, Mary. 1978. *Gyn/ecology: The Metaethics of Radical Feminism.* Boston: Beacon Press.

Dickinson, Robert Latou. 1941. The Gynecology of Homosexuality, Appendix VI. In *Sex Variants: A Study of Homosexual Patterns,* ed. George W. Henry. New York, London: Paul B. Hoeber.

Dixson, Alan. 1998. *Primate Sexuality: Comparative Studies of the Prosimians, Monkeys, Apes, and Human Beings.* Oxford: Oxford University Press.

Fausto-Sterling, Anne. 1995. Gender, race, and nation: The comparative anatomy of "Hottentot" women in Europe, 1815–1817. In *Deviant Bodies: Critical Perspectives on Difference in Science and Popular Culture,* ed. Jennifer Terry and Jacqueline Urla. Bloomington: Indiana University Press.

Federation of Feminist Women's Health Centers. 1981. *A New View of a Woman's Body: A Fully Illustrated guide; illustrations by Suzann Gage; photographs by Sylvia Morales.* New York: Simon and Schuster.

Ferrier, James F. 1854. *Institutes of Metaphysic.* Edinburgh: Blackwood.

Foucault, Michel. 1980. *Power/knowledge: Selected Interviews and other Writings. 1972–1977.* Ed. and trans. Colin Gordon. New York: Pantheon Books.

———. 1989. Friendship as a way of life. In *Foucault Live.* Trans. John Johnston. Ed. Sylvere Lotringer. New York: Semiotext(e).

———. 1990. *The History of Sexuality, Volume I: An Introduction.* Trans. Robert Hurley. New York: Random House.

Freud, Sigmund. 1962. *Three Essays on the Theory of Sexuality.* Trans. and Ed. James Strachey. New York: Avon.

———. 1964. Femininity. In *Standard Edition of the Complete Psychological Works.* Volume 22. Trans. and Ed. James Strachey. London: Hogarth Press.

Gallagher, Catherine and Thomas Laqueur, eds. 1987. *The Making of the Modern Body: Sexuality and society in the nineteenth century.* Berkeley: University of California Press.

Goodall, Jane. 1988. *In the Shadow of Man.* Boston: Houghton Mifflin.

Grafenburg, Ernst. 1950. The role of the urethra in female orgasm. *The International Journal of Sexology* 3: 145–48.

Hamilton, William. 1858–60/2001. Lectures on metaphysics and logic. In *Works of William Hamilton,* ed. Savina Tropea. Bristol: Thoemmes Press.

Haraway, Donna J. 2000. *How like a Leaf: An interview with Thyrza Nichols Goodeve.* New York, London: Routledge.

Harding, Sandra. 1998. *Is Science Multi-Cultural? Postcolonialisms, Feminisms, and Epistemologies.* Bloomington: Indiana University Press.

Hesiod. 1983. *Theogony, Works and Days, and the Shield.* Trans. Apostolos Athanassakis. Baltimore: Johns Hopkins Press.

Hite, Shere. 1976. *The Hite report: A Nationwide Study of Female Sexuality.* New York: Dell.

Hume, David. 1978. *A Treatise of Human Nature.* Ed. Lewis Amherst Selby-Bigge. New York: Oxford University Press.

Inanna: Queen of Heaven and Earth, her Stories and Hymns from Sumer. 1983. Trans. Diane Wolkstein and Samuel Noah Kramer. New York: Harper and Row.

Irigaray, Luce. 1985. *Speculum of the Other Woman.* Trans. Gillian C. Gill. Ithaca: Cornell University Press.

Kelly, Gary F. 1988, 1994, 1998, 2001. *Sexuality Today: The Human Perspective.* Boston: McGraw Hill.

Kimber, Diana Clifford, Carolyn E. Gray, Caroline E. Stackpole, Lutie C. Leavell, Marjorie A. Miller. 1966. *Anatomy and Physiology* 15th ed. New York: Macmillian.

Kinsey, Alfred C., and the staff of the Institute for Sex Research, Indiana University. 1953. *Sexual Behavior in the Human Female.* Philadelphia: Saunders.

Kitzinger, Sheila. 1985. *Women's Experience of Sex: The Facts and Feelings of Female Sexuality at every Stage of Life.* New York: Penguin Books.

Koedt, Ann. 1970. The myth of the vaginal orgasm. In *Notes from the Second Year: Women's Liberation,* ed. Shulamith Firestone and Ann Koedt. New York: Radical Feminism.

Laqueur, Thomas. 1986. Orgasm, generation, and the politics of reproductive biology. *Representations* 14: 1–41.

———. 1989. 'Amor Veneris, vel Dulcedo Appeleur.' In *Fragments for a History of the Human Body,* ed. Michel Feher. New York: Zone.

———. 1990. *Making Sex: Body and Gender from the Greeks to Freud.* Cambridge: Harvard University Press.

Laumann, Edward O., John H. Gagnon, Robert T. Michael, and Stewart Michaels. 1994. *The Social Organization of Sexuality: Sexual Practices in the United States.* Chicago: University of Chicago Press.

Lehrer, Keith. 1990. *Theory of Knowledge.* Boulder: Westview Press.

Lloyd, Elisabeth A. 1993. "Pre-theoretical assumptions in evolutionary explanations of female sexuality." *Philosophical Studies* 69:139–53.

Margulis, Lynn, and Dorion Sagan. 1991. *Mystery Dance: On the Evolution of Human Sexuality.* New York: Summit Books.

Masters, William H., and Virginia E. Johnson. 1966. *Human Sexual Response.* Boston: Little, Brown.

McAnulty, Richard D., and M. Michele Burnette. 2001. *Exploring Human Sexuality: Making Healthy Decisions.* Boston: Allyn and Bacon.

McWhorter, LaDelle. 1999. *Bodies & Pleasures: Foucault and the Politics of Sexual Normalization.* Bloomington: Indiana University Press.

Mills, Charles S. 1997. *The Racial Contract.* Ithaca, N.Y.: Cornell University Press.

Moore, Lisa Jean, and Adele E. Clarke. 1995. Clitoral conventions and transgressions: Graphic representations in anatomy texts, cl900–1991. *Feminist Studies* 21(2): 255–301.

Paré, Ambroise. 1968. *The Collected Works of Ambroise Paré.* Trans. Thomas Johnson. New York: Milford House.

Perry, John Delbert, and Beverly Whipple. 1981. Pelvic muscle strength of female ejaculators: Evidence in support of a new theory of orgasm. *Journal of Sex Research* 17(1): 22–39.

Proctor, Robert N. 1995. *Cancer Wars: How Politics Shapes What We Know and Don't Know About Cancer.* New York: Basic Books.

Rathus, Spencer A., Jeffrey S. Nevid, and Lois Fichner-Rathus. 1993, 2000, 2002. *Human Sexuality in a World of Diversity.* 5th Ed. Boston: Allyn and Bacon.

Rosen, Raymond, and Linda Reich Rosen. 1981. *Human Sexuality.* New York: Alfred A. Knopf.

Schiebinger, Londa L. 1989. *The Mind Has No Sex? Women in the Origins of Modern Science,* Cambridge: Harvard University Press.

Sedgwick, Eve Kosofsky. 1990. *Epistemology of the Closet.* Berkeley, Los Angeles: University of California Press.

Shulman, Alix. 1971. Organs and orgasms. In *Women in Sexist Society,* ed. Vivian Gornick and Barbara K. Moran. New York: New American Library.

Singer, Josephine, and Irving Singer. 1972. Types of female orgasm *Journal of Sex Research* 8 (4): 2550–267.

Small, Meredith F. 1995. *What's Love Got to do with it? The Evolution of Human Mating.* New York: Anchor Books.

Sprecher, Susan, Anita Barbee, and Pepper Schwartz. 2001. "Was it good for you, too?": Gender differences in first sexual intercourse experience. In *Social Psychology and Human Sexuality,* ed. Roy F. Baumeister. Philadelphia: Taylor and Francis.

Symons, Donald. 1979. *The Evolution of Human Sexuality.* New York: Oxford University Press.

Terry, Jennifer. 1995. Anxious slippages between "us" and "them": A brief history of the scientific search for homosexual bodies. In *Deviant bodies: Critical Perspectives on Difference in Science and Popular culture,* ed. Jennifer Terry and Jacqueline Urla. Bloomington: Indiana University Press.

———. 1999. *An American Obsession: Science, Medicine, and Homosexuality in Modern Society.* Chicago: University of Chicago Press.

Tuana, Nancy. 1988. "The Weaker Seed: The Sexist Bias of Reproductive Theory." *Hypatia: A Journal of Feminist Philosophy,* 3 (1): 35–39.

———. 1993. *"The Less Noble Sex: Scientific, Religious and Philosophical Conceptions of Woman's Nature.* Bloomington: Indiana University Press.

———. 1996a. "Fleshing Gender, Sexing the Body: Refiguring the Sex/Gender Distinction," *Spindel Conference Proceedings. Southern Journal of Philosophy.* Vol. XXXV.

———. 1996b. "Re-valuing Science." In *Feminism, Science, and the Philosophy of Science,* ed. Lynn Hankinson Nelson and Jack Nelson. Dordrecht, Netherlands: Kluwer.

———. 2001. "Material locations: An Interactionist Alternative to Realism/Social Constructivism." In *Engendering Rationalities,* ed. Nancy Tuana and Sandra Morgen. Bloomington: Indiana University Press.

Whipple, Beverly. 1995. "Research Concerning Sexual Response in Women." *The Health Psychologist* 17 (1): 16–18.

FOR FURTHER READING

Alcoff, Linda Martín, and Elizabeth Potter, eds. *Feminist Epistemologies.* New York: Routledge, 1993.

Antony, Louise M., and Charlotte E. Witt, eds. *A Mind of One's Own: Feminist Essays on Reason and Objectivity.* 2nd ed. Boulder: Westview Press, 2002.

Belenky, Mary Field, Blyth M. Clinchy, Nancy R. Goldberger, and Jill M. Tarutle. *Women's Ways of Knowing: The Development of Self, Voice and Mind.* New York: Basic Books, 1986.

Bleier, Ruth. *Science and Gender: A Critique of Biology and Its Theories on Women.* London: Pergamon Press, 1984.

Chodorow, Nancy. *The Reproduction of Mothering.* Berkeley: University of California Press, 1978.

Code, Lorraine. *What Can She Know? Feminist Theory and the Construction of Knowledge.* Ithaca, NY: Cornell University Press, 1981.

Code, Lorraine. *Rhetorical Spaces: Essays on Gendered Locations.* New York: Routledge, 1995.

Collins, Patricia Hill. *Black Feminist Thought.* New York: Routledge, 1990.

Duran, Jane. *Toward a Feminist Epistemology.* Savage, MD: Rowman and Littlefield, 1991.

Haraway, Donna. *Simians, Cyborgs, and Women: The Reinvention of Nature.* New York: Routledge, 1991.

Harding, Sandra, and Merrill Hintikka, eds. *Discovering Reality: Perspectives on Epistemology, Metaphysics, Methodology, and Philosophy of Science.* Dordrecht, Holland: D. Reidel, 1983.

Harding, Sandra. *Whose Science? Whose Knowledge?* Ithaca, NY: Cornell University Press, 1991.

Harding, Sandra, ed. *The "Racial" Economy of Science: Toward a Democratic Future.* Bloomington, IN: Indiana University Press, 1993.

Hartsock, Nancy. "The Feminist Standpoint: Developing the Ground for a Specifically Feminist Historical Materialism." In *Discovering Reality: Perspectives on Epistemology, Metaphysics, Methodology, and Philosophy of Science,* edited by Harding and Hintikka. Dordrecht, Holland: D. Reidel, 1983.

Hartsock, Nancy. *The Feminist Standpoint Revisited and Other Essays.* Boulder: Westview Press, 1998.

Heckman, Susan. *Gender and Knowledge.* Boston: Northeastern University Press, 1990.

Keller, Evelyn Fox. *A Feeling for the Organism: The Life and Work of Barbara McClintock.* San Francisco: W. H. Freeman, 1983.

Keller, Evelyn Fox. *Reflections on Gender and Science.* New Haven: Yale University Press, 1985.

Lloyd, Genevieve. *The Man of Reason: "Male" and "Female" in Western Philosophy.* Minneapolis: University of Minnesota Press, 1984.

Longino, Helen. *Science as Social Knowledge.* Princeton, NJ: Princeton University Press, 1990.

Mills, Charles. *The Racial Contract.* Ithaca, NY: Cornell University Press, 1997.

Nelson. Lynn Hankinson. *Who Knows?: From Quine to Feminist Empiricism.* Philadelphia: Temple, 1990.

Nelson, Lynn Hankinson. "The Very Idea of Feminist Epistemology." *Hypatia* 10(3) (1995): 31–50.

Rooney, Phyllis. "Gendered Reason: Sex Metaphor and Conceptions of Reason." *Hypatia* 6(2) (1991): 77–103.

Rooney, Phyllis. *Feminism and Epistemology.* New York: Routledge, 2006.

Rose, Hilary. "Hand, Brain, and Heart: A Feminist Epistemology of the Natural Sciences." *Signs* 9(1) (1983): 73–90.

Scheman, Naomi. *Engenderings: Constructions of Knowledge, Authority, and Privilege.* New York: Routledge, 1993.

Smith, Dorothy. *The Everyday World as Problematic.* Toronto: University of Toronto Press, 1987.

Tanesini, Alessandra. *An Introduction to Feminist Epistemologies.* Malden, MA: Blackwell Publishers, 1999.

Tuana, Nancy. *The Less Noble Sex: Scientific, Religious, and Philosophical Conceptions of Human Nature.* Bloomington, IN: Indiana University Press, 1993.

Tuana, Nancy, and Sandra Morgan. *Engendering Rationalities.* Albany, NY: SUNY Press, 2001.

MEDIA RESOURCES

Evelyn Fox Keller: Science and Gender. VHS. Produced by Leslie Clark (US, 1994). PBS World of Ideas Video Series, Public Affairs Television, Inc. In this 30-minute interview with Bill Moyers, Evelyn Fox Keller discusses how gender plays a significant role in the language that scientists use to describe their work. Available: Films Media Group at http://www.films.com/Home.aspx?BrandType=F or by calling 1–800–257–5126.

Epistemology: What Can We Know? DVD. (US, 2004). This 46-minute program travels from Plato's cave to Gettier's papier-mâché barns as a way of addressing questions such as: What does it mean to really know something? How do I know what I know? And is seeing the same thing as believing? Rutgers University's Alvin Goldman and Peter Klein and Princeton University's Alexander Nehamas and Daniel Garber deconstruct the basic principles of epistemology. A good background for students unfamiliar with basics of traditional epistemology, and a good way of illustrating how epistemology is done in "apolitical" ways. Available: Films for the Humanities and Sciences, http://www.films.com/, or 1–800–257–5126.

CHAPTER 10

FEMINIST ONTOLOGIES

Ontology refers to the study of being, which in the history of philosophy is often understood as a set of abstract questions about the logic of existence (as opposed to nonexistence). Ontology is another area of inquiry where feminist philosophical investigations have made significant and unique contributions, for feminist thinkers are particularly interested in "be-ing" as a verb to be explored phenomenologically, through theory based in experience, rather than a noun to be defined abstractly.[1] In feminist theory central questions about being therefore involve what some have called the "metaphysics of self." That is, the main ontological questions raised by feminists involve human existence as conscious bodies that are necessarily and deeply relational, or "formed" to some degree by social and ecological relations, and that are physically and psychologically constituted in relation to dominant categorizations, such as sex and race. Such questions about the fundamental qualities of human selves call for more than navel-gazing, because understanding even one's own body fully involves understanding much about relationships, specific contexts, and human biological, psychological, and technological possibilities.

The emphasis in feminist ontologies on the relational and embodied aspects of human selves marks a significant departure from philosophical approaches that have been dominant in Western academic conversations. As Sally Haslanger writes, "Dominant frameworks for representing the world, especially the social world, purport to classify things on the basis of intrinsic properties when in fact the classifications are (or should be) crucially dependent on relational properties." By focusing on the "important relational aspects" of subjectivity, agency, and physical being, feminist philosophy makes key contributions to metaphysics and ontology in general. For example, Diana Meyers argues that feminist philosophy's "appreciation of the psycho-corporeal attributes and capabilities embedded in the embodied self and the relational self," can correct mistaken assumptions about the "disembedded, disembodied

---

[1] Phenomenological traditions are an exception here, and feminist philosophers have often drawn on the work of existential and other phenomenological theorists. This use of "be-ing" is from Mary Daly.

self" evident in contemporary analytic philosophy (2005, 200).

Beyond drawing attention to fundamental features of embedded and embodied selves, feminist philosophers analyze the qualities and experience of being from various social positions, raising questions about what it is to be embodied, gendered, raced (etc.), *political* beings, in particular historical and cultural contexts. So in addition to articulating being in the context of oppression, they articulate and explore revolutionary forms of being, and resistant subjectivities within and beyond the constraints of heteropatriarchal, ableist, racist, and capitalist understandings of what a "self" or "subject" is supposed to be. Themes explored in feminist ontologies include hybridity and "mixed" forms of being, such as the state of being a conscious object that is both natural and cultural, both biological and technological, and both "insider" and "outsider" to dominant realities. Feminist philosophy emphasizes the limits of dominant categorizations, such as dualistic formulations of reality, and the potential for transformation through radical consciousness and bodily practices, so feminist ontologies make important contributions to our understanding of the complexities of embodied consciousness in the midst of various fields of meaning and influence.

The ontological explorations collected here challenge the assumption that human selves are homogenous, atomistic, independent, timeless creatures. They characterize being as social, hybrid, ecological, and emergent, yet they also capture the power and persistence of individual consciousness and selfhood. They explore the beginnings of personhood, the impacts of violent oppressive power on experiences of selfhood, and the potential for new forms of being and consciousness. It is worth noting that feminist philosophical work in ontology can be quite "located" in real circumstances and experiences (such as the experience of being disabled in America today), yet also quite speculative about abstract matters (such as the nature of souls).

One question about being and existence that has probably always been interesting and important to women is about when human life begins. Mary Anne Warren's widely read essay "The Moral Significance of Birth" contends that birth is the most appropriate place to mark the existence of a new legal person. Warren begins by unpacking the intrinsic-property and single-criterion assumptions that liberal philosophers have used to ground moral rights. She rejects all fetal rights based arguments rooted in those assumptions because they frame the abortion debate in ways that ignore the moral significance of the event of birth. Instead, a socially perceptive alternative account of rights grounded in relationships rather than abstract individualism is possible. But that account requires answers to two key questions: why should we protect infants, and why does birth matter? Warren argues that birth is morally significant because it marks the end of the fetus-woman relationship and the beginning of the infant's existence as a social person. Because there is room for only one person with full rights inside a single human skin, birth, rather than sentience, viability, or some other pre-natal feature must mark the beginning of legal personhood.

Another fundamental feature of female experience is the threat of rape. In "A Phenomenology of Fear: The Threat of Rape and Female Bodily Comportment," Ann Cahill argues that, although bodies are not blank slates onto which social forces inscribe value and meaning, gendered and raced bodies do develop habits, practices, desires, and tendencies through living in hierarchical social systems. Blending Foucault's analysis of how power produces social bodies and realities, Iris Young's observations on female motility, and Sandra Bartky's analysis of feminine social practices (e.g., dieting, exercise, and makeup), Cahill provides a clear and compelling account of how the fear of rape disciplines female bodies. Because rape is a pervasive practice maintaining the hierarchies of patriarchy, feminists must continue to explore the ways in which the threat of sexual violence disciplines and constructs feminine bodies.

In "Toward a Feminist Theory of Disability," Susan Wendell draws on her own experience with a disabling chronic illness to argue for an integration of a greater understanding of disability into feminist theory, and a specifically feminist theory of disability. The experience of disability makes obvious the fact that social worlds are structured "for people who have no weaknesses," which is an injustice to disabled people, but also alienates the able-bodied from the fact of their own physical vulnerability and contingency. Wendell illustrates how feminism's radical thinking about cultural attitudes toward bodies benefits theories of disability. For example, the universal paradigm of human physical being as young, healthy, and independent, fostered by patriarchal desire for control of bodies, is illusory. All bodies are dependent, and as we age all bodies must face diminished capacities and the possibility of pain.

Though her characteristically creative discourse, in "Be-Longing: The Lust for Happiness," Mary Daly calls on "Nags" (feminists) to participate in the "unfolding of be-ing," a life-affirming route to happiness. In contrast with the theology of happiness put forth by medieval Christian philosopher Thomas Aquinas, which describes happiness as attainable only after death "and then only through divine intervention," for those who resist patriarchy happiness is a life of activity committed to continuing and ever-evolving affirmations of life on earth. Daly crafts several concepts to describe the commitments she recommends. One is "metapatterning," which involves breaking through paternal patterns and transcending patriarchal thinking, speaking, and acting. Another is a notion of soul that is both intellectual and coextensive with the body, and therefore physical rather than metaphysical. For Daly, be-ing is a matter of conscious commitment, and feminist be-ing is in defiance of patriarchal "civilization."

Like Mary Daly, Rosi Braidotti expresses feminist knowledge about the possibilities of existence in ways that refuse to mime dominant and dominating discourses. In "Mothers, Monsters, and Machines," she traces the conceptual connections between these three threatening forms of being in order to uncover the status of difference in rationality, and to frame a new conception of feminist subjectivity. While mothers represent women and the subjects of feminism, monsters symbolize the bodily incarnation of difference, and machines help determine female futures, especially in the form of new reproductive technologies. She addresses the reader as collaborator in the feminist project of research and experimentation toward those ends.

"*La Conciencia de la Mestiza:* Towards a New Consciousness" is probably the most celebrated section of Gloria Anzaldúa's influential *Borderlands/La Frontera: The New Mestiza* (1987). This is a *mestiza,* or "mixed" text in which borderland identities are voiced in a seamless blend of Nahuatl, Mexican Spanish, and English languages, and Chicano/a histories are told through a blend of theory, autobiography, norteña song lyrics, and poetry. The so-called "real world" and the spirit world commingle in Anzaldúa's ontologies, and her perspective challenges the dualistic thinking and love of purity at the heart of traditional Anglo thinking about categories and identities. Anzaldúa presents the view that a "massive uprooting of dualistic thinking" can only be led by the *mestiza,* who sits between the worlds and from there is able to communicate across borders. Writing theory from *mestiza* knowledge also makes visible the transcultural experiences of those living in between different worlds of meaning. The possibility of resistance is revealed by perceiving one face of the self in the process of being oppressed, as another face is in the process of resisting oppression. A radical oppositional *mestiza* consciousness is therefore born from conscious interplay between oppression and resistance.

THE MORAL SIGNIFICANCE OF BIRTH

Mary Anne Warren

Does birth make a difference to the moral rights of the fetus/infant? Should it make a difference to its legal rights? Most contemporary philosophers believe that birth cannot make a difference to moral rights. If this is true, then it becomes difficult to justify either a moral or a legal distinction between late abortion and infanticide. I argue that the view that birth is irrelevant to moral rights rests upon two highly questionable assumptions about the theoretical foundations of moral rights. If we reject these assumptions, then we are free to take account of the contrasting biological and social relationships that make even relatively late abortion morally different from infanticide.

English common law treats the moment of live birth as the point at which a legal person comes into existence. Although abortion has often been prohibited, it has almost never been classified as homicide. In contrast, infanticide generally is classified as a form of homicide, even where (as in England) there are statutes designed to mitigate the severity of the crime in certain cases. But many people—including some feminists—now favor the extension of equal legal rights to some or all fetuses (S. Callahan 1984, 1986). The extension of legal personhood to fetuses would not only threaten women's right to choose abortion, but also undermine other fundamental rights. I will argue that because of these dangers, birth remains the most appropriate place to mark the existence of a new legal person.

SPEAKING OF RIGHTS

In making this case, I find it useful to speak of moral as well as legal rights. Although not all legal rights can be grounded in moral rights, the right to life can plausibly be so construed.

This approach is controversial. Some feminist philosophers have been critical of moral analyses based upon rights. Carol Gilligan (1982), Nell Noddings (1984), and others have argued that women tend to take a different approach to morality, one that emphasizes care and responsibility in interpersonal relationships rather than abstract rules, principles, or conflicts of rights. I would argue, however, that moral rights are complementary to a feminist ethics of care and responsibility, not inconsistent or competitive with it. Whereas caring relationships can provide a moral ideal, respect for rights provides a moral floor—a minimum protection for individuals which remains morally binding even where appropriate caring relationships are absent or have broken down (Manning 1988). Furthermore, as I shall argue, social relationships are part of the foundation of moral rights.

Some feminist philosophers have suggested that the very concept of a moral right may be inconsistent with the social nature of persons. Elizabeth Wolgast (1987) argues convincingly that this concept has developed within an atomistic model of the social world, in which persons are depicted as self-sufficient and exclusively self-interested individuals whose relationships with one another are essentially competitive. As Wolgast notes, such an atomistic model is particularly inappropriate in the context of pregnancy, birth, and parental responsibility. Moreover, recent feminist research has greatly expanded our awareness of the historical, religious, sociological, and political forces that shape contemporary struggles over reproductive rights, further underscoring the need for approaches to moral theory that can take account of such social realities (Harrison 1983; Luker 1984; Petchesky 1984).

But is the concept of a moral right necessarily incompatible with the social nature of human beings? Rights are indeed individualistic, in that they can be ascribed to individuals, as well as to groups. But respect for moral rights need not be based upon an excessively individualistic view of human nature. A more socially perceptive account of moral rights is possible, provided that we reject two common assumptions about the theoretical foundations of moral rights. These assumptions are widely accepted by mainstream philosophers, but rarely stated and still more rarely defended.

The first is what I shall call the intrinsic-properties assumption. This is the view that the only facts that can justify the ascription of basic moral rights[1] or moral standing[2] to individuals are facts about *the intrinsic properties of those individuals.* Philosophers who accept this view disagree about which of the intrinsic properties of individuals are relevant to the ascription of rights. They agree, however, that relational properties—such as being loved, or being part of a social community or biological ecosystem—cannot be relevant.

The second is what I shall call the single-criterion assumption. This is the view that there is some single property, the presence or absence of which divides the world into those things which have moral rights or moral standing, and those things which do not. Christopher Stone (1987) locates this assumption within a more general theoretical approach, which he calls "moral monism." Moral monists believe that the goal of moral philosophy is the production of a coherent set of principles, sufficient to provide definitive answers to all possible moral dilemmas. Among these principles, the monist typically assumes, will be one that identifies some key property which is such that, "Those beings that possess the key property count morally . . . [while those] things that lack it are all utterly irrelevant, except as resources for the benefit of those things that do count" (1987, 13).

Together, the intrinsic-properties and single-criterion assumptions preclude any adequate account of the social foundations of moral rights. The intrinsic-properties assumption requires us to regard all personal or other relationships among individuals or groups as wholly irrelevant to basic moral rights. The single-criterion assumption requires us

to deny that there can be a variety of sound reasons for ascribing moral rights, and a variety of things and beings to which some rights may appropriately be ascribed. Both assumptions are inimical to a feminist approach to moral theory, as well as to approaches that are less anthropocentric and more environmentally adequate. The prevalence of these assumptions helps to explain why few mainstream philosophers believe that birth can in any way alter the infant's moral rights.

THE DENIAL OF THE MORAL SIGNIFICANCE OF BIRTH

The view that birth is irrelevant to moral rights is shared by philosophers on all points of the spectrum of moral views about abortion. For the most conservative, birth adds nothing to the infant's moral rights, since all of those rights have been present since conception. Moderates hold that the fetus acquires an equal right to life at some point after conception but before birth. The most popular candidates for this point of moral demarcation are (1) the stage at which the fetus becomes viable (i.e., capable of surviving outside the womb, with or without medical assistance), and (2) the stage at which it becomes sentient (i.e., capable of having experiences, including that of pain). For those who hold a view of this sort, both infanticide and abortion at any time past the critical stage are forms of homicide, and there is little reason to distinguish between them either morally or legally.

Finally, liberals hold that even relatively late abortion is sometimes morally acceptable, and that at no time is abortion the moral equivalent of homicide. However, few liberals wish to hold that infanticide is not—at least sometimes—morally comparable to homicide. Consequently, the presumption that being born makes no difference to one's moral rights creates problems for the liberal view of abortion. Unless the liberal can establish some grounds for a general moral distinction between late abortion and early infanticide, she must either retreat to a moderate position on abortion, or else conclude that infanticide is not so bad after all.

To those who accept the intrinsic-properties assumption, birth can make little difference to the moral standing of the fetus/infant. For birth does not seem to alter any intrinsic property that could reasonably be linked to the possession of a strong right to life. Newborn infants have very nearly the same intrinsic properties as do fetuses shortly before birth. They have, as L. W. Sumner (1983, 53) says, "the same size, shape, internal constitution, species membership, capacities, level of consciousness, and so forth."[3] Consequently, Sumner says, infanticide cannot be morally very different from late abortion. In his words, "Birth is a shallow and arbitrary criterion of moral standing, and there appears to be no way of connecting it to a deeper account" (52).

Sumner holds that the only valid criterion of moral standing is the capacity for sentience. Prenatal neurophysiology and behavior suggest that human fetuses begin to have rudimentary sensory experiences at some time during the second trimester of pregnancy. Thus, Sumner concludes that abortion should be permitted during the first trimester but not thereafter, except in special circumstances.[4]

Michael Tooley (1983) agrees that birth can make no difference to moral standing. However, rather than rejecting the liberal view of abortion, Tooley boldly claims that neither late abortion nor early infanticide is seriously wrong. He argues that an entity cannot have a strong right to life unless it is capable of desiring its own continued existence. To be capable of such a desire, he argues, a being must have a concept of itself as a continuing subject of conscious experience. Having such a concept is a central part of what it is to be a person, and thus the kind of being that has strong moral rights. Fetuses certainly lack such a concept, as do infants during the first few months of their lives. Thus, Tooley concludes, neither fetuses nor newborn infants have a strong right to life, and neither abortion nor infanticide is an intrinsic moral wrong.

These two theories are worth examining, not only because they illustrate the difficulties generated by the intrinsic-properties and single-criterion assumptions, but also because each includes valid insights that need to be integrated into a more comprehensive account. Both Sumner and Tooley are partially right. Unlike "genetic humanity"—a property possessed by fertilized human ova—sentience and self-awareness are properties that have some general relevance to what we may owe another being in the way of respect and protection. However, neither the sentience criterion nor the self-awareness criterion can explain the moral significance of birth.

THE SENTIENCE CRITERION

Both newborn infants and late-term fetuses show clear signs of sentience. For instance, they are apparently capable of having visual experiences. Infants will often turn away from bright lights, and those who have done intrauterine photography have sometimes observed a similar reaction in the late-term fetus when bright lights are introduced in its vicinity. Both may respond to loud noises, voices, or other sounds, so both can probably have auditory experiences. They are evidently also responsive to touch, taste, motion, and other kinds of sensory stimulation.

The sentience of infants and late-term fetuses makes a difference to how they should be treated, by contrast with fertilized ova or first-trimester fetuses. Sentient beings are usually capable of experiencing painful as well as pleasurable or affectively neutral sensations.[5] While the capacity to experience pain is valuable to an organism, pain is by definition an intrinsically unpleasant experience. Thus, sentient beings may plausibly be said to have a moral right not to be deliberately subjected to pain in the absence of any compelling reason. For those who prefer not to speak of rights, it is still plausible that a capacity for sentience gives an entity some moral standing. It may, for instance, require that its interests be given some consideration in utilitarian calculations, or that it be treated as an end and never merely as a means.

But it is not clear that sentience is a sufficient condition for moral equality, since there are many clearly-sentient creatures (e.g., mice) to which most of us would not be prepared to ascribe equal moral standing. Sumner examines the implications of the sentience criterion primarily in the context of abortion. Given his belief that some compromise is essential between the conservative and liberal viewpoints on abortion, the sentience criterion recommends itself as a means of drawing a moral distinction between early abortion and late abortion. It is, in some ways, a more defensible criterion than fetal viability.

The 1973 *Roe v. Wade* decision treats the presumed viability of third-trimester fetuses as a basis for permitting states to restrict abortion rights in order to protect fetal life in the third trimester, but not earlier. Yet viability is relative, among other things, to the medical care available to the pregnant woman and her infant. Increasingly sophisticated neonatal intensive care has made it possible to save many more premature infants than before, thus altering the average age of viability. Someday it may be possible to keep even first-trimester fetuses alive and developing normally outside the womb. The viability criterion seems to imply that the advent of total ectogenesis (artificial gestation from conception to birth) would automatically eliminate women's right to abortion, even in the earliest stages of pregnancy. At the very least, it must imply that as many aborted fetuses as possible should be kept alive through artificial gestation. But the mere technological possibility of providing artificial wombs for huge numbers of human fetuses could not establish such a moral obligation. A massive commitment to ectogenesis would probably be ruinously expensive, and might prove contrary to the interests of parents and children. The viability criterion forces us to make a hazardous leap from the technologically possible to the morally mandatory.

The sentience criterion at first appears more promising as a means of defending a moderate view of abortion. It provides an intuitively plausible distinction between early and late abortion. Unlike the viability criterion, it is unlikely to be undermined by new biomedical technologies. Further investigation of fetal neurophysiology and behavior might refute the presumption that fetuses begin to be capable of sentience at some point in the second trimester. Perhaps this development occurs slightly earlier or slightly later than present evidence suggests. (It is unlikely to be much earlier or much later.) However, that is a consequence that those who hold a moderate position on abortion could live with; so long as the line could still be drawn with some degree of confidence, they need not insist that it be drawn exactly where Sumner suggests.

But closer inspection reveals that the sentience criterion will not yield the result that Sumner wants. His position vacillates between two versions of the sentience criterion, neither of which can adequately support his moderate view of abortion. The strong version of the sentience criterion treats sentience as a sufficient condition for having full and equal moral standing. The weak version treats sentience as sufficient for having some moral standing, but not necessarily full and equal moral standing.

Sumner's claim that sentient fetuses have the same moral standing as older human beings clearly requires the strong version of the sentience criterion. On this theory, any being which has even minimal capacities for sensory experience is the moral equal of any person. If we accept this theory, then we must conclude that not only is late abortion the moral equivalent of homicide, but so is the killing of such sentient nonhuman beings as mice. Sumner evidently does not wish to accept this further conclusion, for he also says that "sentience admits of degrees . . . [a fact that] enables us to employ it both as an inclusion criterion and as a comparison criterion of moral standing" (144). In other words, all sentient beings have some moral standing, but beings that are more highly sentient have greater moral standing than do less highly sentient beings. This weaker version of the sentience criterion leaves room for a distinction between the moral standing of mice and that of sentient humans—provided, that is, that mice can be shown to be less highly sentient. However, it will not support the moral equality of late-term fetuses, since the relatively undeveloped condition of fetal brains almost certainly means that fetuses are less highly sentient than older human beings.

A similar dilemma haunts those who use the sentience criterion to argue for the moral equality of nonhuman animals. Some animal liberationists hold that all sentient beings are morally equal, regardless of species. For instance, Peter Singer (1981) maintains that all sentient beings are entitled to equal consideration for their comparably important interests. Animal liberationists are primarily concerned to argue for the moral equality of vertebrate animals, such as mammals, birds, reptiles and fish. In this project, the sentience criterion serves them less well than they may suppose. On the one hand, if they use the weak version of the sentience criterion then they cannot sustain the claim that all nonhuman vertebrates are our moral equals—unless they can demonstrate that they are all sentient to the same degree that we are. It is unclear how such a demonstration would proceed, or what would count as success. On the other hand, if they use the strong version of the sentience criterion, then they are committed to the conclusion that if flies and mosquitos are even minimally sentient then they too are our moral equals. Not even the most radical animal liberationists have endorsed the moral equality of such invertebrate animals,[6] yet it is quite likely that these creatures enjoy some form of sentience.

We do not really know whether complex invertebrate animals such as spiders and insects have sensory experiences, but the evidence suggests that they may. They have both sense organs and central nervous systems, and they often act as if they could see, hear, and feel very well. Sumner says that all invertebrates are probably nonsentient, because they lack certain brain structures—notably forebrains—that appear to be essential to the processing of pain in vertebrate animals. But might not some invertebrate animals have neurological devices for the processing of pain that are different from those of vertebrates, just as some have very different organs for the detection of light, sound, or odor? The capacity to feel pain is important to highly mobile organisms which guide their behavior through perceptual data, since it often enables them to avoid damage or destruction. Without that capacity, such organisms would be less likely to survive long enough to reproduce. Thus, if insects, spiders, crayfish, or octopi can see, hear, or smell, then it is quite likely that they can also feel pain. If sentience is the sole criterion for moral equality, then such probably-sentient entities deserve the benefit of the doubt.

But it is difficult to believe that killing invertebrate animals is as morally objectionable as homicide. That an entity is probably sentient provides a reason for avoiding actions that may cause it pain. It may also provide a reason for respecting its life, a life which it may enjoy. But it is not a sufficient reason for regarding it as a moral equal. Perhaps an ideally moral person would try to avoid killing any sentient being, even a fly. Yet it is impossible in practice to treat the killing of persons and the killing of sentient invertebrates with the same severity. Even the simplest activities essential to human survival (such as agriculture, or gathering wild foods) generally entail some loss of invertebrate lives. If the strong version of the sentience criterion is correct, then all such activities are morally problematic. And if it is not, then the probable sentience of late-term fetuses and newborn infants is not enough to demonstrate that either late abortion or infanticide is the moral equivalent of homicide. Some additional argument is needed to show that either late abortion or early infanticide is seriously immoral.

THE SELF-AWARENESS CRITERION

Although newborn infants are regarded as persons in both law and common moral conviction, they lack certain mental capacities that are typical of persons. They have sensory experiences, but, as Tooley points out, they probably do not yet think, or have a sense of who they are, or a desire to continue to exist. It is not unreasonable to suppose that these facts make some difference to their moral standing. Other things being equal, it is surely worse to kill a self-aware being that wants to go on living than one that has never been self-aware and that has no such preference. If this is true, then it is hard to avoid the conclusion that neither abortion nor infanticide is quite as bad as the killing of older human beings. And indeed many human societies seem to have accepted that conclusion.

Tooley notes that the abhorrence of infanticide which is characteristic of cultures influenced by Christianity has not been shared by most cultures outside that influence. Prior to the present century, most societies—from the gatherer-hunter societies of Australia, Africa, North and South America, and elsewhere, to the high civilizations of China, India, Greece, Rome, and Egypt—have not only tolerated occasional instances of infanticide but have regarded it as sometimes the wisest course of action. Even in Christian Europe there was often a *de facto* toleration of infanticide—so long as the mother was married and the killing discreet. Throughout much of the second millennium in Europe, single women whose infants failed to survive were often executed in sadistic ways, yet married women whose infants died under equally suspicious circumstances generally escaped legal penalty (Piers 1978). Evidently, the sanctions against infanticide had more to do with the desire to punish female sexual transgressions than with a consistently held belief that infanticide is morally comparable to homicide.

If infanticide has been less universally regarded as wrong than most people today believe, then the self-awareness criterion is more consistent with common moral convictions than it at first appears. Nevertheless, it conflicts with some convictions that are almost universal, even in cultures that tolerate infanticide. Tooley argues that infants probably begin to think and to become self-aware at about three months of age, and that this is therefore the stage at which they begin to have a strong right to life. Perhaps this is true. However the customs of most cultures seem to have required that a decision about the life of an infant be made within, at most, a few days of birth. Often, there was some special gesture or ceremony—such as washing the infant, feeding it, or giving it a name—to mark the fact that it would thenceforth be regarded as a member of the community. From that point on, infanticide would not be considered, except perhaps under unusual circumstances. For instance, Margaret Mead gives this account of birth and infanticide among the Arapesh people of Papua New Guinea:

> While the child is being delivered, the father waits within ear-shot until its sex is determined, when the midwives call it out to him. To this information he answers laconically, "Wash it," or "Do not wash it." If the command is "Wash it," the child is to be brought up. In a few cases when the child is a girl and there are already several girl-children in the family, the child will not be saved, but left, unwashed, with the cord uncut, in the bark basin on which the delivery takes place. (Mead [1935] 1963, 32–33)

Mead's account shows that among the Arapesh infanticide is at least to some degree a function of patriarchal power. In this, they are not unusual. In almost every society in which infanticide has been tolerated, female infants have been the most frequent victims. In patriarchal, patrilineal and patrilocal societies, daughters are usually valued less than sons, e.g., because they will leave the family at marriage, and will probably be unable to contribute as much as sons to the parents' economic support later. Female infanticide probably reinforces male domination by reducing the relative number of women and dramatically reinforcing the social devaluation of females.[7] Often it is the father who decides which infants will be reared. Dianne Romaine has pointed out to me that this practice may be due to a reluctance to force women, the primary caregivers, to decide when care should not be given. However, it also suggests that infanticide often served the interests of individual men more than those of women, the family, or the community as a whole.

Nevertheless, infanticide must sometimes have been the most humane resolution of a tragic dilemma. In the absence of effective contraception or abortion, abandoning a newborn can sometimes be the only alternative to the infant's later death from starvation. Women of nomadic gatherer-hunter societies, for instance, are sometimes unable to raise an infant born too soon after the last one, because they can neither nurse nor carry two small children.

But if infanticide is to be considered, it is better that it be done immediately after birth, before the bonds of love and care between the infant and the mother (and other persons) have grown any stronger than they may already be. Postponing the question of the infant's acceptance for weeks or months would be cruel to all concerned. Although an infant may be little more sentient or self-aware at two weeks of age than at birth, its death is apt to be a greater tragedy—not for it, but for those who have come to love it. I suspect that this is why, where infanticide is tolerated, the decision to kill or abandon an infant must usually be made rather quickly. If this consideration is morally relevant—and I think it is—then the self-awareness criterion fails to illuminate some of the morally salient aspects of infanticide.

PROTECTING NONPERSONS

If we are to justify a general moral distinction between abortion and infanticide, we must answer two questions. First, why should infanticide be discouraged, rather than treated as a matter for individual decision? And second, why should sentient fetuses not be given the same protections that law and common sense morality accord to infants? But before turning to these two questions, it is necessary to make a more general point.

Persons have sound reasons for treating one another as moral equals. These reasons derive from both self-interest and altruistic concern for others—which, because of our social nature, are often very difficult to distinguish. Human persons—and perhaps all persons—normally come into existence only in and through social relationships. Sentience may begin to emerge without much direct social interaction, but it is doubtful that a child reared in total isolation from human or other sentient (or apparently sentient) beings could develop the capacities for self-awareness and social interaction that are essential to personhood. The recognition of the fundamentally social nature of persons can only strengthen the case for moral equality, since social relationships are undermined and distorted by inequalities that are perceived as unjust. There may be many nonhuman animals who have enough capacity for self-awareness and social interaction to be regarded as persons, with equal basic moral rights. But, whether or not this is true, it is certainly true that if any things have full and equal basic moral rights then persons do.

However we cannot conclude that, because all persons have equal basic moral rights, it is always wrong to extend strong moral protections to beings that are not persons. Those who accept the single-criterion assumption may find that a plausible inference. By now, however, most thoughtful people recognize the need to protect vulnerable elements of the natural world—such as endangered plant and animal species, rainforests, and rivers—from further destruction at human hands. Some argue that it is appropriate, as a way of protecting these things, to ascribe to them legal if not moral rights (Stone 1974). These things should be protected not because they are sentient or self-aware, but for other good reasons. They are irreplaceable parts of the terrestrial biosphere, and as such they have incalculable value to human beings. Their long-term instrumental value is often a fully sufficient reason for protecting them. However, they may also be held to have inherent value, i.e., value that is independent of the uses we might wish to make of them (Taylor 1986). Although destroying them is not murder, it is an act of vandalism which later generations will mourn.

It is probably not crucial whether or not we say that endangered species and natural habitats have a moral right to our protection. What is crucial is that we recognize and act upon the need to protect them. Yet certain contemporary realities argue for an increased willingness to ascribe rights to impersonal elements of the natural world. Americans, at least, are likely to be more sensitive to appeals and demands couched in terms of rights than those that appeal to less familiar concepts, such as inherent value. So central are rights to our common moral idiom, that to deny that trees have rights is to risk being thought to condone the reckless destruction of rainforests and redwood groves. If we want to communicate effectively about the need to protect the natural world—and to protect it for its own sake as well as our own—then we may be wise to develop theories that permit us to ascribe at least some moral rights to some things that are clearly not persons.

Parallel issues arise with respect to the moral status of the newborn infant. As Wolgast (1987) argues, it is much more important to understand our responsibilities to protect and care for infants than to insist that they have exactly the same moral rights as older human beings. Yet to deny that infants have equal basic moral rights is to risk being thought to condone infanticide and the neglect and abuse of infants. Here too, effective communication about human moral responsibilities seems to demand the ascription of rights to beings that lack certain properties that are typical of persons. But, of course, that does not explain why we have these responsibilities towards infants in the first place.

WHY PROTECT INFANTS?

I have already mentioned some of the reasons for protecting human infants more carefully than we protect most comparably-sentient nonhuman beings. Most people care deeply about infants, particularly—but not exclusively—their own. Normal human adults (and children) are probably "programmed" by their biological nature to respond to human infants with care and concern. For the mother, in particular, that response is apt to begin well before the infant is born. But even for her it is likely to become more intense after the infant's birth. The infant at birth enters the human social world, where, if it lives, it becomes involved in social relationships with others, of kinds that can only be dimly foreshadowed before birth. It begins to be known and cared for, not just as a potential member of the family or community, but as a socially present and responsive individual. In the words of Loren Lomansky (1984, 172), "birth constitutes a quantum leap forward in the process of establishing . . . social bonds." The newborn is not yet self-aware, but it is already (rapidly becoming) a social being.

Thus, although the human newborn may have no intrinsic properties that can ground a moral right to life stronger than that of a fetus just before birth, its emergence into the social world makes it appropriate to treat it as if it had such a stronger right. This, in effect, is what the law has done, through the doctrine that a person begins to exist at birth. Those who accept the intrinsic-properties assumption can only regard this doctrine as a legal fiction. However, it is a fiction that we would have difficulty doing without. If the line were not drawn at birth, then I think we would have to draw it at some point rather soon thereafter, as many other societies have done.

Another reason for condemning infanticide is that, at least in relatively privileged nations like our own, infants whose parents cannot raise them can usually be placed with people who will love them and take good care of them. This means that infanticide is rarely in the infant's own best interests, and would often deprive some potential adoptive individual or family of a great benefit. It also means that the prohibition of infanticide need not impose intolerable burdens upon parents (especially women). A rare parent might think it best to kill a healthy[8] infant rather than permitting it to be reared by others, but a persuasive defense of that claim would require special circumstances. Far instance, when abortion is unavailable and women face savage abuses for supposed sexual transgressions, those who resort to infanticide to conceal an "illegitimate" birth may be doing only what they must. But where enforcement of the sexual double standard is less brutal, abortion and adoption can provide alternatives that most women would prefer to infanticide.

Some might wonder whether adoption is really preferable to infanticide, at least from the parent's point of view. Judith Thomson (1971, 66) notes that, "A woman may be utterly devastated by the thought of a child, a bit of herself, put out for adoption and never seen or heard of again." From the standpoint of narrow self-interest, it might not be irrational to prefer the death of the child to such a future. Yet few would wish to resolve this problem by legalizing infanticide. The evolution of more open adoption procedures which permit more contact between the adopted child and the biological parent(s) might lessen the psychological pain often associated with adoption. But that would be at best a partial solution. More basic is the provision of better social support for child-rearers, so that parents are not forced by economic necessity to surrender their children for adoption.

These are just some of the arguments for treating infants as legal persons, with an equal right to life. A more complete account might deal with the effects of the toleration of infanticide upon other moral norms. But the existence of such effects is unclear. Despite a tradition of occasional infanticide, the Arapesh appear in Mead's descriptions as gentle people who treat their children with great kindness and affection. The case against infanticide need not rest upon the questionable claim that the toleration of infanticide inevitably leads to the erosion of other moral norms. It is enough that most people today strongly desire that the lives of infants be protected, and that this can now be done without imposing intolerable burdens upon individuals or communities.

But have I not left the door open to the claim that infanticide may still be justified in some places, e.g., where there is severe poverty and a lack of accessible adoption agencies or where women face exceptionally harsh penalties for "illegitimate" births? I have, and deliberately. The moral case against the toleration of infanticide is contingent upon the existence of morally preferable options. Where economic hardship, the lack of contraception and abortion, and other forms of sexual and political oppression have eliminated all such options, there will be instances in which infanticide is the least tragic of a tragic set of choices. In such circumstances, the enforcement of extreme sanctions against infanticide can constitute an additional injustice.

WHY BIRTH MATTERS

I have defended what most regard as needing no defense, i.e., the ascription of an equal right to life to human infants. Under reasonably favorable conditions that policy can protect the rights and interests of all concerned, including infants, biological parents, and potential adoptive parents.

But if protecting infants is such a good idea, then why is it not a good idea to extend the same strong protections to sentient fetuses? The question is not whether sentient fetuses ought to be protected: of course they should. Most women readily accept the responsibility for doing whatever they can to ensure that their (voluntarily continued) pregnancies are successful, and that no avoidable harm comes to the fetus. Negligent or malevolent actions by third parties which result in death or injury to pregnant women or their potential children should be subject to moral censure and legal prosecution. A just and caring society would do much more than ours does to protect the health of all its members, including pregnant women. The question is whether the law should accord to late-term fetuses *exactly the same* protections as are accorded to infants and older human beings.

The case for doing so might seem quite strong. We normally regard not only infants, but all other postnatal human beings as entitled to strong legal protections *so long as they are either sentient or capable of an eventual return to sentience.* We do not also require that they demonstrate a capacity for thought, self-awareness, or social relationships before we conclude that they have an equal right to life. Such restrictive criteria would leave too much room for invidious discrimination. The eternal propensity of powerful groups to rationalize sexual, racial, and class oppression by claiming that members of the oppressed group are mentally or otherwise "inferior" leaves little hope that such restrictive criteria could be applied without bias. Thus, for human beings past the prenatal stage, the capacity for sentience—or for a return to sentience—may be the only pragmatically defensible criterion for the ascription of full and equal basic rights. If so, then both theoretical simplicity and moral consistency may seem to require that we extend the same protections to sentient human beings that have not yet been born as to those that have.

But there is one crucial consideration which this argument leaves out. It is impossible to treat fetuses *in utero* as if they were persons without treating women as if they were something less than persons. The extension of equal rights to sentient fetuses would inevitably license severe violations of women's basic rights to personal autonomy and physical security. In the first place, it would rule out most second-trimester abortions performed to protect the woman's life or health. Such abortions might sometimes be construed as a form of self-defense. But the right to self-defense is not usually taken to mean that one may kill innocent persons just because their continued existence poses some threat to one's own life

or health. If abortion must be justified as self-defense, then it will rarely be performed until the woman is already in extreme danger, and perhaps not even then. Such a policy would cost some women their lives, while others would be subjected to needless suffering and permanent physical harm.

Other alarming consequences of the drive to extend more equal rights to fetuses are already apparent in the United States. In the past decade it has become increasingly common for hospitals or physicians to obtain court orders requiring women in labor to undergo Caesarean sections, against their will, for what is thought to be the good of the fetus. Such an extreme infringement of the woman's right to security against physical assault would be almost unthinkable once the infant has been born. No parent or relative can legally be forced to undergo any surgical procedure, even possibly to save the life of a child, once it is born. But pregnant women can sometimes be forced to undergo major surgery, for the supposed benefit of the fetus. As George Annas (1982) points out, forced Caesareans threaten to reduce women to the status of inanimate objects—containers which may be opened at the will of others in order to get at their contents.

Perhaps the most troubling illustration of this trend is the case of Angie Carder, who died at George Washington University Medical Center in June 1987, two days after a court-ordered Caesarean section. Ms. Carder had suffered a recurrence of an earlier cancer, and was not expected to live much longer. Her physicians agreed that the fetus was too undeveloped to be viable, and that Carder herself was probably too weak to survive the surgery. Although she, her family, and the physicians were all opposed to a Caesarean delivery, the hospital administration—evidently believing it had a legal obligation to try to save the fetus—sought and obtained a court order to have it done. As predicted, both Carder and her infant died soon after the operation.[9] This woman's rights to autonomy, physical integrity, and life itself were forfeit—not just because of her illness, but because of her pregnancy.

Such precedents are doubly alarming in the light of the development of new techniques of fetal therapy. As fetuses come to be regarded as patients, with rights that may be in direct conflict with those of their mothers, and as the *in utero* treatment of fetuses becomes more feasible, more and more pregnant women may be subjected against their will to dangerous and invasive medical interventions. If so, then we may be sure that there will be other Angie Carders.

Another danger in extending equal legal protections to sentient fetuses is that women will increasingly be blamed, and sometimes legally prosecuted, when they miscarry or give birth to premature, sick, or abnormal infants. It is reasonable to hold the caretakers of infants legally responsible if their charges are harmed because of their avoidable negligence. But when a woman miscarries or gives birth to an abnormal infant, the cause of the harm might be traced to any of an enormous number of actions or circumstances which would not normally constitute any legal offense. She might have gotten too much exercise or too little, eaten the wrong foods or the wrong quantity of the right ones, or taken or failed to take certain drugs. She might have smoked, consumed alcohol, or gotten too little sleep. She might have "permitted" her health to be damaged by hard work, by unsafe employment conditions, by the lack of affordable medical care, by living near a source of industrial pollution, by a physically or mentally abusive partner, or in any number of other ways.

Are such supposed failures on the part of pregnant women potentially to be construed as child abuse or negligent homicide? If sentient fetuses are entitled to the same legal protections as infants, then it would seem so. The danger is not a merely theoretical one. Two years ago in San Diego, a woman whose son was born with brain damage and died several weeks later was charged with felony child neglect. It was said that she had been advised by her physician to avoid sex and illicit drugs, and to notify the hospital immediately if she noticed any bleeding. Instead, she had allegedly had sex with her husband, taken some inappropriate drug, and delayed getting to the hospital for what might have been several hours after the onset of bleeding.

In this case, the charges were eventually dismissed on the grounds that the child protection law invoked had not been intended to apply to cases of this kind. But the multiplication of such cases is inevitable if the strong legal protections accorded to infants are extended to sentient fetuses. A bill recently introduced in the Australian state of New South Wales would make women liable to criminal prosecution if they are found to have smoked during pregnancy, eaten unhealthful foods, or taken any other action which can be shown to have adversely affected the development of the fetus (*The Australian,* July 5, 1988, 5). Such an approach to the protection of fetuses authorizes the legal regulation of virtually every aspect of women's public and private lives, and thus is incompatible with even the most minimal right to autonomy. Moreover, such laws are apt to prove counterproductive, since the fear of prosecution may deter poor or otherwise vulnerable women from seeking needed medical care during pregnancy. I am not suggesting that women whose apparent negligence causes prenatal harm to their infants should always be immune from criticism. However, if we want to improve the health of infants we would do better to provide the services women need to protect their health, rather than seeking to use the law to punish those whose prenatal care has been less than ideal.

There is yet another problem, which may prove temporary but which remains significant at this time. The extension of legal personhood to sentient fetuses would rule out most abortions performed because of severe fetal abnormalities, such as Down's Syndrome or spina bifida. Abortions performed following amniocentesis are usually done in the latter part of the second trimester, since it is usually not possible to obtain test results earlier. Methods of detecting fetal abnormalities at earlier stages, such as chorion biopsy, may eventually make late abortion for reasons of fetal abnormality unnecessary; but at present the safety of these methods is unproven.

The elimination of most such abortions might be a consequence that could be accepted, were the society willing to provide adequate support for the handicapped children and adults who would come into being as a result of this policy. However, our society is not prepared to do this. In the absence of adequate communally-funded care for the handicapped, the prohibition of such abortions is exploitative of women. Of course, the male relatives of severely handicapped persons may also bear heavy burdens. Yet the heaviest portion of the daily responsibility generally falls upon mothers and other female relatives. If fetuses are not yet persons (and women are), then a respect for the equality of persons should lead to support for the availability of abortion in cases of severe fetal abnormality.[10]

Such arguments will not persuade those who deeply believe that fetuses are already persons, with equal moral rights. How, they will ask, is denying legal equality to sentient fetuses different from denying it to any other powerless group of human beings? If some human beings are more equal than others, then how can any of us feel safe? The answer is twofold.

First, pregnancy is a relationship different from any other, including that between parents and already-born children. It is not just one of innumerable situations in which the rights of one individual may come into conflict with those of another; it is probably the *only* case in which the legal personhood of one human being is necessarily incompatible with that of another. Only in pregnancy is the organic functioning of one human individual biologically inseparable from that of another. This organic unity makes it impossible for others to provide the fetus with medical care or any other presumed benefit, except by doing something to or for the woman. To try to "protect" the fetus other than through her cooperation and consent is effectively to nullify her right to autonomy, and potentially to expose her to violent physical assaults such as would not be legally condoned in any other type of case. The uniqueness of pregnancy helps to explain why the toleration of abortion does not lead to the disenfranchisement of other groups of human

beings, as opponents of abortion often claim. For biological as well as psychological reasons, "It is all but impossible to extrapolate from attitudes towards fetal life attitudes toward [other] existing human life" (D. Callahan 1970, 474).

But, granting the uniqueness of pregnancy, why is it *women's* rights that should be privileged? If women and fetuses cannot both be legal persons then why not favor fetuses, e.g., on the grounds that they are more helpless, or more innocent, or have a longer life expectancy? It is difficult to justify this apparent bias towards women without appealing to the empirical fact that women are already persons in the usual, nonlegal sense—already thinking, self-aware, fully social beings—and fetuses are not. Regardless of whether we stress the intrinsic properties of persons, or the social and relational dimensions of personhood, this distinction remains. Even sentient fetuses do not yet have either the cognitive capacities or the richly interactive social involvements typical of persons.

This "not yet" is morally decisive. It is wrong to treat persons as if they do not have equal basic rights. Other things being equal, it is worse to deprive persons of their most basic moral and legal rights than to refrain from extending such rights to beings that are not persons. This is one important element of truth in the self-awareness criterion. If fetuses were already thinking, self-aware, socially responsive members of communities, then nothing could justify refusing them the equal protection of the law. In that case, we would sometimes be forced to balance the rights of the fetus against those of the woman, and sometimes the scales might be almost equally weighted. However, if women are persons and fetuses are not, then the balance must swing towards women's rights.

CONCLUSION

Birth is morally significant because it marks the end of one relationship and the beginning of others. It marks the end of pregnancy, a relationship so intimate that it is impossible to extend the equal protection of the law to fetuses without severely infringing women's most basic rights. Birth also marks the beginning of the infant's existence as a socially responsive member of a human community. Although the infant is not instantly transformed into a person at the moment of birth, it does become a biologically separate human being. As such, it can be known and cared for as a particular individual. It can also be vigorously protected without negating the basic rights of women. There are circumstances in which infanticide may be the best of a bad set of options. But our own society has both the ability and the desire to protect infants, and there is no reason why we should not do so.

We should not, however, seek to extend the same degree of protection to fetuses. Both late-term fetuses and newborn infants are probably capable of sentience. Both are precious to those who want children; and both need to be protected from a variety of possible harms. All of these factors contribute to the moral standing of the late-term fetus, which is substantial. However, to extend equal legal rights to fetuses is necessarily to deprive pregnant women of the rights to personal autonomy, physical integrity, and sometimes life itself. *There is room for only one person with full and equal rights inside a single human skin.* That is why it is birth, rather than sentience, viability, or some other prenatal milestone that must mark the beginning of legal parenthood.[11]

NOTES

1. Basic moral rights are those that are possessed equally by all persons, and that are essential to the moral equality of persons. The intended contrast is to those rights which arise from certain special circumstances—for instance, the right of a person to whom a promise has been made that that promise be kept. (Whether there are beings that are not persons but that have similar basic moral rights is one of the questions to be addressed here.)
2. "Moral standing," like "moral status," is a term that can be used to refer to the moral considerability of individuals, without being committed to the existence of moral rights. For instance,

Sumner (1983) and Singer (1981) prefer these terms because, as utilitarians, they are unconvinced of the need for moral rights.
3. It is not obvious that a newborn infant's "level of consciousness" is similar to that of a fetus shortly before birth. Perhaps birth is analogous to an awakening, in that the infant has many experiences that were previously precluded by its prenatal brain chemistry or by its relative insulation within the womb. This speculation is plausible in evolutionary terms, since a rich subjective mental life might have little survival value for the fetus, but might be highly valuable for the newborn, e.g., in enabling it to recognize its mother and signal its hunger, discomfort, etc. However, for the sake of the argument I will assume that the newborn's capacity for sentience is generally not very different from that of the fetus shortly before birth.
4. It is interesting that Sumner regards fetal abnormality and the protection of the woman's health as sufficient justifications for late abortion. In this, he evidently departs from his own theory by effectively differentiating between the moral status of sentient fetuses and that of older humans—who presumably may not be killed just because they are abnormal or because their existence (through no fault of their own) poses a threat to someone else's health.
5. There are evidently some people who, though otherwise sentient, cannot experience physical pain. However, the survival value of the capacity to experience pain makes it probable that such individuals are the exception rather than the rule among mature members of sentient species.
6. There is at least one religion, that of the Jains, in which the killing of any living thing—even an insect—is regarded as morally wrong. But even the Jains do not regard the killing of insects as morally equivalent to the killing of persons. Laypersons (unlike mendicants) are permitted some unintentional killing of insects—though not of vertebrate animals or persons—when this is unavoidable to the pursuit of their profession. (See Jaini 1979, 171–3.)
7. Marcia Guttentag and Paul Secord (1983) argue that a shortage of women benefits at least some women, by increasing their "value" in the marriage market. However, they also argue that this increased value does not lead to greater

freedom for women; on the contrary, it tends to coincide with an exceptionally severe sexual double standard, the exclusion of women from public life, and their confinement to domestic roles.

8. The extension of equal basic rights to infants need not imply the absolute rejection of euthanasia for infant patients. There are instances in which artificially extending the life of a severely compromised infant is contrary to the infant's own best interests. Competent adults or older children who are terminally ill sometimes rightly judge that further prolongation of their lives would not be a benefit to them. While infants cannot make that judgment for themselves, it is sometimes the right judgment for others to make on their behalf.

9. See *Civil Liberties* 363 (Winter 1988), 12, and Lawrence Lader, "Regulating Birth: Is the State Going Too Far?" *Conscience* IX: 5 (September/October, 1988), 5–6.

10. It is sometimes argued that using abortion to prevent the birth of severely handicapped infants will inevitably lead to a loss of concern for handicapped persons. I doubt that this is true. There is no need to confuse the question of whether it is good that persons be born handicapped with the very different question of whether handicapped persons are entitled to respect, support, and care.

11. My thanks to Helen Heise, Helen B. Holmes, Laura M. Purdy, Dianne Romaine, Peter Singer, and Michael Scriven for their helpful comments on earlier versions of this paper.

REFERENCES

Annas, George. 1982. Forced cesareans: The Most Unkindest Cut. *Hastings Center Report,* June 12: 3.

The Australian, Tuesday, July 5, 1988, 5.

Callahan, Daniel. 1970. *Abortion: Law, Choice and Morality.* New York: Macmillan.

Callahan, Sydney. 1984. Value Choices in Abortion. In *Abortion: Understanding Differences.* Sydney Callahan and Daniel Callahan, eds. New York and London: Plenum Press.

Callahan, Sydney. 1986. Abortion and the Sexual Agenda. *Commonweal,* April 25, 232–238.

Gilligan, Carol. 1982. *In a Different Voice: Psychological Theory and Women's Development.* Cambridge, Massachusetts: Harvard University Press.

Guttentag, Marcia, and Paul Secord. 1983. *Too Many Women: The Sex Ratio Question.* Beverly Hills: Sage Publications.

Harrison, Beverly Wildung. 1983. *Our Right to Choose: Toward a New Ethic of Abortion.* Boston: Beacon Press.

Jaini, Padmanab S. 1979. *The Jaina Path of Purification.* Berkeley, Los Angeles, London: University of California Press.

Lomansky, Loren. 1984. Being a Person—does it Matter? In *The Problem of Abortion.* Joel Feinberg, ed. Belmont, California.

Luker, Kristen. 1984. *Abortion and the Politics of Motherhood.* Berkeley, Los Angeles and London: University of California Press.

Manning, Rita. 1988. *Caring For and Caring About.* Paper presented at conference entitled *Explorations in Feminist Ethics,* Duluth, Minnesota. October 8.

Mead, Margaret. [1935] 1963. *Sex and Temperament in Three Primitive Societies.* New York: Morrow Quill Paperbacks.

Noddings, Nell. 1984. *Caring: A Feminine. Approach to Ethics and Moral Education.* Berkeley, Los Angeles and London: University of California Press.

Petchesky, Rosalind Pollack. 1984. *Abortion and Women's Choice.* New York, London: Longman.

Piers, Maria W. 1978. *Infanticide.* New York: W. W. Norton and Company.

Singer, Peter. 1981. *The Expanding Circle: Ethics and Sociobiology.* New York: Farrar, Straus and Giroux.

Stone, Christopher. 1974. *Should Trees Have Standing: Towards Legal Rights for Natural Objects.* Los Altos: William Kaufman.

Stone, Christopher. 1987. *Earth and Other Ethics.* New York: Harper & Row.

Sumner, L. W. 1983. *Abortion and Moral Theory.* Princeton, New Jersey: Princeton University Press.

Taylor, Paul W. 1986. *Respect for Nature: A Theory of Environmental Ethics.* Princeton, New Jersey: Princeton University Press.

Thomson, Judith Jarvis. 1971. A Defense of Abortion. *Philosophy and Public Affairs* 1(1): 47–66.

Tooley, Michael. 1983. *Abortion and Infanticide.* Oxford: Oxford University Press.

Wolgast, Elizabeth. 1987. *The Grammar of Justice.* Ithaca & London: Cornell University Press.

A PHENOMENOLOGY OF FEAR: THE THREAT OF RAPE AND FEMININE BODILY COMPORTMENT

Ann J. Cahill

The body of the embodied subject is not be understood as a purely natural blank slate on which social forces inscribe their values, meanings, and narratives. Nevertheless, individual bodies develop their habits, tendencies, desires, and particularities in the context of a social immersion. Given that rape is a pervasive social phenomenon that affects all women, individual experiences of rape are imposed on an embodied subject who has already been influenced by that social phenomenon. We need to explore the significance rape has in forming the body, and specifically the feminine body, itself. As ensuing analysis will demonstrate, the threat of rape is a formative movement in the construction of the distinctly feminine body, such that even bodies of women who have not been raped are likely to carry themselves in such a way as to express the truths and values of a rape culture.

During a 1977 roundtable discussion concerning, among other matters, his work that was later published in English as *Discipline and Punish* (1979), Michel Foucault commented on the problem of rape. His analysis was inspired by questions posed to him by a French commission concerned with the reform of the penal code:

> One can always produce the theoretical discourse that amounts to saying: in any case, sexuality can in no circumstances be the object of punishment. And when one punishes rape one should be punishing physical violence and nothing but that. And to say that it is nothing more than an act of aggression: that there is no difference, in principle, between sticking one's fist into someone's face or one's penis into their sex. . . . [T]here are problems [if we are to say that rape is more serious than a punch

in the face], because what we're saying amounts to this: sexuality as such, in the body, has a preponderant place, the sexual organ isn't like a hand, hair, or a nose. It therefore has to be protected, surrounded, invested in any case with legislation that isn't that pertaining to the rest of the body. . . . It isn't a matter of sexuality, it's the physical violence that would be punished, without bringing in the fact that sexuality was involved. (1988, 200–202)

At first glance, it would appear that Foucault's suggestion was remarkably in keeping with the current feminist wisdom, which sought to define rape solely as a violent crime. It is perhaps surprising, then, that both the women who were present at the discussion and subsequent feminist thinkers responded vehemently, and negatively, to his position. Yet the philosophical motivation behind Foucault's support of the desexualization of the crime of rape (and its legal redefinition as merely an example of assault) is significantly different from the impetus behind Brownmiller's (admittedly incomplete) solution of a "gender-free, non–activity-specific" law (Brownmiller 1975, 378). Whereas feminist thinkers were seeking to purge rape of its sexual content in order to render moot the legal question of victim (i.e., female) culpability, Foucault viewed the desexualization of rape as a liberating blow against the disciplining discourse that constructed sexuality as a means of social and political power.

Despite this difference in motivation, one could still expect Foucault's position to be largely in agreement with feminist theories that also located sexuality as one means by which a patriarchal culture maintained control over women. Judging by the response of various feminist theorists to his assertions, however, this was not the case. It is important to note at this juncture that Foucault's comments were relatively spontaneous and not fully developed; nevertheless, they at least appear to be generally consistent with his larger concern with the separation of sexuality from disciplinary power, and therefore cannot be dismissed out of hand. The challenge represented by his remarks was immediately taken up by Monique

Plaza (1981), and later most directly by Winifred Woodhull (1988) and Vikki Bell (1991), although several other feminist works on Foucault (including Martin [1988]) have mentioned the problem in passing. Most recently, Laura Hengehold (1994) has attempted a new analysis by locating the crime of rape in the overall system of hysterization of women that Foucault himself posited. While her argument succeeds in doing just that, it and other feminist theories seem unable to answer the question posed by Foucault: why should an assault with a penis be distinguished legally from an assault with any other body part?

Even this particular posing of this question leads us to a distinction that will prove crucial to the following discussion. Foucault here is considering rape as something done by a penis, that is, accomplished by a distinctly male and masculinized body. Because Foucault's implied definition is centered around the male physiology, it does not include a consideration of the multiple ways a woman can be violated sexually (see Tong 1984, 92–94). To redefine rape not as something a man does, but something a woman experiences shifts the conversation in important ways. This provisional redefining of the act of rape also has its problems, for women are not the only beings who can be raped. Yet while men are capable of being raped, they are not subjected to the pervasive threat of rape that faces women in the present culture. Nor are they raped at the horrifying (if controversial) numbers that women are. The fact that men can be, but are not often, raped emphasizes the extent to which rape enforces a systematic (i.e., consistent, although not necessarily conscious), sexualized control of women. Thus Monique Plaza writes:

Rape is an oppressive act exercised by a (social) man against a (social) woman, which can be carried out by the introduction of a bottle held by a man into the anus of a woman; in this case rape is not sexual, or rather it is not genital. It is very sexual in the sense that it is frequently a sexual activity, but above all in the sense that it opposes men and women: it is social

sexing which underlies rape. (1981, 29; emphasis in the original)

Extending Plaza's logic to the phenomenon of male-on-male rape emphasizes the implicit womanizing that occurs on the victim, who is placed in the role of the sexually submissive and helpless. He is, at that moment, a "social woman."

To return to the question as formulated by Foucault: how is an assault with a penis different from an assault with a fist? The answer to this question, I will argue, is dependent not only on the bodily phenomenon of rape, as Foucault seems to assume, but also on the social production of the feminine body. Winifred Woodhull points to this necessity when she claims, "If we are seriously to come to terms with rape, we must explain how the vagina becomes coded—and experienced—as a place of emptiness and vulnerability, the penis as a weapon, and intercourse as violation, rather than naturalize these processes through references to 'basic' physiology" (1988, 171).

However, Woodhull here has neglected to consider seriously enough Foucault's concern with the construction of the particularly sexual body, a historical process he documents in his first volume of *The History of Sexuality* (1990). In that work, as well as its sequels, Foucault details the various ways sexuality has been constructed in the context of other overarching social demands, particularly the demand for self-mastery. The centrality of sexual identity to the subject was a means of the exercise of power:

[Sex] was at the pivot of the two axes along which developed the entire political technology of life. On the one hand it was tied to the disciplines of the body: the harnessing, intensification, and distribution of forces, the adjustment and economy of energies. On the other hand, it was applied to the regulation of populations, through all the far-reaching effects of its activity. It fitted in both categories at once, giving rise to infinitesimal surveillances, permanent controls, extremely meticulous orderings of space, indeterminate medical or psychological examinations, to an entire micro-power concerned with the body. (1990, 145–46)

Because the construction of the sexual body, whose sexuality was grounded strictly in the genitals, was fundamental to the disciplines that formed both the body and the subject's place in society, Foucault locates one important possibility for resistance in a process of extricating sexuality both from its limited, genital definition and from direct, oppressive legislation. In *Power/Knowledge,* Foucault praises feminist movements for their attempt at desexualization:

> The real strength of the women's liberation movements is not that of having laid claim to the specificity of their sexuality and the rights pertaining to it, but that they have actually departed from the discourse conducted within the apparatuses of sexuality. . . . What has their outcome been? Ultimately, a veritable movement of de-sexualisation, a displacement effected in relation to the sexual centering of the problem, formulating the demand for forms of culture, discourse, language, and so on, which are no longer part of that rigid assignation and pinning-down to their sex which they had initially in some sense been politically obliged to accept in order to make themselves heard. (1980, 219–20)

Foucault questions the definition of rape as sexual because such a definition retains sexuality as an appropriate target and expression of disciplinary power. Resistance to that disciplinary power demands a desexualisation of rape, just as feminist movements have resisted the "sexual centering of the problem." Moreover, Foucault infers from the sexual definition of rape a continuation of the privileging of the genitals with regard to sexuality, a privileging that supports the "naturalness" of the sexual body and therefore serves to veil the intricate relation of sexuality and power. Foucault suggests the desexualization of rape on the basis of an analysis of the social construction of the sexual body, a construction that privileges the genitals and sexuality in general as a primary seat of identity.

A critique of this conclusion must begin with a more detailed consideration of the Foucauldian analysis of the body. From there, I shall argue that the act of rape is distinct from other types of assault not solely because of the body parts involved in the act, but more importantly, because of the role rape—or, more precisely, the threat of rape—plays in the production of the specifically (and socially recognizable) feminine body. Moreover, I will assert that the legal reform suggested by Foucault—that is, the redefinition of rape as assault and the eradication of rape as a distinctly sexual crime—would serve to veil aspects of the crime that impinge directly on women's experience and bodies and that constitute the current phenomenon of rape itself in important ways.

THE BODY FOR FOUCAULT

Perhaps one of the most well-known aspects of Foucault's work is his compelling analysis of power.[1] Refusing the traditional description of power as primarily repressive and imposed solely from a position of authority, Foucault claims instead that power actually produces social bodies and realities, and does not emanate from one central source, but rather is diffused throughout the social structure:

> [P]ower would be a fragile thing if its only function were to repress, if it worked only through the mode of censorship, exclusion, blockage and repression, in the manner of a great Superego, exercising itself only in a negative way. If, on the contrary, power is strong this is because, as we are beginning to realize, it produces effects at the level of desire—and also at the level of knowledge. Far from preventing knowledge, power produces it. If it has been possible to constitute a knowledge of the body, this has been by way of an ensemble of military and educational disciplines. It was on the basis of power over the body that a physiological, organic knowledge of it became possible. (1980, 59)

For Foucault, the structures and dynamics of power actually create the possibilities of various social discourses by constituting the subjects who will undertake them. In this model, what is significant is not merely, or perhaps even primarily, who has power over whom, but how power has produced the specific and characteristic moments of a discursive reality.

If power is not solely a punishing, authoritarian force that seeks to control the actions of subjects primarily by prohibiting certain ones, if instead it is a subtle, pervasive, creative force that seeks to influence actions on the level of desire and identity, then it is not surprising to find the body as its privileged site. Indeed, as Foucault claims, "[N]othing is more material, physical, corporal than the exercise of power" (1980, 57–58). The body, far from being in any sense natural or primary, is the location of the inscription of power discourses. Specifically, Foucault is concerned with the power dynamics that construct the body as sexual:

> What I want to show is how power relations can materially penetrate the body in depth, without depending even on the mediation of the subject's own representations. If power takes hold on the body, this isn't through its having first to be interiorised in people's consciousness. There is a network or circuit of bio-power, or somato-power, which acts as the formative matrix of sexuality itself as the historical and cultural phenomenon within which we seem at once to recognise and lose ourselves. (1980, 186)

As a theoretical moment in Foucault's analysis of power, the body and its corresponding abilities, desires, and habits are the results of the inscription of power dynamics that renders knowledge as well as agency possible. Through this inscription, individual bodies are produced with certain powers, capabilities, and expectations. As Jana Sawicki describes it, "Disciplinary power is exercised on the body and soul of individuals. It increases the power of individuals at the same time as it renders them more docile (for instance, basic training in the military)" (1991, 22). Any limitations imposed on the body are always concomitant with certain, delimited powers, but both the limitations and the endowed capabilities are directly related to and supportive of the overall power dynamic.

Moreover, the sexuality of the body is central to its construction and to its vulnerability to discursive power. Because power is not ultimately or merely repressive, but also productive, sexuality

cannot be understood as an innocent, underlying set of desires, dynamics, and practices that various power structures attempt to suppress or deny. Rather, sexuality is produced as a moment within a network of power itself.

> But I said to myself, basically, couldn't it be that sex—which seems to be an instance having its own laws and constraints, on the basis of which the masculine and feminine sexes are defined—be something which on the contrary is *produced* by the apparatus of sexuality? What the discourse of sexuality was initially applied to wasn't sex but the body, the sexual organs, pleasures, kinship relations, interpersonal relations, and so forth. (Foucault 1980, 210)

Foucault's *History of Sexuality* in its entirety is a historical exploration of sexuality in relation to other workings of power, for example, in the construction of the self that is capable of self-mastery. However, given that the diffuse, decentralized, productive power Foucault describes is particularly bodily (one of its salient characteristics is its ability to produce bodies of particular types, with particular abilities), sexuality is not just another site of discursive power, but a particularly trenchant one. "I believe that the political significance of the problem of sex is due to the fact that sex is located at the point of intersection of the discipline of the body and the control of the population" (1980, 125). Not only is sexuality not a force outside the realm of power that calls for its own liberation from oppressive forces, but in fact, precisely because of its bodily significance and grounding, it is a major site for the expression and production of power itself. Resisting the norms that are imposed through and by power dynamics does not demand sexual liberation, but a decentering of the significance of sexuality with regard to pleasure and subjectivity:

> [I]n the West this systematisation of pleasure according to the "laws" of sex gave rise to the whole apparatus of sexuality. And it is this that makes us believe that we are "liberating" ourselves when we "decode" all pleasure in terms of a sex shorn at last

of disguise, whereas one should aim instead at a desexualisation, at a general economy of pleasure not based on sexual norms. (1980, 191)

The possibility of such a desexualization leads us to the question of resistance with regard to Foucault's theory of power. To a certain extent, the concept that power is not only repressive but productive implies that the produced or constructed (sexual) body of the subject is entirely reducible to the purposes and values of that particular network of power. However, that the body is the result of power dynamics does not necessarily imply that the body is wholly or predictably determined. Even as Foucault terms the body "docile," referring to its status as reflection or projection of the dominant discourse, he insists that the body as constructed is not incapable of resisting or defying some (if not all) of the demands of that discourse. Because power is diffuse and lacking a single source as well as a single object, its effects are scattered and uneven with regard to individual bodies, even as its predominant claims may be coherent and consistent. For Foucault, resistance is the necessary counterpart to power, for while power produces bodies as subjects with certain and different capabilities, it cannot always control the ways those abilities are utilized. As pervasive as the play of power is, its control is not omnipotent. Excess persists.

> [T]here is always something in the social body, in classes, groups and individuals themselves which in some sense escapes relations of power, something which is by no means a more or less docile or reactive primal matter, but rather a centrifugal removement, an inverse energy, a discharge. . . . This measure . . . is not so much what stands outside relations of power as their limit, their underside, their counter-stroke, that which responds to every advance of power by a movement of disengagement. (1980, 138)

The fact that the body is socially constructed by the play of power does not necessitate its own powerlessness. Rather, its ability to resist certain expressions of power is itself related to the nature of power. Concomitantly, just as the power that Foucault describes is not omnipotent, the resistance that is possible is not limitless. No embodied subject is capable of resisting any and all expressions of power, for the simple reason that to do so would be to undermine that subject's ability to act at all.

The meanings and codings of the body differ radically in various historical and social situations, and indeed, Foucault's point is that the sole commonly held characteristic or property of bodies of varying environments is that of effecthood. The only stable point about the body is its relationship to power; in all other matters, it is necessarily in flux, subject to change, lacking any ontological status (see McWhorter 1989).[2] Yet liberation *of a sort* is certainly possible. At any given moment, certain aspects of the dominant discourse are vulnerable, and subjects are capable of questioning and undermining them. With regard to real, live bodies themselves, and the disciplinary power that shapes them and their possibilities, the only hope of so-called liberation lies in our ability to see them precisely as a site of this inscription and production of power dynamics—as long as we understand their inscribed status as not utterly determinative. An analysis of these dynamics can serve to loosen certain aspects of the discourses of power imposed upon actual bodily persons.

To complain that such bodies would then be reinscribed with different discourses is to forget Foucault's analysis of power, which insists that power involves not only oppression, but also production. If to "liberate" bodies is to render them wholly independent from the various discourses that exist in the particular historical and cultural context, then indeed such a goal is, within the context of Foucault's project, impossible. There is no purely "natural" or "free" body to reclaim. If, however, one seeks to liberate individual bodies from particular moments of the relevant dominant discourses, then precisely this type of analysis is necessary. To recognize that virtually no aspect of bodies can be described in terms of universally true, objective discourses (for example, the scientific discourse), that is, to recognize them as *fundamentally* nonnatural, does not weaken familiar feminist insights concerning various cultural and bodily methods of expressing and enforcing women's inferiority. It is rather to say that the effects of power do not stop at such blatant practices as corseting, foot binding, clitoridectomies, and forced sterilization, but that these are only the most obvious results of a discourse whose influence is far deeper and more subtle than originally thought. Whereas some early feminist thought relied on the objective and ostensibly value-free realm of the "natural" to serve as a contrast to the artificial aspects of femininity (Wollstonecraft [1792] 1983 is a prime example), Foucault's model allows no such easy opposition. In fact, it allows no totality of any sort, so that while resistance is possible (that is, while subjects can express and effect their objections to certain aspects of the dominant discourse, and can even eradicate some), *total* resistance, that is, a wholesale resistance to the power structure *as such,* is not. Because the body is always already implicated in the play of power, because the inscription of power occurs at the moment at which the body enters culture, the body never exists as a *tabula rasa.* For Foucault, the body only and always exists as a social and cultural entity.

If, as Foucault claims, individual bodies are produced with certain identifiable characteristics that relate directly to power dynamics, then bodies are texts that we may read in order to discern the (sometimes implicit) claims of the dominant discourse. Given the admittedly complex but always central role of the body in the political oppression of women, the feminine body is a particularly crucial text. Indeed, much feminist scholarship has been devoted to reading the details of the feminine body for precisely such purposes. The specifics of the feminine body, particularly feminine bodily comportment, reflect the power relations that have produced them and the myriad ways this production is accomplished.

A closer look at the behavior and habits of bodies typically described and recognized as feminine is therefore warranted. The work of two feminist theorists is invaluable here: Iris Marion Young's "Throwing Like a Girl" (1990) and Sandra Lee Bartky's "Foucault, Femininity, and the Modernization of Patriarchal Power" (1988).[3]

THE FEMININE BODY

Describing "the" feminine body in a distinctly phenomenological sense presents, of course, a host of difficulties. Strictly speaking, there is no one feminine body, no single incarnation that fulfills perfectly the ideal set up for it. Moreover, it would appear doubtful that even within the confines of a particular culture and a particular historical period, there is one static ideal of the feminine body. Femininity has never been that simple. Certainly in current times, the ideal is somewhat of a moving target, whereby women are at once exhorted to be thin but muscular, slender but buxom, fit but not overly strong. Definitions of "feminine" behavior, appearance, and character vary widely among classes and ethnicities, and gender is only one means by which bodies are constructed and categorized. Finally, each individual woman is affected differently by the demands of femininity. While a largely consistent definition of the elements of that femininity may be possible, there will always be individual women (and perhaps groups of women) for whom such definitions will not hold. Given these multiple and varied factors, phenomenological attempts to discern that which is feminine can run the risk of ignoring other factors in the construction of the feminine body, thus implicitly holding up one ideal of femininity to the exclusion of all others. Iris Marion Young defends against just this kind of criticism when she writes,

> I take "femininity" to designate not a mysterious quality or essence that all women have by virtue of their being biologically female. It is, rather, a set of structures and conditions that delimit the typical *situation* of being a woman in a particular society,

as well as the typical way in which this situation is lived by the women themselves. Defined as such, it is not necessary that *any* women be "feminine"—that is, it is not necessary that there be distinctive structures and behavior typical of the situation of women. This understanding of "feminine" existence makes it possible to say that some women escape or transcend the typical situation and definition of women in various degrees and respects. I mention this primarily to indicate that the account offered here of the modalities of feminine bodily existence is not to be falsified by referring to some individual women to whom aspects of the account do not apply, or even to some individual men to whom they do. (1990, 143–44)

Young is answering only one part of the problem (namely, that however femininity is articulated, there will be individual women whose experiences are not included within the stated parameters), and insofar as her argument is so limited, I find it a useful one. However, she does not address the alleged singularity of the femininity that she then proceeds to describe. Her description of the feminine body is notoriously unraced, which suggests that there is only one standard of femininity, which, however complex and contradictory, nevertheless provides a continuum upon which most, if not all, women can be placed. It may be argued that, to the contrary, there are many different standards of femininity that are particular to economic classes or ethnic groups, and that to assume that there is only one once again reinscribes the dominance of the European American in contemporary U.S. society by claiming that the experiences of that group are the parameters that "delineate the typical" (Huggins 1991; hooks 1981; Spelman 1988).

While I am sympathetic to such criticisms of Young's work—criticisms to which, it seems to me, most if not all phenomenological analyses are vulnerable—I do not consider them ultimately fatal. The femininity which Young (and Bartky too, for that matter) describes is a distinctly white one, and it should be delimited as such. However, in the context of a racist political

structure, the construction of white femininity was, and in many ways still is, the construction of the ideal femininity. White femininity has held a privileged place in the construction of gender, and as such holds significance not only for those women it includes, but also for those whom it excludes. The significances, obviously, differ, and it is these differences that the theories of Young, at least those concerning typical feminine bodily comportment, are incapable of approaching. But it is precisely the dominance of a white femininity that has often served to define women of certain ethnicities or classes out of their femininity (and thus, importantly, out of their humanity); Barbara Smith notes that "when you read about Black women being lynched, they aren't thinking of us as females. The horrors that we have experienced have absolutely everything to do with them *not even viewing us as women*" (Smith quoted in Spelman 1988, 37). African American women have certainly not, historically, been accorded the chivalrous courtesy allegedly commanded by those of the fairer sex—hence the paradoxical and unanswerable question traditionally attributed to Sojourner Truth. Insofar as the particularities of the dominant white femininity have been utilized to construct women of color as not "really" women, they have constituted the standard of femininity itself and are significant (although in different ways) to women of all races.

That being said, any analysis that takes as its basis the racially limited work of Young will inevitably be similarly limited. While the ensuing discussion will concern itself with the construction of the typically or socially recognizable feminine body, it is important to keep in mind that this body is also, simultaneously, raced. Moreover, the raced quality of the recognizably feminine body has particular import for the matter of rape, in that women of color who do not exemplify the ideals of white femininity (passivity, submission, etc.) may have their status as "victim" doubted even more strenuously than white victims. It is quite possible, even likely, that the conclusions reached in this essay apply not to women in general, but to a racially specific and dominant subset of women, a limitation that demonstrates the need for phenomenological analyses of feminine ways of being that are excluded by the distinctly white standards.

In her essay, Young is primarily concerned with the limited scope of feminine motility. Although she focuses her analysis on goal-oriented actions and therefore claims to avoid "sexual being" (1990, 143), her conclusions shed considerable light on the bodily fear that constricts the sphere of feminine physical experience. One of her central claims is that the feminine body is treated by the woman as an object, a thing that exists separate from (and often opposed to) the aims of the woman as subject. "[T]he modalities of feminine bodily existence have their root in the fact that feminine existence experiences the body as a mere thing—a fragile thing, which must be picked up and coaxed into movement, a thing that exists as *looked at and acted upon*" (Young 1990, 150; emphasis in the original). The woman experiences her body as an alien, unwieldy, weak object that, depending on the particular goal, needs either massive transformation or kid-glove treatment. As it stands, it seems, a woman's body is good for very little.

To experience the body as itself *essentially* weak is to necessitate placing it under constant surveillance. Dangers are rife, and the woman attempts to protect her appallingly vulnerable body by restricting its spatial scope. Limiting the area into which the body extends is a means of reducing possible risks, and thus "the space . . . that is *physically* available to the feminine body is frequently of greater radius than the space that she uses and inhabits" (1990, 151). Similarly, given the assumed fragility of the female bones, muscles, and tissues, the girl learns to throw not with her whole arm (an action that demands, after all, faith), but rather with a mere portion of it. Feminine bodily comportment is marked by an odd economy, where any given action is undertaken not by the entirety of physical capabilities that

could be gathered, but rather only with the necessary minimum. "Women often do not perceive themselves as capable of lifting and carrying heavy things. . . . We frequently fail to summon the full possibilities of our muscular coordination, position, poise and bearing" (145).

Young emphasizes that this disciplining of the female body is not merely prohibitive, but also linked to the acquiring of positive habits and capacities (1990, 154). By constituting one's body as essentially and irrevocably weak and vulnerable, the person becomes a card-carrying woman, with all the rights and responsibilities assigned thereto. Her position in the larger society is established securely (although perhaps not as securely as may appear at first glance, for femininity, and masculinity too for that matter, demands constant maintenance). "The more a girl assumes her status as feminine, the more she takes herself to be fragile and immobile and the more she actively enacts her own body inhibition" (154).

Unlike Young, Bartky is working explicitly out of a Foucauldian analysis of the body, although she decries his failure, in *Discipline and Punish* (1979), to account sufficiently for the implications of sexual difference (Bartky 1988, 63). She attempts to answer this omission by examining "those disciplinary practices that produce a body which in gesture and appearance is recognizably feminine" (64). In her analysis of the social practices of dieting, exercise, and makeup, she reveals a systematic and simultaneous vilification and disempowering of the female body. In the case of makeup, the impetus to transform one's body into something beautiful by means of cosmetic force transforms the body into a hostile entity, constantly threatening to revert to its natural, that is to say, unbeautiful, state, and in so doing manifesting itself to be directly oppositional to the wishes of the woman. Note that while the *ideal* feminine body may be believed to be "naturally" beautiful, *individual* female bodies are subjected to a host of intrusive, expensive, and high-maintenance practices in order to be rendered beautiful. Left on its own, the female face is plain, common, unremarkable (and, perhaps worst of all, subject to the process of aging). In order to be femininely beautiful, it needs paint, if not surgery. The war against unwanted weight is an even more confrontational phenomenon. One's appetites and desires must be carefully guarded against, lest unwanted pounds find their way onto the hard-won slender frame. The body is constituted again, perhaps even more insidiously, as that which the woman needs to struggle against, to control, to whip into shape, in an effort to counteract its inherent tendencies to lapse into an unattractive appearance.

Bartky remarks that one crucial aspect of the ideal feminine body that inspires these social practices is precisely its unrealizability. Constant and inevitable failure is necessary to the perpetuation of the ideal. The power of the cosmetic, diet, and exercise industries lies precisely in their ability to promise beauty while always defining the horizon as just beyond reach. If the ideal were actually within the grasp of individual women, innovative techniques would be rendered unnecessary. The beautiful woman is never finished, but is constantly adapting to changing and sometimes contradictory definitions of attractiveness. Not only, in Simone de Beauvoir's (1974) famous formulation, does one become a woman, but one is *always* in a state of becoming.

One interesting point about this process of creating the beautifully feminine self that Bartky doesn't address directly is its significantly individualistic nature. Despite the fact that the project of beautification provides women with all-women or mostly-women spaces within which to achieve their goal (one thinks immediately of the intimacy of the beauty salon), the pervasive sense of having failed to achieve the desired image is relentlessly personalized. Even as women commiserate about the difficulty of weight loss, for example, each individual woman is more likely to recognize her own particular lack of thinness while assuring her friends that they are really quite all right. Not only is the woman's body vilified for failing to live up to the desired image (both

of society and of the individual woman), but that failure is experienced as unique to that particular body. As long as the failure is personalized, as long as the enemy is *this particular body* with its particular faults, stubbornness, or weakness, the culture-wide "disciplinary project of femininity" that is at work is successfully concealed (Bartky 1988, 71). Yet if the body is the site of the failure to beautify, of alienation and hostility, it can also be experienced as the site for success, mutual admiration, and creativity. The creation of the beautiful feminine appearance has its poignant and self-affirming moments, and the process of getting "dressed up," especially if it is a communal, girls- or women-only undertaking, can be intensely pleasurable. In this case, the project of creating feminine beauty exists briefly as an artistic challenge, and it is the process of doing, rather than the result of being seen, that is momentarily emphasized.[4]

If the feminine body is constituted and experienced as the enemy of the womanly subject—not a docile body in relation to power dynamics, but a hostile one in relation to the social desires of the woman—it is also a paradoxically weak one. Bartky describes the limitations of feminine motility as the results of bodily fear. The woman experiences her body not as a means by which to accomplish a variety of physical tasks, but rather as a barrier to those accomplishments. In a point that Young takes up in greater detail, Bartky claims that "woman's space is not a field in which her bodily intentionality can be freely realized but an enclosure in which she feels herself positioned and by which she is confined" (1988, 66). Here the body is not so much an enemy as an assumed hindrance, plagued by weakness, uncertainty, and fragility. Of course, these two aspects of Bartky's analysis—body as enemy and body as hindrance—find a common source in the ideal feminine image. "An aesthetic of femininity, for example, that mandates fragility and a lack of muscular strength produces female bodies that can offer little resistance to physical abuse, and the physical abuse of women by men, as we know, is widespread" (1988, 72). To approach success in the realm of beauty is to abandon a degree of physical strength, and it is the mutual exclusiveness between beauty and strength that increases the vulnerability of women's bodies. The ideal feminine image is, of course, constantly shifting, and in its metamorphoses we occasionally encounter an image that is more muscular than its predecessor. However, it is safe to say that while images of contemporary Western beauty at times invoke physical strength, it is never beautiful for a woman to be as strong as she possibly can. A male bodybuilder is the epitome of masculinity, a female bodybuilder at best a borderline woman and at worst (i.e., at her most muscular), a monstrosity.[5]

Both Young's and Bartky's analyses describe a feminine bodily comportment that is marked by fear: fear of bodily desires (so strong they threaten to undo all the subject's best efforts) and fear of harm (so likely that the subject constructs a small "safety zone" around the body). What is significant about these analyses is that they stress the degree to which the woman experiences her own individual body as culpable for producing all these dangers. It appears that the feminine body is not only essentially weak; but also somehow accountable for its own vulnerability.

The feminine body that Young and Bartky describe is that of a pre-victim. If it attempts something beyond its highly limited capacities, if it wanders beyond its safety zone, it—*by virtue of its own characteristics*—can expect to be hurt. The woman who experiences her body in this way does not locate the dangers presented to her body as originating from outside her body. Rather, they have as their source the fact and nature of her body itself. If that body is hurt or violated, the blame must rest on the woman's failure to sufficiently limit its movements.[6]

This typically (white) feminine experience of the body, while not universally or similarly applicable to every individual woman, is related to the constitution of the feminine body as that which is alien to the female subject. Considering the body

as a force or element somehow fundamentally separated from the wishes and desires of the female subject confirms its status as a source of impending danger. Likewise, perceiving the body as a liability positions it outside the female subjectivity in such a way at to endow it with a degree of ontological alienation. If the body is so distanced from the female subject, we may wonder whether that subject can be held at all responsible for the control of her charge. Who could hope to control this wild and weak mass of flesh? Yet insofar as it is able to be controlled at all, that responsibility rests squarely on the female subject. Only she can take that flesh, mold it in the image of the beautiful, and shelter it from the ramifications of its own countless failings. Even when a degree of the responsibility is abdicated to a man, still the (adult) woman bears the responsibility of finding a suitable protector. If control is lost and violence or harm ensues, she bears the blame.

Note too that this bodily alienation pits the female subject against her own body, such that her ability to be and move in the world is directly contingent on her successful control of that barbaric flesh. Women thus experience the "unbearable weight" (Bordo 1993) of their bodies, a weight that continually hampers their full and free inclusion in society.

RAPE AND FEMININE BODILY COMPORTMENT

The feminine habits and motility described by Bartky and Young clearly imply a constant state of danger for the feminine body, and indeed find the source of the danger within the feminine body itself. But what specific dangers do all the hard-won feminine habits seek to counteract? In refusing to call on the totality of physical abilities present in the feminine body, the woman attempts to reduce the risk of self-inflicted bodily harm. To throw with her whole arm may cause her slender muscles to snap; to run fast, hard, for an extended period of time may overtax her tender heart.

However, woman's limitation of the space within which her body can move seems to gesture not toward self-inflicted harm, but rather toward harm inflicted by other bodies. Within the invisible wall she throws up around her, a woman may consider herself safe; in this space, she has maximum control over her body. To go beyond that space is to enter an arena where her body is in danger of being violated.[7] This limited, individual safety zone, which determines the smallness of a woman's step, the gathering-in of her sitting body, and the daintiness of her gestures, mirrors in fact the larger hampering of her mobility. For a woman, the travellable world is a small place. Entire portions of each twenty-four-hour day are deemed unsafe, and unless accompanied by a man (or, alternatively, many women), a woman should spend these hours in the safety of her own home. Geographical areas that may be considered completely accessible to men are, for women, sites of possible (even likely) harassment, molestation, or rape.

What is important in this comparison is that where women are encouraged or mandated to restrict their movement for safety's sake, the danger described is not to the body *in general*. That danger is almost always specifically sexualized. The reason that men can travel where women ought not to is only that women can be and are raped (whereas men can be, but are not often), not that women can be and are mugged or beaten up (as in fact men can be, and are). For the male subject, the threat presented is one of destruction of the body, whereas for the female subject, the trenchant harm concerns her sexual being and freedom. Women's individual restrictions of their bodily movements reflect an attempt to deny unwanted sexual access. Paradoxically, this denial serves to highlight their persistent vulnerability.

> In an extraordinary series of over two thousand photographs, many candid shots taken in the street, the German photographer Marianne Wex has documented differences in typical masculine and feminine body posture. Women sit waiting for trains with arms close to the body, hands folded together in their laps, toes pointing straight ahead or turned inward, and legs pressed together. The women in these photographs make themselves small and narrow, harmless; they seem tense; they take up little space. Men, on the other hand, expand into the available space; they sit with legs far apart and arms flung out at some distance from the body. Most common in these sitting male figures is what Wex calls the "proffering position": the men sit with legs thrown wide apart, crotch visible, feet pointing outward, often with an arm and a casually dangling hand resting comfortably on an open, spread thigh. (Bartky 1988, 67)

The men's sex is expressed freely, almost defiantly, while the women cover theirs, for fear of its being stolen, violated, consumed. The women, conscious of the sexual dangers that surround them, attempt to make themselves even tinier, as if the safest status they could hold would be invisibility. Not only is this self-protection illusory, but it actually serves to reiterate women's vulnerability. It produces and presents women as pre-victims expecting to be victimized (not because men are rapists, but because women's bodies are rapable). Even more worrisome, this attempt at invisibility is in direct contradiction to the importance of beautification to the distinctly feminine body. We have here a strange situation indeed, where women spend inordinate amounts of time and money on creating an image designed to attract male desire, and then, on entering the public world, find it necessary to protect themselves from that desire. Attracting the male gaze is, in the context of a patriarchal society, necessary to achieve social status and worth, yet that attraction is in itself a trenchant threat.[8]

The hesitancy with which women enter the bodily world, the assumption of responsibility regarding the behavior of men, the locating of danger within the facticity of the feminine body: all these express the power dynamic that blames women for the sexual assaults inflicted upon them. That rape is experienced as a fate as frightening as death demonstrates the privileged role which the threat of sexual violence plays in the production of the feminine body (according to a study performed by Mark Warr [1984], most women in most age groups fear rape significantly more than they fear death; see also Gordon and Riger [1989]). If we claimed previously that the socially produced feminine body is that of a pre-victim, we may also claim that it is the body of the *guilty* pre-victim. In the specific moments and movements of this body are written the defense of the sexual offender: she was somewhere she should not have been, moving her body in ways she should not have, carrying on in a manner so free and easy as to convey an utter abdication of her responsibilities of self-protection and self-surveillance.

Returning to our Foucauldian analysis of the body, we are compelled to ask, What power relations are inscribed on this feminine body? To what purpose has it been created, and whom does it serve? In feminine gestures and bodily comportment, we see the effects of a power dynamic that holds women responsible for their own physical, sexual victimization. Insofar as the assaults considered most dangerous and most pervasive are precisely sexual assaults, we may also recognize the production of culpable feminine sexuality, which by its existence alone incites men, who remain allegedly powerless in the presence of its overwhelming temptation, to violence. Hence Lynne Henderson writes:

> [A] primary impediment to recognition that rape is a real and frequent crime is a widely accepted cultural "story" of heterosexuality that results in an unspoken "rule" of male innocence and female guilt in law. By "male innocence and female guilt", I mean an unexamined belief that men are not morally responsible for their heterosexual conduct, while females are morally responsible both for their conduct and for the conduct of males. (1992, 130–31)

The "story" to which Henderson refers is not only believed, not only implied, not only stated, it is in fact lived in the bodily habits of feminine subjects.

Let us be exact about this process. In acquiring the bodily habits that render the subject "feminine," habits that are inculcated at a young age and then constantly redefined and maintained, the woman learns to accept her body as dangerous, willful, fragile, and hostile. *It* constantly poses the possibility of threat, and only persistent vigilance can limit the risk at which it places the woman. The production of such a body reflects and supports a status quo that refuses, in the particular case of sexual assault, to consider the victim innocent until proven guilty; rather, the opposite is assumed.

The threat of rape, then, is a constitutive and sustained moment in the production of the distinctly feminine body. It is the pervasive danger that renders so much public space off-limits, a danger so omnipresent, in fact, that the "safety zone" women attempt to create rarely exceeds the limits of their own limbs and quite often falls far short of that radius. Women consider their flesh not only weak and breakable, but also violable. The truth inscribed on the woman's body is not that, biologically, all men are potential rapists. It is rather that, biologically, all women are potential rape victims. Note, too, that this bodily inscription may take place without the explicit articulation of the concept of "rape" or the actual experience of sexual assault. Girls especially may know that their bodies are inherently dangerous without being clear as to the precise nature of the danger they present. They may only sense that something very bad and very hurtful will befall them should their surveillance falter, and, correspondingly, that all sorts of social opportunities will be open to them should their project of femininity be successful.[9]

THE PROBLEM OF RESISTANCE

With the feminine body described as the expression of a distinct power discourse that includes at a fundamental level the threat of rape, the question of resistance again becomes pertinent. Foucault, it will be remembered, insisted on both the constitutive role of power and the necessarily concurrent force of resistance. With regard to rape, Foucault's suggestions seem to imply that a legal redefinition of the crime would constitute a major change in the discourse, thus helping to free women's bodies from the defining elements that produce them as pre-victims.

Yet in this suggestion Foucault has seemed to forget, or perhaps underestimate, the force of his analysis of power. A mere change in the legal definition of rape is not nearly sufficient to answer the constitutive and productive effects of this particular discourse. To believe that such a change would have the desired result is to accept the legal realm as a privileged source of power with determinative effects. It is obvious that the legal world is a source of political and social power, as well as a reflection and extension of the dominant discourses that Foucault describes. However, it is but one node in a complex matrix of relationships and institutions. It not only expresses dominant discourses, but is subject to them.

Here we see one significant result of the differing motivations behind the similar claims of Foucault and feminist theorists. In seeking primarily to liberate sexuality from a disciplinary discourse, and doing so in a way that, as many feminist criticisms have stated, does not sufficiently take into consideration the differing power positions related to sex and gender, Foucault suggests that the legal discourse refrain from passing judgment on the sexual content of the act of rape. In making that suggestion, Foucault remains focused on the sexual content of an act that a man performs. His primary concern, with regard to rape, is in protecting a certain aspect of male sexuality from the disciplinary force of the law. Were rape to be redefined as primarily a crime of assault, the *sexual* behavior and meanings inherent in the crime would be legally invisible.

A significant element of the woman victim's experience of rape is directly related to the constitutive element of a power discourse that produces her body as violable, weak, and alien to her subjectivity. From the rape victim's perspective, although not necessarily consciously (in fact,

precisely in a bodily way), these meanings too are part of the crime, insofar as that particular action is perceived as a threat fulfilled. To redefine the crime as primarily an assault would mask these meanings. Moreover, given the historical relationship of the law and women's bodies, it seems dubious (although not impossible) that the categories, language, and concepts found in the legal world could be effectively wielded to change significantly the character of the produced feminine body.

Foucault's suggested decriminalization of rape as a sexual crime underestimates the degree to which the bodies of rape *victims* (overwhelmingly feminine bodies) are themselves expressions of a given power discourse. It also fails to recognize that the act of rape itself, especially given its pervasive occurrence, is fundamental to the discourse that defines women as inferior and socially expendable. The real, live, living, breathing women who experience rape and the threat of rape on a daily basis, and whose bodily behavior and being are to a significant degree formed by the presence of the threat of rape, will not be liberated by a redefinition of rape that ignores its constitutive and oppressive effects on their existence.

Where, then, is resistance to be found against this pervasive and constitutive discourse of power? Given that rape is, among other things, a crime recognized by society (even as it is implicated in fundamental social dynamics and beliefs), it has a specific legal status that should be preserved. Regardless of how rape is defined or understood, it is widely recognized as a behavior worthy of legal recriminations, and despite feminist concerns with the means of law enforcement in the United States (especially its distinctly racist results), It would seem all but impossible to imagine a feminism that did not urge that serious legal action be taken against the rapist. Foucault, after all, does not wish to render rape itself legal, but merely wishes to punish only one particular aspect of rape, that pertaining to its status as assault. The analysis of rape's role with regard to women's bodily comportment and experience suggests that one way of resisting this particular discourse would be to urge the legal world to recognize not only the violence inherent in rape but also its sexually specific meanings insofar as it is a sexually differentiated enforcement of a set of patriarchal, misogynist values. The legal definition of rape should include, therefore, an understanding of the bodily and sexual meanings central to the action of rape, and should take those meanings into consideration when considering the appropriate legal response to a rapist.

Such an inclusion in the legal world constitutes resistance to the particular discourse of power that underscores rape by rendering that discourse visible. A great deal of the power behind the particular discourses that constitute and produce the feminine body is due to their allegedly biological and hence irrefutable claims. What is needed is an explicit recognition of the roles of those discourses within an overarching and markedly unnatural, system of oppression by which women were reduced to an inferior status. Such a recognition does not, importantly, deny the validity of women's experiences of such bodily comportment and behavior; the distinctly feminine body does not need to be wholly natural in order to be a valid source of knowledge. However, that recognition does render nonsensical any defensive invocation of a "natural"—and naturally culpable—women's sexuality (especially a sexuality oriented around the erotic appeal of being dominated). The sexual meanings of rape from the perspective of the victim have everything to do with the construction of the particularly feminine body, and as such are fundamental to the crime as experienced by the victim. An emphasis on the implication of the construction of the feminine body within a larger system of sexual hierarchization would account for women's feelings of shame and self-blame while refusing to hold the victim accountable for the assault. Foucault's strategy, on the other hand, by silencing any and all sexual meanings relating to rape, would allow assumptions concerning women's culpability to remain intact, if, perhaps, unsaid in the courtroom itself.

In other words, given that rape is a constitutive element of women's experience and that it is a social means of sexual differentiation (such that it has radically different meanings for men and women), it must be approached legally in such a way so that its sex-specific meanings may be articulated. Foucault's analysis of power, especially the way power discourses act on real, live, living bodies, should remind us that the individual women rape victims who prosecute their cases were marked by the threat of rape long before their bodies were actually violated, and that their experience of rape is not exhausted, although it is certainly dominated, by the particular incident that commands the court's attention.

THE ACT OF RAPE

The location of the threat of rape as a basic source of feminine bodily comportment has specific ramifications for the individual experience of being sexually assaulted. On a bodily level, a woman will be likely to experience a rape in some important sense as a threat fulfilled. The typical reactions of a rape victim, marked by overwhelming guilt and self-loathing, are the reactions of a person who should have known but temporarily forgot that she was constantly at risk. To have believed for even a moment that she was not in danger, for whatever reason, is felt to be the cause of the attack. Those assumptions that were prevalent in the production of her bodily comportment have been confirmed, and the attack itself may well be considered a reminder of the need for increased self-surveillance.

Why is an attack on a woman by a man with a penis (or its substitute) distinct from an attack with any other body part? Why is, in Foucault's terms, sticking one's fist into someone's face different from sticking one's penis into their sex? Precisely because the attack with the penis, the particularly sexual (and usually male) assault of and into one's (usually female) sex, is a danger that is fundamental to the specifics of feminine bodily comportment. To desexualize the act of rape, to consider it legally only as any other assault, would be to obfuscate—not weaken—its role in the production of the sexual hierarchy through the inscription of individual bodies. Rather than resisting the insistent process of sexualization that Foucault describes and decries, it would support the equally insistent process of sexual hierarchization which places women's bodies at such daily risk. As Teresa de Lauretis observes,

> In the terms of Foucault's theoretical analysis, his proposal may be understood as an effort to counter the technology of sex by breaking the bond between sexuality and crime; an effort to enfranchise sexual behaviors from legal punishments, and so to render the sexual sphere free from intervention by the state. Such a form of "local resistance" on behalf of the men imprisoned on, or subject to, charges of rape, however, would paradoxically but practically work to increase and further to legitimate the *sexual* oppression of women. (1987, 37)

Brownmiller's analysis of rape as primarily violent rather than sexual, that is, as a means of the expression of sheer power by which one group of people dominated another, failed to explicate sufficiently the ways rape was distinctly sexual and the ways sex and power were co-implicated. Although Foucault arrives at a similar conclusion as Brownmiller, his error lies not in a failure to consider the interplay between sex and power, but in his interpretation of rape only as something a man does, for which a man may be punished, and not as something experienced by a feminine body. His analysis remains solidly focused on the *masculine* body and its vulnerability to disciplinary discourses. However, in locating the man as central to the phenomenon, he has forgotten to ask the question of the bodily significance of the experience of being raped, an experience that occurs disproportionately to women. If we make the bodily experiences of women central to the question, it is possible to claim that an assault with a penis is distinct not because of what it claims about the masculine body, but rather because of what it claims about the feminine body, and how those claims are located in an overall power structure. To challenge that set of cultural assumptions, the discourse that produces the feminine body, necessitates not a desexualization of rape, but rather a recognition of its sexual meanings.

Interestingly enough, our analysis may lead us to quite the opposite conclusion than Foucault's in another way as well. While the threat of rape is, I have argued, the threat most feared by women, more compelling even than the threat of death, it is not the only threat. Other assaults, including those made with fists, and especially those that occur in the context of sexual relationships, may be experienced as sexual in nature precisely insofar as they confirm the assumptions about the feminine body discussed above. In some ways, these assaults may be perceived as precursors to the act of rape; if this is the case, then this analysis would call for a serious reconsideration of domestic violence not merely as an act of assault, but rather as an act with an underlying set of sexual meanings as well.

If the feminine body is a location whereon the tenets of a sexually hierarchical culture are written, it is also the site where they may be fought. Working out the Foucauldian notion of resistance, Lois McNay writes, "[T]he sexed body is to be understood not only as the primary target of the techniques of disciplinary power, but also as the point where these techniques are resisted and thwarted" (1992, 39). When women's bodies are constituted not as objects that incite other, more innocent bodies to violence, but rather as powerful means of counteracting that violence, the power structures that support the all too pervasive phenomenon of rape will be seriously undermined.

NOTES

1. For three particularly interesting discussions of the role of power in Foucault's thought, see Ladelle McWhorter (1990), Annie Bunting (1992), and Mary Rawlinson (1987). Judith Butler (1987) briefly considers some of Foucault's assertions regarding power and the body specifically in relation to the theories of Simone de Beauvoir and Monique Wittig.

2. Ladelle McWhorter (1989), Lois McNay (1991; 1992, 11–47), and Judith Butler (1989) have challenged this concept of the body. For McWhorter, it leaves moot the possibility of liberty; if the body is marked only by its function to be formed according to power relations, "he leaves us with nothing to liberate" (1989, 608), and surely, as Foucault's emphasis on the project of desexualization implies, liberation seems fundamental to his purposes. McNay, while for the most part accepting Foucault's theory of the "docile" body, also argues that it fails to account sufficiently for a variety of experiences central not only to women's experience, but also to the development of a feminist consciousness. Butler takes Foucault to task because his analysis seems to imply, contrary to his asserted purpose, that the body does in fact exist prior to power's inscription, precisely as a blank surface—for, after all, power must have something to write on, and thus "it would appear that 'the body,' which is the object or surface on which construction occurs, is itself prior to construction" (1989, 601). McNay and McWhorter, I would argue, fail to acknowledge sufficiently the deeply implicated relationship between power and resistance that I discuss above; Butler overemphasizes the inscriptive capabilities of power, which do not contradict, but coexist with, its productive abilities.

3. For a compelling Foucauldian analysis of a group of disorders usually associated with the female body and/or psyche, see Bordo (1991).

4. I thank Mary Rawlinson for this telling insight.

5. In contemporary U.S. society, there is much pressure on women to exercise and get "in shape"; however, the purpose of such exercise is not so much to build muscle and strength, but to lose weight and inches. One reason the female bodybuilder is so monstrous is that her muscles are so big (and her breasts, assuming they have not been surgically enlarged, so small). It is interesting to note that while female bodybuilding is suspect, cosmetic plastic surgery is not, and in fact is often praised by women as being a way of raising self-esteem. See Kathy Davis (1995) for an exploration of why women, even feminists, seek cosmetic surgery to mold their bodies to a more appealing shape; see also Kathryn Pauly Morgan (1991). Susan Bordo (1993, 245–75) notes that the postmodern emphasis on the plasticity of bodies, especially the ability of the (often female) subject to willfully shape one's body into a preferred shape, obscures the political content of the norms that are idealized. As Bordo points out, despite the promises and exhortations of choice, "one cannot have any body that one wants—for not every body will do" (230).

6. As an aside, we may note that this description of feminine bodily being provides a direct challenge to the Merleau-Pontian notion of the lived body on the basis of sexual difference. The body Merleau-Ponty (1981) describes as an openness to the surrounding world, a means not only of achieving certain projects but also, and more importantly, of perceiving those projects as feasible and attainable, seems distinctly male. The analyses of Young and Bartky suggest that the feminine lived body speaks more of limitation, failure, and harm than of achievement.

7. Over 88 percent of people who suffer from agoraphobia are women (Thorpe and Burns 1983, 20). Robert Seidenberg and Karen DeCrow write:

We believe that in a culture that has consistently doled out punishment to women who travel away from home (from unequal pay in the workplace to blame for children who turn to drugs to actual physical assault on the streets), it is no surprise that certain women, sensing the existential irony of their situation, refuse to leave the home. We see agoraphobia as a paradigm for the historical intimidation and oppression of women. The self-hate, self-limitation, self-abnegation, and self-punishment of agoraphobia is a caricature of centuries of childhood instructions to women. . . . Only when society gives just value to the work women do at home, and makes it easier for them to leave the home to do fully accepted and compensated work, will women no longer need to be agoraphobic. (1983, 6)

8. I thank Eva Feder Kittay for the formulation of this particular contradiction.

9. Mary Pipher has explored the traumatic transformation which many adolescent girls undergo,

and has located the difficulty of the transition within the demands of a patriarchal culture: Something dramatic happens to girls in early adolescence. Just as planes and ships disappear mysteriously into the Bermuda Triangle, so do the selves of girls go down in droves. They crash and burn in a social and developmental Bermuda Triangle. In early adolescence, studies show that girls' IQ scores drop and their math and science scores plummet. They lose their resiliency and optimism and become less curious and inclined to take risks. They lose their assertive, energetic and "tomboyish" personalities and become more deferential, self-critical and depressed. They report great unhappiness with their own bodies. (Pipher 1994, 19)

TOWARD A FEMINIST THEORY OF DISABILITY

Susan Wendell

In 1985, I fell ill overnight with what turned out to be a disabling chronic disease. In the long struggle to come to terms with it, I had to learn to live with a body that felt entirely different to me—weak, tired, painful, nauseated, dizzy, unpredictable. I learned at first by listening to other people with chronic illnesses or disabilities; suddenly able-bodied people seemed to me profoundly ignorant of everything I most needed to know. Although doctors told me there was a good chance I would eventually recover completely, I realized after a year that waiting to get well, hoping to recover my healthy body, was a dangerous strategy. I began slowly to identify with my new, disabled body and to learn to work with it. As I moved back into the world, I also began to experience the world as structured for people who have no weaknesses.[1] The process of encountering the able-bodied world led me gradually to identify myself as a disabled person, and to reflect on the nature of disability.

Some time ago, I decided to delve into what I assumed would be a substantial philosophical literature in medical ethics on the nature and experience of disability. I consulted *The Philosopher's Index,* looking under "Disability," "Handicap," "Illness," and "Disease." This was a depressing experience. At least 90% of philosophical articles on these topics are concerned with two questions: Under what conditions is it morally permissible/right to kill/let die a disabled person and how potentially disabled does a fetus have to be before it is permissible/right to prevent its being born? Thus, what I have to say here about disability is not a response to philosophical literature on the subject. Instead, it reflects what I have learned from the writings of other disabled people (especially disabled women), from talking with disabled people who have shared their insights and experiences with me, and from my own experience of disability. It also reflects my commitment to feminist theory, which offers perspectives and categories of analysis that help to illuminate the personal and social realities of disability, and which would, in turn, be enriched by a greater understanding of disability.

We need a theory of disability. It should be a social and political theory, because disability is largely socially-constructed, but it has to be more than that; any deep understanding of disability must include thinking about the ethical, psychological and epistemic issues of living with disability. This theory should be feminist, because more than half of disabled people are women and approximately 16% of women are disabled (Fine and Asch 1988), and because feminist thinkers have raised the most radical issues about cultural attitudes to the body. Some of the same attitudes about the body which contribute to women's oppression generally also contribute to the social and psychological disablement of people who have physical disabilities. In addition, feminists are grappling with issues that disabled people also face in a different context: Whether to stress sameness or difference in relation to the dominant group and in relation to each other; whether to place great value on independence from the help of other people, as the dominant culture does, or to question a value-system which distrusts and de-values dependence on other people and vulnerability in general; whether to take full integration into male dominated/able-bodied society as the goal, seeking equal power with men/able-bodied people in that society, or whether to preserve some degree of separate culture, in which the abilities, knowledge and values of women/the disabled are specifically honoured and developed.[2]

Disabled women struggle with both the oppressions of being women in male-dominated societies and the oppressions of being disabled in societies dominated by the able-bodied. They are bringing the knowledge and concerns of women with disabilities into feminism and feminist perspectives into the disability rights movement. To build a feminist theory of disability that takes adequate account of our differences, we will need to know how experiences of disability and the social oppression of the disabled interact with sexism, racism and class oppression. Michelle Fine and Adrienne Asch and the contributors to their 1988 volume, *Women and Disabilities,* have made a major contribution to our understanding of the complex interactions of gender and disability. Barbara Hillyer Davis has written in depth about the issue of dependency/independence as it relates to disability and feminism (Davis 1984). Other important contributions to theory are scattered throughout the extensive, primarily experiential, writing by disabled women;[3] this work offers vital insights into the nature of embodiment and the experience of oppression.

My purpose in writing this essay is to persuade feminist theorists, especially feminist philosophers, to turn more attention to constructing a theory of disability and to integrating the experiences and knowledge of disabled people into feminist theory as a whole. Toward this end I will discuss physical disability[4] from a theoretical perspective, including: some problems of defining it (here I will criticize the most widely-used definitions—those of the United Nations); the social construction of disability from biological reality on analogy with the social construction of gender; cultural attitudes toward the body which oppress disabled people while also alienating the able-bodied from their own experiences of embodiment; the "otherness" of disabled people; the knowledge that disabled people could contribute to culture from our diverse experiences and some of the ways this knowledge is silenced and invalidated. Along the way, I will describe briefly three issues discussed in disability theory that have been taken up in different contexts by feminist theory: sameness vs. difference, independence vs. dependency and integration vs. separatism.

I do not presume to speak for disabled women. Like everyone who is disabled, I have a particular standpoint determined in part by both my physical condition and my social situation. My own disability may be temporary, it could get better or worse. My disability is usually invisible (except when I use a walking stick). I am a white university professor who has adequate medical and long-term disability insurance; that makes me very privileged among the disabled. I write what I can see from my standpoint. Because I do not want simply to describe my own experience but to understand it in a much larger context, I must venture beyond what I know first-hand. I rely on others to correct my mistakes and fill in those parts of the picture I cannot see.

WHO IS PHYSICALLY DISABLED?

The United Nations offers the following definitions of and distinctions among impairment, disability and handicap:

> *"Impairment:* Any loss or abnormality of psychological, physiological, or anatomical structure or function. *Disability:* Any restriction or lack (resulting from an impairment) of ability to

perform an activity in the manner or within the range considered normal for a human being. *Handicap:* A disadvantage for a given individual, resulting from an impairment or disability, that limits or prevents the fulfillment of a role that is normal, depending on age, sex, social and cultural factors, for that individual."

Handicap is therefore a function of the relationship between disabled persons and their environment. It occurs when they encounter cultural, physical or social barriers which prevent their access to the various systems of society that are available to other citizens. Thus, handicap is the loss or limitation of opportunities to take part in the life of the community on an equal level with others. (U.N. 1983:I.c. 6-7)

These definitions may be good-enough for the political purposes of the U.N. They have two advantages: First, they clearly include many conditions that are not always recognized by the general public as disabling, for example, debilitating chronic illnesses that limit people's activities but do not necessarily cause any visible disability, such as Crohn's Disease. Second, the definition of "handicap" explicitly recognizes the possibility that the primary cause of a disabled person's inability to do certain things may be social—denial of opportunities, lack of accessibility, lack of services, poverty, discrimination—which it often is.

However, by trying to define "impairment" and "disability" in physical terms and "handicap" in cultural, physical and social terms, the U.N. document appears to be making a shaky distinction between the physical and the social aspects of disability. Not only the "normal" roles for one's age, sex, society, and culture, but also "normal" structure and function, and "normal" ability to perform an activity, depend on the society in which the standards of normality are generated. Paradigms of health and ideas about appropriate kinds and levels of performance are culturally-dependent. In addition, within each society there is much variation from the norm of any ability; at what point does this variation become disability? The answer depends on such

factors as what activities a society values and how it distributes labour and resources. The idea that there is some universal, perhaps biologically or medically-describable paradigm of human physical ability is an illusion. Therefore, I prefer to use a single term, "disability," and to emphasize that disability is socially constructed from biological reality.

Another objection I have to the U.N. definitions is that they imply that women can be disabled, but not handicapped, by being unable to do things which are not considered part of the normal role for their sex. For example, if a society does not consider it essential to a woman's normal role that she be able to read, then a blind woman who is not provided with education in Braille is not handicapped, according to these definitions.

In addition, these definitions suggest that we can be disabled, but not handicapped, by the normal process of aging, since although we may lose some ability, we are not handicapped unless we cannot fulfill roles that are normal *for our age*. Yet a society which provides few resources to allow disabled people to participate in it will be likely to marginalize *all* the disabled, including the old, and to define the appropriate roles of old people as very limited, thus handicapping them. Aging is disabling. Recognizing this helps us to see that disabled people are not "other," that they are really "us." Unless we die suddenly, we are all disabled eventually. Most of us will live part of our lives with bodies that hurt, that move with difficulty or not at all, that deprive us of activities we once took for granted or that others take for granted, bodies that make daily life a physical struggle. We need an understanding of disability that does not support a paradigm of humanity as young and healthy. Encouraging everyone to acknowledge, accommodate and identify with a wide range of physical conditions is ultimately the road to self-acceptance as well as the road to liberating those who are disabled now.

Ultimately, we might eliminate the category of "the disabled" altogether, and simply talk about individuals' physical abilities in their social context. For the present, although "the disabled" is a category of "the other" to the able-bodied, for that very reason it is also a politically useful and socially meaningful category to those who are in it. Disabled people share forms of social oppression, and the most important measures to relieve that oppression have been initiated by disabled people themselves. Social oppression may be the only thing the disabled have in common;[5] our struggles with our bodies are extremely diverse.

Finally, in thinking about disability we have to keep in mind that a society's labels do not always fit the people to whom they are applied. Thus, some people are perceived as disabled who do not experience themselves as disabled. Although they have physical conditions that disable other people, because of their opportunities and the context of their lives, they do not feel significantly limited in their activities (see Sacks 1988); these people may be surprised or resentful that they are considered disabled. On the other hand, many people whose bodies cause them great physical, psychological and economic struggles are not considered disabled because the public and/or the medical profession do not recognize their disabling conditions. These people often long to be perceived as disabled, because society stubbornly continues to expect them to perform as healthy people when they cannot and refuses to acknowledge and support their struggles.[6] Of course, no one wants the social stigma associated with disability, but social recognition of disability determines the practical help a person receives from doctors, government agencies, insurance companies, charity organizations, and often from family and friends. Thus, how a society defines disability and whom it recognizes as disabled are of enormous psychological, economic and social importance, both to people who are experiencing themselves as disabled and to those who are not but are nevertheless given the label.

There is no definitive answer to the question: Who is physically disabled? Disability has social, experiential and biological components, present and recognized in different measures for different people. Whether a particular physical condition is disabling changes with time and place, depending on such factors as social expectations, the state of technology and its availability to people in that condition, the educational system, architecture, attitudes towards physical appearance, and the pace of life. (If, for example, the pace of life increases without changes in other factors, more people become disabled simply because fewer people can keep up the "normal" pace.)

THE SOCIAL CONSTRUCTION OF DISABILITY

If we ask the questions: Why are so many disabled people unemployed or underemployed, impoverished, lonely, isolated; why do so many find it difficult or impossible to get an education (Davis and Marshall 1987; Fine and Asch 1988, 10-11); why are they victims of violence and coercion; why do able-bodied people ridicule, avoid, pity, stereotype and patronize them?, we may be tempted to see the disabled as victims of nature or accident. Feminists should be, and many are, profoundly suspicious of this answer. We are used to countering claims that insofar as women are oppressed they are oppressed by nature, which puts them at a disadvantage in the competition for power and resources. We know that if being biologically female is a disadvantage, it is because a social context makes it a disadvantage. From the standpoint of a disabled person, one can see how society could minimize the disadvantages of most disabilities, and, in some instances, turn them into advantages.

Consider an extreme case: the situation of physicist Stephen Hawking, who has had Amyotrophic Lateral Sclerosis (Lou Gehrig's Disease) for more than 26 years. Professor Hawking can no longer speak and is capable of only the smallest muscle movements. Yet, in his context of social and technological support, he is able to function as a professor of physics at Cambridge University; indeed he says his disability has given him the *advantage* of having more time to think, and he is one of the foremost theoretical physicists of our time. He is a courageous and talented man, but he is able to live the creative life he has only because of the help of his family, three nurses, a graduate student who travels with him to maintain his computer-communications systems, and the fact that his talent had been developed and recognized before he fell seriously ill (*Newsweek* 1988).

Many people consider providing resources for disabled people a form of charity, superogatory in part because the disabled are perceived as unproductive members of society. Yet most disabled people are placed in a double-bind: they have access to inadequate resources because they are unemployed or underemployed, and they are unemployed or underemployed because they lack the resources that would enable them to make their full contribution to society (Matthews 1983; Hannaford 1985). Often governments and charity organizations will spend far more money to keep disabled people in institutions where they have no chance to be productive than they will spend to enable the same people to live independently and productively. In addition, many of the "special" resources the disabled need merely compensate for bad social planning that is based on the illusion that everyone is young, strong, healthy (and, often, male).

Disability is also frequently regarded as a personal or family problem rather than a matter for social responsibility. Disabled people are often expected to overcome obstacles to participation by their own extraordinary efforts, or their families are expected to provide what they need (sometimes at great personal sacrifice). Helping in personal or family matters is seen as superogatory for people who are not members of the family.

Many factors contribute to determining whether providing a particular resource is regarded as a social or a personal (or family) responsibility.[7] One such factor is whether the majority can identify with people who need the resource.

Most North Americans feel that society should be organized to provide short-term medical care made necessary by illness or accident, I think because they can imagine themselves needing it. Relatively few people can identify with those who cannot be "repaired" by medical intervention. Sue Halpern makes the following observation:

> Physical health is contingent and often short-lived. But this truth eludes us as long as we are able to walk by simply putting one foot in front of the other. As a consequence, empathy for the disabled is unavailable to most able-bodied persons. Sympathy, yes, empathy, no, for every attempt to project oneself into that condition, to feel what it is like not to be ambulatory, for instance, is mediated by an ability to walk (Halpern 1988, 3).

If the able-bodied saw the disabled as potentially themselves or as their future selves, they would be more inclined to feel that society should be organized to provide the resources that would make disabled people fully integrated and contributing members. They would feel that "charity" is as inappropriate a way of thinking about resources for disabled people as it is about emergency medical care or education.

Careful study of the lives of disabled people will reveal how artificial the line is that we draw between the biological and the social. Feminists have already challenged this line in part by showing how processes such as childbirth, menstruation and menopause, which may be represented, treated, and therefore experienced as illnesses or disabilities, are socially-constructed from biological reality (Rich 1976; Ehrenreich and English 1979). Disabled people's relations to our bodies involve elements of struggle which perhaps cannot be eliminated, perhaps not even mitigated, by social arrangements. *But*, much of what is *disabling* about our physical conditions is also a consequence of social arrangements (Finger 1983; Fine and Asch 1988) which could, but do not, either compensate for our physical conditions, or accommodate them so that we can participate fully, or support our struggles and integrate us into the community *and our struggles into the cultural concept of life as it is ordinarily lived.*

Feminists have shown that the world has been designed for men. In North America at least, life and work have been structured as though no one of any importance in the public world, and certainly no one who works outside the home for wages, has to breast-feed a baby or look after a sick child. Common colds can be acknowledged publicly, and allowances made for them, but menstruation cannot. Much of the world is also structured as though everyone is physically strong, as though all bodies are "ideally shaped," as though everyone can walk, hear and see well, as though everyone can work and play at a pace that is not compatible with any kind of illness or pain, as though no one is ever dizzy or incontinent or simply needs to sit or lie down. (For instance, where could you sit down in a supermarket if you needed to?) Not only the architecture, but the entire physical and social organization of life, assumes that we are either strong and healthy and able to do what the average able-bodied person can do, or that we are completely disabled, unable to participate in life.

In the split between the public and the private worlds, women (and children) have been relegated to the private, and so have the disabled, the sick and the old (and mostly women take care of them). The public world is the world of strength, the positive (valued) body, performance and production, the able-bodied and youth. Weakness, illness, rest and recovery, pain, death and the negative (de-valued) body are private, generally hidden, and often neglected. Coming into the public world with illness, pain or a de-valued body, we encounter resistance to mixing the two worlds; the split is vividly revealed. Much of our experience goes underground, because there is no socially acceptable way of expressing it and having our physical and psychological experience acknowledged and shared. A few close friends may share it, but there is a strong impulse to protect them from it too, because it seems so private, so unacceptable. I found that,

after a couple of years of illness, even answering the question, "How are you?" became a difficult, conflict-ridden business. I don't want to alienate my friends from my experience, but I don't want to risk their discomfort and rejection by telling them what they don't want to know.[8]

Disabled people learn that many, perhaps most, able-bodied people do not want to know about suffering caused by the body. Visibly disabled women report that curiosity about medical diagnoses, physical appearance and the sexual and other intimate aspects of disability is more common than willingness to listen and try to understand the experience of disability (Matthews 1983). It is not unusual for people with invisible disabilities to keep them entirely secret from everyone but their closest friends.

Contrary to what Sue Halpern says, it is not simply because they are in able bodies that the able-bodied fail to identify with the disabled. Able-bodied people can often make the imaginative leap into the skins of people physically unlike themselves; women can identify with a male protagonist in a story, for example, and adults can identify with children or with people much older than themselves. Something more powerful than being in a different body is at work. Suffering caused by the body, and the inability to control the body, are despised, pitied, and above all, feared. This fear, experienced individually, is also deeply embedded in our culture.

THE OPPRESSION OF DISABLED PEOPLE IS THE OPPRESSION OF EVERYONE'S REAL BODY

Our real human bodies are exceedingly diverse—in size, shape, colour, texture, structure, function, range and habits of movement, and development—and they are constantly changing. Yet we do not absorb or reflect this simple fact in our culture. Instead, we idealize the human body. Our physical ideals change from time to time, but we always have ideals. These ideals are not just about appearance; they are also ideals of strength and energy and proper control of the body. We are per-petually bombarded with images of these ideals, demands for them, and offers of consumer prod-ucts and services to help us achieve them.⁹ Ide-alizing the body prevents everyone, able-bodied and disabled, from identifying with and loving her/his real body. Some people can have the illu-sion of acceptance that comes from believing that their bodies are "close enough" to the ideal, but this illusion only draws them deeper into identi-fying with the ideal and into the endless task of reconciling the reality with it. Sooner or later they must fail.

Before I became disabled, I was one of those people who felt "close enough" to cultural ideals to be reasonably accepting of my body. Like most feminists I know, I was aware of some alienation from it, and I worked at liking my body better. Nevertheless, I knew in my heart that too much of my liking still depended on being "close enough." When I was disabled by illness, I experienced a much more profound alienation from my body. After a year spent mostly in bed, I could barely identify my body as my own. I felt that "it" was torturing "me," trapping me in exhaustion, pain and inability to do many of the simplest things I did when I was healthy. The shock of this experi-ence and the effort to identify with a new, disa-bled body, made me realize I had been living a luxury of the able-bodied. The able-bodied can postpone the task of identifying with their *real* bodies. The disabled don't have the luxury of de-manding that their bodies fit the physical ideals of their culture. As Barbara Hillyer Davis says: "For all of us the difficult work of finding (one's) self includes the body, but people who live with disability in a society that glorifies fitness and physical conformity are forced to understand more fully what bodily integrity means" (Davis 1984, 3).

In a society which idealizes the body, the phys-ically disabled are marginalized. People learn to identify with their own strengths (by cultural standards) and to hate, fear and neglect their own weaknesses. The disabled are not only de-valued

for their de-valued bodies (Hannaford 1985), they are constant reminders to the able-bodied of the negative body—of what the able-bodied are trying to avoid, forget and ignore (Lessing 1981). For example, if someone tells me she is in pain, she reminds me of the existence of pain, the imperfection and fragility of the body, the possibility of my own pain, the *inevitability* of it. The less willing I am to accept all these, the less I want to know about her pain; if I cannot avoid it in her presence, I will avoid her. I may even blame her for it. I may tell myself that she *could have* avoided it, in order to go on believing that I *can* avoid it. I want to believe I am not like her; I cling to the differences. Gradually, I make her "other" because I don't want to confront my real body, which I fear and cannot accept.¹⁰

Disabled people can participate in marginal-izing ourselves. We can wish for bodies we do not have, with frustration, shame, self-hatred. We can feel trapped in the negative body; it is our inter-nalized oppression to feel this. Every (visibly or invisibly) disabled person I have talked to or read has felt this; some never stop feeling it. In addi-tion, disabled women suffer more than disabled men from the demand that people have "ideal" bodies, because in patriarchal culture people judge women more by their bodies than they do men. Disabled women often do not feel seen (be-cause they are often not seen) by others as whole people, especially not as sexual people (Campling 1981; Matthews 1983; Hannaford 1985; Fine and Asch 1988). Thus, part of their struggle against oppression is a much harder version of the strug-gle able-bodied women have for a realistic *and positive* self-image (Bogle and Shaul 1981). On the other hand, disabled people who cannot hope to meet the physical ideals of a culture can help reveal that those ideals are not "natural" or "nor-mal" but artificial social creations that oppress everyone.

Feminist theorists have probed the causes of our patriarchal culture's desire for control of the body—fear of death, fear of the strong impulses and feelings the body gives us, fear of nature, fear and resentment of the mother's power over the infant (de Beauvoir 1949; Dinnerstein 1976; Griffin 1981). Idealizing the body and wanting to control it go hand-in-hand; it is impossible to say whether one causes the other. A physical ideal gives us the goal of our efforts to control the body, and the myth that total control is possible deceives us into striving for the ideal. The consequences for women have been widely discussed in the literature of feminism. The consequences for disabled people are less often recognized. In a culture which loves the idea that the body can be controlled, those who cannot control their bodies are seen (and may see themselves) as failures.

When you listen to this culture in a disabled body, you hear how often health and physical vigour are talked about as if they were moral virtues. People constantly praise others for their "energy," their stamina, their ability to work long hours. Of course, acting on behalf of one's health can be a virtue, and undermining one's health can be a vice, but "success" at being healthy, like beauty, is always partly a matter of luck and therefore beyond our control. When health is spoken of as a virtue, people who lack it are made to feel inadequate. I am not suggesting that it is always wrong to praise people's physical strength or accomplishments, any more than it is always wrong to praise their physical beauty. But just as treating cultural standards of beauty as essential virtues for women harms most women, treating health and vigour as moral virtues for everyone harms people with disabilities and illnesses.

The myth that the body can be controlled is not easily dispelled, because it is not very vulnerable to evidence against it. When I became ill, several people wanted to discuss with me what I thought I had done to "make myself" ill or "allow myself" to become sick. At first I fell in with this, generating theories about what I had done wrong; even though I had always taken good care of my health, I was able to find some (rather far-fetched) accounts of my responsibility for my illness. When a few close friends offered hypotheses as to how *they* might be responsible

for my being ill, I began to suspect that something was wrong. Gradually, I realized that we were all trying to believe that nothing this important is beyond our control.

Of course, there are sometimes controllable social and psychological forces at work in creating ill health and disability (Kleinman 1988). Nevertheless, our cultural insistence on controlling the body blames the victims of disability for failing and burdens them with self-doubt and self-blame. The search for psychological, moral and spiritual causes of illness, accident and disability is often a harmful expression of this insistence on control (see Sontag 1977).

Modern Western medicine plays into and conforms to our cultural myth that the body can be controlled. Collectively, doctors and medical researchers exhibit very little modesty about their knowledge. They focus their (and our) attention on cures and imminent cures, on successful medical interventions. Research, funding and medical care are more directed toward life-threatening conditions than toward chronic illnesses and disabilities. Even pain was relatively neglected as a medical problem until the second half of this century. Surgery and saving lives bolster the illusion of control much better than does the long, patient process of rehabilitation or the management of long-term illness. These latter, less visible functions of medicine tend to be performed by nurses, physiotherapists and other low-prestige members of the profession. Doctors are trained to do something to control the body, to "make it better" (Kleinman 1988); they are the heroes of medicine. They may like being in the role of hero, but we also like them in that role and try to keep them there, because *we* want to believe that someone can always "make it better."[11] As long as we cling to this belief, the patients who cannot be "repaired"—the chronically ill, the disabled and the dying—will symbolize the failure of medicine and more, the failure of the Western scientific project to control nature. They will carry this stigma in medicine and in the culture as a whole.

When philosophers of medical ethics confine themselves to discussing life-and-death issues of medicine, they help perpetuate the idea that the main purpose of medicine is to control the body. Life-and-death interventions are the ultimate exercise of control. If medical ethicists looked more closely at who needs and who receives medical help, they would discover a host of issues concerning how medicine and society understand, mediate, assist with and integrate experiences of illness, injury and disability.

Because of the heroic approach to medicine, and because disabled people's experience is not integrated into the culture, most people know little or nothing about how to live with long-term or life-threatening illness, how to communicate with doctors and nurses and medical bureaucrats about these matters, how to live with limitation, uncertainty, pain, nausea, and other symptoms when doctors cannot make them go away. Recently, patients' support groups have arisen to fill this gap for people with nearly every type of illness and disability. They are vitally important sources of knowledge and encouragement for many of us, but they do not fill the cultural gulf between the able-bodied and the disabled. The problems of living with a disability are not private problems, separable from the rest of life and the rest of society. They are problems which can and should be shared throughout the culture as much as we share the problems of love, work and family life.

Consider the example of pain. It is difficult for most people who have not lived with prolonged or recurring pain to understand the benefits of accepting it. Yet some people who live with chronic pain speak of "making friends" with it as the road to feeling better and enjoying life. How do they picture their pain and think about it; what kind of attention do they give it and when; how do they live around and through it, and what do they learn from it? We all need to know this as part of our education. Some of the fear of experiencing pain is a consequence of ignorance and lack of guidance. The effort to avoid pain contributes to such widespread problems as drug and alcohol addiction, eating disorders, and sedentary lives. People with painful disabilities can teach us about pain, because they *can't* avoid it and have had to learn how to face it and live with it. The pernicious myth that it is possible to avoid almost all pain by controlling the body gives the fear of pain greater power than it should have and blames the victims of unavoidable pain. The fear of pain is also expressed or displaced as a fear of people in pain, which often isolates those with painful disabilities. All this is unnecessary. People *in* pain and knowledge *of* pain could be fully integrated into our culture, to everyone's benefit.

If we knew more about pain, about physical limitation, about loss of abilities, about what it is like to be "too far" from the cultural ideal of the body, perhaps we would have less fear of the negative body, less fear of our own weaknesses and "imperfections," of our inevitable deterioration and death. Perhaps we could give up our idealizations and relax our desire for control of the body; until we do, we maintain them at the expense of disabled people and at the expense of our ability to accept and love our own real bodies.

DISABLED PEOPLE AS "OTHER"

When we make people "other," we group them together as the objects of *our* experience instead of regarding them as fellow *subjects* of experience with whom we might identify. If you are "other" to me, I see you primarily as symbolic of something else—usually, but not always, something I reject and fear and that I project onto you. We can all do this to each other, but very often the process is not symmetrical, because one group of people may have more power to call itself the paradigm of humanity and to make the world suit its own needs and validate its own experiences.[12] Disabled people are "other" to able-bodied people, and (as I have tried to show) the consequences are socially, economically and psychologically oppressive to the disabled and psychologically oppressive to the able-bodied.

Able-bodied people may be "other" to disabled people, but the consequences of this for the able-bodied are minor (most able-bodied people can afford not to notice it). There are, however, several political and philosophical issues that being "other" to a more powerful group raises for disabled people.

I have said that for the able-bodied, the disabled often symbolize failure to control the body and the failure of science and medicine to protect us all. However, some disabled people also become symbols of heroic control against all odds; these are the "disabled heroes," who are comforting to the able-bodied because they re-affirm the possibility of overcoming the body. Disabled heroes are people with visible disabilities who receive public attention because they accomplish things that are unusual even for the able-bodied. It is revealing that, with few exceptions (Helen Keller and, very recently, Stephen Hawking are among them), disabled heroes are recognized for performing feats of physical strength and endurance. While disabled heroes can be inspiring and heartening to the disabled, they may give the able-bodied the false impression that anyone can "overcome" a disability. Disabled heroes usually have extraordinary social, economic and physical resources that are not available to most people with those disabilities. In addition, many disabled people are not capable of performing physical heroics, because many (perhaps most) disabilities reduce or consume the energy and stamina of people who have them and do not just limit them in some particular kind of physical activity. Amputee and wheelchair athletes are exceptional, not because of their ambition, discipline and hard work, but because they are in better health than most disabled people can be. Arthritis, Parkinsonism and stroke cause severe disability in far more people than do spinal cord injuries and amputations (Bury 1979). The image of the disabled hero may reduce the "otherness" of a few disabled people, but because it creates an ideal which most disabled people cannot meet, it *increases* the "otherness" of the majority of disabled people.

One recent attempt to reduce the "otherness" of disabled people is the introduction of the term, "differently-abled." I assume the point of using this term is to suggest that there is nothing *wrong* with being the way we are, just different. Yet to call someone "differently-abled" is much like calling her "differently-coloured" or "differently-gendered." It says: "This person is not the norm or paradigm of humanity." If anything, it increases the "otherness" of disabled people, because it reinforces the paradigm of humanity as young, strong and healthy, with all body parts working "perfectly," from which this person is "different." Using the term "differently-abled" also suggests a (polite? patronizing? protective? self-protective?) disregard of the special difficulties, struggles and suffering disabled people face. We are *dis-abled*. We live with particular social and physical struggles that are partly consequences of the conditions of our bodies and partly consequences of the structures and expectations of our societies, but they are struggles which only people with bodies like ours experience.

The positive side of the term "differently-abled" is that it might remind the able-bodied that to be disabled in some respects is not to be disabled in all respects. It also suggests that a disabled person may have abilities that the able-bodied lack in virtue of being able-bodied. Nevertheless, on the whole, the term "differently-abled" should be abandoned, because it reinforces the able-bodied paradigm of humanity and fails to acknowledge the struggles disabled people face.

The problems of being "the other" to a dominant group are always politically complex. One solution is to emphasize similarities to the dominant group in the hope that they will identify with the oppressed, recognize their rights, gradually give them equal opportunities, and eventually assimilate them. Many disabled people are tired of being symbols to the able-bodied, visible only or primarily for their disabilities, and they want nothing more than to be seen as individuals rather than as members of the group, "the disabled." Emphasizing similarities to the

able-bodied, making their disabilities unnotice-
able in comparison to their other human qualities
may bring about assimilation one-by-one. It does
not directly challenge the able-bodied paradigm
of humanity, just as women moving into traditionally male arenas of power does not directly
challenge the male paradigm of humanity, although both may produce a gradual change in the
paradigms. In addition, assimilation may be very
difficult for the disabled to achieve. Although
the able-bodied like disabled tokens who do not
seem very different from themselves, they may
need someone to carry the burden of the negative
body as long as they continue to idealize and try
to control the body. They may therefore resist the
assimilation of most disabled people.

The reasons in favour of the alternative solution to "otherness"—*emphasizing difference*
from the able-bodied—are also reasons for emphasizing similarities among the disabled, especially social and political similarities. Disabled
people share positions of social oppression that
separate us from the able-bodied, and we share
physical, psychological and social experiences
of disability. Emphasizing differences from the
able-bodied demands that those differences be
acknowledged and respected and fosters solidarity among the disabled. It challenges the able-
bodied paradigm of humanity and creates the
possibility of a deeper challenge to the idealization of the body and the demand for its control. Invisibly disabled people tend to be drawn
to solutions that emphasize difference, because
our need to have our struggles acknowledged is
great, and we have far less experience than those
who are visibly disabled of being symbolic to the
able-bodied.

Whether one wants to emphasize sameness
or difference in dealing with the problem of being "the other" depends in part on how radically
one wants to challenge the value-structure of the
dominant group. A very important issue in this
category for both women and disabled people is
the value of independence from the help of others, so highly esteemed in our patriarchal culture

and now being questioned in feminist ethics (see,
for example, Sherwin 1984, 1987; Kittay and
Meyers 1987) and discussed in the writings of
disabled women (see, for example, Fisher and
Galler 1981; Davis 1984; Frank 1988). Many
disabled people who can see the possibility of
living as independently as any able-bodied person, or who have achieved this goal after long
struggle, value their independence above everything. Dependence on the help of others is
humiliating in a society which prizes independence. In addition, this issue holds special complications for disabled women; reading the stories
of women who became disabled as adults, I was
struck by their struggle with shame and loss of
self-esteem at being transformed from people
who took physical care of others (husbands and
children) to people who were physically dependent. All this suggests that disabled people need
every bit of independence we can get. Yet there
are disabled people who will always need a lot of
help from other individuals just to survive (those
who have very little control of movement, for
example), and to the extent that everyone considers independence necessary to respect and
self-esteem, those people will be condemned to
be de-valued. In addition, some disabled people
spend tremendous energy being independent in
ways that might be considered trivial in a culture
less insistent on self-reliance; if our culture valued *interdependence* more highly, they could use
that energy for more satisfying activities.

In her excellent discussion of the issue of
dependency and independence, Barbara Hillyer
Davis argues that women with disabilities and
those who care for them can work out a model
of *reciprocity* for all of us, if we are willing to
learn from them. "Reciprocity involves the difficulty of recognizing each other's needs, relying
on the other, asking and receiving help, delegating responsibility, giving and receiving empathy,
respecting boundaries" (Davis 1984, 4). I hope
that disabled and able-bodied feminists will join
in questioning our cultural obsession with independence and ultimately replacing it with such a

model of reciprocity. If *all* the disabled are to be fully integrated into society without symbolizing failure, then we have to change social values to recognize the value of depending on others and being depended upon. This would also reduce the fear and shame associated with dependency in old age—a condition most of us will reach.

Whether one wants to emphasize sameness or difference in dealing with the problems of being "other" is also related to whether one sees anything valuable to be preserved by maintaining, either temporarily or in the long-run, some separateness of the oppressed group. Is there a special culture of the oppressed group or the seeds of a special culture which could be developed in a supportive context of solidarity? Do members of the oppressed group have accumulated knowledge or ways of knowing which might be lost if assimilation takes place without the dominant culture being transformed?

It would be hard to claim that disabled people as a whole have an alternative culture or even the seeds of one. One sub-group, the deaf, has a separate culture from the hearing, and they are fighting for its recognition and preservation, as well as for their right to continue making their own culture (Sacks 1988). Disabled people do have both knowledge and ways of knowing that are not available to the able-bodied. Although ultimately I hope that disabled people's knowledge will be integrated into the culture as a whole, I suspect that a culture which fears and denigrates the real body would rather silence this knowledge than make the changes necessary to absorb it. It may have to be nurtured and cultivated separately while the able-bodied culture is transformed enough to receive and integrate it.

THE KNOWLEDGE OF DISABLED PEOPLE AND HOW IT IS SILENCED

In my second year of illness, I was reading an article about the psychological and philosophical relationship of mind to body. When the author painted a rosy picture of the experience of being embodied, I was outraged at the presumption of the writer to speak for everyone from a healthy body. I decided I didn't want to hear *anything* about the body from anyone who was not physically disabled. Before that moment, it had not occurred to me that there was a world of experience from which I was shut out while I was able-bodied.

Not only do physically disabled people have experiences which are not available to the able-bodied, they are in a better position to transcend cultural mythologies about the body, because they *cannot* do things that the able-bodied feel they *must* do in order to be happy, "normal" and sane. For example, paraplegics and quadriplegics have revolutionary things to teach about the possibilities of sexuality which contradict patriarchal culture's obsession with the genitals (Bullard and Knight 1981). Some people can have orgasms in any part of their bodies where they feel touch. One man said he never knew how good sex could be until he lost the feeling in his genitals. Few able-bodied people know these things, and, to my knowledge, no one has explored their implications for the able-bodied.

If disabled people were truly heard, an explosion of knowledge of the human body and psyche would take place. We have access to realms of experience that our culture has not tapped (even for medical science, which takes relatively little interest in people's *experience* of their bodies). Like women's particular knowledge, which comes from access to experiences most men do not have, disabled people's knowledge is dismissed as trivial, complaining, mundane (or bizarre), *less than* that of the dominant group.

The cognitive authority (Addelson 1983) of medicine plays an important role in distorting and silencing the knowledge of the disabled. Medical professionals have been given the power to describe and validate everyone's experience of the body. If you go to doctors with symptoms they cannot observe directly or verify independently of what you tell them, such as pain or weakness or numbness or dizziness or difficulty concentrating, and if they cannot find an objectively observable cause of those symptoms, you are likely to be told that there is "nothing wrong with you," no matter how you feel. Unless you are very lucky in your doctors, no matter how trustworthy and responsible you were considered to be *before* you started saying you were ill, your experience will be invalidated.[13] *Other* people are the authorities on the reality of your experience of your body.

When you are very ill, you desperately need medical validation of your experience, not only for economic reasons (insurance claims, pensions, welfare and disability benefits all depend upon official diagnosis), but also for social and psychological reasons. People with unrecognized illnesses are often abandoned by their friends and families.[14] Because almost everyone accepts the cognitive authority of medicine, the person whose bodily experience is radically different from medical descriptions of her/his condition is invalidated as a knower. Either you decide to hide your experience, or you are socially isolated with it by being labelled mentally ill[15] or dishonest. In both cases you are silenced.

Even when your experience is recognized by medicine, it is often re-described in ways that are inaccurate from your standpoint. The objectively observable condition of your body may be used to determine the severity of your pain, for instance, regardless of your own reports of it. For example, until recently, relatively few doctors were willing to acknowledge that severe phantom limb pain can persist for months or even years after an amputation. The accumulated experience of doctors who were themselves amputees has begun to legitimize the other patients' reports (Madruga 1979).

When you are forced to realize that other people have more social authority than you do to describe your experience of your own body, your confidence in yourself and your relationship to reality is radically undermined. What can you know if you cannot know that you are experiencing suffering or joy; what can you communicate to people who don't believe you know

even this?[16] Most people will censor what they tell or say nothing rather than expose themselves repeatedly to such deeply felt invalidation. They are silenced by fear and confusion. The process is familiar from our understanding of how women are silenced in and by patriarchal culture.

One final caution: As with women's "special knowledge," there is a danger of sentimentalizing disabled people's knowledge and abilities and keeping us "other" by doing so. We need to bring this knowledge into the culture and to transform the culture and society so that everyone can receive and make use of it, so that it can be fully integrated, along with disabled people, into a shared social life.

CONCLUSION

I have tried to introduce the reader to the rich variety of intellectual and political issues that are raised by experiences of physical disability. Confronting these issues has increased my appreciation of the insights that feminist theory already offers into cultural attitudes about the body and the many forms of social oppression. Feminists have been challenging medicine's authority for many years now, but not, I think, as radically as we would if we knew what disabled people have to tell. I look forward to the development of a full feminist theory of disability.[17] We need a theory of disability for the liberation of both disabled and able-bodied people, since the theory of disability is also the theory of the oppression of the body by a society and its culture.

NOTES

1. Itzhak Perlman, when asked in a recent CBC interview about the problems of the disabled, said disabled people have two problems: the fact that the world is not made for people with any weaknesses but for supermen and the attitudes of able-bodied people.
2. An excellent description of this last issue as it confronts the deaf is found in Sacks 1988.

3. See Matthews 1983; Hannaford 1985; Rooney and Israel (eds.) 1985, esp. the articles by Jill Weiss, Charlynn Toews, Myra Rosenfield, and Susan Russell; and, for a doctor's theories, Kleinman 1988.

4. We also need a feminist theory of mental disability, but I will not be discussing mental disability in this essay.

5. In a recent article in *Signs,* Linda Alcoff argues that we should define "woman" thus: "woman is a position from which a feminist politics can emerge rather than a set of attributes that are 'objectively identifiable.' " (Alcoff 1988, 435). I think a similar approach may be the best one for defining "disability."

6. For example, Pelvic Inflammatory Disease causes severe prolonged disability in some women. These women often have to endure medical diagnoses of psychological illness and the skepticism of family and friends, in addition to having to live with chronic severe pain. See Moore 1985.

7. Feminism has challenged the distribution of responsibility for providing such resources as childcare and protection from family violence. Increasingly many people who once thought of these as family or personal concerns now think of them as social responsibilities.

8. Some people save me that trouble by *telling me* I am fine and walking away. Of course, people also encounter difficulties with answering. "How are you?" during and after crises, such as separation from a partner, death of a loved one, or a nervous breakdown. There is a temporary alienation from what is considered ordinary shared experience. In disability, the alienation lasts longer, often for a lifetime, and, in my experience, it is more profound.

9. The idealization of the body is clearly related in complex ways to the economic processes of a consumer society. Since it pre-dated capitalism, we know that capitalism did not cause it, but it is undeniable that idealization now generates tremendous profits and that the quest for profit demands the reinforcement of idealization and the constant development of new ideals.

10. Susan Griffin, in a characteristically honest and insightful passage, describes an encounter with the fear that makes it hard to identify with disabled people. See Griffin 1982, 648–649.

11. Thanks to Joyce Frazee for pointing this out to me.

12. When Simone de Beauvoir uses this term to elucidate men's view of women (and women's view of ourselves), she emphasizes that Man is considered essential, Woman inessential; Man is the Subject, Woman the Other (de Beauvoir 1952, xvi). Susan Griffin expands upon this idea by showing how we project rejected aspects of ourselves onto groups of people who are designated the Other (Griffin 1981).

13. Many women with M.S. have lived through this nightmare in the early stages of their illness. Although this happens to men too, women's experience of the body, like women's experience generally, is more likely to be invalidated (Hannaford 1985).

14. Accounts of the experience of relatively unknown, newly-discovered, or hard-to-diagnose diseases and conditions confirm this. See, for example, Jeffreys 1982, for the story of an experience of Chronic Fatigue Syndrome, which is more common in women than in men.

15. Frequently people with undiagnosed illnesses are sent by their doctors to psychiatrists, who cannot help and may send them back to their doctors saying they must be physically ill. This can leave patients in a dangerous medical and social limbo. Sometimes they commit suicide because of it (Ramsay 1986). Psychiatrists who know enough about living with physical illness or disability to help someone cope with it are rare.

16. For more discussion of this subject, see Zaner 1983 and Rawlinson 1983.

17. At this stage of the disability rights movement, it is impossible to anticipate everything that a full feminist theory will include, just as it would have been impossible to predict in 1970 the present state of feminist theory of mothering. Nevertheless, we can see that besides dealing more fully with the issues I have raised here, an adequate feminist theory of disability will examine all the ways in which disability is socially constructed; it will explain the interaction of disability with gender, race and class position; it will examine every aspect of the cognitive authority of medicine and science over our experiences of our bodies; it will discuss the relationship of technology to disability; it will question the

belief that disabled lives are not worth living or preserving when it is implied in our theorizing about abortion and euthanasia; it will give us a detailed vision of the full integration of disabled people in society, and it will propose practical political strategies for the liberation of disabled people and the liberation of the able-bodied from the social oppression of their bodies.

REFERENCES

Addelson, Kathryn P. 1983. "The man of professional wisdom." In *Discovering Reality.* Sandra Harding and Merrill B. Hintikka, eds. Boston: D. Reidel.

Alcoff, Linda. 1988. "Cultural Feminism Versus Poststructuralism: The Identity Crisis in Feminist Theory." *Signs: Journal of Women in Culture and Society* 13(3):405–436.

Bullard, David G. and Susan E. Knight, eds. 1981. *Sexuality and Physical Disability.* St. Louis: C.V. Mosby.

Bury, M.R. 1979. "Disablement in Society: Towards an Integrated Perspective." *International Journal of Rehabilitation Research* 2(1): 33–40.

Beauvoir, Simone de. 1952. *The Second Sex.* New York: Alfred A. Knopf.

Campling, Jo, ed. 1981. *Images of Ourselves—Women with Disabilities Talking.* London: Routledge and Kegan Paul.

Davis, Barbara Hillyer. 1984. "Women, Disability and Feminism: Notes Toward a New Theory." *Frontiers: A Journal of Women Studies* VIII(1):1–5.

Davis, Melanie and Catherine Marshall. 1987. "Female and Disabled: Challenged Women in Education." *National Women's Studies Association Perspectives* 5: 39–41.

Dinnerstein, Dorothy. 1976. *The Mermaid and the Minotaur: Sexual Arrangements and Human Malaise.* New York: Harper and Row.

Ehrenreich, Barbara and Dierdre English. 1979. *For Her Own Good: 150 Years of the Experts' Advice to Women.* New York: Anchor.

Fine, Michelle and Adrienne Asch, eds. 1988. *Women with Disabilities: Essays in Psychology, Culture and Politics.* Philadelphia: Temple University Press.

Finger, Anne. 1983. "Disability and Reproductive Rights." *off our backs* 13(9):18–19.

Fisher, Bernice and Roberta Galler. 1981. "Conversation Between Two Friends about Feminism and Disability." *off our backs* 11(5):14–15.

Frank, Gelya. 1988. "On Embodiment: A Case Study of Congenital Limb Deficiency in American Culture." In *Women with Disabilities.* Michelle Fine and Adrienne Asch, eds. Philadelphia: Temple University Press.

Griffin, Susan. 1981. *Pornography and Silence: Culture's Revenge Against Nature.* New York: Harper and Row.

Griffin, Susan. 1982. "The Way of All Ideology." *Signs: Journal of Women in Culture and Society* 8(3):641–660.

Halpern, Sue M. 1988. "Portrait of the Artist." Review of *Under the Eye of the Clock* by Christopher Nolan. *The New York Review of Books,* June 30:3–4.

Hannaford, Susan. 1985. *Living Outside Inside. A Disabled Woman's Experience. Towards a Social and political perspective.* Berkeley: Canterbury Press.

Jeffreys, Toni. 1982. *The Mile-High Staircase.* Sydney: Hodder and Stoughton Ltd.

Kittay, Eva Feder and Diana T. Meyers, eds. 1987. *Women and Moral Theory.* Totowa, NJ: Rowman and Littlefield.

Kleinman, Arthur. 1988. *The Illness Narratives: Suffering, Healing, and the Human Condition.* New York: Basic Books.

Lessing, Jill. 1981. "Denial and Disability." *off our backs* 11(5):21.

Madruga, Lenor. 1979. *One Step at a Time.* Toronto: McGraw-Hill.

Matthews, Gwyneth Ferguson. 1983. *Voices From the Shadows: Women with Disabilities Speak Out.* Toronto: Women's Educational Press.

Moore, Maureen. 1985. "Coping with Pelvic Inflammatory Disease." In *Women and Disability.* Frances Rooney and Pat Israel, eds. *Resources for Feminist Research* 14(1).

Newsweek. 1988. "Reading God's Mind." June 13. 56–59.

Ramsay, A. Melvin. 1986. *Postviral Fatigue Syndrome, the Saga of Royal Free Disease.* London: Gower Medical Publishing.

Rawlinson, Mary C. 1983. "The Facticity of Illness and the Appropriation of Health." In *Phenomenology in a Pluralistic Context.* William L. McBride and Calvin O. Schrag, eds. Albany: SUNY Press.

Rich, Adrienne. 1976. *Of Woman Born: Motherhood as Experience and Institution.* New York: W.W. Norton.

Rooney, Frances and Pat Israel, eds. 1985. *Women and Disability. Resources for Feminist Research* 14(1).

Sacks, Oliver. 1988. "The Revolution of the Deaf." *The New York Review of Books,* June 2, 23–28.

Shaul, Susan L. and Jane Elder Bogle. 1981. "Body Image and the Woman with a Disability." In *Sexuality and Physical Disability.* David G. Bullard and Susan E. Knight, eds. St. Louis: C.V. Mosby.

Sherwin, Susan. 1984–85. "A Feminist Approach to Ethics." *Dalhousie Review* 64(4):704–713.

Sherwin, Susan. 1987. "Feminist Ethics and In Vitro Fertilization." In *Science, Morality and Feminist Theory.* Marsha Hanen and Kai Nielsen, eds. Calgary: The University of Calgary Press.

Sontag, Susan. 1977. *Illness as Metaphor.* New York: Random House.

U.N. Decade of Disabled Persons 1983–1992. 1983. *World Programme of Action Concerning Disabled Persons.* New York: United Nations.

Whitbeck, Caroline. "Afterword to the Maternal Instinct." In *Mothering: Essays in Feminist Theory.* Joyce Trebilcot, ed. Totowa: Rowman and Allanheld.

Zaner, Richard M. 1983. "Flirtations or Engagement? Prolegomenon to a Philosophy of Medicine." In *Phenomenology in a Pluralistic Context.* William L. McBride and Calvin O. Schrag, eds. Albany: SUNY Press.

BE-LONGING: THE LUST FOR HAPPINESS

Mary Daly

Supernatural: "Transcending nature in degree and in kind or concerned with what transcends nature (a divine order which directs history from outside and keeps man in touch with the eternal world through the Church and the sacraments—*Times Lit. Supp.*"

Webster's Third New International Dictionary of the English Language

Super Natural: "Unfolding Nature in degree and in kind or concerned with what Unfolds Nature (an Elemental order which directs history from inside and keeps women and all biophilic creatures in Touch with the real world through the senses—*Tidal Times*."

Websters' First New Intergalactic Wickedary of the English Language

The word *happiness* has been banalized/travestied beyond belief/relief by the Bosses of Boredom. Repeated and regurgitated by the verbiage vendors, it is phallicism's formalized label for fullfillment. Images of "happy" fembots file through the Foreground of fatherdom's dumb shows/fantasies, erasing Rage, setting the stage for numberless mummified/numb-ified copies. Xeroxed First Ladies parade through commercials and soaps. Mechanical toys applauding the boys, televised numbots nod their agreement to all of His speeches and smile while He preaches His Nuclear Sermons. Like Daisy with Donald, like Nancy with Ronald, the doll-women duckspeak their memorized scripts. "Everything's fine." So goes the Line. "There's happiness for all in store, in nineteen hundred eighty-four."*

---

* The following is my own rendering of a typical Numbot Chorus number, which conveys something of the style and thought content of these man-made manikins' performances:

> Four score and seven years ago, our fathers made a T.V. show.
> It's time to switch the dial again, time to watch and smile again.
> We've always smiled and watched our men.
> We'll smile and watch our men again. Again. Again.
> When acid falling from the sky was just a gleam in Daddy's eye.
> We never asked the reason why; we'll never ask again.
> When nukes were just a big boys' plot, we smiled and watched a lot.
> It's 1984 again. We'll smile and watch our men again.
> Amen.
> (Applause, as the Numbots fade in time for the Nightly News.)

Happiness has Wholly Other meanings from all this, however. The following discussion launches a Nag-Gnostic ontological exploration of such Other dimensions.

PHILOSOPHICAL AND THEOLOGICAL CONSIDERATIONS OF HAPPINESS

The word *happiness,* deeply understood, is radiant with ontological meaning. Uncovering its philosophical meaning is an important task for Wonderers seeking/Lusting for Wisdom. Our exorcism and ecstasy can be aided by exploration of this philosophical background. Indeed, such investigation is a catalyst for Metamorphic movement into our own Background of Metabeing. Moreover, Nag-Gnostic examination of the medieval theological tradition concerning happiness (or what was known as "man's last end") is vital for this exploit/exploration. Theologians have believed that "grace" is necessary for the attainment of happiness, and the reasons that led them to this conclusion shed light upon our Metamorphic movement.

In Aristotelian philosophy, happiness is *eudaimonia,* which in Greek means having a good attendant or indwelling spirit. As a philosophical term employed by Aristotle and his disciples it means "a life of activity governed by reason." In the highest sense, happiness is a life of activity of the mind, or contemplation.[1]

Clearly, then, within this tradition, happiness is not equatable with some passing emotion. Rather, the emotion of joy—popularly identified with happiness—is a consequence of the life of activity that constitutes happiness. The experience of joy is a psychic manifestation of happiness.

Following the tradition of Aristotle, Aquinas taught that "man's happiness," which he identified as "man's last end" consists in an operation of the intellect. Consistent with his own logic, moreover, he concluded that the happiness of "man" must consist in the operation of

his highest power—the intellect—in relation to its highest object. For Aquinas, the highest object of knowledge is the "Divine Essence." He writes:

> For perfect happiness the intellect needs to reach the very Essence of the First Cause. And thus it will have its perfection through union with God as with that object, in which alone man's happiness consists.[2]

This conclusion presented a problem to its author. For he believed that man could not attain such union through his natural powers. For:

> Every knowledge that is according to the mode of created substance falls short of the vision of the Divine Essence, which infinitely surpasses all created substance. Consequently neither man nor any creature, can attain final Happiness by his natural powers.[3]

Man, then, would seem doomed to eternal frustration. God, however, has the solution. By infusing grace into the soul, god elevates the capacities of Man, so that Man can merit eternal happiness in the next life. Yet one problem remains, namely, that the created intellect after death still lacks the capacity to see the "Divine Essence," even after this reward has been "merited" with the aid of grace. Aquinas maintains that this is resolved by the infusion of a "supernatural disposition," that is, a special supernatural light, which is added to the intellect "in order that it may be raised up to such a great and sublime height."[4]

Although some Hags and Harpies may feel a bit hysterical after hearing of all these additives and erections, it is important not to succumb to the urge to roll on the floor or fly away before considering the fascinating insights which can be gleaned from such texts. For, as representative of mainstream traditional christian belief, Aquinas was conveying overt and subliminal messages of importance. I shall note some of these.

First, there is the notion that happiness is fully attainable only after death. Second, this presupposes that the spiritual faculties (intellect and will) of the Happy Dead Ones were elevated supernaturally by grace when they were still alive, so that they could merit eternal happiness. Third, the Happy Creature, in order to have the Beatific Vision in heaven, must be in a permanently passive condition in relation to "God," who has all of the power in this relationship. The Aristotelian idea of happiness as a life of activity of the mind has been converted into an afterlife of passivity. Since the "operation" or "activity" is utterly supernatural, artifactual, the Happy State is one of essential impotence. This afterlife of perpetual union/copulation with the Divine Essence is an absolutely artificial operation.

One could see this doctrine of happiness, then, as a confession and legitimation of male impotence. It is by no means a woman-originated doctrine. Women do not experience a need for a supernaturally stimulated eternal erection. As impotent beings, patriarchal males do have this need, which they have erected religiously as the requirement for happiness. It will be noticed that the eternal copulation under scrutiny here is a male homoerotic relationship. The sons seek union with their male god, who is frozen forever as the dominant partner in this pathetically unequal union.

One might ask what all this has to do with women. In one sense, it would seem, the answer is "not much." Women have never concocted such a bizarre scenario of eternal full-fillment, although many have succumbed to intolerable pressures to swallow such myths. Women do feel blocked/fixed by forces which they often cannot Name, and which are experienced as impediments to the unfolding of our own native capacities. Since patriarchal propaganda is everywhere, even within women's minds, and since phallo-institutions impose sanctions throughout father-land, the lives of many women have indeed been made so miserable that they have been able to accept the bore-ophilic belief that happiness is attainable only after death. They have even been bored/gored into believing that their powers need

supernatural elevation (grace) in this life in order to have any hope of happiness in the next.

As the mind-bindings come loose, however, women become increasingly aware that the impediments to our attainment of happiness are not innate deficiencies. Wild women do not share the phallocratic male's problem of impotence and thus do not have the need to fantasize an eternal connection with an omnipotent being. Metamorphosing women recognize that our happiness is indeed a *life of activity*. In a special way happiness is activity of the mind, or contemplation. It can include many activities: artistic creation, political action, development of spiritual powers, athletic activities. These are a few facets of our many-sided Unfolding, our holistic Realization of Be-Longing, that is, our Happiness.

METAPATTERNING

As we have seen, the theology of eternal happiness implies the need for supernatural extensions of man's powers, so that he can connect eternally with god. It is not hard to detect which organ in a phallocentric religion, is subliminally the focus of this attention/extension. Nags will note also, on the basis of previous discussion, that theological language about supernatural "raising up" of the intellect "to a great and sublime height" so that it can connect with god has analogs in phallotechnology's erections. The explosions of nuclear weapons are also supernatural/artificial emissions—attempts of impotent males to connect eternally with their omnipotent killer-god. Since the impotent patriarchal male's own organ "falls short" (to use the expression of Aquinas concerning man's intellect) of attaining the "Divine Essence," he needs to build and use technological extensions of that organ.

Given this context, male pronouncements concerning a new stage of "spiritual evolution" that requires the acquisition of "new organs" are suspect in the eyes of Metamorphosing women. Thus the statements of the master Rumi of Balkh and of the sufis that are cited by Doris Lessing reflect this perspective of male obsession with impotence.* When women adapt this kind of language uncritically, it becomes easy to slide into other phallic assumptions.

Feminists also sometimes have used this kind of language. For example, Barbara Starrett's presents the concept of a new "organ" which "enables us to will our own further evolution." There is nothing whatsoever that is phallic about Starrett's ideas, and indeed it is a valid mode of speculation to ask whether women are developing such a faculty. However, it is important for Nags to question where and under what circumstances we began to employ certain words to convey ideas that are new to us, and whether they can be misleading.**

The use of such a term as "organ" to designate the Metamorphosing Powers of metapatriarchal women could carry with it subliminal associations not intended by the speaker/writer. It could suggest, for example, that Lusty women's Be-Longing is somehow parallel or comparable to the patriarchal killer males' felt need to transcend their physical and ontological sense of impotence by acquiring supernatural or technological extensions. Wonderlusting Voyagers do not need such extensions. Wild women Realize our will to further evolution, our Lust for participation in the Unfolding of Be-ing, our Happiness. Our primary problem now is the overcoming of the unnatural obstacles—both external and embedded—to this ontological Passion.

There are Elemental powers in each woman's psyche that are covered by the embedded codes of her captors. In her process of breaking the embedded code, she uncovers her own powers. One way of describing this process is to call it *metapatterning*.

The Dreaming/Musing that engenders Metamorphosis is a process of metapatterning. This process presupposes Seeing through the paternal patterns, the moldy molds intended to stunt our lives. It is thought-provoking for Searchers to find that the word *pattern* is derived from the Middle Latin *patronus,* meaning patron of a benefice, patron saint, master, pattern. *Patronus,* of course, is derived from *pater,* meaning father. Indeed, there is an odor of paternalism about the definition of the word *pattern,* which means "a fully realized form, original, or model accepted or proposed for imitation: something regarded as a normative example to be copied: ARCHETYPE, EXEMPLAR." Metapatriarchal Erratic movement is hardly according to patriarchal pattern. Metamorphosing women do not imitate/copy some "fully realized" paternal form or model. Rather, we are Realizing/Forming/Originating.

When metamorphosing Muses use the term *metapatterning,* we mean to Name the process of breaking through paternal patterns.[5] Nag-identified metapatterning involves real transcending of patriarchal patterns of thinking, speaking, acting. It is weaving our way through and out of these patterns. Erratic women weave our lives, our works, not as imitations of models, nor as models for others, but as unique diversified creations.

Rather than seeking to develop new "organs" (an old pattern), then, metapatterning women recognize that we already have the powers to will our own further evolution. The idea of a new "organ" is too limiting to Name the source of the metapatterning powers which myriad consciously mutating women are now discovering in multiform ways. That source is something like a Telic Focusing Principle that is all-pervasive within the organism that is entirely present in all parts of the organism. This Telic Focusing Principle

---

* The fact that these "spiritual teachers" were not christians is irrelevant to this point. Whether the "spiritual teacher" is Aquinas or the master Rumi, the over-riding "sacred canopy" of legitimations is constructed of the symbols of phallicism. See Balbara Starrett, "I Dream in Female: The Metaphors of Evolution," *Amazon Quartery* 3(1), Nov. 1974.

** My earlier use of the word *androgyny* to signify woman-identified integrity is a case in point. When I was writing *Beyond God the Father* this word was suggested by a male colleague. Although it sounded a bit alien, I adopted it without enough critical evaluation. Subsequent experiences made it clear that the word was completely inadequate, conveying something like the images of Ronald and Nancy Reagan scotch-taped together.

enables us to assimilate what we need from the environment, to grow, to adapt, to change. It is a re-membering principle as well as a metapatterning principle. Our analysis of Metamorphospheric Movement requires that we give further attention to the workings of this principle.

FOCUSING/CENTERING

When a woman is deeply in touch with her creative powers, her powers of metapatterning, she can, of course, recall other times of feeling at a distance from these powers and from this kind of activity. The Presence of her metapatterning Self accentuates her awareness of the alienation she experienced in times of foreground fixation. She may, at these peak moments, be able to acknowledge the alienation of "normal" times during which she could not fully experience her own experience of alienation. She may then ask her Self in astonishment where she was at those other times, when, it seems, she had fallen away from her Center.

She had, in fact, been dragged away from her Center by the fragmentation of foreground "living," that is, dying. The process of dislocation/splintering, however, may have been subtle, subliminal. Sometimes, therefore, a woman will describe her experience of being connected once more with her metapatterning Presence as suddenly coming home again after an unexplained and inexplicable absence.

Metapatterning can take many forms. The activities involved are multiform, for example, traveling in a foreign country, riding a bicycle, being engaged in a Spinning discussion of ideas, walking on the beach. The process of writing a book of feminist philosophy can be a useful illustration. This is particularly so because the effort of metapatterning is sustained over a somewhat lengthy period of time and because the process itself of metapatterning is the object of attention.

So, then, a woman may be in the process of writing a book, an activity that requires telic centering/focusing. In the course of this prolonged activity she assimilates all kinds of events into the writing process. The book she is writing participates in the deep purposefulness of her living. Her Lust to write this particular work becomes part of her Be-Longing, and writing it is one dimension of writing the book of her life. It is a Metaphor of her Journey into Metabeing. The focus required for bringing forth a work in this dimension, and of these dimensions, encourages the writer into a state of heightened awareness. Many apparent "coincidences" then begin to happen. For example, although the author of this book does not often watch television, she turns on the T.V. set one day just in time to see/hear a "news" story that evokes a whole chain of metaphors. Or again, she is thinking about a Foresister—Elizabeth Cady Stanton—and wishing she had a particular piece of information at her fingertips. A few minutes later she opens her mailbox and finds that a publisher has sent her a complimentary, unsolicited copy of a book on Stanton, containing just the information wanted. Moreover, she "just happens" to open the book immediately to the right place. Or again, in the course of a telephone conversation a friend mentions an article that is exactly what is needed to support the argument she is developing at the moment.

The sensory aliveness that accompanies such a process is complex/gynaesthetic. A typo turns out to be the truly accurate and subliminally intended word. This aliveness is a consequence of deep telic focusing/centering. Even the tedious distractions of daily life can sometimes be assimilated into this process by the telic principle. A boring committee meeting occasionally can provide material for radical analysis. A trip to the supermarket can suddenly supply a missing clue. The Presence of the creative telos, then, keeps a woman fiercely focused. Since the author here described is a radical feminist, she is involved in the creative communal process of decoding the prevailing codes and of creating out of her own Code, that is, metapatterning. The material for her Search, therefore, is Everywhere.

Yet the forces of fragmentation lie in ambush. As Dragons, as Gorgons, women must guard and foster the Flame of telic focus. For poor women, for women of color, and for others whose individual circumstances are particularly oppressive, the struggle against the fragmentation of energy that brings physical disease and psychic paralysis is often unspeakably hard. For all women, particularly in times and places of extreme repression, the creative telos within the Self is in conflict with the agendas of the sadostate. Some counterforce is provided by the communal telos of the feminist movement, and the constant weaving of this net of knowledge and commitment is both the primary act and the necessary condition for the macromutation that is the Elemental Metamorphic Movement of women.

THE "SOUL" AS METAPHOR FOR TELIC PRINCIPLE

One traditional way of naming the principle of telic focus has been to call this the "soul." Shrewds can use this as a starting point for our analysis. Since my intent is to wrench this concept out of its traditional context, using it in a Nag-Gnostic context. I am employing it not simply as an analytic concept but also as Metaphor.

Soul, as springboard word, then, refers here to the animating principle of an organism. Specifically, it means the "substantial form" of a living body, as this is understood in Aristotelian philosophy.[6] Soul, then, as the word is used here, is not intended in a Platonic sense, as if it were a distinct entity loosely connected with the body, or imprisoned in the body. Certainly I do not mean it in any sort of Cartesian sense, as if it were "mind" or *res cogitans* vaguely connected with matter. Rather, I use the word *soul* to mean an animating principle that is intimately united with/present to the body, in a union that traditionally has been called a "hylomorphic union." According to this theory, in human beings the "intellectual principle" is united to the body as the body's form.[7]

To speak of the soul in this sense, then, is not to convey the naive, dualistic notion that soul and body are two united entities. The soul, conceived as the animating and unifying principle of the organism, is the radical source of life functions and activities. It is the source of telic centering—of the purposiveness of the organism.

The soul, understood in this tradition, is wholly present in each part of the body.[8] It is not a mere quantitative whole. An example of the latter would be a house, which is composed of foundation, walls, and roof. (Obviously, the entire house is not in each of its parts.) Moreover, the soul is not just a generic or logical whole, as a whole definition is made up of all of its parts. Rather, it is a "potential whole." Explaining this concept, Aquinas wrote that the whole soul is divided into "virtual parts." That is:

> The whole soul is in each part of the body, by totality of perfection and of essence, but not by totality of power. . . . with regard to sight, it is in the eye; and with regard to hearing, it is in the ear, and so forth.[9]

Since this concept of unity (of essence) at the root of multiplicity (of parts/powers) was not comprehended by all philosophers, Aquinas had to refute the position that "besides the intellectual soul there are in man other souls essentially different from one another."[10]

This seemingly simple position, namely, that there are not many souls in one person, but rather one soul, wholly present everywhere within that person, can be a Metaphoric springboard for Metamorphosing women. It can function as an aid to Amazons seeking the meaning of our Be-Longing in the face/faces of the fear-full fragmentation of women that is inflicted in the fatherland. Some of the implications may be more obvious if the Searcher substitutes the word *Self* for *soul,* thereby constructing the statement: There are not many Selves in one woman, but rather, one Self, wholly present in that woman. I am not asserting here that Self and soul are precisely equivalent terms; in fact, they are not. My point is that one obvious consequence of the idea that a woman has one soul wholly present in all of her "parts," is that there is an essential integrity at the very core of her Self.

Be-Longing implies the Unfolding, the Realization, of this inherent integrity. It is Realized as a woman becomes wholly Present in all of her activities. The phenomenological manifestation of this integrity and pervasive Presence of her soul is a radical consistency in her behavior. She does not seem to be "one person one day and someone else the next." This is not to say that she lacks complexity and variety of skills, activities, and experiences. Quite the opposite is the case; she manifests a high degree of differentiation. Moreover, she is spontaneous. This is possible because her energy is focused; it is not dissipated in the maintenance of masks, of fragmented false selves—splintered personae parading on the periphery of her Self.

The Unfolding/Realizing of this integrity is be-ing beyond such reified beings, the solidified pseudo-selves. It is participation in Metabeing. The Lust for this intensely focused ontological activity, or Be-Longing, is the Lust for Happiness.

Souls and Holograms/Holographs

The concept of the unity of the soul, as presented in Aristotelian philosophy and developed in the doctrine of Aquinas, can not easily be dismissed as completely absurd and irrelevant. To one who has long been familiar with this doctrine, it is both fascinating and funny to find contemporary scientific thinkers using language that in some ways is reminiscent of this idea, when they write of the universe and of the mind as "holograms."

According to David Bohm, for example, who often uses the holographic analogy, the information of the entire universe is contained in each of its parts. As Larry Dossey describes holograms:

> A hologram is a specially constructed image which, when illuminated by a laser beam, seems eerily suspended in three-dimensional space. The most

incredible feature of holograms is that any *piece* of it, if illuminated with coherent light, provides an image of the *entire* hologram. The information of the whole is contained in each part.[11]

Dossey—and others before him—asks whether, as part of the universe, we have holographic features ourselves that permit us to comprehend a holographic universe. Stanford neurophysiologist Karl Pribam has answered the question in the affirmative, proposing the hologram as a model of brain function.[12] Putting together the ideas of Bohm and Pribam, Dossey suggests that the brain is a hologram "that is a part of an even larger hologram—the universe itself."[13]

The holographic analogy is, of course, just that—an analogy.* It has provided a language for these scientists to speak of an idea of the mind and of its relation to the universe that is really not entirely new. Comparable themes have recurred in the history of philosophy.[14] Bearing this in mind, Brewsters may wish to use holograms/holographs as variant metaphors pointing to integrity/wholeness. This is not to suggest that contemporary scientific jargon legitimates the classical philosophical language, concerning the soul, for example. It may be, however, that the holographic metaphor can render more accessible some of the potentially helpful concepts that are contained/captured within the contexts of philosophical treatises.

The holographic metaphor, moreover, as applied to the idea of the soul, can suggest a telic centering principle which is an unfolding potential whole—one that is changing in harmony with the universe. Prudes can use this combination of metaphors to point to the internal source of the unfolding integrity of metapatriarchal women. Such integrity is manifested in the whole spectrum of a woman's activities and characterizes her presentiating Presence.

---

* Robin Morgan uses the holographic analogy in a thought-provoking way to view feminism. See *The Anatomy of Freedom* (Garden City, N.Y.: Doubleday and Company, 1982).

COMMUNICATION BEYOND THE
CELLS OF SICKNESS

Since Metamorphosing women are Gyn/Ecological, we do not evolve/mutate as isolated units, nor do our powers develop in isolation from each other. Recalling the metaphor of the hologram, we reflect upon the fact that "any *piece* of it, if illuminated with coherent light, provides an image of the *entire* hologram." Women who are Realizing any of our powers, that is, illuminating such powers with the coherent light of our own reason, find that this process implies Realizing the telic principle (soul) in its entirety/integrity. Metamorphosing women are Unfolding as *whole* intellectual/passionate/sentient Selves as we move out of the Numbed State. No other than holistic change is desirable. To speak of it another way, this mutation is organic. The powers of Crones evolve in harmony with each other, in *communication* with each other.

David Bakan discusses communication on a biological level in a way that can be helpful for the analysis of metapatriarchal processes. After distinguishing conscious communication between two persons from internal communication that takes place when something previously unconscious becomes conscious within an individual, he discusses internal biological communication:

> Within the human organism there are varieties of forms of communication evident when what happens in one part of the body affects what happens in other parts. There are numerous mechanisms in such internal communication, the neural and hormonal being particularly conspicuous. . . . The mechanisms are remarkably diverse. The fact that communication takes place, by whatever mechanism, pervades all biological phenomena.[15]

The reduction of such internal communication results in disease and death. Identifying this anti-process as telic decentralization, Bakan discusses lack of communication in cancer cells:

> It turns out that the cells of cancer, which are radically and manifestly removed from the telos of any higher level of the hierarchical order, are precisely those cells which are distinguishable from their cellular counterparts by a gross inability to communicate with other cells, as indicated both by their growth behavior and by the lack of ionic transfer.[16]*

Nags are very much aware of the "gross inability to communicate" which characterizes those who manufacture and maintain the imprisoning cells of snooldom. Those who construct and sell these cells (homes, schools, hospitals, doctrines, myths, et cetera) are precisely those who cannot communicate in biophilic and ontological dimensions. They attempt, however, to invade and man-ipulate those whom they imprison and poison, and this predatory P-R impedes Elemental communication. The result, of course, is a sick social "organism," and a widespread sickness unto death among members of that society.

Bakan reminds us that *"a degree of telic decentralization is the essential underlying characteristic of the diseased organism."*[17] Metamorphosing women are determined to leave the diseased organism of fatherland. The way out is precisely telic centering/focusing, which implies quantum leaps of conscious communication within our Selves, among each other, and with the universe. This consciously willed centered Unfolding implies macroevolution.

MACROEVOLUTION

Having affirmed the Aristotelian doctrine of the soul as one viable starting point for discussion of our transformation, Soothsayers will assess some of its liabilities as well as its assets. There is, first of all, the problem of its dualism. We have seen that the dualism of Aristotle and Aquinas was not merely a crude belief in form (soul) and matter as if these were two "things." Rather, these were understood to be intimately connected principles of a living creature. There

---

* Bakan's choice of the words *higher* and *hierarchical* order is perhaps unfortunate, but this does not invalidate his point.

is hardly a more abstract concept in the history of philosophy than Aristotle's notion of "prime matter," which was by no means believed to be sense perceptible, but rather was thought to be knowable only through a complex reasoning process. Yet dualism, however subtle, is recognized as inadequate by Nag-Gnostic critics, for Naming the reality of our Selves. It is more in accord with the experience of women breaking free of *feminitude*[18] to view "soul" and "body" as ways of talking about different aspects of the same Self. Moreover, there are more than two aspects of such experience. Words such as *spirit* and *aura,* for example, name other aspects of Self-definition, as does *Elemental be-ing.*[19]

Nags also criticize the *essential* unchangeableness of the Aristotelian soul. It is true that change was believed to take place on an "accidental" level. The intellect, for example, could acquire new knowledge. In the view of Aquinas, the essence of the soul is something like a root or source of many faculties, which are distinguished from each other by their acts and objects. The powers flow from the essence of the soul and are interconnected with each other.[20] The activities proceeding from these powers of the soul, thus conceived, were understood to bring about individual and social development. No matter how highly these faculties are developed, however, according to this tradition, this brings about no essential change in the individual or the species. The worldview of Aristotelianism, then, was static, nonevolutionary.

It was, perhaps, a glimmer of intuition and yearning for more than this stasis that prompted the christian doctrine of grace—especially the doctrine of sanctifying grace. The latter, conceived as "supernatural life" infused into the soul, was believed to make possible a "heightening" or intensification of the soul's spiritual capacities, so that these could attain higher levels or dimensions. Unfortunately, the higher levels all converged into/boiled down to "God."

The intimations of quantum leaps beyond the prevailing static state were potted into a belief in a "supernatural" Static State, the eternal stagnation of the blessed.

Hags find this kind of eternal retirement plan ineffably resistible. Dismissing christian supernaturalism as the Kiss of Death, we catch our breath and return to the Aristotelian concept of the soul, considering other aspects of this theory. The treatment of sexual differentiation, for example, is another important topic, although seemingly not very important to Aristotle, for sexual difference is considered "accidental" to the "human species." Although to the uninitiated, "accidental" may sound like a joke term, it was intended seriously. Taken in this context, it did not mean "happening by chance or causing injury." Rather, it was intended to convey that the difference of gender is nonessential, that it does not change the species of individuals. In other words, women were considered to be "human"—in abstract theory though not in the actual society legitimated by Aristotle. That is, women were said to belong to the fixed species called MAN.[21]

Metamorphosing women are not flattered but rather are horrified at the idea of such belonging. Moreover, the experience of such a woman is that she does not "belong." Her Erraticism essentially implies breaking the molds of the Fixed Species. Her psychic/physical Living requires Macroevolution.

Macroevolution is defined as "evolutionary change involving relatively large and complex steps (as transformation of one species to another)." Such evolution is now intended, with varying degrees of explicitness, by many Crones. Metapatriarchal women experience as ineffably accidental our connection with the species that has planned and executed witchcrazes, death camps, slavery, torture, racism in all of its manifestations, world famine, chemical contamination, animal experimentation, the nuclear arms race. This differentiation is affirmed by a series of conscious choices.

Metapatriarchally moving women not only experience now but continue to choose to develop our differences from those who consciously and willingly perpetrate these horrors and we recognize these differences as not merely accidental, but rather *essential*. The traditional concept of "species," especially of "the human species" does not adequately encompass the differently oriented lives supposedly contained therein. I refer primarily to its grotesque blurring of differences between those whose intent and behavior is radically biophilic and those whose desensitized/decentralized, soulless and berserk (dis)orientation manifests "gross inability to communicate" and fundamental enmity toward Life itself.*

Alice Walker has expressed an almost inexpressably enraged awareness of these differences in her article "Nuclear Exorcism" (first delivered as a speech at an anti-nuclear arms rally). After reciting a curse prayer that was collected by Zora Neale Hurston in the 1920s, Walker discusses the hope for revenge that she believes to be at the heart of people of color's resistance to joining the anti-nuclear movement. She writes:

> And it would be good, perhaps, to put an end to the species in any case, rather than let white men continue to subjugate it and continue their lust to dominate, exploit and despoil not just our planet but the rest of the universe, which is their clear and oft-stated intention, leaving their arrogance and litter not just on the moon but on everything else they can reach.[22]

After presenting a strong argument for "fatally irradiating ourselves" and for "accepting our demise as a planet as a simple and just preventive medicine administered to the universe," Alice Walker decides against passive acceptance of extinction:

> Life is better than death, I believe, if only because it is less boring, and because it has fresh peaches in it. In any case, earth is my home—though for centuries white people have tried to convince me that I have no right to exist, except in the dirtiest, darkest corners of the globe.
>
> So let me tell you: I intend to protect my home.[23]

I suggest that the decision not to allow nuclear maniacs "to put an end to the species" logically implies rejection of the idea that there is a "human species." The gynocidal, genocidal, biocidal aggressors whose lust is for destruction are deciding in one direction. It is possible to decide in Other directions through the consciously willed and continual affirmation of Ongoing Life that is Pure Lust. This lived decision as it is carried out in everyday events constitutes not only more than an accidental difference; it is also greater than a specific difference. *It renders the old philosophical concept of "species" obsolete,* especially as a tool for conceptualizing and Naming the be-ing of biophilic creatures. Such ones cannot be confined to any static species, for our essences are changing, metapatterning.

When I write Metaphorically of the "souls" of women as our telic focusing and metapatterning principle, then, I am not restricting the term to express the classical Aristotelian idea of substantial form determining an individual as a member of a fixed species. For such a species can conceivably contain/encompass other "members" whose telos (if the privation can be designated by an affirmative name) is really anti-telos, that is, ultimate destruction of meaning and purpose. Indeed, the concept of such a species is contradictory, nonsensical. It would attempt to embrace creatures whose conscious behavior is wholly oriented in opposite directions.

Yet the term *soul* can be heard with the Third Ear by one who listens in an Other context. Springing off from the Aristotelian structure, and from the language of modern science as well, the Spirited Searcher may speak of the soul not as that

---

* Wise readers will recognize that this sort of distinction is not a simplistic bifurcation on the basis of gender. Patriarchy here is seen as a disease attacking the core of consciousness in females as well as males.

which confines an individual within a "species," but rather as a principle of uniqueness/diversity.*

Since Metamorphosing women can view our bodies as transmutable to and from energy, the soul can be seen as the centering principle of this energy/gynergy. It is, as the ancients believed, the form of the body, but this is translated by Wanton/Wandering women to mean the meta-patterning principle through which we direct our shape-shifting, our transfiguration/mutation.

This telic principle of uniqueness/diversity by no means has the effect of undermining unity, manifested in community, commonality, and bonding. Rather, it expands and intensifies the possibilities of Living the realities designated by these words. The deep connections that are rooted in one's individuality as an intentional creator of her be-ing are more significant than are accidental connections in space and time, that is, of geographical and/or temporal proximity. They are more radical even than familial, ethnic, and class ties, and ties of religious and educational "background."

To affirm this connectedness that is rooted in Self-creation is hardly to overlook these other ties, in all their complexity and depth. It is to begin to understand these givens in the context of metapatriarchal becoming. The confrontation and exploration of the effects of these bonds of "background" has been an important concern of many feminists. Crones are also re-membering a more radical Background of diversity and connectedness that moves women into Meta-morphospheres. Bonding in relation to the final cause—the cause of causes—is focused upon where we are going. It is focused also upon where we came from, in the most radical sense, for it is rooted in Elemental origins.

This bonding of women as deeply connected with our final cause takes place in a world of vibrations, of resonances, of ribbons of rhythm weaving through rivers, sands, trees, winds, flames, seas. Our thoughts respond to the music of plants and animals, oceans and stars. Women sense, too, that animals and plants respond to our thought-forms, that nothing is done in isolation. We are participants not only in what is commonly called the dance of life, but also in what Prudes might prefer to call the Prance of Life. For macroevolution, we recall, requires "relatively large and complex steps." This is especially the case as we continue to transform from one species to another.

The intensity/immensity of individual women's steps—our prancing, metapatterning movements of individuation—augments our capacity and Lust for participation. The Lusty longing for ontological participation is an intrinsic aspect of Be-Longing. It is a longing to live in connectedness that already is, but is not yet Realized. Realizing such ontological participation requires conjuring metamemories, the memories that aid our Prancing, that spring and bound into the deep past, thereby carrying our vision forward.

BE-LONGING AND METAMEMORY

Women's yearning for experiencing our ontological connectedness with all that is Elemental implies a longing to mend, to weave together the Elemental realities that have been severed from consciousness, that is, forgotten. The deep significance of forgetting and re-membering is suggested in Greek myth. According to Hesiod, Lethe (Forgetting) is the daughter of Eris (Strife).[24] It is clear that the amnesia of women is in large measure the product of strife/conflict. From the earliest beginnings of our lives all of the agents of patriarchal patterning work unceasingly to destroy women's Elemental Wildness. The suffering involved in the struggle to survive this battering certainly induces forgetfulness.

---

* Haggard Searchers will relish recalling that according to medieval theology, *each* angel is a distinct species. (See Thomas Aquinas, *Summa theologiae*, I, q. 50, a. 4.) Each Metamorphosing Journeyer experiences moments in which she recognizes her Self and Others who *live* biophilically as many distinct species.

There is much more to be understood about deep forgetfulness, however. As we have seen, in Greek mythology Mnemosyne, the Goddess of Memory, was the mother of all art. Poetry, then, was the child of Memory. Reflecting upon Plato's banning of poetry from his ideal state, Ernest Schachtel recalls that since that philosopher was concerned with planning the future rather than with evoking the past, he chose to impose a taboo upon memory in its most potent forms.[25] Comparing the story of Ulysses' strategy for withstanding the irresistible song of the Sirens with Plato's banning of the poets, Schachtel reminds us that "the profound fascination of memory of past experience . . . with its promise of happiness and pleasure" poses a "threat to the kind of activity, planning, and purposeful thought and behavior encouraged by modern Western civilization."[26]

Unfortunately, Schachtel does not have very clear intimations of what it is about deep Memory that promises happiness and pleasure. Nor can he really say *what* it is, exactly, about "the kind of purposeful thought and behavior encouraged by modern Western civilization" that makes it radically inimical to such Memory. Metapatriarchal women, however, are dis-covering what sort of Memory is so potent, so promising, and so threatening to modern civilization's "purposeful" thought and behavior. Nags Nag each other into recurrent awareness of what is wrong with the purposes of the Memory-hating civilization. We know that truly focused purposefulness is rooted in deep Memory, which we might now call Metamemory. For this is beyond and transformative of ordinary "memories," and it is a source of the Lust for Happiness, that is, Be-Longing.

Crones, therefore, are keenly cognizant of the urgency of the task—implied in Be-Longing itself—of overcoming our amnesia. For as long as vaster expanses of Metamemory still elude us, the energy of our Lusting is slowed down, potted, deflected. Clues for our Memory-Searching can be gleaned from Schachtel's analysis of "childhood amnesia." He writes:

> The categories (or schemata) of adult memory are not suitable receptacles for early childhood experiences and therefore not fit to preserve these experiences and enable their recall.[27]

Developing this thesis, Schachtel points out the inadequacy of the Freudian assumption that a repression of sexual experience accounts for the repression of nearly all experience of early childhood. Rather, the problem of amnesia is also associated with the fact that there is a quality and intensity typical of early childhood experience that cannot be contained in the adult's categories for retaining memories. Muses hardly need to be persuaded of Schachtel's point that the average adult memory is incapable of reproducing "anything that resembles a really rich, full, rounded, and alive experience."[28] As he points out:

> Even the most "exciting" events are remembered as milestones rather than as moments filled with the concrete abundance of life. Adult memory reflects life as a road with occasional signposts and milestones rather than as the landscape through which this road has led.... And even these signposts themselves do not usually indicate the really significant moments in a person's life; rather they point to the events that are conventionally supposed to be significant, to the clichés which society has come to consider as the main stations of life.[29]

Thus the memories of most people come to resemble "the stereotyped answers to a questionnaire."

While agreeing with this point, Crone-logical critics find it imperative to point out the inadequacy of Schachtel's analysis and description of the average adult's poverty of memory. For the categories of "adult memory" in patriarchy are the categories of androcentric memory. The "milestones" of this artificial memory are male milestones, and all too frequently function for women as millstones. Thus, for example, religious and national holidays conjure memories of servitude—shopping, cooking, cleaning, et cetera. Patriarchal weddings imply the legal and ritualized loss of one's own name and autonomy. Going to work commonly means accepting a dead-end, low paying, Self-erasing job. Birthdays are reminders of aging and subsequent patriarchal devaluation. While the milestones of adult "life" may be dreary for individual males, they are at the same time a collective boost to the male ego, to the Mythic Male with whom each man identifies. Thus Christmas, Easter, Veterans' Day, Washington's Birthday, a marriage in the family are designed to be "uppers" for men and "downers" (disguised as uppers) for women.

Moral outrage at the degradation/erasure of women implied in all of these milestones/ millstones can propel a woman to the gateways of Metamemory. The quest to re-member the qualitatively Other, vivid, richly significant experiences of our past is especially urgent for women, for Realizing of such realities gives us the strength to exorcise the patriarchal categories. A woman who can evoke her childhood experiences of gazing at the moon and stars on clear nights, or lying on the grass, or listening to the sea, or watching the sunset is Elementally inspired. When she can recall early experiences of the smell of leaves on an October day, the taste of raspberries at a picnic, the feel of sand warmed by the sun, she is empowered. Energized by her own unique Elemental memories, she can break through the maze of "adult categories." Her reawakened, recharged aura expands its rays, shining through the film of societally imposed schemata, rendering visible the deep connections.

Enormous breakthroughs to the spheres of deep Memory can be occasioned by the accidental recurrence of a body posture. Feminists becoming aware of our bodies in new/ancient powerful ways know that this far-from-accidental process reconnects us with Metamemory. Women who study self-defense and various forms of the martial arts, for example, sometimes describe a vivid re-membering of bodily integrity and coordination which they had known as young girls, before the heavy indoctrination of adolescence forced feminization upon them.[30] Through the living of physical as well as spiritual intimacy with other Deviant/Defiant women, Hags experience gestures, postures, acts reminiscent of earliest woman-loving experiences with our mothers. Craftswomen who are deeply absorbed in such crafts as pottery, spinning, and weaving sometimes describe the experience of their work in words that evoke Metamemory.

DEVIANT/DEFIANT WOMEN AS METAMEMORY-BEARING GROUP

The memories accessible to Crones are not simply of physical closeness to our mothers. The charged memories of childhood carry with them in a complex and condensed way the vivid Elemental perceptions of the world that we experienced as children. Virginia Woolf expresses this quality of Elemental memory, in describing what she calls her first memory, which is a combination of two memories. The first part is a recollection of being on her mother's lap on a train or in an omnibus. This blends with the other part. She writes:

> If life has a base that it stands upon, if it is a bowl that one fills and fills and fills—then my bowl without a doubt stands upon this memory. It is of lying half asleep, half awake, in bed in the nursery at St. Ives. It is of hearing the waves breaking, one, two, one, two, and sending a splash of water over the beach; and then breaking, one, two, one, two, behind a yellow blind. It is of hearing the blind draw its little acorn across the floor as the wind blew the blind out. It is of lying and hearing this splash and seeing this light, and feeling, it is almost impossible that I should be here, of feeling the purest ecstasy I can conceive.[31]

Of crucial importance is the blending of being on her mother's lap with "the most important of all memories." This memory of lying in the nursery of St. Ives is an illustration of Metamemory. It is Elemental, filled with rhythmic sounds of the sea and the wind, suffused with light.

Such memories are Taboo. Their ecstasy and fullness can be more real than the present moment. They beckon to the ways of escape from the prison cells that are constructed of the schemata of "adult," that is, male-controlled, memory. Sirens/Sibyls insist that the Taboo against woman-bonding is connected with the Taboo against such memories. For commitment to women and breaking of the Total Taboo implies breaking through the blocks that stop us from re-membering the ecstatic spheres of Metamemory. Woman-bonding be-ing, then, is the opening of Pandora's box, which is filled with the richest treasures.

The ecstatic memories that become accessible do not induce passivity, but rather they are catalysts of intense activity which is qualitatively Other than that desired by the patriarchal planners. They are catalysts of macroevolution. Viragos' violations of Taboo, by transcending as well as including the sexual sphere, imply a constant Quest. This Quest requires creative living of the promise of Happiness that is inherent in Metamemory. Refusal to conform to hetero-relational norms is, in effect, refusal to be re-minded by the re-formers of Memory.

In a special way, then, Deviant/Defiant women are the Metamemory-bearing group among women.* This is the logical consequence of a radical choice to re-member Happiness, of a Great Refusal to be re-minded by obedience to the deadening rules of the Ruling Caste. This Choice to recall the empowering memories and to create in our daily lives future memories of Happiness is a continuing act of deviant defiance. It is a macroevolutionary leap that is fueled by Be-Longing.

Some years ago Herbert Marcuse wrote, concerning Freudian theory:

Theoretically, the difference between mental health and neurosis lies only in the degree and effectiveness of resignation: mental health is successful, efficient resignation—normally so efficient that it shows forth as moderately happy satisfaction.[32]

Further developing his exposition of this theme, Marcuse explained Freud's view:

> Repression and unhappiness *must be* if civilization is to prevail. . . . In the long run, the question is only how much resignation the individual can bear without breaking up. In this sense, therapy is a course in resignation.[33]

It is precisely this resignation to "civilization" with its numbing schemata that is defied and transcended by deviant Hags whose re-membering is the root of metapatterning, of metamorphosis.

Of course, some of patriarchy's therapists have attempted to offer their clients something more than resignation to everyday unhappiness. Discussing these pathetic efforts, Marcuse continues:

> Over and against such a "minimum program," Fromm and the other revisionists proclaim a higher goal of therapy: "optimal development of a person's potentialities and the realization of his individuality." Now it is precisely this goal which is essentially unattainable—not because of limitations in the psychoanalytic techniques but because the established civilization itself, in its very structure, denies it.[34]

Radical feminism, insofar as it is true to itself, is the Denial of this denial. As the Metamemory-bearing group, Taboo-breaking women, insofar as we are true to our Selves, are Deniers of this denial. This deviant Denying is radical unmasking of the spheres of Metamemory which are the rightful heritage of all women.

RE-MEMBERING BEYOND CIVILIZATION

Freud, that apostle of adjustment to common, everyday unhappiness, defined the foreground conditions of forget-full father-land:

---

* This is why patriarchal professionals work to control/channel female deviance. The "encouragement" of female sickness is one means to this end. As Denise Connors has demonstrated, "women's sickness can be seen as a means of channeling women's potential deviance away from a collective, system-destructive route and into a more privatized and self-destructive path." She shows that "the sick role has served to neutralize and contain women's rage, their subversive force and potential to envision and create a new way of life." ("The Social Construction of Women's Sickness," paper delivered in the Feminist Lecture Series, Smith College. Northampton, Mass., February 17, 1983.)

The programme of becoming happy, which the pleasure principle imposes on us, cannot be fulfilled; yet we must not—indeed, we cannot—give up our efforts to bring it nearer to fulfillment by some means or other.... Happiness, in the reduced sense in which we recognize it as possible, is a problem of the economics of the individual's libido.[35]

Shrewish Prudes parody this paternal patter, and in the process of reversing its reversals come up with a bit of Soothsaying. Thus:

The Elemental power of becoming happy, which our memories recall to us, can be Realized. Therefore, we must not—indeed we cannot—give up our efforts to bring it nearer to actualization by our own means.... Happiness, in the ecstatic sense in which we recognize it as possible, is the project of Metamemory-bearing women.

Feminism essentially means commitment to our past and future memories of Happiness in defiance of civilization.[*] Bearing in mind that an "obsolete" meaning of *civilization* is "the act of making a criminal process civil," Sibyls suggest that phallic civilization is essentially a criminal process, parading as "civil." Singing into conscious awareness our childhood and ancestral memories, Sirens lure women into our Past and therefore into our Future, awakening Be-Longing.

------

[*] Lillian Smith, discussing Freud's view that woman is retarded as a civilized person, wrote: "I think that what he mistook for her lack of civilization is woman's lack of *loyalty* to civilization." See "Autobiography as a Dialogue between King and Corpse," in *The Winner Names the Age,* ed. by Michelle Cliff (New York: W. W. Norton and Company, 1978). Developing this theme, Adrienne Rich has written of the problematic intertwining of racism and the oppression of women as these evils affect the lives of women, especially in the United States. This theme of choosing to be disloyal to civilization is essential in the development of feminist theory which takes on the task of realistic assessment of the multiple oppression of women under patriarchy. See Adrienne Rich, "Disloyal to Civilization: Feminism, Racism, Gynephobia," in *On Lies, Secrets, and Silence: Selected Prose 1966–1978* (New York: W. W. Norton and Company, 1979), pp. 275–310.

A simple and telling comment on civilization is recorded in *Daughters of Copper Woman,* a remarkable collection of stories from native women of Vancouver Island, women who are "members of a secret society whose roots go back beyond recorded history to the dawn of Time itself."[36] The specific statement is:

Civilization brought measles, whooping cough, chicken pox, diphtheria, small pox, tuberculosis, and syphilis.[37]

In a wide sense, all of the stories in *Daughters of Copper Woman* are comments on civilization. The white christian conquerors of the native people decimated their population. When vast numbers of the "memorizers," the women of this matriarchal, matrilineal society, who were living history books, were killed by the disease-carrying, raping, white male invaders, much of the knowledge and wisdom of these women died with them. Yet some of the knowledge remains. The voice of Old Woman, speaking to the young girl Ki-Ki through her "Granny," explained:

"We must reach out to our sisters, all of our sisters, and ask them to share their truth with us, offer to share our truth with them.... The last treasure we have, the secrets of the matriarchy, can be shared and honored by women, and be proof there is another way, a better way, and some of us remember it."[38]

Expressing a vision of universal female remembering, Old Woman said:

"Women are bringing the pieces of truth together. Women are believing again that we have a right to be whole. Scattered pieces from the black sisters, from the yellow sisters, from the white sisters, are coming together, trying to form a whole, and it can't form without the pieces we have saved and cherished."[39]

Metamemory is deep and vast. Women who "are bringing the pieces of the truth together" are moving beyond civilization. This moving implies Natural Grace. Since the Graceful leaps of Be-Longing women cannot be accomplished in isolation, it is essential now to explore more deeply the problem of communication, which is Be-Friending.

NOTES

1. See Aristotle, *Nicomachean Ethics* X, 6, 7.
2. Thomas Aquinas, *Summa theologiae* I–II, q. 3, a. 8c.
3. Ibid., I–II, q. 5, a. 5c.
4. Ibid., I, q. 12, a. 5c.
5. Gregory Bateson, in *Mind and Nature: A Necessary Unity* (New York: E. P. Dutton, 1979), uses the term *metapattern,* but not in this metapatriarchal sense. See pp. 11ff.
6. Aquinas, *Summa theologiae* I, q. 75, 76. See Aristotle, *De Anima* II, ch. 1 and 2.
7. Aquinas, *Summa theologiae* I, q. 76, a. 1c. See Aristotle, *De Anima* II, 2.
8. Aquinas, *Summa theologiae* I, q. 76, a. 8c.
9. Ibid., I, q. 76, a. 8c.
10. Ibid., I, q. 76, a. 3c.
11. Larry Dossey, M.D., *Space, Time and Medicine* (Boulder & London: Shambhala Publications, 1982), p. 103.
12. Karl Pribam, interviewed by Daniel Goleman, "Holographic Memory," *Psychology Today,* February 1979, pp. 71–84.
13. Dossey, *Space, Time and Medicine,* p. 107. See David Bohm, *Wholeness and the Implicate Order* (London: Routledge and Kegan Paul, Ltd., 1980).
14. According to Leibniz (1646–1716), for example, the universe is composed of a hierarchy of "monads," each of which is a microcosm reflecting the world with differing degrees of clarity. See Gottfried Wilhelm von Leibniz, *The Monadology and Other Philosophical Writings,* trans. by Robert Latta (London: Oxford University Press, 1925).
15. David Bakan, *Disease, Pain, and Sacrifice* (Boston: Beacon Press, 1968), p. 34.
16. Ibid., p. 37.
17. Ibid., p. 38.
18. This word was invented by Françoise d'Eaubonne, a French feminist theoretician, in her book *Le Féminisme ou la mort* (Paris: Pierre Horay, 1974).
19. Jane Roberts describes the principle of unity in diversity through using the concept of "focus personality." See *Psychic Politics* (Englewood Cliffs, N.J.: Prentice-Hall, Inc., 1976).
20. Aquinas, *Summa theologiae* I, q. 77, a. 6.
21. Both Aristotle and Aquinas believed women to be defective and misbegotten males. Aquinas explained that this is only according to the "individual nature" (of all women). Nevertheless, "as regards human nature in general" women are not misbegotten, but are included in nature's intention for the work of generation. *Summa theologiae* I, q. 92, a. 1 ad 1. See Aristotle, *De Generatione Animalium* IV, 2.
22. Alice Walker, "Nuclear Exorcism," *Mother Jones,* September/October 1982, p. 21.
23. Ibid.
24. Hesiod, *Theogony,* 227.
25. Ernest G. Schachtel, *Metamorphosis* (New York: Basic Books, Inc., 1959), pp. 279–80.
26. Ibid., p. 280.
27. Ibid., p. 284.
28. Ibid., p. 287.
29. Ibid.
30. Emily Culpepper has described her own experience of this phenomenon in "Philosophia in a Feminist Key: Revolt of the Symbols" (unpublished Th.D. dissertation, Harvard University, 1983), chapter 8.
31. Virginia Woolf, *Moments of Being: Unpublished Autobiographical Writings,* ed. and with an introduction by Jeanne Schulkind (New York: Harcourt Brace Jovanovich, 1976), pp. 64–65.
32. Herbert Marcuse, *Eros and Civilization* (New York: Alfred A. Knopf, Vintage Books, 1955), p. 224.
33. Ibid., p. 225.
34. Ibid., p. 235.
35. Sigmund Freud, *Civilization and Its Discontents,* trans. and ed. by James Strachey (New York: W. W. Norton and Company, 1961), p. 30.
36. Anne Cameron, *Daughters of Copper Woman* (Vancouver, British Columbia: Press Gang Publishers, 1981), preface.
37. Ibid., p. 12.
38. Ibid., p. 146.
39. Ibid., p. 145.

MOTHERS, MONSTERS, AND MACHINES

Rosi Braidotti

FIGURING OUT

I would like to approach the sequence "mothers, monsters, and machines" both thematically and methodologically, so as to work out possible connections between these terms. Because women, the biological sciences, and technology are conceptually interrelated, there can not be only one correct connection but, rather, many, heterogeneous and potentially contradictory ones.

The quest for multiple connections—or conjunctions—can also be rendered methodologically in terms of Donna Haraway's "figurations."[1] The term refers to ways of expressing feminist forms of knowledge that are not caught in a mimetic relationship to dominant scientific discourse. This is a way of marking my own difference: as an intellectual woman who has acquired and earned the right to speak publicly in an academic context, I have also inherited a tradition of female silence. Centuries of exclusion of women from the exercise of discursive power are ringing through my words. In speaking the language of man, I also intend to let the silence of woman echo gently but firmly; I shall not conform to the phallogocentric mode.[2] I want to question the status of feminist theory in terms not only of the conceptual tools and the gender-specific perceptions that govern the production of feminist research but also of the form our perceptions take.

The "nomadic" style is the best suited to the quest for feminist figurations, in the sense of adequate representations of female experience as that which cannot easily be fitted within the parameters of phallogocentric language.

The configuration of ideas I am trying to set up: mothers, monsters, machines, is therefore a case study—not only in terms of its propositional content but also in defining my place of enunciation and, therefore, my relationship to the readers who are my partners in this discursive game. It is a new figuration of feminist subjectivity.

Quoting Deleuze,[3] I would like to define this relationship as "rhizomatic"; that is to say not only cerebral, but related to experience, which implies a strengthened connection between thought and life, a renewed proximity of the thinking process to existential reality.[4] In my thinking, "rhizomatic" thinking leads to what I call a "nomadic" style.

Moreover, a "nomadic" connection is not a dualistic or oppositional way of thinking[5] but rather one that views discourse as a positive, multilayered network of power relations.[6]

Let me develop the terms of my nomadic network by reference to Foucauldian critiques of the power of discourse: he argues that the production of scientific knowledge works as a complex, interrelated network of truth, power, and desire, centered on the subject as a bodily entity. In a double movement that I find most politically useful, Foucault highlights both the normative foundations of theoretical reason and also the rational model of power. "Power" thus becomes the name for a complex set of interconnections, between the spaces where truth and knowledge are produced and the systems of control and domination. I shall unwrap my three interrelated notions in the light of this definition of power.

Last, but not least, this style implies the simultaneous dislocation not only of my place of enunciation as a feminist intellectual but also accordingly of the position of my readers. As my interlocutors I am constructing those readers to be "not just" traditional intellectuals and academics but also active, interested, and concerned participants in a project of research and experimentation for new ways of thinking about human subjectivity in general and female subjectivity in particular. I mean to appeal therefore not only to a requirement for passionless truth but also to a passionate engagement in the recognition of the theoretical and discursive implications of sexual difference. In this choice of a theoretical style that leaves ample room for the exploration of subjectivity, I am following the lead of Donna Haraway, whose plea for "passionate detachment" in theory making I fully share.[7]

Let us now turn to the thematic or propositional content of my constellation of ideas: mothers, monsters and machines.

For the sake of clarity, let me define them: "mothers" refers to the maternal function of women. By *WOMEN* I mean not only the biocultural entities thus represented, as the empirical subjects of sociopolitical realities, but also a discursive field: feminist theory. The kind of feminism I want to defend rests on the presence and the experience of real-life women whose political consciousness is bent on changing the institution of power in our society.

Feminist theory is a two-layered project involving the critique of existing definitions, representations as well as the elaboration of alternative theories about women. Feminism is the movement that brings into practice the dimension of sexual difference through the critique of gender as a power institution. Feminism is the question; the affirmation of sexual difference is the answer.

This point is particularly important in the light of modernity's imperative to think differently about our historical condition. The central question seems to be here: how can we *affirm* the positivity of female subjectivity at a time in history when our acquired perceptions of "the subject" are being radically questioned? How can we reconcile the recognition of the problematic nature of the notion and the construction of the subject with the political necessity to posit female subjectivity?

By *MACHINES* I mean the scientific, political, and discursive field of technology in the broadest sense of the term. Ever since Heidegger the philosophy of modernity has been trying to come to terms with technological reason. The Frankfurt School refers to it as "instrumental reason": one that places the end of its endeavors well above the means and suspends all judgment on its inner logic. In my work, as I mentioned in the previous chapter, I approach the technology issue from

within the French tradition, following the materialism of Bachelard, Canguilhem, and Foucault.

By *MONSTERS* I mean a third kind of discourse: the history and philosophy of the biological sciences, and their relation to difference and to different bodies. Monsters are human beings who are born with congenital malformations of their bodily organism. They also represent the in between, the mixed, the ambivalent as implied in the ancient Greek root of the word "monsters," *teras,* which means both horrible and wonderful, object of aberration and adoration. Since the nineteenth century, following the classification system of monstrosity by Geoffroy Saint-Hilaire, bodily malformations have been defined in terms of "excess," "lack," or "displacement of organs."[8] Before any such scientific classification was reached, however, natural philosophy had struggled to come to terms with these objects of abjection. The constitution of teratology as a science offers a paradigmatic example of the ways in which scientific rationality dealt with differences of the bodily kind.

The discourse on monsters as a case study highlights a question that seems to me very important for feminist theory: the status of difference within rational thought. Following the analysis of the philosophical ratio suggested by Derrida[9] and other contemporary French philosophers, it can be argued that Western thought has a logic of binary oppositions that treats difference as that which is other-than the accepted norm. The question then becomes: can we free difference from these normative connotations? Can we learn to think differently about difference?[10]

The monster is the bodily incarnation of difference from the basic human norm; it is a deviant, an a-nomaly; it is abnormal. As Georges Canguilhem points out, the very notion of the human body rests upon an image that is intrinsically prescriptive: a normally formed human being is the zero-degree of monstrosity. Given the special status of the monster, what light does he throw on the structures of scientific discourse? How was the difference of/in the monster perceived within this discourse?

When set alongside each other, mothers/monsters/machines may seem puzzling. There is no apparent connection among these three terms and yet the link soon becomes obvious if I add that recent developments in the field of biotechnology, particularly artificial procreation, have extended the power of science over the maternal body of women. The possibility of mechanizing the maternal function is by now well within our reach; the manipulation of life through different combinations of genetic engineering has allowed for the creation of new artificial monsters in the high-tech labs of our biochemists. There is therefore a political urgency about the future of women in the new reproductive technology debate, which gives a polemical force to my constellation of ideas—mothers, monsters, and machines.

The legal, economic, and political repercussions of the new reproductive technologies are far-reaching. The recent stand taken by the Roman Catholic church and by innumerable "bioethics committees" all across Western Europe against experimentation and genetic manipulations may appear fair enough. They all invariably shift the debate, however, far from the power of science over the women's body in favor of placing increasing emphasis on the rights of the fetus or of embryos. This emphasis is played against the rights of the mother—and therefore of the woman—and we have been witnessing systematic slippages between the discourse against genetic manipulations and the rhetoric of the antiabortion campaigners. No area of contemporary technological development is more crucial to the construction of gender than the new reproductive technologies. The central thematic link I want to explore between mothers, monsters, and machines is therefore my argument that contemporary biotechnology displaces women by making procreation a high-tech affair.

CONJUNCTION 1: WOMAN/MOTHER AS MONSTER

As part of the discursive game of nomadic networking I am attempting here, let us start by associating two of these terms: let us superimpose the image of the woman/mother onto that of the monstrous body. In other words, let us take the case study of monsters, deviants, or anomalous entities as being paradigmatic of how differences are dealt with within scientific rationality. Why this association of femininity with monstrosity?

The association of women with monsters goes as far back as Aristotle who, in *The Generation of Animals*, posits the human norm in terms of bodily organization based on a male model. Thus, in reproduction, when everything goes according to the norm a boy is produced; the female only happens when something goes wrong or fails to occur in the reproductive process. The female is therefore an anomaly, a variation on the main theme of man-kind. The emphasis Aristotle places on the masculinity of the human norm is also reflected in his theory of conception: he argues that the principle of life is carried exclusively by the sperm, the female genital apparatus providing only the passive receptacle for human life. The sperm-centered nature of this early theory of procreation is thus connected to a massive masculine bias in the general Aristotelian theory of subjectivity. For Aristotle, not surprisingly, women are not endowed with a rational soul.[11]

The *topos* of women as a sign of abnormality, and therefore of difference as a mark of inferiority, remained a constant in Western scientific discourse. This association has produced, among other things, a style of misogynist literature with which anyone who has read *Gulliver's Travels* must be familiar: the horror of the female body. The interconnection of women as monsters with the literary text is particularly significant and rich in the genre of satire. In a sense, the satirical text is implicitly monstrous, it is a deviant, an aberration in itself. Eminently transgressive, it can afford to express a degree of misogyny that might shock in other literary genres.

Outside the literary tradition, however, the association of femininity with monstrosity points to a system of pejoration that is implicit in the binary logic of oppositions that characterizes the phallogocentric discursive order. The monstrous as the negative pole, the pole of pejoration, is structurally analogous to the feminine as that which is other-than the established norm, whatever the norm may be. The actual propositional content of the terms of opposition is less significant for me than its logic. Within this dualistic system, monsters are, just like bodily female subjects, a figure of devalued difference; as such, it provides the fuel for the production of normative discourse. If the position of women and monsters as logical operators in discursive production is comparable within the dualistic logic, it follows that the misogyny of discourse is not an irrational exception but rather a tightly constructed system that requires difference as pejoration in order to erect the positivity of the norm. In this respect, misogyny is not a hazard but rather the structural necessity of a system that can only represent "otherness" as negativity.

The theme of woman as devalued difference remained a constant in Western thought; in philosophy especially, "she" is forever associated to unholy, disorderly, subhuman, and unsightly phenomena. It is as if "she" carried within herself something that makes her prone to being an enemy of mankind, an outsider in her civilization, an "other." It is important to stress the light that psychoanalytic theory has cast upon this hatred for the feminine and the traditional patriarchal association of women with monstrosity.

The woman's body can change shape in pregnancy and childbearing; it is therefore capable of defeating the notion of fixed *bodily form*, of visible, recognizable, clear, and distinct shapes as that which marks the contour of the body. She is morphologically dubious. The fact that the female body can change shape so drastically is troublesome in the eyes of the logocentric economy within which to see is the primary act of knowledge and *the gaze* the basis of all epistemic awareness.[12] The fact that the male sexual organ does, of course, change shape in the limited time span of the erection and that this operation—however precarious—is not exactly unrelated to the changes of shape undergone by the female body during pregnancy constitutes, in psychoanalytic

theory, one of the fundamental axes of fantasy about sexual difference.

The appearance of symmetry in the way the two sexes work in reproduction merely brings out, however, the separateness and the specificity of each sexual organization. What looks to the naked eye like a comparable pattern: erection/pregnancy, betrays the ineluctable difference. As psychoanalysis successfully demonstrates, reproduction does not encompass the whole of human sexuality and for this reason alone anatomy is *not* destiny. Moreover, this partial analogy also leads to a sense of (false) anatomical complementarity between the sexes that contrasts with the complexity of the psychic representations of sexual difference. This double recognition of both proximity and separation is the breeding ground for the rich and varied network of misunderstandings, identifications, interconnections, and mutual demands that is what sexual human relationships are all about.

Precisely this paradoxical mixture of "the same and yet other" between the sexes generates a drive to denigrate woman in so far as she is "other-than" the male norm. In this respect hatred for the feminine constitutes the phallogocentric economy by inducing in both sexes the desire to achieve order, by means of a one-way pattern for both. As long as the law of the One is operative, so will be the denigration of the feminine, and of women with it.[13]

Woman as a sign of difference is monstrous. If we define the monster as a bodily entity that is anomalous and deviant vis-à-vis the norm, then we can argue that the female body shares with the monster the privilege of bringing out a unique blend of *fascination and horror*. This logic of attraction and repulsion is extremely significant; psychoanalytic theory takes it as the fundamental structure of the mechanism of desire and, as such, of the constitution of the neurotic symptom: the spasm of the hysteric turns to nausea, displacing itself from its object.

Julia Kristeva, drawing extensively on the research of Mary Douglas, connects this mixture[14] to the maternal body as the site of the origin of life and consequently also of the insertion into mortality and death. We are all of woman born, and the mother's body as the threshold of existence is both sacred and soiled, holy and hellish; it is attractive and repulsive, all-powerful and therefore impossible to live with. Kristeva speaks of it in terms of "abjection"; the abject arises in that gray, in between area of the mixed, the ambiguous. The monstrous or deviant is a figure of abjection in so far as it trespasses and transgresses the barriers between recognizable norms or definitions.

Significantly, the abject approximates the sacred because it appears to contain within itself a constitutive ambivalence where life and death are reconciled. Kristeva emphasizes the dual function of the maternal site as both life- and death-giver, as object of worship and of terror. The notion of the sacred is generated precisely by this blend of fascination and horror, which prompts an intense play of the imaginary, of fantasies and often nightmares about the ever-shifting boundaries between life and death, night and day, masculine and feminine, active and passive, and so forth.

In a remarkable essay about the head of the Medusa, Freud connected this logic of attraction and repulsion to the sight of female genitalia; because there is *nothing to see* in that dark and mysterious region, the imagination goes haywire. Short of losing his head, the male gazer is certainly struck by castration anxiety. For fear of losing the thread of his thought, Freud then turns his distress into the most overdetermined of all questions: "what does woman want?"

A post-Freudian reading of this text permits us to see how the question about female desire emerges out of male anxiety about the representation of sexual difference. In a more Lacanian vein, Kristeva adds an important insight: the female sex as the site of origin also inspires awe because of the psychic and cultural imperative to separate from the mother and accept the Law of the Father. The incest taboo, the fundamental law of our social system, builds on the mixture

of fascination and horror that characterizes the feminine/maternal object of abjection. As the site of primary repression, and therefore that which escapes from representation, the mother's body becomes a turbulent area of psychic life.

Obviously, this analysis merely describes the mechanisms at work in our cultural system; no absolute necessity surrounds the symbolic absence of Woman. On the contrary, feminists have been working precisely to put into images that which escapes phallogocentric modes of representation. Thus, in her critique of psychoanalysis, Luce Irigaray points out that the dark continent of all dark continents is the mother-daughter relationship. She also suggests that, instead of this logic of attraction and repulsion, sexual difference may be thought out in terms of recognition and wonder. The latter is one of the fundamental passions in Descartes' treatise about human affectivity: he values it as the foremost of human passions, that which makes everything else possible. Why Western culture did not adopt this way of conceptualizing and experiencing difference and opted instead for difference as a sign of negativity remains a critical question for me.

It is because of this phallogocentric perversion that femininity and monstrosity can be seen as isomorphic. Woman/mother is monstrous by excess; she transcends established norms and transgresses boundaries. She is monstrous by lack: woman/mother does not possess the substantive unity of the masculine subject. Most important, through her identification with the feminine she is monstrous by displacement: as sign of the in between areas, of the indefinite, the ambiguous, the mixed, woman/mother is subjected to a constant process of metaphorization as "other-than."

In the binary structure of the logocentric system, "woman," as the eternal pole of opposition, the "other," can be assigned to the most varied and often contradictory terms. The only constant remains her "becoming-metaphor," whether of the sacred or the profane, of heaven or hell, of life or death. "Woman" is that which is assigned and has no power of self-definition. "Woman" is the anomaly that confirms the positivity of the norm.

CONJUNCTION 2: TERATOLOGY AND THE FEMININE

The history of teratology, or the science of monsters, demonstrates clearly the ways in which the body in general and the female body in particular have been conceptualized in Western scientific discourse, progressing from the fantastic dimension of the bodily organism to a more rationalistic construction of the body-machine. The monster as a human being born with congenital malformations undergoes a series of successive representations historically, before it gives rise, in the latter part of the eighteenth century, to an acceptable, scientific discourse.

The work of French epistemologist and philosopher of science Georges Canguilhem and of his disciple Michel Foucault is extremely useful in studying the modes of interaction of the normal and the pathological, the normative and the transgressive in Western philosophy. For Canguilhem, the stakes in theory of monstrosity are the questions of reproduction, of origins: "how can such monstrous creatures be conceived?" The conception of monsters is what really haunts the scientific imagination. Whereas psychoanalysts like Lacan and Irigaray argue that the epistem(ophil)ic question of the origin lies at the heart of *all* scientific investigation, Canguilhem is interested in providing the historical perspective on how the scientific discourse about monsters emerged. He argues that teratology became constituted as a discipline when it required the conceptual and technological means of mastering the pro/reproduction of monsters. In other words, the scientific and technological know-how necessary for the artificial reproduction of human anomalies is the precondition for the establishment of a scientific discipline concerned with abnormal beings.

This means that on the discursive level, the monster points out the major epistemological function played by anomalies, abnormalities, and pathology in the constitution of biological sciences. Historically, biologists have privileged phenomena that deviate from the norm, in order to exemplify the normal structure of development. In this respect the study of monstrous births is a forerunner of modern embryology. Biologists have set up abnormal cases in order to elucidate normal behavior; psychoanalysis will follow exactly the same logic for mental disorders. The proximity of the normal and the pathological demonstrates the point Foucault made in relation to madness and reason: scientific rationality is implicitly normative, it functions by exclusion and disqualification according to a dualistic logic.

The history of discourse about monsters conventionally falls into three chronological periods. In the first, the Greeks and Romans maintained a notion of a "race" of monsters, an ethnic entity possessing specific characteristics. They also relied on the notion of "abjection," seeing the monster not only as the sign of marvel but also of disorder and divine wrath. The practice of exposing monstrous children as unnatural creatures was inaugurated by the Greeks. Thus Oedipus himself—"swollen foot"—was not "normal," and his destruction should have been in the order of things.

More generally, classical mythology represents no founding hero, no main divine creature or demigod as being of woman born. In fact, one of the constant themes in the making of a god is his "unnatural" birth: his ability, through subterfuges such as immaculate conceptions and other tricks, to short-circuit the orifice through which most humans beings pop into the spatio-temporal realm of existence. The fantastic dimension of classical mythological discourse about monsters illustrates the paradox of aberration and adoration that I mentioned earlier, and it therefore inscribes an antimaternal dimension at the very heart of the matter.

We can make a further distinction between the baroque and enlightened or "scientific" discourses on monsters. In the sixteenth and seventeenth centuries, the monster still possesses the classical sense of something wonderful, fantastic, rare, and precious. Just like the madman, the dwarf and other marvels, it participates in the life of his/her town and enjoys certain privileges. For instance, dwarves as court jesters and fools can transgress social conventions, can say and do things that "normal" human beings cannot afford to say or do.

The imagination of the times runs wild as to the origins of monsters as objects of horror and fascination, as something both exceptional and ominous. The question of the origins of monsters accompanies the development of the medical sciences in the prescientific imagination; it conveys an interesting mixture of traditional superstitions and elements of reflection that will lead to a more scientific method of enquiry. Out of the mass of documentary evidence on this point, I will concentrate on one aspect that throws light on my question about the connection between monstrosity and the feminine. Ambroise Paré's treatise[15] on wondrous beings lists among the causes for their conception various forms of unnatural copulation ranging from bestiality to everyday forms of immorality, such as having sexual intercourse too often, or on a Sunday night (sic), or on the night of any major religious holiday. As a matter of fact, all sexual practices other than those leading to healthy reproduction are suspected to be conducive to monstrous events. Food can also play a major role; the regulation of diet is extremely important and implicitly connected to religious regulations concerning time, season and cycles of life.[16]

Bad weather can adversely affect procreation, as can an excess or a lack of semen; the devil also plays an important role, and he definitely interferes with normal human reproduction. Well may we laugh at such beliefs; many still circulate in rural areas of Western Europe. Besides, the whole fantastic discourse about the origins of monsters becomes considerably less amusing when we consider that women paid a heavy price for these wild notions. The history of women's relationship to "the devil" in Western Europe is a history too full of horrors for us to take these notions lightly.

It is not surprising, therefore, that the baroque mind gave a major role to the maternal imagination in procreation generally and in the conception of monsters particularly.[17] The mother was said to have the actual power of producing a monstrous baby simply by: (a) *thinking* about awful things during intercourse (it's the close-your-eyes-and-think-of-England principle); (b) *dreaming* very intensely about something or somebody; or (c) *looking* at animals or evil-looking creatures (this is the Xerox-machine complex: if a woman looked at a dog, for instance, with a certain look in her eyes, then she would have the power of transmitting that image to the fetus and reproducing it exactly, thus creating a dog-faced baby).

I let you imagine the intense emotion that struck a village in Northern France in the seventeenth century when a baby was born who looked remarkably like the local bishop. The woman defended herself by claiming gazing rights: she argued that she had stared at the male character in church with such intense devotion that . . . she xeroxed him away! She saved her life and proved the feminist theory that female gaze as the expression of female desire is always perceived as a dangerous, if not deadly, thing.

In other words, the mother's imagination is as strong as the force of nature; in order to assess this, one needs to appreciate the special role that the *imagination* plays in the seventeenth century theories of knowledge. It is a fundamental element in the classical worldview, and yet it is caught in great ambivalence: the imagination is the capacity to draw connections and consequently to construct ideas and yet it is potentially antirational.

The Cartesian *Meditations* are the clearest example of this ambivalence, which we find projected massively onto the power of the mother.

She can direct the fetus to normal development or she can de-form it, un-do it, de-humanize it.

It is as if the mother, as a desiring agent, has the power to undo the work of legitimate pro-creation through the sheer force of her imagina-tion. By deforming the product of the father, she cancels what psychoanalytic theory calls "the Name-of-the-Father." The female "signature" of the reproductive pact is unholy, inhuman, illegiti-mate, and it remains the mere pre-text to horrors to come. Isn't the product of woman's creativity always so?

This belief is astonishing however, when it is contextualized historically: consider that the de-bate between the Aristotelian theory of concep-tion, with its sperm-centered view of things, and mother-centered notions of procreation, has a long history. The seventeenth century seems to have reached a paroxysm of hatred for the feminine; it inaugurated a flight from the female body in a desire to master the woman's generative powers.

Very often feminist scholars have taken this point as a criticism of classical rationalism, es-pecially in the Cartesian[18] form, far too provoca-tively. The feminist line has been "I think therefore *he* is," thus emphasizing the male-centered view of human nature that is at work in this discourse. Whatever Descartes' responsibility for the flight from womanhood may be—and I maintain that it should be carefully assessed—for the purpose of my research what matters is the particular form that this flight took in the seventeenth century.

CONJUNCTION 3: THE FANTASY OF MALE-BORN CHILDREN

The flight from and rejection of the feminine can also be analyzed from a different angle: the his-tory of the biological sciences in the prescientific era, especially the sixteenth and seventeenth cen-turies. I argue that the flight from the feminine, and particularly from the monstrous power of the maternal imagination and desire, lies at the heart of the recurring fantasy of a child born from man alone.

We find, for instance, alchemists busy at work to try to produce the philosopher's son—the ho-munculus, a man-made tiny man popping out of the alchemists' laboratories, fully formed and end-owed with language. The alchemists' imagina-tion pushes the premises of the Aristotelian view of procreation to an extreme, stressing the male role in reproduction and minimizing the female function to the role of a mere carrier. Alchemy is a *reductio ad absurdum* of the male fantasy of self-reproduction.

How can a child be of man born? In a recent article, S. G. Allen and J. Hubbs[19] argue that al-chemical symbolism rests on a simple process— the appropriation of the womb by male "art," that is to say the artifact of male techniques. Paracel-sus, the master theoretician of alchemy, is certain that a man should and could be born outside a woman's body. Womb envy, alias the envy for the matrix or the uterus, reaches paradoxical dimen-sions in these texts—art being more powerful than nature itself.

The recipe is quite simple, as any reader of *Tristram Shandy* will know. It consists of a mix-ture of sperm and something to replace the uterus, such as the alchemist's jars and other containers so efficiently described in Mary Shelley's *Frank-enstein*. At other times the matrix is replaced by an ox-hide, or by a mere heap of compost or ma-nure. The basic assumption is that the alchemists can not only imitate the work of woman, they can also do it much better because the artifact, the ar-tificial process of science and technique, perfects the imperfection of the natural course of events and thus avoids mistakes. Once reproduction be-comes the pure result of mental efforts, the ap-propriation of the feminine is complete.

On the imaginary level, therefore, the test-tube babies of today mark the long-term triumph of the alchemists' dream of dominating nature through their self-inseminating, masturbatory practices. What is happening with the new re-productive technologies today is the final chapter in a long history of fantasy of self-generation by and for the men themselves—men of science, but men of the male kind, capable of producing new monsters and fascinated by their power.

Ever since the mid nineteenth century, the abnormal monstrous beings, which had been objects of wonder, have fallen prey to the massive medicalization of scientific discourse. The marvelous, imaginary dimension of the monster is forgotten in the light of the new technologies of the body. Michel Foucault's analysis of modern rationality describes the fundamental shift that has taken place in scientific discourse of the modern era.

By the late eighteenth century, the monster has been transferred to hospital or rather, to the newly established institution of the anatomy clinic, where it could be analyzed in the context of the newly evolved practice of comparative anatomy and experimental biomedicine. Thus is born the science of teratology. Founded by G. Saint-Hilaire, by the end of the century it had become an experimental science. Its aim was to study malformations of the embryo so as to understand in the light of evolutionary theory the genesis of monstrous beings. Notice that the initial curiosity as to the origin of such horrendous creatures remains, but it is expressed differently.

The experimental study of the conditions that would lead to the production of anomalous or monstrous beings provides the basic epistemological structure of modern embryology. Foucault's analysis of modernity emphasizes the epistemological shifts between the normal and the pathological, reason and madness, in terms of the understanding of the body, the bodily roots of human subjectivity. The biomedical sciences occupy a very significant place in the discursive context of modernity.

Two institutions of learning appear in the modern era—the clinic and the hospital. The appearance of these structures is in turn related to a major theoretical breakthrough—the medical practice of anatomy. In Foucault's archaeological mode, for comparative clinical anatomy to come into being as a scientific discourse, a century-old taboo had to be lifted, the one that forbade the dissection of corpses for the purpose of scientific investigation.

Western culture had respected a fundamental taboo of the body up until then—the medical gaze could not explore the inside of the human body because the bodily container was considered as a metaphysical entity, marked by the secrets of life and death that pertain to the divine being. The anatomical study of the body was therefore forbidden until the fifteenth century and after then was strictly controlled. The nineteenth century sprang open the doors of bodily perception; clinical anatomy thus implies a radical transformation in the epistemological status of the body. It is a practice that consists in deciphering the body, transforming the organism into a text to be read and interpreted by a knowledgeable medical gaze.

Anatomy as a theoretical representation of the body implies that the latter is a clear and distinct configuration, a visible and intelligible structure. The dead body, the corpse, becomes the measure of the living being, and death thus becomes one of the factors epistemologically integrated into scientific knowledge.

Today, the right to scrutinize the inside of the body for scientific purposes is taken for granted, although dissections and the transferal of organs as a practice are strictly regulated by law. As a matter of fact, contemporary molecular biology is making visible the most intimate and minute fires of life.

Where has the Cartesian passion of wonder gone? When compared to the earlier tradition, the medicalization of the body in the age of modernity and its corollary, the perfectibility of the living organism and the gradual abolition of anomalies, can also be seen—though not exclusively—as a form of denial of the sense of wonder, of the fantastic, of that mixture of fascination and horror I have already mentioned. It marks the loss of fascination about the living organism, its mysteries and functions.

Psychoanalytic theory has explained this loss of fascination as the necessary toll that rational theory takes on human understanding. In the psychoanalytic perspective, of Freudian and Lacanian inspiration, the initial curiosity that prompts the drive and the will to know is first and foremost *desire,* which takes knowledge as its object.

The desire to know is, like all desires, related to the problem of representing one's origin, of answering the most childish and consequently fundamental of questions: "where did I come from?" This curiosity, as I stated in the previous chapter, is the matrix for all forms of thinking and conceptualization. Knowledge is always the desire to know about desire, that is to say about things of the body as a sexual entity.

Scientific knowledge becomes, in this perspective, an extremely perverted version of that original question. The desire to go and see how things work is related to primitive sadistic drives, so that, somewhere along the line, the scientist is like the anxious little child who pulls apart his favorite toy to see how it's made inside. Knowing in this mode is the result of the scopophilic drive—to go and see, and the sadistic one—to rip it apart physically so as to master it intellectually. All this is related to the incestuous drive, to the web of curiosity and taboos surrounding the one site of certain origin—the mother's body.

From a psychoanalytic perspective the establishment of clinical comparative anatomy in the modern era is very significant because it points out the rationalistic obsession with visibility, which I have analyzed earlier. Seeing is the prototype of knowing. By elaborating a scientific technique for analyzing the bodily organs, Western sciences put forward the assumption that a body is precisely that which can be seen and looked at, no more than the sum of its parts. Modern scientific rationality slipped from the emphasis on visibility to the mirage of absolute transparence of the living organism, as I have argued previously.

Contemporary biological sciences, particularly molecular biology, have pushed to the extreme these assumptions that were implicit in the discourse of Western sciences. When compared to the clinical anatomy of the nineteenth century, contemporary biomedical sciences have acquired the right and the know-how necessary to act on the very structure of the living matter, on an infinitely small scale.

Foucault defined the modern era as that of biopower; power over life and death in a worldwide extension of man's control of outer space, of the bottom of the oceans as well as of the depths of the maternal body. There are no limits today for what can be shown, photographed, reproduced— even a technique such as echography perpetuates this pornographic re-presentation of bodily parts, externalizing the interior of the womb and its content.

The proliferation of images is such that the very notion of the body, of its boundaries and its inner structure is being split open in an everregressing vision. We seem to be hell bent on xeroxing even the invisible particles of matter.

Philosophers of science, such as Kuhn and Fayarabend, have stressed the modern predicament in scientific discourse. Kuhn points out the paradoxical coincidence of extreme rationalism of the scientific and technological kind, with a persisting subtext of wild fantastic concoctions. In the discourse of monstrosity, rational enquiries about their origin and structure continue to coexist with superstitious beliefs and fictional representations of "creeps." The two registers of the rational and the totally nonrational seem to run alongside each other, never quite joined together.

The question nevertheless remains—where has the wonder gone? What has happened to the fantastic dimension, to the horror and the fascination of difference? What images were created of the bodily marks of difference, after they became locked up in the electronic laboratories of the modern alchemists?

Was there another way, other than the phallogocentric incompetence with, and antipathy to, differences—its willful reduction of otherness, to negativity? Is there another way out, still?

CONJUNCTION 4: THE AGE OF FREAKS

As the Latin etymology of the term *monstrum* points out, malformed human beings have always been the object of display, subjected to the public gaze. In his classic study, *Freaks,* Leslie Fiedler[20] analyses the exploitation of monsters for purposes of entertainment. From the county fairs, right across rural Europe to the Coney Island sideshows, freaks have always been entertaining.

Both Fiedler and Bogdan[21] stress two interrelated aspects of the display of freaks since the turn of the century. The first is that their exhibition displays racist and orientalist undertones: abnormally formed people were exhibited alongside tribal people of normal stature and bodily configuration, as well as exotic animals.

Second, the medical profession benefited considerably by examining these human exhibits. Although the freak is presented as belonging to the realm of zoology or anthropology, doctors and physicians examined them regularly and wrote scientific reports about them.

Significantly, totalitarian regimes such as Hitler's Germany or the Stalinist Soviet Union prohibited the exhibition of freaks as being degenerate specimens of the human species. They also dealt with them in their campaigns for eugenics and race or ethnic hygiene, by preventing them from breeding.

Fiedler sees a connection between the twentieth-century medicalization of monsters, the scientific appropriation of their generative secrets, and an increased commodification of the monster as freak, that is, the object of display.

Contemporary culture deals with anomalies by a fascination for the freaky. The film *Freaks* by Tod Browning (1932) warns us that monsters are an endangered species. Since the sixties a whole youth culture has developed around freaks, with special emphasis on genetic mutation as a sign of nonconformism and social rebellion. Whole popular culture genres such as science fiction, horror, rock'n'roll comics, and cyberpunk are about mutants.

Today, the freaks are science fiction androids, cyborgs, bionic women and men, comparable to the grotesque of former times; the whole rock'n'roll scene is a huge theater of the grotesque, combining freaks, androgynes, satanies, ugliness, and insanity, as well as violence.

In other words, in the early part of our century we watch the simultaneous formalization of a scientific discourse about monsters and their elimination as a problem. This process, which falls under the rationalist aggression of scientific discourse, also operates a shift at the level of representation, and of the cultural imaginary. The dimension of the "fantastic," that mixture of aberration and adoration, loathing and attraction, which for centuries has escorted the existence of strange and difficult bodies, is now displaced. The "becoming freaks" of monsters both deflates the fantastic projections that have surrounded them and expands them to a wider cultural field. The whole of contemporary popular culture is about freaks, just as the last of the physical freaks have disappeared. The last metaphorical shift in the status of monsters—their becoming freaks—coincides with their elimination.

In order not to be too pessimistic about this aspect of the problem, however, I wish to point out that the age of the commodification of freaks is also the period that has resulted in another significant shift: abnormally formed people have organized themselves in the disabled political movement, thereby claiming not only a renewed sense of dignity but also wider social and political rights.[22]

IN TRANSIT; OR, FOR NOMADISM

Mothers, monsters, and machines. What is the connection, then? What con/dis-junctions can we make in telling the tale of feminism, science, and technology? How do feminist fabulations or figurations help in figuring out alternative paradigms? To what extent do they speak the language of sexual difference? Where do we situate our-selves in order to create links, construct theories, elaborate hypotheses? Which way do we look to try and see the possible impact modern science will have on the status of women? How do we assess the status of difference as an ontological category at the end of the twentieth century? How do we think about all this?

The term *transdisciplinary* can describe one position taken by feminists. Passing in between different discursive fields, and through diverse spheres of intellectual discourse. The feminist theoretician today can only be "in transit," moving on, passing through, creating connections where things were previously dis-connected or seemed un-related, where there seemed to be "nothing to see." In transit, moving, dis-placing—this is the grain of hysteria without which there is no theorization at all.[23] In a feminist context it also implies the effort to move on to the invention of new ways of relating, of building footbridges between notions. The epistemic nomadism I am advocating can only work, in fact, if it is properly situated, securely anchored in the "in between" zones.

I am assuming here a definition of "rigor" away from the linear Aristotelian logic that domi-nated it for so long. It seems to me that the rigor feminists are after is of a different kind—it is the rigor of a project that emphasizes the necessary interconnection-connections between the theo-retical and the political, which insists on putting real-life experience first and foremost as a cri-terion for the validation of truth. It is the rigor of passionate investment in a project and in the quest of the discursive means to realize it.

In this respect feminism acts as a reminder that in the postmodern predicament, rationality in its classical mode can no longer be taken as representing the totality of human reason or even of the all-too-human activity of thinking.

By criticizing the single-mindedness and the masculine bias of rationality I do not intend to fall into the opposite and plead for easy ready-made irrationalism. Patriarchal thought has for too long confined women in the irrational for me to claim such a non-quality. What we need in-stead is a redefinition of what we have learned to recognize as being the structure and the aims of human subjectivity in its relationship to differ-ence, to the "other."

In claiming that feminists are attempting to redefine the very meaning of thought, I am also suggesting that in time the rules of the discursive game will have to change. Academics will have to agree that thinking adequately about our histori-cal condition implies the transcendence of disci-plinary boundaries and intellectual categories.

More important, for feminist epistemologists, the task of thinking adequately about the histori-cal conditions that affect the medicalization of the maternal function forces upon us the need to reconsider the inextricable interconnection of the bodily with the technological. The shifts that have taken place in the perception and the representation of the embodied subject, in fact, make it imperative to think the unity of body and machine, flesh and metal. Although many fac-tors point to the danger of commodification of the body that such a mixture makes possible, and although this process of commodification con-ceals racist and sexist dangers that must not be underestimated, this is not the whole story. There is also a positive side to the new interconnection of mothers, monsters, and machines, and this has to do with the loss of any essentialized definition of womanhood—or indeed even of motherhood. In the age of biotechnological power motherhood is split open into a variety of possible physiologi-cal, cultural, and social functions. If this were the best of all possible worlds, one could celebrate the decline of one consensual way of experienc-ing motherhood as a sign of increased freedom for women. Our world being as male-dominated as it is, however, the best option is to construct a *nomadic* style of feminism that will allow women to rethink their position in a postindustrial, post-metaphysical world, without nostalgia, paranoia, or false sentimentalism. The relevance and po-litical urgency of the configuration "mothers, monsters and machines" makes it all the more urgent for the feminist nomadic thinkers of the world to connect and to negotiate new boundaries for female identity in a world where power over the body has reached an implosive peak.

NOTES

I wish to thank Margaret R. Higonnet, of the Center for European Studies at Harvard, and Sissel Lie, of the Women's Research Center at Trondheim, Norway, for their helpful comments on an earlier draft of this paper.

1. Donna Haraway, "'Gender' for a Marxist Dictionary: The Sexual Politics of a Word," in *Simians, Cyborgs, and Women*, pp. 127–48 (London: Free Association Books, 1991).
2. For an enlightening and strategic usage of the notion of "mimesis," see Luce Irigaray, *Ce sexe qui n'en est pas un* (Paris: Minuit, 1977).
3. To refer to the concept elaborated by the French philosopher of difference, see Gilles Deleuze in collaboration with Felix Guattari, *Rhizome* (Paris: Minuit, 1976).
4. The notion of "experience" has been the object of intense debates in feminist theory. See for example, Teresa de Lauretis, *Alice Doesn't* (Bloomington: Indiana University Press, 1984); Sandra Harding, *The Science Question in Feminism* (London: Open University, 1986), and *Feminism and Methodology* (London: Open University, 1987); Joan Scott, "Experience," in Joan Scott and Judith Butler, eds., *Feminists Theorize the Political* (London and New York: Routledge, 1992), pp. 22–40.
5. Genevieve Lloyd, *The Man of Reason* (London: Methuen, 1985).
6. Cf. Michel Foucault, *L'ordre du discours* (Paris: Gallimard, 1971); *Surveiller et punir* (Paris: Gallimard, 1975); "Les intellectuels et le pouvoir," *L'Arc*, no. 49 (1972).
7. This expression, originally coined by Laura Mulvey in film criticism, has been taken up and developed by Donna Haraway in a stunning exploration of this intellectual mode; see "Situated Knowledges: The Science Question in Feminism and the Privilege of Partial Perspective," and "A Cyborg Manifesto: Science, Technology,

and Socialist-Feminism in the Late Twentieth Century," in *Simians, Cyborgs, and Women*, pp. 183–202 and 127–48.
8. I explored this notion of monstrosity at some length in a seminar held jointly with Marie-Jo Dhavernas at the College international de Philosophie in Paris in 1984–1985. The report of the sessions was published in *Cahier du College International de Philosophie*, no. 1 (1985): 42–45.
9. See Jacques Derrida, *L'écriture et al différence* (Paris: Seuil, 1967); *Marges de la philosophie* (Paris: Minuit, 1972); *La carte postale* (Paris: Flammarion, 1980).
10. On this point, see Alice Jardine, *Gynesis: Configurations of Woman in Modernity,* (Ithaca: Cornell University Press, 1984).
11. For a feminist critique of Aristotle, see Sandra Harding and Maryl Hintikka, eds., *Discovering Reality* (Boston: Reidel, 1983).
12. The most enlightening philosophical analysis of the scopophilic mode of scientific knowledge is Michel Foucault's *Naissance de la clinique* (Paris: Gallimard, 1963).
13. This is the fundamental starting point for the work of feminist philosopher of sexual difference Luce Irigaray; see, for instance *L'éthique de la différence sexuelle* (Paris: Minuit, 1984).
14. Julia Kristeva, *Pouvoirs de l'horreur* (Paris: Seuil, 1980).
15. Ambroise Paré, *Des monstres et prodiges* (1573; Geneva: Droz, 1971).
16. The second and third volume of Foucault's *History of Sexuality* (New York: Pantheon, 1987–1988) outline quite clearly all these regulations in the art of existence.
17. Pierre Darmon, *Le mythe de la procreation à l'âge baroque,* (Paris: Seuil, 1981).
18. See for instance Susan Bordo, "The Cartesian Masculinization of Thought," *Signs* 11, no. 3 (1986); Evelyn Fox Keller, *Reflections on Gender and Science* (New Haven: Yale University Press, 1985).
19. S. G. Allen and J. Hubbs, "Outrunning Atlanta: Destiny in Alchemical Transmutation," *Signs* 6, no. 2 (Winter 1980): 210–29.
20. Leslie Fiedler, *Freaks* (New York: Simon & Schuster, 1978).
21. Robert Bogdan, *Freak Show* (Chicago and London: University of Chicago Press 1988).

22. David Hevey, ed., *The Creatures Time Forgot: Photography and Disability Imagery* (London and New York: Routledge, 1992).

23. As Monique David-Menard argues in *L'Hystérique entre Freud et Lacan* (Paris: Ed. Universitaire, 1983).

LA CONCIENCIA DE LA MESTIZA/ TOWARDS A NEW CONSCIOUSNESS

Gloria Anzaldúa

*Por la mujer de mi raza
bablará el espíritu.*[1]

José Vasconcelos, Mexican philosopher, envisaged *una raza mestiza, una mezcla de razas afines, una raza de color—la primera raza síntesis del globo.* He called it a cosmic race, *la raza cósmica,* a fifth race embracing the four major races of the world.[2] Opposite to the theory of the pure Aryan, and to the policy of racial purity that white America practices, his theory is one of inclusivity. At the confluence of two or more genetic streams, with chromosomes constantly "crossing over," this mixture of races, rather than resulting in an inferior being, provides hybrid progeny, a mutable, more malleable species with a rich gene pool. From this racial, ideological, cultural and biological cross-pollinization, an "alien" consciousness is presently in the making—a new *mestiza* consciousness, *una conciencia de mujer.* It is a consciousness of the Borderlands.

UNA LUCHA DE FRONTERAS / A STRUGGLE OF BORDERS

Because I, a *mestiza,*
continually walk out of one culture
and into another,
because I am in all cultures at the same time,
alma entre dos mundos, tres, cuatro,
me zumba la cabeza con lo contradictorio.
Estoy norteada por todas las voces que me hablan
simultáneamente.

The ambivalence from the clash of voices results in mental and emotional states of perplexity. Internal strife results in insecurity and indecisiveness. The *mestiza's* dual or multiple personality is plagued by psychic restlessness.

In a constant state of mental nepantilism, an Aztec word meaning torn between ways, *la mestiza* is a product of the transfer of the cultural and spiritual values of one group to another. Being tricultural, monolingual, bilingual, or multilingual, speaking a patois, and in a state of perpetual transition, the *mestiza* faces the dilemma of the mixed breed: which collectivity does the daughter of a darkskinned mother listen to?

El choque de un alma atrapado entre el mundo del espíritu y el mundo de la técnica a veces la deja entullada. Cradled in one culture, sandwiched between two cultures, straddling all three cultures and their value systems, *la mestiza* undergoes a struggle of flesh, a struggle of borders, an inner war. Like all people, we perceive the version of reality that our culture communicates. Like others having or living in more than one culture, we get multiple, often opposing messages. The coming together of two self-consistent but habitually incompatible frames of reference[3] causes *un choque,* a cultural collision.

Within us and within *la cultura chicana,* commonly held beliefs of the white culture attack commonly held beliefs of the Mexican culture, and both attack commonly held beliefs of the indigenous culture. Subconsciously, we see an attack on ourselves and our beliefs as a threat and we attempt to block with a counterstance.

But it is not enough to stand on the opposite river bank, shouting questions, challenging patriarchal, white conventions. A counterstance locks one into a duel of oppressor and oppressed; locked in mortal combat, like the cop and the criminal, both are reduced to a common denominator of violence. The counterstance refutes the dominant culture's views and beliefs, and, for this, it is proudly defiant. All reaction is limited by, and dependent on, what it is reacting against. Because the counterstance stems from a problem with authority—outer as well as inner—it's a step towards liberation from cultural domination. But it is not a way of life. At some point, on our way to a new consciousness, we will have to leave the opposite bank, the split between the two mortal combatants somehow healed so that we are on both shores at once and, at once, see through serpent and eagle eyes. Or perhaps we will decide to disengage from the dominant culture, write it off altogether as a lost cause, and cross the border into a wholly new and separate territory. Or we might go another route. The possibilities are numerous once we decide to act and not react.

A TOLERANCE FOR AMBIGUITY

These numerous possibilities leave *la mestiza* floundering in uncharted seas. In perceiving conflicting information and points of view, she is subjected to a swamping of her psychological borders. She has discovered that she can't hold concepts or ideas in rigid boundaries. The borders and walls that are supposed to keep the undesirable ideas out are entrenched habits and patterns of behavior; these habits and patterns are the enemy within. Rigidity means death. Only by remaining flexible is she able to stretch the psyche horizontally and vertically. *La mestiza* constantly has to shift out of habitual formations; from convergent thinking, analytical reasoning that tends to use rationality to move toward a single goal (a Western mode), to divergent thinking,[4] characterized by movement away from set patterns and goals

and toward a more whole perspective, one that includes rather than excludes.

The new *mestiza* copes by developing a tolerance for contradictions, a tolerance for ambiguity. She learns to be an Indian in Mexican culture, to be Mexican from an Anglo point of view. She learns to juggle cultures. She has a plural personality, she operates in a pluralistic mode—nothing is thrust out, the good the bad and the ugly, nothing rejected, nothing abandoned. Not only does she sustain contradictions, she turns the ambivalence into something else.

She can be jarred out of ambivalence by an intense, and often painful, emotional event which inverts or resolves the ambivalence. I'm not sure exactly how. The work takes place underground—subconsciously. It is work that the soul performs. That focal point or fulcrum, that juncture where the *mestiza* stands, is where phenomena tend to collide. It is where the possibility of uniting all that is separate occurs. This assembly is not one where severed or separated pieces merely come together. Nor is it a balancing of opposing powers. In attempting to work out a synthesis, the self has added a third element which is greater than the sum of its severed parts. That third element is a new consciousness—a *mestiza* consciousness—and though it is a source of intense pain, its energy comes from continual creative motion that keeps breaking down the unitary aspect of each new paradigm.

En unas pocas centurias, the future will belong to the *mestiza.* Because the future depends on the breaking down of paradigms, it depends on the straddling of two or more cultures. By creating a new mythos—that is, a change in the way we perceive reality, the way we see ourselves, and the ways we behave—*la mestiza* creates a new consciousness.

The work of *mestiza* consciousness is to break down the subject-object duality that keeps her a prisoner and to show in the flesh and through the images in her work how duality is transcended. The answer to the problem between the white race and the colored, between males and females, lies in healing the split that originates in the very foundation of our lives, our culture, our languages, our thoughts. A massive uprooting of dualistic thinking in the individual and collective consciousness is the beginning of a long struggle, but one that could, in our best hopes, bring us to the end of rape, of violence, of war.

LA ENCRUCIJADA / THE CROSSROADS

A chicken is being sacrificed
at a crossroads, a simple mound of earth
a mud shrine for *Eshu,*
Yoruba god of indeterminacy,
who blesses her choice of path.
She begins her journey.

Su cuerpo es una bocacalle. La mestiza has gone from being the sacrificial goat to becoming the officiating priestess at the crossroads.

As a *mestiza* I have no country, my homeland cast me out: yet all countries are mine because I am every woman's sister or potential lover. (As a lesbian I have no race, my own people disclaim me; but I am all races because there is the queer of me in all races.) I am cultureless because, as a feminist, I challenge the collective cultural/ religious male-derived beliefs of Indo-Hispanics and Anglos; yet I am cultured because I am participating in the creation of yet another culture, a new story to explain the world and our participation in it, a new value system with images and symbols that connect us to each other and to the planet. *Soy un amasamiento,* I am an act of kneading, of uniting and joining that not only has produced both a creature of darkness and a creature of light, but also a creature that questions the definitions of light and dark and gives them new meanings.

We are the people who leap in the dark, we are the people on the knees of the gods. In our very flesh, (r)evolution works out the clash of cultures. It makes us crazy constantly, but if the center holds, we've made some kind of evolutionary step forward. *Nuestra alma el trabajo,* the opus, the great alchemical work; spiritual *mestizaje,* a "morphogenesis,"[5] an inevitable un-

folding. We have become the quickening serpent movement.

Indigenous like corn, like corn, the *mestiza* is a product of crossbreeding, designed for preservation under a variety of conditions. Like an ear of corn—a female seed-bearing organ—the *mestiza* is tenacious, tightly wrapped in the husks of her culture. Like kernels she clings to the cob; with thick stalks and strong brace roots, she holds tight to the earth—she will survive the crossroads.

Lavando y remojando el maíz en agua de cal, despojando el pellejo. Moliendo, mixteando, amasando, haciendo tortillas de masa.[6] She steeps the corn in lime, it swells, softens. With stone roller on *metate,* she grinds the corn, then grinds again. She kneads and moulds the dough, pats the round balls into *tortillas.*

We are the porous rock in the stone *metate*
    squatting on the ground.
We are the rolling pin, *el maíz y agua,*
la masa harina. Somos el amasijo.
Somos lo molido en el metate.
We are the *comal* sizzling hot,
the hot *tortilla,* the hungry mouth.
We are the coarse rock.
We are the grinding motion,
the mixed potion, *somos el molcajete.*
We are the pestle, the *comino, ajo, pimienta,*
We are the *chile colorado,*
the green shoot that cracks the rock.
We will abide.

EL CAMINO DE LA MESTIZA / THE MESTIZA WAY

Caught between the sudden contraction, the breath sucked in and the endless space, the brown woman stands still, looks at the sky. She decides to go down, digging her way along the roots of trees. Sifting through the bones, she shakes them to see if there is any marrow in them. Then, touching the dirt to her forehead, to her tongue, she takes a few bones, leaves the rest in their burial place.

She goes through her backpack, keeps her journal and address book, throws away the muni-bart metromaps. The coins are heavy and they go next, then the greenbacks flutter through the air. She keeps her knife, can opener and eyebrow pencil. She puts bones, pieces of bark, *hierbas,* eagle feather, snakeskin, tape recorder, the rattle and drum in her pack and she sets out to become the complete *tolteca.*

Her first step is to take inventory. *Despojando, desgranando, quitando paja.* Just what did she inherit from her ancestors? This weight on her back—which is the baggage from the Indian mother, which the baggage from the Spanish father, which the baggage from the Anglo?

Pero es difícil differentiating between *lo here-dado, lo adquirido, lo impuesto.* She puts history through a sieve, winnows out the lies, looks at the forces that we as a race, as women, have been a part of. *Luego bota lo que no vale, los des-mientos, los desencuentos, el embrutecimiento. Aguarda el juicio, hondo y enraizado, de la gente antigua.* This step is a conscious rupture with all oppressive traditions of all cultures and religions. She communicates that rupture, documents the struggle. She reinterprets history and, using new symbols, she shapes new myths. She adopts new perspectives toward the darkskinned, women and queers. She strengthens her tolerance (and intol-erance) for ambiguity. She is willing to share, to make herself vulnerable to foreign ways of see-ing and thinking. She surrenders all notions of safety, of the familiar. Deconstruct, construct. She becomes a *nahual,* able to transform herself into a tree, a coyote, into another person. She learns to transform the small "I" into the total Self. *Se hace moldeadora de su alma. Según la concepción que tiene de sí misma, así será.*

QUE NO SE NOS OLVIDEN LOS HOMBRES

"Tú no sirves pa' nada—
you're good for nothing.
Eres pura vieja."

"You're nothing but a woman" means you are defective. Its opposite is to be *un macho.* The modern meaning of the word "machismo," as well as the concept, is actually an Anglo inven-tion. For men like my father, being "macho" meant being strong enough to protect and sup-port my mother and us, yet being able to show love. Today's macho has doubts about his ability to feed and protect his family. His "machismo" is an adaptation to oppression and poverty and low self-esteem. It is the result of hierarchical male dominance. The Anglo, feeling inadequate and inferior and powerless, displaces or transfers these feelings to the Chicano by shaming him. In the Gringo world, the Chicano suffers from excessive humility and self-effacement, shame of self and self-deprecation. Around Latinos he suffers from a sense of language inadequacy and its accompanying discomfort; with Native Amer-icans he suffers from a racial amnesia which ig-nores our common blood, and from guilt because the Spanish part of him took their land and op-pressed them. He has an excessive compensatory hubris when around Mexicans from the other side. It overlays a deep sense of racial shame.

The loss of a sense of dignity and respect in the macho breeds a false machismo which leads him to put down women and even to brutalize them. Coexisting with his sexist behavior is a love for the mother which takes precedence over that of all others. Devoted son, macho pig. To wash down the shame of his acts, of his very being, and to handle the brute in the mirror, he takes to the bottle, the snort, the needle, and the fist.

Though we "understand" the root causes of male hatred and fear, and the subsequent wound-ing of women, we do not excuse, we do not con-done, and we will no longer put up with it. From the men of our race, we demand the admission/acknowledgment/disclosure/testimony that they wound us, violate us, are afraid of us and of our power. We need them to say they will begin to eliminate their hurtful put-down ways. But more than the words, we demand acts. We say to them: We will develop equal power with you and those who have shamed us.

It is imperative that *mestizas* support each other in changing the sexist elements in the Mexican-Indian culture. As long as woman is put down, the Indian and the Black in all of us is put down. The struggle of the *mestiza* is above all a feminist one. As long as *los hombres* think they have to *chingar mujeres* and each other to be men, as long as men are taught that they are superior and therefore culturally favored over *la mujer,* as long as to be a *vieja* is a thing of derision, there can be no real healing of our psyches. We're halfway there—we have such love of the Mother, the good mother. The first step is to un-learn the *puta/virgen* dichotomy and to see *Coatlalopeuh-Coatlicue* in the Mother, *Guadalupe.*

Tenderness, a sign of vulnerability, is so feared that it is showered on women with verbal abuse and blows. Men, even more than women, are fettered to gender roles. Women at least have had the guts to break out of bondage. Only gay men have had the courage to expose themselves to the woman inside them and to challenge the current masculinity. I've encountered a few scattered and isolated gentle straight men, the beginnings of a new breed, but they are confused, and entangled with sexist behaviors that they have not been able to eradicate. We need a new masculinity and the new man needs a movement.

Lumping the males who deviate from the general norm with man, the oppressor, is a gross injustice. *Asombra pensar que nos hemos quedado en ese pozo oscuro donde el mundo encierra a las lesbianas. Asombra pensar que hemos, como femenistas y lesbianas, cerrado nuestros corazónes a los hombres, a nuestros hermanos los jotos, desheredados y marginales como nosotros,* Being the supreme crossers of cultures, homosexuals have strong bonds with the queer white, Black, Asian, Native American, Latino, and with the queer in Italy, Australia and the rest of the planet. We come from all colors, all classes, all races, all time periods. Our role is to link people with each other—the Blacks with Jews with Indians with Asians with whites with extraterrestrials.

It is to transfer ideas and information from one culture to another. Colored homosexuals have more knowledge of other cultures; have always been at the forefront (although sometimes in the closet) of all liberation struggles in this country; have suffered more injustices and have survived them despite all odds. Chicanos need to acknowledge the political and artistic contributions of their queer. People, listen to what your *jotería* is saying.

The *mestizo* and the queer exist at this time and point on the evolutionary continuum for a purpose. We are a blending that proves that all blood is intricately woven together, and that we are spawned out of similar souls.

SOMOS UNA GENTE

Hay tantísimas fronteras
que dividen a la gente,
pero por cada frontera
existe también un puente.
—Gina Valdés[7]

Divided Loyalties   Many women and men of color do not want to have any dealings with white people. It takes too much time and energy to explain to the downwardly mobile, white middleclass women that it's okay for us to want to own "possessions," never having had any nice furniture on our dirt floors or "luxuries" like washing machines. Many feel that whites should help their own people rid themselves of race hatred and fear first. I, for one, choose to use some of my energy to serve as mediator. I think we need to allow whites to be our allies. Through our literature, art, *corridos,* and folktales we must share our history with them so when they set up committees to help Big Mountain Navajos or the Chicano farmworkers or *los Nicaragüenses* they won't turn people away because of their racial fears and ignorances. They will come to see that they are not helping us but following our lead.

Individually, but also as a racial entity, we need to voice our needs. We need to say to white society: We need you to accept the fact that Chicanos are different, to acknowledge your rejection and negation of us. We need you to own the fact that you looked upon us as less than human, that you stole our lands, our personhood, our self-respect. We need you to make public restitution: to say that, to compensate for your own sense of defectiveness, you strive for power over us, you erase our history and our experience because it makes you feel guilty—you'd rather forget your brutish acts. To say you've split yourself from minority groups, that you disown us, that your dual consciousness splits off parts of yourself, transferring the "negative" parts onto us. (Where there is persecution of minorities, there is shadow projection. Where there is violence and war, there is repression of shadow.) To say that you are afraid of us, that to put distance between us, you wear the mask of contempt. Admit that Mexico is your double, that she exists in the shadow of this country, that we are irrevocably tied to her. Gringo, accept the doppelganger in your psyche. By taking back your collective shadow the intracultural split will heal. And finally, tell us what you need from us.

BY YOUR TRUE FACES WE WILL KNOW YOU

I am visible—see this Indian face—yet I am invisible. I both blind them with my beak nose and am their blind spot. But I exist, we exist. They'd like to think I have melted in the pot. But I haven't, we haven't.

The dominant white culture is killing us slowly with its ignorance. By taking away our self-determination, it has made us weak and empty. As a people we have resisted and we have taken expedient positions, but we have never been allowed to develop unencumbered—we have never been allowed to be fully ourselves. The whites in power want us people of color to barricade ourselves behind our separate tribal walls so they can pick us off one at a time with their hidden weapons; so they can whitewash and distort history. Ignorance

splits people, creates prejudices. A misinformed people is a subjugated people.

Before the Chicano and the undocumented worker and the Mexican from the other side can come together, before the Chicano can have unity with Native Americans and other groups, we need to know the history of their struggle and they need to know ours. Our mothers, our sisters and brothers, the guys who hang out on street corners, the children in the playgrounds, each of us must know our Indian lineage, our afro-*mestizaje,* our history of resistance.

To the immigrant *mexicano* and the recent arrivals we must teach our history. The 80 million *mexicanos* and the Latinos from Central and South America must know of our struggles. Each one of us must know basic facts about Nicaragua, Chile and the rest of Latin America. The Latinoist movement (Chicanos, Puerto Ricans, Cubans and other Spanish-speaking people working together to combat racial discrimination in the marketplace) is good but it is not enough. Other than a common culture we will have nothing to hold us together. We need to meet on a broader communal ground.

The struggle is inner: Chicano, *indio,* American Indian, *mojado, mexicano,* immigrant Latino, Anglo in power, working class Anglo, Black, Asian—our psyches resemble the bordertowns and are populated by the same people. The struggle has always been inner, and is played out in the outer terrains. Awareness of our situation must come before inner changes, which in turn come before changes in society. Nothing happens in the "real" world unless it first happens in the images in our heads.

EL DÍA DE LA CHICANA

> I will not be shamed again
> Nor will I shame myself.

I am possessed by a vision: that we Chicanas and Chicanos have taken back or uncovered our true faces, our dignity and self-respect. It's a validation vision.

Seeing the Chicana anew in light of her history. I seek an exoneration, a seeing through the fictions of white supremacy, a seeing of ourselves in our true guises and not as the false racial personality that has been given to us and that we have given to ourselves. I seek our woman's face, our true features, the positive and the negative seen clearly, free of the tainted biases of male dominance. I seek new images of identity, new beliefs about ourselves, our humanity and worth no longer in question.

Estamos viviendo en la noche de la Raza, un tiempo cuando el trabajo se hace a lo quieto, en lo oscuro. El día cuando aceptamos tal y como somos y para donde vamos y porque—ese día será el día de la Raza. Yo tengo el conpromiso de expresar mi visión, mi sensibilidad, mi percepción de la revalidación de la gente mexicana, su mérito, estimación, honra, aprecio, y validez.

On December 2nd when my sun goes into my first house, I celebrate *el día de la Chicana y el Chicano.* On that day I clean my altars, light my *Coatlalopeuh* candle, burn sage and copal, take *el baño para espantar basura,* sweep my house. On that day I bare my soul, make myself vulnerable to friends and family by expressing my feelings. On that day I affirm who we are.

On that day I look inside our conflicts and our basic introverted racial temperament. I identify our needs, voice them. I acknowledge that the self and the race have been wounded. I recognize the need to take care of our personhood, of our racial self. On that day I gather the splintered and disowned parts of *la gente mexicana* and hold them in my arms. *Todas las partes de nosotros valen.*

On that day I say, "Yes, all you people wound us when you reject us. Rejection strips us of self-worth; our vulnerability exposes us to shame. It is our innate identity you find wanting. We are ashamed that we need your good opinion, that we need your acceptance. We can no longer camouflage our needs, can no longer let defenses and fences sprout around us. We can no longer

withdraw. To rage and look upon you with contempt is to rage and be contemptuous of ourselves. We can no longer blame you, nor disown the white parts, the male parts, the pathological parts, the queer parts, the vulnerable parts. Here we are weaponless with open arms, with only our magic. Let's try it our way, the *mestiza* way, the Chicana way, the woman way."

On that day, I search for our essential dignity as a people, a people with a sense of purpose—to belong and contribute to something greater than our *pueblo.* On that day I seek to recover and reshape my spiritual identity. *¡Anímate! Raza, a celebrar el día de la Chicana.*

EL RETORNO

*All movements are
accomplished in six stages,
and the seventh brings return.*
—I Ching[8]

*Tanto tiempo sin verte casa mía,
mi cuna, mi hondo nido de la huerta.*
—"Soledad"[9]

I stand at the river, watch the curving, twisting serpent, a serpent nailed to the fence where the mouth of the Rio Grande empties into the Gulf.

I have come back. *Tanto dolor me costó el alejamiento.* I shade my eyes and look up. The bone beak of a hawk slowly circling over me, checking me out as potential carrion. In its wake a little bird flickering its wings, swimming sporadically like a fish. In the distance the expressway and the slough of traffic like an irritated sow. The sudden pull in my gut, *la tierra, los aguaceros.* My land, *el viento soplando la arena, el lagartijo debajo de un nopalito. Me acuerdo como era antes. Una región desértica de vasta llanuras, costeras de baja altura, de escasa lluvia, de chaparrales formados por mesquites y huizaches.* If I look real hard I can almost see the Spanish fathers who were called "the cavalry of Christ" enter this valley riding their *burros,* see the clash of cultures commence.

Tierra Natal   This is home, the small towns in the Valley, *los pueblitos* with chicken pens and goats picketed to mesquite shrubs. *En las colonias* on the other side of the tracks, junk cars line the front yards of hot pink and lavender-trimmed houses—Chicano architecture we call it, self-consciously. I have missed the TV shows where hosts speak in half and half, and where awards are given in the category of Tex-Mex music. I have missed the Mexican cemeteries blooming with artificial flowers, the fields of aloe vera and red pepper, rows of sugar cane, of corn hanging on the stalks, the cloud of *polvareda* in the dirt roads behind a speeding pickup truck, *el sabor de tamales de rez y renado.* I have missed *la yegua colorada* gnawing the wooden gate of her stall, the smell of horse flesh from Carito's corrals. *Hecho menos las noches calientes sin aire, noches de linternas y lechuzas* making holes in the night.

I still feel the old despair when I look at the unpainted, dilapidated, scrap lumber houses consisting mostly of corrugated aluminum. Some of the poorest people in the U.S. live in the Lower Rio Grande Valley, an arid and semi-arid land of irrigated farming, intense sunlight and heat, citrus groves next to chaparral and cactus. I walk through the elementary school I attended so long ago, that remained segregated until recently. I remember how the white teachers used to punish us for being Mexican.

How I love this tragic valley of South Texas, as Ricardo Sánchez calls it; this borderland between the Nueces and the Rio Grande. This land has survived possession and ill-use by five countries: Spain, Mexico, the Republic of Texas, the U.S., the Confederacy, and the U.S. again. It has survived Anglo-Mexican blood feuds, lynchings, burnings, rapes, pillage.

Today I see the Valley still struggling to survive. Whether it does or not, it will never be as I remember it. The borderlands depression that was set off by the 1982 peso devaluation in Mexico resulted in the closure of hundreds of Valley businesses. Many people lost their homes, cars, land. Prior to 1982, U.S. store owners thrived on retail sales to Mexicans who came across the border for groceries and clothes and appliances. While goods on the U.S. side have become 10, 100, 1000 times more expensive for Mexican buyers, goods on the Mexican side have become 10, 100, 1000 times cheaper for Americans. Because the Valley is heavily dependent on agriculture and Mexican retail trade, it has the highest unemployment rates along the entire border region; it is the Valley that has been hardest hit.[10]

"It's been a bad year for corn," my brother, Nune, says. As he talks, I remember my father scanning the sky for a rain that would end the drought, looking up into the sky, day after day, while the corn withered on its stalk. My father has been dead for 29 years, having worked himself to death. The life span of a Mexican farm laborer is 56—he lived to be 38. It shocks me that I am older than he. I, too, search the sky for rain. Like the ancients, I worship the rain god and the maize goddess, but unlike my father I have recovered their names. Now for rain (irrigation) one offers not a sacrifice of blood, but of money.

"Farming is in a bad way," my brother says. "Two to three thousand small and big farmers went bankrupt in this country last year. Six years ago the price of corn was $8.00 per hundred pounds," he goes on. "This year it is $3.90 per hundred pounds." And, I think to myself, after taking inflation into account, not planting anything puts you ahead.

I walk out to the back yard, stare at *los rosales de mamá.* She wants me to help her prune the rose bushes, dig out the carpet grass that is choking them. *Mamagrande Ramona también tenía rosales.* Here every Mexican grows flowers. If they don't have a piece of dirt, they use car tires, jars, cans, shoe boxes. Roses are the Mexican's favorite flower. I think, how symbolic—thorns and all.

Yes, the Chicano and Chicana have always taken care of growing things and the land. Again

I see the four of us kids getting off the school bus, changing into our work clothes, walking into the field with Papi and Mami, all six of us bending to the ground. Below our feet, under the earth lie the watermelon seeds. We cover them with paper plates, putting *terremotes* on top of the plates to keep them from being blown away by the wind. The paper plates keep the freeze away. Next day or the next, we remove the plates, bare the tiny green shoots to the elements. They survive and grow, give fruit hundreds of times the size of the seed. We water them and hoe them. We harvest them. The vines dry, rot, are plowed under. Growth, death, decay, birth. The soil pre-pared again and again, impregnated, worked on. A constant changing of forms, *renacimientos de la tierra madre.*

> This land was Mexican once
> was Indian always
> and is.
> And will be again.

NOTES

1. This is my own "take off" on José Vasconcelos' idea. José Vasconcelos, *La Raza Cósmica: Misión de la Raza lbero-Americana* (México: Aguilar S.A. de Ediciones, 1961).
2. Vasconcelos.
3. Arthur Koestler termed this "bisociation." Albert Rothenberg, *The Creative Process in Art, Science, and Other Fields* (Chicago, IL: University of Chicago Press, 1979), 12.
4. In part, I derive my definitions for "convergent" and "divergent" thinking from Rothenberg, 12–13.
5. To borrow chemist Ilya Prigogine's theory of "dissipative structures." Prigogine discovered that substances interact not in predictable ways as it was taught in science, but in different and fluctuating ways to produce new and more complex structures, a kind of birth he called "morphogenesis," which created unpredictable innovations. Harold Gilliam, "Searching for a New World View," *This World* (January, 1981), 23.
6. *Tortillas de masa harina:* corn tortillas are of two types, the smooth uniform ones made in a tortilla press and usually bought at a tortilla factory or supermarket, and *gorditas,* made by mixing *masa* with lard or shortening or butter (my mother sometimes puts in bits of bacon or *chicharrones*).
7. Gina Valdés, *Puentes y Fronteras: Coplas Chicanas* (Los Angeles, CA: Castle Lithograph, 1982), 2.
8. Richard Wilhelm, *The I Ching or Book of Changes,* trans. Cary F. Baynes (Princeton, NJ: Princeton University Press, 1950), 98.
9. *"Soledad"* is sung by the group *Haciendo Punto en Otro Son.*
10. Out of the twenty-two border counties in the four border states. Hidalgo County (named for Father Hidalgo who was shot in 1810 after instigating Mexico's revolt against Spanish rule under the banner of *la Virgen de Guadalupe*) is the most poverty-stricken county in the nation as well as the largest home base (along with Imperial in California) for migrant farmworkers. It was here that I was born and raised. I am amazed that both it and I have survived.

FOR FURTHER READING

Antony, Louise M., and Charlotte E. Witt, eds. *A Mind of One's Own: Feminist Essays on Reason and Objectivity.* Cambridge: Westview Press, 2002.

Anzaldúa, Gloria. *Borderlands/la Frontera: The New Mestiza.* 2nd ed. San Francisco: Spinsters/Aunt Lute, 1999.

Bordo, Susan. *Unbearable Weight: Feminism, Western Culture and the Body.* Berkeley: University of California Press, 1993.

Braidotti, Rosi. 2002. *Metamorphoses: Towards a materialist theory of becoming.* Malden. MA: Blackwell.

———. *Nomadic Subjects: Embodiment and Sexual Difference in Contemporary Feminist Theory.* New York: Columbia University Press, 1994.

Brison, Susan J. *Aftermath: Violence and the Remaking of the Self.* Princeton: Princeton University Press, 2002.

Callahan, Joan, and James W. Knight. *Preventing Birth: Contemporary Methods and Related Moral*

Controversies. Salt Lake City: Univ. of Utah Press, 1989.

Frye, Marilyn. "The Necessity of Differences: Constructing a Positive Category of Women." *Signs* 21, no. 4 (1996): 991–1010.

Gatens, Moira. *Imaginary Bodies.* New York: Routledge, 1996.

Galler, Roberta. "The Myth of the Perfect Body." In *Pleasure and Danger: Exploring Female Sexuality,* edited by Carole Vance. Hammersmith, England: Pandora Press, 1984.

Haraway, Donna. "A Cyborg Manifesto: Science, Technology and Socialist Feminism in the Late Twentieth Century." In *Simians, Cyborgs and Women: The Reinvention of Nature.* New York: Routledge, 1991.

Haslanger, Sally. "Feminism and Metaphysics: Unmasking Hidden Ontologies." *APA Newsletter on Feminism and Philosophy* 99(2) (2000).

Haslanger, Sally. "Ontology and Social Construction." *Philosophical Topics* 23(2) (1995): 95–125.

Hoagland, Sarah L., and Marilyn Frye. *Feminist Interpretations of Mary Daly.* University Park: The Pennsylvania State University Press, 2000.

Keith, Lois, ed. *What Happened to You?: Writing by Disabled Women.* London: The Women's Press, 1994.

Kittay, Eva, Alexa Schriempf, Anita Silvers, and Susan Wendell, eds. "Feminism and Disability, Part I." Special issue of *Hypatia* 16(4) (Fall 2001).

Kittay, Eva, Alexa Schriempf, Anita Silvers, and Susan Wendell, eds. "Feminism and Disability, Part II." Special issue of *Hypatia* 17(3) (2002).

Meyers, Diana Tietjens. "Who's There? Selfhood, Self-Regard, and Social Relations." *Hypatia* 20(4) (2005): 200–15.

Meyers, Diana Tietjens, ed. *Feminists Rethink the Self.* Boulder, CO.: Westview Press, 1997.

Shrage, Laurie J. *Abortion and Social Responsibility: Depolarizing the Debate.* New York: Oxford University Press, 2003.

Silvers, Anita, David Wasserman, and Mary B. Mahowald. *Disability, Difference, Discrimination: Perspectives on Justice in Bioethics and Public Policy.* Lanham, MD: Rowman and Littlefield, 1998.

Silvers, Anita. "Reconciling Equality to Difference: Caring (f)or Justice for People with Disabilities." In *Feminist ethics and social policy,* edited by Patrice DiQuinzo and Iris Marion Young. Indianapolis: Indiana University Press, 1995.

Weir, Allison. *Sacrificial Logics: Feminist Theory and the Critique of Identity.* New York: Routledge, 1996.

Witt, Charlotte. "Feminist Metaphysics." In *A Mind of One's Own,* edited by Louis Antony and Charlotte Witt, pp. 273–88. Boulder, CO.: Westview Press, 1993.

Witt, Charlotte. "Anti-Essentialism in Feminist Theory." *Philosophical Topics* 23, no. 2 (1995): 321–44.

Young, Iris. *On Female Body Experience: "Throwing Like a Girl" and Other Essays.* Oxford University Press, 2005.

Young, Iris. "Gender as Seriality: Thinking About Women as a Social Collective." *Signs* 19, no. 3 (1994): 733–34.

MEDIA RESOURCES

Dating Rites: Gang Rape on Campus. VHS. Produced by Alison Stone and Stonescape Productions (US, 1992). A compelling view of sexual assault on college campuses. Available: Filmaker's Library, www.filmakers.com, or 1–212–808–4980.

Positive Images: Portraits of Women with Disabilities. VHS. Produced and directed by Julie Harrison and Harilyn Rousso (US, 1989). People with disabilities constitute nearly twenty percent of the American population. Sexism and often racism compound discrimination based on disability. Designed to provide positive, realistic pictures of the lives of women with disabilities and the social, economic, and political issues they face, this film locates disability as a women's issue of concern to us all by discussing education, employment and careers, sexuality, family life and parenting, and societal attitudes. Available: Women Make Movies, http://www.wmm.com/, or 1–800–343–5540.

From the Back-Alleys to the Supreme Court and Beyond. VHS. Produced by Dorothy Fadiman, Daniel Meyers, and Beth Seltzer (US, 1996). This three-part series provides a comprehensive look at abortion in the United States. Combining interviews and archival footage, it covers the *Roe v. Wade* decision and current climate surrounding legalized abortion. In "Part One: When Abortion was Illegal: Untold Stories," women and doctors speak frankly about the era of back-alley abortions, revealing the physical, legal, and emotional dimensions of abortion when it was a crime. "Part Two:

From Danger to Dignity: The Fight for Safe Abortion" recounts the national movement to decriminalize abortion. "Part Three: The Fragile Promise of Choice: Abortion in the U.S. Today" examines how restrictive legislation, funding cutbacks, and anti-choice violence affect abortion's availability and how activists and clinicians are working to preserve abortion access. Available: Women Make Movies, http://www.wmm.com/, or 1–800–343–5540.

Leona's Sister Gerri. VHS. Directed and Produced by Jane Giooly (US, 1995). No one can forget the photography of the naked woman, dead from a botched illegal abortion, lying on a motel room floor. The picture appeared in *Ms.* magazine in April 1973, and quickly became a symbol for the abortion rights movement. This video tells the story of Gerri Santoro, a mother of two and the "real person" in the now famous photo. What circumstances led to Gerri's tragic death? Powerfully addressing issues of reproductive rights and domestic violence, this video is a moving portrait of Gerri Santoro's life and society's response to her death. Available: Transit Media, http://www.transitmedia.net, or 1–800–343–5540.

Tank Girl. Directed by Rachel Talalay (US, 1995). Tank Girl and her friends are the only remaining citizens living in the wasteland that is Earth, where all the water is controlled by Water and Power, the mega corporation/government that runs the territory. While incarcerated at W + P, Tank Girl and her new friend Jet Girl break out and steal . . . a tank and a jet. After meeting some mutant kangaroo/humans, and rescuing a young girl, the kangaroos and the girls kick Water and Powers' butt. A good example of hybridity and resistance from pop culture. Feature film.

In Harm's Way. Directed by Jan Krawitz (US, 1996). The film's introductory narration sets the stage for an inquiry into societal "truths" advanced during the 1950s and the subsequent violation of the world view they established. Prompted by her adult experience as a random victim of sexual assault, the filmmaker revisits her childhood's fragile myths to examine a belief system gone awry. Utilizing images from a generation's collective past, this personal memoir questions assumptions instilled in children growing up in the late 1950s. As evocative as it is cautionary, the film thoughtfully juxtaposes formative experiences of the world with the legacy of anonymous violence encountered as an adult woman. Available: Women Make Movies, http://www.wmm.com/, or 1–800–343–5540.

CREDITS

Linda Martin Alcoff, "How is epistemology political?" from *Radical Philosophy: Tradition, Counter-tradition, Politics,* edited by Roger S. Gottlieb. Copyright © 1993. Reprinted with the permission of Temple University Press.

American Anthropological Association, statement on "Race" (1998), **www.aaanet.org/stmts/racepp.htm.** Copyright © 1998 by the American Anthropological Association. Reprinted with permission.

Gloria Anzaldúa, "La conciencia de la mestiza: Toward a new consciousness" from *Borderlands/La Frontera: The New Mestiza, Second Edition.* Copyright © 1987, 1999 by Gloria Anzaldúa. Reprinted with the permission of Aunt Lute Books.

Alison Bailey, "Locating traitorous identities: Towards a theory of white character formation" from *Hypatia* 13.3 (1998). Copyright © 1998. Reprinted with the permission of Indiana University Press.

Sandra Bartky, "On psychological oppression" from *Femininity and Domination: Studies in the Phenomenology of Oppression.* Copyright © 1990 by Routledge, Chapman and Hall, Inc. Reprinted with the permission of Routledge/Taylor & Francis Group, LLC.

Simone de Beauvoir, Introduction from *The Second Sex,* translated by H.M. Parshley. Copyright 1952 and renewed © 1980 by Alfred A. Knopf, Inc. Reprinted with the permission of Alfred A. Knopf, a division of Random House, Inc.

Seyla Benhabib, "The generalized and the concrete other: The Kohlberg-Gilligan Controversy and Moral Theory" from *Situating the Self.* Copyright © 1992 by Seyla Benhabib. Reprinted with the permission of Routledge/Taylor & Francis.

Jessica Benjamin, "A desire of one's own: Psychoanalytic feminism and intersubjunctive space" from *Feminist Theories/Critical Studies* (Bloomington: Indiana University Press, 1986). Copyright © 1986 by Jessica Benjamin. Reprinted with the permission of the author.

Susan Bordo, "Purification and transcendence" from *The Flight to Objectivity: Essays on Cartesianism and Culture.* Copyright © 1987 by State University of New York. Reprinted with the permission of the State University of New York Press. All rights reserved.

Rosi Braidotti, "Mothers, Monsters, and Machines" from *Nomadic Subjects: Embodiment and Sexual Difference in Contemporary Feminist Theory.* Copyright © 1994 by Columbia University Press. Reprinted with the permission of Columbia University Press.

Judith Butler, "Performative acts and gender constitution: An essay in phenomenology and feminist theory" from *Performing Feminism: Feminist Critical Theory and Theater,* edited by Sue Ellen Case. Copyright © 1988 by The Johns Hopkins University Press. Reprinted with the permission of The Johns Hopkins University Press.

Ann J. Cahill, "A phenomenology of fear: The threat of rape and female bodily comportment" from *Rethinking Rape.* Copyright © 2001 by Ann J. Cahill. Reprinted with the permission of Cornell University Press.

Claudia Card, "The moral powers of victims" from *The Atrocity Paradigm: A Theory of Evil.* Copyright © 2002 by Claudia Card. Reprinted with the permission of Oxford University Press, Ltd.

Lorraine Code, "Taking Subjectivity into Account" from *Feminist Epistemologies,* edited by Linda Martin Alcoff and Elizabeth Potter. Copyright © 1993 by Routledge, Chapman and Hall, Inc. Reprinted with the permission of Routledge/Taylor & Francis Group, LLC.

Kimberlé Crenshaw, "Mapping the Margins: Intersectionality, Identity Politics, and Violence Against Women of Color" from *Stanford Law Review* 1241 (1991). Reprinted with the permission of the *Stanford Law Review,* Stanford University School of Law.

Chris J. Cuomo, "Dignity and the Right to Be Lesbian or Gay" from *Philosophical Studies* 132, no. 1 (January 2007): 75–85. Reprinted with the permission of Springer.

Mary Daly, "Be-longing: The lust for happiness" from *Pure Lust: Elemental Feminist Philosophy* (Boston: Beacon Press, 1984). Copyright © 1984 by Mary Daly. Reprinted with the permission of the author.

Angela Y. Davis, "The Prison Industrial Complex" from *Are Prisons Obsolete?* Copyright © 2003 by Angela Y. Davis. Reprinted with the permission of Seven Stories Press.

Cynthia Enloe, "Updating the Gendered Empire: Where are the Women in Occupied Afghanistan and Iraq?" from *The Curious Feminist: Searching for Women in a New Age of Empire.* Copyright © 2006 by the Regents of the University of California. Reprinted with the permission of the University of California Press.

Anne Fausto-Sterling, "Should there be only two sexes?" from *Sexing the Body: Gender Politics and the Construction of Sexuality.* Copyright © 2000 by Anne Fausto-Sterling. Reprinted with the permission of Basic Books, a member of Perseus Books, L.L.C.

Ann Ferguson, "Sex war: The debate between radical and libertarian feminists" from *Signs: A Journal of Women and Culture* (1984): 106–112.

Nancy Fraser, excerpts from "After the family wage: Gender equity and the welfare state" from *Political Theory* 22:4 (1994). Copyright © 1994 by. Reprinted with the permission of Sage Publications, Inc.

Marilyn Friedman, "Autonomy, Social Disruption and Women" from *Relational Autonomy: Feminist Perspectives on Autonomy, Agency, and the Social Self,* edited by Catriona Mackenzie and Natalie Stoljar. Copyright © 2000 by. Reprinted with the permission of Oxford University Press, Ltd.

Marilyn Frye, "Oppression" from *The Politics of Reality: Essays in Feminist Theory.* Copyright © 1983 by Marilyn Frye. Reprinted with the permission of The Crossing Press, a division of Ten Speed Press, Berkeley, CA. www.tenspeed.com.

Carol Gilligan, "Moral Orientation and Moral Development" from *Women and Moral Theory,* edited by Eva F. Kittay and Diana T. Meyers. Copyright © 1987 by Rowman & Littlefield Publishers. Reprinted with the permission of the publisher.

Judith Halberstam, "Transgender Butch" from *Female Masculinity.* Copyright © 1998 by Duke University Press. All rights reserved. Used by permission of the publisher.

Evelynn Hammonds, "Toward a genealogy of black female sexuality" from *Feminist Theory and the Body: A Reader,* edited by Janet Price and Margaret Shildrick. Copyright © 1997 by Routledge. Reprinted with the permission of Routledge/Taylor & Francis Group, LLC.

Sandra Harding, "Strong objectivity" from *Whose Science? Whose Knowledge: Thinking from Women's Lives.* Copyright © 1991 by Cornell University. Reprinted with the permission of Cornell University Press.

Virginia Held, "Moral theory from a feminist perspective" from *Feminist Morality: Transforming Culture, Society, and Politics.* Copyright © 1993. Reprinted with the permission of the author and The University of Chicago Press.

Sarah Hoagland, "Separating from heterosexualism" from *Lesbian Ethics: Toward a New Value* (Institute of Lesbian Studies, PO Box 25568, Chicago, IL 60625). Copyright © 1988. Reprinted with the permission of the author.

ILLUSTRATION CREDITS

INDEX